2006

Poet's
Market®

Nancy Breen, Editor
Erika Kruse O'Connell, Assistant Editor

WRITER'S DIGEST BOOKS
CINCINNATI, OH

Managing Editor, Writer's Digest Market Books: Alice Pope
Senior Editor, Writer's Digest Market Books: Kathryn S. Brogan
Supervisory Editor, Writer's Digest Market Books: Donna Poehner
Writer's Market website: www.writersmarket.com
Writer's Digest Books website: www.writersdigest.com

International Standard Serial Number 0883-5470
International Standard Book Number 1-58297-400-4

Cover design by Kelly Kofron

Interior design by Clare Finney

Production coordinated by Robin Richie

Attention Booksellers: This is an annual directory of F+W Publications. Return deadline for this edition is December 31, 2006.

Contents

From the Editor

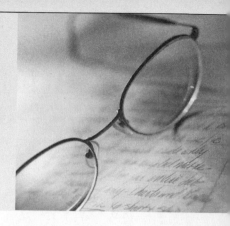

Every so often I get a letter or phone call. "I've written over 300 poems. I know they'd make a great book. Can you suggest a publisher?" Or "I think my manuscript could be a bestseller. How can I find an agent?" Or "Can I get rich and famous writing poetry?"

I have to tell them the truth—and the truth hurts. No one's going to publish a 300-poem volume by an unknown. Poetry books are rarely bestsellers, and agents won't handle them. Poetry will not make you rich and famous. I imagine the disappointment my letter will bring when the recipient opens the envelope, and I wince as I hear the hope and enthusiasm evaporate from a caller's voice. Despite my best intentions, I've trampled on a dream.

That's when I have to remind myself that dreams worth pursuing can't be rooted in self-deception. In *The Poetry Home Repair Manual* (University of Nebraska Press, 2005), Ted Kooser, our U.S. Poet Laureate, says, "You'll never be able to make a living writing poems . . .I don't want you to have any illusions."

At *Poet's Market*, we don't want you to have any illusions, either. We can't guarantee you fame and fortune, or even that the publishing process won't have its curves and speed bumps. However, we do want to encourage your dreams—by providing as many publishing opportunities as possible, through magazine, press, and contest listings. And we try to help you keep those dreams in perspective by providing solid how-to information and advice from experienced poets and editors.

In this 2006 edition, **Ann Gasser**, **Greg Kosmicki**, **Mary Harwell Sayler**, **Vijaya Schartz**, and **Ronald Wallace**, editors and judges, offer their viewpoints in a roundtable discussion of poetry contests. **Naomi Shahib Nye** is one of several experts who examine how poets can cultivate young readers through classroom programs. And in our Insider Reports, **Robert Stewart**, **Sandra Alcosser**, **David Tucker**, **Jessie Lendennie**, **Keith Taylor**, and **Alessio Zanelli** discuss a range of interesting and helpful topics: a look at the history of the journal *New Letters* and the writing it publishes; the new poetry installation in the Central Park Zoo; strategies for studying markets and submitting work; poetry publishing in Ireland; the lifestyle commitments a poet makes; and the challenges of an Italian-language poet writing in English.

We all have our dreams—but we also need to equip ourselves with the instincts and expertise necessary to make our dreams come true. I hope this edition of *Poet's Market* plays a part in helping make you a better, smarter—and published—poet.

Nancy Breen
poetsmarket@fwpubs.com

Getting Started

(and Using This Book)

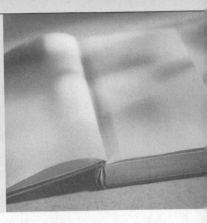

Delving into the pages of *Poet's Market* indicates a commitment—you've decided to take that big step and begin submitting your poems for publication. Good for you! How do you *really* begin, though? Here are eight quick tips to help make sense of the marketing/submission process. Follow these suggestions, study the markets in this book carefully, and give proper attention to the preparation of your manuscript. And remember, you're already pursuing your dream of seeing your poems in print.

1. Read. And read. Then read some more. You'll never develop your skills if you don't immerse yourself in poetry of all kinds. It's essential to study the masters; however, from a marketing standpoint, it's equally vital to read what your contemporaries are writing and publishing. Read journals and magazines, chapbooks and collections, anthologies for a variety of voices; scope out the many poetry sites on the Internet. Develop an eye for quality, then use that eye to assess your own work. Don't rush to publish until you know you're writing the best poetry you're capable of producing.

2. Know what you like to write—and what you write best. Ideally you should be experimenting with all kinds of poetic forms, from free verse to villanelles. However, there's sure to be a certain style with which you feel most comfortable, that conveys your true "voice." Whether you favor more formal, traditional verse or avant-garde poetry that breaks all the rules, you should identify which markets publish work similar to yours. Those are the magazines and presses you should target to give your submissions the best chance of being read favorably—and accepted. (See the Subject Index beginning on page 528 to see how some magazines and presses specify their needs.)

3. Learn the "biz." Poetry may not be a high-paying writing market, but there's still a right way to go about the "business" of submitting and publishing poems. Learn all you can by reading writing-related books and magazines. Read the articles and interviews in this book for plenty of helpful advice. Surf the Internet for a wealth of sites filled with writing advice, market news, and informative links. (See Additional Resources on page 479 for some leads.)

4. Research those markets. Start by studying the listings in *Poet's Market*. Each gathers the names, addresses, editorial preferences, and other pertinent information in one place. (The Publishers of Poetry section begins on page 38, with the Contests & Awards section following on page 400. Also, the indexes at the back of this book provide insights to what a publication or publisher might be looking for.)

You should be reading a variety of published poetry (see #1 above). That's the best way to gauge the kinds of poetry a market publishes. However, you need to go a step further. Study several issues of a magazine/journal or several of a press's books to get a feel for the

Submission Tracker

Poem Title	Publication/ Contest	Editor/Contact	Date Sent	Date Returned	Date Accepted	Date Published	Pay Received	Comments

2006 POET'S MARKET KEY TO SYMBOLS

 this market is recently established and appearing for the first time in *Poet's Market*

 this market did not appear in the previous edition of *Poet's Market*

 this market is located in Canada

 this market is located outside the U.S. and Canada

$ this market pays a monetary amount

 this market welcomes submissions from beginning poets

 this market prefers submissions from skilled, experienced poets; will consider work from beginning poets

 this market prefers submissions from poets with a high degree of skill and experience

 this market has a specialized focus

 this market is currently closed to *all* submissions

● indicates market information of special note

ms, mss manuscript(s)

b&w black & white (art/photo)

SASE self-addressed, stamped envelope

IRC International Reply Coupon (replaces return postage when mailing to countries other than your own)

(For words and expressions relating specifically to poetry and submissions, see the Glossaries in the back of this book.)

Find a handy pull-out bookmark, a quick reference to the icons used in this book, right inside the front cover.

style and content of each. If the market has a Web address (when available, websites are included in the contact information for each listing in this book), log on and take a look. Check out the site for poetry samples, reviews and other content, and especially guidelines. If a market isn't online, send for guidelines and sample copies. Guidelines give you the lowdown on what an editor expects of submissions, the kind of "insider information" that's too valuable to ignore.

5. Start slowly. As tempting as it may be to send your work straight to *The New Yorker* or *Poetry*, try to adopt a more modest approach if you're just starting out. Most listings in this book show symbols that reflect the level of writing a magazine or publisher would prefer to receive. The (□) symbol indicates a market that welcomes submissions from beginning or unpublished poets. As you gain confidence and experience (and increased skill in your writing), move on to markets coded with the (◖) symbol. Later, when you've built a publication history, submit to the more prestigious magazines and presses (the ● markets). Although it may tax your patience, slow and steady progress is a proven route to success.

6. Be professional. Professionalism is not something you should "work up to." Make it show in your first submission, from the way you prepare your manuscript to the attitude you project in your communications with editors.

Follow guidelines. Submit a polished manuscript. (See "Frequently Asked Questions" on page 7 for details on manuscript formatting and preparation.) Choose poems carefully with the editor's needs in mind. *Always* include a SASE (self-addressed stamped envelope) with any submission or inquiry. Such practices show respect for the editor, the publication, and the process; and they reflect *your* self-respect and the fact that you take your work seriously. Editors love that; and even if your work is rejected, you've made a good first impression that could help your chances with your next submission.

7. Keep track of your submissions. First, do *not* send out the only copies of your work. There are no guarantees your submission won't get lost in the mail, misplaced in a busy editorial office, or vanish into a black hole if the market winds up closing down. Create a special file folder for poems you're submitting. Even if you use a word processing program and store your manuscripts on disk, keep a hard copy file as well.

Second, establish a tracking system so you always know which poems are where. This can be extremely simple: index cards, a chart made up on the computer, or even a simple notebook used as a log. (You can photocopy an enlarged version of the Submission Tracker on page 3 or use it as a model to design your own.) Note the titles of the poems submitted (or the title of the manuscript, if submitting a collection); the name of the publication, press, or contest; date sent; and date returned *or* date accepted. Additional information you may want to log includes the name of the editor/contact, date the accepted piece is published, the pay received, rights acquired by the publication or press, and any pertinent comments.

Without a tracking system, you risk forgetting where and when pieces were submitted. This is even more problematic if you simultaneously send the same poems to different magazines. And if you learn of an acceptance at one magazine, you *must* notify the others that the poem you sent them is no longer available. You run a bigger chance of overlooking someone without an organized approach. This causes hard feelings among editors you may have inconvenienced, hurting your chances with these markets in the future.

Besides, a tracking system gives you a sense of accomplishment, even if your acceptances are infrequent at first. After all, look at all those poems you've sent out! You're really working at it, and that's something to be proud of.

8. Learn from rejection. No one enjoys rejection, but every writer faces it. The best way to turn a negative into a positive is to learn as much as you can from your rejections. Don't let them get you down. A rejection slip isn't a permission slip to doubt yourself, condemn your poetry, or give up.

Look over the rejection. Did the editor provide any comments about your work or reasons why your poems were rejected? Probably he or she didn't. Editors are extremely busy and don't necessarily have time to comment on rejections. If that's the case, move on to the next magazine or publisher you've targeted and send your work out again.

If, however, the editor *has* commented on your work, pay attention. It counts for something that the editor took the time and trouble to say anything, however brief, good, or bad. And consider any remark or suggestion with an open mind. You don't have to agree, but you shouldn't automatically disregard it, either. Tell your ego to sit down and be quiet, then use the editor's comments to review your work from a new perspective. You might be surprised how much you'll learn from a single scribbled word in the margin; or how encouraged you'll feel from a simple "Try again!" written on the rejection slip.

Keep these eight tips in mind as you prepare your poetry manuscript, and keep *Poet's Market* at hand to help you along. Believe in yourself and don't give up! As the wealth of listings in this book show, there are many opportunities for beginning poets to become published poets.

GUIDE TO LISTING FEATURES

On page 6 is an example of the market listings you'll find in the Publishers of Poetry section. Note the callouts that identify various format features of the listing. A key to the symbols used at the beginning of all listings is located on page 4 and on the inside covers of this book.

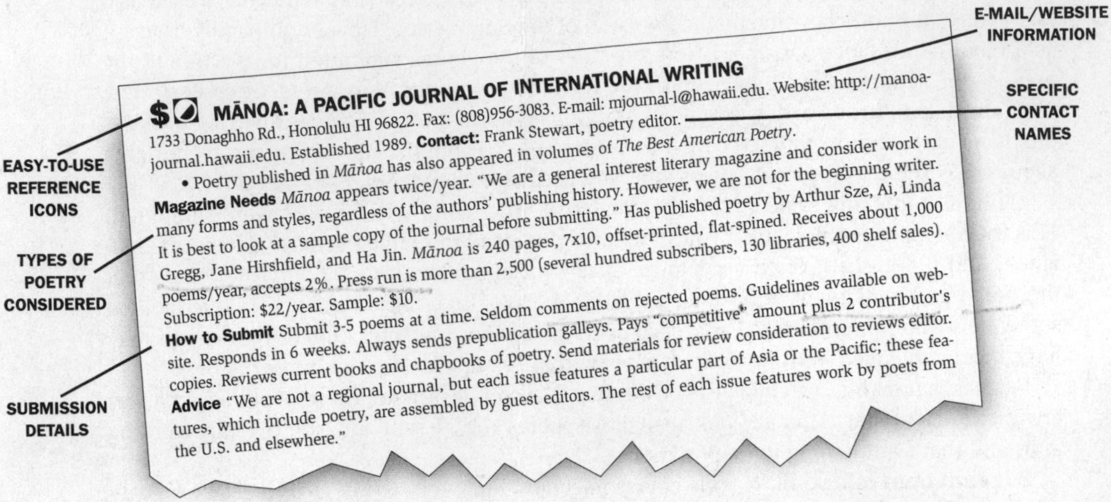

Articles & Information

EASY-TO-USE
REFERENCE
ICONS

TYPES OF
POETRY
CONSIDERED

SUBMISSION
DETAILS

E-MAIL/WEBSITE
INFORMATION

SPECIFIC
CONTACT
NAMES

$⦸ MĀNOA: A PACIFIC JOURNAL OF INTERNATIONAL WRITING

1733 Donaghho Rd., Honolulu HI 96822. Fax: (808)956-3083. E-mail: mjournal-l@hawaii.edu. Website: http://manoa-journal.hawaii.edu. Established 1989. **Contact:** Frank Stewart, poetry editor.

• Poetry published in *Mānoa* has also appeared in volumes of *The Best American Poetry*.

Magazine Needs *Mānoa* appears twice/year. "We are a general interest literary magazine and consider work in many forms and styles, regardless of the authors' publishing history. However, we are not for the beginning writer. It is best to look at a sample copy of the journal before submitting." Has published poetry by Arthur Sze, Ai, Linda Gregg, Jane Hirshfield, and Ha Jin. *Mānoa* is 240 pages, 7x10, offset-printed, flat-spined. Receives about 1,000 poems/year, accepts 2%. Press run is more than 2,500 (several hundred subscribers, 130 libraries, 400 shelf sales). Subscription: $22/year. Sample: $10.

How to Submit Submit 3-5 poems at a time. Seldom comments on rejected poems. Guidelines available on website. Responds in 6 weeks. Always sends prepublication galleys. Pays "competitive" amount plus 2 contributor's copies. Reviews current books and chapbooks of poetry. Send materials for review consideration to reviews editor.

Advice "We are not a regional journal, but each issue features a particular part of Asia or the Pacific; these features, which include poetry, are assembled by guest editors. The rest of each issue features work by poets from the U.S. and elsewhere."

ARTICLES & INFORMATION

Frequently Asked Questions

A t *Poet's Market*, we hear certain essential questions on a regular basis. The following FAQ section ("frequently asked questions") provides the expert knowledge you need to submit your poetry like a pro.

Important Note: Most basic questions such as "How many poems should I send?", "How long should I wait for a reply?", and "Are simultaneous submissions okay?" can be answered by simply reading the listings in the Publishers of Poetry section. See the introduction to that section for an explanation of the information contained in the listings. Also, see the Glossary of Listing Terms on page 490.

Is it okay to submit handwritten poems?

Usually, no. Now and then a publisher or editor makes an exception and accepts handwritten manuscripts. However, check the preferences stated in each listing. If no mention is made of handwritten submissions, assume your poetry should be typed or computer-printed.

How should I format my poems for submission to magazines and journals?

If you're submitting poems by regular mail (also referred to as *land mail*, *postal mail*, or *snail mail*), follow this format (also see sample on page 8):

Poems should be typed or computer-printed on white 8½×11 paper of at least 20 lb. weight. Left, right, and bottom margins should be at least one inch. Starting ½ inch from the top of the page, type your name, address, telephone number, e-mail address (if you have one), and number of lines in the poem in the *upper right* corner, individual lines, single-spaced. Space down about six lines and type the poem title, either centered or flush left. The title may appear in all caps or in upper and lower case. Space down another two lines (at least) and begin to type your poem. Poems are usually single-spaced, although some magazines may request double-spaced submissions. (Be alert to each market's preferences.) Double-space between stanzas. Type one poem to a page. For poems longer than one page, type your name in the *upper left* corner; on the next line type a key word from the title of your poem, the page number, and indicate whether the stanza begins or is continued on the new page (i.e., BAILEY'S FAREWELL, Page 2, continue stanza *or* begin new stanza).

If you're submitting poems by e-mail (also see sample on page 9):

First, make sure the publication accepts e-mail submissions. This information, when available, is included in all *Poet's Market* listings. In most cases, include poems within the body of your e-mail, *not* as attachments. This is the preference of many editors accepting e-mail submissions because of the danger of viruses, the possibility of software incompatibility, and other concerns. Editors who consider e-mail attachments taboo may even delete the message without ever opening the attachment.

Most Impd. w/ Emails —

Mailed Submission Format

DO leave ¹/₂" margin on top, at least 1" on sides and bottom.

DO list contact information and number of lines in upper right corner.

DO space down about 6 lines.

DO type title in all caps or upper/lower case. Center it or type flush with left margin.

DON'T type a by-line but **DO** space down at least 2 lines.

DO double-space between stanzas.

DO type poems single-spaced unless guidelines specify double spacing.

For multi-page poems, **DO** show your name, key word(s) from title, page number, and "continue stanza" or "new stanza."

DO space down at least 3 lines before resuming poem.

S. T. Coleridge
1796 Ancient Way
Mariner Heights, OH 45007
(852)555-5555
albatross@strophe.vv.cy
54 lines

KUBLA KHAN

In Xanadu did Kubla Khan
a stately pleasure dome decree:
where Alph, the sacred river, ran
through caverns measureless to man
down to a sunless sea.
So twice five miles of fertile ground
with walls and towers were girdled round:
and there were gardens bright with sinuous rills,
where blossomed many an incense-bearing tree;
and here were forests ancient as the hills,
enfolding sunny spots of greenery.

But oh! that deep romantic chasm which slanted
down the green hill athwart a cedarn cover!
A savage place! as holy and enchanted
as e'er beneath a waning moon was haunted
by woman wailing for her demon lover!
And from this chasm, with ceaseless turmoil seething,
as if this earth in fast thick pants were breathing,
a mighty fountain momently was forced:
amid whose swift half-intermitted burst
huge fragments vaulted like rebounding hail,
or chaffy grain beneath the thresher's flail:
And 'mid these dancing rocks at once and ever
it flung up momently the sacred river.

S. T. Coleridge
KUBLA KAHN, Page 2, continue stanza

Five miles meandering with a mazy motion
through wood and dale the sacred river ran,
then reached the caverns measureless to man,
and sank in tumult to a lifeless ocean:
and 'mid this tumult Kubla heard from afar
ancestral voices prophesying war!

The shadow of the dome of pleasure
floated midway on the waves;
where was heard the mingled measure
from the fountain and the caves.
It was a miracle of rare device,
a sunny pleasure dome with caves of ice!

A damsel with a dulcimer
in a vision once I saw:
It was an Abyssinian maid,

E-mail Submission Format

DO use a basic typeface and point size.

DO use the appropriate e-mail address.

DO consult guidelines for special instructions about formatting the subject line.

DO follow basic guidelines for a good cover letter.

DO provide contact information, including regular mail address.

DO be aware that formatting can become lost in an electronic submission. Keep it simple.

DO paste all poems within one message, one after the other, unless guidelines specify otherwise.

DON'T send submissions by e-mail unless editor says it's okay (in market listing or guidelines).

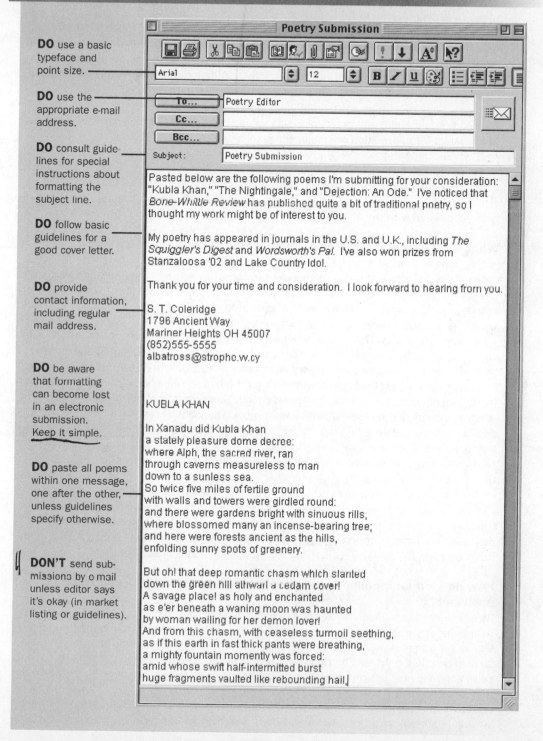

Poetry Submission

Arial   12   B / U

To...   Poetry Editor
Cc...
Bcc...
Subject :   Poetry Submission

Pasted below are the following poems I'm submitting for your consideration: "Kubla Khan," "The Nightingale," and "Dejection: An Ode." I've noticed that *Bone-Whittle Review* has published quite a bit of traditional poetry, so I thought my work might be of interest to you.

My poetry has appeared in journals in the U.S. and U.K., including *The Squiggler's Digest* and *Wordsworth's Pal.* I've also won prizes from Stanzaloosa '02 and Lake Country Idol.

Thank you for your time and consideration. I look forward to hearing from you.

S. T. Coleridge
1796 Ancient Way
Mariner Heights OH 45007
(852)555-5555
albatross@strophe.w.cy

KUBLA KHAN

In Xanadu did Kubla Khan
a stately pleasure dome decree:
where Alph, the sacred river, ran
through caverns measureless to man
down to a sunless sea.
So twice five miles of fertile ground
with walls and towers were girdled round:
and there were gardens bright with sinuous rills,
where blossomed many an incense-bearing tree;
and here were forests ancient as the hills,
enfolding sunny spots of greenery.

But oh! that deep romantic chasm which slanted
down the green hill athwart a cedarn cover!
A savage place! as holy and enchanted
as e'er beneath a waning moon was haunted
by woman wailing for her demon lover!
And from this chasm, with ceaseless turmoil seething,
as if this earth in fast thick pants were breathing,
a mighty fountain momently was forced:
amid whose swift half-intermitted burst
huge fragments vaulted like rebounding hail,

Of course, other editors do accept, and even prefer e-mail submissions as attachments. This information should be clearly stated in the market listing. If it's not, you're probably safer submitting your poems in the body of the e-mail. (All the more reason to pay close attention to details given in the listings.)

Note, too, the number of poems the editor recommends including in the e-mail submission. If no quantity is given specifically for e-mails, go with the number of poems an editor recommends submitting in general. Identify your submission with a notation in the subject line. Some editors simply want the words ''Poetry Submission'' while others want poem titles. Check the market listing for preferences. **Note:** Because of spam, filters, and other concerns, some editors are strict about what must be printed in the subject line and how. If you're uncertain about any aspect of e-mail submission formats, double-check the website (if available) for information or contact the publication for directions.

If you're submitting poems by disk:

Submit poems by disk *only* when the publication indicates this is acceptable. Even then, if no formatting preferences are given, contact the publisher for specifics before sending the disk. Make sure your disk is virus-free. Always include a hard copy (i.e., printed copy) of your submission with the disk.

What is a chapbook? How is it different from a regular poetry book?

A chapbook is a booklet averaging 24-50 pages in length (some may be shorter), usually digest-sized ($5^1/_2 \times 8^1/_2$, although chapbooks can come in all sizes, even published within the pages of a magazine). Typically, a chapbook is saddle-stapled with a soft cover (card or special paper); however, chapbooks can also be produced with a plain paper cover the same weight as the pages, especially if the booklet is photocopied.

A chapbook is a much smaller collection of poetry than a full-length book (which runs anywhere from 50 pages to well over 100 pages, longer for ''best of'' collections and retrospectives). There are probably more poetry chapbooks being published than full-length books, and that's an important point to consider. Don't think of the chapbook as a poor relation to the full-length collection. While it's true a chapbook won't attract big reviews, qualify for major prizes, or find national distribution through large bookstores, it's a terrific way for a poet to build an audience (and reputation) in increments, while developing the kind of publishing history that may attract the attention of a book publisher one day.

Although some presses consider chapbook-length submissions, many choose manuscripts through competitions. Check each publisher's listing for requirements, send for guidelines or visit the website (absolutely vital if a competition is involved), and check out some sample chapbooks the press has already produced (these are usually available from the publisher). Chapbook publishers are usually just as choosy as book publishers about the quality of work they accept. Submit your best work in a professional manner. (See the Chapbook Publishers Index on page 496 for markets that consider chapbook manuscripts.)

How do I format a collection of poems to submit to a book/chapbook publisher?

Before you send a manuscript to a book/chapbook publisher, request guidelines (or consult the publisher's website, if one is available). Requirements vary regarding formatting, query letters and samples, length, and other considerations. Usually you will be using $8^1/_2 \times 11$, 20 lb. paper; left, right, and bottom margins of at least one inch; your name and title of your collection in the top left corner of every page; one poem to a page (although poems certainly may run longer than one page); and pages numbered consecutively. Individual publisher requirements may include a title page, table of contents, credits page (indicating where previously published poems originally appeared), and biographical note.

If you're submitting your poetry book or chapbook manuscript to a competition, you *must* read and follow the guidelines. Failure to do so could disqualify your manuscript. Guidelines for a competition may call for a special title page, a minimum and maximum number of pages, the absence of the poet's name anywhere in the manuscript, and even a special entry form to accompany the submission.

What is a cover letter? Do I have to send one? What should it say?

A cover letter is your introduction to the editor, telling him a little about yourself and your work. Most editors indicate their cover letter preferences in their listings in the Publishers of Poetry section. If an editor states that a cover letter is "required," absolutely send one! It's also better to send one if a cover letter is "preferred." Experts disagree on the necessity and appropriateness of cover letters, so use your own judgment when preferences aren't clear in the listing.

A cover letter should be professional but also allow you to present your work in a personal manner. (See the fictional cover letter on page 12 as an example.) Keep your letter brief, no more than one page. Address your letter to the correct contact person. (Use "Poetry Editor" if no contact name appears in the listing.) Include your name, address, phone number, and e-mail address (if available). If a biographical note is requested, include 2-3 lines about your job, interests, why you write poetry, etc. Avoid praising yourself or your poems in your letter (your submission should speak for itself). Include titles (or first lines) of the poems you're submitting. List a few of your most recent publishing credits, but no more than five. (If you haven't published any poems yet, you may skip this. However, be aware that some editors are interested in and make an effort to publish new writers.) Show your familiarity with the magazine to which you're submitting—comment on a poem you saw printed there, tell the editor why you chose to submit to her magazine, mention poets the magazine has published. Use a business-style format for a professional appearance, and proofread carefully; typos, misspellings, and other errors make a poor first impression. Remember that editors are people, too. Respect, professionalism, and kindness go a long way in poet/editor relationships.

What Is a SASE? An IRC (with SAE)?

A SASE is a self-addressed, stamped envelope. Don't let your submission leave home without it! You should also include a SASE if you send an inquiry to an editor. If your submission is too large for an envelope (for instance, a bulky book-length collection of poems), use a box and include a self-addressed mailing label with adequate return postage paper-clipped to it.

An IRC is an International Reply Coupon, enclosed with a self-addressed envelope for manuscripts submitted to foreign markets. Each coupon is equivalent in value to the minimum postage rate for an unregistered airmail letter. IRCs may be exchanged for postage stamps at post offices in all foreign countries that are members of the Universal Postal Union (UPU). When you provide the adequate number of IRCs and a self-addressed envelope (SAE), you give a foreign editor financial means to return your submission (U.S. postage stamps cannot be used to send mail *to* the United States from outside the country). Purchase price is $1.75 per coupon. Call your local post office to check for availability (sometimes only larger post offices sell them).

Important note about IRCs: Foreign editors sometimes find the IRCs have been stamped incorrectly by the U.S. post office when purchased. This voids the IRCs and makes it impossible for the foreign editor to exchange the coupons for return postage for your manuscript. When buying IRCs, make sure yours have been stamped correctly before you leave the counter. (The Postal Service clerk must place a postmark in the block with the heading *control stamp of the country or origin*.) More information about International Reply Coupons is available on the USPS website (www.usps.com).

Important

Preparing Your Cover Letter

DO type on one side of 8 1/2 x 11 20-pound paper.

DO proofread carefully.

DO use a standard 12-point typeface (like Times New Roman).

DO list the poems you're submitting for consideration.

DO mention something about the magazine and about yourself.

DO be brief!

Perry Lineskanner
1954 Eastern Blvd.
Pentameter, OH 45007
(852) 555-5555
soneteer@trochee.vv.cy

April 24, 2006

Spack Saddlestaple, Editor
The Squiggler's Digest
Double-Toe Press
P.O. Box 54X
Submission Junction, AZ 85009

Dear Mr. Saddlestaple:

Enclosed are three poems for your consideration for *The Squiggler's Digest*: "Josh's Complaint," "Sydney in July," and "Erika's Wedding."

Although I'm a long-time reader of *The Squiggler's Digest*, this is my first submission to your publication. However, my poetry has appeared in other magazines, including *The Bone-Whittle Review*, *Bumper-Car Reverie*, and *Stock Still*. I've won several awards through the annual Buckey Versefest! contests, and my chapbook manuscript was a finalist in the competition sponsored by Hollow Banana Press. While I devote a great deal of time to poetry (both reading and writing), I'm employed as a website editor — which inspires more poetry than you might imagine.

Thank you for the opportunity to submit my work. Your time and attention are much appreciated, and I look forward to hearing from you.

Sincerely,

Perry Lineskanner

Note: The names used in this letter are intended to be fictional; any resemblance to real people, publications, or presses is purely coincidental.

To save trouble and money, poets sometimes send disposable manuscripts to foreign markets and inform the editor to discard the manuscript after it's been read. Some enclose an IRC and SAE for reply only; others establish a deadline after which they will withdraw the manuscript from consideration and market it elsewhere.

How much postage does my submission need?

As much as it takes; you do *not* want your manuscript to arrive postage due. Purchase a postage scale or take your manuscript to the post office for weighing. Remember, you'll need postage on two envelopes: the one containing your submission and SASE, and the return envelope itself. Submissions without SASEs usually will not be returned (and possibly may not even be read).

First-Class Postage is 37 cents for the first ounce, 23 cents for each additional ounce up to 13 ounces. So, if your submission weighs in at five ounces, you'll need to apply $1.29 in postage. Note that three pages of poetry, a cover letter, and a SASE can be mailed for one First-Class stamp using a #10 (business-size) envelope; the SASE should be either a #10 envelope folded in thirds or a #9 envelope. Larger envelopes may require different rates, so check with your post office.

Mail over 13 ounces is sent Priority Mail automatically. Priority Mail Flat Rate, using the envelope provided by the Postal Service, costs $3.85 regardless of weight or destination. If sending a bulky manuscript (a full-length book manuscript, for instance), check with the post office for rates.

For complete U.S. Postal Service information, including rates and increases, a postage calculator, and the option to buy stamps online with a credit card, see their website at www.usps.gov. Canadian Postal Service information is available at www.canadapost.ca.

What does it mean when an editor says "no previously published" poems? Does this include poems that have appeared in anthologies?

If your poem appears *anywhere* in print for a public audience, it's considered "previously" published. That includes magazines, anthologies, websites and online magazines, and even programs (say for a church service, wedding, etc.). See the following explanation of rights, especially *second serial (reprint) rights* and *all rights* for additional concerns about previously published material.

What rights should I offer for my poems? What do these different rights mean?

Editors usually indicate in their listings what rights they acquire. Most journals and magazines license *first rights* (a.k.a. *first serial rights*), which means the poet offers the right to publish the poem for the first time in any periodical. All other rights to the material remain with the poet. (Note that some editors state that rights to poems "revert to authors upon publication" when first rights are acquired.) When poems are excerpted from a book prior to publication and printed in a magazine/journal, this is also called *first serial rights*. The addition of *North American* indicates the editor is the first to publish a poem in a U.S. or Canadian periodical. The poem can still be submitted to editors outside of North America or to those who acquire reprint rights.

When a magazine/journal licenses *one-time rights* to a poem (also known as *simultaneous rights*), the editor has *nonexclusive* rights to publish the poem once. The poet can submit that same poem to other publications at the same time (usually markets that don't have overlapping audiences).

Editors/publishers open to submissions of work already published elsewhere seek *second serial (reprint) rights*. The poet is obliged to inform them where and when the poem previously appeared so they can give proper credit to the original publication. In essence, chap-

Postage Information

First-Class Mail Rates

First ounce	$0.37
Each addit'l ounce	$0.23

First-Class Mail Rates

Weight not over (ounces)	Rate	Weight not over (ounces)	Rate
1	$0.37	8	1.98
2	0.60	9	2.21
3	0.83	10	2.44
4	1.06	11	2.67
5	1.29	12	2.90
6	1.52	13	3.13
7	1.75		

Source: Website of the United States Postal Service (www.usps.com)

U.S. and Canadian Postal Codes

AL	Alabama	MN	Minnesota	VA	Virginia
AK	Alaska	MS	Mississippi	WA	Washington
AZ	Arizona	MO	Missouri	WV	West Virginia
AR	Arkansas	MT	Montana	WI	Wisconsin
CA	California	NE	Nebraska	WY	Wyoming
CO	Colorado	NV	Nevada		
CT	Connecticut	NH	New Hampsire	**Canada**	
DE	Delaware	NJ	New Jersey	AB	Alberta
DC	District of	NM	New Mexico	BC	British Columbia
	Columbia	NY	New York	MB	Manitoba
FL	Florida	NC	North Carolina	NB	New Brunswick
GA	Georgia	ND	North Dakota	NL	Newfoundland &
GU	Guam	OH	Ohio		Labrador
HI	Hawaii	OK	Oklahoma	NS	Nova Scotia
ID	Idaho	OR	Oregon	NT	Northwest
IL	Illinois	PA	Pennsylvania		Territories
IN	Indiana	PR	Puerto Rico	NU	Nunavut
IA	Iowa	RI	Rhode Island	ON	Ontario
KS	Kansas	SC	South Carolina	PE	Prince Edward
KY	Kentucky	SD	South Dakota		Island
LA	Louisiana	TN	Tennessee	QC	Quebec
ME	Maine	TX	Texas	SK	Saskatchewan
MD	Maryland	UT	Utah	YT	Yukon
MA	Massachusetts	VT	Vermont		
MI	Michigan	VI	Virgin Islands		

book or book collections license reprint rights, listing the magazines in which poems previously appeared somewhere in the book (usually on the copyright page or separate credits page).

If a publisher or editor requires you to relinquish *all rights*, be aware that you are giving up ownership of that poem or group of poems. You cannot resubmit the work elsewhere, nor can you include it in a poetry collection without permission or negotiating for reprint rights to be returned to you. Before you agree to this type of arrangement, ask the editor first if he or she is willing to acquire first rights instead of all rights. If you receive a refusal, simply write a letter withdrawing your work from consideration. Some editors will reassign rights to a writer after a given amount of time, such as one year.

With the growth in Internet publishing opportunities, *electronic rights* have become very important. These cover a broad range of electronic media, including online magazines, CD recordings of poetry readings, and CD-ROM editions of magazines. When submitting to an electronic market of any kind, find out what rights the market acquires upfront (many online magazines also stipulate the right to archive poetry they've published so it's continually available on their websites).

What is a copyright? Should I have my poems copyrighted before I submit them for publication?

Copyright is a proprietary right that gives you the power to control your work's reproduction, distribution, and public display or performance, as well as its adaptation to other forms. In other words, you have legal right to the exclusive publication, sale, or distribution of your poetry. What's more, your "original works of authorship" are protected as soon as they are "fixed in a tangible form of expression," or written down. Since March 1989, copyright notices are no longer required to secure protection, so it's not necessary to include them on your poetry manuscript. Also, in many editors' minds, copyright notices signal the work of amateurs distrustful and paranoid about having work stolen.

If you still want to indicate copyright, use the © symbol or the word *copyright*, your name, and the year. Furthermore, if you wish, you can register your copyright with the Copyright Office for a $30 fee. (Since paying $30 per poem is costly and impractical, you may prefer to copyright a group of poems for that single fee.) Further information is available from the U.S. Copyright Office, Library of Congress, 101 Independence Ave. S.E., Washington DC 20559-6000. You can also call the Copyright Public Information Office at (202)707-3000 between 8:30 a.m. and 5:00 p.m. weekdays (EST). Copyright forms can be downloaded from or requested through www.copyright.gov (includes advice on filling out forms, general copyright information, a "Copyright Forms by Mail" request page, and links to copyright-related websites).

Special note regarding Copyright Office mail delivery: The "effective date of registration" for copyright applications is usually the day the Copyright Office actually receives all elements of the application (application form, fee, and copies of work being registered). Because of security concerns, all USPS and private-carrier mail is being screened off-site prior to arrival at the Copyright Office. This can add 3-5 days to delivery time and could, therefore, impact the effective date of registration.

Roundtable: Poetry Contests

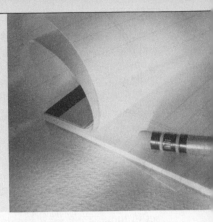

by Will Allison

Editor's note: At press time (April 2005) Foetry.com's founder was identified publicly; he took down the site, then reactivated it, with forums closed to new members. The comments in this roundtable reflect developments within Foetry's first year of existence.

Since its launch in April 2004, a website called Foetry.com has been shaking up the poetry world with allegations that numerous poetry contests—including some of the country's most highly regarded competitions—employ unfair judging and screening practices. Adding to the controversy is the fact that Foetry.com is anonymous, giving the site, in the eyes of some, a witch-hunt taint.

Whether Foetry.com is good or bad for American poetry has been a subject of spirited debate. Meanwhile, it's making contest directors more self-conscious about their guidelines, and prompting poets to closely scrutinize contests before mailing in their entry fees.

In an effort to help poets better understand how contests are conducted, *Poet's Market* asked sponsors of five contests to discuss how they ensure the integrity of their competitions, and what poets should look for in choosing a contest. The following interview includes two sponsors of contests for book-length manuscripts (The Backwaters Press and University of Wisconsin Press) and three sponsors of contests for individual poems (Arizona Authors Association, Florida Freelance Writers Association, and Pennsylvania Poetry Society).

Ann Gasser began writing poetry in 1981 and has written more than 2,700 poems, winning 784 awards. She serves as recording secretary for the Pennsylvania Poetry Society and as editor of the PPS' newsletter, its annual book of prize poems, and its booklet of winning student poems from the Pegasus contest. Ann frequently serves as a judge for state and national poetry contests. She is the author of *Awakening the Poet Within* (AGEE Keyboard Press, 1995), as well as numerous volumes of poetry.

Greg Kosmicki is editor and publisher of The Backwaters Press, which he founded in 1988. His press established The Backwaters Prize in 1998 and the Weldon Kees Chapbook Award in 2003. His own poetry has been published in *Paris Review*, *New Letters*, *Cimarron*

WILL ALLISON is a staff member at the Squaw Valley Community of Writers and teaches creative writing at Indiana University-Purdue University at Indianapolis. His short stories have appeared in *Zoetrope: All-Story*, *Kenyon Review*, *One Story*, *Shenandoah*, *American Short Fiction*, *Atlanta*, and other magazines.

Review, Connecticut Review, and numerous other magazines. He is the author of one book and five chapbooks of poems, the most recent of which is *The Patron Saint of Lost and Found* (Lone Willow Press, 2003). A new collection, *we have always been coming to this morning,* is due out in 2005 from Sandhills Press.

Mary Harwell Sayler chairs and judges the annual poetry contest for Florida Freelance Writers Association. For over 20 years she worked with students through her correspondence course, which became the book *Poetry: Taking Its Course* (Ocean Publishing, 2004). (Information about that title and her other ''helps for poets'' can be found at www.poetryof course.com.)

Vijaya Schartz is president of Arizona Authors Association, editor of *Arizona Literary Magazine,* a fiction reviewer for various magazines, and the former host of a radio program for writers. Her award-winning novel, *Ashes for the Elephant God* (Blue Planet Books, 2000), set in India, is in the process of becoming a feature film. Her current project is a historical fantasy series based on authentic medieval legends.

Ronald Wallace is the author of 12 books of poetry, fiction, and criticism, including, most recently, *Long for This World: New and Selected Poems* (University of Pittsburgh Press, 2003). He co-directs the creative writing program at the University of Wisconsin-Madison and serves as editor for the University of Wisconsin Press poetry series. He divides his time between Madison and a 40-acre farm in Bear Valley, Wisconsin.

How does a poet know if he is ready to enter contests?

Gasser: There are a number of state poetry organizations that sponsor contests and print the poems that win money. Get a copy of one of these books, and see if you are writing poetry similar to these winning poems. Study the winning poems and see if you can figure out why they won. For a SASE, Pennsylvania Poetry Society will send you a ''Judges' Criteria Sheet'' to show what judges look for in choosing winning poems. If you're a novice, my book, *Awakening the Poet Within,* will give you all the basic information you need to grow in the craft.

Kosmicki: Success in getting your poems published in at least a couple prestigious literary magazines (and there are many) will give you an indication that your work is at a level skilled enough to win a contest. You must have an entire manuscript strong as your very best work. One or two clunkers in a manuscript will knock you out of competition.

Sayler: When you ''feel good'' about your work, it's time. Entering reputable contests provides an opportunity for positive feedback. For instance, an honorable mention will let you know your poem has outstanding qualities that have now been noticed and recognized by an informed reader of poetry.

Schartz: If you have this fantastic poem you feel the urge to enter in a contest, you are ready. If nothing else, it will give you an idea of where you stand in your poetry writing.

Wallace: A poet is ready to begin submitting work to magazines (and contests) when they've written a lot and read a lot, and they're prepared to get rejection after rejection without despairing.

What factors should a poet consider when choosing a contest?

Gasser: Find contests that seem to be geared to your type of writing. Avoid the huge commercial contests run by poetry businesses that are primarily out to make money by flattering the poet's ego. I know a couple of poets who have won money in these contests, but they're definitely the exception. Most poets are given an honorable mention and urged to buy an expensive anthology and other material.

Contests sponsored by state organizations are legitimate, and there are many other poetry contests that may or may not be on the level. Contests sponsored by academic sources usually award prizes to academics only. If you are not an academic poet, you will probably not win in one of their contests. Our Pennsylvania Poetry Society newsletter lists contests we feel are worth entering.

The National Federation of State Poetry Societies' annual contest of 50 categories is a good place to test the waters. Go to www.nfsps.com and click on "poetry contests." The site will also tell you how to buy the most recent edition of *Encore*, the NFSPS anthology of prize poems, so you can see which poems recently won.

Kosmicki: Poets just starting out shouldn't enter contests—save your money; work on your writing for several years. Buy some of the past contest-winning books and read them to see if your poetry is like them at all. If you know the name of the final judge, read some of the judge's own writing to see if it's at least remotely like yours. If it's not, don't enter that contest.

Sayler: Contest sponsors need to be checked out. For example, anyone who looks into the Florida Freelance Writers Association will know this group works hard for writers, poets, and editors—not only by offering professional guidance, but encouragement, too.

Besides reputation, another factor is the level of competition. Prestigious awards or ones with large prizes will usually be highly competitive. More modest but reputable contests, such as those sponsored by FFWA, offer good possibilities for published poets and also beginners or novices with a skillfully crafted poem.

Be wary of contests that offer big prizes with no entry fees. Someone has to pay for those awards, and often it's by making everyone a "winner" who pays to attend ceremonies or to purchase exorbitantly priced anthologies. An exception would be a company, such as a perfume manufacturer, who wants a prize poem to assist an advertising campaign.

Schartz: For a beginner, a contest that offers critiques might be a better choice. Whether you win or lose, you get something valuable in return. For a confirmed poet, the widespread reputation of the contest and the number of entries should prevail when choosing.

Wallace: The contest should be legitimate. There are still vanity operations out there, and winning one of those can actually damage, rather than enhance, one's reputation. A poet should ideally submit only to contests that have published work he or she admires. Some presses are more prestigious than others, and a poet might want to submit only to the "best" publisher. However, because the odds of winning any particular contest these days are so small, given the large number of submissions, it's probably wise to submit to as many legitimate competitions as a writer can afford.

How might a poet gauge her odds of winning a particular contest?

Gasser: To win any poetry contest takes a combination of skill and luck. You need to follow the rules precisely, enter well-crafted poems, and hope you hit a judge who likes your subject and style. Enter as many categories in a contest as possible to give yourself the best chance of winning. Many times the poem you think has the least chance turns up a winner, and vice versa.

Kosmicki: No way to gauge odds, except if you enter a smaller contest, you have a better chance, mathematically speaking. The strength of your writing is your gauge—how does it compare with the best writing you know?

Sayler: Trust your instincts! If you feel something in your poem is "off," correct it. Your best work stands as good a chance as anyone else's. Also, if you know who will judge a competition, look for information on that person. For instance, anyone familiar with my work probably knows I don't like vulgarity or words that demean any person or group.

Schartz: If winning is your goal, you might not be ready. No matter how educated the judges, judging is always subjective, and you're setting yourself up for rejection. Enter only your very best—a poem that will evoke deep emotions among the judges.

Wallace: The odds are small in any competition that invites national and international submissions, as does the University of Wisconsin Press. We receive up to 900 book-length submissions annually, and a large number of them are serious contenders. Poets who have published work in good magazines can be more confident about the quality of that work. My own first book, *Plums, Stones, Kisses & Hooks*, was rejected 99 times before the University of Missouri Press accepted it on the 100th submission.

What's your opinion of Foetry.com, a website that bills itself as the "American poetry watchdog" and promises to expose fraudulent and unfair contests?

Gasser: I'm not familiar with Foetry.com.

Kosmicki: It's good to have integrity monitored. Whoever runs the Foetry.com site should practice what they preach and not keep their identities secret as though they were a vigilante group, however.

Sayler: I would have welcomed their warnings before wasting time and fees on one or more of the unfair competitions mentioned but am concerned about the potentiality of jumping to conclusions. For example, if former students win the competition I judge, I'll be thrilled by their success but worried that my high ethical standards would then be suspect!

Schartz: It's good someone is watching and keeping track. Scams are easy to set up on the Internet. But not all complaints reported are reliable. One bitter loser doesn't make a contest bad. Take everything with a grain of salt, and do your own research. But if there are many complaints about a particular contest, stay away from it.

Wallace: I'm in favor of exposing fraudulent and unfair contests when the facts merit it, and I've seen enough cases of mismanagement to be sympathetic with Foetry.com's goals. I do worry a bit about the stringency of the guidelines the site favors. In the early years of our competition at Wisconsin, I refused to accept any submissions from anyone I'd had any contact with at all. I wanted to avoid even the appearance of bias.

Some years ago I began to discover I knew so many writers, however, and my judges had had contact with so many writers, many of the best were being excluded from our competition. It seemed unfair to penalize (by exclusion) those writers who had pursued their craft by taking workshops and attending conferences and consulting with fellow poets. At Wisconsin, we no longer exclude anyone (other than Wisconsin employees or current students) from submitting manuscripts. However, our reading process is so painstaking and meticulous I believe we run one of the fairest and most open contests around.

What steps do you take to ensure the fairness and integrity of your contest?

Gasser: Our policy is to choose judges who aren't members of our state society, but who have shown their skill in the craft by winning in NFSPS contests or other prestigious places. We never use the same judges two years in a row.

Kosmicki: Manuscripts are read "blind" at every step—neither the screeners nor the judge know the identity of the poet. Manuscripts in which the poet includes his own name in the body of the text are disqualified, as stated in the published guidelines. Since the integrity controversy became widely known enough that it finally caught my attention, thanks to Foetry.com, I inserted wording into my contest guidelines to guard against cronyism. My contests always have been conducted with the highest standards of integrity, but I thought it better to avoid even the slightest appearance of impropriety.

Sayler: As contest judge, I receive only blind entries with the name of the poet omitted, so I don't know who has sent what until winning names are announced. My former students or poets whose work I critique are clearly told not to submit a poem I've seen. If an entry seems even vaguely familiar to me, it's immediately disqualified. So far, "familiarity" happened only because a couple of poets sent poems they had previously entered!

Schartz: Our contest is international, and the judging totally blind, handled by several different sets of judges. Our judges have no possible connection with the entrants. They are published authors in their own right, volunteering their time to reward emerging writers. In 2004, our winners were from Scotland, England, Canada, and Florida, whereas most of our judges live in the western United States.

Wallace: We accept submissions from anyone other than current University of Wisconsin-Madison staff and students. Six or more screening readers read the approximately 900 submissions we receive each year. I then personally read at least something in each of the 900 manuscripts myself. On the basis of these readings, I pass approximately 100-150 manuscripts on to a second set of screening readers, who each carefully read approximately 15 manuscripts. These readers each recommend two finalists to me for a total of about 20-25 finalists. I reread these manuscripts carefully myself before sending them to an outside judge. Thus, each finalist manuscript has been positively read by three separate readers before the judge sees it and judges it blind. Judges remain anonymous until the competition is over, to ensure contestants don't contact judges about their submissions. Screening readers and judges rotate annually. My initial screeners and the final judge are paid a modest honorarium; I, and my secondary screeners, work on a volunteer basis. It's a very time-consuming process.

How many entries do you typically receive?

Gasser: The number of entries varies. The total would be somewhere between 500 and 1,000.

Kosmicki: Around 400 the last three years.

Sayler: We usually get a few more each year as word continues to get out, but generally expect at least 100 poems.

Schartz: It varies from year to year and from category to category. Poetry and short story are the most popular categories, and both receive several hundred entries each year.

Wallace: Up to 900.

How would you characterize the overall quality of the entries you receive?

Gasser: The quality of poems we receive is more or less consistent from year to year. There are always some that are easily passed over, some that are good but not exceptional, and some that are truly excellent, making the judges' decisions difficult.

Kosmicki: The quality is very high and consistent year to year. Lots of people—with MFAs and PhDs and several book publications and awards and tons of poems published in every magazine from *The New Yorker* on down to the tiniest literary magazine Xeroxed off in someone's apartment—submit manuscripts. A plethora of great writing programs are teaching poets the "craft," so it can be very difficult, almost painfully so, to decide against one manuscript and for another. There are also thousands of writer's groups not in academia, working with each other to increase the quality of their participants' writing. There seems to be an immense and growing interest in poetry overall throughout the world.

Sayler: Entries do vary and, overall, improve each year. To help writers develop their own judgment about their work, we post tips and guidelines at www.writers-editors.com. When time permits, I send notes to poets who win or who receive honorable mentions to provide feedback on what worked well. Hopefully, that helps them improve their poems—and my reading material!

Schartz: Like the number of entries, the quality varies, but it seems to improve from year to year. We have many returnees among our contestants. Each year we also see an increasing number of very young writers, and we love to see their amazed faces at the awards ceremony.

Wallace: The quality is remarkably similar from year to year, though my impression is it keeps improving. Nearly all the manuscripts are competent; very few can be rejected easily.

Many of the manuscripts are excellent. Many of the poets have published extensively in good magazines or have published previous books.

In 2004, poet, critic, and publisher Kevin Walzer of WordTech Communications told the *Boston Globe*, "There seem to be more people willing to pay for a chance to have their own book published (i.e., via a contest reading fee) than there are people willing to buy a book of poetry by someone else." Do you agree?

Gasser: Absolutely! Books of poetry generally do not sell well unless they're written by a celebrity. Nearly all poets want to publish their poetry, but few are interested in reading poetry written by someone else, and the general public is generally apathetic to the genre.

Kosmicki: I don't know the numbers, but lots of poetry books are sold, and lots of contests entered. Sure, poetry doesn't sell like novels because it attracts a specialized audience. A lot of contests give every entrant a copy of the winning book (my press does), so the reading/contest entry fee actually is buying a book, too.

Sayler: I'm sorry to say, I do agree. For example, I recently led a poetry workshop hosted by another group and was surprised to see most of the conferees had self-published their work. Actually, I've done that myself with chapbooks. However, I studied heavily, established publishing credits, and had a ready audience, so I could "hawk" self-published products at a writer's conference or other place where I had been asked to speak. Also, the poems were selected with other people in mind, such as one might do in self-publishing a family history. For poets who are serious about their work, I recommend writing lots of poems, studying poetry techniques, and reading poems by others—all of which inevitably take poets and their poems to a higher level of professionalism.

Schartz: It may seem that way, but as the editor of the *Arizona Literary Magazine*, I can tell you each year our readers are eager to appreciate the talent of the Arizona Literary Contest finalists, and some poetry anthologies are doing very well with the public. All the poets I know are also avid poetry readers.

Wallace: Well, no I don't agree. At any given time, I'd estimate maybe several thousand poets are actively submitting manuscripts to contests. While poetry is rarely a bestseller, many more poetry books than that are being sold these days. The average sales figure for most poetry books is 500-1,500; hundreds of poetry books are published annually.

For more information on the contests highlighted in this interview, see the listings on pages 403, 462 (Arizona Authors Association); page 404 (The Backwaters Press); page 407 (Florida Freelance Writers Association); page 423 (Pennsylvania Poetry Society); and page 375 (University of Wisconsin Press).

Opening Doors to Poetry

by Vivé Griffith

T hose of us who write, read, and revel in poetry also tend to feel concerned about poetry's future. Our reasons are myriad: Each year new media hits the market to distract us from the written word. Small presses that publish poetry are struggling against increasingly large publishing conglomerates. Pop culture is obsessed with reality without giving much consideration to what's real.

The hope for poetry's future lies in our ability to reach the next generation of writers and readers. One of the most exciting ways that happens is by poets stepping directly into school classrooms.

Since 1964, when California Poets in the Schools started placing poets in Bay Area class-rooms to read poetry to children, programs matching accomplished writers with school-age children have sprung up all over the country. From large urban classrooms to one-room schoolhouses, after-school workshops to extended residencies, poets are reaching out to cultivate the next generation of poetry lovers. Their work serves as a call to all poets to do their part to bring poetry to youth.

Kids need poetry

Writing-in-the-schools programs do a lot to keep creative writing alive, but that's generally not the impetus behind the programs. The driving force is the belief that kids need poetry. They need it for the way it fosters imagination and a love of language, for the way it allows for mystery and reflection. The lack of emphasis on poetry in the standard curriculum, and the dry way it is often taught, may be bad for poetry, but it's even worse for kids.

"In the classroom, the artistic part of writing often gets overwhelmed by the academic needs," says Nancy Shapiro, director of New York City's Teachers & Writers Collaborative (TWC), one of the foremost writing-in-the-schools programs in the nation. "Our program aims to counteract that by bringing back passion and creativity and a commitment to the writing process."

TWC was formed when a group of writers and teachers joined forces to look at how they could improve writing in the classroom. Shapiro emphasizes the program was designed by both sides—those who write and those who teach kids to write—and continues to serve both sides. Today TWC reaches more than 30,000 students in the New York City area and publishes

VIVÉ GRIFFITH's poetry, stories, and essays have appeared in *Gettysburg Review*, *Antioch Review*, *Black Warrior Review*, and other magazines. She lives in Austin, Texas, where she's taught poetry to writers ranging from kindergart-ners to retirees.

an amazing array of books, as well as the tremendous resource *Teachers & Writers Magazine*.

One of the things Shapiro thinks kids gain from working with poets is the sense that there's not an answer to every question—an idea hardly embraced in the traditional school curriculum.

"We use adult poetry in the classroom with the belief children are capable of understanding and being insightful about poetry written for adults," she says. "You can take a complicated poet like Wallace Stevens and children will just go with it. They learn that it's okay to do that.

"Schools are not set up for kids to take risks. They're set up for kids to be successful. They want them to have answers."

Nowhere is this more obvious than in the move toward standardized testing in schools across the nation. The more teachers are pushed to focus their classes on the tests, the more they need help in bringing the creative back into their curriculums.

According to poet Naomi Shihab Nye, in a world of tests that deaden language, poetry is one of the things that keep kids awake. Nye has achieved veteran status after working for three decades with children in classrooms nationwide and publishing seven anthologies aimed at adolescent and teen audiences, in addition to her own poetry and prose. When Nye looks at schools today, she finds poetry particularly essential.

"The need for it is profoundly greater now than it was when I started out, even with all the efforts going on across the country, because of the emphasis on standardized testing and the belief that those tests give a sense of where students are. Many teachers are saddened by the fact they have to teach to a test, and more than ever before they need support to encourage their own students' voices."

When visiting with students, Nye reads her own poems as well as work by other poets. She often talks of growing up Palestinian-American, or of the characters she meets on airplanes, hikes, or in the streets of her own downtown neighborhood. And she gets students to write, asking them questions like "What have you lost?" and "Where do you come from?" The responses can be amazing.

Nye jokes that students sometimes tell her she would fail the state language arts test if she had to take it. (She stretches language out, and she doesn't obey the rules.) However, teachers tell Nye their students do better on the standardized tests if they have poetry and creative writing integrated into their curriculums.

"Kids will write better if we give them a chance to write in interesting ways," Nye says. "By sharing poetry with them, we give them a sense that there is a land of language—fascinating, textural, delicious language beyond the formulaic language of those tests."

Writers benefit, too

Even established writers can lose touch with the wonders of the land of language. Working with kids has a way of reminding them why they fell in love with poetry in the first place. In any program, there are those who will tell you—the people who benefit most are the writers themselves.

It's not only because writers are paid. (And in most programs they are. In fact, some programs are able to pay well enough to provide poets the rare opportunity to earn a living because they are practicing poets, rather than in spite of it. Other programs may provide supplemental income or other perks.) The more valuable gift to writers may be the wealth of surprises that comes from working with kids.

Children are still capable of simply delighting in a poem. Put a silly rhyme about smelly socks in front of a group of kindergartners, the rhythmic "The Love Song of J. Alfred Prufrock" in front of middle schoolers, or a tender poem about a first date in front of high school students, and the response is often pure appreciation. Instead of taking a poem apart, kids simply relish it. Adults, on the other hand, can forget this is still an option.

"Something magical happens between a writer and kids in the classroom, and that's a core situation we're re-creating over and over," says Robin Reagler, executive director of the Houston-based Writers in the Schools (WITS). "Kids are seeing the world as brand new, and writers are a lot like kids. So there's something really joyful about the way writers approach them.

"Our mission statement is 'WITS engages children in the pleasure and power of reading and writing,' " Reagler points out. "What a great thing if children's enjoyment of the writing process leads them to become lifelong readers of poetry."

While writers working with kids might find their own writing reinvigorated, they might discover an expanded literary community, too.

The formation of Austin, Texas-based Badgerdog Literary Publishing was driven in part because founder Melanie Moore missed being involved in a literary community. After finishing graduate work in creative writing, Moore entered the corporate world, where she stayed for years, exchanging novels for management manuals and poems for technology. In 2002, on the way home from a business trip, she read a novel for the first time in years. Within 90 days she had quit her job. Soon thereafter she created Badgerdog.

Badgerdog's program Youth Voice in Ink matches writers with students in area middle and high schools for twice-weekly after-school programs.

"I've always said I think we're serving two levels of writers here, the new and the experienced," Moore says. "I'm humbled by the caliber of talent that continues to accumulate around this project. And I think the people involved are creating a community you don't get when you're not in a graduate program."

In addition to training and support, Badgerdog supplies reading lists to keep writers on their toes, and conversation through periodic gatherings and a blog. Moore says she hopes to help writers participate on many levels in the national conversation about literary writing and reading. For her part, she's back in the world she loves, and her blood pressure is a lot lower.

Poetry in the everyday classroom

It would be naïve to suggest that all it takes is a visiting poet to keep poetry alive for the next generation. Visiting poets help, but so do teachers and parents.

While the standard curriculum may not place much emphasis on poetry, many teachers love poetry and make sure it has a place in the classroom, to the benefit of their students. For example, Jaynelle Nestle, a fifth-grade teacher at Casis Elementary in Austin, Texas, grew up loving words. Her mother writes poetry, and poetry is still part of her family gatherings. Nestle recalls a recent holiday visit when she and her mother rode a city bus across snowy Regina, Saskatchewan, and read Longfellow's "Evangeline" aloud.

It's not surprising, then, that poetry and literature are an integrated part of her classroom.

"Poetry is often kind of thought of as a unit," Nestle says, "and I don't like that it's something you just visit, because it can be something that really enriches your life."

Nestle starts the school year with a quote on the board, often a fragment of a poem or something from literature. When she calls class meetings, she has students sit in a circle and discuss different topics, one of which is the quote. As the year goes on, other quotes may appear. So will poems kids have written and Nestle has saved, or particularly penetrating lines from something the class has read.

"When my students write, I tell them writing is holy time," Nestle says. "It's a time set apart to be silent and to really treat as sacred. If you let kids and adults write whatever they want, often it comes out as poetry."

Attracting Young Readers to Poetry

1. **Find a writing-in-the-schools program in your area** and get involved. The Internet is a good source of information on such programs, and Houston's Writers in the Schools has formed a consortium of similar programs, with links available on their website (www.writersintheschools.org). If you don't want to teach in a program, support one financially.

2. **Look for opportunities** at state and local arts organizations. Many programs offer funding for individuals to work with children in schools and other community-based centers.

3. **Volunteer at a school in your area**, even if just for an hour each semester. Most teachers welcome visitors who can bring a skill and some enthusiasm to their classrooms.

4. **Look for other programs** that would enable you to bring poetry to youth—through libraries, youth centers, churches and synagogues, scouts—anywhere kids gather.

5. **Donate books of poems.** Poet Al Young suggests people donate poetry books to juvenile detention centers. Think about safe-place shelters, after-school programs for disadvantaged youth, and programs for teenage parents.

6. **Make sure poetry is part of your everyday world**, not set aside in a sanctified place. We all have a realm. Naomi Shihab Nye talks about office workers who post a poem a week on their bulletin boards. Read a poem to your family each night at the dinner table. Tuck poems into birthday cards. Think about infusing your life with lyricism. Others will notice.

What's important for Nestle is students leave her class having had the opportunity to look deeper into language, with a sense of the power of their own words.

She admits to a fear of poetry, and that her academic training didn't prepare her to teach poetry. Nestle has benefited, however, from professional development training with the New Jersey Writing Project in Texas (NJWPT), one of many programs across the country offering workshops that help teachers teach writing better. In some sense, such training is an extension of more traditional writing-in-the-schools programs. It acknowledges that teachers, interacting with their students every day, are best poised to get them writing.

"I started liking poetry because I liked writing it," Nestle says, "and I probably didn't even know it was poetry, except for the format I wrote it in. I definitely didn't know who Robert Frost or any other poets were, but writing was a door that opened and led me to reading them."

Opening doors

Nye uses the metaphor of opening a door as well, acknowledging you never really know how you'll affect children when you give them the chance to write in their own voices.

"Now and then someone comes back and says to me, 'I've always wanted to tell you what poetry has done for me,' " Nye says. "And I know *I* didn't make that happen. I just turned the doorknob. The door was already there."

Moore tells the story of a student that Badgerdog poet Farid Matuk worked with last year. The middle-school girl was diffident at the start of the program, Moore says. She was angry and excessively proud of her time spent in detention. Then one day Matuk gave the class an exercise to write about their mothers.

The girl started writing, kept writing after the rest of the class stopped, then took her journal home and continued writing. At the end of the program, she shared a long, sophisticated poem broken into sections, titled "All About My Mother," which she read at her school and the following fall at the Texas Book Festival.

"It would just rip your heart out," Moore says. "It had lines like, 'My mother gave me to my father like a gift, like a toy.' We found out later that for years her father had tried to get her to talk to him about her mother, who had abandoned her, but she wouldn't. Through the writing process, she was able to start to move through the experience."

The student has come back to Badgerdog's after-school workshops each semester since, and she and her friends can be seen in their middle-school hallways carrying their journals. Not all stories will be that dramatic, of course, and not all will end so successfully. But with each encounter with a young person, the possibility exists to leave a mark.

"Writing helps children take agency over the things happening in their worlds," Moore says. "They can't control very much in their lives, but they can control what happens on the page."

If we're lucky, taking young people to the page will help them see poetry not as an exercise in finding rhymes and counting meter, but as a source of enjoyment and maybe even transformation. It's the best bet we have for ensuring that poetry is a vital part of our cultural future. And with it comes the possibility of better test scores, a richer appreciation of language, and maybe even a perk or two we hadn't expected.

"All of us who have grown up loving poetry have the sense it's made us better people," Nye says. "It's given us a comfort and a satisfaction that the language of media and journalism has not. It's important we're creating students who can feel for others."

Armed with that belief, what else is there to do but step into a classroom and begin?

For more resources, see the Poets in Education section on page 488.

Mistakes Poets Make

In putting together listings for *Poet's Market*, we ask editors for any words of advice they want to share with our readers. Often the editors' responses include comments about what poets should and shouldn't do when submitting work—the same comments, over and over. That means there are a lot of poets repeating similar mistakes when they send out their poems for consideration.

The following list includes the most common of those mistakes—the ones poets should work hardest to avoid.

Not reading a publication before submitting work

Researching a publication is essential before submitting your poetry. Try to buy a sample copy of a magazine (by mail, if necessary) or at least see if an issue is available at the library. It may not be economically feasible for poets to purchase a copy of every magazine they target, especially if they send out a lot of poems. However, there are additional ways to familiarize yourself with a publication.

Read the market listing thoroughly. If guidelines are available, send for them by e-mail or regular mail, or check for them online. A publication's website often presents valuable information, including sample poems, magazine covers—and guidelines.

Submitting inappropriate work

Make good use of your research so you're sure you understand what a magazine publishes. Don't rationalize that a journal favoring free verse might jump at the chance to consider your long epic poem in heroic couplets. Don't convince yourself your experimental style will be a good fit for the traditional journal filled with rhyming poetry. Don't go into denial about whether a certain journal and your poetry are made for each other. It's counterproductive and ultimately wastes postage (not to mention your time and the editor's).

Submitting an unreasonable number of poems

If an editor recommends sending between three and five poems (a typical range), don't send six. Don't send a dozen poems and tell the editor to pick the five she wants to consider. If the editor doesn't specify a number (or the listing says "no limit"), don't take that as an invitation to mail off 20 poems. The editors and staff of literary magazines are busy enough as it is, and they may decide they don't have time to cope with you. (When submitting book or chapbook manuscripts to publishers, make sure your page count falls within the range they state.)

Don't go to the other extreme and send only *one* poem, unless an editor says it's okay (which is rare). One poem doesn't give an editor much of a perspective on your work, and it doesn't give you very good odds on getting the piece accepted.

Ignoring the editor's preferences regarding formats

If an editor makes a point of describing a preferred manuscript format, follow it, even if that format seems to contradict the standard. (Standard format includes using $8\frac{1}{2} \times 11$ white paper and conventional typeface and point size; avoid special graphics, colors, or type flourishes; put your name and address on every page.) Don't devise your own format to make your submission stand out. Keep everything clean, crisp, and easy to read (and professional).

Be alert to e-mail submission formats. Follow directions regarding what the editor wants printed in the subject line, how many poems to include in a single e-mail, whether to use attachments or paste work in the body of the message, and other elements. Editors have good reasons for outlining their preferences; ignoring them could mean having your e-mail deleted before your poems are even read.

Omitting a self-addressed, stamped envelope (SASE)

Why do editors continuously say "include a SASE with your submission"? Because so many poets don't do it. Here's a simple rule: Unless the editor gives alternate instructions, include a #10 SASE, whether submitting poems or sending an inquiry.

Writing bad cover letters (or omitting them completely)

Cover letters have become an established part of the submission process. There are editors who remain indifferent about the necessity of a cover letter, but many consider it rude to be sent a submission without any other communication from the poet.

Unless the editor says otherwise, send a cover letter. Keep it short and direct, a polite introduction of you and your work. (See page 11 in "Frequently Asked Questions" for more tips on cover letters, and an example.) Here are a few important Don'ts:

- **Don't** list all the magazines where your work has appeared; limit yourself to five magazine titles. The work you're submitting has to stand on its own.
- **Don't** tell the editor what a good poet you are—or how good someone else thinks you are.
- **Don't** tell the editor how to edit, lay out, or print your poem. Some of those decisions are up to the editor, assuming she decides to accept your poem in the first place.
- **Don't** point out the poem is copyrighted in your name or include the copyright symbol. All poems are automatically copyrighted in the poet's name as soon as they're "fixed" (i.e., written down), and editors know this.

Not maintaining good editor/poet relations

Most editors are hard-working poetry lovers dedicated to finding and promoting good work. They aspire to turn submissions around as quickly as possible and to treat all poets with respect. They don't want to steal your work. They often aren't paid for their labor and probably are lucky if they don't have to dip into their own pockets just to keep their magazines going.

Poets should finesse their communications with editors regarding problems, especially in initial letters and e-mail. Editors (and their magazines and presses) aren't service-oriented businesses, like the phone company. Getting huffy with an editor as if arguing with your cable provider about an overcharge is inappropriate. Attitude isn't going to get you anywhere; in fact, it could create additional obstacles.

That's not to say poets shouldn't feel exasperated when they're inconvenienced or ill treated. None of us likes to see our creations vanish, or to pay good money for something we're never going to receive (like a subscription or sample copy). However, exasperated is one thing; outraged is another. Too often poets go on the offensive with editors and make matters worse. Experts on making effective complaints recommend you keep your cool and stay professional, no matter what kind of problem you're trying to work out.

For additional advice on editor/poet relations, see "Dealing With Problem Editors" on page 30.

Articles & Information

Dealing With Problem Editors

There *are* problem editors out there, and we've all encountered them at one time or another. Some rip people off, prey on poets' desires to be published, or treat poets and their work with flagrant disregard. Fortunately, such editors are very much in the minority.

Now and then you may discover the disorganized editor or the overwhelmed editor; these two cause heartache (and heartburn) by closing up shop without returning manuscripts, or failing to honor paid requests for subscriptions and sample copies. More often than not, their transgressions are rooted in chaos and irresponsibility, not malicious intent. Frustrating as such editors are, they're not out to get you.

There are many instances, too, where larger circumstances are beyond an editor's control. For example, a college-oriented journal may be student-staffed, with editors changing each academic year. Funds for the journal may be cut unexpectedly by administration belt-tightening, or a grant could be cancelled. The editorial office may be moved to another part of the university. An exam schedule could impact a publishing schedule. All of these things cause problems and delays.

Then again, a literary journal may be a one-person, home-based operation. The editor may get sick or have an illness in the family. Her regular job may suddenly demand lots of overtime. There may be divorce or death with which the editor has to cope. A computer could crash. Or the editor may need to scramble for money before the magazine can go to the printer. Emergencies happen, and they take their toll on deadlines. The last thing the editor wants is to inconvenience poets and readers, but sometimes life gets in the way.

Usually, difficulties with these kinds of "problem" editors can be resolved satisfactorily through communication and patience. There are always exceptions, though. Here are a few typical situations with problem editors and how to handle them:

An editor is rude. If it's a matter of bad attitude, take it with a grain of salt. Maybe he's having a rotten day. If there's abusive language and excessive profanity involved, let us know about it. (See the complaint procedure on page 31.)

An editor harshly criticizes your poem. If an editor takes time to comment on your poetry, even if the feedback seems overly critical, consider the suggestions with an open mind and try to find something valid and useful in them. If, after you've given the matter fair consideration, you think the editor was out of line, don't rush to defend your poetry or wave your bruised ego in the editor's face. Allow that the editor has a right to her opinion (which you're not obligated to take as the final word on the quality of your work), forget about it, and move on.

An editor is slow to respond to a submission. As explained above, there may be many reasons why an editor's response takes longer than the time stated in the market listing or guidelines. Allow a few more weeks to pass beyond the deadline, then write a polite inquiry about the status of your manuscript. (Include a SASE if sending by regular mail.) Understand an editor may not be able to read your letter right away if deadlines are pressing or if he is embroiled in a personal crisis. It's hard, but try to be patient. However, if you haven't received a reply to your inquiry after a month or so, it's time for further action.

An editor won't return your manuscript. Decide whether you want to invest any more time in this journal or publisher. If you conclude you've been patient long enough, write a firm but professional letter to the editor withdrawing your manuscript from consideration. Request the manuscript be returned; but know, too, a truly indifferent editor probably won't bother to send it back or reply in any way. Keep a copy of your withdrawal letter for your files, make a new copy of your manuscript, and look for a better market.

Also, contact *Poet's Market* by letter or e-mail with details of your experience. We always look into problems with editors, although we don't withdraw a listing on the basis of a single complaint unless we discover further evidence of consistent misbehavior. We do, however, keep complaints on file and watch for patterns of unacceptable behavior from any specific market.

An editor takes your money. If you sent a check for a subscription or sample copy you haven't yet received, review your bank statement to see if the check has been cashed. If it has, send the editor a query mentioning she has cashed your check, but you have yet to receive the material you were expecting. Give the editor the benefit of the doubt: an upcoming issue of a magazine could be running late, your subscription could have been overlooked by mistake, or your copy could have been lost in transit or sent in error to the wrong address.

If your check has *not* been cashed, query the editor to see if your order was ever received. It may have been lost (in the mail or on the editor's desk), the editor may be holding several checks to cash at one time, or the editor may be waiting to cash checks until a tardy issue is finally published.

In either case, if you get an unsatisfactory response from the editor (or no response at all), wait a few weeks and try again. If the matter still has not been resolved, let us know about it. We're especially interested in publishers who take money from poets but don't

Complaint Procedure

If you feel you have not been treated fairly by a market listed in *Poet's Market*, we advise you to take the following steps:

Important

- First, try to contact the market. Sometimes one phone call or letter can quickly clear up the matter. Document all your communications with the market.

- When you contact us with a complaint, provide the details of your submission, the date of your first contact with the market, and the nature of your subsequent communication.

- We will file a record of your complaint and further investigate the market.

- The number and severity of complaints will be considered when deciding whether or not to delete a market from the next edition of *Poet's Market*.

deliver the goods. Be sure to send us all the details of the transaction, plus copies of any correspondence (yours and the editor's). We can't pursue your situation in any legal way, but we can ban an unscrupulous publisher from *Poet's Market* and keep the information as a resource in case we get later complaints.

Should you continue trying to get your money back from such editors? That's your decision. If your loss is under $10 (say, for a subscription or sample copy), it might cost you less in the long run to let the matter go. And the fee for a "stop payment" order on a check can be hefty—possibly more than the amount you sent the editor in the first place. Yes, it's infuriating to be cheated, but sometimes fighting on principle costs more than it's worth.

If your monetary loss is significant (for instance, you shelled out a couple hundred dollars in a subsidy publishing agreement), consider contacting your state attorney general's office for advice about small claims court, filing a complaint, and other actions you can take.

Are You Being Taken?

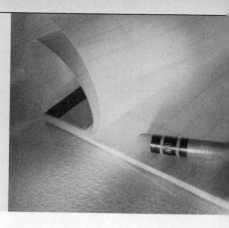

There are many publishing opportunities for poets, from traditional magazines and journals to contests, websites, and anthologies. Along with that good news comes this warning: There are also many opportunities for poets to be taken. How do you know whether an opportunity is legitimate? Listed below are some of the most common situations that cost poets disappointment, frustration—and cash. Watch out for them when you're submitting your work, and *don't* let your vanity be your guide.

ANTHOLOGIES

Has this happened to you? You see an ad in a perfectly respectable publication announcing a poetry contest with big cash prizes. You enter, and later you receive a glowing letter congratulating you on your exceptional poem, which the contest sponsor wants to include in his deluxe hardbound anthology of the best poetry submitted to the contest. The anthology costs only $55 (or whatever, could be more). You don't have to buy it—they'll still publish your poem—but wouldn't you be proud to own one? And wouldn't it be nice to buy additional copies to give to family and friends? And for an extra charge you can include a biographical note. And so on . . .

Of course, when the anthology arrives, you may be disappointed. The quality of the poetry isn't what you were expecting, with several poems crammed unattractively onto a page. It turns out everyone who entered the contest was invited to be published; you basically paid cash to see your poem appear in a phone book-like volume with no literary merit at all.

Are you being taken? Depends on how you look at it. If you bought into the flattery heaped on you and believed you were being published in an exclusive, high-quality publication, no doubt you feel duped. On the other hand, if all you were after was seeing your poem in print, even knowing you'd have to pay for the privilege, then you got what you wanted. (Unless you've deceived yourself into believing you've truly won an honor and now have a worthy publishing credit; you don't).

You'll really feel taken if you fall for additional spiels, like having your poem printed on coffee mugs and t-shirts (you can do this yourself through print shops or online services like www.cafepress.com.) or spending large sums on awards banquets and conferences. Also, find out what rights the contest sponsor acquires before you submit a single line of poetry. You may be relinquishing all rights to your poem simply by mailing it in or submitting it through a website. If the poem no longer belongs to you, the publisher can do whatever he wishes with it. Don't let your vanity propel you into a situation you'll always regret.

READING AND CONTEST FEES

Suppose you notice a promising market for your poetry, but the editor requires a set fee just to consider your work. You see a contest that interests you, but you have to pay the sponsor fee just to enter. Are you being taken?

In the case of reading fees, keep these points in mind: Is the market so exceptional that you feel it's worth risking the cost of the reading fee to have your work considered? What makes it so much better than markets that do *not* charge fees? Has the market been around awhile, with an established publishing schedule? What are you paid if your work is accepted? Are reasonably priced samples available so you can judge the production values and quality of the writing?

Reading fees don't necessarily signal a suspicious market. In fact, they're increasingly popular as editors struggle with the costs of publishing books and magazines, including the man-hours required to read loads of (often bad) submissions. However, fees represent an additional financial burden on poets, who often don't receive any monetary reward for their poems to begin with. It's really up to individual poets to decide whether paying a fee is beneficial to their publishing efforts. Think long and hard about fee-charging markets that are new and untried, don't pay poets for their work (at the very least a print publication should offer a contributor's copy), charge high prices for sample copies, or set fees that seem unreasonable ($1/poem is an average fee).

Entry fees for contests often are less worrisome. Usually, these funds cover prizes, judges' fees, and expenses of running and promoting the contest (including publishing a "prize" issue of a magazine). Other kinds of contests charge entry fees, from Irish dancing competitions to bake-offs at a county fair. Why not poetry contests?

That's not to say you shouldn't be cautious. Watch out for contests that charge higher-than-average fees, especially if the fees are out of proportion to the amount of prize money being given. (Look through the Contests & Awards section beginning on page 400 to get a sense of what most competitions charge; you'll also find contests in listings throughout the Publishers of Poetry section, beginning on page 38.) Try to find out how long the contest has been around, and verify whether prizes have been awarded each year and to whom. In the case of book and chapbook contests, send for a sample copy to confirm the publisher puts out a quality product. Beware any contest that tells you you've won something, then demands payment for an anthology, trophy, or other item. (It's okay if a group offers an anthology for a modest price without providing winners with free copies. Most state poetry societies have to do this; but they also present cash awards in each category of the contest, and their entry fees are low.) See "Roundtable: Poetry Contests" on page 16 for more advice on evaluating poetry contests.

SUBSIDY PUBLISHERS

Poetry books are a hard sell to the book-buying public. Few of the big publishers handle them, and those that do feature the "name" poets (major prize winners and contemporary masters with breathtaking reputations). Even the small presses publish only so many books per year—far less than the number of poets writing.

No wonder poets feel desperate enough to turn to subsidy publishers (also called "vanity publishers"). These operations charge a sum to print a given number of copies of a poetry book. They promise promotion and distribution; the poet receives a certain percentage of the print run, along with a promise of royalties after the printing costs are met.

Are you being taken? The situation sounds okay, but the whole picture is painted rosier than it really is. Often the sum the publisher charges is inflated, and the finished books may be of dubious quality. Bookstores won't stock subsidy-published books (especially poetry), and promotion efforts often consist of sending review copies far and wide, even though such volumes are rarely reviewed. In some particularly tricky situations, the poet may not even own rights to his or her work any more. Regardless, the poet is left with a stack of unsold books (it's not unusual for the publisher to offer the balance of the print run to the poet for a certain price). What appeared to be a dream realized turns out to be a dead end.

Before shelling out huge sums of money to a subsidy publisher for more books than you'll ever need, consider self-publishing. Literary history is starred with great poets who published their own works (Walt Whitman is one of the most well known). Talk to some local printers about the kind of book you have in mind, see what's involved, and get some price quotes. If the cost is too high for your budget, consider doing a more modest publication. Chapbooks (about 24 pages) are an ideal length and can be produced attractively, softbound and saddle-stapled, for a reasonable cost. (You can even lay out and typeset the whole chapbook on your computer.) You'll have something beautiful to share with family and friends, to sign and sell at readings, and you might be able to persuade a supportive local bookstore to put a few copies on its shelves. Best of all, you'll still own and control your work; and if you turn a profit, every cent goes to you.

Obviously, poets who don't stay on their toes may find themselves preyed upon. And a questionable publishing opportunity doesn't have to be an out-and-out rip-off for you to feel cheated. In every situation, you have a choice *not* to participate. Exercise that choice, or at least develop a healthy sense of skepticism before you fling yourself and your poetry at the first smooth talker who compliments your work. Poets get burned because they're much too impatient to see their work in print. Calm your ego, slow down, and devote that time, energy, and money toward reading other poets and improving your own writing. You'll find that getting published will eventually take care of itself.

Helpful Websites

For More Info

The following websites include specific information about questionable poetry publishers and awards. For more websites of value to poets, see Additional Resources on page 479.

- Answers to frequently asked questions about poetry awards from the Academy of American Poets: *www.poets.org/awards/faq.cfm*

- Poets will find warnings and other valuable publishing information on the Preditors & Editors website: *www.anotherealm.com/prededitors/*

- Writer Beware tracks contests, publishers, and literary agents: *www.sfwa.org/beware*

- "Literary Contest Caution" at http://windpub.com/literary.scams

Self-Promotion

A Chance to Share

These days, all writers have to become involved in promoting themselves and their work. This is especially true for poets. Does the idea of "putting yourself out there" make you uncomfortable? Think of self-promotion as a means of sharing poetry as well as promoting it. Here are a few suggestions to get you started:

Meet the public

Do poetry readings and book signings. Get in touch with bookstores and coffeehouses: call, send postcards (see below) or press releases, let them know you're available. Find out when and where open mic readings are scheduled. Sign up, read your poems. If you've published a book or chapbook, be creative about handselling your collection. It's hard to break into the big chain bookstores, but the small, independent stores may be happy to stock your publication (especially if you're a local author) and arrange a book signing.

Widen your scope: Would the local historical society be interested in an appearance? Is there a community group who might enjoy having you read and sign books as part of their meeting program? Would a friend be willing to sponsor a "poetry night" house party with you as the featured reader?

Do postcards

Think specially designed postcards, not the plain ones you buy at the post office. You can create postcards on your computer, or paste up a master design from typewritten copy and clip art. If you design the postcards on your computer, you can print them out yourself as well. (Special perforated postcard stock for home printers is available in various sizes at your local office supply store.) Or you can take your master design to a quick-print shop and have the postcards printed there. (If you're printing a lot of postcards, this might be the less expensive option.)

Postcards can be informational (i.e., used to announce a reading or new publication). They can also be used to share your poetry. Simply type one of your poems on one side of the card, using an attractive, readable font. Leave the other side blank; or, if the poem is from a book or chapbook you want to promote, indicate the title of the collection and include ordering information. Keep all text and design elements on the far left side of the postcard back so they don't interfere with the addressee portion of the card.

Postcard mailings get results, but remember that postcards don't have to be mailed to be effective. Don't be shy about giving out postcards at readings, especially your poem postcards. Offer to sign them. Your audience will enjoy having a personalized souvenir of your reading, and they may decide later to order your book or chapbook.

Use your poem postcards for personal communications, too. Turn a simple note into a chance to enhance someone's day with poetry.

Step into the media spotlight

It doesn't have to be a *big* spotlight. Your community newspaper probably prints "news-maker" tidbits like award and publication announcements, and it may even be interested in doing a feature on a "local poet." (Regional magazines are another possibility.) Newspapers usually have calendar sections where you can list a reading or bookstore appearance. (Be sure to provide all the necessary details.) TV and radio stations may also broadcast arts and entertainment calendars, and locally produced programs may be very happy to schedule a poet for an interview segment or to promote a reading. You never know until you ask. (Be polite, never pushy.)

Create a website

It's helpful to have a URL to list on press releases, business cards, and postcards. A website is a shortcut for anyone who wants to know more about you, from biographical information to samples of your poetry. Your website can be as complicated or as simple as you wish. There are plenty of books and software programs available to help, even if you're a first-timer with limited computer skills. There's also a lot of free information on the Web, from tutorials to HTML guides. Enter the words "basic web development" or "beginner web development" in your favorite search engine to call up all the resources you'll need. (Also, the word processing software on your computer may provide how-tos and automatic formatting for web page development.)

Whether you try these approaches or come up with some new, creative techniques of your own, don't hesitate to promote yourself and your work. Every reading, book signing, interview, and website is an opportunity to attract new readers to poetry.

Important Market Listing Information

Important

- Listings are based on questionnaires completed by editors and on subsequent verified copy. Listings are not advertisements, *nor* are markets necessarily endorsed by the editors of this book.

- Information in the listings comes directly from the publishers and is as accurate as possible. However, publications and editors come and go, and poetry needs fluctuate between the publication date of this directory and the date of purchase.

- If you are a poetry publisher and would like to be considered for a listing in the next edition, send a SASE (or SAE and IRC) with your request for a questionnaire to *Poet's Market*—QR, 4700 East Galbraith Road, Cincinnati OH 45236, or e-mail us at poetsmarket@fwpubs.com. Questionnaires and questionnaire requests received after February 7, 2006, will be held for the 2008 edition.

- *Poet's Market* reserves the right to exclude any listing that does not meet its requirements.

Publishers of Poetry

In today's literary world, poetry is published in a variety of ways: in magazines; in literary and academic journals; in books and chapbooks produced by both large and small presses; in anthologies assembled by poetry societies and other groups; on CDs and tapes that feature poets reading their own work; and on the Internet in sites ranging from individual web pages to sophisticated digital publications.

In *Poet's Market*, we strive to gather as much information about these markets as possible. Each listing in the Publishers of Poetry section gives an overview of the various activities for a single operation as described by the editors/publishers who replied to our queries. These include magazines/journals, books/chapbooks, contests, workshops, readings, organizations, and whatever else each editor/publisher thinks will be of interest to our readers. For those publishers with projects at different addresses, or who requested their activities be broken out into other sections of the book, we've cross-referenced the listings so the overview will be complete.

HOW LISTINGS ARE FORMATTED

To organize all this information within each listing, we follow a basic format:

Symbols. Each listing begins with symbols that reflect various aspects of that operation: (**N**) this market is recently established and new to *Poet's Market*; (**⚄**) this market did not appear in the 2005 edition; (**✿**) this market is located in Canada or (**⊕**) outside the U.S. and Canada; (**$**) this market pays a monetary amount (as opposed to contributor's copies); (**□**) this market welcomes submissions from beginning poets; (**◪**) this market prefers submissions from skilled, experienced poets, will consider work from beginning poets; (**◉**) this market prefers submissions from poets with a high degree of skill and experience; (**◎**) this market has a specialized focus (listed in parentheses after title); and (**⊘**) this market is currently closed to *all* submissions. (Keys to these symbols are listed on the inside covers of this book and on page 4.)

Contact Information. Next you'll find all the information you need to contact the market, as provided by each editor/publisher: names (in bold) of all operations associated with the market (with areas of specialization noted in parentheses where appropriate); regular mail address; telephone number; fax number; e-mail address; website address; year the market was established; the name of the person to contact; and membership in small press/publishing organizations (when provided).

Magazine Needs: This is an important section to study as you research potential markets. Here you'll find the editor's overview of the operation and stated preferences (often in his or her own words), plus a list of recently published poets; production information about the market (size of publication, printing/binding methods, art/graphics); statistics regarding the number of submissions the market receives vs. the number accepted; and distribution and price information.

How to Submit: Another important section. This one gets down to specifics—how many poems to send; minimum/maximum number of lines; preferences regarding previously published poems and simultaneous submissions, as well as electronic submissions; payment, rights, and response times; and a lot more.

Book/Chapbook Needs & How to Submit: Same as the information for magazines with added information tailored to book/chapbook publishers.

Contest/Award Offerings: Information about prizes and competitions associated with the market.

Also Offers: Check this section for conferences/workshops, readings and other activities, or organizations sponsored by or affiliated with the market.

Advice: Offers direct quotes from editors and publishers about everything from pet peeves to tips on writing to views on the state of poetry today.

GETTING STARTED, FINDING MARKETS

If you don't have a publisher in mind, just begin reading through the listings, possibly making notes as you go (don't hesitate to write in the margins, underline, use highlighters; it also helps to flag markets that interest you with Post-it Notes). Browsing the listings is an effective way to familiarize yourself with the information presented and the publishing opportunities available.

If you have a specific market in mind, however, begin with the General Index. This is where *all* listings are alphabetized (i.e., all the markets included within a single listing). For instance, what if you want to check out Frith Press? If you turn to the "F" listings in the Publishers of Poetry section, you won't find this publisher. The information appears as part of the *Ekphrasis* listing (along with the *Ekphrasis* Prize). In the General Index, though, Frith Press is listed individually along with the page number for *Ekphrasis* so you can go straight to the source for the information you need. (Sound confusing? Try it, it works.)

The General Index also lists markets from the 2005 edition that don't appear in this book, along with a two-letter code explaining the absence (see the introduction to the General Index on page 544 for an explanation of these codes). In addition, markets that have changed names since the 2005 edition are listed in the General Index, cross referenced to the new titles.

REFINE YOUR SEARCH

In addition to the General Index, we provide several more specific indexes to help you refine your marketing plan for your poems. The editors/publishers themselves have indicated how and where they want their listings indexed, and not every listing appears in one of these specific indexes. Therefore, use them only to supplement your other research efforts:

Chapbook Publishers Index provides a breakdown of markets that publish chapbooks.

Book Publishers Index indicates markets looking for book-length collections of poetry.

Openness to Submissions Index breaks out markets according to the symbols (⬓ ◑ ◐ ◉) that appear at the beginning of each listing—signposts indicating the level of writing a market prefers to see. (For an explanation of these symbols, see page 4 or the inside covers of this book.)

Geographical Index sorts markets by state and by countries outside the U.S. Some markets are more open to poets from their region, so use this index when you're pinpointing local opportunities.

Subject Index groups markets into categories according to areas of interest. These include all specialized markets (appearing with the ◉ symbol) as well as broader categories such as online markets, poetry for children, markets that consider translations, and others. Save time when looking for a specific type of market by checking this index first.

THE NEXT STEP

Once you know how to interpret the listings in this section and identify markets for your work, the next step is to start submitting your poems. See "Getting Started (and Using This Book)" on page 2 and "Frequently Asked Questions" on page 7 for advice, guidelines about preparing your manuscript, and proper submission procedures.

ADDITIONAL INFORMATION

The Publishers of Poetry section includes six Insider Reports: **Robert Stewart**, poet, essayist, and editor of *New Letters*, discusses the 70-year history of his magazine and the transformative power of great writing; **Sandra Alcosser**, poet and activist, talks about her work on the poetry installation at New York City's Central Park Zoo; **David Tucker**, a career journalist as well as an award-winning poet, shares his perspectives on exploring the everyday in his poems; **Jessie Lendennie**, co-founder and managing editor of Salmon Publishing, comments on the press and its impact on the poetry scene in Ireland; **Keith Taylor**, poet and editor, examines the lifestyle of a poet and the commitments it demands; and **Alessio Zanelli**, an Italian poet who publishes internationally, explains the challenges and rewards of adopting English as his language of literary expression.

This section also includes the covers of nine literary magazines that reflect the range of print publications being produced today. Such images tell a lot about a publication's style and content, as do the accompanying comments by editors regarding why the cover images were selected. (When evaluating a potential market for your work, consider everything that makes up the product—the poets being published, style and quality of content, guidelines, editorial comments, cover art, and even ads.)

And remember, the opportunities in the Publishers of Poetry section are only part of the picture. Study the sections that follow (Contests & Awards, Conferences & Workshops, Organizations, and Additional Resources) for more market leads, competitions, and educational and informational sources of special interest to poets.

◐ A SMALL GARLIC PRESS (ASGP); AGNIESZKA'S DOWRY (AgD)

5445 N. Sheridan Rd., #3003, Chicago IL 60640. E-mail: marek@enteract.com and ketzle@ketzle. net (send submissions to both e-mail addresses simultaneously). Website: http://asgp.org. Established 1995. **Contact:** Marek Lugowski and katrina grace craig, co-editors.

Magazine Needs *Agnieszka's Dowry (AgD)* is "a magazine published both in print and as a permanent Internet installation of poems and graphics, letters to Agnieszka. The print version consists of professionally crafted chapbooks. The online version comprises fast-loading pages employing an intuitive if uncanny navigation in an interesting space, all conducive to fast and comfortable reading. No restrictions on form or type. We use contextual and juxtapositional tie-ins with other material in making choices, so visiting the online *AgD* or reading a chapbook of an *AgD* issue is required of anyone making a submission." Single copy: $2 plus $2 shipping, if ordered from website by an individual. Make checks payable to A Small Garlic Press.

How to Submit Submit 5-10 poems at a time, by e-mail to Katja and Marek simultaneously. "Please inform us of the status of publishing rights." Accepts e-mail submissions only (pasted into body of message in plain text), "unless you are in prison—prisoners may make submissions by regular mail, and we will waive the requirement that they read a print issue." Sometimes comments on rejected poems. Guidelines and annotated catalog available on website only. Responds online or by SASE usually in 2 months. Pays one contributor's copy. Acquires one-time rights where applicable.

Book/Chapbook Needs & How to Submit A Small Garlic Press (ASGP) publishes up to 3 chapbooks of poetry/year. Query with a full online ms, ASCII (plain text) only.

◐ ◎ THE AARDVARK ADVENTURER; THE ARMCHAIR AESTHETE; PICKLE GAS PRESS (Specialized: humor)

31 Rolling Meadows Way, Penfield NY 14526. (585)388-6968. E-mail: bypaul@netacc.net. Established 1996. **Contact:** Paul Agosto, editor.

Magazine Needs *The Aardvark Adventurer* is "a quarterly family-fun newsletter-style zine of humor, thought, and verse. Very short stories (less than 500 words) are sometimes included." Prefers "light, humorous verse; any style; any 'family-acceptable' subject matter. Nothing obscene, overly forboding; no graphic gore or violence." Has published poetry by Paul Humphrey, Ray Gallucci, Max Gutmann, and Theone DiRocco. *The Aardvark Adventurer* is 6-12 pages, $8\frac{1}{2} \times 14$, photocopied, corner-stapled. Receives about 500 poems/year, accepts about 40%. Press run is 150 (100 subscribers). Single copy: $2; subscription: $5. Make checks payable to Paul Agosto. "Subscription not required, but subscribers given preference."

Magazine Needs Also publishes *The Armchair Aesthete*, a quarterly zine of "thoughtful, well-crafted, concise fiction and poetry. Interested in more fiction submissions than poetry though." *The Armchair Aesthete* is 40-60 pages, digest-sized, quality desktop-published, photocopied, with card cover, includes ads for other publications and writers' available chapbooks. Receives about 300 poems/year, accepts about 25-30%. Subscription: $10/year. Sample postpaid: $3. Make checks payable to Paul Agosto.

How to Submit Lines/poem: 32 maximum (*Aardvark*); 30 maximum (*Armchair*). For both publications, accepts previously published poems and simultaneous submissions, if indicated. Accepts e-mail submissions (pasted into body of message). Cover letter is preferred. Time between acceptance and publication is up to 9 months. Seldom comments on rejected poems. *The Aardvark Adventurer* occasionally publishes theme issues, but *The Armchair Aesthete* does not. Guidelines for both magazines available for SASE. Responds in 2 months. Pays one contributor's copy. Acquires one-time rights. The staff of *The Aardvark Adventurer* reviews books and chapbooks of poetry in 100 words. The staff of *The Armchair Aesthete* occasionally reviews chapbooks. Send materials for review consideration.

Advice "*The Aardvark Adventurer,* a newsletter-style publication with a very playful format, is a perfect opportunity for the aspiring poet."

◐ ABBEY; ABBEY CHEAPOCHAPBOOKS

5360 Fallriver Row Court, Columbia MD 21044. E-mail: greisman@aol.com. Established 1970. **Contact:** David Greisman, editor.

Magazine Needs & How to Submit *Abbey*, "a more-or-less quarterly informalzine looking for poetry that does for the mind what the first sip of Molson Ale does for the palate. No pornography or politics." Has published poetry and artwork by Richard Peabody, Robin Merrill, Patricia Rourke, Ruth Moon Kempher, D.E. Steward, Carol Hamilton, Harry Calhoun, Wayne Hogan, and Edmund Conti. With the exception of landmark issues like 2004's *Abbey* #100, a 100-plus-page extravaganza, the usual *Abbey* is 20-26 pages, magazine-sized, photocopied, and held together with one low-alloy metal staple in the top left corner. Receives about 1,000 poems/year, accepts about 150. Press run is 200. Subscription: $2. Sample: 50¢. Responds in one month "except during baseball season." Pays 1-2 contributor's copies.

Book/Chapbook Needs & How to Submit *Abbey Cheapochapbooks* come out once or twice every 5 years, averaging 10-15 pages. For chapbook consideration, query with 4-6 samples, bio, and list of publications. Responds in 2 months "including baseball season." Pays 25-50 author's copies.

Advice The editor says he is "definitely seeing poetry from two schools—the nit'n'grit school and the textured/reflective school. I much prefer the latter."

✪ ◙ ◎ ABRAXAS MAGAZINE; GHOST PONY PRESS (Specialized: lyric poetry)

P.O. Box 260113, Madison WI 53726-0113. (608)238-0175. E-mail: abraxaspress@hotmail.com or ghostponypress@hotmail.com. Website: www.geocities.com/Paris/4614. *Abraxas* established in 1968 by James Bertolino and Warren Woessner; Ghost Pony Press established in 1980 by editor/publisher Ingrid Swanberg. **Contact:** Ingrid Swanberg (for both presses).

Magazine Needs & How to Submit *Abraxas* **no longer considers unsolicited material**, except as announced as projects arise. Interested in poetry that is "contemporary lyric, experimental, and poetry in translation." Does not want to see "political posing; academic regurgitations. When submitting translations, please include poems in the original language as well." Has published poetry by William Stafford, Ivan Argüelles, Denise Levertov, César Vallejo, and Andrea Moorhead. *Abraxas* is up to 80 pages (160 pages, double issues), digest-sized, flat-spined (saddle-stapled with smaller issues), litho-offset, with original art on matte card cover. Appears "irregularly, 9- to 12-month intervals or much longer." Press run is 600 (500 subscribers, 150 libraries). Subscription: $16/4 issues (US), $20/4 issues (Canada, Mexico, and overseas). Sample: $4 ($8 double issues). *Abraxas* will announce submission guidelines as projects arise. Pays one contributor's copy plus 40% discount on additional copies.

Book/Chapbook Needs & How to Submit To submit to Ghost Pony Press, inquire with SASE plus 5-10 poems and cover letter. Accepts previously published material for book publication by Ghost Pony Press. Editor sometimes comments briefly on rejected poems. Submissions by post only; no e-mail submissions. No promised response time. "We currently have a considerable backlog." Payment varies per project. Send SASE for catalog to buy samples. Has published three books of poetry by próspero saíz including *the bird of nothing & other poems*: 168 pages, 7×10, with sewn and wrapped binding; paperback available for $20 (signed and numbered edition is $35). Also published *Zen Concrete & Etc.* by d.a. levy: 268 pages, magazine-sized, perfect-bound, illustrated; paperback available for $27.50.

Advice "Ghost Pony Press is a small press publisher of poetry books; *Abraxas* is a literary journal publishing contemporary poetry, criticism, and translations. Do not confuse these separate presses!"

⊕ ◐ ACUMEN MAGAZINE; EMBER PRESS

6 The Mount, Higher Furzeham, Brixham, South Devon TQ5 8QY England. Website: www.acumen-poetry.co.uk. Press established 1971. *Acumen* established 1984. **Contact:** Patricia Oxley, poetry editor.

Magazine Needs *Acumen* appears 3 times/year (in January, May, and September) and is a "general literary magazine with emphasis on good poetry." Wants "well-crafted, high-quality, imaginative poems showing a sense of form. No experimental verse of an obscene type." Has published poetry by Ruth Padel, William Oxley, Hugo Williams, Peter Porter, Danielle Hope, and Leah Fritz. *Acumen* is 100 pages, A5, perfect-bound. "We aim to publish 120 poems out of 12,000 received." Press run is 650 (400 subscribers, 20 libraries). Subscription: $45 surface/$50 air. Sample: $15.

How to Submit Submit 5-6 poems at a time. Accepts simultaneous submissions, if not submitted to UK magazines; no previously published poems. Responds in one month. Pays "by negotiation" and one contributor's copy. Staff reviews books of poetry in up to 300 words (single-book format) or 600 words (multi-book format). Send materials for review consideration to Glyn Pursglove, 25 St. Albans Rd., Brynmill, Swansea, West Glamorgan SA2 0BP Wales. "If a reply is required, please send IRCs. One IRC for a decision, 3 IRCs if work is to be returned."

Advice "Read *Acumen* carefully to see what kind of poetry we publish. Also read widely in many poetry magazines, and don't forget the poets of the past—they can still teach us a great deal."

ADASTRA PRESS

16 Reservation Rd., Easthampton MA 01027-1227. Established 1980. **Contact:** Gary Metras, publisher.

Book/Chapbook Needs "Adastra is primarily a chapbook publisher using antique equipment and methods, i.e., hand-set type, letterpress printing, hand-sewn bindings. Any titles longer than chapbook length are by special arrangement and are from poets who have previously published a successful chapbook or two with Adastra. Editions are generally released with a flat-spine paper wrapper, and some titles have been bound in cloth. Editions are limited, ranging from 200- to 400-copy print runs. Some of the longer titles have gone into reprint, and these are photo-offset and perfect-bound. Letterpress chapbooks by themselves are not reprinted as single titles. Once they go out of print, they are gone. I am biased against poems that rhyme and/or are religious in theme. Sequences and longish poems are always nice to present in a chapbook format. Competition is keen. Less than .5% of submissions are accepted." Published chapbooks include *Poetic License* by Susan Terris, *Digger's Blues* by Jim Daniels, *Behind Our Memories* by Michael Hettich, and *Three* by Stephen Philbrick. Publishes 2-4 chapbooks/year. Sample hand-crafted chapbook: $6 postpaid.

How to Submit Chapbook mss should be 12-18 pages, double-spaced. No full-length mss will be considered. Submit in February of each year. Responds by April. Time between acceptance and publication can be as long as 2 years. Pays 10% of press run.

Advice "Adastra Press is a one-man printer/publisher but releases more poetry titles per year than Random House, one of the largest trade book publishers in the world. I approach book-making as an art, and design each chapbook to fit the poetry. As *The Virginia Quarterly Review* wrote, Adastra is 'one of our most interesting smaller press.' "

ADEPT PRESS; SMALL BRUSHES

P.O. Box 5, Allamuchy NJ 07820. Established 1999. **Contact:** Jan Epps Turner and John Chadsey Turner, editors.

Magazine Needs Published twice/year in April and October, *Small Brushes* "looks for poetry of literary quality, including humor and nostalgia. We value unity, coherence, emphasis, accessibility, and want to see poetry expressed without the use of vulgarity. Striving for universality and ageless connections of the human spirit, we avoid issues of a narrow religious, social, or political character as well as overly sentimental or personal poems." Has published poetry by John P. Kristofco, Christy Berlowitz, Kurt Krumpholz, Laverne Frith, Carol Hamilton, and Clemens Schoenebeck. *Small Brushes* is 28 pages, digest-sized, desktop-published, photocopied, saddle-stapled, with heavyweight paper cover. Receives more than 1,000 poems/year, accepts about 8%. Press run is 100. Single copy: $3; subscription: $10/2 years (4 issues). Make checks payable to Adept Press. "Subscriptions are for a few loyal readers and a way for contributors to get extra copies at a savings by specifying the issues or any 4 copies they want. Otherwise, we neither require nor expect contributors to subscribe. Subscription purchase does not affect our choice of poetry, so please do not send a check with first submissions. Samples (old issues), with our guidelines enclosed, can be obtained by sending a self-addressed catalog envelope (6×9) with 83¢ postage attached.''

How to Submit Submit 3-4 poems at a time. No previously published poems or simultaneous submissions. Cover letter is required. ''Please include a brief bio in your cover letter, and place your name and address at the top of each manuscript page. Send SASE if you want any manuscript returned (standard envelope and first-class postage only).'' Time between acceptance and publication is up to 18 months. Guidelines available for SASE. Responds in up to 3 months. Pays one contributor's copy. Rights remain with authors and artists.

Advice ''Read carefully our needs and preferences in this listing. Submit poetry to us only if your style and subject matter are an exact fit. Please send submissions to us in regular-size envelopes.''

ADVOCATE, PKA's PUBLICATION

1881 Little West Kill Rd., Prattsville NY 12468. (518)299-3103. Established 1987.

Magazine Needs *Advocate* is a bimonthly advertiser-supported tabloid (12,000 copies distributed free) using ''original, previously unpublished works, such as feature stories, essays, 'think' pieces, letters to the editor, profiles, humor, fiction, poetry, puzzles, cartoons, or line drawings.'' Wants ''nearly any kind of poetry, any length, but not religious or pornographic. Poetry ought to speak to people and not be so oblique as to have meaning only to the poet. If I had to be there to understand the poem, don't send it. Now looking for horse-related poems, stories, drawings, and photos.'' Accepts poetry written by children when included with release form signed by adult. Accepts about 25% of poems received. Subscription: $16.50 (6 issues). Sample: $4.

How to Submit No previously published poems or simultaneous submissions. Time between acceptance and publication is up to 6 months. ''Occasionally'' comments on rejected poems. Responds in 2 months. Guidelines available with sample copy ($4). Pays 2 contributor's copies. Acquires first rights only.

Advice ''Send your submission with a SASE; no postcards, please.''

$ AGNI

Creative Writing Program, Boston University, 236 Bay State Rd., Boston MA 02215. (617)353-7135. Fax: (617)353-7134. E-mail: agni@bu.edu. Website: www.agnimagazine.org. Established 1972. **Contact:** Sven Birkerts, editor.

• Work published in *AGNI* has been included regularly in *The Best American Poetry* and *Pushcart Prize* anthologies.

Magazine Needs *AGNI* is a biannual journal of poetry, fiction, and essays ''by both emerging and established writers. We publish quite a bit of poetry in forms as well as 'language' poetry, but we don't begin to try and place parameters on the 'kind of work' that *AGNI* selects.'' Wants readable, intelligent poetry—mostly lyric free verse (with some narrative and dramatic)—that somehow communicates tension or risk. Has published poetry by Adrienne Rich, Seamus Heaney, Maxine Scates, Rosanna Warren, Chinua Achebe, and Ha Jin. *AGNI* is typeset, offset-printed, perfect-bound. Circulation is 3,000 for subscriptions, mail orders, and bookstore sales. Subscription: $17. Sample: $10, $12 for 30th Anniversary Poetry Anthology.

How to Submit ''Our reading period runs from September 1st until May 31st. Please submit no more than 5 poems at a time. No fancy fonts, gimmicks. Send SASE, no preformatted reply cards. No work accepted via e-mail. Brief, sincere cover letters.'' Accepts simultaneous submissions; no previously published poems. Pays $10/page ($150 maximum) plus 2 contributor's copies, a one-year subscription, and 4 gift copies. Acquires first serial rights.

THE AGUILAR EXPRESSION

1329 Gilmore Ave., Donora PA 15033. (724)379-8019. E-mail: xyz0@access995.com. Established 1986. **Contact:** Xavier F. Aguilar, editor/publisher.

Magazine Needs *The Aguilar Expression* appears semiannually in summer and winter. ''In publishing poetry, I try to exhibit the unique reality that we too often take for granted and acquaint as mediocre. We encourage poetics that deal with *now*, which our readers can relate to." Has published poetry by Martin Kich and Gail Ghai. *The Aguilar Expression* is 4-20 pages, photocopied on 8½×11 sheets. Receives about 10-15 poems/month, accepts about 10-15/year. Circulation is 200. Sample: $8. Make checks payable to Xavier Aguilar.

How to Submit "We insist that all writers send a SASE for writer's guidelines before submitting." Submit up to 3 poems at a time in a clear, camera-ready copy, any topic/style. Lines/poem: 30 maximum. Does not accept e-mail submissions. Cover letter (including writing background) and SASE (for contact purposes) required with submissions. Reads mss in December, January, February, and March. Manuscripts received in any other months will be discarded unopened. "Send copies; manuscripts will not be returned." Responds in 2 months. Pays 2 contributor's copies.

AHSAHTA PRESS; SAWTOOTH POETRY PRIZE

MFA Program in Creative Writing, Boise State University, 1910 University Dr., Boise ID 83725-1525. (208)426-2195. Fax: (208)426-4373. E-mail: ahsahta@boisestate.edu. Website: http://ahsaht apress.boisestate.edu. **Contact:** Editor. Director: Janet Holmes.

Book/Chapbook Needs Ahsahta Press has been publishing contemporary poetry of the American West since 1976. "It has since expanded its scope to publish poets nationwide, seeking out and publishing the best new poetry from a wide range of aesthetics—poetry that is technically accomplished, distinctive in style, and thematically fresh." Has published *Oriflamme* by Sandra Miller, *Fence Above the Sea* by Brigitte Byrd, *Island* by Charles O. Hartman, *Cur aliquid vidi* by Lance Phillips, *Spell* by Dan Beachy-Quick, *Leave the Room to Itself* by Graham Foust, as well as work by Wyn Cooper, Craig Cotter, Sandra Alcosser, and Cynthia Hogue.

How to Submit Accepts multiple and simultaneous submissions. Submit only during March 1 through May 31 reading period. Send complete ms and letter-sized SASE for reply. Responds in up to 3 months. Forthcoming, new, and backlist titles available from website. Most backlist titles: $9.95; most current titles: $14.95.

Contest/Award Offerings Sponsors the Sawtooth Poetry Prize, offering a $1,500 award and publication of a book-length collection of poetry judged by a nationally recognized poet (2005 judge was Carolyn Forche).

Also Offers Publishes a letterpress broadside series drawn from Ahsahta Press authors. Query first.

Advice "Ahsahta seeks distinctive, non-imitative, unpredictable, and innovatively crafted work. Please check our website for examples of what we publish."

$ AIM MAGAZINE (Specialized: social issues; ethnic; political)

P.O. Box 1174, Maywood IL 60153. (773)874-6184. Fax: (206)543-2746. E-mail: apiladoone@aol.c om. Website: www.aimmagazine.org. Established 1974. **Contact:** Ruth Apilado, poetry editor.

Magazine Needs *Aim* appears quarterly, "dedicated to racial harmony and peace." Uses 3-4 poems ("poetry with social significance mainly"—average 32 lines) in each issue. Accepts poetry written by high school students. Has published poetry by J. Douglas Studer, Wayne Dowdy, Ned Pendergast, and Maria DeGuzman. *Aim* is magazine-sized with glossy cover. Receives about 30 submissions/year, accepts about half. Press run is 10,000 (3,000 subscribers including the libraries of K-12 schools, colleges, and universities). Single copy: $7.50, subscription: $20. Sample: $5.

How to Submit Accepts simultaneous submissions. List of upcoming themes available for SASE. Responds in 6 weeks. Pays $3/poem and one contributor's copy. Does not send an acceptance notice: "We simply send payment and magazine copy."

Advice "Read the work of published poets."

ALASKA QUARTERLY REVIEW

University of Alaska Anchorage, 3211 Providence Dr., Anchorage AK 99508. Phone/fax: (907)786-6916. E-mail: ayaqr@uaa.alaska.edu. Website: www.uaa.alaska.edu/aqr. Established 1981. **Contact:** Ronald Spatz, executive editor.

Publishers of Poetry

• Poetry published in *Alaska Quarterly Review* has been selected for inclusion in *The Best American Poetry*, *Pushcart Prize*, and *Beacon's Best* anthologies.

Magazine Needs *Alaska Quarterly Review* "is a journal devoted to contemporary literary art. We publish both traditional and experimental fiction, poetry, literary nonfiction, and short plays." Has published poetry by Kim Addonizio, Pattiann Rogers, John Balaban, Albert Goldbarth, Billy Collins, and Dorianne Laux. Wants all styles and forms of poetry, "with the most emphasis perhaps on voice and content that displays 'risk,' or intriguing ideas or situations." Publishes 2 double-issues/year, each using between 40-125 pages of poetry. *Alaska Quarterly Review* is 224-300 pages, digest-sized, professionally printed, perfect-bound, with card cover with color or b&w photo. Receives up to 5,000 submissions/year, accepts 40-90. Press run is 3,500 (500 subscribers, 32 libraries). Subscription: $10. Sample: $6.

How to Submit Does not accept fax or e-mail submissions. Manuscripts are *not* read from May 15 through August 15. Responds in up to 4 months, sometimes longer during peak periods in late winter. Pay depends on funding. Acquires first North American serial rights. Guest poetry editors have included Stuart Dybek, Jane Hirshfield, Stuart Dischell, Maxine Kumin, Pattiann Rogers, Dorianne Laux, Peggy Shumacher, Nancy Eimers, Michael Ryan, and Billy Collins.

◑ ◎ ALBATROSS; THE ANABIOSIS PRESS (Specialized: nature)

2 S. New St., Bradford MA 01835. (978)469-7085. E-mail: rsmyth@anabiosispress.org. Website: www.anabiosispress.org. **Contact:** Richard Smyth, editor.

Magazine Needs *Albatross* appears "as soon as we have accepted enough quality poems to publish an issue—about one per year. We consider the albatross to be a metaphor for the environment; the journal's title is drawn from Coleridge's *The Rime of the Ancient Mariner* and is intended to invoke the allegorical implications of that poem. This is not to say that we publish only environmental or nature poetry, but that we are biased toward such subject matter. We publish mostly free verse, and we prefer a narrative style. We seek poetry written in a strong, mature voice that conveys a deeply felt experience or makes a powerful statement. We rarely accept rhyming poetry or haiku." Has published poetry by Catherine Carter, E.G. Burrows, Kate Chadbourne, T.P. Perrin, and Don Russ. *Albatross* is 28 pages, digest-sized, laser-typeset, with linen cover. Subscription: $5/2 issues. Sample: $3.

How to Submit Submit 3-5 poems at a time. Lines/poem: 200 maximum. "Poems should be typed single-spaced, with name, address, and phone number in upper left corner." No simultaneous submissions. Accepts e-mail submissions if included in body of message. Name and address must accompany e-mail submissions. Cover letter not required; "We do, however, need bio notes and SASE for return or response." Time between acceptance and publication is up to 6 months to a year. Guidelines available for SASE or on website. Responds in up to one month. Pays one contributor's copy. Acquires all rights. Returns rights provided that "previous publication in *Albatross* is mentioned in all subsequent reprintings."

Contest/Award Offerings Sponsors an annual chapbook contest. Winner receives $100 and at least 50 copies of his/her published chapbook. All entrants receive a free copy of the winning chapbook. Submit 16-20 pages of poetry, any theme, any style. Include name, address, and phone number on the title page. **Deadline:** June 30 of each year. **Reading fee:** $10 (check payable to Anabiosis Press).

Advice "We expect a poet to read as much contemporary poetry as possible. We want to be moved. When you read our poetry, we hope that it moves you in the same way that it moves us. We try to publish the kind of poetry that you would want to read again and again."

✪ ◑ ALDEN ENTERPRISES; POETIC VOICES MAGAZINE

Hartselle AL. E-mail: editor@poeticvoices.com (for Robin Travis-Murphree) or ursula@poeticvoices.com (for Ursula T. Gibson). Website: www.poeticvoices.com. Established 1997. **Contact:** Ursula T. Gibson, submissions editor (*Poetic Voices*). Executive Editor (Alden): Robin Travis-Murphee.

Magazine Needs *Poetic Voices* is "informational and educational in content. Articles include feature interviews, columns on the mechanics of writing, questions on writing and publishing, information on organizations useful to poets, contest and award opportunities, publishing opportunities, workshops and conferences, book reviews and more. We are open to most forms, styles, and subjects. No pornography, scatology, racial slurs, or dehumanizing poems." Has published poetry by Lyn Lifshin, David Lehman, Michael McClure, Kevin Stein, Molly Peacock, Afaa Weaver, and others. *Poetic Voices* is an electronic magazine. Receives more than 3,000 poems/year, accepts about 10%. Circulation is "more than 50,000 poets in more than 30 countries each month."

How to Submit Submit up to 4 poems/month by e-mail (pasted into body of message) to Ursula T. Gibson. Accepts previously published poems and simultaneous submissions. Guidelines available on website. Responds in 2 months. Acquires one-time rights. Reviews books and chapbooks of poetry and other magazines in 200-500 words. Send materials for review consideration to Robin Travis-Murphree.

Advice "Make sure you read and follow guidelines. Make sure your work is neatly presented. There is nothing worse than receiving messy work or work that does not conform to the guidelines."

$🖉 ◎ ALIVE NOW (Specialized: spiritual formation; themes)

1908 Grand Ave., P.O. Box 340004, Nashville TN 37203-0004. E-mail: AliveNow@upperroom.org. Website: www.alivenow.org or www.upperroom.org. **Contact:** Melissa Tidwell, editor.

Magazine Needs *Alive Now* is a bimonthly devotional magazine that invites readers to enter an ever-deepening relationship with God. "*Alive Now* seeks to nourish people who are hungry for a sacred way of living. Submissions should invite readers to see God in the midst of daily life by exploring how contemporary issues impact their faith lives. Each word must be vivid and dynamic and contribute to the whole. We make selections based on a list of upcoming themes. Manuscripts which do not fit a theme will be returned." Considers avant-garde and free verse. *Alive Now* is 64 pages. Accepts 20 poems/year. Circulation is 70,000. Subscription: $14.95/one year (6 issues); $23.95/2 years (12 issues). Additional subscription information, including foreign rates, available on website.

How to Submit Submit 5 poems at a time. Lines/poem: 10 minimum, 45 maximum. "Submissions should be typed, double-spaced, on $8^{1}/_{2} \times 11$ paper; include SASE. If you are submitting material for more than one theme, send a SASE for each theme represented. On each page you submit, include your name, address, and the theme for which the piece is being sent. You may also submit via e-mail; copy and paste single-spaced, plain-text poems into message. Send up to 5 poems per theme in single e-mail. Put theme in subject line." **All poems must relate to themes.** List of upcoming themes and guidelines available for SASE or on website. "We will notify contributors of manuscript status when we make final decisions for a theme, 3 months before the issue date. We place manuscripts on hold for specific issues; authors are free to request their manuscripts be returned to them at any time." Pays $40 and up on acceptance. Purchases newspaper, periodical, and electronic rights; may purchase one-time use.

Advice "*Alive Now* is ecumenical, including both lay persons and church professionals. Our readers are primarily adults, from young adults to older adults, and include persons of many cultures and ethnic backgrounds."

$🖉 ALLIGATOR JUNIPER

Prescott College, 301 Grove Ave., Prescott AZ 86301. (928)350-2012. E-mail: aj@prescott.edu. Website: www.prescott.edu/highlights/alligator_juniper.html. Established 1995. **Contact:** Poetry Editor.

Magazine Needs *Alligator Juniper* is a contest publication appearing annually in May. "We publish work based only on artistic merit." Has published poetry by Elton Glaser and Fatima Lim-Wilson. *Alligator Juniper* is 200 pages. Receives about 1,200-1,500 poems/year, accepts about 6-20. Press run is 1,500 (600 subscribers); 200 distributed free to other reputable journals, MFA programs, and writers' colonies. Subscription: $12/2 years (2 issues). Sample: $7.50. "We publish one issue per year and it's always a contest, requiring a $10 fee which allows us to pay a $500 first prize in each

Publishers of Poetry

category—fiction, poetry, creative nonfiction, and photography. All entrants receive a copy of the next issue."

How to Submit Submit up to 5 poems at a time with reading fee. Include SASE for response only; mss are not returned. "All entrants receive a personal letter from one of our staff regarding the status of their submissions." Accepts simultaneous submissions; no previously published poems. No e-mail or fax submissions. Cover letter is required. **Postmark Deadline:** October 1. "We read and select what we will publish from all the work submitted so far that calendar year." **Reading fee:** $10/entry (5 poems or 5 pages of poetry). Time between acceptance and publication is 3-5 months. "Finalists are selected in-house and passed on to a different guest judge each year." Occasionally publishes theme issues. Guidelines available for SASE, by e-mail, or on website. Responds in 5 months. Each year, one winner receives $500 plus 4 contributor's copies; all other poets whose work is selected for publication receive payment in contributor's copies only.

◐ ◎ AMAZE: THE CINQUAIN JOURNAL (Specialized: American cinquain)

10529 Olive St., Temple City CA 91780. E-mail: cinquains@hotmail.com. Website: www.amaze-cinquain.com. Established 2002. **Contact:** Deborah P. Kolodji, editor. Webmaster: Lisa Janice Cohen.
Magazine Needs *Amaze: The Cinquain Journal* is a biannual literary journal (in both print and online webzine formats) devoted to the cinquain poetry form. "The webzine is published on a continuous flow basis as we accept submissions for the current issue. The print version is published 2 months after submissions close for the webzine." Wants American cinquains as invented by Adelaide Crapsey (5 lines with a 2-4-6-8-2 syllable pattern) and cinquain variations (mirror cinquains, crown cinquains, cinquain sequences, etc.). Does not want any poetry not based upon the American cinquain, nor "grammar-lesson" cinquains based upon parts of speech. Nothing hateful, racist, or sexually explicit. Has published poetry by an'ya, Ann K. Schwader, Michael McClintock, naia, and Denis Garrison. The print version of *Amaze* is 40-50 pages, digest-sized, photocopied, saddle-stapled, with card stock cover with photograph/artwork. Receives about 1,500 poems/year, accepts about 200. Press run is 100-200 (25 subscribers). Single copy: $6 U.S., $7.50 non-U.S.; subscription: $12 U.S., $15 non-US. Make checks payable to Deborah P. Kolodji, or pay online through PayPal.
How to Submit Submit 1-10 poems at a time. Lines/poem: 5. Accepts previously published poems; no simultaneous submissions. Accepts e-mail submissions; no fax or disk submissioins. "E-mail submissions preferred, with poems in the body of the e-mail. Do not send attachments." Include SASE with postal submissions. Reads submissions "on a continuous flow." Time between acceptance and publication is 3 weeks for webzine, up to 8 months for print journal. "Poems are evaluated on quality, form, and content." Often comments on rejected poems. Guidelines available for SASE or on website. Responds in up to 6 weeks. Acquires one-time rights.

⊕ ◐ AMBIT

17 Priory Gardens, Highgate, London N6 5QY England. Phone: 020 8340 3566. Website: www.ambit magazine.co.uk. **Contact:** Martin Bax, Carol Ann Duffy, and Henry Graham, poetry editors.
Magazine Needs *Ambit* is a 96-page quarterly of avant-garde, contemporary, and experimental work. Subscription: £25 UK, £27/€48 rest of Europe, £29/$56 overseas (individuals); £36 UK, £38/€64 rest of Europe, £40/$73 overseas (institutions). Sample: £6.50 UK, £7/€15 rest of Europe, £8/$18 overseas.
How to Submit Submit up to 6 poems at a time, typed double-spaced. No previously published poems or simultaneous submissions. Guidelines available in magazine or on website. Pay is "variable plus 2 contributor's copies. SAE vital for reply." Staff reviews books of poetry. Send materials for review consideration to review editor.
Advice "Read a copy of the magazine before submitting!"

✪ ◐ ◎ THE AMERICAN DISSIDENT (Specialized: engaged writing)

1837 Main St., Concord MA 01742. E-mail: enmarge@aol.com. Website: www.geocities.com/enma rge. Established 1998. **Contact:** G. Tod Slone, editor.

Magazine Needs *The American Dissident* appears 2 times/year to, "amongst other things, provide a forum for examing the dark side of the academic/literary industrial complex." Wants "poetry and short (250-750 words) essays in English, French, or Spanish, written on the edge with a dash of personal risk and stemming from personal experience, conflict with power, and/or involvement." Submissions should be "iconoclastic and parrhesiastic in nature." *The American Dissident* is 56-64 pages, digest-sized, offset-printed, perfect-bound, with card cover. Press run is 200. Single copy: $8. Subscription: $16.

How to Submit Submit 3 poems at a time. Accepts simultaneous submissions; no previously published poems. No e-mail submissions. "Include SASE and cover letter containing not credits, but rather personal dissident information and specific events that may have pushed you to reject indoctrination and 'go upright and vital, and speak the rude truth in all ways' (Emerson)." Time between acceptance and publication is up to 9 months. Almost always comments on rejected poems. Guidelines available for SASE. Responds in one month. Pays one contributor's copy. Acquires first North American serial rights. Reviews books and chapbooks of poetry and other magazines in 250 words, single-book format. Send materials for review consideration.

Advice "For the sake of deomcracy, poetry needs to be much more than safe, comfortable, diversionary intellectual entertainment, and poets much more than public court jesters. If only the latter endeavored to be more than just working the poem and filling out applications for grants, fellowships, and contests. If only they questioned and challenged, rather than accepted. If only they heeded Villon ('Estoit-il lors temps de moy taire'), Thoreau ('Let your life be a counter friction to stop the machine'), Wole Soyinka ('Criticism, like charity, starts at home'), Solzhenitsyn ('Poetry under a tombstone, truth under a stone'), Parra ('La poesía morirá si no se la ofende, hay que poseerla y humillarla en público'), and James Baldwin ('The peculiar nature of this [the writer's] responsibility is that he must never cease warring with it [society], for its sake and for his own'). Do not be afraid to name names!"

AMERICAN LITERARY REVIEW

University of North Texas, P.O. Box 311307, Denton TX 76203-1307. (940)565-2755. E-mail: americanliteraryreview@yahoo.com. Website: www.engl.unt.edu/alr. **Contact:** Bruce Bond and Corey Marks, poetry editors.

Magazine Needs *American Literary Review* is a biannual publishing all forms and modes of poetry and fiction. "We are especially interested in originality, substance, imaginative power, and lyric intensity." Has published poetry by Kathleen Pierce, Mark Irwin, Nance Van Winkle, William Olsen, Eric Pankey, and Nancy Eimers. *American Literary Review* is about 120 pages, digest-sized, attractively printed, perfect-bound, with color card cover with photo. Subscription: $10/year, $18/2 years. Sample: $6 US, $8 ROW.

How to Submit Submit up to 5 typewritten poems at a time. No fax or e-mail submissions. Cover letter with author's name, address, phone number, and poem titles is required. Reads mss September 1 to May 1. Guidelines available for SASE or on website. Responds in up to 4 months. Pays 2 contributor's copies.

Contest/Award Offerings Sponsors poetry and fiction contest in alternating years. Most recent poetry contest was in 2004. Send SASE for details.

THE AMERICAN POETRY JOURNAL; THE AMERICAN POET PRIZE

P.O. Box 4041, Felton CA 95018. E-mail: editor@americanpoetryjournal.com. Website: www.americanpoetryjournal.com. Established 2004. **Contact:** J.P. Dancing Bear, editor.

Magazine Needs *The American Poetry Journal*, published biannually (January and July), "seeks to publish work using poetic device, favoring image, metaphor, and good sound. We like alliteration, extended metaphors, image, movement, and poems that can pass the 'so what' test. *The American Poetry Journal* has in mind the reader who delights in discovering what a poem can do to the tongue and what the poem paints on the cave of the mind." Wants poems "that exhibit strong, fresh imagery, metaphor, and good sound." Does not want "narratives about family, simplistic verse, annoying word hodge-podges." Has published poetry by C.J. Sage, Hailey Leithauser, Margaret F. Gibson, Lynne Knight, Hannah Stein, and Rob Carney. *The American Poetry Journal* is 60 pages, digest-sized. Accepts about 1% of poems submitted. Single copy: $6; subscription: $10. Make checks payable to J.P. Dancing Bear.

How to Submit Submit 3-5 poems at a time. Accepts simultaneous submissions; no previously published poems. No e-mail or disk submissions. Cover letter is preferred. Reads submissions all year. Time between acceptance and publication is 6 months. "Poems are read first for clarity and technique, then read aloud for sound quality." Seldom comments on rejected poems. Guidelines available on website. Responds in 6 weeks. Pays one contributor's copy. Acquires first rights.

Contest/Award Offerings "We offer The American Poet Prize, awarding $300 and publication. All entries will be considered for publication and all entrants receive a year's subscription. Send 3 original, unpublished poems without identifiers on the page, a cover letter with poem titles, author's name, contact information, optional stamped postcard for delivery confirmation, and SASE." **Entry fee:** $10. Make checks payable to J.P. Dancing Bear. **Deadline:** was June 30 for 2004.

Advice "Know your target before submitting. It's not that difficult, but it helps your odds when the editor can tell that you get what the magazine is about. Reading an issue is the easiest way to do this."

AMERICAN RESEARCH PRESS (Specialized: paradoxism)

P.O. Box 141, Rehoboth NM 87322. E-mail: M_L_Perez@yahoo.com. Website: www.gallup.unm.edu/~smarandache/ebooksliterature.htm. Established 1990. **Contact:** Minh Perez, publisher.

Book/Chapbook Needs American Research Press publishes 2-3 poetry paperbacks/year. Wants experimental poetry dealing with paradoxism. No classical poetry. See website for poetry samples. Has published poetry by Al. Florin Tene, Anatol Ciocanu, Nina Josu, and Al Bantos.

How to Submit Submit 3-4 poems at a time. No previously published poems or simultaneous submissions. Cover letter is preferred. Submit seasonal poems one month in advance. Time between acceptance and publication is one year. Seldom comments on rejected poems. Responds to queries in one month. Pays 100 author's copies. Order sample books by sending SASE.

Also Offers Free e-books available on website.

AMERICAN TANKA (Specialized: form/style—tanka)

P.O. Box 120-024, Staten Island NY 10312. E-mail: info@americantanka.com or submissions@americantanka.com. Website: www.americantanka.com. Established 1996. **Contact:** Editor.

Magazine Needs *American Tanka* appears annually in spring and is devoted to single English-language tanka. Wants "concise and vivid language, good crafting, and echo of the original Japanese form." Does not want anything that is not tanka. Has published poetry by Sanford Goldstein, Marianne Bluger, Michael McClintock, Michael Dylan Welch, Jane Reichhold, and George Swede. *American Tanka* is 95-120 pages, digest-sized, perfect-bound, with glossy cover. Single copy: $12; subscription: $20.

How to Submit Submit up to 5 poems at a time; "submit only once per reading period." No previously published poems or simultaneous submissions. Accepts submissions by e-mail (pasted into body of message) and through online submission form. Reads mss from September 15 to February 15. Guidelines available for SASE, by e-mail, or on website. Responds in up to 2 months. Acquires first North American serial rights.

Advice "Become familiar with the tanka form by reading both translations and English-language tanka. In your own tanka, be natural and concrete and vivid. Avoid clichés, overcrowded imagery, or attempting to imitate Japanese poems."

THE AMHERST REVIEW

Box 2172, Amherst College, P.O. Box 5000, Amherst MA 01002-5000. E-mail: review@amherst.edu. **Contact:** Janet Lydecker, editor-in-chief.

Magazine Needs *The Amherst Review*, appearing in late spring, is an annual international literary magazine seeking quality submissions of fiction, poetry, nonfiction, and photography/artwork. "All kinds of poetry welcome." *The Amherst Review* is 80 pages, 5×8, with soft cover with photography, art, and graphics. Receives 800-900 mss/year, accepts about 30. Sample: $6. Make checks payable to *The Amherst Review*.

How to Submit Accepts simultaneous submissions; no previously published poems. No e-mail submissions. Reads submissions from September through March only. Magazine staff makes democratic decision. Guidelines available for SASE. Responds in April. Pays one contributor's copy.

$ ◻ ◎ ANCIENT PATHS (Specialized: religious/Christian)

P.O. Box 7505, Fairfax Station VA 22039. E-mail: SSBurris@msn.com. Website: www.editorskylar.com. Established 1998. **Contact:** Skylar H. Burris, editor.

Magazine Needs *Ancient Paths* is published annually in September "to provide a forum for quality Christian literature. It contains poetry, short stories, art, and chapbook reviews." Wants "traditional rhymed/metrical forms and free verse; subtle Christian themes. I seek poetry that makes the reader both think and feel. No 'preachy' poetry, inconsistent meter, or obtrusive rhyme; no stream of conscious or avant-garde work; no esoteric academic poetry." Has published poetry by Giovanni Malito, Ida Fasel, Diane Glancy, Walt McDonald, and Donna Farley. *Ancient Paths* is 48 pages, digest-sized, photocopied, perfect-bound, with cardstock cover. Receives about 600 poems/year, accepts about 7%. Press run is 175 (55 paid subscribers, 30 individual copy sales); 80 distributed free to churches, libraries, and authors. Subscription: $5/year (1 issue); $9.50/2 years (2 issues). Sample: $3.50 back issue, $5 current issue. Make checks payable to Skylar Burris.

How to Submit Submit up to 5 poems at a time, single-spaced. Lines/poem: 60 maximum. Accepts previously published poems and simultaneous submissions. Accepts e-mail submissions "only if you reside outside the U.S. E-mail submissions should be pasted directly into the message, single-spaced, one poem per message, using a small or normal font size, with name and address at the top of each submission. Use subject heading: ANCIENT PATHS SUBMISSION, followed by your title. Always include name, address, and line count on first page of all submissions, and note if the poem is previously published and what rights (if any) were purchased." Time between acceptance and publication is up to one year. Often comments on rejected poems. Guidelines available for SASE or on website. Responds in "3-4 weeks if rejected, longer if being seriously considered." Pays $1/poem and one contributor's copy. Acquires one-time or reprint rights. Reviews religious poetry chapbooks in 100 words.

Advice "Read the great religious poets: John Donne, George Herbert, T.S. Eliot, Lord Tennyson. Remember not to preach. This is a literary magazine, not a pulpit. This does not mean you do not communicate morals or celebrate God. It means you are not overbearing or simplistic when you do so."

⭐ ◻ ◎ THE ANTHOLOGY OF NEW ENGLAND WRITERS; ROBERT PENN WARREN AWARDS (Specialized: form/free verse); NEW ENGLAND WRITERS CONFERENCE; VERMONT POETS ASSOCIATION; NEWSCRIPT (Specialized: membership/subscription)

P.O. Box 5, Windsor VT 05089. (802)674-2315. Fax: (802)674-5767. E-mail: newvtpoet@aol.com. Website: www.newenglandwriters.org. Established 1986. **Contact:** Frank Anthony, editor. Associate Editor: Susan Anthony.

Magazine Needs *The Anthology of New England Writers* appears annually in November. All poems published in this annual are winners of contest. Wants "unpublished, original, free verse poetry only." Open to *all* poets, not just New England. Also accepts poetry written by teenagers. Has published poetry by Richard Eberhart, Rosanna Warren, David Kirby, and Vivian Shipley. *Anthology* is 56 pages, digest-sized, professionally printed, perfect-bound, with colored card cover. Press run is 450. Single copy: $5.50. Make checks payable to New England Writers.

How to Submit Submit 3-9 poems at a time with contest reading fee (3 poems: $5; 6 poems: $10; 9 poems: $15). Lines/poem: 10 minimum, 30 maximum. Include 3×5 card with name, address, and titles of poems. No previously published poems or simultaneous submissions. Reads submissions postmarked January through June 15 only. Guidelines available for SASE, by e-mail, or on website. Responds 6 weeks after June 15 **deadline**. Sends prepublication galleys. Pays one contributor's copy. All rights revert to author upon publication.

Contest/Award Offerings Sponsors an annual free verse contest: The Robert Penn Warren Awards. Offers 1st Prize: $300; 2nd Prize: $200; 3rd Prize: $100. Also awards 10 Honorable Mentions ($20 each), 10 Commendables, and 10 Editor's Choice. **Entry fee:** $5/3 poems. Winners announced at the New England Writers Conference in July. All submissions are automatically entered in contest.

Also Offers The New England Writers/Vermont Poets Association was established in 1986 "to encourage precision and ingenuity in the practice of writing and speaking, whatever the form and style." Currently has 500 members. Writing information is included in the biannual newsletter, *NewScript*. Meetings are held several times/year. Membership dues: $10, $7 senior citizens and students. Additional information available for SASE, by e-mail, or on website. Also sponsors the annual New England Writers Conference with nationally known writers and editors involved with workshops, open mike readings, and a writer's panel. Annual conference date: third Saturday of July. Conference lasts one afternoon and is "affordable" and open to the public.

✪ $ANTIETAM REVIEW

Washington County Arts Council, 41 S. Potomac St., Hagerstown MD 21740-5512. (301)791-3132. Fax: (240)420-1754. E-mail: antietamreview@washingtoncountyarts.com. Website: http://washingtoncountyarts.com. Established 1982. **Contact:** Paul Grant, poetry editor. Managing Editor: Mary Jo Vincent.

• Public Radio's series *The Poet and the Poem* recognized *The Antietam Review* as an "outstanding contributor to American Letters."

Magazine Needs *The Antietam Review* appears annually in June and looks for "well-crafted, literary-quality poems." Has published poetry by Ace Boggess, Joshua Poteat, and Susan Printz Robb. *Antietam Review* is 76 pages, magazine-sized, saddle-stitched, with glossy card cover. Press run is 1,000. Sample: $6.30 back issue, $8.40 current.

How to Submit Submit no more than 3 poems. "We prefer a cover letter stating other publications, although we encourage new and emerging writers. We do not accept previously published poems and reluctantly take simultaneous submissions." No fax or e-mail submissions accepted. "We read from September 1 through December 1 annually." Guidelines available for #10 SASE or on website. Pays $25/poem, plus 2 contributor's copies. Acquires first North American serial rights.

Contest/Award Offerings Sponsors a literary contest. Send #10 SASE or see website for details.

✪ ⊘ THE ANTIGONISH REVIEW

P.O. Box 5000, Antigonish NS B2G 2W5 Canada. (902)867-3962. Fax: (902)867-5563. E-mail: TAR@stfx.ca. Website: www.antigonishreview.com. Established 1970. **Contact:** Peter Sanger, poetry editor. Co-Editors: Jeanette Lynes and Gerald Trites.

Magazine Needs *The Antigonish Review* appears quarterly and "tries to produce the kind of literary and visual mosaic that the modern sensibility requires or would respond to." Wants poetry "not over 80 lines, i.e., 2 pages; subject matter can be anything; the style is traditional, modern, or post-modern limited by typographic resources. Purpose is not an issue." No "erotica, scatalogical verse, excessive propaganda toward a certain subject." Has published poetry by Andy Wainwright, W.J. Keith, Michael Hulse, Jean McNeil, M. Travis Lane, and Douglas Lochhead. *The Antigonish Review* is 144 pages, digest-sized, offset-printed, flat-spined, with glossy card cover with art. Receives 2,500 submissions/year, accepts about 10%. Press run is 1,000 (950 subscribers). Subscription: $24 Canadian, $30 US elsewhere. Sample: $6.

How to Submit Submit 5-10 poems at a time. No simultaneous submissions or previously published poems. Include SASE (or SAE and IRCs if outside Canada). "We cannot use U.S. postage." Accepts fax submissions; no e-mail submissions. Time between acceptance and publication is up to 8 months. Editor sometimes comments on rejected poems. Guidelines available for SASE, by e-mail, or on website. Responds in up to 6 months. Pays 2 contributor's copies. Acquires first North American serial rights.

✪ $◙ THE ANTIOCH REVIEW

P.O. Box 148, Yellow Springs OH 45387. (937)769-1365. Website: www.review.antioch.edu. Established 1941. **Contact:** Judith Hall, poetry editor.

● Work published in this review has been frequently included in *The Best American Poetry* and *Pushcart Prize* anthologies.

Magazine Needs *The Antioch Review* "is an independent quarterly of critical and creative thought . . . For well over 50 years, creative authors, poets, and thinkers have found a friendly reception . . . regardless of formal reputation. We get far more poetry than we can possibly accept, and the competition is keen. Here, where form and content are so inseparable and reaction is so personal, it is difficult to state requirements or limitations. Studying recent issues of *The Review* should be helpful. No 'light' or inspirational verse." Has published poetry by Edward Hirsch, David Lehman, W.S. Merwin, and Harryette Mullen. Receives about 3,000 submissions/year. Circulation is 5,000 (70% distributed through bookstores and newsstands); large percentage of subscribers are libraries. Subscription: $40. Sample: $7.

How to Submit Submit 3-6 poems at a time. No previously published poems or simultaneous submissions. Include SASE with all submissions. Reads submissions September 1 through May 1 only. Guidelines available on website. Responds in 2 months. Pays $10/published page plus 2 contributor's copies; additional copies available at 40% discount. Reviews books of poetry in 300 words, single-book format.

Ⓝ $▢ ◎ AOIFE'S KISS (Specialized: fantasy; science fiction)

P.O. Box 782, Cedar Rapids IA 52406-0782. E-mail: aoife@samsdotpublishing.com. Website: www. samsdotpublishing.com. Established 2002. **Contact:** Tyree Campbell, managing editor. Member: The Speculative Literature Foundation (http://SpeculativeLiterature.org.)

Magazine Needs *Aoife's Kiss* is a quarterly print and online journal (the two versions are different) "publishing fantasy, science fiction, sword and sorcery, alternate history, horror short stories, poems, illustrations, and movie and book reviews." Wants "fantasy, science fiction, spooky horror, and speculative poetry with minimal angst." Does not want "horror with excessive blood and gore." Has published poetry by Bruce Boston, Karen A. Romanko, Mike Allen, Erin Donahoe, Julie Shiel, and Marge B. Simon. *Aoife's Kiss* (print version) is 32 pages, magazine-sized, offset-printed, saddle-stapled, with color paper cover, includes ads. *Aoife's Kiss* is also published online. Receives about 300 poems/year, accepts about 50 (17%). Press run is 100/issue (40 subscribers, 30 shelf sales); 5 distributed free to reviewers. Single copy: $7; subscription: $18/year, $34/2 years. Make checks payable to Tyree Campbell/Sam's Dot Publishing.

How to Submit Submit up to 5 poems at a time. Lines/poem: prefers less than 100. Accepts previously published poems; no simultaneous submissions. Accepts e-mail submissions (pasted into body of message); no disk submissions. "Submission should include snail mail address and a short (1-2 lines) bio." Reads submissions year round. Submit seasonal poems 6 months in advance. Time between acceptance and publication is 2-5 months. Often comments on rejected poems. Guidelines available on website. Responds in 4-6 weeks. Pays $5/poem, $3/reprint, and one contributor's copy. Acquires first North American serial rights. Reviews books and chapbooks of poetry. Send materials for review consideration to Tyree Campbell.

Advice "It's up to the writer to take the first step and submit work. Some of our best poems have come from poets who weren't sure if they were good enough. Horror poetry is a difficult sell with us."

✪ ◳ APALACHEE REVIEW; APALACHEE PRESS

P.O. Box 10469, Tallahassee FL 32302. Established 1971. **Contact:** Laura Newton, Mary Jane Ryals, and Michael Trammell, editors.

Magazine Needs Has published poetry by Rita Mae Reese and Charles Harper Webb. *Apalachee*

Review is 160 pages, digest-sized, professionally printed, perfect-bound, with card cover. Press run is 700 (350 subscribers, 75 libraries). Subscription: $15. Sample: $5.

How to Submit Submit clear copies of 3-5 poems, with name and address on each. Accepts simultaneous submissions. Accepts submissions by postal mail only. Reads submissions year round. Sometimes comments on rejected poems. Guidelines available for SASE. Pays 2 contributor's copies. Staff reviews books of poetry. Send materials for review consideration.

✪ ⊕ ⊘ AQUARIUS

Flat 4, Room B, 116 Sutherland Ave., Maida-Vale, London W9 2QP England. Website: www.geocities.com/eddielinden. **Contact:** Eddie Linden, poetry editor.

Magazine Needs & How to Submit *Aquarius* is a literary biannual publishing poetry, fictional prose, essays, interviews, and reviews. "Please note the magazine will not accept work unless writers have bought the magazine and studied the style/form of the work published." Single copy: $10; subscription: $50 (US); special issue on the poets/writers George Barker and W.S. Graham available for £6 plus £1.25 p&p in United Kingdom. Payment is by arrangement.

Ⓝ ⊘ ARABLE: A LITERARY JOURNAL; ARABLE PRESS

514 Washburn Ave., Louisville KY 40222. E-mail: arable@insightbb.com. Website: www.arablepress.com. Established 2004. **Contact:** Edmund August, editor.

Arable

a Literary Journal

Arable editor Edmund August is also the cover photographer and designer for the Volume I, Number 2 issue. "The theme is the interplay of nature, art, and ideas. The purpose of this magazine is to provide a place where ideas can take root."

Magazine Needs *Arable: A Literary Journal* appears 3 times/year and publishes accessible, quality poetry, fiction, and creative nonfiction. "Our only requirement is good writing." Does not want "poetry from people who write more than they read." Has published poetry by Annette Allen, Reid Bush, Kathleen Driskell, Amelia Blossom Pegram, W. Loren Smith, and Pamela Steele. *Arable* is 100 pages, digest-sized, offset-printed, perfect-bound, with glossy paper cover, includes ads. Press run is 500 (37 subscribers, 3 libraries, 300+ shelf sales); 70 distributed free to contributors and press. Single copy: $10; subscription: $27. Make checks payable to Arable Press.

How to Submit Submit up to 10 poems at a time. Lines/poem: 3-300. Accepts simultaneous submissions; no previously published poems. Accepts e-mail submissions (pasted into body of message); no disk submissions. Cover letter is preferred. "Include SASE for reply only. All manuscripts are recycled." Reads submissions year round. Time between acceptance and publication is 3 months. Sometimes comments on rejected poems. Guidelines available on website. Responds in 2 months. Pays one contributor's copy. Acquires one-time rights.

Advice "Read everything. Write clearly and without pretention."

⊕ ⊘ ARC PUBLICATIONS

Nanholme Mill, Shaw Wood Rd., Todmorden, Lancashire OL14 6DA United Kingdom. E-mail: arc.publications@btconnect.com. Website: www.arcpublications.co.uk. Established 1969. **Contact:** Tony Ward, managing editor/senior partner.

Book/Chapbook Needs & How to Submit ARC Publications "specializes in the publication of contemporary poetry from new and established writers in the UK and abroad, with special emphasis on the work of world poets writing in English, and the work of overseas poets in translation." Has published *Row!* by Thomaz Salamun (Slovenia), *Far from Sodom* by Inna Lisnianskaya (Russia), *Star Light* by David Baker (USA), *Bluegrass Wasteland* by Terry Hummer (USA), *The Readers Under the City* by Saskia Hamilton (Canada), and *A Sinner Saved by Grace* by Michael Haslam (UK). **"Please note that our publication schedule is full for the next two years and that we are not at present accepting unsolicited manuscripts."**

ARCTOS PRESS; HOBEAR PUBLICATIONS

P.O. Box 401, Sausalito CA 94966-0401. (415)331-2503. E-mail: runes@aol.com. Website: http://members.aol.com/RUNES. Established 1997. **Contact:** CB Follett, editor.

Book/Chapbook Needs Arctos Press, under the imprint HoBear Publications, publishes 1-2 paperbacks/year. "We publish quality, perfect-bound books and anthologies of poetry, usually theme-oriented, in runs of 1,500." Has published *GRRRRR, A Collection of Poems About BEARS* (anthology); *Prism*, poems by David St. John; *Fire Is Favorable to the Dreamer*, poems by Susan Terris; and others.

How to Submit "We do not accept unsolicited manuscripts unless a current call has been posted in *Poets & Writers* and/or elsewhere, at which time up to 5 poems related to the theme should be sent." Accepts previously published poems (if author holds the rights) and simultaneous submissions ("if we are kept informed"). Accepts submissions by postal mail only. List of upcoming themes and guidelines available for SASE or on website. Pays one author's copy; discounts available on additional copies.

Also Offers *Runes, A Review of Poetry* (see separate listing in this section).

ARJUNA LIBRARY PRESS; JOURNAL OF REGIONAL CRITICISM (Specialized: surrealism; science fiction/fantasy; spirituality; symbols)

1404 E. Bijou St., Colorado Springs CO 80909-5520. Website: http://hometown.aol.com/druphoff/myhomepage/newsletter.html. Library established 1963; press established 1979. **Contact:** Count Prof. Joseph A. Uphoff, Jr., executive director.

Magazine Needs "The Arjuna Library Press is avant-garde, designed to endure the transient quarters and marginal funding of the literary phenomenon (as a tradition) while presenting a context for the development of current mathematical ideas in regard to theories of art, literature, and performance; photocopy printing allows for very limited editions and irregular format. Quality is maintained as an artistic materialist practice." Publishes "surrealist prose poetry, visual poetry, dreamlike, short and long works; no obscene, profane (will criticize but not publish), unpolished work." Has published work by B.Z. Niditch, Dr. Shari O'Brien, David Lawrence, Holly Day, John Grey, and Woodrow G. Moore, II. *Journal of Regional Criticism* is published on loose photocopied pages of collage, writing, and criticism, appearing frequently in a varied format. Reviews books of poetry "occasionally." Send materials for review consideration. "Upon request will treat material as submitted for reprint, one-time rights."

Book/Chapbook Needs & How to Submit Arjuna Library Press publishes 6-12 chapbooks/year, averaging 50 pages each. Sample: $2.50. Currently accepting one or two short poems, with a cover letter and SASE, to be considered for publication. Accepts submissions by postal mail only. Guidelines available for SASE.

Advice "Website exhibition of visual poetics and literature has proceeded through the Mail Art phenomenon. This is an excellent means of contacting the public in an impersonal way; it remains true that there are other venues to develop the commercial profile. As a general rule, we should use principles of scientific observation (minimum interference) such that the preferred dimensions are not strained or reconfigured. If the membership grows too large, rather than excluding contributors by pyramidal elitism, more organization can be founded. In this way an accurate assessment can be maintained as to how many individuals are requesting service. Instead of redesigned organization, the pyramidal elitism can be established by supplemental organization. It follows that acceptance then rises to the level of competency of the artist or writer within a system that provides continuing adequate support for newcomers and advancing practitioners. Thus, we do not need a surrender by vulgar insults: irony can be separated from the other reputable constructs. The audience can gravitate to protected interests.''

☐ ◎ ARKANSAS REVIEW: A JOURNAL OF DELTA STUDIES (Specialized: regional)

P.O. Box 1890, State University AR 72467-1890. (870)972-3043. Fax: (870)972-3045. E-mail: tswillia @astate.edu. Website: www.clt.astate.edu/arkreview. Established 1968 (as *Kansas Quarterly*). **Contact:** Tom Williams, general editor & creative materials editor.

Magazine Needs Appearing 3 times/year, the *Arkansas Review* is ''a regional studies journal devoted to the 7-state Mississippi River Delta. Interdisciplinary in scope, we publish academic articles, relevant creative material, interviews, and reviews. Material must respond to or evoke the experiences and landscapes of the 7-state Mississippi River Delta (St. Louis to New Orleans).'' Has published poetry by Greg Fraser, Jo McDougall, and Catherine Savage Brosman. *Arkansas Review* is 92 pages, magazine-sized, photo offset-printed, saddle-stapled, with 4-color cover. Receives about 500 poems/year, accepts about 5%. Press run is 600 (400 subscribers, 300 libraries, 20 shelf sales); 50 distributed free to contributors. Subscription: $20. Sample: $7.50. Make checks payable to ASU Foundation.

How to Submit Submit any number of poems at a time. No previously published poems or simultaneous submissions. Accepts submissions by postal mail, e-mail (pasted into body of message/as attachment), and on disk. Cover letter with SASE is preferred. Time between acceptance and publication is about 6 months. ''The Creative Materials Editor makes the final decision based—in part—on recommendations from other readers.'' Often comments on rejected poems. Occasionally publishes theme issues. Guidelines available for SASE or by e-mail. Responds in 4 months. Pays 5 contributor's copies. Acquires first rights. Staff reviews books and chapbooks of poetry in 500 words, single- and multi-book format. Send materials for review consideration to Tom Williams. (''Inquire in advance.'')

$ ◎ ARTFUL DODGE

Dept. of English, College of Wooster, Wooster OH 44691. E-mail: dbourne@wooster.edu. Website: www.wooster.edu/artfuldodge/. Established 1979. **Contact:** Philip Brady, poetry editor.

Magazine Needs *Artful Dodge* is an annual literary magazine that ''takes a strong interest in poets who are continually testing what they can get away with successfully in regard to subject, perspective, language, etc., but who also show mastery of current American poetic techniques—its varied textures and its achievement in the illumination of the particular. What all this boils down to is that we require high craftsmanship as well as a vision that goes beyond one's own storm windows, grandmothers, or sexual fantasies—to paraphrase Hayden Carruth. Poems can be on any subject, of any length, from any perspective, in any voice, but we don't want anything that does not connect with both the human and the aesthetic. Thus, we don't want cute, rococo surrealism, someone's warmed-up, left-over notion of an avant-garde that existed 10-100 years ago, or any last bastions of rhymed verse in the civilized world. On the other hand, we are interested in poems that utilize stylistic persuasions both old and new to good effect. We are not afraid of poems that try to deal with large social, political, historical, and even philosophical questions—especially if the poem emerges from one's own life experience and is not the result of armchair pontificating. We often offer encouragement to writers whose work we find promising, but *Artful Dodge* is more a journal for the already emerging writer than for the beginner looking for an easy place to publish. We also have a sustained commitment to translation, especially from Polish and other East European literatures, and we feel the interchange between the American and foreign works on our pages is of great interest to our readers. We also feature interviews with outstanding literary figures.'' Has published poetry by Gregory Orr, Julia Kasdorf, Denise Duhamel, Tess Gallagher, and William Heyen. *Artful Dodge* is digest-sized, professionally printed, perfect-bound, with glossy cover, includes ads. Receives at least 2,000 poems/year, accepts about 60. Press run is 1,000 (100 subscribers, 30 libraries). Single copy: $7; subscription: $7/year, $14/2 years, $25/4 years. Sample (back issue): $5.

How to Submit "Simultaneous submissions are fine, if we are informed of acceptance elsewhere. Please limit submissions to 6 poems. Long poems may be of any length, but send only one at a time. We encourage translations, but we ask for original text and statement from translator that he/she has copyright clearance and permission of author." Responds in up to one year. Pays 2 contributor's copies, plus (currently) $5/page honorarium because of grants from the Ohio Arts Council. Send materials for review consideration; however, "there is no guarantee we can review them!"

$⬤ ARTS & LETTERS JOURNAL OF CONTEMPORARY CULTURE

Campus Box 89, Georgia College & State University, Milledgeville GA 31061. (478)445-1289. E-mail: al@gcsu.edu. Website: http://al.gcsu.edu. Established 1999. **Contact:** Alice Friman, poetry editor. Editor: Martin Lammon.

● Work published in *Arts & Letters Journal* has received two Pushcart Prizes.

Magazine Needs *Arts & Letters Journal of Contemporary Culture* is a biannual journal devoted to contemporary arts and literature, featuring ongoing series such as The World Poets, Translation Series, and The Mentors Interview Series. Wants work that is of the highest literary and artistic quality. Does not want genre fiction, light verse. Has published poetry by Margaret Gibson, Marilyn Nelson, Stuart Lishan, R.T. Smith, Laurie Lamon, and Miller Williams. *Arts & Letters Journal of Contemporary Culture* is 180 pages, offset-printed, perfect-bound, with glossy cover with varied artwork, includes ads. Receives about 4,000 poems/year, accepts about .5%. Press run is 1,500 (1,000 subscribers, 20 libraries). Single copy: $8 plus $1 postage for current issue; subscription: $15 for 2 issues (one year). Sample: $5 plus $1 postage for back issue. Make checks payable to Georgia College & State University.

How to Submit Submit 5 poems at a time. No previously published poems. "Simutaneous submissions are accepted if we are notified immediately of publication elsewhere." No fax, e-mail, or disk submissions. Cover letter is preferred. Include SASE. Reads submissions September 1 through April 1. "Poems are screened, discussed by group of readers, then if approved, submitted to poetry editor for final approval." Seldom comments on rejected poems. Guidelines available in magazine, for SASE, by e-mail, or on website. Responds in 1-2 months. Always sends prepublication galleys. Pays $10/published page ($50 minimum) plus 2 contributor's copies. Acquires one-time rights. Reviews books of poetry in 500 words, single-book format. Query first to Martin Lammon.

Also Offers Annual Arts & Letters Prize for Poets ($1,000, publication, and visit to campus for awards program) and annual Arts & Letters Workshops (May of each year, one-week residential workshops in several genres, including poetry).

🔲 ⬤ ASCENT: ASPIRATIONS FOR ARTISTS MAGAZINE

1560 Arbutus Dr., Nanoose Bay BC V9P 9C8 Canada. (250)468-7313. E-mail: ascentaspirations@shaw.ca. Website: www.bcsupernet.com/users/ascent. Established 1997. **Contact:** David Fraser, editor.

Magazine Needs *Ascent: Aspirations for Artists Magazine* appears quarterly and is "a quality electronic publication specializing in poetry, short fiction, essays, and visual art. *Ascent* is dedicated to encouraging aspiring poets and fiction writers. We accept all forms of poetry on any theme. Poetry needs to be unique and touch the reader emotionally with relevant human, social, and philosophical imagery." Does not want poetry "that focuses on mainstream overtly religious verse." Has published poetry by Janet Buck and Taylor Graham. *Ascent* is published online; however, the magazine will launch its first annual print edition in Fall 2005. Funding for the print version will come from contest entries (see below). Receives about 1,000 poems/year, accepts about 10%.

How to Submit Submit 1-5 poems at a time. Accepts previously published poems and simultaneous submissions. Prefers e-mail submissions (pasted into body of message or as attachment in Word); no disk submissions. "If you must submit by postal mail because it is your only avenue, provide a SASE with IRCs or Canadian stamps." Reads submissions all year on a quarterly basis. Time between acceptance and publication is 3 months. Editor makes decisions on all poems. Seldom comments on rejected poems. Occasionally publishes theme issues. List of upcoming themes available on website. Responds in 3 months. Acquires one-time rights.

Contest/Award Offerings To fund the printing of an annual anthology, *Ascent* offers a contest for poetry and fiction. 1st Prize: $100; 2nd Prize: $75; 3rd Prize: $50; 4th Prize: $25; 5 Honorable Mentions: $10 each (all prizes in Canadian dollars); all winners and honorable mentions receive 2 copies of anthology; all other entrants published in anthology receive one free copy. **Entry fee:** $5/poem or $10/3 poems. **Deadline:** July 31. Guidelines available for SASE, by e-mail, or on website.

Advice "Write with passion for your material. In terms of editing, always proofread to the point where what you submit is the best it can possibly be. Never be discouraged if your work is not accepted; it may be just not the right fit for the current publication."

ASHEVILLE POETRY REVIEW

P.O. Box 7086, Asheville NC 28802. (828)649-0217. E-mail: editor@ashevillereview.com. Website: www.ashevillereview.com. Established 1994. **Contact:** Keith Flynn, founder/managing editor.

Magazine Needs *Asheville Poetry Review* appears "every 200 days. We publish the best regional, national, and international poems we can find. We publish translations, interviews, essays, historical perspectives, and book reviews as well." Wants "quality work with well-crafted ideas married to a dynamic style. Any subject matter is fit to be considered so long as the language is vivid with a clear sense of rhythm. We subscribe to the Borges dictum that great poetry is a combination of 'algebra and fire.' " Has published poetry by Sherman Alexie, Eavan Boland, Gary Snider, Colette Inez, Robert Bly, and Fred Chappell. *Asheville Poetry Review* is 160-180 pages, digest-sized, perfect-bound, laminated, with full-color cover. Receives about 8,000 poems/year, accepts about 5%. Press run is 1,000. Subscription: $22.50/2 years, $43.50/4 years. Sample: $13. "We prefer poets purchase a sample copy prior to submitting."

How to Submit Submit 3-5 poems at a time. Accepts simultaneous submissions; no previously published poems. No submissions by e-mail. Cover letter is required. Include comprehensive bio, recent publishing credits, and SASE. Submission deadlines: January 15 and July 15. Time between acceptance and publication is up to one year. Poems are circulated to an editorial board. Seldom comments on rejected poems. Occasionally publishes theme issues. Guidelines and upcoming themes available for SASE. Responds in up to 7 months. Pays one contributor's copy. Rights revert back to author upon publication. Reviews books and chapbooks of poetry. Send materials for review consideration.

ASININE POETRY (Specialized: humor; satire); MONGREL PUBLICATIONS

P.O. Box 1349, New York NY 10276. E-mail: editor@asininepoetry.com. Website: www.asininepoetry.com. Established 1998 (print), 2001 (online). **Contact:** R. Narvaez, editor.

• Voted Cool Site of the Month, February 2003.

Magazine Needs *the journal of asinine poetry*, a weekly online publication, "features 3-4 new poems each week. We specialize in poems and poets that do not take themselves too seriously. Our poems are best described as silly, saucy, and/or satirical." Wants "any form of poetry, but for us the poetry must be in a humorous, parodic, or satirical style. Many submissions to our site are slapdash, too broadly funny, or funny on just one snickering level. We prefer well-crafted poems that may contain serious elements or cover serious subjects—but which are also slyly amusing, blatantly absurd, or hilarious." Does not want serious, straightforward poems. Has published poetry by Hal Sirowitz, William Trowbridge, Allan Planz, Graham Everett, and Colonel Drunky Bob. Receives about 600 poems/year, accepts about 20%.

How to Submit Submit 3-4 poems at a time. Lines/poem: 50 maximum. Accepts previously published poems and simultaneous submissions. Accepts e-mail (pasted into body of message) and disk submissions. "Attachments are okay—once we've gotten to know you." Cover letter is preferred. "Please send us a brief bio with your submission. If accepted, you may be asked a series of questions to help us cobble a biography that fits in with the site's philosophy." Reads submissions year round. Submit seasonal poems 2 months in advance. Time between acceptance and publication is 2 months. "Poems are circulated to an editorial board that meets once or twice a month in a bar and reads the poems out loud. If you are in a bar and hear your poem being read, feel free to come over and read it to us yourself, so we can hear it the way you intended. Buying us a round also helps." Sometimes comments on rejected poems. Regularly publishes theme issues. List of upcoming themes available by e-mail. Guidelines available on website. Responds in 1-2 months. No payment. "Poet retains rights. If we wish to use the poem in a printed publication, the terms will be negotiated." Reviews books of poetry. Send materials for review consideration to the editor.

Book/Chapbook Needs & How to Submit: Mongrel Publications publishes chapbook collections and compilations of prolific poets from the *asinine poetry* website. Publishes 4 chapbooks/year and one anthology/year. Manuscripts are selected through open submission. "Our anthologies are generally selected from the best poems on the site. Our chapbooks are compilations of the works of individual poets who have more than 12 poems of high quality on the site. Basically, we assemble a greatest hits chapbook for promotional purposes for the poet and the website. Only 50-100 copies are printed. The books are combinations of poems from the site and new submissions." Chapbooks are 12-16 pages, laser-printed, saddle-stapled, with heavy stock covers with art/graphics "depending on the subject matter." Chapbook mss may include previously published poems. Responds to mss in 1-2 weeks. Pays (for chapbook) 20 author's copies (out of a press run of 100) or (for book) 2 author's copies (press run varies). Order sample chapbooks by sending $1.50/chapbook. "Send cash cleverly hidden in envelope; we should have a checking account soon, but for now this is the only way we can accept money."

Contest/Award Offerings Biannual contests "are geared toward certain subjects—for example, erotica, food, politics, holidays—but the poems must fit into our style, i.e., be asinine." Offers 1st Prize: $50-100. **Entry fee:** $1-5. **Deadline:** check website. Guidelines available on website. "The finalists and winners of our past contests are archived on the site. Read through those to see what kinds of poems our guest judges tend to rate highly."

Also Offers "We link to a large array of other humorous poetry sites."

Advice "We find there are two ways of approaching asinine poetry. One, think funny first, and see where the poem takes you. Two, pick a serious topic and take it to a place no one would expect it to go."

☑ ATLANTA REVIEW; ATLANTA REVIEW POETRY 2006

P.O. Box 8248, Atlanta GA 31106. E-mail: dan@atlantareview.com. Website: www.atlantareview.com. Established 1994. **Contact:** Dan Veach, editor.

 • Work published in this review has been included in *Pushcart Prize* anthologies.

Magazine Needs *Atlanta Review* is a semiannual primarily devoted to poetry, but also features fiction, interviews, essays, and fine art. Wants "quality poetry of genuine human appeal." Has published poetry by Seamus Heaney, Billy Collins, Derek Walcott, Maxine Kumin, and Thomas Lux. *Atlanta Review* is 128 pages, digest-sized, professionally printed on acid-free paper, flat-spined, with glossy color cover. Receives about 10,000 poems/year, accepts about 1%. Press run is 2,500 (1,000 subscribers, 50 libraries, 1,000 shelf sales). Single copy: $6; subscription: $10. Sample: $5.

How to Submit No previously published poems. No e-mail submissions unless outside North America. Issue deadlines are June 1 and December 1. Time between acceptance and publication is 6 months. Seldom comments on rejected poems. Guidelines available for SASE. Responds in 2 weeks. Pays 2 contributor's copies plus author's discounts. Acquires first North American serial rights.

Contest/Award Offerings *Atlanta Review* sponsors POETRY 2006, an annual international poetry competition. Prizes: $1,000; 5 $100 awards; 20 International Publication Awards; 30 International Merit Awards. Winners announced in leading literary publications. All entries considered for publication in *Atlanta Review*. **Entry fee:** $5 for the first poem, $3 for each additional. **Postmark deadline:** May 15, 2006. No entry form or guidelines necessary.

◪ THE AURОREAN: A POETIC QUARTERLY; THE UNRОREAN; ENCIRCLE PUBLICATIONS

P.O. Box 187, Farmington ME 04938. (207)778-0467. E-mail: Cafpoet37@aol.com (cannot review submissions or reply to mss by e-mail). Press established 1992; magazine established 1995. **Contact:** Cynthia Brackett-Vincent, editor.

Magazine Needs *The Aurorean* has been published continuously every March, June, September, and December since December 1995. Wants poetry "that is inspirational (not overly religious), meditational, or reflective of the Northeast. Seasonal focus. Need short (up to 6 lines) poems, haiku, and well-done humor. We use mostly free verse, only occasional rhyme. We welcome the beginner and the well published. No ranting, swearing for shock value alone. Nothing hateful." Will publish poetry by children "if it works." Has published poetry by Barry Ballard, Dr. Jim Brosnan, Joanna Nealon, and Christine Klocek-Lim. *The Aurorean* is digest-sized, professionally printed, perfect-bound, with seasonal design. Press run is 500-550. Single copy: $6 US, $7 international; subscription: $21 US, $25 international (for 4 issues). Sample (back issue): $3. Make checks payable to *The Aurorean*.

How to Submit "Please note that our mailing address has changed! As well, the December 2005 issue is our 10th Anniversary issue. For that issue only, submissions are closed for a special celebration. So, except for the reading period of August 16 to November 15, 2005, submit as usual." Lines/poem: 40 maximum. Accepts previously published poems and simultaneous submissions if notified at time of submission ("if they are simultaneous, be aware that none can be withdrawn once we have gone to press"). Cover letter is required. "Fold cover letter separately and fold poems together. Poems folded individually are a nightmare for editors, and we are unable to review them. Include SASE with sufficient postage for return/reply. All manuscripts are acknowledged with a postcard or by e-mail upon receipt. Deadlines are always the 15th of February, May, August, and November. Notice of acceptance and proofs are always sent; poets will be asked to return a 50-word bio upon acceptance. (We cannot edit a long bio and will not use information from a cover letter for a bio.) Poets may specifically send a 50-word bio with their submission if they choose." Pays 3 contributor's copies/accepted poem. Requests one-time rights only; appreciates credit if later published elsewhere.

Contest/Award Offerings 1) Features a "Poet-of-the-Quarter" (a body of work that best captures the season of that issue); awards publication of up to 3 poems with a 100-word bio, 10 copies of magazine, and a one-year subscription. 2) "Also, in each issue, an independent judge picks 'Best Poem'; winner receives $20. 3) Anyone may send entries for 'Poetic-Quote-of-the-Season.' Send 4 lines maximum from a not-too-obscure poet. Source MUST be cited to verify quote, which cannot be acknowledged or returned. Winner receives 2 free issues. 4) Editor recommends one chapbook per issue (small blurb and ordering information; we do not publish reviews). For chapbook to be considered, it must be published within the last 6 months. Cannot be acknowledged or returned."

Also Offers *The Unrorean*, a broadsheet, appears twice/year, publishing poems too long, experimental, or dark for the magazine. "Still, nothing hateful." Broadsheet is 2-4 pages, 11×17, laser-printed. Sample: $2 postpaid. Include SASE for return/reply. No proofs, acknowledgments, or bios; open submission dates. Pays one contributor's copy/poem. "Poets may submit for the magazine or broadsheet individually. Work sent to the magazine will also be considered for the broadsheet, unless otherwise requested in cover letter."

Advice "Be familiar with your markets. Keep writing. Try to support the markets that support poets. *Poet's Market* is your best friend."

$◪ AUSABLE PRESS

1026 Hurricane Rd., Keene NY 12942-9719. E-mail: editor@ausablepress.org. Website: www.ausablepress.org. Established 1999. **Contact:** Chase Twichell, editor. Member: CLMP.

Book Needs & How to Submit Ausable Press wants poetry "that investigates and expresses human consciousness in language that goes where prose cannot." Interested in work by new poets. Does not want children's poetry or poetry for children, chapbooks, light verse, inspirational poetry, illustrated poetry, or journal entries. Has published poetry by C.K. Williams, Steve Orlen, Julianne Buchsbaum, Patrick Donnelly, Karen Whalley, and James Richardson. Publishes 4-6 paperback or hardback titles/year. Number of pages varies; offset-printed, paper and cloth editions. Guidelines available for SASE or on website. Accepts unsolicited mss in June only. **Charges reading fee of $25.** Responds to queries in one week; to mss in up to 4 months. Pays royalties of 10%, advance of $1,000, and 10 author's copies (out of a press run of 1,000).

Advice "This is not a contest. Ausable Press is under no obligation to publish any of the manuscripts submitted. Response time can be as long as 3-4 months, so please be patient."

AVOCET, A JOURNAL OF NATURE POEMS (Specialized: nature; spirituality)

P.O. Box 8041, Calabasas CA 91372-8041. Website: www.csun.edu/~pjs44945/avocet.html. First issue published fall 1997. **Contact:** Patricia Swenson, editor. Chief Associate Editor: Nancy A. Taylor.

Magazine Needs *Avocet* is a quarterly poetry journal "devoted to poets seeking to understand the beauty of nature." Wants "poetry that shows man's interconnectedness with nature; discovering the Divine in nature." Does not want "poems that have rhyme or metrical schemes, cliché, abstraction, or sexual overtones." Has published poetry by Barbara Bennett, Gary Every, Greg Gregory, John Grey, Suzanne Murray, and Lorraine Vail. *Avocet* is 30 pages, $4\frac{1}{4} \times 5\frac{1}{2}$, professionally printed, saddle-stapled, with card cover. Single copy: $5; subscription: $20. Make checks payable to Patricia Swenson.

How to Submit Submit 3-5 poems at a time. Accepts previously published poems if acknowledged; no simultaneous submissions. Cover letter is required. Include SASE for reply only; mss will not be returned. Time between acceptance and publication is up to 6 months. Responds in up to 3 months. Pays one contributor's copy.

THE AWAKENINGS REVIEW (Specialized: people living with mental illness)

5 Forest Hill Dr., Suite 201, Glen Ellyn IL 60137. E-mail: awakeningsreview@aol.com. Website: www.theawakeningsproject.org. Established 1999. **Contact:** Robert Lundin, editor.

Magazine Needs *The Awakenings Review* appears biannually in March and December to publish works by people living with mental illness: consumers, survivors, family members, ex-patients. Wants "meaningful work, good use of the language. Need not be about mental illness." Has published poetry by Joan Rizzo, Wanda Washko, Ben Beyerlein, and Trish Evers. *The Awakenings Review* is 150 pages, digest-sized, perfect-bound, with glossy b&w cover. Receives about 800 poems/year, accepts about 20%. Press run is 1,000 (100 subscribers, 2 libraries, 600 shelf sales); 300 are distributed free to contributors, friends. Single copy $16; subscription: $32. Sample: $10. Make checks payable to *Awakenings Review*.

How to Submit Poet "must live with mental illness: consumer, survivor, family member, ex-patient." Submit 5 poems at a time. No previously published poems or simultaneous submissions. Does not accept e-mail submissions. Cover letter is preferred. Include SASE and short bio. Submit seasonal poems 6 months in advance. Time between acceptance and publication is 8 months. Poems are read by a board of editors. Often comments on rejected poems. Occasionally publishes theme issues. Guidelines available in magazine, for SASE, by e-mail, or on website. Responds in one month. Always sends prepublication galleys. Pays 2 contributor's copies. Acquires first rights. Send materials for review consideration.

Advice "Write a cover letter outlining your relationship to mental illness: consumer, survivor, ex-patient, family member, therapist."

AXE FACTORY REVIEW; CYNIC PRESS

P.O. Box 40691, Philadelphia PA 19107. E-mail: cynicpress@yahoo.com. *Axe Factory* established 1986. Cynic Press established 1996. **Contact:** Joseph Farley, editor/publisher.

Magazine Needs *Axe Factory* is published 1-4 times/year to "spread the disease known as literature. The content is mostly poetry and essays. We now use short stories, too." Wants "eclectic work. Will look at anything but suggest potential contributors purchase a copy of the magazine first to see what we're like. No greeting card verse. If children wish to submit poetry, parents should read the magazine to see if they want their children in it, as much material is adult in nature." Has published *River Architecture: poems from here & there* by Louis McKee, and poetry by Taylor Graham, A.D. Winans, Normal, and John Sweet. *Axe Factory* is 20-40 pages, magazine-sized, saddle-stapled, neatly printed, with light card cover. Press run is 200. Single copy: $9 (current issue); subscription: $24 for 4 issues. Sample: $8 (back issue). Make checks payable to Cynic Press or Joseph Farley.

How to Submit Submit up to 10 poems at a time. Accepts previously published poems ("sometimes, but let me know up front") and simultaneous submissions. Cover letter is preferred, "but not a form letter; tell me about yourself." Often comments on rejected poems. Pays 1-2 contributor's copies. " 'Featured poet' receives more." Reserves right to anthologize poems under Cynic Press; all other rights returned. Several anthologies planned; upcoming themes available for SASE, by e-mail, and in publication. Reviews books of poetry in 10-1,000 words. Send materials for review consideration.

Book/Chapbook Needs & How to Submit Cynic Press occasionally publishes chapbooks. Has published *Childhood* by B.Z. Niditch, *Rule of Thumb* by Kelley Jean White, M.D., *Yellow Flower Girl* by Xu Juan, *Under the Dogwoods* by Joseph Banford, *Ceiling of Mirrors* by Shane Allison, and *13 Ways of Looking at Godzilla* by Michael Hafer. **Reading fee:** $20. Make checks payable to Cynic Press. No guarantee of publication. Contest information available by e-mail.

Advice "Writing is a form of mental illness, spread by books, teachers, and the desire to communicate."

⭐ ◑ ◎ **BABEL: The multilingual, multicultural online journal and community of arts and ideas (Specialized: bilingual/foreign language)**
E-mail: malcolm@towerofbabel.com. Website: www.towerofbabel.com. Established 1995. **Contact:** Malcolm Lawrence, editor-in-chief.

Magazine Needs "*Babel* is an electronic zine that publishes regional reports from international stringers all over the planet, as well as features, round table discussions, fiction, columns, poetry, erotica, travelogues, and reviews of all the arts and editorials. We are an online community involving an extensive group of over 50 artists, writers, and programmers, and over 150 translators representing (so far) 36 of the world's languages. We encourage poetry from all over the planet, especially multicultural poetry as well as multilingual poetry or poetry that has been translated into or from another language, so long as it is in English at least. We also encourage gay/lesbian, bisexual, and pansexual writers. Please, God, no more Bukowski wannabes. Poetry is not a Darwinian competition. It is an expression of who you are. We're not interested in male-bashing or female-bashing poetry. There's a difference between the person who broke your heart and half of the human race. Please don't confuse poetry with therapy. If you do have to bash something, bash the real enemy: corporations. The more they keep us bashing each other, the more they know we won't have the energy to bash them." Has published poetry by Federico Garcia Lorca, Leila Imam-Kulieva, Yves Jaques, and Suzanne Gillis. Receives about 100 poems/year, accepts about 5%.

How to Submit Submit no more than 10 poems at a time. Accepts previously published poems and simultaneous submissions. Accepts e-mail submissions only. Cover letter is required. "Please send submissions with a résumé/cv or bio as a Microsoft Word or RTF document attached to e-mail." Time between acceptance and publication varies; "usually no more than a month or two depending on how busy we are." Seldom comments on rejected poems. Guidelines available on website. Responds in 2-4 weeks. Reviews books and chapbooks of poetry and other magazines, single- and multi-book format. Open to unsolicited reviews. Send materials for review consideration.

Advice "We would like to see more poetry with first-person male characters written by female poets as well as more poetry with first-person female characters written by male poets. The best advice we can give to writers wanting to be published in our publication is simply to write passionately.''

✦ ☐ BABYSUE®

P.O. Box 3360, Cleveland TN 37320-3360. Established 1985. Website: www.babysue.com and www. LMNOP.com. **Contact:** Don W. Seven, editor/publisher.

Magazine Needs *babysue* appears twice/year publishing obtuse humor for the extremely openminded. ''We are open to all styles, but prefer short poems.'' No restrictions. Has published poetry by Edward Mycue, Susan Andrews, and Barry Bishop. *babysue* is 32 pages, offset-printed. ''We print prose, poems, and cartoons. We usually accept about 5% of what we receive.'' Subscription: $16 for 4 issues. Sample: $5.

How to Submit Accepts previously published poems and simultaneous submissions. Deadlines are March 30 and September 30 of each year. Seldom comments on rejected poems. Responds ''immediately, if we are interested.'' Pays one contributor's copy. ''We do occasionally review other magazines.''

Advice ''We have received no awards, but we are very popular on the underground press circuit and sell our magazine all over the world.''

☑ THE BALTIMORE REVIEW

P.O. Box 36418, Towson MD 21286. E-mail: susan@susanmuaddidarraj.com. Website: www.baltimorereview.org. Established 1996. **Contact:** Susan Muaddi Darraj, editor. Founding Editor: Barbara Westwood Diehl.

Magazine Needs *The Baltimore Review*, ''an eclectic collection of writing from Baltimore and beyond,'' appears twice/year (winter and summer) and showcases creative nonfiction, short fiction, poetry, and book reviews. ''We invite submissions from writers in the Baltimore region as well as nationally and internationally.'' Does not want ''sentimental-mushy, loud, or very abstract poetry; corny humor; poorly crafted or preachy poetry.'' *The Baltimore Review* is 144 pages, 6×9, offsetlithograph-printed, perfect-bound, with 10-pt. CS1 cover. Subscription: $15/year, $28/2 years. Sample: $10 (includes $2 p&h). Make checks payable to *The Baltimore Review*.

How to Submit Submit 1-4 poems at a time. No previously published poems. Accepts simultaneous submissions, ''but notify us immediately if your work is accepted elsewhere.'' No fax or e-mail submissions. Cover letter is preferred. SASE required for response. Reads submissions year round. Time between acceptance and publication is up to 6 months. ''Poems are circulated to at least 2 reviewers.'' Sometimes comments on rejected poems. Guidelines available on website. Responds in up to 4 months. Pays 2 contributor's copies, reduced rate for additional copies.

Contest/Award Offerings Sponsors an annual poetry contest. Offers 1st Prize: $300 plus publication in *The Baltimore Review*; 2nd Prize: $150; 3rd Prize: $50. ''Submit 1-4 poems, no more than 5 pages total. All forms and styles accepted, including prose poems.'' **Entry fee:** $12 (includes copy of issue in which 1st-Prize winner is published) or $20 (includes one-year subscription). See website for complete details.

☐ BARBARIC YAWP; BONEWORLD PUBLISHING

3700 County Rt. 24, Russell NY 13684. (315)347-2609. Established 1996. **Contact:** John and Nancy Berbrich, editors.

Magazine Needs *Barbaric Yawp* appears quarterly, ''publishing the best fiction, poetry, and essays available''; encourages beginning writers. ''We are not preachers of any particular poetic or literary school. We publish any type of quality material appropriate for our intelligent and wide-awake audience; all types considered: blank, free, found, concrete, traditional rhymed and metered forms. We do not want any pornography, gratuitous violence, or any whining, pissing, or moaning.'' Has

Robert Stewart

Work that stays new

New Letters, based at the University of Missouri-Kansas City, is one of the premier journals of the Midwest, with a national reputation. It was established in 1934 as *The University Review* and became *New Letters* in 1971. Poet, essayist, and editor Robert Stewart, who has been involved with the magazine since the 1980s, took over as editor-in-chief of *New Letters, New Letters on the Air*, and BkMk Press in September 2002. His latest book is *Outside Language: Essays* (Helicon Nine Editions, 2003).

The 2004 and 2005 issues celebrate the 70th year of *New Letters*. Please tell us about the history of the magazine and your involvement with it.
New Letters magazine, over its 70-year life, has helped define American writing; that's a big claim, but take a look. Any writing student has heard of William Carlos Williams' dictum, "No ideas but in things." That appears in a poem Williams published in *New Letters* in 1944 when it was still called *The University Review. New Letters* has brought forth writers such as e.e. cummings, Edgar Lee Masters, Robinson Jeffers, J.D. Salinger, and Richard Wright. We just published a breakthrough interview with former poet laureate Billy Collins that was excerpted around the country.

My involvement with *New Letters* started as a volunteer in the mid-1970s, under David Ray's editorship. I left the magazine early in the 1980s and returned in 1985, part-time, when James McKinley succeeded Ray and asked me to work with him. During Ray's tenure, he and his wife, Judy, began the national radio show *New Letters on the Air*, and a lot of my own work went into establishing that program. Now the radio program has more than a thousand half-hour programs with writers discussing their work—everyone from Joseph Brodsky and Rita Dove to up-and-comers. I took over in September 2002 as editor-in-chief of the magazine and the radio program.

How many people are involved with *New Letters*, including editors, production staff, etc.? Where do you get your funding?
My role at the magazine continues to be part-time, since I also teach writing in the English Department. Our administrative director, Betsy Beasley, and our editorial assistant, Amy Lucas, both support more than the magazine here at the university, so we sometimes get spread thin. That's our staff, including typesetting and production, which is all in-house. The magazine receives support from the University of Missouri-Kansas City, but is expected to generate most of its own revenue through subscriptions, sales, grants, private gifts, and the like.

In a recent editorial, you wrote: "As our title implies, we seek to publish work that is new; but more than that, we seek work that stays new. Great writing sustains itself after the circumstances of its creation have changed." What do you look for in submissions that identify them as "new"? Can you give some examples?

By "new," I mean more than work that appears in the magazine for the first time; I mean eccentricity, individuality, what Shelley identifies as the "before unapprehended relations of things." One can't really define "new" until it arrives. The job of the literary artist is to reshape our expectations. Who could have predicted Richard Wilbur's poem "Love Calls us to the Things of This World"? A work "stays new" when it has integrity: whole, authentic, complete unto itself, and does not rely on the news item or sentiment of the day to complete its story. I want a story or a poem to engage a moral dilemma, something that matters, which I can carry with me. The possibilities are endless and might range from a single image ("I look into the dragonfly's eye / and see / mountains over my shoulder," Basho) to the strange and secretive life of a man called "The Skull Hunter," which is a story by Robert Day in our January 2005 issue.

As an editor you are clearly interested in the "rediscovery" of writers and artists. A recent example is the prose of Vincent Carter. Can you tell us more about this interest?

The best example is the way *New Letters* revived the reputation of the great Proletarian writer and editor Jack Conroy. Conroy had written folk tales and stories in the 1930s and 1940s, and his novel *The Disinherited* was the definitive novel of the Great Depression until *The Grapes of Wrath* came along. After Conroy left Chicago to retire in his hometown of Moberly, Missouri, David Ray, editor at the time, began to publish Conroy's stories and memoirs in *New Letters*. Then, in 1991, James McKinley and I created a special issue of all new Conroy material, called *The People, Yes*, all of which is fascinating and important. We do things like that In small and large ways all the time—the 1940s-era murals by the artist Luis Quintanilla, for example, in our summer 2004 issue.

Like all editors, I'm over-familiar with the cover letter detailing the writer's hundreds of publications and awards. How much attention do you give to the "credentials" of the writer?

Given the volume of manuscripts most magazines receive, an editor cannot help but be drawn, hopefully, to a cover letter that cites major awards and publications. What counts, however, is the writing itself, and no cover letter can mask a weak story or poem. I will tell you I read every manuscript, looking for greatness; to find greatness by a relative newcomer is often more gratifying than to find greatness by an established writer. "Great" writing to me, by the way, means it is fresh and authentic.

How do you divide your time between your own creative work and editing? Do you find your own work is inspired by what you're considering for *New Letters*?

Richard Wright once said the perfect job for a writer would be as night watchman in a warehouse. What a writer needs is time. I presently have almost none for my own writing, except what I steal from the night or from a department meeting. Somehow, I manage to write poems, which have begun to feel more and more like miracles. "Where did that come from?" However, my prose writing suffers most, because it requires more sustained time.

Being editor of *New Letters* and its affiliate operations—*New Letters on the Air*, BkMk Press, along with the teaching I do—does inspire me intellectually; it puts me into the national discussion of ideas and aesthetics. I also work in my office on Thanksgiving and Christmas, trying to meet deadlines. It's the job I want, my version of the perfect job. It's eating me alive.

Every editor puts his or her "mark" on their publication. In what direction are you taking *New Letters*?

There are two phenomena in this process: the phenomenon of submissions—monsoons of manuscripts to consider for publication—and there is the phenomenon of reading new work by well-established writers. An editor has to move fast, and, ultimately, all that matters is great writing. That's all. The volume of manuscripts forces an editor to respond first of all, instinctively, to what he loves. There's a quality of voice that emerges now and then, that has distinctiveness. That voice I think of as authenticity. Push aside the jargon, conventional phrases, journalistic clichés, academic pretension, self-absorbed bar talk, and once in a while a voice will emerge that sounds like the writer actually has an interest in something other than himself. The subject is life.

How would you characterize your audience? How aware are you of them when you're making editorial choices?

I believe in the transformative power of great writing; and if this magazine can deliver to its audience, both the MFA creative writing student and the retired farmer (both of whom exist among our readers), then they'll be delighted and changed.

What work published in *New Letters* has given you the most pleasure?

I get pleasure from publishing the kind of short stories, poems, essays, and art that our readers do not expect to see in the magazine. What is a typical *New Letters* story? Is it "What Does God Care About Your Dignity, Victor Travesty?" by Thomas E. Kennedy, about a crime boss who confronts God in a warehouse? Is it the poem "Ella" by Gary Gildner, about killing a dog? Every piece of writing that succeeds as literary art finds its own way to beauty.

Please tell us about the literary awards sponsored by *New Letters* and their significance to the magazine.

Our annual literary awards—$1,000 prizes, plus publication—have, over their 20-year tenure, had the amazing ability to find great writing we otherwise would not have found. Most of the winners have been virtually unknown writers; the vast majority have been women. This is true, even though we scrupulously maintain anonymity in the judging process. The Awards function as a separate and complimentary level of editorial discovery.

What position do you think serious literature and art in general hold in 21st-century American society?

The National Endowment for the Arts recently conducted a survey that shows literary reading on the decline (from 1980 to 2000); but there are still millions of literary readers, even for poetry. More important, literary writers need to take the long view when thinking about audience. Basho and Keats, Dickinson and Gelhorn, and all the other masters still are being read. My own poem "Ice and Freezing Rain" might well matter to someone who experiences the ice storm of 2105.

—*Brian Daldorph*

Brian Daldorph, editor of *Coal City Review*, teaches at the University of Kansas in Lawrence. He has taught in Japan, Senegal, Zambia, and England. His third full-length book of poems is *Senegal Blues* (219 Press).

published poetry by Nancy Henry, Mark Spitzer, and Jeff Grimshaw. *Barbaric Yawp* is a 60-page booklet, stapled, with 67-lb. cover. Receives 1,000 poems/year, accepts about 5%. Press run is 120 (40 subscribers, 4 libraries). Single copy: $4; subscription: $15/year (4 issues). Make checks payable to John Berbrich.

How to Submit Submit up to 5 poems at a time. Lines/poem: 50 maximum. Accepts previously published poems and simultaneous submissions. Accepts submissions by postal mail only. One-page cover letter is preferred; include a short publication history (if available) and a brief bio. Include SASE. No deadlines; reads year round. Time between acceptance and publication is up to 6 months. Often comments on rejected poems. Guidelines available for SASE. Responds in up to 2 months. Pays one contributor's copy. Acquires one-time rights.

Advice "Read a lot—Dead White Males and Living Black Females—and everyone in between. Write often, summon the Muse, and don't fear rejection!"

☑ BARDSONG, THE JOURNAL FOR CELEBRATING THE CELTIC SPIRIT (Specialized: Celtic-themed)

P.O. Box 775396, Steamboat Springs CO 80477-5396. Fax: (970)879-2657. E-mail: agilpin@bardson gpress.com. Website: www.bardsongpress.com. Established 1997. **Contact:** Ann Gilpin, editor. Member: SPAN, PMA, CIPA.

Magazine Needs *Bardsong* is a Celtic-themed literary magazine appearing semi-annually. "Our quest is to encourage and celebrate Celtic heritage and culture through poetry, short stories, essays, creative nonfiction, reviews, interviews, and artwork. We are looking for work that reflects the ageless culture, history, symbolism, mythology, and spirituality that belongs to Celtic heritage. Any style or format is welcome. If it is not Celtic themed, don't submit it." *Bardsong* is laser-printed, saddle-stitched. Sample: $6.50. Make checks payable to Bardsong Press.

How to Submit Submit up to 3 poems at a time (2 pages/poem maximum). No book-length poetry collections. Accepts simultaneous submissions ("notify us if the piece is published elsewhere before acceptance with us"). Accepts e-mail submissions (at submissions@bardsongpress.com); no fax submissions. Cover letter is preferred; include brief bio and publication credits. Guidelines available for SASE or on website. Responds in 4 months. Pays 2 contributor's copies/contribution.

Advice "Please follow the publisher's guidelines; professionalism counts."

$☑ BARNWOOD PRESS; BARNWOOD

P.O. Box 146, Selma IN 47383. (765)288-0149. E-mail: tkoontz@bsu.edu. Website: www.barnwood press.org. Established 1975. **Contact:** Tom Koontz, editor.

Magazine Needs *Barnwood* appears online "to serve poets and readers by publishing excellent poems." Does not want "expressions of prejudice such as racism, sexism." Has published poetry by Bly, Goedicke, Friman, and Stafford. Receives about 3,000 poems/year, accepts about 1%.

How to Submit Submit 1-3 poems at a time. Accepts simultaneous submissions; no previously published poems. Accepts submissions by postal mail only. "SASE or no response." Reads submissions September 1 through May 31 only. Time between acceptance and publication is one day. Seldom comments on rejected poems. Responds in one month. Pays $25/poem. Acquires one-time rights.

Book/Chapbook Needs & How to Submit Barnwood Press publishes one paperback and one chapbook of poetry/year. Has recently published *Gone So Far* by Martha Collins and *Whatever You Can Carry* by Stephen Herz. Chapbooks are usually 12-32 pages, offset-printed, saddle-stapled, with paper covers with art; size varies. Query first with a few sample poems and cover letter with brief bio and publication credits. Responds to queries and mss in one month. Order sample books or chapbooks from website.

Advice "Emphasize imagination, passion, engagement, artistry."

Publishers of Poetry

☑ BARROW STREET; BARROW STREET PRESS; BARROW STREET PRESS BOOK CONTEST

P.O. Box 1831, New York NY 10156. E-mail: info@barrowstreet.org. Website: www.barrowstreet.org. Established 1998. **Contact:** Patricia Carlin, Peter Covino, Lois Hirshkowitz, and Melissa Hotchkiss, editors.

- Poetry published in *Barrow Street* has been selected for inclusion in *The Best American Poetry 2000, 2001, 2002,* and *2003.*

Magazine Needs "*Barrow Street,* a poetry journal appearing twice/year, is dedicated to publishing new and established poets." Wants "poetry of the highest quality; open to all styles and forms." Has published poetry by Kim Addonizio, Lyn Hejinian, Marie Ponsot, Jane Hirshfield, Donald Revell, and Charles Bernstein. *Barrow Street* is 96-120 pages, digest-sized, professionally printed, perfect-bound, with glossy cardstock cover with color or b&w photography. Receives about 3,000 poems/year, accepts about 3%. Press run is 1,000. Subscription: $15/year, $28/2 years, $42/3 years. Sample: $8.

How to Submit Submit up to 5 poems at a time. Accepts simultaneous submissions (when notified); no previously published poems. Cover letter with brief bio is preferred. Reads submissions year round. Poems are circulated to an editorial board. Seldom comments on rejected poems. Occasionally publishes theme issues. Guidelines available for SASE or on website. Responds in up to 6 months. Always sends prepublication galleys. Pays 2 contributor's copies. Acquires first rights.

Contest/Award Offerings Barrow Street Press was established in 2002. Recently published *Selah* by Joshua Corey, *Hiatus* by Evelyn Reilly, and *Hat on a Bed* by Christine Scanlon. Submit ms to Barrow Street Press Book Contest. Publication of ms in book form and $1,000 awarded to "best previously unpublished manuscript of poetry in English." Manuscript should be single-spaced on white 8½×11 paper. Photocopies acceptable. Include 2 title pages and an acknowledgments page listing any poems previously published in journals or anthologies. Author's name, address, and daytime phone number should appear on first title page only. Include SASE for notification. **Entry fee:** $25. Make checks payable to Barrow Street. **Deadline:** was June 30 in 2005. See website for current guidelines.

Advice "Submit your strongest work."

☐ BATHTUB GIN; PATHWISE PRESS

P.O. Box 2392, Bloomington IN 47402. E-mail: charter@bluemarble.net. Website: http://home.bluemarble.net/~charter/btgin.htm. Established 1997. **Contact:** Christopher Harter, editor.

Magazine Needs *Bathtub Gin,* a biannual appearing in April and October, is "an eclectic aesthetic . . . we want to keep you guessing what is on the next page." Wants poetry that "takes a chance with language or paints a vivid picture with its imagery . . . has the kick of bathtub gin, which can be experimental or a sonnet. No trite rhymes . . . Bukowski wannabes (let the man rest) . . . confessionals (nobody cares about your family but you)." Has published poetry by Kell Robertson, Mark Terrill, Mike James, and Lindsay Wilson. *Bathtub Gin* is about 60 pages, digest-sized, laser-printed, saddle stapled, with 80-lb. coverstock cover. "We feature a 'News' section where people can list their books, presses, events, etc." Receives about 1,200 poems/year, accepts about 5%. Press run is 250 (70 subscribers, 30 shelf sales); 10 distributed free to reviewers, other editors, and libraries. Subscription: $8. Sample: $5; foreign orders add $2; back issues: $3.50. Make checks payable to Christopher Harter.

How to Submit Submit 4-6 poems at a time. Include SASE. Accepts previously published poems and simultaneous submissions. Accepts submissions by postal mail and by e-mail (pasted into body of message). Cover letter is required. "Three- to five-line bio required if you are accepted for publication . . . if none [provided], we make one up." Reads submissions June 1 through September 15 only, but accepts contributions for 2 issues. Time between acceptance and publication is up to 8 months. Often comments on rejected poems. Guidelines available in magazine, for SASE, by e-mail, or on website. Responds in up to 2 months. Pays 2 contributor's copies. "We also sell extra copies to contributors at a discount, which they can give away or sell at full price."

Book/Chapbook Needs & How to Submit Pathwise Press's goal is to publish chapbooks, broadsides, and "whatever else tickles us." Has published *The Levelling Wind* by Kell Robertson, *Nothing But Love* by Mike James, *The United Colors of Death* by Mark Terrill, and *Living Room, Earth* by Carmen Germain. For publishing guidelines, send SASE or visit website.

Advice "Press will probably be moving; destination unknown. Query via e-mail to check current address."

BAY AREA POETS COALITION (BAPC); POETALK

P.O. Box 11435, Berkeley CA 94712-2435. E-mail: poetalk@aol.com. Website: http://hometown.aol.com/poetalk/myhomepage/index.html. Established 1974.

Magazine Needs *Poetalk*, the quarterly poetry journal of the BAPC, publishes about 65 poets in each issue. "BAPC has 150 members, 30 subscribers, but *Poetalk* is open to all. No particular genre. Rhyme must be well done." *Poetalk* is 36 pages, digest-sized, photocopied, saddle-stapled, with heavy card cover. Circulation is 300+ for members, subscribers, and contributors. Subscription: $8/year. Sample: SASE with 83¢ postage. BAPC Membership: $15/year, includes subscription to *Poetalk* and other privileges; extra outside US.

How to Submit Submit up to 4 poems at a time, no more than twice/year. Lines/poem: under 35 preferred; longer poems of outstanding quality accepted. Accepts previously published poems and simultaneous submissions, but must be noted. Cover letter and SASE are required. "Manuscripts should be clearly typed, single-spaced, and include author's name and mailing address on every page. Include e-mail address if you have one." Responds in up to 4 months. Pays one contributor's copy. All rights revert to authors upon publication.

Contest/Award Offerings Sponsors yearly contest. Guidelines available in early September for SASE or by e-mail.

Also Offers BAPC holds monthly readings (in Berkeley, CA).

Advice "If you don't want suggested revisions, you need to say so clearly in your cover letter or indicate on each poem submitted."

BAY WINDOWS (Specialized: gay/lesbian)

637 Tremont St., Boston MA 02118. E-mail: rkikel@baywindows.com. Website: www.BayWindows.com. Established 1983. **Contact:** Rudy Kikel, poetry editor.

Magazine Needs *Bay Windows* is a weekly gay and lesbian newspaper published for the New England community, regularly using "short poems of interest to lesbians and gay men. Poetry that is 'experiential' seems to have a good chance with us, but we don't want poetry that just 'tells it like it is.' Our readership doesn't read poetry all the time. A primary consideration is giving pleasure. We'll overlook the poem's (and the poet's) tendency not to be informed by the latest poetic theory, if it does this: pleases. Pleases, in particular, by articulating common gay or lesbian experience, and by doing that with some attention to form. I've found that a lot of our choices were made because of a strong image strand. Humor is always welcome—and hard to provide with craft. Obliquity, obscurity? Probably not for us. We won't presume on our audience." Has published poetry by Patrick Donnelly, Renee Dragoset, Shawn Fawson, Bob McCranie, and Judith Saunders. Receives about 300 submissions/year, accepts about 10%. *Bay Windows* is published online as well as in print. Single copy: 50¢; subscription: $40. Sample: $3.

How to Submit Submit 3-5 poems at a time. Lines/poem: up to 30. "Include short biographical blurb and SASE. No submissions via e-mail, but poets may request info via e-mail." Editor "often" comments on rejected poems. Responds in up to 6 months. Pays one contributor's copy "unless you ask for more." Acquires first rights. Reviews books of poetry in about 750 words—"Both single and omnibus reviews (the latter are longer)."

BAYOU

Dept. of English, University of West Florida, 11000 University of West Florida, Pensacola FL 32514 *(for spring deadline)* **or** Dept. of English, University of New Orleans, Lakefront, New Orleans LA 70148 *(for fall deadline)*. E-mail: bayou@uwf.edu **or** bayou@uno.edu. Established 1975 as *The*

Panhandler (University of West Florida); 2002 as *Bayou* (co-published by University of West Florida and University of New Orleans). **Contact:** Reginald Shepherd, editor (University of West Florida) **or** Joanna Leake, editor (University of New Orleans, Lakefront). Member: CLMP (Council of Literary Magazines and Presses).

Magazine Needs *Bayou*, formerly known as *The Panhandler*, is "a semiannual literary journal of poetry and prose, a collaborative project between the University of New Orleans and the University of West Florida. The University of New Orleans publishes the Fall issue, and the University of West Florida publishes the Spring issue." Wants "sophisticated, intelligent, well written poetry that takes full advantage of the resources of the English language and literary tradition; besides that, we have no particular stylistic biases." Does not want "amateur poetry; vague, clichéd, or preachy poetry." Has published poetry by Marilyn Hacker, Brenda Hillman, Laura Mullen, and Cole Swensen. *Bayou* is 76 pages, digest-sized, professionally printed, perfect-bound, with matte cardstock cover (artwork varies). Receives "hundreds of submissions," accepts "very few." Press run is 500 (150 subscribers, 15 libraries, 50 shelf sales); distributed free to students and faculty of University of West Florida and University of New Orleans. Single copy: $5; subscription: $10. Make checks payable to "University of West Florida **or** UNO Foundation (for University of New Orleans), depending on where you send your subscription request."

How to Submit Submit 4 poems at a time. Lines/poem: "We have no strict length restrictions, though obviously it is harder to fit in very long poems." Accepts simultaneous submissions; no previously published poems. No e-mail or disk submissions. "A brief cover letter is appropriate, but don't tell us your life story, explain your poems, or tell us how wonderful your poems are." Submission deadlines are October 31 and February 15. "Send to the University of New Orleans for the fall deadline, and to the University of West Florida for the spring deadline. We do not read submissions outside of our reading periods, and we do not read over the summer." Time between acceptance and publication is 6 months. Poems are circulated to an editorial board. Never comments on rejected poems. Guidelines available in magazine, for SASE, or by e-mail. Responds in 3 months. Pays 2 contributor's copies. Acquires first North American serial rights.

🔲 ◎ BEAR CREEK HAIKU (Specialized: haiku/senryu; poems under 15 lines)

P.O. Box 3787, Boulder CO 80307. Established 1991. **Contact:** Ayaz Daryl Nielsen, editor.

Magazine Needs *bear creek haiku* appears in a small format. Wants especially haiku/senryu in addition to poetry of any form/style. Has published poetry by Ed Markowski, Amitava Dasgupta, Kelley Jean White, and Vivian Bolland Schroeder. *bear creek haiku* is 24 pages, photocopied on legal-sized colored paper that is cut in thirds lengthwise, stacked 3-high, folded in the middle, and stapled. Receives about 3,000 poems/year, accepts about 8%. Press run is about 150 (50+ subscribers); others distributed free to poets and a homeless person who occasionally sells copies at a traffic interchange for spare coins. Single copy: free for SASE; subscription: $5/year. Make checks payable to Daryl Nielsen or the Humane Society of Boulder Valley.

How to Submit Submit 5-20 poems at a time. Accepts previously published poems and simultaneous submissions. "Name, address, and several haiku on each page. Keep your postage expenses at 2 first-class stamps, one of which is on the SASE." Reads submissions year round. Time between acceptance and publication is about 2 months. "Appreciate poetic interaction, albeit usually brief." Guidelines available for SASE. Responds within one month. Pays 2 contributor's copies. Acquires first rights.

Also Offers Continuing yearly, will publish an anthology of poets published the prior year, with one copy going to each poet the first quarter of following year. Also, will contact potential victims about chapbooks.

Advice "We appreciate receiving your own personal favorites, be they simultaneously submitted or published elsewhere or never seen before. Write, create your poems—the heart, spirit, shadow, ancestors, an occasional editor, etc., will benefit deeply."

$ ◎ THE BEAR DELUXE (Specialized: nature/ecology)

P.O. Box 10342, Portland OR 97296-0342. (503)242-1047. E-mail: bear@orlo.org. Website: www.orl o.org. Established 1993. **Contact:** Casey Bush, poetry editor. Editor: Tom Webb.

- Note: *The Bear Deluxe* is published by Orlo, a nonprofit organization exploring environmental issues through the creative arts.

Magazine Needs *The Bear Deluxe* is a quarterly that "provides a fresh voice amid often strident and polarized environmental discourse. Street-level, non-dogmatic, and solution-oriented, *The Bear Deluxe* presents lively creative discussion to a diverse readership." Wants poetry with "innovative environmental perspectives, not much longer than 50 lines. No rants." Has published poetry by Judith Barrington, Robert Michael Pyle, Mary Winters, Stephen Babcock, Carl Hanni, and Derek Sheffield. *The Bear Deluxe* is 48 pages, 9×12, newsprint with brown Kraft paper cover, saddle-stapled. Receives about 1,200 poems/year, accepts about 20-30. Press run is 20,000 (750 subscribers, 20 libraries); 18,000 distributed free on the streets of the Western US and beyond. Subscription: $16. Sample: $3. Make checks payable to Orlo.

How to Submit Submit 3-5 poems at a time. Lines/poem: 50 maximum. Accepts previously published poems and simultaneous submissions, "so long as noted." Accepts e-mail submissions, "in body of message. We can't respond to e-mail submissions but do look at them." Poems are reviewed by a committee of 3-5 people. Publishes one theme issue/year. List of upcoming themes and guidelines available for SASE. Responds in 6 months. Pays $20/poem, one contributor's copy (more if willing to distribute), and subscription. Acquires first or one-time rights.

$ ☐ ◎ BEAR STAR PRESS; DOROTHY BRUNSMAN POETRY PRIZE (Specialized: regional)

185 Hollow Oak Dr., Cohasset CA 95973. (530)891-0360. E-mail: bspencer@bearstarpress.com. Website: www.bearstarpress.com. Established 1996. **Contact:** Beth Spencer, editor/publisher.

Book/Chapbook Needs & How to Submit Bear Star Press accepts work by poets from Western and Pacific states ("Those west of Central time zone"). "Bear Star is committed to publishing the best poetry it can attract." Wants "well-crafted poems. No restrictions as to form, subject matter, style, or purpose." Has published *The Soup of Something Missing* by Rick Bursky, *Keel Bone* by Maya Khosla, *Nowhere Near Moloka'i* by Gary Chang, *The Book of Common Betrayals* by Lynne Knight, and *The Bandsaw Riots* by Arlitia Jones. Publishes 1-2 paperbacks/year, and occasionally chapbooks. Books are usually 35-75 pages, professionally printed, perfect-bound; size varies. Chapbooks are usually $7; full-length collections, $12. "Poets should enter our annual book competition (see below). Other books are occasionally solicited, sometimes from among contestants who didn't win."

Contest/Award Offerings The annual Dorothy Brunsman Poetry Prize is "open to poets from Western and Pacific states (including Alaska and Hawaii), although other eligibility requirements change depending on the composition of our list up to that point. From time to time we add to our list other poets from our target area whose work we admire." Awards $1,000 and 25 author's copies (out of a press run of up to 750). Submit ms of 50-65 pages. Accepts previously published poems ("with permissions") and simultaneous submissions. "Any form or subject is acceptable, but I prefer single-spaced manuscripts in a plain, 10- to 12-point font such as Times New Roman. Name, address, and phone number should appear on a separate cover sheet only. Manuscripts are not returned but are recycled." Generally reads submissions September through November. Guidelines available for SASE or on website. Time between acceptance and publication is up to 9 months. "I occasionally hire a judge. More recently I have taken on the judging with help from poets whose taste I trust." Seldom comments on rejected poems. Responds to queries regarding competitions in 1-2 weeks. **Entry fee:** $20. **Postmark deadline:** was November 30 for 2004. Contest winner notified on or before February 1.

Advice "Send your best work; consider its arrangement. A 'Wow' poem early on keeps me reading."

☐ ◎ BELHUE PRESS (Specialized: gay)

2501 Palisade Ave., Suite A1, Riverdale, Bronx NY 10463. E-mail: belhuepress@earthlink.net. Website: www.perrybrass.com. Established 1990. **Contact:** Tom Laine, editor.

Book/Chapbook Needs A small press specializing in gay male poetry, publishing 3 paperbacks/year—no chapbooks. "We are especially interested in books that get out of the stock poetry market." Wants "hard-edged, well-crafted, fun and often sexy poetry. No mushy, self pitying, confessional, boring, indulgent, teary, or unrequited love poems—yuck! Poets must be willing to promote book through readings, mailers, etc. We have a $10 sample and guideline fee. Please send this before submitting any poetry. We have had to initiate this due to a deluge of bad, amateur, irrelevant submissions. After fee, we will give constructive criticism when necessary."

How to Submit Query first with 6 pages of poetry and cover letter. Accepts previously published poems and simultaneous submissions. Time between acceptance and publication is one year. Often comments on rejected poems. Will request criticism fees "if necessary." Responds "fast" to queries and submitted mss. No payment information provided.

Advice "The only things we find offensive are stupid, dashed off, 'fortune cookie' poems that show no depth or awareness of poetry. We like poetry that, like good journalism, tells a story."

◘ BELLINGHAM REVIEW; THE 49TH PARALLEL POETRY AWARD

Western Washington University, M.S. 9053, Bellingham WA 98225. (360)650-4863. E-mail: bhreview@cc.wwu.edu. Website: www.wwu.edu/~bhreview. Established 1975. **Contact:** Poetry Editor. Editor: Brenda Miller.

Magazine Needs *Bellingham Review* appears twice/year. "We want well-crafted poetry but are open to all styles." No specifics as to form. Has published poetry by David Shields, Tess Gallagher, Gary Soto, Jane Hirshfield, Albert Goldbarth, and Rebecca McClanahan. *Bellingham Review* is digest-sized, perfect-bound, with matte cover. Circulation is 1,500. Subscription: $14/year, $27/2 years, $41/3 years; $20/year for libraries and institutions. Sample: $7. Make checks payable to The Western Foundation/*Bellingham Review*.

How to Submit Submit 1-3 poems at a time, with SASE. Accepts simultaneous submissions with notification. Accepts submissions by postal mail only. General submissions must be postmarked October 1 through February 1 only. Guidelines available for SASE or on website. Responds in 2 months. Pays 2 contributor's copies, a year's subscription, plus monetary payment (if funding allows). Acquires first North American serial rights.

Contest/Award Offerings The 49th Parallel Poetry Award offers $1,000 annually for 1st Prize, plus publication in and a year's subscription to the *Bellingham Review*. Runners-up and finalists may be considered for publication. Submissions must be unpublished and not accepted for publication elsewhere; work under consideration elsewhere must be withdrawn from the competition if accepted for publication. Submit up to 3 poems. "Poems within a series will each be treated as a separate entry." For each entry, include a 3 × 5 index card stating the title of the work, the category (poetry), the author's name, phone number, address, and e-mail. "Make sure writing is legible on this card. Author's name must not appear anywhere on the manuscript." Include SASE for announcement of winners. Manuscripts will not be returned. Guidelines available for SASE or on website. **Entry fee:** $15 for first entry (up to 3 poems); $10 each additional poem. Make checks payable to The Western Foundation/*Bellingham Review*. "Everyone entering the competition will receive a complimentary 2-issue subscription to the *Bellingham Review*." **Postmark deadline:** between December 1 and March 15. Winners will be announced in summer. 2004 winner was Christopher Bursk for "Epluribus Unum." 2004 contest judge was Lucia Perillo.

◘ BELLOWING ARK; BELLOWING ARK PRESS

P.O. Box 55564, Shoreline WA 98155. (206)440-0791. E-mail: bellowingark@bellowingark.org. Website: www.bellowingark.org. Established 1984. **Contact:** Robert R. Ward, editor.

Magazine Needs *Bellowing Ark* is a bimonthly literary tabloid that "publishes only poetry which demonstrates in some way the proposition that existence has meaning or, to put it another way, that life is worth living. We have no strictures as to length, form, or style; only that the work we publish is, to our judgment, life-affirming." Does not want "academic poetry, in any of its manifold forms." Has published poetry by James Hobbs, Len Blanchard, Paula Milligan, Esther Cameron,

Margaret Hodge, and Jacqueline Hill. *Bellowing Ark* is 32 pages, tabloid-sized, printed on electro-bright stock. Press run is 1,000 (275 subscribers, 500 shelf sales). Subscription: $18/year. Sample: $4.

How to Submit Submit 3-6 poems at a time. "Absolutely *no* simultaneous submissions." Accepts submissions by postal mail and on disk only. Guidelines available for SASE or on website. Responds to submissions in up to 3 months and publishes within the next 2 issues. Occasionally will criticize a ms if it seems to "display potential to become the kind of work we want." Sometimes sends prepublication galleys. Pays 2 contributor's copies. Reviews books of poetry. Send materials for review consideration.

Book/Chapbook Needs & How to Submit Bellowing Ark Press publishes collections of poetry by *invitation only*.

BELL'S LETTERS POET (Specialized: subscribers)

P.O. Box 2187, Gulfport MS 39505-2187. E-mail: jimbelpoet@aol.com. Established 1956. **Contact:** Jim Bell, editor/publisher.

Magazine Needs *Bell's Letters Poet* is a quarterly that you must buy if you wish to be published in it. "Many say they stop everything the day it arrives," and judging by the many letters from readers, that seems to be the case. Though there is no payment for poetry accepted, many patrons send cash awards to the poets whose work they especially like. Poems are "four to 20 lines in good taste." Wants "clean writing; no vulgarity, no artsy vulgarity." Has published poetry by Betty Wallace, Paul Pross, Carrie Quick, and Kalman Gayler. *Bell's Letters Poet* is about 60 pages, digest-sized, photocopied on plain bond paper (including cover), and saddle-stapled. Single copy: $6; subscription: $24. Sample: $5. "Send a poem (20 lines or under, in good taste) with your sample order, and we will publish it in our next issue."

How to Submit Submit 4 poems at a time. No simultaneous submissions. Accepts previously published poems "if cleared by author with prior publisher." Accepts submissions by postal mail only. Accepted poems by subscribers are published immediately in the next issue. Guidelines available in magazine or for SASE. Deadline for poetry submissions is 2 months prior to publication. Reviews books of poetry by subscribers. "The Ratings" is a competition in each issue. Readers are asked to vote on their favorite poems, and the "Top 40" are announced in the next issue, along with awards sent to the poets by patrons. News releases are then sent to subscriber's hometown newspaper. *Bell's Letters Poet* also features a telephone and e-mail exchange among poets, a birth-date listing, and a profile of its poets.

Advice "Tired of seeing no bylines this year? Subscription guarantees a byline in each issue."

BELOIT POETRY JOURNAL; CHAD WALSH POETRY PRIZE

P.O. Box 151, Farmington ME 04938. (207)778-0020. E-mail: sharkey@maine.edu (for information only). Website: www.bpj.org. Established 1950. **Contact:** John Rosenwald and Lee Sharkey, editors.

- Poetry published in the *Beloit Poetry Journal* has been included in *The Best American Poetry* and *Pushcart Prize* anthologies.

Magazine Needs *Beloit Poetry Journal* is a well-known, long-standing quarterly of quality poetry and reviews. "For 55 years of continuous publication, we have been distinguished for the extraordinary range of our poetry and our discovery of strong new poets. We publish the best poems we receive, without bias as to length, school, subject, or form. To diversify our offerings, we occassionally publish chapbooks (most recently *Poets Under Twenty-Five*); these are almost never the work of a single poet." Wants "visions broader than the merely personal; fresh music; language that makes us laugh and weep, recoil, resist—and pay attention. We tend to prefer poems that make the reader share an experience rather than just read about it; these we keep for up to 4 months, circulating them among our readers, and continuing to winnow. At the quarterly meetings of the Editorial Board, we read aloud all the surviving poems and put together an issue of the best we have." Has published poetry by Lucille Clifton, Albert Goldbarth, Patricia Goedicke, Karl Elder, John Haines, and Peter Streckfus. *Beloit Poetry Journal* is about 48 pages, digest-sized, saddle-stapled, attractively printed, with card cover with tasteful art. Circulation is 1,250 (725 subscribers, 225 libraries). Subscription: individuals $18/year, institutions $23/year. Sample (including guidelines): $5. Guidelines without sample available for SASE.

How to Submit "Submit any time, without query, in any legible form; no bios necessary. Any length of manuscript, but most poets send what will go in a business envelope for one stamp. Don't send your life's work." No previously published poems or simultaneous submissions. No e-mail submissions. Pays 3 contributor's copies. Acquires first serial rights. Editor for Reviews and Excanges reviews books by and about poets in an average of 500 words, usually single-book format. Send materials for review consideration to Marion Stocking, 24 Berry Cove Rd., Lamoine ME 04605.

Contest/Award Offerings The journal awards the Chad Walsh Poetry Prize ($3,000 in 2004) to a poem or group of poems published in the calendar year. "Every poem published in 2006 will be considered for the 2006 prize."

Advice "We are always watching for fresh insights, live forms, and language."

N $◎ ⊘ BELTWAY: A POETRY QUARTERLY (Specialized: regional/Washington DC)

E-mail: beltway@mac.com. Website: http://washingtonart.com/beltway.html. Established 2000. **Contact:** Kim Roberts, editor.

Magazine Needs *Beltway: A Poetry Quarterly* "features poets who live or work in the greater Washington, DC metro region. Extensive links give information on area grants, member organizations, presses, reading series, libraries, individual poets, and more. *Beltway* showcases the richness and diversity of Washington, DC authors, with poets from different backgrounds, races, ethnicities, ages, and sexual orientations represented. We have included Pulitzer Prize winners and those who have never previously published. We publish academic, spoken word, and experimental authors—and those whose work defies categorization." Does not want unsolicited submissions. Has published poetry by Cornelius Eady, Anthony Hecht, E. Ethelbert Miller, Jane Shore, Sharan Strange, and Hilary Than. *Beltway* is published online.

How to Submit Considers poems by invitation only. "We publish 4-8 poems by each author featured (typically 5 poets per issue)." Never comments on rejected poems. Sometimes publishes theme issues. List of upcoming themes and guidelines available on website. Pays $150/contributor.

Also Offers "Monthly Poetry News section has information on new publications, calls for entries, workshops, readings and performances. Extensive links also include the most complete listing anywhere of artist residency programs in the U.S."

N $☐ ◎ BETWEEN KISSES NEWSLETTER (Specialized: fantasy; science fiction; horror)

P.O. Box 782, Cedar Rapids IA 52406-0782. E-mail: betweenkisses@samsdotpublishing.com. Website: www.samsdotpublishing.com. Established 2002. **Contact:** Tyree Campbell, editor. Member: The Speculative Literature Foundation (http://SpeculativeLiterature.org).

Magazine Needs *Between Kisses Newsletter* is an online quarterly publishing fantasy, science fiction, sword and sorcery, alternate history, horror short stories, poems, illustrations, and movie and book reviews. Wants fantasy, science fiction, spooky horror, and speculative poetry. Does not want "horror with excessive blood and gore." Has published poetry by Bruce Boston, Karen A. Romanko, Erin Donahoe, Cythera, Kristine Ong Muslim, and Aurelio Rico Lopez III. Receives about 150 poems/year, accepts about 35 (23%).

How to Submit Submit up to 5 poems at a time. Lines/poem: prefers less than 100. Accepts previously published poems; no simultaneous submissions. Accepts e-mail submissions (pasted into body of message); no disk submissions. "Submission should include snail mail address and a short (1-2 lines) bio." Reads submissions year round. Submit seasonal poems 6 months in advance. Time between acceptance and publication is 1-2 months. Often comments on rejected poems. Guidelines available on website. Responds in 4-6 weeks. Pays $2/poem, $1/reprint. Acquires first North American serial rights. Reviews books and chapbooks of poetry. Send materials for review consideration to Tyree Campbell.

Advice "*Between Kisses* is a good place for beginning writers to submit their work."

Ⓝ $□ ◎ BEYOND CENTAURI (Specialized: fantasy, science fiction, and mild horror for older children and teens)

P.O. Box 782, Cedar Rapids IA 52406-0782. E-mail: beyondcentauri@samsdotpublishing.com. Website: www.samsdotpublishing.com. Established 2003. **Contact:** Tyree Campbell, managing editor. Member: The Speculative Literature Foundation (http://SpeculativeLiterature.org).

Magazine Needs *Beyond Centauri* is a quarterly print publication containing "fantasy, science fiction, sword and sorcery, very mild horror short stories, poetry, and illustrations for readers ages 9-18." Wants "fantasy, science fiction, spooky horror, and speculative poetry for younger readers." Does not want "horror with excessive blood and gore." Has published poetry by Bruce Boston, Bobbi Sinha-Morey, Andy Miller, Dorothy Imm, Cythera, and Terrie Leigh Relf. *Beyond Centauri* is 32 pages, magazine-sized, offset-printed, saddle-stapled, with paper cover with color art, includes ads. Receives about 200 poems/year, accepts about 50 (25%). Press run is 100/issue (20 subscribers, 50 shelf sales); 5 distributed free to reviewers. Single copy: $6; subscription: $17/year, $33/2 years. Make checks payable to Tyree Campbell/Sam's Dot Publishing.

How to Submit Submit up to 5 poems at a time. Lines/poem: prefers less than 100. Accepts previously published poems; no simultaneous submissions. Accepts e-mail submissions (pasted into body of message); no disk submissions. "Submission should include snail mail address and a short (1-2 lines) bio." Reads submissions year round. Submit seasonal poems 6 months in advance. Time between acceptance and publication is 1-2 months. Often comments on rejected poems. Guidelines on website. Responds in 4-6 weeks. Pays $2 for original poems and one contributor's copy. Acquires first North American serial rights. Reviews books and chapbooks of poetry. Send materials for review consideration to Tyree Campbell.

Advice "We like to see submissions from younger writers."

$✉ ◎ BIBLE ADVOCATE (Specialized: religious/Christian)

P.O. Box 33677, Denver CO 80233. E-mail: bibleadvocate@cog7.org. Website: www.cog7.org/BA. Established 1863. **Contact:** Sherri Langton, associate editor.

Magazine Needs *Bible Advocate*, published 8 times/year, features "Christian content—to be a voice for the Bible and for the church." Wants "free verse, some traditional, with Christian/Bible themes." Does not want "avant garde poetry." *Bible Advocate* is 32 pages, magazine-sized. Receives about 30-50 poems/year, accepts about 10-20. Press run varies (13,500 subscribers); all distributed free.

How to Submit Submit no more than 5 poems at a time. Lines/poem: 5 minimum, 20 maximum. Accepts previously published poems (with notification) and simultaneous submissions. Accepts e-mail submissions (pasted into body of message; no attachments). "No fax or handwritten submissions, please." Cover letter is preferred. Time between acceptance and publication is up to one year. "I read them first and reject those that won't work for us. I send good ones to editor for approval." Seldom comments on rejected poems. Publishes theme issues. List of upcoming themes and guidelines available for SASE or on website. Responds in 2 months. Pays $20 and 2 contributor's copies. Acquires first, reprint, electronic, and one-time rights.

Advice "Avoid trite or forced rhyming. Be aware of the magazine's doctrinal views (send for doctrinal beliefs booklet)."

◎ ✉ BIBLIOPHILOS (Specialized: bilingual/foreign language; ethnic/nationality; nature/ecology; social issues)

200 Security Building, Fairmont WV 26554. Established 1981. **Contact:** Gerald J. Bobango, editor. (For CA, OR, WA submissions, send to Susanne Olson, P.O. Box 39843, Griffith Station, Los Angeles CA 90039.)

Magazine Needs "*Bibliophilos* is an academic journal for the literati, illuminati, amantes artium, and those who love animals; scholastically oriented, for the liberal arts. Topics include fiction and nonfiction, literature and criticism, history, art, music, theology, philosophy, natural history, educational theory, contemporary issues and politics, sociology, and economics. Published in English, French, German, and Romanian." Also publishes one all-poetry issue per year, containing the winners of an annual poetry contest (see below). Wants "traditional forms, formalism, structure, rhyme; also blank verse. Aim for concrete visual imagery, either in words or on the page. No inspirational verse, or anything that Ann Landers or Erma Bombeck would publish." Accepts poetry written by children ages 10 and up. Has published poetry by Anselm Brocki, Esther Cameron, Paul Bray, Jack C. Wolf, Eugene C. Flinn, and Bernie Bernstein. *Bibliophilos* is 72 pages, digest-sized, laser-photography-printed, saddle-stapled, with light card cover, includes ads. Receives about 200 poems/year, accepts about 30%. Press run is 300 (200 subscribers). Subscription: $18/year, $35/2 years. Sample: $5.25. Make checks payable to *The Bibliophile*. West Virginia residents, please add 6% sales tax.

How to Submit Closed to unsolicited submissions. Query first with SASE and $5.25 for sample and guidelines. Then, if invited, submit 3-5 poems at a time, with name and address on each page. Accepts previously published poems and simultaneous submissions. Cover letter with brief bio is preferred. Time between acceptance and publication is up to one year. Often comments on rejected poems. Guidelines available for SASE. Responds in 2 weeks. Pays 2 contributor's copies. Acquires first North American serial rights. Staff reviews books and chapbooks of poetry in 750-1,000 words, single-book format. Send materials for review consideration.

Contest/Award Offerings Sponsors an annual poetry contest. 1st Prize: $25 plus publication. Send SASE for guidelines.

Advice "Do not send impressionistic, 'Why did he/she leave me, I can't live without him/her' poems about 'relationships,' which have no meaning beyond the author's psyche. Send poetry lamenting the loss of millions of acres of farmland to miserable Wal-Marts, or the lives lost by industrial rape and pollution."

N ◪ BIG TOE REVIEW

E-mail: submissions@bigtoereview.com. Website: www.bigtoereview.com. Established 2004. **Contact:** Joshua Michael Stewart, editor.

Magazine Needs *Big Toe Review*, an online journal, will consider "all types of poems, but we really, really want prose poems. If you write in traditional forms, you better be doing something new with them." Does not want "anything trite." Has published poetry by Ellen Doré Watson, Ryan G. Van Cleave, David Dodd Lee, and Mary Koncel.

How to Submit Submit 3-5 poems at a time. Lines/poem: "the shorter the poem, the better your chances." Accepts previously published poems and simultaneous submissions. Accepts e-mail submissions (pasted into body of message; "never, never attach document"); no disk submissions. Cover letter is required. "We take *only* e-mail submissions. A new issue goes up when there are enough strong poems to warrant a new issue." Reads submissions year round. Sometimes comments on rejected poems. Guidelines available by e-mail or on website. Responds "as soon as possible." No payment. Acquires first North American serial rights.

Also Offers "There is a page dedicated to giving *free* advertisement for the books/chapbooks of poets who are contributors to the magazine, with links to where to buy the book in question."

Advice "Buy as much poetry and read as much poetry as you write."

N ◪ ◎ THE BIG UGLY REVIEW (Specialized: themes)

2703 Seventh St., Box 345, Berkeley CA 94710. E-mail: info@biguglyreview.com (inquiries); poetry@biguglyreview.com (sumissions). Website: www.biguglyreview.com. Established 2004. **Contact**: Miriam Pirone, poetry editor.

Magazine Needs *The Big Ugly Review*, an online literary magazine, appears 3 times/year showcasing "emerging and established writers, photographers, and musicians. Each issue includes fiction (short stories and flash fiction), creative nonfiction, poetry, photo-essays, and downloadable songs, all related to that issue's theme." Wants "vivid and accurate poetry of any style, form, or length." Has published poetry by Edward Smallfield, Jennifer C. Chapis, Stephen Hemenway, and James Cihlar. Receives about 750-1,000 poems/year, accepts about 20.

How to Submit Submit no more than 6 poems at a time. Lines/poem: open. Accepts previously published poems and simultaneous submissions. Accepts e-mail submissions (pasted into body of message *and* as attachment); no disk submissions. "Send documents in Word or Word-readable attachments. Also paste the poems into the body of the e-mail text. Include your name, address, phone number, and e-mail on the first page." Cover letter is preferred. Reads submissions year round. Time between acceptance and publication is 1-2 months. Sometimes comments on rejected poems. Regularly publishes theme issues. List of upcoming themes and guidelines available on website. Responds "approximately one month after close of the issue's submission deadline." No payment. Author retains all rights.

Also Offers: Publishes an annual hard copy "best of" issue.

$⊘ ◎ BIRCH BROOK PRESS (Specialized: anthologies; nature; sports/recreation; popular culture)

P.O. Box 81, Delhi NY 13753. Fax: (607)746-7453. E-mail: birchbrook@usadata.net (no submissions). Website: www.birchbrookpress.info. Established 1982. **Contact:** Poetry Editor. Member: American Academy of Poets, Small Press Center, Publishers Marketing Association, American Typefounders Fellowship.

Book/Chapbook Needs Birch Brook "is a letterpress book printer/typesetter/designer that uses monies from these activities to publish several titles of its own each year with cultural and literary interest." Specializes in literary work, flyfishing, baseball, outdoors, anthologies, translations of classics, books about books. Has published *The Hungarian Sea* by Hollace Lee Gruhn, *Rome Burning* by Helen Barolini, *Daimonion Sonata* by Steven Owen Shields, and *The Architect, The Poet & The Physician* by Rolf Sigfond. Publishes 4 paperbacks and/or hardbacks per year. The press specializes "mostly in anthologies with specific subject matter." Books are "handset letterpress editions printed in our own shop."

How to Submit Query first with sample poems, or send entire ms. No e-mail submissions. Accepts submissions by postal mail *only*. "Must include SASE with submissions." Occasionally comments on rejected poems. Guidelines available for SASE. Pays from $5-25 for publication in anthology. Order sample books by sending SASE for free catalog.

Advice "Send your best work, and see other Birch Brook Press books."

⊘ THE BITTER OLEANDER; FRANCES LOCKE MEMORIAL AWARD

4983 Tall Oaks Dr., Fayetteville NY 13066-9776. (315)637-3047. Fax: (315)637-5056. E-mail: info@b itteroleander.com. Website: www.bitteroleander.com. Established 1974. **Contact:** Paul B. Roth, editor/publisher.

• Poetry published in *The Bitter Oleander* has been included in *The Best American Poetry*.

Magazine Needs *The Bitter Oleander* appears biannually in April and October, publishing "imaginative poetry; poetry in translation; serious language." Wants "highly imaginative poetry whose language is serious." Particularly interested in translations. Has published poetry by Robert Bly, Alan Britt, Duane Locke, Silvia Scheibli, Anthony Seidman, and Charles Wright. *The Bitter Oleander* is 128 pages, digest-sized, offset-printed, perfect-bound, with glossy 4-color cover with art, includes ads. Receives about 10,000 poems/year, accepts about 1%. Press run is 2,000 (1,600 shelf sales). Single copy: $8; subscription: $15. Make checks payable to Bitter Oleander Press.

How to Submit Submit up to 8 poems at a time, with name and address on each page. Lines/poem: 30 maximum. No previously published poems or simultaneous submissions. No e-mail submissions unless outside US. Cover letter is preferred. Does not read mss during July. Time between acceptance and publication is 6 months. Guidelines available for SASE or on website. "All poems are read by the editor only, and all decisions are made by this editor." Often comments on rejected poems. Responds within one month. Pays one contributor's copy.

Contest/Award Offerings Sponsors the Frances Locke Memorial Award, offering $1,000 and publication. Submit any number of poems. **Entry fee:** $10/5 poems, $2 each additional poem. **Postmark deadline:** March 15 through June 15.

Advice "We simply want poetry that is imaginative and serious in its performance of language. So much flat-line poetry is written today that anyone reading one magazine or another cannot tell the difference."

N ◯ BLACK BOOK PRESS

1608 Wilmette Ave., Wilmette IL 60091. (847)302-9547. E-mail: krvanheck@noctrl.edu. Established 2004. **Contact:** Kyle Van Heck, founder/editor.

Magazine Needs *Black Book Press* is a monthly "independent zine, aiming to give small and unpublished authors and artists a place to call home." Prefers "non-rhyming free verse poetry, anything daring, out of the ordinary, or offbeat." Does not want "anything sounding like Robert Frost; no nature poetry, no greeting card verse." *Black Book Press* is about 6 pages, magazine-sized, photocopied, stapled, with plain white paper cover with b&w artwork. Receives about 50 poems/year, accepts about 90%. Press run is 50 (10 subscribers, 10 shelf sales); 20 distributed free to possible contributors and interested writers. Single copy: $1; subscription: $8 ("pays for stamps and paper only!"). Sample: free for SASE. "Promotional stickers are available, 2/$1. Please make any and all checks payable to Kyle Van Heck."

How to Submit Submit any number of poems at a time. Lines/poem: 2 minimum, up to 3 pages maximum. Accepts previously published poems and simultaneous submissions. Accepts e-mail submissions (as attachment in MS Word or WordPerfect); no disk submissions. Cover letter is required. "Always include short (3 lines) bio, SASE. Please type poems and include name, address, phone number, and e-mail on each page." Reads submissions year round. Submit seasonal poems 2 months in advance. Time between acceptance and publication is 1-2 months. "I am the editor (and a struggling writer). If the work is good and/or if I like it, I'll publish it. If it's interesting, strange, original, or different, I'll publish it." Often comments on rejected poems. "I ask (but don't require) that contributors purchase a copy for $1 or a subscription for $8." Guidelines available in magazine, for SASE, or by e-mail. Responds ASAP. Pays one contributor's copy. Acquires one-time rights. Reviews books and chapbooks of poetry and other magazines/journals in 500 words. Send materials for review consideration to Kyle Van Heck.

Advice "Getting published can be tough and frustrating, but it will never happen if you don't try. Just send your work!"

$ ◻ BLACK WARRIOR REVIEW

P.O. Box 862936, Tuscaloosa AL 35486-0027. (205)348-4518. E-mail: bwr@ua.edu. Website: http://webdelsol.com/bwr. Established 1974. **Contact:** Kimberly Campanello, poetry editor. Editor: Aaron Welborn.

● Poetry published in *Black Warrior Review* has been included in volumes of *The Best American Poetry* and *Pushcart Prize* anthologies.

Magazine Needs *Black Warrior Review* is a biannual review appearing in March and October. Has published poetry by W.S. Merwin, Anne Carson, Mark Doty, Jane Miller, Medbh McGuckian, C.D. Wright, and Tomaz Salamun. *Black Warrior Review* is 180 pages, digest-sized. Press run is 2,000. Subscription: $14/year, $25/2 years, $30/3 years. Sample: $8. Make checks payable to the University of Alabama.

How to Submit Submit 3-6 poems at a time. Accepts simultaneous submissions if noted. No electronic submissions. Responds in up to 5 months. Pays up to $50 and one-year subscription. Acquires first rights. Reviews books of poetry in single- or multi-book format. Send materials for review consideration.

Advice "Subscribe or purchase a sample copy to see what we're after. For 30 years, we've published new voices alongside Pulitzer Prize winners. Freshness and attention to craft, rather than credits, impress us most."

✪ ◻ BLACKWIDOWS WEB OF POETRY

4240 Sean St., Eugene OR 97402. E-mail: sunris2set@aol.com. Website: www.geocities.com/black widowswebofpoetry. Established 2001. **Contact:** J. Koffler, chief editor. Editor: Maureen Bush.

Magazine Needs *Blackwidows Web of Poetry* appears 3 times/year. "We are a growing magazine striving to open the door to beginning poets, dedicated to publishing great poetry. We now also accept short stories (less than 2 pages)." Wants well-crafted poetry, all styles and forms. "We love unique, strong imagery; love, nature, humor, etc. Rhyming must be great. We encourage all subject matters. Art accompanied by poems is welcome. We would like to see more art work." Does not want overly religious, sexual, political poems; no racist/violent poetry. Has published poetry by G.A. Scheinoha, Dale Neuman, Tim Reedy, Michael J. Rivet, and Carrie Russ. *Blackwidows Web of Poetry* is 40-60 pages, digest-sized, laser-printed, photocopied, saddle-stapled, with color cover on 65-lb. cardstock with smooth finish. Receives about 500 poems/year, accepts about 40%. Press run is 200 (50 subscribers); 25 distributed free to coffeehouses, local areas of interest. Single copy: $7; subscription: $17. Make checks payable to J. Koffler.

How to Submit Submit 5 poems at a time. Lines/poem: 3 minimum, 30 maximum. Accepts previously published poems and simultaneous submissions. No fax, e-mail, or disk submissions. Cover letter is required, "should include a brief bio, name, address, and phone number. SASE is required. Overseas poets will receive an e-mail response *only*; no SASE is needed, and no payment is able to be made due to funds, though copies are available for purchase." Reads submissions all year. Submit seasonal poems 3 months in advance. Time between acceptance and publication is 4 months. "Do not send unfinished work for critique. Read the guidelines carefully! We do not accept careless submissions. Poems are in review for opinion, style, content, originality, punctuation, etc." Often comments on rejected poems ("we like personal contact with each poet"). "We recommend you invest in a copy to see what we're all about, but it's not required. We appreciate all your support now and in the future." Guidelines are stated in this listing. Responds in one month or less. Sometimes sends prepublication galleys. Pays one contributor's copy. Acquires one-time rights with future credit to *Blackwidow's Magazine*. Reviews other magazines/journals.

Advice "Trust yourself, write what you know, keep your pen alive, and revise, revise!"

THE BLIND MAN'S RAINBOW; THE BLIND PRESS BIANNUAL POETRY CONTEST; THE BLIND PRESS

P.O. Box 18219, Denver CO 80218-0219. E-mail: editor@bmrpoetry.com. Website: www.bmrpoetry .com. Established 1993. **Contact:** Melody Sherosky, editor. Assistant Editor: Nate Condron.

Magazine Needs *The Blind Man's Rainbow* is a quarterly publication "creating a diverse collection of art and poetry from around the world." Wants "all forms of poetry (Beat, rhyme, free verse, haiku, etc.). All subject matter accepted." *The Blind Man's Rainbow* is 24-30 pages, magazine-sized, photocopied, saddle-stitched, with paper cover with art. Receives about 500 submissions/month. Subscription: $14 US, $18 foreign. Sample: $4 US, $5 foreign. Make checks payable to The Blind Man's Rainbow or The Blind Press.

How to Submit Submit 2-10 poems at a time, with name and address on each poem. Accepts previously published poems and simultaneous submissions, "but it is nice to let us know." Accepts submissions by postal mail only; no e-mail submissions. Cover letter is preferred. Include SASE. "Submissions returned only if requested and with adequate postage." Time between acceptance and publication is up to one year. Often comments on rejected poems. Guidelines available for SASE, by e-mail, or on website. Responds in up to 6 months. Pays one contributor's copy. Acquires one-time rights.

Contest/Award Offerings The Blind Press Biannual Poetry Contest awards 3 cash prizes (1st Prize of at least $100). Winners and honorable mentions will be printed in *The Blind Man's Rainbow*. Submit up to 10 poems. No line limit for poems. Contest submissions must include a short poet bio. Mark contest submissions clearly; send to the attention of Melody Sherosky at the address above. Manuscripts will not be returned. Include a SASE if you would like to be notified of contest winners; winners will be contacted directly and announced in the magazine and on the website. **Entry fee:** $4 for first poem, $2 each additional poem. **Deadlines:** May 15 and November 15. Entries postmarked after the contest deadline will be held for the next contest. Guidelines available on website.

Also Offers Additional services offered include designing and distributing advertising and promotional materials for artists and writers. "We design, produce, and distribute chapbooks, postcards, bookmarks, and flyers. Interested parties should contact us with project ideas for a price quote."

✖ ◪ ◎ BLUE COLLAR REVIEW; PARTISAN PRESS; WORKING PEOPLE'S POETRY COMPETITION (Specialized: social issues; working class)

P.O. Box 11417, Norfolk VA 23517. E-mail: red-ink@earthlink.net. Website: www.partisanpress.org. *Blue Collar Review* established 1997; Partisan Press established 1993. **Contact:** A. Markowitz, editor. Co-Editor: Mary Franke.

Magazine Needs *Blue Collar Review* (*Journal of Progressive Working Class Literature*) is published quarterly and contains poetry, short stories, and illustrations "reflecting the working class experience—a broad range from the personal to the societal. Our purpose is to promote and expand working class literature and an awareness of the connections between workers of all occupations and the social context in which we live. Also to inspire the creativity and latent talent in 'common' working people." Wants "writing of high quality which reflects the working class experience from delicate internal awareness to the militant. We accept a broad range of style and focus—but are generally progressive, political/social. Nothing racist, sexist-misogynist, right wing, or overly religious. No 'bubba' poetry, nothing overly introspective or confessional, no academic/abstract or 'Vogon' poetry. No simple beginners rhyme or verse." Has published poetry by Jeff Vande Zande, Joya Lonsdale, Kathryn Kirkpatrick, Marge Piercy, Alan Catlin, and Rob Whitbeck. *Blue Collar Review* is 60 pages, digest-sized, offset-printed, saddle-stapled, with colored card cover, includes literary ads. Receives hundreds of poems/year, accepts about 30%. Press run is 500 (350 subscribers, 8 libraries). Subscription: $15/year, $25/2 years. Sample: $5. Make checks payable to Partisan Press.

How to Submit Submit up to 4 poems at a time; "no complete manuscripts, please." Accepts previously published poems; no simultaneous submissions. Accepts submissions by postal mail only. Cover letter is preferred. Include full-size SASE for response. "Poems should be typed as they are to appear upon publication. Author's name and address should appear on every page. Overly long lines reduce chances of acceptance as line may have to be broken to fit the page size and format of the journal." Time between acceptance and publication is 3 months to a year. Poems are reviewed by editor and co-editor. Seldom comments on rejected poems. Responds in 3 months. Sends prepublication galleys only upon request. Pays 1-3 contributor's copies. Reviews of chapbooks and journals accepted.

Book/Chapbook Needs & How to Submit Partisan Press looks for "poetry of power that reflects a working class consciousness and which moves us forward as a society. Must be good writing reflecting social/political issues." Publishes about 3 chapbooks/year; **not presently open to unsolicited submissions**. "Submissions are requested from among the poets published in the *Blue Collar Review*." Has published *Dictation* by Anne Babson and *American Sounds* by Robert Edwards. Chapbooks are usually 20-60 pages, digest-sized, offset-printed, saddle-stapled or flat-spined, with card or glossy covers. Sample chapbooks are $5 and listed on website.

Contest/Award Offerings Sponsors the annual Working People's Poetry Competition. Prize: $100 and one-year subscription to *Blue Collar Review*. **Entry fee:** $15 per entry. **Deadline:** May 1. Winner of the 2004 Working People's Poetry Competition was Rob Whitbeck. "Include cover letter with entry, and make check payable to Partisan Press."

Advice "Don't be afraid to try. Read a variety of poetry and find your own voice. Write about reality, your own experience, and what moves you."

◪ BLUE LIGHT PRESS; THE BLUE LIGHT POETRY PRIZE AND CHAPBOOK CONTEST

P.O. Box 642, Fairfield IA 52556. (641)472-7882. E-mail: bluelightpress@aol.com. Established 1988. **Contact:** Diane Frank, chief editor.

Book/Chapbook Needs Blue Light Press publishes 3 paperbacks, 2 chapbooks/year. "We like poems that are imagistic, emotionally honest, and that push the edge—where the writer pushes through the imagery to a deeper level of insight and understanding. No rhymed poetry." Has published poetry by Xue Di, Laurie Kuntz, Viktor Tichy, Tom Centolella, Michaelangelo Tata, Christopher Buckley, and Alice Rogoff. Xue Di's *Forgive* is 32 pages, digest-sized, professionally printed with Chinese calligraphy and elegant matte card cover. Cost is $8 plus $2 p&h. A new anthology of visionary poets is in production.

How to Submit Does not accept e-mail submissions. Guidelines available for SASE or by e-mail. Has an editorial board. "We work in person with local poets, have an ongoing poetry workshop, give classes, and will edit/critique poems by mail—$40 for 4 poems. We also have an online poetry workshop. Send an e-mail for info."

Contest/Award Offerings Sponsors the Blue Light Poetry Prize and Chapbook Contest. "The winner will be published by Blue Light Press and receive a $100 honorarium and 50 copies of his or her book, which can be sold for $8 each, for a total of $500." Submit ms of 10-24 pages, typed or printed with a laser or inkjet printer. Include SASE. No ms will be returned without a SASE. **Entry fee:** $10. Make checks payable to Blue Light Press. Send SASE for more information.

Advice "Read some of the books we publish, especially one of the anthologies. We like to publish poets with a unique vision and gorgeous or unusual language; poems that push the edge. Stay in the poem longer and see what emerges in your vision and language."

☑ THE BLUE MOUSE; SWAN DUCKLING PRESS

P.O. Box 586, Cypress CA 90630. E-mail: swduckling@aol.com. Established 1998. **Contact:** René Diedrich, poetry editor. Editor: Mark Bruce.

Magazine Needs *The Blue Mouse* appears quarterly. Wants "poetry based on personal experience; short poems in which common experience is related in an uncommon way." Does not want "abstract, philosophical musings, literary rehashes, Gramma's oven poetry, doggerel, cowboy poetry, smut, Bukowski imitators. Do not send anti-gay or racist material." Has published poetry by Katya Giritsky, Lyn Lyfshin, Michael Kramer, Rachel Rose, and B.Z. Niditch. *The Blue Mouse* is 32 pages, copied, stapled, with blue cover. Receives about 200 poems/year, accepts about 40. Press run is 350 (20 subscribers); 320 distributed free to coffeehouses and poetry readings. Single copy: $1.50; subscription: $6. Make checks payable to Swan Duckling Press.

How to Submit Submit 4 poems at a time. Lines/poem: 2 minimum, 35 maximum. "Do not send epic poems; please respect the line limit." No previously published poems or simultaneous submissions. Accepts e-mail submissions; no disk submissions. Cover letter is preferred. "Remember SASE. One poem per page, typed or typeset." Time between acceptance and publication is 6 months. "We only have 2 editors. If we like it, it goes in. Be prepared to edit." Sometimes comments on rejected poems "if the poems are close but missing something." Guidelines available for SASE or by e-mail. Responds in 6 months. Pays 2 contributor's copies. "Poet keeps copyrights."

Contest/Award Offerings Swan Duckling Press publishes 4 chapbooks/year. Some mss are selected through annual competition. **Deadline:** Competition opens in July, ends October 31. **Entry fee:** $15, includes subscription to *Mouse* and copy of winning chapbook. Chapbook mss may include previously published poems. "Other than contest, chapbooks are published by invitation *only*."

Advice "Don't think we're related to that cartoon mouse down the road. Our mouse is gaining respect because we choose good, compelling poems. Don't send mediocre stuff."

☑ BLUE UNICORN, A TRIQUARTERLY OF POETRY; BLUE UNICORN POETRY CONTEST

22 Avon Rd., Kensington CA 94707. (510)526-8439. Website: www.blueunicorn.org. Established 1977. **Contact:** Ruth G. Iodice, John Hart, and Fred Ostrander, editors.

Magazine Needs *Blue Unicorn* appears in October, February, and June. Wants "well-crafted poetry of all kinds, in form or free verse, as well as expert translations on any subject matter. We shun the trite or inane, the soft-centered, the contrived poem. Shorter poems have more chance with us because of limited space." Has published poetry by James Applewhite, Kim Cushman, Patrick Worth Gray, Joan LaBombard, James Schevill, and Gail White. *Blue Unicorn* is "distinguished by its fastidious editing, both with regard to contents and format." *Blue Unicorn* is 56 pages, narrow digest-sized, finely printed, saddle-stapled. Receives over 3,500 submissions/year, accepts about 200. Single copy: $7, foreign add $3; subscription: $18/3 issues, foreign add $6.

How to Submit Submit 3-5 typed poems on 8½×11 paper. No simultaneous submissions or previously published poems. "Cover letter OK, but will not affect our selection." Guidelines available for SASE. Responds in 3 months (generally within 6 weeks), sometimes with personal comment. Pays one contributor's copy.

Contest/Award Offerings Sponsors an annual (spring) contest with prizes of $150, $75, $50, and sometimes special awards; distinguished poets as judges; publication of top 3 poems and 6 honorable mentions in the magazine. **Entry fee:** $6 for first poem, $3 for each additional poem. Guidelines available for SASE.

Advice "We would advise beginning poets to read and study poetry—both poets of the past and of the present; concentrate on technique; and discipline yourself by learning forms before trying to do without them. When your poem is crafted and ready for publication, study your markets and then send whatever of your work seems to be compatible with the magazine you are submitting to."

◎ BLUELINE (Specialized: regional)

English Dept., Potsdam College, Potsdam NY 13676. Fax: (315)267-2043. E-mail: blueline@potsda m.edu. Established 1979. **Contact:** Rick Henry, editor-in-chief. Member: CLMP.

Magazine Needs Appearing in May, *Blueline* "is an annual literary magazine dedicated to prose and poetry about the Adirondacks and other regions similar in geography and spirit." Wants "clear, concrete poetry that goes beyond mere description. We prefer a realistic to a romantic view. We do not want to see sentimental or extremely experimental poetry." Uses poems on "nature in general, Adirondack Mountains in particular. Form may vary, can be traditional or contemporary." Has published poetry by L.M. Rosenberg, John Unterecker, Lloyd Van Brunt, Laurence Josephs, Maurice Kenny, and Nancy L. Nielsen. *Blueline* is 200 pages, digest-sized. Press run is 600. Sample: $7 for back issues.

How to Submit Submit 3 poems at a time. Lines/poem: 75 maximum; "occasionally we publish longer poems." No simultaneous submissions. Submit September 1 through November 30 only. Include short bio. Poems are circulated to an editorial board. Sometimes comments on rejected poems. Guidelines available for SASE or by e-mail. Responds in up to 3 months. Pays one contributor's copy. Acquires first North American serial rights. Reviews books of poetry in 500-750 words, single- or multi-book format.

Advice "We are interested in both beginning and established poets whose poems evoke universal themes in nature and show human interaction with the natural world. We look for thoughtful craftsmanship rather than stylistic trickery."

$☑ BOA EDITIONS, LTD.; A. POULIN, JR. POETRY PRIZE

260 East Ave., Rochester NY 14604. (585)546-3410. Website: www.boaeditions.org. Established 1976. **Contact:** Thom Ward, poetry editor.

Book/Chapbook Needs & How to Submit Has published poetry by W.D. Snodgrass, John Logan, Isabella Gardner, Richard Wilbur, and Lucille Clifton. Also publishes introductions by major poets of those less well-known. For example, Gerald Stern wrote the foreword for Li-Young Lee's *Rose*. Guidelines available for SASE or on website. Pays advance plus 10 author's copies.

Contest/Award Offerings Sponsors the A. Poulin, Jr. Poetry Prize for a first-book ms. **Deadline:** August–December annually. Guidelines available on website in May.

◪ BOGG PUBLICATIONS; BOGG: A JOURNAL OF CONTEMPORARY WRITING

422 N. Cleveland St., Arlington VA 22201-1424. Established 1968. **Contact:** John Elsberg (USA), Wilga Rose (Australia: 13 Urara Rd., Avalon Beach, NSW 2107 Australia), and Sheila Martindale (Canada: 36114 Talbot Line, Shedden ON N0L 2E0 Canada), poetry editors.

Magazine Needs Appearing twice/year, *Bogg* is "a journal of contemporary writing with an Anglo-

American slant. Its content combines innovative American work with a range of writing from England and the Commonwealth. It includes poetry (to include haiku and tanka, prose poems, and experimental/visual poems), very short experimental or satirical fiction, interviews, essays on the small press scenes (both in America and in England /the Commonwealth), reviews, review essays, and line art. We also publish occasional free-for-postage pamphlets." The magazine uses a great deal of poetry in each issue (with featured poets)—"poetry in all styles, with a healthy leavening of shorts (under 10 lines). Seeks original voices." Accepts all styles, all subject matter. "Some have even found the magazine's sense of play offensive. Overt religious and political poems have to have strong poetical merits—statement alone is not sufficient." *Bogg* started in England and in 1975 began including a supplement of American work; it is now published in the US and mixes US, Canadian, Australian, and UK work with reviews of small press publications from all of those areas. Has published work by Richard Peabody, Ann Menebraker, John M. Bennett, Marcia Arrieta, Kathy Ernst, and Steve Sneyd. *Bogg* is 56 pages, typeset, saddle-stapled, in a digest-sized format "that leaves enough white space to let each poem stand and breathe alone." Receives over 10,000 American poems/year, accepts about 100-150. Press run is 1,750 (400 subscribers, 20 libraries). Single copy: $6; subscription: $15 for 3 issues. Sample: $4.

How to Submit Submit 6 poems at a time. No simultaneous submissions. "We will occasionally reprint previously published material, but with a credit line to a previous publisher." No fax or e-mail submissions. Cover letter is preferred; "it can help us get a 'feel' for the writer's intentions/slant." SASE required or material discarded ("no exceptions.") Prefers typewritten manuscripts, with author's name and address on each sheet. Guidelines available for SASE. Responds in one week. Pays 2 contributor's copies. Acquires one-time rights. Reviews books and chapbooks of poetry in 250 words, single-book format. Send materials to relevant editor (by region) for review consideration.

Book/Chapbook Needs & How to Submit Occasionally publishes pamphlets and chapbooks **by invitation only**, with the author receiving 25% of the print run. Recent chapbooks include *Cleft Brow Totem* by Dave Wright and *South Jersey Shore* by David Check and John Elsberg. Obtain free chapbook samples by sending digest-sized SASE "with at least 2 ounces worth of postage."

Advice "Become familiar with a magazine before submitting to it. Long lists of previous credits irritate me. Short notes about how the writer has heard about *Bogg* or what he or she finds interesting or annoying in the magazine I read with some interest."

◖ BOMBAY GIN

Naropa University, 2130 Arapahoe Ave., Boulder CO 80302. (303)546-3540. Fax: (303)546-5297. E-mail: bgin@naropa.edu. Website: www.naropa.edu/writingandpoetics/bombaygin.html. Established 1974. **Contact:** Samantha Wall.

Magazine Needs "*Bombay Gin*, appearing in June, is the annual literary journal of the Jack Kerouac School of Disembodied Poetics at Naropa University. Produced and edited by MFA students, *Bombay Gin* publishes established writers alongside those who have been previously unpublished. It has a special interest in works that push conventional literary boundaries. Submission of poetry, prose, visual art, translation, and works involving hybrid forms and cross-genre exploration are encouraged." Has published poetry by Amiri Baraka, Joanne Kyger, Jerome Rothenberg, Lawrence Ferlinghetti, Edwin Torres, and Edward Sanders. *Bombay Gin* is 150-200 pages, digest-sized, professionally printed, perfect-bound, with color card cover. Receives about 300 poems/year, accepts about 5%. Press run is 500 (400 shelf sales); 100 distributed free to contributors. Single copy: $12.

How to Submit "Submit up to 3 pages of poetry (12-pt. Times New Roman). Translations are also accepted. Guidelines are the same as for original work. Translators are responsible for obtaining any necessary permissions." No previously published poems or simultaneous submissions. Accepts submission by postal mail, on disk (PC format), and by e-mail (attachment). Cover letter is preferred. Reply with SASE only. Submissions are accepted September 1 through December 1 only. Notification of acceptance/rejection: April 15. Guidelines available for SASE, by e-mail, or on website. Pays 2 contributor's copies. Acquires one-time rights.

◑ ◎ BORDERLANDS: TEXAS POETRY REVIEW (Specialized: regional; bilingual); WRITERS' LEAGUE OF TEXAS

P.O. Box 33096, Austin TX 78764. E-mail: borderlands_tpr@hotmail.com. Website: www.borderlands.org. Established 1992. **Contact:** Editor.

Magazine Needs *Borderlands* appears twice/year publishing "high-quality, outward-looking poetry by new and established poets, as well as brief reviews of poetry books and critical essays. Cosmopolitan in content, but particularly welcomes Texas and Southwest writers." Wants "outward-looking poems that exhibit social, political, geographical, historical, feminist, or spiritual awareness coupled with concise artistry. We also seek poems in two languages (one of which must be English), where the poet has written both versions. Please, no introspective work about the speaker's psyche, childhood, or intimate relationships." Has published poetry by Walter McDonald, Naomi Shihab Nye, Mario Susko, Wendy Barker, Larry D. Thomas, and Reza Shirazi. *Borderlands* is 100-150 pages, digest-sized, offset, perfect-bound, with 4-color cover. Receives about 2,000 poems/year, accepts about 120. Press run is 1,000. Subscription: $18/year, $34/2 years. Sample: $12.

How to Submit Submit 4 typed poems at a time. No previously published poems or simultaneous submissions. No e-mail submissions. Include SASE (or SAE and IRCs) with sufficient postage to return poems. Seldom comments on rejected poems. Guidelines available for SASE or on website. Responds in 4-6 months. Pays one contributor's copy. Acquires first rights. Reviews books of poetry in one page. Also uses 3- to 6-page essays on single poets, and longer essays (3,500-word maximum) on contemporary poetry in some larger context (query first). Address submissions to "Editors, *Borderlands*."

Also Offers The Writers' League of Texas is a state-wide group open to the general public. Established in 1981, the purpose of the Writers' League of Texas is "to provide a forum for information, support, and sharing among writers; to help members improve and market their skills; and to promote the interests of writers and the writing community." Currently has 1,600 members. Annual membership dues are $45. Send SASE for more information to: The Writers' League of Texas, 1501 W. 5th St., Suite E-2, Austin TX 78703. "For non-editorial questions, e-mail borderlandspoetry@gbronline.com."

◐ BORN MAGAZINE

P.O. Box 1313, Portland OR 97207-1313. E-mail: editor@bornmagazine.org. Website: www.bornmagazine.org. Established 1996. **Contact:** Anmarie Trimble, editor. Contributing Editors: Jennifer Grotz, Bruce Smith, and Tenaya Darlington.

Magazine Needs *Born Magazine* appears quarterly as "an experimental online revue that marries literary arts and interactive media. We publish 6-8 multimedia 'interpretations' of poetry and prose in each issue, created by interactive artists in collaboration with poets and writers." Wants poems suited to "interpretation into a visual or interactive form. Due to the unusual, collaborative nature of our publication, we represent a variety of styles and forms of poetry." Has published poetry by Edward Hirsch, Michele Glazer, Crystal Williams, Major Jackson, Joyelle McSweeney, and Bruce Beasley. *Born Magazine* is published online only.

How to Submit Submit 2-5 poems at a time. Accepts previously published poems; no simultaneous submissions. Accepts e-mail submissions. "We prefer electronic submissions as Word documents or .txt files but also accept hard copies; electronic format on disk or via e-mail will be required upon acceptance." Reads submissions year round. Submit seasonal poems 4 months in advance. Time between acceptance and publication is 1-3 months. "Poems must be accepted by the editor and one contributing editor. Selected works are forwarded to our art department, which chooses an artist partner to work with the writer. Artist and writer collaborate on a concept, to be realized by the artist." Never comments on rejected poems. Guidelines available on website. Responds in 3 weeks to e-mail queries. Always sends prepublication galleys. No pay; "We can offer only the experience of participating in a collaborative community, as well as a broad audience (we average 32,000 readers to our site per month)." Acquires one-time rights.

Advice "We accept new and previously published work. *Born*'s mission is to nurture creativity and co-development of new literary art forms on the Web."

$⬛ BOSTON REVIEW; BOSTON REVIEW POETRY CONTEST

E53-407, MIT, 30 Wadsworth St., Cambridge MA 02139-4307. (617)258-0805. Fax: (617)252-1549. E-mail: review@mit.edu. Website: www.bostonreview.net. Established 1975. **Contact:** Timothy Donnelly, poetry editor.

● Poetry published in this review has been included in volumes of *The Best American Poetry*.

Magazine Needs *Boston Review* is a bimonthly tabloid-format magazine of arts, culture, and politics. "We are open to both traditional and experimental forms. What we value most is originality and a strong sense of voice." Has published poetry by Heather McHugh, Richard Howard, Allen Grossman, Cole Swenson, Tan Lin, and Claudia Rankine. Receives about 3,000 submissions/year, accepts about 30 poems/year. Circulation is 20,000 nationally, including subscriptions and newsstand sales. Single copy: $3.50; subscription: $17. Sample: $4.50.

How to Submit Submit 3-5 poems at a time. Submissions and inquiries are accepted via postal mail only. Cover letter with brief bio is encouraged. Time between acceptance and publication is 6 months to one year. Responds in 3 months. Pays $40/poem plus 5 contributor's copies. Acquires first serial rights. Reviews books of poetry. Only using *solicited* reviews. Send materials for review consideration.

Contest/Award Offerings Sponsors an annual poetry contest. Awards publication and $1,000. Submit up to 5 unpublished poems, no more than 10 pages total, with postcard to acknowledge receipt. **Entry fee:** $15. **Deadline:** June 1. Guidelines available for SASE or on website.

✚ ▢ ◎ BOTTOM DOG PRESS, INC. (Specialized: regional/Midwest; working lives; Zen Buddhism)

P.O. Box 425, Huron OH 44839. (419)433-3573. E-mail: LsmithDog@aol.com. Website: http://members.aol.com/lsmithdog/bottomdog. **Contact:** Larry Smith, director. Associate Editors: David Shevin and Laura Smith.

Book/Chapbook Needs & How to Submit Bottom Dog Press, Inc. "is a nonprofit literary and educational organization dedicated to publishing the best writing and art from the Midwest." Has published poetry by Jeff Gundy, Ray McNiece, Maj Ragain, Diane di Prima, and Sue Doro. Publishes the Midwest Series, Working Lives Series, and Harmony Series (91 books to date). Also plans to publish a Family Poems anthology. Guidelines available on website.

Advice "Please read some of our books and send us a query before submitting anything."

$▢ BOULEVARD; BOULEVARD EMERGING POETS CONTEST

PMB 325, 6614 Clayton Rd., Richmond Heights MO 63117. (314)862-2643. E-mail: ballymon@hotmail.com. Website: www.boulevardmagazine.com. Established 1985. **Contact:** Richard Burgin, editor.

● Poetry published in *Boulevard* has been frequently included in *The Best American Poetry* and *Pushcart Prize* anthologies.

Magazine Needs *Boulevard* appears 3 times/year. "*Boulevard* strives to publish only the finest in fiction, poetry, and nonfiction (essays and interviews; we do not accept book reviews). While we frequently publish writers with previous credits, we are very interested in publishing less experienced or unpublished writers with exceptional promise. We've published everything from John Ashbery to Donald Hall to a wide variety of styles from new or lesser known poets. We're eclectic. We are interested in original, moving poetry written from the head as well as the heart. It can be about any topic. Do not want to see poetry that is uninspired, formulaic, self-conscious, unoriginal, insipid." No light verse. Has published poetry by Albert Goldbarth, Molly Peacock, Bob Hicok, Alice Friman, Dick Allen, and Tom Disch. *Boulevard* is 175-250 pages, digest-sized, professionally printed, flat-spined, with glossy card cover. Press run is 3,500 (1,200 subscribers, 200 libraries).

Subscription: $12/3 issues, $20/6 issues, $25/9 issues. Sample: $8 plus 5 first-class stamps and SASE. Make checks payable to Opojaz, Inc.

How to Submit Submit up to 5 poems at a time. Lines/poem: 200 maximum. No previously published poems. *"Boulevard* does allow, even encourages, simultaneous submissions, but we want to be notified of this fact." Does not accept fax or e-mail submissions. All submissions must include SASE. Author's name and address must appear on each submission, with author's first and last name on each page. Cover letters are encouraged but not required. Reads submissions October 1 through April 30 only. Editor sometimes comments on rejected poems. Guidelines available for SASE, by e-mail, or on website. Responds in less than 2 months. Pays $25-300/poem (sometimes more), depending on length, plus one contributor's copy. Acquires first-time publication and anthology rights.

Contest/Award Offerings Sponsors an annual poetry contest, awarding $1,000 and publication in *Boulevard* for the best group of 3 poems by a poet who has not yet published a book of poetry with a nationally distributed press. Accepts simultaneous submissions; no previously published poems. Manuscripts will not be returned. **Entry fee:** $15 per group of 3 poems, $15 for each additional group of poems (includes one-year subscription to *Boulevard*). **Deadline:** was May 15 for 2005. "All entries will be considered for publication and payment at our regular rates." Guidelines available on website.

Advice "Write what you really want to, the best way you know how, instead of trying to write what you think editors want."

✪ BRANCHES; UCCELLI PRESS; BEST OF BRANCHES

P.O. Box 85394, Seattle WA 98145-1394. E-mail: editor@branchesquarterly.com (inquiries); submit @branchesquarterly.com (submissions). Website: www.branchesquarterly.com. Established 2001. **Contact:** Toni La Ree Bennett, editor.

Magazine Needs *Branches* is a quarterly online journal "dedicated to publishing the best of known and unknown artists and authors, presenting, when possible, verbal and visual art together in a way that expands their individual meanings." Wants poetry that is "educated but not pretentious. Seeking an eclectic, sophisticated mix of poetry, short prose, art, photos, fiction, essays, and translations. No rhyming unless specific form. No greeting card verse or openly sectarian religious verse (spirituality okay)." Has published poetry by John Amen, Janet Buck, A.E. Stallings, Richard Jordan, Corrine de Winter, and John Sweet. *Branches* is published online, equivalent to about 30 pages in print. *Best of Branches* is an annual print version. Receives about 2,000 poems/year, accepts about 5%.

How to Submit Submit 3-5 poems at a time. Accepts simultaneous submissions; no previously published poems, "unless by invitation." Accepts e-mail submissions (pasted into body of message); no disk or fax submissions. Cover letter is strongly encouraged; include poem titles in cover letter. "Preferred method of submission is to e-mail work in body of message to submit@branchesq uarterly.com. Send art/photos as jpeg attachments. Submitters must be willing to have their work appear with visual art of editor's choosing." Reads submissions continually; see website for issue deadlines. Submit seasonal poems 3 months in advance. Time between acceptance and publication is up to 3 months. Seldom comments on rejected poems. Guidelines available on website. Responds in up to 6 months. Always sends prepublication galleys (online only). Pays one contributor's copy of *Best of Branches* annual print version to those who will be published in it. Acquires first rights and retains right to archive online unless otherwise negotiated.

Advice *"Branches* is a place where 'the undefined and exact combine' (Verlaine). Artists live in a privileged, neglected place in our society. We are expected to make concrete the fluid, to tell the future, to work without recompense, and walk around naked. I'm looking for solid craftsmanship and an honest attempt to articulate the undefined."

✦ ✦ ◉ THE BREAD OF LIFE MAGAZINE (Specialized: religious/Catholic)

P.O. Box 395, Hamilton ON L8N 3H8 Canada. (905)529-4496. Fax: (905)529-5373. E-mail: info@the breadoflife.ca. Website: www.thebreadoflife.ca. Established 1977. **Contact:** Fr. Peter Coughlin, editor.

Magazine Needs *The Bread of Life* is "a Catholic charismatic magazine, published bimonthly and designed to encourage spiritual growth in areas of renewal in the Catholic Church today." It includes articles, poetry, and artwork. *The Bread of Life* is 34 pages, magazine-sized, professionally printed, saddle-stapled, with glossy paper cover. Receives about 50-60 poems/year, accepts about 25%. Press run is 2,500 (subscribers only). "It's good if contributors are members of The Bread of Life Renewal Centre, a non-profit, charitable organization."

How to Submit Accepts previously published poems and simultaneous submissions. Cover letter is preferred. Publishes theme issues. Send SAE with IRCs for upcoming themes.

◉ THE BRIAR CLIFF REVIEW

Briar Cliff College, 3303 Rebecca St., Sioux City IA 51104-2340. E-mail: jeanne.emmons@briarclif f.edu. Website: www.briarcliff.edu/bcreview/. Established 1989. **Contact:** Jeanne Emmons, poetry editor. Managing Editor: Tricia Currans-Sheehan. Member: CLMP; American Humanities Index.

- *The Briar Cliff Review* has received the Columbia Scholastic Association Gold Crown and the Associated Collegiate Press Pacemaker Award.

Magazine Needs *The Briar Cliff Review*, appearing annually in April, is an attractive "eclectic literary and cultural magazine focusing on (but not limited to) Siouxland writers and subjects." Wants "quality poetry with strong imagery; especially interested in regional, Midwestern content with tight, direct, well-wrought language." Has published poetry by Gaylord Brewer, James Doyle, and Michael Carey. *The Briar Cliff Review* is 96 pages, magazine-sized, professionally printed on 80-lb. dull text paper, perfect-bound, with 4-color cover on dull stock. Receives about 600 poems/year, accepts about 30. Press run is 1,000. Sample: $15.

How to Submit Submissions should be typewritten or letter quality, with author's name and address on each page. Accepts simultaneous submissions, but expects prompt notification of acceptance elsewhere; no previously published poems. No fax or e-mail submissions. Cover letter with short bio is required. "No manuscripts returned without SASE." Reads submissions August 1 through November 1 only. Time between acceptance and publication is up to 6 months. Seldom comments on rejected poems. Responds in 6 months. Pays 2 contributor's copies. Acquires first serial rights.

Contest/Award Offerings Sponsors an annual contest. Awards $500 and publication. Send 3 poems for consideration. **Entry fee:** $15. **Deadline:** November 1.

◉ BRICK & MORTAR REVIEW; BRICK & MORTAR REVIEW'S BIANNUAL POETRY CONTEST

P.O. Box 21, Santa Barbara CA 93102. E-mail: submit@bmreview.com. Website: www.bmreview.c om. Established 2003. **Contact:** Jack Stull, senior editor.

Magazine Needs *Brick & Mortar Review* appears quarterly. Wants poetry "that is grounded in concrete language, i.e., that evokes images. Avoid the use of empty, fluffy language such as 'beauti-ful,' 'freedom,' 'amazed,' 'spectacular,' 'love,' etc. Of course, these words can be used in the right context, but sparingly. Also, avoid over-rhyming. We don't mind an occasional rhyme if it's natural, but we don't want poetry that is forced into rhyme schemes (unless it is exceptional)." *Brick & Mortar Review* is published online only.

How to Submit Submit 3 or more poems, up to 10 at a time. Accepts simultaneous submissions; no previously published poems. Accepts e-mail submissions (pasted into body of message); no disk submissions. Cover letter is preferred. "For regular mail, include a SASE or indicate that you would like an e-mail response. For e-mail submissions, we respond by e-mail. On your cover page, please include a brief bio (a few sentences about yourself), and make sure your name is on every page you submit." Reads submissions year round. Time between acceptance and publication can be months. "The editors independently review the submissions and then meet to discuss and vote."

Publishers of Poetry

Seldom comments on rejected poems. Guidelines available on website. Responds in 2 months. No payment. Acquires one-time rights.

Contest/Award Offerings Offers biannual award of 1st Prize: $1,000; 2nd Prize: $250; 3rd Prize: $100; plus 3 Honorable Mentions. All winning poetry is published on the website. Pays winners from other countries by International Money Order. Submissions may be entered in other contests (with notification of acceptance elsewhere). Submit 3 or more poems of any length. "If submitting by e-mail, make sure it's clear where each poem begins and ends; also write 'contest' in the subject box (see website for more details on submitting electronically). If submitting by ground mail, please type 'contest' on your cover page. Both e-mail and ground mail submissions should include a brief bio (2-3 sentences about yourself)." **Entry fee:** $5/poem. "We accept U.S. dollars and International Money Orders, but credit cards online are the best way for foreign entries." **Deadline:** "We accept entries year round. Awards are given at the beginning of winter and summer." Judges are the editors. Winners will be announced on the website and possibly other places, such as *Poets & Writers*. "Avoid the overuse of empty language. This means we want poetry that evokes images, that shows rather than tells. An occasional rhyme is okay, but we're not interested in poetry that conforms to rhyme schemes." Guidelines available on website.

BRICKHOUSE BOOKS, INC.; NEW POETS SERIES, INC./CHESTNUT HILLS PRESS; STONEWALL SERIES (Specialized, Stonewall only: gay/lesbian/bisexual)

306 Suffolk Rd., Baltimore MD 21218. (410)235-7690. E-mail: charriss@towson.edu. Website: www. towson.edu/~harriss/!bhbwebs.ite/bhb.htm. Established 1970. **Contact:** Clarinda Harriss, editor/director.

● New Poets Series, Chestnut Hills Press, and Stonewall are imprints of BrickHouse Books.

Book/Chapbook Needs BrickHouse Books, Inc. "is open to submissons of all kinds (poetry, novellas, plays, etc.), so long as they do not exceed 128 pages." New Poets Series brings out first books by promising new poets. Poets who have previously had book-length mss published are not eligible. Prior publication in journals and anthologies is strongly encouraged. Wants "excellent, fresh, nontrendy, literate, intelligent poems. Any form (including traditional), any style." BrickHouse Books and New Poets Series pay 20 author's copies (out of a press run of 500), the sales proceeds going back into the corporation to finance the next volume. "BrickHouse has been successful in its effort to provide writers with a national distribution; in fact, The New Poets Series was named an Outstanding Small Press by the prestigious Pushcart Awards Committee, which judges some 5,000 small press publications annually." Chestnut Hills Press publishes author-subsidized books—"High-quality work only, however. Chestnut Hills Press has achieved a reputation for prestigious books, printing only the top 10% of manuscripts Chestnut Hills Press and New Poets Series receive." Chestnut Hills Press authors receive proceeds from sale of their books. The Stonewall series publishes work with a gay, lesbian, or bisexual perspective. New Poets Series/Chestnut Hills Press has published books by Chester Wickwire, Jim Elledge, Brad Sachs, Rane Aroyo, and Richard Fein. BrickHouse publishes 42- to 128-page works. Chapbooks: $10. Full-length books: $15.

How to Submit "Do not query by phone or fax; e-mail or postal mail queries only. Send a 50- to 55-page manuscript, $10 **reading fee**, and cover letter giving publication credits and bio. Indicate if manuscript is to be considered for BrickHouse, New Poets Series, Chestnut Hills Press, or Stonewall." Accepts simultaneous submissions. No e-mail submissions. "Cover letters should be very brief, businesslike, and include an accurate list of published work." Editor sometimes comments briefly on rejected poems. Responds in up to one year. Manuscripts "are circulated to an editorial board of professional, publishing poets. BrickHouse is backlogged, but the best 10% of the manuscripts it receives are automatically eligible for Chestnut Hills Press consideration," a subsidy arrangement. Send $5 and a 7×10 SASE for a sample volume.

◗ **BRIGHT HILL PRESS; BRIGHT HILL PRESS POETRY BOOK AWARD; BRIGHT HILL PRESS POETRY CHAPBOOK AWARD; WORD THURSDAYS READING SERIES; WORD THURSDAYS LITERARY WORKSHOPS; RADIO BY WRITERS; SHARE THE WORDS HIGH-SCHOOL POETRY COMPETITION; WORD AND IMAGE GALLERY**

P.O. Box 193, 94 Church St., Treadwell NY 13846-0193. (607)829-5055. Fax: (607)829-5056. E-mail: wordthur@stny.rr.com. Website: www.brighthillpress.org. Established 1992. **Contact:** Bertha Rogers, editor-in-chief/founding director. Member: Council of Literary Magazines and Presses, NYC.

Book/Chapbook Needs Bright Hill Press publishes 2-3 paperbacks and one chapbook annually, chosen through competition. **Considers mss submitted through competition only** (see below). Also publishes an anthology. No beginners; no unpublished poets/writers. Has published poetry by Barry Ballard, Richard Deutch, Shelby Stephenson, Lisa Rhoades, Victoria Hallerman, and Naton Leslie.

Contest/Award Offerings 1) **Bright Hill Press Poetry Book Award** offers an annual award of $1,000 and publication for a poetry ms of 48-64 pages. Prize includes 25 author's copies. Pays winners from other countries by certified check or International Money Order. Submissions may be entered in other contests. Submit ms of 48-64 pages, paginated (include bio, contents, acknowledgments, 2 title pages—one with name, address, and phone number, one with title of manuscript only) and secured with bulldog clip. Include SASE for results only; mss not returned. Guidelines available for SASE or by e-mail. **Entry fee:** $20. Does not accept entry fees in foreign currencies; U.S. International Money Order only. **Postmark deadline:** November 30. Competition receives over 300 entries/year. Past winners include Lisa Rhoades (2002), Barbara Hurd (2001), and Richard Deutch (2000). Winners will be announced in summer of the year following the contest. Copies of winning books available for $12 plus $3.85 postage from BHP Sample Books at the address above. "Publish your poems in literary magazines before trying to get a whole manuscript published. Publishing individual poems is the best way to hone your complete manuscript." 2) **Bright Hill Press Poetry Chapbook Award** offers an annual award of $300 and publication for a poetry ms of 16-24 pages. Prize includes 25 author's copies. Pays winners from other countries by certified check or International Money Order. Submissions may be entered in other contests. Submit ms of 16-24 pages, paginated (include bio, contents, acknowledgments, 2 title pages—one with name, address, and phone number, one with title of manuscript only) and secured with bulldog clip. Include SASE for results only; mss not returned. Guidelines available for SASE or by e-mail. **Entry fee:** $10. Does not accept entry fees in foreign currencies; U.S. International Money Order only. **Postmark deadline:** July 31. Competition receives over 300 entries/year. Past winners include Tom Lavazzi (2003), Shelby Stephenson (2002), Barry Ballard (2001), and Matthew J. Spireng (2000). Winners will be announced in summer of the year following the contest. Copies of winning chapbooks available for $6 plus $2.50 postage from BHP Sample Books at the address above.

Also Offers Words Thursdays (reading series); Radio by Writers (a Catskills radio series heard on WJFF, the Sullivan Co. NPR affiliate); Share the Words High-School Poetry Competition; Word and Image gallery at the Bright Hill Center; Speaking the Words Tour and Festival; and the Word Thursdays Literary Workshops for Kids and Adults. See website for further information. (Also administers the New York State Literary Map and the New York State Council on the Arts Literary Curators website at www.nyslittree.org.)

Advice "Read poetry; read fiction. Send your poetry/fiction out for publication; when it comes back, revise it and send it out again."

◳ ◎ **BRILLIANT CORNERS: A JOURNAL OF JAZZ & LITERATURE (Specialized: jazz-related literature)**

Lycoming College, Williamsport PA 17701. (570)321-4279. Fax: (570)321-4090. E-mail: bc@lycoming.edu. Website: www.lycoming.edu/BrilliantCorners. Established 1996. **Contact:** Sascha Feinstein, editor.

Magazine Needs *Brilliant Corners*, a biannual, publishes jazz-related poetry, fiction, and nonfiction. "We are open to length and form, but want work that is both passionate and well crafted—work worthy of our recent contributors. No sloppy hipster jargon or improvisatory nonsense." Has published poetry by Amiri Baraka, Jayne Cortez, Yusef Komunyakaa, Philip Levine, Colleen McElroy, and Al Young. *Brilliant Corners* is 100 pages, digest-sized, commercially printed, perfect-bound, with color card cover with original artwork, includes ads. Accepts about 5% of work received. Press run is 800 (200 subscribers). Subscription: $12. Sample: $7.

How to Submit Submit 3-5 poems at a time. Previously published poems "very rarely accepted, and only by well established poets"; no simultaneous submissions. No e-mail or fax submissions. Cover letter is preferred. Reads submissions September 1 through May 15 only. Seldom comments on rejected poems. Responds in 2 months. Pays 2 contributor's copies. Acquires first North American serial rights. Staff reviews books of poetry. Send materials for review consideration.

☑ BRYANT LITERARY REVIEW

Faculty Suite F, Bryant University, Smithfield RI 02917. Website: http://web.bryant.edu/~blr. Established 2000. **Contact:** Tom Chandler, editor. Member: CLMP.

Magazine Needs *Bryant Literary Review* appears annually in May and publishes poetry, fiction, photography, and art. "Our only standard is quality." Has published poetry by Michael S. Harper, Mary Crow, Denise Duhamel, and Baron Wormster. *Bryant Literary Review* is 125 pages, digest-sized, offset-printed, perfect-bound, with 4-color cover with art or photo. Receives about 3,000 poems/year, accepts about 1%. Press run is 2,500. Single copy: $8; subscription: $8.

How to Submit Submit 3-5 poems at a time. Cover letter is required. "Include SASE; please submit only *once* each reading period." Reads submissions September 1 through December 31. Time between acceptance and publication is 5 months. Seldom comments on rejected poems. Guidelines available in magazine or on website. Responds in 3 months. Pays 2 contributor's copies. Acquires one-time rights.

Advice "No abstract expressionist poems, please. We prefer accessible work of depth and quality."

✪ ☑ BUFFALO CARP

1715 Second Ave., Rock Island IL 61201. (309)793-1213. Fax: (309)793-1265. E-mail: twhite@quadc ityarts.com. Website: www.quadcityarts.com. Established 1998. **Contact:** Tracy Alan White, managing editor.

Magazine Needs *Buffalo Carp* is "a national literary journal featuring the best unpublished writing in the genres of poetry, fiction, and narrative nonfiction." Wants "any style of poetry as long as it is well crafted, vivid, and accessible." Has published poetry by John E. Smelcer, Jack R. Ridl, Carolyn Brook Morrell, Terry Savoie, and Matt Schumacher. *Buffalo Carp* is 50 pages, digest-sized, offset-printed, perfect-bound, with coated, full-color cover with jury-selected, original artwork. Press run is 500; distributed free to selected libraries and schools. Single copy: $10. Sample: $4. Make checks payable to Quad City Arts.

How to Submit Submit 5 poems at a time (maximum/annual reading period). Lines/poem: 1-2 pages/poem; "longer if excellent work." Accepts simultaneous submissions "if notified immediately of other acceptance"; no previously published poems. No fax, e-mail, or disk submissions. Cover letter is preferred. "All submissions must include SASE to be returned and/or acknowledged." Time between acceptance and publication is about 6 months. Poems are circulated to an editorial board. Sometimes comments on rejected poems. "Although we can't comment on all submissions, we do offer advice to writers whose work shows promise." Sometimes publishes theme issues. Guidelines available in magazine. Pays 2 contributor's copies. Acquires first North American serial rights.

Advice "Good writing contains the same qualities found in a breeze-blown Midwestern lake; the surface exudes a sparkle and liveliness which compels deeper examination. Soon many details, movements, and meanings are discovered, and a clarity surprising for the depth."

$ ☑ ◎ BUGLE: JOURNAL OF ELK COUNTRY AND THE HUNT (Specialized: elk conservation; nature/ecology)

Rocky Mountain Elk Foundation, P.O. Box 8249, Missoula MT 59807-8249. (406)523-4538. Fax:

(406)543-7710. E-mail: bugle@rmef.org. Website: www.elkfoundation.org. Established 1984. **Contact:** Paul Queneau, assistant editor.

Magazine Needs *Bugle* is the bimonthly publication of the nonprofit Rocky Mountain Elk Foundation, whose mission is to ensure the future of elk, other wildlife, and their habitats. "The goal of *Bugle* is to advance this mission by presenting original, critical thinking about wildlife conservation, elk ecology, and hunting." Wants "high-quality poems that explore the realm of elk, the 'why' of hunting, or celebrate the hunting experience as a whole. Free verse preferred. No 'Hallmark' poetry." Has published poetry by Mike Fritch, John Whinery, and Ted Florea. *Bugle* is 130 pages, magazine-sized, professionally printed on coated stock, saddle-stapled, with full-color glossy cover with photo or illustration, includes ads. Receives about 50 poems/year, accepts about 10%. Press run is 132,000. Subscription: $30 membership fee. Sample: $5.95. Make checks payable to Rocky Mountain Elk Foundation.

How to Submit "Poets may submit as many poems as they'd like at a time." Prefers that each poem is not longer than one page. Accepts simultaneous submissions. Accepts e-mail (prefers attached file in Word), fax, and disk submissions. Cover letter is preferred. Time between acceptance and publication varies. "Poems are screened by assistant editor first; those accepted are then passed to editorial staff for review and comment; final decision based on their comments. We will evaluate your poem based on content, quality, and our needs for the coming year." Rarely comments on rejected poems. Publishes special sections. Guidelines available for SASE, by fax, by e-mail, or on website. Responds in 3 months. "The Rocky Mountain Elk Foundation is a nonprofit conservation organization committed to putting membership dollars into protecting elk habitat. So we appreciate, and still receive, donated work. However, if you would like to be paid for your work, our rate is $100/poem, paid on acceptance. Should your poem appear in *Bugle*, you will receive 3 complimentary copies of the issue." Acquires first North American serial rights. Staff reviews other magazines.

Advice "Although poetry has appeared periodically in *Bugle* over the years, it has never been a high priority for us, nor have we solicited it. A lack of high-quality work and poetry appropriate for the focus of the magazine has kept us from making it a regular feature. However, we've decided to attempt to give verse a permanent home in the magazine . . . Reading a few issues of *Bugle* prior to submitting will give you a better sense of the style and content of the magazine."

☑ BURNSIDE REVIEW

P.O. Box 1782, Portland OR 97207. E-mail: sid@burnsidereview.com. Website: www.burnsidereview.com. Established 2004. **Contact:** Sid Miller and Bill Bogart, co-editors.

Magazine Needs The editors of *Burnside Review* "look to publish writers from throughout the country, while featuring an individual poet from the Northwest." Feature includes interview and poems. Translations are welcome. "We tend to publish poetry that finds beauty in truly unexpected places; that combines urban and natural themes; that breaks the heart." Open to all forms. Would like to see more poetry that combines narrative and lyric language. "Anything over two pages must be exceptional. If you can't say it with the images and language, then you surely can't with the line breaks and fonts." Has published poetry by Dorriane Laux, Virgil Suárez, Paul Guest, T.E. Ballard, Rebecca Loudon, and Robyn Art. *Burnside Review* is 40-48 pages, digest-sized, professionally printed, saddle-stitched, with cardstock cover with photography. Receives about 2,500 poems/year. Press run is 200 (25 subscribers, 50 shelf sales). Single copy: $6; subscription: $10. Make checks payable to *Burnside Review*.

How to Submit Accepts simultaneous submissions; no previously published poems. Accepts e-mail submissions, "but strongly prefer submissions sent by ground mail. Check website for details." Cover letter is required. "Include bio and SASE. Please include your name and address on every page." Reads submissions year round. Submit seasonal poems 3-6 months in advance. Time between acceptance and publication is up to 6 months. "Editors read all poems." Seldom comments on rejected poems. Guidelines available on website. Responds in up to 2 months. Pays one contributor's copy. Acquires first rights.

◖ BUTTON MAGAZINE

P.O. Box 26, Lunenburg MA 01462. E-mail: aiolia@worldnet.att.net. Website: http://moonsigns.n et. Established 1993. **Contact:** Maude Piper, poetry editor. Editor: Sally Cragin.

Magazine Needs *Button* "is New England's tiniest magazine of fiction, poetry, and gracious living." Wants "poetry that incises a perfect figure eight on the ice, but also cuts beneath that mirrored surface. No sentiment; minimal use of vertical pronoun; no 'musing' on who or what done ya wrong." Has published poetry by Amanda Powell, Brendan Galvin, Jean Monahan, Mary Campbell, Kevin McGrath, and Ed Conti. *Button*, published annually, is 30 pages, 4¼×5½, saddle-stapled, with card stock offset cover with illustrations that incorporate one or more buttons. Press run is 1,200 (more than 500 subscribers, 750 shelf sales). Subscription: $5/4 issues, $25/lifetime. Sample: $2 and a first-class stamp.

How to Submit Submit no more than 2 poems at a time. No previously published poems. "Do not submit more than twice in one year." Cover letter is required. Time between acceptance and publication is up to 6 months. Poems are circulated to an editorial board. Often comments on rejected poems. Guidelines available by e-mail. Responds in 4 months. Pays honorarium, subscription, and at least 5 contributor's copies. Acquires first North American serial rights.

Advice "Writing as therapy is fine. Publishing as therapy is not. Take the vertical pronoun (I) and write your poem without it. Still got something to say? Also, *Button* tries to reflect a world one would want to live in—this does not mean we make the space for various uncatalogued human vices (self-pity, navel gazing). If you can be really amusing about those, that's another story. Finally, writers who need to say they've published 1,200 poems in various magazines and then name all of the magazines. . . . well, we don't really need to know. Aim high, write often, but refine, refine, refine."

$ ◖ ◎ BYLINE MAGAZINE; BYLINE LITERARY AWARDS (Specialized: writing)

P.O. Box 5240, Edmond OK 73083-5240. (405)348-5591. E-mail: MPreston@bylinemag.com. Website: www.bylinemag.com. Established 1981. **Contact:** Sandra Soli, poetry editor. Editor: Marcia Preston.

Magazine Needs *ByLine* is a magazine for the encouragement of writers and poets, using 8-10 poems/issue about writers or writing. Has published poetry by Judith Tate O'Brien, Katharyn Howd Machan, and Harvey Stanbrough. *ByLine* is magazine-sized, professionally printed, includes ads. Receives about 2,500 poetry submissions/year, accepts about 100. Subscription: $24. Sample: $5.

How to Submit Submit up to 3 poems at a time. No previously published poems. No e-mail or fax submissions. Guidelines available for SASE or on website. Responds within 6 weeks. Pays $10/ poem. Acquires first North American serial rights.

Contest/Award Offerings Sponsors up to 20 poetry contests, including a chapbook competition open to anyone. Send #10 SASE for details. Also sponsors the *ByLine* Short Fiction and Poetry Awards, open only to subscribers. Prize: $250. Send SASE for guidelines.

Advice "We are happy to work with new writers, but please read a few samples to get an idea of our style. We would like to see more serious poetry about the creative experience (as it concerns writing)."

◖ CALIFORNIA QUARTERLY; CALIFORNIA STATE POETRY SOCIETY

P.O. Box 7126, Orange CA 92863-7126. (949)854-8024. E-mail: jipalley@aol.com. Website: www.ca liforniaquarterly.blogspot.com. Established 1972. **Contact:** Julian Palley and Kate Ozbirn, editors.

Magazine Needs *California Quarterly* is the official publication of the California State Poetry Society (an affiliate of the National Federation of State Poetry Societies) and is designed "to encourage the writing and dissemination of poetry." Wants poetry on any subject. "No geographical limitations. Quality is all that matters." Has published poetry by Michael L. Johnson, Lyn Lifshin, and Joanna C. Scott. *California Quarterly* is 64 pages, digest-sized, offset-printed, perfect-bound, with heavy paper cover with art. Receives 3,000-4,000 poems/year, accepts about 5%. Press run is 500 (300 subscribers, 24 libraries, 20-30 shelf sales). Membership in CSPS is $25/year and includes a subscription to *California Quarterly*. Sample (including guidelines): $6.

How to Submit Submit up to 6 poems at a time, with name and address on each sheet. Lines/poem: 60 maximum. No previously published poems. Accepts submissions by postal mail only; no e-mail submissions. Include SASE. Seldom comments on rejected poems. Guidelines available for SASE. Responds in up to 8 months. Pays one contributor's copy. Acquires first rights. Rights revert to poet after publication.

Contest/Award Offerings CSPS also sponsors an annual poetry contest. Awards vary. All entries considered for *California Quarterly*. For inquiries about the contest, write to Maura Harvey, Annual Contest Chair, P.O. Box 2672, Del Mar CA 92014; include SASE.

Advice "Since our editor changes with each issue, we encourage poets to resubmit."

☐ ◎ CALYX, A JOURNAL OF ART & LITERATURE BY WOMEN (Specialized: women; lesbian; multicultural); CALYX BOOKS

P.O. Box B, Corvallis OR 97339-0539. (541)753-9384. Fax: (541)753-0515. E-mail: calyx@proaxis.com. Established 1976. **Contact:** Beverly McFarland, senior editor.

Magazine Needs *Calyx*, appearing 3 times every 18 months, is a journal edited by a collective editorial board. Publishes poetry, prose, art, book reviews, essays, and interviews by and about women. Wants "excellently crafted poetry that also has excellent content." Has published poetry by Maurya Simon, Diane Averill, Carole Boston Weatherford, and Eleanor Wilner. *Calyx* is 6×8, handsomely printed on heavy paper, flat-spined, with glossy color cover. Poems tend to be lyric free verse that makes strong use of image and symbol melding unobtrusively with voice and theme. Single copy: $9.50. Sample: $11.50.

How to Submit Send up to 6 poems with SASE and short bio. "We accept copies in good condition and clearly readable. We focus on new writing, but occasionally publish a previously published piece." Accepts simultaneous submissions, "if kept up-to-date on publication." No fax or e-mail submissions. *Calyx* is open to submissions October 1 through December 31 only. Manuscripts received outside of reading period will be returned unread. Guidelines available for SASE or by e-mail. Responds in 9 months. Pays one contributor's copy plus subscription. Send materials for review consideration.

Book/Chapbook Needs & How to Submit Calyx Books publishes one book of poetry/year. All work published is by women. Has published *Black Candle* by Chitra Divakaruni. However, Calyx Books is closed for ms submissions until further notice.

Advice "Read the publication and be familiar with what we have published."

☒ $☐ ◎ CANADIAN WRITER'S JOURNAL (Specialized: writing)

White Mountain Publications, Box 1178, New Liskeard ON P0J 1P0 Canada. (705)647-5424. Fax: (705)647-8366. E-mail: cwj@cwj.ca. Website: www.cwj.ca. **Contact:** Deborah Ranchuk, editor.

Magazine Needs *Canadian Writer's Journal* is a digest-sized bimonthly, publishing mainly short "how-to" articles of interest to writers at all levels. Uses a few "short poems or portions thereof as part of 'how-to' articles relating to the writing of poetry, and occasional short poems with tie-in to the writing theme. We try for 90% Canadian content but prefer good material over country of origin or how well you're known." Subscription: $35/year, $67.50/2 years (add 7% gst in Canada). Sample: $8.

How to Submit Submit up to 5 poems ("poems should be titled"). Include SASE ("U.S. postage accepted; do not affix to envelope"). No previously published poems. Accepts fax and e-mail ("Include in body of message, not as attachment. Write 'Submission' in the subject line.") submissions. Hard copy and SASE (or SAE and IRC) required if accepted. Responds in 3-6 months. Token payment. Pays $2-7.50 and one contributor's copy/poem.

⊠ $⊘ THE CAPILANO REVIEW

2055 Purcell Way, North Vancouver BC V7J 3H5 Canada. (604)984-1712. E-mail: tcr@capcollege.bc
.ca. Website: www.capcollege.bc.ca/thecapilanoreview. Established 1972. **Contact:** Sharon
Thesen, editor.

Magazine Needs *The Capilano Review* is a literary and visual arts review appearing 3 times/year.
Wants "avant-garde, experimental, previously unpublished poetry of sustained intelligence and
imagination. We are interested in poetry that is new in concept and in execution." Has published
poetry by bill bissett, Phyllis Webb, and Michael Ondaatje. *The Capilano Review* comes in a hand-
some digest-sized format, 90-100 pages, perfect-bound, finely printed, with glossy full-color card
cover. Circulation is 800. Sample: $9 prepaid.

How to Submit Submit 5-6 poems, minimum, with cover letter and SAE and IRC. "Submissions with
U.S. postage will not be considered." No simultaneous submissions. No e-mail or disk submissions.
Responds in up to 5 months. Pays $50-200, plus subscription and 2 contributor's copies. Acquires
first North American serial rights.

Advice "The best advice we can offer is to read the magazine before you submit. *The Capilano
Review* receives several manuscripts each week; unfortunately the majority of them are simply
inappropriate for the magazine."

$☐ ◎ CAPPER'S; BRAVE HEARTS (Specialized: inspirational; humor; themes)

1503 SW 42nd St., Topeka KS 66609-1265. (785)274-4300. Fax: (785)274-4305. Website: www.capp
ers.com or www.braveheartsmagazine.com. Established 1879. **Contact:** Ann Crahan, editor.

Magazine Needs & How to Submit *Capper's* is a biweekly tabloid (newsprint) going to 240,000
mail subscribers, mostly small-town and rural families. Wants short poems (4-16 lines preferred,
lines of one-column width) "relating to everyday situations, nature, inspirational, humorous. Most
poems used in *Capper's* are upbeat in tone and offer the reader a bit of humor, joy, enthusiasm,
or encouragement." Accepts poetry written by children ages 12 and under. Has published poetry
by Elizabeth Searle Lamb, Robert Brimm, Margaret Wiedyke, Helena K. Stefanski, Sheryl L. Nelms,
and Claire Puneky. Not available on newsstand. Send $1.95 for sample. Submit 5-6 poems at a
time. Lines/poem: 14-16. No simultaneous submissions. No e-mail or fax submissions. Returns
mss with SASE. Publishes seasonal theme issues. Guidelines available for SASE or on website.
Responds in 3 months. Pays $10-15/poem; additional payment of $5 if poem is used on website.
Acquires one-time rights.

Magazine Needs & How to Submit *Brave Hearts* is an inspirational magazine appearing quarterly
in February, May, August, and November. Features themes and humorous or inspirational poems.
"Poems should be short (16 lines or less)." Does not accept poetry written by children. Sample:
$4.95. Accepts submissions by postal mail only. List of upcoming themes available in magazine or
for SASE. Guidelines available for SASE or on website. Pays $5-12/poem; additional payment of
$2 if poem is used on website.

Advice "Poems chosen are upbeat, sometimes humorous, always easily understood. Short poems
of this type fit our format best."

☐ ◎ THE CARIBBEAN WRITER (Specialized: regional)

University of the Virgin Islands, RR 02, P.O. Box 10,000, Kingshill, St. Croix USVI 00850. (340)692-
4152. Fax: (340)692-4026. E-mail: qmars@uvi.edu. Website: www.TheCaribbeanWriter.com. Established 1987. **Contact:** Ms. Quilin Mars. Editor: Marvin E. Williams.

• Poetry published in *The Caribbean Writer* was included in the 2002 *Pushcart Prize* anthology.

Magazine Needs *The Caribbean Writer* is a literary anthology, appearing in July, with a Caribbean
focus. The Caribbean must be central to the literary work, or the work must reflect a Caribbean
heritage, experience, or perspective. Has published poetry by Virgil Suárez, Thomas Reiter, Kamau
Brathwaite, and Opal Palmer Adisa. *The Caribbean Writer* is 300 + pages, digest-sized, handsomely
printed on heavy stock, perfect-bound, with glossy card cover. Press run is 1,200. Single copy: $12

plus $4 postage; subscription: $20. Sample: $7 plus $4 postage. (Note: postage to and from the Virgin Islands is the same as within the US.)

How to Submit Submit up to 5 poems. Accepts simultaneous submissions; no previously published poems. Accepts e-mail (as attachment), disk, and postal submissions; no fax submissions. Blind submissions only: name, address, phone number, e-mail address, and title of ms should appear in cover letter along with brief bio. Title only on ms. Deadline is September 30 of each year. Guidelines available in magazine, for SASE, by e-mail, or on website. Pays 2 contributor's copies. Acquires first North American serial rights. Reviews books of poetry and fiction in 1,000 words. Send materials for review consideration.

Contest/Award Offerings All submissions are eligible for the Daily News Prize ($300) for the best poem or poems, The Marguerite Cobb McKay Prize to a Virgin Island author ($200), the David Hough Literary Prize to a Caribbean author ($500), the Canute A. Brodhurst Prize for Fiction ($400), and the Charlotte and Isidor Paiewonsky Prize ($200) for first-time publication.

CAROLINA WREN PRESS (Specialized: women; ethnic; gay/lesbian; social issues)
120 Morris St., Durham NC 27701. (919)560-2738. Fax: (919)560-2759. E-mail: carolina@carolinaw renpress.org. Website: www.carolinawrenpress.org. Established 1976. **Contact:** Andrea Selch, president.

Book/Chapbook Needs Publishes one book/year "usually through our chapbook series. Primarily women and minorities, though men and majorities also welcome." Has published *Churchboys and Other Sinners* by Presten L. Allen, as well as poetry by George Elliott Clarke, jaki shelton green, Evie Shockley, and Erica Hunt.

How to Submit Accepts submissions by fax, e-mail (pasted into body of message), on disk, and by postal mail. "We read manuscripts twice/year, but your best bet is to submit as part of our biannual poetry contest. See website for current guidelines." Guidelines also available for SASE or by e-mail. Payment varies.

CAVEAT LECTOR
400 Hyde St., Apt. 606, San Francisco CA 94109-7445. Phone/fax: (415)928-7431. E-mail: editors@c aveat-lector.org. Website: http://caveat-lector.org. Established 1989. **Contact:** Christopher Bernard, Ho Lin, and Adam Sass, editors.

Magazine Needs Appearing 2 times/year, "*Caveat Lector* is devoted to the arts and to cultural and philosophical commentary. We publish visual art and music as well as literary and theoretical texts. Our website includes a multimedia section offering video and audio. We are looking for accomplished poems, something that resonates in the mind long after the reader has laid the poem aside. We want work that has authenticity of emotion and high craft, whether raw or polished, that rings true—if humorous, actually funny, or at least witty. Classical to experimental." Has published poetry by Deanne Bayer, Simon Perchik, Alfred Robinson, and E.S. Hilbert. *Caveat Lector* is 24-32 pages, $11 \times 4\frac{1}{4}$, photocopied, saddle-stapled, with color cover. Receives 200-600 poems/year, accepts about 2%. Press run is 300 (20 subscribers, 200 shelf sales). Single copy: $3.50; subscription: $15/4 issues. Sample: $3.

How to Submit "Submit up to 6 short poems (up to 50 lines each), 3 medium-length poems (51-100 lines), or one long poem (up to 500 lines) at a time on any subject, in any style, as long as the work is authentic in feeling and appropriately crafted. Place name, address, and (optional) telephone number on each page. Include SASE, cover letter, and brief bio (100 words or less)." Accepts simultaneous submissions, "but please inform us." Reads submissions from January through June. Time between acceptance and publication is one year. Sometimes comments on rejected poems. Guidelines available for SASE. Responds in one month. Pays 2 contributor's copies. Acquires first publication rights.

Advice "The two rules of writing are: 1. Rewrite it again. 2. Rewrite it again. The writing level of most of our submissions is pleasingly high. A rejection by us is not always a criticism of the work, and we try to provide comments to our more promising submitters."

⚁ $⊘ CC. MARIMBO

P.O. Box 933, Berkeley CA 94701-0933. Established 1996. **Contact:** Peggy Golden, editor. **"We are currently closed to all submissions as we are scheduled into 2008!"**

Book/Chapbook Needs CC. Marimbo "promotes the work of underpublished poets/artists by providing a well-crafted, cheap (people's prices), and therefore affordable/accessible, collection." Publishes 2-3 poetry titles per year. "Books are issued as 'minichaps' to introduce underpublished poets/artists to the public. Runs done by alphabet, lettered A-Z, AA-ZZ, etc. Short poems for the small format, styles, and content welcome in whatever variation. We do not want to see already published work, unless poems previously in print in magazines (attributed), i.e., poems OK, reprintable books not OK." Has published poetry by Guy R. Beining, Joan McNair Gatten, and Mark Schwartz. Chapbooks are usually 40 pages, 4¼×5¼, offset-printed, photocopied, with matte covers.

How to Submit Query first, with a few sample poems and cover letter with brief bio and publication credits. Include SASE. Lines/poem: 25 maximum. Responds in 3 months to queries; 6 months to mss. Pays 5 author's copies (out of a press run of 26), additional copies paid for larger press runs. "Author gets 10% of cover price on all copies sold, except for copies sold to author." Order sample chapbooks by sending $5 (5¢ for p&h).

Ⓝ ◻ CELLAR DOOR

503 Salyers Branch, Hueysville KY 41640. E-mail: cellardoormag@yahoo.com. Website: www.geocities.com/cellardoormag. Established 2004. **Contact:** Jarrid Deaton, editor/publisher; Sheldon Compton, editor/publisher.

Magazine Needs *Cellar Door* is a quarterly journal publishing "poetry and fiction that pushes boundaries and inspires growth in contemporary literature." Wants "poets and writers who have developed their own style and are not afraid to push boundaries and go against conventional literature. We are looking for the new voices in the writing world, and we want to help them become a part of the new movement in contemporary literature." Does not want "anything boring or that your grandparents would approve of (unless your grandfather was Charles Bukowski)." Has published poetry by George Eklund, Matt St. Amand, GC Smith, and Laura Perry. *Cellar Door* is 65-100 pages, magazine-sized, perfect-bound, with glossy cover with b&w photography. Receives about 400 poems/year, accepts about 25-30. Press run is 250. Single copy: $7; subscription: $20. Make checks payable to *Cellar Door Magazine*.

How to Submit Submit up to 3 poems at a time. Lines/poem: 5-100 ("nothing epic, but no real restrictions"). Accepts previously published poems and simultaneous submissions. Accepts e-mail (pasted into body of message) and disk submissions. Cover letter is preferred. "Just let us know a little about who you are and, if you have been published before, a list of publications. None of this is required, but it makes things easier for the compilations of contributor's notes if your work is accepted." Reads submissions year round. Time between acceptance and publication is "months." Poems are circulated to an editorial board. Often comments on rejected poems. Guidelines available in magazine or on website. Responds in 1-3 weeks. Pays one contributor's copy. Acquires first rights.

Advice "We here at *Cellar Door* are very excited about the current state of literature and hope to be able to help the future leaders of poetry and fiction to grow as writers. We recommend reading Chuck Palahniuk, Joey Goebel, Charles Bukowski, George Eklund, Craig Clevenger, Will Christopher Baer, and others whom we think represent where great literature and poetry are heading. These writers found their own voice and were not afraid to go against the grain. We hope to inspire others to do the same."

⊘ CENTER: A JOURNAL OF THE LITERARY ARTS

202 Tate Hall, University of Missouri-Columbia, Columbia MO 65211-1500. (573)882-4971. E-mail: cla@missouri.edu. Website: www.missouri.edu/~center. Established 2000. **Contact:** Poetry Editor.

Magazine Needs *Center: A Journal for the Literary Arts* appears annually in April. Wants well-crafted verse of any kind. Also interested in seeing sequences, part or whole. Has published poetry by Annie Finch, Eric Pankey, Maura Stanton, Floyd Skloot, Simon Perchik, and Barbara Lefcowitz. *Center: A Journal* is 100+ pages, digest-sized, perfect-bound, with 4-color card cover, includes 3 ads for literary journals. Receives about 1,000 poems/year, accepts about 30. Press run is 500 (100 subscribers). Single copy: $6 (current issue). Sample: $3 (back issue). Make checks payable to *Center: A Journal*.

How to Submit Submit 3-6 poems at a time. Simultaneous submissions OK with notification; no previously published poems. Accepts e-mail submissions from international poets only. Cover letter is preferred. Reads submissions July 1 through November 30. "Submissions received outside of the reading period will be returned unread." Time between acceptance and publication is up to 5 months. "An editorial board of experienced writers in our creative writing program reviews all submission as they arrive." Seldom comments on rejected poems. Guidelines available for SASE or on website. Responds in up to 4 months. Acquires first North American serial rights. Rights revert to poets upon publication.

☑ CHAFFIN JOURNAL

Dept. of English, Case Annex 467, Eastern Kentucky University, Richmond KY 40475-3102. (859)622-3080. Website: www.english.eku.edu/chaffin_journal. Established 1998. **Contact:** Robert W. Witt, editor.

Magazine Needs *The Chaffin Journal* appears annually in December. Publishes quality short fiction and poetry by new and established writers/poets. Wants any form, subject matter, or style. Does not want "poor quality." Has published poetry by Taylor Graham, Diane Glancy, Judith Montgomery, Simon Perchik, Philip St. Clair, and Virgil Suárez. *The Chaffin Journal* is 120 pages, digest-sized, offset-printed, perfect-bound, with plain cover with title only. Receives about 500 poems/year, accepts about 10%. Press run is 300 (65 subscribers, 4 libraries, 180 shelf sales); 40-50 are distributed free to contributors. Single copy: $6; subscription: $6 annually. Sample (back issue): $5. Make checks payable to *The Chaffin Journal*.

How to Submit Submit 5 poems at a time. Accepts simultaneous submissions (although not preferred); no previously published poems. No fax, e-mail, or disk submissions. Cover letter is preferred. "Submit typed pages with only one poem per page. Enclose SASE." Reads submissions June 1 through October 1. Time between acceptance and publication is 6 months. Poems are reviewed by the general editor and 2 poetry editors. Never comments on rejected poems. Guidelines available in magazine or on website. Responds in 3 months. Pays one contributor's copy. Acquires one-time rights.

Advice "Submit quality work during our reading period; include cover letter and SASE."

Ⓝ $⊚ CHAMPAGNE SHIVERS (Specialized: horror poetry only); EXPRESSIONS

E-mail: ChampagneShivers@hotmail.com (accepts submissions by e-mail only). Website: www.samsdotpublishing.com/champagne/cover.html. Established 2002. **Contact:** Cathy Buburuz, editor.

Magazine Needs *Champagne Shivers* "is a classy horror magazine. This is not the place to submit offensive language. We prefer poetic, well-written horror." Wants "horror poetry only. We prefer poems that do not rhyme, but all verse will be considered. Long poems stand the best chance for acceptance, especially if they're scary and entertaining. Do not send anything that isn't horror related, and always proof and edit before you send your submission. If your work does not have high entertainment or high impact, do not send it here." Has published poetry by R. J. Michaelz, Nancy Bennett, Tao Rae Tasmaine, W. B. Vogel III, and Keith W. Sikora. *Champagne Shivers* is 40-60 pages, magazine-sized, professionally-printed, saddle-stapled, with b&w cover with scary art. Receives about 1,200 poems/year, accepts about 5%. Press run and subscriber base vary; the only free copies go to reviewers and contributors. Single copy: $12 US and Canada. Sample: $10 US and Canada (foreign countries please inquire about cost). Make checks payable to Tyree Campbell,

Sam's Dot Publishing, P.O. Box 782, Cedar Rapids IA 52406-0782 (for subscriptions and sample copies only; DO NOT SEND SUBMISSIONS TO THIS ADDRESS).

How to Submit Submit one poem at a time. Lines/poem: 20-30. Accepts previously published poems; no simultaneous submissions. Accepts e-mail submissions (pasted into body of message; DO NOT SEND ATTACHMENTS); no disk submissions. Cover letter is preferred. "Submit one poem with a bio written in the third person, your mailing address, and your e-mail address." Reads submissions year round. Submit seasonal poems 4 months in advance. Time between acceptance and publication is less than 6 months. Always comments on rejected poems. Guidelines available by e-mail or on website. Pays 10 cents/line for unpublished poems; 5 cents/line for previously published poems (let the editor know where and when the poem appeared). Pays one contributor's copy. Acquires "First North American Serials Rights to unpublished poems, one-time rights to previously published poems. All rights revert back to the writer upon publication."

Contest/Award Offerings Sam's Dot Publishing offers The James Award (Trophy) annually. "Submit one poem per e-mail, but submit as often as you like." **Entry fee:** "None—it's free." **Deadline:** December 31. Guidelines available on website. "Never send snail mail submissions; always submit in the body of an e-mail after reading the information under How to Submit above."

Also Offers *Expressions (A Newsletter for Creative People Worldwide)*, edited by Cathy Buburuz (visit the website at www.samsdotpublishing.com/expressions.htm).

Advice "Submit horror poems only. I love psychological horror poetry, horror poetry about the Old West, horror poems about asylums, or anything that's just plain scary. I do not want poems about werewolves, vampires, ghosts, or traditional monsters. I want to read poetry that's fresh and exciting. Most of all, send me something that's high in entertainment, that's never been done before. Send poems that will give me and my audience the shivers."

🌐 🖥 ◎ CHAPMAN (Specialized: ethnic/nationality); CHAPMAN PUBLISHING

4 Broughton Place, Edinburgh EH1 3RX Scotland. Phone: (0131)557-2207. Fax: (0131)556-9565. E-mail: chapman-pub@blueyonder.co.uk. Website: www.chapman-pub.co.uk. Established 1970. **Contact:** Joy Hendry, editor. Assistant Editor: Edmund O'Connor.

Magazine Needs *Chapman*, published 3 times/year, "is controversial, influential, outspoken, and intelligent. Established in 1970, it has become a dynamic force in Scottish culture covering theatre, politics, language, and the arts. Our highly-respected forum for poetry, fiction, criticism, review, and debate makes it essential reading for anyone interested in contemporary Scotland. *Chapman* publishes the best in Scottish writing—new work by well-known Scottish writers in the context of lucid critical discussion. It also, increasingly, publishes international writing. With our strong commitment to the future, we energetically promote new writers, new ideas, and new approaches." Also interested in receiving poetry dealing with women's issues and feminism. Has published poetry and fiction by Liz Lochhead, Sorley MacLean, Edwin Morgan, Willa Muir, Tom Scott, and Una Flett. *Chapman* is 144 pages, digest-sized, perfect-bound, professionally printed in small type on matte stock, with glossy card cover. Press run is 2,000 (1,500 subscribers, 300 libraries). Receives "thousands" of poetry submissions/year, accepts about 200. Single copy: £6.50; subscription: £20. Sample: £5 (overseas).

How to Submit Submit 4-10 poems at a time, one poem/page. "We do not usually publish single poems." No simultaneous submissions. Cover letter is required. "Submissions must be accompanied by a SASE/IRC. Please send sufficient postage to cover the return of your manuscript. Do not send foreign stamps." Responds "as soon as possible." Always sends prepublication galleys. Pays contributor's copies. Staff reviews books of poetry. Send materials for review consideration.

Book/Chapbook Needs Chapman Publishing is currently not accepting submissions.

Advice "Poets should not try to court approval by writing poems especially to suit what they perceive as the nature of the magazine. They usually get it wrong and write badly."

$ 🖥 CHAPULTEPEC PRESS

4222 Chambers, Cincinnati OH 45223. (513)681-1976. E-mail: chapultepecpress@hotmail.com. Website: www.TokyoRoseRecords.com. Established 2001. **Contact:** David Garza.

Book/Chapbook Needs & How to Submit Chapultepec Press publishes books of poetry/literature, essays, social/political issues, art, music, film, history, popular science; library/archive issues and bilingual works. Wants "poetry/literature that works as a unit, that is caustic, fun, open-ended, worldly, mature, relevant, stirring, evocative. Bilingual. No poetry/literature collections without a purpose, that are mere collections. Also looking for broadsides/posters/illuminations." Publishes 3-5 books/year. Books are usually 1-100 pages, with art/graphics. Query first with a few sample poems, or a complete ms, and cover letter with brief bio and publication credits. Responds to queries and mss in up to 2 months. Pays advance of $5-15 and 3-5 author's copies. Order sample books by sending $3 payable to "David Garza."

$◯ THE CHARITON REVIEW

English Dept., Brigham Young University, Provo UT 84602. (801)422-1503. Established 1975. **Contact:** Jim Barnes, editor.

Magazine Needs *The Chariton Review* began in 1975 as a biannual literary magazine and in 1978 added the activities of the press (now defunct). The poetry published in the magazine is "open and closed forms—traditional, experimental, mainstream. We do not consider verse, only poetry in its highest sense, whatever that may be. The sentimental and the inspirational are not poetry for us. Also, no more 'relativism': short stories and poetry centered around relatives." Has published poetry by Michael Spence, Kim Bridgford, Sam Maio, Andrea Budy, Wayne Dodd, and J'laine Robnolt. *The Chariton Review* is 100+ pages, digest-sized, flat-spined, professionally printed, with glossy cover with photographs. Receives 8,000-10,000 submissions/year, accepts about 35-50. Press run is about 600 (400 subscribers, 100 libraries). Subscription: $9/year, $15/2 years. Sample: $5.

How to Submit Submit 3-5 poems at a time, single-spaced typescript. No simultaneous submissions. Do *not* write for guidelines. Responds quickly; accepted poems often appear within a few issues of notification. Always sends prepublication galleys. Pays $5/printed page. Acquires first North American serial rights. **Contributors are expected to subscribe or buy copies.**

▨ ◯ CHASE PARK

% David Harrison Horton, Foreign Affairs Dept., Nanjing University of Finance and Economics, 128 Tie Lu Bei Jie, Nanjing 210003 China. E-mail: twentymule@yahoo.com. Website: www.geocities.com/twentymule/index.html. Established 2000. **Contact:** David Harrison Horton, editor.

- "*Chase Park* **is currently on an extended hiatus and not reading manuscripts at this time. Please check** *Poets & Writers* **or our website for status updates.**"

$◯ THE CHATTAHOOCHEE REVIEW

Georgia Perimeter College, 2101 Womack Rd., Dunwoody GA 30338. (770)551-3019. Website: www.chattahoochee-review.org. Established 1980. **Contact:** Lawrence Hetrick, editor-in-chief.

Magazine Needs *The Chattahoochee Review* is a quarterly of poetry, short fiction, essays, reviews, and interviews, published by Georgia Perimeter College. "We publish a number of Southern writers, but *Chattahoochee Review* is not by design a regional magazine. All themes, forms, and styles are considered as long as they impact the whole person: heart, mind, intuition, and imagination." Has published poetry by A.E. Stalling, Carolyne Wright, Coleman Barks, Ron Rash, and Fred Chappell. *Chattahoochee Review* is 140 pages, digest-sized, professionally printed on cream stock, flat-spined, with one-color card cover. Press run is 1,250; 300 are complimentary copies sent to editors and "miscellaneous VIPs." Subscription: $16/year. Sample: $6.

How to Submit Writers should send one copy of each poem and a cover letter with bio material. No simultaneous submissions. Time between acceptance and publication is up to 4 months. Publishes theme issues. Guidelines and a list of upcoming themes available for SASE. Responds to queries in 2 weeks; to mss in 3 months. Pays $50/poem and 2 contributor's copies. Acquires first rights. Staff reviews books of poetry and short fiction in 1,500 words, single- or multi-book format. Send materials for review consideration.

☑ CHAUTAUQUA LITERARY JOURNAL; CHAUTAUQUA LITERARY JOURNAL ANNUAL CONTEST

P.O. Box 613, Chautauqua NY 14722. E-mail: CLJEditor@aol.com. Established 2003. **Contact:** Richard Foerster, editor.

Magazine Needs *Chautauqua Literary Journal* is an annual magazine of poetry, short fiction, creative nonfiction, and book reviews, published in June. "We welcome poems that exhibit the writer's craft and attention to language, employ striking images and metaphors, engage the mind as well as the emotions, and reveal insights into the larger world of human concerns. The editor invites traditional as well as experimental work." Does not want "hackneyed inspirational versifying; poems typed in all capitals or on pastel paper." Has published poetry by Betty Adcock, Ellen Bass, William Heyen, Colette Inez, Margaret Gibson, and Gabriel Welsch. *Chautauqua Literary Journal* is 196 pages, digest-sized, offset-printed, with notch adhesive binding and glossy cover with original artwork, includes ads. Receives about 2,000 poems/year, accepts about 50. Press run is 2,000 (1,200 subscribers, 500 shelf sales); 300 distributed free to contributors and VIPs. Single copy: $12.95; subscription: $10. Make checks payable to The Writers' Center at Chautauqua, Inc.

How to Submit Submit a maximum of 4 poems at a time. Accepts simultaneous submissions (if notified); no previously published poems. No e-mail or disk submissions. Cover letter is preferred. "Prefer single-spaced manuscripts in 12-pt. font. Cover letters should be brief and mention recent publications (if any). SASE is mandatory." Reads submissions year round. Time between acceptance and publication is up to one year. "The editor is the sole arbiter, but we do have advisory editors who periodically make recommendations." Sometimes comments on rejected poems. Guidelines available for SASE or by e-mail. Responds in 3 months or less. Always sends prepublication galleys. Pays 2 contributor's copies. Acquires first rights plus one-time non-exclusive rights to reprint accepted work in an anniversary issue. Reviews books and chapbooks of poetry in 750-1,000 words, single- and multi-book format. Send materials for review consideration to *Chautauqua Literary Journal*/Reviews, P.O. Box 2039, York Beach ME 03910.

Contest/Award Offerings Annual contest awards two $1,500 prizes (payable upon publication), one for best poem or group of poems, one for best prose work. Winners selected in anonymous competitions by the magazine's editor and advisory staff. Winning entries are published in *Chautauqua Literary Journal*, and all work entered is considered for publication. Submit up to 6 poems or a maximum of 500 lines. Each entry will be judged for overall artistic excellence; the poems do not have to be related by theme. Only original, previously unpublished work is eligible. See guidelines (available for SASE) for formatting instructions. **Entry fee:** $15 U.S./entry. Make checks payable to The Writers' Center at Chautauqua, Inc. Each entrant will receive a copy of *Chautauqua Literary Journal* that contains the prize-winning entries. **Postmark deadline:** September 30. Winners will be announced in early January. **Mail to:** *Chautauqua Literary Journal* Annual Contests, P.O. Box 2039, York Beach ME 03910 (do not mail entries to Chautauqua, NY address).

Also Offers The Writers' Center at Chautauqua (see separate listing in the Conferences & Workshops section).

Advice "Poets who are not avid readers of contemporary poetry will most likely not be writing anything of interest to us."

$ ☑ CHELSEA; CHELSEA AWARD FOR POETRY

P.O. Box 773, Cooper Station, New York NY 10276-0773. Established 1958. **Contact:** Alfredo de Palchi, editor. Associate Editor: Andrea Lockett.

- Work published in *Chelsea* has been included in *The Best American Poetry*, *Beacon's Best*, and *Pushcart Prize* anthologies.

Magazine Needs *Chelsea* is a long-established, high-quality literary biannual, appearing in June and December, that aims to promote intercultural communication. "We look for intelligence and sophisticated technique in both experimental and traditional forms. We are also interested in translations of contemporary poets. Although our tastes are eclectic, we lean toward the cosmopolitan avant-garde. We would like to see more poetry by writers of color. Do not want to see 'inspirational' verse, pornography, or poems that rhyme merely for the sake of rhyme." *Chelsea* is 192-240 pages, digest-sized, perfect-bound, offset-printed, with full-color art on card cover, includes ads. Press run is 2,100 (900 subscribers). Subscription: $13 domestic, $16 foreign. Sample: $6.

How to Submit "Submissions of 5-8 pages of poetry are ideal; long poems should not exceed 10 pages. Must be typed double-spaced; include brief bio." No previously published poems or simultaneous submissions. Reads submissions from September to June. Guidelines available for SASE. Responds within up to 5 months. Always sends prepublication galleys. Pays $15/page and 2 contributor's copies. Acquires first North American serial rights and one-time non-exclusive reprint rights.

Contest/Award Offerings The *Chelsea* Award for Poetry offers an annual award of $1,000 and publication in *Chelsea* for the best group of poems selected by the editors in anonymous competition. All work entered is considered for publication. Submissions must be unpublished; may not be under consideration elsewhere or scheduled for book publication within 8 months of the competition deadline. Submit 4-6 poems, the entire entry not to exceed 500 lines. Poems do not need to be related thematically. Manuscripts must be typed (single-spaced for poetry). Poet's name should not appear on the ms itself; include a single, separate cover sheet with title(s), poet's name, address, and telephone number, plus e-mail address. No entries or inquiries by phone, fax, or e-mail. Manuscripts cannot be returned; include SASE for competition results. Guidelines available for SASE. **Entry fee:** $10 (includes subscription to *Chelsea*). **Cannot accept fees by personal check; only money order or bank check will be accepted.** Make fee payable to Chelsea Associates, Inc. **Postmark deadline:** December 15. Winners will be announced about 2 months after the deadline.

CHILDREN, CHURCHES AND DADDIES; SCARS PUBLICATIONS

829 Brian Court, Gurnee IL 60031. E-mail: ccandd96@scars.tv. Website: http://scars.tv. Established 1993. **Contact:** Janet Kuypers, editor/publisher.

Magazine Needs *Children, Churches and Daddies (The Unreligious, Non-Family-Oriented Literary Magazine)* is published "monthly and contains poetry, prose, art, and essays. We specialize in electronic issues and collection books. We accept poetry of almost any genre, but we're not keen on rhyme for rhyme's sake, and we're not keen on religious poems (look at our current issue for a better idea of what we're like). We are okay with gay/lesbian/bisexual, nature/rural/ecology, political/social issues, women/feminism. We do accept longer works, but within 2 pages for an individual poem is appreciated. We don't go for racist, sexist (therefore we're not into pornography, either), or homophobic stuff." Has published poetry by Rochelle Holt, Angeline Hawkes-Craig, Cheryl Townsend, Kurt Nimmo, Pete McKinley, and Janine Canan. Print versions of *Children, Churches and Daddies* have ranged from 30 to 100 pages, have been both digest-sized and standard-sized, photocopied, saddle-stapled, with art and ads. Receives hundreds of poems/year, accepts about 40%. Press run "depends." Sample: $6. Make checks payable to Janet Kuypers.

How to Submit Accepts submissions by e-mail (pasted into body of message or as attachment) or on disk only. "When submitting via e-mail in body of message, explain in preceding paragraph that it is a submission; for disk submissions, mail floppy disk with ASCII text, or Macintosh disk." Accepts previously published poems and simultaneous submissions. Comments on rejected poems if asked. Guidelines available for SASE, by e-mail, or on website. Responds in 2 weeks.

Also Offers Scars Publications sometimes sponsors a book contest. Write or e-mail (Editor@scars.tv) for information. "The website is a more comprehensive view of what *Children, Churches and Daddies* does. All the information is there." Also able to publish chapbooks. Write for more information.

CHIRON REVIEW; CHIRON BOOKS; KINDRED SPIRIT PRESS

522 E. South Ave., St. John KS 67576-2212. (620)786-4955. E-mail: chironreview@hotmail.com. Website: www.geocities.com/SoHo/Nook/1748/. Established 1982 as *The Kindred Spirit*. **Contact:** Michael Hathaway, editor.

Magazine Needs *Chiron Review* is a quarterly tabloid using photographs of featured writers. No taboos. Has published poetry by Sam Pierstorff, Linda Rocheleau, Will Inman, Ian Young, and Shane Allison. Press run is about 1,000. Subscription: $15 US, $30 overseas. Sample: $5 US, $10 overseas or institutions.

How to Submit *Chiron Review* **will be closed to submissions through 2006.** Guidelines available for SASE or on website. Responds in 2 months. Pays one contributor's copy, discount on additional copies. Acquires first-time rights. Reviews books of poetry in 500-700 words.

Book/Chapbook Needs & How to Submit For book publication, query. Publishes 1-3 chapbooks/ year, flat-spined, professionally printed. Pays 25% of press run of 100-200 copies.

Also Offers Personal Publishing Program is offered under the Kindred Spirit Press imprint. "Through special arrangements with a highly specialized printer, we can offer extremely short run publishing at unbelievably low prices." Information available for SASE.

$☑ ◎ THE CHRISTIAN CENTURY (Specialized: Christian; social issues)

104 S. Michigan Ave., Suite 700, Chicago IL 60603. (312)263-7510. Fax: (312)263-7540. Website: www.ChristianCentury.org. Established 1884; named *The Christian Century* 1900, established again 1908, joined by *New Christian* 1970. **Contact:** Jill Peláez Baumgaertner, poetry editor.

Magazine Needs This "ecumenical weekly" is a liberal, sophisticated journal of news, articles of opinion, and reviews from a generally Christian point-of-view, using approximately one poem/ issue, not necessarily on religious themes but in keeping with the literate tone of the magazine. Wants "poems that are not statements but experiences, that do not talk about the world but show it. We want to publish poems that are grounded in images and that reveal an awareness of the sounds of language and the forms of poetry even when the poems are written in free verse." Does not want "pietistic or sentimental doggerel." Has published poetry by Jeanne Murray Walker, Ida Fasel, Kathleen Norris, Luci Shaw, J. Barrie Shepherd, and Wendell Berry. *Christian Century* is about 30 pages, magazine-sized, saddle-stapled, printed on quality newsprint, includes ads. Sample: $3.

How to Submit Submit poems typed, double-spaced, one poem/page. Include your name, address, and phone number on each page. Lines/poem: 20 maximum. "Prefer shorter poems." No simultaneous submissions. Submissions without SASE or SAE and IRCs will not be returned. Pays usually $20/poem plus one contributor's copy and discount on additional copies. Acquires all rights. Inquire about reprint permission. Reviews books of poetry in 300-400 words, single-book format; 400-500 words, multi-book format.

☑ ◎ CHRISTIAN GUIDE (Specialized: Christian)

P.O. Box 14622, Knoxville TN 37914. Established 1989. **Contact:** J. Brian Long, poetry editor.

Magazine Needs *The Christian Guide* is a regional, quarterly publication featuring articles, announcements, advertisements, photographs, and poetry. "We seek positive, accessible poetry that concerns itself with the interaction between God and the nature of (and surrounding) mankind in micro- or macrocosm. All poems themed to the gentler tenets of the devotion reciprocated between Heaven and Earth are welcomed, but only the most well-crafted will be accepted." Does not want forced, trite rhyme. Has published poetry by Jill Alexander Essbaum, C.E. Chaffin, Teresa White, and Charles Semones. *The Christian Guide* has a varied number of pages, is magazine-sized, with full-color cover with photographs and/or artwork, includes b&w and full-color ads. Press run is 25,000. Single copy or subscription: free for SASE.

How to Submit Submit 1-5 poems at a time. Lines/poem: 200 maximum. Accepts previously published poems and simultaneous submissions. No e-mail, fax, or disk submissions. Cover letter is required. "Include brief bio, list of publishing credits, and a SASE." Reads submissions year round. Submit seasonal poems 6 months in advance. Seldom comments on rejected poems. Guidelines available for SASE. Responds in 3 months. Pays 2 contributor's copies. Acquires one-time rights.

Advice "Subtlety. Subtlety. Subtlety. We are seeking poems that inspire awe, but do so by speaking to (and through) the reader with that 'small, still voice.'"

◪ ◎ **CHRISTIANITY AND LITERATURE (Specialized: religious/Christian; spirituality/ inspirational)**

Dept. of Humanities, Pepperdine University, 24255 Pacific Coast Highway, Malibu CA 90263. **Contact:** Maire Mullins, poetry editor.

Magazine Needs *Christianity and Literature* is a quarterly scholarly journal publishing about 6-8 poems/issue. Press run is 1,350 (1,125 subscribers, 525 libraries). Single copy: $7; subscription: $25/year, $45/2 years. Make checks payable to CCL.

How to Submit Submit 1-6 poems at a time. No previously published poems or simultaneous submissions. Accepts submissions by surface mail only. Cover letter is required. Submissions must be accompanied by SASE. Time between acceptance and publication is 6 months. "Poems are chosen by our poetry editor." Responds within 4 months. Pays 2 contributor's copies "and a dozen offprints to poets whose work we publish." Rights revert to poets upon written request. Reviews poetry collections in each issue (no chapbooks).

Advice "We look for poems that are clear and surprising. They should have a compelling sense of voice, formal sophistication (though not necessarily rhyme and meter), and the ability to reveal the spiritual through concrete images. We cannot return submissions that are not accompanied by SASE."

◪ **CIDER PRESS REVIEW; CIDER PRESS REVIEW BOOK AWARD**

777 Braddock Lane, Halifax PA 17032. E-mail: editor@ciderpressreview.com. Website: http://cider pressreview.com. Established 1997. **Contact:** Caron Andregg and Robert Wynne, co-editors.

Magazine Needs *Cider Press Review* appears annually and features "the best new work from con- temporary poets." Wants "thoughtful, well-crafted poems with vivid language and strong images. We prefer poems that have something to say. We would like to see more well-written humor. No didactic, inspirational, greeting-card verse; empty word play, therapy, or religious doggerel." Has published poetry by Jackson Wheeler, Janet Holmes, W.D. Snodgrass, Diane Lockward, Charles Harper Webb, and Eileen Doherty. *Cider Press Review* is 120 pages, digest-sized, offset-printed, perfect-bound, with 2-color coated card cover. Receives about 1,500 poems/year, accepts about 5%. Press run is 750. Subscription: $22/2 issues (one journal, one book award). Library subscrip- tions, $30 annually. Sample (journal): $10.

How to Submit Submit up to 5 poems at a time. No previously published poems or simultaneous submissions. Accepts submissions by postal mail only; "Authors outside North America may send *queries* by e-mail. Do not send unsolicited disk or e-mail submissions." Cover letter with short bio is preferred. "Please include SASE." Reads submissions from April to August only. Time between acceptance and publication is 6-9 months. Poems are circulated to an editorial board. Guidelines available for SASE or on website. Responds in 1-4 months. Always sends prepublication galleys. Pays one contributor's copy. Acquires first North American serial rights.

Contest/Award Offerings Sponsors the annual Cider Press Review Book Award. Offers 1st Prize: $500 and publication. Submit book-length ms of 48-80 pages. Include 2 cover sheets—one with title, author's name and complete contact information; one with title only—bound with a spring clip. Inlcude SASE for notification of winner; mss cannot be returned. All entrants will receive a copy of the winning book. **Entry fee:** $25. **Postmark Deadline:** between September 1 and November 30. Judge announced each year on website and in newsletter. 2004 judge was Cecilia Woloch.

◪ $◪ **CIMARRON REVIEW**

205 Morrill Hall, Oklahoma State University, Stillwater OK 74078-0135. E-mail: cimarronreview@ya hoo.com. Website: http://cimarronreview.okstate.edu. Established 1967. **Contact:** Lisa Lewis, Al- fred Corn, and Ai, poetry editors. Editor: E.P. Walkiewicz.

Magazine Needs *Cimarron* is a quarterly literary journal. "We take pride in our eclecticism. We like evocative poetry (lyric or narrative) controlled by a strong voice. No sing-song verse. No restrictions as to subject matter. We look for poems whose surfaces and structures risk uncertainty and which display energy, texture, intelligence, and intense investment." Has published poetry by

William Stafford, Gerry LaFemina, Phillip Dacey, Holly Prado, Mark Halliday, and Kim Addonizio. *Cimarron Review* is 100-150 pages, digest-sized, perfect-bound, with color cover and attractive printing. Circulation is 600 (one-third of subscribers are libraries). Single copy: $7; subscription: $24/year ($28 Canada), $65/3 years ($72 Canada).

How to Submit Submit 3-5 poems, with name and address on each, typed single- or double-spaced. Simultaneous submissions welcome, "but please note in cover letter." Accepts submissions by postal mail only. "Writers outside North America may *query* by e-mail." No response without SASE. Guidelines available on website. Responds in up to 6 months. Pays 2 contributor's copies. Acquires first North American serial rights only. Reviews books of poetry in 500-900 words, single-book format, occasionally multi-book. All reviews are assigned.

$☑ THE CINCINNATI REVIEW

P.O. Box 210069, Cincinnati OH 45221-0069. (513)556-3954. E-mail: editors@cincinnatireview.com. Website: www.cincinnatireview.com. Established 2003. **Contact:** Don Bogen, poetry editor.

Magazine Needs *The Cincinnati Review* is a biannual journal "devoted to publishing the best new poetry and literary fiction, as well as book reviews, essays, and interviews. Open to any schools, styles, forms—as long as the poem is well made and sophisticated in its language use and subject matter." *The Cincinnati Review* is 180-200 pages, digest-sized, perfect-bound, with matte paperback cover with full-color art, includes ads. Press run is 1,500. Single copy: $7; subscription: $12.

How to Submit Submit up to 10 pages of poetry at a time. Accepts simultaneous submissions with notification; no previously published poems. No e-mail or disk submissions. Cover letter is preferred. SASE required. Reads submissions September 1 through May 31. Time between acceptance and publication is 6 months. "First-round reading by small, trained staff. Final decisions made by genre editors." Seldom comments on rejected poems. Guidelines available for SASE or on website. Responds in one month. Always sends prepublication galleys. Pays $30/page and 2 contributor's copies. Acquires first North American serial rights. Reviews books of poetry in 1,500 words, single-book format.

☐ THE CIRCLE MAGAZINE; HIGHWIRE PRESS

173 Grandview Rd., Wernersville PA 19565. (610)678-6650. Fax: (610)678-6550. E-mail: circlemag @aol.com. Website: www.circlemagazine.com. Established 1998. **Contact:** Penny Talbert, editor.

Magazine Needs *The Circle Magazine* is a quarterly literary magazine "where culture and subculture meet. Read the poetry we currently publish" for style and content. Does not want anything religious or predictable. Has published poetry by Ace Boggess, Virgil Suárez, and Janet Buck. *The Circle Magazine* is 48-52 pages, digest-sized, offset-printed, saddle-stapled, with 2-color glossy cover. Receives about 4,000 poems/year, accepts about 1%. Press run varies. Single copy: $4; subscription: $15.

How to Submit Submit 3-5 poems at a time. Lines/poem: 4 minimum, 50 maximum. Accepts previously published poems and simultaneous submissions. Accepts e-mail submissions (pasted into body of message); no fax or disk submissions. Cover letter is preferred. Include name, address, and e-mail address with all submissions. Reads submissions year round. Time between acceptance and publication is 3-5 months. Poems are circulated to an editorial board. Seldom comments on rejected poems. Guidelines available on website. Responds in up to 4 months. Pays one contributor's copy. Acquires one-time rights. Reviews books and chapbooks of poetry.

Book/Chapbook Needs & How to Submit Highwire Press publishes 1-2 poetry chapbooks/year. Manuscripts are selected through open submission. Chapbooks are 40-52 pages, offset-printed, perfect-bound, with glossy covers. Query first, with a few sample poems and a cover letter with brief bio and publication credits. Chapbook mss may include previously published poems. "We normally solicit poets we're interested in publishing." Responds to queries in up to 2 months; to mss in up to 8 months. **Approximately 50% of chapbooks are author-subsidy published.**

Contest/Award Offerings Sponsors an annual poetry contest. Offers cash prizes of $100, $50, and

$25, plus subscription and publication. Previously published poems OK. No e-mail submissions. Include SASE. **Entry fee:** $3/poem, $5/2 poems. See website for deadline and guidelines.

✿ ☑ ◎ THE CLAREMONT REVIEW (Specialized: teens/young adults)

4980 Wesley Rd., Victoria BC V8Y 1Y9 Canada. Website: www.theClaremontReview.ca. Established 1991. **Contact:** Susan Stenson.

Magazine Needs *The Claremont Review* is a biannual review that publishes poetry and fiction by writers ages 13 to 19. Each Fall issue also includes an interview with a prominent Canadian writer. Wants "vital, modern poetry and fiction with a strong voice and living language. We prefer works that reveal something of the human condition. No clichéd language nor copies of 18th- and 19th-century work." Has published poetry by Claire Battershill, Danielle Hubbard, and Jennifer Slade. *The Claremont Review* is 110 pages, digest-sized, professionally printed, perfect-bound, with an attractive color cover. Receives 600-800 poems/year, accepts about 120. Press run is 700 (200 subscribers, 50 libraries, 250 shelf sales). Subscription: $18/year, $35/2 years. Sample: $10.

How to Submit Submit poems typed one to a page with author's name at the top of each. Accepts simultaneous submissions; no previously published poems. Cover letter with brief bio is required. Reads submissions September through June only. Always comments on rejected poems. Guidelines available in magazine or on website. Responds in up to 6 weeks (excluding July and August). Pays one contributor's copy, and funds when grants allow it. Acquires first North American serial rights.

Advice "Read excerpts on the website, and content of back issues."

✦ $☑ THE CLARION REVIEW

21293 Cameron Hunt Place, Ashburn VA 20147. (717)968-7787. E-mail: Price@clarionreview.edu. Website: http://clarionreview.com. Established 2002. **Contact:** Jonathan Price, editor-in-chief.

Magazine Needs *The Clarion Review* appears quarterly. "We are open to all forms of poetry, including translations." Has published poetry by Adrienne Su, Daniel Klotz, and Ralph Slotten. *The Clarion Review* is magazine-sized, offset-printed, perfect-bound, with 80-lb. velour cover, includes ads. Receives about 50 poems/year, accepts about 20%. Press run is 1,000 (300 subscribers, 100 libraries, 500 shelf sales); 100 distributed free to authors. Single copy: $8.50; subscription: $26.50. Make checks payable to Classic Culture, Inc.

How to Submit Submit 10 poems at a time. Lines/poem: 200 maximum. Accepts previously published poems and simultaneous submissions. Accepts e-mail (pasted into body of message) and disk submissions. Include SASE. Reads submissions year round. Submit seasonal poems 3 months in advance. Time between acceptance and publication is 10 weeks. Poems are circulated to an editorial board ("4 editors—¾ consensus"). Often comments on rejected poems. Regularly publishes theme issues. List of upcoming themes available for SASE or by e-mail. Guidelines available on website. Responds in one month. Sometimes sends prepublication galleys. Pays $50 and 3 contributor's copies. Acquires one-time rights. Reviews books and chapbooks of poetry and other magazines/journals in 750 words. Send materials for review consideration to Jonathan Price.

☾ ◎ CLARK STREET REVIEW (Specialized: form/style—narrative and prose poetry)

P.O. Box 1377, Berthoud CO 80513. E-mail: clarkreview@earthlink.net. Established 1998. **Contact:** Ray Foreman, editor.

Magazine Needs Appearing 8 times/year, *Clark Street Review* publishes narrative poetry and short shorts—"to give writers and poets cause to keep writing by publishing their best work." Wants "narrative poetry under 100 lines that reaches readers who are mostly published poets and writers. Subjects are open. No obscure or formalist work." Has published poetry by Louis McKee, Mariann Ritzer, Alan Catlin, Al De Genova, and Laurel Speer. *Clark Street Review* is 20 pages, digest-sized, photocopied, saddle-stapled, with paper cover. Receives about 1,000 poems/year, accepts about 10%. Press run is 200 (150 subscribers). Single copy: $2; subscription: $10 for 10 issues postpaid for writers. Make checks payable to R. Foreman.

How to Submit Submit 1-5 poems at a time. Lines/poem: 20 minimum, 75 maximum. Accepts previously published poems and simultaneous submissions. "Disposable sharp copies. Maximum width—65 characters. Include SASE for reply. No cover letter." Time between acceptance and publication is 4 months. "Editor reads everything with a critical eye of 30 years of experience in writing and publishing small press work." Often comments on rejected poems. Guidelines available for SASE or by e-mail. Responds in 3 weeks. Acquires one-time rights.

Advice "*Clark Street Review* is geared to the more experienced poet and writer deeply involved in the writer's life. There are tips and quotes throughout each issue writers appreciate. As always, the work we print speaks for the writer and the magazine. We encourage communication between our poets by listing their e-mail addresses. Publishing excellence and giving writers a reason to write is our only aim. Well-crafted, interesting, and accessible human narrative poems will see ink in *CSR*."

☑ COAL CITY REVIEW

English Dept., University of Kansas, Lawrence KS 66045. E-mail: briandal@ku.edu. Established 1989. **Contact:** Brian Daldorph, editor.

Magazine Needs Published in the fall, *Coal City Review* is an annual publication of poetry, short stories, reviews, and interviews—"the best material I can find." As for poetry, the editor quotes Pound: " 'Make it new.' " Does not want to see "experimental poetry, doggerel, 5-finger exercises, or beginner's verse." Has published poetry by Michael Gregg Michaud, Phil Miller, Walt McDonald, Thomas Zri Wilson, Virgil Suárez, and Denise Low. *Coal City Review* is 100 pages, digest-sized, professionally printed on recycled paper, perfect-bound, with light, colored card cover. Accepts about 5% of material received. Press run is 200 (50 subscribers, 5 libraries). Subscription: $10. Sample: $6.

How to Submit Submit 6 poems at a time with name and address on each page. Occasionally accepts previously published poems; prefers not to receive simultaneous submissions. No e-mail submissions. "Please do not send list of prior publications." Seldom comments on rejected poems. Guidelines available for SASE. Responds in up to 3 months. Pays one contributor's copy. Reviews books of poetry in 300-1,000 words, mostly single-book format. Send materials for review consideration.

Book/Chapbook Needs & How to Submit *Coal City Review* also publishes occasional chapbooks and books as issues of the magazine, but does not accept unsolicited chapbook submissions. Most recent book is *Notes to the Man Who Shot Me: Vietnam War Poems* by John Musgrave.

Advice "Care more (much more) about writing than publication. If you're good enough, you'll publish."

◖ COFFEE HOUSE PRESS

27 N. Fourth St., Suite 400, Minneapolis MN 55401. (612)338-0125. Established 1984. **Contact:** Christopher Fischbach, senior editor.

> ● Coffee House Press books have won numerous honors and awards. As an example, *The Book of Medicines* by Linda Hogan won the Colorado Book Award for Poetry and the Lannan Foundation Literary Fellowship.

Book Needs Publishes 4-5 poetry books/year. Wants poetry that is "challenging and lively; influenced by the Beats, the NY School, LANGUAGE and post-LANGUAGE, or Black Mountain." Has published poetry collections by Victor Hernandez Cruz, Anne Waldman, Eleni Sikelianos, and Paul Metcalf.

How to Submit Submit 8-12 poems at a time. Accepts previously published poems. Cover letter and bio are required. "Please include a SASE for our reply and/or the return of your manuscript." Seldom comments on rejected poems. Responds to queries in one month; to mss in up to 8 months. Always sends prepublication galleys. Send SASE for catalog. "Absolutely no phone, fax, or e-mail queries."

◢ COLD MOUNTAIN REVIEW

English Dept., Appalachian State University, Boone NC 28608. (828)262-2313. Fax: (828)262-2133. E-mail: coldmountain@appstate.edu. Website: www.coldmountain.appstate.edu. **Contact:** John Crutchfield, editor.

Magazine Needs *Cold Mountain Review* is published twice/year (January and July) by the English Department at Appalachian State University and features poetry, interviews with poets, book reviews, and b&w line drawings and photographs. "We're open to diverse perspectives and styles." Wants experimental poetry; humor. Has published poetry by Sarah Kennedy, Robert Morgan, Susan Ludvigson, Aleida Rodríguez, R.T. Smith, and Virgil Suárez. *Cold Mountain Review* is about 72 pages, digest-sized, neatly printed with one poem/page (or 2-page spread), perfect-bound, with light card stock cover. Accepts about 3% of the submissions received. For sample, send SASE or make donation to ASU *Cold Mountain Review.*

How to Submit Submit 3-5 poems at a time. No simultaneous submissions or previously published poems. Accepts submissions by postal mail only. "Please include name, address, phone number, and (if available) e-mail address on each poem." Cover letter with short bio is required. Reads submissions year round, "though response is slower in summer." Guidelines available fo SASE. Responds in up to 3 months. Pays 2 contributor's copies.

$◢ COLORADO REVIEW; COLORADO PRIZE FOR POETRY

Dept. of English, Colorado State University, Ft. Collins CO 80523. (970)491-5449. E-mail: creview@ colostate.edu. Website: http://coloradoreview.colostate.edu. Established 1956 as *Colorado State Review,* resurrected 1967 under "New Series" rubric, renamed *Colorado Review* 1985. **Contact:** Jorie Graham and Donald Revell, poetry editors. Editor: Stephanie G'Schwind.

● Poetry published in *Colorado Review* has been frequently included in volumes of *The Best American Poetry.*

Magazine Needs *Colorado Review* is a journal of contemporary literature that appears 3 times/year combining short fiction, poetry, and personal essays. Has published poetry by Robert Creeley, Rebecca Wolff, Robert Haas, Mark Strand, Lucie Brock-Broido, Jane Miller, and Fanny Howe. *Colorado Review* is about 224 pages, digest-sized, professionally printed, notch-bound, with glossy card cover. Press run is 1,300 (1,000 subscribers, 100 libraries). Receives about 10,000 submissions/year, accepts about 2%. Subscription: $24/ year. Sample: $10.

How to Submit Submit about 5 poems at a time. No previously published poems. Simultaneous submissions OK, "but you must notify *CR* immediately if accepted elsewhere." No e-mail submissions. SASE required for response. Reads submissions September 1 through May 1 only. Responds in 2 months, "often sooner." Pays $5/printed page for poetry. Acquires first North American serial rights. Reviews books of poetry, fiction, and nonfiction. "Most book reviews are solicited, but feel free to query." Send materials for review consideration.

Contest/Award Offerings Also sponsors the annual Colorado Prize for Poetry, established in

The Fall/Winter 2004 cover of *Colorado Review* features Teri Dixon's evocative "Chair in an Abandoned Schoolhouse" (© Getty Images).

1995. Offers an honorarium of $1,500 and publication. Book as a whole must be unpublished, though individual poems may have been published elsewhere. Submit a book-length ms on any subject in any form. Guidelines available for SASE or via e-mail. **Entry fee:** $25 (includes subscription). **Deadline:** January 15. Winner announced in May. Most recent award winner (2004) was Rusty Morrison; judge was Forrest Gander.

◙ COLUMBIA: A JOURNAL OF LITERATURE AND ART

415 Dodge Hall, Columbia University, New York NY 10027. (212)854-4216. Fax: (212)854-7704. E-mail: columbiajournal@columbia.edu. Website: www.columbia.edu/cu/arts/journal. Established 1977. **Contact:** Mark Bowen and Margaret Monaghan, poetry editors. Editor: Thomas Blaylock.

Magazine Needs *Columbia* appears semiannually and "will consider any poem that is eclectic and spans from traditional to experimental genre." Has published poetry by Joshua Beckman, Miranda Field, Eamon Grennan, Mary Jo Salter, Matthew Rohrer, and Yuse Komunyakaa. *Columbia* is 176 pages, digest-sized, offset-printed, notch-bound, with glossy cover, includes ads. Receives about 2,000 poems/year, accepts about 2%. Press run is 2,000 (200 subscribers, 30 libraries). Subscription: $15/year, $25/2 years. Sample: $10; back issue: $5+. Make checks payable to *Columbia Journal*.

How to Submit Submit up to 5 poems at a time. Accepts simultaneous submissions when noted; no previously published poems. Cover letter is preferred. Reads submissions year round. Poems are circulated to an editorial board. Seldom comments on rejected poems. Guidelines available in magazine or on website. Responds in 3-4 months. Pays 2 contributor's copies. Acquires first North American serial rights.

Contest/Award Offerings Sponsors annual contest with an award of $500. **Entry fee:** $10. See website or recent journal issue for submission deadline. Submit no more than 5 poems/entry. All entrants receive a copy of the issue publishing the winners.

◙ COMMON GROUND REVIEW; COMMON GROUND POETRY CONTEST

21 Primrose St., West Springfield MA 01089. Website: www.cgreview.org. Established 1999. **Contact:** Larry O'Brien, editor.

Magazine Needs *Common Ground Review* appears biannually, publishing poetry and original artwork. Wants poetry with strong imagery; well-written free or traditional forms. No greeting card verse; overly sentimental or political poetry. Has published poetry by James Doyle, Martin Galvin, Lyn Lifshin, Virgil Suárez, and Rennie McQuilken. *Common Ground Review* is 40-58 pages, digest-sized, high-quality photocopied, saddle-stapled, with card cover. Receives about 1,000 poems/year, accepts less than 10%. Press run is 125-150. Single copy: $6.50. Make checks payable to *Common Ground Review*.

How to Submit Submit 1-5 poems at a time. Lines/poem: 40 maximum. No previously published poems or simultaneous submissions. No fax, e-mail, or disk submissions. Cover letter is required. "Poems should be single-spaced; include name, address, phone, e-mail address, brief biography, and SASE (submissions without SASE will be discarded)." Reads submissions all year. Submit seasonal poems 6 months in advance. Time between acceptance and publication is 4-6 months. "Editor reads and culls submissions. Final decisions made by editorial board." Seldom comments on rejected poems. Guidelines available in magazine or on website. Responds in 2 months. Pays one contributor's copy. Acquires one-time rights.

Contest/Award Offerings Sponsors an annual poetry contest. Offers 1st Prize: $100; 2nd Prize: $50; 3rd Prize: $25; honorable mentions. **Entry fee:** $10 for 1-3 unpublished poems. **Deadline:** February 28. All contest submissions are considered for publication in *Common Ground Review*.

Advice "Read journal before submitting. Beginning poets need to read what's out there, get into workshops, and work on revising. Attend writers' conferences. Listen and learn."

❑ ◉ COMMON THREADS; OHIO HIGH SCHOOL POETRY CONTESTS (Specialized: membership; students)

3520 State Route 56, Mechanicsburg OH 43044. (937)834-2666. Website: www.geocities.com/theoh

iopoetryassociation/. Established 1928. **Contact:** Amy Jo Zook, editor. Ohio Poetry Association is a state poetry society open to members from outside the state, an affiliate of the National Federation of State Poetry Societies. (See separate listing for Ohio Poetry Association in the Organizations section.)

Magazine Needs *Common Threads* is the Ohio Poetry Association's biannual poetry magazine, appearing in April and October. **Only members of OPA may submit poems.** Does not want to see poetry that is highly sentimental, overly morbid, religiously coercive, or pornograpic—and nothing over 40 lines (unless it is exceptional, and still not over 50 lines). "We use beginners' poetry, but would like it to be good, tight, revised. In short, not first drafts. Too much is sentimental or prosy when it could be passionate or lyric. We'd like poems to make us think as well as feel something." Accepts poetry written by teens "if members or high school contest winners." Has published poetry by Bill Reyer, Michael Bugeja, Timothy Russell, Yvonne Hardenbrook, and Dalene Stull. *Common Threads* is 52 pages, digest-sized, computer-typeset, with matte card cover. "*Common Threads* is a forum for our members, and we do use reprints so new members can get a look at what is going well in more general magazines." Annual dues, including 2 issues of *Common Threads*: $15; seniors (over age 65): $12. Single copies: $2, $5 for students (through college).

How to Submit Accepts previously published poems, if "author is upfront about them. All rights revert to poet after publication." Accepts submissions by postal mail only. Reads submissions year round. Frequently publishes seasonal poems. Guidelines available for SASE or on website.

Contest/Award Offerings The Ohio Poetry Association sponsors an annual contest for unpublished poems written by high school students in Ohio, with categories for traditional and modern, plus several other categories. Offers 3 cash awards in each category. **March deadline.** For contest information, write Ohio Poetry Association, % Janeen Lepp, 1798 Sawgrass Dr., Reynoldsburg OH 43068. "We publish student winners in a book of winning poems. Also, we have a quarterly (on soltices and equinoxes) contest open to all poets. Themes change." Offers 2 cash awards; winners published in following issue of magazine. **Entry fee:** $1/poem for up to 5 poems (first poem free for OPA members). Contact Nora Holt at 404 Thurber Dr. W., Apt. 3, Columbus OH 43216 for themes and deadlines.

Advice "Read a lot to see what is being done by good poets nationally. Write what you know and love. Revise!!"

⬚ $ ⬚ ◎ COMMONWEAL (Specialized: religious/Catholic)

475 Riverside Dr., Room 405, New York NY 10115. E-mail: editors@commonwealmagazine.org. Website: www.commonwealmagazine.org. **Contact:** Rosemary Deen, poetry editor.

Magazine Needs *Commonweal*, a Catholic-published general interest magazine for college-educated readers, appears every 2 weeks. Prefers serious, witty, well-written poems. Does not publish inspirational poems. Circulation is 20,000. Subscription: $47. Sample: $7.

How to Submit Lines/poem: 75 maximum. No simultaneous submissions. Accepts e-mail submissions (prefers MS Word attachments). Reads submissions September 1 through June 30 only. Pays 50¢/line plus 2 contributor's copies. Acquires all rights. Returns rights when requested by the author. Reviews books of poetry in 750-1,000 words, single- or multi-book format.

◪ THE COMSTOCK REVIEW; COMSTOCK WRITERS' GROUP, INC.; MURIEL CRAFT BAILEY MEMORIAL AWARD; JESSE BRYCE NILES MEMORIAL CHAPBOOK AWARD

4956 St. John Dr., Syracuse NY 13215. (315)488-8077. E-mail: poetry@comstockreview.org. Website: www.comstockreview.org. Established 1987 as *Poetpourri*, published by the Comstock Writers' Group, Inc. **Contact:** Peggy Sperber Flanders, managing editor.

Magazine Needs *The Comstock Review* appears biannually: Volume I in summer, Volume II in winter. Wants "well-written free and traditional verse. Metaphor and fresh, vivid imagery encouraged. Poems over 40 lines discouraged. No obscene, obscure, patently religious, or greeting card verse. Few Haiku." Has published poetry by Jim Daniels, Keith Flynn, Alison Luterman, Marilyn Bates, Lois McKee, and Susan Terris. *The Comstock Review* is about 100 pages, digest-sized, professionally printed, perfect-bound. Press run is 600. Single copy: $9; subscription: $16/year; $28/2 years. Samples through year 2002: $6.

How to Submit Submit 3-6 poems at a time with name, address, and phone number or e-mail address on each page. No previously published poems. Simultaneous submissions discouraged. No e-mail submissions. Cover letter with short bio is preferred. Reads submissions January 1 through March 15 only (at present; check website). Acceptances mailed out 4-6 weeks after close of reading period. "Rejections may receive editorial commentary and may take slightly longer." Guidelines available in magazine, for SASE, or on website. Pays one contributor's copy. Acquires first North American serial rights.

Contest/Award Offerings 1) The annual **Muriel Craft Bailey Memorial Award** offers 1st Prize: $1,000; 2nd Prize: $250; 3rd Prize: $100; Honorable Mentions; publication of all finalists. May offer discounted awards edition to entrants. **Postmark deadline:** July 1. Before submitting, send SASE or check website for current rules. 2005 judge: Cornelius Eady. 2) The **Jesse Bryce Niles Memorial Chapbook Award** offers $1,000 plus publication and 50 author's copies; one copy to each entrant. Offered every other year. "Submission deadlines vary; usually late summer." Query with SASE or check website for complete rules, which must be followed.

CONCHO RIVER REVIEW; FORT CONCHO MUSEUM PRESS

P.O. Box 10894, Angelo State University, San Angelo TX 76909. (915)942-2273. Fax: (915)942-2155. E-mail: bradleyjw@hal.lamar.edu. Website: www.angelo.edu/dept/english/concho_river_review.htm. Established 1984. **Contact:** Jerry Bradley, poetry editor. Editor: Mary Ellen Hartje.

Magazine Needs *Concho River Review* is a literary journal published twice/year. "Prefer shorter poems, few long poems accepted; particularly looking for poems with distinctive imagery and imaginative forms and rhythms. The first test of a poem will be its imagery." Short reviews of new volumes of poetry are also published. Has published poetry by Walt McDonald, Robert Cooperman, Mary Winters, William Wenthe, and William Jolliff. *Concho River Review* is 120-138 pages, digest-sized, professionally printed, flat-spined, with matte card cover. Receives 600-800 poems/year, accepts 35-40. Press run is 300 (200 subscribers, 10 libraries). Subscription: $14. Sample: $5.

How to Submit "Please submit 3-5 poems at a time. Use regular legal-sized envelopes—no big brown envelopes; no replies without SASE. Type must be letter-perfect, sharp enough to be computer-scanned." Accepts submissions by e-mail (as attachment). Responds in 2 months. Pays one contributor's copy. Acquires first rights.

Advice "We're always looking for good, strong work—from both well-known poets and those who have never been published before."

CONCRETE WOLF; CONCRETE WOLF POETRY CHAPBOOK CONTEST

P.O. Box 730, Amherst NH 03031-0730. E-mail: editors@concretewolf.com. Website: http://concretewolf.com. Established 2001. **Contact:** Brent Allard, Lana Ayers, and Martha D. Hall, editors. Member: CLMP.

- Concrete Wolf no longer publishes a quarterly poetry journal. The press now publishes chapbooks only through its annual contest and cannot respond to submissions outside of the contest.

Book/Chapbook Needs Concrete Wolf publishes one poetry chapbook/year through its annual competition. "We prefer chapbooks that have a theme, either obvious (i.e., chapbook about a divorce) or understated (i.e., all the poems mention the color blue). We like a collection that feels more like a whole than a sampling of work. We have no preference as to formal or free verse. We probably slightly favor lyric and narrative poetry to language and concrete, but excellent examples of any style get our attention. We like to see fresh perspectives on common human experiences, with careful attention to words; poems that give the impression the poet is in the room." Does not want "poetry that is all head, or preaches rather than speaks." Has published poetry by Martha Miller, Brian Moreau, Jeanne Kent, Frank Bogan, Gertrude F. Bantle, and Nancy Brady Cunningham. Manuscripts are selected through competition only (see below). Contest receives about 200 entries. Chapbooks are 20-24 pages, duplex-printed, perfect-bound, with matte card stock covers with b&w art. Press run is usually 500-1,000. Order sample chapbooks by sending $7 payable to Concrete Wolf.

Contest/Award Offerings Annual poetry chapbook contest offers honorarium plus 50 author's copies. **Entry fee:** $15. **Deadline:** January 15 for 2005. "Follow submission guidelines on website." Contest is judged by editors and an anonymous guest judge, announced after the contest.

Also Offers Website will occasionally post writing exercises. Future plans include a supplementary CD of poets reading their work.

Advice "Poetry exists for everyone, not just the academic. Remember that poetry is work that requires crafting."

$◨ CONFRONTATION MAGAZINE

English Dept., C.W. Post Campus of Long Island University, Brookville NY 11548-1300. (516)299-2720. Fax: (516)299-2735. E-mail: martin.tucker@liu.edu. Established 1968. **Contact:** Michael Hartnett, poetry editor. Editor-in-Chief: Martin Tucker.

Magazine Needs *Confrontation Magazine* is "a semiannual literary journal with interest in all forms. Our only criterion is high literary merit. We think of our audience as an educated, lay group of intelligent readers. We prefer lyric poems. Length generally should be kept to 2 pages. No sentimental verse." Has published poetry by David Ray, T. Alan Broughton, David Ignatow, Philip Appleman, Jane Mayhall, and Joseph Brodsky. *Confrontation* is about 300 pages, digest-sized, professionally printed, flat-spined. Receives about 1,200 submissions/year, accepts about 150. Circulation is 2,000. Subscription: $10/year. Sample: $3.

How to Submit Submit no more than 10 pages, clear copy. No previously published poems. "Prefer single submissions." Accepts queries by e-mail, but not submissions. Do not submit mss June through August. Publishes theme issues. Upcoming themes available for SASE. Responds in 2 months. Sometimes sends prepublication galleys. Pays $5-50 and one contributor's copy with discount available on additional copies. Staff reviews books of poetry. Send materials for review consideration.

Also Offers Basically a magazine, they do on occasion publish "book" issues or "anthologies." Their most recent "occasional book" is *Clown at Wall*, stories and drawings by Ken Bernard.

Advice "We want serious poetry, which may be humorous and light-hearted on the surface."

$◨ THE CONNECTICUT POETRY REVIEW

P.O. Box 818, Stonington CT 06378. Established 1981. **Contact:** J. Claire White and Harley More, poetry editors.

Magazine Needs *The Connecticut Poetry Review* is a "small press annual magazine. We look for poetry of quality that is both genuine and original in content. No specifications except length: 10-40 lines." Has published poetry by John Updike, Robert Peters, Diane Wakoski, and Marge Piercy. *The Connecticut Poetry Review* is 45-60 pages, flat-spined, digest-sized, "printed letterpress by hand on a Hacker Hand Press from Monotype Bembo." Receives over 2,500 submissions/year, accepts about 20. Press run is 400 (80 subscribers, 35 libraries). Sample: $3.50.

How to Submit Lines/poem: 10 minimum, 40 maximum. Reads submissions April through June and September through December only. Responds in 3 months. Pays $5/poem plus one contributor's copy.

Advice "Study traditional and modern styles. Study poets of the past. Attend poetry readings and write. Practice on your own."

◨ CONNECTICUT REVIEW

Southern Connecticut State University, 501 Crescent St., New Haven CT 06515. (203)392-6737. Fax: (203)392-5748. E-mail: ctreview@southernct.edu. Website: www.southernct.edu/projects/ctr eview. Established 1968. **Contact:** Vivian Shipley, editor.

● Poetry published in this review has been included in *The Best American Poetry* and *The Pushcart Prize* anthologies; has received special recognition for Literary Excellence from Public Radio's series *The Poet and the Poem*; and has won the Phoenix Award for Significant Editorial Achievement from the Council of Editors of Learned Journals (CELJ).

Magazine Needs *Connecticut Review*, published biannually, contains essays, poetry, articles, fiction, b&w photographs, and color artwork. Has published poetry by Jack Bedell, Colette Inez, Maxine Kumin, Tony Fusco, Dana Gioia, and Marilyn Nelson. *Connecticut Review* is 208 pages, digest-sized, offset-printed, perfect-bound, with glossy 4-color cover. Receives about 2,500 poems/year, accepts about 5%. Press run is 3,000 (400 libraries); 1,000 distributed free to Connecticut State libraries and high schools. Sample: $8. Make checks payable to Connecticut State University.

How to Submit Submit 3-5 typed poems at a time with name, address, and phone number in the upper left corner, with SASE for reply only. Accepts submissions by postal mail only. Guidelines available for SASE. Pays 2 contributor's copies. Acquires first or one-time rights.

◪ ✦ CONNECTICUT RIVER REVIEW; ANNUAL CONNECTICUT RIVER REVIEW POETRY CONTEST; BRODINSKY-BRODINE CONTEST; WINCHELL CONTEST; LYNN DECARO HIGH SCHOOL COMPETITION; CONNECTICUT POETRY SOCIETY

P.O. Box 4053, Waterbury CT 06704-0053. Established 1978. **Contact:** Tony Fusco, editor.

Magazine Needs Published by the Connecticut Poetry Society, *Connecticut River Review* appears annually in July or August. Wants "original, honest, diverse, vital, well-crafted poetry; any form, any subject. Translations and long poems welcome." Has published poetry by Marilyn Nelson (CT Poet Laureate), Claire Zoghb, and Vivian Shipley. *Connecticut River Review* is digest-sized, attractively printed, perfect-bound. Receives about 2,000 submissions/year, accepts about 100. Press run is about 300 (175 subscribers, 5% libraries). CPS membership: $25/year (includes *CRR* and *Long River Run*, a members-only magazine).

How to Submit Submit up to 3 poems at a time. "Complete contact information typed in upper right corner; SASE required." No previously published poems. Accepts simultaneous submissions if notified of acceptance elsewhere. Cover letter with current bio is appreciated. Reads submissions from October 1 to April 15. Guidelines available for SASE. Responds in up to 6 weeks. Pays one contributor's copy. "Poet retains copyright."

Contest/Award Offerings 1) The Annual *Connecticut River Review* Poetry Contest. **Entry fee:** $10/3 poems. **Deadline:** April 30. 2) The Brodinsky-Brodine Contest awards publication in *Connecticut River Review*. **Entry fee:** $10/3 poems. **Deadline:** postmarked between May 1 and July 31. 3) The Winchell Contest awards publication in *Connecticut River Review*. **Entry fee:** $10/3 poems. **Deadline:** postmarked between October 1 and December 31. 4) The Lynn Decaro High School Competition **(for CT high school students only)** awards publication in *Long River Run*. **Entry fee:** none. **Deadline:** postmarked between December 1 and February 27.

Also Offers Affiliated with the National Federation of State Poetry Societies, the Connecticut Poetry Society currently has about 150 members. Sponsors conferences, workshops, open-mike readings. Publishes *Newsletter*, a bimonthly publication for members, also available to nonmembers for SASE. Members and nationally known writers give readings that are open to the public. Members meet monthly. Annual dues are $25. Send SASE for more information.

Advice "Read as much good poetry as you can before you write."

Ⓝ ✦ CONVERGENCE

P.O. Box 1127, Magalia CA 95954. (408)515-9204. E-mail: editor@convergence-journal.com. Website: www.convergence-journal.com. Established 2003. **Contact:** Lara Gularte, editor.

Magazine Needs *Convergence*, an online quarterly, "seeks to unify the literary and visual arts and draw new interpretations of the written word by pairing poems and flash fiction with complementary art. We are open to many different styles, but we do not often publish formal verse. Read a couple of issues to get a sense of what we like; namely, well-crafted work with fresh images and a strong voice." Does not want "poetry with trite, unoriginal language or unfinished work." Has published poetry by Lola Haskins, Grace Cavalieri, Molly Fisk, and Renato Rosaldo. Receives about 250 poems/year, accepts about 5-25/issue. Has about 400 subscribers.

How to Submit Submit 5 poems at a time. Lines/poem: 60 maximum. Accepts previously published poems; no simultaneous submissions. Accepts e-mail submissions only (as Word attachment); no disk submissions. Cover letter is required. Reads submissions year round. Time between acceptance and publication is 2 weeks. Poems are circulated to an editorial board. Sometimes comments on rejected poems. Guidelines available on website. Responds in 4 months. No payment. Acquires first rights.

◑ COPPER CANYON PRESS; HAYDEN CARRUTH AWARD

P.O. Box 271, Port Townsend WA 98368. (877)501-1393. Fax: (360)385-4985. E-mail: poetry@copp ercanyonpress.org. Website: www.coppercanyonpress.org. Established 1972. **Contact:** Sam Hamill, editor.

Book/Chapbook Needs Copper Canyon publishes books of poetry. Has published collections by Lucille Clifton, Hayden Carruth, Carolyn Kizer, Olga Broumas, Ruth Stone, and Jim Harrison.

How to Submit Currently accepts no unsolicited poetry. E-mail queries and submissions will go unanswered.

Contest/Award Offerings Copper Canyon Press publishes one volume of poetry each year by a new or emerging poet through its Hayden Carruth Award. "For the purpose of this award, an emerging poet is defined as a poet who has published not more than 2 books." Winner receives $1,000 advance, book publication with Copper Canyon Press, and a one-month residency at the Vermont Studio Center. Each unbound ms submitted should be a minimum of 46 typed pages on white paper, paginated consecutively with a table of contents. Author's name or address must not appear anywhere on ms (this includes both title and acknowledgments pages). Please do not staple or paper-clip ms. Include **$25 handling fee** (check payable to Copper Canyon Press), submission form (available on website), and SASE for notification (mss will be recycled, not returned). **Deadline:** postmarked between November 1 and November 30, 2005. No entries by e-mail or fax. Winner announced February 21, 2006. Past winners include Sascha Feinstein's *Misterioso*, Rebecca Wee's *Uncertain Grace*, Jenny Factor's *Unraveling at the Name*, Peter Pereira's *Saying the World*, Ben Lerner's *Lichtenberg Figures*, and Scott Hightower's *Part of the Bargain*. Past judges include Jane Miller (2000), Marilyn Hacker (2001), and Gregory Orr (2002). Further guidelines available for SASE or on website.

✪ ↯ $◑ ◎ COTEAU BOOKS; THUNDER CREEK PUBLISHING CO-OP (Specialized: regional/Canada; children)

401-2206 Dewdney Ave., Regina SK S4R 1H3 Canada. (306)777-0170. Fax: (306)522-5152. E-mail: coteau@coteaubooks.com. Website: www.coteaubooks.com. Established 1975. **Contact:** Acquisitions Editor. Managing Editor: Nik L. Burton. Publisher: Geoffrey Ursell.

Book/Chapbook Needs Coteau is a "small literary press that publishes poetry, fiction, drama, anthologies, criticism, young adult novels—by Canadian writers only." Has published *A Secret Envy of the Unsaved* by Rebecca Frederickson, *Silence of the Country* by Kristjana Gunnars, and *The Names Leave the Stones* by Steven Michael Berzensky.

How to Submit Submit 30-50 poems "and indication of whole manuscript," typed with at least 12-point font; simultaneous and American submissions not accepted. Accepts e-mail submissions (send as .txt file attachments, maximum 20 pages). No fax submissions. Cover letter is required; include publishing credits and bio, and SASE for return of ms. Queries will be answered and mss responded to in 4 months. Always sends prepublication galleys. Authors receive 10% royalty and 10 author's copies. Catalog (for ordering samples) free for 9 × 12 SASE.

Also Offers Website includes title and ordering information, author interviews, awards, news and events, submission guidelines and links.

Advice "Generally, poets should have a number of publishing credits (single poems or series) in literary magazines and anthologies before submitting a manuscript."

✪ ◑ CRAB CREEK REVIEW

P.O. Box 840, Vashon Island WA 98070. E-mail: editors@crabcreekreview.org. Website: www.crab creekreview.org. Established 1983. **Contact:** Editors.

Magazine Needs Appearing biannually, *Crab Creek Review* publishes "an eclectic mix of energetic poems, free or formal, and more interested in powerful imagery than obscure literary allusion. Wit? Yes. Punch? Sure. Toast dry? No thank you. Translations are welcome—please submit with a copy of the poem in its original language, if possible." Has published poetry by Pauls Toutonghi, Molly Tenenbaum, Judith Skillman, Derek Sheffield, David Lee, and Kevin Miller. *Crab Creek Review* is an 80- to 120-page, perfect-bound paperback. Subscription: $10 (2 issues). Sample: $5.

How to Submit Submit up to 5 poems at a time. No fax or e-mail submissions. Include SASE ("without one we will not consider the work"). Responds in up to 4 months. Pays 2 contributor's copies. Guidelines available for SASE or on website.

$☑ CRAB ORCHARD REVIEW; CRAB ORCHARD SERIES IN POETRY OPEN COMPETITION AWARDS; CRAB ORCHARD SERIES IN POETRY FIRST BOOK AWARD; THE RICHARD PETERSON POETRY PRIZE

Dept. of English, Southern Illinois University, Carbondale IL 62901-4503. Website: www.siu.edu/ ~crborchd. Established 1995. **Contact:** Allison Joseph, poetry editor. Managing Editor: Jon C. Tribble.

- *Crab Orchard Review* received a 2003 Literary Award and a 2004 Operating Grant from the Illinois Arts Council. Poetry from *Crab Orchard Review* has also appeared in *The Best American Poetry* and *Beacon's Best of 1999* and *2000*.

Magazine Needs *Crab Orchard Review* appears biannually in February and August. "We are a general interest literary journal publishing poetry, fiction, creative nonfiction, interviews, book reviews, and novel excerpts." Wants all styles and forms from traditional to experimental. No greeting card verse; literary poetry only. Has published poetry by Francisco Aragón, Ned Balbo, Betsy Sholl, Shara McCallum, and Camille Dungy. *Crab Orchard Review* is 280-300 pages, digest-sized, professionally printed, perfect-bound, with (usually) glossy card cover with color photos. Receives about 10,000 poems/year, accepts about 1%. Press run is 2,500 (2,000 subscribers, 400 libraries); 100 exchanged with other journals; remainder in shelf sales. Subscription: $15. Sample: $8.

How to Submit Submit up to 5 poems at a time. Accepts simultaneous submissions with notification; no previously published poems. Accepts submissions by postal mail only. Cover letter is preferred. "Indicate stanza breaks on poems of more than one page." Reads submissions April to November for Summer/Fall special theme issue, December to April for regular, non-thematic Winter/Spring issue. Time between acceptance and publication is 6 months to a year. "Poems that are under serious consideration are discussed and decided on by the managing editor and poetry editor." Seldom comments on rejected poems. Publishes theme issues. List of upcoming themes available in magazine, for SASE, or on website. Guidelines available for SASE or on website. Responds in up to 9 months. Pays $15/page ($100 minimum) plus 2 contributor's copies and one year's subscription. Acquires first North American serial rights. Staff reviews books of poetry in 500-700 words, single-book format. Send materials for review consideration to Managing Editor Jon C. Tribble.

Contest/Award Offerings 1) **Crab Orchard Series in Poetry Open Competition Awards:** 1st Prize: $3,500 and publication of a book-length ms; 2nd Prize: $1,500 and publication of a book-length ms. "Cash prize totals reflect a $1,500 honorarium for each winner for a reading at Southern Illinois University at Carbondale. Publication contract is with Southern Illinois University Press. Entrants must be U.S. citizens or permanent residents. Individual poems may have been previously published, but collection as a whole must be unpublished, written in English. May be under consideration elsewhere, but series editor must be informed immediately upon acceptance. Manuscripts should be typewritten or computer generated (letter quality only, no dot matrix), single-spaced; clean photocopy is recommended as manuscripts are not returned." See guidelines for deadline and complete formatting instructions. Guidelines available for SASE or on website. **Entry fee:** $25/ submission (includes subscription to *Crab Orchard Review*). Make checks payable to Crab Orchard Award Series. 2004 winners: Victoria Chang (1st prize, *Circle*) and Greg Pape (2nd prize, *American Flamingo*). 2) **Crab Orchard Series in Poetry First Book Award:** $2,500 ($1,000 prize plus $1,500 honorarium for a reading at Southern Illinois University at Carbondale) and publication. "Manuscripts should be 50-75 pages of original poetry, in English, by a U.S. citizen or permanent resident who has neither published, nor committed to publish, a volume of poetry 40 pages or more in length (individual poems may have been previously published). Current students and employees of Southern Illinois University and authors published by Southern Illinois University Press are not eligible.'' See guidelines for deadline and complete formatting instructions. Guidelines available for SASE or on website. **Entry fee:** $25/submission (includes subscription to *Crab Orchard Review*). Make checks payable to Crab Orchard Award Series. 2004 winner: A. Loudermilk (*Strange Valentine*). 3) **The Richard Peterson Poetry Prize:** $1,500 plus publication in Winter/Spring issue of *Crab Orchard Review*. ''Submissions must be unpublished original work not under consideration elsewhere, written in English by a U.S. citizen or permanent resident. Name, address, telephone number, and/or e-mail address should appear only on the title page of manuscript; author's name should not appear on any subsequent pages. Mark 'poetry' on outside of envelope. Include #10 SASE for notification of winners.'' See guidelines for deadline and complete formatting instructions. Guidelines available for SASE or on website. **Entry fee:** $15/entry (1-5 pages, no more than one poem per page; poet may submit up to 3 separate entries if not entering the fiction or nonfiction categories of the literary contest). Each fee entitles entrant to a one-year subscription, extension of current subscription, or gift subscription; indicate choice and include complete address. Make checks payable to *Crab Orchard Review*.

Advice ''Do not send any submissions via e-mail! Include SASE (#10 or larger) with all submissions and all queries. Before you send work, check the website to see what issue we are currently reading submissions for. Being familiar with our reading schedule will help you submit appropriate work at the right time.''

CRAZYHORSE; CRAZYHORSE FICTION AND POETRY AWARDS

Dept. of English, College of Charleston, 66 George St., Charleston SC 29424. (843)953-7740. E-mail: crazyhorse@cofc.edu. Website: http://crazyhorse.cofc.edu. Established 1960. **Contact:** Paul Allen and Carol Ann Davis, poetry editors.

- Richard Jackson's *This* won a 2004 Pushcart Award for *Crazyhorse*; Dinty Moore's *Son of Mr. Green Jeans* was reprinted in *Harper's* magazine.

Magazine Needs *Crazyhorse* appears biannually and publishes fine fiction, poetry, and essays. ''Send your best words our way. We like to print a mix of writing regardless of its form, genre, school, or politics. We're especially on the lookout for writing that doesn't fit the categories.'' Does not want ''writing with nothing at stake. Before sending, ask 'What's reckoned with that's important for other people to read?' '' Has published poetry by David Wojahn, Mary Ruefle, Nance Van Winkle, Dean Young, Marvin Bell, and A.V. Christie. *Crazyhorse* is 160 pages, 8¾×8½, perfect-bound, with 4-color glossy cover. Receives about 8,000 poems/year. Press run is 2,000. Single copy: $8.50; subscription: $15/year, $25/2 years, $40/3 years. Sample: $5. Make checks payable to *Crazyhorse*.

How to Submit Submit 3-5 poems at a time. Accepts simultaneous submissions; no previously published poems. No fax, e-mail, or disk submissions. Cover letter is preferred. Reads submissions year round. ''We read slower in summer.'' Time between acceptance and publication is 6 months. Seldom comments on rejected poems. Guidelines available in magazine, for SASE, or by e-mail. Responds in 3 months. Sometimes sends prepublication galleys. Pays 2 contributor's copies plus one-year subscription (2 issues). Acquires first rights.

Contest/Award Offerings The Crazyhorse Fiction and Poetry Awards: $1,000 and publication in *Crazyhorse*. Guidelines available for SASE or on website.

Advice ''Feel strongly; then write.''

THE CREAM CITY REVIEW

Dept. of English, University of Wisconsin at Milwaukee, P.O. Box 413, Milwaukee WI 53201. (414)229-4708. E-mail: creamcity@uwm.edu. Website: www.uwm.edu/Dept/English/ccr/index.htm. **Contact:** Oody Petty and Jen Collins, poetry editors. Editor: Erica Wiest.

• Poetry published in this review has been included in volumes of *The Best American Poetry*.

Magazine Needs *The Cream City Review* is a nationally distributed literary magazine published twice/year by the university's Creative Writing Program. "We seek to publish all forms of writing, from traditional to experimental. We strive to produce issues that are challenging, diverse, and of lasting quality. We are not interested in sexist, homophobic, racist, or formulaic writings." Has published poetry by William Harrold, Maxine Chernoff, Kate Braverman, Billy Collins, Bob Hicok, and Allison Joseph. *The Cream City Review* is about 200 pages, digest-sized, perfect-bound, with full-color cover on 70-lb. paper. Press run is 1,000 (450 subscribers, 40 libraries). Single copy: $12; subscription: $22/year, $41/2 years; institutional subscription: $30/year. Sample: $7.

How to Submit "Include SASE when submitting, and please submit no more than 6 poems at a time." Accepts simultaneous submissions when notified. Accepts submissions by postal mail only. "Please include a few lines about your publication history and other information you think of interest." Reads submissions August 1 through April 1 only. Sometimes comments on rejected poems. Publishes theme issues; "inquire regularly." Guidelines available for SASE. Responds in 6-8 months. Payment includes one-year subscription. Acquires first rights. Reviews books of poetry in 1-2 pages. Send materials for review consideration to the book review editor.

Contest/Award Offerings Sponsors an annual poetry contest. Awards $100 plus publication. Submit 3 poems/entry. **Entry fee:** $10. **Deadline:** November 1. All entries considered for publication.

$☐ ◎ CRICKET; SPIDER, THE MAGAZINE FOR CHILDREN; LADYBUG, THE MAGAZINE FOR YOUNG CHILDREN; BABYBUG, THE LISTENING AND LOOKING MAGAZINE FOR INFANTS AND TODDLERS (Specialized: children); CICADA (Specialized: teens)

P.O. Box 300, Peru IL 61354-0300. Website: www.cricketmag.com. *Cricket* established 1973. *Ladybug* established 1990. *Spider* established 1994. *Babybug* established 1994. *Cicada* established 1998. **Contact:** Marianne Carus, editor-in-chief.

Magazine Needs *Cricket* (for ages 9-14) is a monthly, circulation 73,000, using "serious, humorous, nonsense rhymes" for children and young adults. Does not want "forced or trite rhyming or imagery that doesn't hang together to create a unified whole." Sometimes uses previously published work. *Cricket* is 64 pages, 8×10, saddle-stapled, with color cover. *Ladybug*, also monthly, circulation 120,000, is similar in format and requirements but is aimed at younger children (ages 2-6). *Spider*, also monthly, circulation 70,000, is for children ages 6-9. Format and requirements similar to *Cricket* and *Ladybug*. *Cicada*, appearing bimonthly, circulation 17,000, is a magazine for ages 14 and up, publishing "short stories, poems, and first-person essays written for teens and young adults." Wants "serious or humorous poetry; rhymed or free verse." *Cicada* is 128 pages, digest-sized, perfect-bound, with full-color cover. *Babybug*, published 10 times/year, circulation 48,000, is a read-aloud magazine for ages 6 months to 2 years. *Babybug* is 24 pages, 6¼×7, printed on cardstock with nontoxic glued spine. The magazines receive over 1,200 submissions/month, accept 25-30. Sample of *Cricket*, *Ladybug*, *Spider*, or *Babybug*: $5; sample of *Cicada*: $8.50.

How to Submit Do not query. Submit no more than 5 poems. Lines/poem: 50 (2 pages) maximum for *Cricket*; 20 maximum for *Spider* and *Ladybug*; 25 maximum for *Cicada*; 8 maximum for *Babybug*. No restrictions on form. Accepts submissions by postal mail only. Guidelines available for SASE or on website. Responds in 4 months. Payment for all is up to $3/line and 6 contributor's copies. "All submissions are automatically considered for all 5 magazines."

Also Offers *Cricket* and *Spider* hold a poetry, story, or art contest each month. *Cricket* accepts entries from readers of all ages; *Spider* from readers ages 10 and under. Current contest themes and rules appear in each issue.

Advice "Read past issues before submitting."

◢ CRUCIBLE; SAM RAGAN PRIZE

Barton College, College Station, Wilson NC 27893. (252)399-6344. E-mail: tgrimes@barton.edu. Established 1964. **Contact:** Terrence L. Grimes, editor.

Magazine Needs *Crucible* is an annual, published in November, using "poetry that demonstrates originality and integrity of craftsmanship as well as thought. Traditional metrical and rhyming poems are difficult to bring off in modern poetry. The best poetry is written out of deeply felt experience which has been crafted into pleasing form. No very long narratives." Has published poetry by Robert Grey, R.T. Smith, and Anthony S. Abbott. *Crucible* is 100 pages, digest-sized, professionally printed on high-quality paper, with matte card cover. Press run is 500 (300 subscribers, 100 libraries, 200 shelf sales). Sample: $7.

How to Submit Submit 5 poems at a time between Christmas and mid-April only. No previously published poems or simultaneous submissions. Responds in up to 4 months. "We require 3 unsigned copies of the manuscript and a short biography including a list of publications, in case we decide to publish the work." Pays contributor's copies.

Contest/Award Offerings The Sam Ragan Prize ($150), in honor of the former Poet Laureate of North Carolina, and other contests (prizes of $150 and $100). Send SASE for guidelines.

Advice Editor leans toward free verse with attention paid particularly to image, line, stanza, and voice. However, he does not want to see poetry that is "forced."

N ☑ CRYING SKY: POETRY & CONVERSATION

164-1 Maple St., Manchester NH 03103. (603)624-2801. Established 2005. **Contact:** W.E. Butts and S Stephanie, editors. Member: CLMP.

Magazine Needs *Crying Sky: Poetry & Conversation*, a biannual literary journal published in March and September, "features new writing from established and emerging poets, as well as interviews and essays." Wants "well crafted, intriguing poetry that is engaged in reflecting the human condition and spirit. We're open to both free verse and traditional forms, but prefer writing that demonstrates a careful attention to language, embodied with metaphor and imagery." Has published poetry by James Haug, Cynthia Huntington, Cleopatra Mathis, Jack Myers, Betsy Sholl, and David Wojahn. *Crying Sky* is 78 pages, digest-sized, saddle-stapled, offset-printed, with glossy card cover with b&w photograph. Press run is 500 for contributors, subscribers, shelf sales, and libraries. Single copy: $9; subscription: $16 (one year). Make checks payable to *Crying Sky*.

How to Submit Submit 3-5 poems at a time. No previously published poems or simultaneous submissions. No disk submissions. "Submissions should be typewritten; include bio and SASE." Reads submissions year round. Time between acceptance and publication is 6 months to one year. Sometimes comments on rejected poems. Guidelines available for SASE. Responds in 4-6 weeks. Always sends prepublication galleys. Pays 2 contributor's copies. All rights revert to author upon publication.

Contest/Award Offerings Sponsors occasional poetry contests. Guidelines available for SASE.

☑ CURBSIDE REVIEW

P.O. Box 667189, Houston TX 77266-7189. (713)529-0198. E-mail: curbsidereview@yahoo.com. Website: www.curbsidereview.org. Established 2000. **Contact:** Carolyn Adams and R.T. Castleberry, co-editors/publishers.

Magazine Needs *Curbside Review* appears monthly. "Our motto on the masthead is from W.B. Yeats: 'Our words must seem to be inevitable.' " Wants mature, crafted poetry in all styles and forms, "though we prefer modern free verse and prose poetry. We like intensity, dark humor, and wit." Has published poetry by Simon Perchik, B.Z. Niditch, Carol Frith, Radames Ortiz, and Dennis Saleh. *Curbside Review* is 4 pages, magazine-sized, copier-printed, folded. Receives about 1,200 poems/year, accepts about 20%. Press run is 400; all distributed free to local poetry groups and events, local independent bookstores. Single copy: free with #10 SASE.

How to Submit Submit 2 copies of 5 poems at a time. Lines/poem: 50 maximum. No simultaneous submissions; no previously published poems. "We have a strict 'don't ask, don't tell' policy on previously published/simultaneous submissions." No fax, e-mail, or disk submissions. Short cover letter is preferred. Reads submissions year round. Submit seasonal poems 4 months in advance. Time between acceptance and publication varies. "We often take more than one poem from writers, so publication is ongoing. Rather than reject, we often ask for revisions on promising poems."

Guidelines available in magazine, for SASE, by e-mail, or on website. Responds in 3 months. Pays 2 contributor's copies. Acquires one-time rights.

Advice "We publish poetry only. Since a sample copy is free, please take advantage of that to read it for a sense of our style. You may also read representative sample poems on our website."

⊕ ◪ CURRENT ACCOUNTS; BANK STREET WRITERS; BANK STREET WRITERS COMPETITION

Regency House, Longworth Rd., Horwich, Bolton BL6 7BA England. Phone/fax: (01204)669858. E-mail: bswscribe@aol.com. Website: http://hometown.aol.co.uk/bswscribe/myhomepage/newsl etter.html. Established 1994. **Contact:** Rod Riesco, editor.

Magazine Needs *Current Accounts* is a biannual, publishing poetry, fiction, and nonfiction by members of Bank Street Writers, and other contributors. Open to all types of poetry. "No requirements, although some space is reserved for members." Has published poetry by Pat Winslow, M.R. Peacocke, and Gerald England. *Current Accounts* is 52 pages, A5, photocopied, saddle-stapled, with card cover with b&w or color photo or artwork. Receives about 300 poems/year, accepts about 5%. Press run is 80 (6 subscribers, 40 shelf sales); 8 distributed free to competition winners. Subscription: UK £4. Sample: UK £2. Make checks payable to Bank Street Writers (sterling checks only).

How to Submit Submit up to 6 poems at a time. Lines/poem: 100 maximum. Unpublished poems preferred; no simultaneous submissions. Accepts e-mail submissions (pasted into body of message). Cover letter is required, and SAE or IRC essential for postal submissions. Time between acceptance and publication is 6 months. Seldom comments on rejected poems. Guidelines available for SASE, by fax, by e-mail, or on website. Responds in 2 months. Pays one contributor's copy. Acquires first rights.

Contest/Award Offerings Sponsors the annual Bank Street Writers Poetry and Short Story Competition. Submit poems up to 40 lines, any subject or style. **Entry fee:** £3/poem. **Deadline:** January 31. Entry form available for SAE and IRC (or download from website).

Also Offers Bank Street Writers meets once/month and offers workshops, guest speakers, and other activities. Write for details.

Advice "We like originality of ideas, images, and use of language. No inspirational or religious verse unless it's also good in poetic terms."

◯ CURRICULUM VITAE; SIMPSON PUBLICATIONS; CV POETRY POSTCARD PROJECT

P.O. Box 1082, Franklin PA 16323. E-mail: simpub@hotmail.com. Established 1995. **Contact:** Amy Dittman, managing editor.

Magazine Needs *Curriculum Vitae* appears biannually in January and July and is "a zine where quality work is always welcome. We'd like to see more metrical work, especially more translations, and well-crafted narrative free verse is always welcome. We're also interested in expanding our list of innovative side projects, books, graphic novels, chapbooks like *The Iowa Monster*, and the CV Poetry Postcard Project. Query with full manuscripts or well-thought-out plans with clips. We do not want to see rambling Bukowski-esque free verse or poetry that overly relies on sentimentality." *Curriculum Vitae* is 40 pages, digest-sized, photocopied, saddle-stapled, with 2-color card stock cover. Receives about 500 poems/year, accepts about 75. Press run is 1,000 (300 subscribers, 7 libraries, 200 shelf sales). Subscription: $6 (4 issues). Sample: $4.

How to Submit Submit 3 poems at a time. "Submissions without a SASE cannot be acknowledged due to postage costs." Accepts previously published poems and simultaneous submissions. Cover letter "to give us an idea of who you are" is preferred. Time between acceptance and publication is 8 months. Poetry is circulated among 3 board members. Often comments on rejected poems. Publishes theme issues. Guidelines available for SASE or by e-mail. Responds within one month. Pays 2 contributor's copies plus one-year subscription.

Book/Chapbook Needs & How to Submit Simpson Publications also publishes about 5 chapbooks/ year. Interested poets should query with full mss and SASE.

Also Offers "We are currently looking for poets who would like to be part of our Poetry Postcard series." Interested writers should query to The *CV* Poetry Postcard Project at the above address for more information.

◙ CUTBANK

English Dept., University of Montana, Missoula MT 59812. (406)243-6156. E-mail: cutbank@selway .umt.edu. Website: www.umt.edu/cutbank. Established 1973. **Contact:** Poetry Editor.

Magazine Needs *CutBank* is a biannual literary magazine that publishes regional, national, and international poetry, fiction, interviews, and artwork. Has published poetry by Richard Hugo, Dara Wier, Sandra Alcosser, and Jane Hirshfield. Press run is 500 (250 subscribers, 30% libraries). Single copy: $6.95; subscription: $12/2 issues. Sample: $4.

How to Submit Submit 3-5 poems at a time, single-spaced with SASE. Simultaneous submissions discouraged but accepted with notification. "We accept submissions from August 15 through March 15 only. Deadlines: Fall issue, November 15; Spring issue, March 15." Guidelines available for SASE or by e-mail. Responds in up to 3 months. Pays 2 contributor's copies. All rights return to author upon publication.

◘ ◙ DALHOUSIE REVIEW

Dalhousie University, Halifax NS B3H 4R2 Canada. (902)494-2541. Fax: (902)494-3561. E-mail: dalhousie.review@dal.ca. Website: http://dalhousiereview.dal.ca. Established 1921. **Contact:** Dr. Robert Martin, editor.

Magazine Needs *Dalhousie Review* appears 3 times/year, is 144 pages, digest-sized. Accepts about 5% of poems received. Press run is 600 (450 subscribers). Single copy: $15; subscription: $22.50 Canadian, $28 US. Make checks payable to *Dalhousie Review*.

How to Submit No previously published poems. "Submissions should be typed on plain white paper, double-spaced throughout. Spelling preferences are those of *The Canadian Oxford Dictionary*: catalogue, colour, program, travelling, theatre, and so on. Beyond this, writers of fiction and poetry are encouraged to follow whatever canons of usage might govern the particular story or poem in question, and to be inventive with language, ideas, and form. Poems should, in general, not exceed 40 lines, but there will of course be valid exceptions to these rules. Initial submissions are by means of hard copy only." Accepts e-mail submissions from outside North America only. "Please enclose a SASE (or SAE and IRC) for response." Reads submissions year round. Seldom comments on rejected poems. Occasionally publishes theme issues. Upcoming themes and guidelines available for SAE and IRC. Pays 2 contributor's copies and 10 off-prints.

$◙ DANA LITERARY SOCIETY ONLINE JOURNAL

P.O. Box 3362, Dana Point CA 92629-8362. Website: www.danaliterary.org. Established 2000. **Contact:** Ronald D. Hardcastle, editor.

Magazine Needs *Dana Literary Society Online Journal* appears monthly. Contains poetry, fiction, nonfiction, and editorials. "All styles are welcome—rhyming/metrical, free verse, and classic—but they must be well-crafted and throught-provoking. We want no pornography. Neither do we want works that consist of pointless flows of words with no apparent significance." Has published poetry by A.B. Jacobs, C. David Hay, Raymond HV Gallucci, and Norma Pain. *Dana Literary Society Online Journal* is equivalent to approximately 75 printed pages. Receives about 900 poems/year, accepts about 10%.

How to Submit Submit up to 3 poems at a time. Lines/poem: 120 maximum. Accepts previously published poems and simultaneous submissions. Accepts submissions by postal mail only. Time between acceptance and publication is 3 months. Poems are selected by Society director and *Online Journal* editor. Often comments on rejected poems. Guidelines available on website. Responds in 2 weeks. Pays $25 for each poem accepted. Acquires right to display in *Online Journal* for one month.

Advice "View the poetry on our website. We favor works that are well-crafted and thought-provoking."

⬚ ▢ ◎ DANCING ON THE DEW (Specialized: paganism; pagan themes)

P.O. Box 295, Nitro WV 25143. (304)533-9608. E-mail: dancing@sacredfountain.org. Website: http://dancing.sacredfountain.org. Established 2004. **Contact:** Holly Cross and Lesley Williams, editors.

Magazine Needs *Dancing on the Dew*, appearing 4 times/year (at Yule, Ostara, Litha, and Mabon), is "a small poetry journal published by pagans, for pagans, with pagan-oriented art and poetry. Each person's spiritual path is unique, and *Dancing on the Dew* wishes to give people a forum to share their individual experiences with others." Considers "all forms of poetry as long as work is pagan themed. Pagan themes include, but are not limited to, the gods, nature, mother earth, the nature of divinity, the seasons, the Sabbats, ghosts, spirits, other dimensions, reincarnation, herbs, feminism, tarot, Kabbalah, esoteric studies, etc." Does not want "anything that bashes other paths, is Satanic or self-indulgent. We welcome poems that explore our darker side, but will not print gratuitous pornography or violence." Accepts poetry written by children, but "we will require a notarized release from a parent or guardian upon publication." *Dancing on the Dew* is "anywhere from 20-40" pages, digest-sized, photocopied, saddle-stapled, with card cover. Press run is 100 (50 subscribers); 25 distributed free to colleges, universities, and coffeehouses. Single copy: $3.50; subscription: $12. Accepts money orders only, payable to Holly Cross (no checks).

How to Submit Submit up to 10 poems at a time. Lines/poem: open. Accepts previously published poems and simultaneous submissions. Accepts e-mail submissions (pasted into body of message); no disk submissions. Cover letter is preferred. "Tell us about yourself and your path in your cover letter. We will be publishing a very short bio if we use your work." Reads submissions year round. Submit seasonal poems 3-4 months in advance. Time between acceptance and publication is 2-6 months. "Poems are discussed and decided on by the co-editors. There is no clearly defined process; we just discuss and make a decision." Always comments on rejected poems. Occasionally publishes theme issues. List of upcoming themes available for SASE, by e-mail, or on website. Guidelines available in magazine, for SASE, by e-mail, or on website. Responds in 2-4 weeks. Sometimes sends prepublication galleys. Pays one contributor's copy. Acquires one-time rights. Reviews books of poetry "written by pagans, or poetry that would appeal to a pagan audience."

Advice "We started this journal because there are no pagan poetry journals, and yet nearly every pagan we know is a poet or writer. *Dancing on the Dew* is named after a line written about the Maenads, known in Greek history and mythology for worshipping Dionysus and celebrating the divinity within themselves. Write from your heart about your path and your relationship to the world and with the Divine. Read as much poetry as you can get your hands on. Yes, your writing is personal, but you can only get a sense of where your work 'fits' into the literary world by knowing what is already out there."

⬚ ▢ ◎ DANDELION ARTS MAGAZINE; FERN PUBLICATIONS (Specialized: membership/subscription)

24 Frosty Hollow, East Hunsbury, Northants NN4 OSY England. Fax: 01604-701730. Established 1978. **Contact:** Mrs. Jacqueline Gonzalez-Marina, M.A, editor/publisher.

• Fern Publications subsidizes costs for their books, paying no royalties.

Magazine Needs *Dandelion Arts Magazine*, published biannually in May and December, is "a platform for new and established poets and prose writers to be read throughout the world." Wants poetry that is "modern but not wild." Does not want "bad language poetry, religious or political, nor offensive to any group of people in the world." Has published poetry by Andrew Duncan, Donald Ward, Andrew Pye, John Brander, and Gerald Denley. *Dandelion Arts* is about 25 pages, A4, with thermal binding and original cover design, includes ads. Receives about 200-300 poems/year, accepts about 40%. Press run is up to 1,000 (about 100 subscribers, 10% are universities and libraries); some distributed free to chosen organizations. Subscription: £14 UK, £20 Europe, £25

US, £25 ROW. Sample: half price of subscription. Make checks payable to J. Gonzalez-Marina.
How to Submit Poets must become member-subscribers of *Dandelion Arts Magazine* and poetry club in order to be published. Submit 4-6 poems at a time. Lines/poem: 35-40 maximum. Accepts simultaneous submissions; no previously published poems. Accepts fax submissions. Cover letter is required. "Poems must be typed out clearly and ready for publication, if possible, accompanied by a SAE or postal order to cover the cost of postage for the reply." Reads submissions any time of the year. Time between acceptance and publication is 2-6 months. "The poems are read by the editor when they arrive, and a decision is taken straight away." Sometimes offers "constructive" comments on rejected poems. Guidelines available for SASE (or SAE and IRC), by fax, or by e-mail. Responds within 3 weeks. Reviews books of poetry. Send materials for review consideration.
Also Offers *Dandelion Arts* includes information on poetry competitions and art events.
Book/Chapbook Needs & How to Submit Fern Publications is a subsidy press of artistic, poetic, and historical books and publishes 2 paperbacks/year. Books are usually 50-80 pages, A5 or A4, "thermal bound" or hand-finished. Query first with 6-10 poems. **Requires authors to subscribe to *Dandelion Arts Magazine.*** Responds to queries and mss in 3 weeks. "All books are published at a cost agreed on beforehand and paid in advance."
Advice "Consider you are submitting material for an international magazine, where subjects such as war or religious issues are not accepted."

$☑ JOHN DANIEL AND COMPANY, PUBLISHER; FITHIAN PRESS

Daniel & Daniel Publishers, Inc., P.O. Box 2790, McKinleyville CA 95519. (707)839-3495. Fax: (707)839-3242. E-mail: dandd@danielpublishing.com. Website: www.danielpublishing.com. Established 1980. Reestablished 1985.
Book/Chapbook Needs John Daniel, a general small press publisher, specializes in literature, both prose and poetry. "Book-length manuscripts of any form or subject matter will be considered, but we do not want to see pornographic, libelous, illegal, or sloppily written poetry." Has published *Yellow Swing* by Rosalind Brackenbury, *Spending the Light* by Tom Smith, and *Littoral Zone* by Barbara Branch Bates. Publishes about 6 flat-spined poetry paperbacks/year. Books average 80 pages. Press runs average between 500-1,000. No longer issues a print catalog, but all books are shown and described on website.
How to Submit Send 12 sample poems and bio. Accepts simultaneous submissions. No fax or e-mail submissions. Responds to queries in 2 weeks, to mss in 2 months. Always sends prepublication galleys. Pays 10% royalties of net receipts. Acquires English-language book rights. Returns rights upon termination of contract.
Also Offers Fithian Press books are subsidized, the author paying production costs and receiving royalties of 60% of net receipts. Books and rights are the property of the author, but publisher agrees to warehouse and distribute for one year if desired.
Advice "We receive over 5,000 unsolicited manuscripts and query letters a year. We publish only a few books a year, of which fewer than half are received unsolicited. Obviously the odds are not with you. For this reason we encourage you to send out multiple submissions, and we do not expect you to tie up your chances while waiting for our response. Also, poetry does not make money, alas. It is a labor of love for both publisher and writer. But if the love is there, the rewards are great."

N ◎ DARKLING PUBLICATIONS; DARKLING MAGAZINE (Specialized: poetry of a dark nature)

RR 3, Box 67, Colome SD 57528. (605)842-1402. E-mail: boxofnothing7@hotmail.com. Established 2005. **Contact:** James C. Van Oort, editor-in-chief; Daniel G. Smethen, publisher.
Magazine Needs *Darkling Magazine*, published annually in May, is "primarily interested in poetry. All submissions should be dark in nature. We do not publish pornography or excessive profanity. Horror poetry is acceptable but not a requisite. All poetry submissions should help expose the darker side of man. Poetry of any form, style, etc., which is either dark or depressing, will be

strongly considered." Does not want "poetry which is aimed at making one feel good or experience the warm fuzzies. Such submissions will be trash-canned and will merit no response." Subscription: $15 with s&h. Make checks payable to Darkling Publications.

How to Submit Submit up to 8 poems at a time. Lines/poem: any length ("epic poems must be of exceptional quality"). Accepts previously published poems and simultaneous submissions. No e-mail or disk submissions. Cover letter is required. Reads submissions year round. Time between acceptance and publication is 2 months. Poems are circulated to an editorial board. Sometimes comments on rejected poems. Sometimes publishes theme issues. Guidelines available in magazine. Responds in 3-6 months. Pays one contributor's copy. All rights revert to author upon publication.

Advice "Find your own voice and develop it. If your voice is a dark one and we like it, we will publish it. We are always looking for new poets who have a voice we feel needs to be heard. Do not be afraid to ask questions. Our editorial staff will be very happy to communicate with you."

☑ ◎ DEAD END: CITY LIMITS (Specialized: dark subjects; failure of religion, society, romance; horror; fallen/dark angels)

The Good Intentions Paving Co., 1875 Century Park East, Suite H-2554, Los Angeles CA 90067. E-mail: goodintentionspaving@hotmail.com. Website: www.goodintentionspaving.com. Established 2003. **Contact:** R.T. St. Claire, editor/publisher.

Magazine Needs "We are a website created primarily to promote our various creative projects such as *No Sleep* (TV show), *CandyAppleBlack* (film and comic book), and our web-based dark poetry page, *Dead End: City Limits*." All styles/forms of poetry welcome, "but it needs to speak to the darkness in our souls. No up-with-people; hey, let's build a teen center; Happy Scrappy Hero Pup; paint a smiley face on a sun-bleached skull; hearts-and-flowers crap. This world is rotten to its core, and we aren't getting any divine help from anyone any time soon, so let's wake up and call a spade a spade. Hope is nothing more than a mean trick used to keep us submissive. If you don't understand what that means, don't submit your work to us." *Dead End: City Limits* is published online only. Receives about 50 poems/year, accepts about 15.

How to Submit Submit 3 poems at a time. Lines/poem: 30 maximum. Accepts previously published poems and simultaneous submissions. Accepts e-mail submissions (pasted into body of message, no attachments); no disk submissions. Reads submissions "all the time." Time between acceptance and publication is "unknown. You mail or e-mail us 3 of your poems; if we like them, we will e-mail you back about featuring your work on the poetry page of our site. If we do not plan on using your work, we will probably not respond to you." Never comments on rejected poems. Guidelines available on website. Response time is "unknown. If we like what you send, you'll hear from us." No payment. Acquires one-time rights.

Advice "Pretty simple. We are The Good Intentions Paving Co. We maintain a poetry page dedicated to dark poets on our website. Go to the site. You'll understand very quickly if we are for you and vice versa. If what you see fits what you write, submit some of your work to us."

☑ DEL SOL PRESS

E-mail: dsp-poetry@webdelsol.com. Website: http://webdelsol.com/DelSolPress. Established 1996. **Contact:** Joan Houlihan, poetry editor. Member: CLMP.

Book Needs & How to Submit Del Sol Press publishes poetry, fiction, and nonfiction. Publishes 2-3 poetry books and one anthology/year. Manuscripts are selected through open submission. Books are 60-100 pages, print-on-demand, perfect-bound, with cloth covers. Curently not accepting unsolicited submissions; however, queries are welcome. Send a few sample poems and a cover letter with brief bio and publication credits. Responds to queries in 2 weeks; to mss in up to 6 months. Order sample books from website.

▓ $◙ ◎ DESCANT (Specialized: themes and miscellanies)

Box 314, Station P, Toronto ON M5S 2S8 Canada. (416)593-2557. E-mail: descant@web.net. Website: www.descant.on.ca. Established 1970. **Contact:** Karen Mulhallen, editor-in-chief.

Magazine Needs *Descant* is "Canada's pre-eminent literary magazine. We publish an assortment of national and international material, which has previously included writers such as Margaret Atwood, P.K. Page, Douglas Glover, and Barbara Gowdy." *Descant* is 120-300 pages, over-sized digest format, elegantly printed and illustrated on heavy paper, flat-spined, with colored glossy cover. Receives 1,200 unsolicited submissions/year, accepts less than 100. Press run is 1,200. Sample: $8.50 plus postage.

How to Submit Submit typed ms of no more than 10 poems, name and address on first page, and last name on each subsequent page. Include e-mail address or SASE with Canadian stamps, or SAE and IRCs. No previously published poems or simultaneous submissions. No e-mail submissions. Guidelines and upcoming themes available for SASE (or SAE and IRC) or on website. Responds within 9-12 months. Pays "approximately $100." Acquires first rights.

Advice "The best advice is to know the magazine you are submitting to. Please read the magazine before submitting."

☑ DESCANT: FORT WORTH'S JOURNAL OF POETRY AND FICTION; THE BETSY COLQUITT AWARD FOR POETRY

English Dept., Box 297270, Texas Christian University, Fort Worth TX 76129. Fax: (817)257-6239. E-mail: descant@tcu.edu. Website: under construction. Established 1956. **Contact:** Dave Kuhne, editor.

Magazine Needs *descant* appears annually during the summer. Wants "well-crafted poems of interest. No restrictions as to subject matter or form. We usually accept poems 60 lines or fewer but sometimes longer poems." *descant* is 100+ pages, digest-sized, professionally printed and bound, with matte card cover. Receives about 3,000 poems/year. Press run is 500 (350 subscribers). Single copy: $12, $18 outside US. Sample: $10.

How to Submit No simultaneous submissions. No fax or e-mail submissions. Reads submissions September through April only. Responds in 6 weeks. Pays 2 contributor's copies.

Contest/Award Offerings Sponsors the annual Betsy Colquitt Award for Poetry. Offers $500 to the best poem or series of poems by a single author in a volume. *descant* also offers a $250 award for an outstanding poem in an issue. Complete contest rules and guidelines available for SASE or by e-mail.

☐ ◎ DESERT VOICES (Specialized: regional/Desert Southwest)

Palo Verde College, One College Dr., Blythe CA 92225. (760)921-5500 or -5449 (Minyard). Fax: (760)922-0230. E-mail: aminyard@paloverde.edu. **Contact:** Applewhite Minyard and Joe Jondrea, co-editors.

Magazine Needs *Desert Voices* is a biannual literary magazine of poetry, art, and short stories especially for the Desert Southwest. Wants poems generally one page or less; especially interested in the Desert Southwest. Does not want "pornography or excessive sexual imagery (erotica OK; profanity in context)." *Desert Voices* is 60 pages, digest-sized, offset-printed, stapled. Receives about 100 poems/year, accepts about 20. Press run is 1,000 (subscribers, 10 libraries); a number are distributed free to students. Single copy: $3. Make checks payable to Palo Verde College.

How to Submit Submit maximum of 3 poems at a time. Accepts simultaneous submissions; no previously published poems. Accepts e-mail (attachment in MS Word or plain text) and disk (MS Word) submissions; no fax submissions. Cover letter is preferred. Include SASE for return or reply. Reads submissions September through June. Time between acceptance and publication is 2-3 months. "Three readers plus editors read and rate submissions. We publish once per semester, and student submissions are considered first." Seldom comments on rejected poems. Occasionally publishes theme issues. Guidelines available for SASE or by e-mail. Responds in 2 months. Pays 2 contributor's copies. Acquires one-time rights.

Advice "Poetry should be real; that is, it should resonate with deeply felt issues that reveal something about the poet. Clichéd pieces and overly romantic or sentimental poems with generalized feelings, or attempting to be 'poetic,' most often are rejected out of hand."

✦ ☻ DEVIL BLOSSOMS

P.O. Box 5122, Seabrook NJ 08302-3511. E-mail: theeditor@asteriuspress.com. Website: www.aste riuspress.com. Established 1997. **Contact:** John C. Erianne, editor.

Magazine Needs *Devil Blossoms* appears irregularly, 1-2 times/year, "to publish poetry in which the words show the scars of real life. Sensual poetry that's occasionally ugly. I'd rather read a poem that makes me sick than a poem without meaning." Wants poetry that is "darkly comical, ironic, visceral, horrific; or any tidbit of human experience that moves me." Does not want religious greetings, 'I'm-so-happy-to-be-alive' tree poetry. Has published poetry by Marie Kazalia, Stephanie Savage, Mitchell Metz, Normal, John Sweet, and Alison Daniel. *Devil Blossoms* is 32 pages, 7×10, saddle-stapled, with matte card cover with ink drawings. Receives about 10,000 poems/year, accepts about 1%. Press run is 750 (200 shelf sales). Single copy: $5; subscription: $14. Make checks payable to John C. Erianne.

How to Submit Submit 2-5 poems at a time. Considers simultaneous submissions "if so informed." Accepts e-mail submissions (pasted into body of message; no attachments). Cover letter is preferred. Time between acceptance and publication is up to one year. "I promptly read submissions, divide them into a 'no' and a 'maybe' pile. Then I read the 'maybes' again." Seldom comments on rejected poems. Guidelines available on website. Responds in up to 2 months. Pays one contributor's copy. Acquires first rights.

Advice "Write from love; don't expect love in return, don't take rejection personally, and don't let anyone stop you."

☻ ◎ DIAL BOOKS FOR YOUNG READERS (Specialized: children/teens)

345 Hudson St., New York NY 10014. Website: www.penguin.com. **Contact:** Submissions.

Book/Chapbook Needs & How to Submit Publishes some illustrated books of poetry for children. Has published poetry by J. Patrick Lewis and Nikki Grimes. Do not submit unsolicited mss. Query first with sample poems and cover letter with brief bio and publication credits. SASE required with all correspondence. Accepts simultaneous submissions; no previously published poems. Responds to queries in up to 4 months. Payment varies.

☻ ◎ JAMES DICKEY NEWSLETTER (Specialized: James Dickey memories/tributes); JAMES DICKEY SOCIETY

Dept. of English, University of South Carolina, 1620 College St., Columbia SC 29208. (803)777-2174. Fax: (803)777-9064. E-mail: greerb@gwm.sc.edu. Website: www.jamesdickey.org. *Newsletter* established 1984; Society established 1990. **Contact:** Ben Greer, poetry editor. Editor: William B. Thesing.

Magazine Needs *James Dickey Newsletter* is a biannual newsletter, published in the spring and fall by the James Dickey Society, "devoted to critical articles/studies of James Dickey's works/biography and bibliography." Publishes "a few poems of high quality. No poems lacking form, meter, or grammatical correctness." Has published poetry by Henry Taylor, Fred Chappell, George Garrett, and Dave Smith. *James Dickey Newsletter* is 50 pages, 8½ × 5½, neatly offset (back and front), saddle-stiched, with card back-cover. Single copy: $8; subscription: $12/year for individuals (includes membership in the James Dickey Society), $14 for US institutions, $15.50 for foreign institutions.

How to Submit "Contributors should follow MLA style and standard manuscript format, sending one copy, double-spaced." Accepts e-mail (pasted into body of message/as attachment) and fax submissions. "However, if poet wants written comments/suggestions line by line, send manuscript by postal mail with SASE." Cover letter is required. Guidelines available in magazine or on website. Pays 2 contributor's copies. Acquires first rights. Reviews "only works on Dickey or that include Dickey."

Advice "Consult issues [of newsletter] and guidelines [before submitting]."

◗ DINER; POETRY OASIS INC.; DINER ANNUAL POETRY CONTEST

P.O. Box 60676, Greendale Station, Worcester MA 01606-2378. (508)853-4143. E-mail: eve@spoken word.to. Website: www.spokenword.to/diner. Established 2000. **Contact:** Eve Rifkah and Michael Milligan, editors.

Magazine Needs *Diner* appears biannually in May and November, publishing 2 feature poets in each issue. "Our taste is eclectic, ranging from traditional forms through all possibilities of style. We want to see poems that take risks, play/push language with an ear to sound." Accepts translations. Has published poetry by Gray Jacobik, Rosmarie Waldrop, Judith Hemschemeyer, and Sandra Kohler. *Diner* is 104 pages, digest-sized, perfect-bound, with glossy card cover with photo. Press run is 1,000. Single copy: $10; subscription: $18. Sample: $8. Make checks payable to Poetry Oasis.

How to Submit Submit no more than 5 poems. Accepts simultaneous submissions; no previously published poems. Accepts e-mail submissions (as attachments) from abroad only. Cover letter and SASE are required. Guidelines available by e-mail or on website. Responds in up to 6 months, "usually faster." Pays one contributor's copy. Reviews books.

Contest/Award Offerings The *Diner* Annual Poetry Contest. Send entries to "CONTEST" at the address above. 1st Prize: $500; 2nd Prize: $100; 3rd Prize: $50; plus 3 honorable mentions. All winning poems published in Fall/Winter edition of *Diner*. "Do not list your name on submitted poems. Send a cover letter with name, address, e-mail, and titles of poems." **Entry fee:** $10 for 3 poems or $22 to include a one-year subscription. **Deadline:** January 31. Past judges include X.J. Kennedy, Mary Ruefle, and Bob Hicok.

◗ DMQ REVIEW

E-mail: editors@dmqreview.com. Website: www.dmqreview.com. **Contact:** Sally Ashton, editor-in-chief.

Magazine Needs *DMQ Review* appears quarterly as "a quality online magazine of poetry presented with visual art. We are interested in finely crafted poetry that represents the diversity of contemporary poetry." Has published poetry by Amy Gerstler, Bob Hicok, Ilya Kaminsky, and Jane Hirshfield, as well as first-time publications. *DMQ Review* is published online; art/photography appears with the poetry. Receives about 3,000-5,000 poems/year, accepts about 1%.

How to Submit Submit 3 poems at a time ("no more than once per quarter"). Accepts simultaneous submissions (with notifications only); no previously published poems. Accepts e-mail submissions only. "Paste poems in the body of an e-mail only; no attachments will be read. Please read and follow complete submission guidelines on our website." Reads submissions year round. Time between acceptance and publication is 1-3 months. Poems are circulated to an editorial board. Never comments on rejected poems. Responds within 3 months. Acquires first rights.

Also Offers Nominates for the Pushcart Prize. "We also consider submissions of visual art, which we publish with the poems in the magazine with links to the artists' websites."

Advice "Read recent issues of *DMQ Review* before submitting, and send your best work."

◗ ◎ DOLPHIN-MOON PRESS; SIGNATURES (Specialized: regional)

P.O. Box 22262, Baltimore MD 21203. Established 1973. **Contact:** James Taylor, president.

Book/Chapbook Needs Dolphin-Moon is "a limited-edition (500-1,000 copies) press that emphasizes quality work (regardless of style), often published in unusual/'radical' format." The writer is usually allowed a strong voice in the look/feel of the final piece. "We've published magazines, anthologies, chapbooks, pamphlets, perfect-bound paperbacks, records, audio cassettes, and comic books. All styles are read and considered, but the work should show a strong spirit and voice. Although we like the feel of 'well-crafted' work, craft for its own sake won't meet our standards either." Has published work by Teller, Michael Weaver, John Strausbaugh, Josephine Jacobsen, and William Burroughs.

How to Submit Send sample of 6-10 pages of poetry and a brief cover letter. No fax or e-mail submissions. Responds to queries, or to submissions of whole work (if invited), in up to one month. Always sends prepublication galleys. Pays in author's copies (negotiable, though usually 10% of the run). Acquires first edition rights. Send SASE for catalog to purchase samples, or send $15 for their "sampler" (which they guarantee to be up to $25 worth of their publications).

Advice "Our future plans are to continue as we have since 1973, publishing the best work we can by local, up-and-coming, and nationally recognized writers—in a quality package."

DOUBLE ROOM: A JOURNAL OF PROSE POETRY AND FLASH FICTION

E-mail: double_room@hotmail.com. Website: www.webdelsol.com/Double_Room. Established 2002. **Contact:** Mark Tursi and Peter Conners, co-editors. Web Designer and Associate Editor: Cactus May. Publisher: Michael Neff, Web del Sol.

Magazine Needs & How to Submit *Double Room* is a biannual online literary journal devoted entirely to the publication and discussion of prose poetry and flash fiction. Each issue also features contemporary artwork, reviews, and special features. Has published poetry by Cole Swensen, Rosmarie Waldrop, Ray Gonzalez, Sean Thomas Dougherty, Holly Iglesias, and Christopher Kennedy. *Double Room* is published online only, with art/graphics solicited by the editors. Guidelines available on website. Acquires first North American serial rights. Reviews books and chapbooks of prose poetry and flash fiction. "See our website for review guidelines."

Advice "In addition to publishing the pp/ff forms, *Double Room* seeks to push them to the forefront of literary consideration by offering a Discussion On The Forms section in which contributors are asked to comment on a question related to the genre. For this reason we are looking for writers who, in addition to writing these forms, are interested in briefly discussing various aspects of them."

DOWN IN THE DIRT; SCARS PUBLICATIONS

829 Brian Court, Gurnee IL 60031. E-mail: alexrand@scars.tv. Website: http://scars.tv. Established 1993. **Contact:** Alexandria Rand, editor.

Magazine Needs & How to Submit *Down in the Dirt* appears "as often as work is submitted to us to guarantee a good-length issue." Does not want smut, rhyming poetry, or poetry already accepted for *Children, Churches and Daddies* (see separate listing in this section). Has published work by I.B. Rad, Jennifer Rowan, Cheryl A. Townsend, Tom Racine, David-Matthew Barnes, and Michael Estabrook. *Down in the Dirt* is published electronically, either on the Web or in e-book form (PDF file). Accepts previously published poems. Prefers e-mail submissions; accepts disk submissions formatted for Macintosh. Guidelines and sample issues available for SASE, by e-mail, or on website.

Also Offers Scars Publications sometimes sponsors a book contest. Write or e-mail (Editor@scars. tv) for information. "The website is a more comprehensive view of what *Down in the Dirt* does. All the information is there." Also able to publish chapbooks. Write for more information.

DREAM HORSE PRESS; DREAM HORSE PRESS NATIONAL POETRY CHAPBOOK PRIZE; THE ORPHIC PRIZE FOR POETRY

P.O. Box 4041, Felton CA 95018. E-mail: dreamhorsepress@yahoo.com. Website: www.dreamhors epress.com. Established 1999.

- **"The press currently reads submissions that are entered in its contests ONLY (see below). Please see website for details and instructions. Do not submit outside of contests; unsolicited submissions will be recycled unread."**

Contest/Award Offerings 1) **Dream Horse Press National Poetry Chapbook Prize** offers an annual award of a cash prize and multiple copies of a handsomely printed chapbook (amounts change yearly, check website for current information; 2003 prize was $300 and 20 copies). Submissions may be previously published in magazines/journals but not in books or chapbooks; may be entered in other contests with notification. "Submit 16-24 paginated pages of poetry in a readable font with acknowledgments, bio, SASE for results, and entry fee." Multiple submissions acceptable (with separate fee for each entry). Poet's name should not appear anywhere on ms. All mss will be recycled. **Entry fee:** changes annually; check website (2003 fee was $13). Fees accepted by check or money order. **Deadline:** check website. All entries will be considered for publication. Recent winners include Amy Holman for *Wait For Me, I'm Gone*, Rob Carney for *New Fables, Old Songs*, and Jason Gray for *Adam & Eve Go to the Zoo*. 2) **The Orphic Prize for Poetry** offers an annual award of $500 and publication of a book-length ms. Submissions may be entered in other contests, "but if your manuscript is accepted for publication elsewhere you must notify Dream Horse Press immediately." Entry fees are non-refundable. Submit 48-80 paginated pages of poetry, table of contents, acknowledgments, bio, and SASE for results (mss will be recycled after judging). Poet's name should not appear anywhere on the ms. Include name and biographical information in separate cover letter, and include e-mail address when available. All entries will be considered for publication. Both free and formal verse styles are welcome. Guidelines available on website. **Entry fee:** $20/ms entered. **Deadline:** was May 1 for 2005; check website for deadlines and details for subsequent years. "Judging will be anonymous." 2004 winner was Penelope Scambly Schott for *Baiting the Void*.

⊘ DREXEL ONLINE JOURNAL

Pennoni Honors College, Drexel University, 3210 Cherry St., Philadelphia PA 19104. (215)895-6469. Fax: (215)895-6288. E-mail: doj@drexel.edu. Website: www.drexel.edu/doj. Established 2001. **Contact:** Valerie Fox and Lynn Levin, poetry editors.

Magazine Needs *Drexel Online Journal* is "a general interest magazine." No limitations as to form. Translations welcome. Has published poetry by Barbara Crooker, Elton Glaser, Marilyn Chin, Lewis Warsh, Lydia Cortes, and Michael McGoolaghan. *Drexel Online Journal* is published online only. Accepts about 5% of poems received. Sample available free on website.

How to Submit Submit up to 5 poems at a time. No previously published poems. "Submit by postal mail with SASE or via e-mail with 'Poetry Submission' in subject field." Time between acceptance and publication is 3 months. "We currently have 3 readers who go by consensus." Occasionally comments on rejected poems. Guidelines available on website. Responds in 2-3 months. Pay varies. Acquires first rights.

Advice "Our tastes are diverse. The *DOJ* is currently not accepting poetry submissions. Please visit the website to read the journal and to find out when we will again be taking poetry submissions."

$⬚ ◎ DSAME; TRACE OF THE HAND: THE ALL-5-SENSES ZINE EXPERIENCE; BNB (Specialized: membership; social issues; women's issues)

Website: www.1dsame.com or www.geocitics.com/loveandunity2020.

Magazine Needs "Two things will cause your submission to be immediately discarded faster than anything else: Numerous misspelled words (except in handwritten diary format poems) and any submission from nonmembers. It is important to realize that in our desire to give voice to the social issues in ignored areas of the world, we are currently open to easy submissions which are basically 'a diary style format of poetry writing.' We are also very interested in other experimental forms of poetry. Examples are poetry written in a comic strip, through surreal paintings, poetry photojournals, etc.; the possibilities are limitless." Wants "all topics and tones of poetry from members, no matter how juvenile or serious, including, but not limited to, non-violent activism and civil disobedience poetry. Also, authors who are fluent in Spanish have the option of submitting a Spanish version of their English material, provided that the English material accompanies it. No translations of author's work. Nothing that promotes, rationalizes, and/or justifies violence (including violent activism), ageism, ableism (which includes the physically and mentally disabled/challenged), classism, racism, sexism, or any form of discrimination against any person's sexual orientation, religion, or lack of religion." *Trace of the Hand: The All-5-Senses Zine Experience* is magazine-sized, "typically photocopied but sometimes offset-printed, using 100% post-consumer recycled paper. The content and texture of the cover greatly varies." Press run greatly varies; 10-100 are distributed free to large zine libraries and zine review publications worldwide. See website for purchase and subscription options and payment methods.

How to Submit Free membership required. No previously published poems or simultaneous submissions; "we accept only new material." No e-mail or disk submissions. Reads submissions year round "from members only." Time between acceptance and publication varies. Never comments on rejected poems. Guidelines available on website (link #9). "It is our desire that our infobook guidelines will be available to female authors of all social classes in the U.S.A. and Canada, even those who don't use computers. Thus, a public librarian can easily go to either of our websites, click on link #7 (for a short infobook) or link #7a (for a long infobook) and print it out for anyone." Response time varies. See website for complete details about payment and Free-Op Circulation for BNB members. "Poet retains ownership of all poems submitted." Reviews chapbooks of poetry and other zines/journals. "Prints 3-D Zine Reviews and 3-D Zine and Chapbook Profiles of non-members only after poets have been specifically invited to do so by the editor. We do not print 3-D Zine reviews of current or former members."

Book/Chapbook Needs & How to Submit Manuscripts are selected through open submission "from members only. Furthermore, each BNB member, throughout the U.S.A. and Canada, will decide individually if they want to circulate another BNB author's publication once accepted." Zines and chapbooks are typically a maximum of 56 pages, "photocopied but sometimes offset-printed. Members individually make that choice." Manuscripts may not include previously published poems. "Please keep in mind that most of the chapbooks we accept are printed 90% 'as is,' all topics and tones including, but not limited to, social issues and non-violent activism that society would rather ignore. We must boldly state that strikingly beautiful layout and astonishingly elegant page design are far more important than content because we want to print poetry that will be treasured, given as gifts, and circulated rather than discarded. Some of the most important issues in the world have been ignored due to poor presentation." **Must be a member.** "Currently, membership is open only to women ages 18 and over in 42 U.S. states, all U.S. territories, and all of Canada." Response time varies. Pays $25 and one author's copy. "If any of your material is selected for a future anthology, your permission will be sought and further payment will be made." Order sample books by sending $10 US, $19 Canada, $30 ROW, "which includes secure, delivery-confirmation shipping where available. (Please print out current subscription prices and order forms found in the infobooks on our website.)"

Also Offers "Link #9 on our website is a printable webpage that gives further detailed information about the benefits of BNB membership."

Advice "We believe poetry should be fresh, alive, and perhaps even spontaneously written from your sincere feelings, rather than limited to the rehearsed and reconstructed confines of rhythm, meter, and the traditional styles of ancient celebrities who established so-called 'rules' of writing poetry. The poetry may express pain, happiness, and/or humor, but it is most important that the emotions are sincere. In this way poetry can act as a vehicle giving voice to the unheard."

⚒ ☑ EAGLE'S FLIGHT; EAGLE'S FLIGHT BOOKS

1505 N. Fifth St., Sayre OK 73662. (580)928-2298. Established 1989. **Contact:** Shyamkant Kulkarni, editor/publisher.

Magazine Needs *Eagle's Flight* is a quarterly "platform for poets and short story writers—new and struggling to come forward." Wants "well-crafted literary-quality poetry, any subject, any form, including translations. Translations should have permission of original poets." No obscene or pornographic material. Accepts poetry written by children over age 10. Has published poetry by Maria Keplinger, Cynthia Ruth Flynn, Jane Stuart, Rekha Kulkarni, and Daniel Green. *Eagle's Flight* is 8-12 pages, 7×8½, printed on colored paper, saddle-stapled, includes ads. Receives about 200 poems/year, accepts about 10%. Press run is 200 (100 subscribers). Subscription: $6. Sample: $1.50.

How to Submit Submit up to 5 poems at a time, with SASE. Lines/poem: 40 maximum. No previously published poems or simultaneous submissions. Cover letter is required; include short bio, up to 4 lines. Reads submissions January 1 through June 30 only. Time between acceptance and publication is up to 2 years. Seldom comments on rejected poems. "All material accepted for publication is subject to editing according to our editorial needs." Guidelines available for SASE. Responds in 6 months. Pays one contributor's copy. Acquires first publication rights. Reviews books of poetry in 250-750 words, single-book format. Send materials for review consideration.

Advice "We expect poets to be familiar with our publication and our expectations and limitations. To be a subscriber is one way of doing this. Everybody wants to write poems and, in his heart, is a poet. Success lies in getting ahead of commonplace poetry. To do this, one has to read, be honest and unashamed, and cherish decent values of life in his heart. Then success is just on the corner of the next block."

✪ ✪ ◑ THE ECLECTIC MUSE; MULTICULTURAL BOOKS

Suite 307, 6311 Gilbert Rd., Richmond BC V7C 3V7 Canada. (604)277-3864. E-mail: jrmbooks@hot mail.com. Website: www.thehypertexts.com. Established 1985. **Contact:** Mr. Joe M. Ruggier, publisher.

Magazine Needs *The Eclectic Muse*, published annually at Christmas, is a poetry journal "devoted to publishing all kinds of poetry (eclectic in style and taste) but specializing in rhyme- and neo-classicist revival." Does not want "bad work (stylistically bad or thematically offensive)." Has published poetry by Mary Keelan Meisel, John Laycock, Philip Higson, Roy Harrison, Michael Burch, and Ralph O. Cunningham. *The Eclectic Muse* is 36 pages, magazine-sized, digitally copied, saddle-stapled, with paper cover. Receives about 300 poems/year, accepts about 15%. Press run is 200 (90 subscribers, 5 libraries); distributed free to all contributing authors plus selected gift subscription recipients. Single copy: $8; subscription: $25. Make checks payable to Joe M. Ruggier.

How to Submit Submit 5 poems at a time. Lines/poem: 60 maximum; "please consult if longer." Accepts previously published poems and simultaneous submissions. Accepts e-mail submissions (as attachment, preferably in Microsoft Word 2000, or else in .rtf) and disk submissions. Cover letter is preferred. "Include brief bio not exceeding 100 words and SASE." Reads submissions year round. Time between acceptance and publication is one year. Poems are circulated to an editorial board. Sometimes comments on rejected poems. **If authors wish to have a manuscript carefully assessed and edited, the fee is $250 U.S.; will respond within 8 weeks."** Guidelines available in magazine or on website. Responds in 2 months. Pays 2 contributor's copies. Reviews books and chapbooks of poetry and other magazines/journals in 900 words. Send materials for review consideration to Joe M. Ruggier, managing editor.

Book/Chapbook Needs & How to Submit Multicultural Books publishes poetry and related literature as well as fiction and various forms of nonfiction. Publishes 1-6 books/year "depending on availability and quality." Manuscripts are selected through open submission. Books are 120+ pages, digitally photocopied, perfect-bound, with heavy color cardstock cover. Query first, with a few sample poems and a cover letter with brief bio and publication credits. Book mss may include previously published poems. "The only criteria is quality of work and excellence." Responds to queries in 2 months; to mss in 2 months. **Offers author-subsidy as well as publisher-subsidy options;** the selection process for the latter is extremely competitive and quality-conscious. "Authors who feel their work may be up to standard are welcome to query us with a sample or else submit an entire manuscript. All interested parties may consult our guidelines as well as our sample publication contract on www.thehypertexts.com." Order sample books/chapbooks by contacting Joe M. Ruggier.

Also Offers "Look us up on www.thehypertexts.com where myself and my services are listed (featured) permanently. The host of this splendid poetry website is my U.S. associate, Mr. Michael Burch. He features, on this site, most of the leading names in contemporary North America."

Advice "An author's style is really the only thing which belongs to him as an artist to manipulate for his own purposes as he pleases. Truths and feelings do not belong to him exclusively and may not be bent or manipulated for his own purposes as he pleases. We do not want bad work where the poet feels that the message matters but the style is bad (not good workmanship), nor do we wish to publish work which seems to us to distort and bend truths and human feelings far too much."

🔄 $ 💬 ◎ ÉCRITS DES FORGES (Specialized: foreign language/French)

1497 Laviolette, Trois-Rivières QC G9A 5G4 Canada. (819)379-9813. Fax: (819)376-0774. E-mail: ecrits.desforges@tr.cgocable.ca. Website: www.ecritsdesforges.com. Established 1971. **Contact:** Gaston Bellemare, président. Directrice Générale: Maryse Baribeau.

Book/Chapbook Needs & How to Submit Écrits des Forges publishes poetry only—45-50 paperback books of poetry/year—and wants poetry that is "authentic and original as a signature. We have published poetry from more than 1,000 poets coming from most of the francophone countries: André Romus (Belgium), Amadou Lamine Sall (Sénégal), Nicole Brossard, Bernard Pozier, Claude Beausoleil, Jean-Marc Desgent, and Jean-Paul Daoust (Québec)." Books are usually 80-88 pages, digest-sized, perfect-bound, with 2-color covers with art. Query first with a few sample poems and cover letter with brief bio and publication credits. Responds to queries in up to 6 months. Pays royalties of 10-20%, advance of 50% maximum, and 25 author's copies. Order sample books by writing or faxing.

Also Offers Sponsors the International Poetry Festival/Festival international de la poésie. "One hundred fifty poets from 30 countries based on the 5 continents read their poems over a 10-day period in 70 different cafés, bars, restaurants, etc.; 30,000 persons attend. All in French." For more information, see website: www.fiptr.com.

◎ EDGZ

Edge Publications, P.O. Box 799, Ocean Park WA 98640. Established 2000. **Contact:** Blaine R. Hammond, editor/publisher. Associate Editor: Debra Brimacombe.

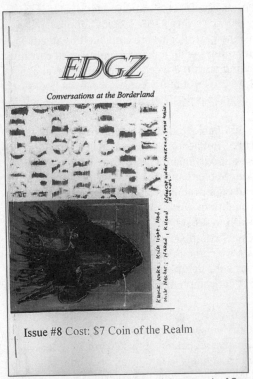

Issue #8 Cost: $7 Coin of the Realm

Editor Blaine R. Hammond featured the artwork of Guy R. Beining in his cover design for *Edgz* #8. "I look for works of art that have an immediate visual impact, but also make you look again. Then again."

Magazine Needs *Edgz* appears semiannually in (or around) March and September and publishes "poetry of all sorts of styles and schools. Our purpose is to present poetry with transpersonal intentions or applications, and to put poets on a page next to other poets they are not used to appearing next to." Wants "a broad variety of styles with a transpersonal intent. *Edgz* has 2 main reasons for existence: Our weariness with the attitude that whatever kind of poetry someone likes is the only legitimate poetry; and our desire to present poetry addressing large issues of life: meaning, oppression, exaltation, and whatever else you can think of. Must be engaged; intensity helps." Does not want "anything with a solely personal purpose; dense language poetry; poetry that does not take care with the basics of language, or displays an ignorance of modern poetry. No clichés, gushing, sentimentalism, or lists of emotions. Nothing vague or abstract. No light verse or doggerel, but humor is fine." Accepts poetry by children, "but not childish poetry; they compete with adult poets on an equal basis." Has published poetry by John Elsberg, Taylor Graham, R. Yurman, Patricia Ann Treat, B.Z. Niditch, and Ruth Moon Kempher. *Edgz* is digest-sized, laser-printed on recycled paper, saddle-stapled, with 80-lb. card stock cover with art/graphics. Single copy: $7; subscription: $13 (2 issues). Sample: $4. Make checks payable to Edge Publications.

How to Submit Submit 3-5 poems at a time; "a

longer poem may be submitted by itself." No limits on line length. Accepts simultaneous submissions; no previously published poems. Accepts submissions by postal mail only. "I don't mind more than one poem to a page or well-traveled submissions; these are ecologically sound practices. I like recycled paper. Submissions without SASE will be gratefully used as note paper. No postcards in place of SASE. Please do not fold poems separately. Handwritten poems OK if poet is poor or incarcerated." Reads submissions year round. **Deadlines:** February 1 and August 1. Time between acceptance and publication is 1-6 months. Comments on rejected poems "as I feel like it. I don't provide criticism services." Guidelines available for SASE. Responds in up to 6 months. Pays one contributor's copy/published poem, with discounts on additional copies. Acquires first rights plus anthology rights ("just in case").

Advice "It is one thing to require subscriptions in order to be published. It is something else to charge reading fees. In a world that considers poetry valueless, reading fees say it is less than valueless—that editors should be compensated for being exposed to it. I beg such editors to cease the practice. I advise everyone else not to submit to them, or the practice will spread. My most common rejection note is 'too personal for my thematic focus.'"

🌙 88: A JOURNAL OF CONTEMPORARY AMERICAN POETRY

% Hollyridge Press, P.O. Box 2872, Venice CA 90294. (310)712-1238. Fax: (310)828-4860. E-mail: T88AJournal@aol.com. Website: www.hollyridgepress.com. Established 1999. **Contact:** Ian Wilson, managing editor. Member: PMA, CLMP.

● Poetry published here was included in the 2003 volume of *The Best American Poetry*.

Magazine Needs *88: A Journal of Contemporary American Poetry* appears annually, publishing poetry, essays on poetry and poetics, as well as reviews. Wants mainstream, experimental, lyric, lyric narrative, and prose poems. "Will consider work that incorporates elements of humor, elements of surrealism. No light verse, limericks, children's poetry." Has published poetry by Tony Hoagland, Thomas Lux, Rosmarie Waldrup, and Matthea Harvey. *88* is 176 pages, digest-sized, printed on-demand, perfect-bound, with 4-color soft cover. Single copy: $13.95.

How to Submit Submit 5 poems at a time. No previously published poems or simultaneous submissions. No fax, e-mail, or disk submissions. Cover letter is required. Poems should be typed, single-spaced on one side of paper; indicate stanza breaks if poem is longer than one page. Name and address should appear on every page. "Unsolicited submissions accompanied by a proof-of-purchase coupon clipped from the back of the journal are read year round. Without proof-of-purchase, unsolicited submissions are considered March 1 through May 31 only. Unsolicited submissions received outside these guidelines will be returned unread. Submissions sent without SASE will be discarded." Time between acceptance and publication is up to one year. "Managing editor has the final decision of inclusion, but every poem is considered by an editorial board consisting of contributing editors whose suggestions weigh heavily in the process." Guidelines available in magazine, for SASE, or on website. Responds in up to 6 months. Sometimes sends prepublication galleys. Pays one contributor's copy. Acquires one-time rights. Reviews books of poetry in 500-1,000 words, single- and multi-book format. Send materials for review consideration to Ian Wilson, managing editor. Also accepts essays on poetics and contemporary American poetry and poets, 5,000 words maximum.

Advice "We believe it's important for poets to support the journals to which they submit. Because of print-on-demand, *88* is always available. We recommend becoming familiar with the journal before submitting."

📄 ⊚ EKPHRASIS (Specialized: ekphrastic verse); THE EKPHRASIS PRIZE; FRITH PRESS

P.O. Box 161236, Sacramento CA 95816-1236. E-mail: frithpress@aol.com. Website: www.hometown.aol.com/ekphrasis1. *Ekphrasis* established 1997; Frith Press established 1995. **Contact:** Laverne Frith and Carol Frith, editors.

● Until further notice, Frith Press will publish occasional chapbooks by invitation only. Poems from *Ekphrasis* have been featured on *Poetry Daily*.

Magazine Needs *Ekphrasis*, appearing in March and September, is a biannual "outlet for the growing body of poetry focusing on individual works from any artistic genre.'' Wants ''poetry whose main content is based on individual works from any artistic genre. Poetry should transcend mere description. Open to all forms. No poetry without ekphrastic focus. No poorly crafted work. No archaic language.'' Has published poetry by Jeffrey Levine, Peter Meinke, David Hamilton, Barbara Lefcowitz, Molly McQuade, and Annie Boutelle. *Ekphrasis* is 40-50 pages, digest-sized, photocopied, saddle-stapled. Subscription: $12/year. Sample: $6. Make checks payable, in US funds, to Laverne Frith.

How to Submit Submit 3-7 poems at a time, with SASE. Accepts previously published poems ''infrequently, must be credited''; no simultaneous submissions. Accepts submissions by postal mail only. Cover letter is required, including short bio with representative credits and phone number. Time between acceptance and publication is up to one year. Seldom comments on rejected poems. Guidelines available for SASE or on website. Responds in 4 months. Pays one contributor's copy. Nominates for Pushcart Prize. Acquires first North American serial or one-time rights.

Contest/Award Offerings The Ekphrasis Prize, $300 and publication for a single poem, is sponsored and judged by the editors of *Ekphrasis*. Guidelines available for SASE or on website. 2004 winner: Gayle Elen Harvey for *Woman, Bird, Stars*.

Advice ''With the focus on ekphrastic verse, we are bringing attention to the interconnections between various artistic genres and dramatizing the importance and universality of language. Study in the humanities is essential background preparation for the understanding of these interrelations.''

Ⓝ ⊘ THE ELEVENTH MUSE; POETRY WEST; POETRY WEST POEM CONTEST; POETRY WEST CHAPBOOK CONTEST

P.O. Box 2413, Colorado Springs CO 80901. E-mail: steveschroeder@gmail.com. Website: www.poetrywest.org/muse.htm. Established 1982. **Contact:** Steven D. Schroeder, editor.

Magazine Needs *The Eleventh Muse* appears annually in March. ''We are open to any type of quality poetry: metrical or free verse, narrative or lyric. We are likely more open to metrical poetry than the average contemporary journal.'' Does not want ''overly 'experimental' or elliptical poems, clumsy greeting card rhymes, or tired subject matter.'' Has published poetry by Ted Kooser, Mary Crow, Timothy Murphy, Philip Dacey, David Keplinger, and Jake Adam York. *The Eleventh Muse* is 50-75 pages, digest-sized, perfect-bound. Receives about 1,000 poems/year, accepts about 5%. Press run is 250. Single copy: $8; subscription: $8 for one year, $5 for each additional year. Sample: $5. Make checks payable to Poetry West.

How to Submit: Submit 3-5 unpublished poems at a time. Lines/poem: 100 maximum. Accepts simultaneous submissions. ''We separately consider previously published poems, but we must receive a copy of the book or journal in which they appeared. Contact us or see website for details.'' No e-mail or disk submissions. Cover letter is preferred. ''Please include e-mail address for reply, if possible, or SASE otherwise.'' Reads submissions ''year round, but the deadline for each issue is December 1.'' Time between acceptance and publication is 1-10 months. Poems are circulated to an editorial board. Sometimes comments on rejected poems. Guidelines available in magazine or on website. Responds in 1-2 months. Pays one contributor's copy. Reviews books and chapbooks of poetry and other magazines/journals. Send materials for review consideration.

Book/Chapbook Needs & How to Submit Poetry West publishes one chapbook/year. Manuscripts are selected through competition (see Contest/Award Offerings below). Chapbooks are 30 pages. Chapbook mss may include previously published poems. Order sample chapbooks by sending $5 to Poetry West.

Contest/Award Offerings Poetry West sponsors 2 annual contests. 1) The **Poetry West Poem Contest** offers 1st Prize: $100; 2nd Prize: $50; 3rd Prize: $25. Submit 1-6 previously unpublished poems, 100 lines or less. **Entry fee:** $5 for the first poem, $2 for each additional poem. **Deadline:** December 1. Guidelines available in magazine or on website. All winning and Honorable Mention poems will be published in *The Eleventh Muse*. 2) The **Poetry West Chapbook Contest** awards $300, publication, and 25 copies for the best ms of 20-28 pages. Submissions must be unpublished as a collection, but individual poems may have been previously published in journals or anthologies. All entries will be considered for publication in *The Eleventh Muse*. **Entry fee:** $15, payable to Poetry West; multiple submissions permitted when accompanied by separate entry fees. All contestants who include an 8½×11 SASE with $1.55 postage affixed (metered postage is not acceptable) will receive a copy of the winning book. **Deadline:** April 30 (postmark). Guidelines available on website.

$⊘ ELLIPSIS MAGAZINE

Westminster College of Salt Lake City, 1840 S. 1300 East, Salt Lake City UT 84105. (801)832-2321. E-mail: Ellipsis@westminstercollege.edu. Website: www.westminstercollege.edu/ellipsis. Established 1967. **Contact:** Poetry Editor (rotating editors). Faculty Advisor: Natasha Sajé.
Magazine Needs *Ellipsis* is an annual appearing in April. Needs "good literary poetry, fiction, essays, plays, and visual art." Has published work by Allison Joseph, Molly McQuade, Virgil Suárez, Maurice Kilwein-Guevara, Richard Cecil, and Ron Carlson. *Ellipsis* is 120 pages, digest-sized, perfect-bound, with color cover. Press run is 2,000; most distributed free through college. Sample: $7.50.
How to Submit Submit 3-5 poems at a time. No previously published poems. Accepts simultaneous submissions if notified of acceptance elsewhere. No fax or e-mail submissions. Include SASE and brief bio. Reads submissions August 1 to November 1. Responds in up to 5 months. Pays $10/poem, plus one contributor's copy.
Contest/Award Offerings "All accepted poems are eligible for the *Ellipsis* Award, which includes a $100 prize. Past judges include Jorie Graham, Sandra Cisneros, Phillip Levine, and Stanley Plumly."
Also Offers Westminster College hosts Writers@Work, an annual literary conference, which sponsors a fellowship competition and features distinguished faculty. (See separate listing for Writers@Work in the Conferences & Workshops section.)

⬚ ⊘ EMPLOI PLUS; DGR PUBLICATION

1256 Principale N. St. #203, L'Annonciation QC J0T 1T0 Canada. Phone/fax: (819)275-3293. Established 1988 (DGR Publication), 1990 (*Emploi Plus*). **Contact:** Daniel G. Reid, publisher.
Magazine Needs *Emploi Plus* is published irregularly. ("Next issue of *Emploi Plus* to be published in 2005 at latest.") Features poems and articles in French or English. Has published *Alexiville*, *Planet Earth* by D.G. Reid as well as poetry by Robert Ott. *Emploi Plus* is 12 pages, 7×8½, photocopied, stapled. Press run is 500; all distributed free. Sample: free.
How to Submit *Does not accept unsolicited submissions.*

⊘ EMRYS JOURNAL

P.O. Box 8813, Greenville SC 29604. E-mail: ldishman@charter.net. Website: www.emrys.org. Established 1982. **Contact:** Poetry Editor. Editor: L.B. Dishman.
Magazine Needs *Emrys Journal* is an annual appearing in April. Wants "literary or narrative poetry less than 36 lines. Rhyming needs to be oustanding to be considered." Has published poetry by Kristin Berkey-Abbott, Adriano Scopino, John Popielaski, J. Morris, and Terri McCord. *Emrys Journal* is up to 120 pages, digest-sized, handsomely printed, flat-spined. Press run is 400 (250 subscribers, 10 libraries). Sample: $12 with SASE (7×10) and 4 first-class stamps.
How to Submit Submit up to 5 poems (per author). Include SASE. No previously published poems. Accepts e-mail submissions (as attachment). Reads submissions August 1 through November 1 only. Time between acceptance and publication is up to 8 months. Guidelines available for SASE or on website. Responds "by the end of the reading period." Pays 5 contributor's copies.
Contest/Award Offerings Sponsors the annual Nancy Dew Taylor Award for excellence in the art of poetry. Offers $250 prize to the author of the best poem published in *Emrys Journal*.

⊘ ENGLISH JOURNAL

College of Education, Columbus State University, Columbus GA 31907-5645. (706)565-3682. Fax: (796)569-3134. E-mail: brewpoem@hotmail.com. Website: www.englishjournal.colostate.edu. **Contact:** James Brewbaker, poetry editor.

Magazine Needs "We encourage poets and readers of *English Journal* to submit their best work—on any subject and in any form or style—for our consideration. Submissions need not be on a topic related to teaching, learning, or the discipline of English itself." A professional education journal published 6 times/year, *EJ* accepts fewer than 10% of submissions.

How to Submit Submit 2 copies of up to 5 poems. Lines/poem: 40 maximum. No previously published poems or simultaneous submissions. No fax or e-mail submissions. Cover letter is required; include phone number, e-mail address, and brief biographical information. "Include your name, address, and e-mail address on each poem. Notification regarding receipt of your poems, acceptances, and rejections is by e-mail. Enclose a SASE for return of manuscripts only; otherwise we will recycle." Pays 2 contributor's copies.

⭐ ◪ ENTROPY MAGAZINE

E-mail: entropymag@gmail.com. Website: www.entropymag.net. Established 1999. **Contact:** Tyson Tate, editor/publisher.

Magazine Needs *Entropy Magazine*, an annual journal, publishes "new and unique literary voices that have a story to tell the world, whether the world wants to hear it or not. *Entropy Magazine* readers find beauty in both progressive and classic literature." Wants "all forms of poetry as long as the work is fresh, interesting, and original. Creative poetry that plays with English and makes the reader smile and think, 'How cool!' is our favorite kind." Does not want "erotica, romance, or angst-ridden depression poems." Has published poetry by Rory Dickenson, Jeremiah Gilbert, and Eugene Combs. *Entropy Magazine* is 40 pages, digest-sized. Single copy: $2.50. Make checks payable to Tyson Tate.

How to Submit Submit no more than 10 poems at a time. Lines/poem: 5-100. Accepts simultaneous submissions; no previously published poems. Accepts e-mail submissions (as attachment); no disk submissions. "Include first and last name, number of words, your personal web page address (if applicable), and a short (50 words) bio." Reads submissions year round. Sometimes comments on rejected poems. **"If requested, I can provide a critique for $1/page."** Guidelines available on website. Responds in 2 months. Pays 1-2 contributor's copies. Acquires first North American serial rights.

Advice "*Entropy Magazine* issues 4 and 5 have poems that can give you a general idea of what we're looking for; but most importantly, your poetry should be creative, original, and fun to read and discover its meaning. Poems with obscure meanings can be fun, too."

$◻ EOTU EZINE OF FICTION, ART & POETRY; CLAM CITY PUBLICATIONS

2102 Hartman, Boise ID 83704. (208)322-3408. E-mail: editor@clamcity.com (inquiries); submissions@clamcity.com (submissions). Website: www.clamcity.com/eotu.html. Established 2000 online; started as print zine in late 1980s. **Contact:** Larry Dennis.

Magazine Needs *EOTU Ezine* appears bimonthly online, specializing in fiction, art, and poetry. "All fiction, art, and poetry needs to be published to have meaning. We do what we can to make that happen. We are open to all genres, though we tend toward literary and speculative work, science fiction, fantasy, and horror, because that's where the editor's tastes lie. Since we are not funded by advertising or subscription sales, we aren't really audience-driven. Each issue is a reflection of what the editor is into at the time. We are more an artistic endeavor than a business." Has published poetry by Bruce Boston, Charles Saplak, Mike Allen, and Ann Schwader. "Present circulation is about 30,000 page views per issue."

How to Submit Lines/poem: 30 maximum. Accepts previously published poems; no simultaneous submissions. Accepts e-mail submissions; "Send in body of e-mail message with no formatting; put title of work, 'poem,' or 'poetry submission' in subject line. Include brief bio." Seldom comments on rejected poems. Occasionally publishes theme issues. "We have been known to do theme issues, but they aren't usually decided upon until 2-4 months before publication. Writers should check our guidelines page on the website for current themes." Responds in up to 3 months. Pays $5/

poem. Acquires one-time online rights; "When a poem is published in an issue, it will remain in the current issue for 2 months and then be archived."

Advice "As far as we have been able to tell through our years of zine publishing, there are only 2 tips a beginning writer must follow to succeed: 1) Read a few issues of any magazine you are thinking of sending work to; 2) Read and follow submission guidelines. If you do only these two things, you will go far."

☑ EPICENTER

P.O. Box 367, Riverside CA 92502. E-mail: poetry@epicentermagazine.org. Website: www.epicentermagazine.org. Established 1994. **Contact:** Rowena Silver.

Magazine Needs *Epicenter* is a biannual literary journal open to all styles. "*Epicenter* is looking for ground-breaking poetry, essays, and short stories from new and established writers. No angst-ridden, sentimental, or earthquake poetry. We are not adverse to graphic images if the work is well presented and contains literary merit." Has published poetry by Virgil Suárez, Alba Cruz-Hacher, B.Z. Niditch, Egon Lass, and Zdravka Evtimova. *Epicenter* is 58 pages, perfect-bound. Receives about 2,000 submissions/year, accepts about 5%. Press run is 800 (250 shelf sales). Single copy: $7. Sample: $7.75. Make checks payable to Rowena Silver.

How to Submit Submit up to 5 poems. Include SASE with sufficient postage for return of materials. Accepts previously published poems and simultaneous submissions. Accepts e-mail submissions (pasted into body of message/as attachment). Seldom comments on rejected poems. Guidelines available in magazine, for SASE, by e-mail, or on website. Pays one contributor's copy. Acquires one-time and electronic rights.

$☑ EPOCH

251 Goldwin Smith, Cornell University, Ithaca NY 14853. (607)255-3385. Website: www.arts.cornell.edu/english/epoch.html. Established 1947. **Contact:** Nancy Vieira Couto, poetry editor. Editor: Michael Koch.

Magazine Needs *Epoch* appears 3 times/year and has a distinguished and long record of publishing exceptionally fine poetry and fiction. Has published poetry by John Bensko, Jim Daniels, Allison Joseph, Maxine Kumin, Heather McHugh, and Kevin Prufer. *Epoch* is 128 pages, digest-sized, professionally printed, flat-spined, with glossy color cover. Accepts less than 1% of the many submissions received each year. Has 1,000 subscribers. Subscription: $11/year domestic, $15/year foreign. Sample: $5.

How to Submit No simultaneous submissions. Reads submissions between September 15 and April 15. Responds in up to 10 weeks. Occasionally provides criticism on mss. Pays 3 contributor's copies and $5-10/page. "We pay more when we have more!" Acquires first serial rights.

Advice "Read the magazine."

$☑ ◎ EVANGEL; LIGHT AND LIFE COMMUNICATIONS (Specialized: religious/Christian)

P.O. Box 535002, Indianapolis IN 46253-5002. Established 1897. **Contact:** J. Innes, editor.

Magazine Needs *Evangel* is a weekly adult Sunday school paper. "Devotional in nature, it lifts up Christ as the source of salvation and hope. The mission of *Evangel* is to increase the reader's understanding of the nature and character of God and the nature of a life lived for Christ. Material that fits this mission and isn't longer than one page will be considered." No rhyming work. *Evangel* is 8 pages, digest-sized (2 8½×11 sheets folded), printed in 4-color, unbound. Accepts about 5% of poetry received. Press run is about 15,000. Subscription: $2.25/quarter (13 weeks). Sample: free for #10 SASE.

How to Submit Submit no more than 5 poems at a time. Accepts simultaneous submissions. Cover letter is preferred. "Poetry must be typed on 8½×11 white paper. In the upper left-hand corner of each page, include your name, address, phone number, and social security number. In the upper right-hand corner of cover page, specify what rights you are offering. One-eighth of the way down the page, give the title. All subsequent material must be double-spaced, with one-inch margins."

Submit seasonal poems one year in advance. Seldom comments on rejected poems. Guidelines available for #10 SASE; "Write 'guidelines request' on your envelope so we can sort it from the submissions." Responds in up to 2 months. Pays $10 plus 2 contributor's copies. Acquires one-time rights.

Advice "Poetry is used primarily as filler. Send for sample and guidelines to better understand what and who the audience is."

⬤ THE EVANSVILLE REVIEW; THE WILLIS BARNSTONE TRANSLATION PRIZE

1800 Lincoln Ave., Evansville IN 47722. Phone/fax: (812)488-1042. Website: http://english.evansville.edu/EvansvilleReview.htm. Established 1989. **Contact:** Lauren Vantuyle, editor.

 • Poetry published in *The Evansville Review* has been included in *Best American Poetry* and the *Pushcart Prize* anthology.

Magazine Needs *The Evansville Review* appears annually in April and publishes "prose, poems, and drama of literary merit." Wants "anything of quality." No excessively experimental work, or erotica. Has published poetry by Joseph Brodsky, J.L. Borges, John Updike, Willis Barnstone, Rita Dove, and Vivian Shipley. *The Evansville Review* is 140-200 pages, digest-sized, perfect-bound, includes art on cover only. Receives about 1,000 poems/year, accepts about 2%. Publishes 45 poems/issue. Press run is 1,500. Sample: $5.

How to Submit Submit 3-5 poems at a time. Considers previously published poems and simultaneous submissions. Accepts submissions by postal mail only. Cover letter with brief bio is required. Include SASE. Reads submissions September 1 through December 10 only. Time between acceptance and publication is 3 months. Poems are circulated to an editorial board. Seldom comments on rejected poems. Guidelines available for SASE or on website. Responds within 3 months of the deadline. Pays 2 contributor's copies. Rights remain with poet.

Contest/Award Offerings The Willis Barnstone Translation Prize offers annual award of $1,000 and publication in *The Evansville Review*. Submissions must be unpublished and may be entered in other contests. Submit 1-10 poems; line limit is 200 lines. Guidelines available for SASE or on website. **Entry fee:** $5 for the first poem; $3 for each subsequent poem. Does not accept entry fees in foreign currencies. **Deadline:** December 1. Competition receives 400 entries/year. 2004 winner was Robert Mezey. Final judge for the 2005 contest is Willis Barnstone. Winner will be announced in April in *The Evansville Review* and through entrants' SASEs.

◎ EXIT 13 (Specialized: geography/travel)

P.O. Box 423, Fanwood NJ 07023-1162. (908)889-5298. E-mail: exit13magazine@yahoo.com. Established 1987. **Contact:** Tom Plante, editor.

Magazine Needs *Exit 13* is a "contemporary poetry annual" using poetry that is "short, to the point, with a sense of geography." Has published poetry by Errol Miller, Adele Kenny, Hugh Fox, Paul Sohar, Kathe Palka, and Joan Digby. *Exit 13*, #12, was 76 pages. Press run is 300. Sample: $7.

How to Submit Accepts simultaneous submissions and previously published poems. Accepts submissions by postal mail and by e-mail (no attachments). Guidelines available in magazine or for SASE. Responds in 4 months. Pays one contributor's copy. Acquires one-time and possible anthology rights.

Advice "*Exit 13* looks for adventure, a living record of places we've experienced. Every state, region, country, and ecosystem is welcome. Write about what you know and have seen. Send a snapshot of an 'Exit 13' road sign and receive a free copy of the issue in which it appears."

ℕ ☑ ◎ EYE (Specialized: poetry by editors and publishers)

% TK, P.O. Box 235, Waterville ME 04903. E-mail: pupil@watchtheeye.com. Website: www.watchtheeye.com. Established 2004. **Contact:** Peter Schwartz, editor.

Magazine Needs *eye* is scheduled to appear annually. "I have a theory that poetry editors and publishers make great poems because they are around poetry the most. Please, if you have proof of this theory, send me a batch of poems. Help put the 'eye' on the people who make poetry available. *eye* will also publish some underground rising stars." Has published poetry by Stellasue Lee of *Rattle*, Robert Dunn of *Medicinal Purposes*, and David Baratier of *Pavement Saw*. *eye* is published both in print and online (as a "pay-per-download" on website).

How to Submit Submit 5-7 poems at a time. Lines/poem: unlimited. Accepts previously published poems and simultaneous submissions. Accepts e-mail submissions (pasted into body of message); no disk submissions. Cover letter is preferred. "Please tell the name of your publication and whether you are an editor or publisher in a short cover letter, along with your HTML link. If you are one of the underground rising star poets, send me a short cover letter about you. Include SASE with submissions." Reads submissions year round. Sometimes comments on rejected poems. Sometimes publishes theme issues. Guidelines available on website. Responds ASAP. Pays one contributor's copy (for print edition). Acquires first rights. Reviews books and chapbooks of poetry and other magazines/journals.

Advice "Poetry is in the hands of people imitating what they think poetry should sound like. Take it back, real poets."

☆ ⌔ EYE DIALECT

E-mail: staff@contemporarypoetry.com. Website: www.contemporarypoetry.com/dialect/. Established 1999. **Contact:** Kristina Van Sant, poetry editor. Editor-in-Chief: RJ McCaffery.

Magazine Needs *Eye Dialect* appears 3 times/year and features "poetry, essays, fiction, reviews, and whatever else we can squeeze in. *Eye Dialect*'s aesthetic is informed by two main goals and its structure: We're interested in juxtaposing emerging voices with more established writers; also, we're not afraid to republish good work if it has only previously appeared in difficult-to-find print media (after all, good writing should not be a disposable single-use flash pop). We've laid out the site to follow a 'ring' structure, in which there are no 'archived issues' per se, but only new works added to an easily accessible body of writing. All types of poetry are welcome but must pay attention to Sound and Sense and thus adhere to Coleridge's dictum of having the Best Words in their Best Order." Has published poetry by Linda Sue Park, Curtis Bauer, Robert Fanning, and Jennifer Wallace. *Eye Dialect* is published online only. Receives about 800 poems/year, accepts about 1%.

How to Submit Submit 4-6 poems at a time. Accepts previously published poems ("but only if previously published in smaller print journals—we do not accept any poems which have already been published/republished on the Web") and simultaneous submissions. Accepts e-mail submissions (pasted into body of message; no attachments); no disk submissions. Cover letter is preferred. Reads submissions year round. Time between acceptance and publication is one month. "Submissions are reviewed by all editors. Final decisions are usually made within a month, and notifications to the writers are made via e-mail." Often comments on rejected poems. Guidelines available on website. Responds in one month. No payment. Acquires first or one-time rights. Reviews books and chapbooks of poetry and other magazines/journals in 2,000 words or less. Send materials for review consideration to RJ McCaffery.

Advice "This is the final stage of your poetry's life cycle—it becomes *for* others, and no longer a private document. Make sure the poem really is for others before you send it out into the world."

⌔ THE FAIRFIELD REVIEW

544 Silver Spring Rd., Fairfield CT 06430-1947. (203)256-1960. E-mail: fairfieldreview@hpmd.com. Website: www.fairfieldreview.org. Established 1997. **Contact:** Janet and Edward Granger-Happ and Pamela Pollak, editors.

Magazine Needs *The Fairfield Review* appears 2 times/year as an e-zine featuring poetry, short stories, and essays from new and established authors. "We prefer free style poems, approachable on first reading, but with the promise of a rich vein of meaning coursing along under the consonants and vowels." Does not want "something better suited for a Hallmark card." Accepts poetry written by children; requires parents' permission/release for children under 18. Has published poetry by Taylor Graham, Lyn Lifshin, and Robert James Berry. *The Fairfield Review* is 20-30 pages, published online (HTML). Receives about 450 poems/year, accepts about 8%.

How to Submit Submit 3 poems at a time. Lines/poem: 75 maximum. Accepts previously published poems with permission; no simultaneous submissions. Accepts e-mail submissions. Cover letter is preferred. "We strongly prefer submissions via e-mail or e-mail attachment. Notifications are sent exclusively via e-mail. An e-mail address is required with all submissions." Reads submissions continually. Time between acceptance and publication is "usually less than 2 months." Poems are circulated to an editorial board. Sometimes comments on rejected poems, if requested and submitted via e-mail. Guidelines available on website. Responds in up to one year. Always sends prepublication galleys (online only). Acquires first rights, right to retain publication in online archive issues, and the right to use in "Best of *The Fairfield Review*" anthologies. Ocassionally reviews books of poetry. "We consider reviews of books from authors we have published or who are referred to us."

Contest/Award Offerings "We select poems from each issue for 'Editor's Choice' awards, plus 'Reader's Choice' awards based on readership frequency."

Advice "Read our article 'Writing Qualities to Keep in Mind.' "

FAT TUESDAY

560 Manada Gap Rd., Grantville PA 17028. (717)469-7159. E-mail: lionelstevroid@yahoo.com. Website: www.yahoogroups.com/FatTuesday. Established 1981. **Contact:** Lionel Stevroid, editor. Editor-in-Chief: F.M. Cotolo.

Magazine Needs & How to Submit *Fat Tuesday* is published irregularly as "a Mardi Gras of literary, visual, and audio treats featuring voices, singing, shouting, sighing, and shining, expressing the relevant to irreverent." Wants "prose poems, poems of irreverence, gems from the gut. Particularly interested in hard-hitting 'autofiction.' " Has published poetry by Chuck Taylor, Charles Bukowski, Mark Cramer, and Cotolo Patrick Kelly. *Fat Tuesday* is up to 60 pages, typeset (large type, heavy paper), saddle-stapled, usually chapbook-style (sometimes magazine-sized, unbound), with card cover, includes ads. Receives hundreds of submissions/year, accepts about 3-5%. All editions are $5, postage paid. Accepts e-mail submissions (pasted into body of message). "Cover letters are fine, the more amusing the better." Publishes theme issues. Responds in up to 3 months. Pays 2 contributor's copies if audio. Rights revert to author after publication. "Please join our web group (see website above) and submit all the material you want. Get read by other writers, non-writers, and wannabes."

Also Offers "In 1998, *Fat Tuesday* was presented in a different format with the production of a stereo audio cassette edition. *Fat Tuesday's Cool Noise* features readings, music, collage, and songs, all in the spirit of *Fat*'s printed versions. *Fat Tuesday* has released other audio projects. In-print magazines will still be produced as planned when funds are available.."

Advice "Support the magazine that publishes your work!"

FAULTLINE

Dept. of English & Comparative Literature, University of California—Irvine, Irvine CA 92697-2650. (949)824-1573. E-mail: faultline@uci.edu. Website: www.humanities.uci.edu/faultline. Established 1991. **Contact:** Poetry Editor. Editors: Sara Joyce Robinson and Lisa P. Sutton.

● Poetry published by this journal has also been selected for inclusion in a *Pushcart Prize* anthology.

Magazine Needs *Faultline* is an annual journal of art and literature occasionally edited by guest editors and published at the University of California—Irvine each Spring. Has published poetry by Larissa Szporluk, Yusef Komunyakaa, Amy Gerstler, and Killarney Clary. *Faultline* is about 200 pages, digest-sized, professionally printed on 60-lb. paper, perfect-bound, with 80-lb. coverstock. Receives about 5,000 poems/year, accepts less than 1%. Press run is 1,000. Single copy: $10. Sample: $5.

How to Submit Submit up to 5 poems at a time. Accepts simultaneous submissions, "but please note in cover letter that the manuscript is being considered elsewhere." No fax or e-mail submissions. Cover letter is required. "To assist anonymous judging, do not include name and address on manuscript." Reads submissions September 1 through March 1 only. Poems are selected by a board of up to 6 readers. Seldom comments on rejected poems. Guidelines available for SASE or on website. Responds in 3 months. Pays 2 contributor's copies. Acquires first or one-time serial rights.

FEATHER BOOKS; THE POETRY CHURCH MAGAZINE; CHRISTIAN HYMNS & SONGS (Specialized: membership/subscription; religious/Christian)

P.O. Box 438, Shrewsbury SY3 0WN United Kingdom. Phone/fax: (01743)872177. E-mail: john@waddysweb.freeuk.com. Website: www.waddysweb.freeuk.com. Feather Books established 1982. *The Poetry Church Magazine* established 1996. **Contact:** Rev. John Waddington-Feather, editor.

Magazine Needs *The Poetry Church Magazine* appears quarterly and contains Christian poetry, prayers, and hymns. Wants "Christian or good religious poetry—usually around 20 lines, but will accept longer." Does not want "unreadable blasphemy." **Publishes subscribers' work only.** Accepts poetry written by children over age 10. Has published poetry by Laurie Bates, Joan Smith, Idris Caffrey, Walter Nash, and Susan Glyn. *The Poetry Church Magazine* is 40 pages, digest-sized, photocopied, saddle-stapled, with laminated cover with b&w art. Receives about 1,000 poems/year, accepts about 500. Press run is 1,000 (400 subscribers, 10 libraries). Single copy free; subscription (4 magazines): £10 ($20 US). Sample: £3.50 ($6 US). Make checks payable in sterling to Feather Books. Payment can also be made through website.

How to Submit *The Poetry Church Magazine* "publishes only subscribers' poems as they keep us solvent." Submit 2 typed poems at a time. Accepts previously published poems and simultaneous submissions. Accepts e-mail submissions (as attachment). Cover letter with information about the poet is preferred. All work must be submitted by postal mail with SASE (or SAE and IRC). Time between acceptance and publication is 4 months. "The editor does a preliminary reading, then seeks the advice of colleagues about uncertain poems." Responds within one week. Poets retain copyright.

Book/Chapbook Needs & How to Submit Feather Books publishes the Feather Books Poetry Series, books of Christian poetry and prayers. Has recently published poetry collections by the Glyn family, Walter Nash, David Grieve, and Rosie Morgan Barry. "We have now published 181 poetry collections by individual Christian poets." Books are usually photocopied, saddle-stapled, with laminated covers. "Poets' works are selected for publication in collections of around 20 poems in our Feather Books Poetry Series. We do not insist, but most poets pay for small run-offs of their work, e.g., around 50-100 copies, for which we charge $270 per 50. If they can't afford it, but are good poets, we stand the cost. We expect poets to read our *Poetry Church Magazine* to get some idea of our standards."

Also Offers Feather Books also publishes *Christian Hymns & Songs*, a quarterly supplement by David Grundy and John Waddington-Feather. Recently published in 2004 was *Seasons and Occasions*, a collection of 50 new songs and hymns for all the church's seasons. And, each winter and summer, selected poems appear in *The Poetry Church Anthology*, the leading Christian poetry anthology used in churches and schools. "We also have a new chapbook collection, the Christianity and Literature Series, which focuses on academic work. The first is a paper by Dr. William Ruleman, of Wesley College, Tennessee, entitled *W.H. Auden's Search for Faith*. Other titles include *Six Contemporary Women Christian Poets* by Dr. Patricia Batstone; *In a Quiet Place: J.B. Priestley & Religion* by Michael Nelson; *'The Dream of the Rood,' 'The Wanderer,' 'The Seafarer': Three Old English Early Christian Poems of the 8th Century*, newly translated by Reverend John Waddington-Feather, with an introduction by Professor Walter Nash; and *Women Hymn-Writers of the 19th Century* by Dr. E.L. Edmonds."

Advice "We find it better for poets to master rhyme and rhythm before trying free verse. Many poets seem to think that if they write 'down' a page they're writing poetry, when all they're doing is writing prose in a different format."

FEELINGS OF THE HEART

116 30th 1/2 St., Gulfport MS 39507. Phone/fax: (228)863-7026 (call to ensure line is free before faxing). E-mail: afitchie2501@aol.com. Website: www.feelingsoftheheart.net. Established 1999. **Contact:** Alice M. Harnisch-Fitchie, editor/publisher/founder.

Magazine Needs *Feelings of the Heart* appears biannually as Winter/Spring and Summer/Fall issues. Wants "*good* poetry from the heart." Has published poetry by Victoria DeLaVergne, Richard Sponaugle, Mark Hurley, Jerry S. Reynolds, and George R. Beck. *Feelings of the Heart* is 50 pages, magazine-sized, computer-printed, stapled, with cover featuring art by poet Carl Stanislaus, includes ads. Receives about 100 poems/year, accepts about 95%. Press run is 100. Single copy: $6; subscription: $18/year, $36/2 years (2-year subscribers receive free gift with order). Make checks payable to Alice M. Fitchie.

How to Submit Submit 5 poems at a time, "with name and address on every poem submitted." Lines/poem: 20-40. Accepts previously published poems and simultaneous submissions. Accepts disk submissions; no e-mail submissions. Cover letter is "important. Please enclose SASE or IRC with all correspondence. No SASE or IRC, no reply!" Submit seasonal poems 2 months in advance. Time between acceptance and publication is less than 2 weeks. Poems "are read by me, the editor, and decided by the poetic intent of poetry submitted." Often comments on rejected poems. Guidelines available for SASE, by e-mail, or on website. Sometimes sends prepublication galleys. Acquires first rights. Reviews books and chapbooks of poetry and other magazines in 200 words or less, single-book format. Send materials for review consideration.

Also Offers Also prints poetry chapbooks for those interested in being self-published. Write for details.

Advice "*Write* poetry for yourself; *publish* for everyone else!"

☑ ◎ FEMINIST STUDIES (Specialized: women/feminism)

0103 Taliaferro Hall, University of Maryland, College Park MD 20742. (301)405-7415. Fax: (301)405-8395. E-mail: info@feministstudies.org. Website: www.feministstudies.org. Established 1969. **Contact:** Creative Writing Editor.

Magazine Needs *Feminist Studies* appears 3 times/year and welcomes "all forms of written creative expression, which may include but is not limited to poetry and short fiction." Has published poetry by Janice Mirikitani, Paula Gunn Allen, Cherrie Moraga, Audre Lorde, Valerie Fox, and Diane Glancy. *Feminist Studies* is 250 pages, elegantly printed, flat-spined, paperback. Press run is 8,000 (7,000 subscribers, 1,500 libraries). Sample: $15.

How to Submit "Authors should send a hard copy of their work, along with a disk version, to the *Feminist Studies* office. Work will not be returned." No simultaneous submissions; will only consider previously published poems under special circumstances. No fax or e-mail submissions. Manuscripts are reviewed twice/year, in May and December. **Deadlines:** May 1 and December 1. Authors will receive notice of the board's decision by July 15 and February 15. Guidelines available on website. Always sends prepublication galleys. Pays 2 contributor's copies. Commissions reviews of books of poetry. Send materials for review consideration to Claire G. Moses.

$☑ FIELD: CONTEMPORARY POETRY AND POETICS; FIELD TRANSLATION SERIES; FIELD POETRY SERIES; FIELD POETRY PRIZE; OBERLIN COLLEGE PRESS

Oberlin College, 50 N. Professor St., Oberlin OH 44074. (440)775-8408. E-mail: oc.press@oberlin.edu (inquiries only). Website: www.oberlin.edu/ocpress. Established 1969. **Contact:** David Young.

● Work published in *FIELD* has been frequently included in volumes of *The Best American Poetry*.

Magazine Needs *FIELD* is a biannual literary journal appearing in October and April, with "emphasis on poetry, translations, and essays by poets." Wants the "best possible" poetry. Has published poetry by Marianne Boruch, Miroslav Holub, Charles Wright, Jon Loomis, Charles Simic, and Sandra McPherson. *FIELD* is 100 pages, digest-sized, printed on rag stock, flat-spined, with glossy color card cover. Subscription: $14/year, $24/2 years. Sample: $7 postpaid.

How to Submit Submit up to 5 poems at a time. No previously published poems or simultaneous submissions. No e-mail submissions. Include cover letter and SASE. Reads submissions year round. Seldom comments on rejected poems. Guidelines available for SASE, by e-mail, or on website. Responds in 4-6 weeks. Always sends prepublication galleys. Pays $15/page plus 2 contributor's copies and one copy of the subsequent issue. Staff reviews books of poetry. Send materials for review consideration.

Book/Chapbook Needs & How to Submit Oberlin College Press publishes books of translations in the *FIELD* Translation Series, flat-spined, hardcover editions averaging 150 pages. Query regarding translations. Also publishes books of poetry in the *FIELD* Poetry Series, by invitation only. Has published *Lie Awake Lake* by Beckian Fritz Goldberg, *Chez Nous* by Angie Estes, *Amnesia* by Jonah Winter, and *The Lightning Field* by Carol Moldaw. Write for catalog or visit website to buy sample books.

Contest/Award Offerings Sponsors the annual *FIELD* Poetry Prize for a book-length collection of poems, awarding $1,000 and publication in the *FIELD* Poetry Series. Submit non-returnable mss of 50-80 pages. **Entry fee:** $22 (includes one-year subscription to *FIELD*). Make checks payable to Oberlin College Press. **Postmark deadline:** during May only. 2004 winner was Beckian Fritz Goldberg. Complete guidelines available for SASE or on website.

Advice "A sampling of 3-5 poems is desirable. Be sure to include enough postage on SASE if you want poems returned. We try to read promptly; please wait to submit poems elsewhere."

⬟ $◻ ◎ THE FIFTH DI . . . (Specialized: fantasy; science fiction)

E-mail: fifth@samsdotpublishing.com. Website: www.samsdotpublishing.com. Established 1994. **Contact:** J. Alan Erwine, editor.

- Honored by *Preditors & Editors* as Best Fiction Zine.

Magazine Needs *The Fifth Di . . .* is an online quarterly featuring fiction and poetry from the science fiction and fantasy genres. Open to most forms, but all poems must be science fiction or fantasy. Does not want horror, or anything that is not science fiction or fantasy. Has published poetry by Bruce Boston, Cathy Buburuz, Marge Simon, Aurelio Rico Lopez III, Terrie Relf, and John Bushore. Receives about 200 poems/year, accepts about 20.

How to Submit Submit one poem at a time. Lines/poem: no limit. No previously published poems or simultaneous submissions. Accepts e-mail submissions *only* (as attachment); no disk submissions. Cover letter is preferred. Reads submissions year round. Time between acceptance and publication is one month. Sometimes comments on rejected poems. Guidelines available on website. Responds in 1-3 months. Pays $5. Acquires first rights.

◙ FINISHING LINE PRESS; MM REVIEW; NEW WOMEN'S VOICES CHAPBOOK SERIES; FINISHING LINE PRESS OPEN CHAPBOOK COMPETITION

P.O. Box 1626, Georgetown KY 40324. (859)514-8966. E-mail: FinishingBooks@aol.com. Website: www.finishinglinepress.com. Established 1998. **Contact:** Poetry Editor. Editor: C.J. Morrison (and occasionally guest editors).

Magazine Needs & How to Submit "We are currently publishing chapbooks only and have suspended publishing of *MM Review* for the next 2 years to focus on chapbook publication."

Book/Chapbook Needs & How to Submit Finishing Line Press seeks to "discover new talent" and hopes to publish chapbooks by both men and women poets who have not previously published a book or chapbook of poetry. Has published *Looking to the East with Western Eyes* by Leah Maines, *Like the Air* by Joyce Sidman, *Startling Art* by Dorothy Sutton, *Foreign Correspondence* by Timothy Riordan, and *Man Overboard* by Steven Barza. Publishes 20-30 poetry chapbooks/year. Chapbooks are usually 25-30 pages, digest-sized, laser-printed, saddle-stapled, with card covers with textured matte wrappers. Submit ms of 16-24 pages with cover letter, bio, acknowledgments, and **$12 reading fee**. Responds to queries and to mss in up to one month. Pay varies; pays in author's copies. "Sales profits, if any, go to publish the next new poet." Order sample chapbooks by sending $6 to Finishing Line Press.

Contest/Award Offerings 1) New Women's Voices Chapbook Competition. **Entry fee:** $12. **Deadline:** January 15. 2) Finishing Line Press Open Chapbook Competition. Open to all poets regardless of past publications. **Deadline:** June 30.

Advice "We are very open to new talent. If the poetry is great, we will consider it for a chapbook."

⊕ ⊘ FIRE

Field Cottage, Old Whitehill, Tackley, Kidlington, Oxfordshire OX5 3AB United Kingdom. Website: www.poetical.org. Established 1994. **Contact:** Jeremy Hilton, editor.

Magazine Needs *Fire* appears biannually in April and October "to publish little-known, unfashionable, or new writers alongside better-known ones." Wants "experimental, unfashionable, demotic work; longer work encouraged. Use of rhyme schemes and other strict forms *not* favored." Has published poetry by Philip Levine, Marilyn Hacker, Adrian C. Louis, Tom Pickard, Allen Fisher, and David Hart. *Fire* is up to 180 pages, A5. Receives about 400 poems/year, accepts about 35%. Press run is 300 (230 subscribers, 20 libraries). Single copy: £5, add £1 postage Europe, £2 postage overseas; subscription: £7 (2 issues), £9 (3 issues), add £2 postage Europe, £4 postage overseas.

How to Submit Accepts previously published poems; no simultaneous submissions. Accepts submissions by postal mail only. Cover letter is preferred. SASE (or SAE with IRCs) required. Time between acceptance and publication "varies enormously." Often comments on rejected poems. Guidelines available for SASE or on website. Responds in 2 months. Sometimes sends prepublication galleys, "but rarely to overseas contributors." Pays one contributor's copy.

Advice "Read a copy first. Don't try to tailor your work to any particular style, format, or formula. Free expression, strongly imaginative work preferred."

⊘ FIRST CLASS; FOUR-SEP PUBLICATIONS

P.O. Box 86, Friendship IN 47021. E-mail: christopherm@four-sep.com. Website: www.four-sep.com. Established 1994. **Contact:** Christopher M., editor.

Magazine Needs *First Class* appears in February and August and "publishes excellent/odd writing for intelligent/creative readers." Wants "short postmodern poems, no traditional work." Has published poetry by Bennett, Locklin, Roden, Splake, Catlin, and Huffstickler. *First Class* is 48-56 pages, 4¼×11, printed, saddle-stapled, with colored cover. Receives about 1,500 poems/year, accepts about 30. Press run is 300-400. Sample (including guidelines): $6, or mini version $1. Make checks payable to Christopher M.

How to Submit Submit 5 poems at a time. Accepts previously published poems and simultaneous submissions. No fax or e-mail submissions. Cover letter is preferred. "Manuscripts will not be returned." Time between acceptance and publication is 2-4 months. Often comments on rejected poems. Guidelines available in magazine, for SASE, or on website. Responds in 3 weeks. Pays one contributor's copy. Acquires one-time rights. Reviews books of poetry and fiction. Send materials for review consideration.

Also Offers Chapbook production available.

Advice "Belt out a good, short, thought-provoking, graphic, uncommon piece."

⊕ FIRST OFFENSE

Syringa, Stodmarsh, Canterbury, Kent CT3 4BA England. E-mail: Tim@firstoffense.co.uk. Website: www.firstoffense.co.uk. Established 1985. **Contact:** Tim Fletcher, editor.

Magazine Needs *First Offense* is published 1-2 times/year. "The magazine is for contemporary poetry and is not traditional, but is received by most ground-breaking poets." Wants "contemporary, language, and experimental poetry and articles." *First Offense* is photocopied, "so we need well typed or word-processed manuscripts." Press run is 300. Subscription: £2.90 plus 75p for postage, or $4.50 plus $5 airmail, or equivalent in Euros. Make checks payable to Tim Fletcher.

How to Submit No previously published poems. "No reply without SAE."

Advice "Always buy a copy before submitting for research so as not to waste everyone's time."

◯ FIRST STEP PRESS; STEPPING STONES MAGAZINE: A LITERARY MAGAZINE FOR THE INNOVATIVE ARTS; CRIMSON RIVERS MAGAZINE

P.O. Box 902, Norristown PA 19404-0902. E-mail: First_Step_Press@hotmail.com. Established 1996 originally, then discontinued publication; re-debuted in 2004. **Contact:** Trinae Angelique Ross, editor.

Magazine Needs *Stepping Stones Magazine* appears 4 times/year and wants "poems written from within the writer's soul. I look at the piece to see if it says something out of the ordinary. Roses are not always red, nor violets blue . . . if you're going to use a cliché, freshen it up a bit and make me think I haven't heard it elsewhere. I want to publish pieces I *want* to share with others. Save the highbrow, stuffy pieces for the academics; this magazine is for those of us still struggling to find our voices. Though free verse is preferred, I will consider rhymed verse if written well.'' Does not want ''short fiction disguised as poetry, poems that say 'I am a poem about . . .', or crazily-formatted poems.'' Has published poetry by Patrick McKinnon, Michael Hathaway, and Maggie Pierce Secara. *Stepping Stones Magazine* is 60 pages, magazine-sized, published electronically on disk in PDF format. Receives about 300 poems/year, accepts about 10-15%. Single copy: free.

Magazine Needs *Crimson Rivers Magazine* is published irregularly but released in October in the year of its creation and explores the darkest regions of the human condition. ''Poetry appearing in *Crimson Rivers* should not be afraid to push the envelope. Visceral writing is a plus. Keep in mind, however, that *Crimson Rivers* will not publish anything dealing with the exploitation of minors or the degradation of any group based on race, religion, gender, or sexual preference. When it comes to *Crimson Rivers*, the goals are simple: **scare the reader**. Do whatever it takes to make the reader afraid to continue reading, and we all will have done our jobs for yet another year.'' Created similarly to *Stepping Stones Magazine* in PDF format.

How to Submit Submit 5 poems at a time for *Stepping Stones*; no more than 4 poems at a time for *Crimson Rivers*. Lines/poem: 100 maximum for both publications. Accepts previously published poems (note where and when ms originally appeared) and simultaneous submissions (with notification of acceptance elsewhere). Accepts e-mail (pasted into body of message) and disk submissions. ''Format electronically as a Microsoft Word document (.doc) or Rich Text File (.rtf); use Times New Roman (12-point) or Courier New (10-point) fonts only.'' Cover letter is required. Reads submissions year round. Submit seasonal poems 6 months in advance. Time between acceptance and publication is 3-6 months. Often comments on rejected poems. Guidelines available for SASE or by e-mail. Responds in one month. Sometimes sends prepublication galleys. Pays one contributor's copy. Acquires one-time rights. ''First Step Press reserves the right to reprint previously published material for future anthologies or a future 'Best of' issue.'' Reviews chapbooks of poetry and other magazines/journals in 500 words.

Also Offers ''Free advertising space is available for those wishing to promote their website, book, or other literary venture. The continuing goal of First Step Press is to provide sanctuary for new and established writers, to hone their skills and commune with one another within the comfort of both publications' electronic pages.''

Advice ''*Stepping Stones Magazine* is created with the intent to instruct, inform, and entertain. Though it is a literal testing ground for writers experimenting with their craft, I still approach publishing as a profession and expect writers to act accordingly. Above all, believe in your worth as a writer. If you do not feel confident about the work you're submitting to the magazine, you cannot honestly expect me to feel confident about my selecting or publishing the piece.''

◑ 5 AM

P.O. Box 205, Spring Church PA 15686. Established 1987. **Contact:** Ed Ochester and Judith Vollmer, editors.

Magazine Needs *5 AM* is a poetry publication that appears twice/year. Open in regard to form, length, subject matter, and style. However, they do not want poetry that is ''religious,'' or ''naive rhymers.'' Has published poetry by Virgil Suárez, Nin Andrews, Alicia Ostriker, Edward Field, Billy Collins, and Denise Duhamel. *5 AM* is a 24-page, offset tabloid. Receives about 5,000 poems/year, accepts about 2%. Press run is 1,200 (650 subscribers, 25 libraries, about 300 shelf sales). Subscription: $15/4 issues. Sample: $5.

How to Submit No previously published poems or simultaneous submissions. Seldom comments on rejected poems. Responds within 6 weeks. Pays 2 contributor's copies plus subscription. Acquires first rights.

Advice ''Read the magazine before submitting.''

◨ FIVE FINGERS REVIEW

P.O. Box 4, San Leandro CA 94577. Phone/fax: (510)632-5769. E-mail: jrobles@aaahawk.com. Website: www.fivefingersreview.org. Established 1987. **Contact:** Jaime Robles, editor.

Magazine Needs *Five Fingers Review* is published annually in September and is "interested in quality work from a wide spectrum of ideas and styles; committed to publishing innovative work by emerging and established writers." Wants "all styles and forms; must be excellent and original work in the chosen form." Has published poetry by Gillian Conoley, Jackson Mac Low, Carl Phillips, Brenda Hillman, Elizabeth Robinson, and Peter Gizzi. *Five Fingers Review* is digest-sized, offset-printed, perfect-bound, with 4-color cover (usually work by contributing artist), includes ads. Press run is 1,000. Single copy: $13; subscription: $16/2 issues. Make checks payable to *Five Fingers Review*.

How to Submit Submit 3-5 poems at a time. Accepts simultaneous submissions; no previously published poems. No fax, e-mail, or disk submissions. Cover letter is preferred. "Don't forget the SASE." Reads submissions June 1 to August 31. "Most poems are solicited by contributing editors. At least two people read unsolicited submissions." Seldom comments on rejected poems. Regularly publishes theme issues. List of upcoming themes and guidelines available for SASE or on website. Responds in up to 6 months. Always sends prepublication galleys. Pays 2 contributor's copies plus discount on additional copies. Acquires one-time rights. Reviews books and chapbooks of poetry and other magazines/journals. Send materials for review consideration to J. Robles.

Contest/Award Offerings Offers contest in poetry and fiction. **Deadline:** June 1. Guidelines available on website.

Also Offers Runs local reading series in San Francisco Bay area.

✪ ⊕ $□ FLARESTACK PUBLISHING; OBSESSED WITH PIPEWORK

41 Buckleys Green, Alvechurch, Birmingham B48 7NG United Kingdom. Phone: 0121 445 2110. E-mail: cannula.dementia@virgin.net. Established 1995. **Contact:** Charles Johnson, editor.

Magazine Needs *Obsessed with Pipework* appears quarterly. "We are very keen to publish strong new voices—'new poems to surprise and delight' with somewhat of a high-wire aspect. We are looking for original, exploratory poems—positive, authentic, oblique maybe—delighting in image and in the dance of words on the page." Does not want "the predictable, the unfresh, the rhyme-led, the clever, the sure-of-itself. No formless outpourings, please." No full-length collection mss. Has published "Searching For Salsa" by Jennifer Ballerini, "Valence" by Sarah Ruth Jacobs, and poetry by David Hart, Jennifer Compton, Susan Wicks, Carol Burns, Lucille Gang Shulklapper, and Maria Jastrzebska. *Obsessed With Pipework* is 49 pages, A5, photocopied, stapled, with card cover, includes ads "by arrangement." Receives about 1,500 poems/year, accepts about 10%. Press run is 70-100. Single copy: £3.50; subscription: £12. Sample: £2 if available. Make checks payable in pounds to Flarestack Publishing.

How to Submit Submit maximum of 6 poems at a time. No previously published poems or simultaneous submissions. Accepts e-mail and fax submissions. "If sending by e-mail, paste a maximum of 3 poems in the body of the message, as attached files may become lost or corrupted." Cover letter is preferred. Often comments on rejected poems. Guidelines available for SASE or by e-mail. Responds in 2 months. Pays one contributor's copy. Acquires first rights.

Book/Chapbook Needs Flarestack Publishing ("talent to burn") aims to "find an audience for new poets, so beginners are welcome, but the work has to be strong and clear." Publishes 8 chapbooks/year. Chapbooks are usually 12-52 pages, A5, photocopied, stapled, with card covers.

How to Submit Query first with a few sample poems (6 maximum) and cover letter with brief bio and publication credits. "Normally we expect a few previous magazine acceptances, but no previous collection publication." Responds to queries in 6 weeks; to mss in 2 months. Pays royalties of 25% plus 6 author's copies (out of a press run of 50-100). Order sample chapbooks by sending £3.50.

Advice "Most beginning poets show little evidence of reading poetry before writing it! Join a poetry workshop. For chapbook publishing, we are looking for *coherent* first collections that take risks, make leaps, and come clean.''

$ ☑ ◎ FLESH AND BLOOD: QUIET TALES OF DARK FANTASY & HORROR (Specialized: horror; dark fantasy; off-beat; supernatural)
121 Joseph St., Bayville NJ 08721. E-mail: HorrorJackF@aol.com. Website: www.fleshandbloodpre ss.com. Established 1997. **Contact:** Jack Fisher, editor-in-chief.
Magazine Needs Appearing 4 times/year, *Flesh and Blood* publishes work of dark fantasy and the supernatural. Wants surreal, bizarre, and avant-garde poetry. No "rhyming or love poems." Has published poetry by Charles Jacob, Mark McLaughlin, China Meiville, TM Wright, and David B. Silva. *Flesh and Blood* is 52-62 pages, full-sized, saddle-stapled, with glossy full-color cover, includes ads. Receives about 200 poems/year, accepts about 10%. Press run is 1,000 (800 subscribers, 200 shelf sales); 50 distributed free to reviewers. Subscription: $16. Sample: $6. Make checks payable to Jack Fisher.
How to Submit Submit up to 5 poems at a time. Lines/poem: 3 minimum, 30 maximum. No previously published poems or simultaneous submissions. Accepts e-mail submissions (pasted into body of message). Cover letter is preferred. "Poems should be on separate pages, each with the author's address. Cover letter should include background writing credits." Time between acceptance and publication is up to 10 months. Guidelines available for SASE or on website. Responds in 2 months. Pays $10-20/poem and one contributor's copy.
Advice "Be patient, professional, and courteous."

☑ FLUME PRESS
California State University at Chico, 400 W. First St., Chico CA 95929-0830. (530)898-5983. E-mail: flumepress@csuchico.edu. Website: www.csuchico.edu/engl/flumepress. Established 1984. **Contact:** Casey Huff, poetry editor.
Book/Chapbook Needs Flume Press publishes poetry chapbooks, selected through competition (see below). "We have few biases about form, although we appreciate control and crafting, and we tend to favor a concise, understated style, with emphasis on metaphor rather than editorial commentary." Has published chapbooks by Tina Barr, Luis Omar Salinas, Pamela Uschuk, Martha M. Vertreace, John Brehm, and David Graham.
Contest/Award Offerings Chapbooks are chosen from a biennial competition. Winner receives $500 and 25 author's copies. Submit 24-32 pages, including title, contents, and acknowledgments. Considers simultaneous submissions. Sometimes sends prepublication galleys. **Entry fee:** $20 (each entrant receives a copy of the winning chapbook). **Postmark deadline:** December 1, 2006. Guidelines available on website. Sample: $8.

☑ FLYWAY, A LITERARY REVIEW
206 Ross Hall, Iowa State University, Ames IA 50011-1201. Fax: (515)294-6814. E-mail: flyway@iast ate.edu. Website: www.flyway.org. Established 1961. **Contact:** Stephen Pett, editor-in-chief.
Magazine Needs Appearing 3 times/year, *Flyway* "is one of the best literary magazines for the money; it is packed with some of the most readable poems being published today—all styles, forms, lengths, and subjects." The editor shuns elite-sounding free verse with obscure meanings, and pretty-sounding formal verse with obvious meanings. *Flyway* is 112 pages, digest-sized, professionally printed, perfect-bound, with matte card cover with color. Press run is 600 (400 subscribers, 100 libraries). Subscription: $18. Sample: $7.
How to Submit Submit 4-6 poems at a time. Cover letter is preferred. "We do not read manuscripts between the end of May and the end of August." May be contacted by fax. Publishes theme issues (Native American, Latino, Arab American). Responds in 6 weeks (often sooner). Pays 2 contributor's copies. Acquires first rights.
Contest/Award Offerings Sponsors an annual award for poetry, fiction, and nonfiction. Details available for SASE or on website.

◙ FOLIO, A Literary Journal at American University

Dept. of Literature, American University, Washington DC 20016. (202)885-2990. Fax: (202)885-2938. E-mail: folio_editors@yahoo.com. Website: www.foliojournal.org. Established 1984. **Contact:** Lauren Fanelli, editor-in-chief.

Magazine Needs *Folio* appears 2 times/year. Wants work "that ignites and endures, is artful and natural, daring and elegant. Will accept formal and free verse." Does not want work of a sexually graphic or discriminatory nature. Has published poetry by Allison Joseph, CJ Sage, Denise Duhamel, Frannie Lindsay, Patrick Rosal, and Kathleen Kirk. *Folio* is 80 pages, digest-sized, with matte cover with graphic art. Receives about 1,000 poems/year, accepts about 25. Press run is 350 (30 subscribers, 5 libraries, 50 shelf sales); 50-60 are distributed free to the American University community and contributors. Single copy: $6; subscription: $12/year. Make checks payable to *Folio*.

How to Submit Submit 4-6 poems at a time. Considers simultaneous submissions "with notice." No fax, e-mail, or disk submissions. Cover letter is preferred. "SASE required for notification only; manuscripts are not returned." Reads submissions September 1 through March 1. Time between acceptance and publication is 2 months. "Poems are reviewed by editorial staff and senior editors." Seldom comments on rejected poems. Occasionally publishes theme issues. Guidelines available in magazine. Pays 2 contributor's copies. Acquires first North American serial rights.

◙ FORPOETRY.COM

E-mail: submissions@forpoetry.com. Website: www.forpoetry.com. Established March 1999. **Contact:** Jackie Marcus, editor.

Magazine Needs *ForPoetry.Com* is a web magazine with daily updates. "We wish to promote new and emerging poets, with or without MFAs. We will be publishing established poets, but our primary interest is in publishing excellent poetry, prose, and reviews. We are interested in lyric poetry, vivid imagery, open form, natural landscape, philosophical themes—but not at the expense of honesty and passion; model examples: Robert Hass, James Wright, Charles Wright's *The Other Side of the River*, Montale, Neruda, Levertov, and Louise Glück. No city punk, corny sentimental fluff, or academic workshop imitations." Has published poetry by Sherod Santos, John Koethe, Jane Hirshfield, Erin Believ, and Kathy Fagan. "We receive lots of submissions and are very selective about acceptances, but we will always try to send a note back on rejections."

How to Submit Submit no more than 2 poems at a time. Accepts simultaneous submissions; no previously published poems. Accepts e-mail submissions only (pasted into body of message, no attachments). Cover letter is preferred. Reads submissions September through May only. Time between acceptance and publication is 2-3 weeks. "We'll read all submissions and then decide together on the poems we'll publish." Comments on rejected poems "as often as possible." Guidelines available on website. Responds in 2 weeks. Reviews books and chapbooks of poetry and other magazines in 800 words.

Advice "As my friend Kevin Hull said, 'Get used to solitude and rejection.' Sit on your poems for several months or more. Time is your best critic."

Ⓝ ◙ 4 AM POETRY REVIEW

11012 Fruitland Dr. #3, Studio City CA 91604. E-mail: fourampoetryreview@gmail.com. Website: http://fourampoetryreview.i8.com. Established 2004. **Contact:** Maria Thibodeau, editor.

Magazine Needs *4 AM*, published annually in August, "exists as an antidote to the usual, publishing poetry of meticulous craft written by word-addicts." Wants "imagery and a skillful interplay of sound and meaning. Narrative and free verse." Does not want "obtrusive rhyming, first drafts, prose with line breaks." *4 AM* is 40-60 pages, digest-sized, laser-copied, thermal-bound, with cardstock cover with photo. Accepts about 40-60 poems/year. Press run is 200. Single copy: $5; subscription: $5. Make checks payable to Maria Thibodeau.

How to Submit Submit 3-5 poems at a time. Accepts simultaneous submissions (with notice); no previously published poems. Accepts e-mail submissions (pasted into body of message); no disk submissions. "For e-mail submissions: one poem/e-mail; include notes regarding any special for-

matting. We accept e-mail submissions as sympathizers to the postage burden but expect poets to exhibit the same care as with postal submissions. For postal submissions: include name and e-mail on each page." Reads submissions year round. Time between acceptance and publication is up to one year. Sometimes comments on rejected poems. Guidelines available in magazine, for SASE, by e-mail, or on website. Responds in 6 weeks. Pays 2 contributor's copies. Acquires first rights. **Also Offers** "I hope to expand into offering audio CDs of featured poets, as well as chapbooks by invitation."
Advice "Read more than you write."

☐ ◎ 4*9*1 NEO-NAIVE IMAGINATION (Specialized: style/neo-naive)

P.O. Box 24306, Lakeland FL 33802. E-mail: stompdncr@aol.com. Website: www.491.20m.com. Established 1997. **Contact:** Donald Ryburn, editor. Assistant Editor: Juan Beauregard-Montez.
Magazine Needs *4*9*1 Neo-Naive Imagination* appears continuously as an online publication featuring poetry, art, photography, essays, and interviews. Wants "poetry of neo-naive genre. No academic poetry; limited and fallacious language." Has published poetry by Duane Locke and Jesus Morales-Montez.
How to Submit Submit 3-6 poems at a time. Accepts previously published poems and simultaneous submissions. Prefers fax, e-mail (pasted into body of message, "submission" in subject box; no attachments accepted or opened), disk, or CD-ROM submissions. "Would like to hear the poet's own words, not some standard format." Cover letter with picture and SASE is preferred. Time between acceptance and publication varies. Response time varies. Payment varies. Acquires first or one-time rights. Reviews books and chapbooks of poetry and other magazines. Send materials for review consideration.
Also Offers Sponsors a series of creative projects. Write or visit the website for details.

◐ FOURTEEN HILLS: THE SFSU REVIEW

Creative Writing Dept., San Francisco State University, 1600 Holloway Ave., San Francisco CA 94132. (415)338-3083. Fax: (415)338-7030. E-mail: hills@sfsu.edu. Website: www.14hills.net. Established 1994. **Contact:** Poetry Editor.
Magazine Needs *Fourteen Hills* is a biannual journal of contemporary literary art. "We are seeking high-quality, innovative work." Has published poetry by Alice Notley, C.D. Wright, Sherman Alexie, and Virgil Suárez. *Fourteen Hills* is 170 pages, digest-sized, professionally printed, perfect-bound, with glossy card cover. Receives about 900 poems/year, accepts about 5-10%. Press run is 600 (125 subscribers, 25 libraries). Single copy: $7; subscription: $12/year, $21/2 years. Sample: $5.
How to Submit Submit 5 poems at a time. Accepts simultaneous submissions, "but please indicate if this is the case"; no previously published poems. Accepts submissions by postal mail only. Cover letter is preferred. Deadline for Winter/Spring issue is September 1; February 1 for Summer/Fall issue. "The editorial staff is composed entirely of graduate students from the Creative Writing Program at SFSU." Seldom comments on rejected poems. Guidelines available in magazine or on website. Responds in 6 months. Always sends prepublication galleys. Pays 2 contributor's copies.
Advice "Please read an issue of *Fourteen Hills* before submitting."

✪ ◐ FOX CRY REVIEW

University of Wisconsin—Fox Valley, 1478 Midway Rd., Menasha WI 54952-1297. (920)832-2664. E-mail: wcurl@uwc.edu. Website: www.fox.uwc.edu/stlife/clubs.html#fcr. Established 1974. **Contact:** Will Curl, editor.
Magazine Needs *Fox Cry Review* is a literary annual, published in September, using poems of any length or style. Has published poetry by Virgil Suárez, Ellen Kort, and Walt McDonald. *Fox Cry Review* is about 100 pages, digest-sized, professionally printed, perfect-bound, with light card cover with b&w illustration. Press run is 200. Single copy: $6 plus $1.50 postage.
How to Submit Submit maximum of 3 poems from September 1 through February 1 only. "Include name, address, and phone number on each poem. Include brief bio and SASE." No previously

published poems or simultaneous submissions. No fax or e-mail submissions. Guidelines available in magazine. Pays one contributor's copy.

◪ FREE LUNCH

P.O. Box 717, Glenview IL 60025-0717. Website: www.poetsfreelunch.org. Established 1988. **Contact:** Ron Offen, editor.

Magazine Needs *Free Lunch* is a "poetry journal interested in publishing the whole spectrum of what is currently being produced by American poets. Features a 'Mentor Series,' in which an established poet introduces a new, unestablished poet. Mentor poets are selected by the editor. Mentors have included Maxine Kumin, Billy Collins, Lucille Clifton, Donald Hall, Carolyn Forché, Wanda Coleman, Lyn Lifshin, Stephen Dunn, and Edward Hirsch. Especially interested in experimental work and work by unestablished poets. Hope to provide all serious poets living in the U.S. with a free subscription. For details on free subscription, send SASE. Regarding the kind of poetry we find worthwhile, we like metaphors, similes, arresting images, and a sensitive and original use of language. We are interested in all genres—experimental poetry, protest poetry, formal poetry, etc. No restriction on form (except no haikus, please), length, subject matter, style, purpose. No aversion to form, rhyme." Has published poetry by Thomas Carper, Jared Carter, Billy Collins, David Wagoner, Donald Hall, D. Nurkse, James Reiss, Lisel Mueller, and Cathy Song. *Free Lunch*, published 2 times/year, is 32-40 pages, digest-sized, attractively printed and designed, saddle-stapled. Press run is 1,200 (1,000 free subscriptions, 200 paid subscriptions, 15 libraries). Subscription: $12 ($15 foreign). Sample: $5 ($6 foreign).

How to Submit "Submissions must be limited to 3 poems and are considered only between September 1 and May 31. Submissions sent at other times will be returned unread. Although a cover letter is not mandatory, I like them. I especially want to know if a poet is previously unpublished, as I like to work with new poets." Accepts simultaneous submissions; no previously published poems. Editor comments on rejected poems and tries to return submissions within 3 months. Guidelines available for SASE or on website. Pays one contributor's copy plus subscription.

Contest/Award Offerings The Rosine Offen Memorial Award, a prize of $200, is awarded to one poem in each issue of *Free Lunch*. Winners are selected solely by the Board of Directors of Free Lunch Arts Alliance, and are announced in the following issue.

Advice "Archibald MacLeish said, 'A poem should not mean/ But be.' I have become increasingly leery of the ego-centered lyric that revels in some past wrong, good-old-boy nostalgia, or unfocused ecstatic experience. Not receptive to poems about writing poems, other poems, poetry reading, etc. Poetry is concerned primarily with language, rhythm, and sound; fashions and trends are transitory and to be eschewed; perfecting one's work is often more important than publishing it."

◪ FREEFALL

Undead Poets Press, 15735 Kerstyn St., Taylor MI 48180. (734)941-8123. E-mail: mauruspoet@yahoo.com. Established 1999. **Contact:** Marc Maurus and T. Anders Carson, editors/publishers.

Magazine Needs *freefall* appears 3 times/year in April, July, and October. *freefall* publishes the quality work of beginners as well as established poets. "Free verse or formal poetry is okay, and our acceptance policy is broad. No concrete, shape, or greeting card verse. No gratuitous language or sex. No fuzzy animals or syrupy nature poems." Has published poetry by B.Z. Niditch, Lyn Lifshin, David Lawrence, Michael Estabrook, and Joe Speer. *freefall* is 40 pages, digest-sized, laser-printed, saddle-stapled, with card stock cover with photographs. Receives about 200 poems/year, accepts about 50%. Press run is 250 (50 subscribers, 10 libraries, 25 shelf sales); 25 are distributed free to small press reviewers. Single copy: $5; subscription: $10. Make checks payable to Marc Maurus.

How to Submit Submit 5-10 poems at a time. Lines/poem: 3 minimum, 80 maximum. Accepts previously published poems with notification; no simultaneous submissions. Accepts e-mail submissions (pasted into body of message, no attachments); no fax or disk submissions. "Snail mail preferred; please send SASE." Cover letter is preferred. Reads submissions all year. Submit seasonal poems 6 months in advance. Time between acceptance and publication is 6 months. "If a poem is high quality, I accept it right away; poor work is rejected immediately, and those on the fence are circulated to as many as 3 other guest editors." Often comments on rejected poems. ***Poems may be sent for critique only for $2 each plus SASE.*** Guidelines available for SASE. Responds in 2 weeks. Pays one contributor's copy. Acquires first rights; rights always revert to author on publication. Reviews chapbooks of poetry and other magazines/journals in 500 words, single-book format. Send materials for review consideration to Marc Maurus.

Advice "We prefer to see crafted work, not unedited one-offs. We welcome as much formal verse as we can because we feel there is a place for it."

$ FREEFALL MAGAZINE

Alexandra Writers' Centre Society, 922 Ninth Ave. SE, Calgary AB T2G 0S4 Canada. Phone/fax: (403)264-4730. E-mail: awcs@telusplanet.net. Website: www.alexandrawriters.org. Established 1990. **Contact:** Vivian Hansen, editor. Assistant Editors: Micheline Maylor and Beth Raugust. Member: AMPA.

Magazine Needs Published in March and October, "*FreeFall's* mandate is to encourage the voices of new, emerging, and experienced writers and provide an outlet for their work. Contains fiction, nonfiction, poetry, interviews related to writers/writing; artwork and photographs suitable for b&w reproduction." Wants "poems in a variety of forms with a strong voice, effective language, and fresh images." Has published poetry by Anne Burke, Lyle Weiss, Myrna Garanis, Liz Rees, Bob Stamp, and Judith Robb. *FreeFall* is 40-44 pages, magazine-sized, xerox-digital-printed, saddle-stapled, with 60-lb. paper cover. Receives about 50-60 poems/year, accepts about 20%. Press run is 350 (270 subscribers, 20 libraries, 80 shelf sales); 30 distributed free to contributors, promotion. Single copy: $8.50 US, $7.50 Canadian; subscription: $14 US, $12 Canadian. Sample: $6.50 US, $5.50 Canadian.

How to Submit Submit 2-5 poems at a time. Lines/poem: 60 maximum. No previously published poems or simultaneous submissions. Accepts disk submissions (ASCII, text format) with hard copy, but no fax or e-mail submissions. Cover letter with 2-line bio and SASE is required. Reads submissions March through April and October through November only. Time between acceptance and publication is 6 months. "All submissions are read by 4 editors." Seldom comments on rejected poems. Occasionally publishes theme issues. Guidelines and upcoming themes available for SAE and IRC, by e-mail, in magazine, or on website. Responds in 3 months. Pays $5 Canadian/page and one contributor's copy. Acquires first North American serial rights.

Contest/Award Offerings Hosts an annual fiction and poetry contest. **Deadline:** October 1.

Also Offers See website for information about the Alexandra Writers' Centre Society activities and services, and for additional information about *FreeFall* magazine.

FREEXPRESSION

P.O. Box 4, West Hoxton NSW 2171 Australia. Phone: (02)9607 5559. Fax: (02)9826 6612. E-mail: freexpression@iprimus.com.au. Website: www.freexpression.net. Established 1993. **Contact:** Peter F. Pike, managing editor.

Magazine Needs *FreeXpresSion* is a monthly publication containing "creative writing, how-to articles, short stories, and poetry including cinquain, haiku, etc., and bush verse." Open to all forms. "Christian themes OK. Humorous material welcome. No gratuitous sex; bad language OK. We don't want to see anything degrading." Has published poetry by Ron Stevens, Ellis Campbell, John Ryan, and Ken Dean. *FreeXpresSion* is 28 pages, magazine-sized, offset-printed, saddle-stapled, with paper cover. Receives about 2,500 poems/year, accepts about 30%. Press run is 500 (400 subscribers, 25 libraries). Single copy: $3.50 AUS; subscription: $42 AUS ($66 overseas airmail). For sample, send large SAE with $1 stamp.

How to Submit Submit 3-4 poems at a time. "Very long poems are not desired but would be considered." Accepts previously published poems and simultaneous submissions. Accepts submissions on disk, by fax, by postal mail, and by e-mail (pasted into body of message). Cover letter is preferred. Time between acceptance and publication is 2 months. Seldom comments on rejected poems. Publishes theme issues. List of upcoming themes available in magazine, by e-mail, or on website. Guidelines available in magazine, for SAE and IRC, by fax, or by e-mail. Responds in 2 months. Sometimes sends prepublication galleys. Pays one contributor's copy; additional copies available at half price. Acquires first Australian rights only. Reviews books of poetry in 500 words. Send materials for review consideration.

Contest/Award Offerings Sponsors an annual contest with 2 categories for poetry: blank verse (up to 60 lines); traditional verse (up to 80 lines). 1st Prize in blank verse: $200; 2nd Prize: $100; 1st Prize in traditional rhyming poetry: $250; 2nd Prize: $150; 3rd Prize: $100.

Also Offers *FreeXpresSion* also publishes books up to 200 pages through subsidy arrangements with authors. "Some poems published throughout the year are used in Yearbooks, annual anthologies."

Advice "Keep it short and simple."

▢ ◉ FRODO'S NOTEBOOK (Specialized: poetry by teens)

P.O. Box 1690, Radio City Station, New York NY 10101. E-mail: editors@frodosnotebook.com. Website: www.frodosnotebook.com. Established 1998. **Contact:** Julia Shields, poetry editor. Editor: Daniel Klotz.

Magazine Needs *Frodo's Notebook* is an online international quarterly of poetry, fiction, and essays by teens. Wants all styles, particularly narrative and personal poems. Does not want unfinished work or work by writers over 19 years of age. *Frodo's Notebook* is published online only. Receives about 1,000 poems/year, accepts about 70. All issues available online at no cost.

How to Submit No previously published poems or simultaneous submissions. Accepts e-mail submissions; no fax or disk submissions. Cover letter is required. "Carefully read submission guidelines available on the website." Reads submissions year round. Time between acceptance and publication is 2-3 months. "Poetry editor makes final selection from a pool of submissions which has been narrowed down by other editors." Always comments on rejected poems. Responds in up to 6 weeks. Acquires first rights. Reviews books of poetry and other magazines/journals in 1,500 words, single-book format. Send materials for review consideration to Daniel Klotz.

Advice "Your chances of acceptance skyrocket if you take the time to revise and edit very carefully, being sure to eliminate clichés."

▦ ◗ THE FROGMORE PAPERS; FROGMORE POETRY PRIZE

18 Nevill Rd., Lewes, East Sussex BN7 1PF England. Website: www.frogmorepress.co.uk. Established 1983. **Contact:** Jeremy Page, poetry editor.

Magazine Needs *The Frogmore Papers* is a biannual literary magazine with emphasis on new poetry and short stories. "Quality is generally the only criterion, although pressure of space means very long work (over 100 lines) is unlikely to be published." Has published "Other Lilies" by Marita Over and "A Plutonian Monologue" by Brian Aldiss, as well as poetry by Carole Satyamurti, John Mole, Linda France, Tobias Hill, Elizabeth Garrett, and John Latham. *The Frogmore Papers* is 46 pages, photocopied in photoreduced typescript, saddle-stapled, with matte card cover. Accepts 3% of poetry received. Press run is 300 (120 subscribers). Subscription: £7 ($20). Sample: £2 ($5). US payments should be made in cash, not check.

How to Submit Submit 5-6 poems at a time. Considers simultaneous submissions. Editor rarely comments on rejected poems. Responds in 6 months. Pays one contributor's copy. Staff reviews books of poetry in 2-3 sentences, single-book format. Send materials for review consideration to Catherine Smith, 24 South Way, Lewes, East Sussex BN7 1LU England.

Contest/Award Offerings Sponsors the annual Frogmore Poetry Prize. Write for information.

Advice "My advice to people starting to write poetry is: Read as many recognized modern poets as you can, and don't be afraid to experiment."

$ ◎ FROGPOND: JOURNAL OF THE HAIKU SOCIETY OF AMERICA; HAIKU SOCIETY OF AMERICA AWARDS/CONTESTS (Specialized: haiku and related forms; translations)

P.O. Box 122, Nassau NY 12123. E-mail: ithacan@earthlink.net. Website: www.hsa-haiku.org. Established 1978. **Contact:** John Stevenson, editor.

Magazine Needs *Frogpond* is the international journal of the Haiku Society of America and is published triannually (February, June, October). Wants "contemporary English-language haiku, ranging from 1-4 lines or in a visual arrangement, focusing on a moment keenly perceived and crisply conveyed, using clear images and non-poetic language." Also accepts "related forms: senryu, sequences, linked poems, and haibun. We welcome translations of any of these forms." Has published work by Cor van den Heuvel, Peggy Willis Lyles, Jim Kacian, and Lee Gurga. *Frogpond* is 96 pages, digest-sized, perfect-bound. Receives about 20,000 submissions/year, accepts about 500. *Frogpond* goes to 800 subscribers, of which 15 are libraries, as well as to over a dozen foreign countries. Sample back issues: $7 US, $9 ROW. Make checks payable to Haiku Society of America.

How to Submit Submit 5-10 poems, with 5 poems per 8½ × 11 sheet. No simultaneous submissions. Accepts submissions by e-mail (as attachment or pasted into body of message), on disk, or by postal mail. Include SASE. Information on the HSA and submission guidelines available for SASE. Responds "usually" in 3 weeks or less. Pays $1/accepted item. Reviews books of poetry, usually in 1,000 words or less. "Authors are urged to send their books for review consideration."

Contest/Award Offerings A "best of issue" prize is awarded to a poem from each issue of *Frogpond* through a gift from the Museum of Haiku Literature, located in Tokyo. The Society also sponsors The Harold G. Henderson Haiku Award Contest, the Gerald Brady Senryu Award Contest, the Bernard Lionel Einbond Memorial Renku Contest, the Nicholas A. Virgilio Memorial Haiku Competition for High School Students, and the Merit Book Awards for outstanding books in the haiku field. See website for guidelines.

Also Offers *HSA Newsletter*, edited by Johnye E. Strickland, appears 4 times/year and contains reports of the HSA quarterly meetings, regional activities, news of upcoming events, results of contests, publications activities, and other information.

Advice "Submissions to *Frogpond* are accepted from both members and nonmembers, although familiarity with the journal will aid writers in discovering what it publishes."

$ ◪ FUGUE

Brink Hall, Room 200, University of Idaho, Moscow ID 83844-1102. E-mail: Fugue@uidaho.edu. Website: www.class.uidaho.edu/english/Fugue. Established 1989. **Contact:** Sara Kaplan, poetry editor.

Magazine Needs *Fugue* is a biannual literary magazine of the University of Idaho, published in summer and winter. "There are no limits on type of poetry; however, we are not interested in trite or quaint verse." Has published poetry by Sonia Sanchez, Simon Perchik, and Denise Duhamel. *Fugue* is up to 200 pages, perfect-bound. Receives about 400 poems/semester, accepts only 15-20 poems/issue. Press run is 250 plus an online version. Sample: $8.

How to Submit No previously published poems or simultaneous submissions. No e-mail submissions. SASE is required; "Submissions without a #10 SASE will not be considered." Reads submissions September 1 through May 1 only. Time between acceptance and publication is up to one year. "Submissions are reviewed by staff members and chosen with consensus by the editorial board. No major changes are made to a manuscript without authorial approval." Publishes theme issues. List of upcoming themes and guidelines available for SASE or on website. Responds in up to 5 months. Pays at least one contributor's copy and honorarium. Acquires first North American serial rights.

Contest/Award Offerings "For information regarding our spring poetry contests, please review our website."

Advice "We are looking for poetry that takes risks while demonstrating powerful voice and careful attention to language and craft. Proper manuscript format and submission etiquette are expected; submissions without proper SASE will not be read or held on file."

⬛ ☑ FULLOSIA PRESS; THE ROCKAWAY PARK PHILOSOPHICAL SOCIETY

P.O. Box 280, Ronkonkoma NY 11779. E-mail: deanofRPPS@aol.com. Website: http://rpps_fullosia _press.tripod.com. Established 1971. **Contact:** jd collins.

Magazine Needs *Fullosia Press* appears online monthly, presenting news, information, satire, and right-conservative perspective. Wants any style of poetry. "If you have something to say, say it. We consider many different points of view." Does not want "anti-American, anti-Christian." Accepts poetry by children with parental approval. Has published poetry by Peter Vetrano, Michael Levy, Dr. Kelley White, John Grey, and Laura Stamps. *Fullosia Press* is published online only. Receives about 50 poems/year, accepts about 40%. Single copy: $15 and SASE (free online); subscription: $25/year (free online). Make checks payable to RPPS-Fullosia Press.

How to Submit Accepts e-mail (pasted into body of message) and disk submissions. "Electronic submission by disk to address; e-mail preferred. Final submission by disk or e-mail only." Cover letter is required. Reads submissions when received. Submit seasonal poems one month in advance. Time between acceptance and publication varies. "I review all poems: (1) Do they say something?; (2) Is there some thought behind it?; (3) Is it more than words strung together?" Always comments on rejected poems. Guidelines and upcoming themes available for SASE, by e-mail, or on website. Responds in one month. Acquires one-time rights. Reviews books and chapbooks of poetry and other magazines/journals. Send materials for review consideration to RPPS-Fullosia Press.

Advice "Say what you have in mind without tripping over your own symbolism. We like poems that are clear, concise, to the point; American traditional heroes; Arthurian legend; American states. Everybody sings about Texas; has anyone written a poem to New Jersey?"

⬛ ☐ THE FUNNY PAPER; F/J WRITERS SERVICE

P.O. Box 455, Lee's Summit MO 64063. E-mail: felixkcmo@aol.com. Website: www.angelfire.com/ biz/funnypaper. Established 1985. **Contact:** Felix Fellhauer, editor.

Magazine Needs *The Funny Paper* appears 4 times/year "to provide readership, help, and the opportunity to write for money to budding authors/poets/humorists of all ages." Accepts poetry written by children ages 8-15. Wants "light verse; humor always welcome. No heavy, dismal, trite work; no pornography." *The Funny Paper* is 10 pages, magazine-sized, photocopied on colored paper, unbound. Receives about 300 poems/year, accepts about 10%. Single copy: $3; subscription: $10/year. Make checks payable to F/J Writers Service.

How to Submit Submit no more than 2 poems at a time. Lines/poem: 16 maximum. Accepts submissions by postal mail and by e-mail (pasted into body of message). "We encourage beginners; handwritten poems OK. Include SASE for acknowledgment only; submissions will not be returned." Seldom comments on rejected poems. Guidelines available in magazine, for SASE, by e-mail, or on website. Pays one contributor's copy. Acquires one-time rights.

Advice "Get guidelines first."

⬛ ☐ THE FURNACE REVIEW

16909 N. Bay Rd. #305, Sunny Isles FL 33160. E-mail: submissions@thefurnacereview.com. Website: www.thefurnacereview.com. Established 2004. **Contact:** Ciara LaVelle, editor.

Magazine Needs *The Furnace Review* is a quarterly online journal of poetry and fiction "dedicated to new writers and unique or groundbreaking work." Wants "all forms, from haiku to sonnets to free verse to totally experimental. Just make it interesting." Has published poetry by Sarah Lynn Knowles, David Gruber, Curtis Evans, and Richard Matthes. Receives about 200 poems/year, accepts about 30.

How to Submit Submit up to 5 poems at a time. Lines/poem: 75 maximum. Accepts simultaneous submissions; no previously published poems. Accepts e-mail submissions (as attachment); no disk submissions. Cover letter is preferred. "Online submissions are free; **if submitting by mail, please include a transcription fee of $2 per manuscript.**" Reads submissions year round. Time between acceptance and publication is 3 months. Poems are circulated to an editorial board. Sometimes comments on rejected poems. Guidelines available on website. Responds in 3 months. Acquires first North American serial rights.

☐ ◎ FURROW—THE UNDERGRADUATE LITERARY AND ART REVIEW (Specialized: undergraduates only); THE ORCHARD PRIZE FOR POETRY

UWM Union Box 194, University of Wisconsin-Milwaukee, P.O. Box 413, Milwaukee WI 53201. (414)229-3405. E-mail: furrow@csd.uwm.edu. Established 1999. **Contact:** Emily Hall, poetry editor. Executive Editor: Dustin Williamson.

Magazine Needs *Furrow—The Undergraduate Literary and Art Review* appears 2 times/year. "We simply want to see poetry that does not take for granted any of the prescribed aesthetic functions of a poem. A poem should have a certain felicity of expression and originality but also be sort of dangerous and fun. We want wild associations, pungent images, and layered meanings. For the most part, we are not interested in poetry that reinforces traditional styles or treats the poem as a derivative of storytelling." Has published poetry by Erika Mueller, Sarah Schuetze, Mike Krull, Michael Hauser, Zack Pieper, and Donald V. Kingsbury. *Furrow* is 45-70 pages, digest-sized, perfect-bound, with card stock cover. Receives about 400 poems/year, accepts about 10%. Press run is 400 (25 subscribers, 5 libraries, 300 shelf sales); one distributed free to each contributor. Sample: free.

How to Submit Submit 3-5 poems at a time. Accepts simultaneous submissions; no previously published poems. Accepts e-mail and disk submissions. "Please include SASE and cover letter stating school, year in school, brief bio note (no more than 5 sentences), and contact information (address, phone, e-mail)." Reads submissions year round. Submit seasonal poems 2 months in advance. Time between acceptance and publication is 1-2 months. "Submissions are read by a single editor, acceptances notified upon approval of undergraduate status." Seldom comments on rejected poems. Guidelines available for SASE. Responds in 2 months. Pays one contributor's copy/accepted piece. Acquires one-time rights. Reviews books and chapbooks of poetry and other magazines in 3,000 words maximum, single-book format. Send materials for review consideration to Dustin Williamson.

Advice "We would like to think that our poets at least have the decency to want to change poetry and make it their own."

◎ ⊘ GENERATOR; GENERATOR PRESS (Specialized: visual poetry)

3503 Virginia Ave., Cleveland OH 44109. (216)351-9406. E-mail: generatorpress@sbcglobal.net. Website: www.generatorpress.com. Established 1987. **Contact:** John Byrum, editor.

Magazine Needs *Generator* is an annual magazine "devoted to the presentation of all types of experimental poetry, focusing on language poetry and 'concrete' or visual poetic modes."

Book/Chapbook Needs Generator Press also publishes the Generator Press chapbook series; approximately one new title/year.

How to Submit Currently not accepting unsolicited mss for either the magazine or chapbook publication.

Advice "Keep it simple."

⚑ ⊘ GEORGETOWN REVIEW

Box 227, 400 East College St., Georgetown KY 40324. (502)863-8308. Fax: (502)868-8888. E-mail: gtownreview@georgetowncollege.edu. Established 1993. **Contact:** Steven Carter, editor. Member: CLMP.

Magazine Needs *Georgetown Review*, published annually in May, is a literary journal of poetry, fiction, and creative nonfiction. "We have no specific guidelines concerning form or content of poetry, but are always eager to see poetry that is insightful, rooted in reality, and human. We rarely publish work that is merely sentimental, political, or inspirational." Has published poetry by Denise Duhamel, X.J. Kennedy, William Greenway, Fred Chappell, John Tagliabue, and Frederick Smock. *Georgetown Review* is 192 pages, digest-sized, offset-printed, perfect-bound, with 60-lb. glossy 4-

color cover with art/graphics, includes ads. Receives about 1,000 poems/year, accepts about 50-60. Press run is 1,000. Single copy: $5; subscription: $5. Make checks payable to *Georgetown Review*.
How to Submit Submit 1-10 poems at a time. Lines/poem: open. Accepts simultaneous submissions; no previously published poems. No fax, e-mail, or disk submissions. Cover letter is preferred. "In cover letter, please include short bio and a list of publications. Also, must include SASE for reply." Reads submissions September 1 through March 15. Submit seasonal poems one year in advance. Time between acceptance and publication is 1-2 months. Poems are circulated to an editorial board. "The first reader passes the poem along to the poetry editor, and then a final decision is made by the poetry editor and the head editor." Seldom comments on rejected poems. Guidelines available for SASE, by e-mail, or on website. Responds in 1-3 months. Pays 2 contributor's copies. Acquires first North American serial rights. Reviews books and chapbooks of poetry in 1,000 words, multi-book format.
Contest/Award Offerings Sponsors annual contest. Offers $1,000 prize. Guidelines available for SASE or by e-mail.

☐ GERONIMO REVIEW; MAOMAO PRESS

E-mail: geronimo@sanjeronimofnd.org. Website: www.sanjeronimofnd.org. Established 1998. **Contact:** S. Bass, editor. Secretary: g. bassetti.
Magazine Needs At this time, *geronimo review* appears "24/7 as an electronic zine. Submit whatever strikes your fancy. Literally. Anything. *geronimo review* will publish on its website virtually everything submitted. Overt pornography, hate speech, etc., taken under editorial advisement." Has 2 submission categories—Open (these submissions are graded "mercilessly" by both editors and readers) and Amateur ("graded on an appropriate scale"). Wants "politics and political satire. *Anything* of unusual excellence, especially the short lyric." Has published poetry by Mark C. Peery, dada rambass, zeninubasho, geronimo bassetti, Élan B. Yergmoul, "and innumerable others."
How to Submit Submit 3 poems at a time. Lines/poem: 100 maximum (or the length demanded by the poem). Accepts simultaneous submissions; no previously published poems. Accepts submissions by e-mail only (as Word attachment or pasted into body of message). Reads submissions all year. Time between acceptance and publication is 2 weeks. Guidelines available on website. Responds in 3 weeks—"maybe." Acquires all rights; returns to poet "on request." Send materials for review consideration.
Book/Chapbook Needs & How to Submit MaoMao Press will publish essays on and reviews of poetry in the future. "Not presently accepting book submissions—watch our website."
Also Offers Plans anthology of *geronimo review* material. Also publishing essays on Shakespearean sonnets which address the question of authorship.
Advice "Don't be Susan Wheeler. Be in the tradition of Yeats, Frost, Carroll, Stevens, and be really original and inspire strong reactions."

$☑ THE GETTYSBURG REVIEW

Gettysburg College, Gettysburg PA 17325. (717)337-6770. Fax: (717)337-6775. E-mail: mdrew@gettysburg.edu. Website: www.gettysburgreview.com. Established 1988. **Contact:** Peter Stitt, editor. Assistant Editor: Mark Drew.
  ● Work appearing in *The Gettysburg Review* has been frequently included in *The Best American Poetry* and *Pushcart Prize* anthologies. As for the editor, Peter Stitt won the first PEN/Nora Magid Award for Editorial Excellence.
Magazine Needs *The Gettysburg Review* is a multidisciplinary literary quarterly considering "well-written poems of all kinds." Has published poetry by Rita Dove, Beckian Fritz Goldberg, Charles Wright, Michelle Boisseau, Mark Doty, and Charles Simic. Accepts 1-2% of submissions received. Press run is 4,500 (2,700 subscriptions). Subscription: $24/year. Sample: $7.
How to Submit Submit 3-5 poems at a time, with SASE. No previously published poems; simultaneous submissions OK. Cover letter is preferred. Reads submissions September through May only. Occasionally publishes theme issues. Response times can be slow during heavy submission periods,

especially in the late fall. Pays $2.50/line, one-year subscription, and one contributor's copy. Essay-reviews are featured in most issues. Send materials for review consideration.

⌂ THE GIHON RIVER REVIEW

Johnson State College, 337 College Hill, Johnson VT 05656. Established 2001. **Contact:** Poetry Editor for submissions; Editor-in-Chief for inquiries (editors are students; contact names change on a yearly basis).

Magazine Needs *The Gihon River Review* is a biannual review of poetry, fiction, and creative nonfiction with a small compliment of art, usually photographs. Has published poetry by Stuart Friebert, Mark Borax, John David Christensen, Julia Shipley, Thomas Dorsett, and William Doreski. *The Gihon River Review* is 80 pages, digest-sized, offset-printed, perfect-bound, with 2-color cover on glossy coverstock. Receives about 1,000 poems/year, accepts about 3%. Press run is 650 (10 subscribers, 2 libraries); 400 are distributed free to US colleges and universities with writing programs. Single copy: $5; subscription: $8 (2 issues). Make checks payable to *The Gihon River Review*.

How to Submit Submit 5 poems at a time. No previously published poems or simultaneous submissions. No disk submissions. Cover letter is required (*"brief* cover letter, with SASE"). Reads submissions all year except summer months; submissions received in late spring are read in fall. Time between acceptance and publication is one month. "All *GRR* staff read poetry. Editorial process is a group effort." Never comments on rejected poems. Occasionally publishes theme issues. List of upcoming themes available for SASE. Guidelines available in magazine. Pays 2 contributor's copies plus one year's subscription (2 issues). Acquires one-time rights.

⌂ GIN BENDER POETRY REVIEW

P.O. Box 150932, Lufkin TX 75915. E-mail: ginbender@yahoo.com (inquiries); submissions@ginbender.com (submissions). Website: www.ginbender.com. Established 2002. **Contact:** T.A. Thompson, founder/chief editor.

Magazine Needs *Gin Bender Poetry Review* is a literary webzine appearing 3 times/year, featuring both experienced and new writers. Wants poetry "from traditional to experimental." Does not want greeting card verse, explicit language ("shock word poetry"), or avant-garde. Has published poetry by Ron Rash, Barry Ballard, Susan H. Case, Robert Wynne, and Janet Buck. *Gin Bender Poetry Review* is published online only. Receives about 400 poems/year, accepts about 10%. Sample: free online.

How to Submit Submit 3-5 poems at a time. No previously published poems or simultaneous submissions. Accepts e-mail submissions; no fax or disk submissions. "We prefer e-mail submissions but also accept snail mail submissions with SASE." Cover letter is preferred. Reads submissions year round. Time between acceptance and publication is 4 months. "Submissions are read by a rotating editorial staff of three." Seldom comments on rejected poems. Guidelines available on website. Responds in up to 6 weeks. Acquires first rights.

Advice "We search for writers who practice their craft. Study the old masters and the new contemporary styles; then read an issue of our magazine before submitting to us."

⊕ $⌂ GINNINDERRA PRESS

P.O. Box 53, Charnwood ACT 2615 Australia. E-mail: smgp@cyberone.com.au. Website: www.ginninderrapress.com.au. Established 1996. **Contact:** Stephen Matthews, publisher.

Book/Chapbook Needs Ginninderra Press works "to give publishing opportunities to new writers." Has published poetry by Alan Gould and Geoff Page. Books are usually up to 72 pages, A5, laser-printed, saddle-stapled or thermal-bound, with board covers.

How to Submit Query first, with a few sample poems and cover letter with brief bio and publication credits. Accepts previously published poems; no simultaneous submissions. No fax or e-mail submissions. Time between acceptance and publication is 2 months. Seldom comments on rejected poems. Responds to queries in one week; to mss in 2 months. Pays royalties of 12.5%.

◪ GOOD FOOT

P.O. Box 681, Murray Hill Station, New York NY 10156. E-mail: info@goodfootmagazine.com. Website: www.goodfootmagazine.com. Established 2000. **Contact:** Amanda Lea Johnson, Katherine Sarkis, and Carmine Simmons, editors.

Magazine Needs *Good Foot* appears biannually and "seeks vibrant, active poetry that is compelling and utterly readable. We invite a wide cross-section of work without restriction in form, style, or subject." Has published poetry by Ander Monson, Matthea Harvey, David Trinidad, Anne Fox, Tony Tost, and Margie Shaheed. *Good Foot* is about 120 pages, 7 × 8.5, professionally offset-printed, perfect-bound, with color matte card cover, includes ads. Receives about 1,200 poems/year, accepts about 8%. Press run is 1,000. Single copy: $8; subscription: $14. Make checks payable to *Good Foot Magazine*.

How to Submit Submit *no more than* 3 poems at a time. Accepts simultaneous submissions ("with timely notice of acceptance elsewhere"); *absolutely* no previously published poems. No e-mail submissions. "Name and contact information should appear on every sheet of paper you submit. Include brief bio in cover letter. Include SASE. Submissions that do not follow these simple guidelines will not be considered." Reads submissions February 1 through October 31. Submissions received during November, December, and January will be returned unread. Time between acceptance and publication "averages" 6 months. "All submissions are read by all 3 editors." Seldom comments on rejected poems. Responds in up to 6 months. Pays one contributor's copy. Acquires first North American serial rights.

◪ ◫ ◎ GOOSE LANE EDITIONS (Specialized: regional/Canada)

469 King St., Fredericton NB E3B 1E5 Canada. (506)450-4251. Fax: (506)459-4991. Website: www.gooselane.com. Established 1954. **Contact:** Ross Leckie, poetry editor. Editorial Director: Laurel Boone.

Book/Chapbook Needs Goose Lane is a small literary press publishing Canadian fiction, poetry, and nonfiction. Writers should be advised that Goose Lane considers mss by Canadian poets only. Receives about 400 mss/year, publishes 10-15 books/year, 4 of which are poetry collections. Has published *The Drunken Lovely Bird* by Sue Sinclair and *The Pallikari of Nesmine Rifat* by David Solway.

How to Submit "Call to inquire whether we are reading submissions." Accepts submissions by postal mail only. Guidelines available for SASE or on website. Always sends prepublication galleys. Authors may receive royalties of up to 10% of retail price on all copies sold. Copies available to author at 40% discount.

Advice "Many of the poems in a manuscript accepted for publication will have been previously published in literary journals such as *The Fiddlehead*, *The Dalhousie Review*, *The Malahat Review*, and the like."

◪ $◫ GRAIN; SHORT GRAIN CONTEST

P.O. Box 67, Saskatoon SK S7K 3K1 Canada. (306)244-2828. Fax: (306)244-0255. E-mail: grainmag @sasktel.net. Website: www.grainmagazine.ca. Established 1973. **Contact:** Gerry Hill, poetry editor. Editor: Kent Bruyneel.

• *Grain* was voted Saskatchewan Magazine of the Year, Western Magazine Awards 2001.

Magazine Needs "*Grain*, a literary quarterly, strives for artistic excellence and seeks poetry that is well-crafted, imaginatively stimulating, distinctly original." Has published poetry by Lorna Crozier, Don Domanski, Cornelia Haeussler, Partrick Lane, Karen Solie, and Monty Reid. *Grain* is 128-144 pages, digest-sized, professionally printed. Press run is 1,800 (1,600 subscribers, 100 libraries). Receives about 1,200 submissions of poetry/year, accepts 80-140 poems. Subscription: $29.95/year, $46/2 years. Sample: $13. (See website for US and foreign postage fees.)

How to Submit Submit up to 8 poems, typed single-spaced on 8½ × 11 paper, one side only. No previously published poems or simultaneous submissions. Accepts submissions by postal mail only; no e-mail submissions. Cover letter is required. "Indicate the number of poems submitted, and include your address (with postal or zip code), phone number, and SASE (or SAE and IRC) or e-mail address for response (if you do not need your submission returned, provide an e-mail address and we will respond electronically and recycle your manuscript)." Reads submissions September through May only. "Manuscripts postmarked and/or received between June 1 and September 1 will be automatically returned to writers, unread." Guidelines available in magazine, for SASE (or SAE and IRC), by fax, by e-mail, or on website. Responds in up to 4 months. Pays $40/page—up to 5 pages or a maximum of $175—and 2 contributor's copies. Acquires first Canadian serial rights only. Copyright remains with the author.

Contest/Award Offerings The annual Short Grain Contest, which includes 3 categories: Prose Poems (a lyric poem written as a prose paragraph, or paragraphs, in 500 words or less); Dramatic Monologues (500 words or less); Postcard Stories (narrative fiction, 500 words or less). Four $500 prizes in each category. **Entry fee:** $28 for 2 entries in the same category (includes a one-year subscription); $8 for up to 3 additional entries. "U.S. and international entrants, pay in U.S. funds and add $6 postage." See website for current guidelines.

Advice "Only work of the highest literary quality is accepted. Read several back issues."

⊡ ☐ GRASSLANDS REVIEW

P.O. Box 626, Berea OH 44017. E-mail: GrasslandsReview@aol.com. Website: www.grasslandsreview.blogspot.com. Established 1989. **Contact:** Laura B. Kennelly, editor.

Magazine Needs *Grasslands Review* is a biannual magazine "to encourage beginning writers and to give adult creative writing students experience in editing fiction and poetry; using any type of poetry; shorter poems stand best chance." Has published poetry by Carol Graser, Marlene Tilton, Don Shockey, Barry Brummett, J.E. McCarthy, and Jennifer Comoll. *Grasslands Review* is 30-50 pages, digest-sized, professionally printed, photocopied, saddle-stapled, with card cover. Accepts 30-50 of 600 submissions received. Press run is 200. Subscription (2 issues): $10 for individuals, $20 for institutions. Sample: $5 for older issues, $6 for more recent.

How to Submit Submit only during October and March, no more than 5 poems at a time. No previously published poems or simultaneous submissions. No e-mail submissions. Short cover letter is preferred. Send #10 SASE for response. Sometimes comments on submissions. Responds in 4 months. Sometimes sends prepublication galleys. Pays one contributor's copy.

⊘ GRAYWOLF PRESS

2402 University Ave., Suite 203, Saint Paul MN 55114. E-mail: wolves@graywolfpress.org (for book catalog requests only). Website: www.graywolfpress.org. Established 1974. **Contact:** Editorial Department.

• Poetry published by Graywolf Press has been included in the *Pushcart Prize* anthology.

Book/Chapbook Needs Graywolf Press does not read unsolicited mss. Considers *only* mss by poets widely published in journals of merit. Has published poetry by Jane Kenyon, David Rivard, Vijay Seshadri, John Haines, Eamon Grennan, Tess Gallagher, Tony Hoagland, William Stafford, Linda Gregg, Carl Phillips, and Dana Gioia. Sometimes sends prepublication galleys. No e-mail submissions or queries.

⊘ GREEN HILLS LITERARY LANTERN

Truman State University, Division of Language & Literature, Kirksville MO 63501. (660)785-4513. E-mail: jbeneven@truman.edu. Website: http://ll.truman.edu/ghllweb/. **Contact:** Joe Benevento, poetry editor.

Magazine Needs *Green Hills Literary Lantern*, an annual journal of Truman State University appearing in summer or early fall, is open to short fiction and poetry of "exceptional quality." Wants "the best poetry, in any style, preferably understandable. There are no restrictions on subject matter, though pornography and gratuitous violence will not be accepted. Obscurity for its own sake is also frowned upon. Both free and formal verse forms are fine, though we publish more free verse overall. No haiku, limericks, or anything over 2 pages." Has published poetry by Jim Thomas,

Phillip Dacey, Susan Terris, Louis Philips, Francine Tolf, and Julie Lechevsky. *Green Hills Literary Lantern* is 200-300 pages, digest-sized, professionally printed, perfect-bound, with glossy 4-color cover. Accepts less than 10% of all poetry received. Press run is 500. Sample: $7.

How to Submit Submit 3-7 poems at a time, typed, one poem/page. Accepts simultaneous submissions, but not preferred; no previously published poems. No fax or e-mail submissions. Cover letter with list of publication credits is preferred. Often comments on rejected poems. Guidelines available for SASE or by e-mail. Responds within 4 months. Always sends prepublication galleys. Pays 2 contributor's copies. Acquires one-time rights.

Advice "Read the best poetry and be willing to learn from what you encounter. A genuine attempt is made to publish the best poems available, no matter who the writer. First-time poets, well-established poets, and those in between, all can and have found a place in the *Green Hills Literary Lantern*. We try to supply feedback, particularly to those we seek to encourage."

⭐ ☑ GREEN MOUNTAINS REVIEW

Johnson State College, Johnson VT 05656. (802)635-1350. Fax: (802)635-1210. E-mail: gmr@jsc.vsc .edu. Website: http://greenmountainsreview.jsc.vsc.edu. Established 1975. **Contact:** Neil Shepard, poetry editor.

- Poetry published in *Green Mountains Review* has been included in *The Best American Poetry* and *Pushcart Prize* anthologies.

Magazine Needs *Green Mountains Review* appears twice/year and includes poetry (and other writing) by well-known authors and promising newcomers. Has published poetry by Carol Frost, Sharon Olds, Carl Phillips, David St. John, and David Wojahn. *Green Mountains Review* is 150-200 pages, digest-sized, flat-spined. Of 3,000 submissions they publish 30 authors. Press run is 1,800 (200 subscribers, 30 libraries). Subscription: $15/year. Sample back issue: $7, current issue $9.50.

How to Submit Submit no more than 5 poems at a time. Accepts simultaneous submissions. Reads submissions September 1 through March 1 only. Editor sometimes comments rejected poems. Publishes theme issues. Guidelines and upcoming themes available for SASE. Responds in up to 6 months. Pays 2 contributor's copies plus one-year subscription. Acquires first North American serial rights. Send materials for review consideration.

⭐ ☑ GREENHOUSE REVIEW PRESS

3965 Bonny Doon Rd., Santa Cruz CA 95060. Established 1975. Publishes a series of poetry chapbooks and broadsides. "Unsolicited manuscripts are not accepted."

☑ THE GREENSBORO REVIEW; GREENSBORO REVIEW LITERARY AWARDS

English Dept., Room 134, McIver Bldg., University of North Carolina at Greensboro, P.O. Box 26170, Greensboro NC 27402. (336)334-5459. E-mail: jlclark@uncg.edu. Website: www.greensbororeview .com. Established 1966. **Contact:** Poetry Editor. Editor: Jim Clark.

- Work published in this review has been consistently anthologized or cited in *Best American Short Stories, New Stories from the South, Pushcart Prize,* and *Prize Stories: The O. Henry Award.*

Magazine Needs *The Greensboro Review* appears twice/year and showcases well-made verse in all styles and forms, though shorter poems (under 50 lines) are preferred. Has published poetry by Stephen Dobyns, Thomas Lux, Stanley Plumly, Alan Shapiro, and Steve Orlen. *The Greensboro Review* is 128 pages, digest-sized, professionally printed, flat-spined, with colored matte cover. Subscription: $10/year, $25/3 years. Sample: $5.

How to Submit "Submissions (no more than 5 poems) must arrive by September 15 to be considered for the Spring issue (acceptances in December), or February 15 to be considered for the Fall issue (acceptances in May). Manuscripts arriving after those dates will be held for consideration for the next issue." No previously published poems or simultaneous submissions. No fax or e-mail submissions. Cover letter is not required but helpful; include number of poems submitted. Guidelines available in magazine, for SASE, or on website. Responds in 4 months. Always sends prepublication galleys. Pays 3 contributor's copies. Acquires first North American serial rights.

Contest/Award Offerings Sponsors an open competition for *The Greensboro Review* Literary Awards, $500 for both poetry and fiction each year. **Deadline:** September 15. Guidelines available in magazine, for SASE, or on website.

Advice "We want to see the best being written regardless of theme, subject, or style."

✪ $⬛ GULF COAST: A JOURNAL OF LITERATURE AND FINE ART

Dept. of English, University of Houston, Houston TX 77204-3012. (713)743-3223. Website: www.gulfcoast.uh.edu. Established 1986. **Contact:** Barbara Duffey, Melanie Jordan, and Brad Telford, poetry editors. Managing Editor: Sasha West. Associate Editor: David Ray Vance.

Magazine Needs *Gulf Coast* is published twice/year in October and April. While the journal features work by a number of established poets, editors are also interested in "providing a forum for new and emerging writers who are producing well-crafted work that takes risks." Each issue includes poetry, fiction, essays, interviews, and color reproductions of work by artists from across the nation. Has published poetry by Anne Carson, Terrance Hayes, Srikanth Reddy, Karen Volkman, Susan Wheeler, and Dean Young. *Gulf Coast* is 230 pages, 7×9, offset-printed, perfect-bound. Single copy: $8; subscription: $14/year, $26/2 years. Sample: $7.

How to Submit Submit up to 4 poems at a time. Accepts simultaneous submissions with notification; no previously published poems. Cover letter with previous publications, "if any," and a brief bio required. Does not read submissions June through August. Guidelines available for SASE or on website. Responds in 6 months. Pays $50/poem and 2 contributor's copies. Returns all rights (except electronic) upon publication.

Contest/Award Offerings Sponsors an annual poetry contest, awarding $1,000 and publication. **Entry fee:** $15 (includes one-year subscription). Make checks payable to *Gulf Coast*. Guidelines available on website.

⬛ GULF STREAM MAGAZINE

English Dept., Florida International University, 3000 NE 151 St., North Miami Campus, North Miami FL 33181. (305)919-5599. E-mail: Gulfstrm@fiu.edu (inquiries only). Website: w3.fiu.edu/gulfstrm. Established 1989. **Contact:** John Dufresne, editor. Associate Editor: Diane Mooney.

Magazine Needs *Gulf Stream* is the biannual literary magazine associated with the creative writing program at FIU. Wants "poetry of any style and subject matter as long as it is of high literary quality." Has published poetry by Gerald Costanzo, Naomi Shihab Nye, Jill Bialosky, and Catherine Bowman. *Gulf Stream* is 96 pages, digest-sized, flat-spined, printed on quality stock, with matte card cover. Accepts less than 10% of poetry received. Press run is 1,000. Subscription: $15. Sample: $5.

How to Submit Submit no more than 5 poems at a time. Accepts simultaneous submissions with notification. "Poets wishing to submit electronically must see website for details. We no longer accept submissions to the above e-mail address." Cover letter is required. Reads submissions September 15 through February 1 only. Publishes theme issues. Guidelines available in magazine or on website. Responds in 3 months. Pays 2 contributor's copies and 2 subscriptions. Acquires first North American serial rights.

✪ $◎ HA!, a humor magazine; WRITERS' HAVEN PRESS

P.O. Box 368, Seabeck WA 98380. (360)830-5772. Fax: (360)830-5772. E-mail: svend@sinclair.net. Established 2002. **Contact:** Sharon Svendsen, poetry editor. Member: SPAN.

Magazine Needs *HA!* is published quarterly. Wants humorous poetry, prose, art, and cartoons. Does not want poetry book mss. Has published poetry by John Engle, Maureen Cannon, Ellen

Sandra Alcosser

Dialogue between poetry and activism

One might say Sandra Alcosser leads the ideal poetic life: She travels the world teaching, writing, and researching poetry—and she gets paid for it. But as much as we would like to imagine a poetic life fed by a wellspring of inspiration alone, and travel guided purely by artistic whimsy, the reality is that Alcosser's work has always been grounded, quite literally, in social and environmental activism. It's these interests that move her from state to state and across the globe. The author of *Except by Nature* (Graywolf Press, winner of the 1998 James Laughlin Award of The Academy of American Poets), Alcosser says, "The world presses upon us—the act of making poems is one part of the epistemological process; the act of being in the world is quite another. Both require energy and vision, but how beautifully they twine and feed each other."

In a time when the "political poem" is blacklisted, and activism in writing is often left to the editorial page, the relationship between poetics and politics might seem dubious at best. How does "argument" live in the lines of a poem? Alcosser says, "Activism is a dialogue we have with our lives, throughout our lives, and it changes as our lives change. One critical question remains in the foreground: As poets, as members of a community, how do we extend our boundaries to include the world in our practice?"

It seems that without even trying, Alcosser keeps her boundaries "extended" in her daily life. For years she has made a habit of going back and forth between her cabin in Montana, where bear and elk roam through her yard, and San Diego, where she's the director of the MFA program in creative writing (a program she founded) at San Diego State University, and where she sleeps beside the ocean, "a 20-billion-year-unconscious." What's more, there is a unique project that shows Alcosser upholding a relationship with the environment to which she committed many years ago.

Alcosser was recently the Poet-in-Residence at the Central Park Zoo in New York City, through a program sponsored by Poets House in partnership with the Wildlife Conservation Society. Though Alcosser's zoo residency inspired many humorous questions and concerns (Would she be an exhibit? Would she live in a cage?), the project was a serious undertaking. For six months Alcosser had the opportunity to work with Dr. Dan Wharton, director of the Central Park Zoo and of the Species Protection Plan for western lowland gorillas and snow leopards.

Alcosser's goal was to help create permanent installations of poetry throughout the zoo. "The poems, spanning cultures and centuries, were selected to inspire visitors to imagine a sustainable future for all life on earth." The poems draw the human experience into the zoo's exhibits, and remind visitors that their lives, and the lives of the animals, are not as distinct as they might seem.

"It actually isn't as much about animals as it is about habitat," Alcosser says. For her, the work meant "spending six months working with a wildlife biologist braiding conservation philosophy and poetry.

"I've worked on wildlife rehabilitation in the past, but this seems like an even greater privilege," she continues, "to be asked to research habitats across centuries and civilizations, to discover what has been honored, to celebrate what is sacred between species." Although the classic ideas of poetry and science seem to place them in different corners of the intellectual sphere, for Alcosser the combination makes perfect sense. "Science and poetry inform the mystery of being. Both praise the complexity of life."

Mare Frigoris

*Coming home late spring night, stars a foreign
Language above me, I thought I would know*

*The moons like family, their dark plains—sea of
Crises, sea of nectar, serpent sea.*

*How quickly a century passes,
Minerals crystallize at different speeds,*

*Limestone dissolves, rivers sneak through its absence.
This morning I learned painted turtles*

*Sleeping inches below the streambank
Freeze and do not die. Fifteen degrees*

*Mare Frigoris, sea of cold, second
Quadrant of the moon's face. I slide toward*

*The cabin, arms full of brown bags, one light
Syrups over drifts of snow. Night rubs*

*Icy skin against me and I warm
Small delicates—cilantro, primrose—*

*Close to the body. A hundred million
Impulses race three hundred miles an hour*

*Through seventeen square feet of skin and
Gravity that collapses stars, lifts earth's*

*Watery dress from her body, touches me
With such tenderness I hardly breathe.*

(© Sandra Alcosser, used with permission)

For the most part, Alcosser's time with the project was spent sifting through the 45,000-book sanctuary at Poets House, and in the New York Public Library researching poets and poems to include. "I wanted each of the poets to have some engagement with the physical world—not just to have written about what they saw around them," she says. "Most of the poets included in the installation have written in service to the natural world, poets like

Birago Diop of Senegal, who, in addition to being an ambassador to Tunisia and an oral archivist for the folktales of the Wolof people, was a veterinary surgeon. Or Judith Wright, an outspoken supporter of Aboriginal rights and environmental integrity, and who was considered for the Nobel Prize.''

Though the sheer amount of research and reading was a challenge, the selection of the poets and poems offered its own hurdles. Since most of the installations included only a portion of a poem, often the lines meant something entirely different when removed from the context of that poem.

For example, there were lines from Lorine Niedecker that read ''throw things / to the flood.'' Alcosser says, ''In the poem it was easy to see Niedecker meant to get rid of things. But there was a little water system running through the zoo, and we quickly realized how easily it would seem that people should toss their garbage, etc., into the waterway! And it had to be changed.''

With the poems permanently installed, visitors see Marianne Moore's lines on the front faces of stairs (a line per stair), Gertrude Stein on a park bench, and Kayobashi Issa in the rainforest. They see poems winding along the banister of one of the bird exhibits, at the foot-level border of a garden, and even on a plaque facing the city. The pieces are intended to unite the human and animal worlds through the medium of poetry, and to encourage a communion with the habitat everyone shares.

The success of this project, and the attention it has attracted, have been exciting. While in residence, Alcosser received a considerable amount of unsolicited interest from editors and publishers, including an invitation from Graywolf Press to work on a book about her collaboration. So, how do things like this appear in the mail or seem to fall into her lap? According to Alcosser, it's the result of a career and a life both focused on the same interests and passions. For her, the Central Park residency was the perfect intersection of writing, wilderness, and social activism. She says, ''Experience in the public world taught me it might be possible to braid pragmatism with aesthetics, activism with poetry.''

For years, Alcosser has traveled as an environmental advocate, reading poems and giving talks on writing and natural history. She teaches each summer at National University of Ireland in Galway and has had environmental residencies at Glacier National Park, Yosemite National Park, University of Minnesota, St. Lawrence University, Canyonlands Field Institute, the Orion Society, and the Sierra Club. On a more grassroots level, she ran poetry workshops and gardens in New York with methadone-to-abstinence patients; directed a program called Poets in the Park, which used Central Park as a classroom; and was a poet in the schools in Montana, where she traveled 50,000 miles to ranches, small communities, and American Indian reservations.

These commitments to poetry and activism speak of a life unified by purpose and drive. As with so many other things (good poetry included), it's the emotional attachment we make that answers the question *Is it good?* Alcosser was asked to include one of her own poems in the Central Park Zoo's installation, and she chose ''What Makes the Grizzlies Dance,'' which ends, ''Have you never wanted / to spin like that / on hairy, leathered feet, / amid swelling berries / as you tasted a language / of early summer—shaping / lazy operatic vowels, / cracking hard-shelled / consonants like speckled / insects between your teeth, / have you never wanted / to waltz the hills / like a beast?''

With lines like these, Alcosser encourages us as readers to identify ourselves with a grizzly bear—something we might not ever have reason to intimately consider. Perhaps it isn't the ''argument'' in the poem, after all, that makes the writing speak of politics or activism. Perhaps it's the attachment we can make to the poem, and to the life of the poet writing it, driven by power, conviction, and most of all, love.

—*Amy Ratto*

Amy Ratto's poems have been widely published, and she's the author of a prize-winning chapbook, *Bread and Water Body*. She received her MFA and MA from the University of Montana and is the former editor-in-chief of *CutBank*. She lives in Missoula, Montana, with her husband and daughter.

Elizabeth, Amy Jo Schoonover, Catherine A. Callaghan, and J. A. Vaneck. *HA!* is 50-60 pages, magazine-sized, saddle-stapled, with 90-lb. colored paper cover with cartoon, includes ads. Receives about 400 poems/year, accepts about 25%. Press run is 225 (13 subscribers). Single copy: $5; subscription: $18/year. Make checks payable to Writers' Haven Press.

How to Submit Submit 5-10 poems at a time. Lines/poem: 2-100. Accepts previously published poems. No fax, e-mail, or disk submissions. Cover letter is preferred. "Include SASE and bio." Reads submissions year round. Submit seasonal poems 6 months in advance. Time between acceptance and publication is 3 months. Sometimes comments on rejected poems. Sometimes publishes theme issues. List of upcoming themes and guidelines available for SASE or by e-mail. Responds in 4 months. Pays $5 and one contributor's copy. Acquires first North American serial, one-time, and reprint rights.

Book/Chapbook Needs & How to Submit Writers' Haven Press publishes one poetry book/year and 6 anthologies/year. Books and anthologies are 50+ pages, digital- or offset-printed, perfect-bound, with laminated paper covers with b&w art/graphics. Query first, with a few sample poems and a cover letter with brief bio and publication credits. Book mss may include previously published poems. "Books are usually by invitation. Poets should have some publication history; not necessarily a book." Responds to queries in 1-2 months; to mss in 4 months. Pays royalties of 10-15% (after publication costs are met) and 50 author's copies (out of a press run of 1,000). Order sample books and anthologies by contacting Writers' Haven Press.

Contest/Award Offerings Writers' Haven Press sponsors a contest every 2 months. Offers 1st Prize: $150; 2nd Prize: $100; 3rd Prize: $50; plus publication in a chapbook anthology of top 3 winners and 10 Honorable Mentions. "There are 6 contests per year, and each contest is different." **Entry fee:** $3/poem. **Deadline:** January 31; March 30; May 31; July 31; September 30; and November 30. Guidelines available for SASE or by e-mail.

Also Offers Writers' Haven Reading Series, monthly in Paulsbo, WA.

Advice "Avoid dirty jokes. No pornography. Keep political humor on the light side."

HAIGHT ASHBURY LITERARY JOURNAL

558 Joost Ave., San Francisco CA 94127. (415)584-8264. E-mail: indigo@haightashbury.zzn.com. Established 1979-1980. **Contact:** Indigo Hotchkiss, Alice Rogoff, and Conyus, editors.

Magazine Needs *Haight Ashbury* is a newsprint tabloid that appears 1-3 times/year. Uses "all forms. Subject matter sometimes political, but open to all subjects. Poems of background—prison, minority experience—often published, as well as poems of protest. Few rhymes." Has published poetry by Dan O'Connell, Diane Frank, Dancing Bear, Lee Herrick, Al Young, and Laura Beausoleil. *Haight Ashbury Literary Journal* is 16 pages with graphics and ads. Press run is 2,500. Subscription: $12/4 issues; $35 for a lifetime subscription, which includes 3 back issues. Sample: $3.

How to Submit Submit up to 6 poems. Accepts submissions by postal mail only. "Please type one poem to a page, put name and address on every page, and include SASE. No bios." Each issue changes its theme and emphasis. Guidelines and upcoming themes available for SASE. Responds in 4 months. Pays 3 contributor's copies, small amount to featured writers. Rights revert to author. An anthology of past issues, *This Far Together*, is available for $15.

Advice "Do not send work that is longer than our magazine!"

$ ☐ ◎ HAIKU HEADLINES: A MONTHLY NEWSLETTER OF HAIKU AND SENRYU (Specialized: haiku and senryu; membership/subscription)

1347 W. 71st St., Los Angeles CA 90044-2505. (323)971-3225. Established 1988. **Contact:** Rengé/ David Priebe, editor/publisher.

Magazine Needs *Haiku Headlines* is "America's oldest monthly publication dedicated to the genres of haiku and senryu *only*." Prefers the 5/7/5 syllabic discipline, but accepts irregular haiku and senryu that display pivotal imagery and contrast. Has published haiku by Dorothy McLaughlin, Emily Romano, Dion O'Donnol, Robert H. Deluty, and Ross Figgins. *Haiku Headlines* is 8 pages, $8^1/_2 \times 11$, corner-stapled, punched for a 3-ring binder. "Each issue has a different color graphic

front page. The back page showcases a Featured Haiku Poet with a photo-portrait, biography, philosophy, and 6 of the poet's own favorite haiku.'' *Haiku Headlines* has 175 subscribers. Single copy: $2 US, $2.25 Canada, $2.50 overseas; subscription: $24 US, $27 Canada, $30 overseas.
How to Submit Haiku/senryu may be submitted with 9 maximum/single page. **Unpublished submissions from subscribers will be considered first.** Nonsubscriber submissions will be accepted only if space permits and SASE is included. Guidelines available in magazine or for SASE. Responds in 2 months. Pays "$1 for haiku/senryu poems and 50¢ for 'haikuisms' to subscribers, deductible from subscription renewal fee.'' Nonsubscribers are encouraged to prepay for issues containing their work.
Contest/Award Offerings Monthly Readers' Choice Awards of $25, $15, and $10 are shared by the "Top Three Favorites.'' The "First Timer'' with the most votes receives an Award of Special Recognition ($5).

▦ ▣ ◎ HANDSHAKE; THE EIGHT HAND GANG (Specialized: science fiction; fantasy; horror)

5 Cross Farm, Station Rd. N., Fearnhead, Warrington, Cheshire WA2 0QG United Kingdom. Established 1992. **Contact:** J.F. Haines.
Magazine Needs *Handshake*, published irregularly, "is a newsletter for science fiction poets.'' Wants "science fiction/fantasy poetry of all styles. Prefer short poems.'' Does not want "epics or foul language.'' Has published poetry by Cardinal Cox, Neil K. Henderson, K.V. Bailey, John Light, and Joanne Tolson. *Handshake* is one sheet of A4 paper, photocopied, includes ads. "It has evolved into being one side of news and information and one side of poetry.'' Receives about 50 poems/year, accepts up to 50%. Press run is 60 (30 subscribers, 5 libraries). Subscription: SAE with IRC. Sample: SAE with IRC.
How to Submit Submit 2-3 poems, typed and camera-ready. No previously published poems or simultaneous submissions. Cover letter is preferred. Time between acceptance and publication varies. Editor selects "whatever takes my fancy and is of suitable length.'' Seldom comments on rejected poems. Publishes theme issues. Responds ASAP. Pays one contributor's copy. Acquires first rights. Staff reviews books or chapbooks of poetry or other magazines of very short length. Send materials for review consideration.
Also Offers *Handshake* is also the newsletter for The Eight Hand Gang, an organization for British science fiction poets, established in 1991. They currently have 60 members. Information about the organization can be found in the newsletter.

$▣ HANGING LOOSE PRESS; HANGING LOOSE

231 Wyckoff St., Brooklyn NY 11217. Website: www.hangingloosepress.com. Established 1966. **Contact:** Robert Hershon, Dick Lourie, and Mark Pawlak, poetry editors.
Magazine Needs *Hanging Loose* appears in April and October and "concentrates on the work of new writers. One section contains poems by high-school-age poets.'' Has published poetry by Sherman Alexie, Paul Violi, Donna Brook, Kimiko Hahn, Ron Overton, and Ha Jin. *Hanging Loose* is 120 pages, offset-printed on heavy stock, flat-spined, with 4-color glossy card cover. Sample: $9.
How to Submit Submit 4-6 "excellent, energetic'' poems. No simultaneous submissions. "Would-be contributors should read the magazine first.'' Responds in 3 months. Pays small fee and 2 contributor's copies.
Book/Chapbook Needs & How to Submit Hanging Loose Press does not accept unsolicited book mss or artwork.
Advice "*Read* the magazine first.''

▢ ◎ HARD ROW TO HOE; POTATO EYES FOUNDATION (Specialized: rural; Native American; environmental)

P.O. Box 541-I, Healdsburg CA 95448. (707)433-9786. **Contact:** Joe E. Armstrong, editor.
Magazine Needs *Hard Row to Hoe*, taken over from Seven Buffaloes Press in 1987, appears 3 times/year as a "book review newsletter of literature from rural America, with a section reserved for

short stories and poetry featuring unpublished authors. The subject matter must apply to rural America, including nature and environmental subjects. No style limits." Does not want "any subject matter not related to rural subjects." Has published poetry by Valory Mitchell, Sandra Lee Stillwell, Dudley Laufman, Greg Tuleja, and John Grey. *Hard Row to Hoe* is 12 pages, magazine-sized, side-stapled. Press run is 300. Subscription: $8/year. Sample: $3.

How to Submit Submit 3-4 poems at a time. "Poems of 40 lines or less given preference, but no arbitrary limit." Accepts previously published poems only if published in local or university papers; no simultaneous submissions. Time between acceptance and publication is "typically" 8-10 months. Guidelines available for SASE. Editor comments on rejected poems "if I think the quality warrants." Pays 2 contributor's copies. Acquires one-time rights. Reviews books of poetry in 600-700 words. Send materials for review consideration.

HARP-STRINGS POETRY JOURNAL; EDNA ST. VINCENT MILLAY "BALLAD OF THE HARP WEAVER" AWARD; VERDURE PUBLICATIONS

P.O. Box 640387, Beverly Hills FL 34464-0387. Fax: (352)746-7817. E-mail: verdure@tampabay.rr.com. Website: www.poetsforum-harpstrings.com. Established 1989. **Contact:** Madelyn Eastlund, editor.

Magazine Needs *Harp-Strings* appears quarterly. Wants "narratives, lyrics, prose poems, haibun, ballads, sestinas, and other traditional forms. Nothing 'dashed off' or trite; no broken prose masquerading as poetry." Has published poetry by Ruth Harrison, Daniel Blackston, Jennifer Pearson, Robert Cooperman, and Barry Ballard. *Harp-Strings* is 16-20 pages, digest-sized, saddle-stapled, professionally printed on quality colored matte stock, with matte card cover. Accepts about 1% of poems received. Press run is 200 (105 subscribers). Subscription: $12. Sample: $3.50.

How to Submit Submit 3-5 poems at a time. Lines/poem: 14 minimum, 80 maximum ("more often find 40- to 60-line poems have best chance"). Accepts previously published poems **by invitation only**. No simultaneous submissions. Accepts e-mail submissions (pasted into body of message or as Word attachment only); no fax or disk submissions. Cover letter is "not necessary, but if enclosed should contain information on poet or poems. *Harp-Strings* does use brief contributor notes. Always include a SASE—lately poets seem to forget." Reads submissions only in February, May, August, and November. Responds at the end of each reading period. Accepted poems will appear in the next issue being planned following each reading period. Seldom comments on rejected poems. "A poem might not be right for us, but right for another publication. Rejection does not necessarily imply poem needs revisions." Pays one contributor's copy. Acquires one-time rights.

Contest/Award Offerings Sponsors the annual Edna St. Vincent Millay "Ballad of the Harp Weaver" Award ($50 and publication for a narrative poem, 40-100 lines). **Entry fee:** $5 for 1-3 poems. Make checks payable to Madelyn Eastlund. **Deadline:** July 15. "We may also sponsor a special contest during each quarter." Contest guidelines available for SASE.

Advice "Some things I've noticed in the past year or 2 are the number of submissions with *no SASE*, submissions stuffed into very small envelopes, failure to put the poet's name on each poem submitted . . . and, evidently, attention not paid to what the magazine lists as 'needs,' because we get haiku, tanka, and other short verse. We also get 8-12 poems submitted with a note that 'this is from my book,' or worse—we get entire manuscripts, especially by e-mail, which we must return because we are not a press. It looks like many poets 'gun shot' their submissions."

HARPUR PALATE; MILTON KESSLER MEMORIAL PRIZE FOR POETRY

Dept. of English, Binghamton University, P.O. Box 6000, Binghamton NY 13902-6000. E-mail: hppoetry@hotmail.com (queries only, no submissions). Website: http://harpurpalate.binghamton.edu. Established 2000. **Contact:** Katy D'Angelo and Ryan Vaughan, poetry editors.

Magazine Needs *Harpur Palate* appears biannually. "We're dedicated to publishing the best poetry and prose, regardless of style, form, and genre." Has published poetry by Marvin Bell, Ryan G. Van Cleave, Jack Ridl, Sascha Feinstein, Allison Joseph, and Ruth Stone. *Harpur Palate* is 100-120 pages, digest-sized, offset-printed, perfect-bound, with matte or glossy cover. Receives about 700 poems/year, accepts about 35. Press run is 1,000. Single copy: $10; subscription: $16/year (2 issues). Sample: $5. Make checks payable to *Harpur Palate*.

How to Submit Submit 3-5 poems at a time. "No line restrictions; entire submission must be 10 pages or less." Accepts simultaneous submissions, "but we must be notified immediately if the piece is taken somewhere else"; no previously published poems. No e-mail submissions. Cover letter is required. Accepts submissions all year. Time between acceptance and publication is 2 months. Poems are circulated to an editorial board. Seldom comments on rejected poems. Guidelines available in magazine, for SASE, or on website. Responds in up to 6 months. Pays 2 contributor's copies. Acquires first North American serial rights.

Contest/Award Offerings The Milton Kessler Memorial Prize for Poetry offers $500 and publication in the Winter issue of *Harpur Palate*. "Poems in any style, form, or genre are welcome. No more than 10 pages total for entry. Must be previously unpublished." **Entry fee:** $15/5 poems. "You may send as many poems as you wish, but no more than 5 poems per entry. Please send checks drawn on a U.S. bank, or money orders, made out to *Harpur Palate*. IMPORTANT: Checks *must* be made out to *Harpur Palate*." Contest opens on August 1. **Postmark deadline:** October 1. Complete guidelines available for SASE or on website.

Also Offers "We publish a Writing By Degrees supplement featuring fiction and poetry in the Winter issue. Writing By Degrees is a creative writing conference run by graduate students in Binghamton's Creative Writing Program."

Advice "We have no restrictions on subject matter or form. Quite simply, send us your highest-quality poetry. Read through all of our submission instructions very carefully before sending out your work (manuscripts that are not properly submitted will be discarded unread). Almost every literary magazine already says this, but it bears repeating: look at a copy of our publication (and other publications as well) to get an idea of the kind of writing published. Do an honest (perhaps even ruthless) assessment of your work to see if it's indeed ready to be submitted."

◎ ☑ HARTWORKS; D.C. CREATIVE WRITING WORKSHOP (Specialized: poetry for teens; African-American issues)

601 Mississippi Ave. SE, Washington DC 20032-3899. (202)297-1957. E-mail: info@dccww.org. Website: www.dccww.org. Established 2000. **Contact:** Nancy Schwalb, executive director.

● Although this journal doesn't accept submissions from the general public, it's included here as an outstanding example of what a literary journal can be (for anyone of any age).

Magazine Needs *hArtworks* appears 3 times/year. "We publish the poetry of Hart Middle School students (as far as we know, Hart may be the only public middle school in the U.S. with its own poetry magazine) and the writing of guest writers such as Nikki Giovanni, Alan Cheuse, Arnost Lustig, Henry Taylor, Mark Craver, and Cornelius Eady, along with interviews between the kids and the grown-up pros. We also publish work by our writers-in-residence, who teach workshops at Hart, and provide trips to readings, slams, museums, and plays." Wants "vivid, precise, imaginative language that communicates from the heart as well as the head." Does not want "poetry that only 'sounds' good; it also needs to say something meaningful." Has published poetry by DeAndre Britten, Rhia Hardman, Shaquiel Jenkins, Jawara Johnson, Raekala Middleton, and Jamal Williams. *hArtworks* is 60 pages, magazine-sized, professionally printed, saddle-stapled, with card cover. Receives about 1,000 poems/year, accepts about 20%. Press run is 500 (75 subscribers, 2 libraries, 100 shelf sales); 100 distributed free to writers, teachers. Single copy: $10; subscription: $25. Make checks payable to D.C. Creative Writing Workshop.

How to Submit "Writers-in-residence solicit most submissions from their classes, and then a committee of student editors makes the final selections. Each year, our second issue is devoted to responses to the Holocaust."

Advice "Read a lot; know something about how other writers approach their craft. Write a lot; build an understanding of yourself as a writer. Don't be so stubborn you settle into the same old poem you perfected in the past. Writing is not some static machine, but a kind of experience, a kind of growing."

◙ HAWAI'I PACIFIC REVIEW

1060 Bishop St., Honolulu HI 96813. (808)544-1108. Fax: (808)544-0862. E-mail: pwilson@hpu.e du. Website: www.hpu.edu. Established 1986. **Contact:** Patrice Wilson, editor.

Magazine Needs Published by Hawai'i Pacific University, *Hawai'i Pacific Review* is an annual literary journal appearing in August or September. Wants "quality poetry, short fiction, and personal essays from writers worldwide. Our journal seeks to promote a world view that celebrates a variety of cultural themes, beliefs, values, and viewpoints. We wish to further the growth of artistic vision and talent by encouraging sophisticated and innovative poetic and narrative techniques." Has published poetry by Wendy Bishop, B.Z. Niditch, Rick Bursky, Virgil Suárez, and Linda Bierds. *Hawai'i Pacific Review* is 80-120 pages, digest-sized, professionally printed on quality paper, perfectbound, with coated card cover. Receives 800-1,000 poems/year, accepts up to 30-40. Press run is about 500 (100 shelf sales). Single copy: $8.95. Sample: $5.

How to Submit Submit up to 5 poems at a time. Lines/poem: 100 maximum. "One submission per issue. No handwritten manuscripts." Accepts simultaneous submissions with notification; no previously published poems. No fax or e-mail submissions. Cover letter with 5-line professional bio including prior publications is required. "Our reading period is September 1 through December 31 each year." Seldom comments on rejected poems. Guidelines available for SASE or by e-mail. Responds within 3 months. Pays 2 contributor's copies. Acquires first North American serial rights.

Advice "We'd like to receive more experimental verse. Good poetry is eye-opening; it investigates the unfamiliar or reveals the spectacular in the ordinary. Good poetry does more than simply express the poet's feelings; it provides both insight and unexpected beauty. Send us your best work!"

◙ HAZMAT REVIEW; CLEVIS HOOK PRESS

P.O. Box 30507, Rochester NY 14603-0507. Website: www.hazmatlitreview.org. Established 1996. **Contact:** Editor.

Magazine Needs *HazMat Review* is a biannual literary review, "about 70% poetry; 25% short story; 5% miscellaneous (essays, reviews, etc.). *HazMat* stands for 'hazardous material,' which we believe poetry most definitely may be!" Wants "your best material; take chances; political pieces welcome; also experimental and/or alternative; especially welcome pieces that show things are not what they appear to be. We think poetry/fiction of the highest quality always has a chance. New Age, witches, ghosts and goblins, vampires—probably not." Has published poetry by Eileen Myles, Marc Olmstead, Steve Hirsch, Thom Ward, Lawrence Ferlinghetti, and Anne Waldman. *HazMat Review* is 96 pages, digest-sized, professionally printed, perfect-bound, with glossy color or b&w cover. Receives about 700 poems/year, accepts up to 20%. Press run is 500 (60 subscribers, 5 libraries, 100 shelf sales); 100 distributed free to coffeehouses for publicity. Single copy: $14; subscription: $25/year. Sample: $7.

How to Submit Submit 3 poems at a time. Accepts previously published poems; no simultaneous submissions. Accepts disk submissions. Cover letter is preferred; SASE requested. Time between acceptance and publication is up to 2 years. "Editors pass promising material to staff readers for second opinion and suggestions, then back to editors for final decision." Often comments on rejected poems. Guidelines available on website. Responds in 3 months. Pays 1-2 contributor's copies. Acquires one-time rights. Staff reviews chapbooks of poetry.

Advice "We are encouraged by the renewed interest in poetry in recent years. If at all possible, read the magazine first before submitting to get a feel for the publication."

✪ $◙ ◎ HEARTLANDS: A MAGAZINE OF MIDWEST LIFE & ART (Specialized: regional; themes)

Firelands Writing Center, BGSU Firelands/One University Rd., Huron OH 44839. (419)433-5560. Fax: (419)433-9696. E-mail: Lsmithdog@aol.com. Website: www.theheartlandstoday.net. Established 1990. **Contact:** David Shevin and Lin Ryan-Thompson, poetry editors. Member: CLMP.

Magazine Needs *Heartlands* is an annual publication of the Firelands Writing Center at Firelands

College. Wants work by Midwestern writers about the Midwest Heartlands, "writing and photography that is set in the Midwest today and deals revealingly and creatively with the issues we face—good writing and art that documents our lives." Each issue has a specific theme. Has published poetry by Alberta Turner, Chris Llewellyn, and Lawrence Ferlinghetti. *Heartlands* is 96 pages, 8½×11, perfect-bound. Accepts 20% of the poetry received. Press run is 800. Single copy: $6.50. Sample: $5.

How to Submit Submit up to 5 poems at a time. Accepts simultaneous submissions. No e-mail submissions, only queries. Cover letter with brief bio is required. Reads submissions January 1 to May 15 only. Often comments on rejected poems. Guidelines and upcoming themes available for SASE. Responds in 2 months once reading period begins. Pays $10 and 2 contributor's copies. Acquires first or second rights.

★ ☑ HEELTAP; PARIAH PRESS

604 Hawthorne Ave. E., St. Paul MN 55101. Established 1985 (Pariah Press), 1997 (*Heeltap*). **Contact:** Richard Houff, editor.

Magazine Needs & How to Submit *Heeltap* appears 2 times/year. Contains "social issues: people connecting with people/surviving chaos and government brain washing/re-establishing a literate society and avoiding the corporate machine." Very open to all kinds of poetry. "We don't believe in censorship." Does not want "early- to mid-19th-century rhyme about mother's lilacs, etc." Has published poetry by Tom Clark, Gerald Locklin, Albert Huffstickler, Theodore Enslin, Charles Plymell, and Marge Piercy. *Heeltap* is 48-64 pages ("varies depending on finances"), digest-sized, laser/high-speed-printed, saddle-stapled, with cardstock cover designed by Mama Rue Day, includes ads. Receives about 10,000 poems/year, accepts about 2-5%. Press run is 500 (50 subscribers, 20 libraries, 300 shelf sales). Single copy: $5; subscription: $18/4 issues. Sample: $5 postage paid. Make checks payable to Richard Houff. "We encourage poets to buy samples before submitting. The amount of inappropriate material we receive is stagnating."

Book/Chapbook Needs & How to Submit Pariah Press publishes *only* solicited material. Has published *Cosmology of Madness* by Albert Huffstickler, *Art & Life* by Gerald Locklin, *Henry's Gift & Other Poems* by Gerald Locklin, *The Clam Diggers & Other Poems* by John Garmon, and *Scorched Hands Anthology*. Published 12 titles in 2000 (number of books published per year "varies depending on cash flow"). Chapbooks are 24 pages, laser/high-speed-printed, saddle-stapled, with covers that vary from 150-lb. glossy to card stock. No unsolicited mss. "We solicit established poets and writers to send a complete manuscript." Responds to queries in 2 months. Pays 50 author's copies (out of a press run of 500). Order sample chapbooks by sending $5 (postage paid) to Richard Houff.

Advice "The beginning poet should study the classics, from the early Greek tradition to the present. On the current scene, try to be yourself. Draw inspiration from others and you'll eventually find your voice. Let Bukowski rest—there are thousands of clones. Buk wouldn't approve."

☑ HELIKON PRESS

120 W. 71st St., New York NY 10023. Established 1972. **Contact:** Robin Prising and William Leo Coakley, poetry editors. "We try to publish the best contemporary poetry in the tradition of English verse. We read (and listen to) poetry and ask poets to build a collection around particular poems. We print fine editions illustrated by good artists. Unfortunately, we cannot encourage submissions."

★ $☑ HERALD PRESS; PURPOSE; STORY FRIENDS; ON THE LINE; WITH (Specialized: religious/Christian; poetry for children and teens)

616 Walnut Ave., Scottdale PA 15683-1999. (724)887-8500. Send submissions or queries directly to the editor of the specific magazine at address indicated.

Magazine Needs & How to Submit *Herald Press*, the official publisher for the Mennonite Church in North America, "seeks also to serve a broad Christian audience. Each of the magazines listed has different specifications, and the editor of each should be queried for more exact information." *Purpose*, edited by James E. Horsch (horsch@mph.org), is a "religious young adult/adult monthly in weekly parts," press run 13,000; its focus: "action-oriented, discipleship living." It is digest-sized with 2-color printing throughout. Buys appropriate poetry up to 12 lines. *Purpose* receives about 2,000 poems/year, accepts 150. Guidelines and sample available for $2 and 9×12 SAE. Mss should be double-spaced, one side of sheet only. Accepts simultaneous submissions. Responds in 2 months. Pays $7.50-20/poem plus 2 contributor's copies. *On the Line*, edited by Mary C. Meyer (mary@mph.org), is a monthly religious magazine for children ages 9-14, "that reinforces Christian values," press run 6,000. Sample available for $2 and 9×12 SAE. Wants poems 3-24 lines. Submit poems "each on a separate 8½×11 sheet." Accepts simultaneous submissions and previously published poems. Responds in one month. Pays $10-25/poem plus 2 contributor's copies. *Story Friends*, edited by Susan Reith Swan (storyfriends@mph.org), is for children ages 4-9; a "monthly magazine that reinforces Christian values," press run 6,500, uses poems 3-12 lines. Send $2 and 9×12 SAE for guidelines/sample copy. Pays $10. *With*, Editorial Team, Box 347, Newton KS 67114, (316)283-5100: This magazine is for teens ages 15-18, focusing on empowering youth to radically commit to a personal relationship with Jesus Christ, and to share God's good news through word and actions." Press run 4,000, uses a limited amount of poetry. Poems should be 4-50 lines. Pays $10-25. Staff reviews books or chapbooks of poetry in 200-800 words. Send materials for review consideration.

HIDDEN OAK

402 S. 25th St., Philadelphia PA 19146. E-mail: hidoak@att.net. Established 1999. **Contact:** Louise Larkins, editor.

Magazine Needs *Hidden Oak* appears 3 times/year. Wants "well-crafted poems which make imaginative use of imagery to reach levels deeper than the immediate and personal. Both traditional forms and free verse are accepted. Especially welcome are poems which include time-honored poetic devices and reveal an ear for the music of language." *Hidden Oak* is 68-72 pages, digest-sized, photocopied, stapled, with original art/photograph on cover. Receives about 600 poems/year, accepts up to 40%. Press run is 100+. Single copy: $5; subscription: $13. Sample: $4. Make checks payable to Louise Larkins.

How to Submit Submit 3-6 poems at a time. Lines/poem: 30 maximum. Occasionally accepts previously published poems; no simultaneous submissions. Accepts e-mail submissions; no disk submissions. Cover letter is preferred. Include SASE. Submit seasonal poems 2-3 months in advance. Time between acceptance and publication is up to 3 months. Seldom comments on rejected poems. Might publish theme issues in the future. Guidelines available for SASE or by e-mail. Responds in one week. Pays one contributor's copy. Does not review books or chapbooks.

$ HIGH PLAINS PRESS (Specialized: regional/American West)

P.O. Box 123, Glendo WY 82213. (307)735-4370. Fax: (307)735-4590. E-mail: editor@highplainspress.com. Website: www.highplainspress.com. Established 1985. **Contact:** Nancy Curtis, poetry editor.

Book/Chapbook Needs High Plains Press considers books of poetry "specifically relating to Wyoming and the American West, particularly poetry based on historical people/events or nature. We mainly publish historical nonfiction, but do publish one book of poetry every year." Has published *Cloud Seeding* by Stacy Coyle, *Close at Hand* by Mary Lou Sanelli, and *Bitter Creek Junction* by Linda Hasselstrom.

How to Submit Query first with 3 sample poems (from a 50-poem ms). Accepts submissions by fax, e-mail (as attachment), postal mail, and on disk. Responds in 2 months. Time between acceptance and publication is up to 2 years. Guidelines available for SASE, by fax, or by e-mail. Always sends prepublication galleys. Pays 10% of sales. Acquires first rights. Catalog available on request; sample books: $5.

Advice "Look at our previous titles."

◑ ◎ HIGHLIGHTS FOR CHILDREN (Specialized: children)

803 Church St., Honesdale PA 18431. (570)253-1080. E-mail: editorial@highlights-corp.com. Website: www.highlights.com. Established 1946. **Contact:** Manuscript Submissions.

Magazine Needs *Highlights* appears every month using poetry for children ages 2-12. Wants "meaningful and/or fun poems accessible to children of all ages. Welcome light, humorous verse. Rarely publish a poem longer than 16 lines, most are shorter. No poetry that is unintelligible to children; poems containing sex, violence, or unmitigated pessimism." Accepts poetry written by children and teens (pays only if 16 years or older). Has published poetry by Ruskin Bond, Aileen Fisher, Eileen Spinelli, and Carl Sandburg. *Highlights* is generally 42 pages, magazine-sized, full-color throughout. Receives about 300 submissions/year, accepts up to 30. Press run is 2.5 million (approximately 2.2 million subscribers). Subscription: $29.64/year (reduced rates for multiple years).

How to Submit "Submit typed manuscript with very brief cover letter. Please indicate if simultaneous submission." No e-mail submissions. Editor comments on submissions "occasionally, if manuscript has merit or author seems to have potential for our market." Guidelines available for SASE. Responds "generally within one month." Always sends prepublication galleys. Payment: "money varies" plus 2 contributor's copies. Acquires all rights.

Advice "We are always open to submissions of poetry not previously published. However, we purchase a very limited amount of such material. We may use the verse as 'filler,' or illustrate the verse with a full-page piece of art. Please note that we do not buy material from anyone under 16 years old."

▦ ◎ HILLTOP PRESS (Specialized: science fiction)

4 Nowell Place, Almondbury, Huddersfield, West Yorkshire HD5 8PB England. Website (online catalog): www.bbr-online.com/catalogue. Established 1966. **Contact:** Steve Sneyd, editor.

Book/Chapbook Needs Hilltop Press publishes mainly science fiction poetry, plus some dark fantasy poetry. Publications include: a series of books on poetry in US and UK SFanzines; collections, new and reprint, by individual science fiction poets including Andrew Darlington, Gavin Salisbury, Mary Ladd, Mark Sonnenfeld, and William Dearden; anthology of SF poetry from Oxford reading that includes Brian Aldiss, etc.; Medusa poems anthology, a cross-section of leading US and UK speculative poets. Orders from the US can be placed through the website of BBR Solutions Ltd. (see above).

How to Submit Does not accept unsolicited mss. Query (with SAE/IRC) with proposals for relevant projects.

Advice "My advice for beginning poets is: a) persist—don't let any one editor discourage you. 'In poetry's house are many mansions,' what one publication hates another may love; b) be prepared for long delays between acceptance and appearance of work—the small press is mostly self-financed and part-time, so don't expect it to be more efficient than commercial publishers; c) *always* keep a copy of everything you send out, put your name and address on *everything* you send, and *always* include adequately stamped SAE."

▦ $◑ ◎ HIPPOPOTAMUS PRESS (Specialized: Modernism); OUTPOSTS POETRY QUARTERLY

22 Whitewell Rd., Frome, Somerset BA11 4EL England. Phone/fax: 01373-466653. *Outposts* established 1943, Hippopotamus Press established 1974. **Contact:** Roland John, poetry editor.

Magazine Needs "*Outposts* is a general poetry magazine that welcomes all work, from either the recognized or the unknown poet." Wants "fairly mainstream poetry. No concrete poems or very free verse." Has published poetry by Jared Carter, John Heath-Stubbs, Lotte Kramer, and Peter Russell. *Outposts* is 60-120 pages, A5, litho-printed, perfect-bound, with laminated card cover, includes ads. Receives about 46,000 poems/year, accepts about 1%. Press run is 1,600 (1,200 subscribers, 400 libraries, 400 shelf sales). Single copy: $8; subscription: $26. Sample (including guidelines): $6. Make checks payable to Hippopotamus Press. "We prefer credit cards because of bank charges."

How to Submit Submit 5 poems at a time. "IRCs must accompany U.S. submissions." Accepts simultaneous submissions; no previously published poems. Accepts fax submissions. Cover letter is required. Time between acceptance and publications is 9 months. Comments on rejected poems "only if asked." Occasionally publishes theme issues. List of upcoming themes available for SASE (or SAE and IRC). Responds in 2 weeks "plus post time." Sometimes sends prepublication galleys. Pays £8/poem plus one contributor's copy. Copyright remains with author. Staff reviews books of poetry in 200 words for "Books Received" page. Also uses full essays up to 4,000 words. Send materials for review consideration to M. Pargitter.

Book/Chapbook Needs & How to Submit Hippopotamus Press publishes 6 books/year. "The Hippopotamus Press is specialized, with an affinity with Modernism. No Typewriter, Concrete, Surrealism." For book publication, query with sample poems. Accepts simultaneous submissions and previously published poems. Responds in 6 weeks. Pays 7½-10% royalties plus author's copies. Send for book catalog to buy samples.

HIRAM POETRY REVIEW

P.O. Box 162, Hiram OH 44234. (330)569-7512. Fax: (330)569-5166. E-mail: greenwoodwp@hiram.edu. Established 1966. **Contact:** Willard Greenwood, poetry editor.

Magazine Needs *Hiram Poetry Review* is an annual publication appearing in spring. "Since 1966, *Hiram Poetry Review* has published distinctive, beautiful, and heroic poetry. We're looking for works of high and low art. We tend to favor poems that are pockets of resistance in the undeclared war against 'plain speech,' but we are interested in any work of high quality." Although most poems appearing here tend to be lyric and narrative free verse under 50 lines, exceptions occur (a few longer, sequence, or formal works can be found in each issue). Circulation is 400 (300 subscribers, 150 libraries). Subscription: $9/year; $23/3 years.

How to Submit Query or send 3–5 poems and a brief bio. Accepts simultaneous submissions. Does not accept e-mail submissions or poems longer than 3 single-spaced pages. Reads submissions year round. Responds in up to 6 months. Pays 2 contributor's copies. Acquires first North American serial rights; returns rights upon publication. Reviews books of poetry in single- or multi-book format, no set length. Send materials for review consideration.

HOGTOWN CREEK REVIEW

4736 Hummingbird Lane, Valdosta GA 31602. E-mail: info@hogtowncreek.org. Website: www.hogtowncreek.org. Established 2000. **Contact:** Michael Martin, founding editor.

Magazine Needs *Hogtown Creek Review*, appearing annually in September, is "a literary/art magazine publishing the best in short fiction, poetry, essays, political commentary, photography, art, and book reviews." Wants "the best poetry being written by poets from around the globe." Has published poetry by Miller Williams, Peter Cooley, Glenn Ingersoll, David Dooley, Michael McFee, and Lola Haskins. *Hogtown Creek Review* is 90 pages, magazine-sized, perfect-bound, with color cover "with artwork, always," includes ads. Receives about 1,000 poems/year, accepts about 1%. Press run is 1,000 (400 subscribers, 5 libraries, 300 shelf sales); 100 distributed free to organizations, writers. Single copy: $10. Sample: $5. Make checks payable to *Hogtown Creek Review*.

How to Submit Submit 3 poems at a time. Lines/poem: open. Accepts simultaneous submissions; no previously published poems. Accepts e-mail submissions (as attachment); no disk submissions. Cover letter is preferred. Include SASE. Reads submissions year round. Time between acceptance and publication is 6 months. Poems are circulated to an editorial board. Sometimes comments on rejected poems. Guidelines available on website. Responds in 3 months. Sometimes sends prepublication galleys. Pays 2 contributor's copies. Acquires first North American serial rights. Reviews books and chapbooks of poetry in 750 words. Send materials for review consideration to Michael Martin.

Advice "Please visit website or purchase back issue before submitting."

⬇ ◎ HOLIDAY HOUSE, INC. (Specialized: children/teens)

425 Madison Ave., New York NY 10017. Website: www.holidayhouse.com. Established 1936. **Contact:** Regina Griffin, editor-in-chief. A trade children's book house. Has published hardcover books for children by John Updike and Walter Dean Myers. Publishes one poetry book/year, averaging 32 pages. "The acceptance of complete book manuscripts of high-quality children's poetry is limited." Send a query with SASE before submitting.

$⬇ THE HOLLINS CRITIC

P.O. Box 9538, Hollins University, Roanoke VA 24020-1538. (540)362-6275. Website: www.hollins. edu/grad/eng_writing/critic/critic.htm. Established 1964. **Contact:** Cathryn Hankla, poetry editor. Editor: R.H.W. Dillard.

Magazine Needs *The Hollins Critic* appears 5 times/year and publishes critical essays, poetry, and book reviews. Uses a few short poems in each issue, interesting in form, content, or both. Has published poetry by William Miller, R.T. Smith, David Huddle, Margaret Gibson, and Julia Johnson. *The Hollins Critic* is 24 pages, magazine-sized. Press run is 500. Subscription: $8/year ($9.50 outside US). Sample: $1.50.

How to Submit Submit up to 5 poems. "Must be typewritten, with SASE." Reads submissions September 1 through December 15. Submissions received at other times will be returned unread. Responds in 6 weeks. Pays $25/poem plus 5 contributor's copies.

⬇ HOME PLANET NEWS

P.O. Box 455, High Falls NY 12440. Established 1979. **Contact:** Donald Lev, editor.

Magazine Needs *Home Planet News* appears 3 times/year. "Our purpose is to publish lively and eclectic poetry, from a wide range of sensibilities, and to provide news of the small press and poetry scenes, thereby fostering a sense of community among contributors and readers." Wants "honest, well-crafted poems, open or closed form, on any subject. Poems under 30 lines stand a better chance. We do not want any work which seems to us to be racist, sexist, agist, anti-Semitic, or imposes limitations on the human spirit." Has published poetry by Enid Dame, Antler, Lyn Lifshin, Gerald Locklin, Hal Sirowitz, and Janine Pommy Vega. *Home Planet News* is a 24-page tabloid, web-offset-printed, includes ads. Receives about 1,000 poems/year, accepts up to 3%. Press run is 1,000 (300 subscribers). Single copy: $4; subscription: $10/3 issues, $18/6 issues.

How to Submit Submit 3-6 poems at a time. No limit on length, "but shorter poems stand a better chance." No previously published poems or simultaneous submissions. Cover letter is preferred. "SASEs are a must." Time between acceptance and publication is one year. Seldom comments on rejected poems. Occasionally publishes theme issues; "We announce these in magazine." Guidelines available for SASE, "however, it is usually best to simply send work." Responds in 4 months. Pays one-year gift subscription plus 3 contributor's copies. Acquires first rights. All rights revert to author on publication. Reviews books and chapbooks of poetry and other magazines in 1,200 words, single- and multi-book format. Send materials for review consideration to Donald Lev. "Note: we do have guidelines for book reviewers; please write for them. Magazines are reviewed by a staff member."

Advice "Read many publications, attend readings, feel yourself part of a writing community, learn from others."

$⬇ HOTEL AMERIKA

360 Ellis Hall, Ohio University, Athens OH 45701. (740)597-1360. E-mail: editors@hotelamerika.n et. Website: www.hotelamerika.net. Established 2002. **Contact:** David Lazar, editor. Managing Editor: Jean Cunningham.

 • Work published in *Hotel Amerika* by Mark Irwin was included in the 2003 *Pushcart Prize* anthology, poems by John Hollander and Nathaniel Mackey were included in *The Best American Poetry 2004*, and poets Cathleen Calbert and Colette Inez had work featured on *Poetry Daily*.

Magazine Needs *Hotel Amerika* is a biannual literary journal open to all genres and schools of writing, "from the most formalistic to the most avant-garde." Has published poetry by Antler, Denise Duhamel, Maureen Seaton, Mark Irwin, Simon Perchik, and Lisa Samuels. *Hotel Amerika* is about 110 pages, magazine-sized, offset-printed, perfect-bound, with cardstock cover with artwork, sometimes includes ads. Receives about 1,500 poems/year, accepts about 100. Press run is 2,000 (100 subscribers, 10 libraries, about 800 shelf sales). Single copy: $9; subscription: $18/year, $34/ 2 years. Make checks payable to *Hotel Amerika*.

How to Submit Submit 3-6 poems at a time. No previously published poems or simultaneous submissions. No e-mail or disk submissions. Cover letter is preferred. "Please include titles of poems in the cover letter, and include a SASE for our response." Reads submissions September 1 through May 1. Manuscripts received outside of the reading period will be returned unread. "The assistant editor and a consulting editor read the poetry submissions and pass their recommendations on to David Lazar, who makes all final decisions." Seldom comments on rejected poems. Guidelines available for SASE or on website. Responds in up to 3 months. Pays "a small honorarium when funds allow" and/or 1-2 contributor's copies. Acquires first North American serial rights; returns rights to poets.

⬛ ⬛ $⬛ ◎ HOUSE OF ANANSI PRESS (Specialized: regional/Canada)

110 Spadina Ave., Suite 801, Toronto ON M5V 2K4 Canada. (416)363-4343. Fax: (416)363-1017. E-mail: online contact and query forms. Website: www.anansi.ca. Established 1967.

Book/Chapbook Needs House of Anansi publishes literary fiction and poetry by Canadian writers. "We seek to balance the list between well-known and emerging writers, with an interest in writing by Canadians of all backgrounds. **We publish Canadian poetry only**, and poets must have a substantial publication record—if not in books, then definitely in journals and magazines of repute. No children's poetry and no poetry by previously unpublished poets." Has published *Power Politics* by Margaret Atwood and *Ruin & Beauty* by Patricia Young. Books are generally 96-144 pages, trade paperbacks with French sleeves, with matte covers.

How to Submit Canadian poets should query first with 10 sample poems (typed double-spaced) and a cover letter with brief bio and publication credits. Accepts previously published poems and simultaneous submissions. Poems are circulated to an editorial board. Often comments on rejected poems. Responds to queries within 3 months, to mss (if invited) within 4 months. Pays 8-10% royalties, a $750 advance, and 10 author's copies (out of a press run of 1,000).

Advice "To learn more about our titles, check our website or write to us directly for a catalog. We strongly advise poets to build up a publishing résumé by submitting poems to reputable magazines and journals. This indicates three important things to us: One, that he or she is becoming a part of the Canadian poetry community; two, that he or she is building up a readership through magazine subscribers; and three, it establishes credibility in his or her work. There is a great deal of competition for only three or four spots on our list each year—which always includes works by poets we have previously published."

⬛ ◎ HQ POETRY MAGAZINE (THE HAIKU QUARTERLY); THE DAY DREAM PRESS

39 Exmouth St., Kingshill, Swindon, Wiltshire SN1 3PU England. Phone: 01793-523927. Website: www.noggs.dial.pipex.com/HQ.htm. Established 1990. **Contact:** Kevin Bailey, editor.

Magazine Needs *HQ Poetry Magazine* is "a platform from which new and established poets can speak and have the opportunity to experiment with new forms and ideas." Wants "any poetry of good quality." Has published poetry by Al Alvarez, D.M. Thomas, James Kirkup, Cid Corman, Brian Patten, and Penelope Shuttle. *HQ Poetry Magazine* is 48-64 pages, A5, perfect-bound, includes ads. Accepts about 5% of poetry received. Press run is 500-600 (500 subscribers, 30 libraries). Subscription: £10 UK, £13 foreign. Sample: £2.80.

How to Submit No previously published poems or simultaneous submissions. Cover letter and SASE (or SAE and IRCs) required. Time between acceptance and publication is 3-6 months. Often comments on rejected poems. Responds "as time allows." Pays one contributor's copy. Reviews books of poetry in about 1,000 words, single-book format. Send materials for review consideration.

Also Offers Sponsors ''Piccadilly Poets'' in London, and ''Live Poet's Society'' based in Bath, Somerset, England. Also acts as ''advisor to *Poetry on the Lake* Annual Poetry Festival in Orta, Italy.''

◖ HUBBUB; VI GALE AWARD; ADRIENNE LEE AWARD; STOUT AWARD; KENNETH O. HANSON AWARD

5344 SE 38th Ave., Portland OR 97202. Established 1983. **Contact:** L. Steinman and J. Shugrue, editors.

Magazine Needs Appearing once/year (usually in December/January), *Hubbub* is designed ''to feature a multitude of voices from interesting contemporary American poets. We look for poems that are well-crafted, with something to say. We have no single style, subject, or length requirement and, in particular, will consider long poems. No light verse.'' Has published poetry by Madeline DeFrees, Cecil Giscombe, Carolyn Kizer, Primus St. John, Shara McCallum, and Alice Fulton. *Hubbub* is 50-70 pages, digest-sized, offset-printed, perfect-bound, with cover art only. Receives about 1,200 submissions/year, accepts up to 2%. Press run is 350 (100 subscribers, 12 libraries, about 150 shelf sales). Subscription: $5/year. Sample: $3.35 (back issues), $5 (current issue).

How to Submit Submit 3-6 typed poems with SASE. No previously published poems or simultaneous submissions. Guidelines available for SASE. Responds in 4 months. Pays 2 contributor's copies. Acquires first North American serial rights. ''We review 2-4 poetry books/year in short (3-page) reviews; all reviews are solicited. We do, however, list books received/recommended.'' Send materials for review consideration.

Contest/Award Offerings Outside judges choose poems from each volume for 4 awards: Vi Gale Award ($100), Adrienne Lee Award ($50), Stout Award ($25), and Kenneth O. Hanson Award ($25). There are no special submission procedures or entry fees involved.

$◖ THE HUDSON REVIEW

684 Park Ave., New York NY 10021. Website: www.hudsonreview.com. **Contact:** Shannon Bond, associate editor. Editor: Paula Deitz.

• Work published in *The Hudson Review* has been included in *The Best American Poetry*.

Magazine Needs *The Hudson Review* is a high-quality, flat-spined quarterly of 176 pages, considered one of the most prestigious and influential journals in the nation. Editors welcome all styles and forms. However, competition is extraordinarily keen, especially since poems compete with prose. Has published poetry by Marilyn Nelson, Hayden Carruth, Louis Simpson, and Dana Gioia. Subscription: $32/year ($36 foreign), institutions $38/year ($42 foreign). Sample: $9.

How to Submit Submit no more than 10 poems at a time. No previously published poems or simultaneous submissions. Nonsubscribers may submit poems between April 1 and June 30 only. ''Manuscripts submitted by subscribers who so identify themselves will be read throughout the year.'' Guidelines available in magazine, for SASE, or on website. Responds in 3 months. Always sends prepublication galleys. Pays 50¢/line and 2 contributor's copies.

Advice ''Read the magazine to ascertain our style/sensibility.''

◖ ◎ HUNGER MAGAZINE; HUNGER PRESS (Specialized: form/language-image experimentation)

1305 Old Route 28, Phoenicia NY 12464. (845)688-2332. E-mail: hunger@hvc.rr.com. Website: www.hungermagazine.com. Established 1997. **Contact:** J.J. Blickstein, editor/publisher.

Magazine Needs *Hunger Magazine* is an international zine based in the Hudson Valley and appears 1-2 times/year. ''*Hunger* publishes mostly poetry but will accept some microfiction, essays, translations, cover art, interviews, and book reviews. Although there are no school/stylistic limitations, our main focus is on language-image experimentation with an edge. We publish no names for prestige, and most of our issues are dedicated to emerging talent. Well-known poets do grace our pages to illuminate possibilities. No dead kitty elegies; Beat impersonators; Hallmark cards; 'I'm not sure if I can write poems'. All rhymers better be very, very good. We have published poetry by Amiri Baraka, Paul Celan, Robert Kelly, Anne Waldman, Janine Pommy Vega, Antonin Artaud, and Clayton Eshleman." *Hunger* is 75-100 pages, magazine-sized, saddle-stapled, with glossy full-color card cover. Accepts about 10% of submissions. Press run is 250-500. Single copy: $8 plus $1 p&h ($11 foreign); subscription: $16 ($21 foreign). Chapbooks: $5. Make checks payable to Hunger Magazine & Press.

How to Submit "Send 3-10 pages and SASE." Accepts simultaneous submissions, if notified; no previously published poems. Accepts e-mail submissions and queries; include text in body of message "unless otherwise requested." Brief cover letter with bio and SASE required. "Manuscripts without SASEs will be recycled. Please proof your work and clearly indicate stanza breaks." Time between acceptance and publication is up to one year. Guidelines available in magazine, for SASE, by e-mail, or on website. Responds in up to 6 months, depending on backlog. Sends prepublication galleys upon request. Pays 1-3 contributor's copies depending on amount of work published. "If invited to be a featured poet, we pay a small honorarium and copies." Acquires first North American serial rights.

Advice "Please follow submission guidelines! Please be familiar with magazine content. The brief descriptions found in *Poet's Market* can only give one a general account of what a journal publishes. Do your research! Young poets, spend as much time reading as you do writing. Please, no unsolicited book-length manuscripts."

⚡ $☑ HUNGER MOUNTAIN, The Vermont College Journal of Arts & Letters; RUTH STONE PRIZE IN POETRY

Vermont College, 36 College St., Montpelier VT 05602. (802)828-8633. Fax: (802)828-8649. E-mail: hungermtn@tui.edu. Website: www.hungermtn.org. Established 2002. **Contact:** Caroline Mercurio, managing editor. Member: CLMP.

Magazine Needs *Hunger Mountain, The Vermont College Journal of Arts & Letters* is a biannual journal "publishing high-quality poetry, prose, and artwork selected by guest editors from the Vermont College MFA in Writing Program." Wants poems "ready for publication." Does not want entire mss, or children's or young adult poetry. Has published poetry by Hayden Carruth, Mark Doty, Carol Muske-Dukes, Maxine Kumin, Charles Simic, and Ruth Stone. *Hunger Mountain* is about 200 pages, 7×10, professionally printed, perfect-bound, with full-bleed color artwork on cover, includes ads (only in back). Receives about 600 poems/year, accepts about 5%. Press run is 1,500 (700 subscribers, 50 libraries, 200 shelf sales); 100 distributed free to writer's centers, book fairs, and other journals. Single copy: $10; subscription: $17/year, $32/2 years, $60/4 years. Make checks payable to *Hunger Mountain*.

How to Submit Submit 3-10 poems at a time. Accepts simultaneous submissions; no previously published poems. No fax, e-mail, or disk submissions. Cover letter is preferred. "Include double copies of everything, including cover letter." Reads submissions year round. Time between acceptance and publication is 6 months. Poems are circulated to an editorial board. Never comments on rejected poems. Guidelines available for SASE, by fax, by e-mail, or on website. Responds in 4 months. Always sends prepublication galleys. Pays $5/page (minimum $30) and 2 contributor's copies. Acquires first North American serial rights.

Contest/Award Offerings Sponsors the annual Ruth Stone Prize in Poetry. Offers $1,000 and publication in magazine; 2 Honorable Mentions also published. Submit 3 poems not to exceed 6 pages. **Entry fee:** $15. **Deadline:** December 10 annually. Guidelines available in magazine, for SASE, by fax, by e-mail, or on website. "Include SASE and index card with poem titles and address; do not put name on poems."

Advice "Always read submission guidelines and make sure your poems are appropriate for the magazine or journal!"

Ⓝ $◻ ◎ HUNGUR MAGAZINE (Specialized: vampires)

P.O. Box 782, Cedar Rapids IA 52406-0782. E-mail: hungurmagazine@yahoo.com. Website: www.s amsdotpublishing.com. Established 2004. **Contact:** L. A. Story Houry, co-editor. Member: The Speculative Literature Foundation (http://SpeculativeLiterature.org).

Magazine Needs *Hungur Magazine* is a biannual print publication "of stories and poems about vampires, and especially about vampires on other worlds." Prefers a "decadent literary style." Does not want "horror with excessive blood and gore." *Hungur Magazine* is 32 pages, magazine-sized, offset-printed, saddle-stapled, with paper cover with color art, includes ads. Receives about 200 poems/year, accepts about 20 (10%). Press run is 100/issue. Single copy: $8; subscription: $14/year. Make checks payable to Tyree Campbell/Sam's Dot Publishing.

How to Submit Submit up to 5 poems at a time. Lines/poem: prefers less than 200. No previously published poems or simultaneous submissions. Accepts e-mail submissions (pasted into body of message); no disk submissions. "Submission should include snail mail address and a short (1-2 lines) bio." Reads submissions year round. Submit seasonal poems 6 months in advance. Time between acceptance and publication is 3-4 months. "Co-Editors L. A. Story Houry and Terrie Leigh Relf jointly review submissions and decide acceptances." Often comments on rejected poems. Guidelines available on website. Responds in 4-6 weeks. Pays $4/poem and one contributor's copy. Acquires first North American serial rights. Reviews books and chapbooks of poetry. Send materials for review consideration to Tyree Campbell.

Advice "It's up to the writer to take the first step and submit work. Some of our best poems have come from poets who weren't sure if they were good enough."

⭐ ☑ ◎ IAMBS & TROCHEES (Specialized: form/metrical verse only); IAMBS & TROCHEES ANNUAL POETRY CONTEST

6801 19th Ave. 5H, Brooklyn NY 11204. Website: www.iambsandtrochees.com. Established 2001. **Contact:** William F. Carlson, editor/publisher.

Magazine Needs *Iambs & Trochees* appears biannually in April and October. Welcomes "poetry written in the great tradition of English and American literature. We will consider rhymed verse, blank verse, and metrically regular verse of any type, along with poems written in the various fixed forms. These include (but are not limited to) the sonnet, the villanelle, the ballade, the triolet, and the ottava rima. We are open to all genres: lyric, elegiac, satiric, narrative, or anything else. We have no restrictions on subject matter, nor do we demand that our writers follow any specific approach or ideology when handling their material. Our concern is strictly with the intrinsic aesthetic merit of a poem." Does not want free verse, syllabic verse. Has published poetry by Alfred Dorn, Rhina Espaillat, Samuel Maio, R.S. Gwynn, Jared Carter, and X.J. Kennedy. *Iambs & Trochees* is 64-124 pages, 7×9, digitally printed, perfect-bound, with paper cover. Single copy: $8; subscription: $15/year (2 issues). Make checks payable to Iambs & Trochees Publishing.

How to Submit Submit no more than 5 poems at a time. No previously published poems or simultaneous submissions. Accepts submissions by postal mail only. Include SASE for return of poems not accepted. Time between acceptance and publication is 2 months. Submission deadlines: December 30 (April) and June 30 (October). Poems are circulated to an editorial board. "We select poems on how well they are crafted." Seldom comments on rejected poems. Guidelines available in magazine. Responds in 2 months. Pays one contributor's copy. Acquires first North American serial rights. Reviews books of poetry *only* in 1,500 words.

Contest/Award Offerings Sponsors annual contest for metrical poetry. Offers 3 awards of $300, $150, and $50. **Entry fee:** none. Guidelines available for SASE or on website.

Advice "Send metrical poems only, and only 5 per submission."

☑ IBBETSON ST. PRESS

25 School St., Somerville MA 02143-1721. (617)628-2313. E-mail: dougholder@post.harvard.edu. Website: http://homepage.mac.com/rconte. Established 1999. **Contact:** Doug Holder, editor. Co-Editors: Dianne Robitaille, Richard Wilhelm, Linda H. Conte, Marc Widershien, Robert K. Johnson, Dorian Brooks, and Lynne Sticklor.

Magazine Needs Appearing biannually in June and November, *Ibbetson St. Press* is "a poetry magazine that wants 'down to earth' poetry that is well-written; has clean, crisp images; with a sense of irony and humor. We want mostly free verse, but are open to rhyme. No maudlin, trite, overly political, vulgar for vulgar's sake work." Has published poetry by Robert K. Johnson, Lo Galluccio, Timothy Gager, Brian Morrissey, Jennifer Matthews, and Deb Priestly. *Ibbetson St. Press* is 30 pages, magazine-sized, desktop-published, with plastic binding and cream coverstock cover, includes ads. Receives about 300 poems/year, accepts up to 40%. Press run is 200 (30 subscribers). Also archived at Harvard, Brown, University of Wisconsin, and Buffalo University Libraries. Single copy: $5; subscription: $10. Make checks payable to *Ibbetson St. Press*.

How to Submit Submit 3-5 poems at a time. Accepts previously published poems and simultaneous submissions. Accepts submissions by postal mail only. Cover letter is required. Time between acceptance and publication is up to 5 months. "Three editors comment on submissions." Guidelines available for SASE. Responds in 2 weeks. Pays one contributor's copy. Acquires one-time rights. Reviews books and chapbooks of poetry and other magazines in 250-500 words. Send materials for review consideration.

Book/Chapbook Needs & How to Submit Does not accept unsolicited chapbook mss. Has published *From the Same Corner of the Bar* by Tim Gager, *Relationships* by Marc Goldfinger, *Hot Rain* by Lo Galluccio, *The Woman Has a Voice* by Deborah M. Priestly, *Fairy Tales and Misdemeanors* by Jennifer Matthews, *Slow as a Poem* by Linda Haviland Conte, *Inaccessibility of the Creator* by Jack Powers, and *Living It* by Joanna Nealon. Responds to queries in one month.

Advice "Please buy a copy of the magazine you submit to—support the small press. In your work, be honest."

$☑ THE ICONOCLAST

1675 Amazon Rd., Mohegan Lake NY 10547-1804. Established 1992. **Contact:** Phil Wagner, editor/publisher. Member: CLMP.

Magazine Needs *The Iconoclast* is a general interest literary publication appearing 6 times/year. Wants "poems that have something to say—the more levels the better. Nothing sentimental, obscure, or self-absorbed. Try for originality; if not in thought, then expression. No greeting card verse or noble religious sentiments. Look for the unusual in the usual, parallels in opposites, the capturing of what is unique or often unnoticed in an ordinary, or extraordinary, moment; what makes us human—and the resultant glories and agonies. Our poetry is accessible to a thoughtful reading public." *The Iconoclast* is 44-96 pages, journal-sized, photo-offset on #45 white wove paper, includes ads. Receives about 2,000 poems/year, accepts up to 3%. Press run is 600-3,000 (380 subscribers). Subscription: $16 for 8 issues. Sample: $2.50.

How to Submit Submit 3-4 poems at a time. Time between acceptance and publication is 4 months to one year. Sometimes comments on rejected poems. Guidelines available for SASE. Responds in one month. Pays one contributor's copy/published page or poem, 40% discount on extras, and $2-5/poem for first North American rights on publication. Reviews books of poetry in 250 words, single-book format.

Advice "If you're spending more time and money on TV, PDAs, and the Internet than on literature, perhaps you're not a small press person and should be sending your work to Time Warner or Newscorp."

⊕ ☐ IDIOM 23; BAUHINIA LITERARY AWARDS

Regional Centre of the Arts, Central Queensland University, Rockhampton 4702 Australia. Established 1988. **Contact:** Leonie Healey, administrator/coordinator.

Magazine Needs "Named for the Tropic of Capricorn, *Idiom 23* is dedicated to developing the literary arts throughout the Central Queensland region. Submissions of original short stories, poems, articles, and b&w drawings and photographs are welcomed by the editorial collective. *Idiom 23* is not limited to a particular viewpoint but, on the contrary, hopes to encourage and publish a broad spectrum of writing. The collective seeks out creative work from community groups with as varied backgrounds as possible. The magazine hopes to reflect and contest idiomatic fictional representations of marginalized or non-privileged positions and values." Accepts poetry written by children

10 years of age and older. *Idiom 23*, published annually, is about 140 pages, $7^3/_4 \times 10$, professionally printed, perfect-bound, with 4-color cover, includes ads. Single copy: $11.

How to Submit Accepts previously published poems. Cover letter is required. Poems are circulated to an editorial board. Reviews books of poetry in single-book format. Send materials for review consideration to Leonie Healey at l.healey@cqu.edu.au.

Contest/Award Offerings Sponsors the Bauhinia Literary Awards for short stories and poetry in 3 categories: Open, Regional, and Student. Submit up to 3 poems, 50 lines maximum each. **Entry fee:** $5. **Postmark deadline:** June 30. Winning entries will be announced at the CQ Multicultural Fair and CQU Open Day in August. Outstanding entries will be published in *The Morning Bulletin* (Australian newspaper). Send SAE and IRC for complete details.

★ ⬛ ◎ THE IDIOT (Specialized: humor)

P.O. Box 69163, Los Angeles CA 90069. E-mail: idiotsubmission@yahoo.com. Website: www.theidiotmagazine.com. Established 1993. President for Life: Sam Hayes. Mussolini to My Hitler: Brian Campbell.

Magazine Needs *The Idiot* is a monthly online humor magazine that publishes a 'Best of' issue every other year. "We mostly use fiction, articles, and cartoons, but will use anything funny, including poetry. Nothing pretentious. We are a magazine of dark comedy. Death, dismemberment, and religion are all subjects of comedy. Nothing is sacred. But it needs to be funny, which brings us to . . . Laughs! I don't want whimsical, I don't want amusing, I don't want some fanciful anecdote about childhood. I mean belly laughs, laughing out loud, fall-on-the-floor funny. If it's cute, give it to your sweetheart or your puppy dog. Length doesn't matter, but most comedy is like soup: It's an appetizer, not a meal; Short is often better. Bizarre, obscure, and/or literary references are often appreciated but not necessary." Has published poetry by Brad Hufford, Denny Spurling, and Andrew Davis. *The Idiot* is 48 pages, digest-sized, professionally printed, staple-bound, with glossy cover. Receives about 250 submissions/year, accepts up to 4-10. Press run is 1,000 + . Subscription: $10. Sample: $6.

How to Submit Accepts previously published poems and simultaneous submissions. Prefers e-mail submissions if included in body of message. Seldom comments on rejected poems. Responds in 1-12 months. Pays one contributor's copy. Acquires one-time rights.

Advice "Gather 'round, my children. Oh, come closer. Closer, don't be shy. Okay, scoot back, that's too close. Now listen carefully as there's something uncle Sammy wants to tell you. Billy, get those fingers out of your ears and listen. I'd like to give you a little advice about submissions. You see, kids, most people send me poems that just aren't funny. We're a *comedy* magazine, emphasis on the word 'comedy.' We're looking for things that make people laugh. Anything less than that demeans us both (but mostly you). So please make sure that whatever you send isn't just amusing or cute, but really, really, really hilarious. Please note that we are only publishing a print copy every other year now. But we need lots of material for the online magazine."

Ⓝ $ ⬛ ◎ ILLUMEN (Specialized: fantasy; science fiction; speculative poetry)

P.O. Box 782, Cedar Rapids IA 52406-0782. E-mail: illumensdp@yahoo.com. Website: www.samsdotpublishing.com. Established 2004. **Contact:** Tyree Campbell, managing editor. Member: The Speculative Literature Foundation (http://SpeculativeLiterature.org).

Magazine Needs *Illumen* is a biannual print publication containing speculative poetry and articles about speculative poetry. "Speculative poetry includes, but is not limited to, fantasy, science fiction, sword and sorcery, alternate history, and horror." Wants "fantasy, science fiction, spooky horror, and speculative poetry with minimal angst." Does not want "horror with excessive blood and gore." Has published poetry by Ian Watson, Bruce Boston, Sonya Taaffe, Mike Allen, Marge B. Simon, and David C. Kopaska-Merkel. *Illumen* is 32 pages, magazine-sized, offset-printed, saddle-stapled, with color paper cover with b&w art, includes ads. Receives about 200 poems/year, accepts about 50 (25%). Press run is 100/issue (20 subscribers, 50 shelf sales); 5 distributed free to reviewers. Single copy: $9; subscription: $15/year. Make checks payable to Tyree Campbell/Sam's Dot Publishing.

How to Submit Submit up to 5 poems at a time. Lines/poem: prefers less than 200. Accepts previously published poems; no simultaneous submissions. Accepts e-mail submissions (pasted into body of message); no disk submissions. "Submission should include snail mail address and a short (1-2 lines) bio." Reads submissions year round. Submit seasonal poems 6 months in advance. Time between acceptance and publication is 1-2 months. Often comments on rejected poems. Guidelines available on website. Responds in 4-6 weeks. Pays 2 cents/word for original poems and one contributor's copy. Acquires first North American serial rights. Reviews books and chapbooks of poetry. Send materials for review consideration to Tyree Campbell.

Advice "It's up to the writer to take the first step and submit work. Some of our best poems have come from poets who weren't sure if they were good enough. Horror poetry is a difficult sell with us."

ILLUMINATIONS, AN INTERNATIONAL MAGAZINE OF CONTEMPORARY WRITING

Dept. of English, College of Charleston, 66 George St., Charleston SC 29424-0001. (843)953-1920. Fax: (843)953-3180. E-mail: lewiss@cofc.edu. Website: www.cofc.edu/Illuminations. Established 1982. **Contact:** Simon Lewis, editor.

Magazine Needs *Illuminations* is published annually "to provide a forum for new writers alongside already established ones." Open as to form and style, and to translations. Does not want to see anything "bland or formally clunky." Has published poetry by Peter Porter, Michael Hamburger, Geri Doran, and Anne Born. *Illuminations* is 64-88 pages, digest-sized, offset-printed, perfect-bound, with 2-color card cover. Receives about 1,500 poems/year, accepts up to 5%. Press run is 400. Subscription: $15/2 issues. Sample: $10.

How to Submit Submit up to 6 poems at a time. No previously published poems or simultaneous submissions. Accepts submissions by fax, e-mail (pasted into body of message, no attachments), postal mail, and on disk. Brief cover letter is preferred. Time between acceptance and publication "depends on when received. Can be up to a year." Publishes theme issues occasionally; "Issue 16 [2000] was a Vietnamese special; Issue 17 [2001] focused on Cuban and Latin American writing." Guidelines available by e-mail. Responds within 2 months. Pays 2 contributor's copies plus one subsequent issue. Acquires all rights. Returns rights on request.

ILLYA'S HONEY; DALLAS POETS COMMUNITY OPEN POETRY COMPETITION

% Dallas Poets Community, P.O. Box 700865, Dallas TX 75370. E-mail: info@dallaspoets.org. Website: www.dallaspoets.org. Established 1994, acquired by Dallas Poets Community in January 1998. **Contact:** Ann Howells, managing editor.

Magazine Needs *Illya's Honey* is a quarterly journal of poetry and micro fiction. "All subjects and styles are welcome, but we admit a fondness for free verse. Poems may be of any length but should be accessible, thought-provoking, fresh, and should exhibit technical skill. Every poem is read by at least 3 members of our editorial staff, all of whom are poets. No didactic or overly religious verse, please." Has published poetry by Lyn Lifshin, Joe Ahern, Seamus Murphy, Robert Eastwood, and Brandon Brown. *Illya's Honey* is 40 pages, digest-sized, saddle-stapled, with glossy card cover with b&w photograph. Receives about 2,000 poems/year, accepts about 5-10%. Press run is 150 (60 subscribers). Single copy: $6; subscription: $18. Sample: $4.

How to Submit Submit 3-5 poems at a time. No previously published poems or simultaneous submissions. Accepts submissions by postal mail only. Cover letter is preferred. Include short biography. Occasionally comments on rejected poems. Guidelines available for SASE. Responds in up to 5 months. Pays one contributor's copy.

Contest/Award Offerings Annual Dallas Poets Community Open Poetry Competition offers 1st prize: $300; 2nd prize: $200; 3rd prize: $100. Winners are published in *Illya's Honey*. Submit one poem/page, any subject, any length to 3 pages; include cover sheet with contact information and name(s) of poem(s). **Entry fee:** $5/poem. **Deadline:** postmark June 1 to August 15.

$ ⚇ ◎ IMAGE: ART, FAITH, MYSTERY (Specialized: religion)

3307 3rd Ave. W., Seattle WA 98119. E-mail: image@imagejournal.org. Website: www.imagejourn al.org. Established 1989. **Contact:** Gregory Wolfe, publisher.

Magazine Needs *Image*, published quarterly, "explores and illustrates the relationship between faith and art through world-class fiction, poetry, essays, visual art, and other arts." Wants "poems that grapple with religious faith, usually Judeo-Christian." Has published poetry by Philip Levine, Scott Cairns, Annie Dillard, Mary Oliver, Mark Jarman, and Kathleen Norris. *Image* is 136 pages, 10×7, printed on acid-free paper, perfect-bound, with glossy 4-color cover, includes ads. Receives about 800 poems/year, accepts up to 2%. Has 5,000 subscribers (100 are libraries). Subscription: $36. Sample: $12.

How to Submit Submit up to 4 poems at a time. No previously published poems. No e-mail submissions. Cover letter is preferred. Time between acceptance and publication is one year. Guidelines available on website. Responds in 3 months. Always sends prepublication galleys. Pays 4 contributor's copies plus $2/line ($150 maximum). Acquires first North American serial rights. Reviews books of poetry in 2,000 words, single- or multi-book format. Send materials for review consideration.

✪ ⚇ IMPLOSION PRESS; IMPETUS; EPITOME

4975 Comanche Trail, Stow OH 44224-1217. (330)688-5210. E-mail: impetus@aol.com. Established 1984. **Contact:** Cheryl Townsend, poetry editor.

Magazine Needs Implosion Press publishes *Impetus*, a "sporadic" literary magazine, and *Epitome*, a regional publication for and by women, as well as chapbooks and special issues. Would like to see "strong social protest with raw emotion. Material should be straight from the gut, uncensored and real. Absolutely no nature poetry or rhyme for the sake of rhyme, or 'kissy, kissy, I love you' poems. Any length as long as it works. All subjects OK, providing there are no 'isms.'" Has published poetry by Sherman Alexie, Ron Androla, Kurt Nimmo, Lyn Lifshin, and Lonnie Sherman. Sample: $5. Make checks payable to Implosion Press.

How to Submit Submit 3-8 poems at a time. "I prefer shorter, to-the-point work." Accepts previously published poems if noted as such (include when and where each poem was originally published). Accepts submissions by e-mail (pasted into body of message) and by postal mail. "I like a cover letter that tells me how the poet found out about my magazine." Include name and address on each page. Time between acceptance and publication is "generally" 5 months. Guidelines available in magazine, for SASE, or by e-mail. Usually responds within 4 months. Acquires one-time rights. Reviews books of poetry. Send materials for review consideration.

Advice "Know your market. Request guidelines and/or a sample copy."

⚇ IN POSSE REVIEW; IN POSSE REVIEW MULTI-ETHNIC ANTHOLOGY

E-mail: in_posse_review@yahoo.com. Website: www.webdelsol.com/InPosse. Established 1998. **Contact:** Ilya Kaminsky, poetry editor. Member: Web del Sol.

- Poetry from *In Posse Review* has been selected for inclusion in *The Best American Poetry*, and also selected regularly for publication at www.versedaily.com, www.mobylives.com, and others.

Magazine Needs *In Posse Review*, published by Web del Sol, appears quarterly. "We publish poetry, fiction, nonfiction, book reviews, and special issues. Many authors we published for the first time later went on to achieve national recognition and awards, such as the Lannan Foundation Fellowship, the Wilson Foundation Fellowship, the Ruth Lilly Fellowship, the Barnes & Noble 'Discover New Writers' Award, and others. We have published the work of poet laureates and high school students. The only criteria for publication is excellence of work submitted." Open to all styles and forms. "We are very selective and accept only about 5-10% of submissions." Has published poetry by Lola Haskins, Jennifer Michael Hecht, David Hinton, Wyn Cooper, Ralf Sneeden, and Walt McDonald. Receives about 5,000 poems/year, accepts about 10. *In Posse Review* is published online.

How to Submit Submit 2-4 poems at a time. Accepts previously published poems; no simultaneous submissions. Accepts e-mail submissions ONLY (pasted into body of message). Acquires one-time rights. Reviews books and chapbooks of poetry. "Write us a letter before submitting your review and ask for specific guidelines."

Also Offers *In Posse Review Multi-Ethnic Anthology*, an ongoing project published along with *In Posse Review*; there is no deadline.

Advice "Read our publication and the editor's own books before submitting. If you are serious about writing and want your work to be considered seriously, you should show it by considering seriously the work we produce and publish."

🗃 ◎ IN THE GROVE (Specialized: regional/California)

P.O. Box 16195, Fresno CA 93755. (559)442-4600, ext. 8105. Fax: (559)265-5756. E-mail: inthegrove @rocketmail.com. Website: http://leeherrick.tripod.com/itg. Established 1996. **Contact:** Lee Herrick, editor/publisher.

Magazine Needs *In the Grove* appears 1-2 times/year and publishes "short fiction, essays, and poetry by new and established writers born or currently living in the Central Valley and throughout California." Wants "poetry of all forms and subject matter. We seek the originality, distinct voice, and craft of a poem. No greeting card verse or forced rhyme. Be fresh. Take a risk." Has published poetry by Andres Montoya, Corrine Hales, Ryan G. Van Cleave, Timothy Liu, Amy Uyematsu, and Renny Christopher. *In The Grove* is 80-100 pages, digest-sized, photocopied, perfect-bound, with heavy card stock cover. Receives about 500 poems/year, accepts up to 10%. Press run is 200 (50 subscribers, 100 shelf sales); 50 distributed free to contributors, colleagues. Subscription: $12. Sample: $6.

How to Submit Submit 3-5 poems at a time. Accepts previously published poems "on occasion" and simultaneous submissions "with notice." Cover letter is preferred. Time between acceptance and publication is up to 6 months. "Poetry editor reads all submissions and makes recommendations to editor, who makes final decisions." Seldom comments on rejected poems. Guidelines available for SASE or on website. Responds in 3 months. Pays 2 contributor's copies. Acquires first or one-time rights. Rights return to poets upon publication.

🗃 ◎ INDEFINITE SPACE (Specialized: experimental)

P.O. Box 40101, Pasadena CA 91114. Established 1992. **Contact:** Marcia Arrieta, editor.

Magazine Needs *Indefinite Space* appears annually. Wants experimental, visual, minimalistic poetry. Does not want rhyming poetry. Has published poetry by Bob Heman, Dan Campion, Elizabeth Kate Switaj, James Doyle, Peter Ganick, and Margarita Engle. *Indefinite Space* is 36 pages, digest-sized. Single copy: $6; subscription: $10/2 issues. Make checks payable to Marcia Arrieta.

How to Submit Accepts simultaneous submissions; no previously published poems. No disk submissions. Seldom comments on rejected poems. Guidelines available for SASE. Responds in up to 3 months. Copyright retained by poets.

🗃 ◎ THE INDENTED PILLOW (Specialized: Tantra, sacred sexuality)

P.O. Box 3502, Camarillo CA 93011. E-mail: rjones@mymailstation.com. Established 2003. **Contact:** Ronald K. Jones, editor/publisher.

Magazine Needs *The Indented Pillow* appears annually in January and publishes poems relating to the Tantric Experience. Wants poems "reflecting sexuality and sex practices of the Eastern philosophical tenets of Tantra, i.e., sex and spirit as one." *The Indented Pillow* is one or more pages ($8\frac{1}{2} \times 11$ single sheets), photocopied, folded, with 67-lb. cover. Receives about 20 poems/year, accepts about 50%. Press run is 200 (30 subscribers); 170 are distributed free to bookstores and relevant organizations. "Since *The Indented Pillow* is a free publication, circulation is often more than stated." Single copy: one first-class stamp; subscription: one first-class stamp.

How to Submit Submit 6 poems at a time. Lines/poem: 20 maximum. Accepts previously published poems and simultaneous submissions. Accepts e-mail submissions (pasted into body of message). Reads submissions all year. Time between acceptance and publication is one year. Often comments on rejected poems. Guidelines available for SASE. Responds in one month. Pays 2 contributor's copies. Acquires one-time rights.

Advice "If you've had a spiritual experience in a sexual encounter, then you already know the meaning of Tantra."

◼ ◎ INDIAN HERITAGE PUBLISHING; INDIAN HERITAGE COUNCIL QUARTERLY; NATIVE AMERICAN POETRY ANTHOLOGY (Specialized: Native American; nature/ecology; spirituality/inspirational; religious)
P.O. Box 752, McCall ID 83638. (208)315-0916. Established 1986. **Contact:** Louis Hooban, CEO.

- *Indian Heritage Council Quarterly* received the Evergreen Award from the Consortium of International Environmental Groups.

Magazine Needs *Indian Heritage Council Quarterly* devotes one issue to poetry with a Native American theme. Wants "any type of poetry relating to Native Americans, their beliefs, or Mother Earth." Does not want "doggerel." Has published poetry by Running Buffalo and Angela Evening Star Dempsey. *Indian Heritage Council Quarterly* is 6 pages, digest-sized ($8\frac{1}{2} \times 11$ folded sheet with $5\frac{1}{2} \times 8\frac{1}{2}$ insert), photocopied. Receives about 300 poems/year, accepts up to 30%. Press run and number of subscribers vary; 50 distributed free to Indian reservations. Subscription: $10. Sample: "negotiable." Make checks payable to Indian Heritage Council.

How to Submit Submit up to 3 poems at a time. Accepts previously published poems (author must own rights only) and simultaneous submissions. Cover letter is required. Time between acceptance and publication is 3 months to one year. "Our editorial board decides on all publications." Seldom comments on rejected poems. Charges criticism fees "depending on negotiations." Publishes theme issues. List of upcoming themes and guidelines available for SASE. Responds within 3 weeks. Pay is negotiable. Acquires one-time rights. Staff reviews books or chapbooks of poetry or other magazines. Send materials for review consideration.

Book/Chapbook Needs & How to Submit Indian Heritage Publishing publishes chapbooks of Native American themes and/or Native American poets. Has published *Crazy Horse's Philosophy of Riding Rainbows*, *Native American Predictions*, and *The Vision: An Anthology of Native American Poetry*. Format of chapbooks varies. Query first, with a few sample poems and cover letter with brief bio and publication credits. Responds to queries within 3 weeks, varies for mss. Pays 33-50% royalties. **Offers subsidy arrangements that vary by negotiations, number of poems, etc.** For sample chapbooks, write to the above address.

Contest/Award Offerings Sponsors a contest for their anthology, "if approved by our editorial board. Submissions are on an individual basis—always provide a SASE."

Advice "Write from the heart and spirit, and write so the reader can understand or grasp the meaning. We seek poets/writers who have strong writing abilities in Native literature."

$ ◼ INDIANA REVIEW
Ballantine Hall 465, 1020 E. Kirkwood Ave., Bloomington IN 47405-7103. (812)855-3439. E-mail: inreview@indiana.edu. Website: www.indiana.edu/~inreview. Established 1976. **Contact:** Grady Jaynes, editor.

- Poetry published in *Indiana Review* has been included in *The Best American Poetry* and *Pushcart Prize* anthologies.

Magazine Needs *Indiana Review* is a biannual of prose, poetry, creative nonfiction, book reviews, and visual art. "We look for an intelligent sense of form and language, and admire poems of risk, ambition, and scope. We'll consider all types of poems—free verse, traditional, experimental. Reading a sample issue is the best way to determine if *Indiana Review* is a potential home for your work. Any subject matter is acceptable if it is written well." Has published poetry by Philip Levine, Sherman Alexie, Marilyn Chin, Alice Friman, Julianna Baggott, and Alberto Rios. *Indiana Review* is 160 pages, digest-sized, professionally printed, flat-spined, with color matte cover. Receives more than 9,000 submissions/year, accepts up to 60. Has 2,000 subscribers. Sample: $8.

How to Submit Submit 4-6 poems at a time; do not send more than 10 pages of poetry per submission. No electronic submissions. Pays $5/page ($10 minimum/poem), plus 2 contributor's copies and remainder of year's subscription. Acquires first North American serial rights only. "We try to respond to manuscripts in 3-4 months. Reading time is often slower during summer and holiday months." Brief book reviews are also featured. Send materials for review consideration.

Contest/Award Offerings Holds yearly poetry and prose-poem contests. Guidelines available for SASE.

$☑ INK POT; LIT POT PRESS, INC.

3909 Reche Rd., Suite 96, Fallbrook CA 92028. Phone/fax: (760)731-3111. E-mail: litpot@veryfast.biz. Website: www.inkpots.net; www.litpotpress.com. Established 2001. **Contact:** Beverly A. Jackson, editor-in-chief. Member: CLMP; Small Press Center.

- Winner of numerous website awards, including Five Star Award, Web 1000 Award, and Best of the Web award.

Magazine Needs *Ink Pot* is a "biannual print literary journal" featuring contemporary poetry, fiction, and essays. Samples of the material published in *Ink Pot* are reprinted on *Ink Pot*'s website. Wants "free verse and experimental forms; classic forms and fresh ideas." Does not want rhymed, children's, or religious poetry. Has published poetry by Simon Perchik, Terri Brown-Davidson, Richard Jackson, Richard Carr, Kate Fetherston, and Roger Weingarten. *Ink Pot* is more than 200 pages, digest-sized, perfect-bound, with color cover. Receives about 300 poems/year, accepts about 50. Press run is 250 (50 subscribers, 150 shelf sales); 50 are distributed free to writers/artists. Single copy: $12; subscription: $22. Make checks payable to Lit Pot Press, Inc.

How to Submit Submit up to 5 poems at a time. Lines/poem: 3 minimum, 100 maximum; prefers shorter poems in free verse. No previously published poems. Accepts submissions by e-mail (as attachment in .rtf, .txt, or .doc format); no disk or snail mail submissions. "E-mail submissions must include 'poetry,' your full name, and number of poems in the subject line. In body of e-mail, include name, address, brief third-person bio, and choice of payment (cash or contributor's copies of *Ink Pot*)." Submit seasonal poems 8 months in advance. Time between acceptance and publication is 8 months to a year. "Poems are read by editor-in-chief and poetry editor before acceptance/rejection." Seldom comments on rejected poems. Guidelines available on website. Responds "in a few days." Always sends prepublication galleys (as electronic proofs). Pays $5/poem or 2 contributor's copies. Acquires first North American serial rights; retains archival rights.

Book/Chapbook Needs & How to Submit "Poetry manuscripts not accepted at this time, except for chapbooks." Chapbooks are 25-40 pages, offset-printed, print-on-demand, with cardstock covers. Query first, with a few sample poems and a cover letter with brief bio and publication credits. Chapbook mss may include previously published poems. "**Chapbooks are author-subsidy efforts right now.** Lit Pot Press has to approve collaborative chapbooks." Responds to queries in one week. Pays royalties of 100%. Order sample books/chapbooks on website.

Advice "See website to get an idea of our style and tastes. Read guidelines and contract on website before submitting."

⚡ $○ INKWELL; INKWELL ANNUAL POETRY COMPETITION

2900 Purchase St., Purchase NY 10577. (914)323-7239. Fax: (914)323-3122. E-mail: inkwell@mville.edu. Website: www.inkwelljournal.org. Established 1995. **Contact:** Christine Adler, editor. Member: CLMP.

Magazine Needs *Inkwell* is a biannual literary journal publishing poetry, fiction, memoir, and essay. Wants "serious work—very well made verse, any form, genre." Does not want "doggerel, light or humorous verse." Has published poetry by Margaret Gibson, Honor Moore, Eamon Grennan, Erica Funkhouser, Elizabeth Alexander, and Philip Byrne. *Inkwell* is 160 pages, digest-sized, press-printed, perfect-bound, with photographs and graphic art on cover, includes ads. Receives about 1,500 poems/year, accepts about 40-50. Press run is 1,000 (200 subscribers, 720 shelf sales). Single copy: $8; subscription: $15/year. Make checks payable to *Inkwell*—Manhattanville College.

How to Submit Submit 6 poems at a time. Lines/poem: open. Accepts simultaneous submissions;

no previously published poems. No fax, e-mail, or disk submissions. Cover letter is required. "Omit name of author from text." Reads submissions August 1 through November 30. Time between acceptance and publication is 4 months. Poems are circulated to an editorial board. Sometimes comments on rejected poems. Sometimes publishes theme issues. List of upcoming themes and guidelines available on website. Responds in 4 months. Pays $5/page and 2 contributor's copies. Acquires first North American serial rights.

Contest/Award Offerings Sponsors the *Inkwell* Annual Poetry Competition. Offers $1,000 and publication for best poem. **Entry fee:** $10 for first poem, $5 for each additional poem. **Deadline:** October 31 annually. Guidelines available on website.

☑ THE INTERFACE; BUTTERMILK ART WORKS

% GlassFull Productions, P.O. Box 57129, Philadelphia PA 19111-7129. E-mail: madlove3000@exci te.com. Website: www.baworks.com/Interface. Established 1997. **Contact:** Earl Weeks, publisher.

Magazine Needs *The INTERFACE* is published online in January and June and covers wrestling, comic books, trading cards, science fiction, and politics. Wants "all kinds of work—romantic, political, social commentary. We want poetry that comes from your heart, that makes tears come to the eye or forces one to want to mobilize the troops. No poems of hate or discrimination." Has published poetry by Mike Emrys, Sheron Regular, Cassandra Norris, Emoni Brisbon, Darren Gilbert, and Monique Frederick. Receives about 20 poems/year, accepts up to 35%.

How to Submit Submit 7 poems at a time. Accepts previously published poems and simultaneous submissions. Accepts submissions by e-mail, through online submission form, and by postal mail. Cover letter is preferred. Send all submissions % Earl Weeks. "We will consider accompanying illustration." Submit seasonal poems 6 months in advance. Time between acceptance and publication is 9 months. Poems are circulated to an editorial board. Occasionally publishes theme issues. Guidelines and upcoming themes available on website. Does not respond to submissions. Acquires two-time rights. "We also have a sister magazine, *The Maelan News*, available only on newsstands in Philly. If you wish not to be printed in the print mag, let us know."

Contest/Award Offerings Interface Positive Poetry Contest; check website for details.

Also Offers "We publish poetry, essays, videogame reviews, book reviews, fashion, science fiction, art, recipes, and more. We are very interested in reviewing your music and passing out any promo materials you have. We are trying to make *The INTERFACE* a meeting place for idea exchanges. We need your opinions and views, so submit them to us."

☐ ◎ INTERNATIONAL BLACK WRITERS; BLACK WRITER MAGAZINE (Specialized: ethnic)

535 Logan Dr. #903, Hammond IN 46320. Established 1970. **Contact:** Mable Terrell, president.

Magazine Needs & How to Submit *Black Writer* is a "quarterly literary magazine to showcase new writers and poets and provide educational information for writers. Open to all types of poetry." *Black Writer* is 30 pages, magazine-sized, offset-printed, with glossy cover. Press run is 1,000 (200 subscribers). Subscription: $19/year. Sample: $1.50. Responds in 10 days. Pays 10 contributor's copies.

Book/Chapbook Needs & How to Submit For chapbook publication (40 pages), submit 2 sample poems and cover letter with short bio. Accepts simultaneous submissions. Pays in author's copies. For sample chapbook, send SASE with book rate postage.

Contest/Award Offerings Offers awards of $100, $50, and $25 for the best poems published in the magazine, and presents them to winners at annual awards banquet. International Black Writers is open to all writers.

⊕ ☑ IOTA; RAGGED RAVEN PRESS

1 Lodge Farm, Snitterfield, Warwicks CV37 0LR United Kingdom. Phone: 44-1789 730358. E-mail: iotapoetry@aol.com. Website: www.iotapoetry.co.uk. Established 1988. **Contact:** Janet Murch and Bob Mee, editors.

Magazine Needs *iota* is a quarterly wanting "any style and subject; no specific limitations as to length.'' Has published poetry by Jane Kinninmont, John Robinson, Tony Petch, Chris Kinsey, Christopher James, and Michael Kriesel. *iota* is 60 pages, professionally printed, perfect-bound, with b&w photograph litho cover. Accepts about 300 of 6,000 poems received. Press run is 300 (170 subscribers, 8 libraries). Single copy: £4.50; subscription: £18. (''UK £ sterling only; payment can also be made by credit card via our website.'')

How to Submit Submit 4-6 poems at a time. Prefers name and address on each poem, typed. No simultaneous submissions or previously published poems. Accepts e-mail submissions (pasted into body of message). Cover letter is required. Responds in 3 weeks (unless production of the next issue takes precedence). ''No SAE, no reply.'' Pays one contributor's copy. Reviews books of poetry. Send materials for review consideration.

Contest/Award Offerings Sponsors an annual poetry competition, offering 1st Prize: £100; 2nd Prize: £50; publication in *iota* and on website. **Entry fee:** free for up to 2 poems for subscribers, £2 for each subsequent poem; £2/poem for non-subscribers. **Deadline:** April 15. Guidelines available on website.

Also Offers ''The editors also run Ragged Raven Press, which publishes poetry collections, nonfiction, and an annual anthology of poetry linked to an international competition.'' Website: www.raggedraven.co.uk.

Advice ''Read poetry, particularly contemporary poetry. Edit your own poems to tighten and polish.''

$ ☑ THE IOWA REVIEW; THE TIM McGINNIS AWARD; THE IOWA AWARD

308 EPB, University of Iowa, Iowa City IA 52242. (319)335-0462. E-mail: iowa-review@uiowa.edu. Website: www.uiowa.edu/~iareview. Established 1970. **Contact:** David Hamilton, editor.

• Poetry published in *The Iowa Review* has been frequently included in *The Best American Poetry* and the *Pushcart Prize* anthologies.

Magazine Needs *The Iowa Review* appears 3 times/year and publishes fiction, poetry, essays, reviews, and, occasionally, interviews. ''We simply look for poems that at the time we read and choose, we find we admire. No specifications as to form, length, style, subject matter, or purpose. Though we print work from established writers, we're always delighted when we discover new talent.'' *The Iowa Review* is 192 pages, professionally printed, flat-spined. Receives about 5,000 submissions/year, accepts up to 100. Press run is 2,900 (1,000 subscribers, about 500 libraries); 1,500 distributed to stores. Subscription: $24. Sample: $8.

How to Submit Submit 3-6 poems at a time. No e-mail submissions. Cover letter (with title of work and genre) is encouraged; SASE required. Reads submissions ''only during the Fall semester, September through November, and then contest entries in the Spring.'' Time between acceptance and publication is ''around a year.'' Occasionally comments on rejected poems or offers suggestions on accepted poems. Responds in up to 4 months. Pays $25/page for the first page and $15 for each subsequent page, 2 contributor's copies, and a one-year subscription. Acquires first North American serial rights, non-exclusive anthology rights, and non-exclusive electronic rights.

Contest/Award Offerings Sponsors the Tim McGinnis Award. ''The award, in the amount of $500, is given irregularly to authors of work with a light or humorous touch. We have no separate category of submissions to be considered alone for this award. Instead, any essay, story, or poem we publish will automatically be under consideration for the McGinnis Award. In 2003, we also instituted an Iowa Award in Poetry, Fiction, and Essay.'' **Entry Fee:** $15. **Postmark Deadline:** February 1. ''Submit in January.'' Outside judges for finalists. Winners will receive $1,000 and publication. Several runners up will also be published. ''Around 100 pages of each December issue are set aside for award winners and finalists.''

✦ ☑ ◎ IRIS: A JOURNAL ABOUT WOMEN (Specialized: women/feminism)

P.O. Box 800588, University of Virginia, Charlottesville VA 22908. (434)924-4500. Fax: (434)982-2901. E-mail: iris@virginia.edu. Website: http://iris.virginia.edu. Established 1980. **Contact:** Pamela Hetherington, editor.

Magazine Needs *Iris* is a biannual magazine appearing in April and November that "focuses on issues concerning women worldwide." It features quality poetry, prose, and artwork—mainly by women, but will also accept work by men "if it illuminates some aspect of a woman's reality." It also publishes translations. Form and length are unspecified. The poetry staff consists of experienced poets with a diversity of tastes who are looking for new and original language and diverse perspectives in well-crafted poems. Has published poetry by Sharon Olds, Mary Oliver, Charlotte Matthews, Rebecca B. Rank, Lisa Russ Spaar, and Gregory Orr. *Iris* is 78 pages, magazine-sized, professionally printed on heavy, glossy stock, saddle-stapled, with full-color glossy card cover. Press run is over 2,000 (about 40 library subscriptions, 1,000 shelf sales). Single copy: $5; subscription: $9/year, $17/2 years. Sample: $6.50.

How to Submit Submit no more than 5 poems at a time. Simultaneous submissions are discouraged. Accepts submissions by postal mail only. "Name, address, and phone number should be listed on every poem. Cover letter should include list of poems submitted and a brief bio." Publishes theme issues. List of upcoming themes available for SASE, on website, and in magazine. Guidelines available for SASE or on website. Responds in 6 months. Pays 5 contributor's copies. Acquires first rights.

Advice "The poetry staff at *Iris* is interested in pieces exploring all aspects of women's lives—especially the lives of younger women. Because many poems are on similar topics, freshness of imagery and style are even more important."

ITALIAN AMERICANA; JOHN CIARDI AWARD (Specialized: ethnic/Italian)

URI/CCE, 80 Washington St., Providence RI 02903-1803. (401)277-5306. Fax: (401)277-5100. E-mail: bonomoal@ital.uri.edu. Website: www.uri.edu/prov/italian/. Established 1974. **Contact:** Michael Palma, poetry editor. Editor: Carol Bonomo Albright.

Magazine Needs *Italian Americana* appears twice/year using 16-20 poems of "no more than 3 pages. No trite nostalgia about grandparents." Has published poetry by Mary Jo Salter and Jay Parini. *Italian Americana* is 150-200 pages, digest-sized, professionally printed, flat-spined, with glossy card cover. Press run is 1,000 (900 subscribers, 175 libraries, 175 shelf sales). Singly copy: $10; subscription: $20/year, $35/2 years. Sample: $6.

How to Submit Submit no more than 3 poems at a time. No previously published poems or simultaneous submissions. Cover letter is not required "but helpful." Name on first page of ms only. Occasionally comments on rejected poems. Responds in 6 weeks. Acquires first rights. Reviews books of poetry in 600 words, multi-book format. Send materials for review consideration to Prof. John Paul Russo, English Dept., University of Miami, Coral Gables FL 33124.

Contest/Award Offerings Along with the National Italian American Foundation, *Italian Americana* co-sponsors the annual $1,000 John Ciardi Award for Lifetime Contribution to Poetry. *Italian Americana* also presents $250 fiction or memoir award annually; and $1,500 in history prizes.

Advice "Single copies of poems for submissions are sufficient."

JACK MACKEREL MAGAZINE (Specialized: surrealism); ROWHOUSE PRESS

P.O. Box 23134, Seattle WA 98102-0434. Established 1992. **Contact:** Greg Bachar, editor.

Magazine Needs *Jack Mackerel*, published annually, features poetry, fiction, and art. Has published poetry by Bill Knott, John Rose, and William D. Waltz. *Jack Mackerel* is 40-60 pages, digest-sized, printed on bond paper, with glossy card coverstock. Press run is 1,000.

How to Submit No previously published poems or simultaneous submissions. Cover letter is preferred. Seldom comments on rejected poems. Responds in one month. Pays 2 contributor's copies.

ALICE JAMES BOOKS; NEW ENGLAND/NEW YORK AWARD; BEATRICE HAWLEY AWARD

University of Maine at Farmington, 238 Main St., Farmington ME 04938. Phone/fax: (207)778-7071. E-mail: ajb@umf.maine.edu. Website: www.alicejamesbooks.org. Established 1973. **Contact:** Aimee Beal, contest coordinator.

Book/Chapbook Needs "The mission of Alice James Books, a cooperative poetry press, is to seek out and publish the best contemporary poetry by both established and beginning poets, with particular emphasis on involving poets in the publishing process." Has published poetry by Jane Kenyon, Jean Valentine, B.H. Fairchild, and Matthea Harvey. Publishes flat-spined paperbacks of high quality, both in production and contents; no children's poetry or light verse. Publishes 6 paperback books/year, 80 pages each, in editions of 1,500. Manuscripts are selected through competition (see below).

Contest/Award Offerings 1) The **New England/New York Award** offers $1,000 and publication; winners become members of the Alice James Books cooperative, with a 3-year commitment to the editorial board. Entrants must reside in New England or New York State. 2) The **Beatrice Hawley Award** offers $2,000 and publication; winners have no cooperative membership commitment. "In addition to the winning manuscript, one or more additional manuscripts may be chosen for publication." Entrants must reside in the US. "No phone queries. Send 2 copies of manuscript (50-70 pages), entry fee, and business-size SASE for notification; manuscripts cannot be returned. Individual poems from the manuscript may have been previously published in magazines, anthologies, or chapbooks of less than 48 pages, but the collection as a whole must be unpublished." Accepts simultaneous submissions, but "we would like to know immediately when a manuscript is accepted elsewhere." **Entry fees:** $25 for each contest. **Deadlines:** early fall and winter (check website). Guidelines available for SASE or on website.

☑ ◎ JEWISH CURRENTS (Specialized: themes; politics; history; religious; ethnic/ nationality)

22 E. 17th St., Suite 601, New York NY 10003-1919. (212)924-5740. Fax: (212)414-2227. E-mail: jewish.currents@verizon.net. Website: www.jewishcurrents.org. Established 1946. **Contact:** Lawrence Bush, editor.

Magazine Needs *Jewish Currents* is a magazine appearing 6 times/year that publishes articles, reviews, fiction, and poetry pertaining to Jewish subjects or presenting a Jewish point of view on an issue of interest, including translations from the Yiddish and Hebrew (original texts should be submitted with translations). *Jewish Currents* is 40 pages, magazine-sized, offset-printed, saddle-stapled. Press run is 2,500 (2,100 subscribers, about 10% are libraries). Subscription: $30/year. Sample: $5.

How to Submit Submit one poem at a time, typed, double-spaced, with SASE. No previously published poems or simultaneous submissions. No fax submissions. Cover letter is required. "Include brief bio with author's publishing history." Time between acceptance and publication is up to 2 years. Often comments on rejected poems. Responds within 3 months. Always sends prepublication galleys. Pays 6 contributor's copies. Reviews books of poetry.

Advice "Be intelligent, original, unexpected, comprehensible."

$ ☑ ◎ JEWISH WOMEN'S LITERARY ANNUAL (Specialized: poetry by Jewish women only)

820 Second Ave., New York NY 10017. (212)751-9223. Established 1994. **Contact:** Dr. Henny Wenkart, editor.

Magazine Needs *Jewish Women's Literary Annual* appears in April and publishes poetry and fiction by Jewish women. Wants "poems by Jewish women on any topic, but of the highest literary quality." Has published poetry by Linda Zisquit, Merle Feld, Helen Papell, Enid Dame, Marge Piercy, and Lesléa Newman. *Jewish Women's Literary Annual* is 160 pages, digest-sized, perfect-bound, with laminated card cover. Receives about 1,500 poems/year, accepts about 10%. Press run is 1,500 (650 subscribers). Subscription: $18/3 issues. Sample: $7.50.

How to Submit No previously published poems. Accepts submissions by postal mail only. Poems are circulated to an editorial board. Often comments on rejected poems. Guidelines available for SASE. Responds in up to 5 months. Pays 3 contributor's copies plus a small honorarium. Rights remain with the poet.

Advice "Send only your very best. We are looking for humor, as well as other things, but nothing cutesy or smart-aleck. We do *no* politics; prefer topics *other than* 'Holocaust'."

◢ ◎ **JOEL'S HOUSE PUBLICATIONS; WILLIAM DEWITT ROMIG POETRY CONTEST** (Specialized: religious/Christian; spirituality; recovery)

P.O. Box 328, Beach Lake PA 18405-0328. (570)729-8709. Fax: (570)729-7246. E-mail: newbeginmin@ezaccess.net. Website: http://newbeginningmin.org. Established 1997. **Contact:** Kevin T. Coughlin, editor.

Magazine Needs *Joel's House Publications* appears annually in December. Produced by New Beginning Ministry, Inc., a nonprofit corporation, *Joel's House Publications* is a newsletter featuring poetry, articles, and original art. Wants poetry that is related to recovery, spirituality; also Christian poetry. Will consider any length, positive topic, and structure. No poetry that is inappropriately sexually graphic or discriminatory in nature. Has published poetry by Cynthia Brackett-Vincent, John Waddington-Feather, Wendy Apgar, K.F. Homer, Melanie Schurr, and William DeWitt Romig. *Joel's House Publications* is 10-20 pages, digest-sized, offset-printed, saddle-stapled, with card stock cover. Receives about 25-50 poems/year, accepts about 25%. Press run is 1,000 (100 subscribers); 200 distributed free to mailing list. Subscription: $5/year (one issue). Sample: $2 plus p&h. Make checks payable to New Beginning Ministry, Inc.

How to Submit Submit 3-5 poems at a time, typed, with name and address on each poem. No previously published poems or simultaneous submissions. Accepts submissions by fax, e-mail, postal mail, and on disk. Cover letter is preferred. "Always include a SASE." Reads submissions all year. Time between acceptance and publication is up to one year. Seldom comments on rejected poems. Guidelines available for SASE. Responds in up to 6 weeks. Always sends prepublication galleys. Pays 2 contributor's copies. Acquires first rights.

Contest/Award Offerings Sponsors annual poetry contest. "Held every December, the William DeWitt Romig Poetry Award will be given to the poet who best demonstrates life through the art of poetry." Guidelines available for SASE.

Also Offers Writing retreats (check website for details).

Advice "Keep writing—revise, revise, revise! If you write poetry, you are a poet. Be true to your craft."

◢ **THE JOHNS HOPKINS UNIVERSITY PRESS**

2715 N. Charles St., Baltimore MD 21218. Website: www.press.jhu.edu. Established 1878. "One of the largest American university presses, Johns Hopkins publishes primarily scholarly books and journals. We do, however, publish short fiction and poetry in the series Johns Hopkins: Poetry and Fiction, edited by John Irwin. Unsolicited submissions are not considered."

⊕ ◢ **THE DAVID JONES JOURNAL; THE DAVID JONES SOCIETY**

48 Sylvan Way, Sketty, Swansea, W. Glam SA2 9JB Wales. Phone: (01792)206144. Fax: (01792)205305. E-mail: anne.price-owen@sihe.ac.uk. Established 1997. **Contact:** Anne Price-Owen, editor.

Magazine Needs *The David Jones Journal* annually publishes "material related to David Jones, the Great War, mythology, and the visual arts." Wants "poetry that evokes or recalls themes and/or images related to the painter/poet David Jones (1895-1974)." Has published poetry by John Mole, R.S. Thomas, Seamus Heaney, and John Montague. The journal is about 160 pages, digest-sized, camera-ready-printed, perfect-bound, with full-color card cover. Receives about 12 poems/year, accepts about 8%. Press run is 400 (300 subscribers). Single copy: $12; subscription: $35. Sample: $10. Make checks payable to The David Jones Society.

How to Submit Submit one poem at a time. Accepts simultaneous submissions; no previously published poems. Accepts e-mail and disk submissions. Cover letter is preferred. Time between acceptance and publication is 6 months. "Two editors agree on publication." Occasionally publishes theme issues. Guidelines available by e-mail. Responds in 6 weeks. Sometimes sends prepublication galleys. Pays 2 contributor's copies. Acquires first rights. Reviews books and chapbooks of poetry and other magazines in 750 words, single-book format. Open to unsolicited reviews. Send materials for review consideration.

$☑ THE JOURNAL

Dept. of English, Ohio State University, 164 W. 17th Ave., Columbus OH 43210. (614)292-4076. Fax: (614)292-7816. E-mail: thejournal@osu.edu. Website: www.english.ohio-state.edu/journals/the_journal/. Established 1972. **Contact:** Kathy Fagan and Michelle Herman, co-editors.

Magazine Needs *The Journal* appears twice/year with reviews, quality fiction and nonfiction, and poetry. "We're open to all forms; we tend to favor work that gives evidence of a mature and sophisticated sense of the language." Has published poetry by Beckian Fritz Goldberg, Terrance Hayes, Bob Hicok, and Linda Bierds. *The Journal* is 128-144 pages, digest-sized, professionally printed on heavy stock. Receives about 4,000 submissions/year, accepts about 200. Press run is 1,900. Subscription: $12. Sample: $7.

How to Submit No fax submissions. Occasionally comments on rejected poems. Occasionally publishes theme issues. Responds in up to 3 months. Pays 2 contributor's copies and an honorarium of $25-50 when funds are available. Acquires all rights. Returns rights on publication. Reviews books of poetry.

Advice "However else poets train or educate themselves, they must do what they can to know our language. Too much of the writing we see indicates poets do not, in many cases, develop a feel for the possibilities of language, and do not pay attention to craft. Poets should not be in a rush to publish—until they are ready."

☆ $◎ JOURNAL OF ASIAN MARTIAL ARTS (Specialized: sports/recreation)

821 W. 24th St., Erie PA 16502. (814)455-9517. Fax: (814)526-5262. E-mail: info@goviamedia.com. Website: www.goviamedia.com. Established 1991. **Contact:** Michael A. DeMarco, editor-in-chief.

Magazine Needs *Journal of Asian Martial Arts* is a quarterly "comprehensive journal on Asian martial arts with high standards and academic approach." Wants poetry about Asian martial arts and Asian martial art history/culture. "No restrictions, provided the poet has a feel for, and good understanding of, the subject." Does not want poetry showing a narrow view. "We look for a variety of styles from an interdisciplinary approach." The journal is 124 pages, magazine-sized, professionally printed on coated stock, perfect-bound, with soft cover, includes ads. Press run is 12,000 (1,500 subscribers, 50 libraries, the rest mainly shelf sales). Single copy: $9.75; subscription: $32/year, $55/2 years. Sample: $10.

How to Submit Accepts previously published poems; no simultaneous submissions. Accepts e-mail submissions. Cover letter is required. Often comments on rejected poems. Guidelines available for SASE, by fax, or by e-mail. Responds in 2 months. Sometimes sends prepublication galleys. Pays $1-100 and/or 1-5 contributor's copies on publication. Buys first world and reprint rights. Reviews books of poetry "if they have some connection to Asian martial arts; length is open." Open to unsolicited reviews. Send materials for review consideration.

Advice "We offer a unique medium for serious poetry dealing with Asian martial arts. Any style is welcome if there is quality in thought and writing."

☑ ◎ JOURNAL OF NEW JERSEY POETS (Specialized: regional/New Jersey)

English Dept., County College of Morris, 214 Center Grove Rd., Randolph NJ 07869-2086. (973)328-5471. Fax: (973)328-5425. E-mail: szulauf@ccm.edu. Established 1976. **Contact:** Sander Zulauf, editor. Associate Editors: North Peterson, Gretna Wilkinson, and Debra DeMattio.

Magazine Needs Published annually in April, *Journal of New Jersey Poets* is "not necessarily about New Jersey—but of, by, and for poets from New Jersey." Wants "serious work that is regional in origin but universal in scope." Has published poetry by Amiri Baraka, X.J. Kennedy, Tina Kelley, Gerald Stern, Kenneth Burke, and Catherine Doty. *Journal of New Jersey Poets* is about 72 pages, digest-sized, offset-printed. Press run is 900. Single copy: $10; subscription: $16/2 issues; institutions: $16/issue. Sample: $5.

How to Submit Submit up to 3 poems at a time; SASE with sufficient postage required for return of mss. Accepts e-mail and fax submissions, "but they will not be acknowledged nor returned." **Annual deadline:** September 1. Responds in up to one year. Time between acceptance and publication is within one year. Guidelines available for SASE or by e-mail. Pays 5 contributor's copies and one-year subscription. Acquires first North American serial rights. Only using solicited reviews. Send materials for review consideration.

Advice "Read the *Journal* before submitting. Realize we vote on everything submitted, and rejection is more an indication of the quantity of submissions received and the enormous number of poets submitting quality work."

◨ ◎ JOURNAL OF THE AMERICAN MEDICAL ASSOCIATION (JAMA) (Specialized: health concerns; themes)

515 N. State, Chicago IL 60610. Fax: (312)464-5824. E-mail: charlene_breedlove@ama-assn.org. Website: www.jama.com. Established 1883. **Contact:** Charlene Breedlove, associate editor.

Magazine Needs *JAMA*, a weekly journal, has a poetry and medicine column and publishes poetry "in some way related to a medical experience, whether from the point-of-view of a health care worker or patient, or simply an observer. No unskilled poetry." Has published poetry by Aimée Grunberger, Floyd Skloot, and Walt McDonald. *JAMA* is magazine-sized, flat-spined, with glossy paper cover. Receives about 750 poems/year, accepts about 7%. Has 360,000 subscribers (369 libraries). Subscription: $66. Sample: free. "No SASE needed."

How to Submit Accepts simultaneous submissions, if identified; no previously published poems. Accepts fax submissions (include postal address in body of message). "Poems sent via fax will be responded to by postal service." Accepts e-mail submissions (pasted into body of message). "I always appreciate inclusion of a brief cover letter with, at minimum, the author's name and address clearly printed. Mention of other publications and special biographical notes are always of interest." Publishes theme issues. Themes include AIDS, violence/human rights, tobacco, medical education, access to care, and end-of-life care. "However, we would rather that poems relate obliquely to the theme." List of upcoming themes available on website. Pays one contributor's copy, more by request. "We ask for a signed copyright release, but publication elsewhere is always granted free of charge."

⊕ ◯ K.T. PUBLICATIONS; THE THIRD HALF; KITE BOOKS; KITE MODERN POETS; KITE MODERN WRITERS

16 Fane Close, Stamford, Lincolnshire PE9 1HG England. Phone: (01780)754193. Established 1989. **Contact:** Kevin Troop, editor.

Magazine Needs *The Third Half* is a literary magazine published regularly. It contains "free-flowing and free-thinking material on most subjects. Open to all ideas and suggestions. No badly written or obscene scribbling." Has published poetry by Gillian Bence-Jones, R. Tomas, Raymond Humphreys, and Mario Petrucci. *The Third Half* is neatly printed, perfect-bound, with glossy cover. Showcases 2 poets/issue. "Each poet has 24 pages with illustrations." Press run is 100-500. Single copy: £5.50 in UK. Sample: £10 overseas. Make checks payable to K.T. Publications.

How to Submit Submit 6 poems at a time. No previously published poems. Accepts submissions by postal mail and on disk; include SAE. Cover letter is preferred. Time between acceptance and publication "depends on the work and circumstances." **There is a £5 reading fee to cover costs.** Seldom comments on rejected poems. Occasionally publishes theme issues ("as themes present themselves"). Responds in 2 days. Always sends prepublication galleys. Pays 1-6 contributor's copies. "Copyright belongs to the poets/authors throughout."

Book/Chapbook Needs & How to Submit K.T. Publications and Kite Books publish "as much as possible each year" of poetry, short stories, and books for children—"at as high a standard as humanly possible." Has published *Freezing the Frame* by Michael Bangerter and *Insect Nights* by Hannah Welfare. Books are usually 50-60 pages, A5, perfect-bound, with glossy covers. Query first, with up to 6 sample poems and a cover letter with brief bio and publication credits. "Also include suitable SAE—so that I do not end up paying return postage every time."

Also Offers Offers a "reading and friendly help service to writers. Costs are reasonable." Write for details.

Advice "Keep writing; be patient."

⚫ ◎ **KAIMANA: LITERARY ARTS HAWAII; HAWAII LITERARY ARTS COUNCIL (Specialized: regional)**

P.O. Box 11213, Honolulu HI 96828. Website: www.hawaii.edu/hlac. Established 1974. **Contact:** Tony Quagliano, editor.

- Poets published in *Kaimana* have received the Pushcart Prize, the Hawaii Award for Literature, the Stefan Baciu Award, the Cades Award, and the John Unterecker Award.

Magazine Needs *Kaimana*, an annual, is the magazine of the Hawaii Literary Arts Council. Poems with "some Pacific reference are preferred—Asia, Polynesia, Hawaii—but not exclusively." Has published poetry by Reuben Tam, Howard Nemerov, Anne Waldman, Joe Balaz, Susan Schultz, and Paul Nelson. *Kaimana* is 64-76 pages, 7½×10, saddle-stapled, with high-quality printing. Press run is 1,000 (600 subscribers, 200 libraries). Subscription: $15, includes membership in HLAC. Sample: $10.

How to Submit Cover letter is preferred. Sometimes comments on rejected poems. Responds with "reasonable dispatch." Guidelines available in magazine. Pays 2 contributor's copies.

Advice "Hawaii gets a lot of 'travelling regionalists,' visiting writers with inevitably superficial observations. We also get superb visiting observers who are careful craftsmen anywhere. *Kaimana* is interested in the latter, to complement our own best Hawaii writers."

$ ◎ **KALEIDOSCOPE: EXPLORING THE EXPERIENCE OF DISABILITY THROUGH LITERATURE AND FINE ARTS (Specialized: disability themes)**

701 S. Main St., Akron OH 44311-1019. (330)762-9755. Fax: (330)762-0912. E-mail: mshiplett@uds akron.org. Website: www.udsakron.org. Established 1979. **Contact:** Gail Willmott, editor-in-chief.

Magazine Needs Published in January and July, *Kaleidoscope* is based at United Disability Services, a not-for-profit agency. Poetry should deal with the experience of disability, but is not limited to that when the writer has a disability. "*Kaleidoscope* is interested in high-quality poetry with vivid, believable images, and evocative language. No stereotyping, patronizing, or offending language about disability." Has published poetry by Jeanne Bryner, Jeff Worley, Barbara Crooker, and Sandra J. Lindow. *Kaleidoscope* is 64 pages, magazine-sized, professionally printed, saddle-stapled, with 4-color semigloss card cover. Press run is 1,500 (libraries, social service agencies, health-care professionals, universities, and individual subscribers). Single copy: $6; subscription: $10 individual, $15 agency.

How to Submit Submit up to 6 poems at a time. Send photocopies with SASE for return of work. Accepts previously published poems and simultaneous submissions, "as long as we are notified in both instances." Accepts fax and e-mail submissions. Cover letter is required. All submissions must be accompanied by an autobiographical sketch and "should be double-spaced, with pages numbered, and with author's name on each page." **Deadlines:** March 1 and August 1. Publishes theme issues. Themes for 2006 include Portrayals of Disability in the Media (July 2006) and Disability and Humor (January 2007). List of upcoming themes and guidelines available for SASE, by fax, by e-mail, and on website. Upcoming themes also announced in magazine. Responds in 3 weeks; acceptance or rejection may take 6 months. Pays $10-25 plus 2 contributor's copies. Rights return to author upon publication. Staff reviews books of poetry. Send materials for review consideration.

$ ▢ ◎ **KALLIOPE, A JOURNAL OF WOMEN'S LITERATURE & ART (Specialized: women writers & artists); SUE SANIEL ELKIND POETRY CONTEST**

South Campus, 11901 Beach Blvd., Jacksonville FL 32246. (904)646-2081. Website: www.fccj.edu/kalliope. Established 1978. **Contact:** Mary Sue Koeppel, editor.

Magazine Needs Appearing in fall and spring, *Kalliope* is a literary/visual arts journal published by Florida Community College at Jacksonville; the emphasis is on women writers and artists. "We like the idea of poetry as a sort of artesian well—there's one meaning that's clear on the surface and another deeper meaning that comes welling up from underneath. We'd like to see more poetry from Black, Hispanic, and Native American women. Nothing sexist, racist, or conventionally sentimental." *Kalliope* publishes fiction, interviews, and visual art in addition to poetry. Has published poetry by Marge Piercy, Ruth Stone, Jill Bialosky, Eleanor Wilner, Maxine Kumin, and Tess Gallagher. *Kalliope* is about 120 pages, 7¼×8¼, flat-spined, handsomely printed on white stock, with glossy card cover. Press run is 1,600 (400-500 subscribers, 100 libraries, 800 shelf sales). Subscription: $16/year or $27/2 years. Sample: $9.

How to Submit Submit poems in batches of 3-5 with brief bio note, phone number, and address. No previously published poems. Accepts submissions by postal mail only; SASE required. Reads submissions September through April only. Because all submissions are read by several members of the editing staff, response time is usually up to 6 months. Publication will be within 6 months after acceptance. Criticism is provided "when time permits and the author has requested it." Publishes theme issues. Guidelines and upcoming themes available for SASE or on website. Pays $10 if grant money available, subscription if not, plus 2 contributor's copies. Acquires first publication rights. Reviews books of poetry, "but we prefer groups of books in one review." Send materials for review consideration.

Editor Olga Obella says artist Joanna Sklan Key "was affected by the images conjured up by the poem 'Hiving' by Claudia Burbank" in the Vol. XIX, No. 1 issue of *Karamu*. Key used old engravings and computer graphics to create her design.

Contest/Award Offerings Sponsors the annual Sue Saniel Elkind Poetry Contest. 1st Prize: $1,000; runners up published in *Kalliope*. **Deadline:** November 1. Details available for SASE or on website.

Advice "*Kalliope* is a carefully stitched patchwork of how women feel, what they experience, and what they have come to know and understand about their lives . . . a collection of visions from or about women all over the world. Send for a sample copy to see what appeals to us—or better yet, subscribe!"

🖉 KARAMU

Dept. of English, Eastern Illinois University, Charleston IL 61920. Website: www.eiu.edu/~k aramu. Established 1966. **Contact:** Olga Abella, editor.

● *Karamu* has received grants from the Illinois Arts Council, and has won recognition and money awards in the IAC Literary Awards competition.

Magazine Needs *Karamu* is an annual journal, usually appearing in May or June, whose "goal is to provide a forum for the best contemporary poetry and fiction that comes our way. We especially like to print the works of new writers. We like to see poetry that shows a good sense of what's being done with poetry currently. We like poetry that builds around real experiences, real images, and real characters, and that avoids abstraction, overt philosophizing, and fuzzy pontifications. In terms of form, we prefer well-structured free verse, poetry with an inner, sub-surface structure as opposed to, let's say, the surface structure of rhymed quatrains. We have definite preferences in terms of style and form, but no such preferences in terms of length or subject matter. Purpose, however, is another thing. We don't have much interest in the openly didactic poem. We don't want poems that preach against or for some political or religious viewpoint. The poem should first be a poem." Has published poetry by Claudia Burbank, Brian Collier, Jennifer Firestone, Jason Koepp, Jan Minich, and George Wallace. *Karamu* is 120 pages, digest-sized, handsomely printed (narrow margins), with matte cover. Receives submissions from about 700 poets each year, accepts 40-50 poems. Press run is 500 (300 subscribers, 15 libraries). Single copy: $8. Sample: $6/2 back issues.

How to Submit Submit no more than 5 poems at a time. No previously published poems. "We don't much like, but do accept, simultaneous submissions. Always include a SASE for reply and return of material. Sufficient postage is necessary for return of work. We read September 1 through February 15 only; for fastest decision, submit January through February 15. Poets should not bother to query. We critique a few of the better poems. We want the poet to consider our comments and then submit new work." Time between acceptance and publication is up to one year. Occasionally publishes theme issues. List of upcoming themes and guidelines available for SASE. Pays one contributor's copy. Acquires first serial rights.

Advice "Follow the standard advice: Know your market. Read contemporary poetry and the magazines you want to be published in. Be patient."

⊘ KATYDID BOOKS

1 Balsa Rd., Santa Fe NM 87508. Website: http://katydidbooks.com. Established 1973. **Contact:** Karen Hargreaves-Fitzsimmons and Thomas Fitzsimmons, editors/publishers.

Book/Chapbook Needs & How to Submit Katydid Books publishes one paperback and one hardback/year. "We publish a series of poetry: Asian Poetry in Translation (distributed by University of Hawaii Press)." Currently not accepting submissions.

▢ ◎ KELSEY REVIEW (Specialized: regional/Mercer County)

Mercer County Community College, P.O. Box B, Trenton NJ 08690. (609)586-4800, ext. 3326. Fax: (609)586-2318. E-mail: kelsey.review@mccc.edu. Website: www.mccc.edu. Established 1988. **Contact:** Robin Schore, editor-in-chief.

Magazine Needs *Kelsey Review* is an annual published in September by Mercer County Community College. It serves as "an outlet for literary talent of people living and working in Mercer County, New Jersey only." Has no specifications as to form, length, subject matter, or style, but does not want to see poetry about "kittens and puppies." Has published poetry by Helen Gorenstein, Winifred Hughes, James Richardson, and Shirley Wright. *Kelsey Review* is about 90 glossy pages, 7×11, with paper cover. Receives about 60 submissions/year, accepts 6-10. Press run is 2,000; all distributed free to contributors, area libraries, bookstores, and schools.

How to Submit Submit up to 6 poems at a time, typed. No previously published poems or simultaneous submissions. No fax or e-mail submissions. **Deadline:** May 1. Always comments on rejected poems. Guidelines available by e-mail. Responds in June of each year. Pays 5 contributor's copies. All rights revert to authors.

$◙ THE KENYON REVIEW; THE WRITERS WORKSHOP

Kenyon College, Gambier OH 43022. (740)427-5208. Fax: (740)427-5417. E-mail: kenyonreview@kenyon.edu. Website: www.KenyonReview.org. Established 1939. **Contact:** David Lynn, editor.

Magazine Needs *Kenyon Review* is a quarterly review containing poetry, fiction, essays, criticism, reviews, and memoirs. It features all styles, forms, lengths, and subject matters, but this market is more closed than others because of the volume of submissions typically received during each reading cycle. Has published poetry by Billy Collins, Diane Ackerman, John Kinsella, Carol Muske-Dukes, Diane di Prima, and Seamus Heaney. *Kenyon Review* is 180 pages, digest-sized, flat-spined. Receives about 4,000 submissions/year. Press run is 6,000. Sample: $12 (includes postage).

How to Submit "Writers may contact us by phone, fax, or e-mail, but may submit manuscripts by postal mail or online submissions program (www.kenyon-review.org/submit) only." Typical reading period is September 1 through March 31. Responds in 3 months. Pays $15-30/page plus 2 contributor's copies. Acquires first North American serial rights. Reviews books of poetry in 2,500-7,000 words, single- or multi-book format. "Reviews are primarily solicited—potential reviewers should inquire first."

Also Offers The Writers Workshop, an annual 8-day event in June. Location: the campus of Kenyon

College. Average attendance is 12 per class. Open to writers of fiction, nonfiction, and poetry. Conference is designed to provide intensive conversation, exercises, and detailed readings of participants' work. Past instructors have included Linda Gregerson, Jonet McAdams, Allison Joseph, P.F. Kluge, Rebecca McClanahan, Margot Livesey, Erin McGrow, Claire Messud, Nancy Zafris, and David Baker. College and non-degree graduate credit is offered. Application available for SASE and on website. Early application is encouraged as the workshops are limited.

Advice "Editor recommends reading recent issues to become familiar with the type and quality of writing being published before submitting your work."

THE KERF (Specialized: animals; nature/ecology)

College of the Redwoods, 883 W. Washington Blvd., Crescent City CA 95531. Established 1995. **Contact:** Ken Letko, editor.

Magazine Needs *The Kerf*, published annually in summer, features "poetry that speaks to the environment and humanity." Wants "poetry that exhibits an environmental consciousness." Has published poetry by Ruth Daigon, Meg Files, James Grabill, and George Keithley. *The Kerf* is 54 pages, digest-sized, printed via Docutech, saddle-stapled, with CS2 coverstock. Receives about 2,000 poems/year, accepts up to 3%. Press run is 400 (150 shelf sales); 100 distributed free to contributors and writing centers. Sample: $5. Make checks payable to College of the Redwoods.

How to Submit Submit up to 5 poems (up to 7 pages) at a time. No previously published poems or simultaneous submissions. Reads submissions January 15 through March 31 only. Time between acceptance and publication is 3 months. "Our editors debate (argue for or against) the inclusion of each manuscript." Seldom comments on rejected poems. Guidelines available for SASE. Responds in 2 months. Sometimes sends prepublication galleys. Pays one contributor's copy. Acquires first North American serial rights.

Advice "Provide insights."

KIDVISIONS (Specialized: fantasy, science fiction, mild horror for older children and teens)

P.O. Box 782, Cedar Rapids IA 52406-0782. E-mail: kidvisions@samsdotpublishing.com. Website: www.samsdotpublishing.com. Established 2002. **Contact:** Lisa M. Bradley, editor. Member: The Speculative Literature Foundation (http://SpeculativeLiterature.org).

Magazine Needs *KidVisions*, an online quarterly, publishes "fantasy, science fiction, sword and sorcery, alternate history, extremely mild horror short stories, poems, illustrations, and movie and book reviews, all for a reading audience of 9-18 years old." Wants "fantasy, science fiction, spooky horror, and speculative poetry" appropriate to age group. Does not want "horror with excessive blood and gore." Has published poetry by Bruce Boston, Karen A. Romanko, Erin Donahoe, Eric Marin, Mikal Trimm, and Dorothy Imm. Receives about 150 poems/year, accepts about 35 (23%).

How to Submit Submit up to 5 poems at a time. Lines/poem: prefers less than 100. Accepts previously published poems; no simultaneous submissions. Accepts e-mail submissions (pasted into body of message); no disk submissions. "Submission should include snail mail address and a short (1-2 lines) bio." Reads submissions year round. Submit seasonal poems 6 months in advance. Time between acceptance and publication is 1-2 months. Often comments on rejected poems. Guidelines available on website. Responds in 4-6 weeks. Pays $2/poem, $1/reprint. Acquires first North American serial rights. Reviews books and chapbooks of poetry. Send materials for review consideration to Tyree Campbell.

Advice "We prefer to see material from younger writers whenever possible."

KING LOG

E-mail: davidcase@earthlink.net. Website: www.angelfire.com/il/kinglog. Established 1997. **Contact:** David Starkey, Carolie Parker-Lopez, or David Case, editors.

Magazine Needs *King Log* appears quarterly. Wants "accomplished poetry by American and Anglophone writers, whether experimental, confessional, or formalist. We are especially interested in poetry that captures the confusion of work/writing, romantic attachments, popular and high culture, history, and political and philosophical idealism and disillusion—comedy, irony, and passion.'' Does not want gushy, sentimental, macho, or precious work. Has published poetry by Jim Daniels, Barry Spacks, Katherine Swiggart, Walt McDonald, Evelyn Perry, and Paul Willis. *King Log* is 30 pages, published online with illustrations from *Aesop's Fables*. Receives about 400 poems/year, accepts about 60.

How to Submit Submit 3-5 poems at a time. No previously published poems or simultaneous submissions. Accepts e-mail submissions; no disk submissions. Cover letter is required. Reads submissions all year. Time between acceptance and publication is 3 months. ''Development of consensus among 3 editors who, broadly, share a sensibility and do not often disagree.'' Seldom comments on rejected poems. Guidelines available on website. Responds in 3 weeks. No payment. Acquires one-time rights.

$☑ THE KIT-CAT REVIEW

244 Halstead Ave., Harrison NY 10528-3611. (914)835-4833. Established 1998. **Contact:** Claudia Fletcher, editor.

Magazine Needs *The Kit-Cat Review* appears quarterly and is ''named after the 18th-century Kit-Cat Club whose members included Addison, Steele, Congreve, Vanbrugh, and Garth. Its purpose is to promote/discover excellence and originality.'' Wants quality work—traditional, modern, experimental. Has published poetry by Coral Hull, Virgil Suárez, Margret J. Hoehn, Louis Phillips, Chayym Zeldis, and Romania's Nobel Prize nominee, Marin Sorescu. *The Kit-Cat Review* is 75 pages, digest-sized, laser-printed/photocopied, saddle-stapled, with colored card cover. Receives about 1,000 poems/year. Press run is 500. ''*The Kit-Kat Review* is part of the collections of the University of Wisconsin (Madison) and the State University of New York (Buffalo).'' Subscription: $25. Sample: $7. Make checks payable to Claudia Fletcher.

How to Submit Submit any number of poems at a time. Accepts previously published poems and simultaneous submissions. ''Cover letter should contain any relevant bio.'' Time between acceptance and publication is 2 months. Responds within 2 months. Pays up to $100/poem plus 2 contributor's copies. Acquires first or one-time rights.

☐ KOTAPRESS; KOTAPRESS LOSS JOURNAL

(206)251-6706. E-mail: editor@kotapress.com. Website: www.kotapress.com. Established 1999. **Contact:** Kara L.C. Jones, editor.

Magazine Needs *KotaPress Loss Journal* is a monthly online magazine ''published in support of the grief and healing process after the death of a child. We publish *only* non-fictional poetry that somehow relates to grief and healing in relation to the death of a child. Please do not make up poems about this kind of loss and send them just to get in the magazine as it is insulting to many of our readers who are living this reality. As always, our interest is more in the content and story rather than one's ability to write in form; more in the ideas of poetry therapy rather than the academic, critique, competitive ideas normally fostered in universities.'' Has published poetry by John Fox, Poppy Hullings, Patricia Wellingham-Jones, Carol Jo Horn, and Sarah Bain.

How to Submit ''Please read current and some archived issues of the *Loss Journal* before sending anything. Then send a letter explaining your interest in contributing. We are interested in knowing how your personal experiences with death, dying, grief, and healing are playing out in the specific poems you are submitting. Include a bio if you wish to see one published with your poems after acceptance. Send your letter, poems, and bio as text all in one e-mail. Multiple e-mails will be ignored. File attachments will be deleted without ever being opened or acknowledged. Make sure the subject line of your e-mail says 'Loss Journal Submission'—we get over 600 e-mails a day, most of them spam, so we sort and read based on the subject line!'' Accepts submissions year round on a rolling basis. Time between acceptance and publication is up to 2 months. More details about guidelines available on website. Responds in 2 months. Acquires one-time electronic rights and archive rights. ''We do not remove works from our archives. Please see our website to find out more about us and about what we offer. We look forward to hearing from you and reading your poetry.''

Advice "If you are interested in contributing to our *Loss Journal*, it is really important that you read the journal first. This will tell you a lot about the voice of the work we publish and how your poems might 'fit the bill' for us. Please understand that while we acknowledge that all losses are difficult, we do not equate pet loss with child loss—and we do not equate fictional ideas about loss with the reality of death and dying. Read the journal first. Then submit your poems if you feel they fit the mission of our journal.''

⊕ ▣ ◎ KRAX (Specialized: humor)

63 Dixon Lane, Leeds, Yorkshire LS12 4RR England. Established 1971. **Contact:** Andy Robson, editor.

Magazine Needs *Krax* appears annually in May and publishes contemporary poetry from Britain and America. Wants "poetry that is light-hearted and witty; original ideas; 2,000 words maximum. Undesired: haiku, religious, or topical politics." All forms and styles considered. Has published poetry by Robert Dunn, Charles Kesler, Trish O'Brien, and Les Merton. *Krax* is 72 pages, digest-sized, offset-printed, saddle-stapled. Receives up to 1,000 submissions/year, accepts about 6%. Single copy: £3.50 ($7); subscription: £10 ($20). Sample: $1 (75p).

How to Submit "Submit maximum of 6 pieces. Writer's name on same sheet as poem. Sorry, we cannot accept material on disk. SASE or SAE with IRC encouraged but not vital." No previously published poems or simultaneous submissions. Brief cover letter is preferred. Responds in 2 months. Pays one contributor's copy. Reviews books of poetry (brief, individual comments; no outside reviews). Send materials for review consideration.

Advice "Writing about writing should not be submitted—too arrogant and introvert—create scenarios of your own, but away from the computer.''

✪ ▣ KUMQUAT MERINGUE; PENUMBRA PRESS

P.O. Box 736, Pine Island MN 55963. (507)288-4464. E-mail: moodyriver@aol.com. Website: www.kumquatcastle.com. Established 1990. **Contact:** Christian Nelson, editor.

Magazine Needs *Kumquat Meringue* appears on an irregular basis, using "mostly shorter poetry about the small details of life, especially the quirky side of love and sex. We want those things other magazines find just too quirky. Not interested in rhyming, meaning of life, or high-flown poetry." The magazine is "dedicated to the memory of Richard Brautigan." Has published poetry by Ianthe Brautigan, T. Kilgore Splake, Lynne Douglas, Denise Duhamel, Shoshauna Shy, and John Clark. *Kumquat Meringue* is 40-48 pages, digest-sized, "professionally designed with professional typography, and nicely printed." Press run is 600 (250 subscribers). Subscription: $12/3 issues. Sample: $6.

How to Submit "We like cover letters but prefer to read things about who you are rather than your long list of publishing credits. Accept previously published and simultaneous submissions, but please let us know." No fax or e-mail submissions. "Please don't forget your SASE or you'll never hear back from us. E-mail address is for 'hello, praise, complaints, threats, and questions' only." Often comments on submissions. Guidelines available for SASE or on website. Usually responds in 3 months. Pays one contributor's copy. Acquires one-time rights.

Advice "Read *Kumquat Meringue* and anything by Richard Brautigan to get a feel for what we want, but don't copy Richard Brautigan, and don't copy those who have copied him. We just want that same feel. We also have a definite weakness for poems written 'to' or 'for' Richard Brautigan. Reviewers have called our publication iconoclastic, post-hip, post-beat, post-antipostmodern; and our poetry, carefully crafted imagery. When you get discouraged, write some more. Don't give up. Eventually your poems will find a home. We're very open to unpublished writers, and a high percentage of our writers had never been published anywhere before they submitted here.''

⬛ ☑ ◎ KWIL KIDS PUBLISHING; MR. MARQUIS' MUSELETTER (Specialized: children/teens/young adults)

Box 29556, Maple Ridge BC V2X 2V0 Canada. E-mail: kmarquis@sd42.ca. Established 1996. **Contact:** Mr. Marquis, editor.

Magazine Needs *Mr. Marquis' Museletter* is a quarterly newsletter "publishing stories/poems to encourage and celebrate writers, readers, and researchers." Wants poetry that is "gentle, with compassionate truth and beauty, peace, humor; for children, by children, about children. No profane, hurtful, violent, political, or satirical work. Has published poetry by Matthew Stasinski Schnitzler, Annunziata Militano, Raanan Burd, Pamela Bond, Bryan Wilson, and Cathy Porter. *Mr. Marquis' Museletter* is 10 pages. Receives about 400 poems/year, accepts about 80%. Press run is 200 (150 subscribers). Subscription: $20 (includes newsletter, newspaper, and greeting card publishing opportunities; a free subscription to Kwil's e-mail poetry list; reading, writing, and publishing tips; and encouragement galore). Sample: $2 and SASE (or SAE and IRC). Make checks payable to Mr. Marquis.

How to Submit Submit 5 poems at a time. Accepts e-mail submissions (pasted into body of message; no attachments). Cover letter is preferred. Include SASE and parent's signature. Submit seasonal poems 3 months in advance. Time between acceptance and publication is up to 3 months. Always comments on rejected poems. "Kwil always provides encouragement and personalized response with SASE (or SAE and IRC)." Occasionally publishes theme issues. Guidelines available for SASE (Canadian-stamped envelope, or IRC, or $1 for Canadian postage) or by e-mail. Responds in April, August, and December. Pays one contributor's copy. Acquires one-time rights.

Advice "Submit best and submit often; provide Canadian-stamped envelope; sign permission card; have fun writing."

☑ LA PETITE ZINE

E-mail: lapetitezine@yahoo.com. Website: www.lapetitezine.org. **Contact:** Jeffrey Salane and Danielle Pafunda, co-editors. Member: CLMP.

● Heidi Peppermint's "Real Toads," published in Issue #13, appears in *The Best American Poetry 2004*, edited by Lyn Hejinian and series editor David Lehman.

Magazine Needs *La Petite Zine* is an online journal appearing about 3 times/year and featuring "new and established voices in poetry, fiction, creative nonfiction, and cross-genre work. While we do not offer parameters for content, form, or style, we ask that writers submit high-quality, well-crafted work. If it's not your best, don't send it." Does not want "writing that employs cliché in place of exploration of language, demonstrates an ignorance of contemporary poetry/literature or (especially) our publication, and/or relies on the sentimentality of its readers." Has published poetry by Joshua Beckman, Tina Celona, Arielle Greenberg, David Lehman, Joyelle McSweeney, and Jonah Winter. *La Petite Zine*'s home page "indexes all authors for each specific issue and offers links to past issues, as well as information about the journal, its interests and editors, and links to other sites. Art and graphics are supplied by Web del Sol. Additionally, we publish graphic poems, excerpts from graphic novels, and the like." Receives about 2,000 poems/year, accepts about 150 (7-8%). Free online; "there is no subscription, but readers are invited to sign up for e-mail notification of new issues at the submission address."

How to Submit Submit 3-5 poems at a time ("please adhere to this guideline"). Accepts simultaneous submissions, "but please notify us immediately if poems are accepted elsewhere"; no previously published poems. Accepts e-mail submissions (pasted into body of message or as attachment—Word document (preferred) or Rich Text Format); no disk submissions. Cover letter is required, with brief bio listing previous publications. "If submitting poems as an attachment, please include all poems in the same document. If we do not accept your work, please wait at least 6 months before resubmitting." Reads submissions all year. Time between acceptance and publication is up to 6 months. "The 2 co-editors make all decisions by consensus." Seldom comments on rejected poems. Occasionally publishes theme issues. List of upcoming themes available on website, when applicable. Guidelines available on website. Responds in up to 2 months "ideally." Always sends electronic prepublication galleys. No payment. Acquires first rights. Reviews books and chapbooks of poetry in 500 words, single- and multi-book format. Send materials for review consideration to Danielle Pafunda, Park Hall, Room 254, English Dept., University of Georgia, Athens GA 30602.

Advice "No matter what sort of writer you are, you should read constantly and always become familiar with publications to which you are submitting: Who are the editors? Who have they published in the past? Is there a discernible aesthetic? Do they take chances on new voices? Always send your best, finished work, accompanied by a brief cover letter including a short bio with any past publications (for those editors who encourage cover letters). Above all, do not let rejections discourage you. If they include comments, decide whether or not those comments are useful to your poetry, but don't let rejection dictate your work. Find those readers who can help you evolve as a writer and refine your voice."

⒩ $◎ LADZ MAGAZINE (Specialized: alternative lifestyles; men's issues)
E-mail: Howell@ladzmagazine.com. Website: www.ladzmagazine.com. Established 2005. **Contact:** Bryon D. Howell, poetry editor.
Magazine Needs *LADZ Magazine* is a "trendy, monthly magazine featuring fashion, pop culture, and queer science from the perspective of the sexually eclectic male under the age of 35." Wants "all styles; prefer contemporary themes. Poetry addressing social issues; fresh use of imagery; gut-wrenching, blood-pumping, heart-churning material which pushes the envelope without being obviously pornographic or obnoxious. Romance, erotica, humor, even angst is acceptable, just do it with originality and feeling while writing from the real world. Traditional, free verse, short prose, experimental, what have you!" Does not want "overtly pornographic, racist, or homophobic [work]. No limericks; no cowboy poetry unless it's about gay cowboys." *LADZ Magazine* is 150+ pages, magazine-sized, stapled, printed full-color on gloss text, includes ads. *LADZ Magazine* also appears online. Receives about 2,000 poems/year, accepts about 3%. Press run is 10,000. Single copy: $2.95; subscription: $24.99/year. Make checks payable to Bryon D. Howell.
How to Submit Submit 3-5 poems at a time. Lines/poem: 75 maximum. Accepts previously published poems; no simultaneous submissions. Accepts e-mail submissions (pasted into body of message); no disk submissions. Cover letter is required. "Please send short bio." Reads submissions year round. Submit seasonal poems 6 months in advance. Time between acceptance and publication is 6 months. Poems are circulated to an editorial board. "Poetry editor makes first cut, then passes the maybes to one or two other staff members for their input." Sometimes comments on rejected poems. **"Will provide detailed, constructive critiques and revision suggestions for a charge of $1/poem."** Regularly publishes theme issues. List of upcoming themes available on website. Guidelines available by e-mail or on website. Responds in 2 weeks. Sometimes sends prepublication galleys. Pays $5/poem and one contributor's copy. Acquires all rights. "Rights returned to the author after publication with the understanding that *LADZ* is to be credited as the first to publish the work. We reserve the right to archive on the website." Reviews books and chapbooks of poetry and other magazines/journals in 500 words, single-book format. See website for information about submitting materials for review.
Advice "Visit the website or order a copy before submitting to gauge our style and tone. Be advised, *LADZ* is not for everybody. It is a sexy, flashy, and often controversial magazine. Send us your best work. Don't be put off by a rejection; rejections from us are never personal. Keep trying! Get used to the fact that some magazines will never publish you, no matter how sensational your poetry is. Any editor who tells you otherwise is not being completely honest with you. There always exist the unspoken realities in literature. To a great degree, it's who you know, where you got your Master's in English (if you have one), and how pretentious you can pretend to be. Consider crossing over to the other side of that reality; and, if you're brave enough, come on in! *LADZ* is your link to poetic immortality!"

◔ LAKE EFFECT

School of Humanities & Social Sciences, Penn State Erie, 5091 Station Rd., Erie PA 16563-1501. (814)898-6281. Fax: (814)898-6032. E-mail: goL1@psu.edu. Established 1978 as *Tempus*; renamed *Lake Effect* in 2001. **Contact:** George Looney, editor-in-chief. Member: CLMP.

Magazine Needs *Lake Effect* is published annually in March/April "to provide an aesthetic venue for writing that uses language precisely to forge a genuine and rewarding experience for our readers. *Lake Effect* wishes to publish writing that rewards more than one reading, and to present side-by-side the voices of established and emerging writers." Wants "poetry aware of, and wise about, issues of craft in forming language that is capable of generating a rich and rewarding reading experience." Does not want "sentimental verse reliant on clichés." Has published poetry by Angie Estes, Chase Twichell, Fleda Brown, Dionisio D. Martinez, and David Kirby. *Lake Effect* is 150 pages, digest-sized, offset-printed, perfect-bound, with gloss-by-flat film lamination cover. Receives about 1,500 poems/year, accepts about 3%. Press run is 800 (300 shelf sales); 300 distributed free to contributors and writing programs. Single copy: $6; subscription: $6. Make checks payable to The Pennsylvania State University.

How to Submit Submit 3-5 poems at a time. Accepts simultaneous submissions; no previously published poems. No fax, e-mail, or disk submissions. Cover letter is required. Reads submissions year round. Time between acceptance and publication is up to 4 months. "The poetry staff reads the poems, meets and discusses them to come to a consensus. Poetry editor, along with editor-in-chief, makes final decisions." Seldom comments on rejected poems. Guidelines available in magazine. Responds in up to 4 months. Pays 2 contributor's copies. Acquires first North American serial rights.

Advice "*Lake Effect* strives to provide an attractive venue for the good work of both established and emerging writers. We care about the integrity of poetry, and care for the poems we accept."

✪ ◻ ◎ LAKE SHORE PUBLISHING; SOUNDINGS (Specialized: anthology)

498 Riverside Dr., Burley ID 83318-5419. (208)678-6378. Established 1983. **Contact:** Carol Spelius, poetry editor.

Magazine Needs *Soundings* is an effort "to put out decent, economical volumes of poetry." Accepts poetry in any form or length, as long as it's "understandable and moving, imaginative with a unique view, in any form. Make me laugh or cry or think. I'm not so keen on gutter language or political dogma—but I try to keep an open mind." Has published poetry by Constance Vogel, Fran Podulka, Tod Palmer, Gertrude Rubin, and June Shipley. *Soundings* is flat-spined, photocopied from typescript, with glossy card cover with art.

How to Submit Submit 5 poems at a time, with **$1/page reading fee**, and a cover letter telling about your other publications, biographical background, personal or aesthetic philosophy, poetic goals and principles. Accepts simultaneous submissions. Accepts submissions by postal mail and on disk. "Reads submissions anytime, but best in fall." Upcoming themes available for SASE. Responds in one year. Pays one contributor's copy, offers half-price for additional copies. "All rights return to poet after first printing."

Book/Chapbook Needs & How to Submit Reads chapbooks, or full-length collections, with the possibility of sharing costs if Lake Shore Publishing likes the book (**$1/page reading fee**). "I split the cost if I like the book." Sample copy of anthology or random choice of full-length collections to interested poets: $5.

⊕ $◎ LANDFALL: NEW ZEALAND ARTS AND LETTERS (Specialized: regional)

University of Otago Press, P.O. Box 56, Dunedin, New Zealand. Phone: 0064 3 479 8807. Fax: 0064 3 479 8385. E-mail: landfall@otago.ac.nz. Established 1947; originally published by Caxton Press, then by Oxford University Press, now published by University of Otago Press. **Contact:** Justin Paton, editor.

Magazine Needs *Landfall* appears twice/year (in May and November). "Apart from occasional commissioned features on aspects of international literature, *Landfall* focuses primarily on New Zealand literature and arts. It publishes new fiction, poetry, commentary, and interviews with

New Zealand artists and writers, and reviews of New Zealand books." Single issue: NZ $29.95; subscription: NZ $45 for 2 issues for New Zealand subscribers, A$30 for Australian subscribers, US $30 for other overseas subscribers.

How to Submit Submissions must be typed and include SASE. No fax or e-mail submissions. "Once accepted, contributions should, if possible, also be submitted on disk." Publishes theme issues. Guidelines and upcoming themes available for SASE. New Zealand poets should write for further information.

◪ LANGUAGE AND CULTURE.NET

4000 Pimlico Dr., Suite 114-192, Pleasanton CA 94588. E-mail: review@languageandculture.net. Website: www.languageandculture.net. Established 2001. **Contact:** Liz Fortini, editor.

Magazine Needs *Language and Culture.net* is a quarterly "exclusively online publication of contemporary poetry." Also includes translations: Spanish, French, German, Italian, and Russian. Other languages under review. Translated poems will be published side by side with the English. No restrictions on form. Has published poetry by John Compton and Susan Wilson. Receives a varied number of poems/year.

How to Submit Submit up to 30 poems. Lines/poem: 70 maximum. Accepts previously published poems and simultaneous submissions. Accepts e-mail submissions (pasted into body of message; no attachments); no fax or disk submissions. "Return e-mail address must be included." Cover letter is optional. Reads submissions "yearly." Time between acceptance and publication is up to 3 months. Poems are circulated to an editorial board. Will comment on rejected poems. No payment. Acquires one-time rights. Reviews chapbooks of poetry.

Chapbook Needs & How to Submit Publishes up to 10 chapbooks/year. Format varies. Send sample poems and a cover letter with brief bio and publication credits. Responds within one month.

Advice "Enrich your lives with different perspectives and poetry styles."

▦ ◪ ◎ LAPWING PUBLICATIONS (Specialized: Irish)

1 Ballysillan Dr., Belfast BT14 8HQ United Kingdom. Phone/fax: 028 90 295 800. E-mail: catherine.g reig1@NTLWorld.com. Website: www.irishreader.com/Pubs/Lapwing.htm. Established 1989. **Contact:** Dennis Greig, editor.

● Lapwing will only produce work if and when resources to do so are available.

Book/Chapbook Needs Lapwing publishes "emerging Irish poets and poets domiciled in Ireland, plus the new work of a suitable size by established Irish writers." Publishes 6-10 chapbooks/year. Wants poetry of all kinds, but, "no crass political, racist, sexist propaganda, even of a positive or 'pc' tenor." Has published Mary O'Donnell (*September Elegies*), Niall McGrath (*Parity*), John Stevenson (*Cherry Tree*), Mary M. Geoghegan (*Bright Unknown*), Philip Quaite (*Life of Zagoba*), and Zlatko Tomicic (*Croatia My Love*). Chapbooks are usually 44-52 pages, A5, Docutech-printed, saddle-stapled, with colored card covers.

How to Submit "Submit 6 poems in the first instance; depending on these, an invitation to submit more may follow." Accepts simultaneous submissions; no previously published poems. Accepts e-mail submissions (pasted into body of message). Cover letter is required. Poems are circulated to an editorial board. "All submissions receive a first reading. If these poems have minor errors or faults, the writer is advised. If poor quality, the poems are returned. Those 'passing' first reading are retained, and a letter of conditional offer is sent." Often comments on rejected poems. Responds to queries in one month; to mss in 2 months. Pays 20 author's copies; no royalties. "After initial publication, irrespective of the quantity, the work will be permanently available using 'print-on-demand' production; such publications will not always be printed exactly as the original, although the content will remain the same."

Advice "Clean; check spelling, grammar, punctuation, layout (i.e., will it fit a book page?); clear text. Due to limited resources, material will be processed well in advance of any estimated publishing date. All accepted material is strictly conditional on resources available, no favoritism. The

Irish domestic market is small, the culture is hierarchical, poet/personality culture predominates, literary democracy is limited.''

☆ ◻ ◎ LAURELS; WEST VIRGINIA POETRY SOCIETY (Specialized: membership)

Rt. 2, Box 13, Ripley WV 25271. E-mail: mbush814@aol.com. Established 1996. **Contact:** Jim Bush, editor.

Magazine Needs *Laurels* is the quarterly journal of the West Virginia Poetry Society containing poetry, line drawings, and a critical article on a poet or form in each issue. Only considers work from WVPS members. Wants traditional forms and good free verse. ''If it's over 39 lines it must be very, very good. No porn, off-color language, shape poems, doggerel, or 'broken prose.' '' Accepts poetry written by children, if members. *Laurels* is 62 pages, saddle-stapled, with paper cover. Receives about 2,000 poems/year, accepts about 80%. Press run is 275 (210 subscribers). Membership: $15 to Natalie J. Doty, 189 Vireo Dr., Wintersville OH 43953-4054 (checks payable to WVPS treasurer). Sample: $4 to Jim Bush at above address.

How to Submit Submit 4-5 poems at a time. Accepts previously published poems. Accepts e-mail submissions. Cover letter is preferred, including brief bio. Issue deadlines are March 15, May 15, August 15, and November 15. Time between acceptance and publication is up to one year. Guidelines available for SASE. *Responds ''only if revision is needed or if poetry is not acceptable.''* Sometimes sends prepublication galleys. Acquires one-time rights.

Contest/Award Offerings Sponsors a 35-category annual contest for members. **Entry fee:** no fee for current WVPS members or K-12 students. Guidelines available to nonmembers for SASE.

Advice ''Our purpose is to encourage and aid amateur poets who believe that words can be used to communicate meaning and to create beauty.''

$◻ ◎ LEADING EDGE (Specialized: science fiction/fantasy only)

3146 JKHB, Provo UT 84602. E-mail: tle@byu.edu. Website: http://tle.byu.edu. **Contact:** Matt Gibbons, poetry director. Editor: Christopher Kugler.

Magazine Needs *Leading Edge* is a magazine appearing in April and October. Wants ''high-quality poetry reflecting both literary value and popular appeal, and dealing with science fiction and fantasy. We accept traditional science fiction and fantasy poetry, but we like innovative stuff. No graphic sex, violence, or profanity.'' Has published poetry by Michael Collings, Tracy Ray, Susan Spilecki, and Bob Cook. *Leading Edge* is 170 pages, digest-sized. Accepts about 4 out of 60 poems received/year. Press run is 500 (100 subscribers, 10 libraries, 400 shelf sales). Single copy: $4.95; subscription: $12.50 (3 issues).

How to Submit Submit one or more poems with name and address at the top of each page. No simultaneous submissions or previously published poems. No e-mail submissions. Cover letter is preferred; include name, address, phone number, length of poem, title, and type of poem. ''Please include SASE with every submission.'' Guidelines available in magazine, for SASE, or on website. Responds in one month. Always sends prepublication galleys. Pays $10 for the first 4 typeset pages, $1.50 for each additional page, plus 2 contributor's copies. Acquires first North American serial rights.

Advice ''Poetry is given equal standing with fiction; it is not treated as filler, but as art.''

☆ ◪ THE LEDGE

40 Maple Ave., Bellport NY 11713. E-mail: tkmonaghan@aol.com. Established 1988. **Contact:** Timothy Monaghan, editor-in-chief/publisher. Co-Editors: George Held and Kim Rohleder.

Magazine Needs ''We seek poems that utilize language and imagery in a fresh, original fashion. We favor poems that speak to the human experience. We seek inspired, well-crafted verse, and are open to all schools and poetic persuasions. Excellence is the ultimate criterion.'' Has published poetry by Elton Glaser, Robert Fanning, Jennifer Perrine, Tony Gloeggler, Neil Carpathios, and Michelle Brooks. *The Ledge* is 220+ pages, digest-sized, typeset, perfect-bound, with b&w glossy cover. Accepts 5% of poetry received. Press run is 1,500 (750 subscribers). Single copy: $10; subscription: $17/2 issues, $30/4 issues, $39/6 issues.

How to Submit Submit 3-5 poems with SASE. Accepts simultaneous submissions; no previously published poems. Reads submissions year round. Responds in 3 months. Pays one contributor's copy. Acquires one-time rights.

Contest/Award Offerings *The Ledge* sponsors an annual poetry chapbook contest, as well as an annual poetry contest. Details available for SASE or by e-mail.

LEFT CURVE (Specialized: political; social issues)

P.O. Box 472, Oakland CA 94604-0472. (510)763-7193. E-mail: editor@leftcurve.org. Website: www.leftcurve.org. Established 1974. **Contact:** Csaba Polony, editor.

Magazine Needs *Left Curve* appears "irregularly, about every 10 months." The journal "addresses the problem(s) of cultural forms, emerging from the crisis of modernity, that strives to be independent from the control of dominant institutions, and free from the shackles of instrumental rationality." Wants poetry that is "critical culture, social, political, 'post-modern'; not purely formal, too self-centered, poetry that doesn't address in sufficient depth today's problems." Has published poetry by Jon Hillson, Devorah Major, W.K. Buckley, and Jack Hirschman. *Left Curve* is 144 pages, magazine-sized, offset-printed, perfect-bound, with Durosheen cover, includes ads. Press run is 2,000 (250 subscribers, 100 libraries, 1,600 shelf sales). Subscription: $30/3 issues (individuals); $45/3 issues (institutions). Sample: $10.

How to Submit Submit up to 5 poems at a time. "Most of our published poetry is one page in length, though we have published longer poems of up to 8 pages. We will look at any form of poetry, from experimental to traditional." Accepts submissions by e-mail or on disk. Cover letter explaining "why you are submitting" is required. Publishes theme issues. Guidelines and upcoming themes available for SASE, by e-mail, or on website. Responds in up to 6 months. Pays 3 contributor's copies. Send materials for review consideration.

LIGHT

P.O. Box 7500, Chicago IL 60680. Website: www.lightquarterly.com. Established 1992. **Contact:** John Mella, editor.

Magazine Needs *Light* is a quarterly of "light and occasional verse, satire, wordplay, puzzles, cartoons, and line art." Does not want "greeting card verse, cloying or sentimental verse." *Light* is 64 pages, perfect-bound. Single copy: $6; subscription: $20. Sample (back issues): $5 plus $2 for first-class postage.

How to Submit Submit one poem/page, with name, address, poem title, and page number on each page. No previously published poems or simultaneous submissions. Seldom comments on rejected poems. Guidelines available for #10 SASE. Responds in 6 months or less. Always sends prepublication galleys. Pays 2 contributor's copies to domestic contributors, one to foreign contributors. Send materials for review consideration.

LILLIPUT REVIEW (Specialized: poems of 10 lines or less)

282 Main St., Pittsburgh PA 15201-2807. Website: http://donw714.tripod.com/lillieindex.html. Established 1989. **Contact:** Don Wentworth, editor.

Magazine Needs *Lilliput Review* appears 8 to 10 times/year, "shipped two issues at a time, every fourth issue being a broadside that features the work of a single poet." Wants poems in any style or form, no longer than 10 lines. Has published *The Future Tense of Ash* by Miriam Sagan and *No Choice* by Cid Corman, as well as poetry by Pamela Miller Ness, Albert Huffstickler, Charlie Mehrhoff, and Jen Besemer. *Lilliput Review* is 12-16 pages, $4^{1}/_{2} \times 3.6$ or $3^{1}/_{2} \times 4^{1}/_{4}$, laser-printed on colored paper, stapled. Press run is 400. Subscription: $5 for 6 issues, $10 for 15 issues; $12 for institutions (12 issues). Sample: $1 or SASE. Make checks payable to Don Wentworth.

How to Submit Submit up to 3 poems at a time. Lines/poem: 10 maximum. Accepts previously published poems if noted as such. SASE required. Editor comments on submissions "occasionally—I always try to establish human contact." Guidelines available for SASE or on website. Responds within 3 months. Pays 2 contributor's copies/poem. Acquires first rights.

Book/Chapbook Needs & How to Submit The Modest Proposal Chapbook Series began in 1994, publishing one chapbook/year, 18-24 pages in length. Has published *Half Emptied Out* by Lonnie Sherman. **Chapbook submissions are by invitation only.** Query with standard SASE. Sample chapbook: $3.

Advice "A note above my desk reads 'Clarity & resonance, not necessarily in that order.' The perfect poem for *Lilliput Review* is simple in style and language, and elusive/allusive in meaning and philosophy. *Lilliput* is open to all short poems in approach and theme, including any of the short Eastern forms, traditional or otherwise."

☑ LIMITED EDITIONS PRESS; ART:MAG

P.O. Box 70896, Las Vegas NV 89170. (702)734-8121. E-mail: magman@iopener.net. Established 1982. **Contact:** Peter Magliocco, editor.

Magazine Needs *ART:MAG* has "become, due to economic and other factors, more limited to a select audience of poets as well as readers. We seek to expel the superficiality of our factitious culture, in all its drive-thru, junk-food-brain, commercial-ridden extravagance—and stylize a magazine of hard-line aesthetics, where truth and beauty meet on a vector not shallowly drawn. Conforming to this outlook is an operational policy of seeking poetry from solicited poets primarily, though unsolicited submissions will be read, considered, and perhaps used infrequently. Sought from the chosen is a creative use of poetic styles, systems, and emotional morphologies other than banally constricting." Has published poetry by Lucille Abato, Michael Bailey, Will Nixon, Kent Kruse, and Barry Ballard. *ART:MAG*, appearing in 1-2 large issues of 100 copies/year, is limited to a few poets. Subscription: $8 (2 issues). Sample: $3 or more. Make checks payable to Peter Magliocco.

How to Submit Submit 5 poems at a time with SASE. "Submissions should be neat and use consistent style format (except experimental work). Cover letters are optional." Accepts simultaneous submissions; sometimes previously published poems. No fax or e-mail submissions. Sometimes comments on rejected poems. Publishes theme issues. Guidelines and upcoming themes available for SASE. Responds within 3 months. Pays one contributor's copy. Acquires first rights. Staff occasionally reviews books of poetry. Send materials for review consideration.

Book/Chapbook Needs & How to Submit Limited Editions Press recently published *The March of Politics* by Neal Wilgus. Query the editor before submitting any ms.

Advice "The mag is seeking a futuristic aestheticism where the barriers of fact and fiction meet, where inner- and outer-space converge in the realm of poetic consciousness in order to create a more productively viable relationship to the coming *Nu-Evermore* of the 21st century."

✪ ✦ $☻ ◎ THE LINK & VISITOR (Specialized: Canadian only; religious; women)

1-315 Lonsdale Rd., Toronto ON M4V 1X3 Canada. (416)544-8550. E-mail: linkvis@baptistwomen.com. Website: www.baptistwomen.com. Established 1878. **Contact:** Esther Barnes, editor.

Magazine Needs *The Link & Visitor* provides bimonthly "encouragement, insight, inspiration for Canadian Christian women; Baptist, mission, and egalitarian slant. Poetry must relate to reader's experience; must be grounded in a biblical Christian faith; contemporary in style and language; upbeat but not naive. We do not want to see anything that has already been better said in the Bible or traditional hymns." *The Link & Visitor* is 24 pages, magazine-sized, offset-printed, with self cover. Receives about 20 poems/year, accepts about 20%. "We have a few poets we use regularly because their work fits our mix." Press run is 4,000. Subscription: $16 Canadian, $25 US and overseas airmail. Sample: $2.75 Canadian.

How to Submit Submit up to 5 poems at a time. Lines/poem: 8 minimum, 30 maximum. Accepts previously published poems and simultaneous submissions. Accepts e-mail submissions. Cover letter is required. Include SASE with Canadian stamps. Time between acceptance and publication is up to 2 years. Seldom comments on rejected poems. Usually publishes theme issues. Guidelines available on website. Pays $10-25 Canadian. Acquires one-time rights.

Advice "Canadian writers only, please."

⊘ LINTEL

24 Blake Lane, Middletown NY 10940. Phone/fax: (845)342-5224. Established 1977.
Book/Chapbook Needs "We publish poetry and innovative fiction of types ignored by commercial presses. We consider any poetry except conventional, traditional, cliché, greeting card types; i.e., we consider any artistic poetry." Has published poetry by Sue Saniel Elkind, Samuel Exler, Adrienne Wolfert, Edmund Pennant, and Nathan Teitel. "Typical of our work" is Teitel's book, *In Time of Tide*, 64 pages, digest-sized, professionally printed in bold type, flat-spined, with hard cover stamped in gold, jacket with art and author's photo on back.
How to Submit Not currently accepting unsolicited mss.

⊘ LIPS

7002 Blvd. East, #2-26G, Guttenberg NJ 07093. (201)662-1303. Fax: (201)861-2888. E-mail: LBOSS7 9270@aol.com. Established 1981. **Contact:** Laura Boss, poetry editor.
Magazine Needs *Lips* "is a quality poetry magazine that is published twice/year and takes pleasure in publishing previously unpublished poets as well as the most established voices in contemporary poetry. We look for quality work: the strongest work of a poet; work that moves the reader; poems that take risks that work. We prefer clarity in the work rather than the abstract. Poems longer than 6 pages present a space problem." Has published poetry by Allen Ginsberg, Maria Gillan, Stanley Barkan, Lyn Lifshin, David Ignatow, and Ishmael Reed. *Lips* is about 150 pages, digest-sized, flat-spined. Receives about 8,000 submissions/year, accepts about 1%. Press run is 1,000 (200 subscribers, 100 libraries). Sample: $10 plus $2 for postage.
How to Submit Poems should be submitted between September and March only; 6 pages maximum, typed; no query necessary. Guidelines available for SASE. Responds in one month (but has gotten backlogged at times). Sometimes sends prepublication galleys. Pays one contributor's copy. Acquires first rights.
Advice "Remember the 2 T's: Talent *and* Tenacity."

⊘ THE LISTENING EYE

Kent State Geauga Campus, 14111 Claridon-Troy Rd., Burton OH 44021. (440)286-3840. E-mail: grace_butcher@msn.com. Website: www.geocities.com/Athens/3716. Established 1970 for student work, 1990 as national publication. **Contact:** Grace Butcher, editor. Assistant Editors: Jim Wohlken and Joanne Speidel.
Magazine Needs *The Listening Eye* is an annual publication, appearing in early fall, of poetry, short fiction, creative nonfiction, and art. Wants "high-literary-quality poetry. Prefer shorter poems (less than 2 pages) but will consider longer if space allows. Any subject, any style. No trite images or predictable rhyme." Accepts poetry written by children if high literary quality. Has published poetry by Alberta Turner, Virgil Suárez, Walter McDonald, and Simon Perchik. *The Listening Eye* is 52-60 pages, digest-sized, professionally printed, saddle-stapled, with card stock cover with b&w or color art. Receives about 200 poems/year, accepts about 5%. Press run is 200. Single copy: $4. Make checks payable to Grace Butcher.
How to Submit Submit up to 4 poems at a time, typed, single-spaced, one poem/page—name, address, phone number, and e-mail address in upper left-hand corner of each page—with SASE for return of work. Previously published poems occasionally accepted; no simultaneous submissions. No e-mail submissions "unless from overseas." Cover letter is required. Reads submissions January 1 through April 15 only. Time between acceptance and publication is up to 6 months. Poems are circulated to the editor and 2 assistant editors who read and evaluate work separately, then meet for final decisions. Occasionally comments on rejected poems. Guidelines available in magazine or for SASE. Responds in one month. Pays 2 contributor's copies. Acquires first or one-time rights.
Contest/Award Offerings Awards $30 to the best sports poem in each issue.
Advice "I look for tight lines that don't sound like prose; unexpected images or juxtapositions; the unusual use of language; noticeable relationships of sounds; a twist in viewpoint; an ordinary idea in extraordinary language; an amazing and complex idea simply stated; play on words and with

words; an obvious love of language. Poets need to read the 'Big 3'—cummings, Thomas, Hopkins—to see the limits to which language can be taken. Then read the 'Big 2'—Dickinson to see how simultaneously tight, terse, and universal a poem can be, and Whitman to see how sprawling, cosmic, and personal. Then read everything you can find that's being published in literary magazines today, and see how your work compares to all of the above."

⚄ ⬗ LITERAL LATTÉ; LITERAL LATTÉ POETRY AWARDS

200 E. 10th St., Suite 240, New York NY 10003. (212)260-5532. E-mail: litlatte@aol.com. Website: www.literal-latte.com. Established 1994. **Contact:** Dorie Davidson, assistant editor. Editor: Jenine Gordon Bockman.

Magazine Needs *Literal Latté* is an online literary journal of "pure prose, poetry, and art. Open to all styles of poetry—quality is the determining factor." Has published poetry by Allen Ginsberg, Carol Muske, Amy Holman, and John Updike. Receives about 3,000 poems/year, accepts 1%. *Literal Latté* is published online only. "We will publish an anthology in book form at the end of each year, featuring the best of our web magazine."

How to Submit Accepts simultaneous submissions; no previously published poems. Accepts submissions by postal mail *only*. Cover letter with bio and SASE required. Time between acceptance and publication is 6 months. Often comments on rejected poems. Guidelines available by e-mail or on website. Responds in 3 months.

Contest/Award Offerings Sponsors the *Literal Latté* Poetry Awards, an annual contest for previously unpublished poems. Offers 1st Prize: $1,000; 2nd Prize: $300; 3rd Prize: $200; all entries considered for publication. **Entry fee:** $10 for 4 poems. Guidelines available for SASE, by e-mail, or on website.

⬗ ◎ LITERARY MAMA (Specialized: writing by mothers about mothering)

E-mail: poetry@literarymama.com (submissions); info@literarymama.com (inquiries). Website: www.literarymama.com. Established 2003. **Contact:** Rachel Iverson, poetry editor. Managing Editor: Amy Hudock.

Magazine Needs *Literary Mama*, a monthly online literary journal, publishes fiction, poetry, and creative nonfiction by writers of all ages who are "self-identified" mothers. "We also publish literary criticism, book reviews, and profiles about mother writers. *Literary Mama* is doing something for mama-centric literature that no one else is doing. The poetry, fiction, and creative nonfiction that may be too long, too complex, too ambiguous, too deep, too raw, too irreverent, too ironic, too body-conscious, and too full of long words for the general reader will find a home with us. While there are plenty of online literary magazines that publish writing like this, none devote themselves exclusively to writing about motherhood." Wants poems of any form that are "extraordinary for their vision, craftsmanship, integrity, and originality; centered around parenting; written by writers who are also self-identified mothers: biological, non-biological, step, transgendered, adoptive." *Literary Mama* is published online only. Receives about 70 poems/month, accepts about 10-15%.

How to Submit Submit a maximum of 4 poems at a time. Accepts previously published poems and simultaneous submissions. Accepts e-mail submissions (pasted into body of message/no attachments); no disk submissions. Cover letter is required. "Please include name, brief bio, and contact information." Reads submissions year round except for December and June. Time between acceptance and publication is 2-8 weeks. "The final decision about all poetry submissions is made by the poetry editor." Sometimes comments on rejected poems. Guidelines available on website. Responds in 4-6 weeks. No payment. Acquires first rights for previously unpublished work, non-exclusive one-time rights for reprints. Reviews books and chapbooks of poetry. Query via e-mail prior to sending materials for review consideration.

⬗ THE LITERARY REVIEW: AN INTERNATIONAL JOURNAL OF CONTEMPORARY WRITING

Fairleigh Dickinson University, 285 Madison Ave., Madison NJ 07940. (973)443-8564. Fax: (973)443-8364. E-mail: tlr@fdu.edu. Website: www.theliteraryreview.org. Established 1957. **Contact:** René Steinke, editor-in-chief.

Magazine Needs *The Literary Review*, a quarterly, seeks "work by new and established poets which reflects a sensitivity to literary standards and the poetic form." No specifications as to form, length, style, subject matter, or purpose. Has published poetry by David Citino, Rick Mulkey, Virgil Suárez, Gary Fincke, and Dale M. Kushner. *The Literary Review* is about 180 pages, digest-sized, professionally printed, flat-spined, with glossy color cover. Receives about 1,200 submissions/year, accepts 100-150. Press run is 2,000 (800 subscribers, one-third are overseas). Sample: $7 domestic, $8 outside US; request a "general issue."

How to Submit Submit up to 5 typed poems at a time. Accepts simultaneous submissions. No fax or e-mail submissions. Do not submit during the summer months of June, July, and August. At times the editor comments on rejected poems. Publishes theme issues. Responds in 4-6 months. Always sends prepublication galleys. Pays 2 contributor's copies. Acquires first rights. Reviews books of poetry in 500 words, single-book format. Send materials for review consideration.

Also Offers Website features original work. Has published poetry by Renée Ashley and Catherine Kasper. Website contact is Louise Stahl.

Advice "Read a general issue of the magazine carefully before submitting."

◖ LONE STARS MAGAZINE; "SONGBOOK" LYRIC POETRY CONTEST

4219 Flint Hill St., San Antonio TX 78230-1619. Established 1992. **Contact:** Milo Rosebud, editor/publisher.

Magazine Needs *Lone Stars*, published 3 times/year, features "contemporary poetry." Wants poetry "that holds a continuous line of thought. No profanity." Has published poetry by Bernie Bernstein, Crayton Moody, Eve J. Blohm, and Cecil Boyce. *Lone Stars* is 25 pages, magazine-sized, photocopied, saddle-stapled, bound with tape. Press run is 200 (100 subscribers, 3 libraries). Single copy: $5.50; subscription: $15. Sample: $4.50.

How to Submit Submit 3-5 poems at a time with "the form typed the way you want it in print." **Charges reading fee of $1 per poem.** Accepts previously published poems and simultaneous submissions. Cover letter is preferred. Time between acceptance and publication is 2 months. Publishes theme issues. List of upcoming themes and guidelines available for SASE. Responds within 3 months. Acquires one-time rights.

Contest/Award Offerings Sponsors annual "Songbook" Lyric Poetry Contest. Details available for SASE.

Advice "Submit poetry that expresses a reasonable train of thought."

⊠ ◖ LONE WILLOW PRESS

P.O. Box 31647, Omaha NE 68131-0647. (402)551-0343. E-mail: lonewillowpress@aol.com. Established 1993. **Contact:** Fredrick Zydek, editor.

Book/Chapbook Needs Publishes 2-3 chapbooks/year. "We publish chapbooks on single themes and are open to all themes. The only requirement is excellence. However, we do not want to see doggerel or greeting card verse." Has published *Cave Poems* by Marjorie Power, *Things Like This Happen All the Time* by Eric Hoffman, *Monsters We Give Our Children* by Carolyn Riehle, and *From the Dead Before* by Clif Mason. Chapbooks are 36-50 pages, digest-sized, neatly printed on fine paper, saddle-stapled, with card stock cover.

How to Submit Query first with 5 sample poems and cover letter with brief bio and publication credits. Accepts previously published poems; no simultaneous submissions. No fax or e-mail submissions. Guidelines available for SASE. Responds to queries in one month; to mss (if invited) in up to 3 months. Pays 25 author's copies. "We also pay a small royalty if the book goes into a second printing." Order sample chapbooks by sending $7.95 via check or money order.

Advice "If you don't know the work of Roethke, DeFrees, and Hugo, don't bother sending work our way. We work with no more than two poets at a time."

⊠ ◎ LONG ISLAND QUARTERLY (Specialized: regional)

P.O. Box 114, Northport NY 11768. E-mail: Liquarterly@aol.com. Website: www.poetrybay.com. Established 1990. **Contact:** George Wallace, editor/publisher.

Magazine Needs *Long Island Quarterly* uses poetry (mostly lyric free verse) by people on or from Long Island. "Surprise us with fresh language. No conventional imagery, self-indulgent confessionalism, compulsive article-droppers." Has published poetry by Edmund Pennant and David Ignatow. *Long Island Quarterly* is 28 pages, digest-sized, professionally printed on quality stock, saddle-stapled, with matte card cover. Press run is 250 (150 subscribers, 15 libraries, 50-75 shelf sales). Subscription: $15. Sample: $4.

How to Submit Submit 3 poems at a time, with name and address on each page. Accepts e-mail submissions (pasted into body of message/no attachments). Cover letter including connection to Long Island region is required. Submissions without SASE are not returned. Responds in 3 months. Sometimes sends prepublication galleys. Pays one contributor's copy. Reviews books and chapbooks of poetry. Send materials for review consideration.

Advice "(1) Go beyond yourself; (2) Don't be afraid to fictionalize; (3) Don't write your autobiography—if you are worth it, maybe someone else will."

⋈ ◑ LONG STORY SHORT, a Magazine for Writers; LONG STORY SHORT CONTESTS

P.O. Box 475, Lewistown MT 59457. E-mail: writingfriend@lewistown.net. Website: www.longstoryshort.us. Established 2003. **Contact:** Gloria Pimentel, poetry editor.

Magazine Needs *Long Story Short* is "an eclectic e-zine open to all forms and styles" of poetry. Does not want "profanity; overly explicit sex." Accepts poetry written by children ages 10 and up. Has published poetry by Carolyn Howard-Johnson, Patricia Wellingham-Jones, Floriana Hall, Glenda Walker-Hobbs, and Jayne Jaudon Ferrer.

How to Submit: Submit 2 poems at a time. Lines/poem: up to 32. Accepts previously published poems and simultaneous submissions. Accepts e-mail submissions (pasted into body of message). "Include a brief biography and permission to use e-mail address for reader contact." Reads submissions year round. Submit seasonal poems 4 months in advance. Time between acceptance and publication is one month. "Poems are reviewed and chosen by the poetry editor." Often comments on rejected poems. Guidelines available on website. Responds in 3 weeks. All rights reserved by author.

Contest/Award Offerings Sponsors poetry contests with cash prizes. Submit 2 poems, up to 32 lines each. **Entry fee:** varies. **Deadline:** varies. "Check the contest page on the website often for changes and updates on contests."

Also Offers Free newsletter with poetry of the month chosen by poetry editor; includes author's bio and web page listed in the e-zine. Also provides resource page on website. Offers light critique of submissions upon request, and a free writing forum.

Advice "*Long Story Short* is an e-zine dedicated to the advancement of women writers, although we do publish work by men as well."

✪ ◑ LOTUS PRESS, INC.; NAOMI LONG MADGETT POETRY AWARD (Specialized: African-American)

P.O. Box 21607, Detroit MI 48221. (313)861-1280. Fax: (313)861-4740. E-mail: lotuspress@aol.com. Website: www.lotuspress.org. Established 1972. **Contact:** Constance Withers. Editor: Naomi Long Madgett.

- "We are presently not accepting submissions except for the Naomi Long Madgett Poetry Award." (See below.)

Contest/Award Offerings Annual award of $500 and publication by Lotus Press, Inc. for a poetry book ms by an African-American poet. Poems in submission may be previously published individually; "no poems published in a collection of your own work, self-published or not, should be included. Please do not submit a manuscript which you have submitted, or which you plan to submit during the period of consideration, to another publisher. However, you may enter another competition as long as you notify us that you have done or plan to do so. If you are notified that your manuscript has won another award or prize, you must inform us of this immediately." Submit 3 complete copies of ms of 60-90 pages, exclusive of table of contents or other optional introductory material. **See guidelines for special formatting instructions.** Enclose stamped, self-addressed post-card to confirm receipt of material; no SASE as mss will not be returned. Mail by First Class Priority; no Certified, Federal Express, or other mail requiring a signature. **Deadline:** entries must be received between January 2 and March 25. Guidelines available for SASE, by e-mail, or on website. Winner and judges announced no later than June 1. Copies of winning books available from Lotus Press at the address above. "If you have already had a book published by Lotus Press, you are ineligible. However, inclusion in a Lotus Press anthology, such as *Adam of Ifé: Black Women in Praise of Black Men*, does not disqualify you."

Advice "Read some of the books we have published, especially award winners. Read a lot of good contemporary poetry. Those who have worked over a period of years at developing their craft will have the best chance for consideration. The work of novices is not likely to be selected."

◨ ◎ LOUISIANA LITERATURE; LOUISIANA LITERATURE PRIZE FOR POETRY (Specialized: regional)

SLU-792, Southeastern Louisiana University, Hammond LA 70402. (504)549-5022. E-mail: lalit@sel u.edu. Website: www.selu.edu/orgs/lalit. **Contact:** Jack Bedell, editor.

Magazine Needs *Louisiana Literature* appears twice/year. "We consider creative work from any-one, though we strive to showcase our state's talent. We appreciate poetry that shows firm control and craft; is sophisticated yet accessible to a broad readership. We don't use highly experimental work." Has published poetry by Claire Bateman, Elton Glaser, Gray Jacobik, Vivian Shipley, D.C. Berry, and Judy Longley. *Louisiana Literature* is 150 pages, $6^3/_4 \times 9^3/_4$, flat-spined, handsomely printed on heavy matte stock, with matte card cover. Single copy: $8 for individuals; subscription: $12 for individuals, $12.50 for institutions.

How to Submit Submit up to 5 poems at a time. No simultaneous submissions. No fax or e-mail submissions. "Send cover letter, including bio to use in the event of acceptance. Enclose SASE and specify whether work is to be returned or discarded." Reads submissions year round, "although we work more slowly in summer." Publishes theme issues. Guidelines and upcoming themes available for SASE or on website. Sometimes sends prepublication galleys. Pays 2 contributor's copies. Send materials for review consideration; include cover letter.

Contest/Award Offerings The Louisiana Literature Prize for Poetry offers a $400 award. Guidelines available for SASE.

Advice "It's important to us that the poets we publish be in control of their creations. Too much of what we see seems arbitrary."

◖ ◎ THE LOUISIANA REVIEW (Specialized: regional)

% Division of Liberal Arts, Louisiana State University at Eunice, P.O. Box 1129, Eunice LA 70535. (337)550-1315. E-mail: bfonteno@lsue.edu. Website: www.lsue.edu/LA-Review/. Established 1999. **Contact:** Dr. Jason Ambrosiano and Dr. Billy Fontenot, editors.

Magazine Needs *The Louisiana Review* appears annually in the fall semester. "We wish to offer Louisiana poets, writers, and artists a place to showcase their most beautiful pieces. Others may submit Louisiana-related poetry, stories, and art, as well as interviews with Louisiana writers. We want to publish the highest-quality poetry, fiction, art, and drama. For poetry, we like strong imagery, metaphor, and evidence of craft, but we do not wish to have sing-song rhymes, abstract, religious, or overly sentimental work." Has published poetry by Gary Snyder, Antler, David Cope, and Catfish McDaris. *The Louisiana Review* is 100-225 pages, magazine-sized, professionally printed, perfect-bound. Receives up to 2,000 poems/year, accepts 40-50. Press run is 300-600. Single copy: $8.

How to Submit Submit up to 5 poems at a time. No previously published poems. No fax or e-mail submissions. "Include cover letter indicating your association with Louisiana. Name and address should appear on each page." Reads submissions January 15 through March 31 only. Time between acceptance and publication is up to 2 years. Pays one contributor's copy. Poets retain all rights.

Advice "Be true to your own voice and style."

◙ LOUISIANA STATE UNIVERSITY PRESS

P.O. Box 25053, Baton Rouge LA 70894-5053. (225)578-6434. Fax: (225)578-6461. Website: www.ls u.edu/lsupress. Established 1935. **Contact:** John Easterly, executive editor. A highly respected publisher of collections by poets such as John Stone, David Kirby, Lisel Mueller, Margaret Gibson, Fred Chappell, Marilyn Nelson, and Henry Taylor. Publisher of the Southern Messenger Poets series edited by Dave Smith. **"Currently accepting poetry submissions, but the lists are full through 2007."**

◙ THE LOUISVILLE REVIEW

Spalding University, 851 S. Fourth St., Louisville KY 40203. (502)585-9911, ext. 2777. E-mail: louisvi llereview@spalding.edu. Website: www.louisvillereview.org. Established 1976. **Contact:** Kathleen Driskell, associate editor.

Magazine Needs *The Louisville Review* appears twice/year. Uses any kind of poetry. Has a section devoted to children's poetry (grades K-12) called The Children's Corner. Has published poetry by Wendy Bishop, Gary Fincke, Michael Burkard, and Sandra Kohler. *The Louisville Review* is 100 pages, digest-sized, flat-spined. Receives about 700 submissions/year, accepts about 10%. Single copy: $8; subscription: $14/year, $27/2 years, $40/3 years (foreign subscribers add $6/year for p&h). Sample: $5.

How to Submit Include SASE; no electronic submissions. "Poetry by children must include permission of parent to publish if accepted." Reads submissions year round. Time between acceptance and publication is up to 3 months. Submissions are read by 3 readers. Guidelines available on website. Pays 2 contributor's copies.

Advice "We look for the striking metaphor, unusual imagery, and fresh language."

◙ LUCID MOON REVIEW POETRY WEBSITE AND NEWSLETTER

Morris Hills Care Center, Room 427 W, 77 Madison Ave., Morristown NJ 07960. (973)993-9744. E-mail: ralphylucidmoon@yahoo.com. Website: www.lucidmoonpoetry.com. Established 1999 (website) and 2003 (newsletter). **Contact:** Ralph Haselmann, Jr., editor

Magazine Needs *Lucid Moon Review Poetry Website and Newsletter* is an online newsletter/journal updated quarterly. Wants "underground Beat poetry; heartfelt, romantic love poetry; humor; moon-themed poetry; and poems with references to pop culture." Does not want "indecipherable experimental poetry, lousy high school poetry, or annoying religious poetry." Has published poetry by Arthur Rimband, Charles Bukowski, Ana Christy, Allen Ginsberg, Kevin M. Hibshman, and Leonard J. Cirino. "All poetry columns have been converted to guestbook-like areas, and you can type in or copy and paste one poem or column per week. Old issues are archived in the newsletter section."

How to Submit Accepts previously published poems and simultaneous submissions. Accepts submissions for the newsletter by e-mail only (as attachment in Microsoft Word or rich-text document). "I do not accept submissions in the body of the e-mail because the lines get broken up. Please do not send snail mail submissions or submissions on disk." Include cover letter (with name, date, address, and e-mail) and a 3-sentence bio. "Please write poem title in 12-pt. Arial Bold font (black), then skip a line and write poem in 12-pt. unbolded Arial black font. Skip a line between each poem." Time between submission and acceptance is 3 months. "In the meantime, type in your poems in my guestbook poetry columns." Guidelines available in FYI section on home page and in poetry section of newsletter.

Advice "Read other poems posted on the website to get a feel for what I'm looking for. Cursing and sexual situations are okay, as long as they are not gratuitous. Let your poetry pen sing, dance, and soar! Check out my website every few months for the new newsletter, and please sign my guestbook."

✪ $◻ LUCIDITY; BEAR HOUSE PRESS

14781 Memorial Dr., #10, Houston TX 77079-5210. (281)920-1795. E-mail: tedbadger1@yahoo.c om. Established 1985. **Contact:** Ted O. Badger, editor.

Magazine Needs *Lucidity* is a semiannual journal of poetry. **Submission fee required**—$1/poem for "juried" selection by a panel of judges, or $2/poem to compete for cash awards of $15, $10, and $5. All winners paid in both cash and copies. Also publishes 6 pages of Succint Verse—poems of 12 lines or less—in most issues. "We expect them to be pithy and significant, and there is no reading/entry fee if sent along with Cash Award or Juried poems. Just think of all poetic forms that are 12 lines or less: cinquain, limerick, etheree, haiku, senryu, lune, etc., not to mention quatrain, triolet, and couplets." In addition, the editor invites a few guest contributors to submit to each issue. Contributors are encouraged to subscribe or buy a copy of the magazine. The magazine is called *Lucidity* because, the editor says, "I have felt that too many publications of verse lean to obscurity." No restrictions on form; space limit do to format. "We look for poetry that is life-related and has clarity and substance. We dedicate our journal to publishing those poets who express their thoughts, feelings, and impressions about the human scene with clarity and substance." Does not want "religious, butterfly, or vulgar poems." Has published poetry by Victoria Black, Ellaraine Lockie, Shari O'Brien, and Lisa Albright Ratnavira. The magazine is 72 pages, digest-sized, photocopied from typescript, saddle-stapled, with matte card cover. Press run is 280 (240 subscribers); some distributed free to selected winners. Subscription: $6. Sample (including guidelines): $2.

How to Submit Submit 3-5 poems at a time in each catagory. Lines/poem: 36 maximum (including spaces). Accepts simultaneous submissions. No e-mail submissions. Time between acceptance and publication is 6 months to a year. Guidelines available for SASE or by e-mail. Responds in 12-18 months. Pays cash plus one contributor's copy. Acquires one-time rights.

Book/Chapbook Needs & How to Submit Bear House Press is "a self-publishing arrangement by which poets can pay to have booklets published in the same format as *Lucidity* (but with perfect binding), with prices beginning at 100 copies of 32 pages for $336." Publishes about 6 chapbooks/year.

Also Offers Sponsors the Lucidity Poets' Ozark Retreat, a 3-day retreat held during the month of April in Eureka Springs, Arkansas.

Advice "Small press journals offer the best opportunity to most poets for publication and recognition."

$◻ ▣ LULLABY HEARSE (Specialized: experimental poetry with an edge)

26 Fifth St., Bangor ME 04401. (207)990-5839. E-mail: editor@lullabyhearse.com. Website: www.lullabyhearse.com. Established 2002. **Contact:** Sarah Ruth Jacobs, editor.

Magazine Needs *Lullaby Hearse* appears quarterly and publishes writing, art, poetry, and vintage movie reviews, with emphasis on work with an edge. Wants "vivid, pained poetry within the genres of horror, experimental, urban, rural, erotic, and personal verse. We read for talent, solidity of voice, and loyalty to vision over fancy." Does not want "poems about writing, bland odes to nature, clumsy/heavy-handed rhyme, self-pitying lyrics, or far-out fantasy. Shocking poetry is fine, when it isn't created from a place of self-imposed ignorance. We prefer crudity over bombast." *Lullaby Hearse* is 50 pages, magazine-sized, photocopied, saddle-stapled, with color card cover with art. Receives about 650 poetry submissions/year, accepts about 30. Press run is 200 (70 subscribers, 10 libraries, 100 shelf sales). Single copy: $5; subscription: $20. Make checks payable to Sarah Ruth Jacobs.

How to Submit Submit 3-10 poems at a time. Accepts simultaneous submissions; no previously published poems. Accepts e-mail submissions. Cover letter is preferred. "Include a SASE with all hard-copy submissions." Reads submissions year round. Time between acceptance and publication is up to 3 months. "I seldom postpone poems for the second upcoming issue. Instead I may delay in replying until all or a substantial amount of submissions have been received." Seldom comments on rejected poems. Guidelines available for SASE or on website. Responds in 6 weeks. Pays $5/poem and one contributor's copy. Acquires one-time rights. Reviews books and chapbooks of poetry and other magazines/journals in 1,000 words. Send materials for review consideration to Sarah Ruth Jacobs.

☑ ◎ LUNA BISONTE PRODS; LOST AND FOUND TIMES (Specialized: experimental/avant-garde)

137 Leland Ave., Columbus OH 43214-7505. Website: www.johnmbennett.net. Established 1967. **Contact:** John M. Bennett, poetry editor.

Magazine Needs *Lost and Found Times* publishes experimental and avant-garde writing. Wants "unusual poetry, naive poetry, surrealism, experimental/visual poetry, collaborations—no poetry workshop or academic pabulum." Has published poetry by J. Leftwich, Sheila Murphy, J.S. Murnet, Peter Ganick, I. Argüelles, and A. Ackerman. *Lost and Found Times* is 60 pages, digest-sized, printed in photo-reduced typescript with wild graphics, with matte card cover with graphics. Press run is 350 (75 subscribers, 30 libraries). Subscription: $30/5 issues. Sample: $7.

How to Submit Submit anytime—preferably camera-ready poems (but this is not required). Responds in 2 days. Pays one contributor's copy. All rights revert to authors upon publication. Staff reviews books of poetry. Send materials for review consideration.

Book/Chapbook Needs & How to Submit Luna Bisonte Prods considers book submissions. Query with samples and cover letter (but "keep it brief"). Chapbook publishing usually depends on grants or other subsidies, and is usually by solicitation. Will also consider subsidy arrangements on negotiable terms. A sampling of various Luna Bisonte Prods products—from posters and audio cassettes to pamphlets and chapbooks—available for $10.

Advice "Be blank."

☑ LUNGFULL! MAGAZINE

316 23rd St., Brooklyn NY 11215. E-mail: lungfull@rcn.com. Website: http://lungfull.org. Established 1994. **Contact:** Brendan Lorber, editor/publisher.

- *LUNGFULL!* was the recipient of a multi-year grant from the New York State Council for the Arts.

Magazine Needs *LUNGFULL!*, published annually, prints "the rough draft of each poem, in addition to the final, so that the reader can see the creative process from start to finish." Wants "any style as long as it's urgent, immediate, playful, probing, showing great thought while remaining vivid and grounded. Poems should be as interesting as conversation." Does not want "empty poetic abstractions." Has published poetry by Alice Notley, Lorenzo Thomas, Tracie Morris, Hal Sirowitz, Eileen Myles, and Bill Berkson. *LUNGFULL!* is 200 pages, 8½×7, offset-printed, desktop-published, perfect-bound, with glossy 2–color cover, includes ads. Receives about 1,000 poems/year, accepts 5%. Press run is 1,000 (150 subscribers, 750 shelf sales); 100 distributed free to contributors. Single copy: $8.95; subscription: $35.80/4 issues, $17.90/2 issues. Sample: $10.50. Make checks payable to Brendan Lorber, or order online.

How to Submit "We recommend you get a copy before submitting." Submit up to 6 poems at a time. Accepts previously published poems and simultaneous submissions (with notification); "However, other material will be considered first and stands a much greater chance of publication." Accepts e-mail submissions. "We prefer hard copy by USPS—but e-submissions can be made in the body of the e-mail itself; submissions with attachments will be deleted unread." Cover letter is preferred. Time between acceptance and publication is up to 8 months. "The editor looks at each piece for its own merit and for how well it will fit into the specific issue being planned based on other accepted work." Guidelines available by e-mail. Responds in one year. Pays 2 contributor's copies.

Also Offers "Each copy of *LUNGFULL! Magazine* now contains a short poem, usually from a series of 6, printed on a sticker—they can be removed from the magazine and placed on any flat surface to make it a little less flat. Innovatively designed and printed in black & white, previous stickers have included work by Sparrow, Rumi, Julie Reid, Donna Cartelli, Joe Maynard, and Jeremy Sharpe, among others."

Advice "Failure demands a certain dedication. Practice makes imperfection and imperfection makes room for the amazing. Only outside the bounds of acceptable conclusions can the astounding transpire, can writing contain anything beyond twittering snack food logic and the utilitarian pistons of mundane engineering.''

✔ ◎ THE LUTHERAN DIGEST (Specialized: humor; nature/rural/ecology; religious/Christian; inspirational)

P.O. Box 4250, Hopkins MN 55343. (952)933-2820. Fax: (952)933-5708. E-mail: tldi@lutherandigest.com. Website: www.lutherandigest.com. Established 1953. **Contact:** David Tank, editor.

Magazine Needs *The Lutheran Digest* appears quarterly ''to entertain and encourage believers and to subtly persuade non-believers to embrace the Christian faith. We publish short poems that will fit in a single column of the magazine. Most are inspirational, but that doesn't necessarily mean religious. No avant-garde poetry or work longer than 25 lines.'' Has published poetry by Kathleen A. Cain, William Beyer, Margaret Peterson, Florence Berg, and Erma Boetkher. *The Lutheran Digest* is 64 pages, digest-sized, offset-printed, saddle-stapled, with 4-color paper cover, includes local ads. Receives about 200 poems/year, accepts 20%. Press run is 100,000; some distributed free to Lutheran churches. Subscription: $14/year, $22/2 years. Sample: $3.50.

How to Submit Submit 3 poems at a time. Lines/poem: 25 maximum. Accepts previously published poems and simultaneous submissions. Accepts submissions by fax, by e-mail (as attachment), and by postal mail. Cover letter is preferred. ''Include SASE if return is desired.'' Time between acceptance and publication is up to 9 months. ''Poems are selected by editor and reviewed by publication panel.'' Guidelines available for SASE or on website. Responds in 3 months. Pays credit and one contributor's copy. Acquires one-time rights.

Advice ''Poems should be short and appeal to senior citizens. We also look for poems that can be sung to traditional Lutheran hymns.''

✖ $◯ LYNX EYE; SCRIBBLEFEST LITERARY GROUP

581 Woodland Dr., Los Osos CA 93402. (805)528-8146. E-mail: pamccully@aol.com. Established 1994. **Contact:** Pam McCully.

Magazine Needs *Lynx Eye* is the quarterly publication of the ScribbleFest Literary Group, an organization dedicated to the development and promotion of the literary arts. *Lynx Eye* is ''dedicated to showcasing visionary writers and artists, particularly new voices.'' Each issue contains a special feature called Presenting, in which an unpublished writer of prose or poetry makes his/her print debut. No specifications regarding form, subject matter, or style of poetry. Has published poetry by Bruce Curley, Dani Montgomery, Michael Neal Morris, and Whitman McGowan. *Lynx Eye* is about 120 pages, digest-sized, perfect-bound. Receives about 2,000 poetry submissions/year. Press run is 500 (250 subscribers, 200 shelf sales). Subscription: $25/year. Sample: $7.95. Make checks payable to ScribbleFest Literary Group.

How to Submit Submissions must be typed and include name, address, and phone number on each page. SASE required. Accepts simultaneous submissions; no previously published poems. No fax or e-mail submissions. Guidelines available for SASE or by e-mail. Responds in up to 3 months. Pays $10/poem and 3 contributor's copies. Acquires first North American serial rights.

✔ THE LYRIC

P.O. Box 110, Jericho Corners VT 05465. Phone/fax: (802)899-3993. E-mail: Lyric@sover.net. Established 1921 (''the oldest magazine in North America in continuous publication devoted to the publication of traditional poetry''). **Contact:** Jean Mellichamp-Milliken, editor.

Magazine Needs *The Lyric* publishes about 55 poems each quarterly issue. ''We use rhymed verse in traditional forms, for the most part, with an occasional piece of blank or free verse. Forty lines or so is usually our limit. Our themes are varied, ranging from religious ecstasy to humor to raw grief, but we feel no compulsion to shock, embitter, or confound our readers. We also avoid poems about contemporary political or social problems—'grief but not grievances,' as Frost put it. Frost is helpful in other ways: If yours is more than a lover's quarrel with life, we are not your best market. And most of our poems are accessible on first or second reading. Frost again: 'Don't hide too far away.' '' Has published poetry by Rhina P. Espaillat, Gail White, Joseph Awad, Alfred Dorn, Ruth Harrison, and Glenna Holloway. *The Lyric* is 32 pages, digest-sized, professionally printed with varied typography, with matte card cover. Press run is 750 (600 subscribers, 40 libraries). Receives about 3,000 submissions/year, accepts 5%. Subscription: $14/year, $24/2 years, $32/3 years (US), $16 for Canada and other countries (in US funds only). Sample: $4.

How to Submit Submit up to 6 poems at a time. ''Will read, but do not prefer, simultaneous submissions; no previously published poems or translations. Cover letters often helpful, but not required.'' Guidelines available for SASE or by e-mail. Responds in 3 months (average); ''inquire after 6 months.'' Pays one contributor's copy, and all contributors are eligible for quarterly and annual prizes totaling $750. ''Subscription will not affect publication of submitted poetry.''

Advice ''Our raison d'être has been the encouragement of form, music, rhyme, and accessibility in poetry. As we witness the growing tide of appreciation for traditional/lyric poetry, we are proud to have stayed the course for 84 years, helping keep the roots of poetry alive.''

☑ LYRIC POETRY REVIEW

P.O. Box 980814, Houston TX 77098. (713)523-4193. E-mail: lyric@lyricreview.org. Website: www.lyricreview.org. Established 2001. **Contact:** Mira Rosenthal, editor. Managing Editor: Heather Bigley. Member: CLMP.

• *Lyric Poetry Review* was a Pushcart Prize winner for 2003.

Magazine Needs *Lyric Poetry Review* appears biannually and presents poetry by Americans, and translations of both little-known and celebrated poets from around the world. Also publishes literary essays. Wants ''poems with singing power; poems with fresh energy to delight and awaken deep feeling; lyric essays that use poetic logic and relate a mosaic of ideas.'' Does not want poems of more than 500 words. Has published poetry by Fanny Howe, Marilyn Hacker, Tony Hoagland, Tomaz Salamun, Czeslaw Milosz, and Jean Valentine. *Lyric Poetry Review* is 96 pages, digest-sized, offset-printed, perfect-bound, with full-color cover with original artwork. Receives about 2,500 poems/year, accepts about 5%. Press run is 1,000. Single copy: $8; subscription: $14/year (subscribers outside US add $5 postage). Make checks payable to *Lyric Poetry Review*.

How to Submit Submit 3-6 poems at a time. Accepts simultaneous submissions if notified; no previously published poems. No fax, e-mail, or disk submissions. Cover letter is required. Reads submissions September through May. Time between acceptance and publication is up to one year. ''Editorial decisions are made collectively by all associated editors. We strongly advise that those submitting work read a recent issue first.'' Seldom comments on rejected poems. Occasionally publishes theme issues. List of upcoming themes available by e-mail. Guidelines available in magazine, for SASE, or on website. Responds in up to 3 months. Always sends prepublication galleys. Pays 2 contributor's copies ''and 2 copies to requested reviewers.'' Acquires first rights. Solicits reviews.

☑ THE MACGUFFIN; NATIONAL POET HUNT

Schoolcraft College, 18600 Haggerty Rd., Livonia MI 48152-2696. (734)462-4400, ext. 5327. Fax: (734)462-4679. E-mail: macguffin@schoolcraft.edu. Website: www.macguffin.org. Established 1984. **Contact:** Steven A. Dolgin, editor.

Magazine Needs *The MacGuffin* is a literary magazine appearing 3 times/year. ''We publish the best poetry, fiction, nonfiction, and artwork we find. We have no thematic or stylistic biases. We look for well-crafted poetry. Avoid pornography, triteness, and sloppy poetry. We do not publish haiku, concrete, or light verse.'' Has published poetry by Linda Nemec Foster, Virgil Suárez, and Susan Terris. *The MacGuffin* is 164+ pages, digest-sized, professionally printed on heavy buff stock, flat-spined, with matte card cover. Press run is 500 (250 subscribers); the rest are local sales, contributor copies, and distribution to college offices. Single copy: $9 regular issue, $15 extended issue; subscription: $22. Sample: $6.

How to Submit Submit up to 5 poems at a time. Lines/poem: 300 maximum. Poems should be typewritten. Accepts submissions by fax, on disk, by e-mail (as attachment), and through postal mail. When submitting by e-mail, "submit each poem as a separate document attachment. Submissions made in the body of an e-mail will not be considered." Occasionally publishes theme issues. Upcoming themes available by fax, by e-mail, and for SASE. Guidelines available for SASE, by fax, by e-mail, or on website. Responds in 3-5 months; publication backlog is 6 months to 2 years. Pays 2 contributor's copies.

Contest/Award Offerings Sponsors the National Poet Hunt, established in 1996, offering 1st Prize: $500; 2nd Prize: $250; 3rd Prize: $100; up to 3 honorable mentions; and publication. Submissions may be entered in other contests. Submit 5 typed poems on any subject in any form. Put name and address on *separate* 3 × 5 index card only. Guidelines available by fax, by e-mail, for SASE, and on website. **Entry fee:** $15/5 poems. **Deadline:** postmarked between April 1 and June 3 for 2005; check website for current deadline. Judge for 2004 contest was Bob Hicok. 2004 winners will be announced in *Poets and Writers* in March/April.

Advice "We will always comment on 'near misses.' Writing is a search, and it is a journey. Don't become sidetracked. Don't become discouraged. Keep looking. Keep traveling. Keep writing."

✪ ⊘ MAD RIVER PRESS

State Road, Richmond MA 01254. (413)698-3184. Established 1986. **Contact:** Barry Sternlieb, editor. Mad River publishes 2 broadsides and one chapbook/year, "all types of poetry, no bias," but none unsolicited.

$⊘ THE MAGAZINE OF FANTASY & SCIENCE FICTION

P.O. Box 3447, Hoboken NJ 07030. E-mail: FandSF@aol.com. Website: www.fsfmag.com. Established 1949. **Contact:** Gordon Van Gelder, editor.

- *The Magazine of Fantasy & Science Fiction* is a past winner of the Hugo Award and World Fantasy Award.

Magazine Needs *The Magazine of Fantasy & Science Fiction* appears monthly, 11 times/year. "One of the longest-running magazines devoted to the literature of the fantastic." Wants only poetry that deals with the fantastic or the science-fictional. Has published poetry by Rebecca Kavaler, Elizabeth Bear, and Robert Frazier. *The Magazine of Fantasy & Science Fiction* is 160 pages, digest-sized, offset-printed, perfect-bound, with glossy cover, includes ads. Receives about 20-40 poems/year, accepts about 1%. Press run is 35,000 (20,000 subscribers). Single copy: $3.95; subscription: $32.97. Sample: $5. Make checks payable to *The Magazine of Fantasy & Science Fiction*.

How to Submit Submit 1-3 poems at a time. No previously published poems or simultaneous submissions. No fax, e-mail, or disk submissions. Time between acceptance and publication is up to 2 years, but usually about 9 months. "I buy poems very infrequently—just when one hits me right." Seldom comments on rejected poems. Guidelines available for SASE or on website. Responds in up to one month. Always sends prepublication galleys. Pays $50/poem and 2 contributor's copies. Acquires first North American serial rights.

$⊘ ◎ THE MAGAZINE OF SPECULATIVE POETRY (Specialized: horror; fantasy; science fiction; science)

P.O. Box 564, Beloit WI 53512. Established 1984. **Contact:** Roger Dutcher, editor.

Magazine Needs *The Magazine of Speculative Poetry* is a biannual magazine that features "the best new speculative poetry. We are especially interested in narrative form, but open to any form, any length (within reason); interested in a variety of styles. We're looking for the best of the new poetry utilizing the ideas, imagery, and approaches developed by speculative fiction, and will welcome experimental techniques as well as the fresh employment of traditional forms." Has published poetry by Mark Rudolph, Bruce Boston, Mario Milosevic, Sandra Lindow, and Laurel Winter. *The Magazine of Speculative Poetry* is 24-28 pages, digest-sized, offset-printed, saddle-stapled, with matte card cover. Accepts less than 5% of some 500 poems received/year. Press run is 150-200 (nearly 100 subscribers). Subscription: $19/4 issues. Sample: $5.

How to Submit Submit 3-5 poems at a time, double-spaced with a "regular old font. We are a small magazine, we can't print epics. Some poems run 2 or 3 pages, but rarely anything longer." No previously published poems or simultaneous submissions. "We like cover letters, but they aren't necessary. We like to see where you heard of us; the names of the poems submitted; a statement if the poetry manuscript is disposable; a big enough SASE; and if you've been published, some recent places." Editor comments on rejected poems "on occasion." Guidelines available for SASE. Responds in up to 2 months. Pays 3¢/word (minimum $5, maximum $25), plus one contributor's copy. Acquires first North American serial rights. "All rights revert to author upon publication, except for permission to reprint in any 'Best of' or compilation volume. Payment will be made for such publication." Reviews books of speculative poetry. Query on unsolicited reviews. Send materials for review consideration.

The Magazine of Speculative Poetry

Volume Six Number Four $5.00   Autumn 2004

Artist Mark Rich has done nearly all the covers for *The Magazine of Speculative Poetry.* Says editor Roger Dutcher of the Volume 6, Number 4 cover, "This one in particular has a dramatic effect. I hope it will 'challenge' a reader to pick up the magazine."

🌣 ◻ ◎ **THE MAGNOLIA QUARTERLY (Specialized: membership); "LET'S WRITE" LITERARY CONTEST; GULF COAST WRITERS ASSOCIATION**
P.O. Box 6445, Gulfport MS 39506. E-mail: gcwriters@aol.com. Website: www.gcwriters.org. Established 1999. **Contact:** John Freeman, poetry editor.

Magazine Needs *The Magnolia Quarterly* publishes poetry, fiction, nonfiction, reviews, and photography. Wants all styles of poetry. Does not want "pornography, racial or religious bigotry, far-left or far-right political poems." Has published poetry by Leonard Cirino, Catharine Savage Brosman, Angela Ball, Jack Bedell, Jack Butler, and Larry Johnson. *The Magnolia Review* is 30 pages, magazine-sized, stapled, with paper cover, includes ads. Single copy: $4; subscription: $15 (or included in $25 GCWA annual dues). Make checks payable to Gulf Coast Writers Assocation.

How to Submit Submit 1-5 poems at a time. Lines/poem: open. Accepts previously published poems and simultaneous submissions. Accepts e-mail (as attachment) and disk submissions. Cover letter is preferred. Reads submissions year round. Time between acceptance and publication is one month. **Membership required to submit to magazine.** Guidelines available in magazine, for SASE, by e-mail, or on website. Responds in 2 weeks. No payment. Acquires first rights. Returns rights to poet upon publication. Reviews books and chapbooks of poetry and other magazines/journals, single-book format. Send materials for review consideration to Victoria Olsen, editor.

Contest/Award Offerings Sponsors annual "Let's Write" Literary Contest, which includes a category for poetry. Offers 1st Prize: $75; 2nd Prize: $50; 3rd Prize: $25; plus publication in *The Magnolia Quarterly.* Submit 1-5 unpublished poems of no more than 36 lines each. Poems may not be submitted to other contests. **Entry fee:** $5/poem for Adult and Young Writer categories. **2005 Deadline:** April 15. Guidelines available on website.

Also Offers The Gulf Coast Writers Association, "a nationally recognized organization which strives to encourage and inspire writers throughout the Mississippi Gulf Coast regional area." Additional information available on website.

🌐 🖊 MAGPIE'S NEST

176 Stoney Lane, Sparkhill, Birmingham B12 8AN United Kingdom. E-mail: magpies-nest@tiscali.co.uk. Established 1979. **Contact:** Mr. Bal Saini, editor.

Magazine Needs *Magpie's Nest* appears quarterly and publishes "cutting-edge, modern poetry and fiction that deals with the human condition. No love poetry or self-obsessed work." *Magpie's Nest* receives about 200 poems/year, accepts about 25%. Press run is 200 (150 subscribers, 50 shelf sales). Single copy: $2.50; subscription: $12.50. Sample: $3.

How to Submit Submit 4 poems at a time. Lines/poem: 10 minimum, 40 maximum. Accepts previously published poems and simultaneous submissions. Accepts e-mail submission (pasted into body of message or as attachment). Cover letter is preferred. "Keep copies of submitted poems as those not used are binned." Reads submissions September 1 through June 30 only. Time between acceptance and publication is 3 months. Seldom comments on rejected poems. Occasionally publishes theme issues. Responds in 3 months. Pays one contributor's copy. Reviews books of poetry and other magazines in 200 words, single-book format. Send materials for review consideration.

Advice "Read past issues of the magazine to assess the editor's taste/preference."

🖊 MAIN STREET RAG; ANNUAL POETRY BOOK AWARD; ANNUAL CHAPBOOK CONTEST

4416 Shea Lane, Charlotte NC 28227. (704)573-2516. E-mail: editor@mainstreetrag.com. Website: www.MainStreetRag.com. Established 1996. **Contact:** M. Scott Douglass, editor/publisher.

Magazine Needs *Main Street Rag* is a quarterly that publishes "poetry, short fiction, essays, interviews, reviews, photos, art, cartoons, (political, satirical), and poetry collections as well as books—we are now a full service bindery with an online bookstore. We like publishing good material from people who are interested in more than notching another publishing credit, people who support small independent publishers like ourselves." *Main Street Rag* "will consider almost anything but prefer writing with an edge—either gritty or bitingly humorous." Has published poetry by Silvia Curbelo, Sean Thomas Dougherty, Denise Duhamel, Cathy Essinger, Ishle Yi Park, and Dennis Must. *Main Street Rag* is about 96 pages, digest-sized, perfect-bound, with 100-lb. laminated color cover. Publishes 30-40 poems and one short story per issue out of 2,500 submissions/year. Press run is about 1,000 (300 subscribers, 15 libraries). "Sold nationally in bookstores." Single copy: $7; subscription: $20/year, $35/2 years.

How to Submit Submit 6 pages of poetry at a time. No previously published poems or simultaneous submissions. E-mail submissions from subscribers only. Cover letter is preferred; "no bios or credits—let the word speak for itself." Time between acceptance and publication is up to one year. Guidelines available for SASE or by e-mail. Responds within 6 weeks. Pays one contributor's copy. Acquires first North American print rights.

Contest/Award Offerings 1) **Annual Poetry Book Award** offers 1st Prize: $1,500 and 50 copies of book; 2nd Prize: $500 and publication; runners-up may also be offered publication. All entrants receive a copy of the winning book. Submit 48-80 pages of poetry, no more than one poem/page. **Entry fee:** $20. **Deadline:** January 31. Guidelines available for SASE, by e-mail, or on website. 2) **Annual Chapbook Contest** offers 1st Prize: $500 and 50 copies of chapbook; 2nd Prize: $100; 3rd Prize: $100; runners-up will also be offered publication, and every ms entered will be considered for publication. All entrants receive a copy of the winning chapbook. Submit 24-32 pages of poetry, no more than one poem/page. **Entry fee:** $15. **Deadline:** May 31. Guidelines available for SASE, by e-mail, or on website. Previous winners include David Chorlton, Alan Catlin, Dede Wilson, Nancy Kenney Connolly, Karla Huston, Pam Bernard, Matt Morris, Sylvia Curbelo, and Jim Ferris.

Advice "Small press independents exist by and for writers. Without their support (and the support of readers), we have no reason to exist. Sampling first is always appreciated."

♻ $🖊 THE MALAHAT REVIEW; LONG POEM PRIZE; FAR HORIZONS AWARD

University of Victoria, P.O. Box 1700, STN CSC, Victoria BC V8W 2Y2 Canada. (250)721-8524. Fax: (250)472-5051. E-mail: malahat@uvic.ca (inquiries only). Website: www.malahatreview.ca. Established 1967. **Contact:** John Barton, editor.

Magazine Needs *The Malahat Review* is "a high-quality, visually appealing literary quarterly which has earned the praise of notable literary figures throughout North America. Its purpose is to publish and promote poetry and fiction of a very high standard, both Canadian and international. We are interested in various styles, lengths, and themes. The criterion is excellence." Has published poetry by Steven Heighton and Jan Zwicky. Receives about 2,000 poems/year, accepts about 100. Has 1,000 subscribers, of which 300 are libraries. Subscription: $40 Canadian for individuals, $50 Canadian for institutions (or US equivalent). Sample: $16.45 US.

How to Submit Submit 5-10 poems. Include SASE with Canadian stamps or IRC with each submission. Guidelines available for SASE (or SAE and IRC). Responds within 3 months. Pays $30 Canadian/printed page plus 2 contributor's copies and one year's subscription. Acquires first world serial rights. Reviews Canadian books of poetry.

Contest/Award Offerings 1) **Long Poem Prize**, offering 2 awards of $400 plus publication and payment at $30 Canadian/page, for a long poem or cycle, 10-20 printed pages (flexible minimum and maximum). **Entry fee:** $35 Canadian or $35 US for foreign entries (includes one-year subscription). **Deadline:** March 1 of alternate years (2005, 2007, etc.). Include name and address on a separate page. 2) **Far Horizons Award**, offering $500 for a poem of 60 lines. Restricted to poets who have not yet published in book-form. **Entry fee:** $25 Canadian or $25 US for foreign entries (includes one-year subscription). **Deadline:** May 1 of alternate years (2006, 2008, etc.). Include name and address on a separate page.

$☑ MAMMOTH BOOKS; MAMMOTH PRESS INC.

7 Juniata St., DuBois PA 15801. Established 1997. **Contact:** Antonio Vallone, publisher.

Book/Chapbook Needs MAMMOTH books, an imprint of MAMMOTH press inc., publishes 2-4 paperbacks/year of creative nonfiction, fiction, and poetry. "We are open to all types of literary poetry." Has published *The House of Sages* by Philip Terman, *The Never Wife* by Cynthia Hogue, *These Happy Eyes* by Liz Rosenberg, and *Subjects for Other Conversations* by John Stigall. Books are usually 5×7 or 6×9, digitally printed, perfect-bound; covers vary (1- to 4-color). **Not currently reading unsolicited mss.** Order sample books by writing to the above address.

Advice "Read big. Write big. Publish small. Join the herd."

★ ☑ ◎ THE MANHATTAN REVIEW (Specialized: translations)

440 Riverside Dr., Apt. 38, New York NY 10027. (212)932-1854. Established 1980. **Contact:** Philip Fried, poetry editor.

Magazine Needs *The Manhattan Review*, "an annual with ambitions to be semiannual, publishes American writers and foreign writers with something valuable to offer the American scene. We like to think of poetry as a powerful discipline engaged with many other fields. We want to see ambitious work. Interested in both lyric and narrative. Not interested in mawkish, sentimental poetry. We select high-quality work from a number of different countries, including the U.S." Has published poetry by Zbigniew Herbert, D. Nurkse, Baron Wormser, Penelope Shuttle, Marilyn Hacker, and Peter Redgrove. *The Manhattan Review* is 64 pages, digest-sized, professionally printed, with glossy card cover. Receives about 300 submissions/year, uses few ("but I do read everything submitted carefully and with an open mind"). Press run is 500 (400 subscribers, 250 libraries). Single copy: $5; subscription: $10. Sample: $6.35 with 6×9 envelope.

How to Submit Submit 3-5 pages of poems at a time. No simultaneous submissions. Cover letter with short bio and publications credits is required. Editor sometimes comments on poems, "but don't count on it." Responds in 3 months if possible. Pays contributor's copies. Staff reviews books of poetry. Send materials for review consideration.

Advice "Always read the magazine first to see if your work is appropriate."

$☑ MĀNOA: A PACIFIC JOURNAL OF INTERNATIONAL WRITING

1733 Donaghho Rd., Honolulu HI 96822. Fax: (808)956-3083. E-mail: mjournal-l@hawaii.edu. Website: http://manoajournal.hawaii.edu. Established 1989. **Contact:** Frank Stewart, poetry editor.

• Poetry published in *Mānoa* has also appeared in volumes of *The Best American Poetry*.

Magazine Needs *Mānoa* appears twice/year. "We are a general interest literary magazine and consider work in many forms and styles, regardless of the author's publishing history. However, we are not for the beginning writer. It is best to look at a sample copy of the journal before submitting." Has published poetry by Arthur Sze, Ai, Linda Gregg, Jane Hirshfield, and Ha Jin. *Mānoa* is 240 pages, 7×10, offset-printed, flat-spined. Receives about 1,000 poems/year, accepts 2%. Press run is more than 2,500 (several hundred subscribers, 130 libraries, 400 shelf sales). "In addition, *Mānoa* is available through Project Muse to about 900 institutional subscribers throughout the world." Subscription: $22/year. Sample: $10.

How to Submit Submit 3-5 poems at a time. Seldom comments on rejected poems. Guidelines available on website. Responds in 6 weeks. Always sends prepublication galleys. Pays "competitive" amount plus 2 contributor's copies. Reviews current books and chapbooks of poetry. Send materials for review consideration to reviews editor.

Advice "We are not a regional journal, but each issue features a particular part of Asia or the Pacific; these features, which include poetry, are assembled by guest editors. The rest of each issue features work by poets from the U.S. and elsewhere. We welcome the opportunity to read poetry from throughout the country, but we are not interested in genre or formalist writing for its own sake, or in casual impressions of the Asia-Pacific region."

✪ ☑ MANY MOUNTAINS MOVING; MANY MOUNTAINS MOVING ANNUAL POETRY BOOK CONTEST

420 22nd St., Boulder CO 80302. (303)545-9942. E-mail: mmm@mmminc.org. Website: www.mm minc.org. Established 1994. **Contact:** Alissa Norton, poetry editor.

• Poetry published in *Many Mountains Moving* has also been included in volumes of *The Best American Poetry* and *The Pushcart Prize*.

Magazine Needs Published 6 times/year, *Many Mountains Moving* is "a literary journal of diverse contemporary voices that welcomes previously unpublished fiction, poetry, nonfiction, and art from writers and artists of all walks of life. We publish the world's top writers as well as emerging talents." Open to any style of poetry, but they do not want any "Hallmark-y" poetry. Accepts poetry by children, "but quality would have to be on par with other accepted work." Has published poetry by Robert Bly, W.S. Merwin, Sherman Alexie, Lawson Fusao Inada, Allen Ginsberg, and Adrienne Rich. *Many Mountains Moving* is about 60 pages, magazine-sized, web-offset, perfect-bound, with 4-color cover. Receives 4,000 poems/year, accepts .1%. Press run is 1,500. Single copy: $6.99; subscription: $18/year.

How to Submit Submit 3-10 poems at a time, typed. Accepts simultaneous submissions; no previously published poems. Accepts submissions by postal mail only; include SASE. Cover letter is preferred. "Poems are first read by several readers. If considered seriously, they are passed to the poetry editor for final decision." Seldom comments on rejected poems. Guidelines available for SASE or on website. Responds within 3 months; "if we are seriously considering a submission, we may take longer." Sends prepublication galleys. Pays 3 contributor's copies, additional copies available at $7/copy. Acquires first North American serial rights and "rights to publish in a future edition of the *Best of Many Mountains Moving Anthology*."

Contest/Award Offerings Sponsors an annual book contest, which awards an honorarium and publication of ms in book form. Details available for SASE.

Advice "Although we have featured a number of established poets, we encourage new writers to submit. However, we recommend that poets read through at least one issue to familiarize themselves with the type of work we generally publish."

☑ MARGIE/THE AMERICAN JOURNAL OF POETRY; THE MARJORIE J. WILSON AWARD FOR EXCELLENCE IN POETRY; "STRONG MEDICINE" AWARD; INTUIT HOUSE POETRY BOOK AWARD CONTEST

P.O. Box 250, Chesterfield MO 63006-0250. Fax: (636)532-0539. E-mail: margiereview@aol.com.

Website: www.margiereview.com. Established 2001. **Contact:** Robert Nazarene, editor-in-chief.
Magazine Needs *MARGIE/The American Journal of Poetry* appears annually in September. *"MARGIE publishes superlative poetry. No limits to school, form, subject matter. Imaginative, risk-taking poetry which disturbs and/or consoles is of paramount interest. A distinctive voice is prized."* Has published poetry by Billy Collins, Emmylou Harris, Ted Kooser, Maxine Kumin, Charles Simic, David Wagoner, and Anne Waldman. *"MARGIE is about 350-400+ pages, digest-sized, professionally printed, perfect-bound, with glossy cover with art/graphics, includes ads. Receives about 30,000-40,000 poems/year, accepts less than 1%. Available by subscription only. Single copy (one-year subscription): $13.95 for individuals, $18.95 for institutions & foreign (prices include shipping & handling). Make checks payable to *MARGIE*.

How to Submit Submit 3-5 poems at a time. Lines/poem: 90 maximum. Accepts simultaneous submissions (notify in cover letter); no previously published poems. No fax, e-mail, or disk submissions. Cover letter is required. *"A short bio is useful, but not required."* Open reading: June 1 through August 1; one submission/poet during open reading period. *"Subscribers only may submit up to 4 times, year round. Identify yourself as 'subscriber' on outside of submission envelope."* Time between acceptance and publication is up to one year. Editor makes final decision. *Sometimes* comments on rejected poems. Guidelines available in magazine, for SASE, or on website. Responds in about 3 weeks. Sometimes sends prepublication galleys. Pays one contributor's copy. Acquires first rights. All rights revert to poet upon publication.

Contest/Award Offerings "The Marjorie J. Wilson Award for Excellence in Poetry" (spring); "Strong Medicine" Award (autumn); IntuiT House Poetry Book Award Contest (winter). Guidelines available for SASE or on website.

Advice "Read, read, read with unwavering discipline. Then, write. Be audacious, innovative, distinctive."

MARGIN: EXPLORING MODERN MAGICAL REALISM (Specialized: magical realism)
321 High School Rd. NE, PMB #204, Bainbridge Island WA 98110. E-mail: magicalrealismmaven@yahoo.com. Website: www.magical-realism.com. Established 2000. **Contact:** Poetry Department.
Magazine Needs *Margin: Exploring Modern Magical Realism* is "the world's only continuous survey of contemporary literary magical realism. We want accessible poetry where metamorphoses are authentic, and where the magical and mundane coexist. Metaphor alone does not qualify as magical realism. No light verse, forced rhyme, or language poetry, and *no* New Age, surrealism, Wiccan, or science fiction." *Margin* is published online ("as we find good poetry—no schedule"). Receives "thousands" of poems/year, accepts about 2%. Circulation is about 5,000 pageviews/month. Subscription: "free, automated, private." Sample: "visit website or send $5 for a copy of *Periphery*, our print zine sample."

How to Submit Submit up to 6 poems at a time. "No preferred line length, but our bias runs to shorter rather than longer." Accepts previously published poems and simultaneous submissions (if notified). Accepts e-mail submissions (*no* attachments). "Poems submitted without SASE will not be read or returned." See website for submission periods. Query regarding translations. Time between acceptance and publication is usually 6 months. Poems are circulated to an editorial board. "Editors live in separate cities in the U.S. and Canada." Seldom comments on rejected poems ("Only when they are good poems but not magical realism. We send reading list of top 10 favorite magical realist poets or authors, plus bio and short definition of 'magical realism.' "). All work is considered for publication in both *Margin* and its print zine sample, *Periphery*. Occasionally publishes theme issues. Guidelines and upcoming themes available on website. Spring 2005 theme: Resurrecting Quixote: Magical Realism from the Iberian Peninsula. Responds in 6 months. Usually sends prepublication galleys as URL form. May offer small payment. Nominates for literary prizes. Rights acquired are negotiable. Reviews books and chapbooks of poetry in under 500 words ("but we are flexible"), single-book and multi-book format. Send materials for review consideration to poetry editor ("Nothing academic!"). Also interested in articles, essays on poetry as magical realism, interviews of magical realist poets, and critical discussions of magical realist work by poets from around the world.

Contest/Award Offerings See website for details of various contests.

Also Offers "Broad global exposure has benefited many of our published writers."

Advice "*Understand* what magical realism is *before* submitting. See website for guidelines."

☑ MARSH HAWK PRESS; MARSH HAWK PRESS PRIZE

P.O. Box 206, East Rockaway NY 11518. E-mail: MarshHawkPress@cs.com. Website: www.Marsh HawkPress.org. Established 2001.

Book/Chapbook Needs & How to Submit Marsh Hawk Press publishes books of "quality poetry of any lineage—post-Imagist-Objectivist, New York School, surrealist, experimental, language, concrete, etc." Has published poetry by Eileen Tabios, Sandy McIntosh, Ed Foster, Harriet Zinnes, Sharon Dolin, and Basil King. Publishes 6 poetry books/year. **Marsh Hawk Press currently accepts submissions only through its annual competition, the Marsh Hawk Press Prize.** Books are 48-152 pages, photo offset-printed, perfect-bound, with 4-color covers. "The press is a collective whose author-members agree to work with the press on all aspects of book production, including editing, design, distribution, sales, advertising, publicity, and fund raising."

Advice "See our website for our manifesto and contest information."

✪ $☐ ☑ THE MARTIAN WAVE (Specialized: science fiction related to exploration/settlement of the Solar System)

P.O. Box 782, Cedar Rapids IA 52406-0782. E-mail: martianwave@samsdotpublishing.com. Website: www.samsdotpublishing.com. Established 1997. **Contact:** J. Alan Erwine, editor. Member: The Speculative Literature Foundation (http://SpeculativeLiterature.org).

Magazine Needs *The Martian Wave* is a quarterly online magazine publishing "science fiction poetry and stories that are related in some way to the exploration and/or settlement of the Solar System." Does not want "anything other than science fiction." Has published poetry by Marge B. Simon, Kristine Ong Muslim, Christina Sng, Aurelio Rico Lopez III, s c. virtes, and Tyree Campbell. Receives about 150 poems/year, accepts about 16 (12%).

How to Submit Submit up to 5 poems at a time. Lines/poem: prefers less than 100. No previously published poems or simultaneous submissions. Accepts e-mail submissions (pasted into body of message); no disk submissions. "Submission should include snail mail address and a short (1-2 lines) bio." Reads submissions year round.

Submit seasonal poems 6 months in advance. Time between acceptance and publication is 1-2 months. Sometimes comments on rejected poems. Guidelines available on website. Responds in 4-6 weeks. Pays $5/poem. Acquires first North American serial rights.

Advice "It's up to the writer to take the first step and submit work. Some of our best poems have come from poets who weren't sure if they were good enough. Most important is our theme. The poem must be related to the exploration and/or settlement of the Solar System."

☑ ☑ MARYMARK PRESS (Specialized: experimental/avant-garde)

45-08 Old Millstone Dr., East Windsor NJ 08520. (609)443-0646. Website: www.experimentalpoet.com. Established 1994. **Contact:** Mark Sonnenfeld, editor/publisher.

Book/Chapbook Needs Marymark Press's goal is "to feature and promote experimental writers. I will most likely be publishing broadsides, give-out sheets, and chapbooks this year. I want to see experimental writing of the outer fringe. Make up words, sounds, whatever, but say something you thought never could be explained. Disregard rules if need be." No traditional, rhyming, or spiritual verse; no predictable styles. Has published poetry by François Marceau, Christopher Robin, Sharlie West, Gyorgy Kostritsky, and Tamara Wyndham.

How to Submit Submit 3 poems at a time. Accepts previously published poems and simultaneous submissions. Cover letter is preferred. "Copies should be clean, crisp, and camera-ready. I do not have the means to accept electronic submissions. A SASE should accompany all submissions, and a telephone number if at all possible." Time between acceptance and publication is one month. Seldom comments on rejected poems. List of upcoming themes and guidelines available for SASE. Responds to queries and mss in up to 2 weeks. Pays at least 10 author's copies (out of a press run of 200-300). May offer subsidy arrangements. "It all depends upon my financial situation at the time. Yes, I might ask the author to subsidize the cost. It could be worth their while. I have good connections in the international small press." Order sample publications by sending a 6×9 SAE. "There is no charge for samples."

Advice "Experiment with thought, language, the printed word."

$🖉 THE MASSACHUSETTS REVIEW

South College, University of Massachusetts, Amherst MA 01003. (413)545-2689. E-mail: massrev@e xternal.umass.edu. Website: www.massreview.org. Established 1959. **Contact:** Deborah Gorlin and Ellen Watson, poetry editors.

- Work published in this review has been frequently included in volumes of *The Best American Poetry*.

Magazine Needs Appearing quarterly, *The Massachusetts Review* publishes "fiction, essays, artwork, and excellent poetry of all forms and styles." Has published poetry by Catherine Barnett, Billy Collins, and Dara Wier. *The Massachusetts Review* is digest-sized, offset-printed on bond paper, perfect-bound, with color card cover. Receives about 2,500 poems/year, accepts about 25. Press run is 1,600 (1,100-1,200 subscribers, 1,000 libraries, the rest for shelf sales). Subscription: $25/ year (US), $33 outside US, $35 for libraries. Sample: $9 (US), $12 outside US.

How to Submit No simultaneous submissions or previously published poems. Reads submissions October 1 through June 30 only. Guidelines available for SASE or on website. Responds in 2 months. Pays minimum of $10, or 35¢/line, plus 2 contributor's copies.

$🖉 ◎ MATURE YEARS (Specialized: senior citizen/aging; Christian)

P.O. Box 801, 201 Eighth Ave. S., Nashville TN 37202. (615)749-6292. Fax: (615)749-6512. E-mail: matureyears@umpublishing.org. Established 1954. **Contact:** Marvin W. Cropsey, editor.

Magazine Needs *Mature Years* is a quarterly. "The magazine's purpose is to help persons understand and use the resources of Christian faith in dealing with specific opportunities and problems related to aging. Poems may or may not be overtly religious. Poems should not poke fun at older adults, but may take a humorous look at them. Avoid sentimentality and saccharine. If using rhymes and meter, make sure they are accurate." *Mature Years* is 112 pages, magazine-sized, perfect-bound, with full-color glossy paper cover. Press run is 55,000. Sample: $5.25.

How to Submit Lines/poem: 16 lines of up to 50 characters maximum. Accepts fax submissions; prefers e-mail submissions. Submit seasonal and nature poems for spring during December through February; for summer, March through May; for fall, June through August; and for winter, September through November. Time between acceptance and publication is up to one year. Guidelines available for SASE or by e-mail. Responds in 2 months. Pays $1/line upon acceptance.

$🖉 ◎ MEADOWBROOK PRESS (Specialized: anthologies; children; humor)

5451 Smetana Dr., Minnetonka MN 55343. Website: www.meadowbrookpress.com. Established 1975. **Contact:** Poetry Editor.

Book/Chapbook Needs Meadowbrook Press "is currently seeking poems to be posted on our website and to be considered for future funny poetry book anthologies for children." Wants humorous poems aimed at children ages 6-12. "Poems should be fun, punchy, and refreshing. We're looking for new, hilarious, contemporary voices in children's poetry that kids can relate to." Accepts poetry written by children and teens (grades 1-12) "only for website contests—not for publication in books." Has published poetry by Shel Silverstein, Jack Prelutsky, Jeff Moss, Kenn Nesbitt, and Bruce Lansky. Anthologies include *Kids Pick the Funniest Poems*, *A Bad Case of the Giggles*, and *Miles of Smiles*.

How to Submit "Please take time to read our guidelines, and send your best work." Submit up to

10 poems; one poem to a page with name and address on each. Lines/poem: 25 maximum. Include SASE with submission. Accepts simultaneous submissions. Time between acceptance and publication is 1-2 years. Poems are tested in front of grade school students before being published. Guidelines available for SASE or on website. Pays $50-100/poem plus one contributor's copy.

◨ MEDICINAL PURPOSES LITERARY REVIEW; MARILYN K. PRESCOTT MEMORIAL POETRY CONTEST; POET TO POET, INC.

75-05 210th St., #6N, Bayside NY 11364. (718)776-8853. E-mail: dunnmiracle@juno.com. Established 1994. **Contact:** Leigh Harrison, associate editor/poetry editor. Executive Editor: Robert Dunn.
Magazine Needs *Medicinal Purposes* appears twice/year and wants "virtually any sort of quality poetry. Please, no pornography, gratuitous violence, or hate mongering." Accepts poetry written by children for the Young Writers' column. Has published poetry by X.J. Kennedy, Rhina P. Espaillat, Ellen Peckham, and Pete Dolack. *Medicinal Purposes* is 32 pages, magazine-sized, professionally printed, perfect-bound, with card stock cover with b&w illustration. Receives 1,200 poems/year, accepts about 10%. "Some submissions are beaten with sticks." Press run is 1,000 (270 subscribers, 6 libraries, 30% shelf sales). Single copy: $7; subscription: $16/year. Sample: $6. Make checks payable to Poet to Poet.
How to Submit Submit 3 poems at a time. Lines/poem: 60 maximum. No previously published poems or simultaneous submissions. Accepts e-mail submissions (pasted into body of message; no attachments). Cover letter is preferred. Include SASE. Time between acceptance and publication is up to 16 months. Often comments on rejected poems. Guidelines available for SASE or by e-mail. Responds in 3 months. Sends prepublication galleys to US contributors. Pays 2 contributor's copies. Acquires first rights.
Contest/Award Offerings Sponsors an annual poetry contest, 1st Prize: $50. Submit 3 poems of 6-16 lines each. **Entry fee:** $5. **Deadline:** June 15. Winners will be published in the year's end issue. Also administers the Marilyn K. Prescott Memorial Poetry Contest. Details available for SASE.
Advice "Over the years, so many people seem to have been attending 'originality through imitation' seminars (go figure), that we were thinking or starting a journal called 'Stop Me If You've Heard This.' We want poets who at least try to make us say, 'Gee, we wish we had said that!' "

◨ MELLEN POETRY PRESS

P.O. Box 450, Lewiston NY 14092-0450. (716)754-2266. Fax: (716)754-4056. Website: www.mellen press.com. Established 1973. **Contact:** Patricia Schultz, poetry editor.
Book/Chapbook Needs "Mellen Poetry Press is a division of The Edwin Mellen Press, a scholarly press. We do not have access to large chain bookstores for distribution, but depend on direct sales and independent bookstores." Pays 5 author's copies, royalties "after 500 copies are sold for 5 years. We require no author subsidies. However, we encourage our authors to seek grants from Councils for the Arts and other foundations because these add to the reputation of the volume." Wants "original integrated work—living unity of poems, preferably unpublished, encompassable in one reading." Has published poetry by Andrew Oerke and James Sutton. Books are up to 128 pages, digest-sized, with hardcover binding; no graphics. Price: $39.95.
How to Submit Submit 70-120 sample poems with cover letter including bio and publication credits. "We do not print until we receive at least 50 prepaid orders. Successful marketing of poetry books depends on the author's active involvement. We send out free review copies to journals or newspapers when requested. An author may, but is not required to, purchase books that count toward the needed pre-publication sales."
Advice "We seek to publish volumes unified in mood, tone, theme."

$◙ THE MENNONITE (Specialized: Christian)

P.O. Box 347, Newton KS 67114-0347. (316)283-5100. Fax: (316)283-0454. E-mail: gordonh@theme nnonite.org. Website: www.themennonite.org. Established 1885. **Contact:** Gordon Houser, associate editor.

Magazine Needs *The Mennonite* is published twice/month and wants "Christian poetry—usually free verse, not too long, with multiple layers of meaning. No sing-song rhymes or poems that merely describe or try to teach a lesson." Has published poetry by Jean Janzen and Julia Kasdorf. *The Mennonite* is 32 pages, magazine-sized, with full color cover, includes ads. Receives about 200 poems/year, accepts about 5%. Press run is 14,000 (13,500 subscribers). Single copy: $2; subscription: $38.75. Sample: $1.

How to Submit Submit up to 4 poems at a time. Accepts previously published poems and simultaneous submissions. Prefers e-mail submissions. Cover letter is preferred. Time between acceptance and publication is up to 6 months. Seldom comments on rejected poems. Occasionally publishes theme issues. List of upcoming themes and guidelines available for SASE. Responds in 2 weeks. Pays $50-75 plus one contributor's copy. Acquires first or one-time rights.

$⊘ MERIDIAN; MERIDIAN EDITORS' PRIZE COMPETITION

University of Virginia, P.O. Box 400145, Charlottesville VA 22904-4145. (434)982-5798. E-mail: meridian@virginia.edu. Website: www.readmeridian.com. Established 1998. **Contact:** Poetry Editor.

Magazine Needs *Meridian* appears biannually, publishing poetry, fiction, interviews, and reviews. Has published poetry by David Kirby, Charles Wright, and Joelle Biele. *Meridian* is 190 pages, digest-sized, offset-printed, perfect-bound, with color cover. Receives about 2,500 poems/year, accepts about 30 (less than 1%). Press run is 1,000 (750 subscribers, 15 libraries, 200 shelf sales); 150 are distributed free to writing programs. Single copy: $7; subscription: $10/year. Make checks payable to *Meridian*.

How to Submit Submit 1-5 poems at a time. Accepts simultaneous submissions; no previously published poems. No fax, e-mail, or disk submissions. Cover letter is preferred. Reads submissions September through May primarily. Time between acceptance and publication is 1-2 months. Seldom comments on rejected poems. Guidelines available on website. Responds in up to 2 months. Always sends prepublication galleys and author contracts. Pays $15/page ($250 maximum, as long as funding is available) and 2 contributor's copies (additional copies available at discount). Reviews books of poetry.

Contest/Award Offerings Annual Editors' Prize offered each December: $1,000 award. All entries must arrive via online system on website. **Entry fee:** $15.

⊘ MERIDIAN ANTHOLOGY OF CONTEMPORARY POETRY

P.O. Box 970309, Boca Raton FL 33497. E-mail: LetarP@aol.com. Website: www.MeridianAnthology.com. Established 2002. **Contact:** Phyliss L. Geller, editor/publisher. Literary Editor: Marilyn Krepf.

Magazine Needs *Meridian Anthology of Contemporary Poetry* appears annually in April and wants "poetry that is contemporary, insightful, and illuminating; that touches the nerves. It should have color, content, and be deciphering of existence." Does not want vulgarity, clichés. Has published poetry by June Owens, John Grey, Richard St. John, Gerald Zipper, and Brenda Serotte. "Volume 3 included the work of Pulitzer Prize winner Philip Levine." *Meridian Anthology* is 96-120 pages, digest-sized, offset-printed, perfect-bound, with soft cover. Press run is 500-1,000. Single copy: $14 for Volume 3, $13 for volume 2, $9 for Volume 1. Make checks payable to *Meridian Anthology*.

How to Submit Submit 1-5 poems at a time. Lines/poem: 78 maximum. Accepts simultaneous submissions and previously published poems. No fax, e-mail, or disk submissions. Cover letter is preferred. Must include SASE. Reads submissions from April to December. Time between acceptance and publication is up to one year. Seldom comments on rejected poems. Guidelines available for SASE or on website. Responds in "3 weeks to 3 months, depending on backlog." Pays one contributor's copy. Acquires one-time rights.

Advice "A poem must have a reason for existence, some universal tendril."

$ ☑ MICHIGAN QUARTERLY REVIEW; LAURENCE GOLDSTEIN POETRY AWARD

University of Michigan, 3574 Rackham Bldg., 915 E. Washington St., Ann Arbor MI 48109. (734)764-9265. E-mail: mqr@umich.edu. Website: www.umich.edu/~mqr. Established 1962. **Contact:** Laurence Goldstein, editor-in-chief.

● Poetry published in *Michigan Quarterly Review* is frequently included in volumes of *The Best American Poetry* and was selected for the 2002 *Pushcart Prize* anthology.

Magazine Needs *Michigan Quarterly Review* is "an interdisciplinary, general interest academic journal that publishes mainly essays and reviews on subjects of cultural and literary interest." Uses all kinds of poetry except light verse. No specifications as to form, length, style, subject matter, or purpose. Has published poetry by Susan Hahn, Carl Phillips, Mary Oliver, and Yusef Komunyakaa. *Michigan Quarterly Review* is 160 pages, digest-sized, flat-spined, professionally printed, with glossy card cover. Receives about 1,400 submissions/year, accepts about 30. Press run is 2,000 (1,200 subscribers, half are libraries). Single copy: $7; subscription: $25. Sample: $4.

How to Submit Prefers typed mss. No previously published poems or simultaneous submissions. No fax or e-mail submissions. Cover letter is preferred; "it puts a human face on the manuscript. A few sentences of biography is all I want, nothing lengthy or defensive." Publishes theme issues. Theme for autumn 2005 is "The Documentary Imagination." Upcoming themes also available in magazine or on website. Guidelines available for SASE or on website. Responds in 6 weeks. Always sends prepublication galleys. Pays $8-12/page. Acquires first rights only. Reviews books of poetry. "All reviews are commissioned."

Contest/Award Offerings The Laurence Goldstein Poetry Award, an annual cash prize of $1,000 given to the author of the best poem to appear in *Michigan Quarterly* during the calendar year. "Established in 2002, the prize is sponsored by the Office of the President of the University of Michigan."

Advice "There is no substitute for omnivorous reading and careful study of poets past and present, as well as reading in new and old areas of knowledge. Attention to technique, especially to rhythm and patterns of imagery, is vital."

$ ☐ ◎ THE MID-AMERICA PRESS, INC.; THE MID-AMERICA POETRY REVIEW (Specialized: regional)

P.O. Box 575, Warrensburg MO 64093-0575. Press established 1976. **Contact:** Robert C. Jones, editor.

Magazine Needs *The Mid-America Poetry Review* appears 3 times/year and publishes "well-crafted poetry primarily from—but not limited to—poets living in Missouri, Illinois, Arkansas, Oklahoma, Kansas, Nebraska, and Iowa. We are open to all styles and forms; what we look for is poetry by writers who know both what they are doing and why." Has published poetry by Charles Guenther, Rhina P. Espaillat, Louis D. Brodsky, David Baker, Kate Northrop, and Gloria Vando. *The Mid-America Poetry Review* is 60-75 pages, digest-sized, offset-printed, perfect-bound, with matte paper cover. Receives about 1,000-2,000 poems/year, accepts about 15%. Press run is 750. Single copy: $6; subscription: $15/year. Make checks payable to The Mid-America Press, Inc.

How to Submit Submit 1-3 poems at a time. Lines/poem: 36 maximum. No previously published poems or simultaneous submissions. Cover letter is useful. "Type submissions, single- or double-spaced, on 8½×11 white paper; include name, address, and telephone number in top left or right corner. Enclose SASE for notification/guidelines. Do not send the only copy of your manuscript—unused submissions are recycled. One-page cover letter (if included) should list items to be considered; contain brief paragraphs of information about author and previous publications." Time between acceptance and publication may be up to one year. Sometimes comments on submissions. Guidelines available for SASE. Responds within 2 months. Sends prepublication galleys. Pays $5/poem on acceptance, 2 contributor's copies on publication, and one-year subscription. Acquires first North American serial rights. Staff occasionally reviews books of poetry. Send materials for review consideration.

Book/Chapbook Needs & How to Submit The Mid-America Press, Inc. publishes 1-5 book-length poetry collections/year. "**At present, the Press is not reading unsolicited book-length poetry manuscripts.** The Mid-America Press Writing Award Competition has been discontinued until further notice." Mid-America Press, Inc. award-winning publications include *From Ink and Sandalwood* (1998) by Cecile M. Franking (winner of the 1999 Thorpe Menn Award for Writing Excellence); *Red Silk* (1999) by Maryfrances Wagner (winner of the 2000 Thorpe Menn Award for Writing Excellence); *Living Off the Land, a Gathering of Writing from The Warrensburg Writers Circle* (1999) edited by Robert C. Jones (First Place in The 2000 Walter Williams Major Work Award, from the Missouri Writers' Guild). Other publications include *Uncurling* (2000) by Jeanie Wilson, *Light and Chance* (2001) by Ardyth Bradley, *Dreaming the Bronze Girl* (2002) by Serina Allison Hearn, and *The Graveyard Picnic* (2002) by William Ford. Order sample books by sending $13.95/book.

Advice "Read several copies of the magazine to see the range of subject matter and forms."

MIDMARCH ARTS PRESS

300 Riverside Dr., New York NY 10025.

Book Needs & How to Submit Midmarch Arts Press publishes 4-6 paperbacks/year (only one poetry paperback/year). **Query prior to submitting anything.** Has recently published *Mirror Mirror*, edited by Isabel Duke; *Split Verse*, edited by Meg Campbell and William Buke; *Solo Crossing* by Meg Campbell; *Sight Lines* by Charlotte Mandel; and *Whirling Round the Sun* by Suzanne Noguerre.

☑ THE MIDWEST QUARTERLY

Pittsburg State University, Pittsburg KS 66762. (620)235-4689. Fax: (620)235-4686. E-mail: smeats @pittstate.edu. Website: www.pittstate.edu/engl/midwest.html. Established 1959. **Contact:** Stephen Meats, poetry editor.

Magazine Needs *The Midwest Quarterly* "publishes articles on any subject of contemporary interest, particularly literary criticism, political science, philosophy, education, biography, and sociology. Each issue contains a section of poetry usually 12 poems in length. I am interested in well-crafted, though not necessarily traditional, poems that explore the inter-relationship of the human and natural worlds in bold, surrealistic images of a writer's imaginative, mystical experience." Has published poetry by Fleda Brown, Jim Daniels, Naomi Shihab Nye, Greg Kuzma, Jeanne Murray Walker, and Peter Cooley. *The Midwest Quarterly* is 130 pages, digest-sized, professionally printed, flat-spined, with matte cover. Press run is 650 (600 subscribers, 500 libraries). Receives about 4,000 poems/year, accepts about 48. Subscription: $15. Sample: $5.

How to Submit Submit no more than 5 poems at a time. Lines/poem: 60 maximum ("occasionally longer if exceptional"). Accepts simultaneous submissions; no previously published poems. No fax or e-mail submissions. Manuscripts should be typed with poet's name on each page. Editor comments on rejected poems "if the poet or poems seem particularly promising." Occasionally publishes theme issues. Guidelines and upcoming themes available for SASE, by fax, or by e-mail. Responds in 2 months, usually sooner. "Submissions without SASE cannot be acknowledged." Pays 2 contributor's copies. Acquires first serial rights. Reviews books of poetry by *Midwest Quarterly*-published poets only.

Advice "Keep writing; read as much contemporary poetry as you can lay your hands on; don't let the discouragement of rejection keep you from sending your work out to editors."

◎ ☑ MIDWEST VILLAGES & VOICES (Specialized: regional/Midwestern)

P.O. Box 40214, St. Paul MN 55104. (612)822-6878. Established 1979.

Book/Chapbook Needs & How to Submit Midwest Villages & Voices is a cultural organization and small press publisher of Midwestern poetry and prose. "We encourage and support Midwestern writers and artists. However, at this time submissions are accepted by invitation only. Unsolicited submissions are not accepted."

⊚ MIDWIFERY TODAY (Specialized: childbirth)

P.O. Box 2672, Eugene OR 97402-0223. (541)344-7438. Fax: (541)344-1422. E-mail: editorial@mid wiferytoday.com. Website: www.midwiferytoday.com. Established 1986. **Contact:** Jan Tritten, editor-in-chief. Editor: Jessica Cagle.

Magazine Needs *Midwifery Today* is a quarterly that "provides a voice for midwives and childbirth educators. We are a midwifery magazine. Subject must be birth or birth profession related." Does not want poetry that is "off subject or puts down the subject." *Midwifery Today* is 75 pages, magazine-sized, offset-printed, saddle-stapled, with glossy card cover with b&w photos and b&w artwork photos, includes ads. Press run is 5,000 (3,000 subscribers, 1,000 shelf sales). Subscription: $50. Sample: $10.

How to Submit No previously published poems. Accepts e-mail submissions (pasted into body of message/as attachment). Cover letter is required. Time between acceptance and publication is 1-2 years. Seldom comments on rejected poems. Publishes theme issues. Upcoming themes and deadlines available on website. Guidelines available for SASE or on website. Responds in 6 months. Pays 2 contributor's copies. Acquires first rights.

Advice "With our publication, *please* stay on the subject."

⊘ MILKWEED EDITIONS

1011 Washington Ave. S., Suite 300, Minneapolis MN 55415-1246. (612)332-3192. Fax: (612)215-2550. E-mail: editor@milkweed.org. Website: www.milkweed.org. Established 1984. **Contact:** Poetry Reader.

Book/Chapbook Needs Milkweed Editions is "looking for poetry manuscripts of high quality that embody humane values and contribute to cultural understanding." Not limited in subject matter. Open to writers with previously published books of poetry or a minimum of 6 poems published in nationally distributed commercial or literary journals. Accepts translations and bilingual mss. Has published *Atlas* by Katrina Vandenberg, *Good Heart* by Deborah Keenan, *Turning Over the Earth* by Ralph Black, and *Song of the World Becoming* by Pattiann Rogers.

How to Submit Submit 60 pages or more, typed on good quality white paper. Do not send originals. No submissions by fax or e-mail. Include SASE for reply. Unsolicited mss read in January and June *only*. "Milkweed can no longer return manuscripts in stamped book mailers. In the event that manuscripts are not accepted for publication, we prefer to recycle them. If you need your work returned, *please enclose a check for $5* rather than a stamped mailer." Guidelines available for SASE. Responds in up to 6 months. Catalog available on request, with $1.50 in postage.

$⊘ MILLER'S POND; LOELLA CADY LAMPHIER PRIZE FOR POETRY; H&H PRESS

RR 2, Box 239, Middlebury Center PA 16935. (570)376-3361. Fax: (570)376-2674. E-mail: cjhoughtal ing@handhpress.com. Website: http://millerspondpoetry.com. Established 1987. **Contact:** C.J. Houghtaling, publisher. Editor: David Cazden. Web Editor: Julie Damerell.

Magazine Needs Published in January, *miller's pond* is an annual magazine featuring contemporary poetry, interviews, reviews, and markets. "We want contemporary poetry that is fresh, accessible, energetic, vivid, and flows with language and rhythm. No religious, horror, pornographic, vulgar, rhymed, preachy, lofty, trite, or overly sentimental work." Has published poetry by Vivian Shipley, Barbara Crooker, Philip Memmer, and Shoshauna Shy. *miller's pond* is 48 pages, digest-sized, offset-printed, saddle-stapled, with cardstock cover. Receives about 200 poems/year, accepts 25-30 poems/issue. Press run is 200. Single copy: $10 plus $3.50 p&h. Sample (back issue) including guidelines: $8. Make checks payable to H&H Press.

How to Submit Submit 3-5 poems at a time. Lines/poem: 40 maximum. Accepts previously published poems and simultaneous submissions. Accepts submissions by postal mail and through online submission form. Cover letter is preferred. "No returns without SASE." Reads submissions February 1 through October 1 only. Submissions received outside of the reading period may be held for the next reading period. Seldom comments on rejected poems. Guidelines available in magazine, for SASE, or on website. Responds in up to 11 months; "although we try to respond sooner, we are not always able to." Sometimes sends prepublication galleys. Pays $2/poem and one contributor's copy for work that appears in hard-copy version. Acquires one-time rights. Pays $5 for poetry book reviews, $10 for interviews with poets. See submission guidelines on website.

Book/Chapbook Needs & How to Submit "H&H Press is a micro-publisher of poetry chapbooks and how-to-write books, with plans to expand into nonfiction and specialty books." Publishes one chapbook/year. Books are usually 24-36 pages, magazine-sized, offset-printed, saddle-stapled, with cardstock covers. Does NOT accept art. **Books published by invitation only; do not query.** My requirements are simple—the poem/poetry must speak to me on more than one level and stay with me for more than just those few brief moments I'm reading it." Responds in 4 months. Pays royalties of 7% minimum, 12% maximum, and 25 author's copies (out of a press run of 200). Books are available for sale via website, phone, or fax.

Contest/Award Offerings H&H Press sponsors the Loella Cady Lamphier Prize for Poetry. Offers 1st Prize: $100; 2nd Prize: $50; 3rd Prize: $25. Guidelines available on website. Accepts submissions through an online submission form only. Contact Julie Damerell, web editor.

Advice "Believe in yourself. Perseverance is a writer's best 'tool.' Study the contemporary masters: Vivian Shipley, Billy Collins, Maxine Kumin, Colette Inez, Hayden Carruth. Please check our website before submitting."

☐ ◎ MINDPRINTS, A LITERARY JOURNAL (Specialized: writers & artists with disabilities)

Learning Assistance Program, Allan Hancock College, 800 South College Dr., Santa Maria CA 93454-6399. (805)922-6966, ext. 3274. Fax: (805)922-3556. E-mail: pafahey@hancockcollege.edu. Website: www.imindprints.com. Established 2000. **Contact:** Paul Fahey, editor.

● *Mindprints* was named one of the Top 30 Short Story Markets by *Writer's Digest* (June 2002 and 2003).

Magazine Needs "*Mindprints, A Literary Journal* is a national annual publication of flash fiction, flash memoir, poetry, and black-and-white artwork. The journal is created as a forum for writers and artists with disabilities, but we also invite those who work in the field or have an interest in the population to submit their work. *Mindprints* takes great pride in showcasing new artists and giving voice to new writers. We also welcome and encourage established writers and artists." Wants all kinds of poetry. "We love anything short: haiku, haibun, cinquain; prose and rhyming poetry with unusual imagery." Has published poetry by Barbara Crooker, LaVonne Schoneman, Margaret Davidson, Marganit Alverez, Denize Lavoie Cain, and Joan C. Fingon. *Mindprints* is digest-sized, perfect-bound, with gloss laminated cover. Receives about 400 submissions/year, publishes about 29 poems/issue. Press run is 600. "We sell copies at book fairs and through our college bookstore." Single copy: $6 plus $2 first-class postage. Make checks payable to Allan Hancock College.

How to Submit Submit up to 3 poems per reading period. Lines/poem: 34 maximum. Accepts previously published poems and simultaneous submissions. Accepts e-mail submissions **only if poet resides outside the US**; accepts disk submissions only once the mss are accepted; no fax submissions. "Please send cover letter and SASE. In cover letter, tell us something about yourself, previous publications, if applicable, and tell us why you are submitting to *Mindprints*." Accepts submissions year round and begins reading collected submissions April 1; contributors are notified in late May. Time between acceptance and publication is 3-4 months. "We have a poetry editor who is an established poet and instructor at the college who reads the poetry and ranks it. (All identifying information has been removed.)" Seldom comments on rejected poems. Guidelines available in magazine, for SASE, or on website. Pays one contributor's copy. Acquires one-time rights.

Advice "We are one of the few national community college journals devoted to celebrating the work of artists and writers with disabilities. We look for a strong voice, unusual point of view, and rich imagery and description."

◔ ◎ THE MINNESOTA REVIEW: A JOURNAL OF COMMITTED WRITING (Specialized: political, social issues)

English Dept., Carnegie Mellon University, 5000 Forbes Ave., Pittsburgh PA 15213-3890. Fax: (412)268-7989. E-mail: editors@theminnesotareview.org. Established 1960. **Contact:** Poetry Editor. Editor: Jeffrey Williams.

Magazine Needs *The Minnesota Review* is a biannual literary magazine wanting "poetry which explores some aspect of social or political issues and/or the nature of relationships. No nature poems, and no lyric poetry without the above focus." Has published poetry by Hollander and Fuentes Lemus. *The Minnesota Review* is about 200 pages, digest-sized, flat-spined, with b&w glossy card cover. Press run is 1,500 (800 subscribers). Subscription: $30/2 years to individuals; $45/year to institutions. Sample: $15.

How to Submit Address submissions to "Poetry Editor" (not to a specific editor). No fax or e-mail submissions. Cover letter including "brief intro with address" is preferred. SASE with sufficient postage required for return of mss. Publishes theme issues. Upcoming themes available for SASE. Responds in up to 4 months. Pays 2 contributor's copies. Acquires all rights. Returns rights upon request.

◻ ◎ MINORITY LITERARY EXPO (Specialized: membership; minorities)

216 Avenue T. Pratt City, Birmingham AL 35214. (205)798-9083. E-mail: kervinfondren@yahoo.com. Established 1990. **Contact:** Kervin Fondren, editor.

Magazine Needs & How to Submit *Minority Literary Expo* is an annual professional literary publication featuring minority poets, writers, and professionals. "Organization membership open to all minority poets nationally. I want poems from minority poets that are holistic and wholesome, less than 24 lines each, any style, any form, any subject matter; no vulgar or hate poetry accepted. Poetry that expresses holistic views and philosophies is very acceptable. Literary value is emphasized. Selected poets receive financial awards, certificates, honorable mentions, critiques, and special poetic honors." Accepts poetry concerning ethnic minorities, homosexuals/bisexuals, students, women/feminism. No fee is charged for inclusion. Single copy: $25. Submit 1-2 poems at a time. Accepts disk submissions; no e-mail submissions. Guidelines and upcoming themes available for SASE or by e-mail. Pays one contributor's copy.

Contest/Award Offerings Sponsors an annual poetry contributor's contest. Offers $150 award. **Deadline:** July annually.

Advice "We're interested in poetry, articles, and literary submissions that can be published in a professional journal."

◔ MISSISSIPPI REVIEW

The University of Southern Mississippi, 118 College Dr., #5144, Hattiesburg MS 39406-0001. (601)266-4321. Fax: (601)266-5757. E-mail: fbx@comcast.net. Website: www.mississippireview.com. **Contact:** Angela Ball, poetry editor. Editor: Frederick Barthelme. Managing Editor: Rie Fortenberry.

Magazine Needs & How to Submit *Mississippi Review* is a publication for those interested in contemporary literature. Publishes 2 issues annually; one, edited by a guest editor, uses only solicited material, while the other publishes contest finalists. "The guest editors for upcoming issues will always be listed on the website. If you can find no editor and issue listed there, then the magazine is not reading new work for the moment." Guidelines available by phone or on website.

Contest/Award Offerings The Mississippi Review Prize, an annual contest open to all US writers except current or former students and employees of USM. Prize: publication and $1,000. Finalists published in prize issue. Each entrant receives a copy of prize issue. Submit up to 3 poems/entry (10 pages maximum). "No limit on number of entries." Does not accept previously published material. "Entrants should put 'MR Prize,' name, address, phone number, e-mail address, and title on page one of entry." Reads submissions April 1 to November 1. **Entry fee:** $15/entry.

Publishers of Poetry

Postmark Deadline: November 1. No mss returned. Winners announced in late January and published in April.

★ ☑ ◎ THE MOCCASIN (Specialized: membership); THE LEAGUE OF MINNESOTA POETS

427 N. Gorman St., Blue Earth MN 56013. (507)526-5321. Established 1937. **Contact:** Meredith R. Cook, editor.

Magazine Needs *The Moccasin*, published annually in October, is the literary magazine of The League of Minnesota Poets. **Membership is required to submit work.** Wants "all forms of poetry. Prefer strong short poems." Does not want "profanity or obscenity." Accepts poetry written by children who are student members of The League of Minnesota Poets (list grade level on poem submitted). Has published poetry by Diane Glancy, Laurel Winter, Susan Stevens Chambers, Doris Stengel, Jeanette Hinds, and Charmaine Donovan. *The Moccasin* is 40 pages, digest-sized, offset-printed, stapled, with 80-lb. linen finish text cover with drawing and poem. Receives about 190 poems/year, accepts about 170. Press run is 250 (144 subscribers, 10 libraries, 96 shelf sales). Single copy: $5.25; subscription: free with LOMP membership. Sample: $2.25 for issues older than 1998. Make checks payable to LOMP and send to James Elberling, LOMP Treasurer, 1766 Karis Way, Eagan MN 55122.

How to Submit Submit 6 or more poems at a time. Lines/poem: 24 maximum (unless poem has won a prize from the National Federation of State Poetry Societies in their annual competition). Accepts previously published poems; no simultaneous submissions. No disk submissions. Cover letter is preferred. "No poems will be returned and no questions answered without a SASE." Reads submissions year round ("deadline for each year's issue is mid-July"). Sometimes comments on rejected poems. **Must be a member of The League of Minnesota Poets to submit. (See membership information below.)** Guidelines available in magazine. No payment; poet receives contributor's copy as part of LOMP membership subscription. Acquires one-time rights.

Also Offers To become a member of The League of Minnesota Poets, send $20 ($10 if high school student or younger) to James Elberling, LOMP Treasurer, 1766 Karis Way, Eagen MN 55122. Make checks payable to LOMP. **You do not have to live in Minnesota to become a member of LOMP.** "Membership in LOMP automatically makes you a member of the National Federation of State Poetry Societies, which makes you eligible to enter their contests at a cheaper (members') rate."

$☑ ◎ MODERN HAIKU (Specialized: translations; haiku/senryu/haibun)

P.O. Box 68, Lincoln IL 62656. Website: www.modernhaiku.org. Established 1969. **Contact:** Lee Gurga, editor. Associate Editor: Charles Trumbull.

Magazine Needs *Modern Haiku* appears 3 times/year (in February, June, and October), and "is the foremost international journal of English-language haiku and criticism. We are devoted to publishing only the very best haiku being written; also publish articles on haiku and have the most complete review section of haiku books." Wants "contemporary haiku in English (including translations into English) that incorporate the traditional aesthetics of the haiku genre, but which may be innovative as to subject matter, mode of approach or angle of perception, and form of expression. Haiku, senryu, and haibun only. No tanka or other forms." Has published haiku by Billy Collins, Lawrence Ferlinghetti, Sharon Olds, Paul Muldoon, and Gary Snyder. *Modern Haiku* is 90 pages (average), digest-sized, printed on heavy quality stock, with full-color cover illustrations. Receives about 12,000-14,000 submissions/year, accepts about 500. Press run is 800. Subscription: $23. Sample: $8.

How to Submit Submit on "8½×11 sheets, any number of haiku per sheet; put name and address on each sheet." Include SASE. No previously published haiku or simultaneous submissions. Guidelines available for SASE. Responds in 2 weeks. Pays $1/haiku (but no contributor's copy). Acquires first North American serial rights. Staff reviews books of haiku in 350-1,000 words, single-book format. Send materials for review consideration with complete ordering information.

Advice "Study what haiku really are. We do not want sentimentality, pretty-pretty, or pseudo-

Japanese themes. Juxtaposition of seemingly disparate entities that nonetheless create harmony is very desirable.''

◻ MONKEY'S FIST; PATHFINDER PRESS

P.O. Box 316, Madison ME 04950-0316. Established 2001. **Contact:** Robin Merrill and Heidi Parker, co-editors.

Magazine Needs *Monkey's Fist* appears sporadically. Wants ''edgy, sassy, accessible poetry that lives in the real world. Have something to say and say it well.'' NOTE: ''Our journal has nothing to do with monkeys, and we have two female editors. Keep these things in mind.'' Has published poetry by Nancy A. Henry, Louis McKee, Jennifer Stanley, and Karl Koweski. *Monkey's Fist* is 60 pages, digest-sized, photocopied, saddle-stapled, with cardstock cover with b&w art. Receives hundreds of poems/year, accepts about 5%. Press run is 100 (50 subscribers). Single copy: $3; subscription: $6. Make checks payable to Robin Merrill.

How to Submit Submit 3 poems at a time. Accepts previously published poems and simultaneous submissions. No disk submissions. Cover letter is ''absolutely mandatory. Have some manners. In your letter, name your favorite small press publication. Poems should be submitted one/page on plain white $8^{1}/_{2} \times 11$ paper, with name and address on each page. Send in white #10 envelope and include SASE. We like creases and dislike big brown envelopes and wasted stamps.'' Reads submissions January 1 through February 28 **only**. Time between acceptance and publication is up to one year. ''Poems are read by 2 editors who duke it out.'' Often comments on rejected poems. Occasionally publishes theme issues. List of upcoming themes and guidelines available in magazine. ''Do not send for guidelines. Just be courteous and professional and follow the guidelines here.'' Responds in up to 2 months. Sometimes sends prepublication galleys. Pays one contributor's copy. Acquires one-time rights. Reviews chapbooks of poetry. Send materials for review consideration to Robin Merrill.

◙ MOTHER EARTH INTERNATIONAL JOURNAL; NATIONAL POETRY ASSOCIATION; POETRY FILM FESTIVAL

% National Poetry Association, 934 Brannan St., 2nd Floor, San Francisco CA 94103. (415)552-9261. Website: www.nationalpoetry.org/npa/mother.html. *Mother Earth International Journal* established 1991, National Poetry Association established 1976. **Contact:** Herman Berlandt, editor/publisher. Sub-Editor: Rob Tricaro.

Magazine Needs ''*Mother Earth International Journal* is the only on-going anthology of contemporary poetry in English translation from all regions of the world. *Mother Earth International Journal* provides a forum for poets to comment in poetic form on political, economic, and ecological issues.'' Wants ''bold and compassionate poetry that has universal relevance with an emphasis on the world's current political and ecological crisis. No self-indulgent or prosaic stuff that lacks imagination.'' Accepts poetry written by children and teens (ages 8-17). Has published poetry by Lawrence Ferlinghetti, Adrienne Rich, Corolyn Kizer, Mary Oliver, Alessio Zanelli, and Abba Korner. *Mother Earth International Journal* is 53 pages, $5^{1}/_{2} \times 8^{1}/_{2}$, offset-printed. Receives about 4,000 poems/year, accepts 15%. Press run is 2,000 (1,200 subscribers, 280 libraries). Subscription: $15/year. Sample: $5. Make checks payable to Uniting the World Through Poetry. ''We encourage the purchase of a copy or a year's subscription.''

How to Submit Submit 4 poems at a time. Accepts previously published poems and simultaneous submissions. No fax or e-mail submissions. Cover letter is preferred. Time between acceptance and publication is 4 months. Occasionally publishes theme issues (humanistic: love, peace, environmental). Guidelines available for SASE. Responds in 3 months. Sometimes sends prepublication galleys. Pays 2 contributor's copies. All rights revert to the author.

Contest/Award Offerings Sponsors a $50 prize for the best of ''Your Two Best Lines,'' a benefit collage poem which will list all entries as a collective poem. As an **entry fee**, ''a $5 check should be enclosed with submission.''

Also Offers National Poetry Association, currently working to establish an International Poetry

Museum in San Francisco. For more information, visit www.internationalpoetrymuseum.org.
Advice "*Mother Earth International Journal* is an ongoing anthology of world contemporary poetry. For subscribers, we reduced the subscription from $18 to $15 per year. While all future issues will include an American section, we hope that all who send in entries will subscribe to *Mother Earth International Journal* to get a truly world perspective of universal concerns."

☑ MOUNT OLIVE COLLEGE PRESS; MOUNT OLIVE REVIEW

634 Henderson St., Mount Olive NC 28365. (919)658-2502. Established 1987 (*Mount Olive Review*), 1990 (Mount Olive College Press). **Contact:** Dr. Pepper Worthington, editor.
Magazine Needs *Mount Olive Review* features "literary criticism, poetry, short stories, essays, and book reviews." Wants "modern poetry." Receives about 2,000 poems/year, accepts 8%. Press run is 500. Single copy: $10. Make checks payable to Mount Olive College Press.
How to Submit Submit 6 poems at a time. No previously published poems or simultaneous submissions. Cover letter is preferred. Time between acceptance and publication varies. Poems are circulated to an editorial board. Seldom comments on rejected poems. Responds in 6 months. Sometimes sends prepublication galleys. Acquires first rights. Reviews books and chapbooks of poetry and other magazines. Send materials for review consideration.
Book/Chapbook Needs & How to Submit Mount Olive Press publishes 2 books/year. Books are usually digest-sized. Submit 12 sample poems. Guidelines available for SASE. Responds to queries and mss in 3 months. Obtain sample books by writing to the above address.

✖ ◎ ☑ MOVING PARTS PRESS (Specialized: bilingual/foreign language; regional)

10699 Empire Grade, Santa Cruz CA 95060-9474. (831)427-2271. E-mail: frice@movingpartspress.com. Website: www.movingpartspress.com. Established 1977. **Contact:** Felicia Rice, poetry editor.
Does not accept unsolicited mss. Published *Codex Espangliensis: from Columbus to the Border Patrol* (1998) with performance texts by Guillermo Gómez-Peña and collage imagery by Enrique Chagoya.

☐ MUDFISH; BOX TURTLE PRESS; MUDFISH POETRY PRIZE AWARD; MUDFISH INDIVIDUAL POET SERIES

184 Franklin St., New York NY 10013. (212)219-9278. E-Mail: mudfishmag@aol.com. Established 1983. **Contact:** Jill Hoffman, editor.
Magazine Needs *Mudfish*, published by Box Turtle Press, is an annual journal of poetry and art. Wants free verse with "energy, intensity, and originality of voice, mastery of style, the presence of passion." Has published poetry by Charles Simic, Jennifer Belle, Stephanie Dickinson, Ronald Wardall, Doug Dorph, and John Ashberry. Press run is 1,200. Single copy: $12 plus $3.50 shipping and handling; subscription: $24 (2 years, including shipping).
How to Submit Submit 4-6 poems at a time. No previously published poems or simultaneous submissions. Accepts submissions by postal mail only. Responds from "immediately to 3 months." Sends prepublication galleys. Pays one contributor's copy.
Contest/Award Offerings Sponsors the Mudfish Poetry Prize Award: $1,000. **Entry fee:** $15 for up to 3 poems, $3 for each additional poem. **Deadline:** varies. Guidelines available for SASE.
Also Offers Mudfish Individual Poet Series 1-4: *Dementia Pugilistica* by David Lawrence, *Black Diaries* by Jill Hoffman, *Too Too Flesh* by Doug Dorph, *Skunk Cabbage* by Harry Waitzman ($14/book plus $2.50 p&h).
Advice "Send your best poems—those with heart and craft."

☑ MUDLARK: AN ELECTRONIC JOURNAL OF POETRY & POETICS

Dept. of English, University of North Florida, Jacksonville FL 32224-2645. (904)620-2273. Fax: (904)620-3940. E-mail: mudlark@unf.edu. Website: www.unf.edu/mudlark. Established 1995. **Contact:** William Slaughter, editor.
Magazine Needs *Mudlark* appears "irregularly, but frequently. *Mudlark* has averaged, from 1995-

David Tucker

The unexplored corners of everyday life

Photo by John Munson, *Star-Ledger*

Poetry has always played a central role in David Tucker's life. "My father recited poetry around the house," he says. "He was a walking sound reel of *Best Loved Poems*: Tennyson, Arnold, passages from the Shakespeare he had to memorize in high school. I also had several good teachers whose love of poetry inspired me to love it and eventually to try to write it in a concerted, persistent way." Those early writing influences clearly inspired Tucker—today he is both an accomplished poet and a career journalist.

Tucker first became serious about writing as a profession when he took classes with acclaimed poets Donald Hall and Robert Hayden at the University of Michigan. According to Tucker, Hall's course "was like getting hit by lightning. After that, I resolved to write every day and to get published." His determined attitude paid off. Tucker has dozens of publishing credits, including poems in magazines such as *Slate*, *Carolina Quarterly*, *New York Quarterly*, *Missouri Review*, *Southern Poetry Review*, and more. His chapbook, *Days When Nothing Happens*, was published in 2003 by Slapering Hol Press, and his book-length collection, *Late for Work* (working title at press time), was chosen by Philip Levine for the 2004 Bakeless Poetry Prize and will be published by Houghton Mifflin.

Examining the unexplored corners of everyday life is a key theme in Tucker's work. "Like poetry x-rays," writes poet Lola Haskins, Tucker's poems "penetrate to where people really live." His work as assistant managing editor for New Jersey's *Star-Ledger* also deeply informs his writing. Former poet laureate Robert Pinsky's endorsement for Tucker's chapbook refers to the influence of the newsroom in his poems, noting they're written "with a reporter's respect for information and a poet's awareness of the undisclosed."

Tucker edited the *Star-Ledger*'s award-winning series on racial profiling in New Jersey, where "State Troopers were stopping motorists based on their skin color, harassing them and abusing their civil rights." More recently he has supervised stories that examined the plight of women and the mentally ill in prison, a millionaire philanthropist who sold fake "rare" violins to the New Jersey Symphony Orchestra, poor security at Newark Airport, and the secret life of New Jersey's gay ex-governor, James McGreevey.

According to Tucker, "The daily grind of putting out a newspaper is great material for poetry. The whole process is so intense sometimes, a little like trying to build a parachute before you hit the ground."

While his newspaper work provides inspiration for his poetry, Tucker is careful to point out that poetry and news writing are two entirely different disciplines. "One is about what the facts tell us, and the other is about what the facts don't tell us." Nevertheless, there are important similarities. "Good stories, like good poems, are quick and clear, with a spareness that makes the language dance," Tucker explains. "Both of them are trying to get at the truth. Both, if they succeed, immerse themselves in their subjects. Good reporters practice their own aggressive brand of what Keats called 'negative capability,' losing all ego for the sake of telling the story."

Tucker's newspaper skills also come in handy when researching markets for his work. For example, Tucker found out about the Slapering Hol chapbook competition by reading *Poet's Market*. He also looks carefully at the acknowledgments page in books by poets he admires, and takes the next step of searching for information about the publisher "to see what else they're taking and whether I stand a chance."

Studying the needs of a specific market is the only way to know if your work truly fits into the market's editorial vision. "You'll never know what they want unless you check out their publications," says Tucker, but he does advise that poets should "start with the assumption that they want clear, original work that reads as though the writer made it with great care, has read many other poets, and knows something about the craft."

To seek out even more publishing opportunities, Tucker subscribes to a variety of journals "to get a feel for 'the scene'—what the tastes of the magazines are, who is getting published." He also uses a poetry calendar to keep track of contests, and recommends poets use one of the poetry calendars available on the Internet to stay on top of deadlines. (Try www.pw.org or enter word combinations such as "poetry contest calendar" or "poetry submissions calendar" for a selection of national and regional results.)

Tucker's investigative skills have taught him the importance of knowing as much as possible about the markets to which he sends his work, something he stresses is crucial for any poet who wants to be published. "Look out for huckster contests," he advises. "Investigate before you send your book; buy a copy of last year's winner to get a sense of whether the publisher is just printing any old junk and whether the books are professionally done."

Like any poet, Tucker remembers his initial publishing success. "I was first published in *Seneca Review* in 1972," he remembers. "They paid me five dollars, and for several days my head was far too big to fit through doors." He started submitting his work during college, "sending poems in batches of three or four at a time, typed and mailed with self-addressed stamped envelopes."

These days, Tucker is much more persistent with his mailings. "I continually send to magazines, and to several contests a year. I send more poems than I used to, twenty to thirty poems in one sweep sometimes, to five or six magazines. I have more luck than I used to, mainly, I think, because I'm a better poet; but getting published creates a little momentum and seems to help get attention from other editors.

"I try to have a lot of poems in the mail to either magazines or contests at any given time. When I was younger, I was less disciplined about sending out my work. I was sporadic and even a little cavalier about sending out my poems and promoting my own work. Only after I became aggressive about it did I begin to make a few breakthroughs."

Tucker believes discipline is the key to getting published. "Keep poems circulating, whether to journals or contests. Try to make the process almost automatic; that way it gets easier and most of the angst of rejection fades away. I think it's important that the sending out process is almost as routine as the daily writing sessions. Just be relentless about it; look at submissions as an essential part of being a poet."

Tucker submitted his chapbook manuscript, *Days When Nothing Happens*, for several years before it was accepted for publication by Slapering Hol Press through their annual chapbook contest. The contest for emerging poets, which was established in 1990, awards winners a cash prize, the publication of their manuscript, and a reading at The Hudson Valley Writers' Center in New York. (See listing for Slapering Hol Press on page 331.)

So how did Tucker know his collection was ready for publication? "I liked the poems and had worked on some of them over a period of several years until I thought they were more or less complete. They seemed to belong together—to say, a little more in sequence than they did just standing alone." He adds, "A good chapbook, in my opinion (and I know the editors at Slapering Hol feel this way), should have thematically tight and interconnected poems. My poems hung together well; they made a real book."

Days When Nothing Happens

On days when nothing happens
a jet loafs overhead, an hourglass of smoke
fanning out behind it.

On days when nothing happens
a paper sack plays in the street, your overcoat sags
and forgets you.

The wind chases the leaves
and they clatter off the porch
like flocks of hands saying "Hurry!"

On days when nothing happens
the mantel clock calls
the small noises back to the house,

a daughter's red sneaker
sits all afternoon on the window sill,
trying to be quiet.

(from *Days When Nothing Happens* [Slapering Hol Press, 2004])

Tucker also knew his manuscript was ready because most of the poems in it had been previously published in literary journals and magazines. "Previous publication certainly helps," he says. "It means other editors liked the poems, but it also means the writer has put in some time and brought the poems through the process of writing, revising, and publishing. They've been through the creative mill."

In order to have a cohesive manuscript, Tucker also included some of his unpublished poems. "I had a sense that some of them worked well together; but when it came time to assemble the manuscript, some poems I had never considered—and a few that had not been published—seemed right for the book."

Tucker believes his editors at Slapering Hol added tremendously to the strength of his final product. "They were all so extremely helpful, cutting some poems, making good edits, and working with the order of the manuscript," he says.

Having someone with a keen editorial eye look at your work is important if you think it's ready to send out. Tucker advises, "Find yourself an editor who knows poetry, who will be tough on you and save you from yourself when you write stupid things, something we all do. My wife, Beth, has been my first and best editor for years, but I have relied on other poets (and friends) as well, such as George Swede, the Canadian haiku poet; Donald Hall; and my friend the poet Joe Salerno, who died in 1996. He was tremendously helpful."

In addition to finding readers who can provide you with constructive criticism, having a network of poets can benefit your writing career in other ways. For example, Tucker has met several important poets by entering contests. Award-winning poets such as Robert Pinsky, Lola Haskins, Carl Dennis, and Dionisio D. Martínez were all judges of contests in which Tucker was either the winner or runner-up. "I asked them for endorsements of my chapbook, and they were all incredibly generous and supportive."

Tucker's final piece of advice for writers is to make poetry as much a part of their lives as possible, and to persevere daily. "Read as much poetry as you can, from the past to the present day," he says. "Not knowing the past is a deal-breaker for would-be poets. You gotta study it if you want to write it. Work hard! Write every day and revise what you write every day, then revise it again and again."

—Donya Dickerson

Donya Dickerson is an editor at McGraw-Hill, focusing on business books. Previously, she was an editor at Writer's Digest Books and the editor of *Guide to Literary Agents*.

2004, 3 issues and 6 posters per year. *Mudlark* publishes in 3 formats: issues of *Mudlark* are the electronic equivalent of print chapbooks; posters are the electronic equivalent of print broadsides; and flash poems are poems that have news in them, poems that feel like current events. The poem is the thing at *Mudlark*, and the essay about it. As our full name suggests, we will consider accomplished work that locates itself anywhere on the spectrum of contemporary practice. We want poems, of course, but we want essays, too, that make us read poems (and write them?) differently somehow. Although we are not innocent, we do imagine ourselves capable of surprise. The work of hobbyists is not for *Mudlark*." Has published poetry by Sheila E. Murphy, John Kinsella, Chris Semansky, Diane Wald, Ian Randall Wilson, and Jeffrey Little. *Mudlark* is archived and permanently on view at www.unf.edu.

How to Submit Submit any number of poems at a time. "Because of our short turn-around time, we'd rather not receive simultaneous submissions. Previously published poems: Inasmuch as issues of *Mudlark* are the electronic equivalent of print chapbooks, some of the individual poems in them might, or might not, have been previously published; if they have been, that previous publication must be acknowledged. Only poems that have not been previously published will be considered for *Mudlark* posters, the electronic equivalent of print broadsides, or for *Mudlark* flash poems." Accepts both e-mail and air-mail submissions. Cover letter is optional. Time between acceptance and publication is up to 3 months. Seldom comments on rejected poems. Guidelines available for SASE, by e-mail, or on website. Responds in "one day to one month, depending . . ." Always sends prepublication galleys, "in the form of inviting the author to proof the work on a private website that *Mudlark* maintains for that purpose." Does not pay. However, "one of the things we can do at *Mudlark* to 'pay' our authors for their work is point to it here and there. We can tell our readers how to find it, how to subscribe to it, and how to buy it . . . if it is for sale. Toward that end, we maintain A-Notes (on the authors) we publish. We call attention to their work." Acquires one time rights.

Advice "*Mudlark* has been reviewed well and often. At this early point in its history, *Mudlark* has established itself, arguably, as one of the few serious rivals in the first generation of the electronic medium, to print versions of its kind. Look at *Mudlark*, visit the website, spend some time there. Then make your decision: to submit or not to submit."

⬧ $⌧ ◎ MYTHIC DELIRIUM (Specialized: science fiction; fantasy; horror; surreal; cross-genre)

P.O. Box 13511, Roanoke VA 24034-3511. E-mail: mythicd2001@yahoo.com. Website: www.mythi

cdelirium.com. Established 1998. **Contact:** Mike Allen, editor. Member: Science Fiction Poetry Association, Science Fiction & Fantasy Writers of America.

Magazine Needs *Mythic Delirium* appears biannually as "a journal of speculative poetry for the new millennium. All forms considered. Must fit within the genres we consider, though we have published some mainstream verse." Does not want "forced rhyme, corny humor, jarringly gross sexual material, gratuitous obscenity, handwritten manuscripts." Has published poetry by Bruce Boston, Theodora Goss, Joe Haldeman, Ursula K. Le Guin, Ian Watson, and Jane Yolen. *Mythic Delirium* is 32 pages, digest-sized, saddle-stapled, with color cover art, includes house ads. Receives about 750 poems/year, accepts about 5%. Press run is 150. Subscription: $9 (2 issues), $16 (4 issues). Sample: $5. Make checks payable to DNA Publications, P.O. Box 2988, Radford VA 24143-2988 (subscription address **only**).

How to Submit No previously published poems or simultaneous submissions. No fax, e-mail, or disk submissions. Cover letter is preferred. Time between acceptance and publication is 9 months. Often comments on rejected poems. Guidelines available for SASE, by e-mail, or on website. Responds in 5 weeks. Pays $5 for poems up to 40 lines, $10 for poems over 40 lines, plus one contributor's copy. Acquires first North American serial rights.

Advice "*Mythic Delirium* isn't easy to get into, but we publish newcomers in every issue. Show us how ambitious you can be, and don't give up."

☑ NAKED KNUCKLE

211 Rowland Ave., Modesto CA 95354. E-mail: gregwords@excite.com. Established 2003. **Contact:** Greg Edwards, editor.

Magazine Needs *Naked Knuckle* appears twice/year (in April and October). Wants "gravel-tongued, side-splittingly funny, gut-wrenching, well-crafted poetry that has something to say." Does not want "predictable rhyme, Hallmark-style junk, or nature poetry that never leaves the forest." Has published poetry by Sam Pierstorff, Dave Church, David J. Thompson, Steve Henn, and Todd Moore. *Naked Knuckle* is up to 40 pages, $4^1/_4 \times 5^1/_2$, photocopied, side-stapled, with cardstock cover with b&w line drawings or computer-generated graphics. Receives about 300 poems/year, accepts about 20%. Press run is 100. Single copy: $3; subscription: $8/3 issues. Make checks payable to Greg Edwards.

How to Submit Submit 3-5 poems at a time. No previously published poems or simultaneous submissions. No e-mail or disk submissions. Cover letter is preferred. "Tell me a little bit about who you are in your cover letter. Such as what you do for a living, where you go to school, stuff like that. Submissions sent without a SASE will not be read." Reads submissions year round. Time between acceptance and publication is 2-6 months. Guidelines available in magazine, for SASE, or by e-mail. Responds in up to 4 months. Pays one contributor's copy. Acquires one-time rights.

Advice "*Naked Knuckle* aims to publish 'poetry that'll bust your mind's eye wide open.' So when submitting, don't be afraid to throw down your gloves and come out swinging raw-fisted. We love a good literary beating."

☑ NASSAU REVIEW

English Dept., Nassau Community College, Garden City NY 11530-6793. (516)572-7792. Established 1964. **Contact:** Editorial Board.

Magazine Needs Appearing in September, *Nassau Review* is an annual "creative and research vehicle for Nassau College faculty and the faculty of other colleges." Wants "serious, intellectual poetry of any form or style. No light verse or satiric verse." Submissions from adults only. "No college students; graduate students acceptable. Want only poems of high quality." Has published poetry by Patti Tana, Dick Allen, David Heyen, Joan Sevick, and Mario Susko. *Nassau Review* is about 190 pages, digest-sized, flat-spined. Receives up to 1,700 poems/year, accepts about 20-25. Press run is 1,100 (about 1,100 subscribers, 200 libraries). Sample: free.

How to Submit Submit *only* 3 poems per yearly issue. "Submit 3 copies of each poem." No previously published poems or simultaneous submissions. SASE required for reply. "Manuscripts will not be returned unless SASE includes sufficient postage." Reads submissions November 1 through March 1 only. Guidelines available for SASE. Responds in up to 4 months. Pays 2 contributor's copies.

Contest/Award Offerings Sponsors a yearly poetry contest with $200 award. **Deadline:** March 31.
Advice "We want professional-level, high-quality work!"

$⬗ THE NATION; "DISCOVERY"/THE NATION POETRY CONTEST

33 Irving Place, New York NY 10003. Established 1865. **Contact:** Grace Schulman, poetry editor.
• Poetry published by *The Nation* has been included in *The Best American Poetry*.

Magazine Needs & How to Submit *The Nation*'s only requirement for poetry is "excellence," which can be inferred from the list of poets they have published: Marianne Moore, Robert Lowell, W.S. Merwin, Maxine Kumin, Donald Justice, James Merrill, Richard Howard, May Swenson, Amy Clampitt, Edward Hirsch, and Charles Simic. Pays $1/line, not to exceed 35 lines, plus one contributor's copy. Accepts submissions by postal mail only; SASE required.

Contest/Award Offerings The magazine co-sponsors the Lenore Marshall Prize for Poetry, an annual award of $10,000 for an outstanding book of poems published in the US. For details, write to the Academy of American Poets, 584 Broadway, #1208, New York NY 10012 (also see separate listing in the Contests & Awards section). Also co-sponsors the "Discovery"/*The Nation* Poetry Contest ($300 each plus a reading at The Unterberg Poetry Center, 1395 Lexington Ave., New York NY 10128). **Deadline:** mid-February. Guidelines available for SASE, at www.92ndsty.org, or by calling (212)415-5759. (See separate listing for Unterberg Poetry Center in the Organizations section.)

⬗ THE NATIONAL POETRY REVIEW; THE ANNIE FINCH PRIZE FOR POETRY; THE NATIONAL POETRY REVIEW CHAPBOOK PRIZE

P.O. Box 4041, Felton CA 95018. Website: www.nationalpoetryreview.com. Established 2003. **Contact:** C.J. Sage, editor.

Magazine Needs "*The National Poetry Review* is a selective journal of contemporary verse appearing twice/year. It is open to well-crafted poetry in both formal and free verse modes but is especially fond of rhyme, rich sound, image, extended metaphor, play *within* form, and unique diction and syntax. *TNPR* balances tradition with innovation and looks for delight, wisdom, and joie de vivre." Does not want "confessional poetry, simple autobiography, narratives without musicality, prose poems, or vulgarity." Has published poetry by Bob Hicok, Debra Bruce, C. Dale Young, Jenny Factor, Emily Rosko, and Ted Kooser. *The National Poetry Review* is 64 pages, perfect-bound, with full-color cover. Accepts less than 1% of submissions. Single copy: $6; subscription: $10/year. Make checks payable to C.J. Sage only.

How to Submit Submit 3-5 poems at a time. Accepts simultaneous submissions with notification ONLY; no previously published poems. No fax, e-mail, or disk submissions. Cover letter is preferred. "Submit poems with brief bio, contact information including e-mail address if you have one (e-mail addresses will be kept confidential), and SASE. Please write *your own* address in the return address area of your SASE as well as in the addressee area." Reads submissions all year. Time between acceptance and publication is no more than 6 months. "The editor makes all publishing decisions." Seldom comments on rejected poems. Guidelines available in magazine or on website. Responds in about 6 weeks. Pays one contributor's copy. Acquires first rights.

Contest/Award Offerings 1) **The Annie Finch Prize for Poetry**, an annual award of $300-500 (check website for current prize information) and publication in *The National Poetry Review*. Pays winners from other countries in US dollars. Submissions must be unpublished; may be entered in other contests, but must be withdrawn if accepted by *TNPR* as a winner, runner up, or honorable mention. Submit 3 poems on any subject, in any form (10-page limit). No name or identifying information on poems. Include a separate cover letter with name, address, e-mail address for results, and brief bio. Guidelines available on website. **Entry fee:** $10 for up to 3 poems. Does not accept entry fees in foreign currencies or money orders; accepts US dollars or personal checks.

Deadline: May 1 (date changes; check website for yearly deadline). 2005 contest judge was Margot Schilpp. Winner will be announced by e-mail. All entries considered for publication in *TNPR*. 2) **The** *National Poetry Review* **Chapbook Prize.** Details available on website.

Advice "Read an issue or two before submitting. Send only your very best work."

⭐ ☑ THE NEBRASKA REVIEW; THE NEBRASKA REVIEW AWARDS

University of Nebraska at Omaha, WFAB 212, Omaha NE 68182-0324. (402)554-3159. Fax: (402)554-3436. E-mail: tnr@zoopress.org. Website: www.zoopress.org/nebraskareview/index.html. Established 1973. **Contact:** Poetry Editor. Editors: Neil Azevedo and Max Watman.

- Poetry published in *The Nebraska Review* has been included in the 2001 *Best American Poetry* and the 2002 *Pushcart Prize* anthology.

Magazine Needs *The Nebraska Review* is a semiannual literary magazine publishing fiction and poetry with occasional essays. Wants "lyric poetry from 10-200 lines, preference being for under 100 lines. Subject matter is unimportant, as long as it has some. Poets should have mastered form, meaning poems should have form, not simply 'demonstrate' it." Doesn't want to see "concrete, inspirational, didactic, or merely political poetry." Has published poetry by Christian Wiman, Greg Williamson, David Barber, A.E. Stallings, Diann Blakely, and Alfred Corn. *The Nebraska Review* is 200 pages, digest-sized, nicely printed, flat-spined, with glossy card cover. It is published by Zoo Press in conjunction with the University of Nebraska at Omaha. Press run is 500 (380 subscribers, 85 libraries). Single copy: $20; subscription: $28/1 year, $48/2 years. Sample: $5.

How to Submit Submit 4-6 poems at a time. "Clean typed copy strongly preferred." Accepts submissions by postal mail only. Reads open submissions January 1 through April 30 only. Time between acceptance and publication is up to one year. Guidelines available on website. Responds in 4 months. Pays one contributor's copy and one-year subscription. Acquires first North American serial rights.

Contest/Award Offerings Submissions for The Nebraska Review Awards are read from September 1 through November 30 only. The Nebraska Review Awards of $500 each in poetry, creative nonfiction, and fiction are published in the spring issue. **Entry fee:** $15, includes discounted subscription. You can enter as many times as desired. **Deadline:** November 30.

Advice "Your first allegiance is to the poem. Publishing will come in time, but it will always be less than you feel you deserve. Therefore, don't look to publication as a reward for writing well; it has no relationship."

☑ THE NEOVICTORIAN/COCHLEA

P.O. Box 55164, Madison WI 53705. E-mail: eacam@execpc.com. Website: www.pointandcircumference.com. Established 1995. **Contact:** Esther Cameron, editor.

Magazine Needs *The Neovictorian/Cochlea* appears biannually and "seeks to promote poetry of introspection, dialogue, and social concern." Wants "poetry of beauty and integrity with emotional and intellectual depth, commitment to subject matter as well as language, and the courage to ignore fashion. Welcome: well-crafted formal verse, social comment (including satire), love poems, philosophical/religious poems, poems reflecting dialogue with other writers (in particular: responses to the work of Paul Celan)." Very rarely accepts poetry by children. Has published poetry by Ida Fasel, Carolyn Stoloff, Richard Moore, Constance Rowell Mastores, Leonard Borenstein, and Michael Burch. *The Neovictorian/Cochlea* is 28-32 pages, magazine-sized, photocopied, saddle-stapled, with cardstock cover. Press run is 275 (60 subscribers). Single copy: $6; subscription: $10.

How to Submit Submit 3-5 poems at a time. Accepts simultaneous submissions and, "on rare occasions, a previously published poem. First-time submissions by surface mail only." Cover letter is "not necessary. Poets whose work is accepted will be asked for titles of books available, to be published in the magazine." Time between acceptance and publication is up to one year. Often comments on rejected poems. Does not offer guidelines because "the tradition is the only 'guideline.' We do encourage contributors to write for a sample." Responds in up to 4 months. Pays 2 contributor's copies. Acquires first rights. *The Neovictorian/Cochlea* publishes the addresses of poets who would welcome correspondence. "Poets can also submit longer selections of work for publication on the 'Point and Circumference' website."

Advice "Like all our social functioning, poetry today suffers from a loss of community, which translates into a lack of real intimacy with the reader. Poets can work against this trend by remaining in touch with the poetry of past generations and by forming relationships in which poetry can be employed as the language of friendship. Publication should be an afterthought."

NERVE COWBOY; LIQUID PAPER PRESS; NERVE COWBOY CHAPBOOK CONTEST

P.O. Box 4973, Austin TX 78765. Website: www.onr.com/user/jwhagins/nervecowboy.html. Established 1995. **Contact:** Joseph Shields and Jerry Hagins, co-editors.

Magazine Needs *Nerve Cowboy* is a biannual literary journal featuring contemporary poetry, short fiction, and b&w drawings. "Open to all forms, styles, and subject matter, preferring writing that speaks directly and minimizes literary devices. We want to see poetry of experience and passion which can find that raw nerve and ride it. We are always looking for that rare writer who inherently knows what word comes next." Has published poetry by Gerald Locklin, Paul Agostino, Ann Mennebroker, Wilma Elizabeth McDaniel, Suellen Luwish, and David J. Thompson. *Nerve Cowboy* is 64 pages, $7 \times 8\frac{1}{2}$, attractively printed, saddle-stapled, with matte card cover with b&w art. Currently accepts about 5% of the submissions received. Press run is 300 (175 subscribers). Subscription: $16/4 issues. Sample: $5.

How to Submit Submit 3-7 poems at a time, with name on each page. Accepts previously published poems with notification; no simultaneous submissions. Informal cover letter with bio and credits is preferred. Seldom comments on rejected poems. Guidelines available for SASE or on website. Responds in 3 months. Pays one contributor's copy. Acquires first or one-time rights.

Contest/Award Offerings Liquid Paper Press publishes 2-3 chapbooks/year but will not be accepting unsolicited chapbook mss in the foreseeable future. Only chapbook contest winners and solicited mss will be published in the next couple of years. For information on *Nerve Cowboy*'s annual chapbook contest, please send a SASE. **Entry fee:** $10. **Deadline:** January 31 of each year. Cash prizes and publication for 1st and 2nd place. Chapbooks are 24-40 pages, digest-sized, photocopied, include some b&w artwork. Recent winners include Michelle Brooks, James Edward O'Brien, Robert Plath, Lori Jakiela, Ralph Dranow, Christopher Jones, and Belinda Subraman. Publications include *When Patti Would Fall Asleep* by Michael Estabrook, *Hoeing Cotton in High Heels* by Wilma Elizabeth McDaniel, *Nothing But Candy* by Jennifer Jackson, *Everyone, Exquisite* by Bob Pajich, *The Back East Poems* by Gerald Locklin, and *Learning to Lie* by Albert Huffstickler. Send SASE for a complete list of available titles.

$ THE NEW CRITERION

The Foundation for Cultural Review, Inc., 900 Broadway, Suite 602, New York NY 10003. Website: www.newcriterion.com. **Contact:** David Yezzi, poetry editor.

Magazine Needs & How to Submit *The New Criterion* is a monthly (except July and August) review of ideas and the arts, publishing poetry of high literary quality. Has published poetry by Donald Justice, Andrew Hudgins, Elizabeth Spires, and Herbert Morris. It is 90 pages, 7×10, flat-spined. Sample: $4.75. Accepts submissions by postal mail only. Cover letter is required. Responds in 3 months. Pays $2.50/line ($75 minimum).

Advice "To have an idea of who we are or what we stand for, poets should consult back issues."

$ NEW ENGLAND REVIEW

Middlebury College, Middlebury VT 05753. (802)443-5075. Fax: (802)443-2088. E-mail: nereview@middlebury.edu. Website: www.middlebury.edu/~nereview/. Established 1978. **Contact:** Poetry Editor. Editor: Stephen Donadio.

● Work published in this review is frequently included in volumes of *The Best American Poetry*.

Magazine Needs *New England Review* is a prestigious, nationally distributed literary quarterly, 180 pages, 7×10, flat-spined, printed on heavy stock, with glossy cover with art. Has published poetry by Nick Flynn, Henri Cole, Debora Greger, and Pimone Triplett. Receives 3,000-4,000 poetry submissions/year, accepts about 70-80 poems/year. Subscription: $25. Sample: $8.

How to Submit Submit up to 6 poems at a time. No previously published poems. All submissions by postal mail; accepts *questions* by e-mail. "Brief cover letters are useful." Address submissions to Poetry Editor. Reads submissions postmarked September 1 through May 31 only. Time between acceptance and publication is 3-6 months. Responds in up to 3 months. Always sends prepublication galleys. Pays $10/page ($20 minimum) plus 2 contributor's copies. Also features essay-reviews. Send materials for review consideration.

Advice "Read a few copies of the magazine before submitting work."

Ⓝ $◨ THE NEW HAMPSHIRE REVIEW

P.O. Box 323, Nashua NH 03061-0322. E-mail: submissions@newhampshirereview.com. Website: www.newhampshirereview.com. Established 2005. **Contact:** Virginia M. Heatter, editor-in-chief; Seth D. Abramson, poetry & politics editor.

Magazine Needs *The New Hampshire Review* is a quarterly online journal of poetry and politics. "We will consider both free and formal verse. Quality is our first concern. We are looking for poems which contemplate the human condition in fresh, interesting, and meaningful ways. Work should aim to reach an intelligent, well-read audience." Does not want "generic voices, poems which adhere too narrowly to a single school, formulaic verse." Has published poetry by Mark Doty, Timothy Liu, Dan Beachy-Quick, David Biespiel, and Peter Campion. Receives about 2,250 poems/year, accepts about 2.5%.

How to Submit Submit 3-5 poems at a time. Accepts simultaneous submissions "if stated in cover letter; we ask that you notify us immediately upon acceptance elsewhere"; no previously published poems. Accepts e-mail submissions; no disk submissions. Cover letter is required. "E-mail submissions without an appropriate cover letter will not receive a response (include in message text). Cover letter must include full name, address, and phone number." Reads submissions year round. Time between acceptance and publication is 3-6 months. Poems are circulated to an editorial board. Sometimes comments on rejected poems. Guidelines available on website. Responds in 2-3 months. Always sends prepublication galleys "as HTML sample page(s)." Pay "varies; see website for details." Acquires first North American serial rights. Reviews books of poetry. Send materials for review consideration to Review Editor.

◨ NEW ISSUES PRESS; NEW ISSUES PRESS POETRY SERIES; GREEN ROSE SERIES; THE NEW ISSUES POETRY PRIZE; THE GREEN ROSE PRIZE IN POETRY

Dept. of English, Western Michigan University, 1903 W. Michigan Ave., Kalamazoo MI 49008-5331. (269)387-8185. Fax: (269)387-2562. E-mail: herbert.scott@wmich.edu. Website: www.wmich.edu/newissues. Established 1996. **Contact:** Herbert Scott, editor.

Book/Chapbook Needs & How to Submit New Issues Press publishes 3-6 first books of poetry/year, one through its annual New Issues Poetry Prize competition (see Contest/Award Offerings below). Additional mss will be selected from those submitted to the competition for publication in the Poetry Series. "A national judge selects the prize winner and recommends other manuscripts. The editors decide on the other books considering the judge's recommendation, but are not bound by it." Past judges include Philip Levine, C.D. Wright, C.K. Williams, Campbell McGrath, Brenda Hillman, and Marianne Boruch. Also publishes the Green Rose Series, a new line of poetry books by established poets. Titles for this series are chosen through the annual Green Rose Prize in Poetry (see Contest/Award Offerings below). Books are printed on acid-free paper in editions of 1,500. New Issues Press does not consider mss outside the context of its competitions.

Contest/Award Offerings 1) **The New Issues Poetry Prize** is open to "poets writing in English who have not previously published a full-length collection of poems in an edition of 500 or more copies." Winner receives $2,000 plus publication of ms. Submit 48- to 72-page ms with one-paragraph bio, publication credits (if any), and $15 **entry fee**. Make checks payable to New Issues

Poetry & Prose. No e-mail or fax submissions. **Deadline:** November 30; reads submissions June 1 through November 30 only. Winner announced the following April. Guidelines available for SASE, by fax, by e-mail, or on website. 2) **The Green Rose Prize in Poetry** offers $2,000 and and publication for a book of poems by an established poet who has published one or more full-length collections of poetry. New Issues may publish as many as 3 additional mss from this competition. **Entry fee:** $20/ms. Make checks payable to New Issues Poetry & Prose. No e-mail or fax submissions. **Deadline:** September 30; reads submissions May 1 through September 30 only. Winner announced the following January. Previous winners include Ruth Ellen Kocher, Christopher Bursk, Gretchen Mattox, Christine Hume, and Hugh Seidman. Other Green Rose poets include Michael Burkard, Maurice Kilwein Guevara, Mary Ann Samyn, Jim Daniels. Guidelines available for SASE, by fax, by e-mail, or on website.

Advice "Our belief is that there are more good poets writing than ever before. Our mission is to give some of the best of these a forum. Also, our books have been reviewed in *Publishers Weekly*, *Booklist*, and the *Library Journal* as well as being featured in the *Washington Post Book World* and the *New York Times Book Review* during 2000 and 2001. New Issues books are advertised in *Poets & Writers*, *APR*, *American Poet*, *The Bloomsbury Review*, etc. We publish 8-12 books of poems per year. New Issues Press is profiled in the May/June 2000 issue of *Poets & Writers*."

✪ ◙ THE NEW LAUREL REVIEW

828 Lesseps St., New Orleans LA 70117. Fax: (504)948-3834. Established 1971. **Contact:** Lee Meitzen Grue and Lenny Emmanuel, editors.

Magazine Needs *The New Laurel Review* "is an annual independent nonprofit literary magazine dedicated to fine art. The magazine is meant to be eclectic, and we try to publish the best we receive, whether the submission is poem, translation, short story, essay, review, or interview. Each issue presents original art, and sometimes photographs, that complement the other genres in the particular issue. We have no domineering preferences in style, and we do consult with invited readers and writers for their opinions. We are seeking original work without hackneyed phrases, indulgent voices, or tired thinking. We love surprises and to see a writer or artists enliven our too often dull, editorial worlds." Has published poetry by Gerald Locklin, Roland John (British), Joyce Odam, Ryan G. Van Cleave, Robert Cooperman, and Dave Brinks. The magazine is usually about 115-130 pages 6×9, laser-printed, perfect-bound, with original art on laminated cover. Receives 400-600 submissions/year, accepts about 30-40 poems. Circulation is about 500. Single copy: $12 for individuals, $14 for institutions. Sample (back issue): $5.

How to Submit Submit 3-5 poems. No simultaneous submissions. "Poems should be typed; no handwritten submissions will be read. Name and address should appear on each poem submitted. Include a brief biography of three or four typed lines of prose, including previous publications. Do not send cover letters, which may or may not distract from the submission. Be sure to include SASE, for manuscripts will not be returned otherwise. If you are submitting from outside the U.S., provide international reply coupons. Because we are totally independent from various funding agencies, we sometimes take an inordinate time to reply. We read submissions between September 1 and May 30 only, and publication date can be as long as a year from acceptance." Pays one contributor's copy. Acquires first rights, but will gladly grant permission for the writer to reprint.

Advice "READ, READ, READ. And it is wise to obtain a copy of any magazine to which you plan to submit work. And also, you might remember that you cannot be cummings, Eliot, Faulkner, or Hemingway. One of the most disheartening aspects of editing is to receive a submission of poems with low caps, no punctuation, or words sprawled all over the page, under the pretense that the work is original and not pseudo-cummings or Yawping Whitman. Find your own voice and techniques."

◙ NEW LETTERS; NEW LETTERS POETRY PRIZE

University of Missouri-Kansas City, Kansas City MO 64110. (816)235-1168. Fax: (816)235-2611. E-mail: newletters@umkc.edu. Website: www.newletters.org. Established 1934 as *University Review*, became *New Letters* in 1971. **Contact:** Robert Stewart, editor.

Magazine Needs & How to Submit *New Letters*, a quarterly, "is dedicated to publishing the best short fiction, contemporary poetry, literary articles, photography, and artwork by both established writers and new talents." Wants "fresh, new writing of all types. Short works are more likely to be accepted than very long ones." Has published poetry by Naomi Shihab Nye, Albert Goldbarth, Quincy Troupe, Ellen Bass, Joseph Millar, and Mia Leonin. *New Letters* is an average of 180 pages, digest-sized, professionally printed, flat-spined, with glossy 4-color cover with art. Press run is 3,600 (2,600 subscriptions, about 40% libraries). Subscription: $17. Sample: $9. Send no more than 4 poems at a time. No previously published poems or simultaneous submissions. Short cover letter is preferred. "We strongly prefer original typescripts." Guidelines available on website.

Contest/Award Offerings The annual New Letters Poetry Prize awards $1,000 to the best group of 3-6 poems published in *New Letters* that year. **Entry fee:** $15; includes one-year subscription. All entries will be considered for publication in the magazine. **Deadline:** May 18. Guidelines available for SASE or on website.

Advice "Write with originality and freshness in language, content, and style. Avoid clichés in imagery and subject."

NEW NATIVE PRESS (Specialized: translations; marginalized and endangered languages)

P.O. Box 661, Cullowhee NC 28723. (828)293-9237. E-mail: newnativepress@hotmail.com. Established 1979. **Contact:** Thomas Rain Crowe, publisher.

Book/Chapbook Needs New Native Press has "selectively narrowed its range of contemporary 20th- and 21st-century literature to become an exclusive publisher of writers in marginalized and endangered languages. All books published are bilingual translations from original languages into English." Publishes about 2 paperbacks/year. Has published *Kenneth Patchen: Rebel Poet in America* by Larry Smith; Gaelic, Welsh, Breton, Cornish, and Manx poets in an all-Celtic-language anthology of contemporary poets from Scotland, Ireland, Wales, Brittany, Cornwall, and Isle of Man, entitled *Writing The Wind: A Celtic Resurgence (The New Celtic Poetry)*; and *Selected Poems* by Kusumagraj (poet from Bombay, India) in the Marathi language. Books are sold by distributors in 4 foreign countries and in the US by Baker & Taylor, Amazon.com, library vendors, and Small Press Distribution. Books are typically 80 pages, offset-printed on glossy 120-lb. stock, perfect-bound, with professionally designed color cover.

How to Submit "Now accepting submissions for translations only (see above)." Authors should query first with 10 sample poems and cover letter with bio and publication credits. Accepts previously published poems and simultaneous submissions. Time between acceptance and publication is up to one year. Always comments on rejected poems. Responds in 2 weeks. Pays author's copies; "Amount varies with author and title."

Advice "We are looking for work indicative of rare and unique talent—and original voices—using language experimentally and symbolically, if not subversively."

NEW ORLEANS POETRY FORUM; GRIS-GRIS PRESS; DESIRE STREET

257 Bonnabel Blvd., Metairie LA 70005-3738. (504)835-8472 or (504)467-9034. Fax: (504)834-2005. E-mail: neworleanspoetryforum@yahoo.com. Poetry forum established 1971, press and magazine established 1994. **Contact:** Andrea S. Gereighty, director. Editor: Chris Hannan.

Magazine Needs *Desire Street* is the quarterly electronic magazine of the New Orleans Poetry Forum. "The Forum, a non-profit entity, has as its chief purpose the development of poets and contemporary poetry in the New Orleans area. To this end, it conducts a weekly workshop in which original poems are presented and critiqued according to an established protocol which assures a non-judgmental and non-argumentative atmosphere. A second aim of the New Orleans Poetry Forum is to foster awareness and support for poetry in the New Orleans area through readings, publicity, and community activities. Promotion is emphasized in order to increase acceptance and support for contemporary poetry." Wants "modern poetry on any topic—one page only. No rhyming verse; no porn, obscenity, or child molestation themes." Has published poetry by Pinkie Gordon Lane, Kay Murphy, John Gery, Richard Katrovas, Yusef Komunyakaa, and Kalamu Ya Salaam.

Desire Street is 30 pages, desktop-published, downloaded, photocopied, and distributed. Receives about 550 poems/year, accepts 10%. Press run is 200 hard copies (200 subscribers). Single copy: $3; subscription: $12/year. Sample (including guidelines): $5. Make checks payable to New Orleans Poetry Forum. Annual fee for members: $30, includes 4 issues of *Desire Street*, 50 3-hour workshops, and one year's free critique of up to 10 poems.

How to Submit Submit 2 poems at a time, 10-poem limit/year. Lines/poem: one $8\frac{1}{2} \times 11$ page only. Accepts previously published poems; no simultaneous submissions. Cover letter is required. Time between acceptance and publication is up to one year. Poems are circulated to an editorial board. "First, poems are read by Andrea Gereighty. Then, poems are read by a board of 5 poets." Comments on rejected poems. Guidelines available for SASE. Responds in one year. Pays one contributor's copy. Acquires one-time rights.

Also Offers The Forum conducts weekly workshops on Wednesday nights in the rear office of 257 Bonnabel Blvd. Also conducts workshops at schools and in prisons. Details available for SASE.

Advice "Read *Desire Street* first. Take your work seriously. Send 2 one-page original poems and bio. Be patient; we are all volunteers."

☑ NEW ORLEANS POETRY JOURNAL PRESS

2131 General Pershing St., New Orleans LA 70115. (504)891-3458. Established 1956. **Contact:** Maxine Cassin, publisher/editor. Co-Editor: Charles de Gravelles.

Book/Chapbook Needs "We prefer to publish relatively new and/or little-known poets of unusual promise or those inexplicably neglected." Does not want to see "cliché or doggerel, anything incomprehensible or too derivative, or workshop exercises. First-rate lyric poetry preferred (not necessarily in traditional forms)." Has published books by Everette Maddox, Charles Black, Malaika Favorite, Martha McFerren, Ralph Adamo, and Charles de Gravelles.

How to Submit This market is currently closed to all submissions.

Advice "Read as much as possible! Write only when you must, and don't rush into print! No poetry should be sent without querying first! Publishers are concerned about expenses unnecessarily incurred in mailing manuscripts. *Telephoning is not encouraged.*"

$☑ NEW ORLEANS REVIEW

Box 195, Loyola University, New Orleans LA 70118. (504)865-2295. Fax: (504)865-2294. Website: www.loyno.edu/~noreview. Established 1968. **Contact:** Sophia Stone, poetry editor. Editor: Christopher Chambers. Book Review Editor: Mary McCay.

Magazine Needs *New Orleans Review* publishes "poetry, fiction, essays, book reviews, and interviews. We're looking for dynamic writing that demonstrates attention to the language and a sense of the medium; writing that engages, surprises, moves us. We suscribe to the belief that in order to truly write well, one must first master the rudiments: grammar and syntax, punctuation, the sentence, the paragraph, the line, the stanza." Has published poetry by Chrisopher Howell, Martha Zweig, Lee Upton, Jeffrey Levine, Carlie Rosemurgy, and D.C. Berry. *New Orleans Review* is 120-200 pages, elegantly printed, perfect-bound, with glossy card cover. Receives about 3,000 mss/year. Press run is 1,500. Single copy: $7. Sample: $5.

How to Submit Submit 3-6 poems at a time. No previously published poems. Accepts simultaneous submissions "if we're notified immediately upon acceptance elsewhere." Does not accept e-mail or fax submissions. Brief cover letter is preferred. Guidelines available on website. Responds in up to 4 months. Pays 2 contributor's copies and honorarium. Acquires first North American serial rights.

♦ ☑ NEW ORPHIC REVIEW; NEW ORPHIC PUBLISHERS

706 Mill St., Nelson BC V1L 4S5 Canada. (250)354-0494. Fax: (250)352-0743. Established 1995 (New Orphic Publishers), 1998 (*New Orphic Review*). **Contact:** Margrith Schraner, associate editor. Editor-in-Chief: Ernest Hekkanen.

Magazine Needs "Appearing in May and October, *New Orphic Review* is run by an opinionated visionary who is beholden to no one, least of all government agencies like the Canada Council or institutions of higher learning. He feels Canadian literature is stagnant, lacks daring, and is terribly incestuous.'' *New Orphic Review* publishes poetry, novel excerpts, mainstream and experimental short stories, and articles on a wide range of subjects. Each issue also contains a *Featured Poet* section. ''*New Orphic Review* publishes authors from around the world as long as the pieces are written in English and are accompanied by a SASE with proper Canadian postage and/or U.S. dollars to offset the cost of postage.'' Prefers ''tight, well-wrought poetry over leggy, prosaic poetry. No 'fuck you' poetry; no rambling pseudo Beat poetry.'' Has published poetry by Robert Cooperman, Step Elder, Louis E. Bourgeios, and Art Joyce. *New Orphic Review* is 120-140 pages, magazine-sized, laser-printed, perfect-bound, with color cover, includes ads. Receives about 400 poems/year, accepts about 10%. Press run is 500 (250 subscribers, 20 libraries). Subscription: $30 (individuals), $35 (institutions). Sample: $20.

How to Submit Submit 6 poems at a time. Lines/poem: 5 minimum, 30 maximum. Accepts simultaneous submissions; no previously published poems. Cover letter is preferred. ''Make sure a SASE (or SAE and IRC) is included.'' Time between acceptance and publication is up to 8 months. ''The managing editor and associate editor refer work to the editor-in-chief.'' Seldom comments on rejected poems. Occasionally publishes theme issues. Guidelines available for SASE (or SAE and IRC). Responds in 2 months. Pays one contributor's copy. Acquires first North American serial rights.

Also Offers New Orphic Publishers publishes 4 paperbacks/year. However, all material is solicited.

Advice ''Read the magazine before submitting.''

$⬚ THE NEW RENAISSANCE; TNR POETRY AWARDS

26 Heath Rd. #11, Arlington MA 02474-3645. E-mail: MarcCreate@aol.com. Website: www.tnrlitmag.net. Established 1968. **Contact:** Frank Finale, poetry editor. Editor-in-Chief: Louise T. Reynolds.

Magazine Needs *the new renaissance* is ''intended for the 'renaissance' person—the generalist, not the specialist. We publish the best new writing and translations and offer a forum for articles on political, sociological topics; feature established as well as emerging visual artists and writers; highlight reviews of small press; and offer essays on a variety of topics from visual arts and literature to science. Open to a variety of styles, including traditional.'' Has published poetry by Anita Susan Brenner, Ann Struther, Marc Widershien, Miguel Torga (trans. Alexis Levetin), Stephen Todd Booker, and Rabindranath Togore (trans. Wendy Barker and S. Togore). *the new renaissance* is 144-182 pages, digest-sized, flat-spined, professionally printed on heavy stock, with glossy color cover. Receives about 650 poetry submissions/year, accepts about 40. Usual press run is 1,500 (760 subscribers, 132 libraries). Single copy: $12.50 (current), $11.50 (recent), $7.50 (back issue); subscription: $30/3 issues US, $35 Canada, $38 all others. ''All checks in U.S. dollars. A 3-issue subscription covers 18-22 months.''

How to Submit Submit 3-6 poems at a time, ''unless a long poem—then one.'' Accepts simultaneous submissions, if notified; no previously published poems ''unless magazine's circulation was under 250.'' Always include SASE or IRC. Accepts submissions by postal mail only; ''when accepted, we ask if a disk is available, and we prefer accepted translations to be available in the original language on disk. All poetry submissions are tied to our Awards Program for poetry published in a 3-issue volume; judged by independent judges.'' **Entry fee:** $16.50 for nonsubscribers, $11.50 for subscribers, ''for which they receive 2 back issues or a recent issue or an extension of their subscription. Submissions without entry fee are *returned unread*.'' Reads submissions January 2 through June 30. Guidelines available for SASE. Responds in 5 months. Pays $21-40 (more for the occasional longer poem), plus one contributor's copy/poem. Acquires all rights but returns rights provided *the new renaissance* retains rights for any *the new renaissance* collection. Reviews books of poetry.

Contest/Award Offerings The Awards Program offers 3 prizes of $250, $125, and $50, with 3-4 Honorable Mentions of $25 each.

Advice ''Read, read, read! And support the literary magazines that support serious writers and poets. In 2002, more than 350 separate submissions came in, all without the required fee. Since our Poetry Awards Program has been in effect since 1995, and since we've notified all markets about our guidelines and entry fee, this just shows an indifferent, careless reading of our magazine's requirements.''

⊕ $⊘ THE NEW WRITER; THE NEW WRITER PROSE AND POETRY PRIZES

P.O. Box 60, Cranbrook TN17 2ZR England. Phone: 01580 212626. Fax: 01580 212041. E-mail: admin@thenewwriter.com. Website: www.thenewwriter.com. Established 1996. **Contact:** Catherine Smith, poetry editor.

Magazine Needs Published 6 times/year, *"The New Writer* is the magazine you've been hoping to find. It's *different* and it's aimed at writers with a serious intent, who want to develop their writing to meet the high expectations of today's editors. The team at *The New Writer* is committed to working with its readers to increase the chances of publication. That's why masses of useful information and plenty of feedback is provided. More than that, we let you know about the current state of the market with the best in contemporary fiction and cutting-edge poetry backed up by searching articles and in-depth features in every issue. We are interested in short and long unpublished poems, provided they are original and undeniably brilliant. No problems with length/form, but anything over 2 pages (150 lines) needs to be brilliant. Cutting edge shouldn't mean inaccessible. No recent disasters—they date. No my baby/doggie poems; no God poems that sound like hymns, dum-dum rhymes, or comic rhymes (best left at the pub).'' *The New Writer* is 56 pages, A4, professionally printed, saddle-stapled, with paper cover. Press run is 1,500 (1,350 subscribers); 50 distributed free to publishers, agents. Single copy: £3.95; subscription: £33 in US. Sample: £3.95 or equivalent in IRCs. "A secure server for subscriptions and entry into the annual Prose & Poetry Prizes on the website. Monthly e-mail newsletter included free of charge in the subscription package.''

How to Submit Submit up to 6 poems at a time. Accepts previously published poems. Accepts e-mail submissions (pasted into body of message). Time between acceptance and publication is up to 6 months. Often comments on rejected poems. Offers criticism service: £12/6 poems. Guidelines available for SASE (or SAE with IRC) or on website. Pays £3 voucher plus one contributor's copy. Acquires first British serial rights. Reviews books and chapbooks of poetry and other magazines. Send materials for review consideration.

Contest/Award Offerings Sponsors the New Writer Prose & Poetry Prizes. An annual prize, "open to all poets writing in the English language, who are invited to submit an original, previously unpublished poem or collection of 6 to 10 poems. Up to 25 prizes will be presented, as well as publication for the prize-winning poets in an anthology, plus the chance for a further 10 shortlisted poets to see their work published in *The New Writer* during the year." Guidelines available by e-mail.

✪ ⊘ NEW YORK QUARTERLY

P.O. Box 693, Old Chelsea Station, New York NY 10113. Website: www.nyquarterly.com. Established 1969. **Contact:** Raymond Hammond, poetry editor.

Magazine Needs *New York Quarterly* appears 3 times/year. It seeks to publish "a cross-section of the best of contemporary American poetry." Has published poetry by Charles Bukowski, James Dickey, Lola Haskins, Lyn Lifshin, Elisavietta Ritchie, and W.D. Snodgrass. *New York Quarterly* is digest-sized, flat-spined, elegantly printed, with glossy color cover. Subscription: $20.

How to Submit Submit 3-5 poems at a time with your name and address; include SASE. Accepts simultaneous submissions with notification. Responds within one month. Pays contributor's copies.

◗ NEW ZOO POETRY REVIEW; SUNKEN MEADOWS PRESS

P.O. Box 36760, Richmond VA 23235. Website: http://members.aol.com/newzoopoet. Established 1997. **Contact:** Angela Vogel, editor.

Magazine Needs *New Zoo Poetry Review* is published annually in January and "tends to publish free verse in well-crafted lyric and narrative forms. Our goal is to publish established poets alongside lesser-known poets of great promise. *New Zoo Poetry Review* wants serious, intellectual poetry of any form, length, or style. Rhyming poetry only if exceptional. No light verse, song lyrics, or greeting card copy. If you are not reading the best of contemporary poetry, then *New Zoo Poetry Review* is not for you." Has published poetry by Heather McHugh, Diane Glancy, D.C. Berry, Natasha Sajé, and Martha Collins. *New Zoo Poetry Review* is 40 pages, digest-sized, photocopied, saddle-stapled, with glossy card cover with b&w photography. Receives about 1,000 poems/year, accepts approximately 4%. Press run is 200. Single copy: $5.

How to Submit Submit 3-5 poems at a time. Accepts simultaneous submissions; no previously published poems. Cover letter with brief bio is required. Seldom comments on rejected poems. Responds in 2 months. Pays one contributor's copy. Acquires first North American serial rights. "Poets are discouraged from submitting more than once in a 12-month period. Please do not write to us for these submission guidelines. We understand and encourage simultaneous submissions and think threatening to 'blacklist' poets who do so responsibly is unfortunate. *NZPR* responds to submissions in an appropriate timeframe and thereby gathers the best work out there."

☐ ◉ NEWSLETTER INAGO (Specialized: form/free verse)

P.O. Box 26244, Tucson AZ 85726-6244. Established 1979. **Contact:** Del Reitz, poetry editor.

Magazine Needs *Newsletter Inago* is a monthly newsletter-format poetry journal. "Free verse and short narrative poetry preferred. Rhymed poetry must be truly exceptional (nonforced) for consideration. Due to format, 'epic' and monothematic poetry will not be considered. Cause-specific, political, or religious poetry stands little chance of consideration. A wide range of short poetry, showing the poet's preferably eclectic perspective, is best for *Newsletter Inago*. No haiku, please." Has published poetry by Dana Thu, Kate Fuller-Niles, Jack Coulehan, Padma Jared-Thornlyre, Corina K. Cook, and Tom Rich. *Newsletter Inago* is 4-5 pages, corner-stapled. Press run is about 200 for subscriptions. No price is given for the newsletter, but the editor suggests a donation of $3.50/issue or $18.50 annually ($3.50 and $21 Canada, £8 and £21 UK). Make checks payable to Del Reitz.

How to Submit Submit 10-15 poems at a time. "Poetry should be submitted in the format in which the poet wants it to appear, and cover letters are always a good idea." Accepts simultaneous submissions and previously published poems. Sometimes comments on rejected poems. Guidelines available for SASE. Responds ASAP (usually within 2 weeks). Pays in contributor's copies. Copyright is retained by authors.

✴ ◐ NEXUS

WO16A Student Union, Wright State University, Dayton OH 45435. (937)775-5533. E-mail: nexus_magazine@hotmail.com. Established 1967. **Contact:** Jim Tarjeft, editor.

Magazine Needs "*Nexus* is a student-operated magazine of mainstream and street poetry; also essays on environmental and political issues. We're looking for truthful, direct poetry. Open to poets anywhere. We look for contemporary, imaginative work." *Nexus* appears 3 times/year—fall, winter, and spring—using about 40 pages of poetry (of 80-96 total pages) in each issue. Receives about 1,000 submissions/year, accepts about 30-50. Circulation is 1,000. Sample: $5 and 10×15 SAE with 5 first-class stamps.

How to Submit Submit 4-6 pages of poetry with bio. Reads submissions September through May only. Accepts simultaneous submissions, "but due to short response time we want to be told it's a simultaneous submission." Editor sometimes comments on rejected poems. Upcoming themes and guidelines available in magazine, for SASE, or by e-mail. Responds in 5 months except during summer months. Pays 2 contributor's copies. Acquires first rights.

◐ NIMROD: INTERNATIONAL JOURNAL OF POETRY AND PROSE; NIMROD/HARDMAN AWARD: PABLO NERUDA PRIZE FOR POETRY

University of Tulsa, 600 S. College, Tulsa OK 74104-3189. (918)631-3080. Fax: (918)631-3033. E-mail: nimrod@utulsa.edu. Website: www.utulsa.edu/nimrod. Established 1956. **Contact:** Manly Johnson, poetry editor. Editor-in-Chief: Francine Ringold.

● Poetry published in *Nimrod* has been included in *The Best American Poetry*.

Magazine Needs *Nimrod* "is an active 'little magazine,' part of the movement in American letters which has been essential to the development of modern literature." *Nimrod* publishes 2 issues/year: an awards issue in the fall, featuring the prize winners of their national competition, and a thematic issue each spring. "Poems in non-award issues range from formal to freestyle with several translations." Wants "vigorous writing that is neither wholly of the academy nor the streets; typed manuscripts." Has published poetry by Diane Glancy, Judith Strasser, Steve Lautermilch, Reeves Kegworth, and Robin Chopman. *Nimrod* is about 190 pages, digest-sized, professionally printed on coated stock, flat-spined, perfect-bound, with full-color glossy cover. Receives about 2,000 submissions/year, accepts 1%. Press run is 3,500 (subscribers, 200 public and university libraries). Subscription: $17.50/year in US, $19 foreign. Sample: $10. "Specific back issues available. Please send check or money order."

How to Submit Submit 5-10 poems at a time. No fax or e-mail submissions. Publishes theme issues. Guidelines and upcoming themes available for SASE, by e-mail, or on website. Responds in up to 3 months. Pays 2 contributor's copies plus reduced cost on additional copies. "Poets should be aware that during the months that the Ruth Hardman Awards Competition is being conducted, reporting time on non-contest manuscripts will be longer."

Contest/Award Offerings The Ruth G. Hardman Award: Pablo Neruda Prize for Poetry offers 1st Prize: $2,000; 2nd Prize: $1,000; plus publication. Entries accepted January 1 through April 30 each year. **Entry fee:** $20, includes 2 issues. Guidelines available for business-sized SASE.

Also Offers Also sponsors the Nimrod/Hardman Awards Workshop, a one-day workshop held annually in October. Cost is about $50. Send SASE for brochure and registration form.

NINETY-SIX PRESS (Specialized: regional/South Carolina)

Furman University, Greenville SC 29613. (864)294-3156. Fax: (864)294-2224. E-mail: bill.rogers@furman.edu. Established 1991. **Contact:** William Rogers and Gilbert Allen, editors.

Book/Chapbook Needs & How to Submit "The name of the press is derived from the old name for the area around Greenville, South Carolina—the Ninety-Six District. The name suggests our interest in the writers, readers, and culture of the region." Publishes 1-2 paperback books of poetry/year. Books are usually 45-70 pages, digest-sized, professionally printed, perfect-bound, with coated stock covers. "We currently accept submissions by invitation only. At some point in the future, however, we hope to be able to encourage submissions by widely published poets who live in South Carolina." For a sample, send $10.

NO EXIT

P.O. Box 454, South Bend IN 46624-0454. Established 1994. **Contact:** Mike Amato, editor.

Magazine Needs *No Exit* is a quarterly forum "for the experimental as well as traditional excellence." Wants "poetry that takes chances in form or content. Form, length, subject matter, and style are open. No poetry that's unsure of why it was written. Particularly interested in long (not long-winded) poems." Has published poetry by David Lawrence, Gregory Fiorini, and Ron Offen. *No Exit* is 32 pages, digest-sized, saddle-stapled, with card cover with art. Accepts 10-15% of the submissions received. Press run is less than 500. Single copy: $5; subscription: $15 ($25 foreign). Sample: $5 postpaid.

How to Submit Submit up to 5 poems ("send more if compelled, but I will stop reading after the fifth"). "No handwritten work, misspellings, colored paper, multiple type faces, typos, or long-winded cover letters and lists of publication credits." Accepts simultaneous submissions; no previously published poems. Time between acceptance and publication can vary from one month to one year. "No themes, but spring issues are devoted to a single poet. Interested writers should submit 24 pages of work. Don't bother unless of highest caliber. There are no other guidelines for single-author issues." Guidelines available for SASE. Responds in up to 3 months. Pays one contributor's copy plus one-year subscription. Acquires first North American serial rights plus right to reprint once in an anthology. "Also looking for articles, critical in nature, on poetry/poets."

Advice "Make your poems sound as if someone wrote them, not as if they just appeared one night under your pillow, a gift from the poetry fairy."

N ⬤ NO TELL MOTEL

E-mail: submit@notellmotel.org. Website: www.notellmotel.org. Established 2004. **Contact:** Reb Livingston, Molly Arden, editors.

Magazine Needs *No Tell Motel* is an online poetry journal featuring a different poet each week and publishing a new poem each weekday. Wants "well-crafted, lively, playful poetry with a hint of decadence. Open to most forms and styles." Has published poetry by Amy Gerstler, Kirsten Kaschock, Jennifer Michael Hecht, Anthony Robinson, Karl Parker, and Shanna Compton. *No Tell Motel* accepts 3-5% of poetry submitted.

How to Submit Submit 5-8 poems at a time. Accepts simultaneous submissions; no previously published poems. Accepts e-mail submissions (pasted into body of message); no disk submissions. Cover letter is preferred. Reads submissions year round. Time between acceptance and publication is 2-5 months. Poems are circulated to an editorial board. Sometimes comments on rejected poems. Guidelines available on website. Responds in 2-6 weeks. Always sends prepublication galleys. No payment. Acquires first rights.

Advice "Please read our submission guidelines and acquaint yourself with the journal before submitting."

✪ ☑ ◎ NOCTURNAL LYRIC, JOURNAL OF THE BIZARRE (Specialized: horror)

P.O. Box 542, Astoria OR 97103. E-mail: nocturnallyric@melodymail.com. Website: www.angelfire.com/ca/nocturnallyric. Established 1987. **Contact:** Susan Moon, editor.

Magazine Needs *Nocturnal Lyric* is an annual journal "featuring bizarre fiction and poetry, primarily by new writers." Wants "poems dealing with the bizarre: fantasy, death, morbidity, horror, gore, etc. Any length. No 'boring poetry.'" Has published poetry by Carrie L. Clark, J. Kevilus, Stan Morner, Richard Geyer, Stephen Kopel, and Linda Rosenkrans. *Nocturnal Lyric* is 40 pages, digest-sized, photocopied, saddle-stapled, with trade ads and staff artwork. Receives about 200 poems/year, accepts about 35%. Press run is 400 (40 subscribers). Single copy: $3 within US, $5 for non-US addresses. Make checks payable to Susan Moon.

How to Submit Submit up to 4 poems at a time. Accepts previously published poems and simultaneous submissions. No e-mail submissions. Seldom comments on rejected poems. Guidelines available in magazine, for SASE, or on website. Responds in up to 6 months. Pays 50¢ "discount on subscription" coupons. Acquires one-time rights.

Advice "Don't follow the trends. We admire the unique."

☑ NOMAD'S CHOIR

% Meander, 30-15 Hobart St., F4H, Woodside NY 11377. Established 1989. **Contact:** Joshua Meander, editor.

Magazine Needs *Nomad's Choir* is a quarterly. Wants "love poems, protest poems, mystical poems, nature poems, poems of humanity, poems with solutions to world problems and inner conflict, poems with hope; simple words, careful phrasing; free verse, rhymed poems, sonnets, half-page parables, myths and legends, song lyrics. No curse words in poems, little or no name-dropping, no naming of consumer products, no 2-page poems, no humor, no bias writing, no poems untitled." Has published poetry by David Lo, Marta Rosario, Tim Divito, and Lily Georgick. *Nomad's Choir* is 12 pages, magazine-sized, typeset, saddle-stapled. Receives about 150 poems/year, accepts 50. Press run is 400; all distributed free. Subscription: $5. Sample: $1.50. Make checks payable to Joshua Meander.

How to Submit Lines/poem: 9 minimum, 30 maximum. Guidelines available for SASE. Responds in 2 months. Pays one contributor's copy.

Advice "Mail 4 poems, each on a different topic. Social commentary with beauty and hope gets first consideration."

$ ◎ NORTH CAROLINA LITERARY REVIEW (Specialized: regional)

Dept. of English, East Carolina University, Greenville NC 27858-4353. (252)328-1537. E-mail: bauer m@mail.ecu.edu. Website: www.ecu.edu/nclr. Established 1992. **Contact:** Margaret Bauer, editor.

• *North Carolina Literary Review* received the CELJ Best Journal Design Award in 1999 and Best New Journal Award in 1994.

Magazine Needs *North Carolina Literary Review* is an annual publication appearing in the summer that "contains articles and other works about North Carolina topics or by North Carolina authors." Wants "poetry by writers currently living in North Carolina, those who have lived in North Carolina, or those using North Carolina for subject matter." Has published poetry by Betty Adcock, James Applewhite, and A.R. Ammons. *North Carolina Literary Review* is 200 pages, magazine-sized. Receives about 250 submissions/year, accepts about 20%. Press run is 1,000 (750 subscribers, 100 libraries, 100 shelf sales); 50 distributed free to contributors. Subscription: $20/2 years, $36/4 years. Sample: $15.

How to Submit Submit 3-5 poems at a time. No e-mail submissions. Cover letter is required. "Submit 2 copies and include SASE or e-mail address for response." Reads submissions August 1 through April 30 only. Time between acceptance and publication is up to one year. Often comments on rejected poems. Guidelines available for SASE, by e-mail, or on website. Responds in 3 months within reading period. Sometimes sends prepublication galleys. Pays with 2-year subscription plus 1-2 contributor's copies. Acquires first or one-time rights. Reviews books of poetry by North Carolina poets in up to 2,000 words, multi-book format. Poets from North Carolina may send books for review consideration. Rarely reviews chapbooks.

◪ ◕ NORTH DAKOTA QUARTERLY

University of North Dakota, Box 7209, Grand Forks ND 58202-7209. E-mail: ndq@und.nodak.edu. Website: www.und.nodak.edu/org/ndq. Established 1910. **Contact:** Robert Lewis, editor.

Magazine Needs *North Dakota Quarterly* is published by the University of North Dakota and includes material related to the arts and humanities—essays, fiction, interviews, poems, and visual art. "We want to see poetry that reflects an understanding not only of the difficulties of the craft, but of the vitality and tact that each poem calls into play." Has published poetry by Edward Kleinschmidt, Alane Rollings, and Robert Wrigley. *North Dakota Quarterly* is about 200 pages, digest-sized, perfect-bound, professionally designed, and often printed with full-color artwork on white card cover. Press run is 850 (650 subscribers). Subscription: $25/year. Sample: $8.

How to Submit Submit 5 poems at a time, typed. No previously published poems or simultaneous submissions. No fax or e-mail submissions. Time between acceptance and publication varies. Responds in up to 6 weeks. Always sends prepublication galleys. Pays one contributor's copy. Acquires first serial rights.

Advice "We look to publish the best fiction, poetry, and essays that, in our estimation, we can. Our tastes and interests are best reflected in what we have been recently publishing, and we suggest that you look at some current numbers."

◕ NORTHEAST; JUNIPER PRESS; JUNIPER BOOKS; CHICKADEE SHORT POEMS SERIES; GIFTS OF THE PRESS

P.O. Box 8037, St. Paul MN 55108-8037. Website: www.ddgbooks.com. Established 1962. **Contact:** Editors.

• "Poets we have published won the Pulitzer Prize, the Posner Poetry Prize, and the Midwest Book Award."

Magazine Needs & How to Submit *Northeast* is an annual literary magazine appearing in February. Has published poetry by Lisel Muller, Alan Broughton, and Bruce Cutler. *Northeast* is digest-sized and saddle-stapled. Subscription: $30/year ($35 for institutions); includes one issue of the magazine, selections from Juniper Books and Chickadees, and some gifts of the press, a total of about 3-5 items. "See our website or send SASE for catalog to order individual items." Sample: $3. No submissions by fax or e-mail. Responds in up to 2 months. Pays 2 contributor's copies.

Book/Chapbook Needs & How to Submit Juniper Press does not accept unsolicited book/chapbook mss.

Advice "Please read us before sending manuscripts. It will aid in your selection of materials to send. If you don't like what we do, please don't submit."

◉ NORTHEAST ARTS MAGAZINE

P.O. Box 4363, Portland ME 04101. Established 1990. **Contact:** Mr. Leigh Donaldson, editor/publisher.

Magazine Needs *Northeast Arts Magazine* is a biannual using poetry, short fiction, essays, reviews, art, and photography that is "honest, clear, with a love of expression through simple language. We maintain a special interest in work that reflects cultural diversity in New England and throughout the world." Has published poetry by Steve Lutrell, Eliot Richman, Elizabeth R. Curry, Bob Begieburg, and Alisa Aran. *Northeast Arts Magazine* is 32 or more pages, digest-sized, professionally printed, with 1-color coated card cover. Accepts 10-20% of submissions. Press run is 500-1,000 (150 subscribers, 75 libraries); 50 distributed to arts organizations. An updated arts information section and feature articles are included. Subscription: $10. Sample: $4.50.

How to Submit Lines/poem: 30 maximum. "A short bio is helpful." Reads submissions November 1 through February 1 only. Guidelines available for SASE. Responds in 3 months. Pays 2 contributor's copies. Acquires first North American serial rights.

◯ NORTHERN STARS MAGAZINE; NORTH STAR PUBLISHING

N17285 Co. Rd. 400, Powers MI 49874. Website: http://hometown.aol.com/Kleiker23/myhomep age/business.html. Established 1997. **Contact:** Beverly Kleikamp, editor.

Magazine Needs *Northern Stars* is published bimonthly and "welcomes submissions of fiction, nonfiction, and poetry on any subject or style. The main requirement is good clean family reading material. Nothing you can't read to your child or your mother. No smut or filth." Has published poetry by Terri Warden, Gary Edwards, Sheila B. Roark, and C.L. Rymer. *Northern Stars Magazine* is 32 pages, magazine-sized, photocopied, saddle-stapled, with cardstock cover. "Send SASE for subscription information." Single copy: $5; subscription: $21. Make checks payable to Beverly Kleikamp or *Northern Stars Magazine*.

How to Submit Submit up to 5 poems at a time. Lines/poem: 25 maximum. "Shorter poems stand a better chance of timely publication." Accepts previously published poems and simultaneous submissions. Cover letter is preferred. "Manuscripts must be typed—please do not submit handwritten material." Often comments on rejected poems. Guidelines available for SASE. "No payment, but nonsubscribers are notified of publication." All rights return to authors on publication.

Chapbook Needs "I also publish chapbooks for an 'affordable' price to the author." Has published *Beholden* by Paul Truttman and *Butterfly Descending Sunlight* by Nancy M. Ryan. Chapbook prices and information available for SASE.

Contest/Award Offerings Sponsors monthly alternating issues contest for poetry and fiction/nonfiction (i.e., poetry contest in March-April issue, fiction/nonfiction in May-June). **Entry fee:** $2.50/poem for non-subscribers, $1/poem for subscribers. **Deadline:** 20th of month preceding publication. Guidelines available for SASE. Publishes an annual chapbook of contest winners and honorable mentions in January. Also sponsors an annual chapbook contest, offering 1st Prize: 50 copies; 2nd Prize: 25 copies; 3rd Prize: 10 copies. Submit 24-page poetry chapbooks only. All copy must be typewritten with name and address at the top of each page. **Entry fee:** $20. **Deadline:** December 31. Winner announced January 30. Guidelines available for SASE.

Also Offers A regular column, "Somewhere In Michigan," featuring people/places/events, etc., tied in with Michigan.

Advice "Keep it clean, short, and interesting."

◙ NORTHWEST REVIEW

369 PLC, University of Oregon, Eugene OR 97403. (541)346-3957. Fax: (541)346-1509. E-mail: jwitte@oregon.uoregon.edu. Website: http://darkwing.uoregon.edu/~nwreview. Established 1957. **Contact:** John Witte, poetry editor.

• Poetry published by *Northwest Review* has been included in *The Best American Poetry*.

Magazine Needs *Northwest Review* "is a triannual publication appearing in May, September, and January. The only criterion for acceptance of material for publication is that of excellence. There are no restrictions on length, style, or subject matter, but we smile on originality." Has published poetry by Alan Dugan, Charles Bukowski, Ted Hughes, Olga Broumas, Gary Snyder, and William Stafford. *Northwest Review* is digest-sized, flat-spined. Receives about 3,500 submissions/year, accepts about 4%. Press run is 1,300 (1,200 subscribers, 600 libraries). Single copy: $8; subscription: $22 (3 issues). Sample: $4.

How to Submit Submit 6-8 poems clearly reproduced. No simultaneous submissions. Accepts submissions by postal mail only. Guidelines available on website. Responds within 3 months. Pays 3 contributor's copies.

Advice "Persist."

▦ ◙ Nthposition

London UK. E-mail: todd@toddswift.com. Website: www.nthposition.com. Established 2002. **Contact:** Todd Swift, poetry editor.

• Readers' poll winner in the 2004 Utne Independent Press Awards.

Magazine Needs *Nthposition* is an eclectic, London-based monthly online journal dedicated to poetry, fiction, and nonfiction "with a weird or innovative edge. *Nthposition* is open to all kinds of poetry—from spoken word to new formalist to linguistically innovative. We also publish political poetry." Does not want poetry from never-before-published authors. Has published poetry by Paul Hoover, Charles Bernstein, Mimi Khalvati, Ruth Fainlight, Bob Holman, and Stephanie Bolster. Receives about 4,000 poems/year, accepts about 10%.

How to Submit Submit 4 poems at a time. No previously published poems or simultaneous submissions. Accepts e-mail submissions (pasted into body of message); no disk submissions. Cover letter is required. "A brief author's bio is appreciated." Reads submissions throughout the year. Time between acceptance and publication is one month. "Poems are read and selected by the poetry editor, who uses his own sense of what makes a poem work online to select." Never comments on rejected poems. Occasionally publishes theme issues. List of upcoming themes available on website. Guidelines available by e-mail or on website. Responds in one week. No pay. Does not request rights.

Also Offers Special theme e-books from time to time, such as *100 Poets Against the War*.

Advice "Never give up; keep writing. Poetry is a life's work."

▢ ◎ NUTHOUSE; TWIN RIVERS PRESS (Specialized: humor)

P.O. Box 119, Ellenton FL 34222. Website: http://hometown.aol.com/Nuthous499/index2.html. Press established 1989, magazine established 1993. **Contact:** Ludwig VonQuirk, editor.

Magazine Needs *Nuthouse*, "your place for humor therapy," appears every 2 months using humor of all kinds, including homespun and political. Wants "humorous verse; virtually all genres considered." Has published poetry by Holly Day, Daveed Garstenstein-Ross, and Don Webb. *Nuthouse* is 12 pages, digest-sized, photocopied from desktop-published originals. Receives about 500 poems/year, accepts about 100. Press run is 100 (50 subscribers). Subscription: $5/4 issues. Sample: $1.25. Make checks payable to Twin Rivers Press.

How to Submit Accepts previously published poems and simultaneous submissions. Time between acceptance and publication is 6 months to one year. Often comments on rejected poems. Responds within one month. Pays one contributor's copy/poem. Acquires one-time rights.

◻ ◎ **THE OAK; THE GRAY SQUIRREL (Specialized: senior citizens); THE ACORN (Specialized: children); THE SHEPHERD (Specialized: religious; inspirational)**

1530 Seventh St., Rock Island IL 61201. (309)788-3980. **Contact:** Betty Mowery, poetry editor.

Magazine Needs & How to Submit *The Oak*, a quarterly established in 1991, is a ''publication for writers, featuring poetry and fiction.'' No restrictions as to types and style, ''but no pornography or love poetry.'' Established in 1991, *The Gray Squirrel* is included in *The Oak* and accepts poetry and fiction from writers 60 years of age and up. Uses more than half of about 100 poems received each year. Press run is 250 (10 libraries). Subscription: $10. Sample: $3. Make all checks payable to *The Oak*. Submit 5 poems at a time. Lines/poem: 35 maximum. ''Include a SASE or manuscripts will not be returned.'' Accepts simultaneous submissions and previously published poems. Responds in one week. ''*The Oak* does not pay in dollars or copies, but you need not purchase to be published.'' Acquires first or second rights.

Magazine Needs & How to Submit *The Acorn*, a quarterly established in 1988, is a ''newsletter for young authors, and teachers or anyone else interested in our young authors.'' Accepts poetry from children in grades K-12. ''Young authors submitting to *The Acorn* should put either age or grade on manuscripts.'' Accepts well over half of submitted mss. Press run is 100 (6 libraries). Subscription: $10. Sample: $3. Make all checks payable to *The Oak*. Submit 5 poems at a time. Lines/poem: 35 maximum. Accepts simultaneous submissions and previously published poems. Responds in one week. ''*The Acorn* does not pay in dollars or copies, but you need not purchase to be published.'' Acquires first or second rights. *The Shepherd*, a quarterly established in 1996, publishes inspirational poetry from all ages. Lines/poem: 35 maximum. ''We want something with a message but not preachy.'' Subscription: $10. Sample: $3. Make all checks payable to *The Oak*. Include SASE with all submissions.

Contest/Award Offerings Sponsors numerous contests. Guidelines available for SASE.

Advice ''Write tight poems with a message; don't write about lost loves or crushes. Study the markets for word limit and subject. Always include SASE, or rejected manuscripts will not be returned. Please make checks for *all* publications payable to *The Oak*.''

⊠ ◰ **OFF THE COAST**

P.O. Box 205, Bristol ME 04539. (207)677-2840. E-mail: arge109@midcoast.com. Website: www.off thecoast.com. Established 1994. **Contact:** George V. Van Deventer, editor.

Magazine Needs *Off the Coast* publishes 3 times/year in January, May, and September. Wants all styles and forms of poetry. Does not want pornography or profanity. Has published poetry by John Balaban, Kate Barnes, Henry Braun, Wesley McNair, Baron Wormser, and Ken Rosen. *Off the Coast* is 68+ pages, digest-sized, copied, perfect-bound, with stock cover with original art. Receives about 350 poems/year, accepts about 80. Press run is 300 (175 subscribers, 6 shelf sales); occasional complimentary copies offered. Single copy: $8; subscription: $25. Make checks payable to *Off the Coast*.

How to Submit Submit 4-6 poems at a time. Lines/poem: prefers 22 maximum. Accepts previously published poems. No e-mail or disk submissions. Cover letter is preferred. ''Put name and address on every page, include SASE.'' Reads submissions year round. Time between acceptance and publication is 2-9 months. Sometimes comments on rejected poems. Guidelines available in magazine or on website. Responds in 4-6 weeks. Pays one contributor's copy. ''The rights to each individual poem and print are retained by each individual artist.'' Reviews books and chapbooks of poetry and other magazines/journals in 800 words. Send materials for review consideration to George V. Van Deventer.

⊠ ◰ ◎ **OFFICE NUMBER ONE (Specialized: form)**

2111 Quarry Rd., Austin TX 78703. Established 1988. **Contact:** Carlos B. Dingus, editor.

Magazine Needs Appearing 2-4 times/year, *Office Number One* is a ''humorous, satirical zine of news information and events from parallel and alternate realities.'' In addition to stories, wants limericks, 3-5-3 or 5-7-5 haiku, and rhymed/metered quatrains. ''Poems should be short (2-12 lines) and make a point. No long rambling poetry about suffering and pathos. Poetry should be technically perfect.'' Accepts poetry written by children, "if it stands on its own." *Office Number One* is 12 pages, magazine-sized, computer-set in 10-pt. type, saddle-stapled, includes ads. Publishes about 40 poems/year. Press run is 2,000 (75 subscribers, 50 shelf sales); 1,600 distributed free locally. Single copy: $1.85; subscription: $8.82/6 issues. Sample: $2.

How to Submit Submit up to 5 pages of poetry at a time. Accepts previously published poems and simultaneous submissions. "Will comment on rejected poems if comment is requested." Occasionally publishes theme issues. List of upcoming themes and guidelines available for SASE. Responds in 2 months. Pays "23¢" and one contributor's copy. Acquires rights for "use in any *Officer Number One* publication."

Advice "Say something that a person can use to change his life."

☆ ◻ THE OLD RED KIMONO

Floyd College, P.O. Box 1864, Rome GA 30162. E-mail: napplega@floyd.edu. Website: www.floyd.edu/ork. Established 1972. **Contact:** Dr. Nancy Applegate, Kimberly Yarborough, and Randie Mayo, poetry editors.

Magazine Needs Appearing annually, *The Old Red Kimono* publishes original, high-quality poetry and fiction. Has published poetry by Walter McDonald, Peter Huggins, Mildred Greear, John Cantey Knight, Kirsten Fox, and Al Braselton. *The Old Red Kimono* is 72 pages, magazine-sized, professionally printed on heavy stock, with colored matte cover with art. Receives about 1,000 submissions/year, accepts about 60-70. Sample: $3.

How to Submit Submit 3-5 poems. Accepts submissions by e-mail (pasted into body of message) and by postal mail. Reads submissions September 1 through March 1 only. Guidelines available for SASE or on website. Responds in 3 months. Pays 2 contributor's copies. Acquires first publication rights.

☆ ◪ ONE TRICK PONY; BANSHEE PRESS

P.O. Box 11186, Philadelphia PA 19136. (215)331-7389. E-mail: lmckee4148@aol.com. Established 1997. **Contact:** Louis McKee, editor.

Magazine Needs *One Trick Pony* is published biannually and contains "poetry and poetry-related reviews and essays (for reviews, essays, interviews, etc.—please query)." Has published poetry by William Heyen, Naomi Shihab Nye, Denise Duhamel, David Kirby, and Michael Waters. *One Trick Pony* is 60 pages, digest-sized, offset printed, saddle-stapled, with glossy cover with art. Receives about 750 poems/year, accepts about 10%. Press run is 400 (more than 150 subscribers, 12 libraries, 150 shelf sales). Single copy: $5; subscription: $10/2 issues. Make checks payable to Louis McKee.

How to Submit Submit 3-6 poems at a time. No simultaneous submissions or previously published poems. Responds in one month. Pays 2 contributor's copies. Acquires first rights. Reviews books and chapbooks of poetry. Send materials for review consideration.

Book/Chapbook Needs Banshee Press publishes one chapbook/year *by invitation only*.

◪ OPEN SPACES

6327 C SW Capitol Hwy., Suite 134, Portland OR 97239. (503)227-5764. Fax: (503)227-3401. E-mail: info@open-spaces.com. Website: www.open-spaces.com. Established 1997. **Contact:** Susan Juve-Hu Bucharest, poetry editor.

Magazine Needs "*Open Spaces* is a quarterly that gives voice to the Northwest on issues that are regional, national, and international in scope. Our readership is thoughtful, intelligent, widely read, and appreciative of ideas and writing of the highest quality. With that in mind, we seek thoughtful, well-researched articles and insightful fiction, reviews, and poetry on a variety of subjects from a number of different viewpoints. Although we take ourselves seriously, we appreciate humor as well. Poetry is presented with care and respect." Has published poetry by Vern Rutsala, Pattiann Rogers, Lou Masson, and William Jolliff. *Open Spaces* is 64 pages, magazine-sized, sheet-fed-printed, with cover art. Press run is 5,000-10,000. Subscription: $25/year. Sample: $10. Make checks payable to Open Spaces Publications, Inc.

How to Submit Submit 3-5 poems at a time. Accepts simultaneous submissions. Accepts submissions by postal mail only; no fax or e-mail submissions. Cover letter is required. Time between acceptance and publication is 2-3 months. Poems are circulated to an editorial board. Seldom comments on rejected poems. Guidelines available on website. Responds in up to 4 months. Payment varies. Reviews books and chapbooks of poetry.

▓ $□ ORBIS: AN INTERNATIONAL QUARTERLY OF POETRY AND PROSE

17 Greenhow Ave., West Kirby, Wirral CH48 5EL United Kingdom. E-mail: carolebaldock@hotmail.com. Established 1968. **Contact:** Carole Baldock, editor.

Magazine Needs *Orbis*, appearing quarterly, is supported by Arts Council England, North West. "We are looking for more work from young people (this includes 20-somethings) and women writers." Features "news, reviews, views, letters, prose, and quite a lot of poetry." *Orbis* is 80 pages, digest-sized, flat-spined, professionally printed, with full-color glossy card cover. Receives "thousands" of submissions/year. Single copy: £4 (£5 overseas, €10, $11); subscription: £15/4 issues (£20 overseas, €30, $36).

How to Submit Submit up to 4 poems by postal mail (one poem/page); enclose SASE (or SAE and 2 IRCs) with *all* correspondence. Accepts e-mail submissions from outside UK only; send no more than 2 poems, pasted into body of message (no attachments). Responds in up to one month. Reviews books and other magazines. Send books for review consideration to Rupert Loydeil, 11 Sylvan Rd., Exeter, Devon EX4 6EW United Kingdom. Send magazines for review consideration to Nessa O'Mahony, 1st Floor Flat, 4 Raglan St., Beaumaris LL58 8BP Wales.

Contest/Award Offerings Prizes in each issue: £50 for featured writer (3-4 poems); £50 Readers' Award for piece receiving the most votes; £50 split among 4 (or more) runners-up.

✪ ⊘ ORCHISES PRESS

P.O. Box 20602, Alexandria VA 22320-1602. E-mail: lathbury@gmu.edu. Website: http://mason.gmu.edu/~rlathbur. Established 1983. **Contact:** Roger Lathbury, poetry editor. **Orchises Press prefers not to receive unsolicited mss.**

⊘ ◎ OSIRIS, AN INTERNATIONAL POETRY JOURNAL/UNE REVUE INTERNATIONALE (Specialized: bilingual; translations)

P.O. Box 297, Deerfield MA 01342-0297. E-mail: amoorhead@deerfield.edu. Established 1972. **Contact:** Andrea Moorhead, poetry editor.

Magazine Needs *Osiris* is a semiannual that publishes contemporary poetry in English, French, and Italian without translation, and in other languages with translation, including Polish, Danish, and German. Wants poetry that is "lyrical, non-narrative, multi-temporal, post-modern, well-crafted. Also looking for translations from non-IndoEuropean languages." Has published poetry by Françoise Hàn (France), George Moore (USA), Flavio Ermini (Italy), Louise Warren (Quebec), Carlos de Oliveira (Portugal), and Ingrid Swanberg (USA). *Osiris* is 48-52 pages, digest-sized, perfect-bound. Press run is 500 (50 subscription copies sent to college and university libraries, including foreign libraries). Receives 200-300 submissions/year, accepts about 12. Single copy: $7.50; subscription: $15. Sample: $3.

How to Submit Submit 4-6 poems at a time. "Poems should be sent by postal mail. Include short bio and SASE with submission. Translators should include a letter of permission from the poet or publisher as well as copies of the original text." Responds in one month. Sometimes sends prepublication galleys. Pays 5 contributor's copies.

Advice "It is always best to look at a sample copy of a journal before submitting work, and when you do submit work, do it often and do not get discouraged. Try to read poetry and support other writers."

OTHER VOICES

P.O. Box 52059, 8210-109 St., Edmonton AB T6G 2T5 Canada. E-mail: info@othervoices.ca. Website: www.othervoices.ca. Established 1988. **Contact:** Poetry Collective.

Magazine Needs *Other Voices* appears 2 times/year in the summer and winter. "We are devoted to the publication of quality literary writing—poetry, fiction, nonfiction; also reviews and artwork. We encourage submissions by new and established writers. Our only desire for poetry is that it is good! We encourage submissions by women and members of minorities, but we will consider everyone's. We never publish popular/sentimental greeting-card-type poetry or anything sexist, racist, or homophobic." Has published poetry by A. Mary Murphy, Myrna Garanis, Sean Howard, Rita Braga, and Kate Marshall Flaherty. *Other Voices* is 100-120 pages, 21½×14cm, professionally printed, perfect-bound, with color cover, includes ads. Receives about 800 poems/year, accepts 4%. Press run is 500 (330 subscribers, 7 libraries, 60 shelf sales). Subscription: $18/year in Canada, $26 US, $28 overseas. Sample: $8. (All prices in Canadian dollars.)

How to Submit Submit 2-6 poems at a time. Include SAE with IRC. "Please limit your submissions to a maximum of 6 pages of poetry, and send only one submission every 6 months." No previously published poems or simultaneous submissions. Accepts submissions by postal mail only. Cover letter is preferred. "Please include short bio. Phone numbers, fax numbers, and e-mail addresses are helpful." **Spring submission deadline:** March 1; **fall deadline:** September 1 (received, not postmarked, by). Time between acceptance and publication is one month. "Poems are read and assessed independently by 3 poetry editors. After the deadline, we gather and 'haggle' over which poems to accept." Seldom comments on rejected poems. Guidelines available for SASE (or SAE with IRC) or on website. Responds in up to 6 months. Pays 2 contributor's copies and one-year subscription, or 4 contributor's copies. Acquires first North American serial rights. Reviews books of poetry in 1,000 words, single- or double-book format. Send materials for review consideration to Editorial Collective.

Contest/Award Offerings "We typically hold one contest per year, but the time, fees, and theme vary. Check our website for details."

Advice "Please take note of our September and March deadlines. If you just miss a deadline, it could take up to 6 months for a reply."

OUTRIDER PRESS

937 Patricia Lane, Crete IL 60417-1362. (708)672-6630. Fax: (708)672-5820. E-mail: outriderpr@aol.com. Website: www.outriderpress.com. Established 1988. **Contact:** Whitney Scott, senior editor.

Book/Chapbook Needs Outrider Press publishes 1-3 novels/anthologies/chapbooks annually in September. Wants "poetry dealing with the terrain of the human heart and plotting inner journeys; growth and grace under pressure. No bag ladies, loves-that-never-were, please." Has published poetry by David T. Lloyd, Albert DeGenova, Vivian Shipley, Michele Cooper, Maureen Connolly, and Lyn Lifshin. Anthologies are 230-260 pages, digest-sized, attractively printed, perfect-bound, with glossy card covers, $15.95 to $17.95.

How to Submit Submit 3-4 poems at a time with SASE. Include name, address, phone/fax number, and e-mail address on every poem. Accepts simultaneous submissions, if specified. Accepts submissions on disk, by e-mail (pasted into body of message), and by postal mail. Cover letter is preferred. Guidelines and upcoming themes available for SASE or by e-mail. Responds to queries in one month, to mss in 2 months. Pays one copy.

Also Offers Outrider publishes a themed anthology annually in September, with cash prizes for best poetry and short fiction. Submit up to 8 poems, no longer than 24 lines in length. **Reading fee:** $16, $12 for Tallgrass Writers Guild members. Guidelines available for SASE. **Deadline:** February 28, 2006. 2006 theme: "Vacations—The Good, The Bad, and The Ugly" (can include spiritual as well as physical). The press is affiliated with the Tallgrass Writers Guild, an international organization open to all who support equality of voices in writing. Annual membership fee: $45. Information available for SASE or on website.

Advice "We look for visceral truths expressed without compromise, coyness, or cliché. Go for the center of the experience. Pull no punches."

⚒ $◙ "OVER THE BACK FENCE" MAGAZINE (Specialized: regional/Ohio)

14 S. Paint St., Suite 169, P.O. Box 756, Chillicothe OH 45601. (740)772-2165. Fax: (740)773-7626. E-mail: backfenc@bright.net. Website: www.pantherpublishing.com/index.html. Established 1994. **Contact:** Sarah Williamson, managing editor.

Magazine Needs A quarterly regional magazine "serving 38 counties in southern Ohio, *Over The Back Fence*' has a wholesome, neighborly style that is appealing to readers from young adults to seniors." Wants rhyming or free-verse poetry; open to subject matter, "but seasonal works well"; friendly or inspirational work. "Since most of our readers are not poets, we want something simple and likeable by the general public. No profanity or erotic subject matter, please." The magazine is 68 pages, printed on high-gloss paper, saddle-stapled, includes ads. Receives less than 200 poems/year, accepts about 4-10. Press run is 15,000 (about 5,000 subscribers in Southern Ohio, 40% shelf sales). Single copy: $2.95; subscription: $9.97/year. Sample: $4. Make checks payable to Panther Publishing, Inc.

How to Submit Submit up to 4 poems at a time. Lines/poem: 24 maximum. Accepts previously published poems and simultaneous submissions, "if identified as such." Cover letter is preferred. Computer disk submissions should be saved in an ASCII text format or Microsoft Word file. Disk should be labeled with your name, address, daytime phone number, name of format, and name of file. Time between acceptance and publication is 6-12 months. Seldom comments on rejected poems. Guidelines available for SASE or on website. Responds in up to 3 months. Pays 10¢/word, $25 minimum. Acquires one-time North American print rights.

Advice "While we truly appreciate the professional poet, most of our published poetry comes from beginners or amateurs. We strive for reader response and solicit poetry contributions through the magazine."

◓ OVER THE TRANSOM

825 Bush St. #203, San Francisco CA 94108. (415)928-3965. E-mail: jsh619@earthlink.net. Established 1997. **Contact:** Jonathan Hayes, editor.

Magazine Needs *Over The Transom*, a free publication of art and literature, appears 2 times/year. Open to all styles of poetry. "We look for the highest quality poetry that best fits the issue." Has published poetry by A.D. Winans, Marie Kazalia, W.B. Keckler, John Grey, Alan Catlin, and Donna Kuhn. *Over The Transom* is 32 pages, magazine-sized, saddle-stapled, with cardstock cover. Receives about 1,000 poems/year, accepts about 5%. Press run is 700 (100 subscribers); 500 distributed free to cafes, bookstores, and bars. Single copy: free. Sample: $3. Make checks payable to Jonathan Hayes.

How to Submit Submit 5 poems at a time. Accepts previously published poems and simultaneous submissions. Accepts e-mail submissions; no fax or disk submissions. Must include a SASE. Reads submissions all year. Time between acceptance and publication is 2-6 months. Never comments on rejected poems. Occasionally publishes theme issues. Guidelines available for SASE or by e-mail. Responds in 2 months. Sometimes sends prepublication galleys. Pays one contributor's copy. Acquires first rights.

Advice "Editors have differing tastes, so don't be upset by rejection. Always send a SASE for response."

ℕ ◓ ◙ OVERTHROW (Specialized: style/Parablism; religious/Christian)

P.O. Box 7868, Gurnee IL 60031-7868. E-mail: parablism@prodigy.net. Established 2004. **Contact:** Douglas J. Ogurek, editor.

Magazine Needs *Overthrow*, a newsletter/journal appearing 3 times/year, features poems, news, essays, and artwork "relating to the literary movement known as 'Parablism.' Form is up to the writer but must support content. Every poem *must* adhere to the Parameters of Parablism: 1) seize and hold attention; 2) achieve universal understanding (including by children); 3) impress the masses and the experts; 4) tell a **secular** story (on the surface); 5) get to the point (500 words or fewer); 6) reinforce a Biblical verse (below the surface)." Does not want "any poetry that the typical American would find boring, unclear, or sappy." *Overthrow* is 4-10 pages, magazine-sized, laser-printed on high-quality yellow paper. Single copy: $7; subscription: $12. Make checks payable to Douglas J. Ogurek.

How to Submit Submit 1-3 poems at a time. Lines/poem: 500 words or fewer. Accepts previously published poems and simultaneous submissions. Accepts disk submissions; no e-mail submissions. Cover letter and SASE required. "Cover letter should include: 1) Biblical verse that poem reinforces; 2) statement detailing why author chose particular verse; 3) what verse means to author; and 4) how parable-poem reinforces meaning of verse." Reads submissions year round. Time between acceptance and publication is 4-6 months. Poems are circulated to an editorial board. Sometimes comments on rejected poems. "Before submitting, **must** send $7 postage and handling for introductory package including brochure, submission guidelines, sample newsletter, and audio cassette explaining Parablism philosophy." Responds in 2-4 months. Sometimes sends prepublication galleys. Pays 5 contributor's copies. Acquires first rights.

Advice "Too many poets neglect the general public with cryptic, overly sentimental works drowned in detail. The Parablistic poet fulfills Christ's two great commands (i.e., love God, love thy neighbor) by writing clear, action-packed story-poems that reinforce Biblical verses to the largest possible audience. Imagine reading your poem to a crowd at a zoo's dolphin show. Then show it to an expert in poetry. What will it take for all of them to understand and enjoy it?"

⭐ ◙ OXFORD MAGAZINE

856 Bachelor Hall, Miami University, Oxford OH 45056. (513)529-1274. E-mail: oxmag@muohio.edu. Website: http://oxmag.muohio.edu. Established 1984. **Contact:** Poetry Editor. Editor: Christopher Michel.

• Work published in *Oxford Magazine* has been included in the *Pushcart Prize* anthology.

Magazine Needs *Oxford Magazine* is an entirely online magazine. "New editions appear on our website annually (in May). We are open in terms of form, content, and subject matter. We have eclectic tastes, ranging from New Formalism to Language poetry to Nuyorican poetry." Has published poetry by Eve Shelnutt, Denise Duhamel, and Walter McDonald.

How to Submit Submit 3-5 poems at a time. Accepts simultaneous submissions; no previously published poems. Accepts submissions by postal mail, on disk, and by e-mail (pasted into body of message or as MS Word attachment). Cover letter is preferred. Reads submissions September 1 through December 31. No payment. Acquires one-time rights.

Advice "We're looking for poetry that shows an attention to craft as well as subject matter. Choice of form—be it a villanelle, an acrostic, a prose poem, or something you've made up—affects the way the poem is received. The best poems tie their subject and delivery together, in a way that equals more than the sum of their parts."

◙ P.D.Q. (POETRY DEPTH QUARTERLY)

5836 North Haven Dr., North Highlands CA 95660. (916)331-3512. E-mail: poetdpth@aol.com. Website: www.poetrydepthquarterly.com Established 1995. **Contact:** Debbie Warrick, publisher.

• "Joyce Odam, our poetry editor, submits nominations for the Pushcart Prize."

Magazine Needs Published quarterly, *P.D.Q.* wants "original poetry that clearly demonstrates an understanding of craft. All styles accepted." Does not want "poetry that is overtly religious, erotic, inflammatory, or demeans the human spirit." Has published poetry by Jane Blue, Taylor Graham, James Mackie, Carol Hamilton, B.Z. Niditch, and Cleo Griffith. *P.D.Q.* is 35-60 pages, digest-sized, coated, saddle-stapled, with glossy color cover. Receives 1,800-2,000 poems/year, accepts about 10%. Press run is 200 (5 subscribers are libraries). Single copy: $5.50; subscription: $20/year, $38/2 years, $56/3 years (add $12/year for foreign subscriptions). Make checks payable to Poetry Depth Quarterly.

Salmon Publishing

Still swimming upstream

O n the west coast of Ireland in County Clare, amidst the natural beauty of the Burren and the 800-foot Cliffs of Moher, lies one of the success stories of contemporary poetry publishing. Salmon Publishing's tale is one of intrepid entrepreneurship, a fierce love of poetry, and a dedication to the idea of giving more women poets a voice.

Arkansas native Jessie Lendennie is the co-founder and managing director of Salmon Publishing, which celebrates its 25th anniversary in 2006. She and designer Siobhan Hutson, who has worked with Lendennie for 15 years, maintain an impressive catalog of poetry titles, as well as one of the publishing world's best websites (www.salmonpoetry.com).

After spending her childhood in Arkansas and Los Angeles, Lendennie moved around the United States before settling in New York for four years. In 1970, she left the U.S. for London, England, where, over the next decade, she obtained her B.A. in philosophy as well as a teaching degree, worked at the Poetry Society in London for a year and a half, and saw her own poetry published.

In 1981, Lendennie married a Welshman of Irish extraction, and they made the decision to move to Ireland. After surveying the scene in the early 1980s, they settled in Galway City on Ireland's west coast.

"We didn't want to be in a big city," Lendennie remembers. "After New York and London, I was more than ready for a quiet life. Galway was smallish and quaint. We joined a writing workshop, which had just started up at Galway University. Ireland was still pretty poor at that time, and most of the young university graduates were leaving; nevertheless, the workshop was very strong and motivational. After a month or so, we all decided to publish a broadsheet [a newspaper-like publication] of our work. This lead, after a little while, to a literary journal, *The Salmon*, and my ex-husband and I became chief editors." The journal's name comes from the Salmon of Knowledge in Celtic mythology.

Asked why she did not choose to set up shop in Dublin, Ireland's legendary historic (and notoriously vicious) literary capital, Lendennie responds, "Because there was very little going on for writers outside Dublin; what we were doing was very important and got a lot of notice. Publishing books was the next step, and it had become really clear to me that Irish women poets weren't represented as they should have been. That became a kind of campaign of mine.

"Also, we wanted to offer a chance of publication to poets outside Dublin, and focused at first on poets in the West of Ireland. Salmon Publishing's first books were by Eva Bourke and Rita Ann Higgins. *The Salmon* literary journal had a 50-50 ratio of men to women, and our initial books were mainly by women poets." That's something of which Lendennie was, and still is, very proud.

After 14 years in Galway, Lendennie moved Salmon Publishing to the rural countryside of County Clare—a place, she says, that "really suits Salmon" and offers a tranquil oasis from the harried pace of Ireland's economic boom, known as the "Celtic Tiger."

"Salmon was, by reputation, very successful," says Lendennie, "but I was stressed and in debt because I was trying to do too much; and it all became too hectic for me: publishing too many books with too little money. As Galway was growing, I was more and more in need of another quiet place.

"I was lucky to find this spot, near the Cliffs, before house prices began to shoot up. Among the many good things technology offers is the possibility of publishing from anywhere, as long as you have a computer. Everything except printing can be done here. Siobhan typesets and designs the books and maintains the website all from the office in my house. We send the files for printing to our printer in Latvia. Yes, *Latvia*."

Ireland's reputation for producing some of the leading poets of the 20th century, such as William Butler Yeats, Patrick Kavanagh, Louis MacNeice, and Seamus Heaney, is well established, but her women poets were not well known. Lendennie saw this as a problem and resolved to amend what she viewed as an oversight.

"When Salmon started," Lendennie recalls, "there just wasn't a lot going on. Women poets weren't tuned in to having their work taken seriously. I think this relates to the idea that Irish poetry was somehow precious and the province of the geniuses and academics (there's still a stand of that here). Yes, there were women publishing (as we found out with *The White Page*), but there wasn't an open literary climate. The women's movement hit Ireland in the 1970s, and there began a slow opening up to women's creativity. Salmon tapped into that."

Salmon's *The White Page/An Bhileog Bhán: Twentieth Century Irish Women Poets* was edited by the poet Joan McBreen and published in 1999 (a new edition will be released in 2005). It's perhaps the most comprehensive collection of contemporary Irish women poets available.

"*The White Page* is unique, and we are extremely proud of having published it. Everyone was amazed at the number of women who had published a volume of poetry between 1910 and 1999 (106 poets). However, most of these were published after 1986; and of those, the majority had been published by Salmon, so they had a lot more encouragement than women in earlier years. We are so glad to be able to highlight the work of the women who braved the status quo in the early part of the century."

While there seems to be a strong focus on Irish women poets at Salmon, there's an amazing diversity in their catalog of both accomplished and new poets from around the world. According to Lendennie, this fits into the overall scheme.

"The international diversity of our list is very much part of how I see Salmon. Almost one third of the books we publish are by American, Canadian, and British poets. We've published Adrienne Rich (a collection of poems spanning 40 years), Ray Bradbury, Carol Ann Duffy, R.T. Smith, Marvin Bell, Richard Tillinghast, Patricia Monaghan, Ethna McKiernan, and Ron Houchin, to name just a few. I'd love to publish a lot more European poets and minority poets. Future titles will definitely be a mixture of Irish and a growing list of international poets. Poetry thrives on diversity."

Over the years, Salmon has introduced a number of outstanding talents who have gone on to international acclaim, such as Rita Ann Higgins, Mary O'Malley, and Joan McBreen. When asked if there were any new "stars" on the horizon, Lendennie could hardly contain her enthusiasm.

"There's Mary O'Donaghue, whose *Tulle* won our first manuscript competition [the Salmon Poetry Publication Prize, which is on hold at the moment] and has sold and been reviewed extremely well; Jude Nutter, widely acclaimed before and after her first collection, *Pictures of the Afterlife*; Alan Jude Moore, who won our second competition with *Black State Cars*; Kevin Higgins, dynamic Galway poet; Mike Begal, American poet who made a splash when he lived in Galway; Emily Wall, Alaskan; Melanie Francis, Canadian . . . oh, and on and on!"

Lendennie fully grasps how significant a role the Internet has played in Salmon's survival.

"The Internet has been essential to our growth. A real boon! In the last five years or so, Irish bookshops have become more and more commercial, and poetry doesn't have the exposure it used to have. A few years ago we placed at least ten copies of each of our new books in around seventy Irish bookshops; now we're 'lucky' to get two copies of each new title placed. This is the same for all the literary presses here, and is a source of much frustrated discussion. I do think that 'literary Ireland' should serve its contemporary poets better.

"With the Internet, there's the thrill of selling a book to someone who would never have seen it without our website. We're also proud of the fact that we're very high on search engines, primarily Google. If you do a search for the word Salmon, we come up in the first ten results (out of over seven million hits)."

Besides its online bookshop, the Salmon Poetry website provides a wealth of information. Visitors will find helpful hints to assist young writers in navigating their way through the vicissitudes of the publishing world, as well as workshops and literary links. When asked if she sees this as part of the Salmon mission, Lendennie remarks, "Absolutely. I want to spend more time at this, as well."

Is there one piece of advice she would like to give fledgling poets? "Well, there's a lot, but what comes immediately to mind: Read the work of other poets. Learn to positively critique your work. If you're sure that your work, as art, is worthy of your aspirations, persevere!"

—Barney F. McClelland

Barney F. McClelland has published numerous short stories, articles, and poems on both sides of the Atlantic, in such publications as *Acorn* (Dublin Writers Group), *Oxford Magazine*, and *The New Formalist*. His poetry chapbooks have been published by An Cailleach Press, KOTA Press, and Seaweed Sideshow Circus. He currently works as a freelance writer and editor in Cincinnati, Ohio.

How to Submit Submit 3-5 poems of any length, "typewritten and presented exactly as you would like them to appear," maximum 52 characters/line (including spaces), with name and address on every page. All submissions require SASE (or SAE with IRC) and cover letter with 3- to 10-line bio. "Manuscripts without SASE or sufficient postage will not be read or returned." No previously published poems or simultaneous submissions. "No download submissions." Accepts e-mail submissions when sent to the publisher, *not to the editor*; include legal name and postal address with each page of poetry. Guidelines available for SASE, by e-mail, or on website. Responds in 3 months. Pays one contributor's copy.

Advice "Read the contemporary poetry publications. Read, read, read. Spell-check before submission. Always offer your best work."

⬛ $⬜ PACIFIC COAST JOURNAL

P.O. Box 56, Carlsbad CA 92018. E-mail: paccoastj@frenchbreadpublications.com. Website: www.frenchbreadpublications.com/pcj. Established 1992. **Contact:** Stillson Graham, editor.

Magazine Needs *Pacific Coast Journal* is an "unprofessional quarterly literary magazine. Whatever you think that means, go with it." Wants "off beat and off-beat. Ask the question 'Why is it poetry?'" Has published poetry by B.Z. Niditch, Lucinda J. Garthwaite, and Gary Hill. *Pacific Coast*

Journal is 40 pages, digest-sized, photocopied, saddle-stapled, with card stock cover. Receives 400-500 poems/year, accepts about 5-10%. Press run is 200 (100 subscribers). Single copy: $3; subscription: $12. Sample: $2.50.

How to Submit Submit up to 6 poems or 12 pages at a time. Accepts simultaneous submissions; no previously published poems. No e-mail submissions; e-mail queries OK. Cover letter is preferred. Encourages the inclusion of e-mail address in lieu of SASE for response. Time between acceptance and publication is up to 18 months. Seldom comments on rejected poems. Guidelines available for SASE or by e-mail. Responds in 9 months. Pays one contributor's copy. Acquires one-time rights.

Advice "Our society is all about reactions because a real objective reality is no longer possible. Evoke and invoke."

$ PAINTED BRIDE QUARTERLY

Rutgers University-Camden, English Dept.-Armitage Hall, 311 N. 5th St., Camden NJ 08102. E-mail: pbq@camden.rutgers.edu. Website: www.webdelsol.com/pbq/. Established 1973. **Contact:** Poetry Editors.

Magazine Needs "*Painted Bride Quarterly* aims to be a leader among little magazines published by and for independent poets and writers nationally. We have no specifications or restrictions. We'll look at anything." Has published poetry by Robert Bly, Charles Bukowski, S.J. Marks, and James Hazen. *Painted Bride Quarterly* is published quarterly online with one hardcopy anthology printed annually. Anthology: $15.

How to Submit Submit up to 5 poems, any length, typed; only original, unpublished work. No e-mail submissions. "Submissions should include a short bio." Time between acceptance and publication is 6-9 months. Seldom comments on rejected poems. Occasionally publishes theme issues. Guidelines and themes available on website. Pays one-year subscription, one half-priced contributor's copy, and $5/accepted piece. Publishes reviews of poetry books. "We also occasionally publish critical essays."

Contest/Award Offerings Sponsors an annual poetry contest and a chapbook competition. **Entry fee** required for both. Send SASE for details.

PARADOXISM; XIQUAN PUBLISHING HOUSE; PARADOXISM ASSOCIATION (Specialized: form/style—avant-garde, experimental)

University of New Mexico, Gallup NM 87301. E-mail: smarand@unm.edu. Website: www.gallup.u nm.edu/ ~ smarandache/a/paradoxism.htm. Established 1990. **Contact:** Florentin Smarandache, editor.

Magazine Needs *Paradoxism* is an annual journal of "avant-garde poetry, experiments, poems without verses, literature beyond the words, anti-language, non-literature and its literature, as well as the sense of the non-sense; revolutionary forms of poetry. Paradoxism, a 1980s movement of anti-totalitarian protest, is based on excessive use of antitheses, antinomies, contradictions, paradoxes in creation." Wants "avant-garde poetry, 1-2 pages, any subject, any style (lyrical experiments). No classical, fixed forms." Has published poetry by Paul Georgelin, Mircea Monu, Ion Rotaru, Michéle de LaPlante, and Claude LeRoy. *Paradoxism* is 52 pages, digest-sized, offset-printed, with soft cover. Press run is 500. "It is distributed to its collaborators, U.S. and Canadian university libraries, and the Library of Congress as well as European, Chinese, Indian, and Japanese libraries."

How to Submit No previously published poems or simultaneous submissions. Do not submit mss in the summer. "We do not return published or unpublished poems or notify the author of date of publication." Responds in up to 3 weeks. Pays one contributor's copy.

Book/Chapbook Needs & How to Submit Xiquan Publishing House also publishes 2 poetry paperbacks and 1-2 chapbooks/year, including translations. "The poems must be unpublished and must meet the requirements of the Paradoxism Association." Responds to queries in 2 months, to mss in up to 3 weeks. Pays 50 author's copies. Sample e-books available on website at www.gallup.unm. edu/ ~ smarandache/ebooksliterature.htm.

Advice "We mostly receive traditional or modern verse, but not avant-garde (very different from any previously published verse). We want anti-literature and its literature, style of the non-style, poems without poems, non-words and non-sentence poems, very upset free verse, intelligible unintelligible language, impersonal texts personalized, transformation of the abnormal to the normal. Make literature from everything; make literature from nothing!''

⚂ PARNASSUS LITERARY JOURNAL

P.O. Box 1384, Forest Park GA 30298-1384. (404)366-3177. Established 1975. **Contact:** Denver Stull, editor.

Magazine Needs ''Our sole purpose is to promote poetry and to offer an outlet where poets may be heard. We welcome well-constructed poetry, but ask that you keep it uplifting, and free of language that might be offensive to one of our readers. We are open to all poets and all forms of poetry, including Oriental.'' No erotica or translations. Has published poetry by B.Z. Niditch, TK Splake, Diane Webster, Jean Calkins, and Louis Cautoni. *Parnassus Literary Journal*, published 3 times/year, is photocopied from typescript, saddled-stapled, with colored card cover. Receives about 1,500 submissions/year, accepts 350. Press run is 200 (150 subscribers, 5 libraries). Circulation includes Japan, England, Greece, India, Korea, Germany, and Netherlands. Single copy: $7 US and Canada, $9.50 overseas; subscription: $18 US and Canada, $25 overseas. Sample: $3. Offers 20% discount to schools, libraries, and for orders of 5 copies or more. Make checks or money orders payable to Denver Stull.

How to Submit Submit up to 3 poems. Lines/poem: 24 maximum. ''Include #10 SASE. Submissions received with postage due will be returned unread. Only one poem per page (haiku excepted).'' Include name and address on each page of ms. ''I am dismayed at the haphazard manner in which work is often submitted. I have a number of poems in my file containing no name and/or address. Simply placing your name and address on your envelope is not enough.'' Accepts previously published poems and simultaneous submissions. Cover letter including something about the writer is preferred. ''Definitely'' comments on rejected poems. ''We do not respond to submissions or queries not accompanied by SASE.'' Guidelines available for SASE or in magazine. Responds within one week. ''We regret that the ever-rising costs of publishing forces us to ask that contributors either subscribe to the magazine or purchase a copy of the issue in which their work appears.'' All rights remain with the author.

Advice ''Write about what you know. Read your work aloud. Does it make sense? Rewrite, rewrite, rewrite.''

⭐ $⚂ PARNASSUS: POETRY IN REVIEW; POETRY IN REVIEW FOUNDATION

205 W. 89th St., #8F, New York NY 10024-1835. (212)362-3492. Fax: (212)875-0148. Website: www.parnassuspoetry.com. Established 1972. **Contact:** Herbert Leibowitz, poetry editor.

Magazine Needs *Parnassus* provides ''comprehensive and in-depth coverage of new books of poetry, including translations from foreign poetry. We publish poems and translations on occasion, but we solicit all poetry. Poets invited to submit are given all the space they wish; the only stipulation is that the style be non-academic.'' Has published work by Alice Fulton, Eavan Boland, Mary Karr, Debora Greger, William Logan, Seamus Heaney, and Rodney Jones. Has 1,250 subscribers (550 are libraries). Subscription: $24/year for individuals, $46/year for libraries.

How to Submit Not open to unsolicited poetry. However, unsolicited essays are considered. In fact, this is an exceptionally rich market for thoughtful, insightful, non-academic essay-reviews of contemporary collections. It is strongly recommended that writers study the magazine before submitting. Multiple submissions ''disliked.'' Cover letter is required. Upcoming themes available for SASE. Responds to essay submissions within 10 weeks (response takes longer during the summer). Pays $25-250 plus 2 gift subscriptions—contributors can also take one themselves. Editor comments on rejected poems—''from one paragraph to 2 pages.'' Send for a sample copy (prices of individual issues can vary) to get a feel for the critical acumen needed to place here.

Advice ''Contributors are urged to subscribe to at least one literary magazine. There is a pervasive ignorance of the cost of putting out a magazine and no sense of responsibility for supporting one.''

⊠ ✑ **PARTING GIFTS; MARCH STREET PRESS**
3413 Wilshire, Greensboro NC 27408. E-mail: rbixby@aol.com. Website: www.marchstreetpress.c om. Established 1987. **Contact:** Robert Bixby, editor.
Magazine Needs *Parting Gifts* is published biannually in July and November. "I want to see everything. I'm a big fan of Jim Harrison, C.K. Williams, Amy Hempel, and Janet Kauffman." Has published poetry by Eric Torgersen, Lyn Lifshin, Elizabeth Kerlikowske, and Russell Thorburn. *Parting Gifts* is 72 pages, digest-sized, photocopied, with colored matte card cover. Press run is 200. Subscription: $18. Sample: $9.
How to Submit Submit in groups of 3-10 with SASE. Accepts simultaneous submissions; no previously published poems. "I like a cover letter because it makes the transaction more human. Best time to submit manuscripts is early in the year." Guidelines available for SASE or on website. Responds in 2 weeks. Sometimes sends prepublication galleys. Pays one contributor's copy.
Book/Chapbook Needs & How to Submit March Street Press publishes chapbooks. **Reading fee:** $20.
Advice "Read our online archives."

⊠ ✑ **PASSAGES NORTH; ELINOR BENEDICT PRIZE**
English Dept., 1401 Presque Isle Ave., Northern Michigan University, Marquette MI 49855. (906)227-1203. E-mail: passages@nmu.edu. Website: http://myweb.nmu.edu/~passages. Established 1979. **Contact:** Austin Hummell, poetry editor. Editor-in-Chief: Kate Myers Hanson.
Magazine Needs *Passages North*, an annual magazine appearing in spring, contains short fiction, poetry, creative nonfiction, essays, and interviews. "The magazine publishes quality work by established and emerging writers." Has published poetry by Jim Daniels, Jack Driscoll, Gabriel Gudding, Ron Rash, Pamela McClure, and Ricardo Pau-Llosa. *Passages North* is 250 pages. Circulation is at 1,000 "and growing." Single copy: $13; subscription: $13/year, $23/2 years. Sample (back issue): $3.
How to Submit Submit 3-6 poems, typed single-spaced. "Poems over 100 lines seldom published." Accepts simultaneous submissions. Time between acceptance and publication is 6 months. Reads submissions September through May only. Responds in 2 months. Pays 2 contributor's copies.
Contest/Award Offerings Sponsors the Elinor Benedict Prize in poetry. Details available for SASE or by e-mail.

$ ☻ ◎ **PASSEGGIATA PRESS (Specialized: ethnic; regional/non-Western; translations; women/feminism)**
420 W. 14th St., Pueblo CO 81003. (719)544-1038. Fax: (719)544-7911. E-mail: passegpress@cs.c om. Established 1973. **Contact:** Margaret Herdeck, editor. Publisher: Donald E. Herdeck.
Book/Chapbook Needs "Published poets only welcomed, and only non-European and non-American poets . . . We publish literature by creative writers from the non-Western world (Africa, the Middle East, the Caribbean, and Asia/Pacific)—poetry by non-Western writers only, or good translations of such poetry if original language is Arabic, French, African vernacular, etc." Has published *An Ocean of Dreams* by Mona Saudi, *Sky-Break* by Lyubomir Levchev, *The Right to Err* by Nina Iskreuko, and *The Journey of Barbarus* by Ottó Orbán. Also publishes anthologies and criticisms focused on relevant themes.
How to Submit Query first, with 4-5 sample poems and a bio with publication credits. Responds to queries in one month, to submissions (if invited) in 1-2 weeks. Always sends prepublication galleys. Offers 7.5% royalty contract (5% for translator). Acquires worldwide English rights. Send SASE for catalog to buy samples.

⊠ ✑ **PATERSON LITERARY REVIEW; ALLEN GINSBERG POETRY AWARDS; THE PATERSON POETRY PRIZE; THE PATERSON PRIZE FOR BOOKS FOR YOUNG PEOPLE; THE POETRY CENTER AT PASSAIC COUNTY COMMUNITY COLLEGE**
Poetry Center, Passaic County Community College, Cultural Affairs Dept., 1 College Blvd., Paterson NJ 07505-1179. (973)684-6555. Fax: (973)684-5843. E-mail: mgillan@pccc.edu. Website: www.pcc

c.edu/poetry. Established 1979. **Contact:** Maria Mazziotti Gillan, editor/executive director.

- The Passaic County Community College Poetry Center Library has an extensive collection of contemporary poetry and seeks small press contributions to help keep it abreast.

Magazine Needs & How to Submit A wide range of activities pertaining to poetry are conducted by the Passaic County Community College Poetry Center, including the annual *Paterson Literary Review*. Wants poetry of "high quality; clear, direct, powerful work." Has published poetry by Diane di Prima, Ruth Stone, Marge Piercy, and Laura Boss. *Paterson Literary Review* is 320 pages, magazine-sized, professionally printed, saddle-stapled, with glossy 2-color card cover. Press run is 1,000 (100 subscribers, 50 libraries). Sample: $10. Submit up to 5 poems at a time. Lines/poem: 100 maximum. Accepts simultaneous submissions. Reads submissions December through March only. Responds within one year. Pays one contributor's copy. Acquires first rights.

Contest/Award Offerings 1) **The Allen Ginsberg Poetry Awards** competition offers annual prizes of $1,000, $200, and $100. All winning poems, honorable mentions, and editor's choice poems will be published in *Paterson Literary Review*. Winners will be asked to participate in a reading that will be held in the Paterson Historic District. **Entry fee:** $15 (includes subscription to *PLR*). **Deadline:** April 1. Guidelines available for SASE or on website. 2) **The Paterson Poetry Prize** of $1,000 is awarded annually to a book of poems (48 or more pages) published in the previous year. The winner will be asked to participate in an awards ceremony and to give a reading at The Poetry Center. **Entry fee:** none; books entered in competition will be donated to The Poetry Center. **Deadline:** February 1. Guidelines and application form available for SASE or on website. 3) **The Paterson Prize for Books for Young People** awards $500 to one book in each of 3 categories: Pre-K-Grade 3; Grades 4-6; Grades 7-12. Books must be published in the previous year and be submitted by the publishers. The authors will be asked to participate in an awards ceremony and to give a reading at The Poetry Center. **Entry fee:** non; books entered in competition will be donated to The Poetry Center. **Deadline:** March 15. Guidelines and application for available for SASE or on website.

Also Offers Also publishes *The New Jersey Poetry Resource Book* ($5 plus $1.50 p&h) and the *New Jersey Poetry Calendar*. The Distinguished Poets Series offers readings by poets of international, national, and regional reputation. Poetryworks/USA is a series of programs produced for UA Columbia-Cablevision. See website for details about these additional resources.

☐ ◎ PATH PRESS, INC. (Specialized: ethnic)

P.O. Box 2925, Chicago IL 60690. (847)424-1620. Fax: (847)424-1623. E-mail: pathpressinc@aol.com. Established 1969. **Contact:** Bennett J. Johnson, president.

Book/Chapbook Needs & How to Submit Path Press is a small publisher of books and poetry primarily "by, for, and about African-American and Third-World people." The press is open to all types of poetic forms; emphasis is on high quality. Submissions should be typewritten in ms format. Accepts submissions by e-mail (as attachment). Writers should send sample poems, credits, and bio. The books are "hardback and quality paperbacks."

Ⓝ ⊕ ☐ PATTAYA POETRY REVIEW (Specialized: subscription required); SOUTH PATTAYA PRESS

Classic Village, 95/31 Moo 10 Nong Phrue, Banglamung, Chonburi 20260, Thailand. Phone: (661)7177 941. E-mail: nasomhong@yahoo.com. Established 2003. **Contact:** Jiraporn Sutta, editor.

Magazine Needs *Pattaya Poetry Review* appears quarterly, publishing poetry, short stories, and reviews. Wants "all types and styles, especially traditional forms." *Pattaya Poetry Review* is 16 pages, digest-sized, with cardstock cover. Receives about 200 poems/year, accepts about 20%. Press run is 70. Single copy: $9; subscription: $16. Make checks payable to Jiraporn Sutta.

How to Submit Submit 3 poems at a time. Accepts previously published poems and simultaneous submissions. No e-mail or disk submissions. Reads submissions year round. Time between acceptance and publication is 3 months. Sometimes comments on rejected poems. **Subscription required to submit work.** Guidelines available for SASE. Responds in 3 months. Always sends prepublication galleys. Pays one contributor's copy. Acquires all rights. Returns rights upon written request. Reviews books and chapbooks of poetry. Send materials for review consideration to Jiraporn Sutta.

Book/Chapbook Needs & How to Submit South Pattaya Press publishes 6 chapbooks/year. Manuscripts are selected through open submission. Chapbooks are 12 pages, stapled, with cardstock covers. Query first, with a few sample poems and a cover letter with brief bio and publication credits. Chapbook mss may include previously published poems. Responds to queries in 3 months. Pays 3 author's copies. **"We publish chapbooks only by partial author subsidy."** Order sample chapbooks by sending $16 to Jiraporn Sutta.

PAVEMENT SAW; PAVEMENT SAW PRESS; TRANSCONTINENTAL POETRY AWARD; PAVEMENT SAW PRESS CHAPBOOK AWARD

P.O. Box 6291, Columbus OH 43206-0291. E-mail: info@pavementsaw.org. Website: www.pavementsaw.org. Established 1992. **Contact:** David Baratier, editor.

Magazine Needs *Pavement Saw*, which appears annually in August, wants "letters and short fiction, and poetry on any subject, especially work. Length: 1-2 pages. No poems that tell, no work by a deceased writer, and no translations." Dedicates 10-15 pages of each issue to a featured writer. Has published poetry by Simon Perchik, Sofia Starnes, Alan Catlin, Adrianne Kalfopoulou, Jim Daniels, and Mary Weems. *Pavement Saw* is 88 pages, digest-sized, perfect-bound. Receives about 9,000 poems/year, accepts less than 1%. Press run is 550 (about 300 subscribers, about 250 shelf sales). Single copy: $6; subscription: $12. Sample: $5. Make checks payable to Pavement Saw Press.

How to Submit Submit 5 poems at a time. "No fancy typefaces." Accepts simultaneous submissions, "as long as poet has not published a book with a press run of 1,000 or more"; no previously published poems. No e-mail submissions. Cover letter is required. Seldom comments on rejected poems. Guidelines available for SASE. Responds in 4 months. Sometimes sends prepublication galleys. Pays 2 contributor's copies. Acquires first rights.

Book/Chapbook Needs & How to Submit The press also publishes books of poetry. "Most are by authors who have been published in the journal." Published "8 titles in 2002 and 7 titles in 2003; 5 are full-length books ranging from 80 to 612 pages."

Contest/Award Offerings 1) **Transcontinental Poetry Award:** "Each year, Pavement Saw Press will seek to publish at least one book of poetry and/or prose poems from manuscripts received during this competition, which is open to anyone who has not previously published a volume of poetry or prose. Writers who have had volumes of poetry and/or prose under 40 pages printed, or printed in limited editions of no more than 500 copies, are eligible. **Submissions are accepted during June and July only.**" Awards publication, $1,000, and a percentage of the press run. **Entry fee:** $18. Include stamped postcard and SASE for acknowledgment of receipt and notification of results. Guidelines available for SASE. 2) **Pavement Saw Press Chapbook Award:** Awards publication, $500, and 10% of print run. Submit up to 32 pages of poetry with a cover letter. **Entry fee:** $12. "All entrants will receive 2 chapbooks. No need for SASE." **Deadline:** December 31. Guidelines available for SASE.

PEACE & FREEDOM; EASTERN RAINBOW; PEACE & FREEDOM PRESS (Specialized: subscribers)

17 Farrow Rd., Whaplode Drove, Spalding, Lincs PE12 0TS England. E-mail: p_rance@yahoo.co.uk. Website: http://uk.geocities.com/p_rance/pandf.htm. Established 1985. **Contact:** Paul Rance, editor.

Magazine Needs *Peace & Freedom* is a magazine appearing 2 times/year. "Those new to poetry are welcome. The poetry we publish is pro-animal rights/welfare, anti-war, environmental; poems reflecting love; erotic, but not obscene; humorous; spiritual, humanitarian; with or without rhyme/meter." Has published poetry by Dorothy Bell-Hall, Freda Moffatt, Bernard Shough, Mona Miller, and Andrew Savage. *Peace & Freedom*'s format varies. Subscription: US $20, UK £10/6 issues. Sample: US $5, UK £1.75. "Sample copies can only be purchased from the above address. Advisable to buy a sample copy before submitting. Banks charge the equivalent of $5 to cash foreign checks in the U.K., so please only send bills, preferably by registered post."

How to Submit Lines/poem: 32 maximum. No simultaneous submissions or previously published poems. "E-mail submissions are now welcome, but no more than 3 poems, please, and no attachments." No fax submissions. Poets are requested to send bios. Reads submissions all year. Publishes theme issues. Upcoming themes available for SAE with IRC, by e-mail, on website, or in magazine. Usually responds to submissions in less than a month, with IRC/SAE. "Work without correct postage will not be responded to or returned until proper postage is sent." Pays one contributor's copy. Reviews books of poetry.

Contest/Award Offerings "*Peace & Freedom* now holds regular poetry contests as does one of our other publications, *Eastern Rainbow*, which is a magazine concerning 20th-century popular culture using poetry up to 32 lines." Subscription: US $20, UK £10/6 issues. Further details of competitions and publications available for SAE and IRC.

Also Offers Also publishes anthologies. Guidelines and details on upcoming anthologies are available for SAE with IRC, by e-mail, on website, or in magazine.

Advice "Too many writers have lost the personal touch that editors generally appreciate. It can make a difference when selecting work of equal merit."

PEARL; PEARL POETRY PRIZE; PEARL EDITIONS

3030 E. Second St., Long Beach CA 90803-5163. (562)434-4523 or (714)968-7530. E-mail: pearlmag @aol.com. Website: www.pearlmag.com. Established 1974. **Contact:** Joan Jobe Smith, Marilyn Johnson, and Barbara Hauk, poetry editors.

Magazine Needs *Pearl* is a literary magazine appearing 2 times/year in April and November. "We are interested in accessible, humanistic poetry that communicates and is related to real life. Humor and wit are welcome, along with the ironic and serious. No taboos, stylistically or subject-wise. We don't want to see sentimental, obscure, predictable, abstract, or cliché-ridden poetry. Our purpose is to provide a forum for lively, readable poetry that reflects a wide variety of contemporary voices, viewpoints, and experiences—that speaks to real people about real life in direct, living language, profane or sublime. Our Fall/Winter issue is devoted exclusively to poetry, with a 12- to 15-page section featuring the work of a single poet." Has published poetry by Fred Voss, David Hernandez, Lisa Glatt, Jim Daniels, Jesse Lee Kercheval, and Judith Vollmer. *Pearl* is 96-121 pages, digest-sized, perfect-bound, offset-printed, with glossy cover. Press run is 700 (150 subscribers, 7 libraries). Subscription: $18/year (includes a copy of the winning book of the Pearl Poetry Prize). Sample: $7.

How to Submit Submit 3-5 poems at a time. Prefers poems no longer than 40 lines, each line no more than 10-12 words, to accommodate page size and format. No previously published poems. "Simultaneous submissions must be acknowledged as such. Handwritten submissions and unreadable printouts are not acceptable." No e-mail submissions. "Cover letters are appreciated." Reads submissions September through May only. Time between acceptance and publication is up to one year. Guidelines available for SASE or on website. Responds in 2 months. Sometimes sends prepublication galleys. Pays one contributor's copy. Acquires first serial rights.

Book/Chapbook Needs Pearl Editions "publishes the winner of the Pearl Poetry Prize only. All other books and chapbooks are *by invitation only*."

Contest/Award Offerings "We sponsor the Pearl Poetry Prize, an annual book-length contest, judged by one of our more well-known contributors." Winner receives $1,000, publication, and 25 author's copies. **Entry fee:** $20 (includes a copy of the winning book). **Deadline:** entries accepted May 1 through July 15 only. Complete rules and guidelines available for SASE or on website. Recent books include *Earth's Ends* by Andrew Kaufman, *How JFK Killed My Father* by Richard M. Berlin, *Traveler in Paradise* by Donna Hilbert, and *Bus Ride to a Blue Movie* by Anne-Marie Levine.

Advice "Advice for beginning poets? Just write from your own experience, using images that are as concrete and sensory as possible. Keep these images fresh and objective. Always listen to the music."

⬿ PEBBLE LAKE REVIEW; PEBBLE LAKE REVIEW FICTION & POETRY CONTEST

15318 Pebble Lake Dr., Houston TX 77095. E-mail: submissions@pebblelakereview.com. Website: http://pebblelakereview.com. Established 2003. **Contact:** Amanda Auchter, editor. Assistant Editor: Jessica McMichael.

Magazine Needs *Pebble Lake Review* is a quarterly online and print literary magazine featuring high-quality poetry, fiction, artwork, and reviews "from contributors around the world." Wants "high-quality, image-rich poetry that demonstrates attention to language, form, and craft." Looking for more experimental work. Does not want "anything cliché, Hallmark-style, racist, or erotic." Has published poetry by Catherine Daly, Jeffrey Greene, Dzvinia Orlowsky, Marge Piercy, and John E. Smelcer. *Pebble Lake Review* (print version) is 82 pages, digest-sized, perfect-bound, with color cover. Receives about 1,000 poems/year, less than 10%. Online circulation: 6,000. Single copy: $6; subscription: $24. Make checks payable to *Pebble Lake Review*.

How to Submit Submit 5 poems at a time. Lines/poem: 40 maximum. Accepts previously published poems and simultaneous submissions. Accepts e-mail submissions (pasted into body of message; attachments accepted if Word documents); no disk submissions. Cover letter is required. "List publication credits, if any. Always include a SASE with postal mail submissions." Reads submissions year round. Time between acceptance and publication is 3-6 months. "Poems are circulated between the editors, and the decision is finalized by the editor-in-chief." Seldom comments on rejected poems. Guidelines available in magazine, for SASE, by e-mail, or on website. Responds in one month. Sometimes sends prepublication galleys. Pays one contributor's copy. Acquires one-time rights; rights are returned to author upon publication. Reviews books and chapbooks of poetry in 350-500 words, single-book format. Send materials for review consideration to Jessica McMichael.

Also Offers Selects poets to read work as part of an online audio project.

Contest/Award Offerings *Pebble Lake* Annual Fiction & Poetry Contest. "Top prizewinner in each category receives $100 plus 5 contributor's copies of the Award Issue and feature in special online version. Submit up to 5 poems or one short story of up to 5,000 words. Include cover letter and SASE for notification." **Entry fee:** $10. "All entrants receive copy of winning issue. Top 3 winners in each category are published in the Award Issue, and all entries will be considered for publication in other issues." **Deadline:** May 31 annually.

N $⬿ THE PEDESTAL MAGAZINE

E-mail: pedmagazine@carolina.rr.com (inquiries only; make submissions through online submission form). Website: www.thepedestalmagazine.com. Established 2000. **Contact:** John Amen, editor-in-chief. Member: CLMP.

Magazine Needs *The Pedestal Magazine* is a bimonthly online journal. "We publish 12-15 poems per issue, as well as fiction, essays, and book reviews. We are open to a wide variety of poetry, ranging from the highly experimental to the traditionally formal." Has published poetry by Sharon Olds, W.S. Merwin, Maxine Kumin, Thomas Lux, Nikki Giovanni, and Hayden Carruth. Receives about 3,600 poems/year, accepts about 2.5 %. "We have a readership of approximately 10,000 per month."

How to Submit Submit up to 6 poems at a time. Lines/poem: open. Accepts simultaneous submissions; no previously published poems. No e-mail or disk submissions. "Submissions are accepted via a submission form provided in the 'Submit' section of the website. Our submissions schedule is posted in the guidelines section." Time between acceptance and publication is 2-4 weeks. Poems are circulated to an editorial board. Sometimes comments on rejected poems. Sometimes publishes theme issues. List of upcoming themes and guidelines available on website. Responds in 4-6 weeks. Always sends prepublication galleys. Pays $30/poem. Acquires first rights. Reviews books and chapbooks of poetry in 750-1,000 words. "Please query via e-mail prior to sending books or related materials."

◪ PEGASUS

P.O. Box 61324, Boulder City NV 89006. Established 1986. **Contact:** M.E. Hildebrand, editor.

Magazine Needs *Pegasus* is a poetry quarterly "for serious poets who have something to say and know how to say it using sensory imagery." Avoid "religious, political, and pornographic themes." Has published poetry by John Grey, Elizabeth Perry, Diana K. Rubin, Lyn Lifshin, Robert K. Johnson, and Nikolas Macioci. *Pegasus* is 32 pages, digest-sized, desktop-published, saddle-stapled, with colored paper cover. Publishes 10-15% of the poetry received. Circulation is 200. Subscription: $20. Sample: $6.

How to Submit Submit 3-5 poems at a time. Lines/poem: 3 minimum, 40 maximum. Accepts previously published poems, provided poet retains rights; no simultaneous submissions. Guidelines available for SASE. Responds in 2 weeks. Publication is payment. Acquires first or one-time rights.

◻ ◎ THE PEGASUS REVIEW (Specialized: themes)

P.O. Box 88, Henderson MD 21640-0088. (410)482-6736. Established 1980. **Contact:** Art Bounds, editor.

Magazine Needs "*The Pegasus Review* is published every other month in a calligraphic format, and each issue is based on a specific theme. Since themes might be changed, poets should inquire as to current themes. With a magazine in this format, strictly adhere to guidelines—brevity is the key. All material must pertain to indicated themes only. Poetry may be in any style (rhyming, free verse, haiku)." Has published poetry by Pearl Mary Wilshaw, Mike James, Barbara Darr, John Fitzpatrick, and Kelley Jean White. Press run is 120 (100 subscribers, 2 libraries). Subscription: $12. Sample: $2.50.

How to Submit Submit 3-5 poems with name and address on each page. Lines/poem: 24 maximum. Accepts previously published poems, if there is no conflict or violation of rights agreement, and simultaneous submissions, but author must notify proper parties once specific material is accepted. "Brief cover letter with specifics as they relate to one's writing background are welcome." Upcoming themes and guidelines available for SASE. Themes planned for 2005 include Adventure (January/February), History (March/April), Imagination (May/June), Parents (July/August), Teaching/Knowledge (September/October), and Music (November/December). Responds within one month, often with a personal response. Pays 2 contributor's copies.

Contest/Award Offerings Offers occasional book awards throughout the year.

Advice "Write and continue to read as well, especially what is being published today. Don't overlook the classics. They have achieved that status for a reason—quality. Seek every opportunity to have your work read at various organizations. The reading of a work can give you a new slant on it. Above all, believe in your craft and stick to it!"

$◪ ◎ PELICAN PUBLISHING COMPANY (Specialized: children; regional)

1000 Burmaster St., Gretna LA 70053. E-mail: editorial@pelicanpub.com. Website: www.pelicanpub.com. Established 1926. **Contact:** Nina Kooij, editor-in-chief.

Book/Chapbook Needs Pelican is a "moderate-sized publisher of cookbooks, travel guides, regional books, and inspirational/motivational books," which accepts poetry for "hardcover children's books only, preferably with a regional focus. However, our needs for this are very limited; we do 12 juvenile titles per year, and most of these are prose, not poetry." Has published *Nurse's Night Before Christmas* by David Davis. Two of their popular series are prose books about Gaston the Green-Nosed Alligator by James Rice and Clovis Crawfish by Mary Alice Fontenot. Has a variety of books based on "The Night Before Christmas," adapted to regional settings such as Cajun, prairie, and Texas. Books are 32 pages, large-format (magazine-sized), include illustrations.

How to Submit *Currently not accepting unsolicited mss.* Query first with cover letter including "work and writing backgrounds and promotional connections." No previously published poems or simultaneous submissions. Guidelines available for SASE or on website. Responds to queries in one month; to mss (if invited) in 3 months. Always sends prepublication galleys. Pays royalties.

Acquires all rights. Returns rights upon termination of contract. Typically, Pelican books sell for $15.95. Write for catalog or go to website to buy samples.

Advice "We try to avoid rhyme altogether, especially predictable rhyme. Monotonous rhythm can also be a problem."

🌐 $⌷ PEN & INC PRESS; REACTIONS; PRETEXT

School of Literature & Creative Writing, University of East Anglia, Norwich, Norfolk NR4 7TJ United Kingdom. Phone: (01603)592783. Fax: (01603)507728. E-mail: info@penandinc.co.uk. Website: www.inpressbooks.co.uk/penandinc. Established 1999. **Contact:** Clare Pollare, editor (*Reactions*); Katri Skala, deputy editor (*Pretext*).

Book/Chapbook Needs & How to Submit "Pen & Inc Press is a small independent publisher that offers a fresh perspective on the writers and writing that are important at the start of the 21st century. We aim to publish good writing, whether it be poetry, short fiction, essays, or criticism." Publishes 3 perfect-bound paperbacks/year, selected through both open submission and commission. Books are usually 150-200 pages, glue-bound, with full-color matte card covers. Submit maximum of 10 poems and cover letter with brief bio and publication credits. Responds to queries in 5 months. Order publications by sending cover price to Pen & Inc Press at the address above; UK Sterling only (transactions by debit/credit card fine also).

Magazine Needs & How to Submit *Reactions* is "an anthology of the best new poets from around the UK and abroad. It features the work of poets who are at a first collection stage or working towards it, and contains work by 30 UK and international poets. The emphasis is on emerging writers." Has published poetry by Helen Ivory, Polly Clark, Margaret Gillio, Owen Sheers, Matthew Hollis, and Henry Shukman. "Submissions are invited from writers who have had a first collection or pamphlet published (but not a second), and from those who have not yet reached that stage. If you are interested in submitting work, please send to Clare Pollard. Must be accompanied by a cover letter which lists the titles of your poems, plus a short biography of no more than 70 words." Single copy: £7.99 (UK), £8.99 (Europe), £9.99 (USA/ROW); all prices include postage and packing. Submit maximum of 10 poems at a time. Accepts original, unpublished poems. "Poems must be your own original work and must not be accepted for publication by any other magazine or anthology. Enclose SAE." Accepts submissions by postal mail only. Reads submissions on an ongoing basis. Time between acceptance and publication is dependent on publication date of anthology. Guidelines available for SAE, by e-mail, or on website. Responds in 4 months. Pays £50 and one contributor's copy.

Magazine Needs & How to Submit *Pretext*, appearing biannually in May and November, is "the international literary magazine from the acclaimed University of East Anglia. With over 200 pages of new poetry, short fiction, essays, criticism, and novel extracts from new and established writers, it provides a cutting-edge platform for creative writing from Great Britain and beyond. There are no editorial restrictions on subject or style, just an insistence on quality. Work must strongly assert itself and be well realized on the page." Has published poetry by Margaret Atwood, Romesh Gunesekera, Alan Jenkins, George Szirtes, Alison Fell, and Egon Schiele. *Pretext* is a book-sized magazine, litho-printed, glue-bound, with full-color matte cover, includes ads. Receives about 100 poems/year, accepts about 10%. Press run is 1,000 (100 subscribers, 10 libraries, 500 shelf sales); 100 distributed free to contributors/reviewers. Single copy: £7.99 (UK), £8.99 (Europe), £9.99 (USA/ROW); subscription: £14 (UK), £16 (Europe), £18 (USA/ROW); all prices include postage and packing. Make checks payable to The University of East Anglia. Submit maximum of 5 poems at a time. "Poems are received and passed to the editorial board for relevant publication. Consultation process involving editors and contributing editors occurs. Poems are accepted or rejected, or passed back to poet for rewriting if deemed necessary." Guidelines available in magazine, for SAE, by e-mail, or on website. Responds in 4 months. Always sends pre-publication galleys. Pays £50 and one contributor's copy.

Advice "Write well and good and do not despair. Try and try again. If you write well, you will be recognized one day."

🌐 ◨ PENNINE INK

% Mid Pennine Arts, The Gallery, Yorke St., Burnley BB11 1HD Great Britain. Phone: (01282)703657. E-mail: sheridans@casanostra.p3online.net. Established 1983. **Contact:** Laura Sheridan, editor.

Magazine Needs *Pennine Ink* appears annually in January using poems and short prose items. Wants "poetry of all kinds." *Pennine Ink* is 48 pages, A5, with b&w illustrated cover, includes small local ads. Receives about 400 poems/year, accepts about 40. Press run is 500. "Contributors wishing to purchase a copy of *Pennine Ink* should enclose £3 ($6 US) per copy."

How to Submit Submit up to 6 poems at a time. Lines/poem: 40 maximum. Accepts previously published poems and simultaneous submissions. Accepts submissions by e-mail. Seldom comments on rejected poems. Responds in 3 months. Pays one contributor's copy.

Advice "Submissions should be accompanied by a suitable SASE (or SAE with IRCs) for return of work."

🌐 ◨ PENNINE PLATFORM

Frizingley Hall, Frizinghall Rd., Bradford, West Yorkshire BD9 4LD United Kingdom. Website: www.pennineplatform.co.uk. Established 1973. **Contact:** Nicholas Bielby, poetry editor.

Magazine Needs *Pennine Platform* appears 2 times/year, in May and November. Wants any kind of poetry but concrete. "All styles—things good of their kind." Has published poetry by Gerard Benson, Miklos Radnoti (trans. Thomas Land), Mike Shields, Sam Smith, William Connely, and Milner Place. *Pennine Platform* is 60 pages, A5, digitally printed, stapled, with matte card cover with graphics. Receives about 1,000 submissions/year, accepts about 100. Circulation is 300 including libraries and universities. Subscription: £8.50 UK, £10 rest of Europe, £12 ROW (all payable in sterling only). Sample: £4.50, £6 ROW.

How to Submit Submit up to 6 poems, typed. Lines/poem: open, "but poems of fewer than 40 lines have a better chance." Editor comments on all poems (*if SAE provided*). Responds in up to 6 months. Pays one contributor's copy. Acquires first serial rights. Reviews books of poetry, multi-book format. Send materials for review consideration.

Advice "Pay attention to technique. Intelligent throughfulness and intelligent humor both appreciated. Religious poetry (but not religiosity) accepted."

◨ PENNSYLVANIA ENGLISH

Penn State DuBois, DuBois PA 15801-3199. (814)375-4814. E-mail: ajv2@psu.edu (inquiries only). Established 1988 (first issue in March 1989). **Contact:** Antonio Vallone, editor.

Magazine Needs *Pennsylvania English*, appearing annually, is "a journal sponsored by the Pennsylvania College English Association." Wants poetry of "any length, any style." Has published poetry by Liz Rosenberg, Walt MacDonald, Amy Pence, Jennifer Richter, and Jeff Schiff. *Pennsylvania English* is up to 200 pages, digest-sized, perfect-bound, with full-color cover. Press run is 500. Subscription: $10/year.

How to Submit Submit 3 or more typed poems at a time. Include SASE. Considers simultaneous submissions but not previously published poems. No e-mail submissions. Guidelines available for SASE. Responds in 6 months. Pays 2 contributor's copies.

Advice "Poetry does not express emotions; it evokes emotions. Therefore, it should rely less on statements and more on images."

⭐ ◨ ◎ PENNY DREADFUL: TALES & POEMS OF FANTASTIC TERROR (Specialized: horror)

P.O. Box 719, Radio City Station, Hell's Kitchen NY 10101-0719. E-mail: MMPendragon@aol.com. Website: www.mpendragon.com. Established 1996. **Conact:** Michael Pendragon, editor/publisher.

● "Works appearing in *Penny Dreadful* have been reprinted in *The Year's Best Fantasy and Horror*." *Penny Dreadful* nominates best tales and poems for Pushcart Prizes.

Magazine Needs *Penny Dreadful* is an irregular publication (published about once/year) of goth-romantic poetry and prose. Publishes poetry, short stories, essays, letters, listings, reviews, and b&w artwork "which celebrate the darker aspects of Man, the World, and their Creator. We're looking for literary horror in the tradition of Poe, M.R. James, Shelley, M.P. Shiel, and LeFanu—dark, disquieting tales and verses designed to challenge the readers' perception of human nature, morality, and man's place within the Darkness. Stories and poems should be set prior to 1910 and/or possess a timeless quality. Avoid references to 20th- and 21st-century personages/events, graphic sex, strong language, excessive gore and shock elements." Has published poetry by Nancy Bennett, Michael R. Burch, Lee Clark, Louise Webster, K.S. Hardy, and Kevin N. Roberts. *Penny Dreadful* is about 170 pages, digest-sized, desktop-published, perfect-bound. Includes market listings "for, and reviews of, kindred magazines." Press run is 200. Subscription: $25/3 issues. Sample: $10. Make checks payable to Michael Pendragon.

How to Submit "Submit up to 12 poems with name and address on opening page, and name/title/page number on all following pages. Poems should not exceed 3 pages; rhymed, metered verse preferred." Accepts previously published poems and simultaneous submissions. Prefers e-mail submissions; "include in body of message with a copy attached. Include cover letter and SASE." Reads submissions all year. Time between acceptance and publication is "indefinite." Poems reviewed and chosen by editor. Guidelines available on website. "Due to the amount of submissions received, the editor cannot always respond. He encourages all contributors to submit work as simultaneous submissions." Always sends prepublication galleys. Pays one contributor's copy. Acquires one-time rights.

Also Offers Publishes *Songs of Innocence & Experience*/Pendragon Publications. See separate listing in this section.

◖◎ THE PENWOOD REVIEW (Specialized: spirituality)

P.O. Box 862, Los Alamitos CA 90720-0862. E-mail: penwoodreview@charter.net. Website: http://webpages.charter.net/penwoodreview/penwood.htm. Established 1997. **Contact:** Lori M. Cameron, editor.

Magazine Needs *The Penwood Review*, published biannually, "seeks to explore the spiritual and sacred aspects of our existence and our relationship to God." Wants "disciplined, high-quality, well-crafted poetry on any subject. Prefer poems be less than 2 pages. Rhyming poetry must be written in traditional forms (sonnets, tercets, villanelles, sestinas, etc.)." Does not want "light verse, doggerel, or greeting card-style poetry. Also, nothing racist, sexist, pornographic, or blasphemous." Has published poetry by Kathleen Spivack, Anne Babson, Hugh Fox, Anselm Brocki, Nina Tassi, and Gary Guinn. *The Penwood Review* is about 40 pages, magazine-sized, saddle-stapled, with heavy card cover. Press run is 50-100. Single copy: $6; subscription: $12.

How to Submit Submit 3-5 poems, one/page with the author's full name, address, and phone number in the upper right corner. No previously published poems or simultaneous submissions. Accepts e-mail submissions (pasted into body of message). Cover letter is preferred. Time between acceptance and publication is up to one year. "Submissions are circulated among an editorial staff for evaluations." Never comments on rejected poems. Responds in up to 4 months. For payment, offers subscription discount of $10 and, with subscription, one additional contributor's copy. Acquires one-time rights.

$◖ THE PEOPLE'S PRESS

4810 Norwood Ave., Baltimore MD 21207-6839. Phone/fax: (410)448-0254. Press established 1997, firm established 1989. **Contact:** Submissions Editor.

Book/Chapbook Needs "The goal of the types of material we publish is simply to move people to think and perhaps act to make the world better than when we inherited it." Wants "meaningful poetry that is mindful of human rights/dignity." Accepts poetry written by children; parental consent is mandatory for publication. Has published *Familiar*, works by various artists; *Late* by Kelley Jean White, MD; *Hard Hooved Hussy* by Mary Alice Ramsey; *Sweet Somethings* by Garrett Flagg and Marvin Pirila; *Braids* by Rasheed Adero Merritt; and *2000 Here's to Humanity* by various artists. Books are at least 50 pages, usually perfect-bound, with soft covers.

How to Submit Query first with 1-5 sample poems and a cover letter with brief bio and publication credits. SASE required for return of work and/or response. No submissions by fax. Time between acceptance and publication is 6 months to one year. Seldom comments on rejected poems. Publishes theme issues. Guidelines available for SASE. Responds to queries within 6 weeks; to mss in within 3 months. Pays royalties of 5-20% and 30 author's copies (out of a press run of 500). Order sample books by sending $8.

Contest/Award Offerings The People's Press sponsors an annual Poetry Month Contest in April. "Prizes and/or publication possibilities vary from contest to contest." Details available for SASE.

Advice "Expound on something that moves you within the realm of human rights/dignity, and hopefully we will be moved also."

★ ◐ PEREGRINE; AMHERST WRITERS & ARTISTS

190 University Dr., Suite 1, Amherst MA 01002. (413)253-3307. E-mail: awapress@aol.com. Website: www.amherstwriters.com. Established 1984. **Contact:** Nancy Rose, editor.

Magazine Needs *Peregrine*, published annually in October, features poetry and fiction. Open to all styles, forms, and subjects except greeting card verse. Has published poetry by Willie James King, Virgil Suárez, Susan Terris, Janet Aalfs, Dianalee Velie, and Ralph Hughes. *Peregrine* is 104 pages, digest-sized, professionally printed, perfect-bound, with glossy cover. Press run is 1,000. Single copy: $12; subscription: $30/3 issues, $45/5 issues, $250/lifetime. Sample: $10. Make checks payable to AWA Press.

How to Submit Submit 3-5 poems. Lines/poem: 50 maximum (including spaces). Accepts simultaneous submissions; no previously published poems. No e-mail submissions. Include cover letter with bio, 40 words maximum. Reads submissions January through May only. "Each manuscript is read by several readers. Final decisions are made by the editor." Guidelines available for #10 SASE or on website. Pays 2 contributor's copies. Acquires first rights.

◐ PERMAFROST: A LITERARY JOURNAL; SUSAN BLALOCK POETRY CHAPBOOK CONTEST

% English Dept., University of Alaska Fairbanks, P.O. Box 755720, Fairbanks AK 99775. E-mail: ftstg@uaf.edu. Website: www.uaf.edu/english/permafrost. Established 1977. **Contact:** Poetry Editor.

Magazine Needs An annual journal published in May, *Permafrost* contains poems, short stories, creative nonfiction, b&w drawings, photographs, and prints. "We survive on both new and established writers, hoping and expecting to see the best work out there. We publish any style of poetry provided it is conceived, written, and revised with care. While we encourage submissions about Alaska and by Alaskans, we also welcome poems about anywhere, from anywhere. We have published work by E. Ethelbert Miller, W. Loran Smith, Peter Orlovsky, Jim Wayne Miller, Allen Ginsberg, Jean Genet, and Andy Warhol." *Permafrost* is about 200 pages, digest-sized, professionally printed, flat-spined. Subscription: $8/year, $16/2 years, $22/3 years. Sample: $4.

How to Submit Submit 3-5 poems, "typed, single- or double-spaced, and formatted as they should appear." Considers simultaneous submissions. **Deadline:** March 15. Does not accept submissions between March 15 and September 1. Editors sometimes comment on poems. Guidelines available for SASE or on website. Responds in about 2 months. Pays 2 contributor's copies; reduced contributor rate on additional copies.

Contest/Award Offerings *Permafrost* sponsors the Susan Blalock Poetry Chapbook Contest, awarding $100 and 30 author's copies. Guidelines available for SASE or on website. **Entry fee:** $10, includes a one-issue subscription to the journal. **Deadline:** March 15.

N ◐ THE PERSISTENT MIRAGE

E-mail: CTPoetryMan@netscape.com. Website: http://freewebs.com/persistentmirage. Established 2005. **Contact:** Bryon D. Howell, editor.

Magazine Needs *The Persistent Mirage* is an online publication. Wants "well-crafted, intelligent, insightful, and enjoyable poetry of all kinds. The editor has a weakness for well-written traditional poetry. Most topics are welcome, although hateful poetry stands no chance. Editor is very liberal in every imaginable way. Right-wing crusaders are encouraged to fly elsewhere." Wants "all styles, but I have a preference for well-written sonnets and other traditional poetry." Does not want "children's poetry, religious poetry, or pornography; occasional profanity might be overlooked if it serves a purpose in the poem." Has published poetry by Mark Gaudet, John Grey, Taylor Graham, Yvette Merton, Christopher Mulrooney, and Maureen Templeton. Receives about 1,000 poems/ year, accepts about 10 %.

How to Submit Submit 3-5 poems at a time. Lines/poem: 100 maximum. Accepts previously published poems and simultaneous submissions. Accepts e-mail submissions (pasted into body of message); no disk submissions. Cover letter is preferred. "Tell me a little about yourself, not just your publication history. Prove to me there is a soul behind the poetry." Reads submissions year round. Submit seasonal poems 3 months in advance. Time between acceptance and publication is 3 months. Always comments on rejected poems. Sometimes publishes theme issues. Guidelines available by e-mail or on website. Responds in 3 weeks. Sometimes sends prepublication galleys. Acquires one-time rights.

Advice "I am in search mainly of those poets who have been published but have not yet received their due recognition. I don't care if you majored in English or if you dropped out of elementary school. If I enjoy your work, it will find a home here at *The Persistent Mirage*. You don't have to be an English major to write remarkable and amazing poetry. Anyone who tells you this is in a very unhealthy state of mind. I will work as well as *network* with beginners who ask for this help. I get rejection letters every day myself. We're all in this together. Read, revise, and above all, never throw poetry away!"

☑ PERSPECTIVES

Dept. of English, Hope College, Holland MI 49422-9000. **Contact:** Francis Fike, poetry editor.

Magazine Needs *Perspectives* appears 10 times/year. The journal's purpose is "to express the Reformed faith theologically; to engage in issues that Reformed Christians meet in personal, ecclesiastical, and societal life; and thus to contribute to the mission of the church of Jesus Christ." Wants "poems excellent in craft and significant in subject, both traditional and free in form. We publish 1-2 poems every other issue, alternating with a Poetry Page on great traditional poems from the past." Has published poetry by Rhoda Janzen, David Middleton, and Frederik Zydek. *Perspectives* is 24 pages, magazine-sized, web offset, saddle-stapled, with paper cover containing b&w illustration. Receives about 50 poems/year, accepts 6-10. Press run is 3,300 (3,000 subscribers, 200 libraries). Subscription: $30. Sample: $3.50.

How to Submit No previously published poems or simultaneous submissions. Accepts submissions by postal mail only. Cover letter is preferred. Include SASE. "Submissions without SASE will not be returned." Time between acceptance and publication is 6 months or less. Occasionally comments on rejected poems. Responds in up to 3 months. Pays 5 contributor's copies. Acquires first rights.

☑ ◎ PERUGIA PRESS; PERUGIA PRESS INTRO AWARD (Specialized: women)

P.O. Box 60364, Florence MA 01062. E-mail: info@perugiapress.com. Website: www.perugiapress. com. Established 1997. **Contact:** Susan Kan, director.

Book/Chapbook Needs "Perugia Press publishes one collection of poetry each year, by a woman at the beginning of her publishing career (first or second books only). Our books appeal to people who have been reading poetry for decades, as well as those who might be picking up a book of poetry for the first time. Slight preference for narrative poetry." Has published *Kettle Bottom* by Diane Gilliam Fisher, *Seamless* by Linda Tomol Pennisi, *Red* by Melanie Braverman, *The Work of Hands* by Catherine Anderson, *A Wound on Stone* by Faye Gore, and *Reach* by Janet E. Aalfs. Manuscripts are selected through competition (see below). Books are an average of 88 pages, offset-printed, perfect-bound. Print run is 500-1,200. Order sample books from website.

Contest/Award Offerings The Perugia Press Intro Award for a first or second book by a woman offers $1,000 and publication. Send 48-72 pages on white paper, "with legible typeface, pagination, and fastened with a removable clip. Include *two* cover pages: one with title of manuscript, name, address, telephone number, and e-mail address, and one with just manuscript title. Include table of contents and acknowledgments page.'' Cover letter and bio not required. Individual poems may be previously published. Accepts simultaneous submissions if notified of acceptance elsewhere. No e-mail submissions. No translations or self-published books. "Poet must be a living U.S. resident." **Entry fee:** $20/ms. Make checks payable to Perugia Press. **Postmark deadline:** between August 1 and November 15; "No FedEx or UPS." Include SASE for April 1 notification only; mss will be recycled. Judges: panel of Perugia authors, booksellers, scholars, etc. Guidelines available on website.

☑ PHI KAPPA PHI FORUM

129 Quad Center, Mell St., Auburn University AL 36849-5306. (334)844-5200. Fax: (334)844-5994. E-mail: kaetzjp@auburn.edu. Website: www.auburn.edu/natforum. Established 1915. **Contact:** Poetry Editors. Editor: James P. Kaetz.

Magazine Needs *Phi Kappa Phi Forum* is the quarterly publication of Phi Kappa Phi using quality poetry. *Phi Kappa Phi Forum* is 48 pages, magazine-sized, professionally printed, saddle-stapled, with full-color paper cover. Receives about 300 poems/year, accepts about 20. Press run is 110,000 (108,000 subscribers, 300 libraries). Subscription: $25.

How to Submit Submit 3-5 short (one page or less in length) poems at a time, including a biographical sketch with recent publications. Accepts e-mail submissions. Reads submissions about every 3 months. Responds in about 4 months. Pays 10 contributor's copies.

☑ PIKEVILLE REVIEW

Humanities Dept., Pikeville College, 147 Sycamore St., Pikeville KY 41501. (606)218-5602. Fax: (606)218-5225. E-mail: sengland@pc.edu (inquiries only). Website: www.pc.edu. Established 1987. **Contact:** Sydney C. England, editor.

Magazine Needs *Pikeville Review* appears annually in July, accepting about 10% of poetry received. "There's no editorial bias, though we recognize and appreciate style and control in each piece. No emotional gushing." *Pikeville Review* is 94 pages, digest-sized, professionally printed, perfect-bound, with glossy card cover with b&w illustration. Press run is 500. Sample: $4.

How to Submit No simultaneous submissions or previously published poems. Accepts submissions by postal mail only. SASE required. Editor sometimes comments on rejected poems. Guidelines available for SASE or on website. Pays 5 contributor's copies.

$ ☑ ◎ PINE ISLAND JOURNAL OF NEW ENGLAND POETRY (Specialized: regional/New England)

P.O. Box 317, West Springfield MA 01090-0317. Established 1998. **Contact:** Linda Porter, editor.

Magazine Needs *Pine Island* appears 2 times/year "to encourage and support New England poets and the continued expression of New England themes." Wants poems of "up to 30 lines; haiku and other forms welcome; especially interested in New England subjects or themes. No horror, no erotica." Has published poetry by X.J. Kennedy, Doug Holder, Carol Purington, and Wanda D. Cook. *Pine Island* is 50 pages, digest-sized, desktop-published, saddle-stapled, with cardstock cover with art. Press run is 200 (80 subscribers). Subscription: $10. Sample: $5. Library rate available. Make checks payable to Pine Island Journal.

How to Submit "Writers must be currently residenced in New England." Submit 5 poems at a time. Lines/poem: 30 maximum. No previously published poems or simultaneous submissions. Cover letter with brief bio is preferred. Include SASE. Time between acceptance and publication is 6 months. Seldom comments on rejected poems. Responds in up to 2 months. Pays $1/poem and one contributor's copy. Acquires first rights. Accepts poetry book/chapbook submissions for books received and books reviewed pages. "Book/chapbook should be less than one year old to be considered, and cannot be returned. Author or editor must currently reside in New England and will receive a copy of the issue in which their listing or review appears."

◻ THE PINK CHAMELEON—ONLINE

E-mail: dpfreda@juno.com. Website: www.geocities.com/thepinkchameleon/index.html. Established 1985 (former print version), 1999 (online version). **Contact:** Dorothy P. Freda, editor.

Magazine Needs *Pink Chameleon—Online* wants "family-oriented, upbeat poetry, any genre in good taste that gives hope for the future. For example, poems about nature, loved ones, rare moments in time. No pornography, no cursing, no swearing, nothing evoking despair." *The Pink Chameleon* is published online. Receives about 50 poems/year, accepts about 50%.

How to Submit Submit 1-4 poems at a time. Lines/poem: 6 minimum, 24 maximum. Accepts previously published poems; no simultaneous submissions. "Only e-mail submissions considered. Please, *no attachments*. Include work in the body of the e-mail itself. Use plain text. Include a brief bio." Reads submissions all year. Time between acceptance and publication is 2 months. "As editor, I reserve the right to edit for grammar, spelling, sentence structure, flow; omit redundancy and any words or material I consider in bad taste. No pornography, no violence for the sake of violence, no curse words. Remember, this is a family-oriented electronic magazine." Often comments on rejected poems. Guidelines available by e-mail or on website. Responds in one month. No payment. Acquires one-time, one-year publication rights. All rights revert to poet one year after publication online.

Advice "Always keep a typed hard copy or a back-up disk of your work for your files. Mail can go astray. And I'm human, I can accidentally delete or lose the submission."

✪ ◪ PINYON

Dept. of Languages, Literature & Communications, Mesa State College, 1100 North Ave., Grand Junction CO 81051. Established 1995. **Contact:** Randy Phillis, editor. Managing Editor: Elizabeth Koepke.

Magazine Needs *Pinyon* appears annually in June and publishes "the best available contemporary American poetry and fiction. No restrictions other than excellence. We appreciate a strong voice. No inspirational, light verse, or sing-song poetry." Has published poetry by Mark Cox, Barry Spacks, Wendy Bishop, and Anne Ohman Youngs. *Pinyon* is about 120 pages, magazine-sized, perfect-bound, cover varies. Receives about 4,000 poems/year, accepts 2%. Press run is 300 (150 subscribers, 5 libraries, 50 shelf sales); 100 distributed free to contributors, friends, etc. Subscription: $8/year. Sample: $4.50. Make checks payable to *Pinyon*, MSC.

How to Submit Submit 3-5 poems at a time. No previously published poems or simultaneous submissions. Cover letter is preferred. "Name, address, e-mail, and phone number on each page. SASE required." Reads submissions August 1 to December 1. "Three groups of assistant editors, led by an associate editor, make recommendations to the editor." Seldom comments on rejected poems. Guidelines available for SASE. Responds in February. Pays 2 contributor's copies. Acquires one-time rights.

Advice "Send us your best work!"

◻ ◎ THE PIPE SMOKER'S EPHEMERIS (Specialized: pipes and pipe smoking)

20-37 120th St., College Point NY 11356-2128. Established 1964. **Contact:** Tom Dunn, editor/publisher.

Magazine Needs "The *Ephemeris* is a limited-edition, irregular quarterly for pipe smokers and collectors and anyone else who is interested in its varied contents. Publication costs are absorbed by the editor/publisher, assisted by any contributions—financial or otherwise—that readers might wish to make." Wants poetry with themes related to pipes and pipe smoking. Issues are 116 pages, magazine-sized, offset, saddle-stapled, with coated stock covers. Has also published collections covering the first and second 15 years of the *Ephemeris*, and issues a triennial "Collector's Directory."

How to Submit Accepts submissions on disk. Cover letter is required with submissions. Pays 1-2 contributor's copies. Staff reviews books of poetry. Send materials for review consideration.

☑ PITT POETRY SERIES; UNIVERSITY OF PITTSBURGH PRESS; AGNES LYNCH STARRETT POETRY PRIZE

Eureka Building, 5th Floor, 3400 Forbes Ave., Pittsburgh PA 15260. Website: www.pitt.edu/~press. Established 1968. **Contact:** Ed Ochester, poetry editor.

Book/Chapbook Needs University of Pittsburgh Press, through the Pitt Poetry Series, publishes at least 4 books/year by established poets, and one by a new poet—the winner of the Starrett Poetry Prize competition (see below). Wants "poetry of the highest quality; otherwise, no restrictions—book manuscripts should be a minimum of 48 pages." Has published books of poetry by Lynn Emanuel, Larry Levis, Billy Collins, and Alicia Ostriker. Their booklist also features such poets as Etheridge Knight, Sharon Olds, Ronald Wallace, David Wojahn, and Toi Derricotte.

How to Submit Unpublished poets or poets "who have published chapbooks or limited editions of less than 750 copies" must submit through the Agnes Lynch Starrett Poetry Prize (see below). Poets who have previously published books should query. For Poetry Series, submit "entire manuscripts only." Accepts simultaneous submissions. Accepts submissions by postal mail only. Cover letter is preferred. Reads submissions from established poets in September and October only. Seldom comments on rejected poems. Always sends prepublication galleys.

Contest/Award Offerings Sponsors the Agnes Lynch Starrett Poetry Prize. "Poets who have not previously published a book should send SASE for rules of the Starrett competition, the only vehicle through which we publish first books of poetry." The Starrett Prize awards $5,000 and book publication. **Entry fee:** $20. **Postmark deadline:** between March 1 and April 30. Competition receives 1,000 entries.

☑ PLAINSONGS

Dept. of English, Hastings College, Hastings NE 68902-0269. (402)461-7352. Fax: (402)461-7756. E-mail: dm84342@alltel.net. Established 1980. **Contact:** Dwight C. Marsh, editor.

Magazine Needs *Plainsongs* is a poetry magazine that "accepts manuscripts from anyone, considering poems on any subject in any style, but free verse predominates. Plains region poems encouraged." Has published poetry by Phillip Belcher, Michael Kriesel, W. Dale Nelson, Judith Tate O'Brien, and Danielle Sellers. *Plainsongs* is 40 pages, digest-sized, set on laser, printed on thin paper, saddle-stapled, with one-color matte card cover with generic black logo. "Published by the English department of Hastings College, the magazine is partially financed by subscriptions. Although editors respond to as many submissions with personal attention as they have time for, the editor offers specific observations to all contributors who also subscribe." The name suggests not only its location on the Great Plains, but its preference for the living language, whether in free or formal verse. *Plainsongs* is committed to poems only, to make space without visual graphics, bio, reviews, or critical positions. Subscription: $12/3 issues. Sample: $5.

How to Submit Submit up to 6 poems at a time, with name and address on each page. Accepts submissions by postal mail only. **Deadlines:** August 15 for fall issue; November 15 for winter; March 15 for spring. Notification is mailed 5-6 weeks after deadlines. Guidlines available for SASE. Pays 2 contributor's copies and one-year subscription, with 3 award poems in each issue receiving $25. "A short essay in appreciation accompanies each award poem." Acquires first rights.

Advice "We like poems that seem to be aware of modernist and post-modernist influences during the last hundred years, not necessarily by imitation or allusion, but by using the tools provided by that rich heritage. Poets need to read and absorb the work of other poets."

⚒ ☑ ◎ PLAN B PRESS (Specialized: style/experimental, concrete, visual); PLAN B PRESS POETRY CHAPBOOK CONTEST

P.O. Box 2080, Philadelphia PA 19103. (215)732-2663. E-mail: teammay@att.net. Website: www.planbpress.com. Established 1999. **Contact:** stevenallenmay, president.

Book/Chapbook Needs & How to Submit Plan B Press publishes poetry and short fiction. Wants "experimental poetry, concrete/visual work." Does not want "sonnets, political or religious poems, work in the style of Ogden Nash." Has published poetry by Lamont B Steptoe, Michele Belluomini,

Jim Mancinelli, Anne Blonstein, Andrew Bradley, and stevenallenmay. Publishes 3-5 poetry books/year and 5 chapbooks/year. Manuscripts are selected through open submission (see also chapbook competition below under Contest/Award Offerings). Books/chapbooks are 24-48 pages, saddle-stapled or perfect-bound, with covers with art/graphics that vary per book. Query first, with a few sample poems and a cover letter with brief bio and publication credits. Book/chapbook mss may include previously published poems. See website for additional information. Responds to queries in one month; to mss in 3 months. Author keeps royalties. Pays varying number of author's copies; press run varies per book. **50-70% of books are author-subsidy published each year.** Order sample books/chapbooks by sending to 3412 Terrace Dr., #173, Alexandria VA 22302.

Contest/Award Offerings Sponsors the annual Plan B Press Poetry Chapbook Contest. Offers $100 plus 60 copies of winner's book. Submit 15-20 poems, no more than 48 pages total. **Entry fee:** $15. **2005 Deadline:** March 15. Guidelines available in magazine or on website. "Include 8½ × 11 SASE for manuscript return; English as primary language, prose acceptable, previously published work acceptable, author retains copyright of poems (although Plan B reserves rights to layout and/or cover art and design)."

Also Offers "Plan B Press is a small publishing company with an international feel. Our intention is to have Plan B Press be part of the conversation about the direction and depth of literary movements and genres. Plan B Press is determined to merge text with image, writing with art."

Advice "Writing reveals the mirror to your soul. Don't think about words until you are in the editing phase, and then only look for errors. Whatever sense your work makes is for the reader to ascertain, not you. You are a beacon, a transmitter. As a Nike ad would put it: Just Do It."

🌐 $💲 PLANET: THE WELSH INTERNATIONALIST

P.O. Box 44, Aberystwyth, Ceredigion SY23 3ZZ Wales. Phone: 01970-611255. Fax: 01970-611197. E-mail: planet.enquiries@planetmagazine.org.uk. Website: http://planetmagazine.org.uk. Established 1970. **Contact:** John Barnie, editor.

Magazine Needs *Planet* is a bimonthly cultural magazine, "centered on Wales, but with broader interests in arts, sociology, politics, history, and science." Wants "good poetry in a wide variety of styles. No limitations as to subject matter; length can be a problem." Has published poetry by Nigel Jenkins, Anne Stevenson, and Mertyl Morris. *Planet* is 128 pages, A5, professionally printed, perfect-bound, with glossy color card cover. Receives about 500 submissions/year, accepts about 5%. Press run is 1,550 (1,500 subscribers, about 10% libraries, 200 shelf sales). Single copy: £3.25; subscription: £15 (overseas: £16). Sample: £4.

How to Submit No previously published poems or simultaneous submissions. Accepts submissions on disk, as e-mail attachment, and by postal mail. SASE or SAE with IRCs essential for reply. Time between acceptance and publication is 6-10 months. Seldom comments on rejected poems. Guidelines available for SASE (or SAE/IRC). Responds within a month or so. Pays £25 minimum. Acquires first serial rights only. Reviews books of poetry in 700 words, single- or multi-book format.

🌐 ◪ ◎ THE PLAZA (Specialized: bilingual)

U-Kan, Inc., Yoyogi 2-32-1, Shibuya-ku, Tokyo 151-0053 Japan. Phone: 81-3-3379-3881. Fax: 81-3-3379-3882. E-mail: plaza@u-kan.co.jp. Website: http://u-kan.co.jp. Established 1985. **Contact:** Leo Shunji Nishida, editor/publisher.

Magazine Needs *The Plaza* is an annual, currently published online only, which "represents a borderless forum for contemporary writers and artists" and includes poetry, fiction, and essays published simultaneously in English and Japanese. Wants "highly artistic poetry dealing with being human and interculturally related. Nothing stressing political, national, religious, or racial differences. *The Plaza* is edited with a global view of mankind." Has published poetry by Al Beck, Antler, Charles Helzer, Richard Alan Bunch, Morgan Gibson, and Kikuzou Hidari. *The Plaza* is 50 full-color pages. Receives about 600 poems/year, accepts 2%. Available free to all readers on the Internet.

How to Submit Accepts simultaneous submissions; no previously published poems. Accepts e-mail (pasted into body of message) and fax submissions. "No e-mail attachments. Cover letter is required. Please include telephone and fax numbers or e-mail address with submissions. As *The Plaza* is a bilingual publication in English and Japanese, it is sometimes necessary, for translation purposes, to contact authors. Japanese translations are prepared by the editorial staff." Seldom comments on rejected poems. Responds within 2 months. "Proofs of accepted poems are sent to the authors one month before online publication." Reviews books of poetry, usually in less than 500 words. Send materials for review consideration.

Advice "*The Plaza* focuses not on human beings but on humans being human in the borderless world."

$☑ PLEIADES; LENA-MILES WEVER TODD POETRY SERIES; PLEIADES PRESS

Dept. of English and Philosophy, Central Missouri State University, Warrensburg MO 64093. (660)543-8106. E-mail: kdp8106@cmsu2.cmsu.edu. Website: www.cmsu.edu/englphil/pleiades. Established 1990. **Contact:** Kevin Prufer, editor.

● Poems from *Pleiades* have been reprinted in *The Best American Poetry 2001, 2002, 2003,* and *2004,* as well as in the 2005 *Pushcart Prize* anthology.

Magazine Needs *Pleiades* is a biannual journal, appearing in April and October, publishing poetry, fiction, literary criticism, belles lettres (occasionally), and reviews. It is open to all writers. Wants "avant-garde, free verse, and traditional poetry, and some quality light verse. Nothing pretentious, didactic, or overly sentimental." Has published poetry by James Tate, Joyce Carol Oates, Brenda Hillman, Wislawa Szymborska, Carl Phillips, and Jean Valentine. *Pleiades* is 160 pages, digest-sized, perfect-bound, with heavy coated cover with color art. Receives about 3,000 poems/year, accepts 1-3%. Press run is 2,500-3,000 (several hundred shelf sales); about 200 distributed free to educational institutions and libraries across the country. Single copy: $6; subscription: $12. Sample: $5. Make checks payable to Pleiades Press.

How to Submit Submit 3-5 poems at a time. Accepts simultaneous submissions with notification; no previously published poems. Cover letter with brief bio is preferred. Time between acceptance and publication can be up to one year. "Each poem published must be accepted by 2 readers and approved by the poetry editor." Seldom comments on rejected poems. Guidelines available for SASE or on website. Responds in up to 3 months. Payment varies. Acquires first and second serial rights.

Contest/Award Offerings Sponsors the Lena-Miles Wever Todd Poetry Series. "We will select one book of poems in open competition and publish it in our Pleiades Press Series. Louisiana State University Press will distribute the collection." Has published *Lure* by Nils Michals, *The Green Girls* by John Blair, and *A Sacrificial Zinc* by Matthew Cooperman. **Entry fee:** $15. **Postmark deadline:** September 30 annually. Complete guidelines available for SASE or on website.

A painting by Dan Namingha, an artist from the Tewa-Hopi tribe, graces the cover of *Ploughshares*, Issue #95, guest-edited by Joy Harjo. *Symbolism VI*, acrylic on canvas, © by Dan Namingha.

$☑ PLOUGHSHARES

Emerson College, 120 Boylston St., Boston MA 02116. (617)824-8753. Website: www.pshares.org. Established 1971.

- Work published in *Ploughshares* is frequently selected for inclusion in volumes of *The Best American Poetry*.

Magazine Needs *Ploughshares* is "a journal of new writing guest-edited by prominent poets and writers to reflect different and contrasting points of view." Editors have included Carolyn Forché, Gerald Stern, Rita Dove, Chase Twichell, and Marilyn Hacker. Has published poetry by Donald Hall, Li-Young Lee, Robert Pinsky, Brenda Hillman, and Thylias Moss. The triquarterly is 250 pages, digest-sized. Receives about 2,500 poetry submissions/year. Press run is 7,000. Subscription: $24 domestic, $36 foreign. Sample: $10.95 current issue, $8.50 back issue.

How to Submit "We suggest you read a few issues (online or in print) before submitting." Accepts simultaneous submissions. Do not submit mss from April 1 to July 31. Responds in up to 5 months. Always sends prepublication galleys. Pays $25/printed page per poem ($50 min, $250 max), plus 2 contributor's copies and a subscription.

⚒ $○ THE PLOWMAN

The Plowman Ministries—A Mission for Christ, Box 414, Whitby ON L1N 5S4 Canada. Established 1988. **Contact:** Tony Scavetta, editor.

Magazine Needs *The Plowman* appears annually in July or August, using "didactic, eclectic poetry; all forms. We will also take most religious poetry except satanic and evil. We are interested in work that deals with the important issues in our society. Social and environmental issues are of great importance." *The Plowman* is 20 pages, magazine-sized, photocopied, unbound. Accepts 70% of the poetry received. Press run is 15,000 (1,200 subscribers, 500 libraries). Subscription: $10. Sample free.

How to Submit Submit up to 5 poems at a time. Lines/poem: 38 maximum. Accepts previously published poems and simultaneous submissions. Cover letter is required. No SASE necessary. Always comments on rejected poems. Guidelines available for SASE. Responds in up to 2 weeks. Always sends prepublication galleys. Pays one contributor's copy. Reviews books of poetry.

Book/Chapbook Needs & How to Submit Also publishes 125 chapbooks/year. Responds to queries and mss in one month. **Reading fee:** $25/book. Pays 20% royalties. Has published *Poems of Joy* by Eva Marie Ippolitio, *A Journey Back to the Light* by Scott J. Miller, *People, Places, Poetry* by Virginia Gomez, and *Silhouettes and Thoughts In Shadow* by Holly Swick.

Contest/Award Offerings Offers monthly poetry contests. **Entry fee:** $2/poem. 1st Prize: 50% of the proceeds; 2nd Prize: 25%; 3rd Prize: 10%. The top poems are published. "Balance of the poems will be used for anthologies."

$○ ◎ POCKETS (Specialized: Christian; children)

1908 Grand Ave., P.O. Box 340004, Nashville TN 37203-0004. E-mail:pockets@upperroom.org. Website:www.pockets.org. **Contact:** Lynn W. Gilliam, editor.

Magazine Needs & How to Submit *Pockets* is an interdenominational magazine for children ages 6-12, published monthly (except February). "Each issue is built around a specific theme, with material (including poetry) that can be used by children in a variety of ways. Submissions do not need to be overly religious; they should help children experience a Christian lifestyle that is not always a neatly wrapped moral package but is open to the continuing revelation of God's will." Lines/poem: 24 maximum. Accepts one-time previously published poems. No fax or e-mail submissions. Submissions should be typed, double-spaced, on 8½×11 paper, accompanied by SASE for return. "Writers who wish to save postage and are concerned about paper conservation may send a SASP for notification of accepted manuscripts; we will recycle the paper the submission is printed on. Please list the name of the submission(s) on the card." Reads submissions year round. Always publishes theme issues ("themes are set each year in December"). List of upcoming themes and guidelines available on website (under "For Adults/Writer's Corner"). Pays $2/line, $25 minimum.

Pays on acceptance; may place mss on long-term hold for specific issues. Acquires newspaper, periodical, and electronic rights.

☑ POEM; HUNTSVILLE LITERARY ASSOCIATION

P.O. Box 2006, Huntsville AL 35804. Established 1967. **Contact:** Rebecca Harbor, editor.

Magazine Needs *Poem* appears twice/year, in May and November, consisting entirely of poetry. "We publish both traditional forms and free verse. We want poems characterized by compression, rich vocabulary, significant content, and evidence of 'a tuned ear and practiced pen.' We want coherent work that moves through the particulars of the poem to make a point. We equally welcome submissions from established poets as well as from less-known and beginning poets." Has published poetry by Kathryn Kirkpatrick, R.T. Smith, and Ronald Wallace. *Poem* is a flat-spined, digest-sized, 90-page journal that contains more than 60 poems, generally featured one to a page, printed on good stock paper, with a clean design and a matte cover. Press run is 500 (all subscriptions, including libraries). Subscription: $20. Sample: $7.

How to Submit "We do not accept translations, previously published poems, or simultaneous submissions. Best to submit December through March and June through September. We prefer to see a sample of 3-5 poems per submission, with SASE. We generally respond in 1-2 months. We are a nonprofit organization and can pay only in contributor's copies." Pays 2 contributor's copies. Acquires first serial rights.

☑ POEMS & PLAYS; THE TENNESSEE CHAPBOOK PRIZE

English Dept., Middle Tennessee State University, Murfreesboro TN 37132. (615)898-2712. Established 1993. **Contact:** Gaylord Brewer, editor.

Magazine Needs *Poems & Plays* is an annual "eclectic publication for poems and short plays," published in the spring. No restrictions on style or content of poetry. Has published poetry by Naomi Wallace, Kate Gale, Richard Newman, and Charles Harper Webb. *Poems & Plays* is 88 pages, digest-sized, professionally printed, perfect-bound, with coated color card cover. "We receive 1,500 poems per issue, typically publish 30-35." Press run is 800. Subscription: $10/2 issues. Sample: $6.

How to Submit No previously published poems or simultaneous submissions (except for chapbook submissions). Reads submissions October through December only. "Work is circulated among advisory editors for comments and preferences. All accepted material is published in the following issue." Sometimes comments on rejected poems. Responds in 2 months. Pays one contributor's copy. Acquires first publication rights only.

Contest/Award Offerings "We accept chapbook manuscripts (of poems or short plays) of 20-24 pages for The Tennessee Chapbook Prize. Any combination of poems or plays, or a single play, is eligible. The winning chapbook is printed within *Poems & Plays*, and the author receives 50 copies of the issue. **SASE and $10 (for reading fee and one copy of the issue) required. Dates for contest entry are the same as for the magazine (October through December).** Past winners include Julie Lechevsky, David Kirby, Gabrielle LeMay, and Rob Griffith. The chapbook competition annually receives over 150 manuscripts from the U.S. and around the world."

Ⓝ $☑ POESIA; OLIVER W. BROWNING POETRY COMPETITION; INDIAN BAY PRESS; DELTA HOUSE PUBLISHING COMPANY

One West Mountain St., Fayetteville AR 72701. (479)444-9323. Fax: (479)444-9326. E-mail: editor@ indianbaypress.com. Website: www.indianbaypress.com. Established 2003. **Contact:** W.R. Mayo, publisher.

Magazine Needs *Poesia* is a literary quarterly of poetry and poetry reviews of all genres. *Poesia* is digest-sized, offset-printed, perfect-bound, includes ads. Receives about 200 poems/year, accepts about 30-40%. Press run is 2,000 (35% subscribers, 15% libraries, 35% shelf sales); 15% distributed free for promotions. Single copy: $3.75; subscription: $12/year, $20/2 years. Make checks payable to Indian Bay Press.

How to Submit Submit 3 poems at a time. No previously published poems or simultaneous submissions. Accepts fax and e-mail (as attachment) submissions; no disk submissions. Cover letter is required. "Include name, address, SASE, and biographical information, including previous publishing credits." Reads submissions year round. Time between acceptance and publication is 3 months. Never comments on rejected poems. Guidelines available on website. Responds in one week. Pays $10/poem and 2 contributor's copies. Acquires one-time rights. Rights revert to author upon publication. Reviews books and chapbooks of poetry in 250-500 words, single-book format. Send materials for review consideration to Attn: Editor, Indian Bay Press.

Contest/Award Offerings Sponsors the annual Oliver W. Browning Poetry Competition. Offers 1st Prize: $500; 2nd Prize: $150; 3rd Prize: Honorable Mention. Submit 3 poems. **Entry fee:** $12 (includes subscription to *Poesia*). **Deadline:** October 15 annually. Guidelines available in magazine or on website.

☑ POESY MAGAZINE

P.O. Box 7823, Santa Cruz CA 95061. (831)460-1048. E-mail: info@poesy.org. Website: www.poesy .org. Established 1991. **Contact:** Brian Morrisey, editor/publisher.

Magazine Needs *POESY Magazine* appears quarterly as "an anthology of American poetry. *POESY*'s main concentrations are Boston, Massachusetts and Santa Cruz, California, 2 thriving homesteads for poets, beats, and artists of nature. Our goal is to unite the 2 scenes, updating poets on what's happening across the country. We like to see original poems that express observational impacts with clear and concise imagery. Acceptence is based on creativity, composition, and relation to the format of *POESY*. Please do not send poetry with excessive profanity. We would like to endorse creativity beyond the likes of everyday babble." Has published poetry by Lawrence Ferlinghetti, Jack Hirschman, Edward Sanders, Linda Lerner, Simon Perchik, and Corey Mesler. *POESY* is 16 pages, magazine-sized, newsprint, glued/folded, includes ads. Receives about 1,000 poems/year, accepts about 10%. Press run is 1,000; most distributed free to local venues. Single copy: $1; subscription: $12/year. Sample: $2. Make checks payable to Brian Morrisey.

How to Submit Submit 4-6 poems at a time. Lines/poem: 32 maximum. No previously published poems or simultaneous submissions. Accepts e-mail and disk submissions; no fax submissions. "Snail mail submissions are preferred with a SASE." Cover letter is preferred. Reads submissions year round. Time between acceptance and publication is one month. "Poems are accepted by the Santa Cruz editor/publisher based on how well the poem stimulates our format." Sometimes comments on rejected poems. Guidelines available in magazine, for SASE, or by e-mail. Responds in one month. Sometimes sends prepublication galleys. Pays 3 contributor's copies. Acquires one-time rights. Reviews books and chapbooks of poetry and other magazines/journals in 1,000 words, single-book format. Send materials for review consideration to *POESY*, % Brian Morrisey.

Advice "Branch away from typical notions of love and romance. Become one with your surroundings and discover a true sense of natural perspective."

☑ POET LORE

The Writer's Center, 4508 Walsh St., Bethesda MD 20815. (301)654-8664. Fax: (301)654-8667. E-mail: postmaster@writer.org. Website: www.writer.org. Established 1889. **Contact:** Jason DeYoung, managing editor. Editors: Rick Cannon, E. Ethelbert Miller, and Jody Bolz.

Magazine Needs *Poet Lore* is a biannual "dedicated to the best in American and world poetry and timely reviews and commentary. We look for fresh uses of traditional forms and devices, but any kind of excellence is welcome." Has published poetry by Adrian Blevins, Fleda Brown, David Wagoner, Martin Galvin, Carrie Etter, and Maria Terrone. *Poet Lore* is 140 pages, digest-sized, professionally printed, perfect-bound, with glossy card cover. Receives about 4,200 poems/year, accepts 125. Press run is at least 800 (600 subscribers, 200 libraries). Single copy: $9; subscription: $18. "Add $1/single copy for shipping; add $5 postage for subscriptions outside U.S."

How to Submit "Submit typed poems, with author's name and address on each page; SASE is required. No electronic submissions. Simultaneous submissions OK with notification in cover letter.'' Guidelines available for SASE or on website. Responds in 3 months. Pays 2 contributor's copies. Reviews books of poetry. Send materials for review consideration.

⊕ ◻ POETIC HOURS

43 Willow Rd., Carlton, Nolts NG4 3BH England. E-mail: erranpublishing@hotmail.com. Website: www.poetichours.homestead.com. Established 1993. **Contact:** Nicholas Clark, editor.

Magazine Needs *Poetic Hours* is published biannually ''to encourage and publish new poets, i.e., as a forum where good but little known poets can appear in print, and to raise money for Third World and other charities. The magazine features articles and poetry by subscribers and others.'' Wants ''any subject, rhyme preferred but not essential; suitable for wide ranging readership, 30 lines maximum.'' Does not want ''gothic, horror, extremist, political, self-interested.'' *Poetic Hours* is 40 pages, A4, printed, saddle-stapled. Receives about 500 poems/year, accepts about 40%. Press run is about 400 (300 subscriptions and shelf sales, 12 libraries). Subscription: £7 sterling, overseas payments in sterling (Europe and EC) or US dollars ($20 from USA or Canada). Subscribe online from website or send bankers checks (UK only) or cash. Sample: £3.75. Make checks payable to Erran Publishing.

How to Submit ''Poets are encouraged to subscribe or buy a single copy, though not required.'' Submit up to 5 nonreturnable poems at a time, via e-mail from website where possible. Accepts previously published poems; no simultaneous submissions. Prefers e-mail submissions (as attachments); accepts disk submissions. Cover letter is required. Time between acceptance and publication is 3 months. ''Poems are read by editors and, if found suitable, are used.'' Always comments on rejected poems. Responds ''immediately, whenever possible.'' Acquires one-time rights.

Also Offers ''Poetic Hours Online'' (at www.poetichours.homestead.com) features original content by invitation of editor only.

Advice ''We welcome newcomers and invite those just starting out to have the courage to submit work. The art of poetry has moved from the hands of book publishers down the ladder to the new magazines. This is where all the best poetry is found.'' *Poetic Hours* is non-profit-making; all proceeds go to various charities, particularly well-building and children's charities. A page of each issue is set aside for reporting how money is spent.

◪ POETIC MATRIX PRESS; POETIC MATRIX, A PERIODIC LETTER; POETIC MATRIX SLIM VOLUME SERIES

P.O. Box 1223, Madera CA 93639. (559)673-9402. E-mail: poeticmatrix@yahoo.com. Website: www. poeticmatrix.com. Established 1997 in Yosemite. **Contact:** John Peterson, editor/publisher.

Magazine Needs *Poetic Matrix, a periodic letteR* appears 2-3 times/year, currently as an online journal. Wants poetry that ''creates a 'place in which we can live' rather than telling us about the place; poetry that draws from the imaginal mind and is rich in the poetic experience—hence the poetic matrix.'' Does not want poetry that talks about the experience. Has published poetry by Lyn Lifshin, Tony White, Gail Entrekin, James Downs, Joan Michelson, and Brandon Cesmat. *Poetic Matrix, a periodic letteR* is currently published online only.

How to Submit Accepts e-mail submissions (pasted into body of message). Guidelines available for SASE, by e-mail, or on website. Pays in contributor's copies. Acquires one-time rights. Reviews books and chapbooks of poetry and other magazines/journals in 500-1,000 words, single- and multi-book format. Send materials for review consideration to John Peterson, editor.

Book/Chapbook Needs & How to Submit Poetic Matrix Press publishes books (70-120 pages), slim volumes (50-60 pages, perfect-bound), and chapbooks (20-30 pages). ''Poetic Matrix Press hosts a Slim Volume Series call for submissions of manuscripts 50-60 pages. The manuscript selected will be published with full-color cover, perfect binding, and ISBN. The selected poet will receive 100 copies of the completed book and a $200 honorarium.'' Full guidelines and submission dates available for SASE or by e-mail. Charges reading fee for Slim Volume Series submissions only. For chapbook and book information, contact the publisher.

Advice ''Write with quality, passion, and intelligence.''

⊠ ◎ **POETICA MAGAZINE, REFLECTIONS OF JEWISH THOUGHT (Specialized: Jewish)**
Box 11014, Norfolk VA 23517. E-mail: poeticamag@aol.com. Website: www.poeticamagazine.c
om. Established 2002. **Contact:** Michal Mahgerefteh, publisher/poetry editor.
Magazine Needs *Poetica* appears 3 times/year. "*Poetica*'s goal is to offer an outlet for the many
writers who draw from their Jewish backgrounds and experiences to create poetry and prose,
giving both emerging and recognized writers the opportunity to share their work with the larger
community." Does not want long pieces, haiku, rhyming poetry. Accepts poetry by young poets,
grades 6-12. *Poetica* is 40-60 pages, digest-sized, desktop-published, saddle-stapled, with glossy
card stock cover with b&w art, includes some ads. Receives about 300 poems/year, accepts about
60%. Press run is 200 (80 subscribers). Single copy: $4; subscription: $12.
How to Submit Submit 3 poems at a time. Lines/poem: 2 pages maximum. Accepts simultaneous
submissions. No e-mail or disk submissions. Cover letter is optional. Reads submissions year round.
Time between acceptance and publication is 6 months to a year. Seldom comments on rejected
poems. Occasionally publishes theme issues. List of upcoming themes and guidelines available for
SASE or on website. Responds in one month. Pays one contributor's copy. Authors retain all rights.
Advice " 'A fierce light beats upon the Jew'—reflect it in your writings. Tikun Olam is encouraged."

$◩ **POETRY; THE POETRY FOUNDATION; BESS HOKIN PRIZE; LEVINSON PRIZE;
FREDERICK BOCK PRIZE; J. HOWARD AND BARBARA M.J. WOOD PRIZE; RUTH LILLY
POETRY PRIZE; RUTH LILLY POETRY FELLOWSHIP; JOHN FREDERICK NIMS MEMORIAL
PRIZE; FRIENDS OF LITERATURE PRIZE; UNION LEAGUE CIVIC AND ARTS POETRY PRIZE**
1030 N. Clark St., Chicago IL 60610. E-mail: poetry@poetrymagazine.org (send Letters to the Editor
to editors@poetrymagazine.org). Website: www.poetrymagazine.org. Established 1912. **Contact:**
Christian Wiman, editor.
● Work published in *Poetry* is frequently selected for inclusion in *The Best American Poetry*
and *The Pushcart Prize: Best of the Small Presses.*
Magazine Needs *Poetry* "is the oldest and most distinguished monthly magazine devoted entirely
to verse. Established in Chicago in 1912, it immediately became the international showcase for
new poetry, publishing in its earliest years, and often for the first time, such giants as Ezra Pound,
Robert Frost, T.S. Eliot, Marianne Moore, and Wallace Stevens. *Poetry* has continued to print the
major voices of our time and to discover new talent, establishing an unprecedented record. There
is virtually no important contemporary poet in the English language who has not, at a crucial stage
in his or her career, depended on *Poetry* to find a public: John Ashbery, Dylan Thomas, Edna St.
Vincent Millay, James Merrill, Anne Sexton, Sylvia Plath, James Dickey, Thom Gunn, David Wagoner, et al. *Poetry* publishes, without affiliation with any movements or schools, what August
Kleinzahler has called 'the most interesting and influential journal for and about poetry in America
right now.' " *Poetry* is an elegantly printed, flat-spined, 5½×9 magazine. Receives 90,000 submis-
sions/year, accepts about 300-350. Press run is 16,000 (11,500 subscribers, 20% libraries). Single
copy: $3.75; subscription: $35, $38 for institutions. Sample: $5.50.
How to Submit Submit up to 4 poems at a time with SASE. No simultaneous submissions. No e-
mail submissions. Guidelines available for SASE. Responds in 1-2 months. Pays $6/line for poetry,
$150/page of prose. Reviews books of poetry in multi-book formats of varying lengths. Send books
for review consideration to the editors.
Contest/Award Offerings Seven prizes (named in heading) ranging from $300 to $5,000 are
awarded annually to poets whose work has appeared in the magazine that year. Only verse already
published in *Poetry* is eligible for consideration, and no formal application is necessary. *Poetry* also
sponsors the Ruth Lilly Poetry Prize, an annual award of $100,000, and the Ruth Lilly Poetry
Fellowship, 2 annual awards of $15,000 to young poets to support their further studies in poetry.
Also Offers For information on Poetry Day and other reading/lecutre series, visit www.poetrymagaz
ine.org.

✪ ☑ ◎ **THE POETRY EXPLOSION NEWSLETTER (THE PEN) (Specialized: ethnic; love; nature)**

P.O. Box 4725, Pittsburgh PA 15206-0725. (866)234-0297. E-mail: arthurford@hotmail.com. Established 1984. **Contact:** Arthur C. Ford, Sr., editor.

Magazine Needs *The Pen* is a "quarterly newsletter dedicated to the preservation of poetry." Wants "all forms and subject matter with the use of good imagery, symbolism, and honesty. Rhyme and non-rhyme. No vulgarity." Accepts poetry written by children; "if under 18 years old, parent or guardian should submit!" Has published poetry by Iva Fedorka. *The Pen* is 12-16 pages, saddle-stapled, mimeographed on both sides. Receives about 300 poems/year, accepts 80. Press run is 850 (735 subscribers, 5 libraries). Subscription: $20/year. Send $4 for sample copy and more information. Make checks payable to Arthur C. Ford.

How to Submit Submit up to 5 poems at a time, with $1 **reading fee**. Lines/poem: 40 maximum. Include large SASE if you want work returned. Accepts simultaneous submissions and previously published poems. No e-mail submissions. Sometimes publishes theme issues. "We announce future dates when decided. July issue is full of romantic poetry." Guidelines and upcoming themes available for SASE. Responds in up to 3 weeks. Editor comments on rejected poems "sometimes, but not obligated." Pays one contributor's copy. Poetry critiques available for 15¢/word. Send materials for review consideration.

Advice "Be fresh, honest, and legible!"

✪ ☑ ◎ **POETRY FORUM; THE JOURNAL (Specialized: subscription; mystery; science fiction/fantasy; social issues); HEALTHY BODY-HEALTHY MIND (Specialized: health concerns)**

5713 Larchmont Dr., Erie PA 16509. E-mail: 75562.670@compuserve.com. Website: www.thepoetryforum.com. **Contact:** Gunvor Skogsholm, editor.

Magazine Needs *Poetry Forum* appears 3 times/year. "We are open to any style and form. We believe new forms ought to develop from intuition. Would like to encourage long themes. No porn or blasphemy, but open to all religious persuasions." Accepts poetry written by children ages 10 and under. Has published poetry by Marshall Myers, Dana Thu, Joseph Veranneau, Ray Greenblatt, Jan Haight, and Mark Young. *Poetry Forum* is 38 pages, $7 \times 8\frac{1}{2}$, photocopied from photoreduced typescript, saddle-stapled, with card cover. Subscription: $26/year. Sample: $4.

How to Submit Submit any number of poems. Lines/poem: 50 maximum. Accepts simultaneous submissions and previously published poems. Accepts submissions by fax, on disk, by postal mail, and by e-mail (pasted into body of message). **Reading fee:** $1/poem. Editor comments on poems "if asked, but respects the poetic freedom of the artist." Publishes theme issues. Guidelines available in magazine, for SASE, by fax, or by e-mail. Sometimes sends prepublication galleys. Gives awards of $25, $15, $10, and 3 honorable mentions for the best poems in each issue. Acquires one-time rights. Reviews books of poetry in 250 words maximum. Send materials for review consideration.

Magazine Needs & How to Submit *The Journal*, which appears twice/year, accepts experimental poetry of any length from subscribers only. Sample: $4. *Healthy Body-Healthy Mind* is a biannual publication concerned with health issues. Accepts essays, poetry, articles, and short-shorts on health, fitness, mind, and soul. Details available for SASE.

Advice "I believe today's poets should experiment more and not feel stuck in the forms that were in vogue 300 years ago. I would like to see more experimentalism—new forms will prove that poetry is alive and well in the mind and spirit of the people."

☑ **POETRY INTERNATIONAL**

Dept. of English, San Diego State University, San Diego CA 92182-8140. (619)594-1523. Fax: (619)594-4998. E-mail: fmoramar@mail.sdsu.edu. Website: http://poetryinternational.sdsu.edu. Established 1996. **Contact:** Fred Moramarco, editor.

Magazine Needs *Poetry International*, published annually in November, is "an eclectic poetry magazine intended to reflect a wide range of poetry being written today." Wants "a wide range of styles and subject matter. We're particularly interested in translations.'' Does not want ''cliché-ridden, derivative, obscure poetry.'' Has published poetry by Adrienne Rich, Robert Bly, Hayden Carruth, Kim Addonizio, Maxine Kumin, and Gary Soto. *Poetry International* is 200 pages, perfect-bound, with coated card stock cover. Press run is 1,200. Single copy: $12; subscription: $24/2 years (plus s&h).

How to Submit Submit up to 5 poems at a time. Accepts simultaneous submissions, ''but prefer not to''; no previously published poems. No fax or e-mail submissions. Reads submissions September 1 through December 30 only. Time between acceptance and publication is 8 months. Poems are circulated to an editorial board. Seldom comments on rejected poems. Responds in up to 4 months. Pays 2 contributor's copies. Acquires all rights. Returns rights ''50/50,'' meaning they split with the author any payment for reprinting the poem elsewhere. ''We review anthologies regularly.''

Advice ''We're interested in new work by poets who are devoted to their art. We want poems that matter—that make a difference in people's lives. We're especially seeking good translations and prose by poets about poetry.''

🌐 $⬚ POETRY IRELAND REVIEW; POETRY IRELAND

120 St. Stephen's Green, Dublin 2, Ireland. Phone: (353)(1)4789974. Fax: (353)(1)4780205. E-mail: poetry@iol.ie. Website: www.poetryireland.ie. Established 1979. **Contact:** Joseph Woods, director.

Magazine Needs *Poetry Ireland Review*, the magazine of Ireland's national poetry organization, ''provides an outlet for Irish poets; submissions from abroad also considered. No specific style or subject matter is prescribed. We strongly dislike sexism and racism.'' Has published poetry by Seamus Heaney, Michael Longley, Denise Levertov, Medbh McGuckian, and Charles Wright. Occasionally publishes special issues. *Poetry Ireland Review* appears quarterly. Receives up to 8,000 submissions/year, accepts about 3%. Press run is 1,200 (800 subscriptions). Single copy: €7.99; subscription: €30.50 Ireland and UK, €40.50 overseas (surface). Sample: $10.

How to Submit Submit up to 6 poems at a time. Include SASE (or SAE and IRC, or an e-mail address). ''Submissions not accompanied by SAEs will not be returned.'' No previously published poems or simultaneous submissions. No e-mail submissions. Time between acceptance and publication is up to 3 months. Seldom comments on rejected poems. Guidelines available on website. Pays €32/poem. Reviews books of poetry in 500-1,000 words.

Also Offers *Poetry Ireland Review* is published by Poetry Ireland, an organization established to ''promote poets and poetry throughout Ireland.'' Poetry Ireland offers readings, an information service, an education service, library and administrative center, and a bimonthly newsletter giving news, details of readings, competitions, etc., for €8/year.

Advice ''Keep submitting: Good work will get through.''

🌐 ⬚ POETRY KANTO

Kanto Gakuin University, Kamariya-cho 3-22-1, Kanazawa-ku, Yokohama 236-8502, Japan. Established 1984 by William I. Elliott. **Contact:** Alan Botsford, editor.

Magazine Needs *Poetry Kanto* appears annually in November and is published by the Kanto Poetry Center. The magazine publishes well-crafted original poems in English, and Japanese poems in English translation. Has published works by Gwyneth Lewis, Vijay Seshadri, Harryette Mullen, Rigoberto Gonzalez, Ellen Bass, and Bruce A. Jacobs. *Poetry Kanto* is 100 pages, 6 × 9, professionally printed on coated stock, perfect-bound, with glossy cover. Press run is 1,000; many are distributed free to schools, poets, and presses. The magazine is unpriced. For sample, send SAE with IRCs.

How to Submit Interested poets should query from February through March with SAE and IRCs before submitting. No previously published poems or simultaneous submissions. Pays 3-5 contributor's copies.

Advice ''From forebears, learn; from the future, write; in the present, live.''

☑ POETRY MIDWEST

(913)469-8500, ext. 4705. E-mail: submit@poetrymidwest.org (submissions); editors@poetrymidwest.org (queries). Website: www.poetrymidwest.org. Established 2000. **Contact:** Matthew W. Schmeer, editor/publisher.

Magazine Needs *Poetry Midwest* appears 3 times/year (winter, spring/summer, fall) and features poetry, nongenre microfiction, and brief creative nonfiction from new and established writers. Wants free verse, traditional Western forms, traditional Asian forms other than haiku and senryu, prose poems, long poems, nongenre microfiction (up to 300 words), and brief creative nonfiction (up to 300 words). Does not want science fiction, fantasy, inspirational, religious, or children's verse or fiction; anything of an overtly political or religious nature; or spoken word poetry. Has published poetry by A.D. Winans, Ryan G. Van Cleave, Robin Reagler, Suzanne Burns, Joseph Somoza, and Richard Garcia. *Poetry Midwest* is 20-100 pages, published online as a (free) downloadable Adobe Acrobat PDF file. Receives about 1,500 poems/year, accepts about 7%.

How to Submit Submit 3 poems at a time. Lines/poem: 3 minimum, 10 pages maximum. Accepts simultaneous submissions; no previously published poems. "Submit via e-mail *only*. Submissions should be pasted into the body of an e-mail message with 'Poetry Midwest Submission' in subject line (omit quotation marks). Absolutely no e-mail file attachments. E-mail messages containing attachments will be deleted upon receipt. Do not send submissions via postal mail; they will be returned unread." Reads submissions year round. Submit seasonal poems 3-6 months in advance. Time between acceptance and publication is 3 months to one year. "I read submissions as they are received, deciding whether or not to use a piece based on its own literary merits and whether it fits in with other poems selected for an issue in progress." Seldom comments on rejected poems. Guidelines available by e-mail or on website. Responds in up to 6 months. Acquires first rights or first North American serial rights as well as First Electronic Rights, Reprint Rights, and Electronic Archival Rights.

Advice "Since *Poetry Midwest* is freely available online, there is no excuse for not reading an issue to sample the type of work the journal tends to feature. Poets should do their research before submitting to any journal; otherwise, they may be wasting not only their time, but the editor's time, too. Online journals are deluged with submissions, and following the posted guidelines will let the editor know you want your submission seriously considered."

☐ POETRY MOTEL; POETRY MOTEL WALLPAPER BROADSIDE SERIES

P.O. Box 202, Kailua-Kona HI 96745. Established 1984. **Contact:** Patrick McKinnon, Bud Backen, and Linda Erickson, editors.

Magazine Needs *Poetry Motel* appears "every 260 days" as a poetry magazine with some fiction and memoire. Wants poetry of "any style, any length." Has published poetry by Adrian C. Louis, Ron Androla, Todd Moore, Albert Huffsticker, Antler, and Serena Fusek. *Poetry Motel* is 52 pages, digest-sized, offset-printed, stapled, with wallpaper cover. Receives about 1,000 poems/year, accepts about 5%. Press run is 1,000 (400 subscribers, 10 libraries). Single copy: $9.95; subscription: $17.95/2 issues, $199/forever. Make checks payable to P. McKinnon.

How to Submit Submit 3-6 pages at a time. Accepts previously published poems and simultaneous submissions. No fax, e-mail, or disk submissions. "Include SASE and brief bio." Reads submissions all year. Time between acceptance and publication varies. Never comments on rejected poems. Guidelines available in magazine or for SASE. Responds in "one week to never." Pays 1-5 contributor's copies. Acquires no rights. Reviews books and chapbooks of poetry and other magazines/journals in varied lengths. Send materials for review consideration to Linda Erickson.

Advice "All work submitted is considered for both the magazine and the broadside series."

🌐 ☑ POETRY NOTTINGHAM; NOTTINGHAM OPEN POETRY COMPETITION

11, Orkney Close, Stenson Fields, Derbyshire DE24 3LW United Kingdom. Established 1946. **Contact:** Adrian Buckner, editor.

Magazine Needs *Poetry Nottingham* is open to submissions from anyone; features articles and reviews in addition to poetry. Has published poetry by Martin Stannard, Edmund Skellings, Helena Nelson, Lorna Dowell, Lucie McKee, and C.J. Allen. *Poetry Nottingham* is 6×8, professionally printed. Receives about 1,500 submissions/year, accepts about 120. Press run is 300 (200 subscribers). Single copy: £2.75 ($9.75 US); subscription: £17 sterling or $34 US.

How to Submit Submit up to 6 poems at any time, or articles up to 1,000 words on current issues in poetry. No previously published poems. Accepts submissions by postal mail only. "Send SAE and 3 IRCs for stamps. No need to query, but cover letter is required." Responds in 2 months. Pays one contributor's copy. Staff reviews books of poetry. Send materials for review consideration.

Contest/Award Offerings The Nottingham Open Poetry Competition offers cash prizes, annual subscriptions, and publication in *Poetry Nottingham*. Open to all. Contact Jeremy Duffield, 71 Saxton Ave., Heanor, Derbyshire DE75 7PZ United Kingdom, or visit http://nottinghampoetrysociety.co.uk for details.

Advice "The new editor is seeking to provide an uncluttered environment for poems of wit, poems of concise lyrical intensity, and poems that are bold enough to expand on a theme."

☐ POETRY OF THE PEOPLE

3341 SE 19th Ave., Gainesville FL 32641. (352)375-0244. E-mail: poetryforaquarter@yahoo.com. Website: www.angelfire.com/fl/poetryofthepeople. Established 1986. **Contact:** Paul Cohen, poetry editor.

Magazine Needs *Poetry of the People* is a leaflet that appears monthly. "We take all forms of poetry, but we like humorous poetry, love poetry, nature poetry, and fantasy. No racist or highly ethnocentric poetry will be accepted. I do not like poetry that lacks images or is too personal or contains rhyme to the point that the poem has been destroyed. All submitted poetry will be considered for posting on website, which will be updated every month." Also accepts poetry written in French and Spanish. Has published poetry by Laura Stamps, Dan Matthews, Jenica Deer, Shannon Dixon, Kristi Castro, and Peggy C. Hall. *Poetry of the People* is 4 pages, magazine-sized, sometimes printed on colored paper. Issues are usually theme oriented. Sample: $4 for 11 pamphlets. "New format is being devised."

How to Submit Submit "as many poems as you want." Include SASE. Accepts submissions on disk, by e-mail, and by postal mail. Cover letter with biographical information is required. "I feel autobiographical information is important in understanding the poetry." Poems are returned within 6 months. Editor comments on rejected poems "often." Upcoming themes available for SASE. Guidelines available by e-mail or on website. Pays 10 contributor's copies. Acquires first rights.

Advice "You should appeal to as broad an audience as possible. Nature makes people happy."

⊠ ⊞ ☑ POETRY SALZBURG; POETRY SALZBURG REVIEW; UNIVERSITY OF SALZBURG PRESS

University of Salzburg, Dept. of English and American Studies, Akademiestrasse 24, A-5020 Salzburg Austria. Phone: 0043 662 8044 4422. Fax: 0043 662 80 44 167. E-mail: editor@poetrysalzburg.com. Website: www.poetrysalzburg.com. Established 1971. **Contact:** Dr. Wolfgang Goertschacher, editor.

Magazine Needs *Poetry Salzburg Review* appears twice/year and contains "articles on poetry, mainly contemporary, and 60 percent poetry. Also includes prose, reviews, interviews, and translations. We tend to publish selections by authors who have not been taken up by the big poetry publishers. Nothing of poor quality." Has published poetry by Desmond O'Grady, James Kirkup, Daniel Weissbrot, Alice Notley, Anne MacLeod, and Rupert Loydell. *Poetry Salzburg Review* is about 200 pages, A5, professionally printed, perfect-bound, with illustrated card cover. Receives about 5,000 poems/year, accepts 10%. Press run is 500 (200 subscribers, 20% libraries). Single copy: about $11; subscription: $20 (cash only for those sending US funds). Make checks payable to Wolfgang Goertschacher. "No requirements, but it's a good idea to subscribe to *Poetry Salzburg Review*."

How to Submit No previously published poems or simultaneous submissions. Accepts submissions by fax, on disk, by e-mail (as attachment), or by postal mail. Time between acceptance and publication is 6 months. Seldom comments on rejected poems. Occasionally publishes theme issues. Responds in 2 months. Payment varies. Acquires first rights. Reviews books and chapbooks of poetry and other magazines. Send materials for review consideration.

Book/Chapbook Needs & How to Submit Poetry Salzburg publishes "collections of at least 100 pages by mainly poets not taken up by big publishers." Publishes 6-20 paperbacks/year. Books are usually 100-700 pages, A5, professionally printed, perfect-bound, with card covers. Query first, with a few sample poems and a cover letter with brief bio and publication credits. Suggests authors publish in *Poetry Salzburg Review* first. Responds to queries in 4 weeks; to mss in about 3 months. Payment varies.

⭐ 🔘 POETRYBAY

P.O. Box 114, Northport NY 11768. (631)427-1950. Fax: (631)367-0038. E-mail: poetrybay@aol.com. Website: www.poetrybay.com. Established 2000. **Contact:** George Wallace, editor.

Magazine Needs *Poetrybay* appears biannually and "seeks to add to the body of great contemporary American poetry by presenting the work of established and emerging writers. Also, we consider essays and reviews." Has published poetry by Robert Bly, Yevgeny Yevtushenko, Marvin Bell, Diane Wakoski, Cornelius Eady, and William Heyen. *Poetrybay* is an online publication.

How to Submit Submit 5 poems at a time. Accepts simultaneous submissions; no previously published poems. Accepts e-mail submissions (pasted into body of message; no attachments); no disk submissions. Time between acceptance and publication is 2 months. Seldom comments on rejected poems. Occasionally publishes theme issues. Guidelines available on website. Sometimes sends prepublication galleys. Acquires first-time electronic rights. Reviews books and chapbooks of poetry and other magazines/journals. Send materials for review consideration.

⭐ $🔘 POETRYLIST LITERARY JOURNAL

628 Lochern Terrace, Bel Air MD 21015. (410)420-8629. E-mail: TheEditors@poetrylist.com. Website: www.poetrylist.com. Established 2001. **Contact:** Robert W. Whetzel II and Michael E. Palmer, editors.

Magazine Needs *Poetrylist Literary Journal* is a bimonthly publication whose "goal is to give voice to writers both accomplished and unknown." Wants "writing rich in imagery and innovation. Details such as line breaks and word/punctuation choices are crucial to a poem's success; poets who understand this, and who calculate their (necessary) risks will do well." Has published poetry by Lyn Coffin and Jim Williams. *Poetrylist Literary Journal* is 40-60 pages, digest-sized, laser-printed, perfect-bound, with b&w cover art, includes ads. Receives about 1,500 poems/year, accepts about 10%. Distributed free to contributors. Single copy: $5; subscription: $30. Make checks payable to *Poetrylist Literary Journal*.

How to Submit Submit 1-6 poems at a time. Accepts previously published poems and simultaneous submissions. Accepts disk submissions; no e-mail submissions. "The preferred method of submission is via the online form, as this negates errors made through copying. All postal submissions must be accompanied by a SASE." Reads submissions year round. Time between acceptance and publication is 2-6 months. Poems are circulated to an editorial board. Often comments on rejected poems. Guidelines available on website. Responds in 6 weeks. Sometimes sends prepublication galleys. Pays $1 and one contributor's copy. Reviews books and chapbooks of poetry and other magazines/journals. Send materials for review consideration to Robert W. Whetzel II.

Advice "Try to spend equal time with classic and contemporary literature. Respect Chaucer and struggle through the Middle English; study e. e. cummings. Then, when you're ready, disregard it all and find your own voice."

⭐ 🔘 THE POET'S ART

171 Silverleaf Lane, Islandia NY 11749. (631)439-0427. E-mail: ngodot1800@aol.com. Established 2000. **Contact:** David Fox and Paul Nachbar, co-editors.

Magazine Needs *The Poet's Art*, published 1-2 times/year, is "a family-style journal, accepting work from the unpublished to the well known and all levels in between." Wants "family-friendly, positive poetry; any form considered. Topics include humor, nature, religion, inspirational, children's poetry, or anything else that fits the family-friendly genre." Does not want "violent, vulgar, pornographic, or overly depressing work. Contributors should keep in mind there are mentally ill people who submit work to this journal." Accepts poetry written by children, "any age, as long as it's good quality; if under 18, get parents' permission." Has published poetry by Ward Kelley, Lyn Lifshin, John Yarbrough, Bob Wambacher, Jr., and Mark Sonnenfeld. *The Poet's Art* is 10 or more pages (varies), magazine-sized, photocopied, paper-clipped or stapled, with computer-paper cover with hand-drawn art or photograph, includes ads. Receives about 25-50 poems/year, accepts about 75%. Press run is 10-15; distributed free "to members of my local poetry group (5 members)." Single copy: $3; subscription: $3. **Only contributors who pay for the magazine receive a copy.** Make checks payable to David Fox.

How to Submit Submit no more than 5 poems at a time. Lines/poem: "Anything less than 2 typed pages, but will include longer, if exceptional quality." Accepts previously published poems and simultaneous submissions. Accepts e-mail submissions (pasted into body of message); no disk submissions. Cover letter is preferred. "It's only polite. List any other *small press* journal publications (if any), poems' titles, and include a SASE—a must!" Reads submissions year round. Submit seasonal poems 2 months in advance. Time between acceptance and publication "depends on the number of poems we receive. We will publish you ASAP. Be patient when you submit." Poems are circulated to an editorial board. "We will review all submissions together to decide what we publish." Sometimes comments on rejected poems. Guidelines available for SASE or by e-mail. Responds "as soon as possible." **Poet must buy contributor's copy to cover mailing costs ($3).** Reviews other magazines/journals "from editors/publishers who submit work to us." Send materials for review consideration to David Fox.

Advice "We enjoy and value loyalty, but remember to send out your work to as many journals as you can. Poetry is *meant* to be shared!"

☐ ◎ POETS AT WORK (Specialized: subscription)

P.O. Box 232, Lyndora PA 16045. Established 1985. **Contact:** Jessee Poet, editor/publisher.

Magazine Needs All contributors are expected to subscribe. "Every poet who writes within the dictates of good taste and within my 20-line limit will be published. I accept all forms and themes of poetry, including seasonal and holiday, but no porn, profanity, horror, bilingual/foreign language, translations, or feminism." Accepts poetry written by children if they are subscribers; "I have a lot of student subscribers." Has published poetry by Dr. Karen Springer, William Middleton, Ann Gasser, Warren Jones, Carolyn Whitaker, and Ralph Hammond. *Poets at Work*, a bimonthly, is generally 36-40 pages, magazine-sized, photocopied from typescript, saddle-stapled, with colored paper cover. Subscription: $23. Sample: $4.

How to Submit If a subscriber, submit 5-10 poems at a time. Lines/poem: 20 maximum. Accepts simultaneous submissions and previously published poems. Guidelines available for SASE. Responds within 2 weeks. No payment. "Because I publish hundreds of poets, I cannot afford to pay or give free issues. Every subscriber, of course, gets an issue."

Contest/Award Offerings Subscribers have many opportunities to regain their subscription money in the numerous contests offered in each issue. Send SASE for flyer for separate monthly and special contests.

Advice "Read others' poetry and then write, revise, subscribe, and submit to *Poets at Work*. I'll be looking for you in Box 232."

Ⓝ ☐ THE POET'S CASTLE

E-mail: poetscastle2005@aol.com. Website: www.poetscastle.com. Established 2004. **Contact:** Lynda G. Anaya, administrator.

• *Poets Castle* won a 2003-2004 Golden Web Award and a 2004 Gold Artsy Award.
Magazine Needs *The Poet's Castle* is "a poetry website devoted to publishing poetry by beginning and experienced poets. *The Poet's Castle* will be accepting all types and styles of poetry (with the exception of questionable material such as profanity or pornographic material due to possible younger members). There will be no fees involved for members. We created this site out of love for the art of poetry!" Has published poetry by Scarlett Wheeler, Adrian Saich, Donald A. McCord, Jacob-erin-cilberto(fog), Che Sarto Francisco, and Larry Powers. Receives about 520 poems/year, accepts about 80%.
How to Submit Submit 3-5 poems at a time. Lines/poem: no limit. Accepts previously published poems and simultaneous submissions. Accepts e-mail submissions (pasted into body of message; or use online form through the "Contact Us" link on website); no disk submissions. "Single-space poems. Include full name, e-mail address, pen name (if other than full name), and brief bio to be published on the website." Reads submissions year round. Submit seasonal poems one month in advance. Time between acceptance and publication is one day to one week. Always comments on rejected poems. "There are no requirements to submit; but if accepted, you would become a member; no charges for membership." Regularly publishes theme issues. List of upcoming themes and guidelines available by e-mail. Responds in one week. Acquires one-time rights.
Contest/Award Offerings Offers monthly contest. Features winner on "Star Page" on website (possibly other prizes to be announced). **Entry fee:** none. **Deadline:** 20th of each month. Guidelines available by e-mail or on website. "Each member receives a monthly newsletter describing the guidelines and theme for that month's contest."
Also Offers "Members will have the ability to comment on posted material, but there will be no scoring system, for we believe in encouraging, not discouraging, poets in their endeavors. We also believe poetry is a work of art, and that art is created by feelings from the heart, not to be judged for style or content by others."
Advice "Never give up your dreams! If you are not accepted by one place, submit again, and again! Read the work on the site or in the magazine for which you are submitting to assure that your submission is suitable. Write from your heart!"

☑ POETS ON THE LINE

P.O. Box 20292, Brooklyn NY 11202-0007. E-mail: llerner@mindspring.com. Website: www.echon yc.com/~poets. Established 1995 (founded by Andrew Gettler and Linda Lerner). **Contact:** Linda Lerner, editor. Currently not accepting unsolicited work.

◨ ◻ POETS' PODIUM

2-3265 Front Rd., E. Hawksbury ON K6A 2R2 Canada. E-mail: kennyel@hotmail.com. Website: http://geocities.com/poetspodium/. Established 1993. **Contact:** Ken Elliott, Catherine Heaney Barrowcliffe, Robert Piquette, and Ron Barrowcliffe, associate editors.
Magazine Needs *Poets' Podium* is a quarterly newsletter published "to promote the reading and writing of the poetic form, especially among those being published for the first time." Poetry specifications are open. However, does not want poetry that is gothic, erotic/sexual, gory, bloody, or that depicts violence. Subscription: $10 (US). Sample: $3 (US). "Priority is given to valued subscribers. Nevertheless, when there is room in an issue we will publish nonsubscribers."
How to Submit Submit 3 poems at a time. Lines/poem: 4 minimum, 25 maximum. Accepts previously published poems and simultaneous submissions. Cover letter is required. Include SASE (or SAE and IRC), name, address, and telephone number; e-mail address if applicable. Time between acceptance and publication varies. Guidelines available for SASE (or SAE and IRC), by fax, or by e-mail. Pays 3 contributor's copies. All rights remain with the author.
Advice "Poetry is a wonderful literary form. Try your hand at it. Send us the fruit of your labours."

◉ PORCUPINE LITERARY ARTS MAGAZINE

P.O. Box 259, Cedarburg WI 53012. E-mail: ppine259@aol.com. Website: www.porcupineliteraryar ts.com. Established 1996. **Contact:** W.A. Reed, managing editor.

Magazine Needs *Porcupine*, published biannually, contains featured artists, poetry, short fiction, and visual art. "There are no restrictions as to theme or style. Poetry should be accessible and highly selective. If a submission is not timely for one issue, it will be considered for another." Has published poetry by Carol Hamilton, James Grabill, and George Wallace. *Porcupine* is 100-150 pages, digest-sized, offset, perfect-bound, with full-color glossy cover. Receives about 500 poems/year, accepts 10%. Press run is 1,500 (500 subscribers, 50 libraries, 500 shelf sales); 100 distributed free. Single copy: $8.95; subscription: $15.95. Sample: $5.

How to Submit Submit up to 3 poems, one/page with name and address on each. Include SASE. "The outside of the envelope should state: 'Poetry.' " No previously published poems or simultaneous submissions. Accepts e-mail submissions (pasted into body of message). Time between acceptance and publication is 6 months. "Poems are selected by editors and then submitted to managing editor for final approval." Seldom comments on rejected poems. Guidelines available for SASE or on website. Responds in 3 months. Pays one contributor's copy. Acquires one-time rights.

⬛ ◪ PORTLAND REVIEW

Portland State University, Box 347, Portland OR 97207-0347. (503)725-4533. Fax: (503)725-4534. Website: www.portlandreview.org ("our website is a general introduction to our magazine, with samples of our poetry, fiction, and art."). Established 1956. **Contact:** Poetry Editor. Editor: Kevin Friedman.

Magazine Needs & How to Submit *Portland Review* is a literary journal published 3 times/year by Portland State University. "We seek submissions exhibiting a unique and compelling voice, and content of substance. Experimental poetry welcomed." Has published poetry by Gaylord Brewer, Richard Bentley, Charles Jensen, Mary Biddinger, and Jerzy Gizella. The journal is about 130 pages. Accepts about 30 of 1,000 poems received each year. Press run is 1,000 (subscribers, libraries, and bookstores nationwide.) Single copy: $9; subscription: $28/year, $54/2 years. Sample: $8. Submit up to 5 poems. Accepts simultaneous submissions. Accepts submissions by postal mail only. Guidelines available for SASE or on website. Responds in up to 4 months. Pays one contributor's copy.

Advice "Include a SASE and specify if submissions need to be returned. Otherwise they will be recycled."

◻ POTLUCK CHILDREN'S LITERARY MAGAZINE (Specialized: children/teens)

P.O. Box 546, Deerfield IL 60015-0546. (847)948-1139. Fax: (847)317-9492. E-mail: susan@potluck magazine.org. Website: http://potluckmagazine.org. Established 1997. **Contact:** Susan Napoli Picchietti, editor.

Magazine Needs *Potluck* is a not-for-profit magazine published quarterly "to provide a forum which encourages young writers to share their voice and to learn their craft. Open to all styles, forms, and subjects—we just want well-crafted poems that speak to the reader. No poems so abstract they only have meaning to the writer. Violent, profane, or sexually explicit poems will not be accepted." *Potluck* is 48 pages, digest-sized, photocopied, saddle-stapled, with 60-lb. glossy paper cover with original artwork. Receives about 350 poems/quarter. Press run is over 1,110 (150 subscribers, 800 shelf sales). Single copy: $5.80 US ($7.80 Canada); subscription: $21.99 US ($31.99 Canada). Sample (including guidelines): $4.25.

How to Submit Submit up to 3 poems at a time. Lines/poem: 30 maximum. No previously published poems or simultaneous submissions. Accepts submissions by fax, by e-mail (pasted into body of message), and by postal mail. Cover letter is optional. "Submissions without a SASE or an e-mail address will not be considered." Poems are circulated to an editorial board. "We each review every poem, make our remarks on them, then discuss our view of each—the best works make the issue." Always comments on rejected poems. Guidelines available in magazine, for SASE, by fax, by e-mail, or on website. Responds 6 weeks after deadline. Pays one contributor's copy. Acquires first rights. Reviews chapbooks of poetry.

Advice "Be present; write what you see, hear, taste, smell, observe, and what you feel/experience. Be honest, clear, and choose your words with great care. Enjoy."

⊘ THE POTOMAC

2020 Pennsylvania Ave. NW, Suite 443, Washington DC 20006. E-mail: the_potomac@cox.net. Website: www.webdelsol.com/The_Potomac. Established 2004. **Contact:** Blake Walmsley, editor. Member: Web del Sol.

Magazine Needs *The Potomac* is a quarterly online literary magazine featuring political commentary, cutting-edge poetry, flash fiction, and reviews. Open to all forms of poetry by new and established writers. Has published poetry by Jim Daniels, Elaine Equi, Maurice Oliver, Holly Iglesias, and Ilya Kaminsky. Receives a "variable" number of poems/year, accepts about 50-60. Free online.

How to Submit Submit any number of poems at a time. Accepts simultaneous submissions; no previously published poems. Accepts e-mail submissions (as attachment); no disk submissions. Cover letter is preferred. Reads submissions year round. Time between acceptance and publication is 3 months. Often comments on rejected poems. Guidelines available on website. Responds in 2 months. Sometimes sends prepublication galleys. No payment. Acquires one-time rights. Reviews books and chapbooks of poetry and other magazines/journals in up to 2,000 words, single- and multi-book format. Send materials for review consideration.

Advice "We welcome the opportunity to read work from new writers."

▣ ⊘ POTOMAC REVIEW: A JOURNAL OF ARTS & HUMANITIES

Montgomery College, Paul Peck Humanities Institute, 51 Mannakee St., Rockville MD 20850. (301)610-4100. Fax: (301)738-1745. E-mail: wattrsedge@aol.com. Website: www.montgomerycoll ege.edu/potomacreview. Established 1994. **Contact:** Christa Watters, editor. Managing Editor: Judith Gaines.

Magazine Needs Appearing in November and May, "*Potomac Review* is a regionally rooted semiannual at the heart of the nation with a national and international range. *Potomac Review* seeks poets from all quarters and focuses." Has published poetry by Judith McCombs, Virgil Suárez, and Hugh Fox. *Potomac Review* is 248 pages, digest-sized, offset-printed, perfect-bound, with medium card cover, includes ads. Receives about 2,500 poems/year, accepts 3%. Subscription: $18/year, $18.90/ year for MD residents (includes 2 double issues), $30/2 years. Sample: $10.

How to Submit Submit up to 3 poems (5 pages maximum) at a time, with SASE. Accepts simultaneous submissions; no previously published poems. Cover letter with brief bio is preferred. Time between acceptance and publication is up to one year. Poems are read "in house," then sent to poetry editor for comments and dialogue. Often comments on rejected poems. Publishes theme issues. List of upcoming themes and guidelines available for SASE or on website. Responds within 6 months. Pays 2 contributor's copies and offers 40% discount on additional copies. Acquires first North American serial rights. Reviews books of poetry; write first for review consideration.

Contest/Award Offerings Sponsors an annual poetry contest. Offers 1st Prize: $500; winner's poem and some runners-up are published. Submit up to 3 poems, any subject, any form. **Entry fee:** $18 ($18.90 for MD residents), includes one-year subscription. **Deadline:** postmarked by January 1, 2006. Guidelines available for SASE, in fall/winter issue, or on website.

▨ $⊘ ◎ THE PRAIRIE JOURNAL; PRAIRIE JOURNAL PRESS (Specialized: regional/prairie; themes)

P.O. Box 61203, Brentwood Post Office, 217-3630 Brentwood Rd. NW, Calgary AB T2L 2K6 Canada. E-mail: prairiejournal@yahoo.com. Website: www.geocities.com/prairiejournal. Established 1983. **Contact:** A. Burke, editor.

Magazine Needs *The Prairie Journal* appears twice/year. Wants poetry of "any length; free verse, contemporary themes (feminist, nature, urban, non-political), aesthetic value, a poet's poetry." Does not want to see "most rhymed verse, sentimentality, egotistical ravings. No cowboys or sage brush." Has published poetry by Liliane Welch, Cornelia Hoogland, Sheila Hyland, Zoe Lendale, and Chad Norman. *Prairie Journal* is 40-60 pages, 7×8½, offset, saddle-stapled, with card cover, includes ads. Receives about 1,000 poems/year, accepts 10%. Press run is 600 (200 subscribers,

50% libraries); the rest are distributed on the newsstand. Subscription: $8 for individuals, $15 for libraries. Sample: $8 ("Use postal money order.").

How to Submit No simultaneous submissions or previously published poems. Does not accept e-mail submissions. Guidelines available for postage (but "no U.S. stamps, please"—get IRCs from the Post Office) or on website. "We will not be reading submissions until such time as an issue is in preparation (twice yearly), so be patient and we will acknowledge, accept for publication, or return work at that time." Sometimes sends prepublication galleys. Pays $10-50 plus one contributor's copy. Acquires first North American serial rights. Reviews books of poetry, "but must be assigned by editor. Query first."

Book/Chapbook Needs & How to Submit For chapbook publication, Canadian poets only (preferably from the region) should query with 5 samples, bio, and publication credits. Responds to queries in 2 months, to mss in 6 months. Payment in modest honoraria. Has published *Voices From Earth*, selected poems by Ronald Kurt and Mark McCawley, and *In the Presence of Grace* by McCandless Callaghan. "We also publish anthologies on themes when material is available."

Also Offers Publishes "Poems of the Month" online. Submit up to 4 poems for $1 reading fee.

Advice "Read recent poets! Experiment with line length, images, metaphors. Innovate."

⚡ ◩ PRAIRIE SCHOONER; STROUSSE AWARD; LARRY LEVIS PRIZE; GLENNA LUSCHEI PRIZE; BERNICE SLOTE PRIZE; VIRGINIA FAULKNER AWARD; HUGH J. LUKE AWARD; EDWARD STANLEY AWARD; JANE GESKE AWARD; READERS' CHOICE AWARDS; PRIZE BOOK SERIES

201 Andrews Hall, University of Nebraska, Lincoln NE 68588-0334. (402)472-0911. Fax: (402)472-9771. E-mail: kgrey@unl.edu. Website: www.unl.edu/schooner/psmain.htm. Established 1926. **Contact**: Hilda Raz, editor-in-chief. Managing Editor: Kelly Grey Carlisle.

- Poetry published in *Prairie Schooner* has been selected for inclusion in *The Best American Poetry 1996* and the *Pushcart Prize* anthology.

Magazine Needs *Prairie Schooner* is "one of the oldest literary quarterlies in continuous publication; publishes poetry, fiction, personal essays, interviews, and reviews." Wants "poems that fulfill the expectations they set up." No specifications as to form, length, style, subject matter, or purpose. Has published poetry by Alicia Ostriker, Marilyn Hacker, D.A. Powell, Stephen Dunn, and David Ignatow. *Prairie Schooner* is about 200 pages, digest-sized, flat-spined. Receives about 4,800 submissions/year, uses about 300 pages of poetry. Press run is 3,100. Single copy: $9; subscription: $26. Sample: $6.

How to Submit Submit 5-7 poems at a time. No simultaneous submissions. No fax or e-mail submissions. "Clear copy appreciated. Submissions must be received between September 1 and June 1. All manuscripts published in *Prairie Schooner* will be automatically considered for our annual prizes." Guidelines available for SASE or on website. Responds in 4 months; "sooner if possible." Always sends prepublication galleys. Pays 3 contributor's copies. Acquires all rights. Returns rights upon request without fee. Reviews books of poetry. Send materials for review consideration.

Contest/Award Offerings The Strousse Award for poetry ($500), the Bernice Slote Prize for beginning writers ($500), the Hugh J. Luke Award ($250), the Edward Stanley Award for poetry ($1,000), the Virginia Faulkner Award for Excellence in Writing ($1,000), the Glenna Luschei Prize for literary distinction ($1,000), the Jane Geske Award ($250), and the Larry Levis Prize for Poetry ($1,000). Also, each year 4-8 Readers' Choice Awards ($250 each) are given for poetry, fiction, and nonfiction. **All contests are open only to those writers whose work was published in the magazine the previous year.** Editors serve as judges. Also sponsors an annual Prize Book Series, offering $3,000 and publication of a book-length collection of poetry by the University of Nebraska Press. **Entry fee:** $25. See website for deadline and guidelines.

Also Offers Editor-in-Chief Hilda Raz also promotes poets whose work has appeared in her pages by listing their continued accomplishments in a special section (even when their work does not concurrently appear in the magazine).

❖ ○ ◎ PRAYERWORKS (Specialized: religious; senior citizen)

P.O. Box 301363, Portland OR 97294-9363. (503)761-2072. E-mail: jay4prayer@aol.com. Established 1988. **Contact:** V. Ann Mandeville, editor.

Magazine Needs Established as a ministry to people living in retirement centers, *PrayerWorks* is a weekly newsletter "encouraging elderly people to recognize their value to God as prayer warriors." Features "prayers, ways to pray, stories of answered prayers, teaching on a Scripture portion, articles that build faith, and poems." *PrayerWorks* is 4 pages, digest-sized, photocopied, desktop-published, folded. Receives about 50 poems/year, accepts about 25%. Press run is 1,000 (1,000 subscribers). Subscription: free.

How to Submit Submit 5 poems, one/page. Accepts previously published poems and simultaneous submissions. Accepts e-mail submissions (WordPerfect or Microsoft Word files). Cover letter is preferred. Time between acceptance and publication is usually within one month. Seldom comments on rejected poems. Publishes theme issues relating to the holidays (submit holiday poetry 2 months in advance). Guidelines available for SASE. Responds in 3 weeks. Pays 5 or more contributor's copies.

◎ PREMIERE GENERATION INK

P.O. Box 2056, Madison WI 53701-2056. E-mail: poetry@premieregeneration.com. Website: www.premieregeneration.com. Established 1998. **Contact:** Poetry Editor.

Magazine Needs & How to Submit *Premiere Generation Ink* publishes "high-quality, honest poetry in a print journal as well as multimedia online. We also publish art, photos, and live audio or video poetry for the website." Has published poetry by Ruth Stone, Liz Rosenberg, Martín Espada, Alix Olson, and Virgil Suárez; interviewed Pulitzer Prize-winning poet Richard Eberhart, Guy Picciotto of the band Fugazi, and Naomi Klein. *Premiere Generation Ink* is 30-40 pages; past covers have been made on a letterpress; the cover of issue #7 was hand painted. Single copy: $5; subscription: $18. *PGI* is currently not accepting submissions. Any submissions received will be recycled.

◙ ◎ PRESS HERE (Specialized: form/haiku and tanka)

22230 NE 28th Place, Sammamish WA 98074-6408. E-mail: WelchM@aol.com. Established 1989. **Contact:** Michael Dylan Welch, editor/publisher.

- ● Press Here publications have won the first-place Merit Book Award and other awards from the Haiku Society of America.

Book/Chapbook Needs Press Here publishes award-winning books of haiku, tanka, and related poetry by the leading poets of these genres, as well as essays, criticism, and interviews about these genres. "We publish work only by those poets who are already frequently published in the leading haiku and tanka journals." Does not want any poetry other than haiku, tanka, and related genres. Has published poetry by Lee Gurga, paul m., Paul O. Williams, Pat Shelley, Cor van den Heuvel, and William J. Higginson. Publishes 2-3 poetry books/year, plus occasional books of essays or interviews. Manuscripts are selected through open submission. Books are 32-112 pages, offset-printed, perfect-bound, saddle-stapled, with glossy paperback covers.

How to Submit Query first, with a few sample poems and a cover letter with brief bio and publication credits. Book mss may include previously published poems ("previous publication strongly preferred"). "All proposals must be by well-established haiku or tanka poets, and must be for haiku or tanka poetry, or criticism/discussion of these genres. If the editor does not already know your work well from leading haiku and tanka publications, then he is not likely to be interested in your manuscript." Responds to queries in up to one month; to mss in up to 2 months. Pays a negotiated percentage of author's copies (out of a press run of 200-1,000). Catalog available for #10 SASE.

Advice "Press Here publishes only 2-3 titles per year by leading haiku and tanka poets. For Press Here to publish your book, you will likely already know other Press Here books and the work of their authors, and the editor would most likely already know you and your work. If not, then establish yourself in these genres first by publishing extensively in the leading haiku or tanka journals."

☐ ◎ THE PRESS OF THE THIRD MIND (Specialized: form/style—Dada/surrealism)

1301 North Dearborn #1007, Chicago IL 60610. E-mail: bradleylastname@lycos.com. Established 1985. **Contact:** Bradley Bonghogger, poetry editor.

Book/Chapbook Needs The Press of the Third Mind is a small press publisher of artist books, poetry, and fiction. "We are especially interested in found poems, Dada, surrealism, written table-scraps left on the floors of lunatic asylums by incurable psychotics, etc." Has published *Oracle Whip* by Bradley Lastname, *Blest This Poet Crest on My Chest* by Robert Pomehrn, and *The Intrusive Ache of Morning* by Patrick Porter. Press run is 1,000, with books often going into a second or third printing.

How to Submit Submit up to 20 sample poems. "No anthologized manuscripts where every poem has already appeared somewhere else." Accepts simultaneous submissions if noted. Accepts submissions by postal mail only. "Cover letter is good, but we don't need to know everything you've published since age 9 in single-spaced detail." Authors are paid "as the publication transcends the break-even benchmark." The press has released an 80-page anthology entitled *Empty Calories*, and published a deconstructivist novel about the repetition compulsion: *The Squeaky Fromme Gets the Grease*. Order sample books by sending $1.43 postage.

Advice "We are the press, of the third mind, an eye for an eye, till the hole whirled is blind."

☑ ◎ PRIMAVERA (Specialized: women)

P.O. Box #37-7547, Chicago IL 60637. Established 1975. **Contact:** Board of Editors.

Magazine Needs *Primavera* is "an irregularly published but approximately annual magazine of poetry and fiction reflecting the experiences of women. We look for strong, original voice and imagery; generally prefer free verse, fairly short length; related, even tangentially, to women's experience." Has published poetry by Margaret Lloyd, Gail Martin, Laurie Lamon, Pamela Gemin, and Andrea Potos. *Primavera* is elegantly printed, flat-spined. Receives over 1,000 submissions of poetry/year, accepts about 25. Press run is 1,000. Single copy: $10. Sample: $7.

How to Submit Submit up to 6 poems at any time; no queries. No previously published poems or simultaneous submissions. Editors comment on rejected poems "when requested or inspired." Guidelines available in magazine or for SASE. Responds in up to 6 months. Pays 2 contributor's copies. Acquires first-time rights.

Advice "Be original with fresh imagery. Read a lot of poetry."

✖ ◎ PRINCETON UNIVERSITY PRESS; LOCKERT LIBRARY OF POETRY IN TRANSLATION (Specialized: bilingual; translations)

41 William St., Princeton NJ 08540. (609)258-4900. Fax: (609)258-6305. Website: www.pupress.princeton.edu. **Contact:** Hanne Winarsky, editor.

Book Needs "In the Lockert Library series, we publish simultaneous cloth and paperback (flat-spine) editions for each poet. Clothbound editions are on acid-free paper, and binding materials are chosen for strength and durability. Each book is given individual design treatment rather than stamped into a series mold. We have published a wide range of poets from other cultures, including well-known writers such as Hölderlin and Cavafy, and those who have not yet had their due in English translation, such as Göran Sonnevi. Manuscripts are judged with several criteria in mind: the ability of the translation to stand on its own as poetry in English; fidelity to the tone and spirit of the original, rather than literal accuracy; and the importance of the translated poet to the literature of his or her time and country."

How to Submit Accepts simultaneous submissions if informed. Accepts submissions by fax and by postal mail. Cover letter is required. Reads submissions year round. "Manuscripts will not be returned." Comments on finalists only. Guidelines available for SASE. Responds in 3 months.

✖ ☑ $☑ PRISM INTERNATIONAL

Creative Writing Program, Buchanan E462-1866 Main Mall, University of British Columbia, Vancouver BC V6T 1Z1 Canada. E-mail: prism@interchange.ubc.ca. Website: http://prism.arts.ubc.ca. Established 1959. **Contact:** Editor (rotating title).

● *PRISM international* is one of the top literary journals in Canada.

Magazine Needs ''*PRISM* is an international quarterly that publishes poetry, drama, short fiction, imaginative nonfiction, and translation into English in all genres. We have no thematic or stylistic allegiances: Excellence is our main criterion for acceptance of manuscripts. We want fresh, distinctive poetry that shows an awareness of traditions old and new. We read everything.'' Accepts poetry by young writers—''Excellence is the only criterion.'' Has published poetry by Marlene Cookshaw, Warren Heiti, Don McKay, Bill Bissett, and Stephanie Bolster. *PRISM international* is 96 pages, digest-sized, elegantly printed, flat-spined, with original color artwork on a glossy card cover. Receives 1,000 submissions/year, accepts about 80. Circulation is for 1,100 subscribers (200 libraries). Subscription: $22, $35/2 years. (Please note: Canadian subscribers add GST; all others, please pay in US $). Sample: $9.95.

How to Submit Submit up to 6 poems at a time, ''any print so long as it's typed.'' Include SASE (or SAE with IRCs); ''Note: American stamps are not valid postage in Canada. No SASEs with U.S. postage will be returned.'' No previously published poems or simultaneous submissions. Cover letter with brief introduction and previous publications is required. ''Translations must be accompanied by a copy of the original.'' Guidelines available for SASE (or SAE with IRCs), by e-mail, or on website. Responds in up to 6 months. Pays $40/printed page plus subscription; plus an additional $10/printed page to selected authors for publication online. Editors sometimes comment on rejected poems. Acquires first North American serial rights.

Advice ''While we don't automatically discount any kind of poetry, we prefer to publish work that challenges the writer as much as it does the reader. We are particularly looking for poetry in translation.''

⊠ ▢ PROSE AX

P.O. Box 22643, Honolulu HI 96823. E-mail: editor@proseax.com. Website: www.proseax.com. Established 2000. **Contact:** J. Salazar, editor.

● *Prose Ax* won Honorable Mention in the *Writer's Digest* Zine Competition for 2000 and 2001.

Magazine Needs *Prose Ax* appears 1-3 times/year, showcasing ''prose, poetry, and visual arts with an edge from emerging and established artists.'' Wants well crafted free verse. ''We usually lean toward poems that 'tell stories' versus poems that 'paint a landscape.' '' Does not want haiku, rhyming poetry, epic poems, or poems in Old English. Has published poetry by Richard Jordan, Eric Paul Shaffer, Cyril Wong, and C.R. Garza. *Prose Ax* is 24-36 pages, $5\frac{1}{2} \times 8\frac{1}{2}$, digital copies, stapled, with 100-lb. b&w cover; excerpts published online. Receives about 240 poems/year, accepts about 30. Press run is 500. Single copy: $2.92/issue; subscription: $7.50 for 3 issues. Make checks payable to *Prose Ax*.

How to Submit Submit 3-6 poems at a time. Accepts previously published poems and simultaneous submissions. Accepts e-mail submissions; no disk submissions. Cover letter is preferred (''but doesn't have to be formal''). ''Prefer e-mail submissions, pasted into body of e-mail, attached if there are formatting issues.'' Reads submissions year round. Time between acceptance and publication is 1-3 months. Poems are reviewed between editor and assistant editor. Often comments on rejected poems (if asked). Guidelines available for SASE, by e-mail, or on website. Responds in up to 4 months. Always sends prepublication galleys. Pays 2 contributor's copies. Acquires one-time rights.

Advice ''At the least, read the poems online to see what our tastes are.''

$ ▣ PROVINCETOWN ARTS; PROVINCETOWN ARTS PRESS

650 Commercial St., Provincetown MA 02657-1725. (508)487-3167. E-mail: cbusa@comcast.net. Website: www.provincetownarts.org. Established 1985. **Contact:** Christopher Busa, editor.

Magazine Needs An elegant annual using quality poetry, ''*Provincetown Arts* focuses broadly on the artists and writers who inhabit or visit the tip of Cape Cod, and seeks to stimulate creative activity and enhance public awareness of the cultural life of the nation's oldest continuous art colony. Drawing upon a century-long tradition rich in visual art, literature, and theater, *Provincetown Arts* publishes material with a view towards demonstrating that the artists' colony, functioning outside the urban centers, is a utopian dream with an ongoing vitality." Has published poetry by Bruce Smith, Franz Wright, Sandra McPherson, and Cyrus Cassells. Published in July, *Provincetown Arts* is about 170 pages, magazine-sized, perfect-bound, with full-color glossy cover. Press run is 10,000 (500 subscribers, 20 libraries, 6,000 shelf sales). Sample: $10.

How to Submit Submit up to 3 typed poems at a time. All queries and submissions should be via postal mail. Reads submissions October through February. Guidelines available for SASE. Responds in 3 months. Usually sends prepublication galleys. Pays $25-100/poem plus 2 contributor's copies. Acquires first rights. Reviews books of poetry in 500-3,000 words, single- or multi-book format. Send materials for review consideration.

Book/Chapbook Needs & How to Submit The Provincetown Arts Press has published 8 volumes of poetry. The Provincetown Poets Series includes *At the Gate* by Martha Rhodes, *Euphorbia* by Anne-Marie Levine (a finalist in the 1995 Paterson Poetry Prize), and *1990* by Michael Klein (co-winner of the 1993 Lambda Literary Award).

☐ THE PUCKERBRUSH PRESS; THE PUCKERBRUSH REVIEW

76 Main St., Orono ME 04473-1430. (207)866-4868. Press established 1971; *Review* established 1978. **Contact:** Constance Hunting, poetry editor.

Magazine Needs & How to Submit *The Puckerbrush Review* is a literary magazine published twice/year. Looks for freshness and simplicity, but does not want to see "confessional, religious, sentimental, dull, feminist, incompetent, derivative" poetry. Has published poetry by Wolly Swist and Muska Nagel. Submit 5 poems at a time. Accepts submissions by postal mail only. Guidelines available for SASE. Pays 2 contributor's copies.

Book/Chapbook Needs & How to Submit The Puckerbrush Press is a small press publisher of flat-spined paperbacks of literary quality. Has published *At Water's Edge* by Margaret Shipley, *Revelation* by Robert Taylor, *At Fifteen* by May Sarton (early journal), and *Catching Beauty* by May Sarton. For book publication, query with 10 sample poems. Prefers no simultaneous submissions. Offers criticism for a fee: $100 is usual. Pays 10% royalties plus 10 author's copies.

Advice "Just write the best and freshest poetry you can."

☑ ◎ PUDDING HOUSE PUBLICATIONS; PUDDING MAGAZINE: THE INTERNATIONAL JOURNAL OF APPLIED POETRY; PUDDING HOUSE CHAPBOOK COMPETITIONS; PUDDING HOUSE INNOVATIVE WRITERS PROGRAMS (Specialized: political; social issues; popular culture reflected in poetry arts)

81 Shadymere Lane, Columbus OH 43213. (614)986-1881. E-mail: info@puddinghouse.com. Website: www.puddinghouse.com. Established 1979. **Contact:** Jennifer Bosveld, editor.

Magazine Needs Pudding House Publications provides "a sociological looking glass through poems that speak to the pop culture, struggle in a consumer and guardian society, and more—through 'felt experience.' Speaks for the difficulties and the solutions. Additionally a forum for poems and articles by people who take poetry arts into the schools and the human services." Publishes *Pudding* every several months; also chapbooks, anthologies, broadsides. Wants "what hasn't been said before. Speak the unspeakable. Don't want preachments or sentimentality. Don't want obvious traditional forms without fresh approach. Long poems OK as long as they aren't windy. Interested in receiving poetry on popular culture, rich brief narratives, i.e. 'virtual journalism' (see website)." Has published poetry by Knute Skinner, David Chorlton, Mary Winters, and Robert Collins. *Pudding* is 70 pages, digest-sized, offset-composed on Microsoft Word PC. Press run is 1,500 (1,100 subscribers). Subscription: $29.95/4 issues. Sample: $8.95.

How to Submit Submit 3-10 poems at a time, with SASE. "Submissions without SASEs will be discarded." No postcards. No simultaneous submissions. Previously published submissions respected, "but include credits." Likes cover letters and "cultivates great relationships with writers." Sometimes publishes theme issues. Guidelines available on website only. Responds on same day (unless traveling). Pays one contributor's copy; $10 and 4 contributor's copies to featured poets. Returns rights "with *Pudding* permitted to reprint." Send materials for review consideration or listing as recommended. "See our website for vast calls for poems for magazine, chapbooks, and anthologies; for poetry and word games; and essays and workshop announcements."

Book/Chapbook Needs & How to Submit Has recently published *The Allegories* by Dan Sicoli, *Barb Quill Down* by Bill Griffin, *Sonnets to Hamlet* by David Rigsbee, *Mischief* by Charlene Fix, and over 120 others last year. Chapbooks considered outside of competitions, no query. **Reading fee:** $10. Send complete ms and cover letter with publication credits and bio. Editor sometimes comments; will critique on request for $4/page of poetry or $85/hour in person.

Contest/Award Offerings Pudding House is the publisher of the nationwide project POETS' GREATEST HITS—an invitational. They have nearly 500 chapbooks and books in print. Pudding House offers an annual chapbook competition. **Entry fee:** $15. **Deadline:** September 30. Guidelines and details available on website.

Also Offers "Our website is one of the greatest poetry websites in the country—calls, workshops, publication list/history, online essays, games, guest pages, calendars, poem of the month, poet of the week, much more." The website also links to the site for The Unitarian Universalist Poets Cooperative and American Poets Opposed to Executions, both national organizations.

Advice "Editors have pet peeves. I won't respond to postcards. I require SASEs. I don't like cover letters that state the obvious, poems with trite concepts, or meaning dictated by rhyme. Thoroughly review our website; it will give you a good idea about our publication history and editorial tastes."

◖ ◎ THE PUDDIN'HEAD PRESS (Specialized: regional/Chicago)

P.O. Box 477889, Chicago IL 60647. (708)656-4900. E-mail: phbooks@compuserve.com. Website: www.puddinheadpress.com. Established 1985. **Contact:** David Gecic, editor-in-chief.

Book/Chapbook Needs & How to Submit The Puddin'head Press is interested in "well-rounded poets who can support their work with readings and appearances. Most of our poets are drawn from the performance poetry community." Wants "quality poetry by active poets. We occasionally publish chapbook-style anthologies and let poets on our mailing lists know what type of work we're interested in for a particular project." Does not want experimental, overly political poetry, or poetry with overt sexual content; no shock or novelty poems. Has published *Inside Job* by Robert Boone and *The Laundromat Girl* by Lee Kitzis. Puddin'head Press publishes one book and one chapbook/year. Books/chapbooks are 30-100 pages, perfect-bound or side-stapled ("we use various formats"). Responds to queries in one month; to mss in 3 months. Poets must include SASE with submission. Pays various royalty rates "depending on the publication. We usually have a press run of 500 books." **About 25% of books are author-subsidy published.** Terms vary. Order sample books/chapbooks by sending $10 (price plus postage) to The Puddin'head Press (also available through Amazon).

Also Offers "We prefer to work closely with poets in the Chicago area. There are numerous readings and events that we sponsor. We do our own distribution, primarily in the Midwest, and also do distribution for other small presses. Please send a SASE for a list of our current publications and publication/distribution guidelines."

Advice "It is difficult to find a quality publisher. Poets must have patience and find a press that will work with them. The most important part of publication is the relationship between poet and publisher. Many good books will never be seen because the poet/publisher relationship is not healthy. If a poet is involved in the literary world, he will find a publisher, or a publisher will find him."

◖ PUERTO DEL SOL

New Mexico State University, Box 30001, Dept. 3E, Las Cruces NM 88003-8001. (505)646-2345. Fax: (505)646-7725. E-mail: puerto@nmsu.edu. Website: www.nmsu.edu/ ~ puerto/welcome.html. Established 1972 (in present format). **Contact:** Kathleene West, poetry editor. Editor-in-Chief: Kevin McIlvoy.

Magazine Needs "We publish a literary magazine twice per year. Interested in poems, fiction, essays, photos, and translations, usually from the Spanish; also (generally solicited) reviews and interviews with writers. We want top-quality poetry, any style, from anywhere; excellent poetry of any kind, any form.'' Has published poetry by Richard Blanco, Maria Ercilla, Pamela Gemin, John Repp, and Lee Ann Roripaugh. *Puerto del Sol* is 150 pages, digest-sized, professionally printed, flat-spined, with matte card cover with art. Receives about 900 poetry submissions/year, accepts about 50. Press run is 1,250 (300 subscribers, 25-30 libraries). Subscription: $10/2 issues. Sample: $8.

How to Submit Submit 3-6 poems at a time, one poem/page. Accepts simultaneous submissions. No e-mail submissions. Brief cover letter is welcome. ''Do not send publication vitae.'' Reads mss September 1 to February 1 only. Offers editorial comments on most mss. Tries to respond within 6 months. Sometimes sends prepublication galleys. Pays 2 contributor's copies.

Advice ''Read the magazine before submitting work.''

PULSAR POETRY MAGAZINE; LIGDEN PUBLISHERS

34 Lineacre, Grange Park, Swindon, Wiltshire SN5 6DA United Kingdom. Phone: (01793)875941. E-mail: pulsar.ed@btopenworld.com. Website: www.pulsarpoetry.com. Established 1992. **Contact:** David Pike, editor. Editorial Assistant: Jill Meredith.

Magazine Needs *Pulsar*, published quarterly, ''encourages the writing of poetry from all walks of life. Contains poems, reviews, and editorial comments.'' Wants ''hard-hitting, thought-provoking work; interesting and stimulating poetry.'' Does not want ''racist material. Not keen on religious poetry.'' Has published poetry by Merryn Williams, Liz Atkin, Li Min Hua, Virgil Suárez, and Michael Newman. *Pulsar* is 36 pages, A5, professionally printed, saddle-stapled, with glossy full-color cover, includes ads. Press run is 300 (100 subscribers, 40 libraries); several distributed free to newspapers, etc. Subscription: $30 (£12 UK). Sample: $7. Make checks payable to Ligden Publishers.

How to Submit Submit 3 poems at a time, ''preferably typed.'' No previously published poems or simultaneous submissions. ''Send no more than 2 poems via e-mail; file attachments will not be read.'' Cover letter is preferred; include SAE with IRCs. ''Poems can be published in next edition if it is what we are looking for. The editor and assistant read all poems.'' Time between acceptance and publication is about one month. Seldom comments on rejected poems. Guidelines available for SASE (or SAE and IRC) or on website. Responds within 3 weeks. Pays one contributor's copy. ''Originators retain copyright of their poems.'' Acquires first rights. Staff reviews poetry books and poetry audio tapes (mainstream); word count varies. Send materials for review consideration.

Advice ''Give explanatory notes if poems are open to interpretation. Be patient and enjoy what you are doing. Check grammar, spelling, etc. (should be obvious). Note: we are a non-profit-making society.''

PULSE ONLINE LITERARY JOURNAL; PULSE POETRY PRIZE

7781 SVL Box, Victorville CA 92395-5117. (760)243-8034. E-mail: mimi47@mac.com. Website: www.heartsoundspress.com. Established 1997. **Contact:** Carol Bachofner, poetry editor.

Magazine Needs *Pulse Online Literary Journal* wants ''your best. Send only work revised and revised again! Open to formal poetry along with free verse. Translations welcome.'' Does not want ''predictable, sentimental, greeting card verse. No gratuitous sexuality or violence. No religious verse or predictable rhyme.'' Has published poetry by Walt McDonald and Lyn Lifshin. Receives about 400 poems/year, accepts about 10-15%.

How to Submit Submit 3-5 poems at a time. Lines/poem: up to 120. Accepts previously published poems. Accepts e-mail submissions (pasted into body of e-mail); no disk submissions. Cover letter is required. ''Send bio of 50-100 words with submission.'' Reads submissions year round. Submit seasonal poems 2 months in advance. Time between acceptance and publication is 3-4 weeks. Sometimes comments on rejected poems. Sometimes publishes theme issues. List of upcoming themes available by e-mail. Guidelines available on website. Responds in 3-4 weeks. Acquires first rights. Reviews books and chapbooks of poetry.

Keith Taylor

Poetry—a lifestyle choice

Canadian-born poet Keith Taylor sits in his Ann Arbor, Michigan, office, surrounded floor-to-ceiling by bookshelves. They spill over with novels, chapbooks, and stacks of papers, leaving little space for his desk or even room to stretch his legs. Behind him the one free wall is covered with a larger-than-life poster of Greek poet C.P. Cavafy. I sit across from Taylor in the chair usually designated for his creative writing students in the University of Michigan's English Department. My former professor (and now friend) is comparing the dimensions of his office to the one-room apartment he inhabited in Paris as a young man. "It was even smaller," he admits.

He describes spending what little money he had in those days on International Reply Coupons, sending out poems from his Parisian closet to journals in Ireland, England, Canada, the United States, "and everywhere else in the English-speaking world." Although he succeeded in publishing a few of his poems, Taylor recalls the countless rejection letters he received, and how he taped them to the wall, completely covering it.

"Before moving out," he says, "I stood at my door, my backpack slung over my shoulder, looking at my small room marked by a wall of rejection letters, and wondered what it would mean to the next person who lived there."

Taylor has come a long way since then. His stories, book reviews, translations, and feature articles have been published widely, and his poems have appeared in many North American and European journals, including *The Beloit Poetry Journal*, *Hanging Loose*, *The Michigan Quarterly Review*, *Mondo Greco*, *New Letters*, and *Poetry Ireland Review*. In addition to having work anthologized by several university presses, Taylor has published five collections of poetry: *Learning to Dance* (Falling Water Books, 1985); *Weather Report* (Ridgeway Press, 1988); *Dream of the Black Wolf: Notes from Isle Royale* (Ridgeway Press, 1993); *Detail from the Garden of Delights* (Limited Mailing Press, 1993); and *Everything I Need* (March Street Press, 1996). His newest book, *Guilty at the Rapture*, a mix of poems, stories, and short essays, is being published by Hanging Loose Press.

Taylor has made a name for himself as an editor as well. With colleague John Knott, he co-edited and wrote for *The Huron River: Voices from the Watershed* (University of Michigan Press, 2000); it was a finalist for the 2001 Great Lakes Book Award for General Nonfiction. With Artemis Leontis and Lauren Talalay, Taylor also co-edited the collection *What These Ithakas Mean: Reading Cavafy* (Athens, Greece: E. L. I. A., 2002), named one of 2002's "Books of the Year" in the *Times Literary Supplement*. In 2003, Taylor began serving as co-editor (with Charles Baxter) of "Sweetwater Fiction: Reintroductions" (University of Michigan Press), a series of reprinted fiction by earlier Midwestern writers.

Taylor has not always worked in the literary realm, however. He put himself through

Bethel College as a housepainter in South Bend, Indiana. Over the years, he's labored as a hunting outfitter, dishwasher, freight handler, teacher, and night attendant at a pinball arcade. Perhaps these unique experiences give his writing genuine honesty and edginess in a pursuit that can be very unglamorous. "None of the arts are fair," says Taylor. "Nor are they democratic. Poetry the least so."

It's fascinating to listen to such a well-respected poet and professor describe his struggles as a starving artist, washing dishes in Paris and using food money for postage. Taylor relates well to his students, who want so desperately to have their voices heard through published work. He admits his path to recognition "was haphazard and slower" than it had to be. Taylor began sending out poems at the age of 18, but it took 14 years before he published his first chapbook. "I wasn't around a major university" he points out, "and I didn't know the rules." Despite the long process, Taylor claims to have known from a young age that writing poetry is a lifestyle choice.

"You begin to write poetry because you are compelled to do it and get down your impressions of the world," he says. "And then, at some point, it becomes the way you see the world. I don't know when it happened, but at some point, pretty early in life, I just couldn't go back."

All Together

We set out all together
riffraff searching for rhymes.
Such a lofty ambition
has become the purpose of our lives.

We replace with sounds and syllables
the feelings in our paper hearts;
we publish our poems
so we can be called "Poets."

We let our hair and our ties fly
in the wind. We strike a pose.
We regard as unbearable prose
the company of pleasant people.
God's creatures, indeed all nature,
exist only for our sake.
In order to send dispatches to Earth
we've ascended to the stars of heaven.

We hang around hungry all day,
we stay up all night under bridges.
We've become sacrificial victims
of "society," of the "times."

(by Kostas Karyotakis, translation by Keith Taylor and William Reader; winner of the 2004 Keeley-Sherrard Translation Award for Poetry)

"Reading and writing are not separate entities," Taylor continues. "Now they're what I do; poetry is how I live. I can imagine going a few weeks without writing a poem, but I would have certainly done something else in the meantime, like written a book review or read a book of poems.''

Taylor finds such commitment lacking in many poets who complain their work's not getting published.

''They're not doing one of two things. Either they're not writing enough; or they're not finding a context for their talent—meaning not reading and researching journals, or only sending their work to a few publications.'' Taylor suggests poets should write a finished poem a week. ''If you're only going to write five poems a year, you don't have enough material.''

Poets also need to work diligently at finding an audience. ''If you're going to make only two or three submissions a year,'' Taylor notes, ''it's going to take you a long time.'' It takes even longer if poets become so distraught over a rejection letter they never send work back to a publication. Taylor knows rejection is part of the process. ''I still get rejected. I even get poems rejected by people who have requested I send them my work!''

As both professor and the director of the University of Michigan's undergraduate creative writing program, Taylor has the perspective of observing students' mistakes: The younger ones ''tend to think their ideas are too important'' instead of valuing sense and emotion. His older students fear sending work out into the world. ''They devalue their work. It's a crisis of confidence.''

As he keeps up on contemporary poetry and reads the countless drafts of aspiring student poets, Taylor finds a considerable change in the aesthetic of the genre since he first began writing. In the 1960s and 1970s, questions of authenticity were at the forefront.

''Honesty was actually used as a critical term,'' he explains. ''The phrase 'plainspoken' in terms of poetry was a form of praise,'' whereas now it's seen as ''dull.'' Taylor describes today's standard as much flashier, focusing on ornate surfaces, wordplay, and disguising meaning. He paraphrases Mark Doty, who once wrote, ''I prefer elaborate surfaces over edgy material.'' Although an admirer of Doty's work, Taylor fears lesser poets might lose something important by stressing the surface and veering away from personal experience. ''Sometimes it's interesting, and sometimes it can become decadent. I still think of 'plainspoken' as an ideal.''

Taylor is also concerned that young writers are not creating their own audiences by starting up new journals and small presses. ''They assume they can find available outlets somewhere, like online, but that's not always a correct assumption.''

Taylor encourages young writers to explore chapbook publication as a way to get work ''out there'' and even make some mistakes. The author of five chapbooks, Taylor advocates organizing material thematically, which is easier to do on a smaller scale. ''The books of poems that have moved me the most are unified books. Chapbooks allow you to do this. If you write twenty poems, then the book becomes the twenty-first poem.''

—*Rebecca Chrysler*

Rebecca Chrysler is a graduate student at the University of Michigan's School of Education. She is former assistant editor of *Children's Writer's & Illustrator's Market* and *Artist's & Graphic Designer's Market*, and her work has appeared in *Novel & Short Story Writer's Market* and *Writer's Digest Handbook of Magazine Article Writing* (all by Writer's Digest Books).

Contest/Award Offerings Sponsors the annual Pulse Poetry Prize. Offers 1st Prize: $100; 2nd Prize: $50; 3rd Prize: $25; plus 3 Honorable Mentions and publication to prizewinners. Submit 3 poems up to 120 lines each. **Entry fee:** $10/entry (multiple entries okay with additional fee for each). **Deadline:** January 30. Guidelines available by e-mail or on website.

Also Offers ''Ask about our Poetry Abroad in London program. E-mail for info. Spend up to 6 weeks visiting and learning your craft in Literary London with possible college credit.''

Advice ''Be relentless in the revision process. Read widely. Write every day.''

🌐 ☑ PURPLE PATCH; THE FIRING SQUAD

25 Griffiths Rd., West Bromwich B7I 2EH England. E-mail: ppatch66@hotmail.com. Website: www. poetrywednesbury.co.uk. Established 1975. **Contact:** Geoff Stevens, editor.

Magazine Needs *Purple Patch* is a quarterly poetry and short prose magazine with reviews, comments, and illustrations. "All good examples of poetry considered, but do not want poor rhyming verse, non-contributory swear words or obscenities, hackneyed themes." Has published poetry by Raymond K. Avery, Bryn Fortey, Bob Mee, B.Z. Niditch, and Steve Sneyd. *Purple Patch* is 24 pages, digest-sized, photocopied, side-stapled, with cover on the same stock with b&w drawing. Receives about 2,500 poems/year, accepts about 8%. Circulation varies. Subscription: £5 UK/3 issues; $20 US (send dollars). Make checks (sterling only) payable to G. Stevens.

How to Submit "Send 2 or more poems with return postage paid." Lines/poem: 40 maximum. Accepts submissions by postal mail only. Cover letter with short "self-introduction" is preferred. Reads submissions year round. Time between acceptance and publication is 4 months. Comments on rejected poems. Occasionally publishes theme issues. List of upcoming themes available for SASE (or SAE and IRCs). Guidelines available in magazine or on website. Responds in one month to Great Britain; can be longer to US. Pays one contributor's copy "to European writers only; overseas contributors must purchase a copy to see their work in print." Acquires first British serial rights. Staff reviews poetry chapbooks, short stories, and tapes in 30-300 words. Send materials for review consideration.

Also Offers *The Firing Squad* is a broadsheet of short poetry of a protest or complaint nature, published at irregular intervals. "All inquiries, submissions of work, etc., must include SASE or SAE and IRCs, or $1 U.S./Canadian for return/reply."

Advice "Don't just send *one* poem. Send *at least* two, and I'll try to like them."

🌐 $☐ QUANTUM LEAP; Q.Q. PRESS

York House, 15 Argyle Terrace, Rothesay, Isle of Bute PA20 0BD Scotland, United Kingdom. Established 1997. **Contact:** Alan Carter, editor.

Magazine Needs *Quantum Leap* is a quarterly poetry magazine. Wants "all kinds of poetry—free verse, rhyming, whatever—as long as it's well written and preferably well punctuated, too. We rarely use haiku." Has published poetry by Pamela Constantine, Ray Stebbing, Leigh Eduardo, Sam Smith, Sky Higgins, Norman Bissett, and Gordon Scapens. *Quantum Leap* is 40 pages, digest-sized, desktop-published, saddle-stapled, with card cover. Receives about 2,000 poems/year, accepts about 15%. Press run is 200 (180 subscribers). Single copy: $12; subscription: $38. Sample: $9. Make checks payable to Alan Carter. "All things being equal in terms of a poem's quality, I will sometimes favor that of a subscriber (or someone who has at least bought an issue) over a nonsubscriber, as it is they who keep us solvent."

How to Submit Submit 6 poems at a time. Lines/poem: 36 ("normally"). Accepts previously published poems (indicate magazine and date of first publication) and simultaneous submissions. Cover letter is required. "Within the UK, send a SASE; outside it, send IRCs to the value of what has been submitted." Time between acceptance and publication is usually 3 months "but can be longer now, due to magazine's increasing popularity." Sometimes comments on rejected poems. Guidelines available for SASE (or SAE and 2 IRCs). Responds in 3 weeks. Pays £2 sterling. Acquires first or second British serial rights.

Book/Chapbook Needs Under the imprint "Collections," Q.Q. Press offers subsidy arrangements "to provide a cheap alternative to the 'vanity presses'—poetry only." Charges £140 sterling (US $280) plus postage for 50 32-page (A4) books. Please write for details. Order sample books by sending $12 (postage included). Make checks payable to Alan Carter.

Contest/Award Offerings Sponsors open poetry competitions and competitions for subscribers only. Send SAE and IRC for details.

Advice "Submit well-thought-out, well-presented poetry, preferably well punctuated, too. If rhyming poetry, make it flow and don't strain to rhyme. I don't bite, and I appreciate a short cover letter, but not a long, long list of where you've been published before! Please do not add U.S. stamps to IRCs. They have no validity here. If you want to increase the value, just send extra IRCs.''

$⬛ QUARTERLY WEST

Dept. of English/LNCO3500, University of Utah, 255 S. Central Campus Dr., Salt Lake City UT 84112-9109. (801)581-3938. E-mail: quarterlywest@yahoo.com. Website: www.utah.edu/quarterl ywest. Established 1976. **Contact:** Mike White and Kathryn Cowles, poetry editors. Editors: Nicole Walker and David Hawkins.

- Poetry published in *Quarterly West* has appeared in *The Best American Poetry* and in numerous *Pushcart Prize* anthologies.

Magazine Needs *Quarterly West* is a semiannual literary magazine that seeks ''original and accomplished literary verse—free or formal. No greeting card or sentimental poetry.'' Also publishes translations. Has published poetry by Robert Pinsky, Eavan Boland, Albert Goldbarth, William Matthews, Agha Shahid Ali, and Heather McHugh. *Quarterly West* is 200 pages, digest-sized, offset-printed, with 4-color cover art. Receives 2,500 submissions/year, accepts less than 1%. Press run is 1,900 (500 subscribers, 300-400 libraries). Subscription: $14/year, $25/2 years. Sample: $7.50.

How to Submit Submit 3-5 poems at a time; if translations, include originals. Accepts simultaneous submissions, with notification; no previously published poems. Accepts submission by postal mail only. Reads submissions from September 1 to May 1. Seldom comments on rejected poems. Guidelines available on website. Responds in up to 6 months. Pays $15-100 plus 2 contributor's copies. Acquires first North American serial rights. Returns rights with acknowledgment and right to reprint. Reviews books of poetry in 1,000-3,000 words.

$□ ◎ ELLERY QUEEN'S MYSTERY MAGAZINE (Specialized: mystery/suspense)

475 Park Ave. S., 11th Floor, New York NY 10016. E-mail: elleryqueen@dellmagazines.com. Website: www.themysteryplace.com. Established 1941. **Contact:** Janet Hutchings.

Magazine Needs *Ellery Queen's Mystery Magazine*, appearing 10 times/year, uses primarily short stories of mystery, crime, or suspense. *Ellery Queen's Mystery Magazine* is 144 pages (double-issue, published twice/year, is 240 pages), digest-sized, professionally printed on newsprint, flat-spined, with glossy paper cover. Subscription: $43.90. Sample: $3.99 (available on newsstands).

How to Submit Accepts simultaneous submissions; no previously published poems. Accepts submissions by postal mail only. Include SASE with submissions. Guidelines available for SASE or on website. Responds in 3 months. Pays $15-65 plus 3 contributor's copies.

⬛ QUERCUS REVIEW; QUERCUS REVIEW PRESS ANNUAL POETRY BOOK AWARD

435 College Ave., Modesto CA 95350. (209)575-6183. E-mail: poetree@juno.com. Website: www.q uercusreview.com. Established 1999. **Contact:** Sam Pierstorff, editor.

Magazine Needs *Quercus Review* is an annual journal of literature and art, appearing in May and publishing ''numerous nationally recognized and award-winning poets from across the nation.'' Wants high-quality poetry, short fiction, and b&w art. Seeks ''writing that reflects a unique voice. No rhyme, religious, or cliché writing.'' Has published poetry by X.J. Kennedy, Gerald Locklin, Naomi Shihab Nye, Amiri Baraka, Charles Harper Webb, and Dorianne Laux. *Quercus Review* is 95 pages, digest-sized, professionally printed, perfect-bound, with full-color cover. Receives about 500 poems/year, accepts about 10-15%. Press run is 500 (50 subscribers, 10 libraries, 350 shelf sales); 100 are distributed free to contributors and local bookstores. Single copy: $7; subscription: $10/2 years. Make checks payable to MJC (QR).

How to Submit Submit 3-5 poems at a time. No previously published poems or simultaneous submissions. No e-mail or disk submissions. Cover letter is required. Include SASE and brief bio. Reads submissions year round, but always responds in March/April. Time between acceptance and publication is usually 3-6 months. ''Poems are selected by 5-person staff of editors, which rotates annually.'' Guidelines available on website. Sometimes sends prepublication galleys. Pays one contributor's copy, plus ½-price discount on additional copies. Acquires first rights.

Contest/Award Offerings Quercus Review Press sponsors an annual poetry book award. Publishes one poetry book/year, selected through competition only (46-80 pages in ms format). **Entry fee:** $20. **Deadline:** submissions accepted May 1 through August 1. Books are 50-80 pages, professionally printed, perfect-bound, with full-color covers. Book mss may include previously published poems. Submission guidelines available on website.

Advice "Avoid overusing the world 'soul,' but feel free to drown us in fresh imagery and bold language. We like poems with a pulse. Make us laugh or cry, but don't bore or try too hard to impress us."

⚐ ☑ QUEST

Freiburger Hall, Lynn University, 3601 N. Military Trail, Boca Raton FL 33431. E-mail: jmorgan@lynn.edu. Established 1997. **Contact:** Dr. Jeff Morgan, editor.

Magazine Needs Quest is an annual literary and arts journal published in April. "We want poems with a clear voice that use careful diction to create poetry in which sound and sense work together, creating fresh perception. We do not want poems that rely on profanity or shock value." Has published poetry by Eugene Martel, Andrea Best, Fred Cichocki, Johanne Perron, Rosalie Schwartz, and Diane Richard-Allerdyce. Quest is digest-sized, laser copy-printed, saddle-stapled, with 32# bright white coverstock cover printed with 4-color process. Receives about 100 poems/year, accepts about 25. Press run is 200 (one library subscriber); 150 distributed free to Lynn University faculty, staff, and students. Single copy: $5. Make checks payable to Jeff Morgan.

How to Submit Submit up to 5 poems at a time. No previously published poems or simultaneous submissions. No fax, e-mail, or disk submissions. Cover letter is preferred. "Include adequate SASE if you want work returned." Reads submissions mid September to mid-January. **Charges $1 reading fee; criticism fee of 15 cents/word.** Time between acceptance and publication is up to 7 months. "English Department faculty review submissions." Seldom comments on rejected poems. Guidelines available for SASE. Responds in up to 2 months. Pays one contributor's copy. Acquires one-time rights.

Advice "Even the freest of verse has its roots in the formal elements."

☑ ◎ RADIX MAGAZINE (Specialized: poetry that expresses a Christian world-view)

E-mail: radixmag@aol.com. Website: www.radixmagazine.com. Established 1969. **Contact:** Luci Shaw, poetry editor. Editor: Sharon Gallagher.

Magazine Needs Radix wants poems "that reflect a Christian world-view, but aren't preachy." Has published poetry by John Leax, Walter McDonald, Evangeline Paterson, and Luci Shaw. Radix is 32 pages, magazine-sized, offset-printed, saddle-stapled, with 60-lb. self cover. Receives about 50 poems/year, accepts about 20%. Press run varies. Sample: $5. Make checks payable to Radix Magazine.

How to Submit Submit 1-4 poems at a time. No previously published poems or simultaneous submissions. **Accepts e-mail submissions only.** Submit seasonal poems 6 months in advance. Time between acceptance and publication is 3 months to 3 years. "We have a serious backlog. The poetry editor accepts or rejects poems and sends the accepted poems to the editor. The editor then publishes poems in appropriate issues. If more than one poem is accepted from any poet, there will probably be a long wait before another is published, because of our backlog of accepted poems." Seldom comments on rejected poems. Occasionally publishes theme issues. Responds in 2 months. Pays 2 contributor's copies. Acquires first rights. Returns rights upon request. Reviews books of poetry.

Advice "Radix has a distinctive voice and often receives submissions that are completely inappropriate. Familiarity with the magazine is recommended before sending any submissions."

☑ RAINBOW CURVE

P.O. Box 93206, Las Vegas NV 89193-3206. E-mail: rainbowcurve@sbcglobal.net. Website: www.rainbowcurve.com. Established 2001. **Contact:** Julianne Bonnet, poetry editor.

Magazine Needs *Rainbow Curve* is a biannual forum for short fiction and poetry. Wants "well-crafted poetry that works both on the surface *and* beneath it." Does not want rhyme, traditional forms, Hallmark greeting card sentiment. Has published poetry by Virgil Suárez and Terry Ehret. *Rainbow Curve* is 100 pages, digest-sized, offset-printed, perfect-bound, with 4-color glossy 10-pt. CIS cover. Receives about 3,500 poems/year, accepts about 2%. Press run is 250. Single copy: $8; subscription: $16. Sample: $6. Make checks payable to *Rainbow Curve*.

How to Submit Submit 3 poems at a time. Accepts simultaneous submissions; no previously published poems. Accepts e-mail submissions (as attachment; must be MS Word 6.0 or higher format only). Cover letter is preferred. "Include SASE with sufficient postage for reply and return of manuscript. If return of manuscript is not desired, we will respond via e-mail, if requested." Reads submissions year round. Time between acceptance and publication is 6 months. Seldom comments on rejected poems. Guidelines available in magazine, for SASE, or on website. Responds in 3 months. Always sends prepublication galleys. Pays one contributor's copy. Acquires first North American serial rights.

Advice "It is always a good idea to read a magazine before submitting to it—that way you have a good idea if your writing style fits with the editorial slant of the publication."

◨ THE RAINTOWN REVIEW

P.O. Box 40851, Indianapolis IN 46240. Website: www.patrickkanouse.com. Established 1996. **Contact:** Patrick Kanouse, editor.

Magazine Needs *The Raintown Review* is published twice/year and contains only poetry. Wants well-crafted poems—metered, syllabic, or free-verse. "While attention is paid to formal verse, *The Raintown Review* does publish all kinds of poetry. The one criterion: quality." Has published poetry by William Baer, Jared Carter, Annie Finch, and Len Roberts. *The Raintown Review* is about 60 pages, chapbook-sized, desktop-published, saddle-stapled, with card cover. Receives about 900 poems/year, accepts 10-15%. Press run is about 100 (most go to subscribers and contributors). Subscription: $24/year. Sample: $7.

How to Submit Submit up to 4 poems at a time. No length restrictions. Accepts previously published poems (with acknowledgment of previous publication) and simultaneous submissions. Accepts submissions by postal mail only. Cover letter is preferred. "We prefer contributors write for guidelines before submitting work." Guidelines available for SASE or on website. Tries to respond in up to 3 months. Pays one contributor's copy and 2-issue subscription. Acquires one-time rights.

$◨ RATTAPALLAX; RATTAPALLAX PRESS

532 La Guardia Place, Suite 353, New York NY 10012. (212)560-7459. E-mail: info@rattapallax.com. Website: www.rattapallax.com. Established 1998. **Contact:** Martin Mitchell, editor-in-chief.

Magazine Needs "A biannual journal of contemporary literature, *Rattapallax* is Wallace Steven's word for the sound of thunder." Wants "extraordinary poetry—words that are well crafted and sing, words that recapture the music of the language, words that bump into each other in extraordinary ways and leave the reader touched and haunted by the experience. We do not want ordinary words about ordinary things." Has published poetry by Anthony Hecht, Sharon Olds, Lou Reed, Marilyn Hacker, Billy Collins, and Glyn Maxwell. *Rattapallax* is 128 pages, magazine-sized, offset-printed, perfect-bound, with 12-pt. CS1 cover. Receives about 5,000 poems/year, accepts 2%. Press run is 2,000 (100 subscribers, 50 libraries, 1,200 shelf sales); 200 distributed free to contributors, reviews, and promos. Single copy: $7.95; subscription: $14/year. Make checks payable to *Rattapallax*.

How to Submit Submit 3-5 poems at a time. Accepts simultaneous submissions; no previously published poems. Accepts e-mail submissions from outside the US and Canada; all other submissions must be sent via postal mail. "SASE is required, and e-mailed submissions should be sent as simple text." Cover letter is preferred. Reads submissions all year; issue deadlines are June 1 and December 1. Time between acceptance and publication is 6 months. "The editor-in-chief, senior editor, and associate editor review all the submissions and then decide on which to accept every week. Near publication time, all accepted work is narrowed, and unused work is kept for the next issue.'' Often comments on rejected poems. Guidelines available by e-mail or on website. Responds in 2 months. Always sends prepublication galleys. Pays 2 contributor's copies. Acquires first rights.

Book/Chapbook Needs & How to Submit Rattapallax Press publishes ''contemporary poets and writers with unique, powerful voices.'' Publishes 5 paperbacks and 3 chapbooks/year. Books are usually 64 pages, digest-sized, offset-printed, perfect-bound, with 12-pt. CS1 covers. Query first with a few sample poems, cover letter with brief bio and publication credits, and SASE. Requires authors to first be published in *Rattapallax*. Responds to queries in one month; to mss in 2 months. Pays royalties of 10-25%. Order sample books by sending SASE and $7.

✒ RATTLE

12411 Ventura Blvd., Studio City CA 91604. (818)505-6777. E-mail: stellasueL@aol.com or timgreen @rattle.com. Website: www.rattle.com. Established 1994. **Contact:** Stellasue Lee and Timothy Green, poetry editors. Editor: Alan Fox. Address submissions to Stellasue Lee.

Magazine Needs *RATTLE* is a biannual poetry publication (appearing in June and December) that also includes interviews with poets, essays, and reviews. Wants ''high-quality poetry of any form, 3 pages maximum. Nothing unintelligible.'' Accepts some poetry written by children ages 10 to 18. Has published poetry by Lucille Clifton, Charles Simic, Mark Doty, Sharon Olds, Billy Collins, and Stephen Dunn. *RATTLE* is 196 pages, digest-sized, neatly printed, perfect-bound, with 4-color coated card cover. Receives about 8,000 submissions/year, accepts 250. Press run is 4,000. Subscription: $28/2 years. Sample: $8. Make checks payable to *RATTLE*.

How to Submit Submit up to 5 poems at a time with name, address, and phone number on each page in upper right hand corner. Include SASE. No previously published poems or simultaneous submissions. Accepts e-mail (pasted into body of message) and fax submissions. Cover letter with e-mail address, if possible, is required as well as a bio. Reads submissions all year. Seldom comments on rejected poems unless asked by the author. Guidelines available in magazine, by e-mail, or on website. Responds in up to 2 months. Pays 2 contributor's copies. Rights revert to authors upon publication. Welcomes essays up to 2,000 words on the writing process, and book reviews on poetry up to 250 words. Send materials for review consideration.

✒ ◎ RAW DOG PRESS; POST POEMS (Specialized: poetry under 7 lines)

151 S. West St., Doylestown PA 18901-4134. Website: http://rawdogpress.bravehost.com. Established 1977. **Contact:** R. Gerry Fabian, poetry editor.

Magazine Needs Raw Dog Press publishes Post Poems annual—a postcard series. ''We want short poetry (3-7 lines) on any subject. The positive poem or the poem of understated humor always has an inside track. No taboos, however. All styles considered. Anything with rhyme had better be immortal.'' Has published poetry by Don Ryan, John Grey, and the editor, R. Gerry Fabian. Send SASE for catalog to buy samples.

How to Submit Submit 3-5 poems at a time. Lines/poem: 3-7. Cover letter is optional; SASE is required. Always comments on rejected poems. Guidelines available on website. Pays contributor's copies. Acquires all rights. Returns rights on mention of first publication. Sometimes reviews books of poetry.

Book/Chapbook Needs & How to Submit Raw Dog Press welcomes new poets and detests second-rate poems from 'name' poets. ''We exist because we are dumb like a fox, but even a fox takes care of its own.'' Send SASE for catalog to buy samples.

Also Offers Offers criticism for a fee; ''if someone is desperate to publish and is willing to pay, we will use our vast knowledge to help steer the manuscript in the right direction. We will advise against it, but as P.T. Barnum said. . . .''

Advice ''I get poems that do not fit my needs. At least one quarter of all poets waste their postage because they do not read the requirements. Also, there are too many submissions without a SASE and they go directly into the trash!''

☑ RB'S POETS' VIEWPOINT

Box 940, Eunice NM 88231. Established 1989. **Contact:** Robert Bennett, editor.

Magazine Needs *RB's Poets' Viewpoint*, published bimonthly, features poetry and cartoons. Wants ''general and religious poetry, sonnets, and sijo with a 21-line limit.'' Does not want ''vulgar language.'' Has published poetry by Robert D. Spector, Ruth Ditmer Ream, Ruth Halbrooks, and Delphine Ledoux. *RB's Poets' Viewpoint* is 34 pages, digest-sized, photocopied, saddle-stapled. Receives about 400 poems/year, accepts about 90%. Press run is 60. Subscription: $8. Sample: $2. Make checks payable to Robert Bennett.

How to Submit Submit 3 poems, typed single-spaced. **Reading fee:** $1.50/poem. Accepts previously published poems and simultaneous submissions. Reads submissions February, April, June, August, October, and December only. Time between acceptance and publication is one month. ''Poems are selected by one editor.'' Often comments on rejected poems. Guidelines available for SASE. Responds in one month. Pays one contributor's copy. Acquires one-time rights.

Contest/Award Offerings Sponsors contests for general poetry, religious poetry, sonnets, and sijo with 1st Prizes of $20, $6, and $5, respectively, plus publication in *RB's Poets' Viewpoint*. **Entry fee:** 50¢/poem (sijo), $1.50/poem (all others). Guidelines available for SASE.

⊞ ☑ ◎ THE RED CANDLE PRESS; CANDELABRUM POETRY MAGAZINE (Specialized: form/style, metrical and rhymed)

% 50 Manbey Grove, London E15 1EX England. E-mail: rcp@poetry7.fsnet.co.uk. Website: www.m embers.tripod.com/redcandlepress. Established 1970. **Contact:** M.L. McCarthy, M.A., editor.

Magazine Needs Red Candle Press ''is a formalist press, specially interested in metrical and rhymed poetry, though free verse is not excluded. We're more interested in poems than poets: that is, we're interested in what sort of poems an author produces, not in his or her personality.'' Publishes the magazine *Candelabrum* twice/year (April and October). Wants ''good-quality metrical verse, with rhymed verse specially wanted. Elegantly cadenced free verse is acceptable. Accepts 5-7-5 haiku. No weak stuff (moons and Junes, loves and doves, etc.). No chopped-up prose pretending to be free verse. Any length up to about 40 lines for *Candelabrum*, any subject, including eroticism (but not porn)—satire, love poems, nature lyrics, philosophical—nothing racist, ageist, or sexist.'' Has published poetry by Pam Russell, Ryan Underwood, David Britton, Alice Evans, Jack Harvey, and Nick Spargo. *Candelabrum* is digest-sized, staple-spined. Receives about 2,000 submissions/year, of which 10% is accepted; usually holds over poems for the next year. Press run is 900 (700 subscribers, 22 libraries). Sample: $6 in bills only; non-sterling checks not accepted.

How to Submit ''Submit anytime. Enclose one IRC for reply only; 3 IRCs if you wish manuscript returned. If you'd prefer a reply by e-mail, without return of unwanted manuscript, please enclose one British first-class stamp, IRC, or U.S. dollar bill to pay for the call. Each poem on a separate sheet please, neat typescripts or neat legible manuscripts. Please, no dark, oily photostats, no colored ink (only black or blue). Author's name and address on each sheet, please.'' No simultaneous submissions. No e-mail submissions. Guidelines available on website. Responds in about 2 months. Pays one contributor's copy.

Advice ''Formalist poetry is much more popular here in Britain, and we think also in the United States, now than it was in 1970, when we established *Candelabrum*. We always welcome new poets, especially formalists, and we like to hear from the U.S.A. as well as from here at home. General tip: Study the various outlets at the library, or buy a copy of *Candelabrum*, or borrow a copy from a subscriber, before you go to the expense of submitting your work. The Red Candle Press regrets that, because of bank charges, it is unable to accept dollar cheques. However, it is always happy to accept U.S. dollar bills.''

⚑ ⊘ RED DANCEFLOOR PRESS; RED DANCEFLOOR

P.O. Box 4974, Lancaster CA 93539-4974. Established 1989.

● **The magazine has suspended publication until further notice. The press is taking a temporary leave of absence from publishing and is not accepting submissions at this time.**

Magazine Needs & How to Submit Red Dancefloor Press publishes the magazine *Red Dancefloor*.

Book Needs & How to Submit Red Dancefloor Press also publishes poetry chapbooks, full-length books, and poetry audiotapes. Has published poetry by Sean T. Dougherty, Gerry Lafemina, Laurel Ann Bogen, Annie Reiner, Gary P. Walton, and Michael Stephans. The editor suggests sampling a book, chapbook, or tape prior to submission. Send 5½×8½ SASE with first-class stamp for catalog.

⊘ RED DRAGON PRESS

P.O. Box 19425, Alexandria VA 22320-0425. Website: www.reddragonpress.com. Established 1993. **Contact:** Laura Qa, editor/publisher.

Book/Chapbook Needs Red Dragon Press publishes 3-4 chapbooks/year. Wants "innovative, progressive, and experimental poetry and prose using literary symbolism and aspiring to the creation of meaningful new ideas, forms, and methods. We are proponents of works that represent the nature of man as androgynous, as in the fusing of male and female symbolism, and we support works that deal with psychological and parapsychological topics." Has published *Spectator Turns Witness* by George Karos and *The Crown of Affinity* by Laura Qa. Chapbooks are usually 64 pages, digest-sized, offset-printed on trade paper, perfect-bound.

How to Submit Submit up to 5 poems at a time with SASE. Accepts previously published poems and simultaneous submissions. Cover letter with brief bio is preferred. **Reading fee:** $5 for poetry and short fiction, $10 for novels; check or money order payable to Red Dragon Press. Time between acceptance and publication is 8 months. "Poems are selected for consideration by the publisher, then circulated to senior editor and/or poets previously published for comment. Poems are returned to the publisher for further action, i.e., rejection or acceptance for publication in an anthology or book by a single author. Frequently, submission of additional works is required before final offer is made, especially in the process for a book by a single author." Often comments on rejected poems. Charges criticism fee of $10/page on request. Responds to queries in 10 weeks, to mss in one year. Purchase sample books at bookstores, or mail-order direct from Red Dragon Press at the above address.

Ⓝ $⊚ RED LIGHTS (Specialized: Oriental forms/tanka)

33 Riverside Dr., Suite 4-G, New York NY 10023-8025. (212)875-9342. E-mail: deucedk@aol.com. Established 2004. **Contact:** Pamela Miller Ness, editor.

Magazine Needs *red lights*, published biannually in January and June, is a journal devoted to English-language tanka and tanka sequences. Wants "print-only tanka, mainly 'free-form' but also strictly syllabic 5-7-5-7-7; will consider tanka sequences and tan-renga." Has published poetry by Sanford Goldstein, Michael McClintock, Laura Maffei, Linda Jeannette Ward, Jane Reichhold, and Michael Dylan Welch. *red lights* is 28-36 pages, 8½×3¾, offset-printed, saddle-stapled, with Japanese textured paper cover with hand-stamped designs within text; copies are numbered. Receives about 400 poems/year, accepts about 15%. Press run is 150. Single copy: $6; subscription: $12 US, $13 Canada, $15 foreign. Make checks payable to Pamela Miller Ness.

How to Submit Submit a maximum of 10 tanka or 2 sequences at a time. No previously published poems or simultaneous submissions. No e-mail or disk submissions. Include SASE. Reads submissions year round. Time between acceptance and publication "depends on submission time." Often comments on rejected poems. Guidelines available for SASE. Responds in 2 weeks. Pays $1/tanka. Acquires first rights.

Contest/Award Offerings "Each biannual issue features a '*red lights* featured tanka' on the theme of 'red lights.' Poet whose poem is selected receives contributor's copy in addition to $1."

Advice "The center 4 pages are devoted to the 'Featured Tanka Poet,' selected by invitation. Twelve previously published poems are featured."

$ ⊠ ◎ RED MOON PRESS; THE RED MOON ANTHOLOGY; CONTEMPORARY HAIBUN (Specialized: haiku and related forms)

P.O. Box 2461, Winchester VA 22604-1661. (540)722-2156. Fax: (708)810-8992. E-mail: redmoon@ shentel.net. Website: www.haikuworld.org/books/redmoon or http://haikuguy.com/redmoonprint.html. Red Moon Press established 1993, *Contemporary Haibun* established 1999 as *American Haibun & Haiga*. **Contact:** Jim Kacian, editor/publisher.

Magazine Needs *Contemporary Haibun*, published annually in April, is the first Western journal dedicated to haibun and haiga. Has published poetry by Luis Cuauhtemoc Berriozabal, Cindy Tebo, Ion Codrescu, Kuniharu Shimizu, Judson Evans, and Noragh Jones. The magazine is 128 pages, digest-sized, offset-printed on quality paper, with 4-color heavy-stock cover. Receives several hundred submissions/year, accepts about 5%. Print run is 1,000 for subscribers and commercial distribution. Subscription: $16.95 plus $4 p&h. Sample available for SASE or by e-mail.

How to Submit Submit up to 3 haibun or haiga at a time with SASE. Considers previously published poems. Accepts submissions by fax, on disk, by e-mail (pasted into body of message or as attachment), and by postal mail. Time between acceptance and publication varies according to time of submission. Poems will be read by editorial board. "Only haibun and haiga will be considered. If you are unfamiliar with the form, consult *Journey to the Interior*, edited by Bruce Ross, or previous issues of *Contemporary Haibun*, for samples and some discussion." Guidelines available in magazine, for SASE, or by e-mail. Pays $1/page. Acquires first North American serial rights.

Book/Chapbook Needs Red Moon Press "is the largest and most prestigious publisher of English-language haiku and related work in the world." Publishes *The Red Moon Anthology*, an annual volume of the finest English-language haiku and related work published anywhere in the world. *The Red Moon Anthology* is offset-printed, perfect-bound, with glossy 4-color heavy-stock cover. Inclusion is by nomination of the editorial board only. The press also publishes 6-8 volumes/ year, usually 3-5 individual collections of English-language haiku, as well as 1-3 books of essays, translations, or criticism of haiku. Under other imprints, the press also publishes chapbooks of various sizes and formats.

How to Submit Query with book theme and information, and 30-40 poems or draft of first chapter. Responds to queries in 2 weeks, to mss (if invited) in 3 months. "Each contract separately negotiated."

Advice "Haiku is a burgeoning and truly international form. It is nothing like what your fourth-grade teacher taught you years ago, and so it is best if you familiarize yourself with what is happening in the genre (and its close relatives) today before submitting. We strive to give all the work we publish plenty of space in which to resonate, and to provide a forum where the best of today's practitioners can be published with dignity and prestige. All our books have either won awards or are awaiting notification. We intend to work hard to keep it that way."

⌨ RED OWL MAGAZINE

35 Hampshire Rd., Portsmouth NH 03801-4815. (603)431-2691. E-mail: RedOwlMag@aol.com. Established 1995. **Contact:** Edward O. Knowlton, editor.

Magazine Needs *Red Owl* is a biannual magazine of poetry and b&w art published in spring and fall. "Ideally, poetry here might stress a harmony between nature and industry; add a pinch of humor for spice. Nothing introspective or downtrodden. Sometimes long poems are OK, yet poems which are 10 to 20 lines seem to fit best." Also open to poems on the subjects of animals, gay/lesbian issues, horror, psychic/occult, nature/ecology, science fiction/fantasy, and women/feminism. Has published poetry by Cynthia Brackett-Vincent, Ken Champion, Gary Every, Rod Farmer, and Pearl Mary Wilshaw. *Red Owl* is about 70 pages, magazine-sized, neatly photocopied in a variety of type styles, spiral-bound, with heavy stock cover. "Out of a few hundred poems received, roughly one third are considered." Single copy: $10; subscription: $20. Sample (including brief guidelines): $10, includes shipping and handling. Make checks payable to Edward O. Knowlton.

How to Submit Submit 3-5 poems at a time. May accept "reworked" previously published poems or simultaneous submissions. "Would rather not receive" e-mail submissions. "Submit in spring for the Fall issue—and vice versa." Cover letter is preferred. "Relay cover letter and each poem separately. I mostly use the 'Net to answer questions; this isn't the best home for 'noetics' or 'noetry.' I'd prefer to receive the submissions I get via the U.S.P.S. since I feel it's more formal—and I'm not in that big of a hurry, nor do I feel that this world has reached a conclusion. . . ." Seldom comments on rejected poems. Guidelines available in magazine. Responds "usually within 3 months." Pays one contributor's copy.

Advice "Try and be bright; hold your head up. Yes, there are hard times in the land of plenty, yet we might try to overshadow them . . ."

✪ ⦸ RED RAMPAN' PRESS; RED RAMPAN' REVIEW; RED RAMPAN' BROADSIDE SERIES

2705 Holly Trails, Apt. #3, Poplar Bluff MO 63901-9775. Established 1981. **Contact:** Larry D. Griffin, poetry editor. Currently not accepting poetry submissions.

⦿ RED WHEELBARROW

De Anza College, 21250 Stevens Creek Blvd., Cupertino CA 95014. (408)864-8600. E-mail: SplitterRandolph@fhda.edu. Website: www.deanza.edu/redwheelbarrow. Established 1976 (as *Bottomfish Magazine*). **Contact:** Randolph Splitter, editor.

• "Note: We are not affiliated with Red Wheelbarrow Press or any similarly named publication."

Magazine Needs *Red Wheelbarrow* is an annual college-produced magazine appearing in spring or summer. Wants "diverse voices." Has published poetry by Mark Brazaitis, Taylor Graham, John Wickersham, Virgil Suárez, Mario Susko, and Morton Marcus. *Red Wheelbarrow* is 140-220 pages, book-sized, well-printed on heavy stock with b&w graphics, perfect-bound. Press run is on demand. Single copy: $10. Sample (back issue): $2.50.

How to Submit Submit 3-5 poems at a time. "Before submitting, writers are strongly urged to purchase a sample copy or visit our website." Accepts e-mail submissions. Best submission times: September through January. Annual deadline: January 31. Include SASE or e-mail address for reply. Responds in 2-6 months, depending on backlog. Pays 2 contributor's copies.

⦿ REDIVIDER

Dept. of Writing, Literature, and Publishing, Emerson College, 120 Boylston St., Boston MA 02118. E-mail: redivider_editor@yahoo.com. Website: http://pages.emerson.edu/publications/redivider. Established (as *Beacon Street Review*) in 1990. **Contact:** Poetry Editor (changes annually, see website). Member: CLMP.

Magazine Needs *Redivider* appears biannually, publishing high-quality poetry, fiction, and creative nonfiction, as well as interviews and book reviews. "All styles of poetry are welcome. Most of all, we look for language that seems fresh and alive on the page, that tries to do something new. Read a sample copy for a good idea. We do not publish greeting card verse or inspirational verse." Has published poetry by Kate Clanchy, William Virgil Davis, Dorianne Laux, David Lawrence, Valerie Nieman, and Jennifer Perrine. *Redivider* is 100 pages, digest-sized, offset-printed, perfect-bound, with 4-color artwork on cover stock. Receives about 1,000 poems/year, accepts about 30%. Press run is 2,000. Single copy: $6; subscription: $10. Make checks payable to *Redivider* at Emerson College.

How to Submit Submit 3-6 poems at a time. Accepts simultaneous submissions ("please notify us *immediately* if your work is taken elsewhere"); no previously published poems. No e-mail or disk submissions. Cover letter is required. Reads submissions year round. Time between acceptance and publication is 6 months. "Poems are read first by poetry editors, then by a board of readers. Final decisions are made by the board." Seldom comments on rejected poems. Guidelines available in magazine, for SASE, or by e-mail. Responds in 5 months. Pays 2 contributor's copies. Acquires first North American serial rights. Reviews books of poetry in 500-2,000 words, single-book format. Send materials for review consideration, Attn: Review Copies.

Advice "Consider subscribing and supporting your fellow writers!"

☑ REFLECTIONS LITERARY JOURNAL

P.O. Box 1197, Roxboro NC 27573. (336)599-1181, ext. 231. E-mail: reflect@piedmontcc.edu. Established 1999. **Contact:** Ernest Avery, editor.

Magazine Needs *Reflections Literary Journal* appears annually in spring, publishing poetry, short fiction, and creative nonfiction. Wants any styles and forms of poetry, including translations, of one page or less. Does not want material using obscenities or culturally insensitive material. Has published poetry by J.E. Bennett, Fred Chappell, Shari O'Brien, Betsy Humphreys, Sheri Narin, and Daniel Green. *Reflections Literary Journal* is 100-150 pages, digest-sized. Receives about 400 poems/year, accepts about 5%. Press run is 250 (20 subscribers, 4 libraries, 150 shelf sales); 75 are distributed free to contributors, editors, advisors, local schools, and cultural sites. Single copy: $7; subscription: $7. Sample: $5 for back issue. Make checks payable to *Reflections Literary Journal*.

How to Submit Submit maximum of 5 poems at a time. Accepts previously published poems and simultaneous submissions (if notified). Accepts e-mail submissions (pasted into body of message or as MS Word attachments); no fax submissions. "Include a 25-word bio with submission. Single-space poetry submissions. Include one copy with name and address and one copy without. Affix adequate postage to SAE for return of manuscript if desired, or use first-class stamps on SAE for notification." Reads submissions September 1 through December 31. "Poems are read by an 8- to 12-member editorial board who rank submissions through 'blind' readings. Board members refrain from ranking their own submissions." Sometimes comments on rejected poems. Guidelines available in magazine, for SASE, or by e-mail. Responds in up to 9 months (in March or April). Pays one contributor's copy. Acquires first North American serial rights (if poem is unpublished) or one-time rights (if poem is previously published).

☑ RENAISSANCE ONLINE MAGAZINE

P.O. Box 3246, Pawtucket RI 02861. E-mail: submit@renaissancemag.com. Website: www.renaissancemag.com. Established 1996. **Contact:** Kevin Ridolfi, editor.

Magazine Needs "Updated monthly, *Renaissance Online* strives to bring diversity and thought-provoking writing to an audience that usually settles for so much less. Poetry should reveal a strong emotion and be able to elicit a response from the reader. No nursery rhymes or profane works." Accepts poetry written by teenagers, "but they must meet the same standard as adults." Has published poetry by Kevin Larimer, Josh May, and Gary Meadows. Receives about 60 poems/year, accepts about 50%.

How to Submit Submit 3 poems at a time. No previously published poems or simultaneous submissions. **Accepts e-mail submissions only (pasted into body of message).** Cover letter is preferred. *Renaissance Online Magazine* is published online only and likes to see potential writers read previous works before submitting. Time between acceptance and publication is 3 months. Poems are circulated to an editorial board. "Poems are read by the editor; when difficult acceptance decisions need to be reached, the editorial staff is asked for comments." Often comments on rejected poems. Occasionally publishes theme issues. Guidelines available for SASE or on website. Responds in 2 months. Acquires all online publishing rights. Reviews books of poetry.

◎ REVISTA/REVIEW INTERAMERICANA (Specialized: ethnic; regional)

Inter-American University of Puerto Rico, Box 5100, San Germán PR 00683. Phone: (787)264-1912, ext. 7229 or 7230. Fax: (787)892-6350. E-mail: reinter@sg.inter.edu. Website: www.sg.inter.edu/revista-ciscla/revista/. **Contact:** Mario R. Cancel, editor.

Magazine Needs Published online and in hard copy, *Revista/Review* is a bilingual (English and Spanish) scholarly journal oriented to Puerto Rican, Caribbean, and Hispanic-American and inter-American subjects. Includes CP, poetry, short stories, essays, and book reviews.

How to Submit See website for details.

☑ RHINO

P.O. Box 591, Evanston IL 60204. Website: www.rhinopoetry.org. Established 1976. **Contact:** Deborah Rosen, Alice George, Kathleen Kirk, and Helen Degen Cohen, editors.

- "*RHINO* has won 7 Illinois Arts Council Literary Awards over the last 4 years."

Magazine Needs *RHINO* is an annual poetry journal, appearing in March, which also includes short-shorts and translations. The editors "delight in work that reflects passion, originality, engagement with contemporary culture, and a love affair with language. We welcome experiments with poetic forms, and other types of risk-taking." Has published poetry by Denise Duhamel, Ray Gonzalez, Aimee Nezhukumatathil, Barry Silesky, Matthew Thorburn, and David Trinidad. *RHINO* is 150 pages, digest-sized, printed on high-quality paper, with card cover with art. Receives 1,500 submissions/year, accepts 60-80. Press run is 1,000. Single copy: $10. Sample: $5 (back issue).

How to Submit Submit 3-5 poems with SASE. Accepts simultaneous submissions with notification; no previously published poems. Submissions are accepted April 1 through October 1. Guidelines available for SASE or on website. Responds in up to 6 months. Pays 2 contributor's copies. Acquires first rights only.

⬛ ◎ RHAPSOIDIA (Specialized: form/style—experimental and metapoetry)

P.O. Box 76, Redlands CA 92373. E-mail: michaelkarman@gmail.com. Website: http://rhapsoidia.com. Established 2002. **Contact:** Michael Karman, poetry editor.

Magazine Needs *Rhapsoidia,* published quarterly, caters to experimental writing. Wants "metapoetry, experimental, fresh, innovative. Generally, we want poetry that emphasizes language over narrative. That is, we're more interested in the shaping than the thing shaped. So poems about personal experience will be considered, but only if they're cunningly written." Has published poetry by Judy Kronenfeld, Christopher Mulrooney, and Paul Kloppenborg. *Rhapsoidia* is 40-56 pages, digest-sized, saddle-stapled, with glossy cover. Receives about 360 poems/year, accepts about 10%. Press run is 350. Single copy: $4.45 ($2.95 plus $1.50 s&h); subscription: $14.20/year. Make checks payable to Mark Manalang. "Or subscribe online via PayPal."

How to Submit Submit 3-5 poems at a time. No previously published poems or simultaneous submissions. Accepts e-mail submissions (pasted into body of message); no disk submissions. "Because formatting is often essential to poetry and e-mail tends to de-format, you may send a snail mail submission to Poetry Editor Michael Karman at the address above, but please include your e-mail address so we can respond to you." Cover letter is preferred. Reads submissions year round. Time between acceptance and publication is 3 months. Seldom comments on rejected poems. Guidelines available in magazine or on website. Pays one contributor's copy. Responds in 3 months. Acquires first North American serial rights.

Advice "Read the poems that have been published in *Rhapsoidia*—preferably more than one issue. Read the poetry in other lit mags that announce themselves as experimental or avant-garde."

⬛ ⬛ $⬛ THE RIALTO

P.O. Box 309, Alysham, Norwich, Norfolk NR11 6LN England. Website: www.therialto.co.uk. Established 1984. **Contact:** Michael Mackmin, editor.

Magazine Needs *The Rialto* appears 3 times/year and "seeks to publish the best new poems by established and beginning poets. *The Rialto* seeks excellence and originality." Has published poetry by Alice Fulton, Jenny Joseph, Les Murray, Penelope Shuttle, George Szirtes, Philip Gross, and Ruth Padel. *The Rialto* is 56 pages, A4, with full-color cover. Receives about 12,000 poems/year, accepts about 1%. Press run is 1,500 (1,000 subscribers, 50 libraries). Subscription: £18. Sample: £6.50. Make checks payable to *The Rialto*. "Checks in sterling only, please. Online payment also available on website."

How to Submit Submit up to 6 poems at a time. Accepts simultaneous submissions; no previously published poems. Cover letter is preferred. "SASE or SAEs with IRCs essential. U.S. readers please note that U.S. postage stamps are invalid in U.K." Time between acceptance and publication is up to 4 months. Seldom comments on rejected poems. Responds in up to 4 months. "A large number of poems arrive every week, so please note that you will have to wait at least 10 weeks for yours to be read." Pays £20/poem. Poet retains rights.

Contest/Award Offerings Sponsors an annual young poets competition. Details available in magazine and on website.

Also Offers "*The Rialto* has recently commenced publishing first collections by poets. Andrew Waterhouse's book *In* won the 2000 Forward/Waterstone's Best First Collection Prize. Please *do not* send book-length manuscripts. Query first."

Advice Before submitting, "you will probably have read many poems by many poets, both living and dead. You will probably have put aside each poem you write for at least 3 weeks before considering it afresh. You will have asked yourself, 'Does it work technically?'; checked the rhythm, the rhymes (if used), and checked that each word is fresh and meaningful in its context, not jaded and tired. You will hopefully have read *The Rialto*."

◯ RIO GRANDE REVIEW

P.M. Box 671, 500 W. University Ave., El Paso TX 79968-0622. E-mail: rgr@utep.edu. Website: www.utep.edu/rgr. **Contact:** Poetry Editor.

Magazine Needs *Rio Grande Review*, a bilingual (English-Spanish) student publication from the University of Texas at El Paso appearing in January and August, contains poetry; flash, short, and nonfiction; short drama; photography and line art. *Rio Grande Review* is 168 pages, digest-sized, professionally printed, perfect-bound, with card cover with line art. Subscription: $8/year, $15/2 years.

How to Submit Submit no more than 5 poems at a time. No simultaneous submissions. Accepts e-mail submissions (pasted into body of message). Include bio; SASE for reply only. "Submissions are recycled regardless of acceptance or rejection." Guidelines available for SASE, by e-mail, or on website. Pays 2 contributor's copies. "Permission to reprint material remains the decision of the author. However, *Rio Grande Review* does request it be given mention."

◐ RIVER CITY

English Dept., University of Memphis, Memphis TN 38152. (901)678-4591. Fax: (901)678-2226. E-mail: rivercity@memphis.edu. Website: www.people.memphis.edu/~rivercity. Established 1980. **Contact:** Kristen Iversen, editor.

Magazine Needs *River City* appears biannually (winter and summer) and publishes fiction, poetry, interviews, essays, and visual art. Has published poetry by Albert Goldbarth, Maxine Kumin, Jane Hirshfield, Terrance Hayes, S. Beth Bishop, and Virgil Suárez. *River City* is 160 pages, 7×10, professionally printed, perfect-bound, with colorful glossy cover. Press run is 2,000. Subscription: $12. Sample: $7.

How to Submit Submit no more than 5 poems at a time. No e-mail submissions. Include SASE. Does not read mss June through August. Guidelines available for SASE or by e-mail. Responds in up to 3 months. Pays 2 contributor's copies.

This intriguing image creates an eye-catching cover for Issue 24:2 of *River City*, a literary journal published through the Creative Writing Program at the University of Memphis.

$ ◐ RIVER CITY PUBLISHING

1719 Mulberry St., Montgomery AL 36106. (334)265-6753. E-mail: jgilbert@rivercitypublishing.com. Website: www.rivercitypublishing.com. Established 1989. **Contact:** Jim Gilbert, editor.

Book/Chapbook Needs "We publish serious or academic poetry; no religious, romantic, or novelty material. Collections from previously published poets only." Publishes 1-2 poetry hardbacks/year. Has recently published *Either/Ur* by Shawn Sturgeon, *The Soft Blare* by Nick Norwood, *Ready to Eat the Sky* by Kevin Pilkington, *How We Came to Stand on That Shore* by Jay Rogoff, and *Necessary Acts* by Peter Huggins.

How to Submit "Experienced poets should submit high-quality collections of at least 40 poems, including information about previous publications in literary journals or chapbooks." Most mss selected by nationally known poet, others by staff. Responds in up to 9 months. "E-mail queries are accepted. Submissions should be hard copy only." Guidelines available for SASE, by fax, by e-mail, or on website. Pays industry-standard royalties and author's copies.

☑ RIVER OAK REVIEW

Elmhurst College, 190 Prospect Ave., Elmhurst IL 60126. (630)617-6483. Website: www.riveroakrev iew.org. Established 1993. **Contact:** Ann Frank Wake, poetry editor.

Magazine Needs *River Oak Review* is an annual literary magazine (will become biannual in 2006) publishing high-quality poetry, short fiction, and creative nonfiction. "We've historically encouraged writers with Midwestern connections, but are dedicated to finding the best established and new talent anywhere." Has published poetry by Wendy Bishop, Jim Elledge, and James Doyle. *River Oak Review* is at least 128 pages, digest-sized, neatly printed, perfect-bound, with glossy color cover with art. Publishes about 5% of poetry received. Press run is 500. Single copy: $10; subscription: $10/year, $20/2 years. Sample: $5. Make checks payable to *River Oak Review*.

How to Submit Submit 4-6 poems at a time. No previously published poems or simultaneous submissions. Sometimes comments on rejected poems. Guidelines available for SASE or on website. Responds in 3 months. Pays 2 contributor's copies.

Contest/Award Offerings Biannual poetry contest offers at least $300 and publication in *River Oak Review*. Submit 4-6 poems at a time, typed, with name, address, phone number on cover letter only. Entries not returned. **Entry fee:** $15. Make checks payable to *River Oak Review*. Guidelines available for SASE or on website.

Advice "Put in the time. Read and study, pay careful attention to craft, and send only excellent work. We agree in principle with Stanley Kunitz, who told his poetry students to 'End on an image and don't explain it!' While we don't mean this literally, we do think that a 'less is more' philosophy usually results in better poems."

$☑ RIVER STYX MAGAZINE; BIG RIVER ASSOCIATION

634 N. Grand Ave., 12th Floor, St. Louis MO 63103. Website: www.riverstyx.org. Established 1975. **Contact:** Richard Newman, editor. Managing Editor: Ryan Stone.

● Poetry published in *River Styx* has been selected for inclusion in past volumes of *The Best American Poetry*, *Beacon's Best*, and *Pushcart Prize* anthologies.

Magazine Needs *River Styx*, published 3 times/year (April, August, December), is "an international, multicultural journal publishing both award-winning and previously undiscovered writers. We feature poetry, short fiction, essays, interviews, fine art, and photography." Wants "excellent poetry—original, energetic, musical, and accessible. Please don't send us chopped prose or opaque poetry that isn't about anything." Has published poetry by Louis Simpson, Molly Peacock, Marilyn Hacker, Yusef Komunyakaa, Andrew Hudgins, and Catie Rosemurgy. *River Styx* is 100 pages, digest-sized, professionally printed on coated stock, perfect-bound, with color cover, includes ads. Receives about 8,000 poems/year, accepts 60-75. Press run is 2,500 (1,000 subscribers, 80 libraries). Subscription: $20/year, $35/2 years. Sample: $7.

How to Submit Submit 3-5 poems at a time, "legible copies with name and address on each page." Accepts submissions by postal mail only. Reads submissions May 1 through November 30 only. Time between acceptance and publication is within one year. Editor sometimes comments on rejected poems. Publishes one theme issue/year. Upcoming themes available in magazine or on website. Guidelines available for SASE or on website. Responds in up to 5 months. Pays 2 contribu-

tor's copies plus one-year subscription, and $15/page if funds available. Acquires one-time rights.
Contest/Award Offerings Sponsors an annual poetry contest. Past judges include Miller Williams, Ellen Bryant Voigt, Marilyn Hacker, Philip Levine, Mark Doty, Naomi Shihab Nye, Billy Collins, and Molly Peacock. **Deadline:** May 31. Guidelines available for SASE or on website.

☑ RIVERSTONE, A PRESS FOR POETRY; RIVERSTONE POETRY CHAPBOOK AWARD

P.O. Box 1421, Carefree AZ 85377. Established 1992. **Contact:** Margaret Holley, editor.
Book/Chapbook Needs Riverstone publishes one chapbook/year through an annual contest (see below). Recent chapbooks include *Reading the Night Sky* by Margo Stever, *A Record* by Anita Barrows, *Dragon Lady: Tsukimi* by Martha Modena Vertreace, *Everything Speaking Chinese* by G. Timothy Gordon, *Balancing on Light* by Margaret Hoen, and *Into Grace* by Lisa Rhoades. The 2003 winner, Julie Lechevsky's *I'm a Serious Something*, is 40 pages, digest-sized, attractively printed on 70-lb. paper, hand-sewn, with gray endleaves and a brick-red card stock cover.
Contest/Award Offerings To be considered for the Riverstone Poetry Chapbook Award, submit chapbook ms of 24-36 pages, "including poems in their proposed arrangement, title page, contents, and acknowledgments. All styles welcome." Accepts previously published poems, multiple entries, and simultaneous submissions. Include 6×9 or larger SASE for notification and copy of last year's chapbook. Guidelines available for SASE. **Entry fee:** $8. **Postmark deadline:** June 30. Winner receives publication, 50 author's copies, and a cash prize of $100. Order sample chapbooks by sending $5.

☑ ROANOKE REVIEW

English Dept., Roanoke College, 221 College Lane, Salem VA 24153. E-mail: review@roanoke.edu. Website: www.roanoke.edu/roanokereview/. Established 1967. **Contact:** Paul Hanstedt, poetry editor.
Magazine Needs *Roanoke Review* is an annual literary review appearing in June, using poetry that is "grounded in strong images and unpretentious language." Has published poetry by David Citino, Jeff Daniel Marion, and Charles Wright. *Roanoke Review* is 200 pages, digest-sized, professionally printed, with matte card cover with full-color art. Receives 400-500 submissions of poetry/year, accepts 40-60. Press run is 250-300 (150 subscribers, 50 libraries). Single copy: $8; subscription: $13/2 years. Sample: $5.
How to Submit Submit original typed mss, no photocopies. Guidelines available on website. Responds in 3 months. Pays 2 contributor's copies "plus cash when budget allows."
Advice "Be real. Know rhythm. Concentrate on strong images."

⊠ ☑ THE ROCKFORD REVIEW; ROCKFORD WRITERS' GUILD

P.O. Box 858, Rockford IL 61105. E-mail: DaveConnieRoss@aol.com. Website: http://writersguild1.tripod.com. Established 1971. **Contact:** David Ross, editor.
Magazine Needs *The Rockford Review* is published by the Rockford Writers' Guild twice/year, featuring poetry and prose by members and other contributors from across the country and abroad. *The Rockford Review* seeks "experimental or traditional poetry that provides fresh insight into the human condition in a literal or satirical voice." Open to veterans and novices alike. "We delight in discovering new talent." *The Rockford Review* is about 100 pages, digest-sized, professionally printed, perfect-bound. Press run is 350. Single copy: $9; subscription: $20 (includes the Guild's monthly newsletter, *Write Away*).
How to Submit Submit up to 3 poems at a time, with SASE. Lines/poem: 50 maximum. Accepts simultaneous submissions; no previously published poems (including those published on Web). Accepts submissions by postal mail only. "Include a cover letter with your name, address, phone number, e-mail address (if available), a three-line bio, and an affirmation that the poems are unpublished electronically or in print." Guidelines available for SASE or on website. Responds in 2 months. Pays one contributor's copy and an invitation to be a guest of honor at annual summer Gala Reading & Reception in July. Acquires first North American serial rights.

Contest/Award Offerings Editor's Choice Prizes of $25 each issue. Also sponsors an Ides of March Poetry and Prose Contest for adults and youth, with cash prizes and publication in the summer *Review*.

Also Offers Rockford Writers' Guild is a nonprofit corporation established 60 years ago "to promote good writing of all forms and to nurture literary artists of all stages." Monthly meetings and newsletters offer practical tips on writing/marketing from professional guest poets, and open mics for contests/works in progress. Membership: $30/year. Further information available for SASE, by e-mail, or on website.

Advice "If the heart/soul of your poetry raises/answers questions about coping with the human condition, try us first—we're on the same page."

◩ ◪ ROMANTICS QUARTERLY (Specialized: form/style—transcendent verse)

318 Indian Trace #183, Weston FL 33326. E-mail: mar62451@aol.com or peekthemorpholux@yahoo.com. Website: www.rqjournal.com. Established 2000. **Contact:** Mary Rae, editor. Rereward: Skadi Abelar.

Magazine Needs "The vision of *Romantics Quarterly*, while continuing the tradition of the Great Romantics such as Blake, Wordsworth, Shelley, Keats, and Housman, is to secure the place of formal verse, both rhymed and blank, in today's poetic arena. We will not consider free verse, and we are not collectors of oddities and discarded flights of fancy. Instead, we ask for well-crafted poetry, poetry in translation, short stories, and essays inspired by the muse and then wrought in the fires of discipline. *Romantics Quarterly* provides a home for the poet who may have been working alone with his or her craft, building an understanding of the past, even in the face of Postmodern critics." Translations must be accompanied by originals. Has published poetry by Margaret Mendus, William F. Bell, Michael Fantina, and M.L. McCarthy. *Romantics Quarterly* is 75 pages, digest-sized, with full-color original art on cover. Accepts less than 10% of poems submitted. Single copy: $7; subscription: $28. Sample: $6.

How to Submit Submit up to 5 poems at a time. Considers but does not encourage previously published poems. Accepts submissions by postal mail; "E-mail submissions are acceptable, but those sent without a courteous note will not be read. We will not acknowledge e-mails redirecting us to a website." Cover letter with brief bio is preferred. Upcoming themes and guidelines available for SASE or on website. Responds in 2 months. Pays one contributor's copy. Acquires one-time rights.

Advice "We advise all contributors to consider subscribing, or to buy a copy of the journal before sending work. We publish many wonderful poets, and are delighted to consider the work of those who actually have a solid idea of what we are looking for."

◩ $◪ ◎ RONSDALE PRESS (Specialized: regional/Canada)

3350 W. 21st Ave., Vancouver BC V6S 1G7 Canada. (604)738-4688. Fax: (604)731-4548. E-mail: ronsdale@shaw.ca. Website: www.ronsdalepress.com. Established 1988. **Contact:** Ronald B. Hatch, director.

Book Needs Publishes 3 flat-spined paperbacks of poetry/year—by Canadian poets only—classical to experimental. "Ronsdale looks for poetry manuscripts which show that the writer reads and is familiar with the work of some of the major contemporary poets. It is also essential that you have published some poems in literary magazines. We have never published a book of poetry when the author has not already published a goodly number in magazines." Has published *Taking the Breath Away* by Harold Rhenisch, *Two Shores/Deux rives* by Thuong Vuong-Riddick, *Cobalt 3* by Kevin Roberts, *Ghost Children* by Lillian Boraks-Nemetz, *Poems for a New World* by Connie Fife, *Steveston* by Daphne Marlatt, and *After Ted & Sylvia* by Crystal Hurdle.

How to Submit Query first, with sample poems and cover letter with brief bio and publication credits. Accepts previously published poems and simultaneous submissions. Often comments on rejected poems. Responds to queries in 2 weeks, to mss in 2 months. Pays 10% royalties and 10 author's copies. Write for catalog to purchase sample books.

Advice "Ronsdale looks for poetry with echoes from previous poets. To our mind, the contemporary poet must be well-read."

$ ◲ ◎ ROOK PUBLISHING (Specialized: form/style—rhyming poetry)

1805 Calloway Dr., Clarksville TN 37042. (931)648-6225. Established 1996. **Contact:** Brad Fischer or E.A. Lawson.

Book/Chapbook Needs & How to Submit Rook Publishing's goal is "to secure and to re-introduce meaningful rhyming poetry in paperback books of 100-150 pages." Wants "rhyming poetry on any subject. We would love poems for children; 10-50 lines seem to work well; open to any style. No profanity, religion-bashing, gay/lesbian subject matter, vampires, gore, aliens, pornography, haiku, free verse, or poems in poor taste." Accepts poetry by children ages 10 and up. Has published poetry by Mary Louise Westbrook, Stephen Scaer, and Byron Von Rosenberg. Recently published *Quothade* by Norman Ball and *The Fruited Plain Anthology*, representing poets from all 50 states. Rook Publishing publishes 2 paperbacks/year. Books are usually 100-120 pages, 5×7, photocopied, perfect-bound, with 4-color covers. Accepts submissions by postal mail only; accepts submissions on disk. "No query letter will be necessary; published poems are fine with us." Guidelines available for SASE. Responds to queries/mss in 10 weeks. Pays royalties of 15-25%, $100, and 3 author's copies (out of a press run of 300-500); or 5 author's copies (out of a press run of 500). Order sample books by sending $8.50 to Rook Publishing.

Advice "Due to high volume, limit single poems to three. We still accept manuscripts along listed themes (available for SASE). Send only your best efforts."

◲ ROSE ALLEY PRESS

4203 Brooklyn Ave. NE, #103A, Seattle WA 98105-5911. (206)633-2725. E-mail: rosealleypress@jun o.com. Website: www.rosealleypress.com. Established 1995. **Contact:** David D. Horowitz, editor/ publisher. "We presently do not read unsolicited manuscripts."

◲ ROSEWATER PUBLICATIONS; THROUGH SPIDER'S EYES

223 Chapel St., Leicester MA 01524-1115. E-mail: rosewaterbooks@yahoo.com. Website: www.ros ewaterpublications.com. Established 1997. **Contact:** April M. Ardito, editor.

Magazine Needs *Through Spider's Eyes*, appearing annually, is "a showcase of the best of what RoseWater Publications receives. The best art is about art or has a strong message. We prefer coffeehouse and slam style poems, work that is just as powerful spoken as written. Multi-layered work always appreciated. Prefer modern and experimental work. Rhymed poetry must be exceptional; biased against 'God is great' and 'See the pretty trees and flowers' poetry." Has published poetry by Timothy McCoy, Gwen Ellen Rider, Ed Fuqua, Jay Walker, Craig Nelson, and Alex Stolis. *Through Spider's Eyes* is 20-36 pages, digest-sized, photocopied b&w. Receives and accepts varied number of poems/year. Press run "varies—minimum of 50 copies." Single copy: $9. Make checks payable to April M. Ardito. Accepts personal checks, money orders, or PayPal for all samples (no longer offers subscriptions).

How to Submit "No minimum/maximum number of poems to submit. Prefer that poets submit a full chapbook-length manuscript." Lines/poem: 3 minimum, 250 maximum. Accepts previously published poems; no simultaneous submissions. Accepts e-mail submissions, either as attachment (.txt or .doc format) or pasted into body of message. Cover letter is preferred. Likes "disposable manuscripts and casual, personal cover letters; SASE required." Reads submissions year round. Does not publish seasonal poems. Time between acceptance and publication is up to 2 years. "Editor always attempts to read all submissions personally, but has a few people who help out when submissions get overwhelming." Seldom comments on rejected poems. Responds in up to one year. Pays one contributor's copy per accepted poem. Acquires one-time rights and reprint rights (possible inclusion in an anthology at a later date). No longer doing book/chapbook reviews.

Book/Chapbook Needs & How to Submit RoseWater Publications "wants to create an aesthically pleasing product for poets who spend as much time on the stage as with the page. Chapbooks are our main business, so more time is spent with full manuscripts than individual poem submissions." Publishes 5-10 chapbooks/year. Chapbooks are usually 20-64 pages, photocopied b&w, stapled, with colored paper, cardstock, or business stock covers with original designs. "Please send full manuscript (16-60 pages). We do not wish to see queries. We would prefer to see a poet's full vision." Responds to mss in up to one year. Pays 50% of copies (out of a press run of 50-100). Order sample books/chapbooks by sending $4.50 to April M. Ardito.

Advice "Spend a lot of time reading and re-reading, writing and re-writing. Always try to keep one finger on the pulse of contemporary poetry, as much to know what isn't working as what is. Stay true to yourself and your vision. Use your words to lure others into your experiences."

☐ ◎ RUAH; POWER OF POETRY; THE NEW EDEN CHAPBOOK COMPETITION (Specialized: spirituality)

Dominican School of Philosophy/Theology, 2401 Ridge Rd., Berkeley CA 94709. Fax: (510)596-1860. E-mail: cjrenzop@yahoo.com. Website: www.popruah.org. Established 1990. **Contact:** C.J. Renz, O.P., general editor.

Magazine Needs *Ruah*, an annual journal published in June, "provides a 'non-combative forum' for poets who have had few or no opportunities to publish their work. Theme: spiritual poetry. The journal has 3 sections: general poems, featured poet, and chapbook contest winners." Wants "poetry that is of a 'spiritual nature,' i.e., describes an experience of the transcendent. No religious affiliation preferences; no style/format limitations. No 'satanic verse'; no individual poems longer than 4 typed pages." Has published poetry by Jean Valentine, Alberto Rios, Luci Shaw, and Wendell Berry. *Ruah* is 60-80 pages, digest-sized, photocopied, perfect-bound, with glossy card stock cover with color photo. Receives about 350 poems/year, accepts 10-20%. Press run is 250 (about 100 subscribers, 7 libraries, 10 shelf sales); 50 distributed free to authors, reviewers, and inquiries. Subscription: donated cost of $10 plus $1.75 p&h. Sample: $5 plus $1.75 p&h. Make checks payable to Power of Poetry/DSPT.

How to Submit Submit 3-5 poems/year. Accepts simultaneous submissions; no previously published poems. Accepts submissions by e-mail (as MS Word 97 file attachments or pasted into body of message), by fax, on disk, and by postal mail. "Do not mail submissions to publisher's address. Contact general editor via e-mail for current address, or send written inquiries to Dominican School." Reads submissions December through March only. Time between acceptance and publication is up to 6 months. "Poems are reviewed by writers and/or scholars in field of creative writing/literature." Guidelines available for SASE or by e-mail. Responds in 2 weeks. Pays one contributor's copy/poem. Acquires first rights.

Contest/Award Offerings Power of Poetry publishes one chapbook of spiritual poetry/year through their annual competition. Chapbooks are usually 24 pages and are included as part of *Ruah*. Winner receives $100 plus publication in a volume of *Ruah* and 25 author's copies (out of a press run of 250). **Entry fee:** $10. **Deadline:** December 30. Responds to queries in up to 6 weeks; to mss in up to 6 months. "Poets should e-mail general editor for contest guidelines and submission address, or write to Dominican School."

Advice "*Ruah* is a gathering place in which new poets can come to let their voices be heard alongside of and in the context of 'more established' poets. The journal hopes to provide some breakthrough experiences of the Divine at work in our world."

◙ RUNES, A REVIEW OF POETRY

Arctos Press, P.O. Box 401, Sausalito CA 94966-0401. (415)331-2503. Fax: (415)331-3092. E-mail: RunesRev@aol.com. Website: http://members.aol.com/Runes. Established 2000. **Contact:** Susan Terris and CB Follett, editors. Member: SPAN, BAIPA.

• Jane Hirshfield's poem "Burlap Sack," first published in *RUNES: Memory*, also appears in *The Best American Poetry 2005*.

Magazine Needs *RUNES, A Review Of Poetry* appears annually. "Our taste is eclectic, but we are looking for excellence in craft." Wants poems that have passion, originality, and conviction. "We are looking for narrative and lyric poetry that is well-crafted and has something surprising to say.'' No greeting card verse. Has published poetry by Lucille Clifton, Norman Dubie, Jane Hirshfield, Shirley Kaufman, Li-Young Lee, and David St. John. *RUNES* is 160 pages, digest-sized, professionally printed, flat-spined, with full-color cover. Receives about 6,000 poems/year, accepts 100. Press run is 1,500 (900 subscribers, 35 libraries). Single copy: $12; subscription: $12. Sample: $10. Make checks payable to Arctos Press.

How to Submit Submit no more than 5 poems at a time. Lines/poem: 100 maximum. Accepts simultaneous submissions if notified; no previously published poems. No e-mail or disk submissions. SASE required. Reads submissions April 1 through May 31 (postmark) only. Time between acceptance and publication is 6 months. Seldom comments on rejected poems. Regularly publishes theme issues. Upcoming themes (''Hearth'' in 2006, ''Connections'' in 2007) and guidelines available in magazine, for SASE, by e-mail, or on website. Responds in 4 months. Sometimes sends prepublication galleys. Pays one contributor's copy. Acquires first North American rights.

Contest/Award Offerings Poetry competition for 2006 will have same theme as magazine—''Hearth.'' 2006 judge will be Mark Doty. **Entry fee:** $15/3 poems, $3 for each additional poem. The entry fee covers a one-year subscription. For publication in *Runes*, it is *not* necessary to enter competition. All submitted poems will be read. Make checks payable to Arctos Press. (See separate listing for Arctos Press in this section.)

Advice ''No one can write in a vacuum. If you want to write good poetry, you must read good poetry—classic as well as modern work.''

S.W.A.G., THE MAGAZINE OF SWANSEA'S WRITERS AND ARTISTS; S.W.A.G. NEWSLETTER

Dan-y-Bryn, 74 CWM Level Rd., Brynhyfryd, Swansea SA5 9DY Wales, United Kingdom. Established 1992. **Contact:** Peter Thabit Jones, chairman/editor.

Magazine Needs *S.W.A.G.* appears biannually and publishes poetry, prose, articles, and illustrations. ''Our purpose is to publish good literature.'' Wants ''first-class poetry—any style.'' Has published poetry by Adrian Mitchell, Alan Llwyd, Mike Jenkins, and Dafydd Rowlands. *S.W.A.G.* is 48 pages, A4, professionally printed on coated paper, saddle-stapled, with glossy paper cover. Press run is 500 (120 subscribers, 50 libraries). Subscription: £5. Sample (including guidelines): £2.50 plus postage.

How to Submit ''Interested poets should obtain sample beforehand (to see what we offer).'' Submit 6 poems, typed. Lines/poem: 40 maximum. No previously published poems or simultaneous submissions. Cover letter is required. Time between acceptance and publication is 4-6 months. Poems are circulated to an editorial board. ''Editor chooses/discusses choices with board.'' Guidelines available for SASE (or SAE with IRCs). Responds ASAP. Pays 2 contributor's copies plus a copy of S.W.A.G.'s newsletter. Staff reviews books and poetry (half page to full page). Send materials for review consideration.

Also Offers The Swansea Writers and Artists Group (S.W.A.G.) also publishes a newsletter containing information on the group's events. Send SASE for details on the organization. ''We also publish Welsh-language poetry.''

SACRED JOURNEY: THE JOURNAL OF FELLOWSHIP IN PRAYER (Specialized: multifaith spirituality)

291 Witherspoon St., Princeton NJ 08542. (609)924-6863. Fax: (609)924-6910. E-mail: editorial@sa credjourney.org. Website: www.sacredjourney.org. Established 1950. **Contact:** Editor.

Magazine Needs *Sacred Journey* is an interfaith bimonthly ''concerned with prayer, meditation, spiritual life, and service to others,'' using short poetry ''with a spiritual and/or religious nature that reflects personal experience and is accessible to people of all faith traditions.'' *Sacred Journey* is 48 pages, digest-sized, professionally printed, saddle-stapled, with glossy card cover. Accepts about 10% of submissions received. Press run is 6,000. Subscription: $18. Sample: free.

How to Submit Submit 1-5 poems at a time, single-spaced. Accepts simultaneous submissions and "sometimes" previously published poems if reprint permission is readily available. Accepts e-mail submissions (pasted into body of message or as MS Word attachment). Cover letter with contact information, "including mailing address, phone number, and e-mail address if applicable," is required. Responds within 2 months. Pays 5 contributor's copies.

$☐ ◎ ST. ANTHONY MESSENGER (Specialized: religious/Catholic; spirituality/inspirational)

28 W. Liberty St., Cincinnati OH 45202-6498. Fax: (513)241-0399. Website: www.americancatholic. org. **Contact:** Christopher Heffron, poetry editor.

- *St. Anthony Messenger* poetry occasionally receives awards from the Catholic Press Association Annual Competition.

Magazine Needs *St. Anthony Messenger* is a monthly 56-page magazine, with a press run of 340,000, for Catholic families, mostly with children in grade school, high school, or college. Some issues feature a poetry page that uses poems appropriate for their readership. Poetry submissions are always welcome despite limited need. Accepts poetry by young writers, ages 14 and up. Sample: free for 9×12 SASE.

How to Submit "Submit seasonal poetry (Christmas/Easter/nature poems) several months in advance. Submit a few poems at a time; do not send us your entire collection of poetry. We seek to publish accessible poetry of high quality. Poems must be original, under 25 lines; spiritual/inspirational in nature a plus, but not required. We do not publish poems that have already been published—must be first run. Please include your social security number with your submission." Accepts submissions by fax, e-mail, and postal mail. Guidelines available on website, by fax, or for standard SASE. Pays $2/line on acceptance plus 2 contributor's copies. Acquires first worldwide serial rights.

$☐ ◎ ST. JOSEPH MESSENGER & ADVOCATE OF THE BLIND (Specialized: religious)

P.O. Box 288, Jersey City NJ 07303. Established 1898. **Contact:** Sister Mary Kuiken, C.S.J.P., poetry editor.

Magazine Needs & How to Submit *St. Joseph Messenger* is a semiannual and publishes "brief but thought-filled poetry; do not want lengthy and issue-filled." Most of the poets they have used are previously unpublished. Receives 400-500 submissions/year, accepts about 50. *St. Joseph Messenger* is 16 pages, magazine-sized. Press run is 14,000. Subscription: $5. Sometimes comments on rejected poems. Publishes theme issues. Guidelines, a free sample, and upcoming themes available for 6½×9½ SASE and 2 stamps. Responds within one month. Pays $5-15/poem plus 2 contributor's copies.

☐ ◎ ST. LINUS REVIEW (Specialized: religious/orthodox Catholicism)

5239 S. Sandusky Ave., Tulsa OK 74135. E-mail: editor@stlinusreview.com. Website: www.stlinusr eview.com. Established 2003. **Contact:** William Ferguson, editor.

Magazine Needs *St. Linus Review* is a biannual journal of poetry and prose written by and for orthodox Catholics. Wants "poetry and prose of diverse subject matter (does not have to be religious) in diverse styles. Prefer quality rhyming verse and structured styles but will accept free verse and other." Does not want "profanity, graphic portrayals of violence or sex, erotica, or works which openly or in general tendency detract from the teachings of the Catholic Church." Has published poetry by Pavel Chichikov, Kate Watkins Furman, Dennis Schenkel, and Sarah DeCorla-Souza. *St. Linus Review* is about 40 pages, digest-sized. Receives about 100 poems/year, accepts about 50%. Press run is 70 (25 subscribers). Single copy: $6; subscription: $12/year. Make checks payable to William Ferguson.

How to Submit Submit up to 5 poems at a time. No previously published poems or simultaneous submissions. Prefers e-mail submissions (as attachment in MS Word); no disk submissions. "We'll accept manuscripts mailed to our physical address; however, manuscripts will not be returned. Include name, city/state, and e-mail address on each submission." Reads submissions year round.

Time between acceptance and publication is 4-6 months. "Poems are read by the editor and 2 associate editors who select poems to be used in the review." Never comments on rejected poems. "Writers are requested to help support the review by subscribing. However, there is no requirement to subscribe." Guidelines available on website. Pays one contributor's copy. Acquires first rights.

Contest/Award Offerings Offers "Best of Review" award (small cash prize) in poetry and prose categories, presented annually.

Advice "Bright, bold orthodoxy in structured verse with strong, engaging words will win our hearts."

Ⓝ Ⓞ SAKANA; FISHHEAD PRESS

11 Bangor Mall Blvd., Suite D, #114, Bangor ME 04401. E-mail: fishheadpress@gmail.com (queries only). Website: www.geocities.com/sakanamag. Established 2004. **Contact:** Johanne LePage, editor.

Magazine Needs *Sakana* is a quarterly literary magazine featuring art and reviews. "Though we don't announce themes to our contributors, as work is accepted the magazine is broken into themed mini-sections derived from the quality work sent to us." Wants "quality works of poetry marked by vision and accomplishment, any style or form." Does not want "derivative poetry or poems lacking insight." Accepts poetry written by children. "Children's work will be held to the same standards as adult contributors, and parents should be advised that some of our magazine may not be suitable for children." Has published poetry by Troy Casa, Catherine Munch, and Catie Joyce. *Sakana* is 40-60 pages, digest-sized, Xeroxed, stapled, with 110-lb. coverstock cover with full-color artwork. Receives about 200 poems/year, accepts about 25. Press run is 100 (16 subscribers, 20 shelf sales). Single copy: $4; subscription: $16. Make checks payable to Jeff McKay.

How to Submit Submit 5-10 poems at a time. Lines/poem: open. Accepts previously published poems and simultaneous submissions. No e-mail or disk submissions. Cover letter is required. "Please always send a SASE with your work and include a bio in your cover letter." Reads submissions year round. Submit seasonal poems 3 months in advance. Time between acceptance and publication is 4 months. Always comments on rejected poems. Guidelines available in magazine, for SASE, by e-mail, or on website. Responds in 2 weeks. Pays one contributor's copy. Acquires one-time rights. Reviews books and chapbooks of poetry. Send materials for review consideration to Johanne LePage.

Also Offers Local poetry readings (central Maine) to kick off issue releases.

Advice "Work very hard, challenge yourself, and let language tell you what it's trying to tell you. No one gets rich (or all that famous) from poetry, so just enjoy it."

Ⓞ THE SAME

P.O. Box 16415, Kansas City MO 64131. E-mail: editor@tsmag.itgo.com. Website: http://tsmag.itgo .com. Established 2000. **Contact:** Carl Bettis and Philip Miller, co-editors.

Magazine Needs *The Same*, a publication of poetry, fiction, essays, and literary criticism, appears irregularly. Wants "eclectic to formal to free verse, traditional to experimental, all subject matter." Does not want misogyny, homophobia, racism, or inspirational. Has published poetry by David Ray, Judy Ray, Gary Lechliter, Phyllis Becker, Stephen Clay Dearborn, and John Mark Eberhart. *The Same* is 24-32 pages, magazine-sized, desktop-published/photocopied, saddle-stapled, with cardstock cover with b&w artwork. Receives about 2,000 poems/year, accepts about 5%. Press run is 150 (125 shelf sales); 25 are distributed free to contributors. Single copy: $5; subscription: $10/ 2 issues, $20/4 issues. Make checks payable to Carl Bettis.

How to Submit Submit 1-7 poems at a time. Lines/poem: 120 maximum. No previously published poems or simultaneous submissions. Accepts e-mail submissions (pasted into body of message); no disk submissions. "Include SASE if you want a response. If you don't want your manuscript returned, you may omit the SASE if we can respond via e-mail." Reads submissions year round. Submit seasonal poems 6 months in advance. Time between acceptance and publication is up to 11 months. Seldom comments on rejected poems. Guidelines available for SASE, by e-mail, or on website. Responds in 6-12 weeks. Pays one contributor's copy. Acquires first North American serial rights and online rights for up to 9 months; returns rights to poet.

Book/Chapbook Needs & How to Submit Publishes 0-3 chapbooks/year. **Solicited mss only.** Chapbooks are 24-32 pages, desktop-published/photocopied, saddle-stapled, with cardstock covers. Pays 25-50 author's copies (out of a press run of 50-100). Order sample chapbooks by sending $5 to *The Same.*

Advice "Our motto is 'Everyone else is different, but we're the same!' We are eclectic and non-doctrinaire."

$☑ SARABANDE BOOKS, INC.; THE KATHRYN A. MORTON PRIZE IN POETRY

2234 Dundee Rd., Suite 200, Louisville KY 40205. (502)458-4028. Fax: (502)458-4065. E-mail: info@sarabandebooks.org. Website: www.SarabandeBooks.org. Established 1994. **Contact:** Sarah Gorham, editor-in-chief.

Book/Chapbook Needs Sarabande Books publishes books of poetry of 48 pages minimum. Wants "poetry that offers originality of voice and subject matter, uniqueness of vision, and a language that startles because of the careful attention paid to it—language that goes beyond the merely competent or functional." Has published poetry by Mark Jarman, Louise Glück, Neela Vaswani, Marjorie Sandor, Charles Wright, and Yolanda Barnes. Guidelines available for SASE, by e-mail, or on website.

Contest/Award Offerings The Kathryn A. Morton Prize in Poetry, Sarabande Books, Inc., P.O. Box 4456, Louisville KY 40204. Awarded to a book-length ms (at least 48 pages). Entry form required. Winner receives $2,000, publication, and a standard royalty contract. All finalists are considered for publication. "At least half of our list is drawn from contest submissions." **Entry fee:** $25. **Deadline:** reads entries January 1 through February 15 only. Competition receives 1,200 entries. 2004 contest winner was Simone Muench for *Lampblack and Ash.* Judge was Carol Muske-Dukes.

Advice "We recommend that you request our catalog and familiarize yourself with our books. Our complete list shows a variety of style and subject matter."

N ☑ THE SARANAC REVIEW

CVH, Plattsburgh State University, English Dept., 101 Broad St., Plattsburgh NY 12901. (518)564-2134. Established 2004. **Contact:** Michael Carrino, poetry editor.

Magazine Needs *The Saranac Review* is published annually in April and "celebrates all aesthetics. We are looking for quality poetry." Does not want "amateurish work." Has published poetry by Valentine, Shephard, and Revell. *The Saranac Review* is magazine-sized, with color cover with photo or painting, includes ads. Press run is 1,000. Single copy: $12; subscription: $10/year. Make checks payable to *The Saranac Review.*

How to Submit Submit 7 poems at a time. Accepts simultaneous submissions; no previously published poems. No e-mail or disk submissions. Cover letter is required. Reads submissions September through May. Submit seasonal poems 6 months in advance. Time between acceptance and publication is 8 months. Poems are circulated to an editorial board. Sometimes comments on rejected poems. Sometimes publishes theme issues. List of upcoming themes available on website. Guidelines available by e-mail or on website. Responds in 3-6 months. Pays 2 contributor's copies. Acquires first rights.

Advice "No greeting card poetry."

✪ ✪ ◯ SAUCYVOX(DOT)COM

E-mail: editor@saucyvox.com. Website: http://saucyvox.com. Established 2001. **Contact:** Feithline Stuart.

Magazine Needs *SaucyVox(Dot)Com* is a monthly online literary magazine of poetry, prose, personal essays, articles, and photography. Wants "free verse by skilled and beginner poets, including erotic poetry." Does not want "verse." Has published poetry by John Sweet, Christopher George, John G. Hall, Laine Perry, and Simchi Cohen.

How to Submit Submit 5 poems minimum at a time; 10 to be considered as Featured Poet. Accepts e-mail submissions (pasted into body of message, no attachments); no disk submissions. "Include a photograph in .jpg format along with a third-person biography. We have no themes or taboos around here, so if it's saucy, we want it." Reads submissions year round. Submit seasonal poems 3 months in advance. Time between acceptance and publication is one month.

Contest/Award Offerings E-mail editor@saucyvox.com for more information.

Also Offers "PAD Challenge, which takes place in our online community. The PAD encourages writers to write a poem a day for 30 days for the purpose of instilling in the writer the habit of writing regularly. Winners of the challenge are featured in the zine. *SaucyVox(Dot)Com* also offers a 'Pay The Writer' program which encourages readers to donate to each individual artist featured on the site. Proceeds are split 50/50 with the site."

Advice "Do use your spell-checker. Do send us anything you want us to look at. Do be patient as we have a very small staff."

⊠ $◎ SCIENCE FICTION POETRY ASSOCIATION; STAR*LINE (Specialized: science fiction; horror); THE RHYSLING ANTHOLOGY

1412 NE 35th St., Ocala FL 34479. E-mail: SFPASL@aol.com. Website: www.sfpoetry.com. Established 1978. **Contact:** Marge Simon, editor.

Magazine Needs The Association publishes *Star*Line*, a bimonthly newsletter and poetry magazine. "Open to all forms—free verse, traditional forms, light verse—so long as your poetry shows skilled use of the language and makes a good use of science fiction, science, fantasy, horror, or speculative motifs." The Association also publishes *The Rhysling Anthology*, a yearly collection of nominations from the membership "for the best science fiction/fantasy long and short poetry of the preceding year." Has published poetry by Lawrence Schimel, Kendall Evans, Charlie Jacob, Terry A. Garey, and Timons Esaias. The magazine and anthology are digest-sized, photocopied, saddle-stapled. Has 250 subscribers (one library). Subscription: $13/6 issues. Sample: $2. Send requests for copies/membership information to Bruce Boston, SFPA Treasurer, at the address above. Submissions to *Star*Line* only. Receives about 300-400 submissions/year, accepts about 80.

How to Submit Send 3-5 poems/submission, typed. Lines/poem: preferably under 50. No simultaneous submissions or queries. Prefers e-mail submissions, "as part of the e-mail message, no attachments." Include brief cover letter. Responds in one month. Pays 10¢/line (minimum $12/poem). Buys first North American serial rights. Reviews books of poetry "within the science fiction/fantasy field" in 50-500 words. Open to unsolicited reviews. Send materials for review consideration.

⊠ $◯ ◎ SCIFAIKUEST (Specialized: forms/scifaiku, horror-ku, tanka, senryu, haibun, and other minimalist poetry forms); SAM'S DOT PUBLISHING

P.O. Box 782, Cedar Rapids IA 52406-0782. E-mail: gatrix65@yahoo.com. Website: www.samsdotp ublishing.com. Established 2003. **Contact:** Tyree Campbell, managing editor. Member: The Speculative Literature Foundation (http://SpeculativeLiterature.org).

- *Scifaikuest* was voted #1 poetry magazine in the 2004 *Preditors & Editors* poll.

Magazine Needs *Scifaikuest*, a quarterly, "publishes science fiction/fantasy/horror minimalist poetry, especially scifaiku, and related forms. We also publish articles about various poetic forms and reviews of poetry collections. *Scifaikuest* is published both online and in print; the 2 versions are different." Wants "scifaiku and speculative minimalist forms such as tanka, haibun, ghazals, senryu. No 'traditional' poetry." Has published poetry by Tom Brinck, Oino Sakai, Deborah P. Kolodji, Aurelio Rico Lopez III, Joanne Morcom, and John Dunphy. *Scifaikuest* (print edition) is 32 pages, digest-sized, offset-printed, saddle-stapled, with color cardstock cover, includes ads. Receives about 500 poems/year, accepts about 160 (32%). Press run is 100/issue (40 subscribers, 30 shelf sales); 5 distributed free to reviewers. Single copy: $7; subscription: $20/year, $37/2 years. Make checks payable to Tyree Campbell/Sam's Dot Publishing.

How to Submit Submit 5 poems at a time. Lines/poem: varies, depending on poem type. No previously published poems or simultaneous submissions. Accepts e-mail submissions (pasted into body of message); no disk submissions. "Submission should include snail mail address and a short (1-2 lines) bio." Reads submissions year round. Submit seasonal poems 6 months in advance. Time between acceptance and publication is 1-2 months. "Co-Editors Teri Santitoro and L. A. Story Houry make joint decisions regarding all acceptances." Often comments on rejected poems. Guidelines available on website. Responds in 6-8 weeks. Pays $1/poem, $4/review or article, and one contributor's copy. Acquires first North American serial rights.

Book/Chapbook Needs & How to Submit Sam's Dot Publishing publishes collections of scifaiku, horror-ku, and minimalist poetry. Publishes 2-3 chapbooks/year and one anthology/year. Manuscripts are selected through open submission. Chapbooks are 32 pages, offset-printed, saddle-stapled, with cardstock covers. Query first, with a few sample poems and a cover letter with brief bio and publication credits. Chapbook mss may include previously published poems. Responds to queries in 2 weeks; to mss in 4-6 weeks. Pays royalties of 12.5 % minimum and 1-2 author's copies (out of a press run of 50-100). Order sample chapbooks by sending $8 to Tyree Campbell/Sam's Dot Publishing.

Advice "It's up to the writer to take the first step and submit work. Some of our best poems have come from poets who weren't sure if they were good enough. A basic knowledge of writing traditional haiku is helpful."

☐ SEAWEED SIDESHOW CIRCUS

P.O. Box 234, Jackson WI 53037. (414)791-1109. Fax: (262)677-0896. E-mail: sscircus@aol.com. Website: http://hometown.aol.com/SSCircus/sscweb.html. Established 1994. **Contact:** Andrew Wright Milam, editor.

Book/Chapbook Needs & How to Submit Seaweed Sideshow Circus is "a place for young or new poets to publish a chapbook." Has published *Main Street* by Steven Paul Lansky and *The Moon Incident* by Amy McDonald. Publishes one chapbook/year. Chapbooks are usually 30 pages, digest-sized, photocopied, saddle-stapled, with cardstock covers. Send 5-10 sample poems and cover letter with bio and credits. Responds to queries in 3 weeks; to mss in 3 months. Pays royalties of 10 author's copies (out of a press run of 100). Order sample chapbooks by sending $6.

▦ ◙ SECOND AEON PUBLICATIONS

19 Southminster Rd., Roath, Cardiff CF23 SAT Wales. Phone/fax: (02920)493093. E-mail: peter@pe terfinch.co.uk. Website: www.peterfinch.co.uk. Established 1966. **Contact:** Peter Finch, poetry editor. Does not accept unsolicited mss.

◙ SEEMS

P.O. Box 359, Lakeland College, Sheboygan WI 53082-0359. (920)565-1276 or (920)565-3871. Fax: (920)565-1206. E-mail: kelder@excel.net. Website: www1.lakeland.edu/seems/. Established 1971. **Contact:** Karl Elder, editor.

Magazine Needs *SEEMS* is published irregularly as a handsomely printed, nearly square ($7 \times 8^{1}/_4$) magazine, saddle-stapled. Two of the issues are considered chapbooks, and the editor suggests sampling *SEEMS #14, What Is The Future Of Poetry?* for $5, consisting of essays by 22 contemporary poets, and "If you don't like it, return it, and we'll return your $5." *Explain That You Live: Mark Strand with Karl Elder* (#29) is available for $3. Has published poetry by Jene Erick Beardsley, William Virgil Davis, William Doreski, Thomas Dorsett, and Joanne Lowery. Print run is 500 (over 250 subscribers, 20 libraries). Single copy: $4; subscription: $16/4 issues.

How to Submit There is a 1- to 2-year backlog. "People may call or fax with virtually any question, understanding that the editor may have no answer." No simultaneous submissions. No fax or e-mail submissions. Guidelines available on website. Responds in up to 3 months (slower in summer). Pays one contributor's copy. Acquires first North American serial rights and permission to publish online. Returns rights upon publication.

Advice "Visit the new *SEEMS* website."

◙ SENECA REVIEW

Hobart and William Smith Colleges, Geneva NY 14456-3397. (315)781-3392. Fax: (315)781-3348. E-mail: senecareview@hws.edu. Website: www.hws.edu/senecareview/. Established 1970. **Contact:** Deborah Tall, editor. Associate Editor: John D'Agata.

- Poetry published in *Seneca Review* has been included in *The Best American Poetry* and *The Pushcart Prize* anthologies.

Magazine Needs *Seneca Review* is a biannual. Wants "serious poetry of any form, including translations. No light verse. Also essays on contemporary poetry and lyrical nonfiction." Has published poetry by Seamus Heaney, Rita Dove, Denise Levertov, Stephen Dunn, and Hayden Carruth. *Seneca Review* is 100 pages, digest-sized, professionally printed on quality stock, perfect-bound, with matte card cover. "You'll find plenty of free verse here—some accessible and some leaning toward experimental—with the emphasis on voice, image, and diction. All in all, poems and translations complement each other and create a distinct editorial mood each issue." Receives 3,000-4,000 poems/year, accepts about 100. Press run is 1,000 (500 subscribers, 250 libraries, about 250 shelf sales). Subscription: $11/year, $20/2 years, $28/3 years. Sample: $5.

How to Submit Submit 3-5 poems at a time. No simultaneous submissions or previously published poems. Reads submissions September 1 through May 1 only. Responds in up to 3 months. Pays 2 contributor's copies and a 2-year subscription.

▣ ◎ SEVEN BUFFALOES PRESS; AZOREAN EXPRESS; BLACK JACK; VALLEY GRAPEVINE; HILL AND HOLLER ANTHOLOGY SERIES (Specialized: rural; regional; anthologies)

Box 249, Big Timber MT 59011. Established 1973. **Contact:** Art Coelho, editor/publisher.

Magazine Needs & How to Submit "I've always thought that rural and working-class writers, poets, and artists deserve the same tribute given to country singers. These publications all express that interest." Wants poetry oriented toward rural and working people; "a poem that tells a story, preferably free verse; poems with strong lyric and metaphor; not romantical; poetry of the heart as much as the head; not poems written like grocery lists or the first thing that comes from a poet's mind; no ivory tower; half my contributors are women." Has published poetry by R.T. Smith, James Goode, Leo Connellan, and Wendell Berry. *Azorean Express* is 35 pages, digest-sized, side-stapled. It appears twice/year. Circulation is 200. Sample: $10 postpaid. Submit 4-8 poems at a time. Lines/poem: 50-100 maximum. No simultaneous submissions. Responds in one month. Pays one contributor's copy. *Black Jack* is an anthology series on Rural America that uses rural material from anywhere, especially the American West; *Valley Grapevine* is an anthology on central California that uses rural material from central California (circulation 750); *Hill and Holler*, Southern Appalachian Mountain series, takes in rural mountain lifestyle and folkways. Sample of any: $10 postpaid.

Book/Chapbook Needs & How to Submit Seven Buffaloes Press does not accept unsolicited mss but publishes books solicited from writers who have appeared in the above magazines.

Advice "Don't tell the editor how great you are. This one happens to be a poet and novelist who has been writing for 30 years. Your writing should not only be fused with what you know from the head, but also from what you know within your heart. Most of what we call life may be some kind of gift of an unknown river within us. The secret to be learned is to live with ease in the darkness, because there are too many things of the night in this world. But the important clue to remember is that there are many worlds within us."

$◙ THE SEWANEE REVIEW

University of the South, 735 University Ave., Sewanee TN 37383-1000. (931)598-1246. E-mail: lcouch@sewanee.edu. Website: www.sewanee.edu/sreview/home.html. Established 1892, thus being our nation's oldest continuously published literary quarterly. **Contact:** George Core, editor.

Magazine Needs "Fiction, criticism, and poetry are invariably of the highest establishment standards. Many of our major poets appear here from time to time." Open to all styles and forms: formal sequences, metered verse, structured free verse, sonnets, and lyric and narrative forms—

all accessible and intelligent. Has published poetry by Wendell Berry, George Bilgere, Catherine Savage Brosman, David Mason, Leslie Norris, and Christian Wiman. *The Sewanee Review* is a hefty paperback of nearly 200 pages, conservatively bound in matte paper, always of the same typography. Press run is 3,100. Sample: $8.50 US, $9.50 foreign. Subscription: $24/year, $30/year (institutions).

How to Submit Submit up to 6 poems at a time. Lines/poem: 40 maximum. No simultaneous submissions. Accepts submissions by postal mail only. "Unsolicited works should not be submitted between June 1 and August 31. A response to any submission received during that period will be greatly delayed." Guidelines available in magazine or on website. Responds in 6 weeks. Pays 70¢/line, plus 2 contributor's copies (and reduced price for additional copies). Also includes brief, standard, and essay-reviews.

Contest/Award Offerings Presents the Aiken Taylor Award for Modern American Poetry to established poets. Poets *cannot* apply for this prize.

Advice "Please keep in mind that for each poem published in *The Sewanee Review*, approximately 250 poems are considered."

SHEMOM (Specialized: motherhood)

2486 Montgomery Ave., Cardiff CA 92007. E-mail: pdfrench@cox.net. Established 1997. **Contact:** Peggy French, editor.

Magazine Needs "Appearing 2-4 times/year, *Shemom* celebrates motherhood and the joys and struggles that present themselves in that journey. It includes poetry, essays, book and CD reviews, recipes, art, and children's poetry. Open to any style, prefer free verse. We celebrate motherhood and related issues. Haiku and native writing also enjoyed. Love to hear from children." *Shemom* is a 10- to 20-page zine. Receives about 100 poems/year, accepts 50%. Press run is 60 (30 subscribers). Single copy: $3.50; subscription: $12/4 issues. Make checks payable to Peggy French.

How to Submit Submit 3 poems at a time. Accepts previously published poems and simultaneous submissions. Accepts e-mail submissions (as attachment or pasted into body of message). "Prefer e-mail submission, but not required; if material is to be returned, please include a SASE." Guidelines available for SASE or by e-mail. Time between acceptance and publication is 3 months. Responds in 2 months. Pays one contributor's copy. Acquires one-time rights.

$ SHENANDOAH; THE JAMES BOATWRIGHT III PRIZE FOR POETRY

Mattingly House, 2 Lee Ave., Washington and Lee University, Lexington VA 24450-0303. (540)458-8765. E-mail: lleech@wlu.edu. Website: http://shenandoah.wlu.edu. Established 1950. **Contact:** R.T. Smith, editor.

● Poetry published in *Shenandoah* has been included in *The Best American Poetry*.

Magazine Needs Published at Washington and Lee University, *Shenandoah* is a triannual literary magazine. Generally, it is open to all styles and forms. Has published poetry by Mary Oliver, Andrew Hudgins, W.S. Merwin, and Rita Dove. *Shenandoah* is 224 pages, digest-sized, professionally printed, perfect-bound, with full-color cover. Press run is 2,000. Subscription: $22/year, $40/2 years, $54/3 years. Sample: $8.

How to Submit All submissions should be typed on one side of the paper only. Your name and address must be clearly written on the upper right corner of the ms. Simultaneous submissions considered "only if we are immediately informed of acceptance elsewhere." No e-mail submissions. Include SASE. Reads submissions September 1 through May 30 only. Responds in 3 months. Pays $2.50/line, one-year subscription, and one contributor's copy. Acquires first publication rights. Staff reviews books of poetry in 7-10 pages, multi-book format. Send materials for review consideration. (Most reviews are solicited.)

Contest/Award Offerings Sponsors the annual James Boatwright III Prize for Poetry, a $1,000 prize awarded to the author of the best poem published in *Shenandoah* during a volume year.

☑ SHIP OF FOOLS; SHIP OF FOOLS PRESS

Box 1028, University of Rio Grande, Rio Grande OH 45674-9989. (740)992-3333. Website: http://meadhall.homestead.com. Established 1983. **Contact:** Jack Hart, editor. Assistant Editor: Catherine Grosvenor. Review Editor: James Doubleday.

Magazine Needs *Ship of Fools* is "more or less quarterly." Wants "coherent, well-written, traditional or modern, myth, archetype, love—most types. No concrete, incoherent, or greeting card poetry." Has published poetry by Rhina Espaillat and Gale White. *Ship of Fools* is digest-sized, offset-printed, saddle-stapled, includes cover art and graphics. Press run is 179 (44 subscribers, 5 libraries). Subscription: $8/4 issues. Sample: $2.

How to Submit No previously published poems or simultaneous submissions. Cover letter is preferred. Often comments on rejected poems. Guidelines available for SASE. Responds in one month. "If longer than 6 weeks, write and ask why." Pays 1-2 contributor's copies. Reviews books of poetry.

Book/Chapbook Needs & How to Submit "We have no plans to publish chapbooks in the next year due to time constraints."

Advice "Forget yourself; it is not you that matters, but the words."

◎ SHIRIM, A JEWISH POETRY JOURNAL (Specialized: ethnic)

259 St. Joseph Ave., Long Beach CA 90803. (310)476-2861. Established 1982. **Contact:** Marc Dworkin, editor.

Magazine Needs *Shirim* appears biannually and publishes "poetry that reflects Jewish living without limiting to specific symbols, images, or contents." Has published poetry by Robert Mezcy, Karl Shapiro, and Grace Schulmon. *Shirim* is 40 pages, 4×5, desktop-published, saddle-stapled, with card stock cover. Press run is 200. Subscription: $7. Sample: $4.

How to Submit Submit 4 poems at a time. No previously published poems or simultaneous submissions. Cover letter is preferred. Seldom comments on rejected poems. Regularly publishes theme issues. Responds in 3 months. Acquires first rights.

$☑ sidereality: a journal of speculative & experimental poetry

Asheville NC. E-mail: managingeditor@sidereality.com. Website: www.sidereality.com. Established 2002. **Contact:** Clayton A. Couch, managing editor.

Magazine Needs *sidereality: a journal of speculative & experimental poetry* appears quarterly as an Internet-only e-journal. "We consider a broad range of styles and forms, but we are looking specifically for poems that challenge reader expectations and imbue the English language with vitality and 'newness.'" Does not want clichéd, non-specific, or vague poetry. Has published poetry by Joel Chace, Bruce Boston, Eileen Tabios, Charles Fishman, Susan Terris, and John Amen. *sidereality* is 80-100 pages, published online, with a web page cover with digital art. Receives about 800-900 poems/year, accepts about 15%.

How to Submit Submit 1-10 poems at a time. No previously published poems or simultaneous submissions. "*sidereality* accepts only e-mail submissions. Send to poetryeditor@sidereality.com with poems in the body of the message or in an attached file (.doc or .rtf format)." Cover letter is preferred. Reads submissions all year. Time between acceptance and publication is 2-5 months. Sometimes comments on rejected poems. Guidelines available on website. Responds in up to 2-3 months. Sometimes sends prepublication galleys. Pays $2-3/poem. "We purchase first printing world exclusive rights for 3 months, after which time you may republish your work elsewhere, so long as *sidereality* is noted as the original publisher. We hope that you will allow *sidereality* to maintain your work in its archives indefinitely, but should you decide to remove it, contact Clayton A. Couch with the request." Reviews books and chapbooks of poetry and other magazines/journals. Send materials for review consideration to managingeditor@sidereality.com.

Advice "Read, read as much as you can. Take risks with your writing, and most importantly, allow your poems room to grow."

☑ SIERRA NEVADA COLLEGE REVIEW

999 Tahoe Blvd., Incline Village NV 89451. E-mail: sncreview@sierranevada.edu. Established 1990. **Contact:** June Sylvester Saraceno, editor.

Magazine Needs *Sierra Nevada College Review* is an annual literary magazine published in May, featuring poetry and short fiction by new writers. "We want image-oriented poems with a distinct, genuine voice. Although we don't tend to publish 'light verse,' we do appreciate, and often publish, poems that make us laugh. We try to steer clear of sentimental, clichéd, or obscure poetry. No limit on length, style, etc." Has published poetry by Virgil Suárez, Amy Gerick, Melissa Staszak, and Alan Britt. *Sierra Nevada College Review* is about 75 pages, with cover art only. "We receive approximately 500 poems/year and accept approximately 50." Press run is 500. Subscription: $10/year. Sample: $5.

How to Submit Submit 5 poems at a time. Accepts simultaneous submissions; no previously published poems. Accepts e-mail submissions (pasted into body of message). Reads submissions September 1 through March 1 only. Sometimes comments on rejected poems. Guidelines available for SASE or by e-mail. Responds in about 3 months. Pays 2 contributor's copies.

Advice "We're looking for poetry that shows subtlety and skill."

$☑ SILVERFISH REVIEW PRESS; GERALD CABLE BOOK AWARD

P.O. Box 3541, Eugene OR 97403. (541)344-5060. E-mail: sfrpress@earthlink.net. Website: www.silverfishreviewpress.com. Established 1979. **Contact:** Rodger Moody, editor.

Contest/Award Offerings Silverfish Review Press sponsors the Gerald Cable Book Award. A $1,000 cash prize and publication is awarded annually to the best book-length ms of original poetry by an author who has not yet published a full-length collection. No restrictions on the kind of poetry or subject matter; translations not acceptable. Has published *Why They Grow Wings* by Nin Andrews, *Odd Botany* by Thorpe Moeckel, *Bodies that Hum* by Beth Gylys, and *Inventing Difficulty* by Jessica Greenbaum. Books are $12 plus $3.50 p&h. A **$20 entry fee** must accompany the ms; make checks payable to Silverfish Review Press. Guidelines available for SASE or by e-mail. Pays 10% of press run (out of 1,000).

☐ SIMPLYWORDS

605 Collins Ave. #23, Centerville GA 31028-1060. (478)953-9482 (between 10 a.m. and 5 p.m. only). E-mail: simplywordspoetry@yahoo.com. Website: http://geocities.com/simplywordspoetry. Established 1991. **Contact:** Ruth Niehaus, editor. Owner/CEO: David Niehaus.

Magazine Needs *SimplyWords* is a quarterly magazine open to all types, forms, and subjects. "No foul language or overtly sexual works." Accepts poetry written by children ages 8 and up; "there are no reading fees for children." Has published poetry by McGuffy Ann Morris, Barbara Cagle Ray, Lois Hayn, Marlie Marks, Donald Harmande, and Sarah LuAnn Jensen. *SimplyWords* is 34-38 pages, magazine-sized, deskjet-printed, spiral-bound, with photo on cover. Receives about 500 poems/year, accepts about 90%. Press run is 60-100 "depending on subscriptions and single-issue orders in-house." Single copy: $7.50; subscription: $23.50/4 issues (includes monthly e-newsletter).

How to Submit "Send SASE for guidelines *before* submitting; write 'GUIDELINES' in big block letters on left-hand corner of envelope." Lines/poem: 28 maximum. No e-mail submissions. Cover letter and SASE are required. "Name, address, phone number, e-mail address (if available), and line count must be on each page submitted." **Reading fee:** $1/poem for non-subscribers, 50¢ for subscribers. Time between acceptance and publication "depends on what issue your work is accepted for." Guidelines available for SASE or by e-mail.

Advice "Send for guidelines!"

☑ SKIDROW PENTHOUSE

44 Four Corners Rd., Blairstown NJ 07825. (908)362-6808 or (212)286-2600. Established 1998. **Contact:** Rob Cook and Stephanie Dickinson, co-editors.

Magazine Needs *Skidrow Penthouse* is published "to give emerging and idiosyncratic writers a new forum in which to publish their work. We are looking for deeply felt authentic voices, whether surreal, confessional, New York School, formal, or free verse. Work should be well crafted: attention to line-break and diction. We want poets who sound like themselves, not workshop professionals. We don't want gutless posturing, technical precision with no subject matter, explicit sex and violence without craft, or abstract intellectualizing. We are not impressed by previous awards and publications." Has published poetry by Lisa Jarnot, Christopher Edgar, Aase Berg, Karl Tierney, James Grinwis, and Robyn Art. *Skidrow Penthouse* is 280 pages, 6×9, professionally printed, perfect-bound, with 4-color cover. Receives about 500 poems/year, accepts 3%. Press run is 300 (50 subscribers); 10% distributed free to journals for review consideration. Single copy: $12.50; subscription: $20. Make checks payable to Rob Cook or Stephanie Dickinson.

How to Submit Submit 3-5 poems at a time. Accepts previously published poems and simultaneous submissions. "Include a legal sized SASE; name and address on every page of your submission. No handwritten submissions will be considered." Time between acceptance and publication is one year. Seldom comments on rejected poems. Responds in 2 months. Pays one contributor's copy. Acquires one-time rights. Reviews books and chapbooks of poetry and other magazines in 1,500 words, single-book format. Send materials for review consideration.

Also Offers "We're trying to showcase a poet in each issue by publishing up-to-60-page collections within the magazine." Send query with SASE.

Advice "We get way too many anecdotal fragments posing as poetry; too much of what we receive feels like this morning's inspiration mailed this afternoon. The majority of those who submit do not seem to have put in the sweat a good poem demands. Also, the ratio of submissions to sample copy purchases is 50:1. Just because our name is *Skidrow Penthouse* does not mean we are a repository for genre work or 'eat, shit, shower, and shave' poetry."

☐ ◎ SKIPPING STONES: A MULTICULTURAL CHILDREN'S MAGAZINE; ANNUAL YOUTH HONOR AWARDS (Specialized: bilingual; children/teens; ethnic/nationality; nature/ ecology; social issues)

P.O. Box 3939, Eugene OR 97403. (541)342-4956. E-mail: editor@skippingstones.org. Website: www.skippingstones.org. Established 1988. **Contact:** Arun Toké, editor.

• Now in its 17th year, *Skipping Stones* is the recipient of EdPress, NAME, and Parent's Guide Awards, among others.

Magazine Needs *Skipping Stones* is an award-winning "nonprofit magazine published bimonthly during the school year (5 issues) that encourages cooperation, creativity, and celebration of cultural and ecological richness." Wants poetry by young writers under age 18, on "nature, multicultural and social issues, family, freedom . . . uplifting. No adult poetry, please." *Skipping Stones* is magazine-sized, saddle-stapled, printed on recycled paper. Receives about 500-1,000 poems/year, accepts 10%. Press run is 2,500 (1,700 subscribers). Subscription: $25. Sample: $5.

How to Submit Submit up to 3 poems at a time. Lines/poem: 30 maximum. Accepts simultaneous submissions; no previously published poems. Accepts e-mail submissions (pasted into body of message). Cover letter is preferred. "Include your cultural background, experiences, and the inspiration behind your creation." Time between acceptance and publication is up to 9 months. Poems are circulated to a 3-member editorial board. "Generally a piece is chosen for publication when all the editorial staff feel good about it." Seldom comments on rejected poems. Publishes theme issues. Guidelines and upcoming themes available for SASE. Responds in up to 4 months. Pays one contributor's copy, offers 25% discount for more. Acquires first serial rights and non-exclusive reprint rights.

Contest/Award Offerings Sponsors Annual Youth Honor Awards for 7- to 17-year-olds. Theme is "Multicultural and Nature Awareness." **Entry fee:** $3 (includes a free issue featuring winners). **Deadline:** June 20 each year. Guidelines available for SASE.

✪ ◢ SKYLINE LITERARY MAGAZINE

P.O. Box 295, Stormville NY 12582-0295. (845)227-5171. E-mail: SkylineEditor@aol.com. Website: www.SkylineMagazines.com. Established 2001. **Contact:** Victoria Valentine, editor.

Magazine Needs *Skyline Literary Magazine* appears online bimonthly, publishing poetry, short stories, art, and special interest columns. "Easy-read, emotional literature for all to enjoy in our free downloadable page-turning ezines." Wants emotional, meaningful, understandable poetry; traditional, free verse, haiku, all styles, all genres. "We seek a smooth, entertaining read for relaxation and enjoyment. Will consider experimental. No porn, religious, political, or racism." Has published poetry by Lynn Stowe, Steven Manchester, Victoria Rose, Dr. Amitabh Mitra, Jan Oskar Hansen, and Richard Fein. Receives about 2,500 poems/year, accepts about 55%.

How to Submit Submit 3-4 poems at a time. Lines/poem: 35 maximum (preferred, with exceptions). Accepts simultaneous submissions; no previously published poems. Accepts e-mail (pasted into body of message) and disk/CD submissions; no fax or snail mail submissions. Short (4-5 lines) bio is required. Seldom comments on rejected poems. Occasionally publishes theme issues. List of upcoming themes available by e-mail or on website. Guidelines available on website. Responds in 3-6 months. Acquires one-time/first electronic rights, "exclusive for 50 days with issues remaining archived."

Also Offers Cash prize contests; see website for details. Nominates for Pushcart Prize.

Advice "Don't expect miracles overnight. Persevere! Scream loud enough and you will be heard, and always . . . reach for the sky, it's closer than you think!"

◢ SLANT: A JOURNAL OF POETRY

Box 5063, University of Central Arkansas, 201 Donaghey Ave., Conway AR 72035-5000. (501)450-5107. Website: www.uca.edu/divisions/academic/english/Slant/HOMPAGE.html. Established 1987. **Contact:** James Fowler, editor.

Magazine Needs *Slant* is an annual journal (appearing in May) using *only* poetry. Wants "traditional and 'modern' poetry, even experimental, moderate length, any subject on approval of Board of Readers; purpose is to publish a journal of fine poetry from all regions of the United States and beyond. No haiku, no translations." Accepts poetry written by children ("although we're not a children's journal.") Has published poetry by Mark Brazactis, Maureen Tolman Flannery, Susan Hazen-Hammond, Sandra Kohler, Parker Towle, and Charles Harper Webb. *Slant* is 120 pages, professionally printed on quality stock, flat-spined, with matte card cover. Receives about 1,500 poems/year, accepts 70-80. Press run is 175 (70-100 subscribers). Sample: $10.

How to Submit Submit up to 5 poems of moderate length, with SASE, between September and mid-November. "Put name, address (including e-mail if available), and phone number on the top of each page." No previously published poems or simultaneous submissions. Editor comments on rejected poems "on occasion." Guidelines available in magazine, for SASE, or on website. Allow 3-4 months from November 15 deadline for response. Pays one contributor's copy.

Advice "We tend to publish those poems whose execution, line by line, does full justice to their conception. Often the decision to accept comes down to the matter of craft, language."

◻ SLAPERING HOL PRESS; SLAPERING HOL PRESS CHAPBOOK COMPETITION

300 Riverside Dr., Sleepy Hollow NY 10591-1414. (914)332-5953. Fax: (914)332-4825. E-mail: info @writerscenter.org. Website: www.slaperingholpress.org. Established 1990. **Contact:** Margo Stever.

Book/Chapbook Needs "Slapering Hol Press is the small press imprint of The Hudson Valley Writers' Center. It was created in 1990 to provide publishing opportunities for emerging poets who have not yet published a book or chapbook, and to publish occasional anthologies. One chapbook is selected for publication on the basis of an annual competition [see below]." Has published *The Last Campaign* by Rachel Loden, *The Landscape of Mind* by Jianqing Zheng, *The Scottish Café* by Susan Case, and *Water Stories* by Brighde Mullins. Slapering Hol Press publishes one or 2 chapbooks/year. Chapbooks are usually less than 40 pages, offset-printed, hand-sewn, with 80-lb. cover-weight covers.

Contest/Award Offerings Slapering Hol Press Chapbook Competition offers annual award of $1,000, publication, 10 author's copies, and a reading at The Hudson Valley Writers' Center. Pays winners from other countries with check in U.S. currency. Open only to poets who have not previously published a book or chapbook. Submit 16-20 pages of poetry, collection or one long poem, any form or style. **Entry fee:** $15. Make checks payable to The Hudson Valley Writers' Center. "Manuscript should be anonymous with separate cover sheet containing name, address, phone number, e-mail address, a bio, and acknowledgments." Manuscripts will not be returned. Include SASE for results only. Guidelines available for SASE, by fax, e-mail, or on website. **Deadline:** May 15. Competition receives more than 300 entries. 2004 contest winner was Nancy Taylor Everett (*Juliet As Herself*). Winner will be announced in September. Copies of winning books available through website and www.amazon.com.

☐ ◎ SLATE & STYLE (Specialized: blind writers)

2704 Beach Dr., Merrick NY 11566. (516)868-8718. E-mail: LoriStay@aol.com. **Contact:** Loraine Stayer, editor.

Magazine Needs *Slate & Style* is a quarterly for blind writers, available on cassette, in large print, in Braille, and by e-mail, "including articles of interest to blind writers, resources for blind writers. Membership/subscription is $10 per year, all formats. Division of the National Federation of the Blind. Prefer contributors to be blind writers, or at least writers by profession or inclination. New writers welcome. No obscenities. Will consider all forms of poetry including haiku. Interested in new talent." Accepts poetry by young writers, "but please specify age." Has published poetry by Mary Brunoli, Kerry Elizabeth Thompson, John Gordon Jr., Katherine Barr, and Nancy Scott. The print version of *Slate & Style* is 28-32 pages, magazine-sized, stapled. Press run is 200 (160 subscribers, 4-5 libraries). Subscription: $10/year. Sample: $2.50.

How to Submit Submit 3 poems once or twice/year. Lines/poem: 5-36. No simultaneous submissions or previously published poems. Accepts submissions by e-mail (pasted into body of message). Cover letter is preferred. "On occasion we receive poems in Braille. I prefer print, since Braille slows me down. Typed is best." Do not submit mss in July. Editor comments on rejected poems "if requested." Guidelines available in magazine, for SASE, by e-mail, or on website. Responds in "2 weeks if I like it." Pays one contributor's copy. Reviews books of poetry. Send materials for review consideration.

Contest/Award Offerings Offers an annual poetry contest. Winners receive $25 and publication. **Entry fee:** $5 for up to 3 poems. **Deadline:** June 1. Write for details.

Advice "Before you send us a poem, read it aloud. Does it sound good to you? We put our poetry into tape format, so we want it to sound and look good."

✖ ◪ SLIPSTREAM

Box 2071, New Market Station, Niagara Falls NY 14301-0071. (716)282-2616 (after 5PM, EST). E-mail: editors@slipstreampress.org. Website: www.slipstreampress.org. Established 1980. **Contact:** Dan Sicoli, Robert Borgatti, and Livio Farallo, poetry editors.

Magazine Needs *Slipstream*, published 1-2 times/year, is a "small press literary mag published in the spring and is about 90% poetry and 10% fiction/prose, with some artwork. We like new work with contemporary urban flavor. Writing must have a cutting edge to get our attention. We like to keep an open forum, any length, subject, style. Best to see a sample to get a feel. Like city stuff as opposed to country. Like poetry that springs from the gut, screams from dark alleys, inspired by experience." No "pastoral, religious, traditional, rhyming" poetry. Has published poetry by Terry Godbey, Gerald Locklin, David Chorlton, Lori Jakiela, Rebecca Cook, and Khan Wong. *Slipstream* is 80-100 pages, $7 \times 8^{1/2}$, professionally printed, perfect-bound. Receives over 2,500 submissions of poetry/year, accepts less than 10%. Press run is 500 (400 subscribers, 10 libraries). Subscription: $20/2 issues and 2 chapbooks. Sample: $7.

How to Submit No e-mail submissions. Editor sometimes comments on rejected poems. Publishes theme issues, but "reading for a general issue through 2006." Guidelines and upcoming themes available for SASE or on website. Responds in up to 2 months, "if SASE included." Pays 1-2 contributor's copies.

Contest/Award Offerings Sponsors annual chapbook contest. Winner receives $1,000 and 50 copies. All entrants receive copy of winning chapbook and an issue of the magazine. Submit up to 40 pages of poetry, any style; previously published work OK with acknowledgments. **Entry fee:** $15. **Deadline:** December 1. Guidelines available for SASE or on website. Most recent winner was Beth Anne Royer for *Radio Dreams*.

Advice "Do not waste time submitting your work 'blindly.' Sample issues from the small press first to determine which ones would be most receptive to your work."

$⬛ SLOPE

340 Richmond Ave., Buffalo NY 14222. E-mail: info@slope.org. Website: www.slope.org. Established 1999. **Contact:** Ethan Paquin, editor-in-chief. Member: CLMP.

• Poetry featured in *Slope* has been included in *The Best American Poetry*.

Magazine Needs *Slope* is a quarterly online journal of poetry "featuring work that is challenging, dynamic, and innovative. We encourage new writers while continuing to publish award-winning and established poets from around the world." Wants "no particular style. Interested in poetry in translation." Has published poetry by Forrest Gander, Paul Hoover, Eleni Sikelianos, James Tate, Bruce Beasley, and Charles Bernstein.

How to Submit Submit 3-6 poems at a time. No previously published poems or simultaneous submissions. Accepts submissions by e-mail only (as attachments). "Submit poems via e-mail to the address on the website." Reads submissions year round. Time between acceptance and publication is 3-6 months. Seldom comments on rejected poems. Guidelines available by e-mail or on website. Responds in 3 months. Acquires one-time rights. Reviews books and chapbooks of poetry in 400 words, single-book format. Send materials for review consideration; "query first."

Contest/Award Offerings Sponsors annual American Sign Language Poetry Prize. See website for details.

⬛ SLOPE EDITIONS; SLOPE EDITIONS BOOK PRIZE

℅ Medaille College, 18 Agassiz Circle, Buffalo NY 14214. E-mail: info@slope.org. Website: www.Sl opeEditions.org. Established 1999. **Contact:** Ethan Paquin, editor-in-chief. Senior Editor: Christopher Janke. Editorial Staff: Jon Link and Brad Flis. Member: CLMP.

Book/Chapbook Needs Slope Editions publishes books of "innovative poetry." Wants "writing of superior quality, of no particular style. As an offshoot of the online journal *Slope*, Slope Editions believes in actively promoting and supporting its authors, especially via the Web." Has published (first books) *The Body* by Jenny Boully, *Maine* by Jonah Winter, *Unfathoms* by Kirsten Kaschock, *Zoo Music* by William Waltz, *Like Wind Loves a Window* by Andrea Baker, and *The Goddess of the Hunt . . .* by Sam White. Manuscripts are selected through competition (see below). Books are 60-120 pages, perfect-bound, professionally printed, with paper covers. Distributed nationally through Baker & Taylor and SPD.

Contest/Award Offerings Sponsors the Slope Editions Book Prize, an annual contest awarding $1,000 and publication. See website for complete guidelines.

✦ ⬜ SLOW TRAINS LITERARY JOURNAL

P.O. Box 4741, Denver CO 80155. E-mail: editor@slowtrains.com. Website: www.slowtrains.com. Established 2001. **Contact:** Susannah Indigo, editor.

Magazine Needs *Slow Trains Literary Journal*, an online quarterly published "on the days the seasons change," provides "a celebration of great writing, with an emphasis on fiction, essays, and poetry that reflect the spirit of adventure, the exploration of the soul, the energies of imagination, and the experience of Big Fun. Music, travel, sex, humor, love, loss, art, spirituality, childhood/coming of age, baseball, and dreams—these are a few of our favorite things—but most of all we are here to share the ideas, the memories, and the visions that our writers are most passionate about.'' Does not want ''genre writing (no sci-fi, erotica, horror, romance, though elements of those may naturally be included).'' Has published poetry by Jessy Randall, Margarita Engle, John Eivaz, Liam Day, Jason Fraley, and Richard Fein. Receives about 1,200 poems/year, accepts about 10%. **How to Submit** Submit 2-4 poems at a time. Lines/poem: less than 200. Accepts previously published poems and simultaneous submissions. Accepts e-mail submissions (pasted into body of message); no disk submissions. Cover letter is preferred. ''Include your name, e-mail address, and a short bio. Please title the subject line of your e-mail with the category and title of your piece.'' Reads submissions year round. Time between acceptance and publication is 1-2 months. Poems are circulated to an editorial board. Never comments on rejected poems. Guidelines available on website. Responds within 2 months. Always sends prepublication galleys. No payment. Acquires one-time electronic rights, with optional archiving. *''Slow Trains* publishes a print volume on an annual basis, and any rights requested for that will be negotiated at that point in time.''

Book/Chapbook Needs & How to Submit ''We also publish online poetry chapbooks—please query with samples of your poetry before submitting an entire chapbook.''

☑ SMARTISH PACE; ERSKINE J. POETRY PRIZE; BEULLAH ROSE POETRY PRIZE

P.O. Box 22161, Baltimore MD 21203. Website: www.smartishpace.com. Established 1999. **Contact:** Stephen Reichert, editor.

Magazine Needs *Smartish Pace*, published in April and October, contains poetry and translations. ''*Smartish Pace* is an independent poetry journal and is not affiliated with any institution.'' No restrictions on style or content of poetry. Has published poetry by Campbell McGrath, Carl Dennis, Paul Muldoon, Maxine Kumin, Alicia Ostriker, and Stephen Dunn. *Smartish Pace* is about 140 pages, digest-sized, professionally printed, perfect-bound, with color heavy stock cover. Receives about 3,000 poems/year, accepts 4%. Press run is 500 (300 subscribers). Subscription: $20. Sample: $10.

How to Submit Submit no more than 6 poems at a time. Accepts simultaneous submissions; no previously published poems. ''Please provide prompt notice when poems have been accepted elsewhere. Cover letter with bio and SASE is required.'' Submit seasonal poems 8 months in advance. Time between acceptance and publication is up to one year. Guidelines available for SASE or on website. Responds in up to 8 months. Pays one contributor's copy. Acquires first rights. Encourages unsolicited reviews, essays, and interviews. Send materials for review consideration. All books received will also be listed in the Books Received section of each issue and on the website along with ordering information and a link to the publisher's website.

Contest/Award Offerings *Smartish Pace* hosts the annual Erskine J. Poetry Prize and the Beullah Rose Poetry Prize (for women). Winners receive cash prizes and publication. Submit 3 poems. **Entry fee:** $5 in either check or money order made payable to *Smartish Pace*. Additional poems may be submitted for $1 per poem. See website for complete details.

Also Offers Also available on website: Poets Q&A, where you can ask questions of poets and read their responses. Recent participants include Robert Pinsky, Jorie Graham, Stephen Dunn, Carl Dennis, Eavan Boland, Campbell McGrath, and Robert Hass.

Advice ''Visit our website. Read a few issues.''

▣ ◻ THE SMITHTOWN POETRY SOCIETY; THE WILLOW

P.O. Box 793, Nesconset NY 11767. (631)656-6690. Fax: (631)656-6690. E-mail: editor@thesmithtownpoetrysociety.com. Website: www.thesmithtownpoetrysociety.com. Established 1991. **Contact:** Sheryl Minter.

Magazine Needs *The Willow*, a quarterly, ''publishes new and upcoming poets alongside known poets. We also feature art, short stories, and poetry, regardless of length, that inspire intelligent thought and originality.'' Wants all forms of poetry. Does not want ''poetry written without thought or in sing-song rhyme.'' Has published poetry by Marian Ford and Najwa Brax. *The Willow* is 20 pages, magazine-sized, photocopied, side-stapled, with color card cover with original artwork, includes ads. Receives about 500 poems/year, accepts about 25%. Press run is 600 (100 subscribers, 200 libraries); 300 distributed free to coffee shops. Single copy: $5; subscription: $20. Make checks payable to S. Minter.

How to Submit Submit 3 poems at a time. Lines/poem: 30 maximum (longer poems are considered but may take longer to publish, depending on magazine space; query before submitting). Accepts previously published poems; no simultaneous submissions. Accepts disk submissions; no fax or e-mail submissions. Cover letter is preferred. "All submissions must be typed, double-spaced, with submitter's name and address clearly printed on it. Please include a SASE for all submissions if you would like your original work returned." Reads submissions year round. Submit seasonal poems 3 months in advance. **Charges $1 reading fee.** Time between acceptance and publication is 3 months. Poems are circulated to an editorial board. Sometimes comments on rejected poems. Guidelines available in magazine, for SASE, by e-mail, or on website. Responds in one month.

Contest/Award Offerings The Smithtown Poetry Society Quarterly Contest is open to all poets and offers 50% of the contest proceeds as first prize; "the other half goes to the distribution of *The Willow*." Submit 3 poems, 20-21 lines maximum/poem. **Entry fee: $5. Deadlines:** March 1, June 1, September 1, December 1 of given year. Guidelines available in magazine, for SASE, or on website. "All submissions may be edited for grammar and punctuation."

🌐 ◐ SMOKE

First Floor, Liver House, 96 Bold St., Liverpool L1 4HY England. Phone: (0151)709-3688. Website: www.windowsproject.demon.co.uk. Established 1974. **Contact:** Dave Ward, editor.

Magazine Needs *Smoke* is a biannual publication of poetry and graphics. Wants "short, contemporary poetry, expressing new ideas through new forms." Has published poetry by Carol Ann Duffy, Roger McGough, Jackie Kay, and Henry Normal. *Smoke* is 24 pages, A5, offset-litho-printed, stapled, with paper cover. Receives about 3,000 poems/year, accepts about 40. Press run is 750 (350 subscribers, 18 libraries, 100 shelf sales); 100 distributed free to contributors/other mags. Subscription: $5 (cash). Sample: $1. Make checks payable to Windows Project (cash preferred/exchanges rate on cheques not viable).

How to Submit Submit 6 poems at a time. Accepts previously published poems and simultaneous submissions. Cover letter is preferred. Time between acceptance and publication is 6 months. Seldom comments on rejected poems. Responds in 2 weeks. Pays one contributor's copy.

$◐ ◎ SNOWY EGRET (Specialized: animals; nature)

P.O. Box 29, Terre Haute IN 47808. Established 1922 by Humphrey A. Olsen. **Contact:** Philip Repp, editor.

Magazine Needs Appearing in spring and autumn, *Snowy Egret* specializes in work that is "nature-oriented: poetry that celebrates the abundance and beauty of nature or explores the interconnections between nature and the human psyche." Has published poetry by Conrad Hilberry, Lyn Lifshin, Gayle Eleanor, James Armstrong, and Patricia Hooper. *Snowy Egret* is 60 pages, magazine-sized, offset-printed, saddle-stapled. Receives about 500 poems/year, accepts about 30. Press run is 400 (250 subscribers, 50 libraries). Sample: $8; subscription: $15/year, $25/2 years.

How to Submit Guidelines available for #10 SASE. Responds in one month. Always sends prepublication galleys. Pays $4/poem or $4/page plus 2 contributor's copies. Acquires first North American and one-time reprint rights.

Advice "First-hand, detailed observation gives poetry authenticity and immediacy."

★ ◐ ◎ SO TO SPEAK: A FEMINIST JOURNAL OF LANGUAGE AND ART (Specialized: women/feminism)

George Mason University, 4400 University Dr., MS 2D6, Fairfax VA 22030-4444. (703)993-3625. E-mail: sts@gmu.edu. Website: www.gmu.edu/org/sts. Established 1991. **Contact:** Heather Holliger, editor.

Magazine Needs *So to Speak* is published 2 times/year. "We publish high-quality work relating to feminism, including poetry, fiction, nonfiction (including book reviews and interviews), photography, artwork, collaborations, lyrical essays, and other genre-questioning texts. We look for poetry that speaks to and/or interconnects with issues of significance to women's lives and movements for equality.''Has published poetry by Eleni Sikelianos, Michelle Tea, Marcella Durand, Jean Donnelly, Heather Fuller, and Carolyn Forché. *So To Speak* is 100-128 pages, digest-sized, photo-offset-printed, perfect-bound, with glossy cover, includes ads. Receives about 800 poems/year, accepts 10%. Press run is 1,000 (75 subscribers, 100 shelf sales); 500 distributed free to students/submitters. Subscription: $12. Sample: $7.

How to Submit Submit 3-5 poems at a time. Accepts simultaneous submissions; no previously published poems. Cover letter is preferred. ''Please submit poems as you wish to see them in print. We do have an e-mail address but do not accept e-mail submissions. Be sure to include a cover letter with full contact info, publication credits, and awards received.'' Reads submissions August 15 through October 15 and December 31 through March 15. Time between acceptance and publication is 6-8 months. Seldom comments on rejected poems. Responds in 3 months if submissions are received during reading period. Pays 2 contributor's copies. Acquires one-time rights.

Contest/Award Offerings *So to Speak* holds an annual poetry contest that awards $500. Guidelines available for SASE or on website.

☐ SO YOUNG!; ANTI-AGING PRESS, INC.

P.O. Box 142174, Coral Gables FL 33114. (305)662-3928. Fax: (305)661-4123. E-mail: julia2@gate.n et. Established 1992 (press), 1996 (newsletter). **Contact:** Julia Busch, editor.

Magazine Needs *So Young!* is a bimonthly newsletter publishing ''anti-aging/holistic health/humorous/philosophical topics geared to a youthful body, attitude, and spirit.'' Wants ''short, upbeat, fresh, positive poetry for the mid-30s and older adult. The newsletter is dedicated to a youthful body, face, mind, and spirit. Work can be humorous, philosophical fillers. No off-color, suggestive poems, or anything relative to first night, maudlin memories, politics, religion, or unrequited love affairs.'' *So Young!* is 16 pages, magazine-sized (8×11 sheets, 3-hole-punched, stapled), unbound. Receives several hundred poems/year, accepts 4-6. Press run is 700 (500 subscribers). Subscription: $35. Sample: $9.

How to Submit Submit up to 5 poems at a time. Accepts previously published poems and simultaneous submissions. Prefers e-mail submissions (pasted into body of message). Cover letter is preferred. Time between acceptance and publication ''depends on poem subject matter—usually 6-8 months.'' Guidelines available for SASE. Responds in 2 months. Pays 10 contributor's copies. Acquires one-time rights.

☑ THE SOCIETY OF AMERICAN POETS (SOAP); IN HIS STEPS PUBLISHING COMPANY; THE POET'S PEN; PRESIDENT'S AWARD FOR EXCELLENCE

309 Cork Pond Rd., Sylvania GA 30467. (912)564-2722. E-mail: DrRev@alltel.net. Established 1984. **Contact:** Dr. Charles E. Cravey, editor.

Magazine Needs *The Poet's Pen* is a literary quarterly of poetry and short stories. ''Open to all styles of poetry and prose—both religious and secular. No gross or 'X-rated' poetry without taste or character.'' Has published poetry by Najwa Salam Brax, Henry Goldman, Henry W. Gurley, William Heffner, Linda Metcalf, and Charles Russ. *The Poet's Pen* uses poetry primarily by members and subscribers, but outside submissions are also welcome. Membership: $30/year ($25 for students). Sample: $10.

How to Submit Submit 3 poems per quarter, with name and address on each page. ''Submissions or inquiries will not be responded to without a #10 business-sized SASE. We do stress originality and have each new poet and/or subscriber sign a waiver form verifying originality.'' Accepts simultaneous submissions and previously published poems, if permission from previous publisher is included. Publishes seasonal/theme issues. Upcoming themes and guidelines available in magazine, for SASE, by fax, or by e-mail. Sometimes sends prepublication galleys. Editor ''most certainly'' comments on rejected poems.

Book/Chapbook Needs & How to Submit In His Steps publishes religious and other books. Also publishes music for the commercial record market. Query for book publication.

Contest/Award Offerings Sponsors several contests each quarter, with prizes totaling $100-250. Editor's Choice Awards each quarter. President's Award for Excellence offers a prize of $50; **Deadline:** November 1. Also publishes a quarterly anthology that has poetry competitions in several categories with prizes of $25-100.

Advice "Be honest with yourself above all else. Read the greats over and again and study styles, grammar, and what makes each unique. Meter, rhythm, and rhyme are still the guidelines that are most acceptable today."

SONG OF THE SAN JOAQUIN (Specialized: regional/San Joaquin Valley); POETS OF THE SAN JOAQUIN

P.O. Box 1161, Modesto CA 95353-1161. E-mail: SSJQ03psj@yahoo.com. Website: www.Chaparral Poets.org/html. Established 2003. **Contact:** Editor.

Magazine Needs *Song of the San Joaquin* appears quarterly and features "subjects about or pertinent to the San Joaquin Valley of Central California. This is defined geographically as the region from Fresno to Stockton, and from the foothills on the west to those on the east." Wants all forms and styles of poetry. "Keep subject in mind." Does not want pornographic, demeaning, vague, or trite approaches. Has published poetry by Susan Wooldridge, debee loyd, Gordon Durham, Marnelle White, Tom Myers, and Nancy Haskett. *Song of the San Joaquin* is 44 pages, digest-sized, direct-copied, saddle-stapled, with cardstock cover with glossy color photo. Press run is 200 ("subscriber base still to be determined," 25 copies to libraries); 40 distributed free to contributors.

How to Submit Submit up to 5 poems at a time. Line length is open; "however, poems under 40 lines have the best chance." Accepts previously published poems; no simultaneous submissions. No e-mail or disk submissions. Cover letter is preferred. "SASE required. All submissions must be typed on one side of the page only. Proofread submissions carefully. Name, address, phone number, e-mail address should appear on all pages. Cover letter should include any awards, honors, and previous publications for each poem, and a biographical sketch of 75 words or less." Reads submissions "periodically throughout the year." Submit seasonal poems at least 3 months in advance. Time between acceptance and publication is 3-6 months. "Poems are circulated to an editorial board of 5 who then decide on the final selections." Seldom comments on rejected poems. Occasionally publishes theme issues. List of upcoming themes available for SASE, by e-mail, or on website. Guidelines available in magazine, for SASE, by e-mail, or on website. Responds in up to 3 months. Pays one contributor's copy. Acquires one-time rights.

Contest/Award Offerings "Poets of the San Joaquin, which sponsors this publication, is a chapter of California Federation of Chaparral Poets, Inc. PSJ holds an annual local young poets' contest as well as regular poetry contests, and publishes an annual anthology of members' works. Information available for SASE or by e-mail."

Advice "Know the area about which you write. Poems do not need to be agricultural or nature-oriented but should reflect the lifestyles of the California Central Valley."

SONGS OF INNOCENCE & EXPERIENCE (Specialized: style/19th-century romantic/ transcendental poetry); PENDRAGONIAN PUBLICATIONS (Specialized: anthologies)

P.O. Box 719, Radio City Station, New York NY 10101-0719. E-mail: mmpendragon@aol.com. Established 1999 (*Songs of Innocence & Experience*); 1995 (Pendragonian Publications). **Contact:** Michael Pendragon, editor/publisher.

• Works appearing in *Songs of Innocence & Experience* have received Honorable Mention in *The Year's Best Fantasy and Horror*.

Magazine Needs *Songs of Innocence & Experience* appears biannually, publishing traditional forms of verse and fiction of a superior quality, in the romantic style. Wants "rhymed, metered, and/or employing traditional poetic elements such as alliteration, internal rhyme, metaphor, etc." Does not want "modern," free verse, quasi-diary-entry, pseudo-poetry. Has published poetry by Louise

Webster, Kevin N. Roberts, Pamela Constantine, Ann K. Schwader, and Wendy Rathbone. *Songs of Innocence & Experience* is about 175 pages, digest-sized, docutech-printed, perfect-bound, with color card cover. Receives about 3,000 poems/year, accepts about 5%. Press run is 200 (150 subscribers, 3 libraries, 22 shelf sales); 25 distributed free to reviewers. Single copy: $10; subscription: $25/3 issues. Make checks payable to Michael Pendragon.

How to Submit Submit up to 5 poems at a time. Accepts previously published poems and simultaneous submissions. Prefers e-mail submissions; no fax or disk submissions. Cover letter is preferred. "Prefer works submitted via e-mail (in body with additional copy attached)." Time between acceptance and publication is up to 2 years. Regularly publishes theme issues. "Themes are determined by content of accepted submissions." Guidelines available in magazine. Due to the amount of submissions received, the editor cannot always respond; he encourages contributors to submit their work as a simultaneous submission. Always sends prepublication galleys. Pays one contributor's copy. Acquires one-time rights. Reviews books and chapbooks of poetry and other magazines/journals. Length of reviews varies. Send materials for review consideration to Michael Pendragon.

Book/Chapbook Needs & How to Submit Pendragonian Publications publishes anthologies of poetry and fiction centered on a given theme. Publishes 1-2 paperbacks/year. Books are usually up to 250 pages, docutech-printed, perfect-bound, with color card covers. Pays one author's copy. Acquires one-time rights. "Books are multi-authored and treated as if they were magazines."

Also Offers See separate listing for *Penny Dreadful: Tales & Poems of Fantastic Terror* in this section.

Ⓝ Ⓜ Ⓜ Ⓘ **SONNETTO POESIA (Specialized: forms/sonnets, quatrains, villanelles)**
297 Blake Boul. #4, Ottawa ON K1L 6L6 Canada. Phone: (613)744-1048. E-mail: laissezmoienpaix@ gmail.com. Website: http://poesieslaissezfaire.ca/. Established 2005. **Contact:** Richard Vallance. Member: The Canadian Federation of Poets; The Canadian Poetry Association; The Association of Formalist Poetry.

Magazine Needs *Sonnetto Poesia* is published quarterly. Wants "highly polished and literate form and rhymed poetry, especially sonnets, quatrains, and villanelles." Does not want "dark, despairing angst poetry, 'fanfare' sensationalist or shock value poetry." Has published poetry by Sondra Ball, Esther Cameron, Jim Dunlap, Üzeyir Lokman Çayci, Sara Russell, and CarrieAnn Thunell. Receives about 1,200 poems/year, accepts about 200 (20%). Single copy: $4 US or Canada; subscription: $10/year US or Canada (4 quarterly issues). Make checks payable to Richard Vallance Janke.

How to Submit Submit 6 poems at a time. Lines/poem: 3-50. Accepts previously published poems; no simultaneous submissions. Accepts e-mail submissions (as attachment; "all poems in one file, 2 files sent, one in .rtf format and one in .txt format ONLY"); no disk submissions. Cover letter is required. "If you snail mail your submissions, please send them in a 9×12 flat manila envelope. Submissions must be in a plain font such as Times New Roman or Arial, 14 point, single-spaced, one poem per page. You may include a brief biography of 3-4 sentences with the link to your poetry home page. You must include your e-mail address so that the editor can contact you. Your poems will not be returned, published or not." Reads submissions "up to one month before the publication date of each quarterly issue (March 21, June 21, September 21, and December 21)." Submit seasonal poems 3 months in advance. Time between acceptance and publication is 3 months. "If I find it difficult to determine whether I should publish a certain poem or not, I shall submit it for preselection to a review board of 4 other internationally acclaimed sonneteers and formalist poets (total 5 reviewers)." Never comments on rejected poems. "It would be considered courtesy and good form for contributors to actually purchase a subscription." Sometimes publishes theme issues. List of upcoming themes available on website. Guidelines available in magazine or on website. Responds in 2 months. Always sends prepublication galleys. Pays one contributor's copy. Acquires all rights. "Poets accepted for publication in *Sonnetto Poesia* must ask the editor permission to republish in other publications, whether in print, on the Internet, or in any format regardless. When such permission is granted, authors/poets must acknowledge in print or online that their poem(s) has/have been previously published in *Sonnetto Poesia*, ISSN 1705-4508, citing complete bibliographic detail (journal title, ISSN, vol. number, issue number, pagination)." Reviews books of poetry and other magazines/journals (devotes 5,000-10,000 words/month to reviews). Send materials for review consideration to Richard Vallance Janke.

Advice "Poets, including myself, should realize that poetry markets are invariably targeted. For instance, I am a bilingual Canadian poet-editor-publisher, with a strong preference for highly polished, culturally appealing formal, rhymed verse, genres such as the sonnet, quatrain, and villanelle. I am not fond of long, discursive poetry. I also willingly accept poetry written in any language I can read, including English, French, Spanish, Italian, and Greek. As a poetry editor, I unabashedly espouse Neo-Romantic ideals, and do not much like angst poetry of alienation that was so commonplace in the 20th century. Editors are like that. Every editor has his or her preferences. Some editors prefer free or blank verse; others do not. I fall in the latter category. However, I will accept extremely competent Neo-Romantic free and blank verse poems up to 50 lines long. As a word of advice, I would suggest aspiring poets who send submissions to poetry editors first familiarize themselves with the editor's preferences. This way, both the submitting poets and the editors concerned are saved a lot of unnecessary work."

✪ ☑ SOUL FOUNTAIN

90-21 Springfield Blvd., Queens Village NY 11428. Phone/fax: (718)479-2594. E-mail: davault@aol. com. Website: www.TheVault.org. Established 1997. **Contact:** Tone Bellizzi, editor.

Magazine Needs *Soul Fountain* is published by The Vault, a not-for-profit arts project of the Hope for the Children Foundation; "committed to empowering young and emerging artists of all disciplines at all levels to develop and share their talents through performance, collaboration, and networking." *Soul Fountain* appears 4 times/year and publishes poetry, art, photography, short fiction, and essays. "Open to all. We publish quality submitted work, and specialize in emerging voices. We are particularly interested in visionary, challenging, and consciousness-expanding material. We are not interested in poems about pets, nature, romantic love, or the occult. Sex and violence themes not welcome. We're hungry for artwork, particularly small black on white drawings." Accepts poetry written by teenage writers. *Soul Fountain* is 28 pages, magazine-sized, offset-printed, saddle stapled. Subscription: $20. Sample: $5. Make checks payable to Hope for the Children Foundation.

How to Submit Submit 2-3 "camera-ready" poems at a time. Lines/poem: one page maximum. No cover letters necessary. Accepts previously published poems and simultaneous submissions. Accepts e-mail submissions (pasted into body of message); "when e-mailing a submission, it is necessary to include your mailing address." Time between acceptance and publication is up to one year. Guidelines available for SASE. Pays one contributor's copy. "There is a release/party/performance, 'Poetry & Poultry in Motion,' attended by poets, writers, artists, etc., appearing in each issue."

✪ ⊕ ☑ SOUTH–A POETRY MAGAZINE FOR THE SOUTHERN COUNTIES

P.O. Box 5369, Poole BH14 0XN United Kingdom. E-mail: south@martinblyth.co.uk. Website: http://martinblyth.co.uk. Established 1990. **Contact:** Poetry Editor.

Magazine Needs *South* is published biannually in April and October. "Poets from or poems about the South region are particularly welcome, but poets from all over the world are free to submit work on all subjects." Has published poetry by Ian Caws, Stella Davis, Lyn Moir, Elsa Corbluth, and Sean Street. *South* is 68 pages, digest-sized, litho-printed, saddle-stapled, with gloss-laminated duotone cover. Receives about 1,500 poems/year, accepts about 120. Press run is 350 (250 subscribers). Single copy: £5.60; subscription: £10/1 year, £18/2 years. Make checks (in sterling) payable to *South Poetry Magazine*.

How to Submit Submit up to 3 poems at a time. No previously published poems or simultaneous submissions. Accepts submissions on disk (if accompanied by hard copy) and by postal mail. "Do not put name or address on manuscript. List poem titles on separate sheet or cover letter with name and address. Deadline for April issue: November 30; for October issue: May 31. "Selection does not begin prior to the deadline and may take 6 weeks or more from that date." Time between acceptance and publication is up to 5 months.

Alessio Zanelli

Poems in another language

Photo by Giorgio Soldi

Like any poet working at his craft, Alessio Zanelli devotes himself to finding the right word and fine-tuning the language of his poems. However, for Zanelli, there's an added challenge: His native language is Italian—but he chooses to compose in English, his adopted (and self-taught) language of literary expression.

A native and resident of Cremona, a small town in Lombardy, northern Italy, Zanelli publishes his work internationally in such magazines as *Main Street Rag* and *Concho River Review* (United States), *The Journal* and *Pulsar* (United Kingdom), *Existere* (Canada), *Paris/Atlantic* (France), and *Poetry Salzburg Review* (Austria). His books include *33 Poesie/33 Poems* (Starrylink Editrice, Italy, 2004), *Small Press Verse & Poeticonjectures* (Xlibris, USA, 2003), and *Loose Sheets* (UpFront Publishing, UK, 2002). Zanelli, a private investment advisor, is a visual artist as well; his photography has appeared on the cover of *Poetry Review*, Britain's leading poetry magazine.

What are the special difficulties of writing poetry in English?

For me, the greatest difficulty is trying to understand and reproduce how a mother-tongue poet would create the same imagery, description, or musing. The goal I set for myself when writing poetry in English, besides communicating my emotions, thoughts, and visions, is that of not letting readers discern or even suspect I am not a native speaker. And, believe me, that's quite a tough assignment!

English, as to grammar and syntax, is structured in a completely different way than Italian and all the Romance Languages, even though differences tend to lessen when we compare the poetical languages. English is way more malleable than Italian, offering an extremely wide assortment of lexical solutions, which allow the poet to find always the perfect word for every need. Italian is a very rich and musical language, but quite less manageable as to the options of its vocabulary. (In Italian, the majority of words end with a vowel sound and follow an almost invariable rule about the position of the tonic accent.) To me, it's easier (and more amusing) to write technically good, ear-and-eye-satisfying poetry in English than in Italian.

How did you first become interested in writing poetry?

I had never been really fond of poetry until I discovered the English language at the beginning of the 1980s, during the last years at high school. The only language I had ever studied at school was German. I happened to become an addict of rock music and to be the singer in the local cover band. I began to get interested in English, in its modern versions (American and British), and in its geographically varied usage (vocabulary, expressions, idioms, and slang from all the English-speaking countries).

I then began to compose lyrics for the band's songs, and to explore the huge richness and mutability of the language, which gradually also led me into the world of English literature, poetry in particular. I've been studying English grammar and usage as an autodidact, and writing my own English poetry (my first poem dates back to 1985).

Describe your first acceptance of a poem by a literary journal. What did it mean to you?

My first acceptance was a poem titled "Dedi," published in December 2000 by a small magazine in California called *Emotions*. To me it was a strong and completely new emotion. I had been writing poems for about 15 years, in a language not mine, but they had inexorably been kept in a drawer 'til then. I was really excited and happy to get the evidence that my work did mean something to someone else, and that it happened on one of my first attempts.

While realizing my works were arousing ever more interest in magazine editors, I've been learning to pay attention to the editors' requirements, needs, and suggestions, and to treasure their comments and critiques. The first acceptances by somewhat more distinguished, bigger-circulation publications spurred me on to try to continuously improve my technique and hone my style and language.

Have you noticed changes in your poetic style as you've become more fluid with English?

Yes, of course. And the deeper and more permanent such changes are, the higher the quality of the publications where my works appear. The way I look at poetry—the very substance of it, what I basically want to say or depict—is not affected in any way by my increasing command of the language, but the style—the structure, the register, the musicality—certainly is.

How would you describe the poetry scene in Italy?

If finding recognition on the English-language scene is not easy, on the Italian scene it's way more arduous. First, potential readers of Italian-written poetry are no more than 60 million in the whole world. Second, poetry publications in Italy are poorly organized, insufficiently backed and financed, hardly promoted, and almost completely invisible to the public. There are many magazines (although much fewer than in the USA or UK), but they are almost completely neglected and often last but a season! Even poetry lovers find it difficult to learn of such magazines or to procure them, and there are no such organizations as the Arts Council of England that support them or contribute to the spreading of poetry. Also, there's no publication like *Poet's Market* in Italy, which means poetry writers can't find help, support, and guidance without applying to an academic institution or a private tutor.

Who are your favorite Italian-language and English-language poets? How have they influenced you?

My favorite Italian poet ever is Ungaretti—so bare, but elegant and powerful at the same time. In my own language, I also like most of the works of Pavese and Cardarelli among the nearly contemporaries; of Leopardi and D'Annunzio among the older ones.

In the English language, my favorites are Blake, Dickinson, and Poe from the past centuries; W. C. Williams, Auden, and Yeats from the modern age; Heaney, Longley, and Creeley from the current masters. Undeniably, they all—and many others—influence my work. The Italian influence tends to have more effect on the subjects and the feelings of my poems, whereas the English influence tends to affect my poetry's overall style and linguistic features.

Do you listen to much English-language poetry (for rhythm, flow, etc.)?

Not really. I know that listening to one's own (or others') poems can be really useful for discovering hidden elements and features or forming a new perspective. Unfortunately, I live in Italy, and for me it's very difficult to attend English-language poetry readings. I'm trying to fill this gap by buying audio collections by living poets in Internet bookshops.

You've said that submitting work to foreign magazines is exciting and exhausting at the same time. What are some of the problems you face in submitting your work?

So far I have sent my work to nearly 400 magazines in over 10 countries (albeit 90 percent of submissions goes to the USA and the UK), and I have to deal with over 50 publications at every time of the year. When you consider many publications accept submissions only by regular mail (which implies a considerable expense for submitters, especially for those overseas), and some editors (with tons of submissions to read and their own life's problems to solve) fail to send a response even after a year has passed and after two or three inquiries, you'll understand why I used the term "exhausting."

Are your friends and family able to read and appreciate your original English-version poems, or do you provide them with Italian translations?

Unfortunately (or fortunately?), very few among my friends and relatives are able to read or appreciate my original texts. My parents don't know English, not a word. My brother and some of my friends do a little, but are hardly interested in poetry! There are just a few friends of mine who take the trouble to read the English works, and most of them live abroad, in the USA, the UK, and Australia (we keep in touch through electronic correspondence). I happen to translate some poems into Italian so my parents can take a look at what I currently write, but I don't like to be the translator of myself very much. My last extensive translation work was done for the publication of *33 Poesie* in Italy, a small bilingual "selected poems" released in early 2004.

Do you attempt to inject Italian culture or sense of place into your poetry, or do you allow the references to come naturally?

I think the imprint of Italian culture and sense of place are certainly present in both my lyrics and prose poems, but it shows forth naturally.

Mid-August Sketch

> *She drained*
> *the last inch of her negroni*
> *only when the sun was culminating,*
> *stood up*
> *without uttering a word and*
> *made off*
> *zigzagging apace through the noontide heat,*
> *swaying her hips down the crowded piazza—*
> *leaving me with*
> *one last bill,*
> *a couple of used straws*
> *and three dripping rocks to suck.*

>   I turned
> my eyes to the dial
> of the renaissance belfry's clock,
>   stared
> at the imperceptible movement of its hands,
> not at the hour indicated,
>   musing
> on her reptile heart and
>   mutely jeering
> at my gander brain.
>
>   I then upped
> in like manner,
> to shake off sultriness,
> and all of a sudden
>   felt
> some fifty looks attached to me,
>   as if I wore
> one of those ludicrous,
> four-coned, multicolored Lappish headgears—
>   I stepped.

(first published in *Italian Americana* [University of Rhode Island, Providence, RI])

Do you give readings in Italy?

No, unfortunately. The only reading I ever gave occurred on the official launch of *33 Poesie*. Readings are just beginning to catch on in Italy. I think it'll take some more time for them to become an established means of circulating poetry. There were plenty of people attending the launch of my book, but nearly all of them had been invited. Drawing people to more general poetry readings is quite another kettle of fish in my country, and things are changing very slowly. Ever more artists are acquainted with English, though (and more than with any other foreign language); but as far as I know, only a few use it as an alternative or optional language for their work. So, I'm still a blue dahlia on the Italian scene, and most people get surprised or puzzled by hearing I'm used to writing and publishing in the tongue of Shakespeare.

Do you see yourself ever turning to Italian more often as you explore and develop your skills as a poet?

Perhaps I will actually turn to Italian in the future, but the time is not yet ripe for that change, nor am I. I like English, and I'm more trained in writing poetry in English. Poetry in Italian, strange to say, would require new study and expertise, and also a great deal of additional patience in order to attain the recognition I have gained in the English language. In any case, I think Italian will never displace English. My own language, more likely, will gradually flank it as an alternative idiom, according to my moods and necessities of expression, as well as the audience I intend to address each time.

—*Nancy Breen*

For more information about Alessio Zanelli, see www.writesight.com/writers/Zanelli/.

Nancy Breen is editor of *Poet's Market*. Her chapbooks include *How Time Got Away* (Pudding House Publications) and *Rites and Observances* (Finishing Line Press). She lives in Loveland, Ohio.

Advice "Buy the magazine. Then it will still be there to consider and publish your work and you'll get the idea of the sort of work we publish. These are basic steps, and both are essential."

☑ SOUTH CAROLINA REVIEW

Center for Electronic & Digital Publishing, 611 Strode Tower, Clemson University, Box 340522, Clemson SC 29634-0522. (864)656-3151 or 656-5399. Fax: (864)656-1345. Website: www.clemson. edu/caah/cedp/scrintro.htm. Established 1968. **Contact:** Wayne Chapman, editor.

Magazine Needs *South Carolina Review* is a biannual literary magazine "recognized by the *New York Quarterly* as one of the top 20 of this type." Will consider "any kind of poetry as long as it's good. No stale metaphors, uncertain rhythms, or lack of line integrity. Interested in seeing more traditional forms. Format should be according to new MLA Stylesheet." Reviews of recent issues back up editorial claims that all styles and forms are welcome; moreover, poems were accessible and well-executed. Has published poetry by Stephen Cushman, Alberto Ríos, and Virgil Suárez. *South Carolina Review* is 200 pages, digest-sized, professionally printed, flat-spined. Receives about 1,000 submissions of poetry/year, accepts about 60. Press run is 600 (400 subscribers, 250 libraries). Sample: $12.

How to Submit Submit 3-10 poems at a time "in an 8×10 manila envelope so poems aren't creased." No previously published poems or simultaneous submissions. No e-mail submissions. "Editor prefers a chatty, personal cover letter plus a list of publishing credits." Do not submit during June, July, August, or December. Publishes theme issues. Responds in 2 months. Pays in contributor's copies. Staff reviews books of poetry.

★ ☑ ◎ SOUTH DAKOTA REVIEW (Specialized: regional; themes)

University of South Dakota, Vermillion SD 57069. (605)677-5184 or 677-5966. Fax: (605)677-6409. E-mail: bbedard@usd.edu. Website: www.usd.edu/SDR. Established 1963. **Contact:** Brian Bedard, editor.

Magazine Needs *South Dakota Review* is a "literary quarterly publishing poetry, fiction, criticism, scholarly and personal essays. When material warrants, an emphasis on the American West; writers from the West; Western places or subjects; frequent issues with no geographical emphasis; periodic special issues on one theme, one place, or one writer. Looking for originality, sophistication, significance, craft—i.e., professional work." Press run is 500-600 (450 subscribers, half are libraries). Single copy: $10; subscription: $30/year, $45/2 years. Sample: $8.

How to Submit Submit 3-6 poems at one time. Reads submissions year round. Editor comments on submissions "occasionally." Publishes theme issues. Guidelines available for SASE. Responds in 2 months. Pays in copies and one-year subscription. Acquires first and reprint rights.

Advice "We tend to favor the narrative poem, the concrete crafted lyric, the persona poem, and the meditative place poem. Yet we try to leave some room for poems outside those parameters to keep some fresh air in our selection process."

★ ◻ THE SOUTHEAST REVIEW

English Dept., Florida State University, 216 Williams Bldg., Tallahassee FL 32306. (850)644-2773. E-mail: southeastreview@english.fsu.edu. Website: http://english.fsu.edu/southeastreview/. Established 1979. **Contact:** James Kimbrell, editor.

Magazine Needs *The Southeast Review* appears twice/year. "We look for the very best poetry by new and established poets." *The Southeast Review* is 160 pages, digest-sized. Receives about 5,000 poems/year, accepts less than 10%. Press run is 1,200 (800 subscribers, 100 libraries, 200 shelf sales); 200 are distributed free. Single copy: $10; subscription: $8/year. Sample: $5. Make checks payable to *The Southeast Review*.

How to Submit Submit 3-5 poems at a time. Accepts simultaneous submissions; no previously published poems. No fax, e-mail, or disk submissions. Cover letter is preferred. Include SASE. Reads submissions September through May. Time between acceptance and publication is up to one year. Seldom comments on rejected poems. Occasionally publishes theme issues. List of upcoming themes available by e-mail. Guidelines available for SASE, by e-mail, or on website. Responds in up to 5 months. Pays 2 contributor's copies. Acquires first North American serial rights. Reviews books and chapbooks of poetry. Send materials for review consideration.

Contest/Award Offerings Sponsors an annual poetry contest. Winner receives $500 and publication; 9 finalists will also be published. **Entry fee:** $10/3 poems. **Deadline:** February 15. Complete guidelines available on website.

🌙 ◎ THE SOUTHERN CALIFORNIA ANTHOLOGY (Specialized: anthology); ANN STANFORD POETRY PRIZES

% Master of Professional Writing Program, WPH 404, University of Southern California, Los Angeles CA 90089-4034. (213)740-3252. Established 1983.

Magazine Needs *The Southern California Anthology* is an "annual literary review of serious contemporary poetry and fiction. Very open to all subject matters except pornography. Any form, style OK." Has published poetry by Robert Bly, Allen Ginsberg, Lisel Mueller, James Ragan, Nikki Giovanni, and John Updike. *The Southern California Anthology* is 144 pages, digest-sized, perfect-bound, with a semi-glossy color cover featuring one art piece. Press run is 1,500 (750 subscribers, 300 libraries, 450 shelf sales). Sample: $5.95.

How to Submit Submit 3-5 poems between September 1 and January 1 only. No simultaneous submissions or previously published poems. All decisions made by mid-February. Guidelines available for SASE. Responds in 4 months. Pays 2 contributor's copies. Acquires all rights.

Contest/Award Offerings Sponsors the Ann Stanford Poetry Prizes (1st: $1,000; 2nd: $200; 3rd: $100) for unpublished poems. **Entry fee:** $10 (5-poem limit). **Deadline:** April 15. Include cover sheet with name, address, and titles, as well as SASE for contest results. All entries are considered for publication, and all entrants receive a copy of *The Southern California Anthology*.

✪ ◑ SOUTHERN HUMANITIES REVIEW; THEODORE CHRISTIAN HOEPFNER AWARD

9088 Haley Center, Auburn University, Auburn AL 36849-5202. E-mail: shrengl@auburn.edu. Website: www.auburn.edu/english/shr/home.htm. Established 1967. **Contact:** Dan Latimer and Virginia M. Kouidis, co-editors.

Magazine Needs *Southern Humanities Review* is a literary quarterly "interested in poems of any length, subject, genre. Space is limited, and brief poems are more likely to be accepted. Translations welcome, but also send written permission from the copyright holder." Has published poetry by Donald Hall, Andrew Hudgins, Margaret Gibson, Stephen Dunn, Walt McDonald, and R.T. Smith. *Southern Humanities Review* is 100 pages, digest-sized. Press run is 800. Subscription: $15/year. Sample: $5.

How to Submit "Send 3-5 poems in a business-sized envelope. Include SASE. Avoid sending faint computer printout." No previously published poems or simultaneous submissions. No e-mail submissions. Responds in 2 months, possibly longer in summer. Always sends prepublication galleys. Pays 2 contributor's copies. Copyright reverts to author upon publication. Reviews books of poetry in approximately 750-1,000 words. Send materials for review consideration.

Contest/Award Offerings Sponsors the Theodore Christian Hoepfner Award, a $50 award for the best poem published in a given volume of *Southern Humanities Review*.

Advice "For beginners we recommend study and wide reading in English and classical literature, and, of course, American literature—the old works, not just the new. We also recommend study of or exposure to a foreign language and a foreign culture. Poets need the reactions of others to their work: criticism, suggestions, discussion. A good creative writing teacher would be desirable here, and perhaps some course work, too; and then submission of work, attendance at workshops. And again, the reading: history, biography, verse, essays—all of it. We want to see poems that have gone beyond the language of slippage and easy attitudes."

✪ ☑ SOUTHERN POETRY REVIEW; GUY OWEN POETRY PRIZE

Armstrong-Atlantic State University, LLP, 11935 Abercorn St., Savannah GA 31419. (912)921-5633. E-mail: smithjam@mail.armstrong.edu. Website: www.spr.armstrong.edu. Established 1958. **Contact:** Robert Parham, editor. Member: CLMP.

 • Work appearing in *Southern Poetry Review* received a 2004 Pushcart Prize.

Magazine Needs *Southern Poetry Review* is a semi-annual poetry journal. Wants "poetry eclectically representative of the genre; no restrictions on form, style, or content." Does not want fiction, essays, or reviews. Has published poetry by Cathy Smith Bowers, Albert Goldbarth, Robert Morgan, Linda Pastan, Margaret Gibson, and R. T. Smith. *Southern Poetry Review* is 70-80 pages, digest-sized, perfect-bound, with 80-lb. matte cardstock cover with b&w photography, includes ads. Receives about 5,000 poems/year, accepts about 2%. Press run is 1,200 (1,000 subscribers). Single copy: $6; subscription: $15 (library). Make checks payable to *Southern Poetry Review*.

How to Submit Submit 3-5 poems at a time. Lines/poem: subject to limitations of space. Accepts simultaneous submissions (with notification in cover letter); no previously published poems. No e-mail or disk submissions. Cover letter is preferred. "Include SASE for reply; manuscript returned only if sufficient postage is included." Reads submissions year round. Time between acceptance and publication is 6 months. Poems are circulated to an editorial board ("multiple readers, lively discussion and decision-making"). Sometimes comments on rejected poems. Guidelines available in magazine, for SASE, by fax, e-mail, or on website. Responds in 2-3 months. Always sends prepublication galleys. Pays 2 contributor's copies and one-year subscription. Acquires one-time rights.

Contest/Award Offerings Sponsors the annual Guy Owen Poetry Prize. Offers $1,000 and publication in *Southern Poetry Review*. Submit 3-5 unpublished poems (10 pages maximum). **Entry fee:** $15 (includes one-year subscription to magazine). **Deadline:** March 1-June 15. Guidelines available in magazine, for SASE, by fax, e-mail, or on website.

Advice "We suggest that before submitting, writers read a current issue to get a feel for our journal."

$☑ THE SOUTHERN REVIEW

43 Allen Hall, Louisiana State University, Baton Rouge LA 70803-5005. (225)578-5108. Fax: (225)578-5098. E-mail: bmacon@lsu.edu. Website: www.lsu.edu/thesouthernreview. Established 1935 (original series), 1965 (new series). **Contact:** Bret Lott, editor. Associate Editor: John Easterly.

 • Work published in this review has been frequently included in *The Best American Poetry* and appeared in *The Beacon's Best of 1999*.

Magazine Needs *The Southern Review* "is a literary quarterly that publishes fiction, poetry, critical essays, and book reviews, with emphasis on contemporary literature in the U.S. and abroad, and with special interest in Southern culture and history. Selections are made with careful attention to craftsmanship and technique and to the seriousness of the subject matter. We are interested in any variety of poetry that is well crafted, though we cannot normally accommodate excessively long poems (i.e., 10 pages and over)." All styles and forms welcome, although accessible lyric and narrative free verse appear most often in recent issues. Has published poetry by Mary Oliver, Sharon Olds, Reynolds Price, and Ellen Bryant Voigt. *The Southern Review* is 240 pages, digest-sized, flat-spined, with matte card cover. Receives about 6,000 submissions of poetry/year. Press run is 2,500 (2,100 subscribers, 70% libraries). Subscription: $25. Sample: $8.

How to Submit Prefers submissions of up to 6 pages. No fax or e-mail submissions. "We do not require a cover letter, but we prefer one giving information about the author and previous publications." Guidelines available for SASE or on website. Responds in one month. Pays $30/printed page plus 2 contributor's copies. Acquires first North American serial rights. Staff reviews books of poetry in 3,000 words, multi-book format. Send materials for review consideration.

$☑ SOUTHWEST REVIEW; ELIZABETH MATCHETT STOVER MEMORIAL AWARD; MORTON MARR POETRY PRIZE

307 Fondren Library West, P.O. Box 750374, Southern Methodist University, Dallas TX 75275-0374.

(214)768-1037. Fax: (214)768-1408. E-mail: swr@mail.smu.edu. Website: www.southwestreview. org. Established 1915. **Contact:** Willard Spiegelman, editor.

- Poetry published in *Southwest Review* has been included in *The Best American Poetry* and the *Pushcart Prize* anthologies.

Magazine Needs *Southwest Review* is a literary quarterly that publishes fiction, essays, poetry, and interviews. "It is hard to describe our preference for poetry in a few words. We always suggest that potential contributors read several issues of the magazine to see for themselves what we like. But some things may be said: We demand very high quality in our poems; we accept both traditional and experimental writing, but avoid unnecessary obscurity and private symbolism; we place no arbitrary limits on length but find shorter poems easier to fit into our format than longer ones. We have no specific limitations as to theme." Has published poetry by Albert Goldbarth, John Hollander, Mary Jo Salter, James Hoggard, Dorothea Tanning, and Michael Rosen. *Southwest Review* is 144 pages, digest-sized, perfect-bound, professionally printed, with matte text stock cover. Receives about 1,000 poetry submissions/year, accepts about 32. "Poems tend to be lyric and narrative free verse combining a strong voice with powerful topics or situations. Diction is accessible and content often conveys a strong sense of place." Circulation is 1,500 (1,000 subscribers, 600 libraries). Subscription: $24. Sample: $6.

How to Submit No simultaneous submissions or previously published poems. Guidelines available for SASE or on website. Responds within one month. Always sends prepublication galleys. Pays cash plus contributor's copies.

Contest/Award Offerings The $250 Elizabeth Matchett Stover Memorial Award is given annually to the author of the best poem or groups of poems (chosen by editors) published in the preceding year. The $1,000 Morton Marr Poetry Prize is awarded annually to a writer who has not yet published a first book; poems submitted should be in a "traditional" form. Guidelines available on website.

ⓩ THE SOW'S EAR POETRY REVIEW: THE SOW'S EAR POETRY COMPETITION; THE SOW'S EAR CHAPBOOK COMPETITION

355 Mount Lebanon Rd., Donalds SC 29638-9115. (864)379-8061. E-mail: errol@kitenet.net. Website: www.sows-ear.kitenet.net. Established 1988. **Contact:** Errol Hess, managing editor. Editor: Kristin Camitta Zimet.

Magazine Needs *The Sow's Ear Poetry Review,* published quarterly, wants fine poetry of all styles and lengths. Black-and-white graphics complement the poems. The editors often take more than one poem by an author they like. "The 'Community of Poets' feature presents group submissions; define 'community' as broadly as you like. The 'Crossover' feature showcases works that marry the written word with another art form (for example, lyrics with music, word collages, or special calligraphy)." Has published poetry by Robert Morgan, Elizabeth Spires, Virgil Suárez, Susan Terris, and Franz Wright. *The Sow's Ear Poetry Review* is 32 pages, magazine-sized, professionally printed, saddle-stapled, with matte card cover. Receives about 3,000 poems/year, accepts about 100. Press run is 700 (600 subscribers, 15 libraries). Subscription: $15. Sample: $5.

How to Submit Submit up to 5 poems at a time, with SASE and a brief bio. Accepts simultaneous submissions "if you tell us promptly when work is accepted elsewhere"; no previously published poems. No e-mail submissions. Guidelines available for SASE or by e-mail. Responds in 3 months. Pays 2 contributor's copies. Acquires first publication rights. Inquire about reviews, interviews, and essays.

Contest/Award Offerings Sponsors an annual contest for unpublished poems. Offers 1st Prize: $1,000; publication for 15-20 finalists. **Entry fee:** $3/poem; submissions of 5 poems/$15 receive a subscription. Submit poems in September/October, with name and address on a separate sheet. Include SASE for notification. Past judges: Dabney Stuart and Elizabeth Spires. Also sponsors a chapbook contest in March/April. **Entry fee:** $15. Guidelines for both contests available for SASE, by e-mail, or on website.

Advice "Four criteria help us judge the quality of submissions: Does the poem make the strange familiar or the familiar strange, or both? Is the form of the poem vital to its meaning? Do the sounds of the poem make sense in relation to the theme? Does the little story of the poem open a window on the Big Story of the human situation?''

SP QUILL QUARTERLY MAGAZINE

Shadow Poetry, 1209 Milwaukee St., Excelsior Springs MO 64024. Fax: (208)977-9114. E-mail: spquill@shadowpoetry.com. Website: www.shadowpoetry.com/magazine/spquill.html. Established 2000 (Shadow Poetry website), 2003 (*SP Quill*). **Contact:** Marie Summers, chief editor. Poetry Editor: Andrea Dietrich.

Magazine Needs *''SP Quill Quarterly Magazine* is an interactive chapbook-style magazine for poets and writers, filled with poetry, short stories, book reviews, articles, contests, interviews, profiles, quotes, and more.'' Wants high-quality poetry, short stories, quotes, and artwork. Does not want ''anything in poor taste, or poorly crafted poetry.'' Accepts poetry, stories, quotes, and artwork from ages 13 and up. *SP Quill Quarterly Magazine* is 56-60 pages, digest-sized, saddle-stapled, with cardstock cover with b&w artwork (cover design remains the same from issue to issue), includes ads related to poetry, writing, and publishing. Receives about 300 poems/quarter, accepts 15%. Single copy: $7.95 US, $8.95 Canada, $9.95 international; subscription: $20/year US, $24/year Canada, $28/year international. Make checks payable to Shadow Poetry.

How to Submit Submit up to 3 poems at a time. ''Submit up to 8 haiku, tanka, and/or cinquain for spring and fall issues only.'' Lines/poem: 3 minimum, 30 maximum. No previously published poems or simultaneous submissions. Accepts fax, e-mail, postal mail, and disk submissions as well as submissions through online form. Cover letter is preferred. ''Name of author, street address, and e-mail address must accompany all submissions, no exceptions. A small author bio may accompany poetry. If work is accepted, participants will be contacted by mail or e-mail before magazine release date. Rejection letters are not sent.'' Submission deadlines are November 20 (Winter issue), February 28 (Spring issue), May 31 (Summer issue), and August 31 (Fall issue). Time between acceptance and publication is 3 weeks. ''Poems are decided upon and edited by the poetry editor and chief editor. Final drafts will be e-mailed or mailed to the accepted poet.'' Never comments on rejected poems. Welcomes seasonal poems for the appropriate issue. Guidelines available in magazine or on website. Acquires first rights. Reviews books and chapbooks of poetry.

Contact/Award Offerings Shadow Poetry sponsors The Little Bitty Poetry Competition, Rhyme Time Poetry Contest, Shadow Poetry Seasonal Poetry Competition, Shadow Poetry's Biannual Chapbook Competition, and Zen Garden Haiku Contest. (See separate listings in the Contests & Awards section.)

SPILLWAY

P.O. Box 7887, Huntington Beach CA 92615-7887. (714)968-0905. E-mail: info@tebotbach.org. Website: www.tebotbach.org. Established 1991. **Contact:** Mifanwy Kaiser and J.D. Lloyd, editors. Associate Editor: Catherine Turner.

Magazine Needs *Spillway* is an annual journal, published in November, ''celebrating writing's diversity and power to affect our lives. Open to all voices, schools, and tendencies. We publish poetry, translations, reviews, essays, and b&w photography.'' Has published poetry by John Balaban, Sam Hamill, Robin Chapman, Richard Jones, and Eleanor Wilner. *Spillway* is about 176 pages, digest-sized, attractively printed, perfect-bound, with 2-color or 4-color card cover. Press run is 2,000. Single copy: $10; subscription: $18/2 issues, $30/4 issues. All prices include s&h. Make checks payable to *Spillway*.

How to Submit Submit 3-6 poems at a time, 10 pages total. Accepts previously published poems (''say when and where'') and simultaneous submissions (''say where also submitted''). Accepts e-mail (as a Word attachment or pasted into body of message) or disk submissions. Cover letter with brief bio and SASE is required. ''No cute bios.'' Reads submissions year round. Responds in up to 6 months. Pays one contributor's copy. Acquires one-time rights. Reviews books of poetry in 500-2,500 words. Send materials for review consideration.

Advice "We have no problem with simultaneous or previously published submissions. Poems are murky creatures—they shift and change in time and context. It's exciting to pick up a volume, read a poem in the context of all the other pieces, and then find the same poem in another time and place. And, we don't think a poet should have to wait until death to see work in more than one volume. What joy to find out that more than one editor values one's work. Our responsibility as editors, collectively, is to promote the work of poets as much as possible—how can we do this if we say to a writer, 'you may only have a piece published in one volume and only one time'? "

⬤ SPINNING JENNY

P.O. Box 1373, New York NY 10276. Website: www.spinning-jenny.com. Established 1994. **Contact:** C.E. Harrison, editor.

Magazine Needs *Spinning Jenny* appears once/year in the fall (usually September). Has published poetry by Tina Cane, Kaya Oakes, Tony Tost, and Ian Randall Wilson. *Spinning Jenny* is 112 pages, digest-sized, perfect-bound, with heavy card cover. "We accept less than 5% of unsolicited submissions." Press run is 1,000. Single copy: $8; subscription: $15/2 issues.

How to Submit No previously published poems or simultaneous submissions. Accepts e-mail (see website for address) submissions (pasted into body of message). Seldom comments on rejected poems. Guidelines available for SASE, by e-mail, or on website. Responds within 4 months. Pays 3 contributor's copies. Authors retain rights.

🌐 ☐ SPLIZZ

4 St. Marys Rise, Burry Port, Carms SA16 OSH Wales. E-mail: splizzmag@yahoo.co.uk. Established 1993. **Contact:** Amanda Morgan, editor.

Magazine Needs *Splizz*, published quarterly, features poetry, prose, reviews of contemporary music, and background to poets. Wants "any kind of poetry. We have no restrictions regarding style, length, subjects." Does not want "anything racist or homophobic." Has published Colin Cross (UK), Anders Carson (Canada), Paul Truttman (US), Jan Hansen (Portugal), and Gregory Arena (Italy). *Splizz* is 60-64 pages, A5, saddle-stapled, includes ads. Receives about 200-300 poems/year, accepts about 90%. Press run is 150 (35 subscribers). Single copy: £2 UK, 6 IRCs or $7 elsewhere; subscription: £8 UK, 24 IRCs or $28 elsewhere. Make checks payable to Amanda Morgan (British checks only).

How to Submit Submit 5 poems; typed submissions preferred. Name and address must be included on each page of submitted work. Include SAE with IRCs. No previously published poems or simultaneous submissions. Accepts e-mail submissions (as attachments). Cover letter with short bio is required. Time between acceptance and publication is 4 months. Often comments on rejected poems. Charges criticism fee: "Just enclose SAE/IRC for response, and allow 1-2 months for delivery. For those sending IRCs, please ensure that they have been correctly stamped by your post office." Guidelines available in magazine, for SASE (or SAE and IRC), or by e-mail. Responds in 2 months. Sometimes sends prepublication galleys. Reviews books or chapbooks of poetry or other magazines in 50-300 words. Send materials for review consideration. E-mail for further enquiries.

Advice "Beginners seeking to have their work published, send your work to *Splizz*, as we specialize in giving new poets a chance to see their work published alongside more established writers."

⬤ THE SPOON RIVER POETRY REVIEW; SPOON RIVER EDITORS' PRIZE CONTEST

4240/English Dept., Illinois State University, Normal IL 61790-4240. Website: www.litline.org/spoon. Established 1976. **Contact:** Lucia Getsi, editor.

Magazine Needs *Spoon River Poetry Review* is a biannual "poetry magazine that features newer and well-known poets from around the country and world." Also features one Illinois poet/issue at length for the magazine's Illinois Poet Series. "We want interesting and compelling poetry that operates beyond the ho-hum, so-what level, in any form or style about anything; language that is fresh, energetic, committed; a poetics aware of itself and of context." Also uses translations of poetry. Has published poetry by Stuart Dybek, David Trinidad, Joyelle McSweeney, Beth Ann

Fennelly, Dorothea Grünzweig, and Alicia Ostriker. *Spoon River Poetry Review* is 128 pages, digest-sized, laser-set, with card cover, includes ads. Receives about 3,000 poems/month, accepts 1%. Press run is 1,500 (800 subscribers, 100 libraries). Subscription: $16. Sample (including guidelines): $10.

How to Submit ''No simultaneous submissions unless we are notified immediately if a submission is accepted elsewhere. Include name and address on every poem.'' Do not submit mss April 15 through September 15. Editor comments on rejected poems ''many times, if a poet is promising.'' Guidelines available in magazine or on website. Responds in 3 months. Pays a year's subscription. Acquires first North American serial rights. Reviews books of poetry. Send materials for review consideration.

Contest/Award Offerings Sponsors the Editor's Prize Contest for previously unpublished work. One poem will be awarded $1,000 and published in the fall issue of *Spoon River Poetry Review*, and two runners-up will receive $100 each and publication in the fall issue. Entries must be previously unpublished. **Entry fee:** $16, includes one-year subscription. **Deadline:** April 15. Write for details. Past winners include Melissa Stein and Susette Bishop.

Advice ''Read. Workshop with poets who are better than you. Subscribe to at least 5 literary magazines a year, especially those you'd like to be published in.''

🌐 $🖉 STAND MAGAZINE

School of English, University of Leeds, Leeds LS2 9JT England. Phone: +44 (0)113 233 4794. Fax: +44 (0)113 233 4791. E-mail: stand@leeds.ac.uk. Website: www.people.vcu.edu/~dlatane/stand.html. **Contact:** Jon Glover, Matthew Welton, John Whale. (US Editor: David Latané, Dept. of English, Virginia Commonwealth University, Richmond VA 23284-2005. E-mail: dlatane@vcu.edu.)

Magazine Needs *Stand*, established by Jon Silkin in 1952, is a highly esteemed literary quarterly. *Stand* seeks more subscriptions from US readers and also hopes that the magazine will be seriously treated as an alternative platform to American literary journals. *Library Journal* calls *Stand* ''one of England's best, liveliest, and truly imaginative little magazines.'' Poet Donald Hall says of it, ''Among essential magazines, there is Jon Silkin's *Stand*, politically left, with reviews, poems, and much translation from continental literature.'' Among better-known American poets whose work has appeared here are John Ashbery, Mary Jo Bang, Brian Henry, and Michael Mott. *Stand* is about 64 pages, A5 (landscape), professionally printed on smooth stock, flat-spined, with matte color cover, includes ads. Press run is 2,000 (1,000+ subscribers, 600 libraries). Subscription: $49.50. Sample: $13.

How to Submit No fax or e-mail submissions. Cover letter is required with submissions, ''assuring us that work is not also being offered elsewhere.'' Publishes theme issues. Always sends prepublication galleys. Pays £20 for first poem and £5 for each subsequent poem over 6 lines, and one contributor's copy. Acquires first world serial rights for 3 months after publication. If work appears elsewhere, *Stand* must be credited. Reviews books of poetry in 3,000-4,000 words, multi-book format. Send materials for review consideration.

🌐 $🖉 STAPLE

Padley Rise, Nether Padley, Grindleford, Hope Valley, Derbys S32 2HE United Kingdom or 74 Rangeley Rd., Walkley, Sheffield S6 5DW United Kingdom. Established 1982 (redesigned 2001). **Contact:** Ann Atkinson and Elizabeth Barrett, co-editors.

Magazine Needs *Staple* appears 3 times/year and ''accepts poetry, short fiction, and articles about the writing process.'' *Staple* is 100 pages, perfect-bound. Press run is 500 (350 subscribers). Single copy: £5; subscription: £20/year. Sample: £3.50.

How to Submit Submit 6 poems at a time. No simultaneous submissions or previously published poems. Cover letter is preferred. Include SAE and 2 IRCs. Submission deadlines are end of March, July, and November. Editors sometimes comment on rejected poems. Responds in up to 3 months. Pays £5/poem.

STEEL TOE BOOKS

Dept. of English, 20C Cherry Hall, Western Kentucky University, 1 Big Red Way, Bowling Green KY 42101-3576. (270)745-5769. E-mail: tom.hunley@wku.edu. Established 2003. **Contact:** Dr. Tom C. Hunley, editor/publisher.

Book/Chapbook Needs & How to Submit Steel Toe Books publishes "full-length, single-author poetry collections. Our books are professionally designed and printed. We look for workmanship (economical use of language, high-energy verbs, precise literal descriptions, original figurative language, poems carefully arranged as a book); a unique style and/or a distinctive voice; clarity; emotional impact; humor (word plays, hyperbole, comic timing); performability (a Steel Toe poet is at home on the stage as well as on the page)." Does not want "dry verse, purposely obscure language, poetry by people who are so wary of being called 'sentimental' they steer away from any recognizable human emotions, poetry that takes itself so seriously that it's unintentionally funny." Has published poetry by James Doyle and Jennifer Gresham. Publishes one poetry book/year. Manuscripts are selected through open submission. Books are 48-64 pages, perfect-bound, with full-color covers with art/graphics. "We have an open reading period during the month of June. There is no reading fee, but we do ask that you purchase one of our titles." Book mss may include previously published poems. Responds to mss in 3 months. Pays 20% royalties and 10 author's copies (out of a press run of 500). Order sample books by sending $12 to Steel Toe Books.

THE WALLACE STEVENS JOURNAL (Specialized: Wallace Stevens)

Arts and Sciences, Clarkson University, Box 5750, Potsdam NY 13699-5750. (315)268-3978. Fax: (315)268-3983. E-mail: serio@clarkson.edu. Website: www.wallacestevens.com. Established 1977. **Contact:** Prof. Joseph Duemer, poetry editor.

Magazine Needs *The Wallace Stevens Journal*, published by the Wallace Stevens Society, appears biannually using "poems about or in the spirit of Wallace Stevens or having some relation to his work. No bad parodies of Stevens's anthology pieces." Has published poetry by David Athey, Jacqueline Marcus, Charles Wright, X.J. Kennedy, A.M. Juster, and Robert Creeley. *The Wallace Stevens Journal* is 80-120 pages, digest-sized, typeset, flat spined, with glossy cover with art. Receives 200-300 poems/year, accepts 15-20. Press run is 800 (600 subscribers, 250 libraries). Subscription: $25, includes membership in the Wallace Stevens Society. Sample: $6.

How to Submit Submit 3-5 poems at a time. "We like to receive clean, readable copy. We generally do not publish previously published material, though we have made a few exceptions to this rule. No fax or e-mail submissions, though requests for information are fine." Responds in up to 10 weeks. Always sends prepublication galleys. Pays 2 contributor's copies. Acquires all rights. Returns rights with permission and acknowledgment. Staff reviews books of poetry. Send materials for review consideration "only if there is some clear connection to Stevens."

Advice "Brief cover letters are fine, even encouraged. Please don't submit to *Wallace Stevens Journal* if you have not read Stevens. We like parodies, but they must add a new angle of perception. Most of the poems we publish are not parodies but meditations on themes related to Wallace Stevens and those poets he has influenced. Those wishing to contribute might want to examine the Fall 1996 issue, which has a large and rich selection of poetry."

$◻ STICKMAN REVIEW: AN ONLINE LITERARY JOURNAL

2890 N. Fairview Dr., Flagstaff AZ 86004. (386)254-8306. E-mail: editors@stickmanreview.com. Website: www.stickmanreview.com. Established 2001.

Magazine Needs *Stickman Review* is a biannual online literary journal dedicated to publishing great poetry, fiction, nonfiction, and artwork. Wants poetry "that is literary in intent; no restrictions on form, subject matter, or style. We would prefer not to see rhyming poetry."

How to Submit Submit 5 poems at a time. Accepts simultaneous submissions; no previously published poems. Accepts e-mail submissions *only*; no fax or disk submissions. Cover letter is preferred. Reads submissions year round. Time between acceptance and publication is 2 months. "Currently, the editors-in-chief review all submissions." Sometimes comments on rejected poems. Guidelines available on website. Responds in up to 4 months. Pays $10/poem, up to $20 per author. Acquires first rights.

Advice "Keep writing and submitting. A rejection is not necessarily a reflection upon the quality of your work. Be persistent, trust your instincts, and sooner or later, good things will come."

$□ ◎ STONE SOUP, THE MAGAZINE BY YOUNG WRITERS AND ARTISTS; THE CHILDREN'S ART FOUNDATION (Specialized: children)

P.O. Box 83, Santa Cruz CA 95063. (831)426-5557. Fax: (831)426-1161. E-mail: editor@stonesoup.com. Website: www.stonesoup.com. Established 1973. **Contact:** Ms. Gerry Mandel, editor.

• *Stone Soup* has received both Parents' Choice and Edpress Golden Lamp Honor Awards.

Magazine Needs *Stone Soup* appears 6 times/year and publishes writing and art by children ages 13 and under. Wants free verse poetry; no rhyming poetry, haiku, or cinquain. *Stone Soup* is 48 pages, 7×10, professionally printed in color on heavy stock, saddle-stapled, with coated ocver with full-color illustration. Receives 5,000 poetry submissions/year, accepts about 12. Press run is 20,000 (14,000 subscribers, 5,000 shelf sales, 1,000 other). Sample: $5. A membership in the Children's Art Foundation at $34/year includes a subscription to the magazine.

How to Submit "Submissions can be any number of pages, any format. Include name, age, home address, and phone number. Don't include SASE; we respond only to those submissions under consideration and cannot return manuscripts." No simultaneous submissions. No e-mail submissions. Guidelines available for SASE, by e-mail, or on website. Responds in up to 6 weeks. Pays $40, a certificate, and 2 contributor's copies plus discounts. Acquires all rights. Returns rights upon request. Open to reviews by children.

☑ STORY LINE PRESS; FREDERICK MORGAN POETRY PRIZE

Three Oaks Farm, P.O. Box 1240, Ashland OR 97520-0055. E-mail: mail@storylinepress.com. Website: www.storylinepress.com. Established 1985. **Contact:** Robert McDowell, editor/publisher.

• Books published by Story Line Press have received such prestigious awards as the Lenore Marshall Prize, the Whiting Award, and the Harold Morton Landon Prize.

Contest/Award Offerings Story Line Press publishes annually the winner of the Frederick Morgan Poetry Prize for a first full-length collection of poetry. Offers $1,000 advance and publication. Submit a ms of original poetry in English, at least 48 pages in length. **Entry fee:** $25 for reading and processing. **Deadline:** October 31. Complete guidelines available for SASE or on website.

Also Offers Story Line Press annually publishes 10-15 books of poetry, literary criticism, memoir, fiction, and books in translation. Has published collections by such poets as Rita Dove, Annie Finch, Donald Justice, Mark Jarman, and David Mason. Query first.

☐ THE STORYTELLER

2441 Washington Rd., Maynard AR 72444. (870)647-2137. E-mail: storyteller1@cox-internet.com. Website: www.freewebs.com/fossilcreekpub. Established 1996. **Contact:** Regina Williams, editor.

Magazine Needs *The Storyteller*, a quarterly magazine, "is geared to, but not limited to new writers and poets." Wants "any form up to 40 lines, any subject, any style, but must have a meaning. Do not throw words together and call it a poem. Nothing in way of explicit sex, violence, horror, or explicit language. I would like it to be understood that I have young readers, ages 9-18." Has published poetry by W.C. Jameson, Bryan Byrd, and Sol Rubin. *Storyteller* is 72 pages, magazine-sized, desktop-published, with slick cover with original pen & ink drawings, includes ads. Receives about 300 poems/year, accepts about 40%. Press run is 600 (over 500 subscribers). Single copy: $6 US, $8 Canada and foreign; subscription: $20 US, $24 Canada & foreign. Sample (if available): $6 US, $8 Canada and foreign.

How to Submit Submit 3 poems at a time, typed and double-spaced. "Make sure name and address are on each page submitted. We are getting many submissions without names." Accepts previously published poems and simultaneous submissions, "but must state where and when poetry first appeared." Accepts submissions by postal mail only. Cover letter is preferred. **Reading fee:** $1/

poem. Time between acceptance and publication is 9 months. "Poems are read and discussed by staff." Sometimes comments on rejected poems. Occasionally publishes theme issues. List of upcoming themes available for SASE. Guidelines available for SASE or on website. Responds in up to 5 weeks. Acquires first or one-time rights. Reviews books and chapbooks of poetry by subscribers only. Send materials for review consideration to Ruthan Riney, associate editor.

Contest/Award Offerings Sponsors a quarterly contest. "Readers vote on their favorite poems. Winners receive copy of magazine and certificate suitable for framing. We also nominate for the Pushcart Prize." See website for yearly contest announcements and winners.

Advice "Be professional. Do not send 4 or 5 poems on one page. Send us poetry written from the heart."

⚔ ◻ ◎ STRUGGLE: A MAGAZINE OF PROLETARIAN REVOLUTIONARY LITERATURE (Specialized: social issues)

P.O. Box 13261, Detroit MI 48213-0261. (313)273-9039. E-mail: timhall11@yahoo.com. Website: www.strugglemagazine.org. Established 1985. **Contact:** Tim Hall, editor.

Magazine Needs *Struggle* is a "literary quarterly; content: the struggle of the working people and all oppressed against the rich. Issues such as: racism, poverty, women's rights, aggressive wars, workers' struggle for jobs and job security, the overall struggle for a non-exploitative society, a genuine socialism." The poetry and songs printed are "generally short, any style; subject matter must criticize or fight—explicitly or implicitly—against the rule of the billionaires. We welcome experimentation devoted to furthering such content. We are open to both subtlety and direct statement." Has published poetry by Rain Wilson, David Campbell, Melissa Shook, Michael Ceraolo, Anne M. Ogle, and Doug Draime. *Struggle* is 36 pages, digest-sized, photocopied. Subscription: $10 for 4 issues. Sample: $3. Make checks payable to "Tim Hall—Special Account."

How to Submit Submit up to 8 poems at a time. "Writers must include SASE. Name and address must appear on the opening page of each poem." Accepts e-mail submissions (pasted into body of message, no attachments), but prefers postal mail. Accepted work usually appears in the next or following issue. Editor tries to provide criticism "with every submission." Tries to respond in 4 months, but often becomes backlogged. Pays one contributor's copy. "If you are unwilling to have your poetry published on our website, please inform us."

Advice "Show passion and fire. Humor also welcome. Prefer powerful, colloquial language over academic timidity. Look to Neruda, Lorca, Bly, Whitman, Braithwaite, Tupac Shakur, Muriel Rukeyser. Experimental, traditional forms both welcome. Especially favor: works reflecting rebellion by the working people against the rich; works against racism, sexism, militarism, imperialism; works critical of our exploitative culture; works showing a desire for—or fantasy of—a non-exploitative society; works attacking the Republican 'anti-terrorism' war frenzy and the Democrats' surrender to it."

◙ STUDIO ONE

Haehn Campus Center, College of St. Benedict, St. Joseph MN 56374. E-mail: studio1@csbsju.edu. Established 1976. Editor changes yearly.

Magazine Needs *Studio One*, an annual literary and visual arts magazine appearing in May, is designed as a forum for local, regional, and national poets/writers. No specifications regarding form, subject matter, or style of poetry submitted. However, poetry no more than 2 pages stands a better chance of publication. Has published poetry by Bill Meissner, Eva Hooker, and Larry Schug. *Studio One* is 50-80 pages, typeset, with soft cover. Receives 600-800 submissions/year. No subscriptions, but a sample copy can be obtained by sending a self-addressed stamped manilla envelope and $6 for p&h. Make checks payable to *Studio One.*

How to Submit Accepts simultaneous submissions, no more than 5 per person. No previously published poems. Accepts e-mail submissions (pasted into body of message); clearly show page breaks and indentations. **Deadline:** January 1 for spring publication. Seldom comments on rejected poems.

◉ SULPHUR RIVER LITERARY REVIEW

P.O. Box 19228, Austin TX 78760-9228. (512)292-9456. Established 1978, reestablished 1987. **Contact:** James Michael Robbins, editor/publisher.

Magazine Needs Appearing in March and September, *Sulphur River* is a biannual of poetry, prose, and artwork. "No restrictions except quality." Does not want poetry that is "trite or religious, or verse that does not incite thought." Has published poetry by Marie C. Jones, E.G. Burrows, Ken Fontenot, Virgil Suárez, Marilyn E. Johnston, and Simon Perchik. *Sulphur River* is digest-sized, perfect-bound, with glossy cover. Receives about 4,000 poems/year, accepts 2%. Press run is 350 (200 subscribers, 100 shelf sales). Subscription: $12. Sample: $7.

How to Submit No previously published poems or simultaneous submissions. Accepts submissions by postal mail only. Often comments on rejected poems, "although a dramatic increase in submissions has made this increasingly difficult." Guidelines available for SASE. Responds in one month. Always sends prepublication galleys. Pays 2 contributor's copies.

Also Offers *Sulphur River* also publishes full-length volumes of poetry; latest book: *Five Fictions* by Joe Ahearn.

Advice "Read everything."

$◉ THE SUN

107 N. Roberson St., Chapel Hill NC 27516. Website: www.thesunmagazine.org. Established 1974. **Contact:** Sy Safransky, editor.

Art director Robert Graham designed the cover for Issue 345 of *The Sun*, which features a photograph by Rita Bernstein. Says Bernstein, "I have photographed these two children frequently . . . I'm drawn to their earnest-ness and their eloquent body language."

Magazine Needs *The Sun* is "noted for honest, personal work that's not too obscure or academic. We avoid traditional, rhyming poetry, as well as limericks and haiku. We're open to almost anything else: free verse, prose poems, short and long poems." Has published poetry by Genie Zeiger, Lee Rossi, Alison Luterman, Richard Newman, Kimberley Pittman-Schultz, and David Budbill. *The Sun* is 48 pages, magazine-sized, offset-printed on 50 lb. paper, saddle-stapled. Circulation is 70,000 (63,000 subscribers, 500 libraries). Receives 3,000 submissions of poetry/year, accepts about 30. Subscription: $34. Sample: $5.

How to Submit Submit up to 6 poems at a time. Poems should be typed and accompanied by a cover letter. Accepts previously published poems, but simultaneous submissions are discouraged. Guidelines available for SASE. Responds within 3 months. Pays $50-250 on publication plus contributor's copies and subscription. Acquires first serial or one-time rights.

◉ SUN POETIC TIMES

P.O. Box 790526, San Antonio TX 78279-0526. (210)325-8122. E-mail: sunpoets@hotmail.com. Established 1994. **Contact:** Rod C. Stryker, editor.

Magazine Needs *Sun Poetic Times*, a literary and visual arts magazine, appears 2-4 times/year to "publish all types of literary and visual art from all walks of life. We take all types. Our only specification is length—one page in length if typed, 2 pages if handwritten (legibly)." Has published poetry by Naomi Shihab Nye, Chris Crabtree, Trinidad Sanchez, Jr., and Garland Lee Thompson, Jr. *Sun Poetic Times* is 24-28 pages, magazine-sized, attractively printed, saddle-stapled, with card stock cover, includes b&w line drawings/halftones. Receives about 300 poems/year, accepts about 20%. Press run is 250 (100 shelf sales). Subscription: $10/2 issues, $20/4 issues. Sample: $5 and SASE. Make checks payable to *Sun Poetic Times*.

How to Submit Submit 3-5 poems at a time. Accepts simultaneous submissions; no previously published poems. Accepts e-mail submissions (pasted into body of message; no attachments. Cover letter is preferred. ''In cover letters, we like to hear about your publishing credits, reasons you've taken up the pen, and general B.S. like that (biographical info).'' Time between acceptance and publication is up to one year. Seldom comments on rejected poems. Occasionally publishes theme issues. Guidelines and upcoming themes available for SASE or by e-mail. E-mail queries welcome. Responds in up to 9 months. Pays one contributor's copy. Rights revert back to author upon publication.

⊠ ⊘ ◎ SUNSTONE (Specialized: religious/Mormon; nature/rural/ecology; social issues; spirituality/inspirational)

343 N. Third W., Salt Lake City UT 84103-1215. (801)355-5926. Established 1974. **Contact:** Dixie Partridge, poetry editor.

Magazine Needs Appearing 5 times/year, *Sunstone* publishes ''scholarly articles of interest to an open, Mormon audience; personal essays; fiction and poetry.'' Wants ''both lyric and narrative poetry that engages the reader with fresh, strong images, skillful use of language, and a strong sense of voice and/or place. No didactic poetry, sing-song rhymes, or in-process work.'' Has published poetry by Susan Howe, Anita Tanner, Robert Parham, Ryan G. Van Cleave, Robert Rees, and Virgil Suárez. *Sunstone* is 80 pages, magazine-sized, professionally printed, saddle-stapled, with semi-glossy paper cover. Receives over 500 poems/year, accepts 40-50. Press run is 5,000 (4,000 subscribers, 300 libraries, 700 shelf sales). Subscription: $36/6 issues. Sample: $8 postpaid.

How to Submit Submit up to 5 poems, with name and address on each poem. Lines/poem: 40 maximum. No previously published poems or simultaneous submissions. Time between acceptance and publication is 2 years or less. Seldom comments on rejected poems. Guidelines available for SASE. Responds in 3 months. Pays 5 contributor's copies. Acquires first North American serial rights.

Advice ''Poems should not sound like a rewording of something heard before. Be original; pay attention to language, sharp imagery. Contents should deepen as the poem progresses. We've published poems rooted strongly in place, narratives seeing life from another time or culture, poems on religious belief or doubt—a wide range of subject matter.''

⊘ ◎ SUPERIOR CHRISTIAN NEWS (formerly *Superior Poetry News*) (Specialized: religions/ Christian; translations; regional/Rocky Mountain West); SUPERIOR POETRY PRESS

P.O. Box 424, Superior MT 59872. Established 1995. **Contact:** Ed and Guna Chaberek, editors.

Magazine Needs *Superior Christian News* appears quarterly and ''publishes the best and most interesting of new Christian poets, as well as mainstream poets, we can find. Also, we encourage lively translation into English from any language.'' Wants ''Christian, Western, or humorous poetry; translations; 40 lines or less.'' Accepts poetry by young writers; the only restriction is quality, not age. Has published poetry by Bob Kimm, Dr. Kelley White, John Grey, makyo, and Charles L. Wright. *Superior Christian News* is 12-24 pages, digest-sized, photocopied. Receives about 1,500 poems/year, accepts 5-10%. Press run is 100 (50 subscribers); 5 distributed free to libraries. Single copy: $2; subscription: $6/4 issues.

How to Submit Submit 3-5 poems at a time. No previously published poems or simultaneous submissions (unless stated). Cover letter with short bio is preferred. Time between acceptance and publication is 3 months. Seldom comments on rejected poems. Guidelines available for SASE. Responds in one week. Pays one contributor's copy. Acquires first rights.

Also Offers *Superior Christian News* is now repositoried at the University of Wisconsin (Madison) Memorial Library.

Advice ''Original—be original.''

☐ ◎ **SUZERAIN ENTERPRISES; LOVE'S CHANCE MAGAZINE** (Specialized: love/romance); **FIGHTING CHANCE MAGAZINE** (Specialized: horror; science fiction/fantasy)
P.O. Box 60336, Worcester MA 01606. Established 1994. **Contact:** Milton Kerr, editor.
Magazine Needs *Love's Chance Magazine* and *Fighting Chance Magazine* are each published 3 times/year to "give unpublished writers a chance to be published and to be paid for their efforts." *Love's Chance* deals with romance; *Fighting Chance* deals with dark fiction, horror, and science fiction. "No porn, ageism, sexism, racism, children in sexual situations." Has published poetry by A.H. Ferguson, Wayne Adams, Robert Donald Spector, Cecil Boyce, and Ellaraine Lockie. Both magazines are 15-30 pages, magazine-sized, photocopied, side-stapled, with computer-designed paper cover. Both receive about 500 poems/year, accept about 10%. Press runs are 100 (70-80 subscribers). Subscription: $12/year for each. Samples: $4 each. Make checks payable to Suzerain Enterprises.
How to Submit For both magazines, submit 3 poems at a time. Lines/poem: 20 maximum. Accepts previously published poems and simultaneous submissions. Cover letter is preferred. "Proofread for spelling errors, neatness; must be typewritten in standard manuscript form. No handwritten manuscripts." Time between acceptance and publication is 3 months. Often comments on rejected poems. Guidelines available for SASE. Responds in 6 weeks. Acquires first or one-time rights.
Advice "Proofread your work. Edit carefully. Send correct postage and always include business-sized SASE. Don't let rejection slips get you down. Keep submitting and don't give up. Don't be afraid to write something different."

$☐ SWAN SCYTHE PRESS

2052 Calaveras Ave., Davis CA 95616-3021. E-mail: sandyjmc@mindspring.com. Website: www.s wanscythe.com. Established 1999. **Contact:** Sandra McPherson, editor/publisher.
- Has been awarded a California Arts Council Multicultural Entry Grant and a Fideicomiso para la Cultura Mexico-EUA/US-Mexico Fund for Culture Grant.

Book/Chapbook Needs & How to Submit Swan Scythe Press publishes "poetry chapbooks, a few full-sized poetry collections, and one anthology. A multi-ethnic press primarily publishing emerging writers, we have also published established poets such as Ted Joans and Jordan Smith." Books should be thematically unified with fresh subject matter. "Every kind of poem from formal to prose poem is welcome." Has published poetry by Emmy Perez, Maria Melendez, John Olivares Espinoza, Karen An-hwei Lee, Pos Moua, and Walter Pavlich. Publishes one poetry book/year, 3 chapbooks/year, and one anthology/year. Manuscripts are selected through open submission. Books/chapbooks are 36-85 pages, commercially printed, perfect-bound, with full-color paper covers. Pays advance of $200 and 50 author's copies (out of a press run of 500). Order sample books/chapbooks by sending $11 to Swan Scythe Press (also available through website).

☐ SWEET ANNIE & SWEET PEA REVIEW

7750 Highway F-24 W, Baxter IA 50028. (641)417-0020. E-mail: sweetann@pcpartner.net. Established 1995. **Contact:** Beverly A. Clark, editor/publisher.
Magazine Needs *Sweet Annie & Sweet Pea Review*, published quarterly, features short stories and poetry. Wants "poems of outdoors, plants, land, heritage, women, relationships, olden times—simpler times." Does not want "obscene, violent, explicit sexual material, obscure, long-winded materials, overly religious materials." Has published poetry by Patricia Rourke, Mary Ann Wehler, Ellaraine Lockie, Patricia Wellingham-Jones, Dick Reynolds, and Susanne Olson. *Sweet Annie & Sweet Pea Review* is 30 pages, digest-sized, offset-printed on bond paper with onion skin page before title page, saddle-stapled, with medium card cover with art. Receives about 200 poems/year, accepts 25-33%. Press run is 40. Subscription: $24. Sample: $7. Make checks payable to Sweet Annie Press.
How to Submit Submit 6-12 poems at a time. **Reading fee:** $5/author submitting. "Strongly recommend ordering a sample issue prior to submitting; preference is given to poets and writers following this procedure and submitting in accordance with the layout used consistently by this press."

Accepts simultaneous submissions; no previously published poems. No e-mail submissions. Cover letter is preferred; "include phone number and personal comments about yourself." Time between acceptance and publication is 9 months. Often comments on rejected poems. Occasionally publishes theme issues. "We select for theme first, content second; narrow selections through editors." Pays one contributor's copy. Acquires all rights. Returns rights with acknowledgment in future publications. Will review chapbooks of poetry or other magazines of short length. Send materials for review consideration.

SYCAMORE REVIEW

Dept. of English, Purdue University, 500 Oval Dr., West Lafayette IN 47907-2038. (765)494-3783. Fax: (765)494-3780. E-mail: sycamore@purdue.edu. Website: www.sla.purdue.edu/sycamore/. Established 1988 (first issue May 1989). **Contact:** Poetry Editor.

● Poetry published by *Sycamore Review* has appeared in the *Pushcart Prize* and *Best American Poetry* anthologies.

Magazine Needs *Sycamore Review* is published biannually in January and June. "We accept personal essays, short fiction, drama, translations, and quality poetry in any form. We aim to publish many diverse styles of poetry from formalist to prose poems, narrative, and lyric." Has published poetry by Denise Levertov, Mark Halperin, Amy Gerstler, Mark Halliday, Dean Young, and Ed Hirsch. *Sycamore Review* is 160 pages, digest-sized, professionally printed, flat-spined, with matte color cover. Press run is 1,000 (200 subscribers, 50 libraries). Subscription: $12; $14 outside US. Sample: $7. Make checks payable to Purdue University (Indiana residents add 5% sales tax.)

How to Submit Submit 3-6 poems at a time, with name and address on each page. Accepts simultaneous submissions, if notified immediately of acceptance elsewhere; no previously published poems except translations. No fax or e-mail submissions. Cover letters not required but invited; include phone number, short bio, and previous publications, if any. "We read August 1 through March 1 only." Guidelines available for SASE. Responds in 4 months. Pays 2 contributor's copies. Acquires first North American rights. After publication, all rights revert to author. Staff reviews books of poetry. Send materials for review consideration to editor-in-chief.

Advice "Poets who do not include a SASE do not receive a response."

$ SYNERGEBOOKS

1235 Flat Shoals Rd., King NC 27021. (336)994-2405. Fax: (336)994-8403. E-mail: inquiries@synerg ebooks.com. Website: www.synergebooks.com. Established 1999. **Contact:** Deb Staples, acquisitions editor. Member: EPPRO; SPAN.

Book/Chapbook Needs SynergEbooks specializes in quality works by talented new writers in every available digital format, including CD-ROMs and paperback. "Poetry must have a very unique twist or theme and must be edited. We are looking specifically for poetry with religious overtones." Does not accept unedited work. Has published poetry by Theresa Jodray, Brenda Roberts, Vanyell Delacroix, Joel L. Young, and Chuck Kelly. SynergEbooks publishes up to 40 titles/year, less than 1% of them poetry. Books are usually 45-150 pages, print-on-demand, with paperback binding.

How to Submit Query by e-mail, with a few sample poems and cover letter with brief bio and publication credits. "We prefer no simultaneous submissions, but inform us if this is the case." Accepts submissions on disk or by e-mail (as attachment) *only*. "Please do not send poetry via postal mail. Valid, working e-mail address is required." Responds to queries in one month; to mss in up to 5 months. Pays royalties of 15-40%.

Advice "We are inundated with more poetry than prose every month; but we will accept the occasional anthology with a unique twist that is original and high quality. New poets welcome."

$ TAKAHE

P.O. Box 13 335, Christchurch, New Zealand. (03)359-8133. Established 1990. **Contact:** James Norcliffe, poetry editor.

Magazine Needs "*Takahe* appears 3-4 times/year and publishes short stories and poetry by both established and emerging writers. The publisher is the Takahe Collective Trust, a nonprofit organization formed to help new writers and get them into print. While insisting on correct British spelling (or recognized spellings in foreign languages), smart quotes, and at least internally consistent punctuation, we, nonetheless, try to allow some latitude in presentation. Any use of foreign languages must be accompanied by an English translation." No style, subject, or form restrictions. Has published poetry by John O'Connor, Owen Bullock, Patricia Prime, Jennifer Compton, David Eggleton, Mark Pirie, and Emma Neale. *Takahe* is 60 pages, A4. Receives about 250 poems/year, accepts about 30%. Press run is 400 (300 subscribers, 30 libraries, 40 shelf sales). Single copy: $6.50 NZ; subscription: $25 NZ within New Zealand, $35 NZ elsewhere.

How to Submit No simultaneous submissions. Cover letter is required. "Advise if you have e-mail." Time between acceptance and publication is 4 months. Often comments on rejected poems. Guidelines available for SASE. Responds in 4 months. "Payment varies but currently NZ$30 total for any and all inclusions in an issue, plus 2 contributor's copies." Acquires first or one-time rights.

⚅ ◻ ◎ TALE SPINNERS; MIDNIGHT STAR PUBLICATIONS (Specialized: country living; being 'one with nature')

R.R. #1, Ponoka AB T4J 1R1 Canada. (403)783-2521. Established 1996. **Contact:** Nellie Gritchen Scott, editor/publisher.

Magazine Needs *Tale Spinners* is a quarterly "'little literary magazine with a country flavor,' for writers who love country and all it stands for." Wants poetry, fiction, anecdotes, personal experiences, etc., "pertaining to country life. Children's poetry welcome." No "scatological, prurient, sexually explicit, or political content." Accepts poetry written by children ages 6 and up. Has published poetry by Dennis K. Ross, Kenneth Rehill, Elizabeth Symon, Daniel Green, John Castagnini, and Harold T. Little. *Tale Spinners* is 48 pages, digest-sized, photocopied, saddle-stapled, with light cardstock cover. Receives about 100 poems/year, accepts about 80%. Press run is 75 (50 subscribers). Subscription: $20. Sample: $5 plus $1 p&h.

How to Submit Submit up to 6 poems at a time. "Short poems preferred, but will use narrative poems on occasion." Accepts previously published poems. Cover letter ensures a reply. Include SAE and IRC. Submit seasonal poems at least 3 months in advance. Time between acceptance and publication varies. Often comments on rejected poems. Guidelines available for SASE. Responds in 2 weeks. Pays one contributor's copy.

Book/Chapbook Needs & How to Submit "Midnight Star Publications is not accepting chapbook manuscripts at present."

Advice "Bear in mind this is a country/farm and ranch oriented magazine. It is a quarterly, so send seasonal material three months in advance—we don't like to return appropriate material simply because it is out of date!"

$ ◻ ◎ TALES OF THE TALISMAN (formerly *Hadrosaur Tales*) (Specialized: science fiction/ fantasy; horror)

P.O. Box 2194, Mesilla Park NM 88047-2194. E-mail: hadrosaur@zianet.com. Website: www.hadrosaur.com. Established 1995. **Contact:** David Lee Summers, editor.

Magazine Needs *Tales of the Talisman* is a quarterly literary journal that publishes "well-written, thought-provoking science fiction and fantasy." Wants science fiction and fantasy themes. No graphic/gory violence. "We like to see strong visual imagery; strong emotion from a sense of fun to more melancholy is good. We do not want to see poetry that strays too far from the science fiction/fantasy genre." Has published poetry by Jean Hull Herman, Christina Sng, K.S. Hardy, John Grey, and Gary Every. *Tales of the Talisman* is 86 pages, $8\frac{1}{2} \times 11$, printed on 60-lb. white paper, perfect-bound, with full-color cardstock cover. Receives about 100 poems/year, accepts up to 25%. Press run is 200 (100 subscribers). Single copy: $8; subscription: $20/year. Make checks payable to Hadrosaur Productions.

How to Submit Submit 1-5 poems at a time. Accepts previously published poems; no simultaneous submissions. Accepts e-mail submissions (pasted into body of message); no disk submissions. "For e-mail submissions, place the word 'Hadrosaur' in the subject line. Submissions that do not include this will be destroyed unread. Postal mail submissions will not be returned unless sufficient postage is provided." Cover letter is preferred. Reads submissions May 1 to June 15 and November 1 to December 15. "Please do not send material outside these ranges." Time between acceptance and publication is one year. Often comments on rejected poems. Guidelines available for SASE or on website. Responds in one month. Sends prepublication galleys on request. Pays $2/poem plus one contributor's copy. Acquires one-time rights.

Advice "Read absolutely everything you can get your hands on, especially poetry outside your genre of choice, and ask 'What if?' This is a great source for original speculative poems."

⬜ ◎ TAPESTRIES (Specialized: senior citizens; anthology)

MWCC Life Program, 444 Green St., Gardner MA 01440. (978)630-9176. Fax: (978)632-6155. E-mail: alanahb@earthlink.net or p_cosentino@mwcc.mass.edu. Website: www.mwcc.mass.edu/LLL/tapestriesGuidelines.html. Established 2001. **Contact:** Patricia B. Cosentino, editor. Life Program Coordinator: Lorraine Wickman.

Magazine Needs *Tapestries* appears annually in November as an anthology for senior citizens of poetry, short stories, features on family, heritage, tradition, and folklore. Wants any style poetry; no restrictions on form. Does not want "political, propaganda, pornographic, or sexually explicit material as this is a 'family' magazine. We do not exclude religious poems, but they must have non-sectarian universality." Has published poetry by Maxine Kumin, Victor Howes, Diana Der-Hovanessian, Marge Piercy, bg Thurston, and FD Reeve. *Tapestries* is 100 pages, magazine-sized, offset-printed, tape-bound, with card stock/offset cover. Receives about 500 poems/year, accepts about 10%. Press run is 500. Single copy: $5 plus $3 postage. Make checks payable to MWCC Life Program.

How to Submit Submit 3-5 poems at a time. Accepts previously published poems and simultaneous submissions. Accepts postal mail and disk submissions; no fax or e-mail submissions. Cover letter is preferred (only if work is previously published). "Prefer hard copy submissions. Submit two copies, with name and address on only one copy. Include SASE." **Deadline:** March 31. Time between acceptance and publication is 4 months. Poems are circulated to an editorial board of 3-4 judges. Occasionally publishes theme issues. List of upcoming themes available on website. Guidelines available in magazine, for SASE, by fax, by e-mail (life@mwcc.mass.edu), or on website. Responds in 3 months. No payment. Acquires first North American serial rights.

Advice "As an anthology we accept original and/or previously published material, but prefer original. Our authors range in age from 50-92. We want humor and wisdom in our writings. Experiment with point of view—too many poems use first-person speaker."

⭐ ◨ TAPROOT LITERARY REVIEW; TAPROOT WRITER'S WORKSHOP ANNUAL WRITING CONTEST

P.O. Box 204, Ambridge PA 15003. (724)266-8476. E-mail: taproot10@aol.com. Established 1986. **Contact:** Tikvah Feinstein, editor.

Magazine Needs Published annually, *Taproot* is "a very respected anthology with increasing distribution. We publish some of the best poets in the U.S. We enjoy all types and styles of poetry from emerging writers to established writers to those who have become valuable and old friends who share their new works with us." Has published poetry by Arlene Atwater, Kurt Saunders, Shoshauna Shy, Vera Schwarcz, Alessio Zanelli, and B.Z. Niditch. *Taproot Literary Review* is about 95 pages, offset-printed on white stock, with one-color glossy cover. Circulation is 500. Single copy: $8.95; subscription: $7.50. Sample: $5.

How to Submit Submit up to 5 poems. Lines/poem: 35 maximum. No previously published poems of simultaneous submissions. Accepts submissions by e-mail (pasted into body of message), but "We would rather have a hard copy. Also, we cannot answer without a SASE." Cover letter with general information is required. Submissions accepted between September 1 and December 31 only. Guidelines available for SASE. Sometimes sends prepublication galleys. Pays 2 contributor's copies; additional copies are $6.50. Open to receiving books for review consideration. Send query first.

Contest/Award Offerings Sponsors the annual Taproot Writer's Workshop Annual Writing Contest. 1st Prize: $25 and publication in *Taproot Literary Review*; 2nd Prize: publication; 3rd Prize: publication. Submit 5 poems of literary quality, any form, any subject except porn. **Entry fee:** $12/5 poems (no longer than 35 lines each), includes copy of review. **Deadline:** December 31. Winners announced the following March.

Advice "We publish the best poetry we can in a variety of styles and subjects, so long as it's literary quality and speaks to us. We love poetry that stuns, surprises, amuses, and disarms."

☑ TAR RIVER POETRY

English Dept., East Carolina University, Greenville NC 27858-4353. (252)328-6046. Website: www.ecu.edu/english/journals. Established 1978. **Contact:** Peter Makuck, editor.

Magazine Needs *Tar River* appears twice/year as an "all-poetry" magazine that accepts dozens of poems in each issue, providing the talented beginner and experienced writer with a forum that features all styles and forms of verse. "We are not interested in sentimental, flat-statement poetry. What we would like to see is skillful use of figurative language, poems that appeal to the senses." Has published poetry by Betty Adcock, Henry Taylor, Mark Cox, Robert Cording, Elisabeth Murawski, and Priscilla Atkins. *Tar River* is 60 pages, digest-sized, professionally printed on salmon stock, with matte card cover with photo. Receives 6,000-8,000 submissions/year, accepts 150-200. Press run is 900 (500 subscribers, 125 libraries). Subscription: $12. Sample: $6.50.

How to Submit Submit 3-6 poems at a time, with name and address on each page. "We do not consider previously published poems or simultaneous submissions. We do not consider manuscripts during summer months." Reads submissions September 1 through April 15 only. Editors will comment "if slight revision will do the trick." Guidelines available for SASE or on website. Responds in 6 weeks. Pays 2 contributor's copies. Acquires first rights. Reviews books of poetry in 4,000 words maximum, single- or multi-book format. Send materials for review consideration.

Advice "Poets are first readers. Read and study traditional and contemporary poetry."

Ⓝ ☑ TAR WOLF REVIEW

P.O. Box 2038, Clarkrange TN 38553. E-mail: tarwolfpoets@hotmail.com. Website: www.tarwolfreview.org. Established 2003. **Contact:** DeAnna Stephens Vaughn, poetry editor.

Magazine Needs *Tar Wolf Review* is a biannual journal of poetry and art. Prefers "free verse that uses innovative language and imagery to discuss unique subjects or to re-see traditional ones, but we'll consider formal verse that meets these standards." Wants "work that expresses a unique perspective and insight. Past issues have featured lyric free verse, lyric-narrative, and prose poetry. We enjoy work that experiments with form, diction, syntax, and juxtaposition of imagery." Does not want "poetry with obvious rhymes and meanings; cliché-ridden, pornographic, or maudlin poetry. Not interested in poems about poems or the process of writing. Multiple submissions will be returned unread or discarded." Has published poetry by Trent Busch, William Doreski, Gayle Elen Harvey, Ruth Holzer, Jacqueline Kolosov, and Gary Metras. *Tar Wolf Review* is 60-80 pages, digest-sized, saddle-stapled, with 110-lb. cover with color or b&w art. Receives about 1,900 poems/year, accepts about 4%. Press run is 80-100. Single copy: $6 plus $1.42 shipping; subscription: $12 plus $2.84 shipping. Make checks or money orders payable to *Tar Wolf Review*.

How to Submit Submit 3-5 poems at a time. Lines/poem: 90 maximum, including spaces. Accepts simultaneous submissions (with notification); no previously published poems. No e-mail or disk submissions. Cover letter is preferred. "Present the poems as you would like them to appear in their published forms. Include name and contact information on each page, and a cover letter with a bio of 40 or fewer words. Submissions without SASEs will be discarded unread." Reads submissions year round. Time between acceptance and publication is one month to one year. Sometimes comments on rejected poems. Guidelines available for SASE or on website. Responds within 4 months. Pays at least one contributor's copy. Acquires first North American serial rights.

Advice "Consider how each line stands on its own and whether it contributes to the poem's effect. Read a diverse selection of poets, especially ones whose work is very different from your own."

TARPAULIN SKY

E-mail: info@tarpaulinsky.com (inquiries) or submissions@tarpaulinsky.com (submissions). Website: www.tarpaulinsky.com. Established 2002. **Contact:** Poetry Editors. Editor: Christian Peet.

Magazine Needs *Tarpaulin Sky* is a quarterly online literary journal, "publishing highest-quality poetry, prose, art, photography, interviews, and reviews. We are open to all styles and forms, providing the forms appear inevitable and/or inextricable from the poems. We are especially fond of inventive/experimental and trans-genre work. The best indication of our aesthetic is found in the journal we produce: Please read it before submitting your work. Also, hardcopy submissions may be received by different editors at different times: check guidelines before submitting." Has published poetry by Jenny Boully, Joshua Corey, Louis Jenkins, Joyelle McSweeney, Juliana Spahr, and Heidi Lynn Staples. *Tarpaulin Sky* is published online only. Receives about 3,000 poems/year.

How to Submit Submit 3 or more poems at a time. Accepts simultaneous submissions; no previously published poems. Accepts e-mail submissions; no fax or disk submissions. "E-mail submissions are best received as attachments in .rtf or .pdf formats." Cover letter is preferred. Reads submissions year round. Time between acceptance and publication is 1-4 months. "All poems are read by four poetry editors. We aim for consensus." Rarely comments on rejected poems. Guidelines available for SASE, by e-mail, or on website. Responds in 1-4 months. Always sends prepublication galleys (electronic). Acquires first rights. Reviews books and chapbooks of poetry.

TATTOO HIGHWAY (Specialized: theme-based)

E-mail: smcaulay@csuhayward.edu. Website: www.tattoohighway.org. Established 1998. **Contact:** Sara McAulay, editor.

Magazine Needs *Tattoo Highway* is a "graphics-heavy biannual online journal of poetry, literary prose, new media, and art. We're open to most styles, including New Media; we like formal poems if well handled. Mainly we want language that is fresh, vivid, and original; writing that is smart and a little edgy, that engages with the world beyond the writer's own psyche." Does not want "self-pity, navel-contemplation, clichés, workshop hackery." Has published poetry by John Gilgun, Walt McDonald, Ian McBryde, Susan H. Case, Erin Murphy, and Corey Mesler. *Tattoo Highway* is published online only. Receives about 800 poems/year, accepts about 50.

How to Submit Accepts previously published poems ("see guidelines on website") and simultaneous submissions. Accepts e-mail submissions (pasted into body of message); no disk or hardcopy submissions. "For hypertext or New Media (Flash, etc.) submissions, please provide a URL where we may view the work." Reading periods vary; "typically last three moths; see guidelines." Poems are circulated to an editorial board. "Blind readings by editorial board. Several rounds of 'triage' during the reading period, usually handled by e-mail. Face-to-face editorial meeting shortly after submission deadline, where final selections are made. Editor and poetry editor have final say." Sometimes comments on rejected poems. "If a poem has its moments, though it doesn't quite work, we try to acknowledge that. We encourage near-misses to try us again." Regularly publishes theme issues. List of upcoming themes and guidelines available on website. Responds in up to 3 months ("within one week of deadline"). Always sends prepublication galleys. No payment. Acquires first electronic rights; rights revert to author 90 days after online publication date.

Contest/Award Offerings "Picture Worth 500 Words" contest for poetry/prose. No entry fee, small prizes. See guidelines on website.

Advice "Read some past issues before submitting."

TEARS IN THE FENCE

38 Hod View, Stourpaine, Nr. Blandford Forum, Dorset DT11 8TN England. Phone: (0044)1258-456803. Fax: (0044)1258-454026. E-mail: westrow@cooperw.fsnet.co.uk. Website: www.wanderingdog.co.uk. Established 1984. **Contact:** David Caddy, general editor.

Magazine Needs *Tears in the Fence* appears 3 times/year and is a "small press magazine of poetry, fiction, interviews, essays, and reviews. We are open to a wide variety of poetic styles. Work that is unusual, perceptive, and risk-taking as well as imagistic, lived, and visionary will be close to our purpose. However, we like to publish a variety of work." Has published poetry by Lori Jakiela, Jeff Martin, Joan Jobe Smith, Jennifer K. Dick, Kim Taplin, and K.M. Dersley. *Tears in the Fence* is 128 pages, A5, docutech-printed on 110-gms. paper, perfect-bound, with matte card cover. Press run is 800 (512 subscribers). Subscription: $20/4 issues. Sample: $7.

How to Submit Submit 6 typed poems with IRCs. Accepts submissions by e-mail (pasted into body of message), on disk, or by postal mail. Cover letter with brief bio is required. Time between acceptance and publication is 10 months "but can be much less." Publishes theme issues. List of upcoming themes available for SASE. Responds in 3 months. Pays one contributor's copy. Reviews books of poetry in 2,000-3,000 words, single- or multi-book format. Send materials for review consideration.

Also Offers The magazine runs a regular series of readings in London, and an annual international literary festival.

Advice "I think it helps to subscribe to several magazines in order to study the market and develop an understanding of what type of poetry is published. Use the review sections and send off to magazines that are new to you."

TEBOT BACH

P.O. Box 7887, Huntington Beach CA 92615-7887. (714)968-0905. E-mail: info@tebotbach.org. Website: www.tebotbach.org. **Contact:** Mifanwy Kaiser, editor/publisher.

Book/Chapbook Needs & How to Submit Tebot Bach (Welsh for "little teapot") publishes books of poetry. Has published *Cantatas* by Jeanette Clough, *48 Questions* by Richard Jones, *The Way In* by Robin Chapman, and *Written in Rain: New and Selected Poems 1985-2000* by M.L. Liebler. Query first with sample poems and cover letter with brief bio and publication credits. Include SASE. Responds to queries and mss, if invited, in one month. Time between acceptance and publication is up to 2 years. Write to order sample books.

Also Offers An anthology of California poets, published annually in April. Must be current or former resident of California in order to submit, but no focus or theme required for poetry. Deadline for submission is in August, annually. Submit up to 6 poems with "California Anthology" written on lower left corner of envelope. Accepts submissions by e-mail (pasted into body of message or as attachment in Word).

$ TEMPORARY VANDALISM RECORDINGS; THE SILT READER

P.O. Box 6184, Orange CA 92863-6184. E-mail: tvrec@yahoo.com. Website: http://home.surewest. net/aphasiapress/. Established 1991 (Temporary Vandalism Recordings), 1999 (*The Silt Reader*). **Contact:** Robert Roden and Barton M. Saunders, editors.

Magazine Needs *The Silt Reader* is published biannually in January and August. "Form, length, style, and subject matter can vary. It's difficult to say what will appeal to our eclectic tastes." Does not want "strictly rants, overly didactic poetry." Has published poetry by M. Jaime-Becerra, Gerald Locklin, Simon Perchik, Margaret Garcia, and Don Winter. *The Silt Reader* is 32 pages, $4\frac{1}{4} \times 5\frac{1}{2}$, saddle-stapled, photocopied, with colored card cover, includes some ads. Accepts less than 5% of poems received. Press run is 500. Sample: $2. Make checks payable to Robert Roden.

How to Submit Submit 5 neatly typed poems at a time. Accepts previously published poems and simultaneous submissions. No e-mail submissions. Cover letter is preferred. Time between acceptance and publication is 9-12 months. "Two editors' votes required for inclusion." Seldom comments on rejected poems. Responds in up to 6 months. Guidelines available for SASE or on website. Pays 2 contributor's copies. Acquires one-time rights.

Book/Chapbook Needs & How to Submit Temporary Vandalism Recordings publishes 2 chapbooks/year. Chapbooks are usually 40 pages, photocopied, saddle-stapled, with an initial press run of 100 (reprint option if needed). Submit 10 sample poems, with SASE for response. "Publication in some magazines is important, but extensive publishing is not required." Responds in 6 months. Pays 50% royalties (after costs recouped) and 5 author's copies (out of a press run of 100). For sample chapbooks, send $5 to the above address.

🌐 🖉 10TH MUSE

33 Hartington Rd., Southampton, Hants SO14 0EW England. E-mail: andyj@noplace.screaming.net. Established 1990. **Contact:** Andrew Jordan, editor.

Magazine Needs *10th Muse* "includes poetry and reviews, as well as short prose (usually no more than 2,000 words) and graphics. My main interest is 'innovative' poetry and the mainstream poetries influenced by it. I have a particular interest in the cultural construction of landscape." Has published poetry by Peter Riley, Andrew Duncan, Richard Caddel, Ian Robinson, John Welch, and Carrie Etter. *10th Muse* is 48-72 pages, A5, photocopied, saddle-stapled, with card cover. Press run is 200. "U.S. subscribers—send $10 in bills for single copy (including postage)."

How to Submit Submit up to 6 poems. Include SASE (or SAE with IRCs). Accepts submissions by postal mail and e-mail (pasted into body of message). Often comments on rejected poems. Responds in 3 months. Pays one contributor's copy. Staff reviews books of poetry. Send materials for review consideration.

Advice "Poets should read a copy of the magazine first."

Ⓝ 🖉 ◎ TEXAS POETRY CALENDAR (Specialized: poems with a TX connection); TEXAS POETRY CALENDAR AWARDS; DOS GATOS PRESS

1310 Crestwood Rd., Austin TX 78722. (512)467-0678. Fax: (408)580-8523. E-mail: scott@dosgatos press.org or david@dosgatospress.org. Website: www.dosgatospress.org. Established 2004 (under current editorship). **Contact:** Scott Wiggerman or David Meischen, co-editors.

Magazine Needs *Texas Poetry Calendar*, published annually in August, features a "week-by-week calendar side-by-side with poems with a Texas connection in a spiral-bound format." Wants "a wide variety of styles, voices, and forms, including rhyme—though a Texas connection is preferred. Humor is welcome! Poetry *only*!" Does not want "children's poetry, erotic poetry, profanity, obscure poems, previously published work, or poems over 30 lines." *Texas Poetry Calendar* is about 130 pages, digest-sized, offset-printed, spiral-bound, with 2-color cardstock cover. Receives about 400 poems/year, accepts about 50. Press run is 1,500; 50 distributed free to contributors. Single copy: $12.95 plus $3 shipping. Make checks payable to Dos Gatos Press.

How to Submit Submit 3 poems at a time. Lines/poem: 30 maximum, including spaces. Accepts simultaneous submissions; no previously published poems. No fax, e-mail, or disk submissions. Cover letter is required. "Include a short bio (50 words or less) and poem titles in cover letter. Do not include poet's name on the poems themselves! Also include e-mail address and phone number." Reads submissions year round. Time between acceptance and publication is 3-4 months. Poems are circulated to an editorial board. Never comments on rejected poems. **"Entry fee for the *Texas Poetry Calendar* Awards is required for all submissions—all poems submitted are eligible for cash awards."** (See Contest/Award Offerings below.) Guidelines available in magazine, by e-mail, or on website. Sometimes sends prepublication galleys. Pays one contributor's copy. Acquires first, electronic, and reprint rights.

Contest/Award Offerings Sponsors the annual *Texas Poetry Calendar* Awards. Offers 1st Prize: $100; 2nd Prize: $50; 3rd Prize: $25. Submit 3 poems. **Entry fee:** $5. **Deadline:** March 15 (postmark). Guidelines available in magazine, by e-mail, or on website. "Award-winning poems receive special recognition in the calendar in which they are printed."

Ⓝ 🖉 TEXAS POETRY JOURNAL

P.O. Box 90635, Austin TX 78709. E-mail: editor@texaspoetryjournal.com. Website: www.texaspoetryjournal.com. Established 2004. **Contact:** Steven Ray Smith, editor.

Magazine Needs *Texas Poetry Journal* appears biannually and publishes poetry, short essays on contemporary poetry, interviews with poets, and photography. "Our journal is high quality and affordable, perfect for readers at home or on-the-go. We also publish a weekly 'Feature Poem' on our website and promote the feature through our e-mail list, which includes readers all over the world. Our goal is to add poetry to the daily lives of busy people, to bring a touch of extraordinary language to each day." Wants "all forms, styles, and subjects as long as the delivery is artistic and makes creative use of the English language. We prefer shorter poems (up to 20 lines). We want poems that are carefully crafted. We especially love formal poetry. All styles should exhibit intentional structure that is suitable for the expression of the particular work." Does not want "prose trying to serve as poetry. So much free verse often looks like a series of declaratives arranged in a random pattern of stanzas. Poetry should be the artistic use of language in verse. We do not care for gratuitous violence, poems about taking revenge on the neighbors, profanity, or vulgarity. We publish very few long (multi-page) poems." Has published poetry by Deborah Warren, Chuck Taylor, Tim Murphy, David Brendan Hopes, Karla Linn Merrifield, and Bonnie Lyons. *Texas Poetry Journal* is 84 pages, digest-sized, offset-printed, perfect-bound, with 80-lb. coated and varnished cover with b&w photo. Receives about 1,000 poems/year, accepts about 8%. Press run is 500. Single copy: $7.50 ($12.50 foreign); subscription: $12 ($22 foreign). Make checks payable to *Texas Poetry Journal*.

How to Submit Submit 4 poems at a time. Lines/poem: 10-20 (occasionally considers longer poems). Accepts simultaneous submissions; no previously published poems. Accepts e-mail (pasted into body of message or as attachment) and disk submissions. Cover letter is preferred. "SASE required with correct postage. We prefer a cover letter or note with any previous publication credits and awards. We welcome simultaneous submissions, though please let us know and please keep us informed if work is accepted elsewhere." Reads submissions year round. Time between acceptance and publication is 6 months. Guidelines available on website. Responds in 2 months. Always sends prepublication galleys. Pays one contributor's copy. Acquires first rights.

Advice "Poets should be craftspeople who understand their art as it interacts with the world into which it must go. Poetry has such great potential to transform the day, as long as it meets the needs of contemporary readers. People are faced with information overload in their daily lives—they are immersed in language and writing, but not poetry. Poetry has the power to add a touch of transcendence and meaning to each day. A well-crafted poem can and will do that."

$ THEMA (Specialized: themes)

Thema Literary Society, P.O. Box 8747, Metairie LA 70011-8747. E-mail: thema@cox.net. Website: http://members.cox.net/thema. Established 1988. **Contact:** Gail Howard, poetry editor. Editor: Virginia Howard.

- *THEMA* is supported by a grant from the Louisiana Division of the Arts, Office of Cultural Development, Department of Culture, Recreation and Tourism, in cooperation with the Louisiana State Arts Council as administered by Art Council of New Orleans.

Magazine Needs *THEMA* is a triannual literary magazine using poetry related to specific themes. "Each issue is based on an unusual premise. Please, please send SASE for guidelines before submitting poetry to find out the upcoming themes." Upcoming themes (and submission deadlines) include: *Just Describe Them to Me* (November 1, 2005), *Rage Over a Lost Penny* (March 1, 2006), *The Perfect Cup of Coffee* (July 1, 2006). "No scatologic language, alternate life-style, explicit love poetry." Poems will be judged with all others submitted. Has published poetry by David Jordan, Steve Dimeo, Linda Elkin, and Ron Vazzano. *THEMA* is 150 pages, digest-sized, professionally printed, with matte card cover. Receives about 400 poems/year, accepts about 8%. Press run is 500 (270 subscribers, 30 libraries). Subscription: $16. Sample: $8.

How to Submit Submit up to 3 poems at a time with SASE. "All submissions should be typewritten and on standard 8½×11 paper. Submissions are accepted all year, but evaluated after specified deadlines." Guidelines and upcoming themes available in magazine, for SASE, by e-mail, or on website. Editor comments on submissions. Pays $10/poem plus one contributor's copy. Acquires one-time rights.

Advice "Do *not* submit to *THEMA* *unless* you have one of *THEMA*'s upcoming themes in mind. And be sure to specify which one!"

THIRD COAST

Dept. of English, Western Michigan University, Kalamazoo MI 49008-5331. (269)387-2675. Website: www.wmich.edu/thirdcoast. Established 1995. **Contact:** Poetry Editors.

Magazine Needs Appearing in March and September, *Third Coast* is a biannual national literary magazine of poetry, prose, creative nonfiction, and translation. Wants "excellence of craft and originality of thought. Nothing trite." Has published poetry by Myronn Hardy, Sean Thomas Dougherty, Terrance Hayes, Margo Schlipp, Mark Halliday, and Philip Levine. *Third Coast* is 176 pages, digest-sized, professionally printed, perfect-bound, with 4-color cover with art. Receives about 2,000 poems/year, accepts about 1%. Press run is 3,000 (650 subscribers, 50 libraries, 1,900 shelf sales). Single copy: $8; subscription: $14/year, $26/2 years, $38/3 years.

How to Submit Submit up to 5 poems at a time. Accepts simultaneous submissions with notification; no previously published poems. No electronic submissions. Cover letter is preferred. "Poems should be typed single-spaced, with the author's name on each page. Stanza breaks should be double-spaced." Poems are circulated to assistant poetry editors and poetry editors; poetry editors make final decisions. Seldom comments on rejected poems. Guidelines available on website. Responds in 4 months. Pays 2 contributor's copies plus one-year subscription. Acquires first rights.

Contest/Award Offerings Sponsors annual poetry award. 1st Prize: $1,000 and publication; 4 finalists receive notification in prize-winning issue (Fall), and possible publication. **Postmark deadline:** November 15. Guidelines available on website.

THORNY LOCUST

P.O. Box 32631, Kansas City MO 64171-5631. E-mail: skoflersilvia@netscape.net. Website: www.thornylocust.com. Established 1993. **Contact:** Silvia Kofler, editor. Managing Editor: Celeste Kuechler.

Magazine Needs *Thorny Locust*, published quarterly, is a "literary magazine that wants to be thought-provoking, witty, and well-written." Wants "poetry with some 'bite,' e.g., satire, epigrams, black humor, and bleeding-heart cynicism." Does not want "polemics, gratuitous grotesques, sombre surrealism, weeping melancholy, or hate-mongering." Has published poetry by Philip Miller, Joanne Lowery, Art Beck, and Gary Lechliter. *Thorny Locust* is 28-32 pages, 7×8½, desktop-published, saddle-stapled, with medium coverstock. Receives about 400-500 poems/year, accepts about 15%. Press run is 120-200 (30 subscribers, 6 libraries); 60 distributed free to contributors and small presses. Single copy: $5; subscription: $15. Sample: $3. Make checks payable to Silvia Kofler.

How to Submit Submit 3 poems at a time. "If you do not include a SASE with sufficient postage, your submission will be pitched!" No simultaneous submissions or previously published poems. Cover letter is preferred. "Poetry must be typed, laser-printed or in a clear dot-matrix." Time between acceptance and publication is 3-5 months. Seldom comments on rejected poems. Guidelines available for SASE or on website. Responds in 3 months. Pays one contributor's copy. Acquires one-time rights.

Advice "Never perceive a rejection as a personal rebuke, keep on trying. Take advice."

THOUGHTS FOR ALL SEASONS: THE MAGAZINE OF EPIGRAMS (Specialized: form/epigrams; humor; themes)

86 Leland Rd., Box 34, Becket MA 01223. Established 1976. **Contact:** Prof. Em. Michel Paul Richard, editor.

Magazine Needs *Thoughts for All Seasons* "is an irregular serial: designed to preserve the epigram as a literary form; satirical. All issues are commemorative. Volume 6 marks the centennial of *Devil's Dictionary* by Ambrose Bierce (circa 1904)." Rhyming poetry and nonsense verse (e.g., original limericks) with good imagery will be considered although most modern epigrams are prose—no haiku. Has published poetry by Kendal Bush, William D. Barney, and Jill Williams. *Thoughts for All Seasons* is 80 pages, offset from typescript, saddle-stapled, with card cover. Accepts about 20%

of material submitted. Press run is 500-1,000. "There are several library subscriptions, but most distribution is through direct mail or local bookstores and newsstand sales." Single copy: $6 (includes p&h).

How to Submit "Submit at least one or two pages of your work, 10-12 epigrams or 2-4 poems." Include SASE and one-paragraph bio. Accepts simultaneous submissions; no previously published epigrams "unless a thought is appended which alters it." Editor comments on rejected poems. Themes for Volume 6 include 1) Satirical Definitions, A-Z, 2) Satirical Tips for Good Health, and 3) New Lyrics for Old Songs. Guidelines available in magazine or for SASE. Responds in one week. Pays one contributor's copy, additional discounted copies.

Advice "Preference given to rhyming poetry, including original limericks. Nonsense verse with good imagery also acceptable. No haiku!"

⬛ THREE CANDLES

E-mail: editor@threecandles.org. Website: www.threecandles.org. Established 1999. **Contact:** Steve Mueske, editor.

Magazine Needs *Three Candles* is published online and posts updates "when qualified poetry is available, generally once or twice a week. Though I am not particular about publishing specific forms of poetry, I prefer to be surprised by the content of the poems themselves. I believe that poetry should have some substance and touch, at least tangentially, on human experience." Does not want poems that are "overtly religious, sexist, racist, or unartful." Has published poetry by Jeffrey Levine, Deborah Keenan, Joyce Sutphen, Ray Gonzalez, and Paul Guest. *Three Candles* is a "high-quality online journal, professionally designed and maintained." Receives about 5,000 poems/year. "Many poems I publish are solicited directly from poets." Receives 40,000 hits/month.

How to Submit Submit 3-5 poems at a time. No simultaneous submissions or previously published poems. Accepts e-mail submissions *only*. Send poems "as the body of the text or, if special formatting is used, as attachments in Word or rich text format. In the body of the e-mail, I want a short bio, a list of a few significant publications, the certification statement that appears on the 'information' page on the website, and a brief note about what writing poetry means to you as an artist." Accepts submissions year round. Time between acceptance and publication is within one week. "Reading the journal is important to get an idea of the level of craft expected." Guidelines available on website. Responds within 2 months. Does not send prepublication galleys but "allows author to make any necessary changes before a formal announcement is e-mailed to the mailing list." No payment "at this time." Acquires first rights. Copyright reverts to author after publication.

Advice "The online poetry community is vital and thriving. Take some time and get to know the journals you submit to. Don't send work that is like what is published. Send work that is as good but different in a way that is uniquely your own."

⬕ ◯ 3 cup morning

13865 Dillabough Rd., R.R. #1, Chesterville ON K0C 1H0 Canada. E-mail: threecupmorning@hotmail.com. Website: http://3cupmorning.topcities.com. Established 1999. **Contact:** Gen O'Neil, editor.

Magazine Needs Published bimonthly online and in print as a 4-page (double-sided) newsletter, *3 cup morning* is "a platform for beginning and novice poets to showcase their work. We firmly believe that seeing your work in print is the single greatest encouragement needed to continue. Every poet should have the opportunity to see their work in print—at least once anyway." Accepts all types of poetry—haiku, traditional, experimental, free form, etc. No graphic violence, hate, profanity, or graphic sex. Has published poetry by Michael Brown, Eve Hall, Kevin Connelly, Linda Bielowski, and John Grey. Subscription: $24 Canadian and US, $30 all others. Sample: $2. Make checks (Canada and US only) or International Money Orders payable to Gen O'Neil.

How to Submit Submit 5 poems at a time. Lines/poem: 3 minimum, 40 maximum. Accepts previously published poems and simultaneous submissions. Prefers e-mail submissions but accepts "anything that is neatly typed or printed. Electronic submissions can be sent in html or plain text (pasted into body of message; no attachments). All 'snail mail' work must be neatly typed on white paper with your name and address on every page. Please include SASE (or SAE with IRCs)." Submit seasonal poems well in advance. Time between acceptance and publication is 2 months. Guidelines available on website. "We guarantee that at least one poem from each submission will be printed in our publication. All work appears in the print copy first, and two weeks later online." Pays one contribtor's copy.

Advice "We look for poetry that is visible—poetry you can see and touch and feel."

⚡ ◻ 360 DEGREES

2012 Edgewater Dr., Charlotte NC 28210. E-mail: threesixtydegreesreview@yahoo.com. Established 1993. **Contact:** Karen Kinnison, managing editor.

Magazine Needs *360 Degrees* is a biannual review containing literature and artwork. "We are dedicated to keeping the art of poetic expression alive. No real limits on poetry, only the limits of the submitter's imagination." However, does not want to see "greeting card verse, simplified emotions, or religious verse." Has published poetry by Sean Brendan-Brown, Lyn Lifshin, and Rochelle Holt. *360 Degrees* is 40 pages, digest-sized, neatly printed, saddle-stapled. Receives about 1,000 poems/year, accepts about 100. Press run is 200 (100 subscribers, one library). Subscription: $10. Sample: $5.

How to Submit Submit 3-6 poems at a time. Include SASE. Accepts simultaneous submissions ("Just let us know if a particular piece you have submitted to us has been accepted elsewhere."); no previously published poems. Accepts submissions by e-mail (as attachment or pasted into body of message). Cover letter is preferred. Seldom comments on rejected poems. Guidelines available in magazine, for SASE, by e-mail, or on website. Responds within 6 months. Pays one contributor's copy.

Advice "The quality of the poetry we publish is often very high, often very innovative, and thought-provoking."

$◻ THE THREEPENNY REVIEW

P.O. Box 9131, Berkeley CA 94709. (510)849-4545. Website: www.threepennyreview.com. Established 1980. **Contact:** Wendy Lesser, poetry editor.

• Work published in this review has also been included in *The Best American Poetry* and *Pushcart Prize* anthologies.

Magazine Needs *Threepenny Review* "is a quarterly review of literature, performing and visual arts, and social articles aimed at the intelligent, well-read (but not necessarily academic) reader. Nationwide circulation." Wants "formal, narrative, short poems (and others). Prefer under 100 lines. No bias against formal poetry, in fact a slight bias in favor of it." Has published poetry by Anne Carson, Frank Bidart, Seamus Heaney, Robert Pinsky, and Louise Glück. Features about 10 poems in each 36-page tabloid issue. Receives about 4,500 submissions of poetry/year, accepts about 12. Press run is 10,000 (8,000 subscribers, 150 libraries). Subscription: $25. Sample: $12.

How to Submit Submit up to 5 poems at a time. Do not submit mss September through December. Guidelines available for SASE or on website. Responds in up to 2 months. Pays $100/poem plus one-year subscription. Acquires first serial rights. "Send for review guidelines (SASE required)."

⚡ $◻ TICKLED BY THUNDER, HELPING WRITERS GET PUBLISHED SINCE 1990

14076-86A Ave., Surrey BC V3W 0V9 Canada. E-mail: info@tickledbythunder.com. Website: www.tickledbythunder.com. Established 1990. **Contact:** Larry Lindner, editor/publisher.

Magazine Needs *Tickled by Thunder* appears up to 4 times/year, using poems about "fantasy particularly; writing or whatever. Require original images and thoughts. Keep them short (up to 40 lines)—not interested in long, long poems. Nothing pornographic, childish, unimaginative. Welcome humor and creative inspirational verse." Has published poetry by Laleh Dadpour Jackson and Helen Michiko Singh. *Tickled by Thunder* is 24 pages, digest-sized, published on Macintosh. Has 1,000 readers/subscribers. Subscription: $12/4 issues. Sample: $2.50.

How to Submit Include 3-5 samples of writing with queries. No e-mail submissions. Cover letter is required with submissions; include "a few facts about yourself and brief list of publishing credits." Editor comments on rejected poems "80% of the time." Guidelines available for SASE or on website. Responds in up to 6 months. Pays 2¢/line, $2 maximum. Acquires first rights. Reviews books of poetry in up to 300 words. Open to unsolicited reviews. Send materials for review consideration.

Contest/Award Offerings Offers a poetry contest 4 times/year. Prize: cash, publication, and subscription. **Entry fee:** $5 for one poem; free for subscribers. **Deadlines:** the 15th of February, May, August, and October.

Also Offers Publishes author-subsidized chapbooks. "We are interested in student poetry and publish it in our center spread: *Expressions*." Send SASE (or SAE and IRC) for details.

◪ TIGER'S EYE PRESS; TIGER'S EYE: A JOURNAL OF POETRY

P.O. Box 2935, Eugene OR 97402. E-mail: tigerseyepoet@yahoo.com. Website: www.tigerseyejourn al.com. Established 2001. **Contact:** Colette Jonopulos and JoAn Osborne, editors.

Magazine Needs *Tiger's Eye: A Journal of Poetry* is a biannual journal featuring both established and unknown poets. "Besides publishing the work of several poets in each issue, we feature 3 poets in interviews, giving the reader insight into their lives and writing habits." Wants "both free verse and traditional forms, no restrictions on subject or length. Poems with distinct imagery and viewpoint are preferred." Does not want overly erotic, violent, or sentimental poetry. Accepts poetry "from young people ages 14 and up; please notify editors if under 18." Has published poetry by David Morse, Andrea L. Watson, Ruth Moon Kempher, and Ace Boggess. *Tiger's Eye* is digest-sized (expanded to accommodate longer lines), saddle-stapled. Receives about 1,000 poems/year, accepts about 100. Press run is 200. Single copy: $5; subscription: $10/2 issues. Make checks payable to Tiger's Eye Press.

How to Submit Submit up to 5 poems at a time. Accepts simultaneous submissions with notification; no previously published poems. No e-mail or disk submissions. Cover letter is required. "We respond only if a SASE is included with submission." Reads submissions year round; deadlines are February 28 and August 31. Time between acceptance and publication is 3 months. "All poems are read by the editors, divided into acceptances, rejections, or maybes. Our 3 featured poets are chosen, then letters and e-mails are sent out." Seldom comments on rejected poems. Guidelines available in magazine or on website. Responds in 6 months. Always sends prepublication galleys. Pays one contributor's copy to each poet, 2 to featured poets. Acquires one-time rights.

Contest/Award Offerings Offers biannual poetry contest with prizes of $100, $50, and $25. Submit 3 poems, 2 copies of each, plus bio, cover letter, and SASE. **Entry fee:** $10. Each entrant receives one copy of *Tiger's Eye* (winners receive 2). **Deadlines:** February 28 and August 31 (same as for journal). Judged by independent judge.

Advice "We accept poems from new poets with as much enthusiasm as from established poets. Poems with clean images, unique subjects, and strong voices have a good chance of being published in *Tiger's Eye*."

◖ TIMBER CREEK REVIEW

8969 UNCG Station, Greensboro NC 27413. E-mail: timber_creek_review@hoopsmail.com. Established 1994. **Contact:** John M. Freiermuth, editor. Associate Editor: Roslyn Willett.

Magazine Needs *Timber Creek Review* appears quarterly, publishing short stories, literary nonfiction, and poetry. Wants all types of poetry. Does not want religious or pornographic poetry. Has published poetry by Louis Bourgeois, Brian Tighe, E.G. Burrows, Louis Phillips, Rowe Carenen, and Tony Barnstone. *Timber Creek Review* is 80-84 pages, digest-sized, laser-printed, stapled, with colored paper cover. Receives about 800 poems/year, accepts about 5%. Press run is 150 (120 subscribers, 2 libraries, 30 shelf sales). Single copy: $4.50; subscription: $16. Make checks payable to J.M. Freiermuth.

How to Submit Submit 3-4 poems at a time. Lines/poem: 3 minimum. Accepts simultaneous submissions; no previously published poems. No fax, e-mail, or disk submissions. Cover letter is required. Reads submissions year round. Submit seasonal poems 10 months in advance. Time between acceptance and publication is 1-3 months. Never comments on rejected poems. Occasionally publishes theme issues. Guidelines available for SASE or by e-mail. Responds in up to 6 months. Pays one contributor's copy. Acquires first North American serial rights.

Advice "Turn off your TV and read that poety magazine that published your last poem, and maybe someone else will read your poem, too!"

☒ $☑ TIMBERLINE PRESS

6281 Red Bud, Fulton MO 65251. (573)642-5035. Website: www.timberlinepress.com. Established 1975. **Contact:** Clarence Wolfshohl, poetry editor.

Book/Chapbook Needs "We do limited letterpress editions with the goal of blending strong poetry with well-crafted and designed printing. We lean toward natural history or strongly imagistic nature poetry but will look at any good work. Also, good humorous poetry." Has published *Annuli* by William Heyen, *Trance Arrows* by James Bogan, *Time Travel Reports* by Charles Fishman, and *Harmonic Balance* by Walter Bargen. Sample copies may be obtained by sending $7.50, requesting sample copy, and noting you saw the listing in *Poet's Market*. Responds in under one month. Pays "50-50 split with author after Timberline Press has recovered its expenses."

How to Submit Query before submitting full ms.

☑ ◎ TIME OF SINGING, A MAGAZINE OF CHRISTIAN POETRY (Specialized: literary religious)

P.O. Box 149, Conneaut Lake PA 16316. E-mail: timesing@zoominternet.net. Website: www.timeof singing.bizland.com. Established 1958-1965, revived 1980. **Contact:** Lora H. Zill, editor.

Magazine Needs *Time of Singing* appears 4 times/year. "Collections of uneven lines, preachy statements, unstructured 'prayers,' and trite sing-song rhymes usually get returned. I look for poems that 'show' rather than 'tell.' The viewpoint is unblushingly Christian—but in its widest and most inclusive meaning." Wants free verse and well-crafted rhyme; would like to see more forms. Has published poetry by John Grey, Luci Shaw, Bob Hostetler, Frances P. Reid, Barbara Crooker, and Charles Waugaman. *Time of Singing* is 44 pages, digest-sized, offset from typescript. Receives over 800 submissions/year, accepts about 175. Press run is 300 (150 subscribers). Subscription: $17 US, $21 (US) for Canada, and $30 (US) for overseas. Sample: $4, or 2 for $6 postage paid.

How to Submit Submit up to 5 poems at a time, single-spaced. "I prefer poems under 40 lines, but will publish up to 60 lines if exceptional." Accepts previously published poems (say when/where appeared) and simultaneous submissions. Accepts e-mail submissions (pasted into body of message). Time between acceptance and publication is up to one year. Editor comments "with suggestions for improvement if close to publication." Guidelines available for SASE, by e-mail, or on website. Responds in 2 months. Pays one contributor's copy.

Contest/Award Offerings Sponsors theme contests for specific issues. Guidelines available for SASE, by e-mail, or on website.

Advice "Study the craft. Be open to critique. A poet is often too close to his/her work and needs a critical, honest eye. *Time of Singing* publishes more literary-style verse, not greeting card style."

☑ TITAN PRESS; MASTERS AWARDS

Box 17897, Encino CA 91416. E-mail: ucla654@yahoo.com. Website: www.titanpress.info. Established 1980. **Contact:** Stephani Wilson, publisher.

Book/Chapbook Needs & How to Submit Titan Press is "a small press presently publishing 6-7 works per year, including poetry, photojournals, calendars, novels, etc. We look for quality, freshness, and that touch of genius." In poetry, "we want to see verve, natural rhythms, discipline, impact, etc. We are flexible, but verbosity, triteness, and saccharine make us cringe. *We now read and publish only manuscripts accepted from the Masters Award.*" Has published books by Bebe Oberon, Walter Calder, Exene Vida, Scott A. Sonders, Carlos Castenada, and Sandra Gilbert. Their tastes are for poets such as Adrienne Rich, Li-Young Lee, Charles Bukowski, Scott A. Sonders, and

Czeslaw Milosz. "We have strong liaisons with the entertainment industry and like to see material that is media-oriented and au courant."

Contest/Award Offerings "We sponsor the Masters Awards, established in 1981, which awards an annual grand prize of $1,000; plus each winner (and the 5 runners-up in poetry) may be published on our website or in a clothbound edition and distributed to selected university and public libraries, news mediums, etc. There is a one-time-only **$15 administration and reading fee** per entrant. Submit a maximum of 5 poems or song lyric pages (no tapes) totaling no more than 150 lines. Any poetic style or genre is acceptable, but a clear and fresh voice, discipline, natural rhythm, and a certain individuality should be evident. Further details and application available for a #10 SASE."

Advice "Please study what we publish before you consider submitting."

TOUCHSTONE LITERARY JOURNAL (Specialized: bilingual/foreign language; form/style; translations); PANTHER CREEK PRESS

P.O. Box 130233, The Woodlands TX 77393-0233. E-mail: panthercreek3@hotmail.com. Website: www.panthercreekpress.com. Established 1975. **Contact:** William Laufer, poetry editor. Managing Editor: Guida Jackson. (Mail for book projects should be sent to Panther Creek Press, P.O. Box 130233, Panther Creek Station, Spring TX 77393-0233, attn: Guida Jackson.)

Magazine Needs *Touchstone Literary Journal* is an annual, appearing in December, that publishes "experimental or well-crafted traditional forms, including sonnets, and translations. No light verse or doggerel." Has published poetry by Paul Christensen, Walter McDonald, Paul Ramsey, Omar Pound, and Christopher Woods. *Touchstone* is 100 pages, digest-sized, flat-spined, professionally printed in small, dark type, with glossy card cover. Subscription: $9.

How to Submit "At present we are overstocked and will accept no new submissions until 2006." Submit 5 poems at a time. "Cover letter telling something about the poet piques our interest and makes the submission seem less like a mass mailing." Sometimes sends prepublication galleys. Pays 2 contributor's copies. Reviews books of poetry. Send materials for review consideration to review editor.

Book/Chapbook Needs & How to Submit Panther Creek Press also publishes an occasional chapbook. Recent titles include *Living on the Hurricane Coast* by Robb Jackson, *The Mottled Air* by Paul Christensen, *Leopards, Oracles, and Long Horns: Three West African Epic Cycles* by chichi layor, *Watching the Worlds Go By, Selected Poems* by Omar Pound, and *Under a Riverbed Sky* by Christopher Woods. "Query first, with SASE. Absolutely no mail is answered without SASE or e-mail address. **At present we are overstocked and will accept no new submissions until 2006.**"

TRANSCENDENT VISIONS (Specialized: people living with mental illness)

251 S. Olds Blvd., 84-E, Fairless Hills PA 19030-3426. (215)547-7159. Established 1992. **Contact:** David A. Kime, editor.

Magazine Needs *Transcendent Visions* appears 1-2 times/year "to provide a creative outlet for psychiatric survivors/ex-mental patients." Wants "experimental, confessional poems; strong poems dealing with issues we face. Any length or subject matter is OK, but shorter poems are more likely to be published. No rhyming poetry." Has published poetry by J. Quinn Brisben, Kelley Jean White, Ruth Deming, and James Michael Ward. *Transcendent Visions* is 24 pages, magazine-sized, photocopied, corner-stapled, with paper cover. Receives about 100 poems/year, accepts 20%. Press run is 200 (50 subscribers). Subscription: $6. Sample: $3. Make checks payable to David Kime.

How to Submit Submit 5 poems at a time. Accepts previously published poems and simultaneous submissions. Cover letter is preferred. "Please tell me something unique about you, but I do not care about all the places you have been published." Time between acceptance and publication is 6 months. Guidelines available for SASE. Responds in 4 months. Pays one contributor's copy. Acquires first or one-time rights. Staff reviews books and chapbooks of poetry and other magazines in 20 words. Send materials for review consideration.

Also Offers "I also publish a zine called *Crazed Nation*, featuring essays concerning mental health issues."

Advice "Find your own voice. Please send camera-ready poems, single-spaced. I don't like poems that go all over the page."

☑ TRESTLE CREEK REVIEW

English Dept., LKH 204-G, North Idaho College, 1000 W. Garden Ave., Coeur d'Alene ID 83814-2199. (208)769-7877. Fax: (208)769-3431. E-mail: lawallin@nic.edu. Established 1982-83. **Contact:** Lori Wallin, editor.

Magazine Needs *Trestle Creek Review* is a "2-year college creative writing program production. Purposes: 1) expand the range of publishing/editing experience for our small band of writers; 2) expose them to editing experience; 3) create another outlet for serious, beginning writers. We're fairly eclectic and accept poetry, fiction, and creative nonfiction. We favor poetry strong on image and sound; spare us the romantic, the formulaic, and the clichéd." Has published poetry by Sean Brendan-Brown, E.G. Burrows, Ron McFarland, and Mary Winters. *Trestle Creek Review* is a 57-page annual, digest-sized, professionally printed on heavy buff stock, perfect-bound, with matte cover with art. Receives 100 submissions/year, accepts about 30. Press run is 300-600. Subscription: $5. Sample: $5.

How to Submit Submit 3-5 poems at a time. No previously published poems or simultaneous submissions. Accepts e-mail submissions (as attachment in Word or .rtf format); no fax submissions. **Deadline:** February 28 (for May publication). Responds by May 30. Pays 2 contributor's copies.

Advice "Be neat; be precise; don't romanticize or cry in your beer; strike the surprising, universal note. Know the names of things."

✪ ☑ ◎ TRIBUTARIES (Specialized: students of Illinois Wesleyan University only)

English Dept., Illinois Wesleyan University, Bloomington IL 61702. E-mail: iwutributaries@hotmail.com. Website: www.iwu.edu/~tribut. Established 2001. **Contact:** Editors.

Magazine Needs *Tributaries* appears biannually in April and December. "We are a magazine meant to showcase the diverse talents of Illinois Wesleyan University's students and add to the greater body of the fine arts. Poetry we have published ranges from the highly experimental to the highly formal. Diversity, originality, and a sense of the poet being comfortable with his or her voice are several criteria we use to distinguish the poetry we select. We are inclusive and accept submissions from all majors, genders, races, grades, and sexual orientations." Has published poetry by Rick Boutcher, Marke Heine, Jessica Kramer, and Rachelle Street. *Tributaries* (print version) is about 100 pages, 8½×5½. Special *Tributaries* material also appears online with color graphics. Press run is 600; distributed free to IWU students and literary magazines.

How to Submit Accepts previously published poems and simultaneous submissions. Accepts e-mail submissions. Cover letter is required. "Include a cover letter with your name and e-mail address if you submit via campus mail." Reads submissions "generally September 1 to October 15 and January 1 to February 15." Time between acceptance and publication is about 2 months. "All work has the author's name removed prior to judging in order to ensure an anonymous selection process." Seldom comments on rejected poems. Guidelines available by e-mail. Responds in one month. Pays 3 contributor's copies.

Advice "Poetry should be well crafted, make no mistake about that. Too many poets today, however, are either accomplished technical writers or very emotional writers. Write poetry that appeals to the emotions as well as the intellect. Always pay attention to the work of other writers and learn what you can from it."

✪ ☐ ◎ TRIBUTARIES: A JOURNAL OF NATURE WRITING; CUYAHOGA VALLEY NATURE WRITERS

c/o Cuyahoga Valley National Park Association, 1403 West Hines Hill Rd., Peninsula OH 44264. Website: www.cvnpa.org. Established 1998.

Magazine Needs *Tributaries: A Journal of Nature Writing* is an annual publication of the Cuyahoga Valley Nature Writers Workshop. Wants "poems addressing some aspect of nature or human relationships with the natural world." Has published poetry by Kathryn Brock, Linda C. Ehrlich, Robert

Farmer, Joseph McLaughlin, Jean Spencer, and Gerald R. Wheeler. *Tributaries* is about 50 pages, digest-sized, saddle-stapled, with color cardstock cover. Single copy: $7. Available from the Cuyahoga Valley National Park Association (see website).

How to Submit Submit 3-5 poems at a time. Accepts simultaneous submissions "if identified as such"; no previously published poems. Cover letter is required. "Give your name, mailing address, phone number, and e-mail address in the cover letter. Do not include your name on the pages containing your poems. Type each poem on a separate 8½×11 page in plain font, single-spaced. Include a SASE **and a $5 reading fee**. Make check payable to Cuyahoga Valley National Park Association. Writers whose work is accepted will be asked to supply a brief biographical note and sign a release certifying the work is their own and has not been published elsewhere." Reads submissions January through July annually. Poems are circulated to a 5-person editorial committee. Guidelines available for SASE. Responds in October of each year by letter.

Also Offers "Cuyahoga Valley Nature Writers is a volunteer group of local and regional writers and provides workshop opportunities for writers in the area to present and discuss their prose and poetry. In keeping with the mission of the park, the principal focus of the group is on the natural world and all living things on our planet. The Cuyhoga Valley Nature Writers Workshop is co-sponsored by the National Park Service at Cuyahoga Valley National Park and Cuyahoga Valley National Park Association."

⊠ ◔ TRUE POET MAGAZINE

P.O. Box 7387, Buffalo Grove IL 60089-7387. (847)229-1622. Fax: (847)919-3846. E-mail: submissions@truepoetmagazine.com. Website: www.truepoetmagazine.com. Established 2003. **Contact:** Michelle Ailene True, managing editor.

Magazine Needs *True Poet Magazine*, published monthly online, is "dedicated to publishing high-quality, insightful poetry by new and established writers." Wants "meaningful poetry that 'says something,' shows good use of metaphor, and is a clever use of words." Has published poetry by Janet Leonard, Susan Rippe, Marie Kazalia, Pat Paulk, Pushpa Ratna Tuladhar, and Aurora Antonovic.

How to Submit Submit no more than 3 poems/month. Lines/poem: 60 maximum, including spaces between stanzas. Accepts previously published poems (include exact name of publication where poem appeared) and simultaneous submissions. Accepts e-mail submissions (pasted into body of message); no fax or disk submissions. Reads submissions year round. "Submissions must be received between the 1st and 25th of the month to be considered for publication in the next month's issue." Submit seasonal poems 2 months in advance. Time between acceptance and publication is 3 weeks. Never comments on rejected poems. Guidelines available on website. No payment. Acquires first, one-time, and/or reprint rights "depending on the circumstances."

Contest/Award Offerings "We may do quarterly theme contests in the future; information will be posted on the website."

Advice "Poets should aspire to be masters of the English language. Your work should reflect that! Before submitting your poetry for publication, make sure you have fine-tuned your poem; eliminate any typos, and correct grammar and punctuation."

◔ TULANE REVIEW

122 Norman Mayer, New Orleans LA 70118. (504)865-5160. Fax: (504)862-8958. E-mail: litsoc@tulane.edu. Website: www.tulane.edu/~litsoc. Established 1988. **Contact:** Jason Horn, editor.

• *Tulane Review* is the recipient of an AWP Literary Magazine Design Award.

Magazine Needs *Tulane Review* is a national biannual literary journal seeking quality submissions of prose, poetry, and art. "We consider all types of poetry, but prefer poems between 1-2 pages. We favor imaginative poems with bold, inventive images." Has published poetry by Virgil Suárez, Tom Chandler, Gaylord Brewer, and Ryan Van Cleave. *Tulane Review* is 80 pages, 7×9, perfect-bound, with 100# cover with full-color artwork. Receives about 1,200 poems/year, accepts about 30. Single copy: $5; subscription: $10. Make checks payable to *Tulane Review*.

How to Submit Submit up to 6 poems at a time. Accepts simultaneous submissions; no previously published poems. No fax, e-mail, or disk submissions. Cover letter is required. "Include brief biography." Reads submissions year round. Time between acceptance and publication is 2 months. "Poems are reviewed anonymously by a review board under a poetry editor's supervision. Recommendations are given to the editor, who makes final publication decisions." Often comments on rejected poems. Guidelines available in magazine, for SASE, by e-mail, or on website. Responds in 2 months. Pays 3 contributor's copies. Acquires first North American serial rights.

TUNDRA: THE JOURNAL OF THE SHORT POEM (Specialized: poetry of 13 or fewer lines, including haiku and tanka)

22230 NE 28th Place, Sammamish WA 98074-6408. E-mail: WelchM@aol.com. Established 1999. **Contact:** Michael Dylan Welch, editor/publisher.

Magazine Needs *Tundra: The Journal of the Short Poem* is a biannual journal showcasing all short poetry, including haiku, tanka, and other genres. Wants "short poetry of 13 or fewer lines rooted in immediate and objective imagery, including haiku and tanka." Does not want religious, topical, or confessional poetry. Has published poetry by Dana Gioia, X.J. Kennedy, Jane Hirshfield, Peter Pereira, Robert Bly, and Madeleine DeFrees. *Tundra* is 128 pages, digest-sized, offset-printed, perfect-bound, with glossy cover. Receives about 14,000 poems/year, accepts about .05%. Press run is 1,200 (700 subscribers, 10 libraries, 50 shelf sales); 10 are distributed free to places such as poetry centers. Single copy: $9; subscription: $21/3issues. Make checks payable to Michael D. Welch.

How to Submit Submit 3-5 poems at a time ("up to 10 is okay if as short as haiku"). No previously published poems or simultaneous submissions. Accepts e-mail submissions (pasted into body of message); no disk submissions. "Please include a #10 SASE with sufficient postage for return of the manuscript or for a response. Cover letters are optional—okay the first time you submit, but unnecessary thereafter unless you write something you are sure the editor needs to know. *Tundra* does not publish bios, so there's no need to include them except for the editor's information. For e-mail submissions, no attached files, please! Always include your full postal address with each e-mail submission." Reads submissions year round. Time between acceptance and publication "varies, but is sometimes up to a year. The editor makes the sole decision, and may occasionally offer suggestions on poems whether accepted or returned. The editor will clearly indicate if he wants to see a revision." Sometimes comments on rejected poems. "I recommend seeing an issue before submitting, but no purchase or subscription is required." Guidelines available for SASE or by e-mail. Responds in up to one month. Sometimes sends prepublication galleys. Pays one contributor's copy. Acquires first rights. "Rights revert to author after publication, but we in future want to include selected poems on a website." Reviews books and chapbooks of poetry in 500-2,000 words, single- and multi-book format. Send materials for review consideration to Michael Dylan Welch.

Advice "If your work centers on immediate and objective imagery, *Tundra* is interested. All submissions must be 13 or fewer lines, with only very rare exceptions (where each line is very short). If you think that a haiku is merely 5-7-5 syllables, then I do not want to see your work (see 'Becoming a Haiku Poet' online at www.haikuworld.org/begin/mdwelch.apr2003.html for reasons why). Due to the excessive volume of inappropriate submissions for *Tundra* in the past, I now encourage only well-established poets to submit."

TURKEY PRESS

6746 Sueno Rd., Isla Vista CA 93117-4904. Website: www.turkeypress.net. Established 1974. **Contact:** Harry Reese and Sandra Reese, poetry editors. "We do not encourage solicitations of any kind to the press. We seek out and develop projects on our own."

24.7; RE-PRESST

30 Forest St., Providence RI 02906. (401)521-4728. Established 1994. **Contact:** David Church, poetry editor. **Currently not accepting submissions**.

⬤ **TWO RIVERS REVIEW: TWO RIVERS REVIEW POETRY PRIZE; TWO RIVERS REVIEW POETRY CHAPBOOK PRIZE**

P.O. Box 158, Clinton NY 13323. E-mail: tworiversreview@juno.com. Website: http://trrpoetry.trip od.com. Established 1998. **Contact:** Philip Memmer, editor.

Magazine Needs *Two Rivers Review* appears biannually and "seeks to print the best of contemporary poetry. All styles of work are welcome, so long as submitted poems display excellence." Has published poetry by Billy Collins, Gary Young, Michael Waters, Meg Kearney, and Reginald Shepherd. *Two Rivers Review* is 44 pages, digest-sized, professionally printed on cream-colored paper, with card cover. Subscription: $10. Sample (current issue): $5. "Poets wishing to submit work may obtain a sample copy for the reduced price of $4."

How to Submit Submit no more than 4 poems at a time, with cover letter (optional) and SASE (required). Simultaneous submissions are considered with notification. No e-mail submissions. Guidelines available for SASE, by e-mail, or on website. Responds to most submissions within one month. Acquires first rights.

Contest/Award Offerings 1) The annual *Two Rivers Review* Poetry Prize; see website for details. 2) The annual *Two Rivers Review* Poetry Chapbook Prize, offering 1st Prize: $100, publication, and 25 author's copies; Editor's Prize: publication and 25 author's copies. Submit 20-25 pages of poetry. **Entry fee:** $10 ($15 outside US and Canada), includes a copy of the winning chapbook. Make checks payable to *Two Rivers Review*. **Deadline:** April 5. Guidelines available on website.

🚫 **THE U.S. LATINO REVIEW; HISPANIC DIALOGUE PRESS**

P.O. Box 150009, Kew Gardens NY 11415. E-mail: andrescastro@aol.com. Established 1999. Managing Editor: Andrés Castro. **U.S. Latino Review has ceased publication "due to illness and lack of financial support."**

📝 📷 **U.S. 1 WORKSHEETS; U.S. 1 POETS' COOPERATIVE (Specialized: regional/New Jersey and area surrounding U.S. 1 corridor)**

P.O. Box 127, Kingston NJ 08528-0127. Website: www.geocities.com/princetonpoets2001/index.ht ml. Established 1973. **Contact:** Nancy Scott, managing editor.

Magazine Needs *U.S. 1 Worksheets* is a literary annual that uses high-quality poetry and fiction. "We prefer complex, well-written work." Has published poetry by Alicia Ostriker, James Richardson, Jean Hollander, Lois Marie Harrod, Winifred Hughes, Charlotte Mandel, and Betty Lies. *U.S. 1 Worksheets* is 76 pages, digest-sized, saddle-stapled, with b&w cover art. "We read a lot but take very few." Subscription: $7/year, $12/2 years.

How to Submit Submit 5 poems at a time. No previously published poems or simultaneous submissions. "We use a rotating board of editors; we read April through June, and can no longer return manuscripts. Enclose SASE for reply." Guidelines available for SASE. Pays one contributor's copy.

Advice "Send us your best. Please note submission dates. We receive many good poems we cannot consider because they arrive far outside our submission dates."

🌐 📝 **UNDERSTANDING MAGAZINE; DIONYSIA PRESS LTD.**

20 A Montgomery St., Edinburgh, Lothian EH7 5JS England. Phone/fax: (0131)4780680. Established 1989. **Contact:** Denise Smith.

Magazine Needs *Understanding Magazine*, published once/year, features "poetry, short stories, parts of plays, reviews, and articles." Wants "original poetry." Has published poetry by Susanna Roxman, D. Zervanou, Thom Nairn, Alexis Stamatis, Byron Leodaris, and Keith Bennett. *Understanding* is A5 and perfect-bound. Receives 2,000 poems/year. Press run is 1,000 (500 subscribers). Single copy: £5.50; subscription: £11. Sample: £3. Make checks payable to Dionysia Press Ltd.

How to Submit Submit up to 5 poems at a time. Accepts simultaneous submissions; no previously published poems. Accepts fax submissions. Time between acceptance and publication is 6 months to a year. Poems are circulated to an editorial board. Often comments on rejected poems. Guidelines available for SASE or by fax. Responds in 6 months or more. Always sends prepublication galleys.

Pays one contributor's copy. Acquires all rights. Returns rights after publication. Staff reviews books or chapbooks of poetry or other magazines. Send materials for review consideration.

Book/Chapbook Needs & How to Submit Dionysia Press Ltd. publishes 2-10 paperbacks and chapbooks of poetry/year. "Sometimes we select from submissions or competitions." Has published *Let Me Sing My Song* by Paul Hullah, *Poems* by Klitos Kyrou (translated by Thom Nairn and D. Zervanou), *Broken Angels* by Susanna Roxman, and *The Feeble Lies of Orestes Chalkiopoulos* by Andreas Mitsou. Books are usually A5, perfect-bound, with hard covers with art. Query first, with a few sample poems and cover letter with brief bio and publication credits. Responds to queries in 2-6 months. Pays author's copies. "We usually get arts council grants, or poets get grants for themselves." For sample books or chapbooks, write to the above address.

Contest/Award Offerings Sponsors poetry competitions with cash prizes. Guidelines and themes available for SASE.

Advice "Be original."

✪ ⊘ THE UNIVERSITY OF CHICAGO PRESS; PHOENIX POETS SERIES

1427 E. 60th St., Chicago IL 60637. (773)702-7700. Fax: (773)702-2705. Website: www.press.uchicago.edu. Established 1891. **Contact:** Randolph Petilos, poetry editor.

Book/Chapbook Needs The University of Chicago Press publishes scholarly books and journals. "We may only publish 4 or 5 books in Phoenix Poets per year, and perhaps 2 or 3 books of poetry in translation per year. We occasionally publish a book of poems outside Phoenix Poets, or as a reprint from other houses." Has published poetry by Anne Winters, Alan Williamson, Susan Stewart, Michael Fried, Jason Sommer, and Gail Mazur.

How to Submit By invitation only. No unsolicited mss.

✪ ⊘ UNIVERSITY OF IOWA PRESS; THE IOWA POETRY PRIZES

100 Kuhl House, 119 West Park Rd., Iowa City IA 52242-1000. (319)335-2000. E-mail: uipress@uiowa.edu. Website www.uiowapress.org.

Contest/Award Offerings The University of Iowa Press offers the annual Iowa Poetry Prizes for book-length mss (50-150 pages) by new or established poets. Winners will be published by the Press under a standard royalty contract. Winning entries for 2004 were *The Waiting* by Megan Johnson and *Ledger* by Susan Wheeler. All writers of English are eligible. Poems from previously published books may be included only in mss of selected or collected poems, submissions of which are encouraged. Accepts simultaneous submissions if press is immediately notified if the book is accepted by another publisher. **Entry fee:** $20. **Deadline:** postmarked during April only. Guidelines available on website.

⊘ UNIVERSITY OF WISCONSIN PRESS; BRITTINGHAM PRIZE IN POETRY; FELIX POLLAK PRIZE IN POETRY

Dept. of English, University of Wisconsin, 600 N. Park St., Madison WI 53706. Website: www.wisc.edu/wisconsinpress/index.html. Brittingham Prize inaugurated in 1985. **Contact:** Ronald Wallace, poetry editor.

Contest/Award Offerings The University of Wisconsin Press publishes primarily scholarly works, but they offer the annual Brittingham Prize and the Felix Pollak Prize, both $1,000 plus publication. These prizes are the only way in which this press publishes poetry. Rules available for SASE or on website. Qualified readers will screen all mss. Winners will be selected by "a distinguished poet who will remain anonymous until the winners are announced in mid-February." Past judges include Rita Dove, Alicia Ostriker, Mark Doty, Ed Hirsch, Kelly Cherry, and Robert Bly. Winners include Tony Hoagland, Stephanie Strickland, Derick Burleson, Cathy Colman, Greg Rappleye, Roy Jacobstein, and Anna Meek. For both prizes, **submit between September 1 and September 30**, unbound ms volume of 50-80 pages, with name, address, and telephone number on title page. No translations. Poems must be previously unpublished in book form. Poems published in journals, chapbooks, and anthologies may be included but must be acknowledged. There is a non-refundable

$25 entry fee which must accompany the ms. (Checks to University of Wisconsin Press.) Mss will not be returned. Contest results available for SASE. "Previous winners of the prizes may submit subsequent book manuscripts between November 1 and November 30."
Advice "Each submission is considered for both prizes (one entry fee only)."

THE UNKNOWN WRITER

P.O. Box 698, Ramsey NJ 07446. E-mail: unknown_writer_2000@yahoo.com. Website: www.fyrefl yjar.net/uw.html. Established 1995. **Contact:** Amy Van Orden, poetry editor. "Please note that we are on hiatus until further notice and will not be able to read the submissions that have come in. Authors who sent submissions via our postal box will receive their work back if return envelopes were provided. We will not be able to reply to submissions sent via e-mail. We do plan to print pieces we accepted before our hiatus, and we will contact those authors about their pieces when we can. Please check our website periodically, as we will post news when our status changes. We thank you for your patience and understanding."

★ ✉ ◐ UNMUZZLED OX

43B Clark Lane, Staten Island NY 10304 or Box 550, Kingston ON K7L 4W5 Canada. (212)226-7170. Established 1971. **Contact:** Michael Andre, poetry editor.
Magazine Needs & How to Submit *Unmuzzled Ox* is a tabloid literary biannual. Each edition is built around a theme or specific project. "The chances of an unsolicited poem being accepted are slight since I always have specific ideas in mind." Has published poetry by Allen Ginsberg, Robert Creeley, and Denise Levertov. Subscription: $20. Only unpublished work will be considered, but poems may be in French as well as English.
Advice "I suggest contributors read carefully an issue before sending in an unsolicited manuscript."

Ⓝ ◯ UP AND UNDER: THE QND REVIEW

93 S. Main St., Medford NJ 08055. E-mail: qndpoets@yahoo.com. Website: www.quickanddirtypoe ts.com. Established 2004. **Contact:** Rachel Bunting, editor.
Magazine Needs *Up and Under: The QND Review*, published annually in March, is "a journal with an eclectic mix of poetry: sex, death, politics, IKEA, Mars, food, and jug handles alongside a smorgasbord of other topics covered in such diverse forms as the sonnet, villanelle, haiku, and free verse. We are interested in excellent poetry with no bias between free verse or traditional forms." Does not want "greeting card verse, graphic pornography." Has published poetry by Dan Maguire, Gina Larkin, Bruce Niedt, and Anna Evans. *Up and Under* is 50-60 pages, digest-sized, laser-printed, saddle-stapled, with card cover with photograph, includes ads. Receives about 300 poems/year, accepts about 30 (or 10%). Press run is 100. Single copy: $7. Make checks payable to Rachel Bunting.
How to Submit Submit up to 5 poems at a time. Lines/poem: no limit. Accepts simultaneous submissions (with notification); no previously published poems. Accepts e-mail submissions (pasted into body of message). Reads submissions September 1 through December 30. Time between acceptance and publication is 3-6 months. Poems are circulated to an editorial board. Sometimes comments on rejected poems. Guidelines available in magazine, for SASE, or on website. Responds in 2-3 months. Pays one contributor's copy. Acquires one-time rights.
Advice "At least read the poems featured on our website before submitting. We prefer poetry that uses concrete imagery to engage all five senses."

⊕ ▨ ◎ URTHONA MAGAZINE (Specialized: Buddhism)

9A Auckland Rd., Cambridge CB5 8DW United Kingdom. Phone: (01223) 309470. E-mail: urthonam ag@onetel.com. Website: www.urthona.com. Established 1992. **Contact:** Poetry Editor.
Magazine Needs *Urthona*, published biannually, explores the arts and Western culture from a Buddhist perspective. Wants "poetry rousing the imagination." Does not want "undigested autobiography, political, or New-Agey poems." Has published poetry by Peter Abbs, Robert Bly, and Peter Redgrove. *Urthona* is 60 pages, A4, offset-printed, saddle-stapled, with 4-color glossy cover,

includes ads. Receives about 300 poems/year, accepts about 40. Press run is 1,200 (200 subscribers, plus shelf sales in Australia and America). "See website for current subscription rates." Sample (including guidelines): $7.99 US, $8.99 Canadian.

How to Submit Submit 6 poems at a time. No previously published poems or simultaneous submissions. Accepts submissions by e-mail (as attachment). Cover letter is preferred. Time between acceptance and publication is up to 8 months. Poems are circulated to an editorial board and read and selected by poetry editor. Other editors have right of veto. Responds within 6 months. Pays one contributor's copy. Acquires one-time rights. Reviews books or chapbooks of poetry or other magazines in 600 words. Send materials for review consideration.

◖ UTAH STATE UNIVERSITY PRESS; MAY SWENSON POETRY AWARD

Logan UT 84322-7800. (435)797-1362. Fax: (435)797-0313. E-mail: michael.spooner@usu.edu. Website: www.usu.edu/usupress. Established 1972. **Contact:** Michael Spooner, poetry editor.

Contest/Award Offerings Utah State University Press publishes poetry books through the annual May Swenson Poetry Award competition only. Has published *Dear Elizabeth* and *May Out West* by May Swenson, *The Owl Question* by Faith Shearin, *The Hammered Dulcimer* by Lisa Williams, *Borgo of the Holy Ghost* by Stephen McLeod, and *She Took Off Her Wings and Shoes* by Suzette Marie Bishop. Guidelines available on website.

◖ VAL VERDE PRESS

30163 Lexington Dr., Castaic CA 91384. E-mail: woeltjen@thevine.net. Established 2003. **Contact:** Lance Woeltjen, editor/publisher. "We publish perfect-bound, quality paperback titles. We are not accepting unsolicited submissions at this time."

⚔ ⚑ $◖ VALLUM: CONTEMPORARY POETRY

P.O. Box 48003, Montreal QC H2V 4S8 Canada. E-mail: vallummag@sympatico.ca. Website: www.vallummag.com. Established 2000. **Contact:** Joshua Auerbach and Helen Zisimatos, editors.

Magazine Needs *Vallum* appears biannually. "We are looking for poetry that's fresh and edgy, something that reflects contemporary experience and is also well-crafted. Open to most styles. We publish new and established poets." Has published poetry by Stephen Dunn, Charles Bernstein, Erin Mouré, Medbh McGuckian, George Elliott Clarke, and Eamon Grennan. *Vallum* is 92 pages, $7 \times 8\frac{1}{2}$, digitally printed, perfect-bound, with color images on coated stock cover. Press run is 2,500. Single copy: $7 US, $8.25 Canadian; subscription: $14 US, $16.50 Canadian. Make checks payable to *Vallum*.

How to Submit Submit 5-8 poems at a time. No previously published poems or simultaneous submissions. No fax or e-mail submissions. Cover letter is preferred. Include SASE (or SAE and IRC). Time between acceptance and publication is up to one year. Sometimes comments on rejected poems. Occasionally publishes theme issues. Guidelines and upcoming themes available on website. Responds in 6-9 months. Pays honorarium and one contributor's copy. Acquires first North American serial rights. Reviews books and chapbooks of poetry in 500-700 words. Send materials for review consideration. Essays on poetics also considered.

Advice "Hone your craft, read widely, be original."

◖ VALPARAISO POETRY REVIEW: CONTEMPORARY POETRY AND POETICS

Dept. of English, Valparaiso University, Valparaiso IN 46383-6493. (219)464-5278. Fax: (219)464-5511. E-mail: vpr@valpo.edu. Website: www.valpo.edu/english/vpr/. Established 1999. **Contact:** Edward Byrne, editor.

Magazine Needs *Valparaiso Poetry Review* is "a biannual online poetry journal accepting submissions of unpublished or previously published poetry, book reviews, author interviews, and essays on poetry or poetics that have not yet appeared online and for which the rights belong to the author. Query for anything else." Wants poetry of any length or style, free verse or traditional forms. Has published poetry by Charles Wright, Jonathan Holden, Reginald Gibbons, Janet McCann, Laurence

Lieberman, Beth Simon, and Margot Schilpp. *Valparaiso Poetry Review* is published online only. Receives about 2,000 poems/year, accepts about 7%.

How to Submit Submit 3-5 poems at a time (no more than 5). Accepts previously published poems ("original publication must be identified to ensure proper credit") and simultaneous submissions. Accepts e-mail submissions (but prefers postal mail; for e-mail, paste into body of message, no attachments); no fax or disk submissions. Cover letter is preferred. Include SASE. Reads submissions year round. Time between acceptance and publication is 6-12 months. Seldom comments on rejected poems. Guidelines available on website. Responds in up to 6 weeks. Acquires one-time rights. "All rights remain with author." Reviews books of poetry in single- and multi-book format. Send materials for review consideration.

🌐 🗐 VAN GOGH'S EAR: BEST WORLD POETRY & PROSE

French Connection Press, 12 rue Lamartine, Paris 75009 France. Phone: (+33)1 40 16 05 35. Fax: (+33)1 40 16 07 01. E-mail: frenchcx@tiscali.fr. Website: www.frenchcx.com. Established 2002. **Contact:** Ian Ayres, founder/editor.

● Poetry published in *VAN GOGH'S EAR* also appears in *The Best American Poetry 2004.*

Magazine Needs *VAN GOGH'S EAR* is an annual anthology series, appearing in January, "devoted to publishing excellent poetry and prose in English by major voices and innovative new talents from around the globe. Without affiliation with specific movements or schools, we seek only to publish the best work being written. The anthology welcomes all poetry, from traditional to experimental; daring, thought-provoking poetry of unusual forms and language genius." Has published poetry by Yoko Ono, John Ashbery, Maya Angelou, Leonard Cohen, Joyce Carol Oates, and John Rechy. *VAN GOGH'S EAR* is 220 pages, digest-sized, digitally-printed, perfect-bound, with 4-color matte cover with commissioned artwork. Receives about 1,000 poems/year, accepts about 10%. Press run is 2,000 (130 subscribers, 13 libraries, 1,750 shelf/online sales); 120 are distributed free to contributors and reviewers. Single copy: $19; subscription: $36/2 years. Make checks payable to Committee on Poetry-VGE, P.O. Box 582, Stuyvesant Station, New York NY 10009.

How to Submit Submit 5 poems at a time, "to the French Connection Press address only!" Lines/poem: 165 maximum. No previously published poems or simultaneous submissions. No disk, fax, or e-mail submissions. Cover letter is preferred. "Please include SASE or e-mail address and a brief biography." Reads submissions January 1 through July 4. **Charges $10 (US) reading fee for nonsubscribers.** Time between acceptance and publication is one year. "Each and every poem is closely read by all members of the editorial board. The members initial each poem and mark an 'E' for excellent, 'G' for good, or an 'OK.' The 'excellent' and 'good' poems are read again with diversity in mind. Another vote is made upon which poems will make the upcoming volume the best one yet." Seldom comments on rejected poems. "Our continued existence, and continued ability to read your work, depends mainly on subscriptions/donations. Therefore, we must ask that you at least purchase a sample copy before submitting work." Guidelines available in anthology or on website. Responds in 9 months. Always sends prepublication galleys. Pays one contributor's copy. Acquires one-time rights.

Advice "We not only encourage the exploration of every possible approach to poetry and creative writing, but also going beyond anything yet imagined. The more daring the subject matter, the better. And we are very open to writers who haven't been published before. Being published isn't as important as the work itself."

◎ VEGETARIAN JOURNAL (Specialized: children/teens; vegetarianism); THE VEGETARIAN RESOURCE GROUP

P.O. Box 1463, Baltimore MD 21203. Website: www.vrg.org. Established 1982.

Magazine Needs The Vegetarian Resource Group is a publisher of nonfiction. *Vegetarian Journal* is a quarterly, 36 pages, magazine-sized, professionally printed, saddle-stapled, with glossy card cover. Press run is 20,000. Sample: $3.

How to Submit "Please, no submissions of poetry from adults; 18 and under only."

Contest/Award Offerings The Vegetarian Resource Group offers an annual contest for ages 18 and under: $50 savings bond in 3 age categories for the best contribution on any aspect of vegetarianism. "Most entries are essay, but we would accept poetry with enthusiasm." **Postmark deadline:** May 1. Details available for SASE.

VEHICLE PRESS; SIGNAL EDITIONS (Specialized: regional/Canada)

P.O. Box 125 Station Place du Parc, Montreal QC H2X 4A3 Canada. (514)844-6073. Fax: (514)844-7543. E-mail: vp@vehiculepress.com. Website: www.vehiculepress.com. **Contact:** Carmine Starnino, poetry editor. Publisher: Simon Dardick.

Book/Chapbook Needs Vehicle Press is a "literary press with a poetry series, Signal Editions, publishing the work of Canadian poets only." Publishes flat-spined paperbacks and hardbacks. Has published *White Stone: The Alice Poems* by Stephanie Bolster (winner of the 1998 Governor-General's Award for Poetry), *Araby* by Eric Ormsby, and *Fielder's Choice* by Elise Partridge. Publishes Canadian poetry that is "first-rate, original, content-conscious."

How to Submit Query before submitting.

VERANDAH

c/o Faculty of Arts, Deakin University, 221 Burwood Hwy., Burwood, Victoria, Australia 3125. Phone: 61.3.9251.7134. E-mail: verandah@deakin.edu.au. Website: www.deakin.edu.au/verandah. Established 1986. **Contact:** Poetry Editor.

Magazine Needs *Verandah* appears annually in September and is "a high-quality literary journal edited by professional writing students. It aims to give voice to new and innovative writers and artists." Has published poetry by Christos Tsiolka, Dorothy Porter, Seamus Heaney, Les Murray, Ed Burger, and Joh Muk Muk Burke. *Verandah* is 120 pages, professionally printed on glossy stock, flat-spined, with full-color glossy card cover. Sample: AU$15.

How to Submit Accepts submissions by postal mail *only*. **Annual deadline:** May 31. **Reading fee:** AU$5 (or AU$10 for 3 poems); Deakin University students exempted ("please provide student number!"). Pays one contributor's copy, "with prizes awarded accordingly." Acquires first Australian publishing rights.

VERSE

Dept. of English, University of Georgia, Athens GA 30602. Website: http://versemag.blogspot.com. Established 1984. **Contact:** Brian Henry and Andrew Zawacki, editors.

- Poetry published in *Verse* has also appeared in *The Best American Poetry* and *Pushcart Prize* anthologies.

Magazine Needs *Verse* appears 3 times/year and is "an international poetry journal which also publishes interviews with poets, essays on poetry, and book reviews." Wants "no specific kind; we look for high-quality, innovative poetry. Our focus is not only on American poetry, but on all poetry written in English, as well as translations." Has published poetry by James Tate, John Ashbery, Barbara Guest, Gustaf Sobin, and Rae Armantrout. *Verse* is 128-416 pages, digest-sized, professionally printed, perfect-bound, with card cover. Receives about 5,000 poems/year, accepts 1%. Press run is 1,000 (600 subscribers, 200 libraries, 200 shelf sales). Single copy: $10; subscription: $18 for individuals, $36 for institutions. Sample: $6.

How to Submit Submit up to 5 poems at a time, no more than twice/year. Accepts simultaneous submissions; no previously published poems. Cover letter is required. Time between acceptance and publication is up to 18 months. Often comments on rejected poems. "The magazine often publishes special features—recent features include younger American poets, Mexican poetry, Scottish poetry, Latino poets, prose poetry, women Irish poets, and Australian poetry—but does not publish 'theme' issues." Guidelines available on website. Responds within 4 months. Always sends prepublication galleys. Pays 2 contributor's copies plus a one-year subscription. Send materials for review consideration.

Publishers of Poetry

Advice "Read widely and deeply. Avoid inundating a magazine with submissions; constant exposure will not increase your chances of getting accepted."

VIA DOLOROSA PRESS; ERASED, SIGH, SIGH. (Specialized: form/free verse; "dark" poetry and death)

701 E. Schaaf Rd., Cleveland OH 44131-1227. E-mail: viadolorosapress@aol.com. Website: www.viadolorosapress.com. Established 1994. **Contact:** Ms. Hyacinthe L. Raven, editor.

Magazine Needs *Erased, Sigh, Sigh.*, appearing biannually in January and July, is a literary journal "showcasing free verse poetry/fiction with a dark tinge. Our theme is death/suicide." Prefers "free verse poetry that is very introspective and dark. We do not publish light-hearted works. No traditional or concrete poetry. Vampire poems will be thrown away." Has published poetry by John Sweet, Karen Porter, Scott Urban, and Lara Haynes. *Erased, Sigh, Sigh.* is about 40 pages, digest-sized, Xerox-printed, saddle-stapled/hand-bound, with parchment paper cover. Receives 500 poems/year, accepts about 10%. Press run is 500-1,000 (75% are shelf sales); 25% are distributed free to "other journals for review and also to charity organizations." Single copy: $5 postpaid; subscription: $8/year US ($9 foreign), $15/2 years US ($17 foreign). Make checks and money orders payable to Via Dolorosa Press.

How to Submit Submit any number of poems at a time. Lines/poem: open. Accepts previously published poems and simultaneous submissions. No fax, e-mail, or disk submissions. Cover letter is preferred. "SASE required for response; we do not respond by e-mail." Reads submissions any time. Submit seasonal poems 6 months in advance. Time between acceptance and publication is up to one year. "Poems are chosen by the editor. Writers will receive an acceptance/rejection letter usually within a month of receipt." Often comments on rejected poems. Guidelines available on website. "Read our submission guidelines! We are strict about our theme and style. We also recommend reading a couple issues prior to considering us." Responds in 2 months. Pays one contributor's copy. Acquires one-time rights.

Book/Chapbook Needs & How to Submit Via Dolorosa Press publishes "poetry, fiction, and nonfiction with an existential/humanist feel. Darker works preferred." Has published *Seasons of Rust* by John Sweet, *Ghostwhispers* by Karen Porter, and *Sestina* by Lara Haynes. Publishes 2-10 chapbooks/year. Chapbooks are usually 10-50 pages, photocopied or offset-printed, saddle-stapled or hand-bound, with card stock, parchment, or other cover. "We ask that poets review our submission guidelines first. Then, if they think their work is fitting, we prefer to read the entire manuscript to make our decision." Responds to queries in 2 months; to mss in 4 months. Pays royalties of 25% plus 10% of press run. "See submission guidelines—our payment terms are listed there." Catalog available on website.

Advice "If you are repeatedly rejected because editors label your work as 'too depressing,' try us before you give up! We want work that makes us feel and that makes us think."

VIGIL; VIGIL PUBLICATIONS

17 Vineys Yard, Bruton, Somerset BA10 0EU England. Established 1979. **Contact:** John Howard Greaves, poetry editor.

Magazine Needs *Vigil* appears 2 times/year. Wants "poetry with a high level of emotional force or intensity of observation. Poems should normally be no longer than 40 lines. Color, imagery, and appeal to the senses should be important features. No whining self-indulgent, neurotic soul-baring poetry. Form may be traditional or experimental." Has published poetry by Michael Newman, Claudette Bass, David Flynn, Sheila Murphy, and Karen Rosenberg. *Vigil* is 40 pages, digest-sized, saddle-stapled, professionally printed, with colored matte card cover. Receives about 400 poems/year, accepts about 60. Press run is 250 (85 subscribers, 6 libraries). Subscription: £8. Sample: £3.

How to Submit Submit up to 6 poems at a time in typed form. No previously published poems. Sometimes comments on rejected poems. Guidelines available in magazine or for SASE (or SAE and IRC). Sometimes sends prepublication galleys. Pays 2 contributor's copies.

Book/Chapbook Needs & How to Submit Query regarding book publication by Vigil Publications. Offers "appraisal" for £10 for a sample of a maximum of 6 poems.

$ 🖰 THE VIRGINIA QUARTERLY REVIEW; EMILY CLARK BALCH PRIZE

1 West Range, P.O. Box 400223, Charlottesville VA 22904-4223. (434)924-3124. Fax: (434)924-1397. Website: www.virginia.edu/vqr. Established 1925. **Contact:** David Lee Rubin (chairman), Angie Hogan, and Karen Kevorkian, poetry board.

Magazine Needs *The Virginia Quarterly Review* uses about 45-50 pages of poetry in each issue. No length or subject restrictions. Issues have largely included lyric and narrative free verse, most of which features a strong message or powerful voice. *The Virginia Quarterly Review* is 200-300 pages, digest-sized, flat-spined. Press run is 4,000. **How to Submit** Submit up to 5 poems, with SASE. "You will *not* be notified otherwise." No simultaneous submissions. Responds in 3 months or longer "due to the large number of poems we receive." Guidelines and upcoming themes available for SASE, by e-mail, or on website; do not request by fax. Pays $5/line.

Contest/Award Offerings Also sponsors the Emily Clark Balch Prize, an annual award of $1,000 given to the best poem published in the *Review* during the year. 2003 winner was Charles Harper Webb.

🌟 🌐 🖰 ◎ VOICES ISRAEL (Specialized: anthology); INTERNATIONAL REUBEN ROSE MEMORIAL POETRY COMPETITION; MONTHLY POET'S VOICE (Specialized: members)

Kibbutz Amiad, Galil Elyon, 12335 Israel. E-mail: berman@amiad.org.il. Website: www.voicesisrael.com. Established 1972. **Contact:** Tom Berman, editor-in-chief.

Magazine Needs The Voices Israel Group of Poets in English publishes *Voices Israel*, "an annual anthology of poetry in English, with contributions worldwide. We consider all kinds of poetry." Has published poetry by Dannie Abse, Shin Shalom, Roger White, Gad Yaacobi, Alan Sillitoe, and Kathleen Raine. *Voices Israel* is about 125 pages, digest-sized, offset from laster output on ordinary paper, flat-spined, with varying cover. Press run is 350. Subscription: $15. Sample $10. "Members receive the anthology with annual dues (US $25)."

How to Submit Submit up to 4 poems/year. Lines/poem: 40 maximum. "Send 7 hard copies, for distribution to the Editorial Board. If possible, poems should also be sent by e-mail. We accept previously published poems, but please include details and assurance that copyright problems do not exist. No reading fee, but a contribution of US $10 for up to 4 poems is requested. This is not mandatory and will not affect acceptance or rejection of poems. Poems must be in English. If you submit a translation, please attach a copy of the original poem." Submissions are read from August 1 to October 31 annually. "We reply to all submissions but do not return poems. We do not guarantee publication of any poem. In poems that we publish, we reserve the right to correct obviously unintentional errors in spelling, punctuation, etc."

Contest/Award Offerings The annual International Reuben Rose Memorial Poetry Competition

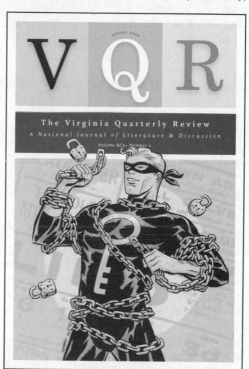

Managing editor Kevin Morrissey says this cover for *The Virginia Quarterly Review* (Volume 80, Number 2) "was chosen for its visual impact. It also reflects the new look of *VQR* in light of its redesign." Artist: Eric Wight. Designer: Percolator Graphic Design.

offers 1st Prize: $300; 2nd Prize $150; 3rd Prize: $100; 4th Prize: $50; Honorable Mentions. Winning poems are published and distributed together with the *Voices Israel* anthology (as a separate booklet). Send poems of up to 40 lines each to John Dicks, P.O. Box 236, Kiriat ATA, 28101 Israel (john_d@netvision.net.il). "Submit 2 copies of each poem: one with name and address, one with no identifying information. Enclose a cover letter providing the name(s) of the poem(s) submitted, your full name, address, and phone number." **Entry fee:** $5/poem. Make checks payable to *Voices*. **Deadline:** September 30. Guidelines available on website.

Also Offers *Monthly Poet's Voice*, a broadside edited by Ezra Ben-Meir, Herzl 45, Nahariya, 22406 Israel (ezrab_m@hotmail.com). "This newsletter is sent only to members of the Voices Israel Group of Poets in English."

⬡ ◖ VOICES LITERARY MAGAZINE; PERSPECTIVES WRITING COMMUNITY

E-mail: editor@1writersway.org. Website: http://1writersway.org. Established 2001. **Contact:** Kristen M. Biss, editor.

Magazine Needs *Voices Literary Magazine* is an online publication "dedicated to the passionate spirit of creation. Each quarterly issue features poetry, art, and photography, available online and in e-book form." Wants "inspired, original poetic expressions. Say something no one has ever said before, or approach a common subject from a new perspective. Poems should be primarily image-driven and concise. Your love of language and sound should be evident in the way you use words in your writing. We consider formal and free verse, with a preference for free verse." Does not want "sing-song verse." Has published poetry by Durlabh Singh, Doug Tanoury, Michael Ladanyi, Bill Chene, and Amanda Auchter. Receives about 700 poems/year, accepts about 7%. Press run is 400 for e-mail subscribers; freely available online.

How to Submit Submit 2-5 poems at a time. Lines/poem: prefers between 10-30. Accepts previously published poems and simultaneous submissions. Accepts e-mail submissions (pasted into body of message; no attachments); no disk submissions. Cover letter is preferred. "If you wish, include 2-3 sentences of bio information (location, previous publications, etc.) with your submission." Reads submissions year round. Submit seasonal poems 8 months in advance. Time between acceptance and publication is 6-8 weeks. Never comments on rejected poems. Guidelines available by e-mail or on website. Responds in 4 months. No payment. Acquires one-time rights and archival rights.

Also Offers "Perspectives Writing Community offers free online poetry and prose workshops. Drop-in and weekly guided workshops for writers of all levels."

◖ VOICINGS FROM THE HIGH COUNTRY; HIGH COUNTRY WORD CRAFTERS

4920 S. Oak St., Casper WY 82601. Established 2000. **Contact:** Ella J. Cvancara, editor.

Magazine Needs *Voicings from the High Country* appears annually in the spring. Wants "poetry with substance, not just pretty words; understandable, rather than obscure; poetry that goes beyond the self. Biased toward free verse that is worldly rather than introspective, tells a story, and uses many/most/all of the 5 senses." Also accepts haiku for a haiku page. No "rhyming, pornography, violent language, 'Hallmark' verse, political poems, or overtly religious poetry. No poetry that's unsure of why it was written, is demeaning to the human spirit, or untitled." Has published poetry by guest poets David Lee, the first poet laureate of Utah, and Robert Roripaugh, former poet laureate of Wyoming. *Voicings from the High Country* is 35-40 pages, digest-sized, computer-generated, stapled, with 110-lb. cardstock cover. Receives about 200 poems/year, accepts about 15%. Press run is 75 (45 shelf sales); 30 distributed free to contributors. Single copy: $5. Make checks payable to Ella J. Cvancara.

How to Submit Submit 3 poems at a time. Lines/poem: 35 maximum. Accepts previously published poems; no simultaneous submissions. No fax, e-mail, or disk submissions. Cover letter is required with a 3- to 5-line bio. "Submit each poem on a separate page with name and address in upper right corner; typed or computer-generated; include SASE for response." Reads submissions July 1 through February 1 *only*. Time between acceptance and publication is 3 months. "Poems are circulated to a 3-member editorial board with the names of the poets removed. They are ranked according to a ranking system." Seldom comments on rejected poems. Guidelines available for SASE. Responds in 6 months. Pays one contributor's copy. Acquires one-time rights.

Advice "Beginners often write about themselves. Reach beyond yourself, avoid clichés, search for fresh language. Use metaphor and simile. Strike a spark with words."

[N] VOX; VOX PROSE POEM AWARD

P.O. Box 527, Oxford MS 38655. E-mail: voxjournal@hotmail.com. Established 2004. **Contact:** Louis E. Bourgeois, Max B. Hipp, and J.E. Pitts, editors.

Magazine Needs *VOX* is published biannually. Wants "lyrical/experimental anti-narrative [poetry]. Originality is key. We are seeking new voices that truly stand out from the crowd." Does not want "workshop conformity, watered-down Dada and Surrealism, or greeting card verse. Rhymed verse is discouraged unless exceptional." Has published poetry by André Breton, Ann Fisher-Wirth, Robert Krut, Gertrude Halstead, and Eve Rifkah. *VOX* is 50 pages, digest-sized, laser-printed, perfect-bound, with glossy color cover with photography (b&w and color), includes ads. Receives about 1,000 poems/year, accepts about 5%. Press run is 500. Single copy: $7.50; subscription: $15. Make checks payable to VOX Publications.

How to Submit Submit 3-5 poems or 3 short prose pieces at a time. Lines/poem: 60 lines maximum for poetry; 1,000 words maximum for prose poetry. Accepts previously published poems and simultaneous submissions. Accepts e-mail submissions (pasted into body of message; no attachments); no disk submissions. Cover letter is preferred. Include SASE. Reads submissions year round. Time between acceptance and publication is 6 months. Poems are circulated to an editorial board. Sometimes comments on rejected poems. Guidelines available in magazine or by e-mail. Responds in up to 4 months. Sometimes sends prepublication galleys. Pays one contributor's copy and a discount on additional issues. Acquires one-time rights. Reviews books and chapbooks of poetry and other magazines/journals in 500 words, single-book format. Send materials for review consideration to J.E. Pitts.

Contest/Award Offerings Sponsors the annual *VOX* Prose Poem Award. Offers 1st Prize: $250; 2nd Prize: $150; 3rd Prize: $50. Submit up to 10 pages of short prose, no single piece more than 1,000 words. **Entry fee:** $12. **Deadline:** September 15. Guidelines available by e-mail. "All finalists will be published in *VOX*, and all submissions to the contest will be considered for publication."

VQONLINE (Specialized: volcanoes and volcanology)

8009 18th Lane SE, Lacey WA 98503. (360)455-4607. E-mail: jmtanaka@webtv.net. Website: http://community.webtv.net/JMTanaka/VQ. Established 1992. **Contact:** Janet M. Cullen Tanaka, editor.

Magazine Needs *VQOnline* is an "interest" publication for professional and amateur volcanologists and volcano buffs. Wants "any kind of poetry as long as it is about volcanoes and/or the people who work on them." Does not want "over-emotive, flowery stuff or anything not directly pertaining to volcanoes." Has published poetry by Margarita Engle and Michael Craig. Published online only.

How to Submit Submit any number of poems. Accepts previously published poems, with permission of the original copyright holder, and simultaneous submissions. Accepts disk (ASCII compatible) and e-mail (pasted into body of message, no attachments) submissions. Time between acceptance and publication is "usually about" 6 months. Always comments on rejected poems. "I try not to outright reject, preferring to ask for a rewrite." Guidelines available for SASE, by e-mail, or on website. Responds in one month. Pays in contributor's copies. "There is as yet no mechanism on the Internet to keep users honest, but we do give you the copyright." Send materials for review consideration if subject is volcanoes.

Advice "I want to concentrate on the positive aspects of volcanoes—gifts from God, 'partners' in creation, resources, beauty, awe, etc."

WAKE UP HEAVY (WUH); WAKE UP HEAVY PRESS

P.O. Box 4668, Fresno CA 93744-4668. E-mail: wuheavy@yahoo.com. Established 1998. **Contact:** Mark Begley, editor/publisher.

Magazine Needs *Wake Up Heavy* is not currently publishing magazine issues, nor accepting submissions for the magazine. The first 4 issues of *Wake Up Heavy* included poetry/prose by Laura Chester, Wanda Coleman, Fielding Dawson, Edward Field, Michael Lally, and Diane Wakoski. ''These out-of-print issues are available through the Web at www.abebooks.com. Many of the poems published have been reprinted in major collections by these authors; most notably, 3 poems by Wanda Coleman that originally appeared in the premier issue of the magazine and were later reprinted in her National Book Award-nominated collection *Mercurochrome* (Black Sparrow Press, 2001). Any other questions about future magazine publications should be sent to the above e-mail address.''

How to Submit *Wake Up Heavy* is currently not accepting submissions of any kind; the magazine has been halted indefinitely.

Book/Chapbook Needs & How to Submit ''Chapbooks and broadsides by single authors have become our main focus. Wake Up Heavy Press has published chapbooks/pamphlets of single poems (Michael Lally's long prose poem *¿Que Pasa Baby?*; Diane Wakoski's *Trying to Convince Robert* and *Inviting John & Barbara*), groups of poems, stories (Wanda Coleman's *Crabs for Breakfast*; Fielding Dawson's *The Dirty Blue Car* and *Backtalk*), memoirs (Wanda Coleman's Pushcart Prize-nominated *Love-ins with Nietzsche*), and chapters from novels (Laura Chester's *Kingdom Come*).'' Wake Up Heavy Press publishes 2-3 chapbooks/pamphlets per year. Chapbooks/pamphlets are usually copied/offset-printed, saddle-stapled, with heavy coverstock, some contain drawings or photos, and most include a signed/numbered edition. ''Again, these titles are available via the Web at www.abebooks.com. Also, you can e-mail about upcoming publications/the availability of past ones. Chapbooks, pamphlets, and broadsides are *strictly from solicitations. Please do not send manuscripts for these publications.*'' Wake Up Heavy Press pays authors in copies, 50% of the press run, which is usually between 130-200 copies. Inquire about samples at the above e-mail address.

★ ☑ WARTHOG PRESS

77 Marlboro St., Belmont MA 02478. (617)484-0336. Established 1979. **Contact:** Patricia Fillingham, poetry editor.

Book/Chapbook Needs Warthog Press publishes paperback books of poetry ''that are understandable, poetic.'' Has published *From the Other Side of Death* by Joe Lackey, *Wishing for the Worst* by Linda Portnay, *Enemies of Time* by Donald Lev, and *Hanging On* by Joe Benevento.

How to Submit Query with 5 samples, cover letter, and SASE. ''A lot of the submissions I get seem to be for a magazine. I don't publish anything but books.'' Accepts simultaneous submissions. Manuscript should be ''readable.'' Comments on rejected poems, ''if asked for. People really don't want criticism.''

Advice ''The best way to sell poetry still seems to be from poet to listener.''

★ ⊞ ◯ ◎ WASAFIRI (Specialized: ethnic/nationality)

Dept. of English, Queen Mary, University of London, Mile End Rd., London E1 4NS United Kingdom. Phone/fax: +44 020 7882 3120. E-mail: wasafiri@qmw.ac.uk. Website: www.wasafiri.org. Established 1984. **Contact:** Susheila Nasta, editor. Managing Editor: Richard Dyer.

Magazine Needs *Wasafiri*, published in March, July, and November, ''promotes new writing and debate on African, Asian, Caribbean, and associated literatures.'' Wants ''African, Asian, Caribbean, diaspora, post-colonial, innovative, high-quality poetry, fiction, reviews, and articles.'' Has published poetry by Vikram Seth, Fred D'Aguiar, Marlene Nourbese Philip, and Kamau Brathwaite. *Wasafiri* is 80 pages, A4, professionally printed on coated stock, perfect-bound, with full-color glossy cover, includes ads. Receives about 350 poems/year, accepts about 30%. Press run is 1,500 (1,000 subscribers, 450 libraries, 300 shelf sales); 50 distributed free to arts council literature panel and education board. Single copy: £7; subscription: £21 individuals, £27 institutions/overseas, £42 UK institutions, £54 overseas institutions.

How to Submit Submit 3 poems at a time. No simultaneous submissions. Accepts submissions by postal mail and on disk (Word or WordPerfect). Cover letter is required. Time between acceptance and publication is 6-12 months. ''Poems are considered by the editor and managing editor. Where guest editors are involved, poetry is considered by them also. Associate editors with expertise are asked to participate also.'' Often comments on rejected poems. Publishes theme issues. Guidelines and upcoming themes available for SAE and IRC, by e-mail, or on website. Themes for future issues include ''Translation and Film'' and ''African Literature.'' Responds in up to 6 months. Sometimes sends prepublication galleys. Pays one contributor's copy. Acquires all rights. Returns rights with editor's permission. Reviews books or chapbooks of poetry or other magazines. Send materials for review consideration.

WASHINGTON SQUARE, A JOURNAL OF THE ARTS

New York University Graduate Creative Writing Program, 19 University Place, Room 219, New York NY 10003. E-mail: washington.square.journal@nyu.edu. Website: http://cwp.fas.nyu.edu/page/wsr. Established 1994 as *Washington Square* (originally established in 1979 as *Ark/Angel*). **Contact:** Maria Filippone, editor.

Magazine Needs Published in December and May, *Washington Square* is ''a non-profit literary journal publishing fiction, poetry, and essays by new and established writers. It's edited and produced by the students of the NYU Creative Writing Program.'' Wants ''all poetry of serious literary intent.'' Has published poetry by Billy Collins, Rick Moody, A.E. Stalling, Dana Levin, Timothy Lin, and Arthur Sze. *Washington Square* is about 150 pages. Press run is 2,000. Subscription: $10/year (individuals), $12/year (institutions). Sample: $6 (current), $5 (back issue).

How to Submit Name and contact information should appear on every page. Accepts simultaneous submissions if noted. Accepts submissions by postal mail only. ''Submit all material with cover letter and SASE.'' Reads submissions year round. Time between acceptance and publication is up to 6 months. ''The editorial staff read all submissions, discuss, and decide which poems to include in the journal.'' Guidelines available for SASE or by e-mail. Responds within 4 months; ''slower during university holidays.'' Pays 2 contributor's copies and a one-year subscription. Acquires first North American serial rights.

Advice ''Keep in mind that the staff changes each academic year.''

WATER MARK PRESS

138 Duane St., New York NY 10013. Established 1978. **Contact:** Coco Gordon, editor. Currently does not accept any unsolicited poetry.

- Note: Please do not confuse Water Mark Press with the imprint Watermark Press, used by other businesses.

WATERWAYS: POETRY IN THE MAINSTREAM (Specialized: themes); TEN PENNY PLAYERS (Specialized: children/teens/young adults); BARD PRESS

393 St. Paul's Ave., Staten Island NY 10304-2127. (718)442-7429. E-mail: tenpennyplayers@SI.RR.com. Website: www.tenpennyplayers.org. Established 1977. **Contact:** Barbara Fisher and Richard Spiegel, poetry editors.

Magazine Needs Ten Penny Players publishes poetry by adult poets in *Waterways*, a magazine that is published 11 times/year. ''We publish theme issues and are trying to increase an audience for poetry and the printed and performed word. The project produces performance readings in public spaces and is in residence year round at the New York public library with workshops and readings. We publish the magazine *Waterways*, anthologies, and chapbooks. We are not fond of haiku or rhyming poetry; never use material of an explicit sexual nature. We are open to reading material from people we have never published, writing in traditional and experimental poetry forms. While we do 'themes,' sometimes an idea for a future magazine is inspired by a submission, so we try to remain open to poets' inspirations. Poets should be guided, however, by the fact that we are children's and animal rights advocates and are a NYC press.'' Has published poetry by Ida Fasel, Albert Huffstickler, Joy Hewitt Mann, and Will Inman. *Waterways* is 40 pages, $4\frac{1}{4} \times 7$, photocopied from various type styles, saddle-stapled, with matte card cover. Accepts 60% of poems submitted. Press run is 150 (58 subscribers, 12 libraries). Subscription: $25. Sample: $2.60.

How to Submit Submit less than 10 poems for first submission. Accepts simultaneous submissions.

Accepts e-mail submissions (pasted into body of message). Guidelines for upcoming themes available for SASE. "Since we've taken the time to be very specific in our response, writers should take seriously our comments and not waste their emotional energy and our time sending material that isn't within our area of interest. Sending for our theme sheet and a sample issue and then objectively thinking about the writer's own work is practical and wise. Manuscripts that arrive without a return envelope are not sent back." Editors sometimes comment on rejected poems. Responds in less than one month. Pays one contributor's copy. Acquires one-time publication rights.

Book/Chapbook Needs & How to Submit Chapbooks published by Ten Penny Players are "by children and young adults only—*not by submission*; they come through our workshops in the library and schools. Adult poets are published through our Bard Press imprint, *by invitation only*. Books evolve from the relationship we develop with writers we publish in *Waterways* and whom we would like to give more exposure."

Advice "We suggest that poets attend book fairs and check our website. It's a fast way to find out what we are publishing. Without meaning to sound 'precious' or unfriendly, the writer should understand that small press publishers doing limited editions and all production work inhouse are working from their personal artistic vision and know exactly what notes will harmonize, effectively counterpoint, and meld. Many excellent poems submitted to *Waterways* are sent back to the writers because they don't relate to what we are trying to create in a given month."

⬤ WAVELENGTH: POEMS IN PROSE AND VERSE

1753 Fisher Ridge Rd., Horse Cave KY 42749-9706. Established 1999. **Contact:** David P. Rogers, editor/publisher.

Magazine Needs *Wavelength: Poems in Prose and Verse* appears 3 times/year. "We want poems that use lively images, intriguing metaphor, and original language. Long poems OK; would like to see more prose poems. Rhyme is almost always a liability. All subjects and styles considered as long as the poem is thought-provoking or uses language in an innovative way." Does not want "rhymed, very religious—anything that sacrifices creativity for convention." Has published poetry by Robert Cooperman, Lyn Lifshin, Francis Blessington, Ann Taylor, Albert Haley, and Virgil Suárez. *Wavelength* is 35 pages, digest-sized, laser-printed, perfect-bound, with heavy cardstock cover with illustration. Receives about 450 poems/year, accepts 5-10%. Press run is 100 (25 subscribers, 20-25 shelf sales); 50 distributed free to the public. Single copy: $6; subscription: $15. Make checks payable to Dr. David P. Rogers.

How to Submit Submit 1-5 poems at a time. Lines/poem: 30 maximum. Accepts previously published poems and simultaneous submissions, "but please do *not* withdraw the poem after we've accepted it." No e-mail or disk submissions. Cover letter is preferred. "SASE or no response. Brief bio preferred. Poet's name and address must appear on every page. Poets who want poems returned should include sufficient postage." Submit seasonal poems 3 months in advance. Time between acceptance and publication is up to one year. Seldom comments on rejected poems. "Please do *not* write for guidelines. Just send a courteous submission following the guidelines in this listing." Responds in 4 months. Pays one contributor's copy. Acquires one-time rights. Reviews books and chapbooks of poetry in 100-150 words, single-book format. Send materials for review consideration.

Advice "Read and write every day. If a poem still seems good a year after you wrote it, send it out. Be original. Say something clever, and ask what will the *reader* get out of it? Editor has a weakness for synesthesia."

⭐ $⬤ WēBER STUDIES—VOICES AND VIEWPOINTS OF THE CONTEMPORARY WEST

Weber State University, 1214 University Circle, Ogden UT 84408-1214. (801)626-6473. E-mail: webe rstudies@weber.edu. Website: http://weberstudies.weber.edu. Established 1983. **Contact:** Brad L. Roghaar, editor.

● Poetry published here has appeared in *The Best American Poetry*.

Magazine Needs *Weber Studies* appears 3 times/year and publishes fiction, poetry, criticism, personal essays, nonfiction, and interviews. It is an interdisciplinary journal interested in relevant works covering a wide range of topics. Wants "three or four poems; we publish multiple poems from a poet." Does not want "poems that are flippant, prurient, sing-song, or preachy." Has published poetry by William Kloefkorn, Gailmarie Pahmeier, Mark Strand, Janet Sylvester, David Lee, Gary Gildner, and Robert Dana. *Weber Studies* is 144 pages, 7½×10, offset-printed on acid-free paper, perfect-bound, with color cover. Receives about 150-200 poems/year, accepts 30-40. Press run is 1,200 (1,000 subscribers, 90 libraries). Subscription: $20, $30 institutions. Sample: $7-8.

How to Submit Submit 3-4 poems, 2 copies of each (one without name). Accepts simultaneous submissions; no previously published poems. Cover letter is preferred. Time between acceptance and publication is 15 months. Poems are selected by an anonymous (blind) evaluation. Seldom comments on rejected poems. Publishes theme issues. Upcoming themes and guidelines available in magazine, for SASE, by e-mail, or on website. Responds in up to 6 months. Always sends prepublication galleys. Pays $30-50/poem (depending on fluctuating grant monies) and 2 contributor's copies. Acquires all rights. Copyright reverts to author after first printing.

Contest/Award Offerings The Dr. Sherwin W. Howard Poetry Award, a $500 cash prize awarded annually to the author of the best set of poems published in *Weber Studies* during the previous year. The competition is announced each year in Spring/Summer issue.

Advice "This journal is referred by established poets—beginners not encouraged."

⚡ ⬙ ◎ THE WELL TEMPERED SONNET (Specialized: form/sonnets)

87 Petoskey St., Suite 120, New Hudson MI 48165. E-mail: welltemperedsonnet@yahoo.com. Established 1998. **Contact:** James D. Taylor II, editor/publisher.

Magazine Needs "Appearing biannually, *The Well Tempered Sonnet* publishes only compositions in sonnet form and caters to those who love and appreciate the form Shakespeare made famous. No erotica, blasphemy, vulgarity, or racism." *The Well Tempered Sonnet* is magazine-sized, desktop-published, spiral-bound, with attractive, heavy stock cover. Subscription: $20/year. Make checks payable to James Taylor. "We encourage submissions requesting subscriptions, details included in guidelines."

How to Submit Submit 4 poems at a time. Accepts previously published poems; no simultaneous submissions. Accepts submissions by postal mail only. Seldom comments on rejected poems. Occasionally publishes theme issues. Guidelines available for SASE. Responds ASAP. Always sends prepublication galleys.

Also Offers "We encourage and try to provide the means for interaction between other sonneteers."

Advice "A well composed sonnet is a piece of art. Understanding word usage is important in the development of the sonnet, as important as colors to a painter."

⚡ ⬙ $ ⬙ ◎ WEST COAST LINE (Specialized: form/style—experimental, innovative)

2027 EAA, Simon Fraser University, Burnaby BC V5A 1S6 Canada. (604)291-4287. Fax: (604)291-4622. E-mail: wcl@sfu.ca. Website: www.westcoastline.ca. Established 1990. **Contact:** Glen Lowry and Jarold Zaslove, editors. Managing Editor: Karen Earl.

Magazine Needs *West Coast Line* is published 3 times/year and "favors work by both new and established Canadian writers, but it observes no borders in encouraging original creativity. Our focus is on contemporary poetry, short fiction, criticism, and reviews of books." Has published poetry by Bruce Andrews, Dodie Bellamy, Clint Burnham, Lisa Robertson, Aaron Vidaver, and Rita Wong. *West Coast Line* is 144 pages, digest-sized, handsomely printed on glossy paper, flat-spined. Receives 500-600 poems/year, accepts about 20. Press run is 800 (500 subscribers, 350 libraries, 150 shelf sales). Single copy: $12; subscription: $30.

How to Submit Submit poetry ". . . in extended forms; excerpts from works in progress; experimental and innovative poems; to 400 lines." No previously published poems or simultaneous submissions. No e-mail submissions. Time between acceptance and publication is up to 8 months. Publishes theme issues. Guidelines available by e-mail or on website. Responds in 4 months. Pays $10 (Canadian)/printed page plus a one-year subscription and 2 contributor's copies. Manuscripts returned only if accompanied by sufficient Canadian postage or IRC.

Advice "We have a special concern for contemporary writers who are experimenting with, or expanding the boundaries of, conventional forms of poetry, fiction, and criticism. That is, poetry should be formally innovative. We recommend that potential contributors send a letter of inquiry before submitting a manuscript."

⬙ ◎ WEST END PRESS (Specialized: social/political concerns; multicultural)

P.O. Box 27334, Albuqueque NM 87125. (505)345-5729. Established 1976. **Contact:** John Crawford, publisher.

Book/Chapbook Needs & How to Submit West End Press publishes poetry, fiction, and drama with a social/cultural interest. Open as to form. Does not want "purely aesthetic, precious, self-involved poetry." Has published poetry by Julia Stein, Ken Waldman, William Witherup, Duane Niatum, and Laura Tohe. Publishes 2 poetry books/year; occasional chapbooks and anthologies. Books/chapbooks are 48-96 pages, offset-printed, perfect-bound, with glossy 4-color covers. Query first, with a few sample poems and a cover letter with brief bio and publication credits. Book/chapbook mss may include previously published poems. Responds to queries in 6 weeks; to mss in 3 months. Pays royalties of 6%; 10% author's copies (out of a press run of 600-1,500). Order sample books/chapbooks postage-free by sending $8.95 to West End Press.

Advice "May you live in interesting times."

▣ $◪ WESTERLY; PATRICIA HACKETT PRIZE

English, Communication, and Cultural Studies, University of Western Australia, Crawley, Western Australia 6009. Phone: (08)6488-2101. Fax: (08)6488-1030. E-mail: westerly@cyllene.uwa.edu.au. Website: http://westerly.uwa.edu.au. Established 1956. **Contact:** Mark Reid, poetry editor. Editors: Dennis Haskell and Delys Bird.

Magazine Needs *Westerly* is a literary and cultural annual, appearing in November, that publishes quality short fiction, poetry, literary critical, socio-historical articles, and book reviews with special attention given to Australia, Asia, and the Indian Ocean region. "We don't dictate to writers on rhyme, style, experimentation, or anything else. We are willing to publish short or long poems. We do assume a reasonably well-read, intelligent audience. Past issues of *Westerly* provide the best guides. Not consciously an academic magazine." *Westerly* is about 200 pages, digest-sized, "electronically printed." Press run is 1,200. Subscription: $16 (US), $23.95 (AUS).

How to Submit Submit up to 6 poems at a time. Accepts submissions by fax and e-mail (in an attached file, Word 6 format; if submission is short, include in body of e-mail). "Please do not send simultaneous submissions. Cover letters should be brief and non-confessional." **Deadline:** June 30. Time between acceptance and publication "can be up to one year depending on when work is submitted." Responds in 3 months. Pays minimum of AU$50 plus one contributor's copy. Acquires first publication rights; requests acknowledgment on reprints. Reviews books of poetry in multi-book format in an annual review essay. Send materials for review consideration.

Contest/Award Offerings The Patricia Hackett Prize (value approx. AU$750) is awarded annually for the best contribution published in the previous year's issue of *Westerly*.

Advice "Be sensible. Write what matters to you, but think about the reader. Don't spell out the meanings of the poems and the attitudes to be taken to the subject matter—i.e., trust the reader. Don't be swayed by literary fashion. Read the magazine, if possible, before sending submissions."

$◪ WESTERN HUMANITIES REVIEW

University of Utah, 255 S. Central Campus Dr., Room 3500, Salt Lake City UT 84112-0494. (801)581-6070. Fax: (801)585-5167. E-mail: whr@mail.hum.utah.edu. Website: www.hum.utah.edu/whr. Established 1947. **Contact:** David McGlynn, managing editor.

    ● Poetry published in this review has been selected for *The Best American Poetry* as well as the 2004 and 2005 *Pushcart Prize* anthologies.

Magazine Needs Appearing in April and October, *Western Humanities Review* is a semiannual publication of poetry, fiction, and a small selection of nonfiction. Wants "quality poetry of any form, including translations." Has published poetry by Scott Cairns, Philip Levine, Bin Ramke, Lucie Brock-Broido, Timothy Liu, John Hollander, and Barbara Hamby. *Western Humanities Review* is 112-144 pages, digest-sized, professionally printed on quality stock, perfect-bound, with coated card cover. Receives about 900 submissions/year, accepts less than 10%. Press run is 1,100 (1,000 subscribers, 900 libraries). Subscription: $16 to individuals in the US. Sample: $10.

How to Submit "We do not publish writer's guidelines because we think the magazine itself conveys an accurate picture of our requirements." Accepts simultaneous submissions; no previously published poems. No fax or e-mail submissions. Reads submissions October 1 through May 31 only. Time between acceptance and publication is 1-4 issues. Managing editor makes an initial cut, then the poetry editor makes the final selections. Seldom comments on rejected poems. Occasionally publishes special issues. Responds in up to 6 months. Pays $5/published page and 2 contributor's copies. Acquires first serial rights.

Contest/Award Offerings Sponsors an annual contest for Utah poets.

WESTVIEW: A JOURNAL OF WESTERN OKLAHOMA

100 Campus Dr., SWOSU, Weatherford OK 73096. Established 1981. **Contact:** James Silver, editor.

Magazine Needs *Westview* is a semiannual publication that is "particularly interested in writers from the Southwest; however, we are open to work of quality by poets from elsewhere. We publish free verse, prose poems, and formal poetry." Has published poetry by Carolynne Wright, Miller Williams, Walter McDonald, Robert Cooperman, Alicia Ostriker, and James Whitehead. *Westview* is 64 pages, magazine-sized, perfect-bound, with full-color glossy card cover. Receives about 500 poems/year, accepts 7%. Press run is 700 (300 subscribers, about 25 libraries). Subscription: $15/2 years. Sample: $5.

How to Submit Submit 5 poems at a time. Cover letter including biographical data for contributor's note is requested with submissions. Accepts submissions by postal mail only. Editor comments on submissions "when close." Manuscripts are circulated to an editorial board; "we usually respond within 4-6 months." Pays one contributor's copy.

$ WESTWARD QUARTERLY; LAUDEMONT PRESS

P.O. Box 250, Kirkland IL 60146. (800)440-4043. E-mail: wwquarterly@aol.com. Website: http://members.aol.com/wwquarterly. Established 1999 (under current name). **Contact:** Shirley Anne Leonard, editor.

Magazine Needs *WestWard Quarterly* is a family-oriented magazine publishing poetry and short stories. Wants "all forms—we welcome rhyming poems, sonnets, etc." Does not want "experimental or avant garde forms, offensive language, depressing or negative poetry." Accepts poetry written by children ("we have a special section for children's poetry each issue"). Has published poetry by Amanda Auchter, Margarita Engle, Phyllis Jean Green, Glenna Holloway, Nancy Martindale, Jane Stuart, and J. Alvin Speers. *WestWard Quarterly* is 24 pages, digest-sized, laser-printed, saddle-stapled, with inkjet color cover with scenic photos, includes ads. Receives about 700 poems/year, accepts about 20%. Press run is 100 (50 subscribers). Single copy: $3; subscription: $12/year, $15 foreign. Make checks payable to Laudemont Press.

How to Submit Submit up to 5 poems at a time. Lines/poem: up to 40. Accepts previously published poems and simultaneous submissions. Accepts e-mail submissions (pasted into body of message); no disk submissions. Reads submissions year round. Submit seasonal poems 3 months in advance. Time between acceptance and publication is "months." Often comments on rejected poems. Guidelines available for SASE, by e-mail, or on website. Responds in weeks. Pays $1-2 plus one contributor's copy. Acquires one-time rights.

Contest/Award Offerings *WestWard Quarterly* offers a quarterly prize of ½ of entry fees/contest. Submit poems up to 40 lines (except when specific forms requested, such as a sonnet). **Entry fee:** $1 for subscribers, $2 for nonsubscribers. **Deadline:** check guidelines (available in magazine, for SASE, by e-mail, or on website).

Advice "Every issue has an article on improving writing skills and/or writing different forms of poetry."

⊡ ⊙ WHISKEY ISLAND MAGAZINE

English Dept., Cleveland State University, Cleveland OH 44115. (216)687-2056. Fax: (216)687-6943. E-mail: whiskeyisland@csuohio.edu. Website: www.csuohio.edu/whiskey_island. Established 1968. Student editors change yearly. **Contact:** Poetry Editor.

Magazine Needs *Whiskey Island* appears biannually and publishes poetry, fiction, nonfiction, and art. Wants "writing that engages the reader immediately. It's always good to be interesting early." Has published poetry by Nin Andrews, Jim Daniels, Denise Duhamel, Alison Luterman, and Maureen McHughm. *Whiskey Island Magazine* is about 80 pages, digest-sized, professionally printed, perfect-bound, with glossy stock cover. Receives 1,000-1,500 poetry mss/year, accepts 6%. Press run is 1,200 (200 subscribers, 20 libraries, about 300 shelf sales). Subscription: $12, $20 overseas. Sample: $6. Make checks payable to *Whiskey Island Magazine*.

How to Submit Submit 3-5 poems. No previously published poems. Include cover letter with brief bio. Include SASE for reply only. Include name, address, e-mail, fax, and phone number on each page. Reads submissions year round. Poems are circulated to an editorial committee. Guidelines available in magazine, for SASE, by e-mail, or on website. Responds within 4 months. Pays 2 contributor's copies and one-year subscription.

Contest/Award Offerings Sponsors an annual poetry contest. 1st Prize: $300; 2nd Prize: $200; 3rd Prize: $100. **Entry fee:** $10. Entries accepted **October 1 through January 31**. Query regarding contest.

⊙ WHITE PELICAN REVIEW

P.O. Box 7833, Lakeland FL 33813. Established 1999. **Contact:** Nancy Wiegel, editor.

Magazine Needs *White Pelican Review* is a biannual poetry journal appearing in April and October, dedicated to publishing poetry of the highest quality. "*White Pelican Review* seeks writing that goes beyond competency to truly masterful acts of imagination and language." Has published poetry by Trent Busch, Denise Duhamel, William Doreski, Virgil Suárez, and Peter Meinke. *White Pelican Review* is about 48 pages, digest-sized, photocopied from typescript, saddle-stapled, with matte cardstock cover. Receives about 5,000 poems/year, accepts 3%. Circulation is 500. Single copy: $4; subscription: $8/year for individuals, $10/year for institutions. Make checks payable to *White Pelican Review*.

How to Submit Submit 3-5 poems at a time. "Optimal length is 32 lines plus title, although longer poems are given full consideration." No previously published poems or simultaneous submissions. Cover letter and SASE are required. "Please include name, address, telephone number, and (if available) e-mail address on each page. No handwritten poems." Reads submissions year round. Time between acceptance and publication is 1-6 months. Poems are circulated to an editorial board. Seldom comments on rejected poems. Guidelines available for SASE. Responds in 6 months. Pays one contributor's copy. Acquires one-time rights.

Contest/Award Offerings The Hollingsworth Prize of $100 is offered to the most distinguished poem in each issue.

WHITE PINE PRESS; THE WHITE PINE PRESS POETRY PRIZE

P.O. Box 236, Buffalo NY 14201. E-mail: wpine@whitepine.org. Website: www.whitepine.org. Established 1973. **Contact:** Dennis Maloney, editor. Managing Director: Elaine LaMattina.

Contest/Award Offerings White Pine Press publishes poetry, fiction, literature in translation, and essays in perfect-bound paperbacks. "**We accept unsolicited work by U.S. poets *only* for our annual competition—the White Pine Press Poetry Prize.** We are always open to submissions of poetry in translation." Competition awards $1,000 plus publication to a book-length collection of poems by a US author. **Entry fee:** $20. **Deadline:** November 30. Guidelines available for SASE or on website. No e-mail submissions. Has published *The Burning Point* by Frances Richey (winner of the White Pine Press Poetry Prize), *In What Disappears* by John Brandi, and *At the Threshold of Memory: New and Selected Poems* by Marjorie Agosín.

☉ TAHANA WHITECROW FOUNDATION; CIRCLE OF REFLECTIONS (Specialized: Native American; animals; nature; spirituality/inspirational)
2350 Wallace Rd. NW, Salem OR 97304. (503)585-0564. Fax: (503)585-3302. E-mail: tahana@open. org. Website: www.open.org/tahana. Established 1987. **Contact:** Melanie Smith, executive director.
Contest/Award Offerings The Tahana Whitecrow Foundation conducts one spring/summer poetry contest on Native American themes in poems up to 30 lines in length. No haiku, Seiku, erotic, or porno poems. No fax or e-mail submissions. **Reading fee:** $3/poem, $10/4 poems. **Deadline:** May 31. Winners, honorable mentions, and selected other entries are published in a periodic anthology, *Circle of Reflections*. Winners receive free copies (at least 2) and are encouraged to purchase others for $6.95 plus $2 handling in order to "help ensure the continuity of our contests." Guidelines available for SASE.
Advice "We seek unpublished Native American writers. Poetic expressions of full-bloods, mixed-bloods, and empathetic non-Indians need to be heard. Future goals include chapbooks. Advice to new writers: Practice, practice, practice to tap into your own rhythm and to hone and sharpen material; don't give up."

☉ WILD PLUM
P.O. Box 4282, Austin TX 78765. Established 2003. **Contact:** Constance Campbell. founder/editor/ publisher.
Magazine Needs *WILD PLUM* is published annually and is "dedicated to bringing readers an array of voices and styles, embracing the best of the new while still honoring tradition and form. We seek to publish poets from the U.S. and abroad." Wants "all styles and voices. We are very open to well-crafted rhyming poems, as well as haiku. Stay away from greeting card verse/sentiments. No pornography. No self-aggrandizing." Has published poetry by Lyn Lifshin, Cyrus Cassels, Toh Hsien Min, Simon Perchik, and Bobbi Lurie. *WILD PLUM* is 48-60 pages, digest-sized, perfect-bound, with cover featuring artwork. Receives about 800-1,000 poems/year, accepts about 5%. Press run is about 300. Single copy: $9; subscription: pre-publication price is $7. Make checks payable to Constance Campbell.
How to Submit Submit 3-5 poems at a time. Lines/poem: 75 maximum. No previously published poems or simultaneous submissions. No e-mail or disk submissions. Cover letter is required. Include specific publishing credits in bio in cover letter, if applicable. Time between acceptance and publication "depends on how close to publication you submitted. The editor reads all submissions carefully and then passes on the ones that seem best to the members of the editorial advisory board. They are then re-read and discussed before we arrive at our final decision." Comments on rejected poems "as often as possible." Guidelines available by e-mail. "Send us a postcard with your e-mail address for our notification list." Responds in 2-6 months. Pays one contributor's copy. Acquires first rights and the right to reprint in future anthologies.
Contest/Award Offerings "We plan to offer contests with cash prizes whenever possible. The editors will nominate poems to the Pushcart Prize committee."
Advice "Refine your work before submitting."

☉ WILD VIOLET
P.O. Box 39706, Philadelphia PA 19106-9706. E-mail: wildvioletmagazine@yahoo.com. Website: www.wildviolet.net. Established 2001. **Contact:** Alyce Wilson, editor.
Magazine Needs *Wild Violet* appears quarterly online. "Our goal is to democratize the arts: to make the arts more accessible and to serve as a creative forum for writers and artists." Wants "poetry that is well crafted, that engages thought, that challenges or uplifts the reader. We have published free verse, haiku, and blank verse. If the form suits the poem, we will consider any form." Does not want "abstract, self-involved poetry; poorly managed form; excessive rhyming; self-referential poems that

do not show why the speaker is sad, happy, or in love." Has published poetry by Erik Kestler, Jules St. John, Sam Vaknin, Leanne Kelly, Jim DeWitt, and Rich Furman. *Wild Violet* is published online with photos, artwork, and graphics. Accepts about 20% of work submitted.

How to Submit Submit 3-5 poems at a time. Accepts simultaneous submissions; no previously published poems. Accepts e-mail submissions (pasted into body of message, or as text or Word attachment); no fax or disk submissions. Cover letter is preferred. Reads submissions year round. Submit seasonal poems 3 months in advance. Time between acceptance and publication is 3 months. "Decisions on acceptance or rejection are made by the editor. Contests are judged by an independent panel." Seldom comments on rejected poems, unless requested. Occasionally publishes theme issues. List of upcoming themes and guidelines available by e-mail. Responds in up to 6 weeks. Pays by providing a bio and link on contributor's page. All rights retained by author. Reviews books and chapbooks of poetry in 250 words, single-book format. Send materials for review consideration.

Contest/Award Offerings Holds an annual poetry contest. 1st Prize: $100 and publication in *Wild Violet*. **Entry fee:** $5. Guidelines available by e-mail or on website.

Advice "Read voraciously; experience life and share what you've learned. Write what is hardest to say; don't take any easy outs."

☑ WILLARD & MAPLE

163 S. Willard St., Box 34, Burlington VT 05401. E-mail: willardandmaple@champlain.edu. Established 1996. **Contact:** Poetry Editor.

Magazine Needs *Willard & Maple* appears annually in April and is "a student-run literary magazine from Champlain College's Professional Writing Program that publishes a wide array of poems, short stories, creative essays, short plays, pen & ink drawings, photos, and computer graphics." Wants "creative work of the highest quality." Does not want any submissions over 5 typed pages in length; all submissions must be in English. Has published poetry by P-R Smith, Robert James Berry, Cheryl Burghdurf, Gerald Zipper, and David Trame. *Willard & Maple* is 125 pages, digest-sized, digitally printed, perfect-bound. Receives about 500 poems/year, accepts about 20%. Press run is 600 (80 subscribers, 4 libraries); 200 are distributed free to the Champlain College writing community. Single copy: $8.50. Make checks payable to Champlain College.

How to Submit Submit up to 5 poems at a time. Lines/poem: 100 maximum. Accepts simultaneous submissions; no previously published poems. Accepts e-mail and disk submissions; no fax submissions. Cover letter is required. "Please provide current contact information including an e-mail address. Single-space submissions, one poem/page." Reads submissions September 1 through March 31. Time between acceptance and publication is less than one year. "All editors receive a blind copy to review. They meet weekly throughout the academic year. These meetings consist of the submissions being read aloud, discussed, and voted upon." Seldom comments on rejected poems. Occasionally publishes theme issues. List of upcoming themes available by e-mail. Responds in 2 months. Pays 2 contributor's copies. Acquires one-time rights. Reviews books and chapbooks of poetry and other magazines/journals in 1,200 words. Send materials for review consideration to the poetry editor.

Advice "Work hard, be good, never surrender!"

☑ THE WILLIAM AND MARY REVIEW

Campus Center, College of William and Mary, P.O. Box 8795, Williamsburg VA 23187-8795. (757)221-3290. E-mail: review@wm.edu. Established 1962. **Contact:** Poetry Editors.

Magazine Needs *The William and Mary Review* is an annual, appearing in May, "dedicated to publishing new work by established poets as well as work by new and vital voices." Has published poetry by Cornelius Eady, Minnie Bruce Pratt, Edward Field, Dan Bellm, Forrest Gander, and Walter Holland. *The William and Mary Review* is about 120 pages, digest-sized, professionally printed on coated paper, perfect-bound, with 4-color card cover. Receives about 5,000 poems/year, accepts 12-15. Press run is 3,500 (250 library subscriptions, about 500 shelf sales). Sample: $5.50.

How to Submit Submit one poem/page, in batches of up to 6 poems, addressed to poetry editors. Cover letter is required; include address, phone number, e-mail address (if available), past publishing history, and brief bio note. Reads submissions September 1 through February 15 *only*. Responds in up to 4 months. Pays 5 contributor's copies.

Advice "If you lie in your cover letter, we usually figure it out. Submit considered, crafted poetry, or don't bother. No guidelines, just send poems."

☑ WILLOW REVIEW; COLLEGE OF LAKE COUNTY READING SERIES

College of Lake County, 19351 W. Washington St., Grayslake IL 60030-1198. (847)543-2956. Fax: (847)543-3956. E-mail: com426@clcillinois.edu. Established 1969. **Contact:** Michael F. Latza, editor.

- The *Willow Review* is partially supported by a grant from the Illinois Arts Council, a state agency.

Magazine Needs "We are interested in poetry, nonfiction, and fiction of high quality with no preferences as to form, style, or subject." Has published poetry by Lisel Mueller, Lucien Stryk, David Ray, Louis Rodriguez, John Dickson, and Garrett Hongo; interviews with Gregory Orr, Diane Ackerman, Patricia Smith, and Li-Young Lee. *Willow Review* is an 88- to 96-page, flat-spined annual, digest-sized, professionally printed, with a 4-color cover featuring work by an Illinois artist. Editors are open to all styles, free verse to form, as long as each poem stands on its own as art and communicates ideas. Press run is 1,000, with distribution to bookstores nationwide. Subscription: $18/3 issues, $30/5 issues. Sample (back issue): $5.

How to Submit Submit up to 5 poems. Accepts submissions on disk and by postal mail. Reads submissions from September to May. Pays 2 contributor's copies. All rights remain with the author.

Contest/Award Offerings Prizes totaling $400 are awarded to the best poetry and short fiction/creative nonfiction in each issue.

Also Offers The College of Lake County Reading Series: 4-7 readings/academic year; has included Angela Jackson, Thomas Lux, Charles Simic, Isabel Allende, Donald Justice, Gloria Naylor, David Mura, Galway Kinnell, Lisel Mueller, Amiri Baraka, Stephen Dobyns, Heather McHugh, Linda Pastan, Tobias Wolff, William Stafford, and others. One reading is for contributors to *Willow Review*. Readings are usually held on Thursday evenings, for audiences of about 150 students and faculty of the College of Lake County and other area colleges, and residents of local communities. They are widely publicized in Chicago and suburban newspapers.

⭐ ☑ ◎ WILLOW SPRINGS (Specialized: translations)

705 W. First Ave., MS 1, Eastern Washington University, Spokane WA 99201. (509)623-4349. Fax: (509)623-4240. E-mail: willow.springs@mail.ewu.edu. Website: http://willowsprings.ewu.edu. Established 1977. **Contact:** Sam Ligon, editor.

Magazine Needs *Willow Springs* is a semiannual publishing "quality poetry, fiction, and nonfiction that is imaginative, intelligent, and has a concern and care for language. We are especially interested in translations from any language or period." Has published poetry by Michael Heffernan, Robert Gregory, Beckian Fritz-Goldberg, and Mark Halliday. *Willow Springs* is 128 pages, digest-sized, professionally printed, flat-spined, with glossy 4-color card cover with art. Receives about 4,000 poems/year, accepts about 1-2%. Press run is 1,500 (700 subscribers, 30% libraries). Subscription: $11.50/year, $20/2 years. Sample: $5.50.

How to Submit Submit year round. Include name on every page, address on first page of each poem. Brief cover letter saying how many poems on how many pages is preferred. Accepts submissions by postal mail only. Guidelines available for SASE. Responds in up to 3 months. Pays 2 contributor's copies, others at reduced rate, and cash when funds available. Acquires all rights. Returns rights on release. Reviews books of poetry and short fiction in 200-500 words.

Contest/Award Offerings Annual poetry and fiction awards ($400 and $500 respectively) for work published in the journal. See website for complete guidelines.

Advice "We like poetry that is fresh, moving, intelligent, and has no spare parts."

$◪ WINDSTORM CREATIVE

P.O. Box 28, Port Orchard WA 98366. E-mail: wsc@windstormcreative.com. (''No submissions or queries; use to follow up on a submission only, please''). Website: www.windstormcreative.com. Established 1989. **Contact:** Ms. Cris DiMarco, senior editor.

Book/Chapbook Needs Windstorm Creative Ltd. publishes ''thoughtful, quality work; must have some depth.'' Wants ''a minimum of 100 (20-50 for chapbooks) publishable, quality poems. You must be familiar with our published poetry before you submit work.'' Has published poetry by Jack Rickard, Vacirca Vaughn, Rudy Kikel, Alden Reimonenq, Lesléa Newman, and Michael Hattersley. Also published (in 2004) *This New Breed: Gents, Bad Boys & Barbarians 2*, an anthology of 30 poets. Publishes 12 paperbacks/year.

How to Submit ''All submissions must include mailing label and submission form found on website. Submission without mailing label and submission form will be discarded unread.'' If invited, send entire ms, 100 poems minimum (for book-length work; 20-50 poems for chapbooks). ''You may include previously published poems as long as there are unpublished pieces as well.'' Manuscripts must be double-spaced, printed on one side of page only, unbound. No e-mail submissions. ''A bio with publishing history, and a page about the collection's focus, theme, etc., will help in the selection process.'' Time between acceptance and publication is 18 months. ''Senior editor reviews all work initially. If appropriate for our press, work is given to editorial board for review.'' Seldom comments on rejected poems. Guidelines available on website. Responds to queries and to mss in 6 months. Pays 15% royalties ''on gross monies received. Contract, contract FAQ, complete title list, and much more available on website.''

◪ ◪ WINGS MAGAZINE, INC.

E-mail: pamwings@juno.com. Website: www.geocities.com/wingsmag2002. Established 1991. **Contact:** Thomas Jones, publisher/poetry editor. Associate Editor: Pamela Malone.

Magazine Needs *Wings* is an exclusively online publication. ''We want to publish the work of poets who are not as widely known as those published in larger journals but who nevertheless produce exceptional, professional material. We also publish personal essays, fiction, and plays.'' Wants ''poetry with depth of feeling. No jingly, rhyming poetry. Rhyming poetry must show the poet knows how to use rhyme in an original way. Poetry on any theme, any style. No requirements, but we encourage poets to check out our website and get an idea of the kind of material we publish.'' Receives about 500 poems/year.

How to Submit Submit up to 5 poems at a time. Lines/poem: 80 maximum. Accepts previously published poems; no simultaneous submissions. ''We take submissions through e-mail only. Send e-mail to the above address. Copy and paste the poem and bio into the e-mail message. The bio should be five lines or less.'' Always responds to submissions. Guidelines available on website. Responds in 2 months. Staff reviews books and chapbooks of poetry in single-book format.

Also Offers Best of Wings CD-ROM.

Advice ''Our needs are eclectic. Content can be on any topic as long as the poet shows mastery of subject matter and craft, as well as penetration into depths. We don't want doggerel. We want sincere, well-crafted work. Poetry has been reduced to second-class status by commercial publishing, and we want to restore it to the status of fiction (novels) or plays.''

◪ ◎ WORCESTER REVIEW; WORCESTER COUNTY POETRY ASSOCIATION, INC. (Specialized: regional)

1 Ekman St., Worcester MA 01607. (508)797-4770. Website: www.geocities.com/Paris/LeftBank/6433. Established 1973. **Contact:** Rodger Martin, managing editor.

Magazine Needs *Worcester Review* appears annually ''with emphasis on poetry. New England writers are encouraged to submit, though work by other poets is used also.'' Wants ''work that is crafted, intuitively honest and empathetic, not work that shows the poet little respects his work or his readers.'' Has published poetry by May Swenson, Robert Pinsky, and Walter McDonald. *Worcester Review* is 160 pages, digest-sized, professionally printed in dark type on quality stock, flat-spined, with glossy card cover. Press run is 1,000 (300 subscribers, 50 libraries, 300 shelf sales). Subscription: $25 (includes membership in WCPA). Sample: $6.

How to Submit Submit up to 5 poems at a time. "I recommend 3 or less for most favorable readings." Accepts simultaneous submissions "if indicated"; previously published poems "only on special occasions." Editor comments on rejected poems "if manuscript warrants a response." Publishes theme issues. List of upcoming themes and guidelines available for SASE. Responds in up to 9 months. Pays 2 contributor's copies. Acquires first rights.

Contest/Award Offerings Has an annual contest for poets who live, work, or in some way (past/present) have a Worcester County connection or are WCPA members.

Advice "Read some. Listen a lot."

☑ THE WORD WORKS; THE WASHINGTON PRIZE

P.O. Box 42164, Washington DC 20015. Fax: (703)527-9384. E-mail: editor@wordworksdc.com. Website: www.wordworksdc.com. Established 1974. **Contact:** Hilary Tham, editor-in-chief.

Book/Chapbook Needs Word Works "is a nonprofit literary organization publishing contemporary poetry in single-author editions, usually in collaboration with a visual artist. We sponsor an ongoing poetry reading series, educational programs, the Capital Collection—publishing mostly metropolitan Washington, D.C. poets, and the Washington Prize—an award of $1,500 for a book-length manuscript by a living American poet." Previous winners include *Biography of Water* by Carrie Bennett, *Survivable World* by Ron Mohring, *Phoenix Suites* by Miles Waggener, *One Hundred Children Waiting for a Train* by Michael Atkinson, *Tipping Point* by Fred Marchant, and *Stalking the Florida Panther* by Enid Shomer. Submission open to any American writer except those connected with Word Works. Entries accepted between January 15 and March 1. **Postmark deadline:** March 1. Winners are announced at the end of June. Publishes perfect-bound paperbacks and occasional anthologies and wants "well-crafted poetry; open to most forms and styles (though not political themes particularly). Experimentation welcomed. We want more than a collection of poetry. We care about the individual poems—the craft, the emotional content, and the risks taken—but we want manuscripts where one poem leads to the next. We strongly recommend you read the books that have already won the Washington Prize. Buy them, if you can, or ask your libraries to purchase them. (Not a prerequisite.)" Most books are $10.

Contest/Award Offerings "Currently we are only reading unsolicited manuscripts for the Washington Prize (see above)." Accepts simultaneous submissions, if so stated. Accepts submissions by first-class postal mail only. Always sends prepublication galleys. Payment is 15% of run (500-1,000 copies). Guidelines and catalog available for SASE or on website. Occasionally comments on rejected poems. "We do have a contest for D.C.-area high school students who compete to read in our Miller Cabin Series." Young poets should submit ms with cover letter (detailing contact info, high school and grade, expected graduation date, and list of submitted poem titles) and SASE from January 1 to March 31. Send to Attn: W. Perry Epes. Two winners will receive an honorarium and a chance to read work.

Advice "Get community support for your work, know your audience, and support contemporary literature by buying and reading the small press."

☑ WORDS OF WISDOM

8969 UNCG Station, Greensboro NC 27413. E-mail: wowmail@hoopsmail.com. Established 1981. **Contact:** Mikhammad Abdel-Ishara, editor.

Magazine Needs *Words of Wisdom* appears quarterly with short stories, essays, and poetry. Wants all types of poetry, except religious or pornographic. Has published poetry by Lyman Grant, Matt Morris, Jene Beardsley, Frederick Zydek, and Dodiemesser Meeks. *Words of Wisdom* is 80-88 pages, digest-sized, laser-printed, saddle-stapled, with cover with art. Receives about 600 poems/year, accepts about 8-10%. Press run is 160 (100 subscribers, 2 libraries, 50 shelf sales). Single copy: $4.50; subscription: $16. Sample: $4.50. Make checks payable to J.M. Freiermuth.

How to Submit Submit 3-5 poems at a time. Lines/poem: 30 maximum. Accepts simultaneous submissions; *absolutely NO previously published poems*. No fax, e-mail, or disk submissions. Cover letter is required. Reads submissions all year. Submit seasonal poems 10 months in advance. Time between acceptance and publication is 6-9 months. Seldom comments on rejected poems. Occasionally publishes theme issues. Guidelines available for SASE or by e-mail. Responds in up to 6 months. Pays one contributor's copy. Acquires first North American serial rights.

Advice ''Turn off the Internet! Surf through a book of poetry.''

$□ ◎ THE WRITE CLUB (Specialized: membership)

P.O. Box 1454, Conover NC 28613. (828)256-3821. E-mail: poetsnet@juno.com. Established 2001. **Contact:** Nettie C. Blackwelder, editor/president.

Magazine Needs *The Write Club* appears quarterly. ''We print *one* original poem from *each* of our members in *each* quarterly club booklet. These poems are voted on by all members. We pay $1 to each member for each vote his/her poem receives. Each booklet also contains 4 assignments for all members who want to do them (usually poetry assignments). Our poetry specifications are open as to form, subject matter, style, or purpose. Just send your best. We don't print anything indecent or offensive.'' Has published poetry by Carolyn Marie Baatz, Raymond Green, Lisa Beck, Doris Nance, and Daniel Lee Walker. *The Write Club* is 32 pages, $4\frac{1}{4} \times 11$, computer-printed, saddle-stapled, with color cardstock cover. Receives about 300 poems/year, accepts about 90%. Press run is 50 (32 subscribers); 12 distributed free to anyone who requests information. Single copy: $2; subscription: $15 (membership). Sample: $1 (or 3 first-class stamps). Make checks payable to Nettie C. Blackwelder.

How to Submit Submit one poem at a time. Lines/poem: 3 minimum, 30 maximum. Accepts previously published poems and simultaneous submissions. No e-mail, fax, or disk submissions. Cover letter is preferred. ''Send SAE and 3 first-class stamps (or $1) for information and sample booklet before submitting poetry.'' Reads submissions all year. Submit seasonal poems 3 months in advance. Time between acceptance and publication is 3 months. ''Poems are voted on by our members. Each vote is worth $1 to that poem's author.'' **Membership required** (all members receive subscription to club booklet). Guidelines available for SASE or by e-mail. Responds in 3 months. Pays $1 per vote, per poem. Acquires one-time rights.

Advice ''Rhythm is the music of the soul and sets the pace of a poem. A clever arrangement of words means very little if they have no sense of 'stop' and 'go.' If you're not sure about the rhythm of a poem, reading it aloud a few times will quickly tell you which words don't belong or should be changed. My advice is rewrite, rewrite, rewrite until you love *every* word and phrase 'as is.' ''

◎ WRITE ON!! POETRY MAGAZETTE

P.O. Box 901, Richfield UT 84701-0901. (435)896-6669. E-mail: jimnipoetry@yahoo.com. Website: www.webspawner.com/users/JimGarman/index.html. Established 1998. **Contact:** Jim Garman, editor.

Magazine Needs *Write On!! Poetry Magazette* appears monthly and features ''poetry from poets around the world.'' Wants poetry of ''any style; all submissions must be suitable for all ages to read. No adult or vulgar material.'' Has published poetry by Carrieann Thunell, Kenneth Rehill, David Lawrence, and Celine Mariotti. *Write On!!* is 24 pages, digest-sized, photostat-copied, saddle-stapled, with color card cover. Receives about 500 poems/year, accepts about 50%. Press run is 50 (10 subscribers, one library, 10 shelf sales). Single copy: $4. Sample: $3. Make checks payable to Jim Garman.

How to Submit Submit 1-6 poems at a time. Lines/poem: 6 minimum, 28 maximum. Accepts previously published poems and simultaneous submissions. Accepts e-mail submissions (pasted into body of message; no attachments); no fax or disk submissions. Reads submissions year round. Submit seasonal poems 2 months in advance. Time between acceptance and publication is one month. Never comments on rejected poems. Occasionally publishes theme issues. List of upcoming themes available by e-mail. Guidelines available on website. Responds in 3 weeks. No payment. Acquires first rights.

Advice ''Send only your best material after it has been refined.''

◢ WRITER'S BLOC

Dept. of Language & Literature, Texas A&M University-Kingsville, MSC 162, Kingsville TX 78363-8202. E-mail: c-downs@tamuk.edu. Website: www.tamuk.edu/langlit/writer's.htm. Established 1980. **Contact:** C. Downs, faculty sponsor.

Magazine Needs *Writer's Bloc* is an annual journal appearing in September, publishing poetry, fiction, creative nonfiction, and graphic art. About half of its pages are devoted to the works of Texas A&M University-Kingsville students and half to the works of writers and artists from all over the world. Wants quality poetry; no restrictions on content or form. *Writer's Bloc* is 80-96 pages, digest-sized. Press run is 300-500. Subscription: $5. Sample: $6.

How to Submit Submit no more than 3 pages of poetry (prose poems OK). Lines/poem: 50 maximum. Accepts simultaneous submissions (encouraged); no previously published poems. Submissions should be typed, double-spaced; SASE required for reply. Reads submissions September through January only. "Manuscripts are published upon recommendation by a staff of students and faculty." Seldom comments on rejected poems. Guidelines available in magazine or for SASE. "Acceptance letters are sent out in September." Pays one contributor's copy.

$◢ WRITERS' JOURNAL

P.O. Box 394, Perham MN 56573-0394. (218)346-7921. Fax: (218)346-7924. E-mail: writersjournal @lakesplus.com. Website: www.writersjournal.com. Established 1980. **Contact:** Esther M. Leiper, poetry editor.

Magazine Needs *Writers' Journal* is a bimonthly magazine "that offers advice and guidance, motivation, and inspiration to the more serious and published writers and poets." Features 2 columns for poets: "Esther Comments," which specifically critiques poems sent in by readers, and "Every Day with Poetry," which discusses a wide range of poetry topics, often—but not always—including readers' work. Wants "a variety of poetry: free verse, strict forms, concrete, Oriental. But we take nothing vulgar, preachy, or sloppily written. Since we appeal to those of different skill levels, some poems are more sophisticated than others, but those accepted must move, intrigue, or otherwise positively capture me. 'Esther Comments' is never used as a negative force to put a poem or a poet down. Indeed, I focus on the best part of a given work and seek to suggest means of improvement on weaker aspects." Accepts poetry written by school-age children. Has published poetry by Lawrence Schug, Diana Sutliff, and Eugene E. Grollmes. *Writers' Journal* is 64 pages (including paper cover), magazine-sized, professionally printed. Receives about 900 submissions/year, accepts about 25 (including those used in columns). Circulation is 26,000. Single copy: $4.99; subscription: $19.97/year (US), Canada/Mexico add $15, Europe add $30, all others add $35. Sample: $5.

How to Submit Submit 3-4 poems at a time. Lines/poem: 25 maximum. Accepts submissions by postal mail only. Responds in up to 5 months. Pays $5/poem plus one contributor's copy.

Contest/Award Offerings The magazine also has poetry contests for previously unpublished poetry. Competitions receive 1,000 entries/year. Winners announced in *The Writers' Journal* and on website. Submit poems on any subject or in any form, 25 lines maximum. "Submit in duplicate: one with name and address, one without." **Reading fee for each contest:** $3/poem. **Deadlines:** April 30, August 30, and December 30. Guidelines available for SASE.

✪ ◢ XAVIER REVIEW

Xavier University, 1 Drexel Dr., New Orleans LA 70125-1098. (504)520-7303. Fax: (504)520-7917. E-mail: rskinner@xula.edu. Established 1961. **Contact:** Robert Skinner, university librarian.

Magazine Needs *Xavier Review* is a biannual that publishes poetry, fiction, nonfiction, and reviews (contemporary literature) for professional writers, libraries, colleges, and universities. Open to writing on any subject. Has published *Three Poets in New Orleans*, featuring Lee Grue, Biljiana Obradovic, Patricia Ward, Stella Nesanovich, and Carole Boston Weatherford, among others. Press run is 300.

How to Submit Submit 3-5 poems at a time with SASE. Accepts submissions by postal mail only. Pays 2 contributor's copies.

☐ YA'SOU! A CELEBRATION OF LIFE

P.O. Box 77463, Columbus OH 43207. Established 2000. **Contact:** David D. Bell, editor.

Magazine Needs *Ya'sou! A celebration of life* appears quarterly. "Our purpose is to celebrate life. We like thought-provoking and uplifting material in any style and subject matter. We would like to see poetry essays, short stories, articles, and b&w artwork." Does not want "sexually explicit, pornographic, or violent poetry. I'd like more poetry written by children; parental consent required." Receives about 200 poems/year, accepts about 75%.

How to Submit Submit 5 poems at a time. Lines/poem: 30 maximum. "Your name and complete address should be at the top left-hand corner of every poem." Accepts previously published poems and simultaneous submissions. Cover letter is preferred. **Reading fee:** $1.50/poem, "or design your own page (8½×11) with as many poems you wish for $5." Work submitted by postal mail should be camera-ready. SASE required. Reads submissions all year. Time between acceptance and publication varies. "All work is read and chosen by the editor." Pays one contributor's copy.

Advice "Let your own unique voice be heard. Remember, express your heart, live your soul, and celebrate life."

⬙ ⊞ ◎ YORKSHIRE JOURNAL (Specialized: regional)

Dalesman Publishing, The Water Mill, Broughton Hall, Skipton, North Yorkshire BD23 3AG England. Phone: (01756)701381. Fax: (01756)701326. E-mail: journal@dalesman.co.uk. Established 1992. **Contact:** Mark Whitley, editor.

Magazine Needs *Yorkshire Journal* is a quarterly general interest magazine about Yorkshire. Wants poetry with strong relevance to Yorkshire. Has published poetry by Vernon Scannell, Anna Adams, Ted Hughes, Andrew Motion, and Simon Armitage. *Yorkshire Journal* is 96 pages, highly illustrated. Receives about 200 poems/year, accepts about 10%. Press run is 5,000 (1,500 subscribers, 2,300 shelf sales). Subscription: £17.50. Sample: £4.50. Make checks payable to Country Publications Ltd.

How to Submit Submit up to 6 poems at a time. Lines/poem: 25 maximum. Accepts previously published poems and simultaneous submissions. Accepts submissions by fax and by e-mail (pasted into body of message). Cover letter including biographical information is required. "Include return postage in sterling." Pays one contributor's copy.

◙ ZILLAH: A POETRY JOURNAL

P.O. Box 202, Port Aransas TX 78373-0202. E-mail: lightningwhelk@msn.com. Established 2001. **Contact:** Pamela M. Smith, editor/publisher.

Magazine Needs Appearing quarterly, *Zillah* is " 'not your mother's poetry.' Simply put, in the year 3999 an archaeologist's dig produces a copy of *Zillah* in situ and, reading it, the treasure hunter knows what it was like to live during the second and third millennia." Does not want pornography, gratuitous violence, evil or devil worship, or anything that lacks quality. *Zillah* is 40-50 pages, 7×8½, stapled, with 80-lb. coverstock. Receives about 1,200 poems/year. Single copy: $4; subscription: $16. Make checks payable to Pamela M. Smith.

How to Submit Submit 5-6 poems at a time, "typed, double-spaced, one poem to a page; SASE essential!" Lines/poem: 60 maximum. Accepts previously published poems and simultaneous submissions. Accepts e-mail submissions. Reads submissions year round. Submit seasonal poems 6 months in advance. Time between acceptance and publication is up to one year. Never comments on rejected poems. Responds in 2 months. Pays one contributor's copy. Acquires first North American serial rights or second reprint rights; rights revert to author after publication.

Advice "Everyone should write, everyone should write poetry. Take a leap of faith. Think of writing as a natural state of being. Let go from a stream of consciousness, from the heart, from depth—edit and refine later."

◙ ZUZU'S PETALS QUARTERLY ONLINE

P.O. Box 4853, Ithaca NY 14852. (607)539-1141. E-mail: info@zuzu.com. Website: www.zuzu.com. Established 1992. **Contact:** T. Dunn, editor.

Magazine Needs "We publish high-quality fiction, essays, poetry, and reviews on our award-winning website, which was featured in *USA Today Online*, *Entertainment Weekly*, *Library Journal*, and *Newsday*. Becoming an Internet publication allows us to offer thousands of helpful resources and addresses for poets, writers, editors, and researchers, as well as to greatly expand our readership. Free verse, blank verse, experimental, visually sensual poetry, etc., are especially welcome here. We're looking for a freshness of language, new ideas, and original expression. No 'June, moon, and spoon' rhymed poetry. No light verse. I'm open to considering more feminist, ethnic, alternative poetry, as well as poetry of place." Has published poetry by Ruth Daigon, Robert Sward, Laurel Bogen, W.T. Pfefferle, and Kate Gale. *Zuzu's Petals* is 70-100 pages, includes full-color artwork, and is an electronic publication available free of charge on the Internet. "Many libraries, colleges, and coffeehouses offer access to the Internet for those without home Internet accounts." Receives about 3,000 poems/year, accepts about 10%. Copies free online; printed sample: $5.

How to Submit Closed to submissions until 2007. Submit up to 4 poems at a time. Accepts previously published poems and simultaneous submissions. Accepts e-mail submissions (pasted into body of message). "Cover letters are not necessary. The work should speak for itself." Seldom comments on rejected poems. Guidelines available for SASE or on website. Responds in up to 2 months. Acquires one-time electronic rights. Staff reviews books of poetry in approximately 200 words. Send materials for review consideration.

Also Offers Publishes digital poetry videos. "Please e-mail for details before sending."

Advice "Read as much poetry as you can. Go to poetry readings, read books and collections of verse. Eat poetry for breakfast, cultivate a love of language, then write!"

Contests & Awards

This section contains a wide array of poetry competitions and literary awards. These range from state poetry society contests with a number of modest monetary prizes to prestigious honors bestowed by private foundations, elite publishers, and renowned university programs. Because these listings reflect such a variety of skill levels and degrees of competitiveness, it's important to read each carefully and note its unique requirements. *Never* enter a contest without consulting the guidelines and following directions to the letter (including manuscript formatting, number of lines or pages of poetry accepted, amount of entry fee, entry forms needed, and other details).

Important note: As we gathered information for this edition of *Poet's Market*, we found that some competitions hadn't yet established their 2006 fees and deadlines. In such cases, we list the most recent information available as a general guide. Always consult current guidelines for updates before entering any competition.

WHERE TO ENTER?

While it's perfectly okay to "think big" and aim high, being realistic may improve your chances of winning a prize for your poetry. Many of the listings in the Contests & Awards section begin with symbols that reflect their level of difficulty:

Contests ideal for beginners and unpublished poets are coded with the (□) symbol. That's not to say these contests won't be highly competitive—there may be a large number of entries. However, you may find these entries are more on a level with your own, increasing your chances of being "in the running" for a prize. Don't assume these contests reward low quality, though. If you submit less than your best work, you're wasting your time and money (in postage and entry fees).

Contests for poets with more experience are coded with the (◩) symbol. Beginner/unpublished poets are still welcome to enter, but the competition is keener here. Your work may be judged against that of widely published, prize-winning poets, so consider carefully whether you're ready for this level of competition. (Of course, nothing ventured, nothing gained—but those entry fees *do* add up.)

Contests for accomplished poets are coded with the (◐) symbol. These may have stricter entry requirements, higher entry fees, and other conditions that signal these programs are not intended to be "wide open" to all poets.

Specialized contests are coded with the (◉) symbol. These may include regional contests; awards for poetry written in a certain form or in the style of a certain poet; contests for women, gay/lesbian, ethnic, or age-specific poets (for instance, children or older adults); contests for translated poetry only; and many others.

There are also symbols that give additional information about contests. The (🆖) symbol indicates the contest is recently established and new to *Poet's Market*; the (◪) symbol indicates this contest did not appear in the 2005 edition; the (◪) symbol identifies a Canadian contest or award and the (🌐) symbol an international listing. Sometimes Canadian and international contests require that entrants live in certain countries, so pay attention when you see these symbols.

ADDITIONAL CONTESTS & AWARDS

When magazines and presses sponsor contests, we include related information in their listings in the Publishers of Poetry section (under **Contest/Award Offerings**). At the end of this section is a cross reference to these additional contest opportunities. For details about a contest associated with a market in this list, go to that market's page number.

WHAT ABOUT ENTRY FEES?

Most contests charge entry fees, and these are usually legitimate. The funds are used to cover expenses such as paying the judges, putting up prize monies, printing prize editions of magazines and journals, and promoting the contest through mailings and ads. If you're concerned about a poetry contest or other publishing opportunity, see "Are You Being Taken?" on page 33 for advice on some of the more questionable practices in the poetry world. Also, read "Roundtable: Poetry Contests" on page 16 for further discussion of this topic, including questions driving the current controversy about some contests.

OTHER RESOURCES

Widen your search for contests beyond those listed in *Poet's Market*. Many Internet writer's sites have late-breaking announcements about competitions old and new (see Additional Resources on page 479). Often these sites offer free electronic newsletter subscriptions, sending valuable information right to your e-mail inbox.

The writer's magazines at your local bookstore regularly include listings for upcoming contests, as well as deadlines for artist's grants at the state and national level. (See Additional Resources on page 479 for a few suggestions; also, Grants on page 442.) The Association of Writers & Writing Programs (AWP) is a valuable resource, including its publication, *Writer's Chronicle*. (See Organizations, page 461.) State poetry societies are listed throughout this book; they offer many contests, as well as helpful information for poets (and mutual support). To find a specific group, search the General Index for listings under your state's name or look under "society"; also consult the Geographical Index on page 516.

Don't overlook your local connections. City and community newspapers, radio and TV announcements, bookstore newsletters and bulletin boards, and your public library can be terrific resources for competition news, especially regional contests.

⊠ $⬚ AKRON POETRY PRIZE

The University of Akron Press, 374B Bierce Library, Akron OH 44325-1703. (330)972-5342. Fax: (330)972-8364. E-mail: uapress@uakron.edu. Website: www.uakron.edu/uapress. **Contact:** Elton Glaser, award director. Offers annual award of $1,000 plus publication. Submissions must be unpublished and may be entered in other contests (with notification of acceptance elsewhere). Submit 60-100 pages maximum, typed, single-spaced or double-spaced, with SASE for results. Mss will not be returned. Do not send mss bound or enclosed in covers. Guidelines available for SASE or by fax or e-mail. **Entry fee:** $25. **Deadline:** entries are accepted May 15 through June 30 only. Competition receives 450-550 entries. Most recent winners were Vern Rutsala, Sharmila Voorakkara, Roger Mitchell, and George Bilgere. 2005 judge: Gerald Stern. Winner will be announced in September by letter (if SASE enclosed with entry) or on website. Copies of winning books are available from UAP or through your local bookstore. The University of Akron Press "is committed to publishing poetry that, as Robert Frost said, 'begins in delight and ends in wisdom.' Books accepted must exhibit three essential qualities: mastery of language, maturity of feeling, and complexity of thought."

$⬚ AGHA SHAHID ALI PRIZE IN POETRY

University of Utah Press, 1795 E. South Campus Dr., Suite 101, Salt Lake City UT 84112. (801)581-6771. Fax: (801)581-3365. Website: www.uofupress.com/Agha-Shahid-Ali. Established 2003. The University of Utah Press and the University of Utah Department of English offer an annual award of $1,000, publication of a book-length poetry ms, and a reading in the Guest Writers Series. Submissions may be previously published and may be entered in other contests. "However, entrants must notify the Press immediately if the collection submitted is accepted for publication elsewhere during the competition." Submit 48-64 typed pages of poetry, with no names or other identifying information appearing on title page or within ms. Include cover sheet with complete contact information (name, address, telephone, e-mail address). Submissions must be in English. Mss will not be returned; include SASE for notification only. Guidelines available on website. **Entry fee:** $25/book submission. **Deadline:** submit March 1-March 31. Competition receives about 500 mss/year. 2004 winner was Jacqueline Berger. 2004 judge: Christopher Merrill. Winner announced in September on the website and through press releases and the Press catalog. Copies of winning books are available from University of Utah Press.

$⬚ THE APR/HONICKMAN FIRST BOOK PRIZE

The American Poetry Review, 117 S. 17th St., Suite 910, Philadelphia PA 19103. (215)496-0439. Fax: (215)569-0808. Website: www.aprweb.org. Established 1972. **Contact:** Elizabeth Scanlon, award director. Offers annual award of $3,000 and publication of a book length ms. Open to U.S. citizens writing in English and who have not yet published a book-length collection of poems. Submissions must be unpublished as a book-length work exceeding 25 pages, although "poems previously published in periodicals or limited-edition chapbooks may be included." Manuscript may be submitted elsewhere, "but please notify us immediately if it is accepted for publication." Submit a poetry ms of 48 pages or more, single-spaced, paginated, with a table of contents and acknowledgments (a good copy is acceptable). Include 2 title pages: 1) first shows name, address, phone number, and the book title; 2) second contains the ms title only. Name or other identifying information should not appear anywhere in the ms besides the first title page. Use a plain file folder for the ms. Mss will not be returned. Include SASE for notification of contest results as well as a SAS postcard for notification of receipt of ms. Guidelines available for SASE or on website. **Entry fee:** $25/book ms. **Deadline:** October 31. Use First Class Mail only to send mss. Competition receives about 1,000 mss/year. Recent winners include James McCorkle (2003), Kathleen Ossip (2002), and Ed Pavlic (2001). 2004 judge: Yusef Komunyakaa. Winner will be announced by January 31 by SASE and in the March/April issue of *The American Poetry Review*. Copies of winning books available from *APR* or most bookstores.

$ ARIZONA LITERARY CONTEST & BOOK AWARDS

Arizona Authors Association, P.O. Box 87857, Phoenix AZ 85080-7857. (602)769-2066. Fax: (623)780-0468. E-mail: info@azauthors.com. Website: www.azauthors.com. **Contact:** Vijaya Schartz, president. Arizona Authors Association sponsors annual literary contest in poetry, short story, essay, unpublished novels, and published books (fiction, nonfiction, and children's literature). Awards publication in *Arizona Literary Magazine*, publication of novel by AuthorHouse, and $100 1st Prize in each category. Pays winners from other countries by International Money Order. Does not accept entry fees in foreign currencies. Poetry submissions must be unpublished and may be entered in other contests. Submit any number of poems on any subject up to 42 lines. Entry form and guidelines available for SASE. **Entry fee:** $10/poem. **Submission period:** January 1 through July 1. Competition receives 1,000 entries/year. Recent poetry winners include Ellaraine Lockie, Lynn Veach Sadler, Don Struble, Ymasumac Maranon, and Betty Brownlow. Judges: Arizona authors, editors, reviewers, and readers. Winners announced at an award banquet in Phoenix by November 15.

$ ARIZONA STATE POETRY SOCIETY ANNUAL CONTEST; THE SANDCUTTERS

4543 E. Via Estrella, Phoenix AZ 85028. Website: www.azpoetry.org. **Contact:** Ernest Griffith, ASPS president. Offers a variety of cash prizes in several categories ranging from $10-125; 1st, 2nd, and 3rd place winners are published in *The Sandcutter*, ASPS's quarterly publication, which also lists names of Honorable Mention winners. See guidelines for detailed submission information (available for SASE or on website). **Entry fee:** varies according to category; see guidelines. **Postmark Deadline:** September 15. Competition receives over 1,000 entries/year. "ASPS sponsors a variety of monthly contests for members. Membership is available to anyone anywhere."

◖ ARKANSAS POETRY DAY CONTEST; POETS' ROUNDTABLE OF ARKANSAS

605 Higdon, Apt. 109, Hot Springs AR 71913. (501)321-4226. E-mail: vernaleeh@hotmail.com. **Contact:** Verna Lee Hinegardner. Over 25 categories, many open to all poets. Brochure available in June; deadline in September; awards given in October. Guidelines available for SASE.

$ ◖ ◎ ARTIST TRUST; ARTIST TRUST GAP GRANTS; ARTIST TRUST/WSAC FELLOWSHIPS (Specialized: regional/WA)

1835 12th Ave., Seattle WA 98122. (206)467-8734. Fax: (206)467-9633. E-mail: info@artisttrust.org. Website: www.artisttrust.org. **Contact:** Fionn Meade, Director of Grant Programs. Artist Trust is a nonprofit arts organization that provides grants to artists (including poets) who are residents of the state. Accepts inquiries by mail, fax, or e-mail. **Deadline:** varies each year. Each competition receives 400-750 entries/year. Most recent winners include Jennifer S. Davis, David Shields, and Gregory Spatz. Also publishes, 3 times/year, a journal of news about arts opportunities and cultural issues.

⊕ $ ◖ AUSTRALIAN-IRISH HERITAGE WRITER'S PRIZE (formerly Catalpa Writer's Prize)

Australian-Irish Heritage Association, P.O. Box 1583, Subiaco, West Australia 6904 Australia. Phone: 08 9384 1368. E-mail: aiha@irishheritage.net. Website: www.irishheritage.net. Established 1997. **Contact:** Pavla Walsh, coordinator. Offers annual awards. See website for current year's entry details.

$ ◪ AUTUMN HOUSE POETRY PRIZE

Autumn House Press, P.O. Box 60100, Pittsburg PA 15211. (412)381-4261. E-mail: simms@duq.edu. Website: http://autumnhouse.org. Established 1999. **Contact:** Michael Simms, editor. Offers annual prize of $1,000 and publication of book-length ms with national promotion. Pays winners by International Money Order in U.S. dollars. Submission must be unpublished as a collection, but individual poems may have been previously published in journals. Submissions may be entered simultaneously in other ms contests. Submit 50-80 pages of poetry ("blind judging—2 cover sheets requested"). Guidelines available for SASE, by e-mail, or on website. **Entry fee:** $25/ms. Does not accept entry fees in foreign currencies; prefers International Money Order or MasterCard/VISA. **Deadline:** June 30 annually. Competition receives 500 entries/year. Most recent winners were Ruth L. Schwartz (2004) and Deborah Slicer (2003). 2005 judge: Jean Valentine. Winners announced through mailings and through ads in *Poets & Writers*, *American Poetry Review*, and *Writer's Chronicle* (extensive publicity for winner). Copies of winning books available from Amazon.com, Barnes & Noble, Borders, and other retailers. "Autumn House is a nonprofit corporation with the mission of publishing and promoting poetry. We have published books by Gerald Stern, Ed Ochester, Julie Suk, Jo McDougall, and others." Advice: "Include only your best poems."

$☐ THE BACKWATERS PRIZE; THE WELDON KEES AWARD

The Backwaters Press, 3502 N. 52nd St., Omaha NE 68104-3506. (402)451-4052. E-mail: gkosm6273 5@aol.com. Website: www.thebackwaterspress.homestead.com. Established 1998. **Contact:** Greg Kosmicki, contest director. **The Backwaters Prize** offers an annual award of $1,000 plus publication, promotion, and distribution for a book-length ms. "Submissions may be entered in other contests, and this should be noted in cover letter. Backwaters Press must be notified if manuscripts are accepted for publication at other presses." Submit up to 80 pages on any subject, any form. "Poems must be written in English. No collaborative work accepted. Parts of the manuscript may be previously published in magazines or chapbooks, but entire manuscript may not have been previously published." Guidelines available for SASE, by e-mail, or on website. **Entry fee:** $25. Does not accept entry fees in foreign currencies; send postal money order or personal check in U.S. dollars. **Deadline:** postmarked by June 4. Competition receives 350-400 entries/year. Most recent contest winner was Aaron Anstett (2004 for *No Accident*). 2004 judge: Philip Devine. **The Weldon Kees Award** offers an annual prize of $125 and publication of a chapbook-length poetry collection for each of 3 winners. Submit 20-30 pages of original poetry by a single poet; no style/content restrictions. Guidelines available for SASE, by e-mail, or on website. **Entry fee:** $20; "you may enter as many manuscripts as you like, but each must be accompanied by the $20 entry fee." **Deadline:** postmarked by December 31. Winners of both contests will be announced in AWP *Writer's Chronicle* ad, in *Poets & Writers'* "Recent Winners," and on the Backwaters website. Copies of winning books available through The Backwaters Press or Amazon.com. "The Backwaters Press is thoroughly committed to safeguarding the integrity of our contests. Judges are instructed to set aside any manuscript in which they recognize the work; in which the judge recognizes he or she has a personal relationship with the poet; or with which manuscript they have had any hand in shaping; or in any instance, for whatever reason, that selecting a particular manuscript might give the appearance of impropriety. The Backwaters Press is a nonprofit press dedicated to publishing the best new literature we can find. Send your best work."

$☑ GEORGE BENNETT FELLOWSHIP

Phillips Exeter Academy, 20 Main St., Exeter NH 03833-2460. Website: www.exeter.edu. Established 1968. **Contact:** Charles Pratt, selection committee coordinator. Provides an annual $10,000 fellowship plus residency (room and board) to a writer with a ms in progress. The Fellow's only official duties are to be in residence while the academy is in session and to be available to students interested in writing. The committee favors writers who have not yet published a book-length work with a major publisher. Application materials and guidelines available for SASE or on website. **Entry fee:** $5. **Deadline:** December 1. Competition receives 190 entries. Recent award winners were Maggie Dietz (2002-2003), Nia Stephens (2003-2004), and Erin Soros (2004-2005). Winners will be announced by mail in March. "Please, no telephone calls or e-mail inquiries."

$☒ BEST OF OHIO WRITERS WRITING CONTEST (Specialized: regional/Ohio residents)

P.O. Box 91801, Cleveland OH 44101. (216)421-0403. E-mail: pwlgc@yahoo.com. Website: www.p wlgc.com/ohiowriter.html. Offers annual contest for poetry, fiction, creative nonfiction, and "Writers on Writing" (any genre). 1st Prize: $150, 2nd Prize: $50, plus publication for first-place winner of each category in a special edition of *Ohio Writer*. Submit up to 3 typed poems, no more than 2 pages each, unpublished mss only. Open only to Ohio residents. "Entries will be judged anonymously, so please do not put name or other identification on manuscript. Attach entry form (or facsimile) to submission. Manuscripts will not be returned." Include SASE for list of winners. Entry form and guidelines available for SASE or by e-mail. **Entry fee:** $15/first entry in each category (includes one-year subscription or renewal to *Ohio Writer*); $2 for each additional entry in same category (limit 3/category). **Deadline:** July 31. Judges have included Larry Smith, Richard Hague, Ron Antonucci, and Sheila Schwartz. Winners announced in the November/December issue of *Ohio Writer*.

$◎ BINGHAMTOM UNIVERSITY MILT KESSLER POETRY BOOK AWARD (Specialized: poets over 40)

Binghamton University Creative Writing Program, P.O. Box 6000, Binghamton NY 13902. (607)777-2713. Fax: (607)777-2408. E-mail: cwpro@binghamton.edu. Website: http://english.binghamton.edu/cwpro. Established 2001. **Contact:** Maria Mazziotti Gillan, award director. Offers annual award of $1,000 and a reading at the university for a book of poetry judged best of those published that year by a poet over the age of 40. "Submit books published that year; do not submit manuscripts." Entry form and guidelines available for SASE, by e-mail, or on website. **Entry fee:** none; "just submit 3 copies of book." **Deadline:** March 1. Competition receives 500 books/year. Most recent winner was John Smelcer (2004). 2004 judge: Marilyn Chin. Winner will be announced in June in *Poets & Writers* and on website, or by SASE if provided. (NOTE: Not to be confused with the Milton Kessler Memorial Prize for Poetry; see listing for *Harpur Palate* in the Publishers of Poetry section.)

✪ $☑ BLUE LYNX POETRY PRIZE; EWU PRESS

Lynx House Press, 705 W. 1st Ave., Spokane WA 99204. (509)623-4285. Fax: (509)623-4283. E-mail: ewupress@ewu.edu. Website: http://ewupress.ewu.edu. **Contact:** Joelean Copeland, managing editor. Offers annual award of $1,500 and publication by EWU Press for a book-length ms. **For U.S. authors only.** Submission must be unpublished as a collection, but individual poems may have been previously published in journals. Submit 48 pages of poetry (minimum) on any subject, in any form. "All U.S. authors are eligible. Manuscripts must contain page numbers and table of contents. No fees or manuscripts will be returned." Guidelines available for SASE, by e-mail, or on website. **Entry fee:** $25. **Deadline:** May 1 annually. Competition receives 400 entries/year. Most recent winners were Randall Watson (2004), Lynn Burris Butler (2003), and Robert Gregory (2002). Past judges: Yusef Komunyakaa, Dorianne Laux, Dara Wier, and Michael Hefferman. Winner announced in fall of contest year. Copies of winning books available from EWU Press. "Lynx House Press has been publishing poetry since 1975 and is now an imprint of Eastern Washington University Press. EWU Press formerly sponsored the Spoken Prize for Poetry. Now the two contests have merged."

$☑ BLUESTEM PRESS AWARD

Emporia State University, English Dept., Box 4019, Emporia KS 66801-5087. (620)341-5216. Fax: (620)341-5547. E-mail: bluestem@esumail.emporia.edu. Website: www.emporia.edu/bluestem/index.htm. Established 1989. **Contact:** Amy Sage Webb, director. Offers annual award of $1,000 and publication for an original book-length collection of poems. Pays in U.S. dollars through electronic transfer. Submissions must be unpublished as a collection and may be entered in other contests (with notification). Submit a typed ms of at least 48 pages on any subject in any form with a #10 SASE for notification. Guidelines and information available for SASE or on website. **Entry fee:** $20. Does not accept entry fees in foreign currencies; send U.S. check or money order. **Deadline:** March 1 annually. Competition receives 500-700 entries/year. Most recent award winner was Matthew Spireng (2004). 2004 judge: Vivian Shipley. Winner will be announced in June by flier in SASE to participants, on website, and in the trade journals. Copies of winning poems or books available from the Bluestem Press at the above address or through website. "Enter early to avoid missing the deadline. Manuscripts will not be returned. Also, looking at the different winners from past years would help.''

⬛ $◎ BP NICHOL CHAPBOOK AWARD (Specialized: regional/Canada)

316 Dupont St., Toronto ON M5R 1V9 Canada. (416)964-7919. Fax: (416)964-6941. Established 1985. Offers $1,000 (Canadian) prize for the best poetry chapbook (10-48 pages) in English published in Canada. Submit 3 copies (not returnable) and a brief curriculum vitae of the author. Accepts inquiries by fax. **Deadline:** March 31. Competition receives between 40-60 entries on average.

⭐ ⬛ $◎ ⊘ CANADIAN AUTHORS ASSOCIATION AWARDS FOR ADULT LITERATURE (Specialized: regional); JACK CHALMERS POETRY AWARD; CANADIAN AUTHORS ASSOCIATION

Box 419, Campbellford ON K0L 1L0 Canada. (705)653-0323. Fax: (705)653-0593. E-mail: admin@CanAuthors.org. Website: www.CanAuthors.org. **Contact:** Alec McEachern, administrator. The CAA Awards for Adult Literature offers $2,500 and a silver medal in each of 5 categories (fiction, poetry, short stories, Canadian history, Canadian biography) to Canadian writers, for a book published during the year. The Jack Chalmers Poetry Award is given for a volume of poetry by one poet. **Entry fee:** $35/title. **Deadline:** December 15; except for works published after December 1, in which case the postmark deadline is January 15. Competition receives 300 entries/year. Most recent poetry award winners were Margaret Avison (2003) and Chris Banks (2004). All awards are given at the CAA Awards Banquet at the annual conference.

$◎ CAVE CANEM POETRY PRIZE (Specialized: ethnic/African American); CAVE CANEM FOUNDATION, INC.

584 Broadway, Suite 508, New York NT 10012. Fax: (212)941-5724. E-mail: ccpoets@verizon.net. Website: www.cavecanempoets.org. Award established 1999; organization 1996. **Contact:** Carolyn Micklem, Cave Canem director. Offers ''annual first book award dedicated to presenting the work of African American poets who have not been published by a professional press. The winner will receive $500 cash, publication, and 50 copies of the book.'' **U.S. poets only.** ''Send 2 copies of manuscript of 50-75 pages. The author's name should not appear on the manuscript. Two title pages should be attached to each copy. The first must include the poet's name, address, telephone, and the title of the manuscript; the second should list the title only. Number the pages. Manuscripts will not be returned, but a SASE postcard can be included for notice of manuscript receipt. Simultaneous submissions should be noted. If the manuscript is accepted for publication elsewhere during the judging, immediate notification is requested.'' Guidelines available for SASE or on website. There is no entry fee. **Deadline:** May 15 of each year. Received 140 entries in 2004. Most recent winners were Amber Thomas (2004), Kyle Dargan (2003), and Tracy K. Smith (2002). 2005 judge: Sonia Sanchez. Winners will be announced by press release in October of year of contest. Copies of winning books are available from ''any bookseller, because the publishers are Graywolf Press (2002, 2005), University of Georgia (2000, 2003), and University of Pittsburgh (2001, 2004). Cave Canem sponsors a week-long workshop/retreat each summer and regional workshops in New York City and Minnesota. (See Cave Canem listing in Conferences & Workshops section.) It sponsors readings in cities in various parts of the country. The winner of the Prize and the judge are featured in an annual reading.'' Recommends being ''at a stage in your development where some of your poems have already been published in literary journals. Manuscripts not adhering to guidelines will not be forwarded to judge nor returned to applicant.''

⬛ $⊘ THE CENTER FOR BOOK ARTS' ANNUAL POETRY CHAPBOOK COMPETITION

28 W. 27th St., 3rd Floor, New York NY 10001. (212)481-0295. E-mail: info@centerforbookarts.org. Website: www.centerforbookarts.org. Established 1995. **Contact:** Alexander Campos, executive director. Offers $500 cash prize, a $500 reading honorarium, and publication of winning manuscript

in a limited edition letterpress-printed and handbound chapbook. Pays winners from other countries in U.S. dollars. Submissions may be previously published and entered in other contests. Submit no more than 500 lines or 24 pages on any subject, in any form; collection or sequence of poems or a single long poem. Entry form and guidelines available for SASE, by e-mail, or on website. **Entry fee:** $20/ms (fee will be credited toward the purchase of the winning chapbook). Does not accept entry fees in foreign currencies; accepts U.S. check, cash, or VISA/MasterCard number. **Postmark deadline:** December 1. Competition receives 500-1,000 entries/year. Most recent contest winner was Jack Ridl. 2004 judges: C.K. Williams and Sharon Dolin. Winner will be contacted in April by telephone. Each contestant receives a letter announcing the winner. Copies of winning chapbooks available for $25. Make checks payable to The Center for Book Arts. "Center for Book Arts is a nonprofit organization dedicated to the traditional crafts of bookmaking and contemporary interpretations of the book as an art object. Through the Center's Education, Exhibition, and Workspace Programs we ensure that the ancient craft of the book remains a viable and vital part of our civilization."

◪ $◩ ◎ CHICANO/LATINO LITERARY PRIZE (Specialized: bilingual/English, Spanish)

Dept. of Spanish & Portuguese, 322 Humanities Hall, University of California at Irvine, Irvine CA 92697-5275. E-mail: cllp@uci.edu. Website: www.humanities.uci.edu/spanishandportuguese/cont est.html. Established 1974. CLLP Director: Prof. Juan Bruce-Novoa. **Contact:** Prize Coordinator. Annual contest focusing on one of 4 genres each year: poetry (2005), drama (2006), novel (2007), and short story (2008). 1st Prize: $1,000, publication of work if not under previous contract, and transportation to Irvine to receive the award; 2nd Prize: $500; 3rd Prize: $250. Work may be in English or Spanish. Only one entry/author. Open to U.S. citizens or permanent residents of the U.S. Guidelines available for SASE, by e-mail, or on website. **Deadline:** June 1. Winners will be notified in October.

$◻ CNW/FFWA FLORIDA STATE WRITING COMPETITION

Florida Freelance Writers Association, P.O. Box A, North Stratford NH 03590-0167. (603)922-8338. E-mail: contest@writers-editors.com. Website: www.writers-editors.com. Established 1978. **Contact:** Dana K. Cassell, award director. Offers annual awards for nonfiction, fiction, children's literature, and poetry. Awards for each category are 1st Prize: $100 plus certificate; 2nd Prize: $75 plus certificate; 3rd Prize: $50 plus certificate; plus Honorable Mention certificates. Submissions must be unpublished. Submit any number of poems on any subject in traditional forms, free verse, or children's. Entry form and guidelines available for SASE or on website. Accepts inquiries by e-mail. **Entry fee:** $3/poem (members), $5/poem (nonmembers). **Deadline:** March 15. Competition receives 350-400 entries/year. Competition is judged by writers, librarians, and teachers. Winners will be announced on May 31 by mail and on website.

$◩ DANA AWARD IN POETRY

200 Fosseway Dr., Greensboro NC 27455. (336)644-8028 (for emergency questions only). E-mail: danaawards@pipeline.com. Website: www.danaawards.com. Established 1996. **Contact:** Mary Elizabeth Parker, award chair. Offers annual award of $1,000 for the best group of 5 poems. Pays winners from other countries by check in U.S. dollars. Submissions must be unpublished and not under promise of publication when submitted; may be simultaneously submitted elsewhere. Submit 5 poems on any subject, in any form; no light verse. Entries by regular mail only. Include SASE for winners list. No mss will be returned. Include separate cover sheet with name, address, phone, e-mail address, and titles of poems. Guidelines available for SASE, by e-mail, or on website. **Entry fee:** $15/5 poems. Does not accept entry fees in foreign currencies; accepts bank draft, International Money Order, or check in U.S. dollars only, drawn on U.S. bank. No personal checks written on foreign banks. **Postmark deadline:** October 31. Competition receives 400-500 poetry entries. Recent judges: Enid Shomer and Michael White. Winner will be announced in early spring by phone, letter, and e-mail.

⭐ $□ DANCING POETRY CONTEST; DANCING POETRY FESTIVAL

Artists Embassy International, 704 Brigham Ave., Santa Rosa CA 95404-5245. (707)528-0912. E-mail: jhcheung@aol.com. Website: www.DANCINGPOETRY.com. Established 1993. **Contact:** Judy Cheung, contest chair. Annual contest offers three Grand Prizes of $100, five 1st Prizes of $50, 10 2nd Prizes of $25, 20 3rd Prizes of $10. The 3 Grand Prize-winning poems will be choreographed, costumed, premiered, and videotaped at the annual Dancing Poetry Festival at Palace of the Legion of Honor, San Francisco; Natica Angilly's Poetic Dance Theater Company will perform the 3 Grand Prize-winning poems. In addition, "all prizes include an invitation to read your prize poem at the festival and a certificate suitable for framing." Pays winners from other countries by International Money Order with U.S. value at the time of the transaction. Submissions must be unpublished or poet must own rights. Submit 2 copies of any number of poems, 40 lines maximum (each), with name, address, phone number on one copy only. Foreign language poems must include English translations. Include SASE for winners list. Entry form available for SASE. No inquiries or entries by fax or e-mail. **Entry fee:** $5/poem or $10/3 poems. Does not accept entry fees in foreign currencies; send International Money Order in U.S. dollars. **Deadline:** June 15. Competition receives about 500-800 entries. 2004 Grand Prize winners were Nancy Jean Carringan, Jabez W. Churchhill, and Carol Frith. Other winners include Sue William Silverman, Jennifer Lemming, Tanya Joyce, Phil Phillips, and Adam David Miller. Judges for upcoming contest: members of Artists Embassy International. Winners will be announced by mail; Grand Prize winners will be contacted by phone. Ticket to festival will be given to all winners. Artist Embassy International has been a nonprofit educational arts organization since 1951, "Furthering intercultural understanding and peace through the universal language of the arts."

$□ THE DOROTHY DANIELS ANNUAL HONORARY WRITING AWARD

The National League of American Pen Women, Inc.—Simi Valley Branch, P.O. Box 1485, Simi Valley CA 93062. E-mail: cdoering@adelphia.net. Established 1980. **Contact:** Carol Doering, award director. Offers annual award of 1st Prize: $100 in each category: poetry, fiction, nonfiction. Pays winners from other countries by check in U.S. currency. Submissions must be unpublished. Submit any number of poems, 50 lines maximum each, on any subject, free verse or traditional. Manuscript must not include name and address. Include cover letter with name, address, phone, title, category of each entry, and line count for each poem. Poem must be titled and typed on $8\frac{1}{2} \times 11$ white paper, single- or double-spaced, one poem/page. Guidelines and winners list available by e-mail. **Entry fee:** $5/poem. Does not accept entry fees in foreign currencies; send "checks which consider the exchange rate, or U.S. cash money." **Deadline:** July 31. Competition receives 1,500 entries/year. Recent award winner was Linda Smith. Winners will be announced by mail in early November. "Request rules and follow them carefully—always include SASE." The National League of American Pen Women, a nonprofit organization headquartered in Washington, DC, was established in 1897 and has a membership of more than 7,000 professional writers, artists, and composers. The Simi Valley Branch, of which noted novelists Dorothy Daniels and Elizabeth Forsythe Hailey are Honorary Members, was established in 1977.

⭐ 🌐 $□ THE DAVID ST. JOHN THOMAS CHARITABLE TRUST COMPETITIONS & AWARDS

The David St. John Thomas Charitable Trust, P.O. Box 6055, Nairn IV12 4YB Scotland. Phone: (01667) 453351. Established 1990. **Contact:** Lorna Edwardson, competition/awards manager. "We run what we believe is the largest single program of writing competitions and awards in the English-speaking world, with prizes totalling £20,000-30,000. There are some regulars, such as the annual ghost story and love story competitions (each 1,600-1800 words with £1,000 first prize) and open poetry competition (poems up to 32 lines, total prize money £1,000). Publication of winning entries is guaranteed, usually in *Writers' News/Writing Magazine*. Awards are led by the annual Self-Publishing Awards, open to anyone who has self-published a book during the preceding calendar year. There are 4 categories, each with £250 prize; the overall winner is declared Self-Publisher of the Year with a total award of £1,000 (established 1993). For full details of these and many others, including an annual writers' groups anthology and Letter-Writer of the Year, please send large SAE.''

$☐ MILTON DORFMAN NATIONAL POETRY PRIZE

% Rome Art & Community Center, 308 W. Bloomfield St., Rome NY 13440. (315)336-1040. Fax: (315)336-1090. E-mail: racc@cnymail.com. Website: www.romeart.org. **Contact:** Chris Galin. Annual award for unpublished poetry. Prizes: $500, $250, and $150. **Entry fee:** $15/poem (American funds only; $20 returned check penalty). Make checks payable to Rome Art & Community Center. Poets must be 18 years of age to enter. **Deadline:** April 30. Include name, address, and phone number on each entry. Poems are published in center's newsletter. Award ceremony and poetry reading in June. Competition receives about 1,000 entries/year. Judge to be announced. Winners notified by May. Results available for SASE.

▦ $◪ T.S. ELIOT PRIZE (Specialized: regional/UK, Ireland)

The Poetry Book Society, Book House, 45 East Hill, London SW18 20Z United Kingdom. Phone: (020)8870 8403. Fax: (020)8870 0865. E-mail: info@poetrybooks.co.uk. Website: www.poetrybook s.co.uk. Established 1993. **Contact:** Chris Holifield, award director. Offers annual award for the best poetry collection published in the UK/Republic of Ireland each year. Prize: £10,000 (donated by Mrs. Valerie Eliot). Submissions must be previously published and may be entered in other contests. **Book/ms must be submitted by publisher** and have been published (or scheduled to be published) the year of the contest. Entry form and guidelines available for SASE or by fax or e-mail. **Deadline:** early August. Competition receives 100 entries/year. Most recent contest winner was Don Paterson. Recent judges: Douglas Dunn, Paul Farley, and Carol Rumens. Winner will be announced in January.

$◪ T.S. ELIOT PRIZE FOR POETRY; TRUMAN STATE UNIVERSITY PRESS

100 E. Normal, Kirksville MO 63501-4221. (660)785-7336. Fax: (660)785-4480. E-mail: tsup@truma n.edu. Website: http://tsup.truman.edu. Press established 1986. **Contact:** Nancy Rediger. Offers annual award of $2,000, publication, and 10 copies as first prize. Submit 60-100 pages, include 2 title pages, one with name, address, phone, and ms title; the other with only the title. Individual poems may have been previously published in periodicals or anthologies, but the collection must not have been published as a book. Include SASE if you wish acknowledgement of receipt of your ms. Manuscripts will not be returned. Guidelines available for SASE or on website. **Entry fee:** $25. **Deadline:** October 31. Competition receives more than 500 entries/year. Recent contest winners were Michael Sowder (2004), Barbara Campbell (2003), and James Gurley (2002).

✪ ◪ ◎ EMERGING VOICES (Specialized: writers from minority, immigrant, and underserved communities)

PEN USA, 672 S. Lafayette Park Place, Suite 42, Los Angeles CA 90057. (213)365-8500. Fax: (213)365-9616. E-mail: ev@penusa.org. Website: www.penusa.org. **Contact:** Literary Programs Coordinator. Annual program offering $1,000 stipend and 8-month fellowship to writers in the early stages of their literary careers. Program includes one-on-one sessions with mentors, seminars on topics such as editing or working with agents, courses in the Writers' Program at UCLA Extension, and literary readings. Participants selected according to potential, experience, and goals. No age restrictions; selection is *not* based solely on economic need. Participants need not be published, but ''the program is directed toward poets and writers of fiction and creative nonfiction with clear ideas of what they hope to accomplish through their writing. Mentors are chosen from PEN's comprehensive membership of professional writers and beyond. Participants are paired with established writers sharing similar writing interests and often with those of the same ethnic and cultural backgrounds.'' Program gets underway in January. **Deadline:** September 2, 2005 (for 2006 cycle). ''All materials must arrive in the PEN offices by the submission deadline—no exceptions.'' See website for brochure and complete guidelines.

⊠ $☑ THE WILLIAM FAULKNER—WILLIAM WISDOM CREATIVE WRITING COMPETITION; MARBLE FAUN PRIZE FOR POETRY; THE DOUBLE DEALER

The Pirate's Alley Faulkner Society, Inc., 624 Pirate's Alley, New Orleans LA 70116. (504)586-1609 or (504)529-3450. E-mail: faulkhouse@aol.com. Website: www.wordsandmusic.org. Established 1992. **Contact:** Rosemary James, award director. Offers annual publication in *The Double Dealer Redux*, cash prize of $750, gold medal, and trip to New Orleans from any continental U.S. city. "Foreign nationals are eligible, but the society pays transportation to awards ceremony from U.S. cities only. Winners must be present at annual meeting to receive award." Submissions must be previously unpublished. Submit one poem of no more than 750 words on any subject in any English-language form. Entry form (required) and guidelines available for SASE or on website. **Entry fee:** $25/entry. **Deadline:** April 1. Competition receives 1,600 (for 7 categories) entries/year. Most recent contest winner was Jan Presley. Winners will be announced on the society's website. "Do not send us multiple poems and expect us to select one. The entry is a single poem. Competition is keen. Send your best work."

⊠ $☑ ◎ FLORIDA INDIVIDUAL ARTIST FELLOWSHIPS (Specialized: regional)

Florida Division of Cultural Affairs, Dept. of State, 1001 DeSoto Park Dr., Tallahassee FL 32301. (850)245-6470. Website: www.florida-arts.org. **Contact:** Erin Long, arts administrator. Offers an undetermined number of fellowships in the amount of $5,000 each biannually. "The Individual Artist Fellowship Program is designed to recognize practicing professional creative artists residing in Florida through monetary fellowship awards. The program provides support for artists of exceptional talent and demonstrated ability to improve their artistic skills and enhance their careers. Fellowships may be awarded in the following discipline categories: dance, folk arts, interdisciplinary, literature, media arts, music, theatre, and visual arts and crafts." Submissions can be previously published or unpublished. Submit 3-5 representative poems, single- or double-spaced. "Reproductions of published work may not be submitted in published format. Open to Florida residents of at least 18 years of age who are not enrolled in undergraduate or graduate programs. Eight copies of the work sample must be included with 8 copies of the application form. Write for entry form and guidelines." **Deadline:** June 2006. Competition receives 500 entries. Most recent winner was Don Stap.

$☑ THE ROBERT FROST FOUNDATION ANNUAL POETRY AWARD

The Robert Frost Foundation, Heritage Place, 439 S. Union St., Lawrence MA 01843. (978)725-8828. E-mail: frostfoundation@comcast.net. Website: www.frostfoundation.org. Established 1997. Offers annual award of $1,000. Pays winners from other countries in U.S. dollars. Submissions may be entered in other contests. Submit up to 3 poems of not more than 3 pages each (2 copies of each poem, one with name, address, and phone number), written in the spirit of Robert Frost. Guidelines available for SASE and on website. **Entry fee:** $10/poem. Does not accept entry fees in foreign currencies. **Deadline:** September 1. Competition receives over 400 entries/year. 2004 winner was Megan Grumbling. Winners will be announced at the annual Frost Festival and by SASE following the Festival (late October). Winning poem can be viewed on website.

$☑ RHEA AND SEYMOUR GORSLINE POETRY COMPETITION

Cloudbank Books, P.O. Box 610, Corvallis OR 97339. (541)752-0075. Website: www.cloudbankbooks.com. Established 2003. **Contact:** Michael Malan, award director. Offers annual award of book publication. Open to poets who have been residents of U.S. or Canada for at least 2 years. Submissions may be previously published individually but ms as a whole must be unpublished (publication credit for each poem should appear on the acknowledgments page). Manuscripts may be entered in other contests, but poet must notify contest if ms is accepted elsewhere. Submit up to 71 pages of poetry (in English); page count includes contents, acknowledgments, section openers, and pages used to present quotation or notes. Type on one side of paper. Include 2 title pages: 1) First should include poet's name, address, telephone number, and title of ms. 2) Second should include ms title only. Poet's name and any other personal information should not appear on pages of ms except first title page. Mss will not be returned; enclose SASP for confirmation of delivery. Hard copy only, no disks. Guidelines available for SASE. **Entry fee:** $10/book ms. **Deadline:** August 15. 2004 judge: Vern Rutsala. Winner will be announced by SASE in December and in the March issue of *Poets & Writers*. Copies of winning books are available from Cloudbank Books and Amazon.

✪ $⌷ GRANDMOTHER EARTH NATIONAL AWARD

Grandmother Earth Creations, P.O. Box 2018, Cordova TN 38088. (901)309-3692. E-mail: Gmoearth @aol.com. Website: www.grandmotherearth.com. Established 1994. **Contact:** Frances Cowden, award director. Offers annual award of $1,250 with varying distributions each year. $1,250 minimum in awards for poetry and prose; $200 first, etc., plus publication in anthology; non-winning finalists considered for anthology if permission is given. Send published or unpublished work. Submissions may be entered in other contests. Submit at least 3 poems, any subject, in any form. Include SASE for winners list. Guidelines available for SASE or on website. **Entry fee:** $10/3 works, $2 each additional work. Entry fee includes a copy of the anthology. **Deadline:** July 15. Most recent award winners were Marilyn Kemph and Maureen Cannon. Judges: Isabel Glaser and Stephen Malin. Winner will be announced in October at the Mid-South Poetry Festival in Memphis. Copies of winning poems or books available from Grandmother Earth Creations.

$⌷ THE GREAT BLUE BEACON POETRY CONTEST; THE GREAT BLUE BEACON

1425 Patriot Dr., Melbourne FL 32940. (321)253-5869. E-mail: ajircc@juno.com. Established 1997. **Contact:** A.J. Byers, award director. Offers prizes approximately 3 times/year, as announced, of 1st Prize: $25; 2nd Prize: $15; 3rd Prize: $10. "Winning poem to be published in *The Great Blue Beacon* (amounts will be increased if sufficient entries are received.)" *The Great Blue Beacon* is a quarterly newsletter for all writers. Sample copy: $1 and 60¢ postage (or IRC). Subscription: $10/year, students $8; $14 outside the U.S. Submissions must be unpublished and may be entered in other contests. Submit up to 3 poems maximum on any subject in any form. "Submit 3 typed copies of each entry, no more than 24 lines/poem. On one copy, place your name, address, and telephone number on the upper left-hand corner of the first page. No name or address on the second or third copies." Guidelines available for SASE or by e-mail. Accepts inquiries by e-mail. **Entry fee:** $3/poem ($2 for subscribers to *The Great Blue Beacon*). Does not accept entry fees in foreign currencies; U.S. dollars only. Make checks payable to Andy Byers. Competition receives 200-300 entries/year. Most recent winners were Anna Evans (NJ), 1st and 2nd places; and Barbara Anton (FL). Winners will be announced approximately 2 months after deadline date. "Contestants must send SASE or e-mail address with entry to receive notification of results. Follow guidelines, particularly line limits. Submit your best work."

✪ $⌷ GROLIER POETRY PRIZE; ELLEN LA FORGE MEMORIAL POETRY FOUNDATION, INC.

6 Plympton St., Cambridge MA 02138. **Note: This is the bookstore address, not the contest address, which changes annually; check guidelines or website for current address.** (617)253-4452. Website: www.grolierpoetrybookshop.com. Established 1974. The Grolier Poetry Prize is open to all poets who have not published either a vanity, small press, trade, or chapbook of poetry. Two poets receive an honorarium of $200 each. Up to 4 poems by each winner and 1-2 by each of 4 runners-up are chosen for publication in the *Grolier Poetry Prize Annual*. Submissions must be unpublished and may not be simultaneously submitted. Submit up to 5 poems, not more than 10 double-spaced pages. Submit one ms in duplicate, without name of poet. On a separate sheet give name, address, phone number, and titles of poems. Only one submission/contestant; mss are not returned. For updated guidelines, send SASE to Ellen La Forge Memorial Poetry Foundation or check website before submitting ms. **Entry fee:** $7, includes copy of *Annual*. Make checks payable to the Ellen La Forge Memorial Poetry Foundation, Inc. Enclose self-addressed stamped postcard for acknowledgement of receipt. Opens January 15 of each year. **Deadline:** May 1. Winners and runners-up will be selected and informed in early June. Competition receives approximately 500

entries. Recent award winners include Maggie Dietz, Natasha Trethewey, and Babo Kamel. The Ellen La Forge Memorial Poetry Foundation sponsors a reading series, generally 10/semester, held on the grounds of Harvard University. Poets who have new collections of poetry available are eligible. Honoraria vary. Such poets as Philip Levine, Susan Kinsolving, Donald Hall, and Molly McQuade have given readings. Foundation depends upon private gifts and support for its activities. Copies of the *Annual* available from the Book Shop at the above address.

✪ $☑ GUGGENHEIM FELLOWSHIPS

John Simon Guggenheim Memorial Foundation, 90 Park Ave., New York NY 10016. (212)687-4470. Fax: (212)697-3248. E-mail: fellowships@gf.org. Website: www.gf.org. Established 1925. Guggenheim fellowships are awarded each year to individuals who have already demonstrated exceptional capacity for productive scholarship or exceptional creative ability in the arts. The amounts of the grants vary. The average grant in 2004 was $37,362. Most recent award winners for poetry were Mary Jo Bang, Olena Kalytiak Davis, Toi Derricotte, Stuart Dischell, Andrew Hudgins, Lawson Fusao Inada, Mary Karr, Kay Ryan, Grace Schulman, and Vijay Seshadri (2004). In 2004, 185 U.S. and Canadian Fellowships were awarded out of 3,268 applications. **Application deadline:** October 1. See webstie for application details.

$☑ THE DONALD HALL PRIZE FOR POETRY; AWP AWARD SERIES

AWP, MS 1E3, George Mason University, Fairfax VA 22030. E-mail: awp@awpwriter.org. Website: http://awpwriter.org. Established 2003. The Association of Writers & Writing Programs (AWP) sponsors an annual competition for the publication of excellent new book-length works, the AWP Award Series, which includes The Donald Hall Prize for Poetry. Offers annual award of $4,000 and publication for the best book-length ms of poetry (book-length defined for this competition as 48 pages minimum of text). Open to published and unpublished poets alike. "Poems previously published in periodicals are eligible for inclusion in submissions, but manuscripts previously published in their entirety, including self-published, are not eligible. As the series is judged anonymously, no list of acknowledgements should accompany your manuscript. You may submit your manuscript to other publishers while it is under consideration by the Award Series, but you must notify AWP immediately in writing if your manuscript is accepted elsewhere. No e-mail or phone calls, please." Manuscripts must be typed and single-spaced on good quality paper, $8\frac{1}{2} \times 11$. Photocopies or copies from letter-quality printers acceptable, but no dot matrix. Manuscripts should not be bound or in a folder; binder-clip or rubber-band mss together. No mss will be returned. Include SASP for confirmation of receipt of ms; SASE for notification of winners. Guidelines, including important formatting information and eligibility requirements, available on website. **Entry fee:** handling fee of $10 (AWP members) or $20 (nonmembers). Does not accept entry fees in foreign currencies; check or money order in U.S. dollars, drawn on U.S. bank, payable to AWP. **Deadline:** mss accepted January 1-February 28. 2005 judge: Ha Jin. AWP is a nonprofit organization of writers, teachers, colleges, and universities. (See separate listing for the Association of Writers & Writing Programs (AWP) in the Organizations section.)

$☑ ◎ J.C. AND RUTH HALLS AND DIANE MIDDLEBROOK FELLOWSHIPS IN POETRY (Specialized: MFA or PhD in creative writing)

Wisconsin Institute for Creative Writing, English Dept., 600 North Park St., Madison WI 53706. Website: http://creativewriting.wisc.edu. Established 1986. **Contact:** Jesse Lee Kercheval, director. Offers annual fellowships, will pay $25,000 for one academic year. Applicants will teach one creative writing class/semester at University of Wisconsin and give a public reading at the end of their stay. Submissions may be entered in other contests. Submit 10 poems maximum on any subject, in any form. *Applicants must have a MFA or PhD in creative writing.* Applicants cannot have published a book (chapbooks will not disqualify an applicant). Guidelines available for SASE or on website. **Reading fee:** $20. Accepts reading fees in foreign currencies. **Deadline:** Applications must be received in the month of February. Competitions receive 200 entries/year. Judges: faculty of the creative writing program. Results will be sent to applicants by May 1. "The fellowships are administered by the Program in Creative Writing at the University of Wisconsin-Madison. Funding is provided by the Jay C. and Ruth Halls Writing Fund and the Carl Djerassi and Diane Middlebrook Fund through the University of Wisconsin Foundation."

$☐ THE ALFRED HODDER FELLOWSHIP

Council of the Humanities, Joseph Henry House, Princeton University, Princeton NJ 08544. E-mail: humcounc@princeton.edu. Website: www.princeton.edu/~humcounc. **Contact:** Lin DeTitta. "Stipends of $54,000 will be given to 2 writers of exceptional promise to pursue independent projects in the humanities at Princeton University during the 2005-2006 academic year. Typically the fellows are poets, playwrights, novelists, creative nonfiction writers, and translators who have published one highly acclaimed work and are undertaking a significant new project that might not be possible without the 'studious leisure' afforded by the fellowship." Preference is given to applicants outside academia. **Candidates for the Ph.D. are not eligible.** Submit a résumé, sample of previous work (10 pages maximum, not returnable), a project proposal of 2-3 pages, and SASE. Guidelines available for SASE or on website. **Postmark deadline:** November 1. Announcement of the Hodder Fellow is posted on the website in March.

$☐ TOM HOWARD/JOHN H. REID POETRY CONTEST

Tom Howard Books, % Winning Writers, 351 Pleasant St., PMB 222, Northampton MA 01060-3961. (866)946-9748. Fax: (413)280-0539. E-mail: johnreid@mail.qango.com. Website: www.winningwriters.com. Established 2003. **Contact:** John H. Reid, award director. Offers annual award of 1st Prize: $1,000; 2nd Prize: $400; 3rd Prize: $200; and 4 Encouragement Awards of $100 each. All prizewinners will be published in an anthology. "Non-U.S. winners will be paid in U.S. currency or via PayPal if a check is inconvenient." Submissions may be published or unpublished, may have won prizes elsewhere, and may be entered in other contests. Submit poems in any form, style, or genre. "There is no limit on the number of lines or poems you may submit." No name on ms pages; type or computer-print on letter-size white paper, single-sided. Submit online or by regular mail. Guidelines available for SASE or on website. **Entry fee:** $5 U.S. for every 25 lines (exclude poem titles and any blank lines from line count). Does not accept entry fees in foreign currencies; "U.S. dollars only, payment accepted by credit card, check, money order, or (last resort) currency." **Deadline:** January 1-September 30. Competition receives about 800 entries/year. 2004 winner was Elaine Winer for "The Dark Room." 2004 judge: Tom Howard. Winners announced in December at WinningWriters.com. Entrants who provide valid e-mail addresses will also receive notification.

$☐ HENRY HOYNS POE/FAULKNER FELLOWSHIPS

Creative Writing Program, 219 Bryan Hall, P.O. Box 400121, University of Virginia, Charlottesville VA 22904-4121. (434)924-6675. Fax: (434)924-1478. E-mail: LRS9E@virginia.edu. Website: www.engl.virginia.edu/cwp. **Contact:** Lisa Russ Spaar, program director. Annual fellowships in poetry and fiction of varying amounts for candidates for the MFA in creative writing. Sample poems/prose required with application. Accepts inquiries by fax and e-mail. **Deadline:** January 1. Competition receives 300-400 entries.

$☐ JOSEPH HENRY JACKSON AWARD; JAMES D. PHELAN AWARD (Specialized: regional/CA, NV)

% Intersection for the Arts, 446 Valencia St., San Francisco CA 94103. (415)626-2787. Fax: (415)626-1636. Website: www.theintersection.org. **Contact:** Awards Coordinator. Offers the **Jackson Award** ($2,000), established in 1955, to the author of an unpublished work-in-progress of fiction (novel or short stories), nonfictional prose, or poetry. Applicants must be residents of northern California or Nevada for 3 consecutive years immediately prior to the January 31 deadline and must be between the ages of 20 and 35 as of the deadline. Offers the **Phelan Award** ($2,000), established in 1935, to the author of an unpublished work-in-progress of fiction (novel or short stories), nonfictional prose, poetry, or drama. Applicants must be California-born (although they may now reside outside of the state), and must be between the ages of 20 and 35 as of the January 31 deadline. See website for complete guidelines and entry form (required). **Deadline:** entries accepted November 15 through January 31. Competitions receive 150-180 entries. 2004 winners were Sandra Stringer and Zakiyyah Alexander. 2004 judges: Paul S. Flores, Susan Griffin, and Kevin Killian.

$□ ◎ HELEN VAUGHN JOHNSON MEMORIAL HAIKU AWARD (Specialized: forms/haiku); POETRY FOR PETS (Specialized: animals)

Women in the Arts, P.O. Box 2907, Decatur IL 62524. Established 2001. **Contact:** Linda Hutton, vice-president. **The Helen Vaughn Johnson Memorial Haiku Award** is awarded annually for traditional haiku. 1st Prize: $25; 2nd Prize: $15; 3rd Prize: $10. Pays winners from other countries by money order. Submissions may be previously published and may be entered in other contests. Submit unlimited number of poems of 5 lines about nature in traditional 5-7-5 haiku format; must not refer to people; no title. Name, address, and phone number should appear in upper righthand corner of each page. Guidelines available for SASE. **Entry fee:** $1/haiku. Make check payable to WITA. Accepts entry fees in foreign currencies. **Postmark Deadline:** January 17 annually. Competition receives 100 entries. 2003 winners were Marilyn Voorhees, Earl Dean, and Lucy Rowan. "Judge is a publishing, professional writer living outside the state of Illinois. New judge annually." Winners will be announced February 20 annually. "Study traditional haiku; we do not accept anything but 5-7-5." Also offers **Poetry for Pets**, an annual prize of $25 each in 2 categories (rhymed and unrhymed poetry). Submissions may be previously published, must be your own work. Submit any number of poems, no more than 24 lines each (excluding title) on the subject of "pets." Entries must be typed and titled, with poet's name and address on back of page. Include #10 SASE for list of winners. **Entry fee:** $2/poem, or 3 poems for $5. Make check payable to WITA. **Postmark Deadline:** June 1. "Two winners will be published in a special flyer. After paying prizes and expenses of contest, the remainder of the entry fees will be donated to a humane society of our choice. Always request complete rules."

⊠ $□ BARBARA MANDIGO KELLY PEACE POETRY CONTEST

Nuclear Age Peace Foundation, PMB 121, 1187 Coast Village Rd., Suite 1, Santa Barbara CA 93108-2794. (805)965-3443. Fax: (805)568-0466. E-mail: wagingpeace@napf.org. Website: www.wagingpeace.org. Established 1996. Offers an annual series of awards "to encourage poets to explore and illuminate positive visions of peace and the human spirit." Awards $1,000 to adult contestants, $200 to youth (13-18), $200 to youth (12 and under), and honorable mentions in each category. Submissions must be unpublished. Submit up to 3 poems in any form. Send 2 copies; maximum 40 lines/poem. Put name, address, phone number, and age (for youth) in upper right-hand corner of one copy of each poem. "Poets should keep copies of all entries as we will be unable to return them." Guidelines available for SASE or on website. **Entry fee:** $15 for up to 3 poems; no fee for youth entries. **Postmark deadline:** July 1. Competition receives over 500 entries. 2004 winners were Colleen Dwyer-Lulf, Lois Beckett (13-18), and Helen Wang (12 and under). Judges: a committee of poets selected by the Nuclear Age Peace Foundation. Winners will be announced through press release and mail notification by October and on website. Winning poems will be posted on the Foundation's website.

$☑ ◎ HAROLD MORTON LANDON TRANSLATION AWARD

The Academy of American Poets, 588 Broadway, Suite 604, New York NY 10012-3210. (212)274-0343. Fax: (212)274-9427. E-mail: rmurphy@poets.org. Website: www.poets.org. Award established 1976. **Contact:** Ryan Murphy, awards coordinator. Offers one $1,000 award each year to a U.S. citizen for translation of a book-length poem, a collection of poems, or a verse-drama translated into English from any language. Guidelines available for SASE or on website. **Deadline:** December 31 of year in which book was published. 2004 winner was Charles Martin for *Metamorphoses*, by

Orid. 2005 judge: Mark Strand. (For further information about The Academy of American Poets, see separate listing in the Organizations section.)

$☯ THE JAMES LAUGHLIN AWARD

The Academy of American Poets, 588 Broadway, Suite 604, New York NY 10012-3210. (212)274-0343. Fax: (212)274-9427. E-mail: rmurphy@poets.org. Website: www.poets.org. Offered since 1954. **Contact:** Ryan Murphy, awards coordinator. Offers $5,000 prize to recognize and support a poet's second book (ms must be under contract to a publisher). Submissions must be made by a publisher in ms form. The Academy of American Poets distributes copies of the Laughlin Award-winning book to its members. Poets must be American citizens. Entry form, signed by the publisher, required. Entry form and guidelines available for SASE or on website. **Deadline:** submissions accepted between January 1 and May 15. Winners announced in August. 2004 winner was Jeff Clark for *Music and Suicide*. Judges: Elizabeth Alexander, Mary Jo Bang, and Susan Stewart. (For further information about The Academy of American Poets, see separate listing in the Organizations section.)

$□ THE LEAGUE OF MINNESOTA POETS CONTEST

310 SW 4th St., Brainerd MN 56401-1173. E-mail: rhyming@gmail.com. **Contact:** Sue Wipperling, contest chair. Annual contest offers 18 different categories, with 3 prizes in each category ranging from $10-125. See guidelines for poem lengths, forms, and subjects. Guidelines available for #10 SASE or by e-mail. **Nonmember fee:** $1/poem per category; $2/poem (limit 6) for Grand Prize category. **Members fee:** $5 for 17 categories; $1/poem (limit 6) for Grand Prize category. Make checks payable to LOMP Contest. **Deadline:** July 31. Nationally known, non-Minnesota judges. Winners will be announced at the October LOMP Conference and by mail.

$□ THE LITTLE BITTY POETRY COMPETITION

Shadow Poetry, 1209 Milwaukee St., Excelsior Springs MO 64024. Fax: (208)977-9114. E-mail: shadowpoetry@shadowpoetry.com. Website: www.shadowpoetry.com. Established 2000. **Contact:** James Summers, award director. Offers quarterly award of 1st Prize: $40; 2nd Prize: $20; 3rd Prize: $10; plus the top 3 winners also receive a certificate, printed copy of winning poem, and a ribbon. Pays winners from other countries in U.S. dollars only by International Money Order or PayPal. Submissions may be previously published and may be entered in other contests. Submit unlimited number of poems of 3-12 lines on any subject, in any form. "Entry form must be present with mail-in entries. Submit entries in duplicate with name, address, phone number, e-mail address (when available) on upper left-hand corner of one sheet. Enclose SASE for winners list. Include an additional SASE for entry receipt (optional). If no SASE is included for receipt, Shadow Poetry will e-mail an entry confirmation to the contestant, if applicable." Entry form and guidelines available for SASE or on website. **Entry fee:** $1.50/poem. Make checks payable to Shadow Poetry. Does not accept entry fees in foreign currencies; accepts International Money Order, cash (U.S. dollars), or payments through PayPal for foreign entries. **Deadlines:** March 31, June 30, September 30, and December 31. Winners will be announced "15 days after each quarterly contest ends, by e-mail and to those who requested a winners list. Results will also be posted on the Shadow Poetry website."

$☯ THE LENORE MARSHALL POETRY PRIZE

The Academy of American Poets, 588 Broadway, Suite 604, New York NY 10012-3210. (212)274-0343. Fax: (212)274-9427. E-mail: rmurphy@poets.org. Website: www.poets.org. Award established 1975. **Contact:** Ryan Murphy, awards coordinator. Offers $25,000 for the most outstanding book of poems published in the U.S. in the preceding year; administered in conjunction with *The Nation*. Contest is open to books by living American poets published in a standard edition (40 pages or more in length with 500 or more copies printed). **Self-published books are not eligible.** Publishers may enter as many books as they wish. Four copies of each book must be submitted and none will be returned. Guidelines, required entry form available for SASE or on website. **Entry**

fee: $25/title. **Deadline:** entries must be submitted between April 1 and June 15. Finalists announced in October; winner announced in November. 2004 winner was Donald Revell for *My Mojave*. 2005 judges: Robert Pinsky, Louise Glück, and Alan Shapiro. (For further information about The Academy of American Poets, see separate listing in the Organizations section.)

⊕ $▢ ◎ MELBOURNE POETS UNION ANNUAL NATIONAL POETRY COMPETITION (Specialized: regional/Australian poets)

Melbourne Poets Union, P.O. Box 266, Flinders Lane, Victoria 8009 Australia. E-mail: shannleon@i hug.com.au. Website: http://home.vicnet.net.au/~mpuinc. Established 1977. **Contact:** Leon Shann. Offers annual prizes of $1,350 AU plus book vouchers, book prizes. Pays winners from other countries "with a draft cheque in Australian currency." Submissions must be unpublished. Submit unlimited number of poems on any subject, in any form, up to 30 lines. "Open to Australian residents living in Australia or overseas." Entry form and guidelines available for SASE (or SAE and IRC). **Entry fee:** AUS $5/poem; AUS $12/3 poems. Accepts entry fees in foreign currencies. **Deadline:** October 31. Competition receives over 500 entries/year. 2004 winners included Heather Marsh, Susan Stanford, and Kerryn Tredrea. Winners announced on the last Friday of November by newsletter, mail, phone, and on website. "The $1,350 prize money comes directly from entry money, the rest going to paying the judge and costs of running the competition."

✪ $◎ MID-LIST PRESS FIRST SERIES AWARD FOR POETRY

Mid-List Press, 4324 12th Ave. S., Minneapolis MN 55407-3218. E-mail: guide@midlist.org. Website: www.midlist.org. Established 1990. Offers the First Series Award for Poetry, an annual contest for poets who have never published a book of poetry. Award includes publication and a $500 advance against royalties. Individual poems within the book ms may be previously published and may be entered in other contests. Submit at least 60 single-spaced pages. Guidelines available for #10 SASE or on website. **Entry fee:** $30 U.S.; must include entry form (available online). **Deadline:** accepts submissions October 1 through February 1 (postmark). Competition receives 350 entries/year. Most recent winner was Lou Suarez for *Ask*. "The First Series Award contest is highly competitive. We are looking for poets who have produced a significant body of work but have never published a book-length collection. (A chapbook is not considered a 'book' of poetry.)"

✪ $▢ MILFORD FINE ARTS COUNCIL NATIONAL POETRY CONTEST; HIGH TIDE

Milford Fine Arts Council, 40 Railroad Ave., South, Milford CT 06460. Established 1976. **Contact:** Roseanne Hoagland, contest chairperson. Offers annual award of 1st Prize: $100; 2nd Prize: $50; 3rd Prize: $25; plus winners will be published in MFAC's annual publication, *High Tide*. Submissions must be unpublished and not under consideration by any other publication or contest. Poems entered may not have won any other prizes or honorable mentions. "Poems must be typed single spaced on white standard paper, 10-30 lines (including title), no more than 48 characters/line, on any subject, in any style, rhymed or unrhymed. Use standard font, clear and legible, one poem/page, no script or fax. No bio or date, only the words 'Unpublished Original' typed above the poem. Type your name, address, and ZIP code in the middle back of the submitted poem, no identifying information on the front of the page. Poems will be judged on form, clarity, originality, and universal appeal. Poems will not be returned, so please keep copies. After winners are notified, poems will be destroyed." Guidelines available for SASE. **Entry fee:** $3 for one poem, $5 for 2 poems, $1 for each additional poem after 2. Contestants may enter an unlimited number of poems. Check or money order accepted, no cash. **Deadline:** March 31. For a list of winners, send SASE with the word NOTIFICATION printed on the bottom left corner of the envelope. "Entries may be considered for publication in *High Tide*. If you do not want your poems considered for publication, then you *must* print on the back of the poem (below your name, address, and ZIP code) 'For National Poetry Contest Only.'"

$☐ MISSISSIPPI VALLEY POETRY CONTEST

Midwest Writing Center, P.O. Box 3188, Rock Island IL 61204. (563)359-1057. **Contact:** Max J. Molleston, chairman. Offers annual prizes of approximately $1,500 for unpublished poems in categories for students (elementary, junior, and senior high), adults, Mississippi Valley, senior citizens, jazz, religious, humorous, rhyming, haiku, ethnic, and history. Submissions must be unpublished. **Entry fee:** $8 for up to 5 poems; no limit to number of entries. **Fee for children:** $5 for up to 5 poems. Send check or U.S. dollars. Professional readers present winning poems to a reception at an award evening in May. **Deadline:** April 1. Competition receives 1,000+ entries.

$☑ ◎ MONEY FOR WOMEN (Specialized: women/feminism); GERTRUDE STEIN AWARD; FANNIE LOU HAMER AWARD

Barbara Deming Memorial Fund, Inc., P.O. Box 630125, Bronx NY 10463. **Contact:** Susan Pliner, executive director. Offers biannual small grants of up to $1,500 to feminists in the arts "whose work addresses women's concerns and/or speaks for peace and justice from a feminist perspective." Pays Canadian winners in U.S. dollars. Submissions may be previously published and entered in other contests. Application form available for SASE. **Entrants must use application form with correct deadline date.** Applicants must be citizens of U.S. or Canada. **Application fee:** $10. Accepts entry fees by postal money order or checks drawn on U.S. funds. **Deadline:** June 30. Competition receives 400 entries/year. Recent award winners were Robin Ekiss, Cynthia Gaver, and Marilyn Johnson. Winners will be announced in November. Also offers the Gertrude Stein Award for outstanding work by a lesbian, and the Fannie Lou Hamer Award for work which combats racism and celebrates women of color.

$☑ JENNY McKEAN MOORE WRITER IN WASHINGTON

Dept. of English, George Washington University, Washington DC 20052. (202)994-6515. Fax: (202)994-7915. E-mail: dmca@gwu.edu. Website: www.gwu.edu/~english. Offers fellowship for a visiting lecturer in creative writing, about $50,000 for 2 semesters. Apply by November 15 with résumé and writing sample of 25 pages or less. Awarded to poets and fiction writers in alternating years.

$☑ SAMUEL FRENCH MORSE POETRY PRIZE

Dept. of English, 406 Holmes, Northeastern University, Boston MA 02115. (617)373-4546. Fax: (617)373-2509. E-mail: g.rotella@neu.edu. Website: www.casdn.neu.edu/~english/pub/morse.htm. **Contact:** Prof. Guy Rotella, editor. Offers annual prize of book publication (ms 50-70 pages) by NU/UPNE and $1,000. Open to U.S. poets who have published no more than one book of poetry. Entry must be unpublished in book form but may include poems published in journals and magazines. Guidelines available on website (under "Publications"). Accepts inquiries by e-mail. **Entry fee:** $15. **Deadline:** August 1 for inquiries; September 15 for single copy of ms. Manuscripts will not be returned. Competition receives approximately 400 entries/year. Recent award winners include Jennifer Atkinson, Ted Genoways, and Dana Roeser. Previous judges: Marilyn Hacker, Rosanna Warren, Robert Cording, and Ellen Bryant Voigt.

$☐ NASHVILLE NEWSLETTER POETRY CONTEST

P.O. Box 60535, Nashville TN 37206-0535. Established 1977. **Contact:** Roger Dale Miller, editor. Offers quarterly prizes of $50, $25, and $10 plus possible publication in newsletter (published poets receive 3 copies of *Newsletter* in which their work appears), and at least 50 Certificates of Merit. Pays winners from other countries with check in U.S. funds. Submit one unpublished poem to a page, any style or subject up to 40 lines, with name and address in upper left corner. Send large #10 SASE for more information and/or extra entry forms for future contests. **Entry fee:** $5 for up to 3 poems. Must be sent all at once for each contest. Does not accept entry fees in foreign currencies; accepts check/money order in U.S. funds. "All other nonwinning poems will be considered for possible publication in future issues." Competition receives over 700 entries/year. Most recent winners were William Beyer, Wayne Frank, Michelle Greenblatt, T. Spinosa, and Lisa Moran. Recent judges: Hazel Kirby and James Lee Miller. Winners will be announced by mail. Sample: $3. Responds in up to 10 weeks.

✪ $◙ NATIONAL BOOK AWARD

The National Book Foundation, 95 Madison Ave., Suite 709, New York NY 10016. (212)685-0261. E-mail: nationalbook@nationalbook.org. Website: www.nationalbook.org. Offers annual grand prize of $10,000 in each of 4 categories plus 4 finalist awards of $1,000 in each category. Presents awards in fiction, nonfiction, poetry, and young people's literature. Submissions must be previously published and **must be entered by the publisher**. General guidelines available on website; interested publishers should phone or e-mail the Foundation. **Entry fee:** $100/title. **Deadline:** early July. 2004 poetry winner was Jean Valentine for *Door in the Mountain: New and Collected Poems, 1965-2003*.

$◻ NATIONAL WRITERS UNION ANNUAL NATIONAL POETRY COMPETITION

P.O. Box 2409, Aptos CA 95001. E-mail: bonnie.thomas@att.net. Website: http://home.earthlink. net/~nwu_local7. Sponsored by Santa Cruz/Monterey Local 7 of the National Writers Union. 1st Prize: $500; 2nd Prize: $300; 3rd Prize: $200. Guidelines available for SASE or on website. **Entry fee:** $4/poem (maximum length 3 pages). **2004 Deadline:** December 31. Competition receives about 1,000 entries/year. 2004 judge: Maxine Kumin. Winners announced in March.

$▣ HOWARD NEMEROV SONNET AWARD

The Formalist, 320 Hunter Dr., Evansville IN 47711. Website: www2.evansville.edu/theformalist. Established 1994. Although *The Formalist* has ceased publication, it continues to sponsor the annual Howard Nemerov Sonnet Award. Offers $1,000 prize; winner and 11 finalists will be published in *The Evansville Review*. Submit original, unpublished sonnets, no translations; sonnet sequences acceptable, but each sonnet will be considered individually. Poets may enter as many sonnets as they wish. Poet's name, address, and phone number should be listed on the back of each entry. Enclose SASE for contest results; entries cannot be returned. Guidelines available for SASE or on website. **Entry fee:** $3/sonnet. **Postmark deadline:** November 15. Past winners include Rhina P. Espaillat, Marion Shore, Deborah Warren, and A. M. Jester. 2005 judge: Charles Martin.

$◻ NEW MILLENNIUM AWARD FOR POETRY; NEW MILLENNIUM WRITINGS

NMW, Room EM, P.O. Box 2463, Knoxville TN 37901. Website: www.newmillenniumwritings.com. **Contact:** Don Williams, editor. Offers 2 annual awards of $1,000 each. Submissions must be unpublished and may be entered in other contests. Submit up to 3 poems, 5 pages maximum. No restrictions on style or content. Include name, address, phone number, and a #10 SASE for notification. All contestants receive the next issue at no additional charge. Printable entry form on website. Manuscripts are not returned. Guidelines available for SASE or on website. Accepts inquiries by e-mail. **Entry fee:** $17. Make checks payable to New Millennium Writings. **Deadlines:** June 17 and November 19 (each deadline may be extended once; check website for updates). Competition receives 2,000 entries/year. "Two winners and selected finalists will be published." Most recent award winner was Renée Ruderman. "Contests are not the only avenues to publication. We also accept—at no cost, no entry fee—general submissions for publication during the months of October, November, and December only. These should be addressed to Poetry Editor. There are no restrictions as to style, form, or content. Submitters should enclose SASE for correspondence purposes."

$◙ NEW RIVER POETS QUARTERLY POETRY AWARDS

New River Poets, 5545 Meadowbrook St., Zephyrhills FL 33541-2715. Established 2000. **Contact:** June Owens, awards coordinator. Offers 1st Prize: $65; 2nd Prize: $45; 3rd Prize: $35 for each quarterly contest, plus 5 Honorable Mentions at $5 each, every quarter. Pays winners from other countries by International Bank Money Order. Submissions may be previously published and may be entered in other contests. Submit 1-4 poems of up to 42 lines each on any subject, in any form. "Send 2 copies each poem on 8½×11 white paper; poet's identification on only one copy of each. If previously published, state where/when. At bottom of each poem, state 'Author owns all rights.' If in a traditional form, state form. Quarter for which work is submitted must appear upper right." Guidelines available for SASE. **Entry fee:** 1-4 poems for $5; $1 each additional; no limit. Prefers U.S. funds. **Deadline:** November 15, February 15, May 15, August 15. Competition receives 800 entries/year. Most recent award winners were Donna Jean Tennis, Gwendolyn Carr, and Theda Bassett. Most recent contest judges were Maureen Tolman Flannery, Dr. John McBride, and Edith Baker. (First Place winners are invited to judge a subsequent competition). Winners will be announced by mail within 45 days of deadline. "New River Poets is a chartered Chapter of Florida State Poets Association, Inc. and member of National Federation of State Poetry Societies (NFSPS). Its purpose is to acknowledge and reward outstanding poetic efforts. NRP's first issue of its anthology, *Watermarks: One*, appeared in Summer 2004; it includes the work of previous winners of NRP Poetry Awards. *Watermarks: Two* is scheduled for Spring 2007, but is not open to general submissions." Copies of New River Poets anthologies are available for $6 plus $1.42 postage each. Advises to "send your best. Always include SASE. Our 'rules' are quite wide open, but please adhere. Remember that competition is not only good for the cause of poetry but for the poetic soul, a win-win situation."

$☑ NEWBURYPORT ART ASSOCIATION ANNUAL SPRING POETRY CONTEST

12 Charron Dr., Newburyport MA 01950. E-mail: espmosk@verizon.net. Website: www.newburyportart.org. Established 1990. **Contact:** Rhina P. Espaillat, contest coordinator. Offers annual awards of 1st Prize: $200, 2nd Prize: $150, 3rd Prize: $100, plus a number of Honorable Mentions and certificates. All winners, including Honorable Mention poets, are invited to read their own entries at the Awards Day Reading in May. Open to anyone over 16 years old. Pays all winners, including those from other countries, with NAA check. Submissions must be previously unpublished, may be entered in other contests. Submit any number of poems, each no more than 3 pages in length. Include SASE for notification of contest results. Any number of poems accepted, but all must be mailed together in a single envelope with one check covering the total entry fee. Guidelines available for SASE, by e-mail, or on website. **Entry fee:** $3/poem. Does not accept entry fees in foreign currencies; send U.S. cash, check, or money order. Make checks payable to NAA Poetry Contest (one check for all entries). **Postmark deadline:** March 15. 2004 winners were Michael Cantor, A.M. Juster, and Midge Goldberg. 2004 judge: William Jay Smith. Do not submit entries without first securing a copy of the guidelines, then follow them carefully.

$☐ ◎ NFSPS COLLEGE/UNIVERSITY LEVEL POETRY AWARDS (Specialized: student writing)

P.O. Box 520698, Salt Lake City UT 84152-0698. (801)484-3113. Fax: (801)606-3444. E-mail: SBSenior@juno.com. Website: www.nfsps.org. **Contact:** N. Colwell Snell, chairman. Offers 2 annual awards of $500 each; one as the Edna Meudt Memorial Award, the second as the Florence Kahn Memorial Award. Award includes publication of winning mss with 75 copies awarded to the respective poet. Recipients will be invited to read at the annual NFSPS (National Federation of State Poetry Societies) convention; NFSPS will provide an additional travel stipend to be presented at the convention to recipients in attendance (winners are responsible for the balance of convention costs). Open to all freshmen, sophomores, juniors, and seniors of an accredited university or college. Submit a ms of 10 original poems, one poem to each page, single-spaced, each poem titled. **Each poem must be no more than 46 lines (including spaces between stanzas) and have no more than 50 characters/line (including spaces between words and punctuation).** Manuscript must be titled and must include cover page with name, address, phone number in upper left-hand corner; ms title centered on page. May include dedication page. No other identification on any page other than cover page. **NOTE:** *A current, official NFSPS application, completed and duly notarized, **must** accompany ms at time of submission.* No e-mail submissions or special deliveries; First Class Mail only. Entry form and guidelines available for SASE or on website. **Entry fee:** none. **2005 Deadline:** notarized applications and mss received on or before February 1 (no entry mailed before January 1). For 2005 competition, winners were selected on or before March 31 and announced after April 15. Each recipient's state poetry society also notified. Copies of published award mss available on NFSPS website. (See separate listing for National Federation of State Poetry Societies in Organizations section and for NFSPS Competitions and Stevens Poetry Manuscript Contest in this section.)

$☐ NFSPS COMPETITIONS; ENCORE PRIZE POEM ANTHOLOGY

Contact: Theda Bassett, Contest Chairperson, 6814 S. 1300 E., #20, Salt Lake City UT 84121. (E-mail: theda_bassett2002@yahoo.com.)Website: www.nfsps.org. NFSPS sponsors a national contest with 50 different categories each year, including the NFSPS Founders Award of 1st Prize: $1,500; 2nd Prize: $500; 3rd Prize: $250. **Entry fees for members:** $1/poem or $8 total for 8 or more categories, plus $5/poem for NFSPS Founders Award (limit 4 entries in this category alone). All poems winning over $15 are published in the *ENCORE Prize Poem Anthology*. Rules for all contests are given in a brochure available from Madelyn Eastlund, editor of *Strophes* newsletter, at 310 South Adams St., Beverly Hills FL 34465 (e-mail: verdure@digitalusa.net); or from Theda Bassett at the address above; or on the NFSPS website. You can also write for the address of your state poetry society. NFSPS also sponsors the annual Stevens Poetry Manuscript Competition and the NFSPS College/University Level Poetry Awards (see separate listings in this section; for further information about the National Federation of State Poetry Societies [NFSPS], see separate listing in the Organizations section.)

Ⓝ $◎ THE NIGHBOAT POETRY PRIZE

Nightboat Books, P.O. Box 656, Beacon NY 12508. E-mail: editor@nightboat.org. Website: www.nightboat.org. Established 2003. **Contact:** Jennifer Chapis or Kazim Ali, editors. Offers annual award of $1,000 plus book publication; announces finalists. Pays international winners by certified check in U.S. currency. Submission must be unpublished as a collection, but individual poems may have been previously published in journals, and collection may be entered simultaneously in other ms contests. Submit 48-100 pages of poetry (suggested length only), single-spaced, paginated, one poem/page, one side only. Manuscript must be typed, bound only by a clip. Include 2 title pages (one with book title, name, address, telephone, and e-mail; one with book title only), table of contents, acknowledgments page. Author's name should *not* appear anywhere in the ms, except on the first title page. Bio optional. Entry form and guidelines available for SASE, by e-mail, or on website. **Entry fee:** $20. Does not accept entry fees in foreign currencies; prefers money order in U.S. dollars. **Postmark Deadline:** November 30. Competition receives 500+ entries/year. 2004 judge: Jean Valentine. Winner announced by March on website, in *Poets & Writers Magazine*, and in a written letter to all entrants. Copies of winning books available from Amazon.com, East and West Coast bookstores, and through the Nightboat Books website. "Nightboat holds no bias based on subject matter, writing style, or previous publication. Please send well-crafted manuscripts that are ready for publication. We look forward to receiving your work."

$☐ ◎ FRANK O'HARA AWARD CHAPBOOK COMPETITION; THORNGATE ROAD PRESS (Specialized: gay/lesbian/bisexual/transgendered)

Dept. of English and Humanities, Pratt Institute, 200 Willoughby Ave., Brooklyn NY 11205. (718)636-3790. E-mail: jelledge@pratt.edu (inquiries only). Established 1996. **Contact:** Jim Elledge, award director/publisher. Offers annual award of $500, publication, and 25 copies. Submissions may be a combination of previously published and unpublished work and may be entered in other contests. Submit 16 pages on any topic, in any form. Another 4 pages for front matter are permitted, making a maximum total of 20 pages. Poets must be gay, lesbian, or bisexual (any race, age, background, etc.). One poem/page. Guidelines available for SASE. Accepts inquiries by e-mail. **Entry fee:** $15/entry. Make checks payable to Thorngate Road Press. **Deadline:** February 1. Competition receives 200-300 entries. Most recent contest winner was Stacey White (*Choke*). Judge: a nationally recognized gay, lesbian, or bisexual poet. Judge remains anonymous until the winner has been announced (by April 15). Copies of winning books may be ordered by sending $6 to the above address made out to Thorngate Road Press. "Thorngate Road publishes at least 2 chapbooks annually, and they are selected by one of 2 methods. The first is through the contest. The second, the Berdache Chapbook Series, is by invitation only. We published chapbooks by Kristy Nielsen, David Trinidad, Reginald Shepherd, Karen Lee Osborne, Timothy Liu, and Maureen Seaton in the Berdache series." Although the contest is open only to gay, lesbian, bisexual, and transgendered authors, the content of submissions does not necessarily have to be gay, lesbian, bisexual, or transgendered.

$☐ OHIO POETRY DAY CONTESTS

Ohio Poetry Day Association, Dept. of English, Heidelberg College, 310 East Market, Tiffin OH 44883. Established 1937. **Contact:** Bill Reyer, contest chair. Offers annual slate of 30-40 contest categories. Prizes range from $75 on down; all money-award poems published in anthology (runs over 100 pages). Pays winners from other countries in cash. "The bank we use does not do *any* exchange at any price." Submissions must be unpublished. Submit one poem/category on topic and in form specified. Some contests open to everyone, but others open only to Ohio poets. "Each contest has its own specifications. Entry must be for a specified category, so entrants *need rules*." Entry form and guidelines available for SASE. **Entry fee:** $8 inclusive, unlimited number of categories. Does not accept entry fees in foreign currencies; cash or checks drawn on U.S. bank only. **Deadline:** usually end of May; see guidelines for each year's deadline. Competition receives up to 4,000 entries/year. Winners and judges for most recent contest listed in winners' book. Judges are never announced in advance. Winners list available in August for SASE (enclose with poem entries); prizes given in October. Copies of winning books available from Bill Reyer for $8.50 (2004 cost; prices can differ from year to year) plus $1.50 postage for one or 2 books. "Ohio Poetry Day is the umbrella. Individual contests are sponsored by poetry organizations and/or individuals across the state. OPD sponsors one, plus Poet of the Year and Student Poet of the Year; have 4 memorial funds." Join mailing list at any time by sending contact information by postcard or letter. Advice: "Revise, follow rules, look at individual categories for a good match."

⊠ $◨ OHIO STATE UNIVERSITY PRESS/THE JOURNAL AWARD IN POETRY

180 Pressey Hall, 1070 Carmack Rd., Columbus OH 43210-1002. (614)292-6930. Fax: (614)292-2065. E-mail: ohiostatepress@osu.edu. Website: www.ohiostatepress.org. **Contact:** David Citino, poetry editor. Each year *The Journal* (see separate listing in the Publishers of Poetry section) selects for publication by Ohio State University Press one full-length (at least 48 pages) book ms. Awards $2,000 cash prize; each entrant receives a one-year subscription (2 issues) to *The Journal*. Some or all of the poems in the collection may have appeared in periodicals, chapbooks or anthologies, but must be identified. Guidelines available by e-mail or on website. **Entry fee:** $25. Check or money order payable to The Ohio State University. **Deadline:** September 30. Has published *Spot in the Dark* by Beth Gylys (2004), *Writing Letters for the Blind* by Gary Fincke (2003), and *Mechanical Cluster* by Patty Seyburn (2002).

⊠ $◙ OHIOANA POETRY AWARD (Helen and Laura Krout Memorial); OHIOANA QUARTERLY; OHIOANA LIBRARY ASSOCIATION (Specialized: regional)

Ohioana Library Association, 274 E. First Ave., Columbus OH 43201. (614)466-3831. Fax: (614)728-6974. E-mail: ohioana@SLOMA.state.oh.us. Website: www.oplin.lib.oh.us/ohioana. **Contact:** Linda Hengst, director. Offers annual Ohioana Book Awards. Up to 6 awards may be given for books (including books of poetry) by authors born in Ohio or who have lived in Ohio for at least 5 years. The Ohioana Poetry Award of $1,000 (with the same residence requirements), made possible by a bequest of Helen Krout, is given yearly "to an individual whose body of published work has made, and continues to make, a significant contribution to poetry, and through whose work as a writer, teacher, administrator, or in community service, interest in poetry has been developed."

Deadline: nominations to be received by December 31. Competition receives several hundred entries. 2004 award winners were Stanley Plumley (poetry award) and William Greenway (book award/poetry). *Ohioana Quarterly* regularly reviews Ohio magazines and books by Ohio authors and is available through membership in Ohioana Library Association ($25/year).

$◎ NATALIE ORNISH POETRY AWARD (Specialized: regional/TX); SOEURETTE DIEHL FRASER TRANSLATION AWARD (Specialized: translations, regional/TX)

% Frances Vick, Texas Institute of Letters, 6335 W. Northwest Highway, #618, Dallas TX 75225. (214)363-7253. Fax: (214)363-6278. E-mail: franvick@aol.com. Website: www.wtamu.edu/til/members.htm. **Contact:** Frances Vick. Established 1947. The Texas Institute of Letters gives annual awards for books by Texas authors, including the **Natalie Ornish Poetry Award**, a $1,000 award for best first volume of poetry. Books must have been first published in the year in question, and entries may be made by authors or by their publishers. One copy of each entry must be mailed to each of 3 judges, with ''information showing an author's Texas association . . . if it is not otherwise obvious.'' Poets must have lived in Texas for at least 3 consecutive years at some time or their work must reflect a notable concern with matters associated with the state. The **Soeurette Diehl Fraser Translation Award** ($1,000) is given for best translation of a book into English. Write during the fall for complete guidelines. Accepts inquiries by fax or e-mail. **Deadlines:** see website. Competitions receive 30 entries/year.

$□ PACIFIC NORTHWEST WRITERS ASSOCIATION (PNWA) LITERARY CONTEST

P.O. Box 2016, Edmonds WA 98020-9516. (425)673-2665. Fax: (425)771-9588. E-mail: pnwa@pnwa.org. Website: www.pnwa.org. Established 1956. **Contact:** Dana Murphy-Love, award director. Offers annual award of 1st Prize: Zola Award and pin, $600 cash, certificate, and reading by performers at a Zola in Performance event; 2nd Prize: $300 cash, certificate; 3rd Prize: $150 cash, certificate. Pays winners from other countries by check in U.S. currency. Submissions must be unpublished but may be entered in other contests. Submit 3 copies of collection of 3 one-page poems in large mailing envelope. Include SASE and entry fee with submission form. Entry form and guidelines available for SASE or on website. **Entry fee:** $35 for PNWA members, $45 for non-PNWA members for each 3-poem collection; only one submission allowed. Does not accept entry fees in foreign currencies; U.S. dollars only. **2006 Deadline:** February 21. Competition receives 75 entries/year. Most recent winners were Julie Gerrard, Ronda Broatch, and Robert Singer. Judges: ''respected members of the literary community.'' Winners will be announced at Awards Banquet at annual PWNA Summer Writers Conference in Seattle, WA. ''The Pacific Northwest Writers Association, a nonprofit organization, is dedicated to Northwest writers and the development of writing talent from pen to publication through education, accessibility to the publishing industry, and participation in an interactive vital writer community. In addition to the annual Literary Contest, PNWA hosts an annual conference each summer in the Seattle area. Members are given opportunities to read their unpublished work through events called The Word is Out.'' See website for further membership and conference details.

$☑ PAUMANOK POETRY AWARD; THE VISITING WRITERS PROGRAM

English Dept., Knapp Hall, Farmingdale State University of New York, 2350 Broadhollow Rd., Farmingdale NY 11735. E-mail: brownml@farmingdale.edu. Website: www.farmingdale.edu. Established 1990. **Contact:** Dr. Margery Brown, director. Offers 1st Prize of $1,000 plus an all-expense-paid feature reading in their 2006-2007 series (*Please note:* travel expenses within the continental U.S. only). Also awards two 2nd Prizes of $500 plus expenses for a reading in the series. Pays winners from other countries in U.S. dollars. Submit cover letter, one-paragraph literary bio, and 3-5 poems (no more than 10 pages total), published or unpublished. Include cover page with name, address, and phone number. **Entry fee:** $25. Make checks payable to Farmingdale State University of New York, VWP. **Postmark deadline:** by September 15. Does not accept entry fees in foreign currencies; send money order in U.S. dollars. Include SASE for results (to be mailed by late December); results also posted on website. Guidelines available for SASE or on website. Competition receives over 600 entries. 2003 contest winners were George Drew (1st Prize) and Richard Michelson and Gerry LaFemina (2nd Prizes).

$ ◎ PEN CENTER USA LITERARY AWARD IN POETRY (Specialized: regional/west of the Mississippi)

PEN Center USA, 672 S. Lafayette Park Place, #42, Los Angeles CA 90057. (213)365-8500. Fax: (213)365-9616. E-mail: awards@penusa.org. Website: www.penusa.org. **Contact:** Awards Coordinator. Offers annual $1,000 cash award to a book of poetry published during the previous calendar year. Open to writers living west of the Mississippi. Submit 4 copies of the entry. Entry form and guidelines available for SASE, by fax, e-mail, or on website. **Entry fee:** $35. **Deadline:** December 17. Most recent award winner was Gabriel Spera. Judges: Eloise Klein Healy, William Archila, and Hilda Raz. Winner will be announced in May and honored at a ceremony in Los Angeles.

$ ◙ ◎ PENNSYLVANIA POETRY SOCIETY ANNUAL CONTEST

(610)374-5848. E-mail: aubade@bluetruck.net. Website: www.nfsps.com/pa/pps-contests.html. **Contact:** Steve Concert, Contest Chairman, 6 Kitchen Ave., Harvey's Lake PA 18618. Offers annual contest with Grand Prize awards of $100, $50, and $25; other categories offer $25, $15, and $10. May enter 3 poems for Grand Prize at $2 each for members and nonmembers alike. Also offers prizes in other categories of $25, $15, and $10 (one entry/category); only one poem accepted in each of remaining categories. A total of 17 categories open to all, 4 categories for members only. **Entry fee:** for members entering categories 2-21, $2.50 inclusive; for nonmembers entering categories 2-15 and 17-21, $1.50 each. Guidelines available for SASE or on website. **Deadline:** January 15. Also sponsors the Pegasus Contest **for PA students only**, grades 5-12. For information, send SASE to Carol Clark Williams, Chairman, 445 North George St., York PA. **Deadline:** February 1. Carlisle Poets Contest open to all poets. **Deadline:** October 31. Guidelines available for SASE from Joy Campbell, Chairman, 10 Polecat Rd., Landisburg PA 17040. The Society publishes a quarterly newsletter with member poetry and challenges, plus an annual soft-cover book of prize poems from the annual contest. Winning Pegasus Contest poems are published in a booklet sent to schools. PPS membership dues: $17/fiscal year. Make checks payable to PPS, Inc., mail to Richard R. Gasser, Treasurer, at 801 Spruce St., West Reading PA 19611-1448.

✪ $ ◎ PEOPLE BEFORE PROFITS POETRY PRIZE (Specialized: peace; social justice; focus on "people before profits"); IN OUR OWN WORDS

Burning Bush Publications, P.O. Box 9636, Oakland CA 94613. (510)434-0385. Website: www.bbbooks.com. **Contact:** Abby Bogomolny, director. Offers annual award of 1st Prize: $200, plus 2 Honorable Mentions; all receive publication in online e-zine, *In Our Own Words*. Pays winners from other countries in U.S. dollars. Submissions may be previously published. Submit 3 poems of any number of lines or in any style on "People Before Profits." "Submit on 8½ × 11 sheets, no name on poem; submit letter or index card with name, titles of poems, your address, phone, and e-mail address." Guidelines available on website. **Entry fee:** $10. Does not accept entry fees in foreign currencies. **Deadline:** May 1 annually. Competition receives 100-200 entries/year. Most recent winners were Jon David Andersen (2004), Leonardo Alishan (2003), and Meliza Bañales (2002). Past Judges: Abby Bogomolny, Michael Calvello, and Carli Schick.

✪ $ ◎ PEW FELLOWSHIPS IN THE ARTS (Specialized: regional/PA)

230 S. Broad St., Suite 1003, Philadelphia PA 19102. (215)875-2285. Fax: (215)875-2276. Website: www.pewarts.org. Established 1991. **Contact:** Melissa Franklin, award director. "The Pew Fellowships in the Arts provide financial support directly to artists so they may have the opportunity to dedicate themselves wholly to the development of their artwork for up to 2 years. Up to 12 fellowships of $50,000 each (in 3 different categories) awarded each year." Must be a Pennsylvania resident of Bucks, Chester, Delaware, Montgomery, or Philadelphia County for at least 2 years;

must be 25 or older. Matriculated students, full or part-time, are not eligible. Application and guidelines available mid-August. **Deadline:** December of the preceding year. Judges: panel of artists and art professionals. Winner will be announced by letter.

$✍ POETIC LICENSE CONTEST; MKASHEF ENTERPRISES

P.O. Box 688, Yucca Valley CA 92286-0688. E-mail: alayne@inetworld.net. Website: www.asidozin es.com. Established 1998. **Contact:** Alayne Gelfand, poetry editor. Offers a biannual poetry contest. 1st Prize: $500, 2nd Prize: $100, 3rd Prize: $40, plus publication in anthology and one copy. Pays winners from other countries in U.S. cash, by money order, or through PayPal. Five honorable mentions receive one copy; other poems of exceptional interest will also be included in the anthology. **Themes and deadlines available for SASE.** Submit any number of poems, any style, of up to 50 lines/poem (poems may have been previously published). Include name, address, and phone number on each poem. Enclose a SASE for notification of winners. Accepts submissions by regular mail, on disk, or by e-mail (attachment or pasted into body of message). "Judges prefer original, accessible, and unforced works." Guidelines available for SASE or by e-mail. **Entry fee:** $1/poem. "We're looking for fresh word usage and surprising imagery. Please keep in mind that our judges prefer non-rhyming poetry. Each contest seeks to explode established definitions of the theme being spotlighted. Be sure to send SASE or e-mail for current theme and deadline."

✪ $✍ THE POETRY CENTER BOOK AWARD

1600 Holloway Ave., San Francisco CA 94132. (415)338-2227. Fax: (415)338-0966. E-mail: poetry@ sfsu.edu. Website: www.sfsu.edu/~poetry. Established 1980. **Contact:** Elise Ficarra, business manager. Offers award to an outstanding book of poems published by an individual author in the current year. Awards one prize of $500 and an invitation to read at The Poetry Center. Books by a single author; no collaborative works, anthologies, or translations. Must be published and copyrighted during year of contest. Publisher, author, or reader may submit entries. **Entry fee:** $10. **2004 deadline:** July 1, 2004-January 31, 2005. Competition receives 200-250 entries. 2002 award winner was Truong Tan for *dust and conscience*. Winner will be announced on website and through press release. "The Poetry Center and American Poetry Archives at San Francisco State University were established in 1954. Its archives include the largest circulating tape collection of writers reading their own work in the United States."

$▢ POETRY IN PRINT CONTEST

P.O. Box 30981, Albuquerque NM 87190-0981. Phone/Fax: (505)888-3937. Established 1991. **Contact:** Robert G. English, award director. Offers annual award of 1st Prize: $1,000; 2nd and 3rd Prize and Honorable Mention awarded plaques with certificates. Pays winners from other countries with cashier's check in U.S. dollars after receiving winner's Social Security number. Submissions may be previously published and may be entered in other contests. Submit unlimited number of poems, 60 lines total. Include name and telephone number on each page of submission. Include SASE for notification of winners. Guidelines available for SASE or by fax. **Entry fee:** $10. Does not accept entry fees in foreign currencies; accepts personal check in U.S. dollars. "Everyone receives a book and one of my personal *Poetry Portfolio* goes to my winners." **Deadline:** August 1. Most recent winners were James K. Larson, Judy Ingersoll-Street, Ted Elden, Russell Pedro, R.J. Ferguson, and Ronnie Maeg. Judge: Robert G. English. Winners announced in August by telephone and through SASEs. "Think TRUTH. I like humanitarian, although I accept any subject."

$POETRY SOCIETY OF AMERICA AWARDS

Poetry Society of America, 15 Gramercy Park, New York NY 10003. (212)254-9628. E-mail: psa@po etrysociety.org. Website: www.poetrysociety.org. Offers the following awards open to PSA members only: **The Writer Magazine/Emily Dickinson Award** ($250, for a poem inspired by Dickinson though not necessarily in her style); **Cecil Hemley Memorial Award** ($500, for a lyric poem that addresses a philosophical or epistemological concern); **Lyric Poetry Award** ($500, for a lyric poem on any subject); **Lucille Medwick Memorial Award** ($500, for an original poem in any form on a humanitarian theme); **Alice Fay Di Castagnola Award** ($1,000 for a manuscript-in-progress of poetry or verse-drama). The following awards are open to both PSA members and nonmembers: **Louise Louis/Emily F. Bourne Student Poetry Award** ($250, for the best unpublished poem by a student in grades 9-12 from the U.S.); **George Bogin Memorial Award** ($500, for a selection of 4-5 poems that use language in an original way to reflect the encounter of the ordinary and the extraordinary and to take a stand against oppression in any of its forms); **Robert H. Winner Memorial Award** ($2,500, to acknowledge original work being done in mid-career by a poet who has not had substantial recognition, open to poets over 40 who have published no more than one book). Entries for the **Norma Farber First Book Award** ($500) and the **William Carlos Williams Award** (purchase prize between $500 and $1,000, for a book of poetry published by a small press, nonprofit, or university press) must be submitted directly by publishers. Complete submission guidelines for all awards are available on website. **Entry fee:** all of the above contests are free to PSA members; nonmembers pay $15 to enter any or all of contests 6-8; $5 for high school students to enter single entries in the student poetry competition; high school teachers/administrators may submit unlimited number of students' poems (one entry/student) to student poetry award for $20. **2005 Deadline:** submissions accepted between October 1 and December 22 (postmarked). Additional information available on website. (See separate listing for Poetry Society of America in the Organizations section and for the PSA Chapbook Fellowships in this section.)

$◻ ◎ THE POETRY SOCIETY OF VIRGINIA ANNUAL CONTESTS (Specialized: forms/ sonnet, haiku, limerick; humor; nature/ecology; students; themes)

E-mail: contest@poetrysocietyofvirginia.org. Website: www.PoetrySocietyOfVirginia.org. **Contact:** Contest Chair. Offers contests for unpublished poems in various categories including the Bess Gresham Memorial (garden or gardeners); Brodie Herndon Memorial (the sea); Judah, Sarah, Grace, and Tom Memorial (inter-ethnic amity); Cenie H. Moon Prize (women); Karma Deane Ogden Memorial (PSV members only); and the Edgar Allan Poe Memorial. (All of the previous categories are open to any form, have limits of 32-48 lines, and some have specific subjects as noted.) The following group of contests require specific forms: the J. Franklin Dew Award (series of 3-4 haiku), Carleton Drewry Memorial (lyric or sonnet about mountains), Handy Andy Prize (limerick), Emma Gray Trigg Memorial (lyric, 64-line limit, PSV members only), Nancy Byrd Turner Memorial (sonnet), plus categories that change annually. Final groups of poems open to students only (no fees required): S-1, Grades 1-2; S-2, Grades 3-4; S-3, Grades 5-6; S-4, Grades 7-8; S-5, Grades 9-10; S-6, Grades 11-12; and S-7, Undergraduate. All poems are open to nonmembers except those noted above. Cash prizes range from $15-500. Contest information available for SASE or on website (guidelines *must* be followed). Does not accept submissions by e-mail. **Entry fee:** $2/poem for adult nonmembers; no fee for students and PSV members. Send **all entries** to Contest Chair at the address above. **Deadline:** January 19 for all contests (Edgar Allan Poe's birthday). Each category averages about 80 entries/year. Winning entries may be published in a booklet unless author indicates otherwise. Also publishes the *Poetry Society of Virginia Newsletter*, which provides PSV members with information about upcoming meetings and local events. Includes some poetry by members, book reviews, and notices of publication/contest opportunities. "Read, revise; read, revise. Follow guidelines to ensure inclusion of poem in contest. Always include SASE for any return information."

$✉ ◎ POETS' CLUB OF CHICAGO; HELEN SCHAIBLE SHAKESPEAREAN/PETRARCHAN SONNET CONTEST (Specialized: form/sonnet)

1212 S. Michigan Ave., Apt. 2702, Chicago IL 60605. **Contact:** Tom Roby, president. The annual Helen Schaible Shakespearean/Petrarchan Sonnet Contest is open to anyone. **For sonnets only!** Offers 1st Prize: $50; 2nd Prize: $35; 3rd Prize: $15; plus 3 Honorable Mentions and 3 Special Recognitions (non-cash). Submit only one entry (2 copies) of either a Shakespearean or a Petrarchan sonnet, which must be original and unpublished. Entry must be typed on 8½ × 11 paper, double-spaced. Name and address in the upper righthand corner on only one copy. *All necessary guidelines appear in this listing.* **Entry fee:** none. **Postmark deadline:** September 1. Competition receives 150 entries/year. Most recent contest winners were Joy Sedgman, Steven Shields, and Mary Anne Burkhart. Judge: June Owens. Winners will be notified by mail by October 31. Include SASE with entry to receive winners' list. The Poets' Club of Chicago meets monthly at the Chicago Cultural Center to critique their original poetry, which the members read at various venues in the Chicago area and publish in diverse magazines and books. Members also conduct workshops at area schools and libraries by invitation. "Read the guidelines—*one* sonnet only!"

$☐ POETS' DINNER CONTEST

2214 Derby St., Berkeley CA 94705-1018. (510)841-1217. **Contact:** Dorothy V. Benson. **Contestant must be present to win.** Submit 3 anonymous typed copies of original, unpublished poems in not more than 3 of the 8 categories (Humor, Love, Nature, Beginnings & Endings, Spaces & Places, People, Theme (changed annually), and Poet's Choice). Winning poems (Grand Prize, 1st, 2nd, 3rd) are read at an awards banquet and Honorable Mentions are presented. Cash prizes awarded; Honorable Mention receives books. The event is nonprofit. Since 1927 there has been an annual awards banquet sponsored by the ad hoc Poets' Dinner Committee, currently at Spenger's in Berkeley. Guidelines available for SASE. **Entry fee:** none. **2005 Deadline:** January 15. Competition receives about 300 entries. Recent contest winners include Charan Sue Wollard (Grand Prize), Anatole Lubovich, Stephen Sadler, Angela Howe, Maria Rosales, Will Landis, Sandra Bozarth, and Sherry Sheehan (1st Prizes). 2004 judges: Janet Wondra, Ruth F. Harrison, Larry K. Richman, Leonard Bischel, Clarence P. Socwell, and Joseph S. Salem. *Remembering*, an anthology of winning poems from the Poet's Dinner over the last 25 years, is available by mail for $10.42 from Dorothy V. Benson at the contest address.

✦ $☐ POETS OF THE VINEYARD CONTEST; VINTAGE

704 Brigham Ave., Santa Rosa CA 95404-5245. E-mail: jhchueng@aol.com. President: Judy Cheung. **Contact:** Kay Renz, contest chair. Offers annual contest sponsored by the Sonoma County Chapter (P.O.V.) of the California Federation of Chaparral Poets. For unpublished poems in various categories. Contest rules and deadline available for SASE from Contest Chair. Prizes in each category are $50, $25, and $15, with a grand prize chosen from category winners ($75). **Entry fee:** nonmembers $5/poem or $10/3 poems; members $3/poem or $10/5 poems. Prize-winning poems will be published in the annual anthology, *Vintage*. Most recent winners were Chris F. Hauge, Joyce Shiver, Maxine Collin Williams, Elizabeth Howard, Judy Stainer, and Victoria Garton. Anthology available for $12 including shipping; past anthologies available for $8 including shipping.

$☑ ◎ THE POETS ON PARNASSUS PRIZE (Specialized: illness and healing, medical writing); THE PHAROS MAGAZINE; POETS ON PARNASSUS

UCSF/*The Pharos Magazine*, P.O. Box 1142, Mill Valley CA 94941. (415)381-8641. E-mail: hdwatts @earthlink.net. Website: http://poetry-and-jazz.com. Established 2000. **Contact:** David Watts, MD; Joan Baranow, award directors. Offers annual award (although sometimes skips a year). 1st Prize: $500 and publication in *The Pharos*; 2-4 runners-up also published. Submissions must be unpublished; may be entered in other contests. Submit up to 5 pages of poetry on a medical subject, in any form. **Entry fee:** $7.50/entry. **Deadline:** May 15. Competition receives 120 submissions/contest. Recent judges: John Stone and Jack Coulehan. Winners announced in *The Pharos* ("we telephone the winners"). "Poets on Parnassus is a campus organization that brings readings, workshops, and special poetry events to a health sciences campus."

$☑ PORTLANDIA CHAPBOOK CONTEST; THE PORTLANDIA GROUP

PMB 225, 6663 SW Beaverton-Hillsdale Hwy., Portland OR 97225. E-mail: braucher@portlandia.c om. Established 1999. **Contact:** Karen Braucher, award director. Offers annual prize of $200, publication of chapbook, and 30 copies. Submit 24 pages of poetry. Submissions must be unpublished as a collection, but individual poems may have been previously published in journals. Submissions may be entered in other contests. Include 2 title pages (one with title and personal info, the other with title only), table of contents, acknowledgments, and bio. Include SASE for results; no mss will be returned. "See guidelines for the year you are submitting." Guidelines available for SASE or by e-mail. **Entry fee:** $12/entry, includes copy of winning chapbook. Does not accept entry fees in foreign currencies; accepts check on U.S. bank or U.S. money order. **Deadline:** check biennial guidelines (was March 1 for 2004). Competition receives about 200 entries/year. Past winners include Ron Drummond, David Biespiel, Eliza A. Garza, John Surowiecki, and Judith Taylor. Copies of winning chapbooks ($8, includes shipping) are available from The Portlandia Group.

$🖉 THE PSA CHAPBOOK FELLOWSHIPS

Poetry Society of America, 15 Gramercy Park, New York NY 10003. (212)254-9628. E-mail: psa@po etrysociety.org. Website: www.poetrysociety.org. Established 2002. Offers the **PSA National Chapbook Fellowships** and the **PSA New York Chapbook Fellowships**, with 4 prizes (2 for each fellowship) of $1,000 and publication of the chapbook ms with distribution by the PSA. National Chapbook Fellowships open to any U.S. resident who has not published a full-length poetry collection; New York Chapbook Fellowships open to any New York City resident (in the 5 boroughs) who is 30 or under and has not published a full-length poetry collection. *Poets may apply to one contest only.* Complete submission guidelines for both fellowships available for SASE or on website. **Entry fee:** $12 for both PSA members and nonmembers. Check or money order to Poetry Society of America. **2005 Deadline:** entries accepted between October 1 and December 22 (postmarked). Does not accept entries by fax or e-mail. Most recent winners were K.E. Allen (*Woman in a Boat*) and Joshua Poteat (*Meditations*) (PSA National Chapbook Fellows); and Andrea Baker (*Gilda*) and Justin Goldberg (*Speaking Past the Tongue*) (PSA New York Chapbook Fellows). Most recent judges: Brenda Hillman and Charles Simic (PSA National Chapbook Fellowships); and Carolyn Forché and Li-Young Lee (PSA New York Chapbook Fellowships). Additional information available on website. (See separate listing for Poetry Society of America in the Organizations section and for the Poetry Society of America Awards in this section.)

$🖉 PULITZER PRIZE IN LETTERS

% The Pulitzer Prize Board, 709 Journalism, Columbia University, New York NY 10027. (212)854-3841. Fax: (212)854-3342. E-mail: pulitzer@www.pulitzer.org. Website: www.pulitzer.org. **Contact:** the Pulitzer Prize Board. Offers 5 prizes of $10,000 and certificate each year, including one in poetry, for books published in the calendar year preceding the award. Entry form and guidelines available for SASE, by fax, or on website. Submit 4 copies of published books (or galley proofs if book is being published after October 15), photo, bio, entry form. **Entry fee:** $50. **Deadlines:** June 15 for books published between January 1 and June 30; October 15 for books published between July 1 and December 31. Competition receives 150 entries/year. 2005 poetry winner was Ted Kooser for *Delights & Shadows* (Copper Canyon Press). 2005 judges: Linda Gregerson, James Baker Hall, and Wesley McNair.

🔀 $🖾 QWF A.M. KLEIN PRIZE FOR POETRY; QUEBEC WRITERS' FEDERATION; QWRITE (Specialized: regional/Quebec; translations)

1200 Atwater Ave., Montreal QC H3Z 1X4 Canada. Phone/fax: (514)933-0878. E-mail: admin@qwf. org. Website: www.qwf.org. **Contact:** Lori Schubert, administrative director. Offers annual awards of $2,000 each for poetry, fiction, nonfiction, first book, and translation. Submissions must be previously published. Open to authors "who have lived in Quebec for at least 3 of the past 5 years." Submit 4 copies of a book of at least 48 pages. Write for entry form. **Entry fee:** $10/submission. **Deadlines:** May 31 for books published between October 1 and May 15; August 15 for books published between May 15 and September 30 (bound proofs are acceptable; the finished book must be received by September 30). Competition receives approximately 50 entries. 2004 winner was Carmine Starnio (*With English Subtitles*). Winners announced in November. "QWF was formed in

1988 to honor and promote literature written in English by Quebec authors." QWF also publishes *QWRITE*, "a newsletter offering information and articles of interest to membership and the broader community."

$☑ ◎ THE RAIZISS/DE PALCHI TRANSLATION AWARD (Specialized: Italian poetry translated into English)

The Academy of American Poets, 588 Broadway, Suite 604, New York NY 10012-3210. (212)274-0343. Fax: (212)274-9427. E-mail: rmurphy@poets.org. Website: www.poets.org. Established 1934. **Contact:** Ryan Murphy, awards coordinator. Awarded for outstanding translations of modern Italian poetry into English. A $5,000 book prize and a $20,000 fellowship are awarded in alternate years. **Book Prize Deadline:** submissions accepted in odd-numbered years September 1 through November 1. **Fellowship Deadline:** submissions accepted in even-numbered years September 1 through November 1. Guidelines and entry form available for SASE or on website. 2004 winner was Ann Snodgrass. Judges: Michael Palma, Phillis Levin, and Charles Martin. Winner announced in January. (For further information about The Academy of American Poets, see separate listing in the Organizations section.)

✪ ◯ REDWOOD ACRES FAIR POETRY CONTEST

P.O. Box 6576, Eureka CA 95502. (707)445-3037. Fax: (707)445-1583. E-mail: ninthdaa@pacbell.n et. Website: www.redwoodacres.com. **Contact:** Diane Fales. Offers an annual contest with various categories for both juniors and seniors. Prizes include Best of Show ribbon and $25; Best of Class ribbon and $5; premiums for 1st-3rd Place. Submissions must be unpublished. "For poems to be returned, entrants *must* enclose a self-addressed stamped envelope. If not picked up, entries will be destroyed." Entry form and guidelines available for SASE. **Entry fee:** 50¢/poem for the junior contests and $1/poem for the senior contests. **Deadline:** May 1. Competition receives 200 entries. Winners will be announced through local newspaper or by SASE.

ℕ $◎ MARGARET REID POETRY CONTEST (Specialized: form/traditional verse)

Tom Howard Books, ℅ Winning Writers, 351 Pleasant St., PMB 222, Northampton MA 01060-3961. (866)946-9748. Fax: (413)280-0539. E-mail: jthreid@gmail.com. Website: www.winningwrit ers.com. Established 2004. **Contact:** John Reid, award director. Offers annual award of 1st Prize: $1,000; 2nd Prize: $400; 3rd Prize: $200; plus 4 Encouragement Awards of $100 each. All prizewinners will be published in an anthology. "Non-U.S. winners will be paid in U.S. currency or via PayPal if a check is inconvenient." Submissions may be published or unpublished, may have won prizes elsewhere, and may be entered in other contests. Submit poems in traditional verse forms, such as sonnets, ballads, odes, blank verse, and haiku. No limit on number of lines or number of poems submitted. No name on ms pages; type or computer-print on letter-size white paper, single-sided. Guidelines available for SASE or on website. Submit online or by mail. **Entry fee:** $5 for every 25 lines (exclude poem title and any blank lines from count). Does not accept entry fees in foreign currencies; "U.S. dollars only, payment accepted by credit card, check, money order, or (last resort) currency." **Deadline:** November 15-June 30. 2004 winner was Guy Kettelhack for "Weather Report" and other poems. 2004 judge: John H. Reid. Winners announced in August at WinningWriters.com; entrants who provide valid e-mail addresses also receive notification.

$◯ ◎ RHYME TIME POETRY CONTEST (Specialized: rhyming poetry)

Shadow Poetry, 1209 Milwaukee St., Excelsior Springs MO 64024. Fax: (208)977-9114. E-mail: shadowpoetry@shadowpoetry.com. Website: www.shadowpoetry.com. Established 2000. **Contact:** James Summers, award director. Offers quarterly awards of 1st Prize: $50; 2nd Prize: $25; 3rd Prize: $10; plus top 3 winners also receive a certificate, printed copy of winning poem, and a ribbon. Pays winners from other countries in U.S. dollars only by International Money Order or PayPal. Submissions may be previously published and may be entered in other contests. Submit unlimited number of poems of 4-28 lines each, on any subject. **All poems must rhyme.** "Entry form must be present with mail-in entries. Submit entries in duplicate with name, address, phone number, and e-mail address (when available) on upper left-hand corner of one sheet. Enclose SASE for winner's list and an additional SASE for entry receipt (optional). If no SASE is included for receipt, Shadow Poetry will e-mail an entry confirmation to the contestant, if applicable.'' Entry form and guidelines available for SASE, by fax, or on website. **Entry fee:** $2/poem. Make checks payable to Shadow Poetry. Does not accept entry fees in foreign currencies; pay by International Money Order, cash (U.S. dollars), or payments through PayPal. **Quarterly deadlines:** March 31, June 30, September 30, and December 31. Competition receives about 150 entries/quarter. Winners will be announced 15 days after each quarterly contest ends by e-mail and to those who requested a winner's list with SASE. Results also will be posted on the Shadow Poetry website.

ROANOKE-CHOWAN POETRY AWARD (Specialized: regional/NC); NORTH CAROLINA LITERARY AND HISTORICAL ASSOCIATION

4610 Mail Service Center, Raleigh NC 27699-4610. (919)807-7290. Fax: (919)733-8807. E-mail: michael.hill@ncmail.net. Website: www.ah.dcr.state.nc.us/affiliates/lit-hist/awards/awards.htm. **Contact:** Michael Hill, awards coordinator. Offers annual award for ''an original volume of poetry published during the 12 months ending June 30 of the year for which the award is given.'' Open to ''authors who have maintained legal or physical residence, or a combination of both, in North Carolina for the 3 years preceding the close of the contest period.'' Submit 3 copies of each entry. Guidelines available for SASE or by fax or e-mail. **Deadline:** July 15. Competition receives about 15 entries. 2004 winner was Kathryn Kirkpatrick (*Beyond Reason*). Winner announced by mail October 15.

$ SARASOTA POETRY THEATRE PRESS; SOULSPEAK; EDDA POETRY CHAPBOOK COMPETITION FOR WOMEN; ANIMALS IN POETRY (Specialized: women/feminism; animals/pets)

P.O. Box 48955, Sarasota FL 34230-6955. (941)366-6468. Fax: (941)954-2208. E-mail: soulspeak1@comcast.net. Website: www.soulspeak.org. Established 1994-1998. **Contact:** Scylla Liscombe, award director. Offers 2 annual contests for poetry with prizes ranging from 1st Prize: $50 plus publication in an anthology to 1st Prize: $100 plus 50 published chapbooks. Honorable Mentions also awarded. Guidelines and details about theater available for SASE, by e-mail, or on website. **Entry fees:** range from $4/poem to $10/ms. **Postmark deadline:** Animals in Poetry, June 30 (winners notified in September); Edda Poetry Chapbook Competition for Women, February 28 (winners notified in May). Competitions receive an average of 600 entries/year. Judges: the staff of the press and ranking state poets. Winners are notified by mail. ''Sarasota Poetry Theatre Press is a division of SOULSPEAK/Sarasota Poetry Theatre, a nonprofit organization dedicated to encouraging poetry in all its forms through the Sarasota Poetry Theatre Press, Therapeutic SOULSPEAK for at-risk youth, and the SOULSPEAK Studio. We are looking for honest, not showy, poetry; use a good readable font. Do not send extraneous materials.''

$ MONA SCHREIBER PRIZE FOR HUMOROUS FICTION & NONFICTION

11362 Homedale St., Los Angeles CA 90049. E-mail: brashcyber@pcmagic.net. Website: www.brashcyber.com. Established 2000. **Contact:** Brad Schreiber. Offers annual awards of 1st Prize: $500; 2nd Prize: $250; 3rd Prize: $100. All winners are posted on website and receive a copy of *What Are You Laughing At?: How to Write Funny Screenplays, Stories & More* by Brad Schreiber. Pays winners from other countries by check in U.S. dollars. Submissions must be unpublished and may be entered in other contests. Submit any number of poems, 750 words maximum/poem. Include contact information on each poem submitted. Guidelines available on website. **Entry fee:** $5/poem. Does not accept entry fees in foreign currencies; prefers cash, check, money order, or cashier's check in U.S. dollars. **Deadline:** December 1 annually. Competition receives 340-350 entries/year. Judge: Brad Schreiber. Winners announced December 24 by phone (if U.S. and Canada) or by e-mail. ''Take risks in form, content, theme, and language.''

✪ $□ ◎ CLAUDIA ANN SEAMAN POETRY AWARD (Specialized: students grades 9-12)

The Community Foundation of Dutchess County, 80 Washington St., Suite 201, Poughkeepsie NY 12601. (845)452-3077. Fax: (845)452-3083. Website: www.communityfoundationdc.org. **Contact:** Nevill Smythe, program vice-president. Established 1983. Offers annual award of $500 (1st Prize) in national contest. Submissions must be unpublished but may be entered in other contests. Submit 1-2 unpublished poems on any subject, in any form. Submissions may be entered in other contests. Open to U.S. students grades 9-12. "Entry must contain student and school names, addresses, and phone numbers and the name of the English or writing teacher." Entry form and guidelines available for SASE or on website. **Deadline:** June 1. 2004 winner was Jennifer Chin. Winner contacted by phone or in writing. Copies of last year's winning poem may be obtained by contacting The Community Foundation by phone or in writing. "The Community Foundation is a nonprofit organization serving Dutchess County, NY; it administers numerous grant programs, scholarship funds, and endowment funds for the benefit of the community. This is an excellent opportunity for young, previously unpublished poets to earn recognition for their work. Since there's no fee, there is little to lose; realize, however, that a national contest will have more entries than a regional competition."

◎ SEASONAL POETRY COMPETITION (Specialized: themes/4 seasons and holidays)

1209 Milwaukee St., Excelsior Springs MO 64024. Fax: (208)977-9114. E-mail: shadowpoetry@shadowpoetry.com. Website: www.shadowpoetry.com. Established 2000. **Contact:** James Summers, award director. Offers biannual award of 1st Prize: $100; 2nd prize: $50; 3rd Prize: $25; plus the top 3 winners also receive a certificate, printed copy of winning poem, and a ribbon. Pays winners from other countries in U.S. dollars only by International Money Order or PayPal. Submissions may be previously published and may be entered in other contests. Submit maximum of 10 poems/poet, 30 line limit/poem, must be written on the topics of the 4 seasons (winter, spring, summer, and/or fall) or the holidays (Christmas, Valentine's Day, Easter, etc.), in any form. "Entry form must be present with mail-in entries. Submit entries in duplicate with name, address, phone number, e-mail address (when available) on upper left-hand corner of one sheet. Enclose SASE for winners list. Include an additional SASE for entry receipt (optional). If no SASE is included for receipt, Shadow Poetry will e-mail an entry confirmation to the contestant, if applicable." Entry form and guidelines available for SASE or on website. **Entry fee:** $3/poem. Does not accept entry fees in foreign currencies; accepts International Money Order, cash (U.S. dollars), or payments through PayPal for foreign entries. **Deadlines:** June 30 and December 31. Winners will be announced "15 days after each contest ends, by e-mail and to those who requested a winners list. Results will also be posted on the Shadow Poetry website."

$□ SHADOW POETRY'S BIANNUAL CHAPBOOK COMPETITION

Shadows Ink Publications, 1209 Milwaukee St., Excelsior Springs MO 64024. Fax: (208)977-9114. E-mail: shadowpoetry@shadowpoetry.com. Website: www.shadowpoetry.com. Established 2000. **Contact:** James Summers, award director. Offers biannual award of $100, 50 copies of published chapbook with ISBN, and 25% royalties paid on each copy sold through Shadow Poetry (retail only). Pays winners from other countries in U.S. dollars only by International Money Order or PayPal. Submissions must be unpublished as a collection and may be entered in other contests. (Winning poet retains copyrights and may publish poems elsewhere later.) Submit ms of 16-40 pages, including poetry and acknowledgments, on any subject, in any form . "Cover letter required with name, address, phone, age, and e-mail address. Enclose cover letter, manuscript, and cover ideas/art, if applicable, in #90 (9 × 12) envelope. Include #10 SASE for winner notification." Guidelines available for SASE or on website. **Entry fee:** $10/ms. Make checks payable to Shadow Poetry. Does not accept entry fees in foreign currencies; accepts International Money Order, cash (U.S. dollars), or payments through PayPal for foreign entries. **Deadlines:** June 30 and December 31. "Notification of winners no later than 20 days after deadline by SASE." Copies of winning or sample chapbooks available from Shadow Poetry for $6.25 (see website for titles).

$▢ SHADOWS INK POETRY CONTEST

Shadows Ink Publications, 1209 Milwaukee St., Excelsior Springs MO 64024. Fax: (208)977-9114. E-mail: shadowpoetry@shadowpoetry.com. Website: www.shadowpoetry.com. Established 2000. **Contact:** James Summers, award director. Offers annual award of 1st Prize: $100 and chapbook publication; 2nd Prize: $75; 3rd Prize: $35; top 3 winners also receive a certificate, printed copy of winning poem, and a ribbon. The top 40 placing poems will be published in a Shadows Ink Poetry Chapbook, and all poets appearing in this publication will receive one free copy (additional copies available for $5 each plus shipping). Pays winners from other countries in U.S. dollars only by International Money Order or through PayPal. Submissions must be unpublished and may be entered in other contests. (Winning poets retain copyrights and may publish poems elsewhere later.) Submit maximum of 10 poems, 24 line limit each, on any subject, in any form. "Entry form must be present with mail-in entries. Submit entries in duplicate with name, address, phone number, and e-mail address (when available) on upper left-hand corner of one sheet. Enclose SASE for winners list. Include an additional SASE for entry receipt (optional). If no SASE is included for receipt, Shadow Poetry will e-mail an entry confirmation to the contestant, if applicable." Entry form and guidelines available for SASE or on website. **Entry fee:** $5/poem. Make checks payable to Shadow Poetry. Does not accept entry fees in foreign currencies; accepts International Money Order, cash (U.S. dollars), or payments through PayPal for foreign entries. **Deadline:** December 31. Competition receives 125 entries/year. "Winners will be announced February 1 by e-mail and to those who requested a winners list. Results will also be posted on the Shadow Poetry website."

$▢ KAY SNOW WRITING AWARDS; WILLAMETTE WRITERS

9045 SW Barbur Blvd., Suite 5A, Portland OR 97219-4027. (503)452-1592. Fax: (503)452-0372. E-mail: wilwrite@teleport.com. Website: www.willamettewriters.com. Established 1986. **Contact:** Marlene Howard, award director. Offers annual awards of 1st Prize: $300, 2nd Prize: $150, 3rd Prize: $50. Pays winners from other countries by postal money order. Submissions must be unpublished. Submit up to 2 poems (one entry fee), maximum 5 pages total, on any subject, in any style or form, single-spaced, one side of paper only. Entry form and guidelines available for SASE or on website. Accepts inquiries by fax or e-mail. **Entry fee:** $10 for members of Willamette Writers; $15 for nonmembers. Does not accept entry fees in foreign currencies; accepts a check drawn on a U.S. bank only. **Deadline:** May 15. Competition receives 150 entries. 2004 poetry winners were Sally Jo Bowman, Erick Mertz, Donovan Reves, Schubert Moore, and Karolyn Boudrealt. Winners will be announced July 31. "Write and send in your very best poem. Read it aloud. If it still sounds like the best poem you've ever heard, send it in."

$▢ RICHARD SNYDER PRIZE

Ashland Poetry Press, English Dept., Ashland University, Ashland OH 44805. (419)289-5979 or (419)289-5110. Website: www.ashland.edu/aupoetry. Established 1997. **Contact:** Stephen Haven, award director. Offers annual award of $1,000 plus book publication in a paper-only edition of 1,000 copies. Submissions must be unpublished in book form and may be entered in other contests. Submit 50-80 pages of poetry. **Reading fee:** $20. Does not accept entry fees in foreign currencies; U.S. dollars only. **Deadline:** June 30. Competition receives 350 entries/year. Most recent winners were Vern Rutsala (2003), Carol Barrett (2002), and Corrinne Clegg Hales (2001). Annual judge: Robert Phillips. Winners will be announced in *Writer's Chronicle* and *Poets & Writers*. Copies of winning books available from Small Press Distribution and directly from the Ashland University Bookstore. The Ashland Poetry Press publishes 2-4 books of poetry/year.

$▢ SOUL-MAKING LITERARY COMPETITION

National League of American Pen Women, Nob Hill, San Francisco Bay Area Branch, 1544 Sweetwood Dr., Colma CA 94015-2029. Phone/fax: (650)756-5279. E-mail: PenNobHill@aol.com. Website: www.soulmakingcontest.us. Established 1993. **Contact:** Eileen Malone, award director. Annual open contest offers cash prizes in each of 9 literary categories, including poetry and prose poem. 1st Prize: $100; 2nd Prize: $50; 3rd Prize: $25. Pays winners from other countries by check drawn on American bank. Submissions in some categories may be previously published. Submit 3 one-page poems on soul-making theme; any form for open poetry category. No names or other identifying information on mss; include 3×5 card with name, address, phone, fax, e-mail, title(s) of work, and category entered. Include SASE for contest results. No mss will be returned. Guidelines available on website. **Entry fee:** $5/entry. Does not accept entry fees in foreign currencies; U.S. dollars only. **Deadline:** November 30. Competition receives 300 entries/year. Names of winners and judges are posted on website. Winners announced in January by SASE and on website. Winners are invited to read at the Koret Auditorium, San Francisco. Event is televised. "National League of American Pen Women is a professional organization of writers, artists, and composers headquartered in Washington, D.C.; includes membership of 6,000. Pen Women are involved in a variety of community arts outreach programs. 'Some say the world is a vale of tears, I say it is a place of soul making.' Use this quote as inspiration."

$▢ SPANISH MOSS LITERARY COMPETITION

New Pike Press, P.O. Box 6620, Banks AL 36005. (334)244-8920. E-mail: poettennis@bellsouth.net. Website: www.alabamapoets.org. Established 2002. **Contact:** John Curbow, award director. Offers annual award in categories of poetry, fiction, and nonfiction. 1st Prize: $100 and publication; 2nd Prize: $50 and publication; 3rd Prize: $25 and publication in each category. Submissions must be unpublished but may be entered in other contests. Submit up to 3 poems, 60 lines maximum, on any subject, in any form. No poems will be returned; send SASE for contest results. Guidelines available for SASE, by e-mail, or on website. **Entry fee:** $10 for 1-3 poems; $3 for additional (single) entries beyond the first 3. Make checks payable to New Pike Press. **2004 deadline:** submit October 1-November 13. Competition receives 200-400 poems/year. Winners announced early in the year following contest deadline by SASE and on website. Copies of winning anthologies available from New Pike Press.

$▢ SPIRE PRESS POETRY CONTEST; SPIRE MAGAZINE

532 LaGuardia Place, Suite 298, New York NY 10012. E-mail: editor@spirepress.org. Website: www.spirepress.org. Established 2002. **Contact:** Shelly Reed, award director. Offers annual award of publication with royalty contract and promotion; sometimes cash prizes (see guidelines for each year). Submissions must be unpublished and may be entered in other contests as long as Spire Press is informed. Submit a chapbook ms of 18-40 pages of poetry in any form (shorter poems preferred). Include SASE. **Entry fee:** $10/ms. Does not accept entry fees in foreign currencies; U.S. dollars only. **Deadline:** December 31. Competition receives 300 entries/year. Most recent winner was Jennifer MacPherson for *In the Mixed Gender of the Sea* (2004). 2005 judge: TBD. Winners will be announced on website one month after contest deadline. Copies of winning chapbooks available through website, Amazon, selected bookstores, and Spire Press. Spire Press also publishes *Spire*, "a biannual magazine of exceptional quality. *Spire* is magazine-sized, perfect-bound, with color cover and artwork. We receive 300 regular submissions per week. Submit 3-5 poems at a time. We pay one contributor's copy. Always check our website for updates. We prefer poetry to be accessible and appeal to the senses. Rhyming poetry is usually rejected."

$▨ WALLACE E. STEGNER FELLOWSHIPS

Creative Writing Program, Stanford University, Stanford CA 94305-2087. (650)725-1208. Fax: (650)723-3679. E-mail: vfhess@stanford.edu. Website: www.stanford.edu/dept/english/cw. **Contact:** Virginia Hess, program administrator. Offers 5 fellowships in poetry of $22,000 plus tuition of over $6,000/year for promising writers who can benefit from 2 years of instruction and criticism at the Writing Center. "We do not require a degree for admission. No school of writing is favored over any other. Chronological age is not a consideration." **Postmark deadline:** December 1. Competition receives about 1,000 entries/year. 2004-2005 fellows in poetry were Shane Book, Jim Fisher, Jeffrey Hoffman, Sara Gail Martin, and Rachel Richardson.

✪ THE WALLACE STEVENS AWARD

The Academy of American Poets, 588 Broadway, Suite 604, New York NY 10012-3210. (212)274-0343. Fax: (212)274-9427. E-mail: academy@poets.org. Website: www.poets.org. Award established 1994. Awards $150,000 annually to recognize outstanding and proven mastery in the art of poetry. **No applications are accepted.** 2004 winner was Mark Strand. Judges: Rosanna Warren, Jonathan Aaron, W.S. Di Piero, Jane Hirshfield, and Lynne McMahon. (For further information about The Academy of American Poets, see separate listing in the Organizations section.)

$☐ STEVENS POETRY MANUSCRIPT CONTEST

1510 S. 7th St., Brainerd MN 56401. E-mail: dpoet@brainerd.net. Website: www.nfsps.org. **Contact:** Doris Stengel. National Federation of State Poetry Societies (NFSPS) offers annual award of $1,000, publication of ms, and 50 author's copies. Individual poems may have been previously published in magazines, anthologies, or chapbooks, but not the entire ms as a collection; accepts simultaneous submissions. Submit 35-60 pages of poetry by a single author, typewritten, one poem or column of poetry to a page. Number pages, but no author identification throughout ms. Include 2 cover/title pages; one with no author identification, the other with name of poet, address, phone number, and state poetry society member affiliation, if applicable. No bulky folders or binders; plain manila folder and/or staples permitted. No illustrations. Include SASE for winner's list. No disk submissions; no certified or registered mail. Manuscripts will not be returned. Guidelines available for SASE or on website. **Entry fee:** $15 for NFSPS members; $20 for nonmembers. Make checks or money orders payable to NFSPS. **Postmark Deadline:** October 15. Winners announced in January following deadline; entrants who include a SASE will be notified of winner. Winning ms will be sold at annual NFSPS convention and winning poet (if present) will read from the ms. Copies of winning mss available through NFSPS website. (See separate listing for National Federation of State Poetry Societies in the Organizations section and for NFSPS Competitions and NFSPS College/University Level Poetry Awards in this section.)

✸ $☑ ◎ THE DAN SULLIVAN MEMORIAL POETRY CONTEST (Specialized: Canadian residents only); WORD WEAVER; THE WRITERS' CIRCLE OF DURHAM REGION

P.O. Box 323, Ajax ON L1S 3C5 Canada. (905)686-0211. E-mail: wcdrinfo@wcdr.org. Website: www.wcdr.org. Established 1995. Offers annual award in 3 categories. *Children:* 1st Prize: $75; 2nd Prize: $50; 3rd Prize: $25. *Youth:* 1st Prize: $150; 2nd Prize: $100; 3rd Prize: $75. *Adult:* 1st Prize: $300; 2nd Prize: $200; 3rd Prize: $100. Winners published in *The Word Weaver* and on WCDR website. Contest open to **Canadian residents only.** Submissions must be unpublished. "Poems may be of any subject matter, type, or style. Length of each entry must not exceed 30 written lines. This may be one poem, or up to 3 short poems whose cumulative total does not exceed 30 lines. There are no limits to the number of entries a person may submit, but each must be submitted separately with the appropriate entry fee." Bios will be solicited from the winners. No submissions by e-mail. Entries will not be returned. Guidelines available on website. **Entry fee:** $10/entry for adults; $5/entry for youth and children. **Deadline:** February 15. Competition receives about 200-250 entries/year. 2004 adult winners were Tina (T.M.) Grabenhorst, Philippa Schmiegelow, and Margaret Malloch Zielinski and Scott Constance (tie). Winners announced in June and winning entries posted on website. "The Writers' Circle of Durham Region is a nonprofit umbrella organization dedicated to encouraging and promoting the art and skill of writing, fostering literacy, and providing moral support to writers through education and networking, both independently and in cooperation with existing organizations." Advice: "Be original in your writing, but follow the rules when submitting."

$☑ ◎ TOWSON UNIVERSITY PRIZE FOR LITERATURE (Specialized: regional/Maryland)

Towson University, College of Liberal Arts, Towson MD 21252. (410)704-2128. Fax: (410)704-6392. E-mail: eduncan@towson.edu. Website: http://towson.edu. **Contact:** Dean of the College of Liberal Arts. Offers annual prize of $1,000 "for a single book or book-length manuscript of fiction, poetry, drama, or imaginative nonfiction by a Maryland writer. The prize is granted on the basis of literary and aesthetic excellence as determined by a panel of distinguished judges appointed by the university. The first award, made in the fall of 1980, went to novelist Anne Tyler." Work must have been published within the 3 years prior to the year of nomination or must be scheduled for publication within the year in which nominated. Submit 5 copies of work in bound form or in typewritten, double-spaced ms form. Entry form and guidelines available for SASE. **Deadline:** June 15. Competition receives 8-10 entries. Most recent contest winners were Michael Waters and Donna Hemans (co-winners).

$ KATE TUFTS DISCOVERY AWARD; KINGSLEY TUFTS POETRY AWARD

Poetic Gallery for the Kingsley Tufts Poetry Awards, Claremont Graduate University, 160 E. 10th St., Harper East B7, Claremont CA 91711-6165. (909)621-8974. Website: www.cgu.edu/tufts. Established 1992 (Kingsley Tufts Award) and 1993 (Kate Tufts Award). **Contact:** Betty Terrell, administrative director. **Kate Tufts Discovery Award** offers $10,000 annually "for a first book by a poet of genuine promise." **Kingsley Tufts Poetry Award** offers $100,000 annually "for a work by an emerging poet, one who is past the very beginning but has not yet reached the acknowledged pinnacle of his/her career." Books for the 2005 prizes must have been published between September 15, 2004 and September 15, 2005. Entry form and guidelines available for SASE or on website. **Deadline:** September 15. Most recent award winners were Henri Cole (Kingsley Tufts, 2004) and Adrian Blevens (Kate Tufts, 2004). Winners announced in February. Check website for updated deadlines and award information.

$ WAR POETRY CONTEST (Specialized: war-themed poetry)

Winning Writers, 351 Pleasant St., PMB 222, Northampton MA 01060-3961. (866)946-9748. Fax: (413)280-0539. E-mail: warcontest@winningwriters.com. Website: www.winningwriters.com. Established 2001. **Contact:** Adam Cohen, award director. Offers annual award of 1st Prize: $1,500; 2nd Prize: $500; 3rd Prize: $250; 10 Honorable Mentions of $75 each. All prizewinners receive online publication at WinningWriters.com; selected finalists may also receive online publication. "Non-U.S. winners will be paid in U.S. currency or via PayPal if a check is inconvenient." Submissions must be unpublished and may be entered in other contests. Submit 1-3 poems of up to 500 lines total on the theme of war, any form, style, or genre. No name on ms pages, typed or computer-printed on letter-size white paper, single-sided. Submit online or by regular mail. Guidelines available for SASE or on website. **Entry fee:** $12 for group of 1-3 poems. Does not accept entry fees in foreign currencies; "U.S. dollars only, payment accepted by credit card, check, money order, or (last resort) currency." **Deadline:** November 15-May 31. Competition receives about 700 entries/year. 2004 winner was Robert Hill Long for "Gulf War News Sign-Off, with Video Tricks." 2004 judge: Jendi Reiter. Winners announced on November 15 at WinningWriters.com. Entrants who provided valid e-mail addresses will also receive notification. (See separate listing for the Wergle Flomp Poetry Contest in this section and for Winning Writers in the Additional Resources section.)

$ WERGLE FLOMP POETRY CONTEST (Specialized: humor/parody of vanity contest entries)

Winning Writers, 351 Pleasant St., PMB 222, Northampton MA 01060-3961. (866)946-9748. Fax: (413)280-0539. E-mail: flompcontest@winningwriters.com. Website: www.winningwriters.com. Established 2001. **Contact:** Adam Cohen, award director. Offers annual award of 1st Prize: $1,190; 2nd Prize: $169; 3rd Prize: $60; plus 5 Honorable Mentions. All prizewinners receive online publication at WinningWriters.com. "Non-U.S. winners will be paid in U.S. currency or by PayPal if a check is inconvenient." Submissions may be previously published and may be entered in other contests. Submit one poem of any length, in any form, but must be "a humor poem that has been submitted to a 'vanity poetry contest' as a joke. See website for examples." Entries accepted **only** through website; no entries by regular mail. Guidelines available on website. **Entry fee:** none. **Deadline:** August 15-April 1. Competition receives about 900 entries/year. 2004 winner was Chris

Kuehn for "The Craven." 2004 judge: Jendi Reiter. Winners announced on August 15 at WinningWr iters.com. Entrants who provided valid e-mail addresses will also receive notification. "Please read the past winning entries and the judge's comments published at WinningWriters.com. Guidelines are a little unusual—please follow them closely." (See separate listing for the War Poetry Contest in this section and for Winning Writers in the Additional Resources section.)

🌐 $ WESTERN AUSTRALIAN PREMIER'S BOOK AWARDS (Specialized: regional/ Western Australia)

State Library of Western Australia, Alexander Library Bldg., Perth Cultural Centre, Perth, Western Australia 6000 Australia. Phone: (61 8)9427 3330. Fax: (61 8)9427 3336. E-mail: jham@liswa.wa.go v.au. Website: www.liswa.wa.gov.au/pba.html. Established 1982. **Contact:** Ms. Julie Ham, award director. Offers annual poetry prize of AUS $7,500 for a published book of poetry. Winner also eligible for Premier's Prize of AUS $20,000. Submissions must be previously published. Open to poets born in Western Australia, current residents of Western Australia, or poets who have resided in Western Australia for at least 10 years at some stage. Entry form and guidelines available by mail or on website. **Entry fee:** none. **Deadline:** January 6. Competition receives about 10-15 entries in poetry category/year (120 overall). Most recent winner was *Peripheral Light* by John Kinsella. Judges: Prof. Brian Dibble, Ms. Suzanne Wyche, Prof. Ed Jaggard, and Ms. Lucille Fisher. Winners announced in June each year (i.e., June 2006 for 2005 awards) at a presentation dinner given by the Premier of Western Australia. "The contest is organized by the State Library of Western Australia, with money provided by the Western Australian State Government to support literature."

✅ WHITING WRITERS' AWARDS; MRS. GILES WHITING FOUNDATION

1133 Avenue of the Americas, 22nd Floor, New York NY 10036-6710. **Contact:** Barbara K. Bristol, director. The Foundation makes awards of $35,000 each to up to 10 writers of fiction, nonfiction, poetry, and plays chosen by a selection committee drawn from a list of recognized writers, literary scholars, and editors. Recipients of the award are selected from nominations made by writers, educators, and editors from communities across the country whose experience and vocations bring them in contact with individuals of unusual talent. The nominators and selectors are appointed by the foundation and serve anonymously. **Direct applications and informal nominations are not accepted by the foundation.**

$ ✅ THE WALT WHITMAN AWARD

The Academy of American Poets, 588 Broadway, Suite 604, New York NY 10012-3210. (212)274-0343. Fax: (212)274-9427. E-mail: rmurphy@poets.org. Website: www.poets.org. Award established 1975. **Contact:** Ryan Murphy, awards coordinator. Offers $5,000 plus publication of a poet's first book by Louisiana State University Press and a one-month residency at the Vermont Studio Center. The Academy of American Poets distributes copies of the Whitman Award-winning book to its members. Submit mss of 50-100 pages. Poets must be American citizens. Entry form required; entry form and guidelines available for SASE or on website. **Entry fee:** $25. **Deadline:** submit between September 15 and November 15. 2004 winner was Geri Doran for *Resin*. Judge: Henri Cole. Winner announced in May. (For further information about The Academy of American Poets, see separate listing in the Organizations section.)

$ ✅ STAN AND TOM WICK POETRY PRIZE

Wick Poetry Center, 301 Satterfield Hall, Kent State University, P.O. Box 5190, Kent OH 44242-0001. (330)672-2067. Fax: (330)672-3152. E-mail: wickpoet@kent.edu. Website: http://dept.kent.edu/ wick. Established 1994. **Contact:** Maggie Anderson, director. Offers annual award of $2,000 and publication by Kent State University Press. Submissions must be unpublished as a whole and may be entered in other contests as long as the Wick Poetry Center receives notice upon acceptance elsewhere. Submit 48-68 pages of poetry. Open to poets writing in English who have not yet published a full-length collection. Entries must include cover sheet with poet's name, address, telephone number, and title of ms. Guidelines available for SASE or on website. **Entry fee:** $20. **Deadline:** May 1. Competition receives 700-800 entries. 2004 contest winner was Anele Rubin. 2004 judge: Philip Levine.

$◎ THE RICHARD WILBUR AWARD (Specialized: American poets)

Dept. of English, University of Evansville, 1800 Lincoln Ave., Evansville IN 47722. (812)479-2963. Website: http://english.evansville.edu/english/WilburAwardGuidelines.htm. **Contact:** William Baer, series director. Offers a biennial award (even-numbered years) of $1,000 and book publication to "recognize a quality book-length manuscript of poetry." Submissions must be unpublished original poetry collections ("although individual poems may have had previous journal publications") and "public domain or permission-secured translations may comprise up to one-third of the manuscript." Submit ms of 50-100 typed pages, unbound, bound, or clipped. Open to all American poets. Manuscripts should be accompanied by 2 title pages: one with collection's title, author's name, address, and phone number; one with only the title. Include SASE for contest results. Submissions may be entered in other contests. Manuscripts are *not* returned. Guidelines available for SASE or on webiste. **Entry fee:** $25/ms. **Deadline:** next competition will be in 2006. Competition receives 300-500 entries. Winning ms is published and copyrighted by the University of Evansville Press.

$◎ WORLD ORDER OF NARRATIVE AND FORMALIST POETS (Specialized: subscription; form/metrical)

P.O. Box 580174, Station A, Flushing NY 11358-0174. Established 1980. **Contact:** Dr. Alfred Dorn, contest chairman. Sponsors biennial contests in a number of categories for traditional and contemporary poetic forms, including the sonnet, blank verse, ballade, sapphics, villanelle, and new forms created by Alfred Dorn. Prizes total at least $5,000. Pays winners from other countries by money order. Submissions must be unpublished and may be entered in other contests. **Entry fee:** None, but only subscribers to *Iambs & Trochees* are eligible for the competition. Complete contest guidelines available for SASE from Alfred Dorn. "Our focus is on metrical poetry characterized by striking diction and original metaphors. We do not want trite or commonplace language." **2005 Deadline:** December 1. Competition receives about 3,000 entries. Past contest winners include Rhina P. Espaillat, Len Krisak, Deborah Warren, Joseph Salemi, and Roy Scheele. Recent judges: William Baer and Gail White. Winners' list will be mailed to contestants after poems have been judged. (For more information on *Iambs & Trochees*, see listing in the Publishers of Poetry section.)

$▢ THE W.B. YEATS SOCIETY ANNUAL POETRY COMPETITION

W.B. Yeats Society of New York, National Arts Club, 15 Gramercy Park S, New York NY 10003. (212)780-0605. Website: www.YeatsSociety.org. Established 1994. **Contact:** Andrew McGowan, president. Offers annual $250 cash prize for 1st Place, $100 cash prize for 2nd Place, and optional Honorable Mentions. Open to beginner as well as established poets. Winners are invited to read their poems at an awards event held each spring in New York; also inducted as Honorary Members of the Society (a 501(c)(3) charitable organization). Submissions must be unpublished and may be entered in other contests. Submit any number of unpublished poems in any style or form, up to 60 lines each, typed on letter-size paper without poet's name. Guidelines available for SASE or on website; no entry form required. **Reading fee:** $8 for first poem, $7 per additional poem. Attach a 3×5 card to each entry containing the poem's title along with the poet's name, address, and phone/fax/e-mail. **Annual deadline:** February 15. Receives 200-300 entries/year. 2004 winners were Barbara Crooker, Diana Ben-Merre, and Zara Raab. 2005 judge: Grace Schulman. Winners selected by March 31 and announced in April. Winning entries and judge's report are posted on the Society's website. Printed report available for SASE. (See separate listing for W.B. Yeats Society of New York in the Organizations section.)

◎ ZEN GARDEN HAIKU CONTEST (Specialized: form/style, haiku)

Shadow Poetry, 1209 Milwaukee St., Excelsior Springs MO 64024. Fax: (208)977-9114. E-mail: shadowpoetry@shadowpoetry.com. Website: www.shadowpoetry.com. Established 2000. **Con-**

tact: James Summers, award director. Offers annual award of 1st Prize: $100; 2nd Prize: $50; 3rd Prize: $25, plus the top 3 winners also receive a certificate, a printed copy of winning haiku, and a ribbon. Pays winners from other countries in U.S. dollars only by International Money Order or through PayPal. Submissions may be previously published and may be entered in other contests. Submit any number of haiku on any subject. "Haiku entries must be typed on $8\frac{1}{2} \times 11$ paper, submitted in duplicate. Poet's name, address, phone number, and e-mail address (if applicable) in the upper left-hand corner of one sheet. If submitting more than one haiku, each poem must be typed on separate sheets (3×5 index card entries welcome). Submit haiku entries in duplicate, neatly handwritten or typed, with poet information on the back of only one card. Repeat method for multiple submissions." Entry form and guidelines available for SASE or on website. **Entry fee:** $2/haiku. Make checks payable to Shadow Poetry. Does not accept entry fees in foreign currencies; accepts International Money Order, cash (U.S. dollars), or payments through PayPal for foreign entries. **Deadline:** December 31. Winners announced February 1 each year "by e-mail and to those who requested a winners list. Results will also be posted on the Shadow Poetry website."

ADDITIONAL CONTESTS & AWARDS

The following listings also contain information about contests and awards. Turn to the page numbers indicated for details about their offerings.

Contests & Awards

Contests & Awards

Grants

State & Provincial

Arts councils in the United States and Canada provide assistance to artists (including poets) in the form of fellowships or grants. These grants can be substantial and confer prestige upon recipients; however, **only state or province residents are eligible**. Because deadlines and available support vary annually, query first (with a SASE) or check websites for guidelines.

UNITED STATES ARTS AGENCIES

Alabama State Council on the Arts, 201 Monroe St., Montgomery AL 36130-1800. (334)242-4076. E-mail: staff@arts.alabama.gov. Website: www.arts.state.al.us.

Alaska State Council on the Arts, 411 W. Fourth Ave., Suite 1-E, Anchorage AK 99501-2343. (907)269-6610 or (888)278-7424. E-mail: aksca_info@eed.state.ak.us. Website: www.educ.state.ak.us/aksca.

Arizona Commission on the Arts, 417 W. Roosevelt, Phoenix AZ 85003. (602)255-5882. E-mail: info@ArizonaArts.org. Website: www.ArizonaArts.org.

Arkansas Arts Council, 1500 Tower Bldg., 323 Center St., Little Rock AR 72201. (501)324-9766. E-mail: info@arkansasarts.com. Website: www.arkansasarts.com.

California Arts Council, 1300 I St., Suite 930, Sacramento CA 95814. (916)322-6555 or (800)201-6201. Website: www.cac.ca.gov.

Colorado Council on the Arts, 1380 Lawrence St., Suite 1200, Denver CO 80204. (303)866-2723. E-mail: coloarts@state.co.us. Website: www.coloarts.state.co.us.

Connecticut Commission on Culture & Tourism, Arts Division, 1 Financial Plaza, 755 Main St., Hartford CT 06103. (860)256-2800. Website: www.cultureandtourism.org.

Delaware Division of the Arts, Carvel State Office Bldg., 820 N. French St., 4th Floor, Wilmington DE 19801. (302)577-8278 (New Castle Co.) or (302)739-5304 (Kent or Sussex Counties). E-mail: delarts@state.de.us. Website: www.artsdel.org.

District of Columbia Commission on the Arts & Humanities, 410 Eighth St. NW, 5th Floor, Washington DC 20004. (202)724-5613. E-mail: cah@dc.gov. Website: http://dcarts.dc.gov.

Florida Arts Council, Division of Cultural Affairs, Florida Dept. of State, 1001 DeSoto Park Dr., Tallahassee FL 32301. (850)245-6470. E-mail: info@florida-arts.org. Website: www.florida-arts.org.

Georgia Council for the Arts, 260 14th St., NW, Suite 401, Atlanta GA 30318. (404)685-2787. E-mail: gaarts@gaarts.org. Website: www.gaarts.org.

Guam Council on the Arts & Humanities Agency, P.O. Box 2950, Hagatna GU 96932. (671)475-4226. E-mail: kaha1@kuentos.guam.net. Website: www.guam.net/gov/kaha.

Hawaii State Foundation on Culture & the Arts, 250 S. Hotel St., 2nd Floor, Honolulu HI 96813. (808)586-0300. E-mail: ken.hamilton@hawaii.gov/sfca. Website: www.state.hi.us/sfca.

Idaho Commission on the Arts, 2410 N. Old Penitentiary Rd., Boise ID 83712. (208)334-2119 or (800)278-3863. E-mail: info@arts.idaho.gov. Website: www.arts.idaho.gov.

Illinois Arts Council, James R. Thompson Center, 100 W. Randolph, Suite 10-500, Chicago IL 60601. (312)814-6750. E-mail: info@arts.state.il.us. Website: www.state.il.us/agency/iac.

Indiana Arts Commission, 150 W. Market St., #618, Indianapolis IN 46204. (317)232-1268. E-mail: IndianaArtsCommission@iac.in.gov. Website: www.in.gov/arts.

Iowa Arts Council, 600 E. Locust, Des Moines IA 50319-0290. (515)281-6412. Website: www.iowaartscouncil.org.

Kansas Arts Commission, 700 SW Jackson, Suite 1004, Topeka KS 66603-3761. (785)296-3335. E-mail: KAC@arts.state.ks.us. Website: http://arts.state.ks.us.

Kentucky Arts Council, Old Capitol Annex, 300 W. Broadway, Frankfort KY 40601-1980. (502)564-3757 or (888)833-2787. E-mail: kyarts@ky.gov. Website: www.kyarts.org.

Louisiana Division of the Arts, P.O. Box 44247, Baton Rouge LA 70804-4247. (225)342-8180. E-mail: arts@crt.state.la.us. Website: www.crt.state.la.us/arts.

Maine Arts Commission, 25 State House Station, 193 State St., Augusta ME 04333-0025. (207)287-2724. E-mail: MaineArts.info@maine.gov. Website: www.mainearts.com.

Maryland State Arts Council, 175 W. Ostend St., Suite E, Baltimore MD 21230. (410)767-6555. E-mail: msac@msac.org. Website: www.msac.org.

Massachusetts Cultural Council, 10 St. James Ave., 3rd Floor, Boston MA 02116-3803. (617)727-3668. E-mail: web@art.state.ma.us. Website: www.massculturalcouncil.org.

Michigan Council for Arts & Cultural Affairs, 702 W. Kalamazoo St., P.O. Box 30705, Lansing MI 48909-8205. (517)241-4011. E-mail: artsinfo@michigan.gov. Website: www.michigan.gov/hal/0,1607,7-160-17445_19272---,00.html.

Minnesota State Arts Board, Park Square Court, 400 Sibley St., Suite 200, St. Paul MN 55101-1928. (651)215-1600 or (800)866-2787. E-mail: msab@arts.state.mn.us. Website: www.arts.state.mn.us.

Mississippi Arts Commission, 239 N. Lamar St., Suite 207, Jackson MS 39201. (601)359-6030. Website: www.arts.state.ms.us.

Missouri Arts Council, Wainwright State Office Complex, 111 N. Seventh St., Suite 105, St. Louis MO 63101-2188. (314)340-6845 or (866)407-4752. E-mail: moarts@ded.mo.gov. Website: www.missouriartscouncil.org.

Montana Arts Council, 316 N. Park Ave., Suite 252, Helena MT 59620-2201. (406)444-6430. E-mail: mac@mt.gov. Website: www.art.state.mt.us.

National Assembly of State Arts Agencies, 1029 Vermont Ave., NW, 2nd Floor, Washington DC 20005. (202)347-6352. E-mail: nasaa@nasaa-arts.org. Website: www.nasaa-arts.org.

Nebraska Arts Council, Joslyn Castle Carriage House, 3838 Davenport St., Omaha NE 68131. (402)595-2122 or (800)341-4067. Website: www.nebraskaartscouncil.org.

Nevada Arts Council, 716 N. Carson St., Suite A, Carson City NV 89701. (775)687-6680. E-mail: jcounsil@clan.lib.nv.us. Website: http://dmla.clan.lib.nv.us/docs/arts.

New Hampshire State Council on the Arts, 2½ Beacon St., 2nd Floor, Concord NH 03301-4974. (603)271-2789. Website: www.nh.gov/nharts.

New Jersey State Council on the Arts, 225 W. State St., P.O. Box 306, Trenton NJ 08625. (609)292-6130. Website: www.njartscouncil.org.

New Mexico Arts, Dept. of Cultural Affairs, P.O. Box 1450, Santa Fe NM 87504-1450. (505)827-6490 or (800)879-4278. Website: www.nmarts.org.

New York State Council on the Arts, 175 Varick St., New York NY 10014. (212)627-4455. Website: www.nysca.org.

North Carolina Arts Council, Dept. of Cultural Resources, Raleigh NC 27699-4632. (919)733-2111. E-mail: ncarts@ncmail.net. Website: www.ncarts.org.

North Dakota Council on the Arts, 1600 E. Century Ave., Suite 6, Bismarck ND 58503. (701)328-7590. E-mail: comserv@state.nd.us. Website: www.state.nd.us/arts.

Commonwealth Council for Arts and Culture, (Northern Mariana Islands), P.O. Box 5553, CHRB, Saipan MP 96950. (670)322-9982 or (670)322-9983. E-mail: galaidi@vzpacifica. net. Website: www.geocities.com/ccacarts/ccacwebsite.html.

Ohio Arts Council, 727 E. Main St., Columbus OH 43205-1796. (614)466-2613. Website: www.oac.state.oh.us.

Oklahoma Arts Council, P.O. Box 52001-2001, Oklahoma City OK 73152-2001. (405)521-2931. E-mail: okarts@arts.state.ok.gov. Website: www.arts.state.ok.us.

Oregon Arts Commission, 775 Summer St. NE, Suite 200, Salem OR 97301-1284. (503)986-0082. E-mail: oregon.artscomm@state.or.us. Website: www.oregonartscommission.org.

Pennsylvania Council on the Arts, Room 216, Finance Bldg., Harrisburg PA 17120. (717)787-6883. Website: www.pacouncilonthearts.org.

Institute of Puerto Rican Culture, P.O. Box 9024184, San Juan PR 00902-4184. (787)724-0700. E-mail: www@icp.gobierno.pr. Website: www.icp.gobierno.pr.

Rhode Island State Council on the Arts, One Capitol Hill, Third Floor, Providence RI 02908. (401)222-3880. E-mail: info@arts.ri.gov. Website: www.arts.ri.gov.

American Samoa Council on Culture, Arts and Humanities, P.O. Box 1540, Office of the Governor, Pago Pago AS 96799. (684)633-4347.

South Carolina Arts Commission, 1800 Gervais St., Columbia SC 29201. (803)734-8696. E-mail: goldstsa@arts.state.sc.us. Website: www.state.sc.us/arts.

South Dakota Arts Council, 800 Governors Dr., Pierre SD 57501. (605)773-3131. E-mail: sdac@state.sd.us. Website: www.state.sd.us/deca/sdarts.

Tennessee Arts Commission, Citizens Plaza Bldg., 401 Charlotte Ave., Nashville TN 37243-0780. (615)741-1701. Website: www.arts.state.tn.us.

Texas Commission on the Arts, E.O. Thompson Office Building, 920 Colorado, Suite 501, Austin TX 78701. (512)463-5535. E-mail: front.desk@arts.state.tx.us. Website: www.arts.state.tx.us.

Utah Arts Council, 617 E. South Temple, Salt Lake City UT 84102. (801)236-7555. Website: http://arts.utah.gov.

Vermont Arts Council, 136 State St., Drawer 33, Montpelier VT 05633-6001. (802)828-3291. E-mail: info@vermontartscouncil.org. Website: www.vermontartscouncil.org.

Virgin Islands Council on the Arts, 41-42 Norre Gade, St. Thomas VI 00802. (340)774-5984. E-mail: adagio@islands.vi. Website: http://vicouncilonarts.org.

Virginia Commission for the Arts, Lewis House, 223 Governor St., 2nd Floor, Richmond VA 23219. (804)225-3132. E-mail: arts@arts.virginia.gov. Website: www.arts.state.va.us.

Washington State Arts Commission, 711 Capitol Way S., Suite 600, P.O. Box 42675, Olympia WA 98504-2675. (360)753-3860. E-mail: info@arts.wa.gov. Website: www.arts.wa.gov.

West Virginia Commission on the Arts, The Cultural Center, 1900 Kanawha Blvd. E., Charleston WV 25305. (304)558-0240. Website: www.wvculture.org/arts.

Wisconsin Arts Board, 101 E. Wilson St., 1st Floor, Madison WI 53702. (608)266-0190. E-mail: artsboard@arts.state.wi.us. Website: www.arts.state.wi.us.

Wyoming Arts Council, 2320 Capitol Ave., Cheyenne WY 82002. (307)777-7742. E-mail: ebratt@state.wy.us. Website: http://wyoarts.state.wy.us.

CANADIAN PROVINCES ARTS AGENCIES

Alberta Foundation for the Arts, 901 Standard Life Centre, 10405 Jasper Ave., Edmonton AB T5J 4R7. Website: www.cd.gov.ab.ca/all_about_us/commissions/arts.

British Columbia Arts Council, P.O. Box 9819, Stn. Prov. Govt., Victoria BC V8W 9W3. (250)356-1718. E-mail: BCArtsCouncil@gems2.gov.bc.ca. Website: www.bcartscouncil.ca.

The Canada Council for the Arts, 350 Albert St., P.O. Box 1047, Ottawa ON K1P 5V8. (613)566-4414 or (800)263-558 (within Canada). Website: www.canadacouncil.ca.

Manitoba Arts Council, 525-93 Lombard Ave., Winnipeg MB R3B 3B1. (204)945-2237. E-mail: info@artscouncil.mb.ca. Website: www.artscouncil.mb.ca.

New Brunswick Arts Board (NBAB), 634 Queen St., Suite 300, Fredericton NB E3B 1C2. (866)460-2787. Website: www.artsnb.ca.

Newfoundland & Labrador Arts Council, P.O. Box 98, St. John's NL A1C 5H5. (709)726-2212 or (866)726-2212. E-mail: nlacmail@nfld.net. Website: www.nlac.nf.ca.

Nova Scotia Arts and Culture Partnership Council, Culture Division, 1800 Argyle St., Suite 402, Halifax NS B3J 2R5. (902)424-4442. E-mail: cultaffs@gov.ns.ca. Website: www.gov.ns.ca/dtc/culture.

Ontario Arts Council, 151 Bloor St. W., 5th Floor, Toronto ON M5S 1T6. (416)961-1660. E-mail: info@arts.on.ca. Website: www.arts.on.ca.

Prince Edward Island Council of the Arts, 115 Richmond St., Charlottetown PE C1A 1H7. (902)368-4410. E-mail: info@peiartscouncil.com. Website: www.peiartscouncil.com.

Quebec Council for Arts & Literature, 79 boul. René-Lévesque Est, 3e étage, Quebéc QC G1R 5N5. (418)643-1707 or (800)897-1707. E-mail: info@calq.gouv.qc.ca. Website: www.calq.gouv.qc.ca.

The Saskatchewan Arts Board, 2135 Broad St., Regina SK S4P 1Y6. (306)787-4056. E-mail: sab@artsboard.sk.ca. Website: www.artsboard.sk.ca.

Yukon Arts Section, Cultural Services Branch, Dept. of Tourism & Culture, Government of Yukon, Box 2703, Whitehorse YT Y1A 2C6. (867)667-8589. E-mail: arts@gov.yk.ca. Website: www.btc.gov.yk.ca/cultural/arts.

Conferences & Workshops

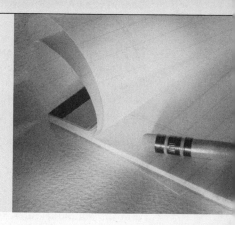

There are times when we want to immerse ourselves in learning. Or perhaps we crave a change of scenery, the creative stimulation of being around other artists, or the uninterrupted productivity of time alone to work.

That's what this section of *Poet's Market* is all about, providing a selection of writing conferences and workshops, artist colonies and retreats, poetry festivals, and even a few opportunities to go travelling with your muse. These listings give the basics: contact information, a brief description of the event, lists of past presenters, and offerings of special interest to poets. Contact an event that interests you for additional information, including up-to-date costs and housing details. **(Please note that most directors had not finalized their 2006 plans when we contacted them for this edition of *Poet's Market*. However, where possible, they provided us with their 2005 dates, costs, faculty names, or themes to give you a better idea of what each event has to offer.)**

Before you seriously consider a conference, workshop, or other event, determine what you hope to get out of the experience. Would a general conference with one or two poetry workshops among many other types of sessions be acceptable? Or are you looking for something exclusively focused on poetry? Do you want to hear poets speak about poetry writing, or are you looking for a more participatory experience, such as a one-on-one critiquing session or a group workshop? Do you mind being one of hundreds of attendees, or do you prefer a more intimate setting? Are you willing to invest in the expense of travelling to a conference, or would something local better suit your budget? Keep these questions and others in mind as you read these listings, view websites, and study conference brochures.

Some listings are coded with symbols to provide certain "information at a glance." The (𝗡) symbol indicates a recently established conference/workshop; the (★) symbol indicates this conference/workshop did not appear in the 2005 edition; the (♦) symbol denotes a Canadian event and the (🌐) symbol one located outside the U.S. and Canada.

⊠ AMERICAN CHRISTIAN WRITERS CONFERENCES

P.O. Box 110390, Nashville TN 37222. (800)21-WRITE. E-mail: ACWriters@aol.com. Website: www.ACWriters.com. **Contact:** Reg Forder, director. Established 1981. Annual 2-day events. Holds 30 conferences/year in cities including Houston, Boston, Minneapolis, Chicago, St. Louis, Detroit, Atlanta, Miami, Phoenix, and Los Angeles. Location: Usually a major hotel chain like Holiday Inn. Average attendance: 40-80.

Purpose/Features Open to anyone. Conferences cover fiction, poetry, writing for children. Offers poets ms critiques.

Costs/Accommodations Cost: $99-169. Participants responsible for all meals. Accommodations available on site.

Additional Info Also sponsors an annual Caribbean Christian Writers Conference Cruise each November. Additional information available for SASE, by e-mail, or on website.

🌐 ANAM CARA WRITER'S AND ARTIST'S RETREAT

Eyeries, Beara, West Cork, Ireland. Phone: 353 (0)27 74441. Fax: 353 (0)27 74448. E-mail: anamcararetreat@eircom.net. Website: www.anamcararetreat.com. **Contact:** Sue Booth-Forbes, director. Offers one-week to one-month individual retreats as well as workshops for writers and artists. Length of workshops varies with subject and leader/facilitator. Location: "Beara is a rural and hauntingly beautiful part of Ireland that is kept temperate by the Gulf Stream. The retreat sits on a hill overlooking Coulagh Bay, the mountains of the Ring of Kerry, and the Slieve Mishkish Mountains of Beara. The village of Eyeries is a short walk away." Average attendance: 5 residents at the retreat when working individually; 12-18 workshop participants.

Purpose/Features "Anam Cara is open to novice as well as professional writers and artists. Applicants are asked to provide a written description on the focus of their work while on retreat. Residencies are on a first-come, first-deposit-in basis." 2004 workshops included Poetry, Painting, and Proprioceptive Writing.

Costs/Accommodations 2004 cost: ranged from €570-670/week for individual retreats, depending on room. Meals and other services, except phone and Internet use, included. Residency fee includes full room and board, laundry, sauna, Jacuzzi, 5 acres of gardens, meadows, riverbank and cascades, river island, swimming hole, and several unique working spots, such as the ruin of a stone mill and a newly created beehive hut. Overflow from workshops stay in nearby B&Bs, a short walk away. Transportation details available on website.

Additional Info Requests for specific information about rates and availability can be made through the website; also available by fax or e-mail. Brochure available on request.

🌐 ART WORKSHOPS IN GUATEMALA

4758 Lyndale Ave. S., Minneapolis MN 55409-2304. (612)825-0747. Fax: (612)825-6637. E-mail: info@artguat.org. Website: www.artguat.org. **Contact:** Liza Fourré, director. Established 1995. Annual 10-day creative writing courses, held in February, March, July, and October. Location: workshops held in Antigua, the old colonial capital of Guatemala. Average attendance: limit 10 students.

Purpose/Features Art Workshops in Guatemala provides "the perfect getaway for creative writers of all skill levels looking for a memorable and inspiring writing/travel experience." For 2005, offered poets "Journey of the Soul" (with Sharon Doubiago, March 14-23) and "Snapshots in Words" (with Roseann Lloyd, July 21-30).

Costs/Accommodations 2005 cost: $2,025. Includes "air transportation from U.S., tuition, lodging in a beautiful old colonial home, a hearty breakfast, and ground transport."

Additional Info Individual poetry critiques included. Call, write, e-mail, fax, or check website.

ASPEN SUMMER WORDS INTERNATIONAL LITERARY FESTIVAL & WRITING RETREAT; ASPEN WRITERS' FOUNDATION

110 E. Hallam St., Suite 116, Aspen CO 81611. (970)925-3122. Fax: (970)920-5700. E-mail: info@asp

enwriters.org. Website: www.aspenwriters.org. Established 1976. Annual 5-day writing retreat and concurrent 5-day literary festival. 2005 dates: June 26-30. Location: The historic Hotel Jerome in Aspen. Average attendance: 90 for the retreat, over 200 for the festival.

Purpose/Features Offers a celebration of words and ideas featuring 17 events for readers and writers. Offers poets workshops, readings, publishing panels, interviews, Q&As, and agent/editor meetings. 2005 poetry faculty included Marie Ponsot.

Costs/Accommodations 2005 cost: $375 for 4-day workshop; $195 for 2-day symposium; $200 for literary festival (5-day pass). Offers $50 discount for registering for both the festival and retreat *or* symposium. Participants responsible for all meals, "though we offer complimentary morning coffee and pastries for students and 2 wine and hors d'oeuvres receptions for ASW registrants." Information on overnight accommodations available on website.

Additional Info Deadline for admission is April 1; deadline for discount housing is May 1. Writing sample required with application. Brochure and application available by phone, fax, e-mail (include regular mailing address with all e-mail inquiries), or on website.

BREAD LOAF WRITERS' CONFERENCE; BAKELESS LITERARY PUBLICATION PRIZES

Middlebury College, Middlebury VT 05753. (802)443-5286. Fax: (802)443-2087. E-mail: blwc@middlebury.edu. Website: www.middlebury.edu/~blwc. Director: Michael Collier. **Contact:** Noreen Cargill, administrative manager. Established 1926. Annual 11-day event. 2005 dates: August 17-28. Location: mountain campus of Middlebury College. Average attendance: 230.

Purpose/Features Conference is designed to promote dialogue among writers and provide professional critiques for students. Offers poets workshops, lectures, faculty readings, and ms critiques. 2005 poetry staff included Michael Collier, Edward Hirsch, Brigit Pegeen Kelly, Yusef Komunyakaa, Tom Sleigh, Arthur Sze, and Ellen Bryant Voigt.

Costs/Accommodations 2005 cost: $2,091 (contributor) or $1,994 (auditor), including tuition, room, and board. Fellowships and scholarships for the conference available. "Candidates for fellowships must have a book published. Candidates for scholarships must have published in major literary periodicals or newspapers. Application and supporting materials due by March 1. See website for further details. Awards are announced in June for the conference in August."

Additional Info Sponsors the Bakeless Literary Publication Prizes, an annual book series competition for new authors of literary works in poetry, fiction, and creative nonfiction. Details, conference brochure, and application form available for SASE or on website.

CAVE CANEM

584 Broadway, Suite 508, New York NY 10012. (212)941-5720. E-mail: ccpoets@verizon.net. Website: www.cavecanempoets.org. **Contact:** Carolyn Micklem, foundation director. Established 1996. Annual weeklong workshop for African-American poets. Usually held last week in June. Location: University of Pittsburgh at Greensburg, PA. Average attendance: 50.

Purpose/Features Open to African-American poets. Participants selected based on a sample of 6-8 poems. Offerings include workshops by fellows and faculty, evening readings. Participants are assigned to groups of about 9 and remain together throughout session, with different faculty leading each workshop. 2005 faculty included Toi Derricotte, Cornelius Eady, Cyrus Cassells, Kwame Dawes, Erica Hunt, Patricia Smith, and Marilyn Nelson.

Costs/Accommodations 2005 cost: $495. Meals and other services included. For complete information, contact Cave Canem.

Additional Information Poets should submit 6-8 poems with cover letter. 2005 postmark deadline: March 15, with accepted poets notified by April 30. Cave Canem Foundation also sponsors the Cave Canem Poetry Prize (see separate listing in Contests & Awards section). Brochure and registration information available for SASE and on website.

CENTRUM'S PORT TOWNSEND WRITERS' CONFERENCE

% Centrum, P.O. Box 1158, Port Townsend WA 98368. (360)385-3102. Fax: (360)385-2470. E-mail: info@centrum.org. Website: www.centrum.org. **Contact:** Rebecca Brown, creative director.

Established 1974. Annual 10-day event. 2005 dates: July 14-24. Location: Fort Worden State Park, historic seaside entrance to Puget Sound. Average attendance: 150 (limit of 16/critiqued workshop). **Purpose/Features** Open to all serious writers. Offers poets limited-enrollment critiqued workshops with private conference or open enrollment workshops, as well as open mic readings, faculty readings, and technique classes. 2005 poetry staff included Kim Addonizio, Peter Pereira, Bhanu Kapil, and Alberto Rios. **Costs/Accommodations** 2005 cost: $525 for critiqued workshop tuition, $425 open enrollment workshop tuition; $285-540 room and/or board options. **Additional Info** Members of critiqued workshops must submit writing samples. Brochure and registration form available for SASE or on website.

CHENANGO VALLEY WRITERS' CONFERENCE

Office of Summer Programs, Colgate University, 13 Oak Dr., Hamilton NY 13346. (315)228-7770. Fax: (315)228-7975. E-mail: info@cvwc.net. Website: www.cvwc.net. **Contact:** Matthew Leone, conference director. Established 1996. Annual weeklong event. 2005 dates: June 19-25. Location: Colgate University, "an expansive campus, with classrooms, dormitories, libraries, and recreational facilities all in close proximity to each other." Average attendance: 75. **Purpose/Features** Open to "all serious writers or aspirants." Offers poets workshops, lectures, readings, and ms critiques. 2005 poetry staff included Bruce Smith, Peter Balakian, and David Thoreen. **Costs/Accommodations** 2005 cost: $995 (tuition, room, and board); $750 for day students. Meal plan available for day students. Accommodations available on-site. **Additional Info** Each applicant must submit a ms with his/her application. Brochures and registration forms available for SASE or on website.

THE CONFERENCE ON TEACHING AND POETRY

The Frost Place, Franconia NH 03580. (603)823-5510. E-mail: rfrost@ncia.net. Website: www.frost place.org. **Contact:** Donald Sheehan and Baron Wormser, co-directors. Annual event. 2005 dates: June 27-July 1. **Purpose/Features** Designed for high school and middle school classroom teachers. Brings together poets and teachers to address how poetry can be taught most effectively. Offers first-hand experience about how poems are created and how poets view their art. 2005 guest poetry faculty included Fleda Brown, Esther Weiner, Major Jackson, and Diane Lockward. **Costs/Accommodations** 2005 cost: $450 ($350 NH residents), plus $70 for daily lunch and 2 dinners. Additional cost of $636 for 3 graduate credits from the University of New Hampshire College for Lifelong Learning. Overnight accommodations available locally. **Additional Info** To apply, send letter describing current teaching situation and literary interests. (See separate listings for Frost Place Annual Festival of Poetry and Frost Place Seminar in this section.)

FINE ARTS WORK CENTER

24 Pearl St., Provincetown MA 02657. (508)487-9960. Fax: (508)487-8873. E-mail: workshops@faw c.org. Website: www.fawc.org. Established 1968. The Fine Arts Work Center in Provincetown "is a nonprofit organization dedicated to providing emerging writers and visual artists with time and space in which to pursue independent work in a community of peers." Seven-month fellowships are awarded to poets and fiction writers in the emerging stages of their careers; professional juries make admissions decisions. Offers 71 weekend and weeklong workshops in poetry, fiction, creative nonfiction, and visual arts. 2005 Summer Workshop Program fees were $480 for each weeklong workshop and $235 for each weekend workshop. Accommodations available in area. See website for details and an application form.

FROST PLACE ANNUAL FESTIVAL OF POETRY

The Frost Place, Franconia NH 03580. (603)823-5510. E-mail: rfrost@ncia.net. Website: www.frost place.org. Executive Director: Donald Sheehan. **Contact:** David Keller, director of admissions. Established 1978. Annual weeklong event. 2005 dates: July 31-August 6. Location: Robert Frost's house and barn, made into a center for poetry and the arts. Average attendance: 50-55.

Purpose/Features Open to poets only. Offers daily lecture/seminar, reading, and organized critique of participant work. 2005 guest faculty included Laura Kasischke, Christopher Merrill, Sarah Gorham, Sydney Lea, Carl Dennis, and Linda Gregerson.

Costs/Accommodations 2005 cost: $775 (participant), plus a $25 reading fee. Auditor fee: $550. Room and board available locally; information sent upon acceptance to program.

Additional Info Application should be accompanied by 3 pages of your own poetry and $25 reading fee (participant). Auditors apply by brief letter describing literary interests. (See separate listings for The Conference on Teaching and Poetry and The Frost Place Seminar in this section.)

FROST PLACE SEMINAR

The Frost Place, Franconia NH 03580. (603)823-5510. E-mail: rfrost@ncia.net. Website: www.frost place.org. **Contact:** Baron Wormser, seminar director. Held annually in early August following the Frost Place Annual Festival of Poetry (see separate listing in this section). 2005 dates: August 8-12. Average attendance: limited to 16 participants.

Purpose/Features Open to those who have participated in the Festival of Poetry at least once prior to the summer for which you are applying. Offers daily lecture/seminar on poetry of the past, workshop focusing on participant poems, reading. 2005 poetry staff included Carol Frost and Richard Frost.

Costs/Accommodations 2005 cost: $710, plus $95 for 2 meals daily and $25 reading fee.

Additional Info Admission competitive. To apply, send cover letter outlining goals for your participation and 3 pages of your own poetry. (See separate listings for Frost Place Annual Festival of Poetry and The Conference on Teaching and Poetry in this section.)

✪ HAYSTACK WRITING PROGRAM SUMMER SESSION

Portland State University, P.O. Box 1491, Portland OR 97207. (800)547-8887, ext. 4186 or (503)725-4186. Fax: (503)725-4840. E-mail: snydere@pdx.edu. Website: www.haystack.pdx.edu. **Contact:** Elizabeth Snyder, coordinator. Established 1969. Annual summer program of weeklong and weekend workshops. Dates: held in July and August. Location: Canon Beach, 80 miles west of Portland on the Oregon coast. Average attendance: 10-15/class; 200 total.

Purpose/Features Open to all writers. Offers poets workshops, lectures, and panels. 2005 poetry staff included Marvin Bell and Judith Barrington.

Costs/Accommodations 2005 cost: was $225-505. Participants pay for their own lodging and meals. Wide range of options for accommodations. List provided upon registration.

Additional Info Brochure and registration form available by mail or on website.

INDIANA UNIVERSITY WRITERS' CONFERENCE

464 Ballantine Hall, Indiana University, Bloomington IN 47405. (812)855-1877. Fax: (812)855-9535. E-mail: writecon@indiana.edu. Website: www.indiana.edu/~writecon. **Contact:** Jacqueline Jones La Mon, associate director. Established 1940. Annual weeklong event. 2005 dates: June 5-10. Location: Bloomington campus of Indiana State University. Average attendance: 100.

Purpose/Features Open to all. Offers poetry workshops, classes, readings, and ms critiques. 2005 poetry staff included Ruth Ellen Kocher, Yusef Komunyakaa, Maura Stanton, and Martha Rhodes.

Costs/Accommodations 2005 cost: $500 for workshop (including all classes); $325 for classes only. $50 application fee. Accommodations available on-site. Information on overnight accommodations available.

Additional Info Poetry workshop applicants must submit up to 10 pages of poetry with application. Brochure and registration form available for SASE, by e-mail, or on website.

IOWA SUMMER WRITING FESTIVAL

C215 Seashore Hall, University of Iowa, Iowa City IA 52242. (319)335-4160. Fax: (319)335-4039. E-mail: iswfestival@uiowa.edu. Website: www.uiowa.edu/~iswfest. **Contact:** Amy Margolis, director. Established 1987. Annual event held in June and July for 6 weeks. Includes one-week and weekend workshops at the University of Iowa campus. Average attendance: 150/week.

Purpose/Features Open to "all adults who have a desire to write." Offers poets workshops, lectures, discussions, and participant readings in either weeklong or weekend formats. 2005 poetry staff included Richard Jackson, Jane Mead, Christine Hemp, Bruce Bond, Jim Heynen, Phil Hey, Michael Morse, Michael Dennis Brown, and Katie Ford.

Costs/Accommodations 2005 cost: $225 for a weekend course and $475-500 for a one-week course. Participants responsible for most meals. Accommodations available on-site and at area hotels. Information on overnight accommodations available by phone or on website.

Additional Info Participants in weeklong workshops have private conference/critique with workshop leader. Brochure and registration form available by e-mail or on website.

THE IWWG SUMMER CONFERENCE

The International Women's Writing Guild, P.O. Box 810, Gracie Station, New York NY 10028. (212)737-7536. Fax: (212)737-9469. E-mail: iwwg@iwwg.org. Website: www.iwwg.org. **Contact:** Hannelore Hahn, executive director. Established 1978. 2005 dates: June 17-24. Location: Skidmore College in Saratoga Springs, NY. Average attendance: 500 maximum.

Purpose/Features Open to all women. Around 70 workshops offered each day. 2005 poetry staff included Barbara Garro, Marj Hahne, D.H. Melhem, Myra Shapiro, and Susan Baugh.

Costs/Accommodations 2005 cost: $945 (single), $810 (double) for IWWG members; $975 (single), $840 (double) for nonmembers. Includes program and room and board for 7 nights, 21 meals at Skidmore College. Shorter conference stays available.

Additional Info Post-conference retreat weekend also available. Additional information available for SASE, by e-mail, or on website.

JENTEL ARTIST RESIDENCY PROGRAM

Jentel Foundation, 130 Lower Piney Creek Rd., Banner WY 82832. (307)737-2311. Fax: (307)737-2305. E-mail: Jentel@jentelarts.org. Website: www.jentelarts.org. **Contact:** Mary Jane Edwards, executive director. Established 2000. One-month residencies throughout the year, scheduled the 15th of one month through the 13th of the following month. Application deadlines are September 15 and January 15 annually. Location: Banner, WY. Average attendance: 2 writers in any genre (also 4 visual artists in any media).

Purpose/Features Residency program for writers and visual artists who are U.S. citizens or from the international community currently residing in the U.S., are 25 years and older, and are not matriculated students. "Set in a rural ranch setting in the foothills of the Big Horn Mountains of North Central Wyoming, Jentel offers unfettered time and space to focus on the creative process, experience of the Wyoming landscape, and interact as desired with a small community of writers and artists." Special features include Jentel Presents, a monthly evening of slide presentations and readings by residents in one of the surrounding communities.

Costs/Accommodations Residents are responsible for travel expenses and personal items. "Jentel provides a private accommodation in a shared living space, a comfortable private studio, and a $400 stipend to help defray the cost of food and personal expenses. Staff takes residents grocery shopping weekly after the stipend is distributed. Staff will pick up and drop off residents at the airport and bus station in Sheridan, 20 miles from the ranch setting of Jentel." Accommodation provided in a large house with common living and dining areas; fully equipped kitchen; library with computer, printer, and Internet access; media room with television, video player, and CD player; special private bedroom; and private studio.

Additional Information Brochure and application form available for self-addressed mailing label and 60 cents postage or on website.

☒ LIFE PRESS CHRISTIAN WRITERS' CONFERENCE; LIFE PRESS CHRISTIAN WRITERS' ASSOCIATION

P.O. Box 2018, Cordova TN 38088. (901)309-3692. E-mail: GMOearth@aol.com. Website: www.grandmotherearth.com. **Contact:** Frances Cowden. Established 1998. Annual one-day event. 2004 date: July 8. Location: Memphis, TN. Average attendance: 45.

Purpose/Features Open to all writers. Offers poets workshops, lectures, readings, and ms critiques. 2004 poetry staff included Florence Bruce and Dr. Malra Treece.

Costs/Accommodations 2004 cost: $35 registration fee (including one contest entry, critique of all entries, continental breakfast); $30 (registration with entries but no critique); or $25 (including food, no entries); $20 fee for spouses. Information on overnight accommodations available.

Additional Info Individual poetry critiques available. Poets should submit a limit of 6 works/category and $10 fee. "One payment for all entries—send with entries." Contest sponsored for "poetry and prose in general, open to all writers. Other contests require attendance." National Awards for poetry (open to everyone, 50-line limit) are $50, $25, $15, and $10. Conference Awards for poetry (open to those who register for the conference, 30-line limit) are $50, $15, and $10. **Entry fee:** "$5 entitles you to one entry; $2 for each additional entry. (Three poems is an entry.)" Critique from the judges is available for $10 for all entries. Guidelines available for SASE or on website.

NAPA VALLEY WRITERS' CONFERENCE

Napa Valley College, 1088 College Ave., St. Helena CA 94574. (707)967-2900. E-mail: writecon@napavalley.edu. Website: www.napavalley.edu/writersconf. **Contact:** Nan Cohen, poetry director. Established 1981. Annual week-long event. 2005 dates: July 24-29. Location: Upper Valley Campus in the historic town of St. Helena, 25 miles north of Napa in the heart of the valley's wine growing community. Average attendance: 48 in poetry and 48 in fiction.

Purpose/Features Conference is "suited to writers who have had some training, but we also encourage enthusiastic beginners to apply." Offers poets workshops, lectures, faculty readings, ms critiques, and meetings with editors. "The poetry session provides the opportunity to work both on generating new poems and on revising previously written ones." 2005 poetry staff included Jane Hirshfield, Brigit Pegeen Kelly, J.D. McClatchy, and C. Dale Young.

Costs/Accommodations 2005 cost: $675, including lunch, 2 dinners, and attendance at all conference events. A limited number of scholarships are available. Information on overnight accommodations available. Limited accommodations in local homes available on a first-come, first-served basis; $30 one-time placement fee.

Additional Info All applicants are asked to submit a qualifying ms with their registration (no more than 5 poems) as well as a brief description of their writing background. Include $10 reading fee and $75 tuition deposit with application. 2005 application deadline: May 20. Brochure and registration form available for SASE or on website.

NATIONAL COWBOY POETRY GATHERING; WESTERN FOLKLIFE CENTER

501 Railroad St., Elko NV 89801. (775)738-7508. Fax: (775)738-2900. E-mail: tbaer@westernfolklife .org. Website: www.westernfolklife.org. **Contact:** Gathering Manager. 2006 dates: January 28-February 4. Location: Western Folklife Center or the Elko Convention Center, plus other venues.

Purpose/Features Early Gathering activities (first weekend and early in week) feature workshops, evening performances, and exhibits. The Gathering swings into full gear on Wednesday with concert and keynote address, followed by 3 days of poetry and music, exhibits, panel discussions, and videos/films.

Costs/Accommodations 2006 advance ticket cost: $35 for 3-day Guest Pass (including program book and guest pass pin); $15 for Single Day Pass (program book purchased separately). Ticket cost does not include handling charge or credit card fee. Advance ticket sale starts in early September. Participants responsible for own meals and housing (there are many motels and casinos in Elko). Advance reservations recommended.

Additional Information The Western Folklife Center distributes books and tapes of cowboy poetry and songs as well as other cowboy memorabilia; also sponsors a variety of other community programs throughout the year. Additional information available about the Center and the Gathering on website.

⚡ OZARK CREATIVE WRITERS CONFERENCE

6817 Gingerbread Lane, Little Rock AR 72204-4738. (501)565-8889. Fax: (501)565-7220. E-mail: pvining@aristotle.net. **Contact:** Peggy Vining, conference counselor. Established 1968. Annual event held the second full weekend in October. 2005 dates: October 13-15. Location: Inn of the Ozarks Convention Center in Eureka Springs, Arkansas. Average attendance: about 200.

Purpose/Features Open to all writers.

Costs/Accommodations 2005 cost: $50 registration fee prior to September 1. "Eureka Springs is a resort town so register early for lodging (say you are with OCWI). Eighty rooms are blocked at the Inn of The Ozarks for the conference." Information on overnight accommodations available from the Chamber of Commerce of Eureka Springs.

Additional Info Various writing contests sponsored as part of conference. Sizeable monetary awards given for all types of writing. Guidelines and brochure/registration form available for #10 SASE after April 1. "If requesting information by e-mail, please include regular mailing address."

PIMA WRITERS' WORKSHOP

Pima College, 2202 W. Anklam Rd., Tucson AZ 85709-0170. (520)206-6084. E-mail: mfiles@pima.edu. **Contact:** Meg Files, director. Established 1987. Annual 3-day event. 2005 dates: May 27-29. Location: Pima College's Center for the Arts, "includes a proscenium theater, a black box theater, a recital hall, and conference rooms, as well as a courtyard with amphitheater." Average attendance: 300.

Purpose/Features Open to all writers, beginning and experienced. Offers poets workshops, ms critiques, writing exercises, and "the workshop's atmosphere—friendly and supportive, practical and inspirational." Past poetry staff has included Peter Meinke, Steve Kowit, David Citino, and others.

Costs/Accommodations 2005 cost: $70. Participants responsible for their own meals. Information on overnight accommodations available.

Additional Info Brochure and registration form available for SASE or by fax or e-mail.

⚡ SAGE HILL SUMMER WRITING EXPERIENCE

P.O. Box 1731, Saskatoon SK S7K 3S1 Canada. Phone/fax: (306)652-7395. E-mail: sage.hill@sasktel.net. Website: www.sagehillwriting.ca. **Contact:** Steven Ross Smith, executive director. Established 1990. Annual 10-day adult summer program. 2005 dates: July 25-August 4. Location: St. Michael's Retreat, Lumsden, Saskatchewan. Average attendance: varies according to specific workshop (usually 6-11 participants).

Purpose/Features Open to writers, 19 years of age and older, who are working in English. No geographic restrictions. Offers poets workshops, labs, colloquia, and readings. 2005 poetry staff included Phil Hall, Sue Goyette, John Steffler, and Nicole Brossard.

Costs/Accommodations 2005 cost: $895, including instruction, accommodations, meals, and all facilities. Accommodations available on-site.

Additional Info Writing sample and $50 deposit required with application. Additional information available for SASE, by phone, e-mail, or on website.

SAN DIEGO STATE UNIVERSITY WRITERS' CONFERENCE

5250 Campanile Dr., San Diego CA 92182-1920. (619)594-2517. Fax: (619)594-8566. E-mail: kicarter @mail.sdsu.edu. Website: www.ces.sdsu.edu. **Contact:** Becky Ryan, coordinator of noncredit community education. Established 1984. Annual 3-day event. 2005 dates: January 21-23. Location: Doubletree Hotel (Mission Valley), 7450 Hazard Center Dr., San Diego. Average attendance: 400.
Purpose/Features Open to writers of fiction, nonfiction, children's books, poetry, and screenwriting. "We have participants from across North America." Offers poets workshops, networking lunch, and editor appointments and consultations.
Costs/Accommodations 2005 cost: $355-475 (through January 4), including one meal. Accommodations available on-site. Information on overnight accommodations available.
Additional Info See website for details. "Editors and agents give awards for favorite submissions." Information and registration form available on website.

SANTA BARBARA WRITERS' CONFERENCE

P.O. Box 6627, Santa Barbara CA 93160. (805)967-1330. Fax: (805)967-8663. E-mail: info@sbwritersc onference.com. Website: www.sbwritersconference.com or www.sbwc.org. **Contact:** Marcia Meier, executive director. Established 1973. Annual event held the last week of June. 2006 dates: June 23-30. Location: Westmont College in Montecito. Average attendance: 350.
Purpose/Features Open to everyone. Covers all genres of writing. Offers poets workshops, lectures, faculty readings, participant readings, ms critiques, and meetings with editors. 2005 poetry staff included Perie J. Longo and Bill Wilkins.
Costs/Accommodations 2005 cost: $1,375 single, $1,075 double (including all workshops and lectures, 2 dinners, and room and board); $425 day students. Participants responsible for some meals. Accommodations available on-site or at area hotels. Information on overnight accommodations available by e-mail or on website.
Additional Info Offers poetry contest as part of conference. Guidelines available on website. Brochure and registration form available on website.

SEWANEE WRITERS' CONFERENCE

310 St. Luke's Hall, 735 University Ave., Sewanee TN 37383-1000. (931)598-1141. E-mail: cpeters@ sewanee.edu. Website: www.sewaneewriters.org. **Contact:** Cheri B. Peters, creative writing programs manager. Established 1990. Annual 12-day event held the last 2 weeks in July. Location: the University of the South ("dormitories for housing, Women's Center for public events, classrooms for workshops, Sewanee Inn for dining, etc."). Attendance: about 105.
Purpose/Features Open to poets, fiction writers, and playwrights who submit their work for review in a competitive admissions process. "Participants belong to a workshop devoted to constructive critique of members' manuscripts; in addition, each participant has a manuscript conference with a faculty member. Readings, craft lectures, panels, and Q&A sessions round out the formal offerings; numerous social functions offer opportunities for informal exchange and networking. Genre, rather than thematic, workshops are offered in each of the 3 areas." 2005 poetry staff included John Hollander, X.J. Kennedy, and Mary Jo Salter.
Costs/Accommodations 2004 cost: $1,325, including room and board. Each year scholarships and fellowships based on merit are available on a competitive basis.
Additional Info A ms should be sent in advance after admission to the conference. Write for brochure and application forms; no SASE necessary. Additional information available on website.

(S.O.M.O.S.) SOCIETY OF THE MUSE OF THE SOUTHWEST; CHOKECHERRIES

P.O. Box 3225, Taos NM 87571. (505)758-0081. Fax: (505)758-4802. E-mail: somos@laplaza.com. Website: www.somostaos.org. **Contact:** Dori Vinella, executive director. Established 1983. "We offer readings, special events, and workshops at different times during the year, many during the summer." Length of workshops varies. Location: various sites in Taos. Average attendance: 10-50.
Purpose/Features Open to anyone. "We offer workshops in various genres—fiction, poetry, nature

writing, etc." Past workshop speakers have included Denise Chavez, Alfred Depew, Marjorie Agosin, Judyth Hill, Robin Becker, and Robert Westbrook. Other special features include the 2-day Annual Taos Storytelling Festival in November, a Winter Writers Series (January-February), and Summer Writer's Series (July-August).

Costs/Accommodations Cost: ranges from $30-175 for workshops, excluding room and board. Information on overnight accommodations available.

Additional Info Additional information available by fax, e-mail, or on website. "Taos has a wonderful community of dedicated and talented writers who make S.O.M.O.S. workshops rigorous, supportive, and exciting." Also publishes *Chokecherries*, an annual anthology.

THE SOUTHAMPTON COLLEGE WRITERS CONFERENCE

239 Montauk Hwy., Southampton NY 11968. (631)287-8175. Fax: (631)287-8253. E-mail: writers@s outhampton.liu.edu. Website: www.southampton.liu.edu/summer. **Contact:** Carla Caglioti, summer director. Established 1976. Annual 11-day event. 2005 dates: July 20-21. Location: Southampton College of Long Island University "in the heart of the Hamptons, one of the most beautiful and culturally rich resorts in the country." Average attendance: 12/workshop.

Purpose/Features Open to new and established writers, graduate students, and upper-level undergraduate students. Offers poets workshops. 2004 poetry staff included Billy Collins and Carol Muske-Dukes.

Costs/Accommodations 2005 cost: was $2,320 for workshop, room and board; $1,890 tuition only. Accommodations available on-site.

Additional Info "Evening events will feature regular faculty and award-winning visiting authors. Participants will also enjoy a rich schedule of formal and informal social gatherings—author receptions, open mic nights, and special literary events. Early registration is encouraged." Brochure and registration form available by e-mail or on website.

SPLIT ROCK ARTS PROGRAM

University of Minnesota, 360 Coffey Hall, 1420 Eckles Ave., St. Paul MN 55108-6084. (612)625-8100. Fax: (612)624-6210. E-mail: srap@cce.umn.edu. Website: www.cce.umn.edu/splitrockarts. Established 1983. Annual summer series of weeklong workshops in creative writing, visual art, design, and creativity enhancement. 2005 dates: June 26-August 6. Location: the University's Twin Cities campus. Average attendance: 550.

Purpose/Features Open to "anyone over 18 years old who has an interest in the visual and literary arts." Offers poets various workshops with intensive, intimate study. 2005 poetry staff included Jim Moore, Joyce Stuphen, Judith Barrington, and Emily Warn.

Costs/Accommodations 2005 cost: $575 (noncredit). Participants responsible for most meals. Accommodations available on-site or at area hotels. Information on overnight accommodations available in catalog or on website.

Additional Info Online and printed catalogs available in late February. Registration also open in late February.

☒ SQUAW VALLEY COMMUNITY OF WRITERS POETRY WORKSHOP

P.O. Box 1416, Nevada City CA 95959. (530)470-8440. Fax: (530)470-8446. E-mail: svcw@oro.net. Website: www.squawvalleywriters.org. **Contact:** Brett Hall Jones, executive director. Established 1969. Annual 7-day event usually held last full week in July. 2003 dates were July 19-26. Location: The Squaw Valley Ski Corporation's Lodge in the Sierra Nevada near Lake Tahoe. "The workshop takes place in the off-season of the ski area. Participants can find time to enjoy the Squaw Valley landscape." Average attendance: 64.

Purpose/Features Open to talented writers of diverse ethnic backgrounds and a wide range of ages. "The Poetry Program differs in concept from other workshops in poetry. Our project's purpose is to help participants break through old habits and write something daring and difficult. Workshops are intended to provide a supportive atmosphere in which no one will be embarrassed, and at the same time to challenge the participants to go beyond what they have done before. Admissions are based on quality of the submitted manuscripts." Offerings include regular morning workshops, craft lectures, and staff readings. "Participants gather in daily workshops to discuss the work they wrote in the previous 24 hours." 2004 poetry staff included Lucille Clifton, Cornelius Eady, Robert Hass, Sharon Olds, and C.D. Wright.

Costs/Accommodations 2004 cost: $750, including regular morning workshops, craft lectures, staff readings, and dinners. Accommodations extra; information on separate accommodations available. "We arrange housing for participants in local houses and condominiums. Participants can choose from a single room for $500/week or a double room for $350/week within these shared houses. We do offer inexpensive bunk bed accommodations on a first come, first served basis."

Additional Info Individual conferences available. "Only work-in-progress will be discussed." Brochure available by e-mail (include mailing address for response) or on website. Also publishes the annual *Squaw Valley Community of Writers Omnium Gatherum and Newsletter* containing "news and profiles on our past participants and staff, craft articles, and book advertising."

STEAMBOAT SPRINGS WRITERS CONFERENCE

P.O. Box 774284, Steamboat Springs CO 80477. (970)879-8079. E-mail: sswriters@cs.com. Website: www.steamboatwriters.com. **Contact:** Harriet Freiberger, director. Established 1982. Annual one-day event. 2004 date: July 17. Location: a "renovated train station, the Depot is home of the Steamboat Springs Arts Council—friendly, relaxed atmosphere." Average attendance: 35-40 (registration limited).

Purpose/Features Open to anyone. Conference is "designed for writers who have limited time. Instructors vary from year to year, offering maximum instruction during a weekend at a nominal cost." 2004 poetry staff included David Mason.

Costs/Accommodations 2004 cost: $45, including luncheon and all seminars. "A variety of lodgings available."

Additional Info Brochure and registration form available for SASE, by e-mail, or on website. Optional: Friday evening dinner (cost not included in registration fee); readings by participants (no cost).

TAOS SUMMER WRITERS' CONFERENCE

University of New Mexico, Dept. of English Language and Literature, MSC03 2170, 1 University of New Mexico, Albuquerque NM 87131-0001. (505)277-6248. Fax: (505)277-5573. E-mail: taosconf@unm.edu. Website: www.unm.edu/~taosconf. **Contact:** Sharon Oard Warner, director. Established 1999. Annual 5-day (weeklong) and 2-day (weekend) workshops usually held mid-July. Location: Sagebrush Inn in Taos. Average attendance: 180 total; 100 places available in weekend, 170 places available in weeklong workshops. Class size limited to 12/class, usually smaller.

Purpose/Features Open to everyone, beginners to experienced. Minimum age is 18. Friendly, relaxed atmosphere with supportive staff and instructors. Offers both weekend and weeklong workshops in such areas as fiction, poetry, memoir, travel narrative, screenwriting, craft, and master classes in novel and poetry. One-on-one consultations with agents and editors available. 2005 workshop presenters included Pam Houston, Antonya Nelson, Greg Martin, Diane Thiel, and John Dufresne. Special features include evening readings and craft panels, open mic sessions, and tours of the D.H. Lawrence Ranch.

Costs/Accommodations 2005 cost: $250 for weekend, $525 for weeklong sessions, $725 combo, including workshop registration and special events. Nearest airport is Albuquerque Sunport. Taos is about 170 miles north of Albuquerque. Information on overnight accommodations available. Sagebrush Inn and Comfort Suites offer special rates.

Additional Info Brochure and registration form available by e-mail or on website. "Taos is a unique experience of a lifetime. The setting and scenery are spectacular; historical and natural beauty abound. Our previous attendees say they have been inspired by the place and by the friendly, personal attention of our instructors."

✪ TENNESSEE MOUNTAIN WRITERS CONFERENCE; TENNESSEE MOUNTAIN WRITERS, INC.

P.O. Box 5435, Oak Ridge TN 37831-5435. E-mail: mail@tmwi.org. Website: www.tmwi.org. Established 1989. Annual event. 2005 dates: April 7-9. Location: Doubletree Hotel in Oak Ridge. Average attendance: 150-200.

Purpose/Features Open to "all aspiring writers, including students." Offers poets workshops, readings, and ms critiques. 2005 poetry staff included Dana Wildsmith.

Costs/Accommodations 2005 cost: $200 for full participants; $170 for day classes only. Participants responsible for all meals except banquet. Accommodations available on-site. Information on overnight accommodations available on website.

Additional Info Offers poetry contest as part of conference. Guidelines available for SASE, by e-mail, or on website. Registration form available on website.

⊕ TŶ NEWYDD WRITERS' CENTRE

Taliesin Trust, Llanystumdwy, Cricieth, Gwynedd LL52 0LW Wales, United Kingdom. Phone: 0441766 522811. Fax: 0441766 523095. E-mail: post@tynewydd.org. Website: www.tynewydd.org. **Contact:** Sally Baker, director. Established 1990. Holds 4½-day courses throughout the year, Monday evening through Saturday morning. Location: Tŷ Newydd, The National Writers' Centre for Wales. Average attendance: 16/course maximum.

Purpose/Features Open to anyone over 16 years of age. Courses are designed to "promote the writing and understanding of literature by providing creative writing courses at all levels for all ages. Courses at Tŷ Newydd provide the opportunity of working intimately and informally with 2 professional writers." Courses specifically for poets of all levels of experience and ability are offered throughout the year.

Costs/Accommodations 2006 cost: check website. 2004 cost for a 4½-day course was £345 (inclusive), shared room; some weekend courses available, cost was £140 (inclusive), shared room. Transportation to and from Centre available if arranged at least a week in advance. Participants stay at Tŷ Newydd House in shared bedrooms or single bedrooms.

Additional Info Brochure and registration form available for SASE. Additional information available on website.

UNIVERSITY OF NORTH DAKOTA WRITERS CONFERENCE

Dept. of English, Box 7117, University of North Dakota, Grand Forks ND 58202-7209. (701)777-3015. Fax: (701)777-3622. E-mail: tami.carmichael@und.nodak.edu. Website: www.undwritersconference.org. **Contact:** Tami Carmichael, director. Established 1970. Annual 4- to 5-day event. 2005 dates: March 29-April 2. Location: the University of Nebraska's Memorial Union. Average attendance: 3,000-5,000. "Some individual events have as few as 20, some over 1,000."

Purpose/Features All events are free and open to the public. Offers poets panel discussions, readings, and book signings. 2005 poetry staff included Carolyn Forché and Marilyn Nelson.

Additional Info Schedule and other information available on website.

✪ VICTORIA SCHOOL OF WRITING

Suite 306-620 View St., Victoria BC V8W 1J6 Canada. (250)595-3000. E-mail: info@victoriaschoolofwriting.org. Website: www.victoriaschoolofwriting.org. **Contact:** Jill Margo, director. Established 1996. Annual 5-day event. 2005 dates: July 17-22. Location: "Residential school in natural, park-like setting. Easy parking, access to university, downtown." Average attendance: 100.

Purpose/Features "A 3- to 10-page manuscript is required as part of the registration process, which is open to all. The general purpose of the workshop is to give hands-on assistance with better writing, working closely with established writers/instructors." Offers poets intensive 5-day workshops (16 hours of instruction and one-on-one consultation). 2005 poetry staff included George Bowering and Sheri-D Wilson.

Costs/Accommodations 2005 cost: $585 Canadian, including opening reception, 5 lunches, and final-night banquet. Other meal/accommodation packages available; see website. "For people who register with payment in full before May 1, the cost is $535 Canadian (2005)."

Additional Info Contest sponsored as part of conference. Guidelines available on website. Brochure and registration form available through online request form.

WESLEYAN WRITERS CONFERENCE

Wesleyan University, Middletown CT 06457. (860)685-3604. Fax: (860)685-2441. E-mail: agreene@ wesleyan.edu. Website: www.wesleyan.edu/writers. **Contact:** Anne Greene, director. Established 1956. Annual 5-day event. 2005 dates: June 19-24. Location: the campus of Wesleyan University "in the hills overlooking the Connecticut River, a brief drive from the Connecticut shore. Wesleyan's outstanding library, poetry reading room, and other university facilities are open to participants." Average attendance: 100.

Purpose/Features "The conference welcomes everyone interested in the writer's craft. Participants are a diverse, international group. Both new and experienced writers are welcome. You may attend all of the seminars, including poetry, the novel, short story, fiction techniques, literary journalism, and memoir." Offers poets workshops, lectures, faculty readings, ms critiques, meetings with editors, and special panel presentations. 2005 poetry staff included Honor Moore, Elizabeth Willis, and Maggie Nelson.

Costs/Accommodations 2005 cost: $780 day student rate (including tuition and meals); $920-950 boarding rate (including tuition, meals, room for 5 nights). Accommodations available on-site or at area hotels. Information on overnight accommodations available on website.

Additional Info Registration for critiques must be made before the conference. Additional information available by phone, fax, or on website.

✖ WHIDBEY ISLAND WRITERS' CONFERENCES; THE WHIDBEY ISLAND WRITERS' ASSOCIATION

P.O. Box 1289, Langley WA 98260. (360)331-6714. E-mail: writers@writeonwhidbey.org. Website: www.writeonwhidbey.org. Established 1997. Annual event. 2006 dates: March 3-5. Location: South Whidbey High School and various sites in the Whidbey Island area. Average attendance: 250.

Purpose/Features Open to writers of every genre and skill level. Offers poets workshops, lectures, readings, author critiques, and "Author Fireside Chats." 2005 poetry staff included Sheila Bender, Katy Lederer, Susan Rich, and Anne Wilson.

Costs/Accommodations 2005 cost: $360 WIWA members, $375 nonmembers. Participants responsible for most meals. Accommodations available at area hotels. Information on overnight accommodations available on website.

Additional Info Offers poetry contest as part of conference. Guidelines available on website. Brochure and registration form available on website.

✖ WINTER POETRY & PROSE GETAWAY IN CAPE MAY

18 North Richards Ave., Ventnor NJ 08406. (609)823-5076. E-mail: info@wintergetaway.com. Website: www.wintergetaway.com. **Contact:** Peter E. Murphy, founder/director. Established 1994. Annual 4-day event. 2006 dates: January 13-16. Location: The Grand Hotel on the Oceanfront in Historic Cape May, NJ. Average attendance: 200 (10 participants in each poetry workshop).

Purpose/Features Open to all writers, beginners and experienced, over the age of 18. "The poetry workshop meets for an hour or so each morning before sending you off with an assignment that will encourage and inspire you to produce exciting new work. After lunch, we gather together to read new drafts in feedback sessions led by experienced poet-teachers who help identify the poem's virtues and offer suggestions to strengthen its weaknesses. The groups are small, and you receive positive attention to help your poem mature. In late afternoon, you can continue writing or schedule a personal tutorial session with one of the poets on staff." 2005 poetry staff included Renee Ashley, Laure-Anne Bosselaar, Michael Broek, Kurt Brown, Toni Brown, Catherine Doty, Stephen Dunn, Douglas Goetsch, Luray Gross, Lois Harrod, Charles Lynch, Laura McCullough, Priscilla Orr, James

Richardson, Mimi Schwartz, Madeline Tiger, J.C. Todd, Angelo Verga, and Paul-Victor Winters.
Costs/Accommodations 2005 cost: $495, including breakfast and lunch for 3 days, all sessions, as well as a double room. Participants responsible for dinner only. Discounts available. ''Early Bard'' Discount: Deduct $25 if paid in full by November 15. Single-occupancy rooms available at additional cost.
Additional Info Individual poetry critiques available. ''Each poet may have a 20-minute tutorial with one of the poets on staff.'' Brochure and registration form available by mail or on website. ''The Winter Getaway is known for its challenging, yet supportive atmosphere that encourages imaginative risk-taking and promotes freedom and transformation in the participants' writing.''

WRITERS@WORK

Conference Registration, P.O. Box 540370, North Salt Lake UT 84054-0370. (801)292-9285. E-mail: contact@writersatwork.org. Website: www.writersatwork.org/conference.html. **Contact:** Lisa Peterson, administrative assistant. Established 1985. Annual event. 2005 dates: June 21-25. Location: Westminster College campus in Salt Lake City. Average attendance: limited to 15/workshop.
Purpose/Features Open to writers of all levels. Offers poets workshops, panel discussions, ms critiques, and readings. 2005 poetry staff included Carol Frost and Crystal Williams.
Costs/Accommodations 2005 cost: $395, including workshop, afternoon sessions, and 30-minute ms consultation. Limited number of rooms available on-site for $150.
Additional Information Schedule and registration information available on website.

Organizations

There are many organizations of value to poets. These groups may sponsor workshops and contests, stage readings, publish anthologies and chapbooks, or spread the word about publishing opportunities. A few provide economic assistance or legal advice. The best thing organizations offer, though, is a support system where poets can turn for a pep talk, a hard-nosed (but sympathetic) critique of a manuscript, or simply the comfort of talking and sharing with others who understand the challenges (and joys) of writing poetry.

Whether national, regional, or as local as your library or community center, each organization has something special to offer. The listings in this section reflect the membership opportunities available to poets with a variety of organizations. Some groups provide certain services to both members and nonmembers.

These symbols may appear at the beginning of some listings: The (N) symbol indicates a recently established organization new to *Poet's Market*; the (★) symbol indicates this organization did not appear in the 2005 edition; the (✦) symbol denotes a Canadian organization and the (🌐) symbol one headquartered outside the U.S. and Canada.

Since some organizations are included in listings in the Publishers of Poetry, Contest & Awards, and Conferences & Workshops sections of this book, we've cross-referenced these listings under Additional Organizations at the end of this section. For further details about an organization associated with a market in this list, go to that market's page number.

To find out more about groups in your area (including those that may not be listed in *Poet's Market*), contact your YMCA, community center, local colleges and universities, public library, and bookstores (and don't forget newspapers and the Internet). If you can't find a group that suits your needs, consider starting one yourself. You might be surprised to find there are others in your locality who would welcome the encouragement, feedback, and moral support of a writer's group.

⭐ 🌐 ACADEMI–YR ACADEMI GYMREIG/THE WELSH ACADEMY; TALIESIN; NWR; A470: WHAT'S ON IN LITERARY WALES

Mount Stuart House, 3rd Floor, Cardiff, Wales CF10 5FQ United Kingdom. Phone: 029 2047 2266. Fax: 029 2049 2930. E-mail: post@academi.org. Website: www.academi.org. **Contact:** Peter Finch, chief executive. Established 1959. "Promotes literature in Wales and assists in the maintaining of its standard." The Welsh National Literature Promotion Agency and Society of Writers is open to "the population of Wales and those outside Wales with an interest in Welsh writing." Currently has 2,000 members. Levels of membership: associate, full, and fellow. Offerings include promotion of readings, events, conferences, exchanges, tours; employment of literature-development workers; publication of a bimonthly events magazine; publication of a literary magazine in Welsh (*Taliesin*) and another (*NWR*) in English. Sponsors conferences/workshops and contests/awards. Publishes *A470: What's On In Literary Wales*, a magazine appearing 5 times/year containing information on Welsh literary events. Available to nonmembers for £15 (annual subscription). Membership dues: £15/year (waged) or £7.50/year (unwaged). Additional information available for SASE (or SAE and IRC), by fax, e-mail, or on website.

THE ACADEMY OF AMERICAN POETS; THE AMERICAN POET

588 Broadway, Suite 604, New York NY 10012-3210. (212)274-0343. Fax: (212)274-9427. E-mail: academy@poets.org. Website: www.poets.org. Executive Director: Tree Swenson. Established 1934. The Academy of American Poets was founded to support the nation's poets at all stages of their careers and to foster the appreciation of contemporary poetry. Administers The Walt Whitman Award; The James Laughlin Award; The Harold Morton Landon Translation Award; The Lenore Marshall Poetry Prize; The Raiziss/de Palchi Translation Award; and The Wallace Stevens Award. (For further details, see individual listings in the Contests & Awards section.) Also awards The Fellowship of the Academy of American Poets ($25,000 to honor distinguished poetic achievement, no applications accepted) and The University & College Poetry Prizes. Publishes *American Poet*, an informative biannual journal sent to those who contribute $35 or more/year. Membership: begins at $35/year "though those who join at higher levels receive complimentary copies of award books and other benefits. The Academy also sponsors National Poetry Month (April), an annual celebration of the richness and vitality of American poetry; the Online Poetry Classroom, an educational resource and online teaching community for high school teachers; and the Poetry Audio Archive, a collection of audio recordings of poetry readings. Additionally, the Academy maintains one of the liveliest and most comprehensive poetry sites on the Internet, at www.poets.org," which includes the National Poetry Almanac, offering monthly themes and daily articles about poetry.

THE AMERICAN POETS' CORNER

The Cathedral Church of St. John the Divine, Cathedral Heights, 1047 Amsterdam Ave., New York NY 10025. (212)316-7540. Website: www.stjohndivine.org. Initiated in 1984 with memorials for Emily Dickinson, Walt Whitman, and Washington Irving. Similar in concept to the British Poets' Corner in Westminster Abbey, was established and dedicated to memorialize this country's greatest writers. A board of electors chooses one deceased author each year for inclusion in The American Poets' Corner; poets and novelists chosen in alternate years. The Cathedral is also home to the Muriel Rukeyser Poetry Wall, a public space for posting poems, which was dedicated in 1976 by Ms. Rukeyser and the Cathedral's Dean. Send poems for the Poetry Wall to the above address. Designated a National Poetry Landmark by the Academy of American Poets.

⭐ ARIZONA AUTHORS ASSOCIATION; ARIZONA LITERARY MAGAZINE; ARIZONA AUTHORS NEWSLETTER

P.O. Box 87857, Phoenix AZ 85080-7857. (602)769-2066. Fax: (623)780-0468. E-mail: info@azauthors.com. Website: www.azauthors.com. **Contact:** Vijaya Schartz, president. Established 1978. Provides education and referral for writers and others in publishing. Statewide organization. Currently has 150 members. Levels of membership: Published, Unpublished (seeking publication), Professional (printers, agents, and publishers), and Student. Sponsors conferences, workshops, contests, awards. Sponsors annual literary contest in poetry, short story, essay, unpublished novels, and published books (fiction and nonfiction). (See separate listing for Arizona Literary & Book Awards in Contests & Awards section.) Publishes *Arizona Literary Magazine* and *Arizona Authors Newsletter*. Membership dues: $45/year for authors, $30/year students, $60/year professionals. Members meet bimonthly. Additional information available on website.

THE ASSOCIATION OF WRITERS AND WRITING PROGRAMS (AWP); THE WRITER'S CHRONICLE

Mailstop 1E3, George Mason University, Fairfax VA 22030. (703)993-4301. E-mail: awp@awpwriter.org. Website: www.awpwriter.org. Established 1967. Offers a variety of services to the writing community, including information, job placement assistance (helps writers find jobs in teaching, editing, and other related fields), writing contests, literary arts advocacy, and forums. Annual individual membership: $59/year; $99/2 years; students who provide photocopy of valid student ID pay $37/year. Membership includes 6 issues of *The Writer's Chronicle* (containing information about grants and awards, publishing opportunities, fellowships, and writing programs) and 7 issues of *AWP Job List* (employment opportunity listings for writers). Other member benefits and opportunities available. *The Writer's Chronicle* is available by subscription only for $20/year (6 issues). Also sponsors the AWP Award Series for poetry, fiction, and creative nonfiction, which includes the Donald Hall Prize for Poetry (see separate listing in Contests & Awards section). Guidelines and additional information available on website.

⍟ THE BEATLICKS; BEATLICK NEWS

1404 Bright Sky Court, La Vergne TN 37086. E-mail: beatlickjoe@yahoo.com. Website: www.beatlick.com. **Contact:** Joe Speer, editor. Established 1988. International organization open to "anyone interested in literature." Currently has 200 members. "There is no official distinction between members, but there is a core group that does the work, writes reviews, organizes readings, etc." Offerings include publication of work (have published poets from Australia, Egypt, India, and Holland) and reviews of books and venues. "We produce an hour show every Friday, Saturday, and Sunday on CATV, Channel 19 in Nashville, TN. Poets submit audio and video tapes from all over. We interview poets about their work and where they are from." Publishes *Beatlick News*, a bimonthly networking tool designed to inform poets of local events and to bring awareness of the national scene. "We include poems, short fiction, art, photos, and articles about poets and venues." Submit short pieces, no vulgar language. "We try to elevate the creative spirit. We publish new voices plus well-established talents." Subscription: $12/year. Additional information available for SASE or by e-mail. "We promote all the arts."

⍟ ⍟ BURNABY WRITERS' SOCIETY

6584 Deer Lake Ave., Burnaby BC V5G 3T7 Canada. E-mail: info@bws.bc.ca. Website: www.bws.bc.ca. **Contact:** Eileen Kernaghan. Established 1967. Corresponding membership in the society, including a newsletter subscription, is open to anyone, anywhere. Currently has 150 members. Yearly dues: $30 regular, $20 students/seniors. Sample newsletter in return for SASE with Canadian stamp. Holds monthly meetings at The Burnaby Arts Centre (located at 6450 Deer Lake Ave.), with a business meeting at 7:30 followed by a writing workshop or speaker. Members of the society stage regular public readings of their own work. Sponsors open mic readings for the public. Sponsors a poetry contest open to British Columbia residents. Competition receives about 200-400 entries/year. Past contest winners include Mildred Tremblay, Frank McCormack, and Kate Braid. Additional information available on website.

⍟ THE WITTER BYNNER FOUNDATION FOR POETRY, INC.

P.O. Box 10169, Santa Fe NM 87504. (505)988-3251. Fax: (505)986-8222. E-mail: bynnerfoundation@aol.com. Website: www.bynnerfoundation.org. **Contact:** Steven Schwartz, executive director.

Awards grants, ranging from $1,000 to $10,000, exclusively to nonprofit organizations for the support of poetry-related projects in the area of: 1) support of individual poets through existing nonprofit institutions; 2) developing the poetry audience; 3) poetry translation and the process of poetry translation; and 4) uses of poetry. "May consider the support of other creative and innovative projects in poetry." Letters of intent accepted annually from August 1 through December 1; requests for application forms should be submitted to Steven Schwartz, executive director. Applications, if approved, must be returned to the Foundation postmarked by February 1. Additional information available by fax or e-mail.

⬛ ⬛ CANADIAN POETRY ASSOCIATION; POEMATA; THE SHAUNT BASMAJIAN CHAPBOOK AWARD; CPA ANNUAL POETRY CONTEST

331 Elmwood Dr., Suite 4-212, Moncton NB E1A 1X6 Canada. Phone/fax: (506)386-2862. E-mail: info@canadianpoetryassoc.com. Website: www.canadianpoetryassoc.com. Established 1985. "We promote all aspects of the reading, writing, publishing, purchasing, and preservation of poetry in Canada. The CPA promotes the creation of local chapters to organize readings, workshops, publishing projects, and other poetry-related events in their area." Membership is open to anyone with an interest in poetry, including publishers, schools, libraries, booksellers, and other literary organizations. Publishes a bimonthly magazine, *Poemata*, featuring news articles, chapter reports, poetry by new members, book reviews, markets information, announcements, and more. Membership dues: $30/year; seniors, students, and fixed income: $20 (all dues Canadian dollars); International: $40 (U.S.). Membership form available for SASE or on website. Also sponsors the following contests: **The Shaunt Basmajian Chapbook Award** offers $100 (Canadian) and publication, plus 50 copies. Guidelines available for SASE and on website. **Annual deadline:** April 30. **The CPA Annual Poetry Contest** offers 3 cash prizes of $75, $50, and $25, with up to 5 Honorable Mentions. **Open to CPA members only.** Winning poems published in *Poemata* and on CPA website. **Postmark deadline:** December 31 annually. Guidelines available for SASE or on website.

COLUMBINE STATE POETRY SOCIETY OF COLORADO

P.O. Box 6245, Westminster CO 80021. (303)431-6774. E-mail: anitajg5@aol.com. Website: http://members.aol.com/copoets. **Contact:** Anita Jepson-Gilbert, secretary/treasurer. Established 1978. Statewide organization open to anyone interested in poetry. Currently has 98 members. An affiliate of the National Federation of State Poetry Societies (NFSPS). Levels of membership: Members at Large, who do not participate in the local chapters but who belong to the National Federation of State Poetry Societies and to the Colorado Society; and local members, who belong to the national, state, and local chapters in Denver or Salida, Colorado. Offerings for the Denver Chapter include weekly workshops and monthly critiques. Sponsors contests, awards for students and adults. Sponsors the Annual Poets Fest where members and nationally known writers give readings and workshops that are open to the public. Membership dues: $12 state and national; $35 local, state, and national. Members meet weekly. Additional information available for SASE, by phone, e-mail, or on website.

GEORGIA POETRY SOCIETY; GEORGIA POETRY SOCIETY NEWSLETTER

P.O. Box 28337, Atlanta GA 30358. E-mail: presidentgps@comcast.net. Website: www.georgiapoetrysociety.com. **Contact:** Steven Owen Shields, president. Established 1979. Statewide organization open to any person who is in accord with the objectives to secure fuller public recognition of the art of poetry, stimulate an appreciation of poetry, and enhance the writing and reading of poetry. Currently has over 200 members. Levels of membership: Active, $20 ($35 family), fully eligible for all aspects of membership; Student, $10, does not vote or hold office, and must be full-time enrolled student through college level; Lifetime, same as Active but pays a one-time membership fee of $300, receives free anthologies each year, and pays no contest entry fees. Offerings include affiliation with NFSPS. At least one workshop is held annually. Contests are sponsored throughout the year, some for members only. "Our contests have specific general rules, which should be followed to avoid the disappointment of disqualification. See the website for details." Publishes *Georgia Poetry Society Newsletter*, a quarterly, also available to nonmembers on website. Also publishes *The Reach of Song*, an annual anthology devoted to contest-winning poems and member works. Each quarterly meeting (open to the public) features at least one poet of high regional prominence. Also sponsors a monthly open mic at a downtown Atlanta bookstore (open to the public). Sponsors Poetry in the Schools project. Additional information available on website.

THE HUDSON VALLEY WRITERS' CENTER

300 Riverside Dr., Sleepy Hollow NY 10591-1414. (914)332-5953. Fax: (914)332-4825. E-mail: info @writerscenter.org. Website: www.writerscenter.org. **Contact:** Dare Thompson, executive director. Established 1988. ''The Hudson Valley Writers' Center is a nonprofit organization devoted to furthering the literary arts in our region. Its mission is to promote the appreciation of literary excellence, to stimulate and nurture the creation of literary works in all sectors of the population, and to bring the diverse works of gifted poets and prose artists to the attention of the public.'' Open to all. Currently has 350 members. Levels of membership: individual, family, senior/student, and donor. Offerings include public readings by established and emerging poets/writers, workshops and classes, monthly open mic nights, paid and volunteer outreach opportunities, and an annual chapbook competition. (See separate listing for Slapering Hol Press in Publishers of Poetry section; see separate listing for Slapering Hol Press Chapbook Competition in the Contests & Awards section.) Membership dues: $35 individual, $45 family, and $20 senior/student. Additional information available for SASE, by fax, e-mail, or on website.

INTERNATIONAL WOMEN'S WRITING GUILD; NETWORK

P.O. Box 810, Gracie Station, New York NY 10028. (212)737-7536. Fax: (212)737-9469. E-mail: dirhahn@aol.com. Website: www.iwwg.org. **Contact:** Hannelore Hahn, founder/executive editor. Established 1976. A network for the personal and professional empowerment of women through writing, the Guild publishes a bimonthly 32-page journal, *Network*, which includes members' achievements, contests, calendar, and publishing information. Other activities and benefits include annual national and regional events, such as the summer conference (see separate listing for The IWWG Summer Conference in the Conferences & Workshops section); ''regional clusters'' (independent regional groups); round robin ms exchanges; agent list; and dental and vision insurance. Membership dues: $45/year (domestic and overseas). Additional information available by fax, e-mail, or on website.

IOWA POETRY ASSOCIATION (Specialized: regional/Iowa residents); IPA NEWSLETTER; LYRICAL IOWA

2325 61st St., Des Moines IA 50322. (515)279-1106. Website: www.iowapoetry.com. **Contact:** Lucille Morgan Wilson, editor. Established 1945. Statewide organization open to ''anyone interested in poetry, with a residence or valid address in the state of Iowa.'' Currently has about 425 members. Levels of membership: Regular and Patron (''same services, but patron members contribute to cost of running the association''). Offerings include ''semiannual workshops to which a poem may be sent in advance for critique; annual contest—also open to nonmembers—with no entry fee; *IPA Newsletter*, published 5 or 6 times/year, including a quarterly national publication listing of contest opportunities; and an annual poetry anthology, *Lyrical Iowa*, containing prize-winning and high-ranking poems from contest entries, available for $10 postpaid. No requirement for purchase to ensure publication.'' Membership dues: $8/year (Regular); $15 or more/year (Patron). ''Semiannual workshops are the only 'meetings' of the Association.'' Additional information (Iowa residents only) available for SASE or on website.

THE KENTUCKY STATE POETRY SOCIETY; PEGASUS; KSPS NEWSLETTER

E-mail: ellengk@yahoo.com. Website: www.kystatepoetrysociety.org. **Contact:** Ellen Kelley, president. Established 1966. Regional organization open to all. Currently has about 215 members. Member of The National Federation of State Poetry Societies (NFSPS). Offerings include association with other poets; information on contests and poetry happenings across the state and nation; annual state and national contests; national and state annual conventions with workshops, selected speakers, and open poetry readings. Sponsors workshops, contests, awards. Membership includes the quarterly *KSPS Newsletter*. Also includes a quarterly newsletter, *Strophes*, of the NFSPS; and the KSPS journal, *Pegasus*, published 3 times yearly: a spring/summer and fall/winter issue which solicits good poetry for publication (need not be a member to submit), and a Prize Poems issue of 1st Place contest winners in over 30 categories. Members or nationally known writers give readings that are open to the public. Membership dues: students $5; adults $20; senior adults $15. Other categories: Life; Patron; Benefactor. Members meet annually. Membership information available by e-mail or on website.

⚔ ⚔ THE LEAGUE OF CANADIAN POETS; GERALD LAMPERT MEMORIAL AWARD; PAT LOWTHER MEMORIAL AWARD

92 Yonge St., Suite 608, Toronto ON M4W 3C7 Canada. (416)504-1657. Fax: (416)504-0096. E-mail: info@poets.ca. Website: www.poets.ca. **Contact:** Andrea Thompson. Established 1966. A nonprofit national association of professional publishing and performing poets in Canada. Its purpose is "to enhance the status of poets and nurture a professional poetic community to facilitate the teaching of Canadian poetry at all levels of education and to develop the audience for poetry by encouraging publication, performance, and recognition of Canadian poetry nationally and internationally. As well as providing members and the public with many benefits and services, the League speaks for poets on many issues such as freedom of expression, Public Lending Right, CanCopy, contract advice, and grievance." Open to all Canadian citizens and landed immigrants; applications are assessed by a membership committee. Currently has 600 members. Levels of membership: Full, Associate, Student, and Supporting. Membership benefits include reading opportunities, promotion of work through the League, a listing in the online membership directory, and other features. Sponsors The Pat Lowther Memorial Award (for a book of poetry by a Canadian woman published in the preceding year; $1,000 prize) and The Gerald Lampert Memorial Award (recognizes the best first book of poetry published by a Canadian in the preceding year; $1,000). Publishes a members' newsletter. Membership dues: $175 Full, $60 Associate, $40 Student, and $100 Supporting. Additional information available on website.

⚔ LIVING SKIES FESTIVAL OF WORDS; THE WORD

217 Main St. North, Moose Jaw SK S6H 0W1 Canada. (306)691-0557. Fax: (306)693-2994. E-mail: word.festival@sasktel.net. Website: www.festivalofwords.com. **Contact:** Lori Dean, operations manager. Established 1996. "The purpose/philosophy of the organization is to celebrate the imaginative uses of languages. The Festival of Words is a registered nonprofit group of over 150 volunteers who present an enjoyable and stimulating celebration of the imaginative ways we use language. We operate year round bringing special events to Saskatchewan, holding open microphone coffeehouses for youth, and culminating in an annual summer festival in July which features activities centered around creative uses of language." National organization open to writers and readers. Currently has 331 members. Offerings include "The Festival of Words programs with readings by poets, panel discussions, and workshops. In addition, poets attending get to share ideas, get acquainted, and conduct impromptu readings. The activities sponsored are held in the Moose Jaw Library/Art Museum complex, as well as in various venues around the city." Sponsors workshops as part of the Festival of Words. "We are also associated with *FreeLance* magazine, a publication of the Saskatchewan Writers' Guild. This publication features many useful articles dealing with poetry writing and writing in general." Also publishes *The Word*, a newsletter appearing approximately 6-7 times/year containing news of Festival events, fund-raising activities, profiles of members, reports from members. Available to nonmembers. First issue is free. Members and nationally known writers give readings that are open to the public. Sponsors open mic readings for members and for the public. Membership dues: $5; $15/3 years. Additional information available for SASE, by fax, e-mail, or on website.

⭐ ◎ THE LOFT LITERARY CENTER (Specialized: Regional/Minnesota); SPEAKEASY; A VIEW FROM THE LOFT

Suite 200, Open Book, 1011 Washington Ave. S, Minneapolis MN 55414. (612)215-2575. Fax: (612)215-2576. E-mail: loft@loft.org. Website: www.loft.org. Established 1974. The largest and most comprehensive literary center in the country, serving both writers and readers with a variety of educational programs, contests and grants, and literary facilites. Membership benefits include discounted tuition, admission charges, and contest fees; check-out privileges at The Loft's resource library; rental access to the Book Club Room and writers' studios; and a year's subscription to *A View from the Loft*. Sponsors classes/workshops, contests, and grants (information available on website). Publishes *Speakeasy*, a literary culture magazine. Sponsors readings by local and national writers. Membership dues: $60/year Individual, $75/year Household, $25 Low Income/Full-Time Student, $125/year Donor. Additional information about The Loft and associated services and programs available on website.

MASSACHUSETTS STATE POETRY SOCIETY, INC.; BAY STATE ECHO; THE NATIONAL POETRY DAY CONTEST; THE GERTRUDE DOLE MEMORIAL CONTEST; AMBASSADOR OF POETRY AWARD; POET'S CHOICE CONTEST; THE NAOMI CHERKOFSKY MEMORIAL CONTEST; OF THEE I SING! CONTEST; ARTHUR (SKIP) POTTER MEMORIAL CONTEST

64 Harrison Ave., Lynn MA 01905. E-mail: jmaes9@aol.com. **Contact:** Jeanette C. Maes, president. Established 1959. Dedicated to the writing and appreciation of poetry and promoting the art form. Statewide organization open to anyone with an interest in poetry. Currently has 200 members. Offerings include critique groups. Sponsors workshops, contests including The National Poetry Day Contest, with prizes of $25, $15, and $10 (or higher) for each of 30 categories. **Entry fee:** $8. **Deadline:** August 1. Competition receives about 2,000 entries/year. Also sponsors these contests: The Gertrude Dole Memorial Contest, with prizes of $25, $15, and $10. **Entry fee:** $3. **Deadline:** March 1. Ambassador of Poetry Award, with prizes of $50, $30, and $20. **Entry fee:** $3/poem. **Deadline:** April 15 annually. The Poet's Choice Contest, with prizes of $50, $25, and $15. **Entry fee:** $3/poem. **Deadline:** November 1. The Naomi Cherkofsky Memorial Contest, with prizes of $50, $30, and $20. **Entry fee:** $3/poem. **Deadline:** June 30. The "Of Thee I Sing!" Contest, with prizes of $50, $25, and $15. **Deadline:** January 15. Arthur (Skip) Potter Memorial Contest with prizes of $50, $30, and $20. **Entry fee:** $3. **Deadline:** December 15 annually. Guidelines available for SASE. Publishes a yearly anthology of poetry and a yearly publication of student poetry contest winners. Also publishes *Bay State Echo*, a newsletter, 5 times/year. Members or nationally known writers give readings that are open to the public. Sponsors open mic readings for members and the public for National Poetry Day. Membership dues: $12/year. Members meet 5 times/year. Additional information available for SASE.

MOUNTAIN WRITERS SERIES; MOUNTAIN WRITERS SERIES NEWSLETTER

Mountain Writers Center, 3624 SE Milwaukie Ave., Portland OR 97202. (503)236-4854. Fax: (503)731-9735. E-mail: pdxmws@mountainwriters.org. Website: www.mountainwriters.org. **Contact:** Scott Bergler, program associate. Established 1973. "Mountain Writers Series is an independent nonprofit organization dedicated to supporting writers, audiences, and other sponsors by promoting literature and literacy through artistic and educational literary arts events in the Pacific Northwest." The Center is open to both members and nonmembers. Currently has about 150 members. Levels of membership: Contributing ($100), Supporting ($500), Patron ($1,000), Basic ($50), Student/Retired ($25), and Family ($75). "Members have access to our extensive poetry library, resource center, and space as well as discounts to most events. Members receive a triannual newsletter. Mountain Writers Series offers intensive one-day and 2-day workshops, weekend master classes, 5-week, 8-week, and 10-week courses about writing." Authors who have participated recently include David James Duncan, Linda Gregg, C.K. Williams, Li-Young Lee, Kim Addonizio, and David St. John. "The Mountain Writers Center is a 100-year-old Victorian house with plenty of comfortable gathering space, a reading room, visiting writers room, library, resource center, garden, and Mountain Writers Series offices." Sponsors conferences/workshops. Publishes the *Mountain Writers Center Newsletter*. Available to nonmembers for $12/year. Sponsors readings that are open to the public. Nationally and internationally known writers are sponsored by the Mountain Writers Series Northwest Regional Residencies Program (reading tours) and the campus readings program (Pulitzer Prize winners, Nobel Prize winners, MacArthur Fellows, etc.). Additional information available for SASE, by fax, e-mail, or on website.

NATIONAL FEDERATION OF STATE POETRY SOCIETIES, INC.; STROPHES

Website: www.nfsps.org. Established 1959. "NFSPS is a nonprofit organization exclusively educational and literary. Its purpose is to recognize the importance of poetry with respect to national cultural heritage. It is dedicated solely to the furtherance of poetry on the national level and serves to unite poets in the bonds of fellowship and understanding." Currently has 7,000 members. Any poetry group located in a state not already affiliated, but interested in affiliating, with NFSPS may contact the membership chairman (see website). In a state where no valid group exists, help may also be obtained by individuals interested in organizing a poetry group for affiliation. Most reputable state poetry societies are members of the National Federation and advertise their various poetry contests through the NFSPS quarterly newsletter, *Strophes* (sample copy available for SASE and $1), edited by Madelyn Eastlund, 310 South Adams St., Beverly Hills FL 34465 (e-mail: verdure@dig italusa.net). **Beware of organizations calling themselves state poetry societies (however named) that are not members of NFSPS,** as such labels are sometimes used by vanity schemes trying to sound respectable. NFSPS holds an annual 3-day convention in a different state each year with workshops, an awards banquet, and addresses by nationally known poets. Sponsors an annual 50-category national contest. (See separate listing for NFSPS College/University Level Poetry Awards, NFSPS Competitions, and the Stevens Manuscript Contest in the Contests & Awards section.) Additional information available by e-mail or on website.

NATIONAL WRITERS ASSOCIATION; AUTHORSHIP

10940 S. Parker Rd., #508, Parker CO 80134. (303)841-0246. Fax: (303)841-2607. Website: www.nation alwriters.com. **Contact:** Sandy Whelchel, executive director. Established 1937. National organization with regional affiliations open to writers. Currently has 3,000 members. Levels of membership: Professional, Regular, and Student. Hosts an annual Summer Conference where workshops, panels, etc., are available to all attendees, including poets. Also offers a yearly poetry writing contest with cash awards of $100, $50, and $25. **Entry fee:** $10/poem. **Deadline:** October 1. Send SASE for judging sheet copies. Publishes *Authorship*, an annual magazine. Sample copy available for 9×12 envelope with $1.21 postage. Available to nonmembers for $20. Membership dues: Professional $85; others $65. Members meet monthly. Additional information available for SASE, by fax, e-mail, or on website.

NEVADA POETRY SOCIETY

P.O. Box 7014, Reno NV 89510. (775)322-3619. **Contact:** Sam Wood, president. Established 1976. Statewide organization. Currently has 30 members. Levels of membership: Active and Emeritus. Offerings include membership in the National Federation of State Poetry Societies (NFSPS), which includes a subscription to their publication, *Strophes*; monthly challenges followed by critiquing of all new poems; lessons on types of poetry. Members of the society are occasionally called upon to read to organizations or in public meetings. Membership dues: $10 (includes membership in NFSPS). Members meet monthly. Additional information available for SASE. "We advise poets to enter their poems in contests before thinking about publication."

⚡ NEW HAMPSHIRE WRITERS' PROJECT; EX LIBRIS

2521 North River Rd., Hooksett NH 03106. (603)314-7980. Fax: (603)314-7981. E-mail: info@nhwrit ersproject.org. Website: www.nhwritersproject.org. **Contact:** Katie Goodman, executive director. Established 1988. Statewide organization open to writers at all levels in all genres. Currently has 800 members. Offerings include workshops, seminars, an annual conference, a literary calendar, and a ms review service. Sponsors day-long workshops and 4- to 6-week intensive courses. Also sponsors biennial awards for outstanding literary achievement. Publishes *Ex Libris*, a bimonthly newsletter for and about New Hampshire writers. Members and nationally known writers give readings that are open to the public. Membership dues: $45/year; $25/year for seniors and students. Additional information available for SASE, by fax, e-mail, or on website.

✕ NORTH CAROLINA WRITERS' NETWORK; THE WRITERS' NETWORK NEWS
P.O. Box 954, Carrboro NC 27510. (919)967-9540. Fax: (919)929-0535. E-mail: mail@ncwriters.org. Website: www.ncwriters.org. Established 1985. Supports the work of writers, writers' organizations, independent bookstores, little magazines and small presses, and literary programming statewide. Membership dues: $75 annually brings members *The Writers' Network News*, a 24-page bimonthly newsletter containing organizational news, national market information, and other literary material of interest to writers; and access to the NCWN Library & Resource Center, other writers, workshops, conferences, readings and competitions, and NCWN's critiquing and editing service. Currently has 1,500 members. Annual fall conference features nationally known writers, publishers, and editors, held in a different North Carolina location each November. Sponsors competitions in short fiction, nonfiction, and poetry for North Carolina residents and NCWN members. Guidelines available for SASE or on website.

OHIO POETRY ASSOCIATION; OHIO POETRY ASSOCIATION NEWSLETTER
Website: www.geocities.com/theohiopoetryassociation. **Contact:** Bob Casey, President, 129 Columbus Rd., Fredericktown OH 43019. (740)694-5013. E-mail: bob@poeticaljourneys.com. Established in 1929 as Verse Writers' Guild of Ohio. Promotes the art of poetry, and furthers the support of poets and others who support poetry. "We sponsor contests, seminars, readings, and publishing opportunities for poets of all ages and abilities throughout and beyond Ohio." Statewide membership with additional members in several other states, Japan, and England. Affiliated with the National Federation of State Poetry Societies (NFSPS). Organization open to "poets and writers of all ages and ability, as well as to nonwriting lovers of poetry in all its forms." Currently has about 215 members. Levels of membership: Regular, Student (including college undergrads), Associate, Senior, Life, and Honorary. Member benefits include regular contests, meeting/workshop participation, assistance with writing projects, networking; twice-yearly magazine, *Common Threads*, 4 state newsletters, 4 NFSPS newsletters, membership in NFSPS, and contest information and lower entry fees for NFSPS contests. Members are automatically on the mailing list for Ohio Poetry Day contest guidelines. "We are cosponsors of Ohio Poetry Day. Individual chapters regularly host workshops and seminars. We publish *Common Threads*, a semiannual, saddle-bound anthology of poetry (open to submission from **members only**)." (See separate listing for *Common Threads* in the Publishers of Poetry section; for Ohio Poetry Day in the Contests & Awards section.) Publishes the *Ohio Poetry Association Newsletter*, a quarterly which includes general news, member accomplishments, publishing opportunities, contests, editorials, items of interest to poets and writers. Members and nationally known writers give readings that are open to the public (at quarterly meetings; public is invited). Sponsors open mic readings for members and the public ("though more likely at local levels"). Past readers have included Lisa Martinovic, David Shevin, Michael Bugeja, David Citino, and Danika Dinsmore. Membership dues: $12 senior; $15 regular; $5 associate and student. Members meet quarterly (September, December, March, May). Additional information available by e-mail or on website. "All poets need an organization to share info, critique, publish, sponsor contests, and just socialize. We do all that."

✕ THE OREGON STATE POETRY ASSOCIATION; VERSEWEAVERS
P.O. Box 602, West Linn OR 97068. (503)655-1274. E-mail: OSPA@oregonpoets.org. Website: www.oregonpoets.org. **Contact:** Eleanor Berry, president. Established 1936. Member of the National Federation of State Poetry Societies, Inc. (NFSPS), sponsors workshops, readings, and seminars around the state and an annual contest for students (K-12). Currently has over 400 members.

Membership dues: $20, $12 (65 and older), $5 (18 and under). Publishes a quarterly *OSPA Newsletter*, annual *Verseweavers* book, and annual *Cascadia* book of Oregon student poetry. Sponsors contests twice yearly, awards prizes in October during Fall Poetry Conference and in April during Spring Poetry Festival, with total cash prizes of $1,000 each. **Entry fee:** $1 for members, $4/poem for nonmembers (out-of-state entries welcome). Themes and categories vary; special category for New Poets. Competition receives 1,600 entries/year. Most recent contest winners include Abigail Brandt, Pat Cason, Sara Jameson, Marvin Lurie, Catherine Moran, Wyn Schoch, Nancy J. Bringhurst, and M.E. Hope. For details send SASE to OSPA, after June 1 and December 1 each year, or check website. Members and nationally known writers give readings that are open to the public. Sponsors public readings in independent bookstores during National Poetry Month (April).

PITTSBURGH POETRY EXCHANGE

P.O. Box 4279, Pittsburgh PA 15203. (412)481-POEM. Website: http://pghpoetryexchange.pghfree. net. **Contact:** Michael Wurster, coordinator. Established 1974. A community-based volunteer organization for local poets, it functions as a service organization and information exchange, conducting ongoing workshops, readings, forums, and other special events. No dues or fees. "Any monetary contributions are voluntary, often from outside sources. We've managed not to let our reach exceed our grasp." Currently has about 30 members (with a mailing list of 300). Reading programs are primarily committed to local and area poets, with honorariums of $25-85. Sponsors a minimum of 3 major events each year in addition to a monthly workshop; includes reading programs in conjunction with community arts festivals, such as the October South Side Poetry Smorgasbord—a series of readings throughout the evening at different shops (galleries, bookstores). Poets from out of town may contact the Exchange for assistance in setting up readings at bookstores to help sell their books. "We have been partnering with Autumn House Press in co-sponsoring events and bringing some of its authors to town." Recent venues include The Hill House (Hill District) and The Bridge Cafe (South Side). Members and nationally known poets give readings that are open to the public. Members meet on an ongoing basis, at least twice monthly. Additional information available for SASE or on website. "Pittsburgh is a very exciting literary town."

POETRY BOOK SOCIETY; THE PBS BULLETIN

Book House, 45 East Hill, London SW18 2QZ England. Phone: +44 (0)20 8870 8403. Fax: +44 (0)20 8870 0865. E-mail: info@poetrybooks.co.uk. Website: www.poetrybooks.co.uk. Established 1953. Promoting "the best newly published contemporary poetry to as wide an audience as possible," the Poetry Book Society is a book club with several membership packages available. Full membership dues are £32 (UK) or £42 (overseas) and include 4 books of new poetry and *The PBS Bulletin*. The selectors also recommend other books of special merit, which are obtainable at a 25% discount. The Poetry Book Society is subsidized by the Arts Council of England. Please write, e-mail, or check website for details.

POETRY IN THE ARTS, INC.; ARDENT!; MOONCROSSED 33/33 (Specialized: zine for teens)

5801 Highland Pass, Austin TX 78731. (512)453-7920. E-mail: jljohns@poetryinarts.org. Website: www.poetryinarts.org. Established 1985. Publishes 2 online zines, *Ardent!* and *MoonCrossed 33/33* (a zine for teens), and an annual anthology, *MoonCrossed*. Sponsors a range of winner-take-all literary competitions and editor's choice awards. Pays a percentage of donor procedes. Additional information available on website.

THE POETRY LIBRARY

Royal Festival Hall, London SE1 8XX United Kingdom. Phone: (0207)921 0943/0664. Fax: (0207)921 0939. E-mail: info@poetrylibrary.org.uk. Website: www.poetrylibrary.org.uk. **Contact:** Simon Smith, librarian. Established 1953. A "free public library of modern poetry. It contains a comprehensive collection of all British poetry published since 1912 and an international collection of poetry from all over the world, either written in or translated into English. As the United Kingdom's national library for poetry, it offers loan and information service and large collections of poetry magazines, tapes, videos, records, poem posters, and cards; also press cuttings and photographs of poets." National center with "open access for all visitors. Those wishing to borrow books and other materials must be residents of U.K." Offerings include "library and information service; access to all recently published poetry and to full range of national magazines; only source of international poetry, including magazines; and information on all aspects of poetry." Offers browsing facilities and quieter area for study; listening facilities for poetry on tape, video record, and CD. Nationally known writers give readings that are open to the public. Additional information available on website. "Our focus is more on published poets than unpublished. No unpublished poems or manuscripts kept or accepted. Donations welcome but please write or call in advance." Open 11-8 Tuesday-Sunday; closed to visitors on Mondays.

POETRY SOCIETY OF AMERICA; CROSSROADS: THE JOURNAL OF THE POETRY SOCIETY OF AMERICA

15 Gramercy Park, New York NY 10003. (212)254-9628. Website: www.poetrysociety.org. Executive Director: Alice Quinn. Established 1910. The PSA is a national nonprofit organization for poets and lovers of poetry. Sponsors readings and lectures as well as programs such as Poetry in Motion; partners with The Favorite Poem Project. Levels of Membership: Student ($25), Member ($45), Supporter ($65), Sustainer ($100), Patron ($250), Benefactor ($500), and Angel ($1,000). All paid members receive *Crossroads: The Journal of the Poetry Society of American*; additional benefits available as membership levels increase. Free to join PSA mailing list for news of upcoming events. PSA also sponsors a number of competitions for members and nonmembers (see separate listing for Poetry Society of America Awards in the Contests & Awards section).

☆ POETRY SOCIETY OF NEW HAMPSHIRE; THE POET'S TOUCHSTONE

31 Reservoir, Farmington NH 03835. (603)332-0732. E-mail: frisella@worldpath.net. **Contact:** Patricia L. Frisella, president. Established 1964. A statewide organization for anyone interested in poetry. Member of the National Federation of State Poetry Societies (NFSPS). Currently has 200 members. Levels of membership: $10, Junior; $20, Regular. Offerings include annual subscription to quarterly magazine, *The Poet's Touchstone*, membership in NFSPS, critiques, contests and workshops, public readings, and quarterly meetings with featured poets. *The Poet's Touchstone* is available to nonmembers for $4.50 (single issue). Members and nationally known writers give readings that are open to the public. Sponsors open mic readings for members and the public. Additional information available for SASE or by e-mail. "We do sponsor a national contest 4 times a year with $100, $50, and $25 prizes paid out in each one. People from all over the country enter and win."

☆ THE POETRY SOCIETY OF TEXAS; POETRY SOCIETY OF TEXAS BULLETIN; A BOOK OF THE YEAR

7059 Spring Valley Rd., Dallas TX 75254. (972)233-6348. E-mail: bmahan@airmail.net. Website: http://members.tripod.com/psttx. **Contact:** Budd Powell Mahan. Established 1921. "The purpose of the society shall be to secure fuller public recognition of the art of poetry, to encourage the writing of poetry by Texans, and to kindle a finer and more intelligent appreciation of poetry, especially the work of living poets who interpret the spirit and heritage of Texas." PST is a member of the National Federation of State Poetry Societies (NFSPS). Has 22 chapters in cities throughout the state. Offers "'Active' membership to native Texans, Citizens of Texas, or former Citizens of Texas who were active members; 'Associate' membership to all who desire to affiliate." Currently has 300 members. Levels of membership: Active Membership, Associate Membership, Sustaining Membership, Benefactors, Patrons of the Poets, and Student Membership. Offerings include annual contests with prizes in excess of $5,000 as well as monthly contests (general and humorous); 8 monthly meetings; annual awards banquet; annual summer conference in a different location each year; round-robin critiquing opportunities sponsored at the state level; and Poetry in Schools with contests at state and local chapter levels. "Our monthly state meetings are held at the Preston Royal Branch of the Dallas

Public Library. Our annual awards banquet is held at the Crown Plaza Suites in Dallas. Our summer conference is held at a site chosen by the hosting chapter. Chapters determine their meeting sites.'' Publishes *A Book of the Year* which presents annual and monthly award-winning poems, coming contest descriptions, minutes of meetings, by-laws of the society, history, and information. Also publishes the *Poetry Society of Texas Bulletin*, a monthly newsletter that features statewide news documenting contest winners, state meeting information, chapter and individual information, news from the National Federation of State Poetry Societies (NFSPS), and announcements of coming activities and offerings for poets. ''*A Book of the Year* is available to nonmembers for $8.'' Members and nationally known writers give readings. ''All of our meetings are open to the public.'' Membership dues: $25 for Active and Associate Memberships, $12.50 for students. Members meet monthly. Additional information available for SASE, by e-mail, or on website.

POETS & WRITERS, INC.; POETS & WRITERS MAGAZINE; A DIRECTORY OF AMERICAN POETS AND FICTION WRITERS

72 Spring St., Suite 301, New York NY 10012. (212)226-3586. Website: www.pw.org. Poets & Writers, Inc., was established in 1970 to foster the development of poets and fiction writers and to promote communication through the literary community. The largest nonprofit literary organization in the nation, it offers information, support, publications, and exposure to writers at all stages in their careers. Sponsors programs such as the Writers Exchange Contest (emerging poets and fiction writers are introduced to literary communities outside their home states), Readings/Workshops, and publication in print and online of *A Directory of American Poets & Fiction Writers*. Publishes *Poets & Writers Magazine* (print), plus *Poets & Writers Online* offers topical information, the Speakeasy writers' message forum, links to over 1,000 websites of interest to writers, and a searchable database of over 5,000 listings from the *Directory*.

POETS' AND WRITERS' LEAGUE OF GREATER CLEVELAND; OHIO WRITER; POETRY: MIRROR OF THE ARTS; WRITERS AND THEIR FRIENDS

12200 Fairhill Rd., Townhouse 3-A, Cleveland OH 44120. (216)421-0403. E-mail: pwlgc@yahoo.com. Website: www.pwlgc.com. **Contact:** Darlene Montonaro, executive director. Established 1974. Founded ''to foster a supportive community for poets and writers throughout Northern Ohio and to expand the audience for creative writing among the general public.'' Currently has 300 members. The Literary Center offers classes, meeting space, and a retreat center for writers. PWLGC conducts a monthly workshop where poets can bring their work for discussion. Publishes a monthly calendar of literary events in NE Ohio; a bimonthly magazine, *Ohio Writer*, which includes articles on the writing life, news, markets, and an annual writing contest in all genres (see separate listing for Best of *Ohio Writer* Writing Contest in the Contests & Awards section); and 2 chapbooks/year featuring an anthology of work by area poets. ''The PWLGC also sponsors a dramatic reading series, *Poetry: Mirror of the Arts*, which unites poetry and other art forms performed in cultural settings; and *Writers & Their Friends*, a biennial literary showcase of new writing (all genres), performed dramatically by area actors, media personalities, and performance poets.'' Membership dues: $25/ year, includes subscription to *Ohio Writer Magazine* and discounts on services and facilities at the Literary Center. Additional information available for SASE, by e-mail, or on website.

POETS HOUSE; DIRECTORY OF AMERICAN POETRY BOOKS; THE REED FOUNDATION LIBRARY; THE POETS HOUSE SHOWCASE; POETRY IN THE BRANCHES; NYC POETRY TEACHER OF THE YEAR

72 Spring St., New York NY 10012. (212)431-7920. Fax: (212)431-8131. E-mail: info@poetshouse.org. Website: www.poetshouse.org. Established 1985. Poets House, a literary center and poetry archive, is a ''home for all who read and write poetry.'' Resources include the 40,000-volume poetry collection, conference room, exhibition space, and a Children's Poets House. Over 50 annual public programs include panel discussions and lectures, readings, seminars and workshops, the New York City Poetry Teacher of the Year award, and The People's Poetry Gathering festival. In addition,

Poets House continues its collaboration with public library systems, Poetry in The Branches, aimed at bringing poetry into communities through collection building, public programs, seminars for librarians, and poetry workshops for young adults (information available upon request). Finally, in April Poets House hosts the Poets House Showcase, a comprehensive exhibit of the year's new poetry releases from commercial, university, and independent presses across the country. (**Note: Poets House is not a publisher.**) Copies of new titles become part of the library collection, and comprehensive listings for each of the books are added to the online version of the *Directory of American Poetry Books*, accessible on www.poetshouse.org. "Poets House depends, in part, on tax-deductible contributions of its nationwide members." Membership levels begin at $40/year; and along with other graduated benefits, each new or renewing member receives free admission to all regularly scheduled programs. Additional information available by fax, e-mail, or on website.

◪ SMALL PUBLISHERS ASSOCIATION OF NORTH AMERICA (SPAN); SPAN CONNECTION

P.O. Box 1306, Buena Vista CO 81211. (719)395-4790. Fax: (719)395-8374. E-mail: span@spannet.org. Website: www.spannet.org. **Contact:** Scott Flora, executive director. Established 1996. Founded to "advance the image and profits of independent publishers and authors through education and marketing opportunities." Open to "authors, small- to medium-sized publishers, and the vendors who serve them." Currently has 1,300 members. Levels of membership: regular and associate vendor. Offers marketing ideas, sponsors annual conference. Publishes *SPAN Connection*, "a 24-page monthly newsletter jam-packed with informative, money-making articles." Available to non-members for $8/issue. Membership dues: $95/year (Regular), $120/year (Associate Vendor). Additional information available for SASE, by fax, or on website.

SOUTH CAROLINA WRITERS WORKSHOP; THE QUILL

P.O. Box 7104, Columbia SC 29202. Website: www.scwriters.com. Established 1990. Offers writers "a wide range of opportunities to improve their writing, network with others, and gain practical 'how to' information about getting published." Statewide organization open to all writers. Currently has 280 members. Offerings include "chapter meetings where members give readings and receive critiques; *The Quill*, SCWW's bimonthly newsletter; a web forum for poets and writers on website; an annual conference with registration discount for members; 2 free seminars each year; and an annual anthology featuring members' work." Chapters meet in libraries, bookstores, and public buildings. Sponsors 3-day annual conference at Myrtle Beach and literary competitions in poetry, fiction, and nonfiction. Members and nationally known writers give readings that are open to the public. Sponsors open mic reading for members and the public at the annual conference. Membership dues: $50/year Individual; $75/year Family. Chapters meet weekly, bimonthly, or monthly. Additional information available on website.

◪ SOUTH DAKOTA STATE POETRY SOCIETY; PASQUE PETALS

Box 398, Lennox SD 57039. (605)647-2447. **Contact:** Verlyss V. Jacobson, membership chair/editor. Established 1926. Regional organization open to anyone. Currently has 200-225 members. Levels of membership: Regular, Patron, Foreign, Student. Sponsors conferences, workshops, and 2 annual contests, one for adults and one for students, with 12 categories. (See separate listing for South Dakota State Poetry Society competitions in Contests & Awards section.) **Deadlines:** August 15 for adults, February 1 for students. Competition receives 300-500 entries/year for both contests. Publishes the magazine *Pasque Petals* 4 times/year. Membership dues: $20 regular, $30 patron, $5 students. Members meet biannually. Additional information available for SASE.

UNIVERSITY OF ARIZONA POETRY CENTER

1600 East 1st St., P.O. Box 210129, Tucson AZ 85721. (520)626-3765. Fax: (520)621-5566. E-mail: poetry@u.arizona.edu. Website: www.poetrycenter.arizona.edu. **Contact:** Gail Browne, executive director. Established 1960. Open to the public, the Center is a contemporary poetry archive and a nationally acclaimed poetry collection that includes over 50,000 items. Programs and services include a library with a noncirculating poetry collection and space for small classes; poetry-related meetings and activities; facilities, research support, and referral information about poetry and poets for local and national communities; the Visiting Poets and Writers Reading Series; community creative writing classes and workshops; bilingual Poets-in-Preschools program; high school poet-in-residence; a one-month summer residency offered each year to an emerging writer selected by jury; and poetry awards, readings, and special events for high school, undergraduate, and graduate students. Publishes a biannual newsletter. Additional information available for SASE, by fax, e-mail, or on website. "One can become a 'Friend of the Poetry Center' by making an annual contribution."

THE UNTERBERG POETRY CENTER OF THE 92ND STREET Y; "DISCOVERY"/THE NATION POETRY CONTEST

1395 Lexington Ave., New York NY 10128. (212)415-5759. E-mail: unterberg@92y.org. Website: www.92y.org/poetry. Offers annual series of readings by major literary figures (weekly readings late September through May), writing workshops, master classes in fiction and poetry, and lectures and literary seminars. Also co-sponsors the "Discovery"/*The Nation* Poetry Contest for poets who have not yet published a book or chapbook (see separate listing for *The Nation* in the Publishers of Poetry section). **Deadline:** mid-January. Competition receives approximately 1,000 entries/year. Additional information available for SASE, on website, or leave name and mailing address on contest voicemail at (212)415-5759.

✪ VIRGINIA WRITERS CLUB; THE VIRGINIA WRITER

P.O. Box 300, Richmond VA 23218. (434)842-1801. Fax: (434)842-6203. E-mail: VWCMail@aol.com. Website: www.virginiawritersclub.org. **Contact:** Linda Layne, editor/executive director. Established 1918. Promotes the art and craft of writing and serves writers and writing in Virginia. Statewide organization with 6 regional chapters open to "any and all writers." Currently has 350 members. Offerings include networking with other poets and writers, discussions on getting published, workshops, an annual conference and symposium, and a newsletter, *The Virginia Writer*, published 4 times/year. Nationally known writers give readings that are open to the public. Membership dues: $30/year. Members meet 4 times/year as well as at workshops, conferences, and monthly chapter meetings. Additional information available for SASE, by fax, e-mail, or on website.

✪ WISCONSIN FELLOWSHIP OF POETS; MUSELETTER; WISCONSIN POETS' CALENDAR

E-mail: kppi2105@sbcglobal.net. Website: www.wfop.org. **Contact:** Peter Piaskoski, Membership Chair, 2105 E. Lake Bluff Blvd., Shorewood WI 53211. President: Peter Sherrill. Established 1950. Statewide organization open to residents and former residents of Wisconsin who are interested in the aims and endeavors of the organization. Currently has 450 members. Levels of membership: Active, Student. Sponsors biannual conferences, workshops, contests and awards. Publishes *Wisconsin Poets' Calendar*, poems of Wisconsin (resident) poets. Also publishes *Museletter*, a quarterly newsletter. Members or nationally known writers give readings that are open to the public. Sponsors open mic readings. Membership dues: Active $25, Student $12.50. Members meet biannually. Additional information available for SASE to WFOP membership chair at the above address, by e-mail, or on website.

THE WRITER'S CENTER; WRITER'S CAROUSEL

4508 Walsh St., Bethesda MD 20815. (301)654-8664. E-mail: postmaster@writer.org. Website: www.writer.org. **Contact:** Gregory Robinson, executive director. Established 1976. "The Writer's Center is a literary crossroads designed to encourage the creation and distribution of contemporary literature. To support these goals, we offer a host of interrelated programs and services, including workshops in all genres; a gallery of books and journals; readings and conferences; publications; desktop publishing center; meeting and work space; and information and communication center. We welcome all genres and levels of skill as well as the other arts. These activities take place 7 days a week in a 12,200 square foot facility, a former community center." Some 2,600 members support the center with annual donations. Publishes *Writer's Carousel*, a quarterly magazine of articles and writing news. Also publishes *Poet Lore*, America's oldest poetry journal. (See separate listing for *Poet Lore* in the Publishers of Poetry section). Membership dues: $40/year general, $25/ year student, $50/year family. Additional information available by e-mail or on website.

⚡ ⚡ WRITERS GUILD OF ALBERTA; WESTWORD

11759 Groat Rd., Edmonton AB T5M 3K6 Canada. (780)422-8174. Fax: (780)422-2663. E-mail: mail@writersguild.ab.ca. Website: www.writersguild.ab.ca. Established 1980. Founder to "provide a community of writers which exists to support, encourage, and promote writers and writing; to safeguard the freedom to write and read; and to advocate for the well-being of writers." Provincial organization open to emerging and professional writers. Currently has over 900 members. Offerings include retreats/conferences, bimonthly newsletter with market section, and the Stephan G. Stephansson Award for Poetry (Alberta residents only). Also publishes *WestWord*, a bimonthly magazine that includes articles on writing, poems, and a market section. Additional information available by phone, e-mail, or on website.

WRITERS INFORMATION NETWORK; THE WIN-INFORMER

The Professional Association for Christian Writers, P.O. Box 11337, Bainbridge Island WA 98110. (206)842-9103. Fax: (206)842-0536. E-mail: WritersInfoNetwork@juno.com. Website: www.christi anwritersinfo.net. **Contact:** Elaine Wright Colvin, director. Established 1983. Founded "to provide a much needed link between writers and editors/publishers of the religious publishing industry, to further professional development in writing and marketing skills of Christian writers, and to provide a meeting ground of encouragement and fellowship for persons engaged in writing and speaking." International organization open to anyone. Currently has 1,000 members. Offerings include market news, networking, editorial referrals, critiquing, and marketing/publishing assistance. Sponsors conferences and workshops around the country. Publishes a 32- to 36-page bimonthly magazine, *The Win-Informer* containing industry news and trends, writing advice, announcements, and book reviews. The magazine will also consider "writing-related poetry, up to 24 lines, with inspirational/Christian thought or encouragement. We accept first rights only." Sample copy: $10. Membership dues: $40 U.S./one year, $75/2 years; $50/year in U.S. equivalent funds for Canada and foreign, $95/2 years. Additional information available for SASE or on website.

THE WRITERS ROOM

740 Broadway, 12th Floor, New York NY 10003. (212)254-6995. Fax: (212)533-6059. E-mail: writers room@writersroom.org. Website: www.writersroom.org. Established 1978. Provides a "home away from home" for any writer who needs a place to work. Open 24 hours a day, 7 days a week, **for members only**. Large loft provides desk space, Internet access, library, and storage. Supported by the National Endowment for the Arts, the New York State Council on the Arts, the New York City Department of Cultural Affairs, and private sector funding. Membership dues: vary from $400 to $600/half year, plus one-time initiation fee of $75. Call for application or download from website.

⚡ THE WRITERS' UNION OF CANADA; THE WRITERS' UNION OF CANADA NEWSLETTER

90 Richmond St. East, Suite 200, Toronto ON M5C 1P1 Canada. (416)703-8982. Fax: (416)504-9090. E-mail: info@writersunion.ca. Website: www.writersunion.ca. Established 1973. Dedicated to advancing the status of Canadian writers by protecting the rights of published authors, defending the freedom to write and publish, and serving its members. National organization open to poets who have had a trade book published by a commercial or university press; must be a Canadian citizen or landed immigrant. Currently has over 1,400 members. Offerings include contact with peers, contract advice/negotiation, grievance support, and electronic communication. Sponsors conferences/workshops. Sponsors Annual General Meeting, usually held in May, where members debate and determine Union policy, elect representatives, attend workshops, socialize, and renew friendships with their colleagues from across the country. Publishes *The Writers' Union of Canada*

Newsletter 6 times/year. Membership dues: $180/year. Regional reps meet with members when possible. For writers not eligible for membership, the Union offers, for a fee, publications on publishing, contracts, and more; a Manuscript Evaluation Service for any level writer; Contract Services, including a Self-Help Package; and 3 annual writing competitions for developing writers. Additional information available for SASE (or SAE and IRC), by fax, e-mail, or on website.

W.B. YEATS SOCIETY OF NEW YORK; POET PASS BY!

National Arts Club, 15 Gramercy Park S, New York NY 10003. Website: www.YeatsSociety.org. **Contact:** Andrew McGowan, president. Established 1990. Founded ''to promote the legacy of Irish poet and Nobel Laureate William Butler Yeats through an annual program of lectures, readings, poetry competition, and special events.'' National organization open to anyone. Currently has 450 members. Offerings include an annual poetry competition (see separate listing for W.B. Yeats Society Annual Poetry Competition in the Contests & Awards section) and *Poet Pass By!*, an annual ''slam'' of readings, songs, and music by poets, writers, entertainers. Also sponsors conferences/workshops. Each April, presents an all-day Saturday program, ''A Taste of the Yeats Summer School in Ireland.'' Nationally known writers give readings that are open to the public. Membership dues: $25/year; $15/year students. Members meet approximately monthly, September to June. Additional information available on website.

ADDITIONAL ORGANIZATIONS

The following listings also contain information about organizations. Turn to the page numbers indicated for details about their offerings.

Resources

Resources

Additional Resources

This section lists publications and websites that focus on information about writing and publishing poetry. While few provide markets for your work, some of these resources do identify promising leads for your submission efforts. You'll also find advice on craft, poet interviews, reviews of books and chapbooks, events calendars, and other valuable material. For print publications, we provide contact information; however, you may also find these publications in your library or bookstore or be able to order them through your favorite online booksellers. (The ✳ symbol at the beginning of a listing denotes a Canadian publication and the ⊕ symbol an international one.)

Internet resources for poetry continue to grow, and there are far too many to list here. However, among the following listings you'll find those key sites every poet should bookmark. Although we confirmed every address at press time, URLs can become outdated quickly; if a site comes up "not found," enter the name of the site in a search engine to check for a new address.

Some listings in the Publishers of Poetry, Contests & Awards, and Conferences & Workshops sections include references to informative print publications (such as handbooks and newsletters). We've cross-referenced these markets in the Additional Publications of Interest list at the end of this section. To find out more about a publication of interest associated with one of these markets, go to that market's page number.

THE ACADEMY OF AMERICAN POETS

Website: www.poets.org. One of the most comprehensive poetry websites on the Internet. (See separate listing in the Organizations section.)

ALIEN FLOWER

Website: www.alienflower.org. An interactive medium for poets to share ideas about poetry and its place in society; includes advice, articles, exercises, and offers a free e-mail newsletter.

ASK JEEVES

Website: www.ask.com. Internet search engine.

ASSOCIATION OF WRITERS AND WRITING PROGRAMS (AWP)

Website: www.awpwriter.org. Home site for AWP, offers membership information, AWP contest guidelines, articles and advice, and career links for writing and publishing. (See separate listing in the Organizations section.)

◼ ◼ CANADIAN POETRY: STUDIES, DOCUMENTS, REVIEWS

Dept. of English, University of Western Ontario, London ON N6A 3K7 Canada. E-mail: canadianpoetry@uwo.ca. Website: www.uwo.ca/english/canadianpoetry. **Contact:** Prof. D.M.R. Bentley, general editor; R.J. Shroyer, associate editor. Established 1977. A refereed journal devoted to the study of poetry from all periods in Canada, published biannually (Spring/Summer and Fall/Winter). Subscription: $15 CAN. **Publishes no poetry except as quotations in articles.** Also offers Canadian Poetry Press Scholarly Editions. Details available for SASE or on website.

CANADIAN POSTAL SERVICE

Website: www.canadapost.ca. Provides all necessary information for mailing to, from, and within Canada. Includes downloadable *Canada Postal Guide(C)*.

CAVE CANEM

Website: www.cavecanempoets.org. Site for the Cave Canem group offers ''A Home for Black Poetry'' on the Internet, including information about Cave Canem programs, poems, and links. (See separate listings in the Contests & Awards, Conferences & Workshops, and Organizations sections.)

DOGPILE

Website: www.dogpile.com. Uses metasearch technology to ''search the search engines'' and return results from Google, Yahoo, AltaVista, Ask Jeeves, About, LookSmart, Overture, Teoma, FindWhat, and others.

DUSTBOOKS; INTERNATIONAL DIRECTORY OF LITTLE MAGAZINES & SMALL PRESSES; DIRECTORY OF POETRY PUBLISHERS; SMALL PRESS REVIEW

P.O. Box 100, Paradise CA 95967. (800)477-6110. Fax: (530)877-0222. E-mail: publisher@dustbooks.com. Website: www.dustbooks.com. **Contact:** Len Fulton. Dustbooks publishes a number of books useful to writers. Send SASE for catalog or check website. Regular publications include *The International Directory of Little Magazines & Small Presses*, published annually with 900 pages of magazine and book publisher listings, plus subject and regional indexes. *Directory of Poetry Publishers* has similar information for over 2,000 poetry markets. *Small Press Review* is a bimonthly magazine carrying updates of listings in *The International Directory*, small press needs, news, announcements, and reviews.

ELECTRONIC POETRY CENTER

Website: http://epc.buffalo.edu. Resource offering links to magazines, poets, and sites of interest on the Internet, including indexes to blogs and sound poetry.

FAVORITE POEM PROJECT

Website: www.favoritepoem.org. Site for the project founded by Robert Pinsky to celebrate, document, and promote poetry's role in American lives.

FIRST DRAFT: THE JOURNAL OF THE ALABAMA WRITERS' FORUM; THE ALABAMA WRITERS' FORUM

Alabama State Council on the Arts, 201 Monroe St., Montgomery AL 36130-1800. (334)242-4076 ext. 233. Fax: (334)240-3269. E-mail: awf@arts.alabama.gov. Website: www.writersforum.org. **Contact:** Jay Lamar, editor. Established 1992. Appears 2 times/year with news, features, book reviews, and interviews relating to Alabama writers. "We do not publish original poetry or fiction." *First Draft* lists markets for poetry, contests/awards, and workshops. Accepts advertising for publishers, conferences, workshops (request ad rates from awf@arts.alabama.gov). Sponsored by the Alabama Writers' Forum. Reviews books of poetry, fiction, and nonfiction by "Alabama writers or from Alabama presses." Subscription: $35/year, includes membership. Sample: $5.

GOOGLE

Website: www.google.com. Internet search engine.

HAIKU SOCIETY OF AMERICA

Website: www.hsa-haiku.org. Includes membership information, contest guidelines, announcements, links, and more.

✵ INDEPENDENT PUBLISHER ONLINE; INDEPENDENT PUBLISHER BOOK AWARDS

Jenkins Group Inc., 400 W. Front St., Suite 4A, Traverse City MI 49684. (800)706-4636 or (231)933-0445 (main). Fax: (231)933-0448. E-mail: jimb@bookpublishing.com. Website: www.independent publisher.com. **Contact:** Jim Barnes, managing editor. For 20 years the mission at *Independent Publisher* has been to recognize and encourage the work of publishers who exhibit the courage and creativity necessary to take chances, break new ground, and bring about change in the world of publishing. The annual Independent Publisher Book Awards, conducted each year to honor the year's best independently published titles (including poetry), accept entries from independent publishers throughout North America, ranging from self-publishers to major university presses. The Awards were launched in 1996 to bring increased recognition to unsung titles published by independent authors and publishers. $5,000 in prize money is divided equally among the Ten Outstanding Books of the Year, and winners and finalists in 49 categories receive plaques, certificates, and gold seals. Winner and finalists appear for an entire year in the *Independent Publisher Online* webzine, which goes out monthly to over 40,000 subscribers worldwide, many of whom are agents, buyers, and librarians.

INTERNAL REVENUE SERVICE (IRS)

Website: www.irs.ustreas.gov. Includes U.S. federal tax information, resources, publications, and forms for individuals and businesses.

THE LIBRARY OF CONGRESS

Website: www.loc.gov. Put "poetry" in the site search engine and retrieve over 2,600 results of interest, including The Poetry & Literature Center of the Library of Congress (www.loc.gov/poetry) and links to the U.S. Poet Laureate and the Poetry 180 Project to promote poetry to high school students.

⭐ 🌐 LIGHT'S LIST; PHOTON PRESS

37 The Meadows, Berwick-Upon-Tweed, Northumberland TD15 1NY England. Phone: (01289)306523. E-mail: photon.press@virgin.net. Website: http://users.cooptel.net/photon.press. **Contact:** John Light, editor. Established 1986. *Light's List* is an annual publication "listing some 1,450 small press magazines publishing poetry, prose, market information, articles, and artwork with addresses, price, page count, frequency, and brief note of interests. All magazines publish work in English. Listings are from the United Kingdom, Europe, United States, Canada, Australia, New Zealand, South Africa, and Asia." *Light's List* is 74 pages, A5-sized, photocopied, saddle-stapled, with card cover. Single copy: $7 (air $8). Accepts inquiries by e-mail.

🌐 MILLENNIUM ARTS MAGAZINE

P.O. Box 71, Prestatyn LL19 7WU North Wales. Phone/fax: 01745 856064. E-mail: mamuk@webspawner.com. Website: www.webspawner.com/users/mamuk/index.html. Established 1995. Primarily an art-associated News-'n'-Information website (Fine Arts, Performing Arts, Literary Arts), plus additional information.

NATIONAL FEDERATION OF STATE POETRY SOCIETIES (NFSPS)

Website: www.nfsps.org. Site for this national umbrella organization includes NFSPS contest information, contact information and links to affiliated state poetry societies, and an online version of the quarterly newsletter, *Strophes*. (See separate NFSPS listings in the Contests & Awards and Organizations sections.)

PARA PUBLISHING

Box 8206-240, Santa Barbara CA 93118-8206. (800)727-2782. E-mail: info@ParaPublishing.com. Website: www.parapublishing.com. Website offers hundreds of pages of valuable book writing, publishing, and promoting information. Author/publisher Dan Poynter's how-to titles on book publishing and self-publishing include *The Self-Publishing Manual: How to Write, Print and Sell Your Own Book*. Also available are Special Reports on various aspects of book production, promotion, marketing, and distribution. Ordering information available on webiste.

PERSONAL POEMS

% F. Jean Hesse, 102 Rockford Dr., Athens GA 30605. (706)208-0420. F. Jean Hesse started a business in 1980 writing poems for individuals for a fee (for greetings, special occasions, etc.). Others started similar businesses after she began instructing them in the process, especially through a cassette tape training program and other materials. Send SASE for free brochure or $20 plus $5.50 p&h for training manual, *How to Make Your Poems Pay*. Has also published a 400-page paperback book, *For His Good Pleasure*, a one-year collection of poems for daily reading "to comfort and inspire." Available for $12.95 plus $3.50 p&h. Make checks payable to F. Jean Hesse.

POETIC VOICES

Website: http://poeticvoices.com. Monthly online poetry journal includes poems, features, news, and advice.

⭐ 🌐 POETRY BOOK SOCIETY; PBS BULLETIN

Book House, 45 East Hill, London SW18 2QZ England. Phone: +44 (0)20 8870 8403. Fax: +44 (0)20 8870 0865. E-mail: info@poetrybooks.co.uk. Website: www.poetrybooks.co.uk. Established 1953 "to promote the best newly published contemporary poetry to as wide an audience as possible." A book club with an annual subscription rate of £45, which covers 4 books of new poetry, the *PBS Bulletin*, and a premium offer (for new members). The selectors also recommend other books of special merit, which are obtainable at a discount of 25%. The Poetry Book Society is subsidized by the Arts Council of England. Please write, fax, or e-mail for details.

POETRY DAILY

Website: www.poems.com. A new poem every day, plus news, reviews, and special features.

⊠ THE POETRY SOCIETY; POETRY REVIEW; POETRY NEWS; NATIONAL POETRY COMPETITION

22 Betterton St., London WC2H 9BX United Kingdom. Phone: 020 7420 9880. Fax: 020 7240 4818. E-mail: npd@poetrysociety.org.uk. Website: www.poetrysociety.org.uk. Established 1909. One of Britain's most dynamic arts organizations, with membership open to all. "The Poetry Society exists to help poets and poetry thrive in Britain today. Our members come from all over the world and their support enables us to promote poetry on a global scale." Publishes *Poetry Review*, Britain's most prominent poetry magazine, and *Poetry News*, the Society's newsletter. Runs the National Poetry Competition.

POETRY SOCIETY OF AMERICA

Website: www.poetrysociety.org. Includes membership and award information, poet resources, and more. (See separate listing in the Organizations section.)

POETS & WRITERS ONLINE

Website: www.pw.org. Includes searchable *A Directory of American Poets & Fiction Writers*, informational resources, and more. (See separate listing for Poets & Writers, Inc. in the Organizations section.)

THE POETS' CORNER

Website: www.theotherpages.org/poems. Text site that includes 6,700 works by 780 poets, plus poet bios and photos, indexes, and The Daily Poetry Break.

PUSHCART PRESS

P.O. Box 380, Wainscott NY 11975. (631)324-9300. Website: www.pushcartprize.com. **Contact:** Bill Henderson, editor. The Pushcart Press, an affiliate publisher of W.W. Norton & Co., publishes the acclaimed annual *Pushcart Prize* anthology, Pushcart Editor's Book Award, and other quality literature, both fiction and nonfiction. "The most-honored literary series in America, *The Pushcart Prize* has been named a notable book of the year by the *New York Times* and hailed with Pushcart Press as 'among the most influential in the development of the American book business' over the past century." *The Pushcart Prize* is available for $35 (cloth) or $17 (paperback).

RAIN TAXI REVIEW OF BOOKS

P.O. Box 3840, Minneapolis MN 55403. E-mail: info@raintaxi.com. Website: www.raintaxi.com. Established 1996. *Rain Taxi Review of Books* is a quarterly publication produced in both print and online versions (the latter with completely different material). The print version is available by subscription and free in bookstores nationwide. "We publish reviews of books that are overlooked by mainstream media, and each issue includes several pages of poetry reviews, as well as author interviews and original essays." Poets and publishers may send books for review consideration. Subscription: $12 domestic, $24 international. Sample: $4. "We DO NOT publish original poetry. Please don't send poems."

⊠ SMALL PRESS CENTER FOR INDEPENDENT PUBLISHING

20 West 44th St., New York NY 10036. (212)764-7021. E-mail: info@smallpress.org. Website: www.smallpress.org. Provides information to and about independent and small publishers and university presses. "The Small Press Center provides access to education and expertise in the field of independent publishing, encouraging excellence and free expression in publishing through workshops, lectures, book fairs, exhibits, and a reference collection. The Center is committed to preserving the

craft and art of publishing through a library dedicated to its history." Website includes resources, publishers news, and member directory.

ℕ THE SPECULATIVE LITERATURE FOUNDATION

P.O. Box 1693, Dubuque IA 52004-1693. Website: http://speculativeliterature.org. Established 2004. A nonprofit organization dedicated to promoting literary quality in speculative fiction. "Speculative literature is a catch-all term meant to inclusively span the breadth of fantastic literature, encompassing literature ranging from hard science fiction to epic fantasy to ghost stories to horror to folk and fairy tales to slipstream to magical realism to modern myth-making—and more." Includes resources and information of value to writers of speculative poetry.

TANKA SOCIETY OF AMERICA

Website: http://hometown.aol.com/tsapoetry/TankaSocietyofAmerica-index.html. Offers membership information, contest guidelines and winning poems, definitions and discussion of tanka.

U.S. COPYRIGHT OFFICE

Website: www.loc.gov/copyright. Offers copyright basics and FAQ, records search, directions for registering work for copyright, and other information.

U.S. POSTAL SERVICE

Website: www.usps.com. Extensive site includes postage rates, mail preparation and mailing directions, domestic and foreign shipping options, and much more.

WEB DEL SOL

Website: http://webdelsol.com. Must-see site for anyone interested in contemporary literary arts. *Web del Sol* "is a collaboration on the part of scores of dedicated, volunteer editors, writers, poets, artists, and staff whose job it is to acquire and frame the finest contemporary literary art and culture available in America, and abroad, and to array it in such a manner that it speaks for itself . . . at WDS we employ the traditional and electronic means necessary to bring a whole new readership to the contemporary literary arts."

WINNING WRITERS.COM

Website: www.winningwriters.com. Resources for poets and writers, including *Poetry Contest Insider* (quarterly, published online, subscription required), links, manuscript tips, "bad contest" warning signs, Winning Writers contests, and free newsletter. (See separate listings in Contests & Awards section.)

WORD WORKS NETWORK (WoW)

Website: www.wow-schools.net. With its mission to "reinvent and restore to prominence the art of writing in American high schools," WoW's site offers resources, links, chat lounge, advice on starting high school literary journals, with links to exceptional journals.

WRITER BEWARE

Website: www.sfwa.org/beware. Science Fiction and Fantasy Writers of American, Inc. offers a page on their website devoted to scam alerts, common publishing practices that take advantage of writers, case studies, and a section on legal recourse for writers.

WRITER'S DIGEST BOOKS

4700 East Galbraith Rd., Cincinnati OH 45236. (800)448-0915. Website www.writersdigest.com. Writer's Digest Books publishes an array of books useful to all types of writers. In addition to *Poet's Market*, books for poets include *You Can Write Poetry* by Jeff Mock, *Creating Poetry* and *The Poetry Dictionary* by John Drury, *The Art and Craft of Poetry* by Michael J. Bugeja, *The Writer's Digest*

Writing Clinic (which includes a poetry segment), and *The Pocket Muse* by Monica Wood (stimulating inspiration for all writers, including poets). Call or write for a complete catalog or log on to www.writersdigest.com, which includes individual web pages for poetry and other genres, plus markets, tips, and special content. **PLEASE NOTE:** *Writer's Digest Books does not publish poetry.*

YAHOO
Website: www.yahoo.com. Internet search engine.

ADDITIONAL PUBLICATIONS

The following listings also contain information about instructive publications for poets. Turn to the page numbers indicated for details about their offerings.

Poets in Education

Whether known as PITS (Poets in the Schools), WITS (Writers in the Schools), or similar names, programs exist nationwide that coordinate residencies, classroom visits, and other opportunities for experienced poets to share their craft with students. Many state arts agencies include such "arts in education" programs in their activities (see Grants on page 442 for contact information). Another good source is the National Assembly of State Arts Agencies (see below), which includes a directory of contact names and addresses for arts education programs state-by-state. The following list is a mere sampling of programs and organizations that link poets with schools. Contact them for information about their requirements (some may insist poets have a strong publication history, others may prefer classroom experience) or check their websites where available. (Don't miss Vivé Griffith's article "Opening Doors to Poetry" on page 22 for a stimulating discussion of poetry in education.)

The Academy of American Poets, 588 Broadway, Suite 604, New York NY 10012-3210. (212)274-0343. E-mail: academy@poets.org. Website: www.poets.org (includes links to state arts in education programs).

Arkansas Writers in the Schools, WITS Director, 333 Kimpel Hall, University of Arkansas, Fayetteville AR 72701. (479)575-4301. E-mail: wits@cavern.uark.edu. Website: www.uar k.edu/ ~ wits.

California Poets in the Schools, 1333 Balboa St., Suite 3, San Francisco CA 94118. (415)221-4201. E-mail: info@cpits.org. Website: www.cpits.org.

e-poets.network, a collective online cultural center that promotes education through video-conferencing (i.e., "distance learning"); also includes the *Voces y Lugares* project. Website: http://learning.e-poets.net (includes online contact form).

Idaho Writers in the Schools, Log Cabin Literary Center, 801 S. Capitol Blvd., Boise ID 83702. (208)331-8000. E-mail: info@logcablit.org. Website: www.logcablit.org/wits.html.

Indiana Writers in the Schools, University of Evansville, Dept. of English, 1800 Lincoln Ave., Evansville IN 47722. (812)479-2962. E-mail: rg37@evansville.edu. Website: http:// english.evansville.edu.

Michigan Creative Writers in the Schools, ArtServe Michigan, 17515 W. Nine Mile Rd., Suite 1025, Southfield MI 48075. (248)557-8288 **OR** 1310 Turner St., Suite C, Lansing MI

48906. (517)371-7029. E-mail: education@artservemichigan.org. Website: www.artserve michigan.org.

National Assembly of State Arts Agencies, 1029 Vermont Ave. NW, 2nd Floor, Washington DC 20005. (202)347-6352. E-mail: nasaa@nasaa-arts.org. Website: www.nasaa-arts.org.

Oregon Writers in the Schools, Literary Arts, 224 NW 13th Ave., Suite 306, Portland OR 97209. (503)227-2583. E-mail: Elizabeth@literary-arts.org. Website: www.literary-arts. org/wits.htm.

PEN in the Classroom (PITC), Pen Center USA, 672 S. Lafayette Park Place, #42, Los Angeles CA 90057. (213)365-8500. E-mail: pitc@penusa.org. Website: www.penusa.org/go/progr ams.

"Pick-a-Poet," The Humanities Project, Arlington Public Schools, 1426 N. Quincy St., Arlington VA 22207. (703)228-6299. Website: www.humanitiesproject.org.

Potato Hill Poetry, 6 Pleasant St., Suite 2, South Natick MA 01760. (888)5-POETRY. E-mail: info@potatohill.com. Website: www.potatohill.com (includes online contact form).

Seattle Writers in the Schools (WITS), Seattle Arts & Lectures, 105 S. Main St., Suite 201, Seattle WA 98104. (206)621-2230. Website: https://secure3.zipcon.net/~lectures/ wits.html.

Teachers & Writers Collaborative, 5 Union Square W., New York NY 10003-3306. (212)691-6590 or (888)BOOKS-TW. E-mail: info@twc.org. Website: www.twc.org. A catalog of T&W books is available online, or call toll-free to request a print copy.

Texas Writers in the Schools, 1523 W. Main, Houston TX 77006. (713)523-3877. E-mail: mail@writersintheschools.org. Website: www.writersintheschools.org.

Writers & Artists in the Schools (WAITS), COMPAS, 304 Landmark Center, 75 W. Fifth St., St. Paul MN 55102. (651)292-3254. E-mail: daniel@compas.org. Website: www.comp as.org.

Youth Voices in Ink, Badgerdog Literary Publishing, Inc., P.O. Box 301209, Austin TX 78703-0021. (512)538-1305. E-mail: info@badgerdog.org. Website: www.badgerdog.org.

Glossary of Listing Terms

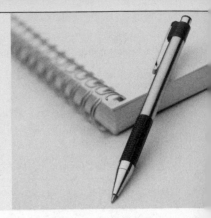

A3, A4, A5. Metric equivalents of $11^{3}/_{4} \times 16^{1}/_{2}$, $8^{1}/_{4} \times 11^{3}/_{4}$, and $5^{7}/_{8} \times 8^{1}/_{4}$ respectively.

Anthology. A collection of selected writings by various authors.

Attachment. A computer file electronically ''attached'' to an e-mail message.

b&w. Black & white (photo or illustration).

Bio. A short biographical statement often requested with a submission.

Camera-ready. Poems ready for copy camera platemaking; camera-ready poems usually appear in print exactly as submitted.

Chapbook. A small book of about 24-50 pages.

Circulation. The number of subscribers to a magazine/journal.

CLMP. Council of Literary Magazines and Presses; service organization for independent publishers of fiction, poetry, and prose.

Contributor's copy. Copy of book or magazine containing a poet's work, sometimes given as payment.

Cover letter. Brief introductory letter accompanying a poetry submission.

Coverstock. Heavier paper used as the cover for a publication.

Digest-sized. About $5^{1}/_{2} \times 8^{1}/_{2}$, the size of a folded sheet of conventional printer paper.

Download. To ''copy'' a file, such as a registration form, from a website.

Electronic magazine. See *online magazine*.

E-mail. Mail sent electronically using computer and modem or similar means.

Euro. Currency unit for the 11 member countries of the European Union; designated by EUR or the € symbol.

FAQ. Frequently Asked Questions.

Font. The style/design of type used in a publication; typeface.

Galleys. First typeset version of a poem, magazine, or book/chapbook.

GLBT. Gay/lesbian/bisexual/transgender (as in ''GLBT themes'').

Honorarium. A token payment for published work.

Internet. A worldwide network of computers offering access to a variety of electronic resources.

IRC. International Reply Coupon; a publisher can exchange IRCs for postage to return a manuscript to another country.

JPEG. Short for *Joint Photographic Experts Group*; an image compression format that allows digital images to be stored in relatively small files for electronic mailing and viewing on the Internet.

Magazine-sized. About $8^{1}/_{2} \times 11$, the size of an unfolded sheet of conventional printer paper.

ms. Manuscript.

mss. Manuscripts.

Multi-book review. Several books by the same author or by several authors reviewed in one piece.

Offset-printed. Printing method in which ink is transferred from an image-bearing plate to a "blanket" and then from blanket to paper.

Online magazine. Publication circulated through the Internet or e-mail.

p&h. Postage & handling.

p&p. Postage & packing.

"Pays in copies." See *contributor's copy.*

PDF. Short for *Portable Document Format*, developed by Adobe Systems, that captures all elements of a printed document as an electronic image, allowing it to be sent by e-mail, viewed online, and printed in its original format.

Perfect-bound. Publication with glued, flat spine; also called "flat-spined."

POD. See *print-on-demand.*

Press run. The total number of copies of a publication printed at one time.

Previously published. Work that has appeared before in print, in any form, for public consumption.

Print-on-demand. Publishing method that allows copies of books to be published as they're requested, rather than all at once in a single press run.

Publishing credits. A poet's magazine publications and book/chapbook titles.

Query letter. Letter written to an editor to raise interest in a proposed project.

Reading fee. A monetary amount charged by an editor or publisher to consider a poetry submission without any obligation to accept the work.

Rich Text Format. Carries the .rtf filename extension. A file format that allows an exchange of text files between different word processor operating systems with most of the formatting preserved.

Rights. A poet's legal property interest in his/her literary work; an editor or publisher may acquire certain rights from the poet to reproduce that work.

ROW. "Rest of world."

Royalties. A percentage of the retail price paid to the author for each copy of a book sold.

Saddle-stapled. A publication folded, then stapled along that fold; also called "saddle-stitched."

SAE. Self-addressed envelope.

SASE. Self-addressed, stamped envelope.

SASP. Self-addressed, stamped postcard.

Simultaneous submission. Submission of the same manuscript to more than one publisher at the same time.

Subsidy press. Publisher who requires the poet to pay all costs, including typesetting, production, and printing; sometimes called a "vanity publisher."

Tabloid-sized. 11×15 or larger, the size of an ordinary newspaper folded and turned sideways.

Text file. A file containing only textual characters (i.e., no graphics or special formats).

Unsolicited manuscript. A manuscript an editor did not ask specifically to receive.

Website. A specific address on the Internet that provides access to a set of documents (or "pages").

Glossary of Poetry Terms

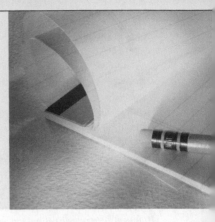

This glossary is provided as a quick-reference only, briefly covering poetic styles and terms that may turn up in articles and listings in *Poet's Market*. For a full understanding of the terms, forms, and styles listed here, as well as common literary terms not included, consult a solid textbook or handbook, such as John Drury's *The Poetry Dictionary* (Writer's Digest Books). (Ask your librarian or bookseller for recommendations.)

Abstract poem: conveys emotion through sound, textures, and rhythm and rhyme rather than through the meanings of words.

Acrostic: initial letters of each line, read downward, form a word, phrase, or sentence.

Alliteration: close repetition of consonant sounds, especially initial consonant sounds. (Also known as *consonance*.)

Alphabet poem: arranges lines alphabetically according to initial letter.

American cinquain: derived from Japanese haiku and tanka by Adelaide Crapsey; counted syllabic poem of 5 lines of 2-4-6-8-2 syllables, frequently in iambic feet.

Anapest: foot consisting of 2 unstressed syllables followed by a stress (- - ').

Assonance: close repetition of vowel sounds.

Avant-garde: work at the forefront—cutting edge, unconventional, risk-taking.

Ballad: narrative poem often in ballad stanza (4-line stanza with 4 stresses in lines 1 and 3, 3 stresses in lines 2 and 4, which also rhyme).

Ballade: 3 stanzas rhymed *ababbcbC* (*C* indicates a refrain) with envoi rhymed *bcbC*.

Beat poetry: anti-academic school of poetry born in '50s San Francisco; fast-paced free verse resembling jazz.

Blank verse: unrhymed iambic pentameter.

Caesura: a deliberate rhetorical, grammatical, or rhythmic pause, break, cut, turn, division, or pivot in poetry.

Chant: poem in which one or more lines are repeated over and over.

Cinquain: any 5-line poem or stanza; also called "quintain" or "quintet." (See also *American cinquain*.)

Concrete poetry: see *emblematic poem*.

Confessional poetry: work that uses personal and private details from the poet's own life.

Consonance: see *assonance*.

Couplet: stanza of 2 lines; pair of rhymed lines.

Dactyl: foot consisting of a stress followed by 2 unstressed syllables (' - -).

Didactic poetry: poetry written with the intention to instruct.

Eclectic: open to a variety of poetic styles (as in "eclectic taste").

Ekphrastic poem: verbally presents something originally represented in visual art, though more than mere description.

Elegy: lament in verse for someone who has died, or a reflection on the tragic nature of life.

Emblematic poem: words or letters arranged to imitate a shape, often the subject of the poem.

Enjambment: continuation of sense and rhythmic movement from one line to the next; also called a "run-on" line.

Envoi: a brief ending (usually to a ballade or sestina) no more than 4 lines long; summary.

Epic poetry: long narrative poem telling a story central to a society, culture, or nation.

Epigram: short, witty, satirical poem or saying written to be remembered easily, like a punchline.

Epigraph: a short verse, note, or quotation that appears at the beginning of a poem or section; usually presents an idea or theme on which the poem elaborates, or contributes background information not reflected in the poem itself.

Epitaph: brief verse commemorating a person/group of people who died.

Experimental poetry: work that challenges conventional ideas of poetry by exploring new techniques, form, language, and visual presentation.

Foot: unit of measure in a metrical line of poetry.

Found poem: text lifted from a non-poetic source such as an ad and presented as a poem.

Free verse: unmetrical verse (lines not counted for accents, syllables, etc.).

Ghazal: Persian poetic form of 5-15 unconnected, independent couplets; associative jumps may be made from couplet to couplet.

Greeting card poetry: resembles verses in greeting cards; sing-song meter and rhyme.

Haibun: originally, a Japanese form in which elliptical, often autobiographical prose is interspersed with haiku.

Haikai no renga: see *renku.*

Haiku: originally, a Japanese form of a single vertical line with 17 sound symbols in a 5-7-5 pattern. In English, typically a 3-line poem with fewer than 17 syllables in no set pattern, but exhibiting a 2-part juxtapositional structure, seasonal reference, imagistic immediacy, and a moment of keen perception of nature or human nature. The term is both singular and plural.

Hokku: the starting verse of a renga or renku, in 5, 7, and then 5 sound symbols in Japanese; or in three lines, usually totaling fewer than 17 syllables, in English; the precursor for what is now called haiku. (See also *haiku*).

Iamb: foot consisting of an unstressed syllable followed by a stress (- ').

Iambic pentameter: consists of 5 iambic feet per line.

Imagist poetry: short, free verse lines that present images without comment or explanation; strongly influenced by haiku and other Oriental forms.

Kyrielle: French form; 4-line stanza with 8-syllable lines, the final line a refrain.

Language poetry: attempts to detach words from traditional meanings to produce something new and unprecedented.

Limerick: 5-line stanza rhyming *aabba*; pattern of stresses/line is traditionally 3-3-2-2-3; often bawdy or scatalogical.

Line: basic compositional unit of a poem; measured in feet if metrical.

Linked poetry: written through the collaboration of 2 or more poets creating a single poetic work.

Long poem: exceeds length and scope of short lyric or narrative poem; defined arbitrarily, often as more than 2 pages or 100 lines.

Lyric poetry: expresses personal emotion; music predominates over narrative or drama.

Metaphor: 2 different things are likened by identifying one as the other (A = B).

Meter: the rhythmic measure of a line.

Modernist poetry: work of the early 20th century literary movement that sought to break with the past, rejecting outmoded literary traditions, diction, and form while encouraging innovation and reinvention.

Narrative poetry: poem that tells a story.

New Formalism: contemporary literary movement to revive formal verse.

Nonsense verse: playful, with language and/or logic that defies ordinary understanding.

Octave: stanza of 8 lines.

Ode: a songlike, or lyric, poem; can be passionate, rhapsodic, and mystical, or a formal address to a person on a public or state occasion.

Pantoum: Malayan poetic form of any length; consists of 4-line stanzas, with lines 2 and 4 of one quatrain repeated as lines 1 and 3 of the next; final stanza reverses lines 1 and 3 of the previous quatrain and uses them as lines 2 and 4; traditionally each stanza rhymes *abab*.

Petrarchan sonnet: octave rhymes *abbaabba*; sestet may rhyme *cdcdcd*, *cdedce*, *ccdccd*, *cddcdd*, *edecde*, or *cddcee*.

Prose poem: brief prose work with intensity, condensed language, poetic devices, and other poetic elements.

Quatrain: stanza of 4 lines.

Refrain: a repeated line within a poem, similar to the chorus of a song.

Regional poetry: work set in a particular locale, imbued with the look, feel, and culture of that place.

Renga: originally, a Japanese collaborative form in which 2 or more poets alternate writing 3 lines, then 2 lines for a set number of verses (such as 12, 18, 36, 100, and 1,000). There are specific rules for seasonal progression, placement of moon and flower verses, and other requirements. (See also *linked poetry*.)

Rengay: an American collaborative 6-verse, thematic linked poetry form, with 3-line and 2-line verses in the following set pattern for 2 or 3 writers (letters represent poets, numbers indicate the lines in each verse): A3-B2-A3-B3-A2-B3 or A3-B2-C3-A2-B3-C2. All verses, unlike renga or renku, must develop at least one common theme.

Renku: the modern term for renga, and a more popular version of the traditionally more aristocratic renga. (See also *linked poetry*.)

Rhyme: words that sound alike, especially words that end in the same sound.

Rhythm: the beat and movement of language (rise and fall, repetition and variation, change of pitch, mix of syllables, melody of words).

Rondeau: French form of usually 15 lines in 3 parts, rhyming *aabba aabR aabbaR* (*R* indicates a refrain repeating the first word or phrase of the opening line).

Senryu: originally, a Japanese form, like haiku in form, but chiefly humorous, satirical, or ironic, and typically aimed at human foibles. (See also *haiku* and *zappai*.)

Sequence: a group or progression of poems, often numbered as a series.

Sestet: stanza of 6 lines.

Sestina: fixed form of 39 lines (6 unrhymed stanzas of 6 lines each, then an ending 3-line stanza), each stanza repeating the same 6 non-rhyming end-words in a different order; all 6 end-words appear in the final 3-line stanza.

Shakespearean sonnet: rhymes *abab cdcd efef gg*.

Sijo: originally a Korean narrative or thematic lyric form. The first line introduces a situation or problem that is countered or developed in line 2, and concluded with a twist in line 3. Lines average 14-16 syllables in length.

Simile: comparison that uses a linking word (*like, as, such as, how*) to clarify the similarities.

Sonnet: 14-line poem (traditionally an octave and sestet) rhymed in iambic pentameter; often presents an argument but may also present a description, story, or meditation.

Spondee: foot consisting of 2 stressed syllables (′ ′).

Stanza: group of lines making up a single unit; like a paragraph in prose.

Strophe: often used to mean "stanza"; also a stanza of irregular line lengths.

Surrealistic poetry: of the artistic movement stressing the importance of dreams and the subconscious, nonrational thought, free associations, and startling imagery/juxtapositions.

Tanka: originally, a Japanese form in one or 2 vertical lines with 31 sound symbols in a 5-7-5-7-7 pattern. In English, typically a 5-line lyrical poem with fewer than 31 syllables in no set syllable pattern, but exhibiting a caesura, turn, or pivot, and often more emotional and conversational than haiku.

Tercet: stanza or poem of 3 lines.

Terza rima: series of 3-line stanzas with interwoven rhyme scheme (*aba, bcb, cdc* . . .).

Trochee: foot consisting of a stress followed by an unstressed syllable (′ -).

Villanelle: French form of 19 lines (5 tercets and a quatrain); line 1 serves as one refrain (repeated in lines 6, 12, 18), line 3 as a second refrain (repeated in lines 9, 15, 19); traditionally, refrains rhyme with each other and with the opening line of each stanza.

Visual poem: see *emblematic poem*.

Waka: literally, "Japanese poem", the precursor for what is now called tanka. (See also *tanka*.)

War poetry: poems written about warfare and military life; often written by past and current soldiers; may glorify war, recount exploits, or demonstrate the horrors of war.

Zappai: originally Japanese; an unliterary, often superficial witticism masquerading as haiku or senryu; formal term for joke haiku or other pseudo-haiku.

Zeugma: a figure of speech in which a single word (or, occasionally, a phrase) is related in one way to words that precede it, and in another way to words that follow it.

Chapbook Publishers

A poetry chapbook is a slim volume of 24-50 pages (although chapbook lengths can vary; some are even published as inserts in magazines). Many publishers and journals solicit chapbook manuscripts through competitions. Read listings carefully, check websites where available, and request guidelines before submitting. See Frequently Asked Questions on page 7 for further information about chapbooks and submission formats.

Special Indexes

Book Publishers Index

The following magazines and publishers consider full-length book manuscripts (over 50 pages, often much longer). See Frequently Asked Questions on page 7 for further information about book manuscript submission.

Special Indexes

Openness to Submissions

In this section, all magazines, publishers, and contests/awards with primary listings in *Poet's Market* are categorized according to their openness to submissions (as indicated by the symbols that appear at the beginning of each listing). Note that some markets are listed in more than one category.

◖ WELCOMES SUBMISSIONS FROM BEGINNING POETS

◑ PREFERS SUBMISSIONS FROM EXPERIENCED POETS, WILL CONSIDER WORK FROM BEGINNING POETS

PREFERS SUBMISSIONS FROM SKILLED, EXPERIENCED POETS, FEW BEGINNERS

◎ MARKET WITH A SPECIALIZED FOCUS

Special Indexes

Special Indexes

Geographical Index

This section offers a breakdown of U.S. publishers and conferences/workshops arranged alphabetically by state or territory, followed by listings for Canada, Australia, France, Ireland, Japan, the United Kingdom, and other countries—a real help when trying to locate publishers in your region as well as conferences and workshops convenient to your area.

Conferences & Workshops

COLORADO
Publishers of Poetry

Conferences & Workshops

CONNECTICUT
Publishers of Poetry

Special Indexes

Conferences & Workshops

NORTH CAROLINA
Publishers of Poetry

MAMMOTH books 217
miller's pond 226
Minnesota Review 228
One Trick Pony 253
PEN, THE 284
Pennsylvania English 270
Pitt Poetry Series 276
Plan B Press 276
Poetry Explosion Newsletter 284
Poetry Forum 284
Poets at Work 289
Raw Dog Press 307
Taproot Literary Review 359
Time of Singing 369
Transcendent Visions 370
Wild Violet 391

Conferences & Workshops
Cave Canem 449

RHODE ISLAND
Publishers of Poetry
Bryant Literary Review 90
Italian Americana 186
Renaissance Online Magazine 312
24.7 373
Wings Magazine, Inc. 394

SOUTH CAROLINA
Publishers of Poetry
Crazyhorse 115
Emrys Journal 133
Illuminations 179
James Dickey Newsletter 124
Ninety-Six Press 247
South Carolina Review 344
Sow's Ear Poetry Review, The 347
Tarpaulin Sky 361

SOUTH DAKOTA
Publishers of Poetry
Darkling Publications 121
South Dakota Review 344

TENNESSEE
Publishers of Poetry
Alive Now 47
babysue® 63
Christian Guide 102

Mature Years 221
Pockets 279
Poems & Plays 280
River City 314
Rook Publishing 318
Sewanee Review, The 326
Tar Wolf Review 360

Conferences & Workshops
American Christian Writers Conf. 448
Life Press Christian Writers' Conf. 453
Sewanee Writers' Conf. 455
Tennessee Mountain Writers Conf. 458

TEXAS
Publishers of Poetry
American Literary Review 49
Borderlands 84
Concho River Review 110
Curbside Review 117
descant 123
Gin Bender Poetry Review 155
Gulf Coast 159
Illya's Honey 179
Lone Stars Magazine 206
Lucidity 209
Lyric Poetry Review 213
Nerve Cowboy 239
Office Number One 252
Pebble Lake Review 267
Poet's Castle, The 289
Rio Grande Review 314
Southwest Review 346
Sulphur River Literary Review 354
Sun Poetic Times 354
Texas Poetry Calendar 363
Texas Poetry Journal 363
Touchstone Literary Journal 370
Wild Plum 391
Writer's Bloc 397
Zillah 398

UTAH
Publishers of Poetry
Chariton Review 99
Ellipsis 133
Leading Edge 201
Quarterly West 304
Sunstone 355

Special Indexes

Conferences & Workshops

VIRGIN ISLANDS
Publishers of Poetry

OTHER COUNTRIES
Publishers of Poetry

Conferences & Workshops

Special Indexes

Subject Index

This index focuses on markets indicating a specialized area of interest, whether regional, poetic style, or specific topic (these markets show a ◎ symbol at the beginning of their listings). It also includes markets we felt offered special opportunities in certain subject areas. Subject categories are listed alphabetically, with additional subcategories indicated under the "Specialized" heading (in parentheses behind the market's name). **Please note:** 1) This index only partially reflects the total markets in this book; many do not identify themselves as having specialized interests and so are not included here. 2) Many specialized markets have more than one area of interest and will be found under multiple categories. 3) When a market appears under a heading in this index, it does not necessarily mean it considers *only* poetry associated with that subject, poetry *only* from that region, etc. It's still best to read all listings carefully as part of a thorough marketing plan.

Bilingual/Foreign Language

Christian

Cowboy Poetry

Form/Style (Oriental)

Gay/Lesbian/Bisexual

Gothic/Horror

Poetry by Children (considers submissions)

Poetry by Teens (considers submissions)

Religious

Science Fiction

Spirituality/Inspirational

Sports/Recreation

Students

Translations

Women's Issues

Writing

General Index

Markets that appeared in the *2005 Poet's Market* but are not included in this edition are identified by two-letter codes explaining their absence. These codes are: *(DS) discontinued; (ED) editorial decision; (HA) on hiatus; (NP) no longer publishing poetry; (NR) no (or late) response to requested verification of information; (OB) out of business* (or, in the case of contests or conferences, cancelled); **(OS) overstocked; (RR) removed by request of the market** (no reason given); **(UF) uncertain future; (UC) unable to contact;** and **(RP) restructuring/purchased.**